SCIENCE FICTION AND FANTASY LITERATURE

SCIENCE FICTION AND FANTASY LITERATURE

A Checklist, 1700-1974

with

Contemporary Science Fiction Authors II

R. Reginald

Volume 2:

Contemporary Science Fiction Authors II

Editorial Associates:
Douglas Menville, Mary A. Burgess

Assistants:
George Locke, Gordon Johnson, Doris Illes,
Barry R. Levin, Michael Grainey

Gale Research Company • Book Tower • Detroit, Michigan 48226

Acknowledgment of previous publication of selected material in "Contemporary Science Fictions Authors II" is made to the following publications:

STELLA NOVA: THE CONTEMPORARY SCIENCE FICTION AUTHORS. Copyright © 1970 by Unicorn & Son, Publishers. Used by permission of the publisher.

CONTEMPORARY SCIENCE FICTION AUTHORS, FIRST EDITION. Copyright © 1974 by R. Reginald. Used by permission of the author.

CONTEMPORARY AUTHORS. Copyright © 1961, 1962, 1963, 1964, 1965, 1966, 1967, 1968, 1969, 1970, 1971, 1972, 1973, 1974, 1975, 1976, 1977, 1978 by Gale Research Company. Used by permission of Gale Research Company.

Library of Congress Catalog Card Number 76-46130

Library of Congress Cataloging in Publication Data

Reginald, R
    Science fiction and fantasy literature.

    The 1st ed. of v. 2 was published separately under title: Contemporary science fiction authors.
    Includes indexes.
    1. Science fiction, American--Bio-bibliography. 2. Science fiction, English--Bio-bibliography. 3. Fantastic literature--Bibliography. 4. Authors, American--20th century --Biography. 5. Authors, English--20th century--Biography. I. Reginald, R. Contemporary science fiction authors. 1979. II. Title
Z1231.F4R42 [PS374.S35] 016.823'0876
ISBN 0-8103-1051-1   76-46130

Contents

Contemporary Science Fiction Authors II

PAUL ABLEMAN

Full Name: Paul Victor Ableman.
   Born June 13, 1927, at Leeds, England. Son of Jack Ableman (a trouser cutter in a factory) and Gertrude Gould (an actress, housewife, and writer). Married Tina Ableman "some seventeen years ago." One son, Martin ("he's fifteen").

Education: King's College, London.
   "I'm not a computer, I just write about them. It was a hell of a long time ago, and I left ingloriously without a degree. Have made it my objective to learn everything, but have not yet achieved this goal."

Career: Author.
   "Have been a writer or author now for eight or nine years."

Literary Agent: Jonathan Clowes, Ltd., 19 Jeffrey Place, London N.W.1, England.

* * * * *

ALEKSANDR ABRAMOV

Full Name: Aleksandr Ivanovich Abramov.
   Born November 30, 1900 at Moskva [Moscow], U.S.S.R. Son of Ivan Abramov (an engineer) and Vera Dormidontova (a housewife). Married Antonina Terekhova. One son, Sergei, born April 10, 1944.

Education: Moscow University.

Career: Writer and newspaper worker; now retired.

First Professional Sale: *Bumazhnik iz Zhelmoi Kozhi*, Molodaia Gvardiia, Moscow, 1926.

Awards:
   Winner of a USSR Writers' Union award for Best Short Story published in the monthly magazine *Moskva* (August, 1960). Member: USSR Writers' Union.

* * * * *

SERGEI ABRAMOV

Full Name: Sergei Aleksandrovich Abramov.
   Born April 10, 1944, at Moskva [Moscow], U.S.S.R. Son of Aleksandr Ivanovich Abramov (a writer) and Antonina Terekhova (a housewife).

Education: Moscow Automobile and Road Construction Institute, 1967. Some preparatory courses in newspaper writing at the Moscow Town House.

Career: Engineer.
   Currently Science Editor for the magazine *Smena*.

First Professional Sale:
   Khozhdenae za Tri Mira; Sbornik "Mir Prikliuchenii" a collection of short stories published by Detgis, Moscow, 1966.

Member: USSR Writers' Union; USSR Journalists' Union.

FORREST J ACKERMAN

Full Name: Forrest James Ackerman.
   Born November 24, 1916, at Los Angeles, California. Son of William Schilling Ackerman (Chief Statistician and Assistant to the Vice-President in Charge of Transportation, Associated Oil Company) and Carroll Cridland Wyman (a housewife). Married Wendayne Wahrmann 1951.

Education: University of California, Berkeley, 1934-1935.

Career: Author, Editor, Literary Agent.
   Civil Service Senior Typist, U.S. Government, 1937; Clerk, Associated Oil Company, 1938; Chief Varitypist, Academy of Motion Pictures Arts and Sciences, 1939-40; Self-employed, 1941; Chief Varitypist, Fluor Drafting Corporation, 1942; S/Sgt., US Army, 1942-45 (edited Ft. MacArthur *Bulletin Alert*, the second most popular of the 2000 wartime military newspapers); established Ackerman Science Fiction Literary Agency, 1947. Editor-in-Chief, *Famous Monsters of Filmland*, 1958-DATE. Managing Editor, Perry Rhodan series, Ace Books, 1969-DATE. Edited all issues of *Monster World* and *Spacemen*. Served as Associate Editor of the one-shot British prozine, *A Book of Weird Tales*. Created the "comicharacter" Vampirella, now featured in comic strips and book series of the same name.

Literary Agent:
   Forrest J Ackerman, 2495 Glendower Avenue, Hollywood CA 90027 [Phone: (213) 666-6326].

Honors and Awards:
   Hugo Award, Number One Fan Personality, 1952 (1953); Fan Guest of Honor, 22nd World Science Fiction Convention (Pacificon II), Oakland, 1964; Guest of Honor, Lunacon, 1974; Guest of Honor, First Annual *Famous Monsters of Filmland* Convention, 1974; Guest of Honor, First Pan-Germanic SF Con, 1957; Guest of Honor, European Perry Rhodan Convention, 1971; Guest of Honor, First International Science Fiction Convention, London, 1951; Guest of Honor, Trieste Science Fiction Film Festival, 1971; Guest of Honor, First SF Filmcon, 1972. Awarded (in tandem with Boris Karloff) the first Ann Radcliffe Award (for Gothic excellence), from the Count Dracula Society; later received a second Radcliffe Award. Member: Science Fiction Writers of America; Science Fiction League (Honorary Member #1); National Fantasy Fan Federation (Honorary Lifetime Member); Los Angeles Science Fantasy Society (Honorary Member); and many others.

Avocations and Interests:
   Esperanto and movies. Ackerman scripted Boris Karloff's narration for the Decca Album, *An Evening with Boris Karloff and His Friends*, and provided liner notes for the albums, *The Phantom of the Organ, Dr. Druid*, and *Vampyre of the Harpsichord*. He also wrote and narrated one side of the record, *Music for Robots*. He is widely sought as a lecturer on science fiction and films.

Ackerman writes:
   "Started reading 'scientifiction' in 1926. First letter published was the first letter in the Readers' Dept. of the first issue of *Science Wonder Quarterly* [Fall 1929]. Created The Boys' Scientifiction Club in 1929. Associate Editor of the world's first fan-

FORREST J ACKERMAN   (cont.)

zine, *The Time Traveller*, 1932. Have been able to
attend every World Science Fiction Convention save
one (a record). Recipient of the very first Hugo
Award. At the World Science Fiction Convention in
Denver (1941), received one of the first awards ever
given in the field (sponsored by Walter J. Daugherty).
Last surviving Charter Member of the Los Angeles
Science Fantasy Society still active in the group.
A Knight of St. Fantony. The LASFS created the
Forry Award in Ackerman's honor, and has given it
to such notables as C. L. Moore, Ray Bradbury, Fritz
Leiber, A. E. van Vogt, and Theodore Sturgeon. Was
Secretary of the pre-SFWA organization, the Science-
Fantasy Writers Association. A portion of memoirs
("A thru B") were recorded for 34 hours on tape about
ten years ago for the Oral History Dept. of UCLA.
Wrote and narrated *Science Fiction Films* (a 70-year
history) for the University of Kansas film series
on SF history. TV appearances include "To Tell the
Truth," "Down Memory Lane," "Merv Griffin Show,"
"Joe Pyne," BBC/TV, and a half-hour non-commercial
public education telecast on science fiction. Films:
The Time Travelers, *Schlock*, *Dracula Vs. Frankenstein*,
Queen (Planet) of Blood. Pseudonyms: Weaver Wright,
Spencer Strong, Jack Erman, Laurajean Ermayne, Fisher
Trentworth, Morris/Norris Chapnick, Dr. Acula,
Vespertina Torgosi, Claire Voyant, Erdstelulov, Fojak,
Clair Helding, Alden Lorraine, Jacques deForest Erman,
Hubert George Wells, Nick Beal, Stone T. Farmington,
Allis Villette, and numerous others. Created names
Nycon, Chicon, and Pacificon; coined the word "egoboo"
and other fanspeak terms; in 1954 introduced the
abbreviation "sci-fi," which has found universal
acceptance in such distant locales as Czechoslovakia
and Hungary, has appeared on the cover of *Playboy*,
is commonly used by *Publishers Weekly* and other media,
and is even included in at least one dictionary. Was
first called "Mr. Science Fiction" in the public
prints in 1949 by the late Willy Ley. My 17-room,
four-storey house contains 75000 stills from imagi-
movies, and perhaps as many prozines, fanzines,
paintings, drawings, manuscripts, pressbooks, motion
picture props, books, etc., all destined to be
preserved for posterity as my life work.

"I got into the field at the age of 9 when the Oct.
'26 *Amazing* jumped off the stands and grabbed hold
of me and shouted its siren song: 'Take me home,
little boy--you'll love me!' Encouraged from that
day forward by my maternal grandparents (Belle &
George Wyman, the last of the Big Time Angels), I
never quit collecting. My major goal has been
realized: to create and maintain the greatest
collection of imaginative memorabilia on this or
(hopefully) any other planet. From HGWells to John
Wyndham to S. Fowler Wright, from Hugo Gernsback
to Frank R. Paul to Fritz Lang; I have met and many
times grown to know most of them all. I have been
A. E. van Vogt's agent for over a quarter of a
century, and represent the estates of Stanley G.
Weinbaum and Ray Cummings, among others. I have
met the Metropolis Robotrix (Brigitte Helm) in her
own home, and slept in the bed in which Wells' sons
were born. I have lectured on 'stf' at high schools
and universities, and constantly welcome students
to view my collection. Surely my cup runneth over.

"Where would I like to go from here? Nowhere. I
just want to stay here. To that end I plan to be

cryogenically preserved, and intend to opt for a time-
travelling come-back if I have enough advance warning
of my death to make the preparations. I regard myself
as a spongeful of scientifictional information, happy
to be squeezed as long as my memory cells hold out,
and I only hope that society or some humanitarian
millionaire gets in the act before long to help me out
with the burden of the finances. Several hundred
individuals have contributed in small ways and large,
all the way up to four figures apiece (Tetsu Yano,
Ronald Graham, James Warren), but the monetary drain
to maintain the museum is enormous. As a 'paleontologist of scientifiction' I would like to leave a lot
of film and Golden Age books as yet unproduced, to be
remembered by. --FJA."

Ackerman never uses a period after his middle initial.

* * * * *

RUTH ADAM

Full Name: Ruth Augusta Adam.
   Born December 14, 1907, Nottingham, England.
Daughter of Rupert William King (a clergyman for the
Church of England) and Annie Wearing. Married Kenneth
Adam (a director of television for BBC) May 24, 1932.
Four children: Corinna, Clive, Piers, Nicholas.

Education: Attended St. Elphin's School for Daughters of the Clergy, Matlock, England, 1919-26.

Career: Author.
   Teacher in primary schools, Nottingham, England,
1926-1932; writer for the British Ministry of Information, 1940-1945. Has also served as a radio broadcaster, and an occasional participant on television
panels.

Literary Agent: David Higham Associates, 5-8 Lower
   John St., London WlR 4HA, England.

Member:
   Society of Authors; P.E.N.; Police Dependent's Trust
Committee; Fisher Committee (children's welfare); Hos-
pital Management Committee.

* * * * *

RICHARD ADAMS

Full Name: Richard George Adams.
   Born May 9, 1920, at Newbury, Berkshire, England.
Married Barbara Elizabeth Acland September 26, 1949.
Two children: Juliet, Rosamond.

Education: M.A., Worcester College, Oxford, 1948.

Career: British Civil Servant; Author.
   Served with the British Ministry of Housing and Local
Government until its amalgamation as part of the Dept.
of Environment, 1948-68; Assistant Secretary, Dept. of
Environment, 1968-74; Full-time Author, 1974-DATE.
Served in the British Army from 1940-45.

Literary Agent: David Higham Associates, 5-8 Lower
   John St., London WlR 4HA, England.

Honors: Guardian Award, 1972; Carnegie Medal, 1972,
   both for *Watership Down*.

MARK ADLARD

Full Name: Peter Marcus Adlard.
  Born June 19, 1932, at Seaton Carew, Durham, England. Son of Arthur Marcus Adlard (an auctioneer) and Ethel Leech (a housewife). Married Sheila Rosemary Skuse October 19, 1968. One daughter, Vanessa Rosemary, born 1971.

Education:
  M.A., Trinity College, Cambridge, 1954; Dip. Ed., Dept. of Education, Oxford, 1955; also has a B.Sc. from the University of London, and has taken various courses in management studies.

Career: Sales Manager.
  "Almost entire working life spent in various management positions in the steel industry."

First Professional Sale:
  "Dead End," in *Penthouse*, November, 1968.

Literary Agent: John Farquharson Ltd., 15 Red
  Lion Square, London WC1R 4QW, England.

Adlard writes:
  "All of my fiction is concerned with the relationships between 'work' and what people used to call the 'good life.' *Volteface* is a kind of sequel to *Interface* (with a similar background and recurring characters), although it can be read independently of it. *Multiface* is a sequel of a similar kind.
  "I think SF is undergoing a cataclysmic change. In my view, future historians will regard what we have learned to call 'science fiction' as a continuous European tradition running from (say) Dante through Stapledon, with the pulp magazines (or genre SF) as a revitalising tributary to the main river of speculative writing."

* * * * *

ROBERT AICKMAN

Full Name: Robert Fordyce Aickman.
  Born June 27, 1914, at London, England. Son of William Arthur Aickman (an architect) and Mabel Violet Marsh (daughter of Richard Marsh, author of the noted supernatural classic, *The Beetle*).

Education:
  Attended Highgate School, London. Also received some training as an architect.

Career: Author and critic.
  Has been a dramatic critic and film critic for various British publications; has also worked for a London literary agency. Aickman has served as chairman of several opera and ballet companies, and has founded a number of important festivals. He is known for his work in the conservation and preservation of of British waterways, and is the Founder and Vice-President of the Inland Waterways Association. He is Director of the Willow Wren Canal Transport Services Ltd., and of various other companies.

First Professional Sale:
  An article in *New Age*.

Literary Agent: Herbert van Thal, London Management, 235 Regent St., London W.1, England.

Avocations & Interests:
  Travel, reading, conventions, walking, all branches of the arts, psychic research.

Awards:
  World Fantasy Award, Best Short Fiction Work, 1973/74 (1975), "Pages from a Young Girl's Diary."

Aickman writes:
  "It seems to me that the ghost story has remained popular in Great Britain because more and more people are rejecting more and more of the alleged answers, in favour of leaving more and more of the questions open.
  "In that direction seems to me to lie the only hope for the world, however slim. There is a limit to the amount of knowledge upon which man thrives: the message of Goethe's *Faust*, and the secret of its continuing power."
  He adds: "I should have been born in 1850 or 1860."

* * * * *

JOAN AIKEN

Full Name: Joan Aiken.
  Born September 4, 1924, at Rye, Sussex, England. Daughter of Conrad Potter Aiken (an author and poet) and Jessie McDonald (Grande Dame). Married Ronald George Brown, July 7, 1945 (since deceased). Two children, John Sebastian, and Elizabeth Delano.

Education: Attended Wychwood School, Oxford, 1936-1941.

Career: Writer.
  Worked for the British Broadcasting Corporation, 1942-43; the United Nations Information Office, London, 1943-49; *Argosy*, 1955-60; J. Walter Thompson Advertising Agency, 1961; Full-time Writer, 1961-DATE.

Literary Agent: Brandt & Brandt, 101 Park Avenue, New York, NY 10017.

Awards:
  Guardian Award, 1969, for *The Whispering Mountain*; Runner-up for the Carnegie Award, 1969, for the same Book; Edgar Award (Mystery Writers of America), 1972, for *Night Fall*.

* * * * *

JOHN AIKEN

Full Name: John Kempton Aiken.
  Born October 10, 1913, at Cambridge, Massachusetts. Son of Conrad Potter Aiken (poet and novelist) and Jessie McDonald (Grande Dame). Married Paddy Street May 10, 1970. One daughter, Alison Mary Delano Leacock, born 1946.

Education: Ph.D. (Chemistry), University College, London, 1936.

Career: Patents Consultant; Information Analyst.
  Research Chemist, Paint Research Station, London, 1936-45; Development Manager, Geigy Company, Manchester 1945-64; Head of Laboratories, M. L. Alkan Ltd., London, 1964-66; Patents Manager, Humphreys & Glasgow Ltd. London, 1967-70.

JOHN AIKEN (cont.)

First Professional Sale:
"Dragon's Teeth," in *New Worlds* #3, 1946.

Literary Agent: Brandt & Brandt, 101 Park Avenue, New World, NY 10017.

Honors:
"The only award I really value is one for a "Probability Zero" entry back in the old *Astounding* days."

Avocations:
Music, chess, gardening, cats, jokes, booze.

Aiken adds:
"I was influenced toward a scientific career by my father, who felt that one poet in the family was enough; so I have only lately climbed aboard the literary wagon to accompany my sisters, Jane and Joan Aiken."

* * * * *

RUTH AINSWORTH

Full Name: Ruth Gallard Ainsworth Gilbert.
Born October 16, 1908, at Manchester, England. Daughter of Percy Clough Ainsworth (a Methodist minister) and Gertrude Fisk. Married Frank Lathe Gilbert (a managing director of a chemical works) March 29, 1935. Three children: Oliver Lathe, Christopher Gallard, Richard Frank.

Education: Attended Ipswich High School and Froebel Training Centre, Leicester, England.

Career: Writer, primarily of juvenile books.

Ainsworth has also written a number of plays and stories for the BBC.

* * * * *

BRIAN ALDISS

Full Name: Brian Wilson Aldiss.
Born August 18, 1925, at East Dereham, Norfolk, England. Son of Stanley Aldiss (an outfitter) and Elizabeth May Wilson (a housewife). Married (2) Margaret Christie Manson December 11, 1965. Four children: Clive (born 1955), Caroline Wendy (born 1959), Timothy Nicholas (born 1967), Charlotte May (born 1969).

Education:
Attended Framlingham College, Suffolk, 1936-39; West Buckland School, 1939-43.

Career: Writer.
Has been an outfitter, soldier, bookseller, art critic, film critic, and reviewer. Literary Editor, *Oxford Mail*, 1957-DATE. Editor, Penguin Science Fiction Series, 1961-64.

First Professional Sale:
"A Book in Time," in *The Bookseller*, February, 1954.
First Science Fiction Sale: "Criminal Record," in *Science Fantasy*, July, 1954.

Literary Agent: Hilary Rubinstein, A. P. Watt, 26/28 Bedford Row, London W.C.1, England.

Honors & Awards:
Guest of Honor, 23rd World Science Fiction Convention (Loncon II), 1965; Nebula Award, Best Novella, 1965 (1966), "The Saliva Tree"; Hugo Award, Best Short Fiction, 1961 (1962), The "Hothouse" Series; Special Plaque, 16th World Science Fiction Convention (Solacon) 1958, as the Most Promising New Author of the Year; British Science Fiction Association Award, Britain's Most Popular Author of Science Fiction, 1969; BSFA Award, 1972, for *The Moment of Eclipse*; Ditmar Award, World's Best Contemporary Science Fiction Author, 1970.

Member:
Science Fiction Writers of America; Society of Authors; British Science Fiction Association (President, 1961-65).

Interests: Writing, travelling, swimming, thinking, painting.

Aldiss was also co-Editor of *SF Horizons*, one of the first serious nonfiction journals devoted to the field; he has been co-Editor (with Harry Harrison) of the *Best SF* annuals since 1966.

Aldiss talks about science fiction:
"Since SF is the sum of the writings of a great many individuals (I can name thirty without trouble in Great Britain alone), it makes more sense to talk about individual writers. Science fiction may be awful at any given period, but one writer may be brilliant enough to compensate for all the rest--like the English theatre in the time of George Bernard Shaw.
"So let me speak up for my own country, and not produce a distorted echo of yours. The feeling over here is extremely creative; I believe the activity is minor on the whole, but that does not necessarily make it less stimulating. Among a number of speculative and science-fictional writers whom I admire are Pamela Zoline, David Masson, Charles Platt, Langdon Jones, and John Sladek. Two of these, you will note, are American. I would certainly add another American, Tom Disch, were he still over here. Cross-fertilization has been going on--and the flower that has attracted the young Americans is *New Worlds*, edited by the legendary but by no means mythical Mike Moorcock.
"The writers I name are noted more for quality than quantity. Of the better-established authors, I need say nothing (Arthur Clarke can speak for himself!). But it is also worth nothing that cross-fertilization has been proceeding in other directions--with several artists, such as Richard Hamilton and Paolozzi, who enjoy reading SF and plough their imagery back into the field; and with several poets, such as D. M. Thomas, Bill Butler, Peter Redgrove, and Robert Conquest.
"The benefits of this cross-fertilization are, I believe, apparent. SF has long been guilty of ancestor-worship; now everyone is looking outwards and forwards instead. A different sort of writing is emerging, which lives in the present-future interface--an evaluative species of fiction more related to movements in the other arts than to the pulp traditions on which the old SF is based. I know that some people find this makes this sort of writing hard to understand; but this is generally because they are more familiar with the pulps; for anyone unfamiliar with the pulps, the conventions there are hard to understand.

BRIAN ALDISS (cont.)

"The only writers whose work means a great deal to me nowadays (once it was otherwise) are Philip K. Dick for his subtilty, my buddy Harry Harrison for his vigor, Vonnegut for his irony, and some of the short stories of J. G. Ballard--oh, and people who are capable of being absolutely outrageous with a straight face, like Alfie Bester, Fred Pohl, William Tenn, and Charles Harness, on occasions. I have an abiding admiration for H. G. Wells, especially his excellently dark *The Island of Dr. Moreau*.

"As for my own role, that's not an easy question for a fairly modest man to answer! But I'll say again--I believe only in the work of individual writers, not in SF as a whole: in the chaps in the corporation, not the corporation itself. And I have always stood for individual work--which is perhaps why I once had a reputation for being obscure; there's little help for anyone, in life or letters, unless he finds and is himself. Fashion is a distraction: yet permanence must move with the times. I have always attempted to write my own thing, and have been helped in this by being as conscious of the general cultural heritage as of the specifically science-fictional one.

"When I began writing SF stories, I was told they were just not SF: presumably because I did not load in technology like an exoskeleton round my characters. Now nobody worries (much, anyway); and perhaps I have softened things up in this way. Perhaps I'm still doing it. I really do not know if my anti-novel, *Report on Probability A*, is also SF, or if my undoubtedly best novel, *Barefoot in the Head*, is also SF; nor do I care; that sort of minute pigeon-holing is for publishers' minds. I'd like to think that my general policy of non-violence was also catching on a bit.

"As an editor, I have been instrumental in securing better payments for authors, and have helped familiarise the general reading public with good SF writers. My Penguin series, for example, brought several unfamiliar American names forward to the British public. I have twice been instrumental in helping Moorcock's *New Worlds* through a crisis, as well as maintaining a fair level of criticism over a number of years.

"This begins to sound like a politician's speech! Well, I believe more and more in the arts of diplomacy. I live, think, and breathe writing, and hate the petty bickering and self-advertisement that writers get up to. Fortunately, in writing one escapes all that: the act of writing is a form of possession, a visionary state that at the moment of involvement has little reference to others.

"As to where SF is going, again, one can only speak of individuals, and I can't see how one writer should presume to speak for others. Some chaps will turn into old hacks, some chaps are hacks, some chaps will stop writing, some will go round the twist, and so on. But SF isn't an army of starship troopers marching on to glory or ignominy; it's just individuals. I don't suffer from the Anxious Ownership Syndrome towards SF that afflicts many of the field's eager beavers.

"Nor do I exactly foresee where I am going personally, though I have all the usual private and stereotyped dreams of success to warm me when my typewriter feels cold. I count success not only in cash terms. At present, my writing is greatly intensifying and gathering strength, and--barring accidents!--nothing can stop me developing. In general terms, I shall continue to explore the human design in times of change. We shall never run out of change!"

MARGARET ALDISS

Full Name: Margaret Christie Aldiss.
  Born May 23, 1933, at Maidstone, Kent, England. Daughter of John Alexander Christie Manson (an aeronautical engineer) and Bethia Robertson Moir (a housewife). Married Brian Wilson Aldiss December 11, 1965. Two children: Timothy Nicholas (born 1967), Charlotte May (born 1969).

Education: Attended Queen Anne's School, Caversham, 1946-51.

Career: Housewife.
  Secretary, Administrative Dept., Royal Opera, Covent Garden, 1954-57; Secretary to the Editor, *Oxford Mail*, 1958-66.

Margaret Aldiss has published two excellent bibliographies of her husband's work, *Item 43*, and the revised edition, *Item 83*.

* * * * *

HOLMES ALEXANDER

Full Name: Holmes Moss Alexander.
  Born January 29, 1906, at Parkersburg, West Virginia. Son of Charles Butler Alexander (an insurance official) and Margaret Moss. Married Mary Barksdale (a schoolteacher) June 24, 1933. Three children: Hunter Holmes, Peter Barksdale, Mary Madge Dufour.

Education:
  B.A., Princeton University, 1928; student at Trinity College, Cambridge University, 1928-29.

Career: Writer.
  English Teacher & Wrestling Coach, McDonogh School, McDonogh, Maryland, 1929-31; Democratic member, Maryland House of Delegates, 1931-35; Free-lance Writer, 1935-DATE; Syndicated political columnist, McNaught Syndicate, 1947-DATE; contributer to various magazines and newspapers. Served in the US Army Air Force from 1942-45.

Honors:
  Litt.D., Salem College, 1971; Freedom Foundation at Valley Forge honor medal, 1973.

Member:
  Overseas Writers Association; Sigma Delta Chi; Society of Lees of Virginia; Society of the Cincinnati; 1925 F Street Club; National Press Club; Metropolitan Club, Washington.

* * * * *

LLOYD ALEXANDER

Full Name: Lloyd Chudley Alexander.
  Born January 30, 1924, at Philadelphia, Pennsylvania. Son of Alan Audley Alexander (an office manager) and Edna Chudley (a housewife). Married Janine Denni in Paris on January 8, 1946. One adopted daughter, Madeleine Khalil (born 1936).

Education: Attended West Chester State, 1941; Lafayette College, 1943; University of Paris, 1946.

LLOYD ALEXANDER (cont.)

Career: Author.

First Professional Sale: *And Let the Credit Go*, T. Y. Crowell Company, 1955.

Awards:
Newbery Medal, 1969, for *The High King*; National Book Award for Best Children's Book of the Year, 1971, for *The Marvelous Misadventures of Sebastien*.

Member: Authors' League of America; P.E.N.

Interests: Violin playing; printmaking.

Alexander talks about Prydain:
"Although I've always been interested in mythology, the Arthurian legend, etc., I suppose what triggered the Chronicles was some of the research I had begun doing in preparation for *Time Cat*, which led me to the history and legends of Wales. At the time, I foresaw only two books, perhaps three at most. But, as the work went on, I grew so immersed and involved, and the books began to take on such personal meanings for me, that the project seemed to grow of itself until it reached five volumes."

* * * * *

MEA ALLAN

Full Name: Mea Allan.
Born June 23, 1909, at Bearsden, Dumbartonshire, Scotland. Daughter of Robert Greenoak Allen and Helen Maitland.

Education: Attended Park School, Glasgow, and Central School of Speech Training and Dramatic Art.

Career: Writer.
Sub-Editor for various Scottish trade journals, 1926-28; editorial writer for Scottish Films Ltd., 1933-35; Sub-Editor of a magazine group, 1938; reporter for the *Sunday Referee*, 1939; reporter for the *Daily Herald*, 1939-48; gossip columnist for the *Lowestoft Journal*, 1948-51; free-lance writer. Allan was the first woman war correspondent permanently accredited to the British Army (in 1944).

Honors: Leverhulme Research Fellow, 1965.

* * * * *

DICK ALLEN

Full Name: Richard Stanley Allen.
Born August 8, 1939, at Troy, New York. Son of Richard Sanders Allen (a writer and historian) and Doris Bishop (a postmaster). Married Lori Negridge, August 13, 1960. Two children: Richard Negridge (born 1963); Tanya Angell (born 1971).

Education:
A.B., College of Liberal Arts, Syracuse University, 1961; M.A., Brown University Graduate School, 1964; two years of post-Masters work.

Career: Professor, writer, poet.
Teaching Assistant, Brown University, 1962-64; Instructor of Creative Writing and American Literature, Wright State University, 1964-68; Assistant Professor of Creative Writing and American Literature, University of Bridgeport, 1968-72; Director of Creative Writing and Associate Professor, University of Bridgeport, 1972-DATE. Editor-in-Chief, *The Mad River Review*, 1966-68; Contributing Editor, *The American Poetry Review*, 1972-DATE; member of the faculty of the Indiana University Writers Conference, in 1967 and 1968.

First Professional Sale: "Death of Adam," in *New York Herald Tribune*, 1961.

Honors and Awards:
A.D.E.-M.L.A. Award for Distinguished Teaching; Academy of American Poets Prize (Brown University); Hart Crane Memorial Poetry Fellowship; Union League Arts and Civic Foundation Prize for Poetry; Robert Frost Poetry Fellowship.

Member:
Modern Language Association; Science Fiction Research Association; World Future Society; MLA Conference on Science Fiction; American Civil Liberties Union; American Association of University Professors.

Avocations:
All aspects of pop culture; mass media; Americana; astronomy; long-distance swimming; research in contemporary ethics.

Allen writes:
"I guess I'm about the only 'recognized' poet, in this country at least, to revel in being called an SF writer. My first submission to a national publication, written when I was eleven, was a one-pager about two space travelers being marooned on Earth. Of course, at the end of the story they turn toward each other, and one says, 'Isn't that right, Adam?' And the other replies, 'Yes, Eve.'
"My first published poem dealt with the last-man-on-Earth theme. Most of my poetry, including *Anon and Various Time Machine Poems*, is of the fantasy and SF variety. I've written poems about hyperspace, tachyons, time machines, black holes and white holes, witches, robots, cyborgs, photo-copy machines, etc., etc. For the past five years I've been writing *The Space Sonnets*, a giant narrative sonnet-sequence which takes place outside America, in the Future, at a place called the 'Space Monastery.' There is a huge telescope, a broken time machine, marijuana fields out in back of the monastery. The sequence is actually extremely 'serious,' though: an entire poetic study of the concept of 'The Future'--from the time of Robert Kennedy's murder until the total doom of the universe, as predicted by St. John and Olaf Stapledon.
"I've been an SF 'fan' since I was eight. I remember vividly how, in a tenth grade Latin class, I predicted man would send up satellites to circle the Earth by 1957. Lennie Brown led the rest of the class, teacher agreeing with him, in laughing: 'Impossible. Gravity would pull them down.'
"When the Russians sent up Sputnik in 1957, I resolved to devote my life's writing to exploring the meanings of the coming Space Ages. In 1966, I attended a Modern Language Association Seminar on SF, looked around, and missed the presence of *young* academic types interested in the genre. There didn't, at that time, seem to be anybody but me. So, what the hell. I began to plan an SF anthology so 'safe' and yet exciting that it could get past reluctant English Department Chairmen,

DICK ALLEN (cont.)

"and allow SF to be taught on the college level. William Pullin, at HBJ, although nervous about publishing a book with a risky market, did take the chance. Hey, it seems to have paid off, the first anthology has been successful, and there are about thirty other SF teaching anthologies on the textbook lists at the time I'm writing this.

"About the same time, by the way, I addressed the New England College English Association on the necessity of SF courses in the college and university curriculums, and wrote an article on serious SF for the *Yale Alumni Magazine*. The article seems to have motivated the *Time* essay on SF which made the genre 'official'--in terms of literary importance--as well as influenced the *New Yorker* into doing an extensive article on SF.

"My major struggle in these past years has been to wear three hats at once--as a full-time college professor, as a poet in the 'traditional' sense, as a science fiction/futurism 'authority.' I work 15-17 hours a day, seven days a week. I smoke a lot, drink a lot, sometimes my hands shake, but I really wouldn't wish to do anything less, be anywhere else, as a writer, than in this amazing, terrible, surrealistic *fin de siècle*."

* * * * *

L. DAVID ALLEN

Full Name: Louis David Allen.
    Born January 24, 1940, at Bemidji, Minnesota. Son of Louis E. Allen (a superintendent of schools) and Irene Simons (a teacher). Married Patricia M. Anderson, March 4, 1961. Two children: Colin David (born 1961); Siobhan Patricia (born 1965).

Education:
    Attended Concordia College, 1958-60; B.S., Moorhead State College, 1960-61; M.A., Bowling Green State University, 1964; Ph.D. candidate, University of Nebraska.

Career: Instructor of English.
    Teacher, Dassel Public Schools, Dassel, Minnesota, 1961-64; Assistant Professor of English, Wayne State College, 1964-69; Instructor in English, University of Nebraska, 1969-DATE.

First Professional Sale: *Science Fiction: An Introduction*, Cliff's Notes, 1973.

Member: Science Fiction Research Association.

Allen notes:
    "Although I remember reading science fiction in high school--our school library had only the worst of space opera at the time--and periodically and in spurts for many years, it was only about seven years ago that I started reading SF extensively and seriously. Since then I've tried to make up for lost time. It seems to me that SF is one of the most viable literary forms going, and I'm interested in what makes it so."

* * * * *

JOHANNES ALLEN

Full Name: Johannes Allen.
    Born May 16, 1916, at Copenhagen, Denmark. Son of Poul Allen and Karen Schleisner. Married Lise Leutzen, December 12, 1941.

Education: Graduate, Oestersoegades Gymnasium, 1935.

Career: Writer.
    Journalist with *Berlingske Tidende*, Copenhagen, 1937-45; writer for *Politiken*, Copenhagen, 1945-49; consultant to Danish television, 1965-DATE; free-lance author.

Literary Agent: Kurt Michaels, Charlottenlund DK-2920, Denmark.

Awards:
    Antonius Prize of Danish Society for Mental Hygiene, 1951, for the film "Cafe Paradize." Member: Danish Journalists' Union; Danish Writers' Association (Member of Board, 1966-70).

* * * * *

M. C. ALLEN

Full Name: Marion C. Allen.
    Born December 12, 1914, at Spartanburg, South Carolina. Son of Albert Mayfield Allen and Caroline Mae Rogers. Married Eleanor Earl Burt (a music teacher), July 31, 1943. Four children: Marian Carol, Burt Mayfield, Robert William, Mary Louise.

Education:
    A.B., Furman University, 1937; B.D., Yale University, 1940; M.A., University of Kansas, 1960; graduate study at Hartford Seminary Foundation.

Career: Teacher and minister.
    Baptist minister in Bristol, Connecticut, 1940-47; in Beaufort, South Carolina, 1947-50; in Clemson, South Carolina, 1950-56; Instructor in Religion, Clemson College, 1952-56; Minister, First Baptist Church, Lawrence, Kansas, 1956-DATE; Teacher of English, University of Kansas, 1958-61; Research Assistant in Modern American Drama, University of Kansas, 1962-DATE. President, Lawrence Council of Churches, 1960-63.

Member: Pi Gamma Mu; Masons; Lions Club; Hand and Torch.

* * * * *

MARGERY ALLINGHAM

Full Name: Margery Louise Allingham.
    Born May 20, 1904, at London, England. Daughter of Herbert John Allingham (a writer) and Emily Jane Hughes. Married Philip Youngman Carter (an artist, and former Editor of the *Tatler*), 1927.

Education: Attended Perse High School for Girls, Cambridge, England.

Career: Author; her first published novel, *Blackkerchief Dick*, was published when she was sixteen.

Allingham is best known for her series of detective novels and stories featuring Mr. Campion, who appeared in twenty books before her death, on June 30, 1966. The series has since been continued by Philip Carter, who collaborated with his wife on many of the stories, and completed a novel left unfinished by her untimely demise.

ROBERT EDMOND ALTER

Full Name: Robert Edmond Alter.
   Born December 10, 1925, at San Francisco, California. Son of Retla Alter and Irene Kerr. Married Maxine Louise Outwater, 1947. One daughter, Sande.

Education: Studied at University of Southern California, 1944, and Pasadena City College, 1946.

Career: Post Office Worker; Writer.
   Migratory worker in Santa Paula, 1942; stock boy for Vroman's Books, Pasadena, 1943-44; farm hand in Hamilton, North Dakota, 1945; carrier, U.S. Post Office, Altadena, California, 1949-62; free-lance writer, 1962-66.

Interests: Skindiving, history, book collecting.

Alter died in Los Angeles on May 26, 1965. A month earlier, he had written his friend and agent Larry Sternig: "I have received the final word. It is malignancy...well rooted in my pelvis, and in order to get it out they have to remove the entire left hip and of course the left leg...They say I have a good 'fighting' chance...I sent Tom [his editor] the rough draft on *First Comes Courage*...I could use some...If I can live and write, then that is just what I shall do." Two days later, in a letter to Carl Rathjen, he wrote: "This is the dark moment... for a quarter of a century now I have been fascinated by the fearful realization that eventually I would have to face the moment of truth...I wrote so many characters in and out of their dark moments...it gives me an obligation to pay back in spirit some part of the courage that I created in print...It is as if I belonged to a large band of brothers...each of them in the end able to face his fate mutely and with a sense of dignity. I am not alone. I am part of a vast brotherhood...." [courtesy of Larry Sternig]

* * * * *

RALPH J. AMELIO

Full Name: Ralph J. Amelio.
   Born January 26, 1939, at Chicago, Illinois. Son of Ernest F. Amelio (a shoemaker) and Carmella Pullano. Married Dorothy Dabrowski (a teacher), June 28, 1964. Two children, Ralph Christopher, and Victoria Ann.

Education: B.S., Loyola University, 1961; M.A., 1964; graduate study at University of Chicago.

Career: Teacher.
   Instructor in English, Willowbrook High School, Villa Park, Illinois, 1961-DATE; Instructor in Film, Wright College, 1971-DATE; film consultant and lecturer.

Member:
   Screen Educators' Society (member of executive board); American Federation of Film Societies; University Film Association; American Film Institute; Illinois Association of Teachers of English.

Amelio has also served as Media Editor for *See Magazine*, and has edited a number of texts and studies on films for educators.

KINGSLEY AMIS

Full Name: Kingsley William Amis.
   Born April 16, 1922, at London, England. Son of William Robert Amis (an office clerk) and Rosa Annie Lucas. Married Hilary Ann Bardwell, 1948 (div. 1965); married Elizabeth Jane Howard (a writer), 1965. Three children: Philip Nicol William, Martin Louis, Sally Myfanwy.

Education:
   B.A., St. John's College, Oxford University, 1947; M.A., Oxford University, 1948; M.A., Cambridge University, 1961.

Career: Writer and teacher.
   Lecturer in English, University College of Swansea, 1949-61; Fellow, Peterhouse, Cambridge University, 1961-63; Full-time writer, 1963-DATE. Visiting Fellow in Creative Writing, Princeton University, 1958; Visiting Professor of English, Vanderbilt University, 1967-68.

Awards: Somerset Maugham Award, 1955, for *Lucky Jim*.

Interests: SF, crime and detective fiction, jazz.

* * * * *

ADRIENNE ANDERSON

Full Name: Adrienne Wynne Barton Anderson.
   Born at Ramsey, Huntingdonshire, England. Daughter of the Rev. F. Barton Horspool (a minister for the Church of England) and Ada Florence Wynne (a pianist). Married Sydney Geddie Anderson (an Assistant Administrator of the Ottawa Civic Hospital), April 24, 1949 in Baghdad.

Education: Educated at various private boarding schools in England.

Career: Nurse.
   "Nursing training at St. Mary's Hospital, Paddington, London, which I had to give up on doctor's orders. After my health improved, I took posts in various schools in England as Matron in charge of health, caring for young children, etc. Later worked as a receptionist in hotels. After the outbreak of World War II in 1939, I obtained an office post in a branch of the War Office. In 1948, I was posted to Baghdad, with the Royal Air Force, where I met my husband."

First Professional Sale:
   "Various poems, articles, and short stories published by several British magazines and publications, from around the year 1925."

Member:
   Canadian Authors Association (Vice President, Ottawa Branch); Inter-denominational Fellowship of Prayer.

Avocations: "A continuing avid interest in life in all its myriad facets, and a driving ambition to learn more about people and things."

Anderson adds: "Before marriage, I changed the locale of my jobs, and switched occupations to obtain local color and experience for my fiction writing. My ambition was always to write novels."

POUL ANDERSON

Full Name: Poul William Anderson.
    Born November 25, 1926, at Bristol, Pennsylvania.
Son of Anton William Anderson (an engineer) and
Astrid Hertz (a librarian). Married Karen June Mil-
lichamp Kruse, 1953. One daughter, Astrid May (born
1954).

Education: B.S., University of Minnesota, 1948.

Career: Writer since 1948.

First Professional Sale: "Tomorrow's Children,"
    in Astounding, March, 1947 (with F. N. Waldrop).

Agent: Scott Meredith, 580 Fifth Avenue, New York,
    NY 10036.

Honors & Awards:
    Guest of Honor, 17th World Science Fiction Conven-
tion (Detention), Detroit, 1959; Nebula Award, Best
Novelette, 1971 (1972), "The Queen of Air and Dark-
ness"; Nebula Award, Best Novelette, 1972 (1973),
"Goat Song"; Hugo Award, Best Short Story, 1960 (1961)
"The Longest Voyage"; Hugo Award, Best Short Fiction,
1963 (1964), "No Truce with Kings"; Hugo Award, Best
Novelette, 1968 (1969), "The Sharing of Flesh"; Hugo
Award, Best Novella, 1971 (1972), "The Queen of Air
and Darkness"; Hugo Award, Best Novelette, 1972 (1973)
"Goat Song"; Macmillan Cock Robin Award for Best
Mystery Novel published by Macmillan in 1959, for
Perish by the Sword; winner of the "Forry" Award of
the Los Angeles Science Fantasy Society; winner of
two Morley-Montgomery prizes for best Sherlock
Holmes scholarship of the year; Knighthood of Mark
Twain; honored by a special issue of The Magazine
of Fantasy and Science Fiction, April, 1971.

Member:
    Science Fiction Writers of America (President, 1972-
1973); Baker Street Irregulars; Mystery Writers of
America; Society for Creative Anachronism, Inc.;
Authors League; American Association for the Advance-
ment of Science; Elves, Gnomes, and Little Men's
Science Fiction, Chowder, and Marching Society.

A Future History, by Poul Anderson:
    "This scheme does not include all my science fiction
stories by any means, nor is it the only set of my
stories which fit together more or less in a single
'history.' However, by now it is the largest such
corpus.
    "In general outline, it presupposes that humankind
will survive its present troubles and, for a while,
enjoy a better day. Earth (and eventually its colo-
nies elsewhere in the Solar System) got a federal
union of nations, the Commonwealth, which gradually
became stronger and more centralized as far as its
own jurisdiction was concerned. Partly because
several of the English-speaking nations continued
particularly influential through the early stages,
and partly because English was, even by the mid-20th
century, the most widely known language of all, this
tongue was the leading one in the Commonwealth (somewhat as Latin was in the western Mediterranean world
and Greek in the eastern, in Classical times). However, peoples remained so diverse and changeable--
what they had in common and what tended to influence
every aspect of their societies was technology--that
that set of institutions and practices was in time
best described as being a whole new civilization, the

Technic, affiliated to but not identical with its Western predecessor.
    "In its vigorous youth, liberated from many old bur-
dens such as war, Technic civilization not only returned to space on a large scale, but made some
astonishing discoveries. Revision of physical theory
opened the way for interstellar travel at pseudospeeds
in excess of light velocity; enormous strides were
made in fields such as gravitics, atomistics, and cy-
bernetics; complex machines and the energy to run them
became comparatively cheap. Thus one person could have
at his fingertips not only the power, but the control
which would formerly have required a large organization
and vast amounts of capital.
    "Early space exploration was explosively expensive,
motivated chiefly by scientific curiosity and a certain
idealism. Interaction with nonhuman cultures stimu-
lated an intellectually and artistically brilliant era.
Individualism burgeoned; elbow room and enormous resources led both to colonization wherever this was possible, and to laissez-faire capitalism. In time, the
companies formed the Polesotechnic League, originally
a voluntary organization for mutual benefit.
    "However, competition tended to grow more and more
cutthroat. And, operating as they did on an interstellar scale and without much restraint, the merchant
princes were often more powerful even as individuals
than any single government. Eventually, through bri-
bery and other means, they were making the Commonwealth
itself their creature and booty. This by itself might
have been correctible, or at least endurable, as long
as the companies remained in free competition with each
other. But more and more, the League degenerated into
a set of cartels. The decision finally to 'establish
internal order,' which in practice meant creating a
super-cartel, can be considered the breakdown point of
Technic civilization.
    "Nicholas van Rijn's career spanned this point.
Breakdowns do not mean immediate chaos (in fact, their
first effect may be to release energies hitherto bound
by tradition, and thus foster a wave of creativity; the
Italian Renaissance is a good example). For most of
his life, he himself was able to operate pretty much as
he wanted. But toward the end, he saw the handwriting
on the wall. Likewise did his protege David Falkayn,
who married a granddaughter of van Rijn, and, late in
life, founded a colony on Avalon, within a sphere belonging to a wholly different and still healthy civilization, that of the nonhuman Ythrians.
    "Within the Technic ambience, strife led increasingly
to chaos. This in turn invited attacks from outside,
especially by various barbarians who had acquired--from
unscrupulous traders--the means of waging modern war.
For a while, Earth itself was the prey of raiders.
Civilized planet dwellers, whether human or nonhuman,
had little to help them survive this Time of Troubles,
except what resources they could muster by themselves.
That fact often forced the growth of a sense of being
independent societies.
    "A human adventurer turned warlord finally succeeded
in unifying a number of systems, giving them rough justice, internal peace, and protection from outsiders.
He went down in history as Manuel the Great, and his
descendants were the first ruling dynasty of the Terran
Empire. It expanded rapidly, mostly by happenstance
rather than design. For example, it seemed wisest to
stay in control of any troublemakers who had been defeated, incorporating them into the Imperial structure.
More often than not, in its earlier phase, the Empire
was welcomed, with governments applying for admission.
    "It was never highly centralized. That would have
been simply impossible. 'Greater Terra' incorporated

POUL ANDERSON (cont.)

the Solar System and certain favored planets elsewhere, whose inhabitants were born to Terran citizenship. Individuals from other worlds might be granted
this as a boon or reward. Otherwise, each inhabited
world had its own special relationship to the Imperium, arising from historical circumstances. It might
only pay a small tribute; indeed, it might not even
do this, and might never be visited by any official.
Or, if more important, it might both contribute and
receive more.

"Imperial governors, backed by units of the Imperial Navy, were responsible for maintaining the Pax in
their various sectors; they had their own sub-gover-
nors, commissioners, etc., as they saw fit. For
inevitably, at a distance from Sol, each such authority had nearly supreme power, to the extent that he
could and would exercise it. The sheer flow of information made centralization impossible; no data systems
could handle it.

"This in turn led to obvious temptations, as well
as obvious suspicions on the part of the Imperium.
Abuses and frictions gradually worsened; the Terran
Empire, the universal state of Technic civilization,
followed the same downward course as many another
universal state in the past.

"It did not exist in a vacuum. Technic man had
never been able to keep track of what was going on
beyond a radius of a few hundred light-years; that
range, tiny on a galactic scale, was inconceivably
huge on the scale of mortal beings, holding millions
of planets, each one an entire world to itself. But
even within this limit, several powerful nonhuman
civilizations had arisen--or had long been present
when man entered space. The inhabitants of giant hy-
drogen-atmosphere planets, such as the Ymirites,
interpenetrated with oxygen breathers; but the differences were so great that there was little contact.
Closer relationships occurred with independent races
like the Ythrians and the Merseians.

"The Merseians in particular became the great ri-
vals of Terra. In former times, the League had saved
them from the lethal effects of a nearby supernova--
but at a high price, humiliating to a proud people.
Driven by an internal logic of their own history, the
Merseians unified under the Roidhun (more a religious
than a secular head), and acquired a sizeable stellar
domain of their own. This presently brought them into conflict with the Terran Empire, whose leaders saw
that it could not afford to let such an aggressive and
ambitious polity grown stronger. But the Empire itself was by now weak, corrupt, divided, beginning to
be shaken by revolt. In that period, Dominic Flandry
was active.

"This is as far as I have brought the continuous
narrative to date. In fact, 'continuous' is hardly
the word, since large gaps remain to fill in, e.g.,
details of the Breakdown of the League and the en-
suing Time of Troubles.

"Basically, though, the scheme is that, while the
Empire makes a recovery for a while, the cost is un-
bearably high (divine autocracy and the like), and
after another couple of centuries it disintegrates
forever. But meanwhile it has worn down Merseia.
Neither race wins; once again, throughout the regions
they controlled, chaos descends--this time, the Long
Night, when both civilizations are dead, though their
ghosts haunt the minds of survivors.

"However, on the far outskirts, and even in en-
claves closer in, new cultures both human and nonhuman have grown up. Though they suffer from the

physical and economic effects of the collapse, they do
not share it spiritually; and it might even be said
that the fall of Empire and Roidhunate sets them free
to grow. A few stories have been published which take
place in this era.

"And throughout history, from time to time various
groups have had occasion to migrate so far that they
completely lost contact with the parent worlds. Some
humans even got into the next arm of the galaxy; and
after thousands of years, some of their descendants
evolved a social order which (perhaps) embodied the
freedom of the League without its potential for cor-
ruption.

"Meanwhile, of course, back in the old regions, new
societies have also appeared. What they are like, I
don't yet know.

"I wish to emphasize that this whole scheme is nothing but a framework for telling stories. I do not
for one instant believe that anything like it will ever
actually come to pass.

"Herewith a list of stories to date which can be
considered to belong to it. I regret that time does
not permit me to arrange them in any order except the
roughly alphabetical one of my notebook:

"A CIRCUS OF HELLS, A MESSAGE IN SECRET, A SUN INVI-
SIBLE, A TWELVEMONTH AND A DAY [aka LET THE SPACEMEN
BEWARE], A TRAGEDY OF ERRORS, [AN] OUTPOST OF EMPIRE,
A LITTLE KNOWLEDGE, A KNIGHT OF GHOSTS AND SHADOWS,
COLLAR OF IRON [published as THE STAR PLUNDERER], ESAU
[published as BIRTHRIGHT], ENSIGN FLANDRY, HIDING PLACE,
HONORABLE ENEMIES, HUNTERS OF THE SKY CAVE [aka A HAND-
FUL OF STARS], HOW TO BE ETHNIC, LODESTAR, MARGIN OF
PROFIT, RESCUE ON AVALON, SUPERNOVA [aka DAY OF BUR-
NING], STARFOG, SATAN'S WORLD, TERRITORY, THE THREE-
CORNERED WHEEL, TIGER BY THE TAIL, THE WARRIORS FROM
NOWHERE, THE GAME OF GLORY, THE MAN WHO COUNTS [aka
WAR OF THE WING-MEN], THE MASTER KEY, THE TROUBLE TWIS-
TERS, THE [A] PLAGUE OF MASTERS, THE REBEL WORLDS, THE
SHARING OF FLESH [aka THE DIPTEROID PHENOMENON], THE
PEOPLE OF THE WIND, THE PROBLEM OF PAIN, THE SEASON OF
FORGIVENESS, THE DAY OF THEIR RETURN, WINGS OF VICTORY,
WINGLESS [ON AVALON].

"Of these, I do have a chronological listing of the
Flandry stories: ENSIGN FLANDRY, A CIRCUS OF HELLS,
THE REBEL WORLDS, TIGER BY THE TAIL, HONORABLE ENEMIES,
THE GAME OF GLORY, A MESSAGE IN SECRET, A PLAGUE OF
MASTERS, A HANDFUL OF STARS, THE WARRIORS FROM NOWHERE,
and A KNIGHT OF GHOSTS AND SHADOWS."

* * * * *

WILLIAM C. ANDERSON

Full Name: William Charles Anderson.
   Born May 7, 1920, at La Junta, Colorado. Son of
Robert Smith Anderson and Fanny Holly. Married Wilma
Y. Duncan, August 17, 1941; Married Dortha Marie Power
July 10, 1948. Three children: Ann Drue Kiessling
(born 1942), Scott (born 1951), Holly (born 1952).

Education: Attended Boise Junior College, 1939; Fort
   Hays College, 1942; University of Maryland, 1948.

Career: Pilot and writer.
   Officer, U.S. Air Force, 1942-64 (retired with rank
of Lieutenant Colonel); Writer, 1964-DATE.

First Professional Sale: *Five, Four, Three, Two,
   One--Pfftt*, Ace Books, 1960.

Literary Agent: William Morris Agency, 1350 Avenue

WILLIAM C. ANDERSON (cont.)

of the Americas, New York, NY 10019.

Honors & Awards:
Knight of Mark Twain, for *The Headstrong Houseboat*. "Most rewarding honor was having *Penelope* and *Adam M-1* reproduced in Braille and tapes for the blind."

Interests:
Flying, bowling, boating, cycling, trailering, swimming, billiards, and beautiful women.

Anderson has written various screenplays, ranging from Disney productions to "Hurricane," an ABC Movie of the Week based upon *Hurricane Hunters*. He adds: "Although I love science fiction, particularly humorous, I have found it the least successful commercially of any of my books. Fantasy, particularly, is a rough commodity to sell in this day and age. It will be a great day when it comes back into the picture."

* * * * *

ENRIQUE ANDERSON IMBERT

Full Name: Enrique Anderson Imbert.
Born February 12, 1910, in Argentina. Son of José Enrique Anderson and Honorina Imbert. Married Margot Di Clerico (a librarian), March 30, 1935. Two children: Carlos, Anabel Himelblau.

Education: Ph.D., National University of Buenos Aires, 1946.

Career: Instructor in Spanish literature.
Professor of Spanish literature, Universidad de Tucuman, 1940-47; Assistant Professor, University of Michigan, Ann Arbor, 1947-48; Associate Professor, 1948-51; Professor, 1951-65; Professor of Hispanic American Literature, Harvard University, 1965-DATE.

Honors: Buenos Aires City Hall literary prize, 1934, for *Vigilia*; Guggenheim Fellowship, 1954-55.

Member:
American Academy of Arts and Sciences; Instituto Internacional de Literatura Iberoamericana.

* * * * *

F. EMERSON ANDREWS

Full Name: Frank Emerson Andrews.
Born January 26, 1902, at Lancaster, Pennsylvania. Son of Harry Andrews and Ellen Wiggins. Married Edith Lilian Severance, July 5, 1932. Three children: Frank M., Peter Bruce, Bryant.

Education: B.A., Franklin and Marshall College, 1923.

Career: Foundation Director.
Manager of advertising printing, Macmillan Co., New York, 1923-28; Director of Publications, Russell Sage Foundation, 1928-56; Director of Philanthropic Research, 1944-56; Director, Foundation Library Center, New York, 1956-64; President, 1964-DATE. Sometime consultant to various foundations.

Honors: First Annual Award, Duodecimal Society; Hon. L.H.D., Franklin and Marshall College, 1952.

Member:
Duodecimal Society of America (President, 1944-50; Chairman of the Board, 1950-64); American Institute of Graphic Arts (Director); Phi Beta Kappa; Authors League of America; National Conference on Social Welfare.

* * * * *

J. S. ANDREWS

Full Name: James Sydney Andrews.
Born December 14, 1934, at Belfast, Northern Ireland. Son of David Andrews (a company director) and Helene L. Baud. Married Judith Ann McCartan, June 1, 1962. Three children: Rona Mary, Susan Helene, Eileen Pamela.

Education: Attended Rossall School, Fleetwood, Lancashire, England.

Career: Company Director.
Director, Isaac Andrews & Sons Ltd. (millers), and various associated companies, Belfast, N. Ireland.

Member:
Society of Authors, Ulster Archaeological Society, Friends of the Ulster Museum, Royal North of Ireland Yacht Club, Amateur Yacht Research Society, Clyde Cruising Club.

* * * * *

CHARLES ANGOFF

Full Name: Charles Angoff.
Born April 22, 1902, at Minsk, Russia. Son of Jacob Joseph Angoff and Anna Pollack. Brought to the US 1908, and naturalized, 1923. Married Sara F. Freedman June 13, 1943. One daughter, Nancy Carol.

Education: A.B., Harvard University, 1923.

Career: Editor and Teacher.
Reporter, *American Mercury*, 1923; Member of editorial staff, 1925-31; Managing Editor, 1931-34, 1943-50; Editor, 1934-35; on board of editors, *Nation*, 1935; Editor of *American Spectator*, 1935-36; Contributing Editor, *North American Review*, 1938-40; Executive Editor, Mercury Publications, 1950-51; Adjunct Professor of English, Wagner College, 1956; Professor of English, Fairleigh Dickinson University, 1957-DATE; Co-Editor, *Literary Review*, 1957-DATE; Adjunct Professor of Literature, New York University, 1958-66; Chairman of the Department of Humanities, 1966-DATE; Research Director, "Meet the Press," 1945-55.

Honors and Awards:
Daroff Memorial Fiction Award for best Jewish novel of 1954, for *In the Morning Light*; special Charles Angoff Collection established at Boston University Library, 1964; Litt.D., Fairleigh Dickinson University, 1966.

Member:
Poetry Society of America, Authors League, International P.E.N.

Angoff has had several plays produced in New York.

PIERS ANTHONY

Full Name: Piers Anthony Dillingham Jacob.
   Born August 6, 1934, at Oxford, England. Son of
Alfred Bennis Jacob and Norma Sherlock. Married Carol
Marble (a computer programmer), June 23, 1956. Two
daughters: Penelope Carolyn (born 1967), Cheryl
(born 1970).

Education:
   B.A., Goddard College, 1956; teacher's certificate,
University of South Florida, 1964.

Career: Writer.
   Technical Writer, Electronics Communications Inc.,
1959-62; English Teacher, Admiral Farragut Academy,
1965-66; Free-lance writer, 1962-63, 1966-DATE.

First Professional Sale: "Possible to Hue," in
   Fantastic, April, 1963.

Literary Agents: Lurton Blassingame, 60 E. 42nd
   Street, New York, NY 10017; (U.K.) Leslie Flood,
   Carnell Agency, 17 Burwash Road, Plumstead, London.

Awards: $5000 Science Fiction Novel Award, given by
   Pyramid/Magazine of Fantasy & Science Fiction/Kent
   Productions, for Sos the Rope.

Anthony comments:
   "I met a fan, via a hostile fanzine, in 1970, and it
changed both of our lives. He was Roberto Fuentes,
with whom I have collaborated on four martial arts/
fantasy novels. As a result, he got into writing, and
I got into judo, at age 40. The knowledge and experience thus gained affect both my writing and my personal health."

* * * * *

BENJAMIN APPEL

Full Name: Benjamin Appel.
   Born September 13, 1907, at New York, New York.
Son of Louis Appel and Bessie Mikofsky. Married
Sophie Marshak, October 31, 1936. Three daughters:
Carla, Willa, Marianna.

Education:
   Attended University of Pennsylvania, 1925-26; New
York University, 1926-27; B.S., Lafayette College,
1929.

Career: Writer.
   Has been a free-lance writer since 1929, with short
breaks as a bank clerk, farmer, lumberjack, tenement
house inspector, aviation mechanic. Visiting author,
University of Pennsylvania, 1974. Died April 3, 1977.

Member: Authors Guild; P.E.N.

* * * * *

MARK J. APPLEMAN

Full Name: Mark Jerome Appleman.
   Born May 4, 1917, at Columbus, Ohio. Son of Philip
Appleman and Rose Singer. Married Marguerite Reinhold (an artists' representative), December 13,
1958.

Education: Attended City College of New York, 1934-
   36, and New York University, 1936-37.

Career: Stock Broker.
   Writer in New York and Hollywood, 1938-41, 1945-46;
Group Head, J. Walter Thompson Co., NY, 1956-61;
General partner, F. I. duPont, Glore, Forgan & Co.,
New York (investment brokers and bankers), 1961-71;
Vice-President, 1971-DATE.

Agent: Phyllis Jackson, International Famous Agency,
   1301 Avenue of the Americas, New York, NY 10019.

Member:
   Authors League; Bankers Club and Downtown Athletic
Club, New York; New York Stock Exchange (member of the
Marketing Advisory Committee and Public Relations Ad-
visory Committee).

* * * * *

E. L. ARCH

Full Name: Rachel Ruth Cosgrove Payes.
   Born December 11, 1922, at Westernport, Maryland.
Daughter of Jacob A. Cosgrove (a mine foreman) and
Martha Pearl Brake (a teacher). Married Norman M.
Payes, September 12, 1954. Two children: Robert N.
(born 1958), Ruth J. (born 1959).

Education: B.S., West Virginia Wesleyan College,
   1943.

Career: Medical Technologist & Writer.
   Medical Technologist at various hospitals, 1943-47;
Research Associate, Pharmacology, American Cyanamid,
Pearl River, New York, 1947-57; Writer, 1957-DATE.

First Professional Sale: Hidden Valley of Oz,
   Reilly & Lee, 1951 (as Rachel Cosgrove).

Member: Science Fiction Writers of America.

Payes writes:
   "About my gothics--I got started writing gothics because I sat beside Don Wollheim at the first Nebula
dinner I attended (#2). Bob Lowndes, who was editing
my SF novels for Avalon, was at the same table, and he
mentioned that I had written an Oz book. Don is an Oz
fan. So, talk went on, and I mentioned that I also
wrote mysteries--so Don asked if I did gothics. I told
him I didn't think I'd care to write gothics. Meanwhile, I'd mentioned doing a string of icky career/
romance/nursies for Avalon. Don 'lowed as how if I
could write nursies, I could write anything. After I
got home, I got thinking about it, and decided he was
right. NOTHING could be worse than writing nursies.
So I did two gothics for Ace. And now I'm doing
gothics for Berkley--my third one is in the works, my
fourth one I should be working on this minute. As
far as the difference between writing SF and gothics
is concerned, writing fiction is writing fiction. I
like to vary what I write for my own sake--keeps it
more interesting. Even my gothics are set both in
18th century and contemporary times. That way I don't
start going stale. My SF novels were all science fictional murders except the first, which had a murder in
it, but was more oriented towards straight adventure.
I am bloodthirsty!"

Payes now uses the byline of Rachel Cosgrove Payes.

TOM ARDIES

Full Name: Tom Ardies.
Born August 5, 1931, at Seattle, Washington. Son of John McIntyre (a salesman) and Irene Nutt. Married Sharon Bernard, April 27, 1963. Two children: Robyn, Sarita.

Education: Attended Daniel McIntyre Collegiate Institute, Winnepeg, Canada.

Career: Reporter & Columnist.
Writer for the *Vancouver Sun*, Vancouver, B.C., 1950-1964; Telegraph Editor, *Honolulu Star Bulletin*, 1964-65; Special assistant to the Governor of Guam, 1965-67; writer.

Interests: Travel.

* * * * *

ROBERT ARDREY

Full Name: Robert Ardrey.
Born October 16, 1908, at Chicago, Illinois. Son of Robert Leslie Ardrey (an editor and publisher) and Marie Haswell. Married Helen Johnson, June 12, 1938 (divorced 1960); married Berdine Grunewald, August 11, 1960. Two children of his first marriage: Ross, Daniel; one step-daughter, Vanessa.

Education: Ph.B., University of Chicago, 1930.

Career: Playwright and screenwriter.
Ardrey began his career with *Star Spangled*, a comedy produced on Broadway in 1936; he recently has turned his talents to anthropology, with such successes as *African Genesis, Territorial Imperative,* and *The Social Contract.*

Literary Agent: Brandt & Brandt, 101 Park Avenue, New York, NY 10017.

Awards:
Guggenheim Fellowship, 1937-38; Sidney Howard Memorial Award, Playwrights Company, 1940, for *Thunder Rock*; Theresa Helburn Memorial Award, Theater Guild, 1961, for *Shadow of Heroes*; Wilkie Brothers Foundation Grant, 1963; Academy Award nomination for best screenplay of 1966, for "Khartoum"; International Forum for Neurological Organization Award, 1970; University of Chicago Award for Professional Achievement, 1972.

Member:
Royal Society of Literature (Fellow); Authors Guild; Dramatists Guild; Writers Guild of America, West; Phi Beta Kappa.

* * * * *

BRUCE ARISS

Full Name: Bruce Wallace Ariss, Jr.
Born October 10, 1911, at Underwood, Washington. Son of Bruce Wallace Ariss (a construction contractor) and Anna Kirwin. Married Jean McLellan Fitch (a writer), July 27, 1934. Five children: Bruce Wallace III (born 1937), Dinah (born 1941), Brien J. (born 1944), Andrea (born 1947), Holly (born 1950).

Education: B.A., University of California, Ber-keley, 1934.

Career: Writer & illustrator.
Editor, *What's Doing*, 1946-50; motion picture art director for various Hollywood studios, 1950-54; supervisor for the TV show, "Bing Crosby," 1954-57; Art Director, Pickering Advertising Agency, San Francisco, 1957-60; Cartoonist, *Dennis the Menace*, 1960-61; Designer and Illustrator, Defense Language Institute, 1961-73; now retired.

First Professional Sale: "The Dreadful Secret of Jonas Harper," in *What's Doing*, November, 1948.

Ariss writes:
"Science fiction has been more of a hobby to me than a vocation. I was primarily an illustrator and mural painter, sometimes doing editorial work for various magazines. In this capacity, I published stories by Alan Nelson, Reg Bretnor, Dave Duncan, John Steinbeck, and others too numerous to mention.
"But mostly I made my living from art, not writing. Now that I'm retired, this may change--I've a contract to write a book about Cannery Row and John Steinbeck, both of whom I knew well in the early days."

* * * * *

MEL ARRIGHI

Full Name: Mel Arrighi.
Born October 5, 1933, at San Francisco, California. Son of Enrico Arrighi (a produce merchant) and Gemma Casentini. Married Patricia Bosworth (a writer and magazine editor), February 15, 1966.

Education:
Attended Reed College, 1951-53; B.A., University of California, Berkeley, 1955.

Career: Actor and writer.
Professional actor in New York, 1956-62; full-time writer, 1962-DATE. Arrighi has acted with the New York Shakespeare Festival, Shakespearwrights, and Irish Players; he toured nationally with the Lunts in "The Great Sebastians."

Agents:
McIntosh & Otis, 18 E. 41st St., New York, NY 10017; (dramatic) Harold Freedman, Brandt & Brandt, 101 Park Avenue, New York, NY 10017.

* * * * *

RUTH M. ARTHUR

Full Name: Ruth Mabel Arthur.
Born May 26, 1905, at Glasgow, Scotland. Daughter of Allan Arthur (an electrical contractor) and Ruth M. Johnston. Married Frederick N. Huggins (a lawyer), September 2, 1932. Six children.

Education: Diploma, Froebel Training College, 1926.

Career: Teacher and writer.
Kingergarten teacher in Glasgow, 1927-30; teacher in Loughton, England, 1930-32; writer, 1932-DATE.

Agent: Curtis Brown Ltd., 60 E. 56th St., New York, NY 10022; and 73 King St., Covent Garden, London WC2E 8HU, England.

ISAAC ASIMOV

Full Name: Isaac Asimov [born Isaak Iudich Azimov].
  Born January 2, 1920, at Petrovichi, U.S.S.R. Came
to the United States 1923, and became a citizen 1928.
Son of Judah Asimov (a candy-store keeper) and Anna
Rachel Berman. Married Gertrude Blugerman, July 26,
1942 (divorced November 16, 1973); married Janet Opal
Jeppson (a writer), November 30, 1973. Two children:
David (born 1951), Robyn Joan (born 1955).

Education:
  B.S., Columbia University, 1939; M.A., Columbia
University, 1941; Ph.D., Columbia University, 1948.

Career: Writer & Professor.
  Instructor, Boston University School of Medicine,
1949-51; Assistant Professor, 1951-55; Associate
Professor, 1955-DATE; Free-lance writer, 1957-DATE.

First Professional Sale: "Marooned off Vesta,"
  in *Amazing Stories*, March, 1939.

Honors and Awards:
  Guest of Honor, 13th World Science Fiction Conven-
tion (Clevention), Cleveland, 1955; Nebula Award,
Best Novel, 1972 (1973), *The Gods Themselves*; Special
Plaque, 21st World Science Fiction Convention (DisCon
I), Washington, 1963, for distinguished contributions
to the field; Hugo Award, Best All-Time Series, 1965
(1966), the *Foundation Trilogy*; Hugo Award, Best
Novel, 1972 (1973), *The Gods Themselves*; numerous
other awards outside of science fiction.

Member: Science Fiction Writers of America.

Asimov has written close to two hundred books, of
which some 35-40 are science fiction works of one
sort or another. Among his own writings, his favorite
books are "*The Gods Themselves* (fiction), and *Asimov's
Guide to Shakespeare* (nonfiction)."

* * * * *

FRANCIS ASKHAM

Full Name: Julia Eileen Courtney Greenwood.
  Born November 4, 1910, at London, England. Mar-
ried (1) Antony Terry; (2) Cecil John Greenwood.
One son.

Career: Journalist and broadcaster.

Agent: A. M. Heath & Co. Ltd., 40 William IV St.,
  London WC2 4DF, England.

* * * * *

MIGUEL ANGEL ASTURIAS

Full Name: Miguel Angel Asturias.
  Born October 19, 1899, at Guatemala City, Guatemala.
Son of Ernesto Asturias (a Supreme Court magistrate)
and Maria Rosales. Married (1) Clemencia Amado; (2)
Blanca Mora y Araujo. Two children: Rodrigo, Miguel
Angel.

Education:
  Doctor of Laws, Universidad de San Carlos de Guate-
mala, 1923; studied at the Sorbonne, University of
Paris, 1923-28.

Career: Diplomat.
  Practiced law after earning his degree; was the European correspondent for various Central American newspapers, 1923-33; returned to Guatemala in 1933, where
he worked as a journalist for *El Diario del Aire*; elected deputy to the Guatemalan National Congress, 1942;
joined the diplomatic service, 1945; Cultural Attache
to Mexico, then to Buenos Aires, 1947-51; Minister-
Counselor in Buenos Aires, 1951-52; served on diplomatic mission to Paris, 1952-53; Ambassador to El
Salvador, 1953-54; lost his citizenship in 1954, due
to his support of the leftist government; moved to
Argentina and became a correspondent for *El Nacional*
(Caracas); left Argentina after the fall of the liberal
government, and moved to Italy, where he participated
in Columbianum, an international exchange program; returned to Guatemala, 1966, and had his citizenship restored; Ambassador to France, 1966-   .

Awards:
  Prix Sylla Monsegur, Paris, 1931, for *Leyendas de
Guatemala*; Prix du Meilleur Roman Etranger, 1952, for
El Senor Presidente; Lenin Peace Prize, 1966; Nobel
Prize for Literature, 1967.

Asturias died June 9, 1974.

* * * * *

JOHN ATKINS

Full Name: John Alfred Atkins.
  Born May 26, 1916, at Carshalton, Surrey, England.
Son of Frank Periam Atkins (a broker) and Bertha
Lovell. Married Dorothy Grey.

Education: B.A., University of Bristol, 1938.

Career: Teacher.
  Interviewer, Mass Observation, London, 1939-41;
Literary Editor, *London Tribune*, 1942-44; District
Organizer, Workers' Educational Association, 1948-51;
Teacher, Sudan Government Ministry of Education, Khar-
toum, 1951-55, 1958-68; Teacher, University of Lodz,
Poland, 1970-DATE.

Agent: David Higham Associates, 5-8 Lower John St.,
  London W1R 4HA, England.

Member: P.E.N. International; Society of Authors.

* * * * *

MICHAEL AVALLONE

Full Name: Michael Angelo Avallone, Jr.
  Born October 27, 1924, at New York, New York. Son of
Michael Angelo Avallone, Sr. Married Frances Weinstein
May 27, 1960. Children: Stephen, Susan, David.

Career: Writer.
  Has been a free-lance writer all of his life. Guest
lecturer on short story and mystery writing at New York
University, Columbia University, and Rutgers University.

Member:
  Mystery Writers of America (has served as National
Director and Chairman of the Motion Picture Awards
Committee).

Avallone writes gothics as Dorothea Nile & Edwina Noone.

JOHN AYLESWORTH

Full Name: John B. Aylesworth.
   Born August 18, 1938, at Toronto, Ontario, Canada.
Son of Fredrick and Marie Aylesworth. Married his
wife, Nancy Aylesworth, July 1, 1961. Four children:
John, Cynthia, William, Thomas.

Education: Attended Forest Hill Collegiate, Toronto.

Career: Television writer & producer.
   Has been a television writer for the CBC in Canada,
the "Perry Como Show," "Judy Garland Show," "Frank
Sinatra--the Man and His Music," "Herb Alpert Special,"
etc. Has also produced the "Jonathan Winters Show"
in Hollywood.

First Professional Sale: *Fee, Fei, Fo, Fum*,
   Avon Books, 1963.

* * * * *

THOMAS AYLESWORTH

Full Name: Thomas Gibbons Aylesworth.
   Born November 5, 1927, at Valparaiso, Indiana. Son
of Carroll Wells Aylesworth (a salesman) and Ruth
Gibbons. Married Virginia L. Boelter (a teacher),
August 13, 1949. Two children: Carol Jean, Thomas
Paul.

Education:
   A.B., Indiana University, 1950; M.S., Indiana University, 1953; Ph.D., Ohio State University, 1959.

Career: Teacher & editor.
   High school teacher in Harvard, Illinois, 1951-52;
junior high school science teacher, New Albany, Indiana, 1952-54; teacher at Battle Creek, Michigan,
1955-57; Assistant Professor of Education, Michigan
State University, 1957-61; Lecturer in Science, and
Senior Editor of *Current Science*, Wesleyan University,
1961-64; Senior Editor, Natural History Press, 1964-
DATE.

Member:
   National Science Teachers Association; National
Association of Biology Teachers; National Association
for Research in Science Teaching; Central Association
of Science and Mathematics Teachers; New York Academy
of Sciences; Phi Delta Kappa.

* * * * *

MICHAEL AYRTON

Full Name: Michael Ayrton.
   Born February 20, 1921, at London, England. Son of
Gerald Gould and Barbara Ayrton. Married Elisabeth
Walshe (a writer), November, 1951.

Career: Painter and sculptor.
   Formerly a teacher; now a writer, primarily in the
field of art; associated with the University of Essex.
Served with the Royal Air Force, 1940-43.

Agent: International Literary Management, 2 Ellis
   St., Sloane Square, London S.W.1, England.

Ayrton died November 17, 1975.

B. B.

Full Name: Denys James Watkins-Pitchford.
   Born July 25, 1905, at Lamport, Northamptonshire,
England. Son of Walter Watkins-Pitchford and Edith
Elizabeth Wilson. Married Cecily Mary Adnitt, August
10, 1939. Two children: Angela June, Robin John.

Education: A.R.C.A., Royal College of Art.

Career: Writer & Illustrator.
   Art Master, Rugby School, Warwickshire, England,
1934-1949; Full-time writer/illustrator, 1949-DATE.

Awards:
   British Library Association Carnegie Medal, for *The
Little Grey Men*. Fellow: Royal Society of Arts.

Literary Agent: David Higham Associates Ltd., 76
   Dean St., London W.1, England.

* * * * *

ASA BABER

Full Name: Asa Baber.
   Born 1936, at Chicago, Illinois. Married Elizabeth
Coe. Two children: James Lawrence, Brendan Patrick.

Education:
   B.A., Princeton University, 1958; M.A., Northwestern
University, 1962; M.F.A., University of Iowa, 1969.

Career: Professor of English.
   Lecturer in English, Roosevelt University, 1962-63;
Instructor in English and Director of the College
Theater, Robert Academy and Robert College, Istanbul,
1963-66; Instructor, University of Hawaii, Honolulu,
1969-71; Asst. Professor of English, 1971-DATE.

Honors: Shubert playwriting fellowship at the University of Illinois, 1967.

* * * * *

RICHARD BACH

Full Name: Richard David Bach.
   Born June 23, 1936, at Oak Park, Illinois. Son of
Roland R. Bach (an American Red Cross chapter manager)
and Ruth Shaw. Married Bette Jeanne Franks, October
15, 1957 (divorced, 1971). Six children: Kristel
Louise, Robert Allen, Erica Lynn, James, Jonathan, Beth.

Education: Attended California State University,
   Long Beach, for one year.

Career: Writer, editor, pilot.
   Captain, United States Air Force, 1956-56, 1961-62;
Associate Editor, *Flying*, 1961-64; Free-lance writer,
1964-DATE.

Literary Agent:
   Kenneth Littauer, Littauer & Wilkinson, 500 Fifth
Avenue, New York, NY 10036.

Bach, a direct descendant of Johann Sebastian Bach,
has contributed over one hundred articles on flying to
such magazines as *Flying, Air Facts, Argosy, Holiday,
Writer*. The enormous popularity of *Jonathan Livingston
Seagull* generated at least three different parodies.

CHARLES W. BAILEY II

Full Name: Charles Waldo Bailey II.
Born April 28, 1929, at Boston, Massachusetts. Son of David Washburn Bailey and Catherine Smith. Married Ann Card Bushnell, 1950. Two children: Victoria Britton, Sarah Tilden.

Education: A.B., Harvard University, 1950.

Career: Reporter.
Reporter, *Minneapolis Star and Tribune*, 1950-54; reporter for Cowles Publications, Washington, 1954-DATE.

Honors:
Honorable mention, Raymond Clapper Award, 1961, 1964.

Member:
White House Correspondents Association; National Press Club; Federal City Club.

* * * * *

J. O. BAILEY

Full Name: James Osler Bailey.
Born August 12, 1903, at Raleigh, North Carolina. Son of Thomas Benjamin Bailey (a city employee) and Nancy Priscilla Smith. Married Mary Ethel Misenheimer, June 12, 1938. One daughter: Nancy Barden Rich (born 1930).

Education:
A.B., University of North Carolina at Chapel Hill, 1924; M.A., 1927; Ph.D., 1934.

Career: Professor of English.
Taught English at the University of North Carolina from 1930 onwards; now a Professor Emeritus (retired).

First Professional Sale: *Pilgrims Through Space and Time*, Argus Books, 1947.

Awards: Pilgrim Award, 1970.

Bailey adds:
"One other item you might wish to mention is my introduction to 'Captain Adam Seaborn's' *Symzonia; A Voyage of Discovery*, published originally in 1820, and reprinted in 1965 by Scholars' Facsimiles and Reprints, of Gainesville, Florida. So far as I know, *Symzonia* was the first piece of science fiction written in America. It is not mentioned in *Pilgrims* because I did not know about the book at that time."

* * * * *

PAUL BAILEY

Full Name: Paul Dayton Bailey.
Born 1906, at American Fork, Utah. Son of Eli Hawkins Bailey and Olive Edith Forbes. Married Evelyn Robison, 1927. Two children: David Paul, Lynn, Robison.

Education: Attended the University of Utah for one year.

Career: Publisher.
Publisher, *Eagle Rock Press-Advertiser*, Eagle Rock,
California, 1938-45; Publisher and Editor, Westernlore Press, 1941-DATE.

Member:
Authors Club, Hollywood; Los Angeles Press Club; Los Angeles Corral of Westerners; E Clampus Vitus; Printing Industry of America; Western Writers of America; Death Valley '49ers; Zamorano.

* * * * *

BETTY BAKER

Full Name: Betty Lou Baker Venturo.
Born June 20, 1928, at Bloomsburg, Pennsylvania. Daughter of Robert Weidler Baker and Mary Wentling. Married Robert George Venturo, 1947 (divorced, 1965). One son: Christopher Patrick.

Education: Attended school in Orange, New Jersey.

Career: Writer.
Has held various jobs as a dental assistant, gift shop owner, lecturer, etc.

Awards:
Western Heritage Award for *Killer-of-Death*; Spur Award, Western Writers of America, 1966, for *Walk the World's Rim*.

Member:
Western Writers of America; Arizona Press Women; Arizona-Sonora Desert Museum.

* * * * *

DENYS VAL BAKER

Full Name: Denys Val Baker.
Born October 24, 1917, at Poppleton, Yorkshire, England. Son of Valentine Henry Baker and Dilys Eames. Married Jess Margaret Bryan (a potter), January 28, 1948. Six children: Martin, Gillian, Jane, Stephen, Demelza, Genevieve.

Career: Writer.
Writer and reporter for British daily and trade newspapers, 1935-41; Free-lance writer, 1941-DATE.

Member: Society of Authors; West Country Writers Association.

* * * * *

MICHAEL BAKER

Full Name: Robert Michael Graham Baker.
Born February 12, 1938, at Northwood, Middlesex, England. Son of Ernest Robert Baker (a civil servant) and Kathleen Muriel Balls. Married Beryl Johnson, April 8, 1967. Two children: Alison, Ruth.

Education: LL.B., University of London, 1959.

Career: Solicitor [attorney].
Solicitor for various law firms in London, 1959-64; Legal Asst. to the Solicitor, Post Office, 1964-DATE.

Member:
Law Society; Civil Service Legal Society; Festiniog Railway Society; Civil Service Motoring Association.

RUSSELL BAKER

Full Name: Russell Wayne Baker.
Born August 14, 1925, in Loudoun County, Virginia. Son of Benjamin Rex Baker and Lucy Elizabeth Robinson. Married Miriam Emily Nash, March 11, 1950. Three children: Kathleen Leland, Allen Nash, Michael Lee.

Education: B.A., Johns Hopkins University, 1947.

Career: Reporter and Author.
Reporter, *Baltimore Sun*, 1947-53; London Bureau Chief for the same newspaper, 1953-54; member of the Washington Bureau of the *New York Times*, 1954-62; author of the column "Observer," 1962-DATE.

Honors:
L.H.D., Hamilton College, Princeton University; LL.D., Union College; L.H.D., Franklin Pierce College.

* * * * *

W. HOWARD BAKER

Full Name: Wilfred Glassford McNeilly.
Born March 8, 1921, in Renfrewshire, Scotland. Son of William Henry McNeilly and Christina Glassford Aitkenhead. Married Margaret Ferguson Macdonald Miller, March 7, 1946. Five children: Colin, John, Christopher, Duncan, Quentin.

Career: Author.
Journalist for the *Northern Whig*, Belfast, 1938-40; journalist on the *Belfast Newsletter*, 1947-52; Full-time author, 1952-DATE. Served in India, 1940-46.

Agent: Scott Meredith Literary Agency, Ltd., 44 Great Russell St., London W.C.1, England.

Member:
Ardglass Town Committee; P.E.N.; Downe Society; Royal Naval Sailing Association; Irish Kennel Club; British Legion; various East Down development and tourist committees.

* * * * *

BRIAN BALL

Full Name: Brian Neville Ball.
Born June 19, 1932, in Cheshire, England. Son of Walter Hope Ball and Elsie Booth. Married Margaret Snead, August 7, 1953. Two children: Jane Nicola, Kathryn Amanda.

Education:
Attended Chester College, 1953-55; B.A., London University, 1960; M.A., Sheffield University, 1968.

Career: Teacher & Author.
Senior Lecturer in English, Doncaster College of Education, 1965-DATE. Has also been a visiting member in the University of British Columbia.

Member: Doncaster Prose and Poetry Society; Rotherdam Golf Club.

First Professional Sale: An article on the Communist invasion of Tibet, *Birmingham Town Crier*, 1948.

Ball writes:
"I've given some thought to *why* I like writing S-F. I think it's the wrestle with metaphysics that excites me. Then there's the topsy-turvy nature of the field. If you recall the Royal Hatcheries of Barsoom as I try to do when I get over-serious, you'll see what I mean: I think didacticism is not for this genre. The S-F writer, if he can preserve his sense of what is and isn't asinine, can intuitively put his finger into lots of interesting plum-filled metaphysical pies, and draw out awesomely rich speculative plums."

* * * * *

JOHN BALL

Full Name: John Dudley Ball, Jr.
Born July 8, 1911, at Schenectady, New York. Son of John Dudley Ball (a research physicist and educator) and Alena Laura Wiles. Married Patricia Hamilton, August 22, 1942. One son: John Dudley Ball III (born 1952).

Education: B.A., Carroll College, 1934.

Career: Author.
Flight Instructor, U.S. Army Air Transport Command, 1942-46; Annotator, Columbia Records, 1946-49; Music Editor, *Brooklyn Eagle*, 1946-50; Daily Columnist, *New York World-Telegram*, 1950-51; Commentator, radio station WOL, Washington, 1951-52; Director of Public Relations, Institute of Aerospace Sciences, 1958-61; Editor-in-Chief, DMS News Services, 1961-63; Full-time author, 1963-DATE.

First Professional Sale: *About Washington Island*, published circa 1936.

Literary Agent: Brandt & Brandt, 101 Park Avenue, New York, NY 10017.

Awards:
In the Heat of the Night, Ball's best-known book, has garnered a number of honors, including an Edgar Award, British Critics Award, New York Critics Award, Cleveland Critics Award, California Writers Award, Golden Globe, an Academy Award for Best Picture of the Year, an Academy Award for Best Story of the Year, etc.

Member:
Japanese-American Citizens League (Chapter President) Committee to Conserve Chinese Culture (National Chairman); Mensa; USAF-Civil Air Patrol (Lt. Col.); Baker Street Irregulars (Chapter President); All America Karate Federation; Akai Kai (Black Belt); Mystery Writers of America; British Crime Writers Association.

Avocations and interests:
"I'm a commercial pilot, collect jade and Oriental art, enjoy music and travel, own and operate in absentia a large Oriental art store established primarily to help charities of the Far East, and Asian craftsmen otherwise unable to reach the American market."

Ball adds:
"I generally specialize in the Far East, and in Far Eastern culture, but write principally mainstream novels based on aviation, various world cultures, etc. I also do an occasional mystery, usually featuring the black Pasadena detective Virgil Tibbs. I've done some SF and spy/espionage for relaxation."

J. G. BALLARD

Full Name: James Graham Ballard.
   Born November 15, 1930, at Shanghai, China. Son of James Ballard and Edna Johnstone. Married Helen Mary Matthews 1954 (died 1964). Three children: James, Fay, Beatrice.

Education: Studied at King's College, Cambridge University.

Career: Author.
   Has been a free-lance author all of his life.

First Professional Sale: "Prima Belladonna," in *Science Fantasy*, December, 1956.

Ballard writes:
   "The current state of SF--extremely interesting, at least in Britain--in the USA less so--American SF writers seem pallid and unadventurous; possibly the commercial publishing scene dominates them--most SF anyway is being produced by other means--science itself, the visual arts, and so on--the sort of imaginative SF that is required now is beyond the range or abilities of most of its present writers, if not all. Where is the new wave headed?--towards becoming the most important literature of the last decades of the C20 [twentieth century], in fact, the new mainstream-- and about time too. Science fiction has been in continuous evolution since Wells--there is nothing particularly unique about modern SF of the 40's and 50's--that has now lost its relevance and vitality, and a new, far more relevant science fiction has appeared."

* * * * *

BILL S. BALLINGER

Full Name: William Sanborn Ballinger.
   Born March 13, 1912. Son of William M. Ballinger and Ella Satia. Married 1) Geraldine Taylor (divorced); 2) Laura Dunham, 1949 (divorced); 3) Lucille Rambeau, 1964. Three children: William B., Bruce R., Constance V.

Education:
   B.A., University of Wisconsin, 1934; LL.D., Northern College, Philippines, 1940.

Career: Writer.
   Magazine, newspaper, and radio writer, 1935-50; Full-time novelist, screen writer, and dramatist, 1950-DATE. University lecturer on creative writing.

Agent: Russell & Volkening, 551 Fifth Avenue, New York, NY 10017.

Awards: Edgar Award, Best Half-Hour Suspense Show in Television, 1960.

Member:
   Authors Guild; Screen Writers Guild (West); Mystery Writers of America; The Lambs (New York); Delta Kappa Epsilon; The Coral Casino, Santa Barbara, Calif.

Ballinger has travelled widely in Europe and the Near East, and speaks French and Spanish. His first novel was published by Harper & Brothers in 1948 [*The Body in the Bed*].

ARTHUR W. BALLOU

Full Name: Arthur W. Ballou.
   Born May 9, 1915, at Brookline, Massachusetts. Married Marjorie Clapp, July 11, 1942. Four children: Sherry, Candace, Julia, Arthur W. Jr.

Education: Attended various business administration schools in New England.

Career: Public relations consultant; writer.
   Employed as a public relations consultant in Boston, 1939-40; petroleum marketer in Boston, 1940-62; Free-lance writer and consultant, 1962-DATE.

* * * * *

DACRE BALSDON

Full Name: John Percy Vyvian Dacre Balsdon.
   Born November 4, 1901, at Bideford, England. Son of Robert Percy Balsdon and Mabel Olive Finlay.

Education: M.A., Exeter College, Oxford University, 1927.

Career: College teacher.
   Fellow of Exeter College and University Lecturer in Ancient History, Oxford University, 1928-40; Assistant Secretary, British Ministry of Labour and National Service, 1940-45; returned to Oxford 1945, and taught there until his death. Died September 18, 1977.

Honors: LL.D., Dalhousie University.

Agent: David Higham Associates, 76 Dean St., Soho, London W.1, England.

* * * * *

GEORGE BAMBER

Full Name: George Everett Bamber.
   Born October 18, 1932, at Ann Arbor, Michigan. Son of George Bamber (a house painter) and Mildred Koch. Married Gayle Boll, November 4, 1967. One son: George Olof.

Education: B.A., University of Michigan, 1955.

Career: Business executive.
   Assistant Manager, U.S. Plywood's Exhibits and Displays Department, 1963-67; President, The Blue Thumb Company [a sales promotion agency], La Crescenta, Cal., 1969-DATE.

First Professional Sale:
   "Like Man, Somebody Dig Me," for the CBS Radio series "Suspense," 1958.

Awards: Avery Hopwood Award for Drama, University of Michigan, 1955.

Member: Model T Club of America.

Interests: "Painting, writing, living."

Bamber adds: "My desire is to write one major work that will have significant social impact--I don't believe I've done that yet."

HENRY BAMMAN

Full Name: Henry A. Bamman.
Born June 13, 1918, at Macon, Missouri. Son of Henry A. Bamman and Ivy McAnally. Married Ruth G. Wiren, June 12, 1948. Two children: Richard, Elin Kristina.

Education:
B.A., Northeast Missouri State Teachers College, 1945; B.S., 1945; M.A., University of Colorado, 1948; Ed.D., Stanford University, 1952.

Career: Professor of Education.
Teacher, Macon County public schools, 1936-41; Instructor in English, University of Colorado, Boulder, 1947-48; Asst. Professor of English, Eastern Washington College of Education, 1948-50; Asst. Director of Counseling Center, Stanford University, 1951-55; Professor of Education, Sacramento State College, 1955-DATE.

Member:
National Council of Teachers of English; National Conference on Research in English; International Reading Association; Kappa Delta Pi; Phi Delta Kappa; Blue Key National Honor Fraternity.

* * * * *

MANLY BANISTER

Full Name: Manly Miles Banister.
Born March 9, 1914, at McCormick, Washington. Son of Charles Edwin Banister (a logger) and Marion Isobell Flowers. Married Eleanor Hammond, 1933 (div. 1935); married Marjorie Grace Houston (an office manager), August 1953. Two children: Nikki Loa, Zoe.

Education: Attended Reed College.

Career: Writer.
General restaurant worker in Oregon and California, 1930-36; messboy, wiper, fireman, oiler on various ships of the Union Oil fleet, sailing out of Los Angeles, 1936-37; employed by WPA, Portland, 1937-40; continuity writer, radio station KCKN, Kansas City, 1940-42, 1945-46; advertising copywriter for Western Auto Supply Co., Kansas City, 1946-53; copywriter for Pacific National Agency, Portland, 1953-54, and for Hugh Dwight Advertising, Portland, 1954-61; Freelance writer, 1961-DATE.

* * * * *

DULAN BARBER

Full Name: Dulan F. Barber.
Born October 11, 1940, at Reading, England. Married Patty Kitchen (a writer), March 27, 1968. Step-son: Dan Bowling.

Education: Attended Leeds University, 1958-59.

Career: Editor & Author.
Editor, Calder & Boyars Ltd., London, 1963-69; Fulltime writer, 1969-DATE.

Award:
Thomas R. Coward Memorial Award in Fiction from Coward-McCann, for A *Lovable Man*.

Literary Agent: Wallace, Aiken, & Sheil, 118 E. 61st St., New York, NY 10021.

Member:
Writers Action Group; Writers Guild of Great Britain; National Council for One Parent Families.

* * * * *

PIERRE BARBET

Full Name: Claude Pierre Avice.
Born May 16, 1925, at Le Mans, France. Son of Léon Avice (a pharmacist) and René Bardet. Married Marianne Brunswick, July 23, 1952. Three children: Brigitte (born 1953), Patrick (born 1955), Olivier (born 1957).

Education:
Docteur en Pharmacie, Diplomé d'études supérieures de Bactériologie, de Sérologie, d'Hématologie, de Parasitologie, Faculté de Pharmacie de Paris et Institut Pasteur de Garches.

Career: Pharmacist and writer.
Pharmacist and laboratory director in Paris; has also been a science fiction writer since 1962.

First Professional Sale: A novel to Librairie Gallimard, 1962.

Member:
Bureau de la Société des Docteurs en Pharmacie; Société d'Astronomie de France.

* * * * *

ALBERT BARKER

Full Name: Albert W. Barker.
Born 1900 at Chicago, Illinois. Son of Edwin L. Barker (an editor) and Jessie Wineman. Married Gertrude Rozan.

Career: Writer.

Literary Agent: Paul R. Reynolds, 597 Fifth Avenue, New York, NY 10017.

* * * * *

SHIRLEY BARKER

Full Name: Shirley Frances Barker.
Born April 4, 1911, at Farmington, New Hampshire. Daughter of Will Tilden Barker and Alta Leighton.

Education:
B.A., University of New Hampshire, 1934; A.M., Radcliffe College, 1938; B.L.S., Pratt Institute Library School, 1941.

Career: Librarian & writer.
Librarian, New York Public Library, 1940-44, 1946-53; Professional writer in New Hampshire, 1954-65. Died November 18, 1965.

Literary Agent:
Mavis McIntosh, McIntosh, McKee & Dodds, 30 E. 60th Street, New York, NY 10022.

JAMES BARLOW

Full Name: James Henry Stanley Barlow.
  Born December 1, 1921, at Birmingham, England. Son of Stanley Barlow (a bank clerk) and Gladys Jones. Married Joyce Margaret Everiss, June 24, 1949. Three children: Stephen, Gillian, Michael.

Education: Attended various English schools, 1927-37.

Career: Writer.
  Worked for Birmingham Water Company, 1939; joined RAF 1940, was invalided out for tuberculosis in 1941, and wrote articles for various magazines until 1946, when he returned to the water company; served as a rate inspector and investigator until 1960, when he moved to the country as a full-time writer. Died January 30, 1973.

Agent: Charles Lavell, Mowbray House, Norfolk St., London WC2, England.

* * * * *

ARTHUR K. BARNES

Arthur Kelvin Barnes was born 1911. He first appeared in the December, 1931 issue of *Wonder Stories* with "Lord of the Lightning," and is best known for a series of eight stories in *Thrilling Wonder Stories* featuring the female character Gerry Carlisle. He collaborated with Henry Kuttner on two science fiction stories. He was a member of the Los Angeles Science Fantasy Society, and a contributor to the SF fanzine *Sweetness and Light*. Biographical sketches appeared in TWS (October, 1939 issue), and in the fanzine *Imagination!* around the end of the 1930s. He died in 1969, presumably in Sunland, CA, where he was last known to be living. [courtesy, Forrest J Ackerman]

* * * * *

DONALD BARR

Full Name: Donald Barr.
  Born August 2, 1921, at New York, New York. Son of Pelham Barr (an economist) and Estelle DeYoung (a psychologist). Married Mary Margaret Ahern, April 22, 1946. Four children: Christopher James (born 1947), William Pelham (born 1950), Hilary Benedict Thomas (born 1952), Stephen Matthew (born 1953).

Education: B.A., Columbia University, 1941; M.A., 1951.

Career: Teacher.
  Literary Editor, *Tomorrow Magazine*, 1945-46; Instructor in English, Columbia University, 1945-56; Asst. to the Dean, and Asst. Dean, Columbia University School of Engineering, 1956-63; Associate Program Director, National Science Foundation, 1963-64; Headmaster, Dalton School, 1964-DATE.

First Professional Sale:
  "But First, a Brief Message from Jeremiah," a poem published in the *New Republic*, 1944.

Literary Agent:
  John Cushman, 23 W. 43rd St., New York, NY 10036;

Lecture Agent: W. Colston Leigh, 1185 Avenue of the Americas, New York, NY 10036.

Honors: Litt.D., St. Francis College, 1974.

Member: Country Day School Headmasters Association.

Interests:
  Reading, chess. Barr adds: "Most of my books have been for or about children, including children's books on atomic energy, building, and prehistoric man. Some others include *Arithmetic for Billy Goats*, a children's book on binary arithmetic; and a book of critical and controversial essays on education, *Who Pushed Humpty Dumpty?* I'm also part-author of various books on college teaching, school underachievement, and classroom organization."

* * * * *

CHARLES BARREN

Full Name: Charles MacKinnon Barren.
  Born December 21, 1913, at London, England. Son of Thomas Bearman Barren and Ada Boone Winfield. Married Vera Dace, November 21, 1936. Three children: Mervyn, Stuart, Dianne.

Education: Attended West Ham Technical College, and Forest Training College.

Career: Teacher.
  Has been a Warden for various youth and community centres; currently Lecturer in English and History, Barking Regional College of Technology, Dagenham, Essex, England (formerly South East Essex Technical College and School of Art).

* * * * *

G. J. BARRETT

Full Name: Geoffrey John Barrett.
  Born September 23, 1928, at Norwich, Norfolk, England. Son of John Barrett (a prison officer) and Violet May Leighton (a domestic servant).

Education: "Elementary."

Career: Writer.

First Professional Sale: *Tully's Return*, Robert Hale & Co., 1962.

Interests:
  Science, philosophy, occult history, piano music, general reading. "I am essentially a kind of 'all purpose' novelist. I have had over a hundred westerns published, and ten thrillers. I should add that this type of writer is becoming increasingly common in G.B., where survival is very difficult on any other terms."

* * * * *

LAURENCE I. BARRETT

Full Name: Laurence I. Barrett.
  Born September 6, 1935, at New York, New York. Son of Harold Barrett (a postman) and Ruth Gaier. Married Paulette Singer, March 9, 1957. Two children: Paul Meyer, David Allen.

LAURENCE I. BARRETT (cont.)

Education: B.A., New York University, 1956; M.S., Columbia University, 1957.

Career: Editor.
Political reporter, columnist, and Washington correspondent, *New York Herald Tribune,* 1958-65; Contributing Editor, *Time,* 1965-67; Associate Editor, 1968-69; Senior Editor, 1970-DATE.

Literary Agent: McIntosh & Otis, 18 E. 41st St., New York, NY 10017.

* * * * *

WILLIAM E. BARRETT

Full Name: William Edmund Barrett.
Born November 16, 1900, at New York, New York. Son of John Joseph Barrett and Eleanor Margaret Flannery. Married Christine M. Rollman, February 15, 1925. Two children: Marjorie Christine, William Edmund Jr.

Education: Attended Manhattan College.

Career: Author.
Advertising Manager, Westinghouse Company, 1923-29; Full-time author, 1929-DATE.

First Professional Sale: "The Music of Madness," in *Weird Tales,* March, 1926.

Literary Agent: Harold Ober Associates, 40 E. 49th St., New York, NY 10017.

Honors: Litt.D., Creighton University, 1961; was given a citation from Regis College, 1956.

Member:
National Press Club; P.E.N.; Colorado Authors League; International Institute of Arts and Letters (Fellow); Denver Athletic Club.

Barrett writes:
"One of my recent books may interest you. It is titled *Lady of the Lotus,* and it is the story of the Princess Yasodhara, who married the Prince Siddharta before he became the Buddha. Yasodhara bore him a son, Rahula, and she was a remarkable woman. Theirs was a great love story. It is amazing that, with hundreds of lives of the Buddha, one looks in vain for a single life of Yasodhara. It was, of course, not easy to trace her through legend and story--but she has always been there for anyone patient enough to seek her. I worked on this book for many years, and I followed the clues and the legends through Nepal, India, Burma, Thailand, the Malay States, Hong Kong, and Japan."

* * * * *

MARJORIE BARROWS

Full Name: Ruth Marjorie Wescott Barrows.
Born at Chicago, Illinois. Daughter of Ransom Moore Barrows (a physician) and Caroline Dixon.

Education: Attended Northwestern University, 1916-17; and University of Chicago, 1917-19.

Career: Editor.
Contributing Editor, *Compton's Encyclopedia,* 1920; Secretary and plots assistant for a short story writer, 1920-21; Associate Editor, and then Editor, *Child Life,* 1922-38; Co-Editor, Consolidated Books, 1943-48; Editor-in-Chief, *Children's Hour,* 1952-62; Editor, *Treasure Trails,* 1954-56; Editor, *Junior Treasure Chest of Family Weekly,* 1954-62; Advisory Editor, *Highlights for Children,* 1956-66; now retired.

Award: Chicago Foundation of Literature Award, 1956.

Member:
P.E.N.; Society of Midland Authors; Chicago Drama League; English-Speaking Union; Evanston Drama Club; Arts Club; Cordon Club.

* * * * *

ALAN FRANK BARTER

Full Name: Alan Frank Barter.
Born August 20, 1933, at Cardiff, South Wales. Son of Edwin Barter (a hospital drugs dispenser) and Irene Thomas (a nurse). Married Susan Pembridge (a school teacher), August 1, 1961. Two children: Andrew (born 1962), Mark (born 1964).

Education: M.A., Cambridge University, 1957.

Career: Schoolmaster.
Has served as a teacher and schoolmaster at various English schools; now Head of English, Poole Grammar School, Dorset, England (since 1973).

First Professional Sale: *Untravelled Worlds,* Macmillan, 1966 (edited with Raymond Wilson).

Interests:
"The Bacon/Shakespeare controversy, reading English literature, both professionally and recreationally, films, theatre, golf, rugby football, tennis. Regarding science fiction and the secondary school, I can say this: certainly children (especially boys) of 13-17 are reading SF more widely than ever before. Some classics in the field have appeared on the list of prescribed books for Public Examinations. There is some resistance from older teachers of English, a consequence of ignorance of the genre and a suspicion that it is all of the "B.E.M." variety. My own teaching of SF stories has met with great enthusiasm from students, and has led them to demand more. As SF is becoming more academically respectable, no doubt the next ten years will see a further change in the attitude of educationalists, so long as there is a plentiful supply of good writing. The present shortage of complex characterizations does make depth teaching difficult."

* * * * *

JOHN BARTH

Full Name: John Simmons Barth.
Born May 27, 1930, at Cambridge, Massachusetts. Son of John Jacob Barth and Georgia Simmons. Married Harriette Anne Strickland, January 11, 1950. Three children: Christine, John, Daniel.

Education: A.B., Johns Hopkins University, 1951; M.A., 1952; also attended Juillard School of Music.

JOHN BARTH (cont.)

Career: Writer & instructor.
Instructor in English, Pennsylvania State University, University Park, 1953-56; Asst. Professor, 1957-60; Associate Professor, 1960-65; Research grant at SUNY Buffalo, 1965-66; Professor of English at SUNY Buffalo 1966-DATE.

Literary Agent: Lurton Blassingame, 60 E. 42nd St., New York, NY 10017.

Honors: National Institute of Arts and Letters grant.

* * * * *

VERNON BARTLETT

Full Name: Vernon Bartlett.
Born April 30, 1894, at Westbury, Wiltshire, England. Son of Thomas Oldfeld Bartlett and Beatrice Jecks. Married Marguerite van den Bemden, September 25, 1917 (died 1966); married Eleanor Needham Ritchie, 1969. Two children: Dennis Oldfeld, Maurice Oldfeld.

Education: Attended Blundell's School, Tiverton, Devonshire.

Career: Reporter and commentator.
Staff member, *London Daily Mail*, 1916; Reporter, Reuters Agency, 1917; Special Correspondent in various European countries, *London Times*, 1919-22; London Director, League of Nations, 1922-32; Radio Broadcaster on Foreign Affairs, British Broadcasting Corp., 1928-34; Staff member, *News Chronicle*, 1934-54; Political Commentator, *Straits Times*, Singapore, 1954-61; Independent Progressive Member of Parliament for the Bridgewater constituency, Somerset, 1938-50; Founder, Vox Mundi Books, 1947; Member, UN Advisory Committee of Experts, 1948.

Honors: Commander of the British Empire, 1956.

Member: Garrick Club, Beefsteak Club, Special Forces Club.

* * * * *

WILLIAM BARTON

Full Name: William Renald Barton III.
Born September 28, 1950, at Boston, Massachusetts. Son of William Renald Barton, Jr. (a geologist) and Hazel Eileen Jones (a cashier). One son, Matthew Benjamin Sandy (born 1974).

Education: Attended Northern Virginia Community College, 1969-72.

Career: Writer.
Fry-cook, Gino's Inc., 1969-70; Free-lance writer, 1972-DATE.

First Professional Sale: *Hunting on Kunderer,* Ace Books, 1973.

Interests:
Music, art, cartography, guitar playing, strenuous dieting, collecting old "78s," carpentry and cabinetmaking, lumbering about on very small mountains, bar-hopping, bicycling, speculative engineering designs, and gourmand cooking.

Barton writes:
"Being the son of a government worker, I grew up all over the United States, rarely spending more than a year (usually less) in one place. Consequently, I had few friends. As a result, I began to turn inward for entertainment, which is quite probably the reason why I eventually became a writer. Upon entering puberty, I was forced to endure my parents' divorce and my own obesity simultaneously, which meant that, although I lived in one place and knew the same people for quite a while, I still had a lousy time of it. With these added annoyances to goad me, I, and a friend who had similar problems, set down to write a number of novels and short stories. We were Edgar Rice Burroughs freaks at the time, so guess what they were? Right. They were lousy.

"So...eventually, I went to college, lost 85 pounds, wrote a novel which sold, and dropped out of college. Oh, well. Then I joined a group marriage, which failed quite abyssmally. Then I went to live with Lois, with whom I collaborated on the authorship of Matthew, and who keeps a foolish grin upon my face at all times. Drug experiences? Well, yes, but not important ones; so now I sit around, broke all the time, writing when I can, and looking for work when I feel up to it. What a boor.

"As for writing, I intend continuing what I'm doing, in the same general way that I'm doing it, until I flip out and depart permanently from reality. Or whatever. From the ideas that I've had, from what I've seen around me, it is reasonable to assume that, in this genre, within ten years, I'll either be a major force or a laughing-stock. Meanwhile, I intend to sit here, with femme and fils, petting my cat and playing with my dog, and lazing about in the warm, mellow sunshine as much as possible.

"Regarding *Hunting on Kunderer*, in the spring of 1972, while boasting about what a good writer I was to a friend, I found that everyone thought that I was just being my usual idiotic self, and I was challenged to prove what I was saying by writing a novel and getting it published. Which I set out to do. After going through my notes on the Starover Series, and finding nothing satisfactory, I set back to consider a wholly new subject, and the germ of an idea began to form. At the time, I was simultaneously reading *Bernard Baruch: My Own Story*, a book about dinosaurs, and a few things on Sumerian mythology, one of which was called *Gilgamesh and the Mulupuu Tree*, I believe. There was, in addition, my usually SF fare, and, as they melded together in my mind, I began to notice a certain commonality of characters, events, and motivations in them. So I read *Beowulf*, the *Bible*, and the *Book of Mormon*. After I had compounded a slush of it all in my mind, I sat down, without referring back, and began to write a tale of how all men seek eternal life, and the surrogates that they put in immortality's place. Like money and power, for instance. As a sub-idea, I also thought: 'Since we don't understand ourselves, how can we possibly understand each other?'

"Some of the other names were derived in equally obvious ways: Maryam represents Mary Magdalene; Scott MacLeod, the Space Angel, represents the failure of interaction between man, culture, and technology. Soring represents Christ and the failure of religion (or science and the failure of technology). Of necessity, of course, not all the names are in parallel. Tikavøi represents the failure of Freud, and so on....

"Told you I was a boor. Maybe Oscar Wilde was right."

OTTO BASIL

Full Name: Otto Basil.
   Born December 24, 1901, at Vienna, Austria. Son of Franz Basil and Leopoldine Hoermann. Married Christine Kuepper, April 3, 1948. One daughter: Jutta; one stepson: Andreas.

Education: Attended University of Vienna, 1921-23.

Career: Writer.
   Clerk, Laenderbank & Marmarosh Blank Banca, Vienna, 1920-22; Clerk, Bohler Steel Works, Vienna, 1924-45; Editor and Member, Board of Directions, Verlag Erwin Mueller, 1945-48; Theatre and Movie Critic, and Book Reviewer, *Neues Oesterreich*, Vienna, 1948-67; Free-lance writer, 1967-DATE.

Honors: Literaturpreis der Stadt Wien, 1964, for his work in literature and journalism.

Member: P.E.N.; International Nestroy Society; Collegium Wiener Dramaturgie.

* * * * *

T. J. BASS

Full Name: Thomas Joseph Bassler.
   Born July 7, 1932, at Clinton, Iowa. Son of Louis Bassler (a shoe repairer) and Faustina Slattery (a registered nurse). Married Gloria Napoli, 1960. Six children: Sara (born 1961), Tom (born 1963), Joan (born 1965), Mary (born 1967), Karl (born 1969), David (born 1971).

Education: B.A., St. Ambrose College, 1955; M.D., State University of Iowa, 1959.

Career: Pathologist.
   Deputy Medical Examiner, Los Angeles, 1961-64; pathologist in private practice, Los Angeles area, 1964-DATE; Editor, *American Medical Joggers Newsletter*, 1972-DATE; Consultant, National Joggers Association.

First Professional Sale: "Star Seeder," in *Worlds of If*, September 1969.

Member:
   Science Fiction Writers of America; American Medical Joggers Association; National Joggers Association; Alpha Omega Alpha (medical honor society).

Interests:
   "Use of marathon running for prevention of coronary heart disease. In *Lancet*, 2:711, 1972, I was the first to publish that immunity to heart disease is associated with the ability to run 42 kilometers (26.2 miles). Since that time, cardiac patients have trained to run marathons after recovering from myocardial infaction. Through the American Medical Joggers Association, founded by Dr. Ronald M. Lawrence, and the National Joggers Association, I hope to encourage large numbers of men to train up to marathon distances and share in this easy protection against coronary heart disease. The life-style of the marathorn runner appears to reduce most risk factors. He does not smoke. His diet is rich in polyunsaturates, vitamins C and E. He avoids the excessive use of alcohol, refined starch, and sucrose.

And while his interest is improved racing performance, not coronary protection, most cardiologists recognise this life-style as beneficial in reducing the incidence of atherosclerosis, and can apply it to their patients. The results of such applications are extraordinary: I've never had a case of my own, or seen one reported in medical literature, where fatal coronary disease occurred in an individual who had finished a 42 km. marathon at any time in his life."

* * * * *

ROBERT BATEMAN

Full Name: Robert Moyes Carruthers Bateman.
   Born June 21, 1922, at Manchester, England. Son of Gerald Ashworth Bateman and Agnes Helen Moyes. Married Margot Winifred Wardle, September 20, 1957. Four children: Geoffrey, Jacqueline, Felicity, Lucy Emma.

Education: Attended Kelly College, Tavistock, England, and Melville College, Edinburgh, Scotland.

Career: Television writer and editor.
   Chief Sub-Editor, and then Sports Editor, for the Independent Television News Ltd., 1955-73. Died at Ifield, Sussex, England, April 12, 1973.

First Professional Sale: "Instructions to Young Athletes," published 1956.

Most of Bateman's writing was children's fiction, with some nonfiction work for both children and adults. He was a member of various philatelic organizations.

* * * * *

JOHN BAXTER

Full Name: John Baxter.
   Born December 14, 1939, at Sydney, Australia. Son of John Archibald William Baxter (a chef) and Cathleen Konrad. Married Merie Elizabeth Brooker, September 1, 1962 (divorced, 1967).

Education: Attended Waverly College, Sydney, 1944-54.

Career: Controller and author.
   Staff Controller, New South Wales State Government, Sydney, 1957-67; Director of Publicity, Australian Commonwealth Film Unit, Sydney, 1967-70; Member of Board, Sydney Film Festival, 1968-69; spent 1970 visiting various European film festivals and archives, and doing film research; free-lance writer.

Awards:
   Bronze Medal, Australian Film Awards, 1969, for his script, "After Proust"; Silver Medal, Kranj Film Festival, Yugoslavia, 1970, for his script, "Golf in Australia"; First Prize, Benson and Hedges Australian Film Competition, 1970, for his television documentary, "No Roses for Michael."

Member:
   Royal Commonwealth Society, London; British Film Institute; Sydney Film Study Group (President, 1967-68).

Agent: E.J. Carnell, 17 Burwash Rd., London SE18.

BARRINGTON J. BAYLEY

Full Name: Barrington John Bayley.
   Born April 9, 1937, at Birmingham, England. Son of John Bayley (a toolmaker) and Clarissa Love. Married Joan Lucy Clarke, October 30, 1969. One son, Sean.

Education: Attended school in Shropshire, England.

Career: Writer.
   Has worked in the civil service, in the Australian public service in London, and as a coal miner; served in the Royal Air Force, 1955-57.

Literary Agent: Scott Meredith, 580 Fifth Avenue, New York, NY 10036.

* * * * *

J. C. BAYLISS

Full Name: John Clifford Bayliss.
   Born October 4, 1919, at Wotton-under-Edge, Gloucester, England. Son of Alfred Edward Macduff Bayliss (a teacher) and Doris Isabel Herrick. Married Amalia Fleischerova. One daughter, Clare Yvonne.

Education: B.A., Cambridge University, 1940; M.A., 1944.

Career: Editor.
   Assistant Principal, Colonial Office, London, 1946-49; Editor, Macmillan & Co., London, 1949-52; Senior Editorial Officer, Northern Rhodesia and Nyasaland Publications Bureau, Lusaka, 1952-59; Principal Information Officer, Central Office of Information, London, 1959-DATE.

* * * * *

PETER S. BEAGLE

Full Name: Peter Soyer Beagle.
   Born April 20, 1939, at New York, New York. Son of Simon Beagle (a teacher) and Rebecca Soyer (a teacher). Married Enid Elaine Nordeen, May 8, 1964. Three children: Vicki Lynn (born 1954), Kalisa (born 1958), Daniel Nordeen (born 1962).

Education: B.A., University of Pittsburgh, 1959; attended Stanford University, 1960-61.

Career: Writer.
   Has been a writer all his life.

First Professional Sale: "Telephone Call," in *Seventeen*, 1956.

Literary Agent: McIntosh & Otis, 475 Fifth Ave., New York, NY 10017.

Honors: Scholastic Writing Scholarship, 1955; Wallace Stegner Writing Fellowship, 1960-61; Guggenheim Foundation Award, 1972-73.

Beagle has been a dishwasher and a coffeehouse singer. His informal education, he says, includes "marriage, libraries, animals, people," and he numbers among his interests "singing, songwriting, guitar, and winemaking." He adds: "My main interest as a writer is the common ground that the Perfectly Serious shares with the Absurd, the matter-of-fact with the terrifying, the costume with the skin, the mask with the face. I don't know if this is the only way to deal with America (which is certainly as fantastic a country as Middle-Earth or Prydain, and almost as real), but it concerns and challenges me right now. If I can get that continually shifting frontier mapped--at least for a moment--then I'll try something else. Fantasy, for me, is a way of seeing, rather than a definite state or style. In a sense, none of my books are fantasies; in another sense, they will all be, even the reportorially 'realistic' ones. It's just the way I see things, all the time."

* * * * *

CARLETON BEALS

Full Name: Carleton Beals.
   Born November 13, 1893, at Medicine Lodge, Kansas. Son of Leon Eli Beals and Elvina S. Blickensderfer. Married Carolyn Kennedy (a farmer), June 30, 1956.

Education: B.A., University of California, 1916; M.A., Columbia University, 1917.

Career: Correspondent.
   Principal, American High School, Mexico City, 1919-20; Correspondent in Spain and Italy for *Nation* and *Current History*, 1921-23; Lecturer, New York School Board, 1924-25; Faculty Lecturer, National University of Mexico, 1927; Correspondent, *Nation*, 1926-27; Lecturer, University of California, Berkeley, 1932; Correspondent, North American Newspaper Alliance, 1934; Correspondent for the *New York Post*, covering the Scottsboro Trial, 1935; Lecturer, New School for Social Research, 1936; President, *Latin American Digest*, during the mid-1930s; Latin American Correspondent for *Nation* in Cuba and Haiti, 1957, 1959, and for the magazine *Independent*, 1960-61; consultant, writer, lecturer.

Literary Agent: Berta Klausner, 130 E. 40th St., New York, NY 10016.

Awards:
   Guggenheim Fellowship, 1931; award from *Arizona Quarterly* for best article of 1961. Member: P.E.N.

* * * * *

NOEL de VIC BEAMISH

Full Name: Annie O'Meara de Vic Beamish.
   Born April 30, 1883, at Dublin, Ireland. Daughter of Frank John de Vic (a military chaplain) and Annie S. Greenfield.

Education:
   Beamish was privately educated at home by tutors and governesses.

Career: Writer.
   Novelist; founder and director of language schools in various parts of Europe.

Agent: John Farquharson Ltd., 15 Red Lion Square, London W.C.1, England. Member: Club Gastronomie, Paris.

C. G. BEARNE

Full Name: Colin Gerald Bearne [pronounced Bee-urn]
   Born November 14, 1939, at Plymouth, Devonshire,
England. Son of Gerald Bearne (an Admiralty execu-
tive officer) and Margaret Child. Married Denise
Dapot, March 30, 1967. Two children: Joseph Edward.
(born 1972), Lucy Emily (born 1973).

Education:
   B.A., Birmingham University, 1962; M.A., 1963;
attended Moscow State University from 1964-65 on a
British Council postgraduate exchange.

Career: Lecturer in Russian.
   Lecturer in Russian, School of European Studies,
University of Sussex, 1965-DATE.

First Professional Sale: *Tales from Thedon*,
   Pergamon Press, 1966.

Member:
   Association of University Teachers; British Universities Association of Slavists; Association of Teachers
of Russian.

Interests:
   Walking, reading, music, birds.

Bearne's anthology of Russian science fiction, *Vortex*, was published in 1970. He writes: "I have been
rather out of touch with the SF world in the Soviet
Union in recent years. The Soviet SF I read between
1966 and 1970 was distinctly different from that
appearing in the West. To begin with, there was much
less interest on the part of authors in machinery
and technological gadgetry. Instead, there seemed a
double stream of approach: a) interest in exploring
the process of human perception of time and time
warps; b) the question of the preservation of certain
basic human reactions, love, fear, pity, under pressure
from technological advances. If this means 'unsophisticated,' then I would have thought American SF is
slightly different from my vision of it.
   "A few years ago, Bradbury and Wyndham were being
translated into Russian, and published in editions of
100,000 or thereabouts. Soviet SF was issued in paperback form, and normally in the same number of
copies. I see no evidence of a crackdown on writers.
On the contrary, if anything there has been an increase in the number of authors in recent years."

* * * * *

JEROME BEATTY JR.

Full Name: Jerome Beatty, Jr.
   Born December 9, 1918, at New Rochelle, New York.

Education: B.A., Dartmouth College, 1939.

Career: Editor & writer.
   Reporter, *Newark News*, 1940-43; Military Service,
US Army, 1943-46, as an interpreter attached to the
Chinese Army; Associate Editor, *Coronet*, 1946-49;
Associate Editor, *Pageant*, 1949-52; Staff Writer for
Collier's Magazine, 1952-57; Free-lance writer, 1957-
DATE.

Beatty's first published book was *I Married a Barracks
Bag*, published in 1944 by the Kaw River Press.

CHARLES BEAUMONT

Full Name: Charles Nutt.
   Born January 2, 1929, at Chicago, Illinois. Son of
Charles Hiram Nutt and Violet Phillips. Married Helen
Louise Broun, 1949. Four children: Christopher,
Catherine, Elizabeth, Gregory.

Education: Self-educated beyond the second year of
   high school.

Career: Writer.
   Beaumont was a free-lance writer all his life. He
died in Los Angeles on February 21, 1967, from a long
and debilitating disease.

Literary Agent: Harold Matson, 22 E. 40th St.,
   New York, NY 10016.

Awards:
   Jules Verne Award, 1954; *Playboy* Award for best nonfiction of the year, 1961.

* * * * *

SIMONE de BEAUVOIR

Full Name: Simone Lucie Ernestine Marie de Beauvoir.
   Born January 9, 1908, at Paris, France. Daughter of
Georges Bertrand de Beauvoir (an advocate to the Court
of Appeal, Paris) and Françoise Brasseur.

Education:
   Attended Institut Normal Catholique Adelina-Désir,
Paris, and Institution Sainte-Marie de Neuilly-sur-
Seine; Licencie ès Lettres, Agrégé des Lettres, Sor-
bonne, University of Paris, 1929.

Career: Writer.
   Teacher of Philosophy, Lycée Montgrand, Marseilles,
1931-33; at Lycée Jeanne d'Arc, Rouen, 1933-37; at
Lycée Molière and Lycée Camille-See, Paris, 1938-43;
Full-time writer, 1943-DATE; Editor, with Jean-Paul
Sartre, *Les Temps Modernes*, 1945-DATE.

Awards: Prix Goncourt, 1945, for *Les Mandarins*; LL.D.
Cambridge University.

Member: International War Crimes Tribunal.

* * * * *

JACK BEECHING

Full Name: Jack Beeching.
   Married Amy Brown (an author and translator), 1950.
Two children: John Rutland, Laura Caroline.

Career: Writer.
   Beeching has been a professional writer all of his
life. He prefers writing poetry, but "other forms
of writing are a means of livelihood." Since the mid-
1950s, he and his wife have lived abroad for long
periods. Many of his novels are juveniles written
with his wife under the joint pseudonym, James Barbery.
He is fluent in French and Spanish.

Literary Agent:
   Hope Leresche & Steele, 11 Jubilee Place, Chelsea,
London S.W.3, England.

HARRY BEHN

Full Name: Harry Behn.
  Born September 24, 1898, in Yavapai County, Arizona.
Son of Henry K. Behn (a miner) and Maren Christensen.
Married Alice Lawrence. Three children: Pamela,
Prescott, Peter.

Education: A.B., Harvard University, 1922.

Career: Teacher & Writer.
  Scenario writer for various motion picture studios,
1925-35; Teacher of Creative Writing, University of
Arizona, Tucson, 1938-47 (Founder and Manager of its
radio bureau, 1938-47; and founder of the University
of Arizona Press, 1960). Died September 4, 1973.

Awards:
  Graduate fellowship in Sweden, 1923-24; Graphic
Arts awards for the book design of *The Little Hill,
All Kinds of Time, The Painted Cave*; Honor Award of
Boys' Clubs of America for *Omen of the Birds*; award
of merit of the Claremont Graduate College, for
Cricket Songs.

Agent: Curtis Brown Ltd., 60 E. 56th St., New York,
  NY 10022.

* * * * *

NORMAN BELL

Full Name: Norman Edward Bell.
  Born July 26, 1899, at Winnemucca, Nevada. Son of
William John Bell (a mine owner) and Freelie Choate.
Married Ysabel Mary Mannix, September 9, 1939. One
daughter, Lucinda Cecile.

Education: B.A., University of Nevada, 1927.

Career: Reporter.
  Worked as a ranch hand, clerk, and delivery truck
driver in Nevada and California, 1920-27; Reporter,
Reno Evening Gazette, 1927; Reporter, *Nevada State
Journal*, 1928-32; Reporter, Editor, and Writer for
the Associated Press, 1932-64.

* * * * *

JOHN BELLAIRS

Full Name: John Bellairs.
  Born January 17, 1938, at Marshall, Michigan. Son
of Frank Edward Bellairs and Virginia Monk. Married
Priscilla Braids, June 24, 1968.

Education: A.B., University of Notre Dame, 1959;
M.A., University of Chicago, 1960.

Career: Instructor in English.
  Instructor in English, College of St. Teresa, 1963-
65; Member of the Humanities Faculty, Shimer College,
Mount Carroll, Illinois, 1966-67; Instructor in Eng-
lish, Emmanuel College, Boston, Massachusetts, 1968-
DATE.

Awards:
Woodrow Wilson Fellowship.

Interests: Archaeology, history, trivia.

LAURA BENET

Full Name: Laura Benét.
  Born June 13, 1884, at Fort Hamilton, Brooklyn, New
York. Daughter of James Walker Benét (an Army officer)
and Frances Neill Rose.

Education: A.B., Vassar College, 1907.

Career: Writer.
  Settlement worker, Spring Street Settlement, New York
1913-16; Inspector, Red Cross Sanitary Commission,
Augusta, Georgia, during World War I; Visitor, St.
Bartholomew's Mission, New York, 1924-25; Asst. Editor,
Book Page, *New York Evening Post*. 1926-28; Assistant
to the Book Page Editor, *New York Sun*, 1928-28; Full-
time writer, 1930-DATE.

Honors: D.Litt., Moravian College, 1967; various
  poetry prizes from *Lyric* and *Voices*.

Member:
  Poetry Society of America; P.E.N.; Women Poets;
Craftsman Group; Pen and Brush Club.

* * * * *

GREG BENFORD

Full Name: Gregory Albert Benford.
  Born January 30, 1941, at Mobile, Alabama. Son of
James Benford (a teacher and military officer) and
Eloise Nelson (a teacher). Married Joan Abbe, August
26, 1967. Two children: Alyson (born 1971); Mark
(born 1973).

Education: B.S., University of Oklahoma, 1963; Ph.D.
  University of California, 1967.

Career: Professor of Physics.
  Physicist, Lawrence Radiation Lab, 1967-71; Professor
of Physics, University of California, Irvine, 1971-DATE

First Professional Sale:
  "Stand-In," in *The Magazine of Fantasy and Science
Fiction*, June, 1965.

Member: Science Fiction Writers of America.

Benford writes:
  "I'm one of the few writers who is a scientist,
which may change the way I view SF. I'm most interested (as a writer) in mysticism, science--and things
in between." Benford won a Nebula Award, Best Novelette
1974 (1975), "The Stars Are Gods."

* * * * *

MARGOT BENNETT

Full Name: Margot Bennett.
  Born 1903 in Scotland. Four children: one daughter,
three sons.

Career: Writer. First Professional Sale: *Time to
  Change Hats*, published in 1943. Agent: David Higham
  Associates, 5 Lower John St., London W.1, England.

Interests: Travel, mythology, psychology, genetics.
  "I am a professional writer, but I write for pleasure.
For years I have switched back and forwards between TV
and books."

DONALD R. BENSEN

Full Name: Donald Roynold Bensen.
Born October 3, 1927, at Brooklyn, New York. Son of Roynold Bensen (an accountant and salesman) and Dorothy Olive Thatcher. Married Anne McCurdy, October 11, 1957. One son, Nicholas Thatcher (born 1965).

Education: A.B., Columbia College, 1950.

Career: Editor.
Production Manager, Wilfred Funk Inc., 1951-52; Editor, Peoples Book Club, 1952-56; Assistant, Advertising Department, American Export Lines, 1956-57; Editor and Editor-in-Chief, Pyramid Books, 1957-68; Executive Editor, Berkley Books, 1968-70; Senior Editor, Ballantine Books and Beagle Books, 1970-DATE.

First Professional Sale: *The Unknown*, an anthology published by Pyramid Books, 1963.

Member: Mystery Writers of America (National Director, 1967-71, 1973).

Bensen talks about fantasy and science fiction:
"I got involved with fantasy before SF. In July, 1940, when I was 12, I chanced to get a copy of *Unknown* to read at the beach, and was hooked right off--first story in that issue was "The Mathematics of Magic," by de Camp and Pratt (part 2 of *The Incomplete Enchanter*), and I think Sturgeon's "It" was in the same issue. I had been reading *Weird Tales* for years, but this stuff was different and better, close to Thorne Smith, whom I'd been devouring since I was seven. I got back issues of the magazine when I could, and all the new ones until it folded. About 1947, I looked at *Astounding*, figuring if Campbell could do so well with fantasy, the SF might be OK; and I liked it, kept buying and reading it, and was delighted when *F&SF* and *Galaxy* started. I was a heavy reader, but not a Fan.
"When I got to Pyramid in '57, they had a minor SF list, with maybe one George O. Smith, and (I think) *The Caves of Steel*. I started buying up a lot of the good stuff I remembered from the magazines, like *Needle*, got a lot of originals going (from Judy Merrill, Sturgeon, Poul Anderson, Gordy Dickson, etc.), and was lucky enough to be offered Cordwainer Smith's novel. There was a lot of stuff around then, much of it published originally by Gnome Press, which was never very aggressive about reprint rights, plus good books from Shasta and so on; so it was rather easy to build up a strong reprint list. Competition was practically nil--only Ace was doing much with SF reprints (Bantam was sticking to safe old Bradbury, and NAL had a bunch of equally safe Heinleins), and Ballantine was strictly original.
"I tended to pick what I liked as a reader (with the exception of Doc Smith's books, which never turned me on), and not bother much about Old Wave/New Wave arguments--would happily publish Raymond Z. Gallun or Harlan Ellison if the books read OK.
"My boss at Pyramid was firmly convinced that SF was pulp, and that the titles had to show this. When they retitled Raymond Jones' *Renaissance*, a classic, to *Man of Two Worlds*, I resolved to come up with SF titles that couldn't be argued with, and commissioned Phil Dick to write *The Zap Gun*, and Jack Vance to do *Space Opera*. 'The Zap Gun? What kind of science fiction title is that?' said my boss--and there was a strong effort to retitle the Vance book to *Space Ritual*. You can't win.

"I know the Pyramid list was very good then--a lot of the books I bought are still in print there and being reissued--and I think the reason was that I was an enthusiastic, but not Fannish, reader, without any scientific background. With no notion of what SF *should* be, and the dimmest understanding of anything technical, I could be pretty sure that what I could understand would be understood by the reader; and that a story that appealed to me when I was twenty, reading it in the magazines, and then again ten years later when I was considering it for Pyramid, probably would hold enough readers to make it worth reprinting."

* * * * *

EVELYN BERCKMAN

Full Name: Evelyn Domenica Berckman.
Born October 18, 1900, at Philadelphia, Pennsylvania. Daughter of Aaron Berckman and Ann Altman.

Career: Writer and musician.
Berckman's compositions have been performed by the Philadelphia Orchestra, Rochester Symphony, and others.

Literary Agent: McIntosh & Otis, 475 Fifth Avenue, New York, NY 10017.

Awards: Red Badge Award, Dodd, Mead & Co., 1954.

Member: Curzon Club, Hamilton Club, West Kent Club.

* * * * *

THOMAS BERGER

Full Name: Thomas Louis Berger.
Born July 20, 1924, at Cincinnati, Ohio. Son of Thomas Charles Berger and Mildred Bubbe. Married Jeanne Redpath, 1950.

Education: B.A., University of Cincinnati, 1948.

Career: Writer.
Librarian, Rand School of Social Science, 1948-51; Staff Member, *New York Times Index*, 1951-52; Assoc. Editor, *Popular Science*, 1952-53; writer, 1953-DATE.

Awards:
Richard and Hinda Rosenthal Award, National Institute of Arts and Letters, 1965, for *Little Big Man*. Member: P.E.N., Authors Guild. Agent: Harold Matson Co., 22 E. 40th St., New York, NY 10016.

* * * * *

BERNARD BERGONZI

Full Name: Bernard Bergonzi.
Born April 13, 1929, at London, England. Son of Charles Ernest Bergonzi and Louisa Lloyd. Married Gabriel Wall, April 19, 1960. Three children: Benet, Clarissa, Lucy.

Education: B.Litt., Oxford University, 1961; M.A., 1962.

Literary Agent: A.D. Peters, 10 Buckingham St., Adelphi, London W.C.2, England.

BERNARD BERGONZI (cont.)

Career: Professor of English.
  Assistant Lecturer, then Lecturer in English, University of Manchester, 1959-66; Senior Lecturer, University of Warwick, 1966-71; Professor of English, 1971-DATE; Visiting Lecturer, Brandeis University, 1964-65; Beckman Summer Lecturer, University of California, Berkeley, 1965.

* * * * *

HUBERT BERMONT

Full Name: Hubert Ingram Bermont.
  Born May 2, 1924, at New York, New York. Son of George J. Bermont (a music teacher) and Naomi Horowitz. Married Aynne Abeles (a radio public relations director), March 9, 1947 (divorced 1967); married Shelly Langston (a child photographer), February 1971. One son: Sheldon.

Education: B.A., New York University.

Career: Business executive.
  Executive Director of Branch Stores, Brentano's, 1957-67; Director of his own book industry consultation firm, 1967-DATE.

* * * * *

CHRISTINE BERNARD

Full Name: Christine Ruth Bernard.
  Born January 28, 1926, at London, England. Daughter of Anthony Bernard (a composer and conductor) and Marie Augustine Jourdan. Married 1) Douglas Jackson; 2) Richard Jennings. Two children: Kit Havinden Jackson (born 1948), Emma Marie Jackson (born 1953).

Education: Attended Reading University in England.

Career: Writer and editor.
  Has been an editor of a children's weekly newspaper; Editor of Fontana Books, London, for eight years; Senior Editor of Studio Vista Paperbacks in London; now a free-lance author.

Interests: Theatre, music, gardening, tennis.

* * * * *

JACK BERTIN

Full Name: John Bertin (originally Giovanni Bertignono Jr.). Born August 11, 1904, at Cigliano, Italy. Son of Mr. and Mrs. Giovanni Bertignono.

Education: Attended Peoples University, New Bedford, Massachusetts.

Career: Writer.

First Professional Sale: Short stories to West Magazine and Black Mask, 1928-29.

Member: Alpine Club, New Bedford, Mass. (Founder).

Bertin died in November, 1963.

PIERRE BERTON

Full Name: Pierre Berton.
  Born July 12, 1920, at Whitehorse, Yukon, Canada. Son of Francis George Berton (a mining recorder) and Laura Thompson. Married Janet Walker, 1946. Six children: Penny, Pamela, Patricia, Peter, Paul, Peggy Ann.

Education: B.A., University of British Columbia, 1941.

Career: Editor.
  City Editor, Vancouver News Herald, 1941-42; Feature Writer, Vancouver Sun, 1946-47; Managing Editor, Maclean's Magazine, 1947-58; Associate Editor and Daily Columnist, Toronto Daily Star, 1958-62; Contributing Editor, Maclean's, 1963-64; Editor-in-Chief, Canadian Centennial Library, 1963-DATE; television commentator and panelist; free-lance writer.

Agent: Willis Kingsley Wing, 24 E. 38th St., New York, NY 10016.

Awards:
  Governor General's Award for Creative Non-Fiction, 1956, The Mysterious North; and, 1958, The Klondike Fever; Stephen Leacock Medal for Humor, 1959, Just Add Water and Stir; J. V. McAree Award for Columnist of the Year, 1959; National Newspaper Awards for Feature Writing and Staff Corresponding, 1960; Film of the Year Award in Canada, and Grand Prix at Cannes for "City of Gold."

Member:
  Authors League of America; Association of Canadian Radio and Television Artists; American Federation of Radio and Television Artists; Toronto Men's Press Club; Celebrity Club.

* * * * *

HERBERT BEST

Full Name: Oswald Herbert Best.
  Born March 25, 1894, at Chester, England. Son of John Dugdale Best (a clergyman) and Julia Deacon. Married Evangel Allena Champlin (an author and illustrator), July 12, 1926.

Education: Attended King's School, Chester; LL.B., Queen's College, Cambridge University, 1914.

Career: Author.
  With the British Colonial Service in Nigeria, 1919-32, holding administrative and judicial posts, including commissioner of the Supreme Court; Full-time author, 1930-DATE.

Member: Royal Geographical Society (Fellow).

* * * * *

ALFRED BESTER

Full Name: Alfred Bester.
  Born December 18, 1913, at New York, New York. Son of James J. Bester (a shoe merchant) and Belle Silverman. Married Rolly Goulko (an advertising executive), September 16, 1936.

ALFRED BESTER (cont.)

Education: B.A., University of Pennsylvania, 1935.

Career: Author & editor.
Was a free-lance writer in the 1940s and 1950s; served as editor of several different popular magazines from the mid-1950s to the early 1970s; returned to writing full-time about 1972.

Awards: Hugo Award, Best Novel, 1952 (1953), *The Demolished Man*.

Member: Science Fiction Writers of America.

* * * * *

H. U. BEVIS

Full Name: Herbert Urlin Bevis.
Born December 27, 1902, at Bascom, Florida. Son of Robert Calhoun Bevis (a grocer) and Mary Augusta Etheridge. Married Jennie Anderson, November 7, 1928. Three children: Herbert A., Patricia Ann, Virginia.

Education: Attended high school in Greenwood, FL.

Career: Seaman and painter.
Farmer during his teen years in Florida; Seaman, U.S. Coast Guard, 1922-23; Sailor, 1923-27; house painter in Florida, 1928-DATE.

* * * * *

CARL BIEMILLER

Full Name: Carl Ludwig Biemiller, Jr.
Born December 16, 1912, at Camden, New Jersey. Son of Carl Ludwig Biemiller (a printer/pressman) and Charlotte Curtis. Married Fanonda Mulvey (a teacher and painter). Four children: John Bennett (born 1937), Carl Ludwig III (born 1939), Gary Mulvey (born 1941), Eric Curtis (born 1945).

Education: Attended Charles Morris Price School, Philadelphia, and Mulvey Institute.

Career: Author & businessman.
Reporter, columnist, and promotion director, *Philadelphia Record*, 1935-39; Assistant Publisher, *Camden Courier-Post*, 1939-44; on public relations staff, National Association of Manufacturers, New York, 1944-45; Associate, then Executive Editor, *Holiday*, 1945-57; Assistant Publisher, *Philadelphia Daily News*, 1957-58; National Director for Public Affairs, National Association of Manufacturers, 1958-61; Free-lance writer, 1961-68; Public relations, Bell & Stanton Inc., New York, 1968-71; Vice President, Ruder & Finn, New York (a public relations firm), 1971-72; full-time author, 1972-DATE; public relations consultant, 1972-DATE.

* * * * *

LLOYD BIGGLE JR.

Full Name: Lloyd Biggle, Jr.
Born April 17, 1923, at Waterloo, Iowa. Son of Lloyd Biggle and Ethel Cruthers. Married Hedwig T. Janiszewski, June 21, 1947. Two children: Donna Helene, Kenneth Lloyd.

Education:
A.B., Wayne University, 1947; M.M., University of Michigan, 1948; Ph.D., University of Michigan, 1953.

Career: Writer, teacher, musicologist.
Teacher of Music Literature and History, University of Michigan, 1948-51; full-time writer, 1951-DATE.

Member: Authors Guild; Science Fiction Writers of America (First Secretary/Treasurer, 1965-67).

Biggle mentions:
"*The World Menders* is a very oblique sequel to *The Still, Small Voice of Trumpets*. There are no characters in common, but the same galactic organizations are involved. *This Darkening Universe* is the third novel in the Jan Darzek series, of which the first two were *All the Colors of Darkness* and *Watchers of the Dark*."

* * * * *

EANDO BINDER

Full Name: Otto Oscar Binder.
Born August 26, 1911, at Bessemer, Michigan. Son of Michael Binder and Marie Payer. Married Ione Frances Turek, November 2, 1940. One daughter, Mary Lorine (died 1967).

Education: Attended Crane City College, Northwestern University, University of Chicago.

Career: Writer.
Free-lance writer, 1930-74, chiefly of comics; Editor and Publisher of *Space World*, 1960-63.

First Professional Sale: "The First Martian," in *Amazing*, October, 1932 (with Earl Binder as Eando Binder).

Agent: Scott Meredith, 580 Fifth Avenue, New York, NY 10036.

Binder writes:
"According to Sam Moskowitz, my single original contribution to science fiction--that is, introducing a new category of stories--is the *first-person robot story*, as per my Adam Link series. They were not the first robot stories, of course, but the first written from the point of view of the robot, giving them a 'humanizing' depth never before attained.
"My impression of the science fiction field today is that the magazines have fallen into some kind of semi-limbo, and show little signs of change, improvement, or appeal, whereas the paperback book market is thriving and boisterous, with many new and quite good novel-length tales appearing with perennial regularity.
"As for where the field of science fiction is headed, I think it will always be a stimulating glimpse into the future, near or far, or into strange lands in unknown universes. By combining both a semi-scientific and therefore 'logical' basis to stories, plus pure entertainment value, I think sci-fi is here to stay-- at least in the paperbacks. The magazines?...who knows?

In talking about his early life, Binder had this to say: "I attended night classes at three different schools, but never obtained a degree, being short too many credits at the time, also short of money. But NASA, on contracting me as a writer in 1965 for one year, to write high school educational material on the Mercury, Gemini, and Apollo programs, told me this in

EANDO BINDER (cont.)

effect gave me an honorary M.S. degree (for my long background in science articles and for the editorship of *Space World* magazine). Also, the Goddard Space Flight Center of NASA offered me a post as public relations technical writer on the basis of my qualifications being roughly equivalent to a master's. I can, today, teach science in any high school if I wish, but not college. Among the various courses I took in college were advanced, quantitative, and organic chemistry, aiming for a chemical engineering degree, or advanced chemical research."

Binder died October 14, 1974.

* * * * *

ADOLFO BIOY CASARES

Full Name: Adolfo Bioy Casares.
Born September 15, 1914, at Buenos Aires, Argentina. Son of Adolfo Bioy and Marta Casares. Married Silvina Ocampo (a writer). One daughter, Marta.

Career: Writer.
Has been a professional author since his late teens.

Awards:
Premio Municipal de la Ciudad de Buenos Aires, 1940, for *La Invencion de Morel*; 2nd Premio Nacional de Literatura, 1963, for *El Lado de la Sombra*; 1st Premio Nacional de Literatura, 1969, for *El Gran Serafin*.

* * * * *

WILLIAM HENRY BIRD

Full Name: William Henry Fleming Bird.
Born March 3, 1896, at Thornton Heath Croydon, Surrey, England. Son of Frederick Edward John Bird (a Congregational Minister) and Caroline Sandison. Married Louie Smith, July 23, 1932.

Education: B.A., Cambridge University, 1920.

Career: Lecturer.
Art Lecturer (sculpture), Southend-on-Sea Education Committee, 1928-58.

First Professional Sale: "Critical Age," in *Futuristic Science Stories*, no. 12, 1953.

Bird exhibited his sculpture at the Royal Academy in London, the Duveen Gallery in Leeds, and at several of the Bradford Spring Exhibitions. His interests included riding and fishing. He served in the British Army during the first World War (Royal Field Artillery), and was a prisoner of war in Germany in 1918. He died at Benfleet, Essex, on July 26, 1971.

* * * * *

CHARLES BIRKIN

Full Name: Sir Charles Lloyd Birkin.
Born September 24, 1907, in England. Son of Charles Wilfred Birkin and Claire Howe. Married Janet Johnson, June 16, 1940. Three children: Jennifer Claire, Amanda Jane, John Christian.

Education: Attended Eton College, 1921-26.

Career: Writer.
Has been an advertising copywriter, a publisher, and professional writer.

Birkin is best known for his horror stories, which he has been writing for the past 45 years. When asked what goes into a good horror tale, he replied quite succinctly: "an unexpected twist of a grand guignol nature at the story's end."

* * * * *

GERALD BISHOP

Full Name: Gerald Vernon Bishop.
Born March 8, 1949, at Newcastle-upon-Tyne, England. Son of Edmund Bishop (a professor of analytical science) and Anna Margaret McIver.

Education: Attended Leeds Polytechnic School of Information Science, 1970-72.

Career: Consultant in Science Fiction.
Audio/lighting technician, Northcott Theater, Exeter, 1968-69; Publisher and Editor, Aardvark House, 1968-DATE; Editor, IMR/ABP, 1972-73; Science Fiction Consultant, Halkett & Laing's *Dictionary of Anonymous and Pseudonymous Publications in the English Language*.

First Professional Sale:
Bibliographies to accompany *The Best of Isaac Asimov*, *The Best of Arthur C. Clarke: 1937-1971*, *The Best of Robert Heinlein*, *The Best of John Wyndham*, published in hardcover by Sidgwick & Jackson, and in paper by Sphere Books, 1973.

Honors: Dip. Treac. Tech. (Dunch) *[Honours Causa]*.

Member:
British Science Fiction Association; Society of Indexers; Faraday Telecommunications Association; Off-Trail Magazine Publishers' Association; Stockport and Intake Dog and Cake Walking Society.

Interests: Films, theatre, audio, drinking.

Bishop writes:
"I have been asked by the editor of this volume for my comments on the current state of bibliographical research in Science Fiction. My thoughts are much as they have always been: with a few exceptions, such as the Great Don Tuck, whose *Encyclopedia* is finally appearing after years of *solid, hard, unremitting devotion to research*, and who can be counted without taking your soxs off, most "researchers'" published material is interesting, but one is unable to say anything more than that."

* * * * *

MORCHARD BISHOP

Full Name: Oliver Stonor.
Born July 3, 1903, at Teddington, Middlesex, England.

Career: Author.
Bishop has been an author, journalist, and critic all his life. Most of his books have been published under the name (E.) Morchard Bishop.

MORRIS BISHOP

Full Name: Morris Bishop.
Born April 15, 1893, at Willard, New York. Son of Edwin Rubergall Bishop and Bessie Gilbert. Married Alison Mason Kingsbury, 1927. One daughter, Alison.

Education: A.B., Cornell University, 1913; M.A., 1914; Ph.D., 1926.

Career: Professor of Romance Languages.
Professor of Romance Languages, Cornell University, 1921-60; Visiting Professor, University of Athens, 1951-52; Member, American Relief Administration Mission to Finland, 1919. Died November 20, 1973.

Awards:
Honorary doctorates from five universities; Order of the White Rose, Finland, 1919; Legion of Honor, 1948; Officer d'Academie, France, 1937; Golden Rose of New England Poetry Club, 1959.

Member:
Modern Language Association (President, 1964); Century Club, New York; American Academy of Arts and Sciences (Fellow); American Association of Teachers of French; Phi Beta Kappa; P.E.N.

* * * * *

JEROME BIXBY

Full Name: Drexel Jerome Lewis Bixby.
Born January 11, 1923, at Los Angeles, California. Son of Rex Vancil Bixby (in real estate and plastics) and Ila Lewis. Married Linda Burman (now divorced). Three sons: Russell Albert (born 1962), Jan Emerson (born 1963), Leonardo Brook (born 1966).

Career: Writer.
Has been an insurance investigator, music clerk, and music autographer. Editor, *Planet Stories*, Summer 1950-July, 1951; Editor, *Two Complete Science-Adventure Books*, Winter, 1950-Summer, 1951. Served as an uncredited Associate Editor for *Galaxy*, *Thrilling Wonder Stories*, and *Startling Stories* during the same period. Owner, Exoterica, Bullhead City, Arizona 1963-64. Free-lance writer since the late 1940s.

Member: Writers Guild of America, West.

Interests:
Architecture, painting, symphonic composition. "My main interest at the present time is psychical research. I've concentrated my writing efforts entirely on film work, and I've lost touch with current SF. I doubt that I've made any contribution to the field, as such...wish I had."

* * * * *

JOHN BLACKBURN

Full Name: John Fenwick Blackburn.
Born June 26, 1923, in Northumberland, England. Son of Charles Eliel Blackburn (a clergyman) and Adelaide Fenwick (a watercolour painter). Married Joan Mary Hepburn Clift (a dancer), July 24, 1950.

Education: B.A., Durham University, 1949.

Career: Writer.
Schoolmaster in London, 1949-51; worked for the Control Commission, Berlin, 1951-52; Director, Red Lion Books, 1952-59; Free-lance writer, 1959-DATE.

First Professional Sale: *A Scent of New-Mown Hay*, Secker & Warburg, 1958.

Agent: A. M. Heath, William IV Street, London W.C.1.

Member: Crime Writers Association.

Interests: Hill walking, gossip, dogs, and public houses.

* * * * *

JOHN BLAINE

Full Name: Harold Leland Goodwin.
Born November 20, 1914, at Ellenburgh, New York. Married Elizabeth Swensk, 1947. Three children: Alan, Christopher, Derek.

Education: Attended Elliot Radio School, 1934-35.

Career: Science administrator.
Director of Atomic Test Operations, Federal Civil Defense Administration, 1951-58; Science Advisor, U.S. Information Agency, 1958-61; administrator and advisor with National Aeronautics and Space Administration, 1961-DATE.

Award: Flemming Award, 1953, as an outstanding young man in federal service.

Member:
Antarctican Society; American Science Film Association (editor and board member); Marine Technology Society; Washington Children's Book Guild.

* * * * *

NICHOLAS BLAKE

Full Name: Cecil Day Lewis.
Born April 27, 1904, at Ballintubber, Ireland. Son of F. C. Day Lewis (a minister) and Kathleen Blake Squires. Married Constance Mary King 1928 (divorced 1951); married Jill Angela Henriette Balcon, April 27, 1951. Children: Sean Francis, Nicholas Charles, Lydia Tamasin, Daniel Michael.

Education: Attended Wadham College, Oxford University.

Career: Teacher and poet.
Assistant Master, various English schools, 1927-35; Editor with the Ministry of Information, 1941-46; Clark Lecturer, Trinity College, Cambridge, 1946; Professor of Poetry, Oxford University, 1951-56; Charles Eliot Norton Professor of Poetry, Harvard University, 1964-65; Member of the Arts Council, Britain, 1962-72; Poet Laureate of Great Britain (appointed by Queen Elizabeth II), 1968-72; Member, Board of Directors, Chatto & Windus (publishers). Died May 22, 1972.

Awards:
Companion, Order of the British Empire, 1950; D.Litt. University of Exeter, 1965; D.Litt., University of Hull 1970; Litt.D., Trinity College, Dublin, 1968.

HARRY BLAMIRES

Full Name: Harry Blamires.
Born November 6, 1916, in England. Son of Tom Blamires (a food merchant) and Clara Size. Married Nancy Bowles, December 26, 1940. Five children: Gabriel, Alcuin, Cyprian, Benedict, Fabian.

Education: M.A., University College, Oxford, 1939.

Career: Lecturer in English.
Principal Lecturer in English, King Alfred's College, 1948-DATE.

* * * * *

WILLIAM PETER BLATTY

Full Name: William Peter Blatty.
Born January 7, 1928, at New York, New York. Son of Peter Blatty (a carpenter) and Mary Mouakad. Married Mary Margaret Rigard, February 18, 1950. Three children: Christine Ann, Michael Peter, Mary Joanne.

Education: A.B., Georgetown University, 1950; M.A., George Washington University, 1954.

Career: Publicity director & writer.
Editor, U.S. Information Agency, 1955-57; Publicity Director, University of Southern California, 1957-58; Public Relations Director, Loyola University of Los Angeles, 1959-60; full-time writer, 1960-DATE; served in the USAF Psychological Warfare Division, 1951-54.

Agent: Brandt & Brandt, 101 Park Avenue, New York, NY 10017.

Member: Writers Guild of America.

Award: August Derleth Award, Best Film, 1974 (1975), "The Exorcist."

* * * * *

JAMES BLISH

Full Name: James Benjamin Blish.
Born May 23, 1921, at Orange, New Jersey. Son of Asa Rhodes Blish (an advertising manager) and Dorothea Schneewind (a pianist). Married Virginia Kidd, 1947 (divorced, 1964); Married Judith Ann Lawrence, 1964. Two children: Elisabeth (born 1956), Charles Benjamin (born 1958).

Education: B.Sc., Rutgers University, 1942; attended Columbia University, 1944-46.

Career: Writer and editor.
Editor of various trade newspapers, 1947-54; Science Editor, Chas. Pfizer & Co, 1955-60; Account Executive, Hill & Knowlton, 1962-68; free-lance writer, 1968-75; Editor, Vanguard Science Fiction, June, 1958 (only issue published). Died in England July 30, 1975.

First Professional Sale: "Emergency Refueling," in Super Science Stories, March, 1940.

Agent: Robert P. Mills Ltd., 156 E. 52nd St., New York, NY 10022.

Honors & Awards:
Guest of Honor, 18th World Science Fiction Convention (Pittcon), Pittsburgh, 1960; Hugo Award, Best Novel, 1958 (1959), A Case of Conscience.

Member: Science Fiction Writers of America (Vice-President, 1966-68).

Blish is best known for his award-winning novel, A Case of Conscience, and for his epic quatrology, Cities in Flight. Concerning the latter, he commented: "A cover on a 1948 Astounding, illustrating a van Vogt story (I don't remember which one), showed a man looking down at a rocket shipyard. I first took the scene to show a city; then when I got a second look, I thought, why not? If you have anti-gravity, there should be no limits to the size or shape of what you can lift with it--why not a whole city?
"I wrote a 15,000 word story around the idea, which Campbell rejected, in a four-page single-spaced letter in which he pointed out all the implications of the idea that I had missed. I mined that letter for years, striking out one sentence at a time as I used up John's ideas. (The original rejected story eventually became the last two chapters of Earthman, Come Home.) One idea led to another, and eventually I had four volumes. Telling the whole cycle as a Spenglerian history was my own idea, as soon as I knew there was going to be a series."

* * * * *

EDWARD BLISHEN

Full Name: Edward Blishen.
Born April 29, 1920, at Whetstone, Middlesex, England. Son of William George Blishen (a civil servant) and Elizabeth Ann Pye. Married Nancy Smith, November 4, 1948. Two sons: Jonathan Edward, Nicholas Martin.

Career: Lecturer & writer.
Journalist in London, 1937-41; teacher of English in secondary schools, 1946-59; Part-time Lecturer in Dept. of Education, University of York, 1963-65; full-time writer, 1965-DATE; conductor for thirteen years of a BBC program directed at young African writers.

Agent: Irene Josephy, 35 Craven St., Strand, London.

Member: P.E.N.; Society of Authors. Award: Carnegie Award, 1971, for The God Beneath the Sea.

* * * * *

ROBERT BLOCH

Full Name: Robert Albert Bloch.
Born April 5, 1917, at Chicago, Illinois. Son of Raphael A. Bloch (a bank cashier) and Stella Loeb (a teacher and social worker). Married Marion Holcombe, October 2, 1940 (divorced, 1963); married Eleanor Alexander, October 16, 1964. One daughter, Sally Ann.

Career: Writer.
Advertising Copy Writer, Gustav Marx Advertising Agency, 1942-53; adapted 39 of his stories for the radio program Stay Tuned for Terror, 1945; television panelist, 1954-59; television and screen writer, 1960-DATE.

ROBERT BLOCH (cont.)

First Professional Sale:
"The Secret in the Tomb," in *Weird Tales*, May, 1935; first professional publication: "The Feast in the Abbey," in *Weird Tales*, January, 1935.

Agent: Scott Meredith, 580 Fifth Avenue, New York, NY 10036.

Honors & Awards:
Guest of Honor, 6th World Science Fiction Convention (Torcon I), Toronto, 1948; Guest of Honor, 31st World Science Fiction Convention (Torcon 2), Toronto, 1973; Guest of Honor, Dallascon, 1972; Guest of Honor, Bouchercon I; Guest of Honor, Comicon, San Diego, 1975; Hugo Award, Best Short Story, 1958 (1959), "The Hell-Bound Train"; World Fantasy Award, Life Award, 1975; Special Mystery Writers of America Scroll for "Psycho," 1961; Ann Radcliffe Award for Television, 1966; Ann Radcliffe Award for Literature, 1969; Trieste Science Fiction Film Festival Award, 1965, for "The Skull"; Cannes Fantasy Film Festival First Prize, for "Asylum"; E. E. Evans Memorial Award; Screen Guild Award.

Member:
Science Fiction Writers of America; Mystery Writers of America (National President, 1971); Writers Guild of America; Motion Pictures Academy of Arts and Sciences; Count Dracula Society.

Interests:
Films, reading, travel, philately, music, theatre.

Bloch writes:
"Science is catching up with science fiction, and science fiction is catching up--stylistically--with mainstream writing. Hopefully, this augurs a wider general audience for the genre, though perhaps the media-shift will be to film and television.
"Through the years, most of my work has been on the peripheral edges of science fiction proper--fantasy, weird-horror, and suspense, together with a smattering of humor. To the extent that psychopathology is classifiable as a branch of medical science, my other novels--*The Scarf, Spiderweb, Shooting Star, The Will to Kill, The Kidnaper, Psycho, The Dead Beat, Firebug, The Couch, The Star-Stalker*, and *The Todd Dossier*-- all contain these elements as they pertain to an examination of subjective reality. I cannot lay claim to playing any significant part in the development of science fiction except insofar as I have attempted in a small way to focus attention on man rather than machines. And I do feel that the exploration of outer space must eventually give way to an exploration of inner space--i.e., the human psyche--if science fiction is to attain maturity. The monsters and marvels moving unnoticed in our midst deserve, I believe, the fuller consideration of writers and readers alike."

* * * * *

URSULA BLOOM

Full Name: Ursula Harvey Bloom.
Born at Chelmsford, Essex, England. Daughter of J. Harvey Bloom (a clergyman) and Mary Bloom. Married Arthur Brownlow Denham-Cookes (an army captain), 1916 (died in battle, 1918); married Charles Gower Robinson (a Royal Naval commander), 1925. One son.

Career: Writer.
Has been writing since the age of seven, producing more than 420 books. She has also served as Beauty Editor of *Woman's Own*, and has worked for the *Sunday Pictorial*.

Member: Royal Historical Society (Fellow); Woman's Press Club, London.

* * * * *

WILFRID BLUNT

Full Name: Wilfrid Jasper Walter Blunt.
Born July 19, 1901, at Ham, Surrey, England. Son of Arthur Stanley Vaughan Blunt (a clergyman) and Hilda Master.

Education:
Attended Marlborough College, 1915-20, and Worcester College, Oxford, 1920-21; A.R.C.A., Royal College of Art, 1923.

Career: Drawing Master & Curator.
Art Master, Haileybury College, 1923-38; Drawing Master, Eton College, 1938-59; Curator, Watts Gallery, Compton, Guildford, England, 1959-DATE.

Agent: Curtis Brown Ltd., 1 Craven Hill, London W.2.

Awards: Veitch Gold Medal for *The Art of Botanical Illustration*. Member: Linnean Society (Fellow).

* * * * *

TOM BOARDMAN

Full Name: Thomas Volney Boardman, Jr.
Born December 20, 1930, at Bronxville, New York. Son of Thomas Volney Boardman (a publishers' representative) and Dorothy Moore Cochran. Married Joyce J. Parkinson, September 20, 1952. Two children: Thomas Volney IV (born 1953), Mary Jean (born 1955).

Education: Attended St. George's College, Quilmes, Argentina, and Haileybury & Imperial Service College.

Career: Publisher & Editor.
Has been a publisher of his own hardcover line in England, an export manager for a large British publishing group, a science fiction reviewer and editor; currently Managing Director, Macdonald Educational (a publisher), London.

First Professional Sale: SF criticism to *Books and Bookmen*, 1959.

Member: Young Publishers; Paternosters; Crime Writers Association; Mystery Writers of America.

* * * * *

JOHN BOLAND

Full Name: Bertram John Boland.
Born February 12, 1913, at Birmingham, England. Son of Albert Edward Boland (a manufacturer) and Elizabeth Mills. Married Philippa Carver (now her husband's secretary), May 29, 1952.

JOHN BOLAND (cont.)

Career: Author.
    Employed variously as a farm hand, laborer, deck-
hand, lumberjack, railroad worker, factory worker,
salesman, 1930-38; manufacturers' agent, selling advertising signs and automobile components, 1946-55;
full-time writer, 1956-DATE; formed his own film company, John Boland Productions Ltd., 1964; Chairman,
Writers' Summer School, 1958-60.

Award: Writers' Guild of Great Britain "Zita," 1968,
    for best radio drama of the year.

Member:
    Writers' Guild of Great Britain; Crime Writers
Association; Mystery Writers of America.

* * * * *

HECTOR BOLITHO

Full Name: Henry Hector Bolitho.
    Born May 28, 1897. Son of Henry Bolitho and Ethel-
red Frances Bregman. Died 1974.

Education: Attended Seddon Memorial College, Auck-
    land, New Zealand.

Career: Author & lecturer.
    Has been a professional author all of his life.

Member:
    Committee for Writing and Reading Aids for the
Paralyzed (Chairman); Royal Society of Arts (Fellow);
Royal Society of Literature (Fellow); Athenaeum Club,
London.

Agent: A.M. Heath, 35 Dover St., London W.1.

* * * * *

DAVID BOLT

Full Name: David Michael Langstone Bolt.
    Born November 30, 1927, at Harrow, England. Son of
Richard Percy William Bolt and Ruby Richardson. Married Louise Virginia O'Hara Hibbert, 1962. Five children: Julian, Vanessa, Stephen, Lucinda, Piers.

Education: Attended Dulwich College, 1939-45.

Career: Literary agent.
    Assistant Superintendent, Malayan Police, 1948-50;
Buyer-Manager, Book Department, Stuttafords, Durban,
South Africa, 1950-53; currently a literary agent
with David Higham Associates, London.

* * * * *

NELSON S. BOND

Full Name: Nelson Slade Bond.
    Born November 23, 1908, at Scranton, Pennsylvania.
Son of Richard Slade Bond (a publicist) and Mary
Beadle. Married Betty Gough Folsom, October 3, 1934.
Two sons: Lynn Nelson, Christopher Kent.

Education: Attended Marshall University, 1932-34.

Career: Writer.
    Public Relations Field Director, Province of Nova
Scotia, 1934-35; full-time writer, 1935-DATE.

Award:
    Citation for valuable contribution to philatelic
literature, International Stamp Exhibition, London,
1960, for *The Postal Stationery of Canada*.

Member:
    Writers Guild of America, East; British North Ameri-
can Philatelic Society (Life Member); Roanoke Writers'
Guild; American Contract Bridge League (national master).

* * * * *

J. F. BONE

Full Name: Jesse Franklin Bone.
    Born June 15, 1916, at Tacoma, Washington. Son of
Homer T. Bone (a U.S. Senator and federal judge) and
Eva K. Wildt (a secretary). Married Jayne M. Clark,
1942 (divorced, 1946); married Faye M. Endter, 1950.
Four children: Janice Lee (born 1942), Brigitta (born
1945), Michael Jay (born 1951), David Franklin (born
1956).

Education:
    B.A., Washington State University, 1937; B.S., 1949;
D.V.M., 1950; M.S., Oregon State University, 1953;
W.D.C., Armed Forces Institute of Pathology; attended
Stanford University, 1969-70.

Career: Professor of Veterinary Medicine.
    Professor of Veterinary Medicine, Oregon State Uni-
versity, 1950-DATE; Editor, *Modern Veterinary Practice*,
1957-58; Associate Editor, 1958-72; Chairman, Board of
Governors, Oregon State University Press, 1972-DATE.

First Professional Sale: "Survival Type," in
    Galaxy, March, 1957.

Agent: Scott Meredith, 580 Fifth Avenue, New York,
    NY 10036.

Awards: Borden Scholarship, 1949; Fulbright Lecturer
    in Veterinary Pathology, Egypt, 1964-65.

Member: Science Fiction Writers of America; numerous
    veterinary and education associations.

Bone writes:
    "I used the veterinary ploy in *The Lani People*, and
have also used it in a couple of shorts. Most of my
yarns (at least those that get published) are biolo-
gically oriented. I've been kicking around an idea
about extra terrestrial veterinary practice, but it
never seems to jell. It'd have to be funny, and I
haven't got the right M.O. yet." He adds: "I'd rather
be sailing!"

* * * * *

PAT BOOTH

Full Name: Patrick John Booth.
    Born September 9, 1929, at Levin, New Zealand. Son
of Frederick Charles Booth & Amelia Johnson. Married
Valerie Lineen, Jan. 24, 1953. Four children: Grant,
Therese, Mark, Sally.

PAT BOOTH (cont.)

Education: Attended Sacred Heart College, Auckland, New Zealand.

Career: Reporter and editor.
Reporter, *Hawera Star*, New Zealand, 1947-50; Reporter, *Auckland Star*, New Zealand, 1950-58; Sub-editor, *Sydney Daily Telegraph*, 1958; Chief Sub-editor, *Auckland Daily Star*, 1960-65; Assistant Editor, 1965-DATE.

Member: Auckland Journalists Association; New Zealand Vintage Car Club.

* * * * *

MARY BORDEN

Full Name: Mary Borden.
Born May 15, 1886, at Chicago, Illinois. Daughter of William Borden and Mary Whiting. Married George Douglas Turner; married second husband, Sir Edward Spears (a major general in the British Army, Member of Parliament, and a historian), 1918. Three Children: Joyce Comfort, Mary Hamilton, Michael.

Education: B.A., Vassar College, 1907.

Career: Author.
Was an organizer and director of field hospitals for the French in both world wars; served as official hostess at the British legations in Beirut and Damascus when her husband was Minister Plenipotentiary to Syria and Lebanon, 1942-44; writer since 1912. Died December 2, 1968.

Awards: British medals for war service; French Legion of Honor, and Croix de Guerre with bar and palms. Member: Society of Authors.

* * * * *

WILLIAM BORDEN

Full Name: William Vickers Borden.
Born January 27, 1938, at Indianapolis, Indiana. Son of Harold R. Borden and Elizabeth Vickers. Married Nancy Lee Johnson, December 17, 1960. Three children: Andrew James, Sara Elise, Rachel Lynne.

Education: A.B., Columbia University, 1960; M.A., University of California, Berkeley, 1962.

Career: Teacher of English.
Instructor, University of North Dakota, 1962-64; Asst. Professor, 1966-70; Associate Professor, 1970-DATE. Member: American Assoc. of University Professors.

Agent: Brandt & Brandt, 101 Park Avenue, New York, NY 10017.

* * * * *

ANTHONY BOUCHER

Full Name: William Anthony Parker White.
Born August 21, 1911, at Oakland, California. Son of James Taylor White (a doctor) and Mary Ellen Parker (a doctor). Married Phyllis Mary Price, May 19, 1938. Two sons: Lawrence Taylor, James Marsden.

Education: B.A., University of Southern California, 1932; M.A., University of California, Berkeley, 1934.

Career: Writer and reviewer.
Free-lance writer, 1934-68. Editor, *The Magazine of Fantasy and Science Fiction*, Fall, 1949-August, 1958 (co-editor with J. Francis McComas from Fall, 1949-August, 1954); Book Editor, September, 1958-January, 1959; Advisory Editor, *Venture Science Fiction*, January 1957-July, 1958; Editor (with J. Francis McComas), *True Crime Detective*, 1952-53; Editor, Mercury Mysteries, 1952-55; Editor, Dell Mystery Series, 1957-60; Editor, Collier Mystery Series, 1962-64; reviewer for the following publications: *United Progressive News*, Los Angeles, 1935-37 (theater and music); *San Francisco Chronicle*, 1942-47 (mysteries and general books); *New York Times Book Review*, 1949-68 (mysteries, science fiction, and general); *Ellery Queen Mystery Magazine*, 1948-50, 1957-68 (mysteries); *Chicago Sun-Times*, 1949-50 (science fiction); *New York Herald-Tribune*, 1951-63 (science fiction reviews under the by-line H.H. Holmes); *Opera News*, 1961-68 (opera); story consultant for various TV shows; music and book reviewer on radio and educational television. Died April 30, 1968.

First Professional Sale: *The Case of the 7 of Calvary*, Simon & Schuster, 1937.

Agent: Collins-Knowlton-Wing, 60 E. 56th St., New York, NY 10022.

Honors & Awards:
Guest of Honor, 8th World Science Fiction Convention (Norwescon), Portland, 1950; Hugo Award, Best Professional Magazine, 1957 (1958), *The Magazine of Fantasy and Science Fiction*; Hugo Award, Best Professional Magazine, 1958 (1959), *The Magazine of Fantasy and Science Fiction*; Edgar Award, Best Critic, 1945, 1949, 1952. Boucher was honored posthumously by two anthologies, *Special Wonder; the Anthony Boucher Memorial Anthology of Fantasy and Science Fiction*, and *Crimes and Misfortunes; the Anthony Boucher Memorial Anthology of Mysteries*, both published by Random House in 1970. A special Anthony Boucher Memorial Library has been established at the New York headquarters of the Mystery Writers of America. And an annual Anthony Boucher mystery convention (Bouchercon) has been held since 1970 in California.

Member:
Science Fiction Writers of America; Mystery Writers of America (National President, 1951); Crime Writers Association; Scowrers and Molly Maguires of San Francisco; Baker Street Irregulars (Scion); San Francisco Opera Guild; Phi Beta Kappa; University of California Alumni Association; California Democratic State Central Committee, 1946-50.

Interests:
Collecting historic vocal recordings, food and drink, poker, spectator sports, puzzles, theater, music, languages, liturgy.

Phyllis White, Anthony Boucher's widow, kindly provided the following reminiscences of her husband:

"Those who are interested in my husband probably know quite a bit about him already, or at least know how to find out, so I'll just try to fill in a few parts of his background.
"I'll begin by skimming over his first 25 years, before he began to make himself known. He was the only child of two doctors. He felt that he was particularly

ANTHONY BOUCHER (cont.)

lucky in his mother, but he never knew his father, who died soon after becoming his father. He did not, however, grow up without masculine influence in the home, and he felt lucky in that respect, too. He had his grandfather, a lawyer and Civil War veteran. He was not lucky as to health. He had asthma from the first, and, throughout his childhood, was bedridden about half the time. Nevertheless, he often told me that in looking back what he remembered was the good times. He said he was like the sundial with the motto, I count only the sunny hours.

"He was a bright, precocious child--one of the so-called gifted group of children selected from California schools for study and follow-up by the Terman project at Stanford. When he was tested for vocational aptitude, it appeared that he should be an architect. (I often thought of that at times when he was, even more than usual, unconscious of his surroundings.) He avoided the problems of rapid promotion into alien age-groups, since he was able to attend school only about half the time. He remained easily at his own age-level, and was always well-supplied with friends.

"In his early school years, his interest was primarily in science, but it eventually shifted to language. (Many years later when he became an editor, it devolved upon him to edit the science content in science fiction stories. He told me then that although he was frequently confronted with matters he knew little about, he had a bell in his head that usually rang when something needed checking.)

"In his high school and college years his health and attendance improved, and he went more into extra-curricular activities, mainly dramatics and journalism. In his spare time, he was a theater-, concert-, and film-goer, and a collector of stamps, coins, and phonograph records. This last was to be a life-time pursuit. He was also writing--stories, plays, translations, poetry. Much of the poetry was in Spanish and German. In the diaries he kept during his high school years, he was already writing reviews. At the University of Southern California his major was Spanish, but he switched to German when he came to the University of California at Berkeley for graduate work.

"This now becomes a first-hand report, because I was simultaneously entering UCB as a freshman. In addition to working towards a master's degree in German, Tony pursued Spanish, Portuguese, Russian, and Sanskrit. He was a brilliant student, but when he did the studying was a mystery to those around him. Much of his time was devoted to writing, acting, and directing; he didn't miss much in the way of theater, films, books, music, or football. And he carried on an eventful social life. In those days, his friends usually called him by his middle initials, A.P. (and some of us still do), but he later preferred Tony.

"When he came to Berkeley, he seemed to be headed for an academic career. Before long, he knew that that way of life was not for him, and he decided that he would try to make it as a writer. He stayed on for a second year, as he had been awarded a fellowship, and felt an obligation to complete the work on his M.A. Having done so with a thesis entitled, *The Duality of Impressionism in the Recent German Drama*, he left. The graduate work was not a blind alley. He was afterwards glad that he had been trained in methods that proved useful in many other connections.

"An additional result of the two years at UCB was the decision that we would get married, but goodness knew when. As it turned out, it took four years,

during which, on top of all the other writing he was vainly producing, we were exchanging letters two or three times a week. The struggles of a beginning writer are a familiar story that doesn't need to be told again. At the same time, the depression was going on, so there weren't any other jobs either.

"His first professionally published writing appeared in a small weekly paper for which he covered both theater and music, but that paid only in passes. His first real sale was a mystery novel. He had written it partly because he thought working within that strict form would be good discipline, and partly because of his admiration for some of the writers in that field. The novel was accepted on its ninth submission. On the strength of that, and of my having meanwhile obtained a certificate in librarianship, we risked getting married.

"Breaking into print at last is not the solution to all a writer's problems, only the onset of new ones, but that's another familiar story. I'll skip ahead now, as the career is all on record. There was behind-the-scenes activity in writers' organizations. He was involved in the beginnings of Mystery Writers of America in New York, and was proud of carrying card #5. He was one of the founders of the Northern California chapter of MWA. In those days, there were Northern California chapters of the Authors' Guild and Radio Writers' Guild, and he was active in both. He was in on some early but unsuccessful attempts to get the science fiction writers organized.

"His interest in improving conditions in his own field expanded, and he entered Democratic politics, eventually serving two terms on the state Central Committee. He endured the heat in the kitchen, but was not altogether sorry when he was finally ordered out of it by his doctor.

"This brings to mind the non-metaphorical kitchen. It's no secret that Tony was a talented gourmet cook, but there is another side to that. A dazzling performer for special occasions may do less well when faced with the daily routine of cooking for a family. This he undertook for a time when our sons were both babies and I had my hands full. The task was trickier than it normally is because of the shortages and rationings of World War II, but he coped resourcefully and successfully.

"For the first eight years that he applied himself to full-time writing, he made Los Angeles his base with the idea of trying to get some work in the film studios. Nothing came of his efforts in that direction, and when he began to sell, it was by mail in New York. A few years later he was writing copiously for Hollywood radio, but was living in Berkeley and commuting. Berkeley suited him as a base. Within walking distance, the University provided a useful library, and the spectator sports and concerts that he enjoyed so much. San Francisco was just far enough away to be a special but frequent treat. In spite of all the local attractions, he had an itching foot, and welcomed any undertaking that involved a trip. For him, New York was indeed a great place to visit, although his health would not have permitted him to live there. In time, he overcame the belief held in those parts that book-reviewing from a distance was impractical. It was also demonstrated that magazine-editing could be decentralized.

"Along with his published book reviews, he wrote additional reviews addressed to himself. They are short and pithy, rarely longer than one side of a file-card, and packed with information, bibliographical and other. These were useful in innumerable ways, both to him, and to those who consulted him. They're fraught with abbreviation and condensation, but not hard to

ANTHONY BOUCHER (cont.)

read once one gets the hand of it. OH, for instance, means 'Our Hero.' IH means 'Idiot Heroine.' That's the girl who, although knowing that menace lurks around the corner, takes it into her head to go prowling in an attic or cave, unaccompanied and without filing a flight plan. When he found errors, he listed them for himself, rather than waste column space enumerating them. The file-card then furnished him with a reply if he received a letter inquiring, 'What do you mean, my law (or my Spanish) was wrong? I checked it with an expert.'

"As well as giving praise in print, A.P. would often express his admiration in person when an occasion arose. He would then try to do it with restraint and credibility, commending something specific, so that his enthusiasm would not be discounted as politeness or the impetus of the moment. He told me he had found that he didn't need to be quite so careful about this with singers as with writers. For a singer, the praise could be laid on a trifle thicker, and still be easily digested.

"In his last few years, he moved into two new areas. He had always been devoted to the Catholic Church, but he became much more active in it during this period. This was the time when the church was suddenly making a great many changes all at once. Some Catholics were upset and confused, but A.P. was delighted, as these changes were just what he had always thought ought to happen. It turned out that he had the combination of talents that could be helpful at this juncture. He filled the newly-added role of lector, which involved more than just reading aloud beautifully. He was sort of an M.C., helping the parishioners to understand what was going on, and encouraging them to take part in it. The rapid conversion from Latin to English sometimes outstripped the availability of suitable translations, and he was able to take care of that too. Tied in with all this was the ecumenical movement, which he also welcomed and worked for, applying his experience as a discussion-moderator, and his knack for making different kinds of people feel comfortable with each other.

"As a reviewer, he moved into a new field, opera. During his lifetime, the production of opera in this country had been moving toward more concern with the dramatic aspects. This was another change that he had always wanted to see. He was able to appreciate and understand equally the vocal and theatrical elements, and so he finally turned pro with what had been a life-long hobby. Back when he was starting in as a mystery reviewer, he said to me in a euphoric moment, 'It's like growing up and owning a candy-store.' That didn't last, of course. As an opera reviewer, however, he was still in the candy-store.

"At the time of his death, he was, as usual, in the midst of a variety of activities. At his requiem, the priest under whose guidance he had been working during the changeover gave the eulogy, and I'll conclude with a quotation from it. He said: 'There is an ancient Christian saying that the glory of God is man fully alive.'"

* * * * *

PIERRE BOULLE

Full Name: Pierre François Marie Louis Boulle.
Born February 20, 1912, at Avignon, France. Son of Eugéne Boulle and Thérèse Seguin. Education: École Supérieure d'Électricité, License és Sciences.

Career: Writer.
Engineer in France, 1933-35; Rubber planter in Malaya, 1936-48; full-time writer, 1949-DATE. Boulle was sent to Malaya in 1941, where he joined the Free French Army, and became a secret agent, using the name Peter John Rule, posing as a Mauritius-born Englishman; he fought in Burma, China, and Indochina, was taken prisoner, and subsequently escaped in 1944; he returned to France and was awarded the French Legion d'Honneur, Croix de Guerre.

Awards:
Prix Sainte-Beuve, 1952, for *Le Pont de Rivière Kwai*; Grand Prix de la Nouvelle, 1953, for *Contes de l'Absurde*.

* * * * *

BEN BOVA

Full Name: Benjamin William Bova.
Born November 8, 1932, at Philadelphia, Pennsylvania. Son of Benjamin Bova (a tailor) and Giove Caporiccio. Married Rosa Cucinotta, November 28, 1953. Two children: Michael Francis, Regina Marie.

Education: B.S., Temple University, 1954.

Career: Writer and editor.
Editor, *Upper Darby News*, 1953-56; Technical Editor, Vanguard Project, Martin Aircraft, 1956-58; Screen Writer, Physical Science Study Committee, MIT, 1958-59; Science Writer, Avco-Everett Research Lab, 1960-64; Manager of Marketing, 1964-1971; Editor, *Analog Science Fiction/Science Fact*, January, 1972-DATE.

First Professional Sale: *The Star Conquerors*, John C. Winston Co., 1959.

Member:
Science Fiction Writers of America; American Association for the Advancement of Science; National Association of Science Writers.

Awards:
Hugo Award, Best Editor, 1972 (1973); Hugo Award, Best Editor, 1973 (1974); Hugo Award, Best Editor, 1974 (1975); Hugo Award, Best Editor, 1975 (1976).

Interests: Fencing, astronomy.

* * * * *

JOHN BOWEN

Full Name: John Griffith Bowen.
Born November 5, 1924, at Calcutta, India. Son of Hugh Griffith Bowen (a works manager) and Ethel Cook (a nurse).

Education: M.A., St. Antony's College, Oxford, 1952.

Career: Writer.
Copy writer, J. Walter Thompson Co., London, 1957-58; Copy chief, St. Garland Advertising, London, 1958-59; Script consultant, Associated Television, London, 1962-68; full-time writer. Asst. Ed., *The Sketch*, 1953-57.

First Professional Sale:
"Living? Try Death!" in *Science Fantasy*, no. 23, June, 1957 (as Justin Blake).

JOHN BOWEN (cont.)

Agent: Elaine Greene, 31 Newington Green, London N16 9PU, England.

Member: P.E.N.

Bowen writes:
"I have read a great deal of science fiction, and written very little, for the excellent reason that I am an ignoramus: I have no physics, no biochemistry, very little sociology. I don't speak the language. My SF output, therefore, has been confined to the novel and play versions of *After the Rain*, in both of which the S is minimal and unlikely, to seven episodes of a television series called *The Guardians*, and to a reworking of Shakespeare called *Heil, Caesar*, both of which are concerned with politics. "Digby," a radio play written with Jeremy Bullmore under the *nom de plume* 'Justin Blake' (and which also appeared as a story called "Living? Try Death!" [not my title]) was a projection of existing practice, but it was about advertising."

* * * * *

JOHN S. BOWMAN

Full Name: John Stewart Bowman.
Born May 30, 1931, at Cambridge, Massachusetts. Son of John Russell Bowman (a teacher) and Anne Stewart. Married Francesca Di Pietro (a social worker) February 11, 1967. One daughter, Michela Ann.

Education: B.A., Harvard University, 1953; attended Cambridge University, 1953-54, Univ. of Munich, 1958.

Career: Writer.
Production Assistant, New England Opera Theatre, Boston, 1957; English Instructor, University of Maryland overseas program, Athens and Crete, 1960; Assoc. Editor, *Natural History*, 1961-62; Associate Editor, Grolier Inc. (a publisher), 1962-63; Free-lance writer, 1963-DATE.

Agent: McIntosh & Otis, 475 Fifth Avenue, New York, NY 10017.

Member: Phi Beta Kappa.

* * * * *

JOHN BOYD

Full Name: Boyd Bradfield Upchurch.
Born October 3, 1919, at Atlanta, Georgia. Son of Ivie Doss Upchurch (a railroad man) and Margaret Blake Barnes. Married Fern Gillaspy Lorts, January 26, 1944.

Education: A.B., University of Southern California, 1947.

Career: Writer.
Salesman, Star Photoengraving Co., 1947-70; Full-time writer, 1970-DATE; Naval officer in World War II.

First Professional Sale: *The Slave Stealer*, Weybright & Talley, 1968 (as Boyd Upchurch). This book was published simultaneously with *The Last Starship from Earth*.

Agent: McIntosh & Otis, 475 Fifth Avenue, New York, NY 10017.

Boyd talks about the origins of his penname:
"In 1967, when I sold my first novel, an antebellum story called *The Slave Stealer*, the then new publishing house, Weybright & Talley, also bought a science fiction novel I had previously written, *The Last Starship from Earth*, which I had not submitted to any other publisher. Since W&T did not wish to publish the two books simultaneously under one name, someone in the publisher's office assigned me the name, John Boyd. Perhaps W&T wanted also to keep the 'lower' genre separate from the 'higher.' Neither I nor my agent ever discovered who actually named me.
"I've found the pseudonym convenient, because I can write in alternate genres without flooding the market. It's a curious fact that many people, particularly the academic folks, feel that a man who publishes often lets the quality of his work suffer, which is about as reasonable as thinking that a pianist who practices every day injures his skills."

* * * * *

MALCOLM BOYD

Full Name: Malcolm Boyd.
Born June 8, 1923, at New York, New York. Son of Melville Boyd (a financier) and Beatrice Lowrie.

Education:
B.A., University of Arizona, 1944; B.D., Divinity School of the Pacific, 1954; attended Oxford University, 1954-55, and later studied at an ecumenical institute in Geneva, Switzerland; S.T.M., Union Theological Seminary, 1956; member of work-study program at the Taize Community in France, 1957.

Career: Priest.
Copywriter, Foote, Cone, & Belding Advertising Agency, Hollywood, 1945-46; director of a homemakers' hour on radio; writer and producer, Republic Pictures and Samuel Goldwyn Productions, 1947-49; with Mary Pickford and Buddy Rogers, established Pickford, Rogers & Boyd, New York, to package television programs, 1949-51; ordained Episcopal priest, 1955, and has served as a chaplain or priest at several different institutions and churches since.

Honors: Selected by *Life* as one of the 100 most important young men and women in the United States.

Member:
Television Producers Association; National Assoc. for the Advancement of Colored People; Episcopal Society for Cultural and Racial Unity.

* * * * *

LEIGH BRACKETT

Full Name: Leigh Douglass Brackett.
Born December 7, 1915, at Los Angeles, California. Daughter of William Franklin Brackett (an accountant) and Margaret Leigh Douglass. Married Edmond Moore Hamilton, December 31, 1946.

Career: Writer.
Was a free-lance writer all of her life, working primarily as a screen writer in recent years. Died March 18, 1978.

LEIGH BRACKETT (cont.)

First Professional Sale: "Martian Quest," in *Astounding Stories*, February, 1940.

Agent: Lurton Blassingame, 60 E. 42nd St., New York, NY 10017.

Honors & Awards:
Co-Guest of Honor, 22nd World Science Fiction Convention (Pacificon II), Oakland, 1964; Jules Verne Fantasy Award, for "Last Days of Shandakor"; Nova Award for distinguished contributions to science fiction and fantasy (with Edmond Hamilton); Golden Spur Award, 1963, for Best Western Novel of the year, *Follow the Free Wind*.

Member:
Science Fiction Writers of America; Western Writers of America; Writers Guild of America, West; Western History Association; Authors League.

Interests: Travel, gardening, photography.

Leigh Brackett is best known in the science fiction field for her stories of Mars and Erik John Stark, whose adventures originally were set primarily on the Red Planet. When questioned about the Martian tales, she had this to say:

"I don't think there ever was a 'proper order' to the Mars stories, which were not really a series at all, in that sense. They were random stories, randomly written; it was simply that I fell in love with that particular imaginary world, and use it repeatedly, so that there is a continuity of background. The Ace collection, *The Coming of the Terrans*, attempted to put the stories in some sort of chronological order.
"As to Eric John Stark, he first appeared in the short novel, "The Immortals of Mars"...sorry, I think that was my title, but *Planet Stories* called it "Queen of the Martian Catacombs." I wrote a second story using Stark, a character I rapidly became very fond of, with a Venusian background, called "The Enchantress of Venus" or "City of the Lost Ones," depending on where you read it, in *Planet* or the later anthology. A third one returned to the Martian background, and was called "Black Amazon of Mars." At that point, fashions were changing, and Malcolm Reiss suggested that we let Stark rest for a while, and do something more in the modern mood. So I didn't use the character again for a long while. Even so, he seemed to have an amazing vitality. Youngsters who hadn't been born when I first wrote about him would ask me when I was going to do some more 'Stark stories.' So I did, fashions having changed again so that that type of story was again acceptable. But some editors still shy away from Mars and the rest of the Solar System...we seem to know too much about them now. So I moved Stark out into the wider galaxy, there being nothing in the earlier stories that says they *didn't* have star-travel. And I am thoroughly enjoying writing about an interstellar Eric John Stark.
"Being a science fiction writer is bountifully rewarding in ways other than financial...lifelong friendships, the pleasure of belonging to a family that stretches right around the globe, so that wherever one goes, one has friends; the pleasure, which does not exist in any other field, of being able to stretch one's imagination 'beyond the farthest star.'"

RAY BRADBURY

Full Name: Ray Douglas Bradbury.
Born August 22, 1920, at Waukegan, Illinois. Son of Leonard Spaulding Bradbury (an electrical lineman) and Esther Marie Moberg. Married Marguerite Susan McClure, September 28, 1947. Four children: Susan Marguerite (born 1949), Ramona Anne (born 1951), Bettina Francion (born 1955), Alexandra Allison (born 1958).

Education: Graduate, Los Angeles High School, 1938; "library educated."

Career: Writer.
"Sold newspapers on a street corner for three years, 1939 thru 1942, when income from writing stories ($20 a week) enabled me to quit selling papers and devote full time to writing."

First Professional Sale: "It's Not the Heat, It's the Hu--", in *Rob Wagner's Script Magazine*, November 2, 1940.

Agent: Harold Matson Company, 22 E. 40th St., New York, NY 10016.

Awards:
Benjamin Franklin Award, 1953, for Best Short Story Published in an American Popular Magazine, for "Sun and Shadow"; American Academy of Arts and Sciences $1,000 Award for Contributing to American Literature, 1954; Commonwealth Club of California Gold Medal, 1954, for *Fahrenheit 451*; Boys Clubs of America Junior Book Award, 1956, for *Switch on the Night*.

Member: Science Fiction Writers of America; Screen Writers Guild of America.

Interests:
"Comic-strip collection from 1929 on; painting, watercolors, oils; collecting masks from various countries." He adds: "I was an apprentice student to Henry Kuttner/ Robert Heinlein/Leigh Brackett/Jack Williamson/Henry Hasse, all of whom taught me how to write."

* * * * *

RUSSELL BRADDON

Full Name: Russell Reading Braddon.
Born January 25, 1921, at Sydney, Australia.

Education:
B.A., Sydney University, 1940; "student from 1946-49, when I abandoned the study of law; I also spent four and a half years in a Japanese P.O.W. camp, which was much more educational than school or university."

Career: Author, lecturer, broadcaster.
Student, 1938-40; soldier, 1941-46; student again, 1946-49; script writer for the BBC, 1949-50; full-time author, 1951-DATE; lecturer, 1953-DATE; broadcaster, 1955-DATE.

Agent: John Farquharson, 15 Red Lion Square, London.

Braddon writes: "I write late at night. If possible I never get up before midday. I dislike morning time and breakfast. I can't type. I answer every letter I receive. I think Richard Nixon is a very typical politician. I look forward to the end of the internal combustion engine, and the drying up of the last oil well."

MARION ZIMMER BRADLEY

Full Name: Marion Eleanor Zimmer Bradley Breen.
    Born June 3, 1930, at Albany, New York. Daughter
of Leslie Raymond Zimmer (a farmer and carpenter) and
Evelyn Parkhurst Conklin (a historian). Married
Robert Alden Bradley, 1949 (divorced, 1964); married
Walter Henry Breen, 1964. Three children: David
Stephen Bradley (born 1950); Patrick Russell Breen
(born 1964); Moira Dorothy Evelyn Breen (born 1966).

Education: B.A., Hardin-Simmons University, 1964;
    attended University of California, 1966.

Career: Writer.
    "I trained for a singer; am a drop-out from three
departments of Education, owing to deep disillusion
with current trends in education; psychologist; parapsychologist; expert on opera, especially Italian;
specialist in Victorian literature, self-taught."
Features Editor, *Sybil Leek's Astrology Journal*, 1970.

First Professional Sale: "Keyhole," in *Vortex*,
    #2, 1953.

Agent: Scott Meredith, 580 Fifth Avenue, New York,
    NY 10036.

Honors: Alpha Chi from Hardin-Simmons University,
    for academic excellence.

Member:
    Science Fiction Writers of America; Mystery Writers
of America; Fantasy Amateur Press Association (has
been President and Official Editor); Society for
Creative Anachronism, Inc. (Member of the Advisory
Board; was previously Seneschal of the East Kingdom).

Interests: Parapsychology, costumery, madrigal
    singing, Gilbert & Sullivan, Gaelic folk music.

Bradley is best known for her series of novels set
on the planet Darkover. In response to questions,
she provided the following short history of the
stories:

"I've never stopped to think it out. The whole
series just grew like Topsy; each successive novel
was a form of self-indulgence, returning to a familiar
milieu instead of doing the hard work of inventing a
new world, new characters, new ecology.
    "Shortly after the discovery of the MAM drive
(Matter Anti Matter), a large number of ships were
sent out from Terra to colonize properly terraformed
worlds. The relatively crude faster-than-light
drives of those days meant that a number of these
ships crashed or were lost somewhere in the Galaxy;
however, a few were marooned on more or less hos-
pitable worlds. One of these ships, whose name has
been lost even to the records of the Terran Empire,
was a primitive MAM-drive ship under the captaincy
of Harry Leicester, first officer Camilla Del Rey.
Its prime purpose, when it was lost, was carrying two
groups of colonists to a recently terraformed planet
known only as the Coronis Colony. One of these two
groups was a standard colony under the auspices of
Earth Expeditionary Forces, under the leadership of
MacDonald Moray; the other, a group of neo-primiti-
vists calling themselves the New Hebrides Commune.
The ethnic makeup of the ship was largely American
and Spanish-America; the colonists were virtually all
Scots or Irish.

"The ship was lost, and vanished from Terran records
for several thousand years. (Several interplanetary
wars intervening, as well as the curiously elastic
nature of time at such distances, make the exact
period indeterminable.) Roughly three thousands years,
Terran reckoning, later, when the Terran Empire had
gone through its first stages of hostility and expansion, and dwindled into a comfortable confederated
bureaucracy, Terran ships located a planet known in
star catalogues only as Cottman Four, having one habi-
table planet with four moons. Several indigenous nonhuman cultures of IBs (Intelligent Beings) were located,
as well as a human culture whose speech retained traces
of Gaelic, Spanish, and English, having a high level
of culture at first considered barbarian, but later
determined to be a post-atomic society, having developed a high level of telepathy and ESP in their ruling
caste, which was known as the Comyn.
    "Their own name for their world was Darkover. They
were reluctant to deal with the Empire, but the Empire,
since they were located conveniently between the Upper
and Lower Arms of the Galaxy, found their location
ideal, and persuaded them to allow the construction
of a large spaceport as a crossroads. The ruling class
stipulated that Darkover remain a Class B Closed World,
with minimal contact with the Empire, and strict en-
forcement of the Darkovan Compact--an ethical proscrip-
tion of any weapon which does not bring its user into
equal danger of death.
    "Virtually all of the Darkover novels deal with the
clash between a deliberately non-technological society
and a society devoted to maximum use of technology.
Virtually all are written from a Darkovan viewpoint
which looks upon the Terran Empire personnel as intru-
ders, interlopers. Most have, as protagonists, members
of the Darkovan telepath castes.
    "The Terran Empire, despite certain discrepancies
in the early books before I began to be committed to
thinking of it as a series, has probably been on Darkover for about 300 of their years. There have been
many intermarriages and personal contacts; these,
shocking at first, are now regarded as inevitable, and
their offspring accepted, although often deplored.
    "Short of giving a plot summary of each book, it must
suffice to say that a mutually intolerant and conflic-
ting set of cultures are being mutually influenced by
one another. Some hint to the actual times between
books is given in the "Note on Chronology," which
appears in the back (pages 157-158) of *The Spell-Sword*.
    "Why did I write them this way? I can only claim
artistic license. Presumably the reason is buried
deep, in my own subconscious, but short of submitting
them to three years of depth psychoanalysis, I don't
know much more about it than the readers do, and they
are always telling me things I didn't know about my
own books, so maybe I know less.
    "The chronology of the series runs like this: *Dark-
over Landfall*, *The Spell-Sword*, *Star of Danger*, *The
Winds of Darkover*, *The Bloody Sun*, *The Heritage of
Hastur*, *The Sword of Aldones*, *The Planet Savers*, *The
World Wreckers*."

Bradley added these additional comments:
    "I seem to have fallen into writing science fiction
as an adjunct of an obsessive passion for SF fandom
in my teens. My first career choice was singing; my
second, teaching. I had no special luck at either.
I never particularly wanted a career as a writer, and
am periodically surprised at the fact that a) I can
make money at it; and b) people seem to like what I
write. I'd rather edit, or teach."

JAMES BRAMWELL

Full Name: James Guy Bramwell.
Born July 25, 1911. Son of Charles Guy Bramwell (a soldier) and Joan Gilkison. One daughter, Teresa Clare.

Education: B.A., Balliol College, Oxford.

Career: Author.
On editorial staff, *London Mercury*, 1934-36; Member, British Council, 1946-51; Lecturer in English, Helsinki University.

Agent: David Higham Associates, 76 Dean St., London W.1, England.

* * * * *

MARC BRANDEL

Full Name: Marc Brandel [orig. Marcus Beresford].
Born March 28, 1919, at London, England. Son of John Davys Beresford (the novelist and critic). Two children: Antonia (born 1958), Vanessa Tara (born 1967).

Education: "Various schools in France, Switzerland, and England."

Career: Writer.
Was a commercial sculptor for some time before first novel accepted; has been a writer ever since. Brandel emigrated to the US at nineteen, and lived there over twenty years, before settling in Ireland.

First Professional Sale: *Rain Before Seven*, Harper & Bros., 1946.

Agent: William Morris, 151 El Camino, Beverly Hills, CA 90212.

Interests:
"Sailing--reading. I worked for over twenty years in television as a script editor-producer-writer. I've written over 150 TV plays, produced by every network in the US and England, and most other countries."

* * * * *

FRANKLYN M. BRANLEY

Full Name: Franklyn Mansfield Branley.
Born June 5, 1915, at New Rochelle, New York. Son of George Percy Branley and Louise Lockwood. Married Margaret Genevieve Lemon (an elementary school teacher), June 26, 1938. Two children: Sandra Kay, Mary Jane.

Education:
Lifetime License, New Paltz Normal School, 1936; B.S., New York University, 1942; M.A., Columbia University, 1948; Ed.D., 1957.

Career: Teacher.
High school teacher in Spring Valley, NY, 1936-42; in Nyack, NY, 1942-44; in New York City, 1944-54; Associate Professor of Science, Jersey State Teachers College, 1954-56; Director of Educational Services,

American Museum of Natural History, Hayden Planetarium, 1956-DATE; Astronomer, 1963-DATE; Chairman, 1968-DATE; Referee, National Science Foundation, 1960-DATE.

Awards:
Edison Award for Outstanding Children's Science Book of 1961, *Experiments in Sky Watching*.

Member:
American Astronomical Society; National Science Teachers Association; American Association for the Advancement of Science; Royal Astronomical Society (Fellow).

* * * * *

PETER ROGER BREGGIN

Full Name: Peter Roger Breggin.
Born May 11, 1936, at Brooklyn, New York. Married Phyllis Lundy, October 13, 1973. Two children: Linda (born 1962), Sharon (born 1964).

Education:
B.A., Harvard College, 1958; M.D., Case Western Reserve Medical School, 1962; Intern and Psychiatric Resident, State University of New York, Syracuse, 1962-63, 1964-66; Teaching Fellow, Harvard Medical School, 1963-64.

Career: Psychiatrist.
Consultant, National Institute of Mental Health, 1966-68; Faculty Member, Washington School of Psychiatry, 1968-73; Director, Center for the Study of Psychiatry, 1973-DATE; Psychiatrist in private practice, 1968-DATE.

First Professional Sale: *The Crazy from the Sane*, Lyle Stuart, 1971.

Member: American Psychiatric Association; Authors Guild.

Breggin has written many scientific and popular articles on the ethical and political implication of psychiatric theory and practice, particularly those aspects which threaten personal and political freedom. He writes: "Over the past two years I have sacrificed my fiction writing in favor of leading a largely succesful international campaign against lobotomy and psychosurgery."

* * * * *

JOSEPH PAYNE BRENNAN

Full Name: Joseph Payne Brennan.
Born December 20, 1918, at Bridgeport, Connecticut. Son of Joseph Payne Brennan (a foreman at New Haven Clock Co.) and Nellie Wilkerson Holborn. Married Doris Philbrick, October 24, 1970.

Education: "Self-educated."

Career: Technical Services Specialist.
Assistant, Advertising Dept., *New Haven Journal-Courier*, 1938-40; Editorial Assistant, *Theatre News*, 1940; soldier, 1943-45; Technical Services Specialist, Yale University Library, 1941-DATE; has also been a part-time book reviewer for the *New Haven Register*.

First Professional Sale: "Endurance," in *Western Short Stories*, 1948. "My first sale to a fantasy

JOSEPH PAYNE BRENNAN (cont.)

magazine was the acceptance of a short story entitled "The Green Parrot" by *Weird Tales* in 1952 (they published it in July of that year). My very first professional sale of any kind was the sale of a verse entitled "When Snow Is Hung" to the *Christian Science Monitor* in 1940--for the staggering sum of $3.50!"

Agent: Kirby McCauley, 220 E. 26th St., New York, NY 10010.

Awards:
Leonora Speyer Memorial Award, Poetry Society of America, for a poem called "New England Vignette"; several other minor awards for verse.

Member: Poetry Society of America; New England Poetry Club.

Interests: Coins, stamps, military miniatures, costume prints, chess.

Brennan writes:
"My work (short stories and poems) has appeared in about fifty anthologies, perhaps more. Stories have been translated into French, German, Dutch, Swedish, Spanish, etc. Two stories were adapted for the old "Thriller" TV program. The late Boris Karloff referred to me as a 'fine master of horror.' I'm very proud of this since I consider Karloff an exceptional editor/critic. I've published over 20 issues of an occasional little magazine, *Macabre*, which has had a very precarious life, but I plan and hope to go on with it."

* * * * *

REGINALD BRETNOR

Full Name: Reginald Bretnor.
Born July 30, 1911, at Vladivostok, Russia. Moved to Japan in 1915, and to the United States in 1920. Married Rosalie Leveille.

Education: "A rather haphazard education in a half dozen private and the same number of public schools and colleges. No degrees."

Career: Writer.
Wrote war propaganda for Office of War Information, and Department of State's OIICA, 1943-47; Free-lance writer, 1947-DATE.

First Professional Sale: "Maybe Just a Little One," *Harper's Magazine*, August, 1947.

Agent: Robert P. Mills Ltd., 152 E. 56th St., New York, NY 10022.

Member:
Science Fiction Writers of America; Mystery Writers of America; American Ordnance Association; National Rifle Association; Japanese Sword Society of the US (served as Chairman for five years); California Society for Psychical Study (served as Director, two years).

Interests:
Japanese swords and related areas of Japanese art; antique and modern weapons; military history.

Bretnor writes:
"My opinion on the relationship between SF and the academic world will depend on how that relationship develops. I believe that the central purpose of academia must be to teach and to assist in conveying a cultural heritage. John Cowper Powys has summed up my own position: 'One rather felicitous definition (of culture) runs as follows--"Culture is what is left over after you have forgotten all you have definitely set out to learn"--and in this sally you get at least a useful warning against associating culture too closely with the academic paraphernalia of education.' In short, I take a dim view of academic literary criticism, with its trendy fashion-making and its persistent attempts to befuddle the literate laity with elaborate private vocabularies, and--having seen what this sort of thing has done to poetry and to the mainstream short story--I can only hope that SF has the strength to resist it. By this I do not mean that members of the teaching profession should abjure all literary criticism, or philosophical speculation, or whatever other intellectual exercise. I do mean, however, that they should do it on their own time, and in a wider and more genuinely competitive marketplace than that offered by the world of tenure."

* * * * *

ROBERT E. BRINEY

Full Name: Robert Edward Briney.
Born December 2, 1933, at Benton Harbor, Michigan. Son of Robert Edward Briney (an electrician) and Catherine Duncan.

Education: A.B., Northwestern University, 1955; Ph.D. Massachusetts Institute of Technology, 1961.

Career: Professor of Mathematics.
Instructor, M.I.T., 1961-62; Asst. Professor, Purdue University, 1962-68; Associate Professor, Salem State College, 1968-70; Professor of Mathematics, 1970-DATE.

Member: American Mathematical Society; Mathematical Association of America; Mystery Writers of America.

Briney has edited *The Rohmer Review* since 1970, and is generally regarded as an expert on the mystery and supernatural genres, and on science fiction bibliography. When questioned about the art of making a good bibliographical study, he had this to say:

"The first requisite is, of course, accuracy and completeness of factual information. Then one decides on the proper format and degree of detail appropriate to the audience and purpose of the bibliography. My own tendency is to prefer too much detail rather than too little, if a choice has to be made. The extreme in this direction is the Rev. Henry Hardy Heins' *Golden Anniversary Bibliography of Edgar Rice Burroughs*, where every conceivable detail about the books was recorded. This was, of course, appropriate for an audience of collectors and bibliophiles. At the opposite pole are works such as Ordean Hagen's *Who Done It?*, or Barzun and Taylor's selected bibliography, *The Catalogue of Crime*, where the bibliographical material is reduced to the barest (and not infrequently incorrect) outline, so that they are really checklists rather than genuine bibliographies." Briney adds: "I have written no fiction under my own name in more than twenty years."

CAROL RYRIE BRINK

Full Name: Carol Ryrie Brink.
    Born December 28, 1895, at Moscow, Idaho. Daughter of Alexander Ryrie and Henrietta Watkins. Married Raymond W. Brink, 1918. Two children: David Ryrie, Nora Caroline.

Education: Attended University of Idaho, 1914-17; B.A., University of California, Berkeley, 1918.

Career: Author.
    Has been an author all of her life.

Awards:
    John Newbery Medal, 1936; Friends of American Writers Award, 1955; D.Litt., University of Idaho, 1965; National League of American Pen Women Fiction Award, 1966, for *Snow in the River*.

Member:
    Phi Beta Kappa; League of American Pen Women; California's Writer's Guild; Faculty Women's Club, University of Minnesota.

* * * * *

HENRY BRINTON

Full Name: Henry Brinton.
    Born July 27, 1901, at Wolverhampton, Staffordshire, England. Son of Henry Brinton. Married Helen Cross Reid Fraser, 1941. Three children: John Richard, Julie Caroline, Alix Veronica.

Career: Author & lecturer.
    Many years in social and political work; full-time writer and lecturer. Member: Royal Astronomical Society (Fellow); British Astronomical Association; P.E.N.

Agent: Curtis Brown Ltd., 60 E. 56th St., New York, NY 10022.

* * * * *

PAT BRISCO

Full Name: Patricia A. Brisco.
    Born July 1, 1927, at San Fernando, California. Daughter of Roy Oliver Ernst and Gladys Gable. Married Marvin Owen Brisco 1946 (divorced); married Clayton Matthews, November 3, 1972. Two children: Michael Arvie Briscoe, David Roy Brisco.

Education: Attended Pasadena Junior College.

Career: Secretary.
    Secretary to the General Manager of Associated Students, California State College, Los Angeles, 1959-DATE.

* * * * *

FENNER BROCKWAY

Full Name: Archibald Fenner Brockway.
    Born November 1, 1888, at Calcutta, India. Son of William George Brockway (a missionary) and Frances Elizabeth Abbey. Married Lilla Harvey-Smith, 1914; Married Edith Violet King, 1946; four children: Audrey, Joan, Olive, Christopher.

Education: Attended School for the Sons of Missionaries (now Eltham College).

Career: Politician.
    Writer and editor for various political magazines, 1907-17; Labour Member of Parliament, 1929-31, 1950-DATE; Organizing Secretary, Independent Labour Party, 1922; General Secretary, 1928, 1933-39; Chairman, 1931-33; Political Secretary, 1939-46; Joint Secretary, British Committee of Indian National Congress, 1919; Chairman, No More War Movement and War Resister's International, 1923-28; Executive Member, Labour and Socialist International, 1926-31; Chairman, British Center for Colonial Freedom, 1942-47; Member, International Committee of Socialist Movement, 1947-52; First Chairman, Congress of Peoples Against Imperialism, 1948-DATE; Chairman, Movement for Colonial Freedom, 1954-DATE; Chairman, British Asian and Overseas Socialist Fellowship, 1959-DATE; Vice-Chairman, Campaign for Nuclear Disarmament, 1964-DATE; Executive Member, Anti-Apartheid Movement, 1964-DATE; Chairman, British Council for Peace in Vietnam, 1965.

Awards: Order of Republic of Tunisia; Honorary Chief, Kikuyu Tribe, Kenya.

* * * * *

CHRISTINE BROOKE-ROSE

Full Name: Christine Brooke-Rose.
    Born at Geneva, Switzerland. Married Jerzy Peterkiewicz (a writer and lecturer).

Education: B.A., Oxford University, 1949; M.A., 1953; Ph.D., University College, London, 1954.

Career: Writer.
    Novelist, critic, and university lecturer.

Awards:
    Society of Authors Travelling Prize, 1965, for *Out*; James Tait Black Prize, 1966, for *Such*; Arts Council Translation Prize, 1969, for *In the Labyrinth*.

* * * * *

DEWEY C. BROOKINS

Full Name: Dewey C. Brookins.
    Born June 4, 1904, at Dothan, Alabama. Son of Frank and Eolin Brookins. Married his wife, Rebecca Brookins, 1951. One daughter, Wanda (born 1952).

Education: Attended U.S. Naval College.

Career: Automobile salesman.
    Automobile salesman in Montgomery, Alabama; has also been a newspaper columnist.

* * * * *

JOHN BROPHY

Full Name: John Brophy.
    Born December 6, 1899, at Liverpool, England. Son of John Brophy and Agnes Bodell. Married Charis Weare Grundy, June 6, 1924. One daughter, Brigid Antonia.

Education: B.A., University of Liverpool, 1922; Diploma in Education, University of Durham, 1923.

JOHN BROPHY (cont.)

Career: Author.
   Taught in Egypt for two years in the 1920s; worked
in a general store; worked as an advertising copywriter in English before becoming full-time author;
critic for various London newspapers and magazines,
and for the BBC; Editor, *John O'London's*, 1940-43.
Died 1965.

Member: P.E.N.; Society of Authors; National Book
   League; Reform Club.

* * * * *

BETH BROWN

Full Name: Beth Brown.
   Born at New York, New York. Daughter of Alex Brown
and Sophia Lane. Married John Barry (divorced). One
daughter, Betty.

Education: Studied at Columbia University, New York
   University, University of Southern California.

Career: Writer.
   Film writer in Hollywood for Metro-Goldwyn-Mayer,
and Paramount Studios; now a full-time writer in Manhattan.

Member: Society of Magazine Writers.

* * * * *

DOUGLAS BROWN

Full Name: Douglas Frank Lambert Brown.
   Born March 25, 1907, at London, England. Son of
Frank Herbert Brown (a journalist) and Clara Pinck-
beck. Married Mary Horn, October 7, 1933. Four
children: Stephen, Anthony, Jennifer, Richard.

Education: Attended King's College, University of
   London, 1924-26.

Career: Reporter and editor.
   Foreign Sub-Editor, *Manchester Guardian*, 1932-35;
Foreign Sub-Editor and Correspondent in Lisbon, *London
Times*, 1935-42; Correspondent in Lisbon, Reuters News
Service, 1942-47; Correspondent in India, Germany,
Africa, and Middle East, *London Daily Telegraph*, 1947-
60; Assistant Editor, *London Sunday Telegraph*, 1960-
DATE.

Member: Catholic Mass Media Commission for England
   and Wales.

* * * * *

FREDRIC BROWN

Full Name: Fredric William Brown.
   Born October 29, 1906, at Cincinnati, Ohio. Son of
Karl Lewis Brown (a newspaper man) and Emma Amelia
Graham. Married Helen Ruth, 1929 (divorced 1947);
married Elizabeth Charlier, October 11, 1948. Two
sons: James Ross (born 1930); Linn Lewis (born 1932).

Education: Attended Hanover College for one year;
   "mostly self-educated."

Career:
   "I was an office worker until 1936 (age 30), when I
became a proofreader, and started selling stories.
Worked at both proofreading and writing, off and on,
until 1947; since then have been a full-time writer.
Have written slightly more in the mystery field than
in science fiction, but prefer the latter." Brown
died March 12, 1972.

First Professional Sale: "The Moon for a Nickel,"
   in *Street & Smith's Detective Story*, c. 1936.

Agent: Scott Meredith, 580 Fifth Avenue, New York,
   NY 10036.   Member: Writers Guild of America.

Awards: Edgar Award, Best First Mystery Novel, 1947
   (1948), *The Fabulous Clipjoint*.

Interests: Chess, music, poker, reading.

Elizabeth Brown provided the following anecdote about
her husband:
   "In 1948, we were living in New York. Fred had had
a few hundred short stories published, and had sold
at least two books, the first of which, *The Fabulous
Clipjoint*, won an Edgar from the Mystery Writers of
America. Fred's then-current publisher asked Fred
to speak at a dinner meeting of a writers' group, and
extended the invitation to me. But the publisher neglected to tell Fred what *kind* of a writers' group it
was, so Fred naturally assumed it was an inexperienced
bunch of amateurs, and prepared accordingly.
   "When we arrived, we found such names as A. E. van
Vogt, Fletcher Pratt, Paul Gallico, Theodore Sturgeon,
and others equally well-known in their respective
fields. At the dinner table, Fred whispered to me,
'My God, Bethie, what'll I do?' Several people spoke.
When Fred was called on, he stood up and said something
to this effect: 'Everything I had planned to say has
already been said, and perhaps better than I could say
it.' He'd had some bad moments!"

* * * * *

HARRISON BROWN

Full Name: Harrison Scott Brown.
   Born September 26, 1917, at Sheridan, Wyoming. Son
of Harrison H. Brown and Agatha Scott. Married Adele
Scrimger, May, 1938 (divorced 1949); married Rudd Owen,
November 11, 1949. One son, Eric Scott.

Education: B.S., University of California, 1938;
   Ph.D., Johns Hopkins University, 1941.

Career: Professor of Geochemistry.
   Assistant Director of Chemistry, Clinton Laboratories,
Oak Ridge, Tenn., 1943-46; Assoc. Professor, Institute
for Nuclear Studies, University of Chicago, 1946-51;
Professor of Geochemistry, California Institute of
Technology, 1951-DATE; Professor of Science and Govern-
ment, California Institute of Technology, 1967-DATE.

Awards:
   Lasker Award, 1958; LL.D., University of Alberta,
1960; D.Sc., Rutgers University, 1964; D.Sc., Amherst
University, 1966.

Member:
   National Academy of Sciences; Philosophical Society;
Phi Beta Kappa; American Chemical Society; American
Association for the Advancement of Science.

J. G. BROWN

Full Name: James Goldie Brown.
Born May 21, 1901, at Christchurch, New Zealand.
Son of James Taylor Brown (an engineer) and Elizabeth
Anne Fraser. Married his wife, Eileen Katharine
Percy, January 21, 1925. Four children: James Gerald
Percy, Elaine Katherine Percy, Juliet Anne Percy,
Andrew Fraser Goldie.

Education:
  M.A., University of Canterbury, Christchurch, N.Z.,
  1922; Certificate in History, 1936.

Career: Schoolmaster.
  Assistant, Wairaraba High School, 1923-24; Head-
master, Western Province School, Nandi, Fiji, 1925-27;
Assistance Housemaster, Mt. Albert Grammar School,
Auckland, N.Z., 1928-67; now retired.

First Professional Sale: *From Frankenstein to
  Andromeda*, B. & J. Paul (N.Z.), 1966 (anthology).

Member: New Zealand Secondary Schools Executive;
  Auckland Cricket Association.

Brown writes:
  "There is some genuine interest in SF here in New
Zealand: ten years ago, I was encouraged to do an
SF anthology for schools, with a decent literary
level, by the late Prof. John Reid of the University
of Auckland, who had a very good SF library. And
some of my own pupils at Mt. Albert Grammar School
had small, but comprehensive collections of science
fiction. I don't know of any native son who special-
ises in SF, but there is no doubt that a market (and
not only a teenage market) exists for good, well-
written materials. Authors like Fred Hoyle, Ray
Bradbury, Arthur C. Clarke, Fritz Leiber, Arthur
Porges, John Brunner, and many others, are well liked
here."

* * * * *

JAMES COOKE BROWN

Full Name: James Cooke Brown.
  Born July 21, 1921, at Tagbilarin, Bohol, Philippine
Islands. Son of Bryan Burtis Brown and Violet Mary
Cooke. Three children: Jefferson (born 1944), Jill
(born 1945), Jennifer (born 1965).

Education: B.A., University of Minnesota, 1946;
  Ph.D., 1948.

Career: Linguist.
  Assistant Professor, University of Florida, until
1953. Invented parlor game, "Careers," in 1955, and
has lived off the royalties ever since. Developed
Loglan, an invented language, in 1960, and is Director
of the Loglan Institute, Palm Springs, California.

First Professional Sale:
  "The Emissary," in *Astounding Science Fiction*,
June, 1952 (as Jim Brown).

Agent: Loglan Institute, P.O. Box 1785, Palm
  Springs, CA 92262.

"Careers," says Brown, "is a frolicsome approach to
job concepts that expressed my own predicament at the
time."

ROSEL GEORGE BROWN

Full Name: Rosel George Brown.
  Born March 15, 1926, at New Orleans, Louisiana.
Daughter of Sam George (a nurseryman) and Elizabeth
Rightor. Married W. Burlie Brown, August 2, 1946.
Two children: Robin Ernest (born 1954); Jennifer Jo
(born 1959).

Education: B.A., Tulane University, 1946; M.A.,
  University of Minnesota, 1950.

Career: Writer & housewife. Died November 26, 1967.

First Professional Sale: "From an Unseen Censor,"
  in *Galaxy*, September, 1958.

Agent: Robert P. Mills, 156 E. 52nd St., New York,
  NY 10022.

Member: Science Fiction Writers of America.

Interests:
  Gardening. "Rosel was an indefatigable student of
the life and literature of 5th century Greece. She
had written a life of Alcibiades, and was at work on
a 'biography' of the heroic little city of Platea when
she died."

W. Burlie Brown had this to say about his wife:
  "Rosel had real fun writing. Her special joy was
fantasy--reflected in most of her short stories. She
died just when her long apprenticeship was beginning
to pay off. Her Sibyl Sue Blue novels may have provided science fiction with a women's lib heroine."

* * * * *

JOHN BRUNNER

Full Name: John Kilian Houston Brunner.
  Born September 24, 1934, at Preston Crowmarsh,
Oxfordshire, England. Son of (Egbert Sidney Houston)
Anthony Brunner (a sales representative) and (Amy
Phyllis Ivy) Felicity Whitaker (a model). Married
Marjorie Rosamond Sauer, July 12, 1958.

Education: Attended Cheltenham College, 1948-51.

Career: Writer.
  Editorial Assistant, *Bulletin of Industrial Diamond
Applications*, 1956; Editorial Assistant, Spring Books,
1956-58; full-time writer, 1958-DATE; Director, Brunner
Fact & Fiction Ltd., 1966-DATE.

First Professional Sale: *Galactic Storm*, Curtis
  Warren, 1951 (as Gill Hunt).

Agents:
  Paul R. Reynolds, 599 Fifth Avenue, New York, NY
10017; John Farquharson Ltd., 15 Red Lion Square, London WC1R 4QW, England.

Awards:
  Hugo Award, Best Novel, 1968 (1969), *Stand on Zanzi-
bar*; British Fantasy Award, 1966; British SF Award
(twice); Prix Apollo.

Member: Science Fiction Writers of America; Society
  of Authors; Crime Writers Association.

Interests: Crossword puzzles, music, dirty limericks.

JOHN BRUNNER (cont.)

Brunner is unique among modern science fiction writers, in that he has consciously revised, rewritten, and (often) retitled many of his early books, thereby reaching a completely new marketplace. In response to questions, he had this reply:
"Why did I revise so many of my early books? I imagine that I've already adumbrated the reason. When I started out, I was furnished with an active and often highly idiosyncratic imagination, but I had virtually no real-world knowledge of human beings, and a restricted acquaintance with the technique of inventing dialogue. Often I hit on a plot which a more competent writer would have treated in a far superior manner. Having (thank goodness) become in the course of time a tolerably well-qualified craftsman, I proceeded to rescue from what would otherwise have been deserved oblivion some of what seemed to me to be my happiest inventions."

* * * * *

D. M. BRYANT

Full Name: Dorothy M. Bryant.
   Born February 8, 1930, at San Francisco, California. Daughter of Joseph Calvetti (a mechanic) and Judith Chiarle (a bookkeeper). Married Louis Ungaretti, June 11, 1949 (divorced, 1963); married Robert K. Bryant (a contractor), October 18, 1968. Two children, John Ungaretti, Lorri Ungaretti; two stepchildren: Evan Bryant, Victoria Bryant.

Education: B.A., San Francisco State College, 1950;
   M.A., 1964.

Career: Instructor in English.
   High School Teacher in San Francisco public schools, 1953-61; Instructor in English, San Francisco State College, 1962; Instructor in English, Golden Gate College, 1963; Instructor in English & Creative Writing, Contra Costa College, 1964-DATE. Alto singer with California Bach Society.

Agent: Seligmann & Collier, 280 Madison Avenue, New
   York, NY 10016.

* * * * *

EDWARD BRYANT

Full Name: Edward Winslow Bryant, Jr.
   Born August 27, 1945, at White Plains, New York. Son of Edward Winslow Bryant (a postal worker) and Anne Harter Van Kleeck (a legal secretary).

Education: B.A., University of Wyoming, 1967; M.A.,
   1968.

Career: Writer.
   Disc jockey, KYCN Radio, 1961-63; News Director, KOWB Radio, 1965; shipping clerk, Blevins Mfg. Co., 1968-69; Teacher, Sherwood Oaks Experimental High School, 1970; full-time writer, 1970-DATE.

First Professional Sale: "The 10:00 Report Is
   Brought to You By..." in Again, Dangerous Visions, an anthology edited by Harlan Ellison, published by Doubleday & Company, 1972.

Agent: Robert P. Mills Ltd., 156 E. 52nd St., New
   York, NY 10022.

Awards:
   General Motors Scholar; Ford Foundation Three-Year Master's Program; First Place, New American Library Fiction Competition, 1971; Nebula Award Finalist, 1974.

Member: Science Fiction Writers of America.

Interests: Travelling, lighter-than-air craft, sharks.

Bryant writes:
   "Although I write as a full-time career, I occasionally get out on the lecture circuit, and have had speaking gigs at local elementary and secondary schools, as well as at the United States Air Force Academy, Northwest Community College, El Paso Community College, and the University of Colorado. I've also conducted an informal but highly productive SF writing workshop in Denver the past few years, based on techniques I learned at the 1968 and 1969 Clarion SF & Fantasy Writers Workshops."

* * * * *

THOMAS G. BUCHANAN

Full Name: Thomas Gittings Buchanan.
   Born March 14, 1919, at Baltimore, Maryland. Son of Thomas Gittings Buchanan and Ellen Gilmor. Married Harriet Dushane Penniman Patterson, 1941. Five children: Vaughn, Jean, Marian, Patricia, Robert.

Education: Attended Yale University, 1936-37; George
   Washington University, 1938-39.

Career: Computer programmer.
   Chief Electronic Computer Programmer, Maryland Casualty Company, Baltimore, 1955-61; Chief Electronic Computer Programmer, Le Matérial Téléphonique, Paris, 1961-62; author.

Agent: McIntosh & Otis, 475 Fifth Avenue, New York,
   NY 10017.

* * * * *

ROBERT BUCHARD

Full Name: Robert Buchard.
   Born December 24, 1931, at Lausanne, Switzerland. Son of Maurice Buchard and Sidonie Decaillet. Married Agnes Ollivier, March 3, 1961. Three sons: Christophe, Eric, Hugues.

Education: Studied law at the University of Paris.

Career: Reporter.
   Reporter, Paris-Presse, 1959-64; reporter for French television, 1964-DATE.

* * * * *

HENRIETTA BUCKMASTER

Full Name: Henrietta Henkle Stephens.
   Daughter of Rae D. Henkle (a publisher) and Pearl Wintermute. Married Peter John Stephens. Education: attended Friends Seminary, and Brearley School.

HENRIETTA BUCKMASTER (cont.)

Career: Writer. Awards: Ohioana Award in Fiction,
1945, for *Deep River*; Guggenheim Fellowship.

Agent: Russell & Volkening, 551 Fifth Avenue, New
York, NY 10017.

* * * * *

ROBERT BUCKNER

Full Name: Robert Henry Buckner.
Born May 28, 1906, at Crewe, Virginia. Son of
Robert Henry Buckner and Inez Katherine James. Mar-
ried Mary Duckett Doyle, 1937. Two children: Robert
Henry Jr., Sharon.

Education: M.A., University of Edinburgh, 1928.

Career: Writer.
Salesman, Alfred A. Knopf, New York, 1928-29; Advertising Manager, Doubleday, Doran Co., New York,
1929-31; Copywriter, Charles Denhard Co., New York,
1931-34; Writer/Producer, Warner Brothers Studios,
Hollywood, 1936-48; Writer/Producer, Universal-Inter-
national Pictures, Hollywood, 1948-52; free-lance
writer, 1952-DATE.

Awards:
Look award for best American film, 1951; twice
nominated for Academy Awards; O'Brien Award for best
American short story, 1936; Screen Writers Guild
Meltzer Award for Best Screenplay, 1952. Member: Pi
Kappa Alpha.

* * * * *

ALGIS BUDRYS

Full Name: Algirdas Jonas Budrys.
Born January 9, 1931, at Konigsberg, East Prussia.
Son of Jonas Budrys and Regina Kashuba. Married Edna
F. Duna, July 24, 1954. Four sons: Jeffrey John,
Steven Paul, Timothy Charles, David James.

Education: Attended University of Miami, 1947-49;
Columbia University, 1951-52.

Career: Writer and editor.
Investigations Clerk, American Express Co., 1950-51;
Asst. Editor, Gnome Press, 1952; Asst. Editor, *Galaxy*,
1953; editor, Pyramid Books, 1958-61; Editor-in-Chief,
Regency Books, 1961-63; Editorial Director, Playboy
Press, 1963-65; President & Creative Director, Com-
mander Publications, 1965-66; Public Relations Account
Executive, Theodore R. Sills, Inc.; Young & Rubicon,
Inc., 1966-DATE; free-lance writer.

Awards: Edgar Award, Best Short Story, 1966. Member:
Old Town Bicycle Club.

* * * * *

KENNETH BULMER

Full Name: Henry Kenneth Bulmer.
Born January 14, 1921, at London, England. Son of
Walter Ernest Bulmer (a chemist) and Hilda Louise Corley. Married Pamela Kathleen Buckmaster, March 7,
1953. Three children: Deborah Louise (born 1960);

Lucy-Ellen (born 1961); Kenneth Laurence (born 1963).

Education: Attended Catford School, London.

Career: Writer.
Representative for various paper merchandising and
office equipment firms, 1947-54; free-lance author,
1954-DATE; Editor, *New Writings in SF*, No. 22- , 1973-
DATE.

First Professional Sale: *Space Treason*, Hamilton
& Co., 1952 (with A. V. Clarke).

Member:
Science Fiction Writers of America; British Science
Fantasy Association; British Fantasy Society; Science
Fiction Foundation; Airship Association.

In addition to books published under his own name, Bulmer writes a series of historical novels about a seaman
named George Abercrombie Fox under the name Adam Hardy,
and a swords-and-sorcery saga, the Dray Prescot series,
under the name Alan Burt Akers. When asked about the
Prescot books, he had this response:

"You ask how one goes about making up an entire world.
There is no quick and easy answer to this, although one
quick and easy reply would be to say that all my life
I have had an interest in worlds of the imagination,
and have studied in fair depth various world civilisa-
tions of different time epochs, and thus a feeling has
been developed that a culture is somewhat like a machine with all its parts relating one to another, where
one mistake will render the whole thing unworkable. For
instance, it would make almost untenable many of the
societies on Kregen if one nation was equipped with a
high-powered rifle with which to arm their warriors.
Equally, the appearance in the stories of metals,
jewels, masonry, etc., of a technology beyond that possible within the context of the society, would likewise
destroy credibility. Also, if a society is, for example, living in a forest of tall trees, and never leave
the trees, then to caparison them with jewels and metals and masonry is likewise not tenable. If these
seem negative points, they are, in my experience, valuable guides as to what not to do. If anything appears
in the stories, it must chime with everything else.
Explanations should be given that will cover the appearance of whatever it is that is desired to be introduced into the story. If this simple and basic
rule is followed, I feel it will obviate inconsisten-
cies. In the case of Dray Prescot, I am dealing with
a single world, so that outside intrusions are not likely to cross-fertilize with any other worlds of the
imagination."

* * * * *

DAVID R. BUNCH

Full Name: David Roosevelt Bunch.
Born at Lowry City, Missouri. Son of David Henry
Bunch and Bessie Edna Barker.

Education: B.S., Central Missouri State College;
M.A., Washington University, St. Louis.

Career: Cartographer.
Cartographer, U.S. Air Force Aeronautical Chart and
Information Center, St. Louis, 1954-DATE.

Member: Science Fiction Writers of America; Alpha
Phi Sigma.

DAVID R. BUNCH (cont.)

Agent: Virginia Kidd, P.O. Box 278, Milford, PA 18337.

Awards:
  Fourth Place ($11,000) in *Promethean Lamp* poetry contest, 1966; First Prize, long poem category, *Scimitar and Song* awards for best poems of the year, 1969.

* * * * *

EUGENE BURDICK

Full Name: Eugene Leonard Burdick.
  Born December 12, 1918, at Sheldon, Iowa. Son of Jack Dale Burdick (a painter) and Marie Ellerbroek. Married Carol Warren, July 3, 1942. Three children: Katherine, Mary, Michael.

Education:
  B.A., Stanford University, 1942; Ph.D., Magdalen College, Oxford University (Rhodes Scholar), 1950.

Career: Professor of Political Theory.
  Professor of Political Theory, University of California, Berkeley, 1950-65; Staff Member, Naval War College, 1950-51. Died July 26, 1965.

Agent: Curtis Brown Ltd., 60 E. 56th St., New York, NY 10022.

Awards:
  Fellowship from the Center for the Advancement of the Study of Behavioral Sciences; O. Henry Prize, 1947; Houghton-Mifflin Literary Fellowship, 1956, for *The Ninth Wave*.

* * * * *

LOLAH BURFORD

Full Name: Lolah Mary Burford.
  Born March 18, 1931, at Dallas, Texas. Daughter of Joseph Michael Egan and Mae Rene Flanary. Married William Burford. Three daughters.

Education: B.A., Bryn Mawr College, 1951; M.A., S.M.U. Graduate School, 1954.

Career: Writer.
  Teacher, Norfleet School of Music and Individual Studies, New York, 1952-53; instructor, S.M.U. English Dept., 1954-56.

First Professional Sale: "Picture of Texaco Capline," *New York Times*, March 24, 1968.

* * * * *

JOANNE BURGER

Full Name: Joanne Denise Burger.
  Born February 13, 1938, at Corpus Christi, Texas. Daughter of Charles Albert Burger (a longshoreman) and Ruth Mae Wilds.

Education: B.S., University of Texas, Austin, 1960; M.S., Texas A. & M. University, 1970.

Career: Research Chemist.
  Chemist, Dow Chemical Company, 1960-DATE.

Member:
  National Fantasy Fan Federation (Member of Directorate, Head of Tape Bureau); Houston Science Fiction Society (President); New England Science Fiction Association.

Interests: Bibliographies; religious education of the young.

* * * * *

ANTHONY BURGESS

Full Name: John Anthony Burgess Wilson.
  Born February 25, 1917, at Manchester, England. Son of Joseph Wilson and Elizabeth Burgess. Married Llewela Isherwood Jones, January 22, 1942 (died March 20, 1968); married Liliana Macellari, September 9, 1968. One son, Paolo Andrea.

Education: B.A. (Honors), Manchester University, 1940.

Career: Writer.
  Lecturer in Phonetics, Ministry of Education, 1948-50; lectured for the Central Advisory Council for Adult Education in the Forces, 1946-48; Educational Officer, Colonial Service, 1954-59; full-time writer, 1959-DATE.

Member: P.E.N.

"Some Views of SF:
  "The form fascinates me as much as it did when I first read H.G. Wells, and, having written two books which I am assured are in the genre, I have often considered writing more. (I have, in fact, written a long SF story published in the *Hudson Review*, but have shied away from anything longer.) The trouble with SF at the moment is that it has been shunted from the main literary stream to a quirky back-channel. It receives the same critical respect as detective fiction receives, and this is over-qualified, merely indulgent. The best SF is literature like Bellow, Malamud, Henry James, or Joyce for that matter. *Lord of the Flies* is SF, so really is *Finnegans Wake*. But SF writers are themselves responsible for the sub-literary regard in which the form is increasingly held. They are interested in language and write extremely well, but they are not much concerned with character, and lack the big architectonic gift. I've just been reading *Pavane* by Keith Roberts, a study of present-day and future England as they might have been if the Counter-Reformation had prevailed in 1588. A wonderful idea, and wonderful writing, but the creator's mind isn't big enough to encompass it. He has to write scrappily, episodically, picking at the theme in short studies. Are not perhaps all our SF writers becoming content to be small, coterie, quirky people, and refusing to compete with the so-called bigger world of 'general fiction?' This worries me."

* * * * *

ERIC BURGESS

Full Name: Eric Alexander Burgess.
  Born September 28, 1912, at London, England. Son of Oliver Burgess (a civil servant) and Lucy Alexander. Married Ena Morley (died 1966). One son, Oliver Mark (born 1941).

ERIC BURGESS (cont.)

Career: Customs Officer.

"After leaving school (age 15), I was successively an office boy, a general hand in the Covent Garden Market, a hop picker, a builder's labourer, and then one of the 3 million odd unemployed at that time. I passed the civil service entrance examination in 1932, and was an Officer of Customs and Excise from 1932-62. During the war, I was a rating in the Fleet Air Arm, serving mainly in Ceylon and India, and editing the magazine *Flip* from 1945-46. Since retiring, I've been a full-time writer."

First Professional Sale: *A Knife for Celeste*, Michael Joseph, 1948.

Agent: Elspeth Gordon, Manor House, Popes Avenue, Strawberry Hill, Middlesex, England.

Interests:
"Reading, walking, talking, drinking in inns and taverns, idling; also trying (largely in vain) to escape from juke boxes, radios, television, traffic, and all the other enemies of tranquility."

Burgess writes:
"Before venturing into the field of science fiction, I had been writing novels of the suspense/detection variety for some time. The printed works in this category were: *A Knife for Celeste*, *The Malice of Monday*, *Accident to Adeline*, *Divided We Fall*, *A Killing Frost* (televised as "Dackson's Wharf"), *Closely Confined*, *Deadly Deceit*, and *Exit Pretty Poll*. I also wrote, with Dick Fagan, the biography of a London lighterman called *Men of the Tideway*.

"Although I had read a good deal of science fiction-- by no means all of it with enjoyment--I had not contemplated turning to this type of story myself until my long-standing friend, Arthur Friggens, came up with an idea that I thought unique, and which stirred the sluggish flow of my imagination to the point of considerable excitement.

"Arthur had not previously written with an eye to getting into print, whereas I was at least to some extent already a professional (albeit in the worst-paid and most ill-recognized profession in the land!). We decided to co-operate, and our first joint production was the novel called *Mortorio*--the name of a distant planet which reverses life and death processes, though only for a selected few. We followed this by the quite different *Anti-Zota*, which deals with the situation that could arise when the perfection of transplant techniques enables half the human race (the donees) to live twice as long as the other half (the donors). We then wrote *Mortorio Two*, a sequel to the first book. Somewhere in between we more or less completed a time-division novel--*The Hounds of Hell*--which awaits some revision; and we have recently started on *Gullible's Travels*, which is intended to be a satire based on what we hope is a hitherto unexplored aspect of the miniaturisation theme.

"Incredible though it may sound, my co-author and myself seldom squabble about anything, and never about writing. Don't ask me why--it is as much a mystery to me as to anyone else. It might have been a different matter had we started our collaboration when we were both much younger and less tolerant, but this can only be guesswork. I suppose that in so far as our books reflect a basic attitude towards life in general, and human problems in particular, our essential attitude is similar, which was certainly not the case when we first met some twenty-five years ago. What happens in practice is something like this:

"In the first place, Arthur presents the main theme. (It is invariably something I could not have dreamt up by myself.) After that, we do a hell of a lot of preliminary talking about its possibilities, playing tennis with derivative notions, tossing them to and fro, developing them, getting a plot outline. We share the first rough drafting in a confused and undisciplined way, outlining characters and situations, rejecting here and modifying there. Mostly the story shapes up in a quite different form from our original expectations. Eventually the result of our mutual labour is sieved through me to give the final version some coherence of style and presentation. It seems to work. And personally--so far--I have found this form of fiction more rewarding intellectually and emotionally than the work I had previously been engaged upon."

* * * * *

JOHN BURKE

Full Name: John Frederick Burke.
Born March 8, 1922, at Rye, Sussex, England. Son of Frederick Goode Burke (a Police Chief Inspector) and Lilian Gertrude Sands. Married Joan Morris (divorced 1963); married Jean Williams, 1963. Seven children: Bronwen, Jennifer, Sally, Jane, Joanna, David, Edmund.

Education: Attended Holt High School, Liverpool.

Career: Writer and editor.
Production Manager, Museum Press, 1955; Editorial Manager, Books for Pleasure Group, London, 1956-59; Public Relations Executive, Shell International Petroleum, 1959-63; European Story Editor, Twentieth-Century Fox Productions, 1963-65; free-lance author, 1965-DATE.

First Professional Sale: "Welcome Home," *Convoy File*, 1945.

Agents:
David Higham Associates, 5-8 Lower John St., London W1R 4HA, England; Harold Ober Associates, 40 E. 49th St., New York, NY 10017.

Awards: Rockefeller Atlantic Award in Literature, 1947, for *Swift Summer*.

Member: Crime Writers Association; Danish Club; East Anglian Writers, Norwich, England.

Interests:
Music: clarinet and piano. "I wrote SF for various UK magazines in the 1950s and 1960s, and various paperback and a few hardcover titles. Nowadays I do mainly book-of-the-film adaptations in this field, like *Moon Zero Two* (Signet, 1969)."

* * * * *

WILLIAM R. BURKETT JR.

Full Name: William Ray Burkett, Jr.
Born August 31, 1943, at Augusta, Georgia. Son of William Ray Burkett and Frances DeLong. Married Wanda Yvonne Kleppe, April 1, 1968.

Education: High school graduate.

WILLIAM R. BURKETT JR. (cont.)

Career: Public relations executive.
  "Student, copyboy, novelist, reporter, feature writer, soldier, Sunday editor, free-lance author, civil service (Navy public relations)."

Member: Authors Guild; National Rifle Association.

* * * * *

BEN LUCIEN BURMAN

Full Name: Ben Lucien Burman.
  Born December 12, 1896, at Covington, Kentucky. Son of Sam and Minna B. Burman. Married Alice Caddy (an illustrator), September 19, 1927.

Education: A.B., Harvard University, 1920.

Career: Writer.
  Reporter, *Boston Herald*, 1920; Assistant City Editor, *Cincinnati Times Star*, 1921; Special Writer, *New York Sunday World*, 1922; Staff Contributor, Newspaper Enterprise Association, 1927; war correspondent, Africa and the Middle East, 1941; free-lance author.

Awards:
  Southern Authors Prize for Most Distinguished Southern Book of the Year, 1938, for *Blow for a Landing*; Thomas Jefferson Memorial Prize, 1945, for *Rooster Crows for Day*; French Legion of Honor for wartime reporting from Africa, 1947; German Young People's Book Festival Prize for *High Water at Catfish Bend*.

Member: Authors League; P.E.N.; Overseas Press Club; Dutch Treat Club.

* * * * *

HALLIE BURNETT

Full Name: Hallie Burnett.
  Born at St. Louis, Missouri. Daughter of John McKnight Southgate (a consulting engineer) and Elizabeth Baker. Married Whitney Ewing Burnett (an author and editor), 1942 (died 1973). Two children: John Southgate; Whitney Ann Stevens.

Career: Editor.
  Co-Editor, *Story*, 1942-70; Editor, Story Press Books, 1942-45; Associate Professor of Literature and Creative Writing, Sarah Lawrence College, 1960-64; Reader, Book-of-the-Month Club, 1957-59; Senior Editor, Prentice-Hall, 1959-60; Fiction Editor, *Yankee*, 1959-60; Conductor of fiction workshop at New York City Writer's Conference, Wagner College, 1955-60; Instructor in short story writing, Hunter College, 1959-61; free-lance author.

Awards: O. Henry Award (third prize), 1942, for "Eighteenth Summer."

Member:
  Authors Guild; American Association of University Professors; Women's National Book Association; P.E.N. (Director, 1951-71); College English Association; New York Junior League Woman Pays Club; Overseas Press; Old York.

SHEILA BURNFORD

Full Name: Sheila Philip Cochrane Burnford.
  Born May 11, 1918, in Scotland. Daughter of Wilfred George Cochrane Every and Ida Philip Macmillan. Married David Burnford, 1941. Three children: Peronelle Philip; Elizabeth Jonquil; Juliet Sheila.

Education: Privately educated in England, France, and Germany.

Career: Writer.

Agent: Harold Ober Associates, 40 E. 49th St., New York, NY 10017.

Member: Society of Authors; Canadian Authors Association; Authors Guild.

* * * * *

ALAN BURNS

Full Name: Alan Burns.
  Born December 29, 1929, at London, England. Son of Harold Burns (a company director) and Anne Marks. Married Carol Lynn (a painter), January 51, 1954. One son, Daniel Paul.

Education: Higher Certificate, Merchant Taylors' School, 1948; Barrister-at-Law, Inns of Court, 1954.

Career: Author and lawyer.
  Barrister in London, 1954-58; Research Assistant, London School of Economics and Political Science, 1959; Libel Lawyer, *London Daily Express*, 1959-62; free-lance author, 1962-DATE.

* * * * *

EDGAR RICE BURROUGHS

Full Name: Edgar Rice Burroughs.
  Born September 1, 1875, at Chicago, Illinois. Son of George Tyler Burroughs (a distiller and battery manufacturer) and Mary Evaline Zeiger. Married Emma Centennia Hulbert, January 1, 1900 (died 1944). Three children, Joan (born 1908), Hulbert (born 1909), John Coleman (born 1913).

Education: Attended Michigan Military Academy, 1891-95.

Career: Author.
  Worked at a variety of jobs, including a period in the Seventh US Cavalry, until selling his first story in 1911; free-lance author, 1911-50; founded Edgar Rice Burroughs, Inc., in 1923; war correspondent in the Pacific during World War II. Died March 19, 1950.

First Professional Sale: "Under the Moons of Mars," serialized in *The All-Story*, Feb.-July, 1912.

Agent: Edgar Rice Burroughs, Inc., P.O. Box 277, Tarzana, CA 91356.

Burroughs purchased the Otis Ranch in the San Fernando Valley in 1919, renamed it the Tarzana Ranch, and later subdivided a portion for homes, calling it the Tarzana Tract; the name was officially adopted for the Tarzana Post Office on December 12, 1930.

JOHN COLEMAN BURROUGHS

Full Name: John Coleman Burroughs.
  Born February 28, 1913, at Chicago, Illinois. Son
of Edgar Rice Burroughs (an author) and Emma Centennia
Hulbert. Married Jane Ralston, December 12, 1936
(divorced, 1961); married Mary Nalon, December 16,
1961. Five children: John Ralston (born 1942),
Danton (born 1944), Dian, Kimberley, Stacy.

Education: Attended Pomona College, 1934.

Career: Author and illustrator.
  Burroughs illustrated many of his father's stories
and books, and has also served as an executive in
the family company, Edgar Rice Burroughs, Inc.

Member: Phi Beta Kappa; Burroughs Bibliophiles
  (Honorary Member).

* * * * *

WILLIAM BURROUGHS

Full Name: William Seward Burroughs.
  Born February 5, 1914, at St. Louis, Missouri. Son
of Perry Mortimer Burroughs (a businessman) and Laura
Lee. Married Joan Vollmer, January 17, 1945 (deceased). One son, William Seward.

Education: A.B., Harvard University, 1936; medical
  studies at the University of Vienna.

Career: Writer.
  Has held a variety of jobs, including advertising
copywriter, newspaper reporter, office employee,
private detective, factory worker, exterminator, and
bartender; now full-time writer.

Burroughs is a grandson of the inventor of the
Burroughs adding machine.

* * * * *

S. H. BURTON

Full Name: Samuel Holroyd Burton.
  Born November 30, 1919, at Caverswall, Stafford-
shire, England. Education: M.A., Queens' College,
Cambridge University, 1945.

Career: Schoolmaster.
  Schoolmaster from 1945-64; currently author and
visiting lecturer in English literature.

First Professional Sale: *The Criticism of Poetry*, Longmans, Green, 1950.

Agent: Peter Janson-Smith, 31 Newington Green,
  London N16 9PU, England.

Interests:
  "Walking the moorlands of England; travelling; watching cricket. I'm an anthologist, critic, writer
of fiction, author of English textbooks and travel
books. I've also edited Shakespeare and English
classics. I write all my books in longhand: can't
stand a typewriter." About science fiction, he had
this to say: "*Good* SF is a great help in secondary
schools. It stirs interest in a wide variety of

topics--sociology, psychology, style, environment, etc.
Nor is it in conflict with the classics; rather, it
complements them. Many students (not all by any means)
are avid readers of SF. Discrimination develops rapidly."

* * * * *

F. M. BUSBY

Full Name: F. M. Busby, Jr.
  Born March 11, 1921, at Indianapolis, Indiana. Son
of F. M. Busby (a personnel director, farmer, teacher,
sports coach) and Clara Irene Nye (an English teacher).
Married Elinor Doub, April 28, 1954. One daughter,
Michele (born 1952).

Education: B.Sc. (Physics), Washington State University, 1946; B.Sc. (Engineering), 1947.

Career: Writer.
  Digital-Communications Engineer, Alaska Communications System, 1947-70; full-time writer, 1970-DATE.

First Professional Sale: "A Gun for Grandfather,"
  in *Future Science Fiction*, #34, Fall, 1957.

Agent: Robert P. Mills Ltd., 156 E. 52nd St., New
  York, NY 10022.

Awards:
  Hugo Award, Best Amateur Publication, 1959 (1960),
Cry of the Nameless; "Here, There, and Everywhere,"
a story in the anthology *Clarion II*, tied for second
prize in the associated New American Library contest,
1971; "Road Map," a story in *Clarion III*, received
second prize in the same contest in 1972.

Member: Science Fiction Writers of America (Vice-
  President, 1974-76); Authors Guild; Authors League.

Interests:
  "Who has time? (Make that--sure, lots of other interests, but nothing major enough to list.) Although
my training and previous career were in 'hard science,'
I find I write 'people' stories, not 'gadget' stories.
My imagination prefers the problems of individuals to
those of groups--'only-child' stories? It fits. I
have been and still may be prone to writing about problems of identity, thinking from inside the head of a
character thrown into a totally-unprecedented identity-
situation. In conclusion, the IRS is much more kind to
free-lance writers than it ever was to communications
engineers!"

* * * * *

STUART J. BYRNE

Full Name: Stuart James Byrne.
  Born October 26, 1913, at St. Paul, Minnesota. Son
of Christopher J. Byrne (an advertiser) and Grace H.
McLean. Married Joey A. Adamo, September, 1935. Two
children: Joanne R. (born 1938); Richard I. (born 1941).

Education: B.A., University of California, Los Angeles; M.A. from same school.

Career: Writer and manager.
  Special Assistant to Supervisor of Manufacturing,

STUART J. BYRNE (cont.)

Douglas Aircraft Company, Santa Monica, 1940-43; Systems Stores Manager, Pan American-Grace Airways, Lima, 1943-47; Administrative Assistant--Procurement, Brown-Pacific-Maxon, Guam, 1948-50; Purchasing Agent, Adamo Company, Los Angeles, 1950-57; screen writer and producer, Hollywood, 1957-59; Senior Writer, Engineering Industries, Hollywood, 1959-61; Chief Writer, Titan II checkouts, Lehigh Engineering, 1961; Engineer and Material Control Manager, Litton Data Systems Division, Van Nuys, 1961-67; Material Control Manager, Scientific Data Systems, El Segundo, 1967-68; Administrative staff, Operations Control, Litton Data Systems Division, Van Nuys, 1968-69; full-time writer, 1969-DATE.

First Professional Sale: "Music of the Spheres," in *Amazing Stories*, August, 1935.

Agent: Forrest J Ackerman, 2495 Glendower Avenue, Hollywood, CA 90027.

Member: Science Fiction Writers of America; Writers Guild.

Byrne writes:
"The sci-fi type of universe building as a lifetime habit has evolved into a 'New Age Consciousness' kind of objective application--where the Inner Space concept is emerging in the form of a planned Foundation: EDRI=Ethical Dynamics Research Institute (one step beyond parapsychology and noetic sciences)."

* * * * *

ELIZABETH CADELL

Full Name: Violet Elizabeth Cadell.
Born November 10, 1903, at Calcutta, India. Daughter of Frederick Reginald Vandyke (a colonial officer) and Elizabeth Lynch. Married Henry Dunlop Raymond Mallock Cadell (a banker), 1928 (deceased). One son, one daughter.

Career: Novelist.
Cadell was raised in India, educated in England, and travelled often to Ireland. After the death of her husband, she turned to writing, and has been a full-time author ever since.

* * * * *

MARTIN CAIDIN

Full Name: Martin Caidin.
Born September 14, 1927, at New York, New York. Married his wife, Grace Caidin, November 1, 1952 (since divorced). Two daughters: Jamie Patrice, Pamela Gale.

Career: Writer.
Nuclear Warfare Specialist, Executive Division, State of New York, 1950-54; expert on World War II aviation history, aerial warfare, rocketry, space exploration, nuclear and biological warfare, etc.; free-lance writer.

Awards:
Numerous writing awards for fiction and nonfiction; has also received awards for "outstanding contribu-

tions to youth."

Member:
Aviation Hall of Fame; British Interplanetary Society (Fellow); Confederate Air Force; Knight of Mark Twain; Aviation/Space Writers Association; Missile, Space & Range Pioneers; United States Naval Institute; American Aviation Historical Society; American Astronautical Society (Founder).

First Professional Sale: *Jets, Rockets, and Guided Missiles*, Robert M. McBride, 1950.

* * * * *

ROGER CAILLOIS

Full Name: Roger Caillois.
Born March 3, 1913, at Reims, France. Children: Catherine. Education: Agrégé de Grammaire, École Normale Supérieure, Paris, 1937; Diploma, École Prades Hautes Études, 1936.

Career: Author and editor.
Founder of French Institute, Buenos Aires, and Editor/Director, *Lettres Francaises*, 1941-45; Editor-in-Chief, *La France Libre*, 1945-47; Member of editorial board of two other journals, *Confluences* and *La Licorne*, 1945-48; with UNESCO, Paris, 1948-DATE; Head of the Division of Letters, Department of Cultural Activities, 1970-DATE.

Awards: International Peace Prize for *Bellone; ou, La Pente de la Guerre*.

* * * * *

JANET CAIRD

Full Name: Janet Caird.
Born April 24, 1913, at Livingstonia, Malawi. Daughter of Peter Scott Kirkwood (a missionary) and Janet Gilmour. Married James Bowman Caird (in Her Majesty's Inspection Service), July 19, 1938. Two daughters: Janet, Elisabeth.

Education: M.A., Edinburgh University, 1935; graduate study at University of Paris, 1935-36.

Career: Teacher and writer.
Teacher of English, French, and Latin in Glasgow and Edinburgh, 1937-38, 1940-43, 1958-61; full-time author.

Agent: A. M. Heath & Co., 35 Dover St., London W1X 4EB, England.

Member:
Royal Overseas League; Society of Authors; Society of Antiquarians of Scotland (Fellow); British Federation of University Women.

* * * * *

ARTHUR CALDER-MARSHALL

Full Name: Arthur Calder-Marshall.
Born August 19, 1908, at Wallington, Surrey, England. Son of Arthur Grotjan Calder-Marshall and Alice Poole. Married Violet Nancy Sales, 1934. Two daughters. Education: B.A., Hertford College, Oxford, 1930.

ARTHUR CALDER-MARSHALL (cont.)

Career: Author.
Schoolmaster, Denstone College, Staffordshire, England, 1931-33; author, biographer, critic, 1933-DATE; Scriptwriter for Metro-Goldwyn-Mayer, Hollywood, 1937.

Agent: Elaine Greene Ltd., 31 Newington Green, London N16 9PW, England.

Member: Royal Society of Literature (Fellow); Savile Club; National Liberal Club.

* * * * *

TAYLOR CALDWELL

Full Name: Janet Miriam Taylor Holland Caldwell.
Born September 7, 1900, at Prestwich, Manchester, England. Daughter of Arthur F. Caldwell (an artist) and Anna Markham. Married William Fairfax Combs, May 27, 1919 (divorced, 1931); married Marcus Reback, May 12, 1931. Two children: Mary Margaret, Judith Ann.

Education: A.B., University of Buffalo, 1931.

Career: Writer.
Court Reporter, New York State Department of Labor, Buffalo, 1923-24; Member, Board of Special Inquiry, U.S. Dept. of Justice, Buffalo, 1924-31; full-time writer.

Awards:
Citation from University of Buffalo, 1949; Award from *Buffalo Evening News*, 1949; Grand Prix Chatrain, 1956, for *Never Victorious, Never Defeated*; Daughters of the American Revolution National Award, 1956; Ph.D. Lit., D'Youville College, 1964; Medal for public service, Marquette University, 1964; citation from Wisdom Society.

Member: American Legion; St. Francis Guild; Nazareth Guild; National Legion of Mary.

* * * * *

MARY CALHOUN

Full Name: Mary Calhoun.
Born August 3, 1926, at Keokuk, Iowa. Daughter of William Clark Huiskamp and Louisa Belle Waples. Married Leon Wilkins (an Episcopalian priest) November 8, 1962. Two children: Mike Calhoun; Gregory Calhoun.

Education: B.A., State University of Iowa, 1948.

Career: Writer.
Reporter, *Omaha World-Herald*, 1948; Society Editor, *Gresham Outlook*, 1948-49; writer, 1949-DATE.

* * * * *

HORTENSE CALISHER

Full Name: Hortense Calisher.
Born December 20, 1911, at New York, New York. Daughter of Joseph Henry Calisher (a manufacturer) and Hedvig Lichtstern. Married Curtis Harnack (a writer) March 23, 1959. Two children: Bennet Heffelfinger (daughter); Peter Heffelfinger.

Education: A.B., Barnard College, 1932.

Career: Teacher of literature.
Adjunct Professor of English, Barnard College, 1956-57; Visiting Lecturer, State University of Iowa, 1957, 1959-60; Visiting Lecturer, Stanford University, 1958; Visiting Lecturer, Sarah Lawrence College, 1962; Visiting Professor of Literature, Brandeis University, 1963-64; writer.

Agent: Brandt & Brandt, 101 Park Avenue, New York, NY 10017.

Awards: Guggenheim Fellow, 1952, 1955; American Specialists Grant, Department of State, 1958. Member: P.E.N.

* * * * *

JULIAN CALLENDER

Full Name: Austin Lee.
Born July 9, 1904, at Cowling, Yorkshire, England. Son of Joseph Nicholas Lee and Gertrude Kershaw.

Education: B.A., Trinity College, Cambridge, 1926; M.A., 1928.

Career: Priest.
Ordained priest, Church of England, 1928; Chaplain, Royal Navy, 1931-36; Vicar of Pampisford, Cambridge, 1935-38; Chaplain to Middlesex Hospital, London, 1938-39; Chaplain, Royal Air Force Motorboats Crew, 1940; Rector of Claxby, and of Willoughby, Lincolnshire; Vicar, Great Paxton, Huntingdonshire, England, 1963-?. Deceased.

Agent: Ursula Winant, 14 Essex St., Strand, London.

Member: Society of Authors; Crime Writers Association; Mystery Writers of America.

* * * * *

ELEANOR CAMERON

Full Name: Eleanor Cameron.
Born March 23, 1912, in Canada. Daughter of Henry Butler and Florence Vaughan. Married Ian Stuart Cameron, 1934. One son, David Gordon.

Education: Attended University of California, Los Angeles, and Art Center School, Los Angeles.

Career: Librarian, writer.
Clerk, Public Library, Los Angeles, 1930-36; Clerk, Board of Education Library, Los Angeles, 1936-42; Research Librarian, Foote, Cone & Belding, Los Angeles, 1943-44; Research Librarian, Honig, Cooper & Harrington, Los Angeles, 1956-58; writer, 1950-DATE.

Member: P.E.N.; Save-the-Redwoods League.

Cameron is best-known for her series of books about Tyco Bass. The first book in the series, *The Wonderful Flight to the Mushroom Planet*, has been translated into Japanese, recorded for the blind, and is regarded by many authorities as one of the best juvenile science fiction stories published in the 1950s. It is one of twelve recommended fantasies in *Library Journal*'s "Growing Up with Books."

LOU CAMERON

Full Name: Lou Cameron.
   Born June 20, 1924, at San Francisco, California.
Son of Louis Arnold Cameron and Ruth Marvin.

Education: Studied at California School of Fine
Arts, San Francisco, 1940-41.

Career: Writer and artist.
   Sergeant, U.S. Army, 1941-50; free-lance artist
for various pulp magazines and comic books, 1950-57;
free-lance writer, 1957-DATE; has also been a movie
extra, private detective, ranch hand, trucker.

Agent: August Lenninger, 11 W. 42nd St., New York,
NY 10036.

Awards: Thomas Edison Award, Best Historical Comic
Book, 1956, *Life of Columbus*.

* * * * *

JOHN W. CAMPBELL

Full Name: John Wood Campbell, Jr.
   Born June 8, 1910, at Newark, New Jersey. Son of
John Wood Campbell and Dorothy Strahern. Married
Dona Stuart, 1931 (divorced, 1950); married Margaret
Winter, 1951. Two children: Philinda, Leslyn S.

Education: B.S., Duke University, 1932.

Career: Writer and editor.
   Free-lance writer, 1932-37; Editor, *Astounding
Science Fiction* (later called *Analog Science Fiction/
Science Fact*), October, 1937-December, 1971; Editor,
Unknown (later called *Unknown Worlds*), March, 1939-
October, 1943. Died July 11, 1971.

First Professional Sale: "When the Atoms Failed,"
   in *Amazing Stories*, January, 1930.

Honors and Awards:
   Guest of Honor, 5th World Science Fiction Convention
(Philcon I), Philadelphia, 1947; Guest of Honor, 12th
World Science Fiction Convention (SFCon), San Francisco, 1954; Guest of Honor, 15th World Science Fiction
Convention (Loncon I), London, 1957; Hugo Award, Best
Professional Magazine, *Astounding Science Fiction*
(later called *Analog Science Fiction/Science Fact*),
for the following years: 1954 (1955); 1955 (1956);
1956 (1957) [Best Professional Magazine, American];
1960 (1961); 1961 (1962); 1963 (1964); 1964 (1965);
1952 (1953).

* * * * *

RAMSEY CAMPBELL

Full Name: John Ramsey Campbell.
   Born January 4, 1946, at Liverpool, England. Son
of Alexander Ramsey Campbell (a policeman and clerk)
and Nora Bernadette Walker. Married Jenny Lynne
Chandler (daughter of A. Bertram Chandler, the science
fiction writer), January 1, 1971.

Education: Attended St. Edward's College, 1957-62.

Career: Writer.
   Clerical officer, Inland Revenue, Liverpool, 1962-66;

Acting Librarian-in-Charge, Liverpool Public Libraries,
1966-73; free-lance writer, 1973-DATE; Film Reviewer,
BBC Radio, Merseyside, 1969-DATE.

First Professional Sale:
   "The Church in High Street," published in the anthology, *Dark Mind, Dark Heart*, Arkham House, 1962 (edited
by August Derleth).

Agent: Kirby McCauley, 220 E. 26th St., New York, NY
10010.

Member: Science Fiction Writers of America; British
   Fantasy Society (President, 1972-73); British Film
   Institute.

Interests:
   Comics, music, (inadvertently) breeding rabbits [my
workroom looks like *Watership Down* right now], psyche-
delics.

"Some thoughts off the top of my head at nine in the
morning (typed, to slow me down):
   "Began writing professionally, or at least for professional publication (after attempts at imitating
Arthur Machen and John Dickson Carr, the manuscripts
of which are now in Liverpool's Local History Library
should anyone want to chortle over them) in 1961,
heavily under the influence of Lovecraft. That influence became lighter once August Derleth satirized it a
little in his reply to my submission. In fact, he
recommended I emulate my favourite author, M. R. James.
Which I gradually did.
   "*Demons by Daylight* took about twice as long to write
as *The Inhabitant of the Lake*, because most of its con-
tents were rewritten completely. Still, that taught
me a lot too. Once that was completed, I continued
writing mostly in the same vein. In 1973, having found
ideas piling up in my mind for a science fiction novel,
I decided I could risk jacking in my full-time job,
and becoming a full-time writer. (If nothing else, I
could stop people sneering when I claimed to be a
writer rather than a librarian.) In June of 1973, I
finally made the break. Took me a long time to stop
feeling guilty at not writing every weekday from 9 to
5. Feeling guilty, I felt depressed; feeling depressed,
I felt unable to write what I'd set out to write. God,
those were a bad few months. Add to that, I discovered
that I felt a first novel and my first SF were too much
all at once to attempt in a single project. Add to
that the horror market seemed to be collapsing. No,
that wasn't a good time of my life.
   "I wrote a few strained SF stories. Then horror
swung up again. I began to feel easier writing SF
once I didn't have to. Same goes for sword-and-sorcery.
I began to realize how important communicating with
the reader was, instead of feeling this was some ir-
relevance editors and agents kept bothering me with.
That's it so far, and here I am.
   "Much of my stuff is autobiographical to a degree.
Particularly "The Cellars," "Napier Court," "Concussion,"
"The Other House." I reckon my best stories are those
which are mostly about their characters, but not everyone agrees with me.
   "I used to write less to cause terror than to dis-
turb. But hardly anyone believed this distinction, so
what the hell. Several of my recent stories were written in a room with seven rabbits. (No, no, good hea-
vens, not hallucinations--real furry, bouncing rabbits,
six of them the product of our own uncaged housepet.)
It doesn't sound much like the way Lovecraft wrote, but
I'm sorry, I can't help that. I suppose they're useful to strengthen my self-discipline. If you examine

RAMSEY CAMPBELL (cont.)

the top left-hand corner of this page, you'll see how high the parent rabbit can jump. I'm surprised she's refrained from helping me type this.

"I do think that horror fiction is capable of a good deal of evolution yet--oh, horror, occult fantasy, science fantasy, whatever you want to call what I write. It has as much life in it as science fiction still, I'm sure. Trouble is, most of the writers in it tend to get discouraged by the limited number of markets. Well, you can't blame the poor buggers. But someone has to make sure that the genre doesn't wither away.

"What perhaps we need is for horror fiction to become acceptable again, to be read as literature, if that's not too strong a word--to become something you're not ashamed of reading, or being seen to read. Maybe the pulps are partly to blame for its fall from grace, as Brian Aldiss suggests was the case with SF. Maybe some of the stories themselves are to blame, but I don't know--a lot of garbage is published in other genres without harming them so seriously. Well, I don't know. But I do reckon that horror fiction can justifiably be written with as much attention to style, technique, insight, as anything else gets. And I'll tell you one more thing--I don't think one need to repress one's sense of humour, one's humanity, anything else about oneself (as Lovecraft certainly did), simply in the service of the dubious discipline of writing A Horror Story. And I don't, if I can help it."

* * * * *

JUDITH CAPE

Full Name: Patricia Kathleen Page.
Born November 23, 1916, at Swanage, Dorsetshire, England. Daughter of Lionel Frank Page and Rose Laura Whitehouse. Married W. Arthur Irwin (a publisher), December, 1950. Stepchildren: Neal A., Patricia J., Shelia A. Emigrated to Canada, 1919.

Education: Attended Art Students' League, New York, and Pratt Institute; studied art privately.

Career: Poet and artist.
Has held jobs as a sales clerk and radio actress in Saint John, New Brunswick, filing clerk and historical researcher in Montreal; script writer, National Film Board, 1946-50. Solo exhibitions of paintings (as P. K. Irwin) at Picture Loan Society, Toronto, 1960; Galeria de Arte Moderna, Mexico City, 1962; Art Gallery of Greater Victoria, 1965.

Awards:
Bertram Warr Award from Contemporary Verse, 1940; Oscar Blumenthal Award from Poetry, 1944; Canadian Governor-General's Award in Poetry, 1954, for The Metal and the Flower.

* * * * *

PAUL CAPON

Full Name: Harry Paul Capon.
Born December 18, 1911, at Kenton, Suffolk, England. Son of Harry Urban Capon (a farmer) and Bessie Martha Gooderham. Married Doreen Evans-Evans (divorced, 1951); married Amy Charlotte Gillam, May 26, 1956. Two children: Felicity-Ann (born 1934); Mark Nicholas (born 1943).

Career: Film writer and editor.
Capon pursued a triple career as a scriptwriter, film editor, and a novelist. He worked for several important film companies, including the Soviet Film Agency, and Walt Disney Productions (England), where he was Supervising Editor. From 1963-67, he was head of the Film Department of Independent Television News. He died in November, 1969. [Courtesy of Amy Capon.]

* * * * *

ERNESTINE GILBRETH CAREY

Full Name: Ernestine Gilbreth Carey.
Born April 5, 1908, at New York, New York. Daughter of Frank Bunker Gilbreth (a consulting engineer) and Lillian Moller (an engineer). Married Charles Everett Carey (a sales executive), September 13, 1930. Two children: Lillian Gilbreth, Charles Everett Jr.

Education: B.A., Smith College, 1929.

Career: Writer and lecturer.
Buyer, R. H. Macy & Co., New York, 1930-44; Buyer, James McCreery & Co., New York, 1947-49; writer, 1949-DATE.

Awards:
Co-recipient (with Frank B. Gilbreth, Jr.) of French International Humor Award, 1950, for Cheaper by the Dozen; McElligett Medallion (with her mother, Dr. Lillian Gilbreth), for professional excellence and integrity in their fields, Marquette University Alumnae, 1966.

Member: P.E.N.; Authors Guild of America; Seven College Conference; Smith College Club.

* * * * *

RUTH CHRISTOFFER CARLSEN

Full Name: Ruth Christoffer Carlsen.
Born February 21, 1918, at Milwaukee, Wisconsin. Daughter of Carl Severin Christoffer (a Milwaukee Railroad official) and Lydia Diefenthaeler. Married George Robert Carlsen, April 5, 1941. Four children: Christopher Robert (born 1942), Kristin Mary (born 1944), Peter Severin (born 1946), Jane Emilie (born 1950).

Education: B.A., University of Minnesota, 1939.

Career: Writer and consultant.
Consultant for Westinghouse Score Tests; full-time author and editor. President, Macbrie Corporation.

First Professional Sale: Mr. Pudgins, Houghton Mifflin, 1951.

Member: Authors Guild; Authors League; Pen Women of America.

Interests:
Travel, designing, making quilts, refinishing furniture, gardening. "There were two prime influences in my life: my father, a great teller of tales, who insisted when I went to college that when I finished, I must be able to get a job. This made me take journalism, which was a great experience, since it knocked out my high-faluting, lugubrious style. My father's

RUTH CHRISTOFFER CARLSEN (cont.)

"formula for story telling was simple: excitement, lots of laughter, and a touch of magic. Okay, call it fantasy. The second influence was my husband, who taught children's lit at the University of Minnesota and the University of Colorado, and got me started writing children's books. He's an able critic, and since he is now Mr. Adolescent Literature, I wonder if I should step my books up to this level?"

* * * * *

DALE CARLSON

Full Name: Dale Carlson.
  Born May 24, 1935, at New York, New York. Daughter of Edgar M. Bick (an orthopedic surgeon) and Estelle Cohen. Married Albert W. D. Carlson (an artist and illustrator), November 24, 1962. Two children: Daniel, Hannah.

Education: B.A., Wellesley College, 1957.

Career: Editor.
  Bookseller, Doubleday & Co. Bookstore, New York, 1958; Assistant, Mel Evans & Co. (editors), 1958-59; Assistant Editor, Thomas Yoseloff, 1959-60; Vice-President and Editor-in-Chief, *Parents League Bulletin*, 1968-69; free-lance editor for other New York publishing houses.

Agent: Toni Mendez, 140 E. 56th St., New York, NY 10022.

* * * * *

CARL CARMER

Full Name: Carl Lamson Carmer.
  Born October 16, 1893, at Cortland, New York. Son of Willis Griswold Carmer (a superintendent of schools) and Mary Lamson. Married Elizabeth Black (an artist and illustrator), December 24, 1928.

Education:
  Ph.B., Hamilton College, 1914; Ph.M., 1917; M.A., Harvard University, 1915.

Career: Instructor and writer.
  Instructor in English, Syracuse University, 1915-16; Asst. Professor of English, University of Rochester, 1916-17; Chairman of Public Speaking Dept., Hamilton College, 1919; Asst. Professor of English, University of Rochester, 1919-21; Assoc. Professor of English, University of Alabama, 1921-24, 1924-27; Columnist, *New Orleans Morning Tribune*, 1927; Asst. Editor, *Vanity Fair*, 1928-29; Assoc. Editor, *Theatre Arts Monthly*, 1929-33; full-time writer and folklorist, 1933-76. Died 1976.

Agent: Harold Ober Associates, 40 E. 49th St., New York, NY 10017.

Awards:
  Litt.D., Elmira College, 1937; L.H.D., Hamilton College, 1941; Litt.D., Susquehanna University, 1944; LL.D., University of Buffalo, 1962; *New York Herald Tribune* Children's Book Festival Award for *Windfall Fiddle*; cited for contributions to children's literature by New York State Association for Curriculum Development; adopted by Wolf Clan of Seneca Nation.

Member:
  Society of American Historians (Councillor); New York State Historical Association; New York State Folklore Society; Authors Guild; American Center of P.E.N.; Poetry Society of America; Edward MacDowell Association; Phi Beta Kappa; Psi Upsilon; Pilgrims Club; Century Association.

* * * * *

JOHN CARNELL

Full Name: Edward John Carnell.
  Born April 8, 1912, at Plumstead, London, England. Son of William John Carnell (an engineer) and Louisa Woollett. Married Irene Cloke, June 17, 1939. Two children: Michael John, Leslyn Hilary.

Education: Attended Bloomfield Secondary School.

Career: Editor.
  Prior to the second World War, Carnell was an apprentice printer, printing house manager, deputy buyer for a commercial printing and stationary company, buyer for a bookstore chain; Publicity Director (and Editor of the *BIS Journal*), British Interplanetary Society, 1936-38; Secretary, British Science Fiction Association, 1937-39; Editor, *New Worlds*, #1-141, October, 1946-April, 1964; Editor, *Science Fantasy*, #3-64, Winter, 1951/52-April, 1964; Editor, *Science Fiction Adventures*, #1-32 (all issues), March, 1958-May, 1963; Director, E. J. Carnell Literary Agency, London, 1964-72; free-lance editor, 1964-72; Editor, *New Writings in SF*, #1-21, 1964-72. Died in London, March 23, 1972. Chairman, 15th World Science Fiction Convention (Loncon I), London, 1957.

Award: Hugo Award, Best Professional Magazine, British, 1956 (1957), *New Worlds*.

First Professional Sale: An article to *Disc* (a jazz magazine), 1937.

Agent: E. J. Carnell Literary Agency, 17 Burwash Road, Plumstead, London SE18 7QY, England.

* * * * *

OTIS CARNEY

Full Name: John Otis Carney.
  Born February, 1922, at Chicago, Illinois. Son of William Roy Carney and Marie Murphy. Married Frederika Fly, 1947. Three sons: Thomas R., John Otis Jr., Peter C.

Education: B.A., Princeton University, 1946.

Career: Writer.
  Writer, Louis de Rochemont Associates, New York, 1947; Reporter, *Minneapolis Star*, 1948-49; Writer, J. Walter Thompson, Chicago, 1950-53; free-lance novelist, television and screenwriter, 1954-DATE.

Agent: Lurton Blassingame, 60 E. 42nd St., New York, NY 10017.

Awards:
  Friends of American Writers Best Book Award, 1960, for *Yesterday's Hero*. Member: Society of Midland Authors; Screen Writers Guild.

JOHN DICKSON CARR

Full Name: John Dickson Carr.
   Born 1906, at Uniontown, Pennsylvania. Son of Wood
Nicholas Carr (a U.S. Congressman and postmaster) and
Julia Carr. Married Clarice Cleaves, 1931. Three
children.

Education: Attended Haverford College.

Career: Writer.
   Full-time writer, 1930-DATE; lived in England, 1931-
48; worked as a writer for the BBC in London during
World War II. Died February 27, 1977.

Member: Mystery Writers of America; London Detective
   Club; Baker Street Irregulars; Savage Club, London.

* * * * *

TERRY CARR

Full Name: Terry Gene Carr.
   Born February 19, 1937, at Grant's Pass, Oregon.
Son of Leslie Clarence Carr (a machinist) and Marcella
Woods Drummond (an office worker). Married Norah
Miriam Dyches, January 31, 1959 (divorced, 1961);
married Carol Ann Stuart, September 7, 1961.

Education: A.A., City College of San Francisco,
   1957; attended University of California, Berkeley,
   1957-59.

Career: Editor.
   Free-lance writer, 1961-62; Associate Editor and
agent, Scott Meredith Literary Agency, 1962-64;
Associate Editor, Ace Books, 1964-67; Editor, 1967-71;
free-lance writer and editor, 1971-DATE.

First Professional Sale:
   "Who Sups with the Devil," in The Magazine of Fantasy and Science Fiction, May, 1962. Carr's first
publication in the science fiction magazines was
"Startling," in Startling Stories, December, 1952,
concerning which he said: "'Startling' was merely
a bit of doggerel verse quoted in the letter column;
no payment was involved. I was paid small sums for
artwork and cartoons in the fanzines Inside and
Abstract, circa 1954. A story, 'Blind Clarinet,'
was sold to an anthology to be published by Regency
Books; half the agreed-upon price was paid immediately.
Regency later rejected the book, however, so the
story never saw professional print. (An earlier
version was published in Lighthouse in 1961.) So
my first real professional sale was 'Who Sups with
the Devil.'"

Agent: Henry Morrison Inc., 58 W. 10th St., New York
   NY 10011.

Awards:
   Hugo Award, Best Amateur Publication, 1958 (1959),
Fanac (with Ron Ellik); Hugo Award, Best Fan Writer,
1972 (1973); "The Dance of the Changer and the Three"
was nominated for both the Hugo and Nebula Awards;
TAFF representative, London, 1965.

Member: Science Fiction Writers of America (edited
   SFWA Bulletin for two years; founded and edited
   SFWA Forum for two years); Fantasy Amateur Press
   Association (since 1952).

Interests:
   Traditional jazz, archeology, sports. Carr adds:
"I founded and edited the (original) Ace Science Fiction Specials series, edited the Universe series of
anthologies, and edited (with Don Wollheim) the World's
Best Science Fiction series for Ace Books." Carr now
edits The Best Science Fiction of the Year series of
annual anthologies for Ballantine Books.

* * * * *

GLADYS HASTY CARROLL

Full Name: Gladys Hasty Carroll.
   Born June 26, 1904, at Rochester, New Hampshire.
Daughter of Warren Verdi Hasty (a sign painter) and
Emma Frances Dow. Married Herbert A. Carroll (now
an emeritus professor of psychology), June 23, 1925.
Two children: Warren H. (born 1932), Sarah L. (born
1941).

Education: A.B., Bates College, 1925.

Career: Writer.
   Free-lance writer, of novels, short stories, nonfiction. Several of her titles have been book club
selections, and one was adapted for motion pictures.

First Professional Sale: "Of Course Not, Doug,"
   in The High Road, 1926.

Awards: Honorary M.A., University of New Hampshire,
   1934; Litt.D., University of Maine, 1940; Litt.D.,
   Bates College, 1945.

Member: Phi Beta Kappa.

Interests:
   Local history, genealogy, antiques. "I believe there
is an element of fantasy in the majority of my books,
more in some than in others, presumably because I see
so much in life which can be presented in no other
terms. I have long been tremendously interested in
the crossing of time tracks, which I am convinced is
much more frequent than is commonly believed."

* * * * *

RUTH CARROLL

Full Name: Ruth Carroll.
   Born September 24, 1899, at Lancaster, New York.
Daughter of Frank Howard Robinson and Sallie Underhill.
Married Latrobe Carroll, January 24, 1928.

Education: A.B., Vassar College, 1922; student, Art
   Students League, 1922-24; student, Cecelia Beaux's
   School of Portrait Painting, New York, 1925.

Career: Author and artist.
   Author, 1934-DATE; artist, often illustrating her
own books; a portfolio of her paintings and drawings
was published in 1964 by Walck.

Awards:
   Juvenile Award, American Association of University
Women (North Carolina Division), 1953, for Peanut;
1955, for Digby, the Only Dog.

Member: Delta Kappa Gamma.

TED CARROLL

Full Name: Thomas Theodore Carroll, Jr.
    Born November 5, 1925, at St. Petersburg, Florida.
Son of Thomas Theodore Carroll (a town clerk) and
Marion Gurerrant. Married Dorothy Lee Sale, June 22,
1951. Two children: Patricia Lee, John DeLorme II.

Education: Attended University of South Carolina,
    The Citadel, University of North Carolina, George
    Washington University.

Career: Editor.
    Reporter, *Roanoke World-News*, 1952-55; Public Rela-
tions Account Executive, MacDonald-Cook Co. (an adver-
tising agency), South Bend, IN, 1955-57; Director of
Public Relations Division, Griffith Advertising
Agency, St. Petersburg, FL, 1957-59; Editor, *Bradenton
Herald*, Bradenton, FL, 1959-61; Editor of Editorial
Page, *Chester Daily Times*, Chester, PA, 1962-DATE.

Agent: Marie Rodell, 141 E. 55th St., New York, NY
    10022.

Awards: Pennsylvania Press Association Best Editor-
    ial Award, 1964, for editorial on Folcroft race
    riots.

* * * * *

JOHN F. CARSON

Full Name: John F. Carson.
    Born August 2, 1920, at Indianapolis, Indiana. Son
of Frederick P. Carson and Mary McKenzie. Married
Beverly V. Carlisle, February 1, 1942. Three children: Jacqueline Ann, John, Bruce.

Education: B.S., Butler University, 1948; M.S.,
    Indiana University, 1954; Ph.D., 1972.

Career: Professor of Secondary Education.
    Biologist, Grassyfork Fisheries, Martinsville, In-
diana, 1948-49; Naturalist, Indianapolis Children's
Museum, 1949-50; teacher of English and biology,
Martinsville High School, 1950-56; magazine editor,
educational coordinator, and field representative,
Indiana Lumber and Builders' Supply Association,
1956-57; Principal, Gosport-Wayne Township School,
1957-58; High School Principal, North Judson Consolidated Schools, 1958-61; High School Principal, Taipei
American Schools, 1961-64; Associate Professor of
Secondary Education, Central Michigan University,
1966-DATE.

Agent: McIntosh & Otis, 475 Fifth Avenue, New York,
    NY 10017.

Member: Phi Delta Kappa; National Association of
    Secondary School Principals.

* * * * *

ANGELA CARTER

Full Name: Angela Olive Carter.
    Born May 7, 1940, at Eastbourne, Sussex, England.
Daughter of Hugh Alexander Stalker (a journalist)
and Olive Farthing. Married Paul Carter, 1960 (divorced, 1972). Children: "None, thank god, though
god had nothing to do with it."

Education: B.A., University of Bristol, 1965.

Career: Writer.
    "I've made some kind of living by writing since
1965, and haven't had a formal job--apart from part-
time teaching, etc. I worked as a reporter on a provincial paper from 1958 more or less until going to
University in 1962."

First Professional Sale: "The Man Who Loved a
    Double Bass," to a small magazine in 1961.

Agent: Deborah Rogers, 29 Goodge St., London W.C.1.

Awards:
    John Llewellyn Rhys Award, 1965, for *The Magic Toy-
shop*; Somerset Maugham Travel Award, 1968, for *Several
Perceptions*.

Memberships: "None. Like Groucho Marx, I'd deeply
    suspect a club that had people like me as members."

Interests: "Politics, painting, music."

"Do you know the first line of the vocal part of Scho-
enberg's first string quartet, which goes: 'I feel the
wind that blows from a new planet...' Sometimes I do,
and sometimes I don't, and being European is like
living in a haunted house, at the best of times.
Nevertheless, I pass much time speculating on that
line, and my work is part of the speculation."

* * * * *

BRUCE CARTER

Full Name: Richard Alexander Hough.
    Born May 15, 1922, at Brighton, England. Son of
George Hough (a banker) and Margaret Esilman. Married
Helen Charlotte Woodyatt (a writer and illustrator),
July 17, 1943. Four children: Sarah, Alexandra,
Deborah, Bryony.

Education: Attended Frensham Heights Schools, 1931-
    40.

Career: Writer.
    RAF pilot, 1941-46; Editor and Manager, Bodley Head
(book publishers), London, 1947-55; subsequently,
Consulting Editor successively to Hamish Hamilton,
and, currently, to William Heinemann Ltd.

First Professional Sale: "The London and Birming-
    ham Railway," in *History Today*, August, 1951.

Award: Best Book of the Sea Award, 1972, for *Captain
    Bligh and Mr. Christian*.

* * * * *

LIN CARTER

Full Name: Linwood Vrooman Carter.
    Born June 9, 1930, at St. Petersburg, Florida. Son
of Raymond L. Carter. Married Noel Vreeland, August
17, 1963.

Education: Attended Columbia University, two years.

Career: Writer.

LIN CARTER (cont.)

First Professional Sale:
"Masters of the Metropolis," in *The Magazine of Fantasy and Science Fiction*, April, 1957 (with Randall Garrett).

Honors and Awards: "Damn few."

Carter is best-known for his series of stories based around the character of Thongor of Lemuria, and for his continuations of the Conan epic with L. Sprague de Camp.

* * * * *

M. L. CARTER

Full Name: Margaret Louise Carter.
Born April 29, 1948, at Norfolk, Virginia. Daughter of John Ervin Greunke (a certified public accountant) and Margaret L. Townsend. Married Leslie Roy Carter, September 21, 1966. Two children: Brian David (born 1967), Richard Alan (born 1971).

Education:
B.A., College of William and Mary, 1972; M.A., University of Hawaii, Honolulu, 1974.

Career: Instructor in English.
Graduate Teaching Assistant, University of Hawaii, 1972-74; free-lance editor and critic.

First Professional Sale: *The Curse of the Undead*, Fawcett, 1970 (anthology).

Agent: Gary M. Bernstein, 4640 282nd St., Toledo, Ohio.

Member: Phi Beta Kappa; Count Dracula Society; Christopher Lee International Club; Civil Air Patrol.

Carter writes:
"I have two great ambitions: 1) to have my script of Stoker's *Dracula* filmed; 2) to write a good vampire novel (an attempt is now in progress)."

* * * * *

DAVID CASE

Full Name: Brian David Case.
Born August 17, 1937, at London, England. Son of Henry Francis Case (in police work) and Ann Davies. Married Pamela Jones (a teacher), March 21, 1964.

Education: B.A., University of Hull, 1961.

Career: Teacher.
Tutor in History, Tutorial Establishment, London, 1963-DATE; served in the RAF, 1956-58.

* * * * *

CURTIS W. CASEWIT

Full Name: Curtis Werner Casewit.
Born May 21, 1922, at Mannheim, Germany. Married Charlotte Fischer-Lamberg, February, 1954. Three children: Carla (born 1954), Stephen (born 1955), Niccolo [Nicky] (born 1960).

Education:
Attended Florence Language School, Firenze, Italy, 1933-38; later studied at University of Denver, and University of Colorado.

Career: Writer.
Book buyer for a department store in Denver, 1959-64; full-time writer, 1964-DATE.

First Professional Sale: "The Mask," in *Weird Tales*, March, 1952.

Awards:
Edgar Award, Best Book Reviewer, 1956; *Writer's Digest* short story contest award, 1955; Dutton Award for article in *Best Articles of 1964*, and *Best Articles of 1966*.

Member: Society of Magazine Writers; Society of American Travel Writers.

* * * * *

BRUCE CASSIDAY

Full Name: Bruce Bingham Cassiday.
Born January 25, 1920, at Los Angeles, California. Son of Robert Maxwell Cassiday and Persis Bingham. Married Doris S. Galloway, 1950. Two children: Bryan Galloway, Cathy Bingham.

Education: B.A., University of California, Los Angeles, 1942.

Career: Editor and writer.
Editor, Popular Publications, 1946-49; Editor, Farrell Publications, 1950-53; Fiction Editor, *Argosy*, 1954-DATE; free-lance author.

Agent: August Lenniger, 11 W. 42nd St., New York, NY 10036.

Member:
Radio Writers of America; Writers Guild; Mystery Writers of America; Overseas Press Club; Authors League; Phi Beta Kappa; Theta Chi; Kap and Bell; California Scholarship Federation; Ephebian Society.

* * * * *

MEL CEBULASH

Full Name: Mel Cebulash.
Born August 24, 1937, at Jersey City, New Jersey. Son of Jack Cebulash (a postman) and Jeanette Duthie. Married Deanna Penn, August 19, 1962. Three children: Glen Harlan (born 1966), Benjamin Farrell (born 1968), Jeanette Mara (born 1971).

Education: B.A., Jersey City State College, 1962; M.A., 1964.

Career: Editor.
Teacher, Jersey City Public Schools, 1962-64; Editorial Director, Dept. of Reading Skills and Career Education, Scholastic Book Services, Inc., 1966-DATE; Associate Editor, *Scope Magazine*, 1968-70.

First Professional Sale: "The Job," in *Junior Challenges*, 1964.

MEL CEBULASH (cont.)

Awards: Author Award, New Jersey Association of Teachers of English, for *Through Basic Training with
Walter Young*.

Member: Mystery Writers of America; Authors Guild.

Interests:
  Literature of the Thirties, James T. Farrell's works,
horse racing. "In addition to writing children's
and teenager's books and stories under my own name,
I also have used other pseudonyms, including Glen
Harlan, Ben Farrell, Jared Jansen, Anthony Carmen-
dolla, and Jeanette Mara."

* * * * *

BENNETT CERF

Full Name: Bennett Alfred Cerf.
  Born May 25, 1898, at New York, New York. Son of
Gustave Cerf (a lithographer) and Fredericka Wise.
Married Sylvia Sidney, 1935 (divorced); married Phyl-
lis Fraser (an editor), 1940. Two children: Chris-
topher Bennett, Jonathan Fraser.

Education: A.B., Columbia University, 1919; Litt.
  B., Columbia School of Journalism, 1920.

Career: Editor.
  Reporter, *New York Herald Tribune*, 1921-23; Vice-
President, Boni & Liveright (publishers), 1923-25;
Founder and President, Modern Library, 1925-71; Co-
Founder (with Donald S. Klopfer), and President,
Random House, 1927-66; Chairman of the Board, Random
House, 1966-71; Director, Bantam Books, 1945-71; Pa-
nelist on TV show "What's My Line," 1952-67; Member,
Peabody Awards Committee, 1950-71 (Chairman, 1955-71);
Member, Board of Directors, Metro-Goldwyn-Mayer, and
Alfred A. Knopf Inc. Died August 27, 1971.

Awards: New York Philanthropic League, Distinguished
  Service Award, 1964.

Member: Pi Lambda Phi; Phi Beta Kappa; Phi Delta Epsilon; Dutch Treat; Overseas Press Club; Century
  Country Club.

* * * * *

CHRISTOPHER CERF

Full Name: Christopher Bennett Cerf.
  Born August 19, 1941, at New York, New York. Son
of Bennett Alfred Cerf (a publisher) and Phyllis
Fraser (an editor).

Education:
  B.A., Harvard College, 1963.

Career: Editor.
  Editor, *Harvard Lampoon*, 1962-63; Editor, Random
House, 1963-1970?; now an editor with the *National
Lampoon*.

First Professional Sale: Parody pieces to the
  magazine *Mademoiselle*, July, 1961.

Member: The Nectarine Organization.

JACK L. CHALKER

Full Name: Jack Laurence Chalker.
  Born December 17, 1944, at Norfolk, Virginia. Son
of Lloyd Allen Chalker, Sr. (an insurance man) and
Nancy Alice Hopkins.

Education: B.S., Towson State College, 1966; M.L.A.,
  Johns Hopkins University, 1969.

Career: History Instructor.
  History instructor, Baltimore City Schools; Editor
and Publisher, Anthem Series, 1961-66; Editor and
Director, Mirage Press, 1966-DATE.

Member:
  Maryland Historical Society; Smithsonian Associates;
Washington Science Fiction Association; New York Sci-
ence Fiction Society; Philadelphia Science Fiction
Society; Baltimore Science Fiction Society (Chairman).

Interests:
  Target shooting, travel, backpacking, gourmet, book
collecting, comic books, old radio, board and card
games (design, play, collect), foreign cars, stereo
systems. "I've ghost-written mystery fiction under a
variety of names, also some minor historical studies
under my name or no byline. I've worked on eight world
science fiction conventions, on the Committee of 3,
and have run Balticon, Disclave, Lunacon at one time
or another. None of these avocations have been consistent, as I need at least a ten-day week to do them all."

Chalker provided the following short history of his
press:

"Mirage Press really began when I discovered the
mimeograph, and, through some fanzine publications, I
also discovered that people were willing to pay money
for material that was interesting, unusual, or unique.
Even so, I published mostly those things I thought
should have been done by somebody.
  "The first of the books was the 1961 Lovecraft bibliography, simply because I was into Lovecraft very
heavily at that time, and thought that a revision and
updating of the Briney/Wetzel 1954 biblio was warranted.
Don Studebaker ran it off on his mimeo, and we presold
the batch. This was followed with a tiny edition of
David H. Keller's last new work, *A Figment of a Dream*,
which Keller subsidized, in 1962. Over the next several years I built up the line, the best of the batch
(and possibly the best to date) being the Clark Ashton
Smith memorial book, which I edited. I'd been one of
Smith's last correspondents, and the note of his death
from Derleth hit me pretty hard. As I had no money and
less facilities, various partners were enlisted for
each item--Studebaker on the biblio, Bill Evans and
Lynn Hickman on the Keller book, Bob Madle and Bob Pav-
lat on the Smith memorial, and then Mark Owings for
the next--the full range of mimeoed books and booklets,
each of which widened the market considerably.
  "In 1967, Bill Osten, who was also a typesetter, got
his family to stake the business to $20,000, and the
Press went pro, first with an underprinted test book-
let, *The Necronomicon: A Study*, and then with the first
hardcover, *The Conan Reader*, in 1968--a project suggested to me by an Owings joke about the publication
of *Pope Conan*. Advent put us onto Malloy Printing and
Lithographing, who have printed almost all of our books,
and we were on the road. With the exception of a
couple of items for the scholarly market we had built
up, all of the books to date have been ones I created,

JACK L. CHALKER (cont.)

"or, hearing about them and reading them, liked. A couple were rejected from other publishers, and were rewritten to my directions. Total editorial and marketing responsibility is in my hands; however, production is solidly in the hands of Bill Osten, who is not very efficient, and who has no business sense, causing us to sometimes wait a year or more for books we have on hand--and leaving me out front, holding the bag, to explain why the books didn't come out when they should. Osten, however, controls production and owns half the corporation, so there is little that can be done.

"Recently, our expanded market has allowed us to distribute some of the books of other houses; and, to get around the perennial production delays, I am considering launching a parallel but independent imprint of my own. The Press employs 4 or 5 people on a more or less permanent basis, although officially we have no employees, but subcontract all work (for tax purposes).

"I have learned how to sell books, and now need to bring production up to demand. The old cry that people aren't reading anymore is ridiculous--specialty publishing is booming, although there will be the high failure rate that's inevitable when the amateurs come in--they don't have 13 years experience, and they have few places to get it."

* * * * *

AIDAN CHAMBERS

Full Name: Aidan Chambers.
Born December 27, 1934, at Chester le Street, Durham, England. Son of George Kenneth Blacklin Chambers (a funeral director) and Margaret Hancock. Married Nancy Lockwood (former editor of *Children's Book News*), March 30, 1968.

Education: Studied at Borough Road College, London, 1955-57.

Career: Writer and editor.
Teacher of English and drama at various English schools, 1957-68; full-time author, 1968-DATE.

Member: Society of Authors.

* * * * *

A. BERTRAM CHANDLER

Full Name: Arthur Bertram Chandler.
Born March 28, 1912, at Aldershot, England. Son of Arthur Robert Chandler (a soldier killed in World War I) and Ida Florence Calver (a domestic servant). Married Joan Margaret Barnard (divorced); married Susan Constance Schlenker, December 23, 1961. Three children: Penelope Anne, Christopher John, Jennifer Lynn (who married Ramsey Campbell, the horror and fantasy author).

Education:
Attended Sir John Leman School, Beccles, Suffolk; Certificate of Competency as Master of a Foreign-Going Steamship, Sir John Cass Nautical School, London.

Career: Ship's Master.
Apprentice and Third Officer, Sun Shipping Co.,

1928-37; with Shaw Savill Line, as a Fourth, Third, Second, and finally, Chief Officer, 1937-56; with Union Steam Ship Company of New Zealand, as a Third, Second, Chief Officer, and now a Master, 1956-DATE.

First Professional Sale: "This Means War!" in *Astounding Science Fiction*, May, 1944.

Agent: Scott Meredith, 580 Fifth Avenue, New York, NY 10036.

Awards: Ditmar (Australia), for *False Fatherland*; Ditmar, for "The Bitter Pill."

Interests: Navigation, harbour pilotage, cookery, naturism.

Chandler is best-known for his stories of Commodore Grimes, and the Rim Worlds, near the edge of the Galaxy. He provided the following history of his saga:

"Grimes and the Rim Worlds:
"I first got the idea of the Rim Worlds when Chief Officer of a vessel engaged upon one of the Union Steam Ship Company's less pleasant trades, running between a small port on the wild west coast of Tasmania, and one of the drearier industrial suburbs of Melbourne (never one of my favourite cities). One had the sense of navigating on the southern edge of the world, with nothing but stormy water between one and the Antarctic wastes. A few years later, I had another spell of Rim Running, when Master of a ship on the Melbourne-South Island (of New Zealand) trade. Rim Runners--the state shipping company of the Rim Worlds--was modelled to a great extent on the Union Steam Ship Company, the vessels of whose Australian fleet were commanded and officered mainly by refugees from the big English shipping companies. Today's shipping companies have Marine Superintendents--so Rim Runners had to have an Astronautical Superintendent. This was Captain Grimes, who, in the earlier Rim Worlds novels, was little more than a background character.

"Somehow, Grimes started taking charge, and he began to have novels all to himself. And Grimes acquired a background of his own. As well as being Rim Runners' Astronautical Superintendent, he was a senior officer in the Rim Worlds Naval Reserve. He was not, however, a native Rim Worlder. He was of Terran birth as well as ancestry. Also, he had a solid reputation as an author of very well-researched books on Terran maritime history. Then too (see *Alternate Orbits*), he had actually sailed as Master of an ocean-going ship on the watery world Aquarius....

"As C. S. Forester went back into Hornblower's career, tracing his rise from Midshipman to Admiral, so I did with Grimes. He started his professional life in the Interstellar Federation's Survey Service (the Federation's space navy), and then something happened that meant his future promotional possibilities were permanently blocked. So he resigned his commission, and went out to the Rim Worlds, not yet broken away from the Federation. He rose in their service, becoming Master of their own survey ship, *Faraway Quest*. As an ex-Terran naval officer, he naturally joined the Rim Worlds Naval Reserve, rising to the rank of Commodore. He made the first landings on the worlds of the Eastern Circuit--Tharn, Mellise, Stree, and Grollor. He made the first contact with the anti-matter systems to the Galactic West, and it was the lightjammer *Flying Cloud*--designed by Grimes, although he did not sail on her maiden voyage--that opened up the trade between the Rim Worlds and the anti-matter planets.

"Insofar as the chronology of Grimes' own career is

A. BERTRAM CHANDLER (cont.)

"concerned, the first novel was *The Road to the Rim*. In it, he is still a very young and innocent Ensign. In *To Prime the Pump*, he has become a junior officer of one of the Federation's battle cruisers, and has already established a reputation for getting into and out of trouble. In *The Hard Way Up* he--still a Lieutenant--has a command of his own, the tiny courier *Adder*. At the finish of this book, he achieves his promotion to Lieutenant Commander by very dubious means. Whilst waiting for his next appointment he, together with Una Freeman, an attractive policewoman, is involved in the very odd adventure of *The Broken Cycle*. While still a Lieutenant Commander, he is appointed Captain of the survey ship *Seeker*, and, in her, discovers the Lost Colony of Sparta (*False Fatherhood*, later reprinted as *Spartan Planet*). In this book, he is a compartively minor character. Later, the *Seeker* makes a landing on Morrowvia (*The Inheritors*), another lost colony, and Grimes tangles with both Drongo Cane (a slave trader), and the representative of the Dog Star Line. Next, as Commander Grimes, he is appointed to the slightly larger ship *Discovery*, in which he acquires *The Big Black Mark* that spells the finish of his Federation Survey Service career. At the finish of the book, he is contemplating emigration to the Rim Worlds.

"He pops up now and again, as a very minor character, in various early Rim Worlds novels. Somehow, in *Catch the Star Winds*, he is Andrew, not John, Grimes, and it is his son who is the maritime historian. But he had yet to develop, to take charge. Then, as Captain (later Commodore) Grimes, he is the major character in *Into the Alternate Universe*, *Contraband from Otherspace*, *Alternate Orbits*, *The Rim Gods*, *The Gateway to Never* (in which Captain Sir Dominic Flandry, borrowed from Poul Anderson, and the ex-Empress Irene, strayed from her own series, also appear). Grimes also clashes with Irene in *Nebula Alert*; she just can't seem to stay in her own universe and stories....

"The Novel on which I am working now is set in the general Rim Worlds framework, but Grimes is being given a rest. But two of his old enemies--Commodore "Handsome Frankie" Delamere, and the villainous Capt. Drongo Kane--are among those present in *Selemsatta Rising*.

"The ex-Empress Irene novels are *Empress of Outer Space*, *Space Mercenaries*, and *Nebula Alert*. They are set in the same general time period as the Grimes novels, but in one of the many alternate universes. *The Deep Reaches of Space* is set in an earlier period during which the cranky gaussjammers were the only means of interstellar transport. *The Coils of Time* and *The Alternate Martians* are put a relatively few years in our future. *The Hamelin Plague*, *The Sea Beasts*, and *The Bitter Pill* are as near as dammit here-and-now. *Glory Planet* was written long before I'd dreamed up the Rim Worlds, and long before various probes had made it obvious that Venus is not the watery, jungly world that we all used to play about on very happily not so very many years ago.

"The cronology of the Grimes saga runs something like this:

The Road to the Rim (1967)	Ensign Grimes on his first Deep Space voyage.
To Prime the Pump (1971)	Lieut. Grimes, junior officer in the cruiser *Aries*, is involved in goings on with the odd people of El Dorado, the planet of the filthy rich.
The Hard Way Up (1972)	Lieut. Grimes, captain of the courier *Adder*, bumbles from misadventure to misadventure, finally achieving undeserved promotion to Lieut. Commander.
Spartan Planet/False Fatherhood (1968)	Lieut. Commander Grimes, captain of the census ship *Seeker*, is involved in the complicated politics of Sparta, a lost colony.
The Inheritors (1972)	Lieut. Commander Grimes, captain of *Seeker*, tries to save the unspoiled (?) people of Morrowvia from the slave trader, Drongo Kane, and from the exploitation of their planet by the Dog Star Line.
The Broken Cycle (1975)	Lieut. Commander Grimes, between appointments, is ordered to assist Sky Marshal Una Freeman, a policewoman, to salvage pirated and abandoned liner *Delta Geminorum*. Grimes and Una are elected by a robot deity to be the Adam and Eve of a new race.
The Big Black Mark (1975)	Grimes, promoted to Commander, puts out in *Discovery* on a lost colony hunt. (For Grimes, read Bligh; for *Discovery* read *Bounty*). After the fun and games are over, Grimes realises that his career in the Federation Survey Service is over, resigns his commission, and emigrates to the Rim Worlds.
Catch the Star Winds (1969)	Grimes, by this time Captain Grimes, Astronautical Superintendent of Rim Runners, designs the lightjammer *Flying Cloud*, which, inadvertently, makes the first landing on one of the anti-matter planets to the Galactic West of the Rim Worlds.
Into the Alternate Universe (1964)	Captain Grimes takes the Rim Worlds survey ship *Faraway Quest* on a voyage to investigate the so-called Rim Ghosts. With him is Commander Sonya Verrill (who has made previous appearances in Rim Worlds novels) of the Intelligence Branch of the Interstellar Federation's Survey Service. Grimes and Sonya get married.
Contraband from Otherspace (1967)	Grimes and Sonya cope with a threatened incursion of highly intelligent mutant rats from an alternate universe.
The Rim Gods (1969)	Commodore Grimes in a series of adventures in and around the various Rim Worlds.
Alternate Orbits (1971)	Commodore Grimes and Sonya in a series of adventures in and around the Rim Worlds.
Nebula Alert (1967)	The ex-Empress Irene (see *Empress of Outer Space* and *Space Mercenaries*) strays from her own time track and tangles briefly with Grimes.
The Gateway to Never (1972)	Commodore Grimes helps the Rim Worlds Customs authorities to stamp out a drug smuggling racket.

A. BERTRAM CHANDLER (cont.)

The Dark Dimensions (1971)   Commodore Grimes takes *Faraway Quest* on an expedition to "the outsider"--a weird alien ship or space station out beyond the Rim. (See *The Ship from Outside*.) All sorts of odd people get involved, including the ex-Empress Irene, another version of Grimes not married to Sonya, but to his old flame Maggie Lazenby (see *Spartan Planet*), and Captain Sir Dominic Flandry, borrowed from Poul Anderson's cosmos. All sorts of odd things happen to everybody. Grimes finishes up hopelessly lost in space and time.

The Way Back (unpublished)   Grimes finds his way back to the Rim Worlds and his own time.

"Grimes, in his capacity as Astronautical Superintendent of Rim Runners, also appears briefly in *The Rim of Space*, *Beyond the Galactic Rim*, and *The Ship from Outside*."

* * * * *

JOY CHANT

Full Name: Eileen Joyce Chant.
Born January 13, 1945, at London, England. Daughter of John Maxwell Chant (a draftsman) and Glenys Sherwell.

Education: Associate, College of Librarianship, Wales, 1970.

Career: Librarian.
Librarian, London borough of Havering, 1966-DATE.

* * * * *

LOUIS CHARBONNEAU

Full Name: Louis Henry Charbonneau.
Born January 20, 1924, at Detroit, Michigan. Son of Louis Henry Charbonneau (an attorney) and Mary Ellen Young. Married Hilda Sweeney, December 15, 1945.

Education: B.A., University of Detroit, 1948; M.A., 1950.

Career: Writer and editor.
Teacher, University of Detroit, 1948-52; advertising copywriter, Mercury Advertising Agency, 1952-56; Staff writer, *Los Angeles Times*, 1956-71; free-lance writer, 1971-74; Book Editor, Security World Publishing Co., Los Angeles, 1974-DATE.

First Professional Sale: *No Place on Earth*, Doubleday & Co., 1958.

Agent: Scott Meredith, 580 Fifth Avenue, New York, NY 10036.

Member: Science Fiction Writers of America; Western Writers of America.

Charbonneau writes:
"Of some 25 published novels, seven are science fiction, which probably puts that area of my writing into fairly accurate perspective. (I used to write more SF, proportionately.) I also write western novels (under the name Carter Travis Young), suspense, and mystery, an occasional contemporary novel, one long historical effort. Years ago, there was radio, children's stories, some TV. Very mixed bag.

"A previous note wondered how science fiction compares with the western and suspense genres. A thoughtful question, not easy to answer. I'm not even sure how I came to wear so many hats, unless it was simply a professional writer's need to sell stories. The stories were there, and I wrote them.

"SF was my first interest, *No Place on Earth* being my first attempt at a novel. I would probably have written more in the field if I hadn't lost an encouraging editor, Dick Roberts, who retired from Bantam some years ago, after I'd written several books for him. Other editors beckoned, in other fictional terrain, and so it goes.

"SF offers the very special challenge of requiring you to create, not only characters and a story, but a whole world. You must recreate a world for the western novel (as with any historical fiction), but you have both the reality of history, and the mythology of the western to draw on. For science fiction, there is only the imagination (fed by logical speculation), at least for my kind of SF (which is more social-science fiction than hard science). For a Clarke or an Asimov, of course, it is quite different. The more you know about a given area of knowledge, the more fruitful the creative play of the mind.

"As for the third of the genres named, suspense or mystery, I believe it is the most difficult to do well (most SF fans will recoil). Also the most difficult to sell, simply because the competition is even fiercer. It leans more directly upon life itself (as it is, not as it might be or might have been), and upon personal experience. (This is a generality, and runs the risk of all such; there are spy stories so fantastic as to make Tolkien resemble Zola. Nevertheless, as a generalization, it remains true.) To capture in words a world of fantasy or of myth is a wonderful thing; to capture reality is no more wonderful, but it is more difficult."

* * * * *

PAUL CHARKIN

Full Name: Paul Samuel Charkin.
Born July 20, 1907, at Muswell Hill, North London, England. Son of Samuel Charkin and Louisa Frances Estelle Walden.

Education: Attended Southoe House, Richmond, Surrey, and County School, Richmond.

Career:
"Started my career as clerk in my father's business, and when that was closed during the industrial depression of the 1930s, became a tramp, door-knocking canvasser, and high pressure salesman, in rapid succession. Entered business as House Agent and Radio Salesman, and failed at both. The War saw me conscripted in A.R.P. duties, which I hated, and then to Red Cross work, which was much more interesting."

First Professional Sale: "The Wrong Glass," in *The Socialist Leader*, 1952.

LESLIE CHARTERIS

Full Name: Leslie Charteris.
  Born Leslie Charles Bowyer Yin, May 12, 1907, at
Singapore, Malaya; legally changed name in 1928 to
Leslie Charteris. Naturalized American citizen, 1946.
Married Pauline Schishkin, 1931 (divorced, 1937); mar-
ried Barbara Meyer, 1938 (divorced, 1943); married
Elizabeth Bryant Borst, 1943 (divorced, 1951); married
Audrey Long, 1952. One daughter, Patricia Ann.

Education: Attended Cambridge University, 1926;
  studied art in Paris.

Career: Author.
  Full-time author, 1928-DATE; Hollywood scenarist
and editor. Editor, *Suspense*, 1946-47; Editor, *The
Saint Mystery Magazine*, 1953-67; Editor, *The Saint
Detective Magazine*, 1953.

* * * * *

RICHARD Z. CHESNOFF

Full Name: Richard Zeltner Chesnoff.
  Born June 4, 1937, at New York, New York. Son of
Lewis Chesnoff (a musician) and Martha Zeltner. Married Yora Yedlin (a ceramicist), June 14, 1959. One
son, Adam Louis.

Education: Studied at New York University, 1955-57,
  and Hebrew University of Jerusalem, 1957-60.

Career: Correspondent.
  Correspondent in Israel for *New York Herald Tribune*,
1964-66, and for *Newsweek* and the National Broadcasting
Company News, 1965-66; Associate Editor for Foreign
News, *Newsweek*, 1966-68; Correspondent, *Newsweek*,
1968-DATE.

Agent: Robert Lescher, 141 E. 55th St., New York,
  NY 10022.

Member: Anglo-American Press Club, Paris.

* * * * *

MICHAEL CHESTER

Full Name: Michael Arthur Chester.
  Born November 23, 1928, at New York, New York. Son
of Arthur Vincent Chester and Irene Greenberg. Married Jacqueline Sapsis, 1950. Three children: Thomas,
Teresa, Barbara.

Education: B.A., University of California, 1952.

Career: Engineer.
  Physicist, Tracerlab, Inc., Berkeley, 1952-53; Research Analyst, Northrop Aircraft Inc., Hawthorne,
California, 1953-55; Engineer, Northrop Aircraft,
1956-57; Engineer, Coleman Engineering Co., Los Angeles, 1955-56; Scientist, Lockheed Missiles and
Space Company, Sunnyvale, California, 1957-DATE.

Member:
  Authors League of America.

Interests:
  Sailing and chess.

R. CHETWYND-HAYES

Full Name: Ronald Henry Glynn Chetwynd-Hayes.
  Born May 30, 1919, at Isleworth, Middlesex, England.
Son of Henry Chetwynd-Hayes (a Master Sergeant, and
cinema manager) and May Rose Cooper.

Education: Attended Hanworth Council School.

Career: Writer and editor.
  "Was employed up to June, 1973 as a showroom manager
in Berkely Street, London; I was connected with the
furnishing trade for many years; now a full-time editor
and writer."

First Professional Sale: "The Empty Grave," in
  Reveille, 1953.

Agent: London Management, 235/241 Regent St., London
  W1A 2JT, England.

Member: Society of Authors.

Interests: Films, books, the Brontes.

Chetwynd-Hayes has established a reputation in
Great Britain as a writer of weird and supernatural
stories. He had this to say about his profession:

  "As to the basic difference between science fiction
and the weird tale, in my youth that was a simple
question to answer. Science fiction dealt with people
who went out into space, and had various adventures
on other planets. Weird stories were mostly about
ghosts, mad scientists who created monsters in mountain laboratories, and so forth. Today, they are all
often lumped under the heading Science Fiction. In
fact, as you have seen, I have edited a book called
Terror Tales from Outer Space. My first long story--
a so-called novel--*The Man from the Bomb*, concerned a
man who was caught in the midst of an atomic explosion,
and emerged as a super-being. The publishers called
it science fiction--I called it fantasy.
  "No, I think SF should deal with science, and be
concerned with events, inventions, and situations that
have their roots in the present day. All else is fantasy, weird or supernatural. But even so, I do agree
that the dividing line is very flexible. My story
"Neighbors" (see *Cold Terror*) is about the people who
move in next door, and turn out to be beautiful human-
shaped machines, which house cold intelligences. Horror story? Yes, but I suppose it is also an SF.
  "But if you still require a straight answer, I will
keep to my original contention. Science fiction must
deal with science carried to its logical conclusion,
and weird stories with the dark world which lurks behind the commonplace."

* * * * *

IRMA CHILTON

Full Name: Irma Chilton.
  Born November 12, 1930, at Loughor, Glamorgan, Wales.
Daughter of Iorwerth Evans (a furnaceman) and Esther
Muxworthy. Married Henry Chilton (a chemist). Two
children: Dafydd Henry (born 1960), Rhiannon Irma
(born 1965).

Education:
  B.A., University of Wales, 1951.

IRMA CHILTON (cont.)

Career: Teacher.

First Professional Sale: *Take Away the Flowers*,
Heinemann, 1967.

Awards:
Several prizes at the National Eisteddfod of Wales
for short stories and children's novels; The Crown
of the Powys Eisteddfod for prose.

Interests:
Hill walking and mountaineering. "I write about
half my work in the Welsh language; this is, of course,
only published in Wales."

* * * * *

AGATHA CHRISTIE

Full Name: Agatha Mary Clarissa Christie.
Born 1890, in Torquay, Devonshire, England. Daugh-
ter of Frederick Alvah and Clarissa Miller. Married
Archibald Christie (a colonel in the Royal Air Corps),
December 24, 1914 (divorced, 1928); married Max Edgar
Lucien Mallowan (an archaeologist), September 11,
1930. One daughter, Rosalind Christie.

Education: Studied singing and piano in Paris.

Career: Writer.
Served as a Voluntary Aid Detachment nurse in a
Red Cross Hospital, during World War I; full-time
writer, 1920-76. After her divorce in 1928, Christie
travelled for several years; she later helped her
second husband at his excavations in Syria and Iraq.
During World War II, she worked in the dispensary for
University College Hospital, London. In the late
1940s, she returned to Mesopotamia to help her husband excavate Assyrian ruins. Died January 12, 1976.

First Professional Sale: *The Mysterious Affair
at Styles*, John Lane, 1920.

Agent: Hughes Massie Ltd., 69 Great Russell St.,
London W.C.1, England.

Awards:
New York Drama Critics' Circle Award, Best Foreign
Play of the Year, 1955, for "Witness for the Prosecu-
tion"; Commander of the British Empire, 1956; D.Litt.,
University of Exeter. Member: Royal Society of
Literature (Fellow).

* * * * *

JOHN CHRISTOPHER

Full Name: Christopher Samuel Youd.
Born April 16, 1922, at Huyton, Lancaster, England.
Christopher married his wife in 1946, and they have
five children, one son, and four daughters.

Education: Attended Peter Symonds' School, Winchester, England.

Career: Writer.
"Army service, 1941-46, Royal Signals, Gibraltar,
North Africa, Italy; started writing seriously in
1947 with the help (still gratefully acknowledged)
of the Rockefeller Foundation."

First Professional Sale: "Christmas Tree," in
Astounding Science Fiction, February, 1949 (as Christopher Youd)

Christopher has always been reticent about his personal life. He writes:

"I think I ought at least to explain my position
more clearly with regard to the questions I did not
answer. To start with, there is a personal aspect.
Many of my friends who are writers, perhaps most, get
an innocent satisfaction out of publicity. I have nothing against this, but I do not share it. I have refused all attempts by publishers to put my photograph
on the jackets of books, and have avoided all but the
simplest biographical details: and even those I have
supplied reluctantly. Where I have given way, I have
found the result embarrassing, and as I get older, I
see less reason to expose myself to embarrassment.
When the *Saturday Evening Post* serialized *No Blade of
Grass*, for instance, they inveigled me into a certain
amount of chat, and also a photograph. I was younger,
then, both grateful to and in awe of this majestic
organization which was paying me so much money. Today
in similar circumstances, I would decline, I hope cour-
teously.
"So much for the personal angle. The argument has
been made that writers are public figures, and have a
duty to the public that supports them. This I do not
accept. If a 'public figure' uses publicity to further his career, then I think they have a case: actors
and actresses are obvious points, and it is true of
some writers. All I do is write books which publishers
risk money on, and which the public may buy or not as
they choose. My goods are offered in the marketplace,
but I do not feel that I must stand there myself. I
would add that there is also a question of what is fit-
ting. An important writer must expect to be got at,
though I would still support his right (as in the case
of J. D. Salinger) to fight for his privacy. Fictional
entertainers like myself are of a different order.
Books like, say, *The Art of Edgar Wallace*, are inevitably written either naively or tongue-in-cheek, and
are an insult to the hard-working craftsman concerned.
"As to why I chose Guernsey as a place to live, this
is difficult to answer, though not through reluctance.
One could say it just happened. I used to live in London, and there worked in an information bureau attached
to a large organization. There came a time when I,
within months, had a lucky break with writing, and an
unexpected promotion to manager of the bureau. I would
have preferred to stay on there, but for the first time
in my life had a chance of capital in place of the
bare exigencies, provided I left England for a couple
of years. My wanderings took in Guernsey, and though
I had planned to go back to England, I did not. I had
five small children who wanted to put down roots, and
this island was better for that than London could have
been...and I had no other roots of my own in England.
I get to London three or four times a year, with a
flight time of less than an hour, and so am not perhaps as isolated as I seem."

In recent years, Christopher has concentrated his efforts on adolescent science fiction and fantasy, including the Tripods Trilogy (*The White Mountains,
The City of Gold and Lead, The Pool of Fire*), and the
Luke Trilogy (*The Prince in Waiting, Beyond the Burning
Lands, The Sword of the Spirits*). One of his recent
books is *Dom and Va*, "an allegory of love and violence
set 500,000 years BC."

R. C. CHURCHILL

Full Name: Reginald Charles Churchill.
Born February 9, 1916, at Bromley, Kent, England.
Son of Edward Wallis Churchill (an accountant) and
Ellen Amelia Culverwell. Married Jeanne Marie Marie,
February 19, 1955.

Education: B.A., Downing College, Cambridge, 1938;
M.A., 1943.

Career: Writer and reviewer.
Various teaching posts in Devonshire and Berkshire,
1940-42; full-time writer and book reviewer, 1942-DATE.
Examiner, Oxford and Cambridge Joint Board, General
Certificate of Education, 1943-63.

* * * * *

PATRICIA CLAPP

Full Name: Patricia Clapp.
Born June 9, 1912, at Boston, Massachusetts. Daughter of Howard Clapp (a dentist) and Elizabeth Blanch-
ford. Married Edward della Torre (a transportation
consultant), March 3, 1933. Three children: Christopher, Patricia, Pamela.

Education: Attended Columbia University, two years.

Career: Writer & playwright.

* * * * *

CARLOS CLARENS

Full Name: Carlos Figueredo y Clarens.
Born July 7, 1936, at Havana, Cuba. Son of Pedro
Figueredo (a financier) and Maria Clarens.

Education:
Studied at Sorbonne, University of Paris, and Institut d'Urbanisme, Paris, 1955-57; Master of Arts
and Architecture, University of Havana, 1958.

Career: Film editor and writer.
Began writing film criticism in 1954 for Latin American periodicals; has been a designer, barman, film
researcher, film editor, producer. Lived in Paris
for many years.

Agent: Peter de Rome, 961 First Ave., New York, NY
10022.

* * * * *

THOMAS D. CLARESON

Full Name: Thomas Dean Clareson.
Born August 26, 1926, at Austin, Minnesota. Son of
Thomas Albert Clareson (a salesman) and Ruth Dalager.
Married Alice Jane Super, December 23, 1954. One son:
Thomas Frederik Reade Clareson (born 1961).

Education:
A.B., University of Minnesota, 1946; M.A., Indiana
University, 1949; Ph.D., University of Pennsylvania,
1956.

Career: Professor of English.
Instructor, New Mexico A & MA, 1949-50; Instructor,

University of Maryland Overseas Program, 1953; Instructor, Norwich University, 1954-55; Professor of English,
College of Wooster, 1955-DATE; Editor, *Extrapolation*,
1959-DATE; Member, Board of Editors, *Victorian Poetry*.

First Professional Sale: "The Evolution of Science Fiction," in *Science Fiction Quarterly*, August,
1953.

Member:
Science Fiction Research Association (Chairman, 1970-
DATE); Ohio College English Association (on Executive
Committee, 1969-71; Vice President, 1974-75); Modern
Language Association; Popular Culture Association;
American Studies Association; First Fandom.

Interests: Photography, travel, collecting old magazines from pre-World War II, novels.

Clareson writes:
"I like both teaching and research. And I do honestly believe that science fiction may provide the best
index there is to the intellectual history of the past
century and a half.
"Academic criticism of science fiction is a healthy
sign, since it recognizes science fiction as a part of
the general body of fiction. I have my doubts on lots
of the critical works. But then, I don't like literary
critics as a type; I prefer literary historians--in the
best sense--which makes them intellectual historians
as well."

* * * * *

CATHERINE ANTHONY CLARK

Full Name: Catherine Anthony Clark.
Born May 5, 1892, at London, England. Daughter of
Edgar Francis Smith (an antique expert) and Catherine
Mary Palmer. Married Leonard Clark (a retired rancher)
December 29, 1919. Two children: Leonard Hugh, Mar-
garet.

Career: Author. Member: Catholic Women's League;
Royal Oak Women's Institute.

Awards: Canadian Librarians' Association Medal, for
The Sun Horse.

* * * * *

LAURENCE CLARK

Full Name: Laurence Walter Clark.
Born May 16, 1914, at Maidstone, Kent, England. Son
of Henry Charles Clark and Gladys Friend. Married
Marion Pies, December 3, 1958. Two sons: Oliver
George, Barnaby Alan.

Education:
B.A., Peterhouse College, Cambridge University, 1935;
M.A., 1940.

Career: Writer.
Free-lance journalist in London, 1935-39; soldier in
the British Army in India and Burma, 1940-46; free-
lance writer, 1947-DATE; Founder and Director, Veracity
Ventures, Rickmansworth, Hertfordshire, 1964-DATE.

Member:
Society of Authors; Special Forces Club, London.

RONALD CLARK

Full Name: William Ronald Clark.
   Born November 2, 1916, at London, England. Son of Ernest and Ethel Clark. Married Irene Tapp, 1938 (divorced, 1953); married Pearla Doris Odden, 1953.

Education: Attended Kings College, Wimbledon.

Career: Writer.

First Professional Sale: "London's Climbing Nursery," in *The Vauxhall Motorist*, c. 1937.

* * * * *

WILLIAM CLARK

Full Name: William Donaldson Clark.
   Born July 28, 1916, at Haltwhistle, England. Son of John McClure Clark and Marion Jackson.

Education: M.A., Oriel College, Oxford, 1938.

Career: Information director.
   Lecturer, University of Chicago, 1938-40; Staff Member, British Information Services, 1942-44; Press Attaché, British Embassy, Washington, 1945-46; London Editor, *Encyclopaedia Britannica*, 1946-49; Diplomatic Correspondent, *Observer*, 1950-55; Public Relations Adviser to Prime Minister Anthony Eden, 1955-56; toured Africa and Asia for BBC, 1957; Editor of "The Week," in the *Observer*, 1958-60; Director, Overseas Development Institute, London, 1960-68; Director of Information and Public Affairs, International Bank for Reconstruction and Development, 1968-DATE.

Member: Athenaeum Club and Savile Club, London; Tavern Club, Chicago.

* * * * *

ARTHUR C. CLARKE

Full Name: Arthur Charles Clarke.
   Born December 16, 1917, at Minehead, Somersetshire, England. Son of Charles Wright Clarke (a farmer) and Nora Mary Jessie Willis. Married Marilyn Mayfield, 1954 (divorced, 1964).

Education: B.Sc., King's College, University of London, 1948.

Career: Author.
   Auditor, British Civil Service, H.M.'s Exchequer and Audit Department, London, 1936-40; Radar Officer, Royal Air Force, 1941-46; Assistant Editor, *Science Abstracts*, 1949-50; full-time writer, 1950-DATE.

First Professional Sale: "Man's Empire of Tomorrow," in *Tales of Wonder*, Winter, 1938.

Agent: Scott Meredith, 580 Fifth Avenue, New York, NY 10036.

Honors & Awards:
   Guest of Honor, 14th World Science Fiction Convention (Newyorcon 2), New York, 1956; Nebula Award, Best Novella, 1972 (1973), "A Meeting with Medusa"; Nebula Award, Best Novel, 1973 (1974), *Rendezvous with Rama*; John W. Campbell Memorial Award for Best

Science Fiction Novel of the Year, 1973 (1974), for *Rendezvous with Rama*; International Fantasy Award, Nonfiction, 1952, *The Exploration of Space*; Hugo Award, Best Short Story, 1955 (1956), "The Star"; Hugo Award, Best Drama, 1968 (1969), for the film version of "2001: A Space Odyssey" (with Stanley Kubrick); Hugo Award, Best Novel, 1973 (1974), *Rendezvous with Rama*; UNESCO-Kalinga Prize, 1961; Stuart Ballantine Gold Medal (Franklin Institute), 1963; Robert Ball Award, Aviation Space-Writers' Association, 1965; AAAS-Westinghouse Science Writing Prize, 1969; Oscar nomination (with Stanley Kubrick), 1969; *Playboy* Editorial Award, 1971; Hon. D.Sc., Beaver College, 1971; AIAA Aerospace Communications Award, 1974.

Member:
   Ceylon Astronomical Association (Patron); Science Fiction Writers of America; British Interplanetary Society (past Chairman); International Academy of Astronautics; World Academy of Art and Science; Royal Astronomical Society; American Institute of Aernautics and Astronautics; Association of British Science Writers; International Science Writers Association; British Sub-Aqua Club; British Astronomical Association; Society of Authors; American Astronautical Association; American Association for the Advancement of Science. Clarke is also Director of Rocket Publishing Company, London; Underwater Safaris, Colombo, Sri Lanka; Spaceward Corporation, New York.

* * * * *

I. F. CLARKE

Full Name: Ignatius [Ian] Frederick Clarke.
   Born July 10, 1918, at Wallasey, Cheshire, England. Son of John Henry Clarke (a broker) and Mabel Bradshaw. Married Margaret Barton (a college lecturer). Three children: Julian (born 1952), Christopher (born 1954), Catherine (born 1962).

Education: B.A., University of Liverpool, 1950; M.A., 1953.

Career: Professor of English.
   University Fellow, University of Liverpool, 1950-53; Head, English Department, Northumberland Education Committee, 1953-56; Professor of English, University of Strathclyde, 1958-DATE; Editor, science fiction reprint program, Cornmarket Press, 1970-73.

First Professional Sale: *The Tale of the Future*, Library Association, 1961.

Agent: A. P. Watt, 26/28 Bedford Row, London WC1R 4HL.

Awards: Pilgrim Award, 1974. Member: Science Fiction Research Association.

Interests:
   Drinking wine, cooking, painting, hill walking.

Clarke is best-known for his two bibliographies, *The Tale of the Future*, and *Voices Prophesying War, 1763-1984*, a listing of imaginary war stories. When asked about the latter book, he had this reply:
   "Regarding the most recent state of this genre, there is hardly any of the old kind written nowadays--the war next year or so with known countries--but our murderous instincts continue to be satisfied with projections into the far future, and into deep space, where the clearly recognisable descendants of twentieth century man perform Capt. Kirk exploits as they wipe out planets and wicked aliens."

PAULINE CLARKE

Full Name: Pauline Clarke.
  Born May 19, 1921, at Kirkby-in-Ashfield, England.
Daughter of Charles Leopold Clark (a minister) and
Dorothy Kathleen Milum. Married Peter Hunter Blair
(a university instructor), February, 1969.

Education: B.A., Somerville College, Oxford, 1943.

Career: Writer.
  Free-lance writer, 1948-DATE; also a lecturer;
adaptor of her own stories for the BBC.

Agent: John Cushman Associates, 24 E. 38th St.,
  New York, NY 10016.

Awards:
  Library Association Carnegie Medal, 1962, Lewis
Carroll Shelf Award, and Deutsche Jugend Buchpreis,
1968, all for *The Twelve and the Genii*.

Member: British Society of Authors; National Book
  League.

* * * * *

HAL CLEMENT

Full Name: Harry Clement Stubbs.
  Born May 30, 1922, at Somerville, Massachusetts.
Son of Harry Clarence Stubbs (an accountant) and
Marjorie Sidney White (a teacher). Married Mary
Elizabeth Myers, July 19, 1952. Three children:
George Clement (born 1953); Richard Myers (born 1954);
Christine (born 1959).

Education:
  B.S., Harvard College, 1943; M.Ed., Boston University, 1947; M.S., Simmons College, 1963.

Career: Science Teacher.
  B-24 copilot and pilot, U.S. Army Air Force, 1943-
45; Technical Instructor, U.S. Air Force, 1951-53;
Science Teacher, Milton Academy, 1949-51, 1953-DATE.

First Professional Sale: "Proof," in *Astounding
  Science Fiction*, June, 1942.

Member: Science Fiction Writers of America; New England Science Fiction Association; New English Association of Chemistry Teachers.

Clement writes:
  "I tend to prefer, and to write, old-fashioned
'idea' science fiction; while some of my personal
concerns such as the energy shortage tend to show up,
I am not as a rule trying to issue a message. I
write for fun, and don't try to make a living at it,
just as I paint (though I sell the paintings also
when anyone is interested). My story ideas are apt
to stem from a slight contrariness; a sentence con-
taining the phrase 'of course' is likely to start me
thinking of a way in which that particular 'of course'
might not be true. My first story, "Proof," was based
on the 'of course' that life is probably chemical,
and needs a solid or liquid environment; *Mission of
Gravity* on the 'of course' that gravity cannot be
greatly different from one part to another of a given
planet. A good deal of slide rule work naturally
followed; this was actually more fun than the writing.

While I naturally regret that some readers--especially
those with access to high-speed computers--have found
detail errors in the Mesklin situation, I do not feel
guilty about it--and I am very happy that the story
gave them not only the fun of reading, but also the
fun of checking out my ideas in detail."
  He adds: "Not everyone seems to have spotted that
Easy Rich, 12 years old in *Close to Critical*, is the
37-year-old Easy Hoffman of *Star Light* (though some
did)."

* * * * *

BRUCE CLEMENTS

Full Name: Bruce Clements.
  Born November 25, 1931, at New York, New York. Son
of Paul Eugene Clements (a salesman) and Ruth Hall (an
editor). Married Hanna Charlotte Margarete Kiep (a
community worker), January 30, 1954. Four children:
Mark, Ruth, Martha, Hanna.

Education:
  A.B., Columbia University, 1954; B.D., Union Theolo-
gical Seminary, 1956; M.A., State University of New
York, Albany, 1962.

Career: Minister and teacher.
  Ordained Minister of United Church of Christ; Pastor,
Schenectady, New York, 1957-64; Teacher, Union College,
1964-67; Teacher, Eastern Connecticut State College,
1967-DATE.

* * * * *

SARAH CLIFFORD

Full Name: Sarah Clifford.
  Born February 10, 1916, at Zaromb, Poland. Daughter
of Morris Pryzant and Rebecca Edel. Married Martin
Clifford (a professional writer), May 2, 1936. Three
children: Kenneth Ian, Paul Ralph, Jerrold Rodger.

Career: Writer.

* * * * *

MILDRED CLINGERMAN

Full Name: Mildred Clingerman.
  Born March 14, 1918, at Allen, Oklahoma. Daughter
of Arthur McElroy (a railroad man) and Meda Bush. Married Stuart Kendall Clingerman (a construction project
manager), May 29, 1937. Two children: Kendall Faye
(daughter, born 1940), Stephen Kurt (born 1942).

Education: Attended University of Arizona, 1941.

Career: Housewife.
  "My only work outside home was during World War II,
when I kept flight-time records at a Ryan flight-train-
ing school, while Stuart was a paratrooper in the army."

First Professional Sale: "Minister without Portfolio," in *The Magazine of Fantasy & Science Fiction*,
February, 1952.

Agent: Collins-Knowlton-Wing, 60 E. 56th St., New
  York, NY 10022.

MILDRED CLINGERMAN (cont.)

Member: Tuscon Press Club; Society of Southwestern Authors.

Interests:
"Travel. I love it. Especially going to England, which we've done for three years in a row. I'm a collector of books, weights (assayer types), Christmas tree ornaments; am fascinated, too, by fine 18th century American furniture." She adds: "I am currently writing and very occasionally selling short stories for the women's magazine market. I had a short story (not fantasy or science fiction) published in the August, 1973 issue of *Good Housekeeping*. I have firmly kept my writing life secondary to other joys. An avocation, really.

"Fantasy is the only fiction that I write easily and playfully--so I tend to disparage it, and yearn to try other kinds (and do). I should like most of all to write a book for children (which includes, of course, children like me, of any age). I have parts of one written. Children's book are still one of my favorite forms of reading-for-pleasure.

"As to the male-oriented nature of the genre, perhaps it's just that there are more male writers of any sort than female. And isn't the male readership of fantasy and science fiction confined, for the most part, to the young man, under 30 years, say? And doesn't that readership (male or female) comprise a small proportion of the reading population--the more intelligent, aware, imaginative, dreaming-wishing, playing-with-ideas group (that is always small)?

"Women, I think, always tend to be more practical-minded--a bit grimmer in outlook than men. Less hopeful, too beset with daily reality--fighting things that are: dirt, budgets, disorder. Planning meals, bringing up children, battling for their rights. Poor dears, most of them grow up too fast. The sense of wonder isn't easy for most of them to maintain. Men (delightful creatures) keep it to the end. Women have made it possible for them to do so."

* * * * *

MARTHA deMEY CLOW

Full Name: Martha deMey Clow.
Born November 16, 1932, at Columbus, Ohio. Daughter of Charles Frederic deMey (an engineer) and Amelia Webster Smith. Married John Warner Clow, April 10, 1956. Five children: John Frederic deMey (born 1957), Gregory Vincent (born 1959), Amelia Bayley (born 1964), Guy Rowan (born 1965), Louise Crankshaw (born 1967).

Education: A.B., Smith College, 1954.

Career: Commercial artist and author.
Layout Artist, Joseph Magnin, 1956-57; free-lance artist and author, 1957-DATE.

First Professional Sale: *Starbreed*, Ballantine Books, 1970.

Honors: Kinsmen Trust Scholarship, Roedean, Brighton, England, 1949-50.

Interests: Immanuel Velikovsky, nutrition.

Clow talks about women and science fiction:
"I am peculiar: I have always had a strong bent for science and math. I think the statistics show that

women in general lean towards the verbal studies more often than the mathematical. I am forever picking flaws out of TV plots and scenarios; the enjoyment ceases when I find the author has been less than factual or logical in his story line. If he has really done his homework, I rejoice; if he is careless or lazy, I become bored.

"My father, the engineer, said that science fiction was the only true fiction that might actually happen. All else was falsity superimposed on history. I suppose this rubbed off on me. The closer one hews to the actual truth, the better I like it. This would apply to an historical romance as well as a scientific tale. There is an obligation to the reader, I think, to supply information as well as entertainment.

"This brings up another point. Science fiction stories, as opposed to fantasy (which I don't care for), should contain one new, creative idea sprung from the author's brain. All else in the story should be as faithful to the truth as he can make it in order to sell the reader on his innovation. He should convince, create belief. The better his idea, the easier to tie it to reality.

"I think women read science fiction as much as men. Perhaps their reluctance to enter the writing field hinges on lack of expertise. I picked up what knowledge I have because of my natural bent. If women were trained more generally in science and math, perhaps their writing would run to that field also."

* * * * *

ROBERT COATES

Full Name: Robert Myron Coates.
Born April 6, 1897, at New Haven, Connecticut. Son of Frederick Coates and Harriet Davidson. Married Elsa Kirpa, 1927 (divorced, 1946); married Astrid Peters, June 14, 1946. One son, Anthony R.

Education: B.A., Yale University, 1919.

Career: Writer. Art Critic, *New Yorker*. Died 1973.

Agent: Harold Ober Associates, 40 E. 49th St., New York, NY 10017.

Member: P.E.N.; Authors League of America; National Institute of Arts and Letters; Century Association.

* * * * *

ELIZABETH COATSWORTH

Full Name: Elizabeth Jane Coatsworth.
Born May 31, 1893, at Buffalo, New York. Daughter of William T. Coatsworth and Ida Reid. Married Henry Beston (a writer), June 18, 1929. Two children: Margaret, Catherine.

Education: B.A., Vassar College, 1915; M.A., Columbia University, 1916; studied at Radcliffe College.

Career: Author.
Has been an author all of her life.

Awards:
Newbery Medal, 1931, for *The Cat Who Went to Heaven*; Litt.D., University of Maine, 1955; L.H.D., New England College, 1958. Member: P.E.N.; North East Poetry Society; Phi Beta Kappa.

STANTON A. COBLENTZ

Full Name: Stanton Arthur Coblentz.
  Born August 24, 1896, at San Francisco, California.
Son of Mayer Coblentz (a life insurance salesman) and
Mattie Arndt. Married Flora Bachrach, June 23, 1922
(died 1974); married Emily Caswell Tiexiera.

Education: A.B., University of Californa, Berkeley,
  1917; M.A., 1919.

Career: Writer.
  Feature Writer, *San Francisco Examiner*, 1919-20;
book reviewer for several different New York newspapers, 1920-38; Editor, *Wings, A Quarterly of Verse*,
and Wings Press, 1933-60; book reviewer, *Los Angeles
Times*, 1959-DATE; free-lance author.

First Professional Sale: A poem to the *New York
  Times*, 1919.

Agents:
  Alex Jackinson, 55 W. 42nd St., New York, NY 10036;
(science fiction) Forrest J Ackerman, 2495 Glendower
Avenue, Hollywood CA 90027.

Awards:
  Lyrical Foundation for Traditional Poetry Award,
1953; Commonwealth Club of California Silver Medal
for Poetry, 1953. Member: Authors League of America.

Coblentz writes:
  "I did not enter writing by accident, but because of
a deep-seated inclination. After a two-year enroll-
ment in the law school at UC Berkeley, I switched to
English when but a year from graduation in law. Owing
to the accident of obtaining a prize for poetry in a
contest conducted by the *San Francisco Chronicle*, I
obtained a position on the *SF Examiner* as a writer of
daily feature poems. Even before that time I had obtained books to review for the San Francisco magazine
Argonaut, a weekly publication in which Ambrose Bierce
had been active. I also was for a time an assistant
editor on *Overland Monthly*. In 1920, I left for New
York, where I managed to make my way as a free-lance
writer, depending largely on book reviewing for the
big dailies and some magazines. Meanwhile, for my
own pleasure, but hoping for book publication, I had
written several science fiction novels without knowing
the term 'science fiction,' or anticipating that work
in that medium would ever become popular. My start
came when one of these, *The Sunken World*, was accepted
by the old *Amazing Stories* in its fledgling days.
This was followed by others, some of which were commissioned, and thus it may be said that my entry into
science fiction, though not into writing in general,
was accidental."

* * * * *

VIRGINIA COFFMAN

Full Name: Virginia Edith Coffman.
  Born July 30, 1914, at San Francisco, California.
Daughter of William M. Coffman (a corporation manager)
and Edythe L. DeuVaul.

Education: A.B., University of California, Berkeley,
  1938.

Career: Writer.
  Secretary and writer in movie and television studios,
including David O. Selznick, Monogram, RKO, Columbia,
and Hal Roach, 1944-56; Secretary and Office Manager,
H. F. "Chick" Bennett Inc. (realty firm), Reno, 1956-
65; full-time writer, 1965-DATE.

Agent: Jay Garon-Brooke Associates, 415 Central Park
  West, 17D, New York, NY 10025.

Member: Mystery Writers of America.

* * * * *

THEODORE R. COGSWELL

Full Name: Theodore Rose Cogswell.
  Born March 10, 1918, at Coatesville, Pennsylvania.
Son of Dewitt Russell Cogswell and Marguerite Rose.
Married Marjorie Mills, 1948 (divorced); married Cora-
lie Norris, 1964 (divorced); married George Rae Williams, August 16, 1972. Two children: Megan Mills
(born 1948); Cathleen Bradford (born 1950).

Education:
  B.A., University of Colorado, 1947; M.A., University
of Denver, 1948; attended University of Minnesota,
1948-52; A.B.L., University of Denver, 1956.

Career: Professor of English.
  Ambulance Driver, Spanish Republican Army, 1937-38;
Statistical Control Officer, U.S. Army Air Force, 1942-
45; Instructor, University of Minnesota, 1949-53; In-
structor, University of Kentucky, 1953-56, 1957-58;
Assistant Professor, Ball State University, 1958-65;
Professor, Keystone Junior College, 1965-DATE; Governor
General, Institute for 21st Century Studies, 1959-DATE.

First Professional Sale: "The Specter General,"
  in *Astounding Science Fiction*, June, 1952.

Agent: "I've had four agents and four wives in the
  last thirty years; maybe there's a connection."

Member:
  Science Fiction Writers of America (Editor, *SFWA
Forum*, 1970-71, 1973-76); Modern Language Association;
American Association for the Advancement of Science;
Mensa; Veterans of the Abraham Lincoln Brigade; Veterans
of Foreign Wars; American Legion; Mayflower Society;
Order of Founders and Patriots.

Interests:
  "Reading pornography, writing science fiction, playing
chess. Whether in the military, in teaching, or in
writing, I've always found myself in the strange position of being paid for work that I enjoyed so much that
I would have been happy to do it for nothing."

* * * * *

WALTER R. COLE

Full Name: Walter Randall Cole.
  Born April 19, 1933, at Brooklyn, New York. Son of
Ernest Tomasuolo (stepfather) and Rose Balgley.

Education: Attended college for two years.

Career:
  "Became active in science fiction in 1946; was connected at various times with *Science Fiction Times*,
and then with *Luna* Publications."

CYRIL COLES

Full Name: Cyril Henry Coles.
  Born June 11, 1899, at London, England. Son of David Coles and Rose Elizabeth Gaite. Married Dorothy Cordelia Smith, 1934. Two sons: Peter, Michael.

Education: Attended school in Petersfield, England.

Career: Writer.
  Apprenticed to a shipbuilding firm, Coles became manager of the millfitting department; he left in the mid-20s to travel around the world, staying for a long period in Australia, where he worked as a garage manager, railway employee, and daily columnist on a Melbourne newspaper; returned to England 1928, and in 1936 began writing detective stories and thrillers with his neighbor, Adelaide Frances Oke Manning, under the joint pseudonym Manning Coles, a partnership that continued until her death in 1959. Died October 9, 1965.

Agent: Curtis Brown Ltd., 60 E. 56th St., New York, NY 10022.

* * * * *

MICHAEL COLLINS

Full Name: Dennis Lynds.
  Born January 15, 1924, at St. Louis, Missouri. Son of John Douglas Lynds and Gertrude Hyem. Married Sheila McErlean, 1961.

Education: B.A., Hofstra College, 1949; M.A., Syracuse University, 1951.

Career: Editor.
  Asst. Editor, Chemical Week, 1951-52; Managing Editor, Chemical Engineering Progress, 1958-61; Editorial Director, Chemical Equipment, 1965-DATE.

* * * * *

T. ALLAN COMP

Full Name: T. Allan Comp.
  Born December 1, 1942, in California. Education: B.A., California State College, Fullerton; M.A., Ph.D., University of Delaware.

Career: Historian.
  Instructor, Boston University, 1971-72; Historian, Historic American Engineering Record, 1973-DATE.

First Professional Sale: The Man in the Moone, Praeger, 1971 (anthology edited with Faith Pizor).

* * * * *

D. G. COMPTON

Full Name: David Guy Compton.
  Born August 9, 1930, at London, England. Son of Gerald Compton (an actor) and Margaret Symonds (an actress). Married Elizabeth Tillotson, February 23, 1952 (divorced, 1968); married Carol Curtis Brown (an editor), January, 1971. Three children: Margaret Jane (born 1951), Hester Josephine (born 1954), James Samuel (born 1959).

Education: Attended Cheltenham College, 1940-48.

Career: Writer and editor.
  Has been a stage electrician, furniture maker, salesman, docker, postman; Editor, Condensed Book Dept., Readers Digest, London, 1969-DATE; free-lance author.

First Professional Sale: "Fully Furnished," a radio play on BBC, 1956.

Member: Authors Society.

Compton writes:
  "For me I think the writing of SF is a sign of weakness. I write about the future because this enables me to write about the present at one remove, and therefore more easily. I am wary of the SF label, partly because in this country among the majority of readers it is still something of a dirty word, and partly because I am wary of labels. Certainly my novel The Palace isn't remotely SF. And anyway, I have till recently thought of myself as a playwright, doing rather experimental things for radio in this country and Germany. That I should have written books still surprises me.
  "Asked for influences, I can only say that I admire and aim to emulate the precise economy and sheer density of meaning of writers like Patrick White (though not his recent misogynism) and E. M. Forster. I like their humour also. My SF hero must be Philip K. Dick. My own books seem to turn out so bloody depressing, which I see as a serious failure."

Interests:
  Keyboard music, bridge, moving house. Compton also writes gothics under the name Frances Lynch.

* * * * *

RICHARD CONDON

Full Name: Richard Thomas Condon.
  Born March 18, 1915, at New York, New York. Son of Richard Aloysius Condon and Martha Irene Pickering. Married Evelyn Hunt, January 14, 1938. Two children: Deborah, Wendy.

Career: Writer.
  Publicist, US film industry, in New York, Hollywood, and Europe, for 21 years; now a novelist. Was a producer on Broadway for two years. Member: Dramatists Guild; Authors Guild.

Agent: Harold Matson, 22 E. 40th St., New York, NY 10016.

* * * * *

MICHAEL G. CONEY

Full Name: Michael Greatrex Coney.
  Born September 28, 1932, at Birmingham, England. Son of Harold Coney (a dentist) and Nora Nettle. Married his wife, Daphne Coney, 1957. Two children: Kevin (born 1958), Sally-Ann (born 1966).

Education: Attended King Edwards School, Birmingham.

Career: Financial analyst.
  Accountant for various firms in England, 1949-69; Hotel Manager, Jabberwock Hotel, Antigua, 1969-72.

MICHAEL G. CONEY (cont.)

First Professional Sale: "Symbiote," in *New Writings in SF 15*, Dennis Dobson, 1969 (edited by John Carnell).

Agent: E. J. Carnell Literary Agency, 17 Burwash Road, Plumstead, London SE18 7QY, England.

Member: Science Fiction Writers of America.

Interests: Sailing, soccer, camping.

"I write for relaxation and escapism only, although the money is useful and helps me relax more. I try to keep to a schedule when writing novels; if a novel takes more than a month to write, I find myself losing interest and concentration. I first got involved in the SF field through reading Wyndham's stories, although I didn't start writing until 1967 or so. I began writing as a challenge more than anything else; I was dissatisfied with the stories I was reading in *New Worlds*, the British magazine, so I tried to do better. I failed miserably, time after time, according to editor Moorcock's little green slips. Then eventaully I wised up, and started to write the type of story the reader wants to read, rather than trying to change the market to suit myself, and this worked. Probably every beginning writer goes through the same thing; I don't know. I do know I wasted two years and god knows how many words writing unsaleable stuff. Now, with the editors and readers knowing my name, I find that I can branch out a bit more, take more chances with style and content, and come up with stories less orthodox and more satisfying. Other advice for the beginning writer? Try to write stories of around 5000 words with more than one plotline. Write them in the style of your own favourite author, without being a slavish copycat. Try to maintain a balance between action, static description, and adequate characterisation. Then, having sold the first couple of stories, forget all that and write in your own style--the one which flows most smoothly."

* * * * *

GROFF CONKLIN

Full Name: Edward Groff Conklin.
Born September 6, 1904, at Glen Ridge, New Jersey. Son of William Bogart Conklin and Sarah Hogate Groff. Married Lucy Tempkin, October 1, 1937 (died November 7, 1954); married Florence Alexander Wohlken, June 5, 1958.

Education: A.B., Columbia University, 1927.

Career: Editor.
Asst. Manager, Doubleday Book Stores, 1930-34; Asst. Editor, University of Chicago Press, 1934-36; Editor, Robert M. McBride Co., 1937; Information Consultant, Bureau of the Census, 1939; Information Specialist, Federal Home Loan Bank Board, 1940; President, Tauxemont Home Builders, 1941-42; Presentation Specialist, Office of Strategic Service, 1943-45; Senior Writer, U.S. Senate Subcommittee on wartime health and education, 1945-46; Deputy Chief, Information Division, Office of Technical Services, U.S. Dept. of Commerce, 1946-47; Senior Information Specialist, National Cancer Institute, 1947-48; Director of Publications, American Diabetes Association, 1950-52; Assoc. Editor,

Living for Young Homemakers, 1959-60; Senior Researcher, Scientific Advisory Board, N. W. Ayer & Son, 1960-61; Senior Writer, American Diabetes Assoc., 1961-64; Science Editor, *American Heritage Dictionary*, 1965-68; free-lance writer and editor, 1930-68. Died July 19, 1968, at Pawling, New York.

Member: Authors Guild; National Association of Science Writers.

* * * * *

ROBERT CONQUEST

Full Name: George Robert Acworth Conquest.
Born July 15, 1917, at Malvern, Worcestershire, England. Son of Robert Folger Westcott Conquest and Rosamund Alys Acworth. Married Joan Watkins, 1942 (divorced 1948); married Tatiana Mihailova, 1948 (divorced 1962); married Caroleen Macfarlane, April 4, 1964. Two sons: John Christopher Arden (born 1943), Richard Charles Pleasanton (born 1945).

Education: B.A., Magdalen College, Oxford, 1939; M.A. 1972.

Career: Writer and editor.
Captain, British Army, 1939-46; with H.M. Diplomatic Service, in Sofia, Great Britain, and the U.S., 1946-56; Fellow, London School of Economics, 1956-58; Lecturer in English, University of Buffalo, 1959-60; Literary Editor, *Spectator*, 1962-63; Senior Fellow, Columbia University Russian Institute, 1964-65; Editor, *Soviet Analyst*, 1971-73; free-lance author.

First Professional Sale: 1938.

Agent: Scott Meredith, 580 Fifth Avenue, New York, NY 10036.

Interests: Student of Roman and sub-Roman Britain, Vinland, and US Civil War; crack rifle shot.

Conquest writes:
"As to the Nouvelle Vague, I have had little patience with it. We all grew up with the experimentalist arts, but everything worth doing had already been done 40 years ago, and tedious repetitions of repetitions, largely of what turned out to be non-viable among the early stuff, simply means unreadability; or, rather, it can only be read by an adolescent on the first step of what he conceives to be thrilling sophistication. As Pasternak, one of the subtlest of experimentalists, remarked after long experience: "The support has been taken out from under that modern trend...this striving, thought true and original in its source, was not self-dependent enough to stand up."
"As practised nowadays, I regard the whole business as largely a piece of self-indulgence by authors, and the taste for it on the part of readers little more than an exercise in self-congratulation on their supposed cleverness and sensitivity.
"This is not to say that occasional bursts of talent may not appear in it, for it has always been the case that some creative authors and other artists have lacked judgment and discipline and have diverted their talents according to the current fashions through weakness or silliness.
"But in fact, by the time the New Wave reached science fiction, it was a pretty tired ripple. It is worth adding that science fiction is particularly

ROBERT CONQUEST (cont.)

"unsuitable area for this sort of thing. It has always been an axiom that logical fantasy must be as clearly expressed as possible, for reasons so obvious they surely don't need developing here.

"Again, while fiction of extreme introspection is perfectly legitimate if one likes that sort of thing, to use of it expressions like 'inner space,' and claim it is anything to do with science fiction, is a mere semantic trick: nor will the use of a few SF properties in otherwise symbolist or far-in fiction transform it into SF.

"Are we really offered Ballard in exchange for Heinlein? They are both capable writers in principle, and both capable of occasional lapses even when doing their best. And Heinlein was always at least as subtle, as cunning, and as imaginative a writer as Ballard. But Ballard is now as often as not just plain silly--and in such a tediously, dreary old way: it might have shocked Queen Victoria, it might have surprised Sinclair Lewis, it might have been thought the last word in novelty by Harriet Monroe. But since shock, surprise, and novelty are the *only* virtues of this method (apart from an implicit claim to be deeply symbolic of everything, which can hardly be taken seriously), once those effects are exhausted all that is left is an empty imitativeness. The semi-educated have always gone for inessential, extrinsic, eye-catching gimmickry in the arts. The fact that many of them still do so should not be taken to be of any significance, except to the sociologist.

"SF proper is already wide-ranging enough. It is perfectly capable of developing wonder and terror, as well as cool satire (in the genuine and original sense), and fantastic naturalism.

"All this may sound a little puritanical, and by all means let people write and read what they like; but it needs saying that the vast fashion-bound novelty trade, in the other arts, only dominates a market not worth having, and has not there achieved the monopoly or even the prestige which it so loudly claims for itself.

"I regard myself as an amateur. But I think I now see what the faults are in the modest efforts at science fiction I have published; when I write some more I would hope particularly to make it livelier, more colourful, and in a sense, more fantastic. However, as in every other field, one shouldn't write in ways that do not really appeal to one--and particularly not by following the mode."

* * * * *

EARL CONRAD

Full Name: Earl Conrad.
  Born December 17, 1912, at Auburn, New York. Son of Eli and Minnie Conrad. Married his wife, Alyse Conrad, 1938. One son, Michael Earl.

Education:
  Attended public schools in Auburn, New York.

Career: Writer.
  Conrad has written for newspapers, has lectured, made radio broadcasts, and has given hundreds of speeches on interracial affairs. He is now a full-time writer of novels and articles.

Member: Authors League.

GLEN COOK

Full Name: Glen Charles Cook.
  Born July 9, 1944, at New York, New York. Son of Charles Albert Cook (in civil service) and Louella Mabel Handy. Married Carol Ann Fritz, June 14, 1971.

Education: Attended University of Missouri, 1962-65.

Career: Grinder, plastic, rework.
  Assembler, Auto, Fisher Body Plant, St. Louis, 1965-67; Munitions Inspector, Chevrolet Army Planet, St. Louis, 1967-70; Material Controller, General Motors, St. Louis, 1970-74; Grinder, plastic, rework, GM, 1974-DATE. "In the matter of employment, all the employers listed are really the same, General Motors, with myself as employee being transferred around as economic conditions varied auto sales. GM is the only full-time employer I've had since leaving college. In part-time and summer work, I've been a cook, a restaurant manager, a janitor, a baker's helper, a waiter, a busboy, a fruit packer, a clerk, a forklift driver, and at least a dozen other things. I spent eight years in the Navy and Navy Reserve, during which time I performed in a broad range of capacities, from flying fighter aircraft to being a forward shore bombardment controller with a Marine Force Recon unit (Marine Corps equivalent of Rangers or commandoes)."

First Professional Sale:
  "Song from a Forgotten Hill," sold to *Worlds of Tomorrow*, but never published there (the magazine failed shortly thereafter); first published in *Clarion*, an anthology edited by Robin Scott Wilson, New American Library, 1971.

Member: Science Fiction Writers of America. Interests: Stamp collecting.

* * * * *

ROBIN COOK

Full Name: Robert William Arthur Cook.
  Born June 12, 1931, at London, England. Son of Arthur Ralph Cook (a company director) and Pamela Florence Pollock. Married Dora Sherwood, Sept. 15, 1959; married Eugene Eva Marie Grossman, October 12, 1963; current wife Sandra Valerie Haggerty (a publicity executive).

Education: Attended Eton College, 1944-48.

Career: Writer.

Agent: Jonathan Clowes, 20 New Cavendish St., London.

* * * * *

CHARLES COOMBS

Full Name: Charles Ira Coombs.
  Born June 27, 1914, at Los Angeles, California. Son of Daniel F. Coombs (a building contractor) and Fleda M. Colf. Married Eleanor H. Evans, Sept. 17, 1939. Three children: Lee Charles (born 1940), Dan William (born 1944), Lynn Eleanor (born 1946).

Education: A.A., Riverside Junior College, 1934; B.A., University of California, Los Angeles, 1939.

CHARLES COOMBS (cont.)

Career: Writer, 1946-DATE.

First Professional Sale: "Hand of Guilt," in
Wild West Weekly, 1940.

Awards:
  Boys' Clubs of America Junior Book Award, 1958, for
  Rockets, Missiles, and Moons; Southern California
  Council on Literature for Young People Award, 1968,
  for "significant contributions to the field of infor-
  mational books." Member: Aviation/Space Writers of
  America.

* * * * *

MICHAEL COONEY

Full Name: Michael Cooney.
  Born April 28, 1921, in Ireland. Married his wife,
Mary Cooney, 1941. Two children: Carol, Terry.

Education: Attended art colleges in Nottingham,
  Leicester, Reading, Maidenhead, and Cheltenham, U.K.

Career: Writer.
  Has been a scriptwriter and copywriter, an advertising manager, and a promotion director; now a full-time
writer.

Agent: Gordon Horbord, 53 St. Martin's Lane, London,
  W.C.2, England.

Member:
  Society of Authors; Royal Society of St. George;
British Legion; Screen Writers Guild.

* * * * *

COLIN COOPER

Full Name: Colin Symons Cooper.
  Born July 5, 1926, at Birkenhead, Cheshire, England.
Son of Frederick Arthur Cooper (a company director)
and Clara Violette Symons. Married Maureen Elizabeth
Goodwin, September 2, 1966. Two children: Daniel
Goodwin (born 1967), Ben Symons (born 1968).

Education: Attended Merchant Venturers Technical
  College, Bristol, 1942-44.

Career: Writer.
  Radio Operator, Royal Corps of Signals, 1944-47;
Assistant Service Manager, Crypton Ltd., 1948-52;
Assistant Sales Manager, John Lysaght Ltd., 1952-59;
Researcher, University of London Institute of Educa-
tion, 1965-70; Features Editor, Guitar Magazine, 1972-
73; full-time writer, 1973-DATE.

First Professional Sale: "Design for Danger,"
  a radio play broadcast in 1956.

Awards:
  Joint third prize in television playwriting contest
organised by the Observer newspaper and London Week-
end Television, 1969.

Member:
  Society of Authors; Writers' Guild of Great Britain;
Radiowriters Association; Writers' Action Group.

Interests:
  "Music, especially classical guitar. Occasional
teacher and contributor to guitar magazines, including
the Journal of the American String Teachers' Association. I was joint founder of Guitar Magazine, and
served as its first Features Editor."

Cooper writes:
  "I believe that SF must continue to extend its boun-
daries. SF must not feel itself to be confined in any
way by antique concepts of style or subject matter.
The best of the science fiction writers have shown
that there is no imaginable subject that cannot be
treated within an SF theme. Far too many people--rea-
ders as well as non-readers--have the impression that
SF is a narrow literary field concerned solely with
spaceships. In Macbeth and Crime and Punishment res-
pectively, Shakespeare and Dostoievsky showed to what
heights a crime story could be pushed. SF has yet to
produce writers of similar calibre, but the time will
come. It must come. Despite the superb work done by
its pioneers, SF is still a very young literary form--
a precocious child, perhaps, but nevertheless one that
still has a long way to go before achieving what I,
personally, am convinced it is capable of."

* * * * *

EDMUND COOPER

Full Name: Edmund Cooper.
  Born April 30, 1926, at Marple, Cheshire, England.
Son of Joseph Cooper (a shopkeeper) and Harriet Fletcher. Married Joyce Plant, April 13, 1946 (divorced,
1963); married Valerie Makin, October 14, 1963. Eight
children: Glynis (born 1947), Daryl (born 1955), Troy
(born 1958), Guy (born 1960), Shaun (born 1960), Justine (born 1962), Regan (born 1963), Jason (born 1964).

Education: Teaching Certificate, Didsbury Training
  College, 1946.

Career: Writer.
  Merchant seaman, 1944-46; Teacher for various Eng-
lish schools, 1947-51; Public Relations Writer, Esso
Petroleum, 1961-66; free-lance writer, 1951-61, 1966-
DATE. Science Fiction Critic, London Sunday Times.

First Professional Sale: "The Unicorn," in Everybody's, 1951.

Member: P.E.N.

Interests:
  Chess, books, music, too much TV, too much drinking,
walking in the English South Downs. "I've raised
laziness to the status of a religion."

Cooper writes:
  "I first started writing poetry--as so many young
people do--in my teens. I did not seriously think in
terms of writing science fiction until my mid-20s. By
that time, I had more or less left poetry behind (I
did have some success), and was making some kind of
living writing magazine short stories. I had always
been interested in science, and had, of course, read
the scientific romances of H. G. Wells. Early in the
1950s, when I had published about forty or fifty magazine stories, it occurred to me that SF was an ideal
medium for disseminating some of my own ideas on science, society, politics, economics, human behaviour,
industry, and so on. In short, it seemed to me to be

EDMUND COOPER (cont.)

"an ideal propaganda medium. I was once told that I was a frustrated Messiah, and there is probably a little truth in this. I have noticed that my best novels are concerned with matters which are rather close to my heart."

* * * * *

LOUISE COOPER

Full Name: Louise Cooper.
 Born May 29, 1952, at Barnet, Hertfordshire, England. Daughter of Erle Antell (an accountant) and Pat Papworth (a newspaper copyreader). Married Gary Richard Cooper, December 5, 1970 (an assistant editor for a rock music magazine).

Education: Attended St. Albans High School for Girls, 1963-67.

Career: Secretary.
 "Very chequered! Largely secretarial work. Various employers. Currently Secretary to a publisher."

First Professional Sale: The Book of Paradox, Delacorte Press, 1973.

Agent: E. J. Carnell Literary Agency, 17 Burward Road, Plumstead, London SE18, England.

Interests:
 "Music (rock/folk/classical)--spent some while as a semi-pro folk singer. Then sang with a local rock band for a few months. Also films, theatre--have studied the occult seriously for several years." She adds: "Writing, for me, is a kind of addiction--if the world fell around my ears tomorrow, I'd still keep scribbling for the sheer enjoyment of it!"

* * * * *

SUSAN COOPER

Full Name: Susan Mary Cooper.
 Born May 23, 1935, at Burnham, Buckinghamshire, England. Daughter of John Richard Cooper and Ethel May Field. Married Nicholas John Grant, August 3, 1963. Two children: Jonathan (born 1966), Katharine (born 1967); three stepchildren: Anne, Bill, Peter.

Education: M.A., Somerville College, Oxford University, 1956.

Career: Writer.
 Reporter and feature writer, London Sunday Times, 1956-63; full-time writer, 1963-DATE.

First Professional Sale: "When Term Is Over," in London Times, August 31, 1956.

Awards:
 Over Sea, Under Stone and The Dark Is Rising were both ALA notable books. The Dark Is Rising won the Boston Globe-Horn Book Award for excellence in Children's Literature, and was runner up for the Newbery Medal, and the Carnegie Medal. The Grey King won a Newbery Medal as best children's book of the year.

Interests: Music and islands.

Member: Society of Authors; Authors Guild.

Susan Cooper is best-known for her five-novel series, The Dark Is Rising, concerning which she wrote:

 "I am presently working on Silver on the Tree, which will probably be published in 1977. This will be the last of a five-book series of fantasies entitled The Dark Is Rising; the volumes have been, in succession, Over Sea, Under Stone, The Dark Is Rising, Greenwitch, and The Grey King. Though the series is published on children's lists in both the U.S. and Great Britain, it has become increasing complex, and copies seem to be turning up more and more often on the adult fiction shelves in libraries. I suppose it's similar to what happened to Tolkien's books, and to Watership Down."

* * * * *

AUDREY COPPARD

Full Name: Audrey Jean Coppard.
 Born May 7, 1931, at London, England. Daughter of Alexander Sherwood Begbie and Doris Beamont. Married Christopher Dirk Coppard (a writer). Three children: Harriet (born 1956), Tim (born 1957), Abbie (born 1959).

Education: English grammar school.

Career: Research Assistant.
 Presently a Research Assistant, London University.

First Professional Sale: Who Has Poisoned the Sea? Heinemann, 1970.

Agent: Bolt & Watson, London.

Coppard mentions: "I'm married to the son of A. E. Coppard, the short story writer."

* * * * *

ALFRED COPPEL

Full Name: Alfredo José de Araña-Marini y Coppel.
 Born November 9, 1921, at Oakland, California. Son of Alfredo José de Marini y Coppel and Ana de Araña. Married Elisabeth Ann Schorr, March 10, 1943. Two children: Alfred III (born 1945), Elisabeth Ann (born 1943).

Education: Attended Stanford University, 1939-42.

Career: Writer.
 Was a technical writer, advertising copywriter, and an advertising executive through 1966; full-time writer, 1966-DATE.

First Professional Sale: "Age of Unreason," in Astounding Science Fiction, December, 1947.

Agent: Robert Lescher, 153 E. 71st St., New York.

Awards: "Distinguished Alumnus," Menlo College, 1968.

Interests: Sailing, scuba, flying, golf.
 "SF allowed the necessary 'freedom to experiment' to break from the inhibitions that plague the new writer. It was then easier to turn to contemporary fiction."

Member: Authors Guild.

BASIL COPPER

Full Name: Basil Copper.
   Born 1924, at London, England. Married Annie
Guerin. Education: Attended a private commercial
college.

Career: Writer.
   Was an editor for 14 years of a Kent newspaper; now
a full-time writer.

Member:
   Society of Authors; Crime Writers Association;
British Film Institute; Tunbridge Wells Vintage Film
Society (Founder); Vintage Film Circle.

Interests: "Old films; one of Britain's leading
   collectors of historic film material."

Copper is best-known as a writer of the macabre; he
has also written 22 novels featuring the private eye,
Mike Faraday (published in England by Robert Hale).

* * * * *

SCOTT CORBETT

Full Name: Scott Corbett.
   Born July 27, 1913, at Kansas City, Missouri. Son
of Edward Roy Corbett and Hazel Marie Emanuelson.
Married Elizabeth Grosvenor Pierce, 1940. One daughter, Florence Lee.

Education: B.J., University of Missouri, 1934.

Career: Writer.

Agent: Collins-Knowlton-Wing, 60 E. 56th St., New
   York, NY.

Awards:
   Edgar Award, 1962, for Cutlass Island. Member:
Authors Guild; Authors League; Alpha Tau Omega; Cape
Cod Chess Club.

* * * * *

ALEXANDER CORDELL

Full Name: Alexander Graber.
   Born September 9, 1914, at Colombo, Ceylon. Son of
Frank Alfred Graber (an English soldier) and Amelia
Young. Married Rosina Wells, 1937. One daughter,
Georgina Elizabeth.

Education: Attended Marist Brothers' College.

Career: Surveyor.
   Civil surveyor, Wales, 1936-39, 1945-DATE; writer.
Member: Cardiff Writers' Club; Leicester Lit. Club.

* * * * *

PAUL COREY

Full Name: Paul Frederick Corey.
   Born July 8, 1903, in Shelby County, Iowa. Son of
Edwin Olney Corey (a farmer) and Margaret Morgan
Brown (a teacher). Married Ruth Lechlitner, February
1, 1928. One daughter, Anne Margaret (born 1941).

Education: A.B., University of Iowa, 1925.

Career: Writer.
   With Encyclopaedia Britannica, 1927-28, and National
Encyclopaedia, 1930-31; guerrilla warfare specialist
with First Service Command Tactical School, 1942; full-
time writer, 1931-DATE.

First Professional Sale: "Their Forefathers Were
   Presidents," in Story, July, 1934.

Agent: E. J. Carnell Literary Agency, 17 Burwash Road,
   Plumstead, London SE18, England.

Member:
   Authors Guild; Science Fiction Writers of America;
National Association for the Advancement of Colored
People; ad hoc Mountain Lion Committee assembled by
the Sierra Club to check the mountain lion population
in the state of California.

Interests:
   "Cats, cats, cats, cats, and at the moment, the mountain lion population in California. The state Fish &
Game had damn-well better not authorize any more tro-
phy-hunter killings."

Corey writes:
   "SF writing is sort of my fourth incarnation. In the
'30s I wrote 'proletarian' short stories, and appeared
in most of the little mags of that decade, including
Blast and The Anvil, and mags that paid, like Story,
and several others. The only sales of any consequence
moneywise were to Scribner's and Farm Journal. One
story from this period had a definite fantasy flavor,
and was called "The Farmer and the Gold Stone."
   "My first Middle Western Farm Novel was published in
September, 1939, and sort of started my second incar-
nation--books, mainly novels. A trilogy (Three Miles
Square, 1939; The Road Returns, 1940; County Seat,
1941), all farm fiction, followed by a fourth, Acres of
Antaeus (1946), and all adult stuff. In 1944, my first
'teenage' novel was published (The Red Tractor), followed by four more: Five Acre Hill, Shad Haul, Corn-
gold Farm, and Milk Flood. The latter, though written
in the '40s, was not published until 1956. Two nonfiction books, Buy an Acre and Build a Home, were
written and published during this period, and had a
do-it-yourself or how-to slant. The only thing I did
at that time with a fantasy or SF flavor was an article
for Look called "Hitler Can Invade America by Air."
This got me into the Guerrilla Warfare act.
   "The Joe McCarthy era brought my novel writing to an
end, and I swung over to the how-to and do-it-yourself
field. I wrote about the houses I had built myself,
in a book titled Homemade Homes (1950). Then I started
designing furniture, photographing the construction
steps, and telling people how-to build such furniture.
Stories of mine of this kind have appeared in all the
mechanics mags, plus Woman's Home Companion, Country
Gentleman, True, etc. And there was also the usual
how-to stuff: how to weather strip, etc. Fawcett
brought out a book of my furniture pieces, Furniture
You Can Build. Also during the '50s, I wrote some SF
stuff in my spare time.
   "Fiction is my first love, and SF, which I have always fancied, seemed to me the only way I could say
some of the things I wanted to say after the J. McC.
era. By the '60s, furniture was so easy to buy that
no one was interested in building it themselves. Other
types of mechanics magazine stuff bored me, so I decided to go all out for SF. However, the only American

PAUL COREY (cont.)

"editor of SF who gave me any encouragement, and he
didn't publish me, was Anthony Boucher. All the
others didn't bother to read me, except one or two
editors of new SF mag names, and they wrote me long,
fatuous criticisms, or even marked up my manuscripts,
and nothing they said can't be said about Clarke or
Bradbury or Heinlein, or the other SF pros. And
they're still doing it; I submit stuff to them for
kicks now. But it was the reaction of the SF stuffed-
shirts here who prompted me to try Britain, and E. J.
Carnell took my first one when he still edited *New
Worlds*; then when he became my agent, he took my
novel *The Planet of the Blind*, and picked up my short
story, "If You're So Smart." I'm not sure that he
really digs me, but everything he's had to say about
my stuff makes a considerable spot of sense to me.

"So my fourth incarnation is now given over pretty
much to SF.

"Just a note on my farm fiction period. *The Middle-
Western Farm Novel in the Twentieth Century* is a doctoral dissertation by a certain Roy Meyer, published
by the University of Nebraska Press in 1966. He
rates me along with Rolvaag, Hamlin Garland, and Willa
Cather, and says that my books have made "the most
important contribution during the past generation to
farm fiction." And Frank Faluka (that's his real
name), Head of Special Collections, University of
Iowa Libraries, wrote me: "You may be interested
to know that one scholar who was here last fall (1965)
and who was much interested in our Corey papers, was a
Mlle. Danine Mouraille, from Nice, France, who is
doing her doctoral disseration for the Sorbonne on
the topic *The Rural World of the Middle West in America
1871 to 1950*." So much for posterity. I can now
enjoy myself with SF writing and reading."

At a later date, he had this to add:
"To paraphrase John Barth, garrulity is always bad
news. When I first wrote you about my life, I should
have admitted only to being born to fit my last
reincarnation: I was born a bastard on July 8, 1943,
grew up in Northern California, graduated from Santa
Rosa J.C., and sold my first SF story to Ted Carnell
of Nova Publications on December 13, 1962—title
"Operation Survival." Then the American Editorial
Queens would think they had a new young SF writer,
and wow! But once discovered to have had three different decades of different kinds of writing previously to SF, the reaction is that the old expletive
can't make it, and we're wasting our time to give him
any attention.

"Since I've become a member of SFWA, and received
free SF books, I've never seen such a flaming, bloody
pile of expletive in my life. There has never been
such an irrelevant and unrelated bunch of expletive
published in the history of the media. The good SF
writers are still good—Clarke, Heinlein, Bradbury,
and the Britishers—but....

"But to your question: my rural background, I
think possibly, gave me an insight into flora and
fauna—the behavior of—that an urban background
doesn't give. Also, I had to learn how to do things
that the urban youngster doesn't, albeit the urban
youngster learns things that the rural doesn't. I
learned 'behaviorism' from the ground up, and not from
Skinner. There is no adequate substitute for the
fellatioism of a month-old suckling calf. All things
seem much cleaner amidst the tasseling corn.

"Anyhow, my first substantial publishing dealt with
the land, and my second with the how-to-do-things

which living on the land taught me. Besides, I really
don't think being born a poor country boy did me any
harm."

* * * * *

EDWIN CORLEY

Full Name: Edwin Corley.
   Born October 22, 1931, at Bayonne, New Jersey. Son
of Gordon Corley and Lillian Neal. Married Elizabeth
Zekauskas, July 5, 1963. Three children: Richard,
Elizabeth, Eugene.

Career: Writer.
   Theatrical stage manager, New York, 1952-54; Publisher, *Off-Broadway*, 1954-58; Advertising copywriter,
New York, 1958-69; Vice-President, Compton Agency,
1966-68, and Dancer-Fitzgerald-Sample, 1969; free-
lance writer, 1969-DATE.

Agent: John Cushman Associates, 24 E. 38th St., New
   York, NY 10016.

Member: Authors Guild.

* * * * *

LEE CORREY

Full Name: George Harry Stine.
   Born March 26, 1928, at Philadephia, Pennsylvania.
Son of Dr. George Haeberle Stine (a physician) and
Rhea Matilda O'Neill. Married Barbara Kauth, June 10,
1952. Three children: Constance Rhea (born 1953),
Eleanor Ann (born 1955), George Willard (born 1960).

Education: B.A., Colorado College, 1952.

Career: Engineer.
   Electronic Scientist/General Engineer, White Sands
Proving Ground, New Mexico, 1952-57; President & Chief
Engineer, Model Missiles, Inc., Denver, 1957-59; Asst.
Director of Research, Huyck Corp., Stamford, CT., 1960-
65; consulting engineer & science writer, New Canaan,
CT., 1965-73; Marketing Manager, Flow Technology, Inc.,
Phoenix, 1973-DATE.

First Professional Sale: "The Galactic Gadgeteers,"
   in *Astounding Science Fiction*, May, 1951 (as Harry
   Stine).

Agent: Lurton Blassingame, 60 E. 42nd St., New York,
   NY 10017.

Honors and Awards:
   Silver Medal, American Space Pioneer, U.S. Army Association, 1965; Special Award, American Rocket Society, 1957, for founding and editing *Missile Away!* magazine, the first general interest astronautic magazine;
Special Award, National Association of Rocketry, 1967;
First recipient, Annual Award, Model Rocketry Division,
Hobby Industry Association of America, 1969; Bendix
Trophy, National Association of Rocketry, 1964, 1965,
1967, 1968; Silver Medal, payload category, First International Model Rocket Competition, Fédération Aéronautique Internationale, Dubnica, Czechoslovakia, 1966.

Member:
   The Explorers Club, New York (Fellow); British Inter-

LEE CORREY (cont.)

planetary Society (Fellow); American Institute of Aeronautics and Astronautics (Associate Fellow); New York Academy of Sciences; National Association of Rocketry (Founder, past President, Honorary Member, and Honorary Trustee); Fédération Aéronautique Internationale, Paris (President, Rocketry Subcommittee, 1962-73); Authors Guild; Academy of Model Aeronautics (Scientific Leader); Phoenix Advertising Club.

Interests: Model rocketry, model aeronautics, photography.

Correy had this to say about future developments in space:
"Look for a permanent Soviet base on Luna within the next ten years. But by that time, private enterprise will have taken over from the NASA program (unless the government decides to 'nationalize' space), and the Western people will be making money out of space."

* * * * *

GEORGE CORSTON

Full Name: Michael George Corston.
Born July 14, 1932, at Kenton, Middlesex, England. Married his wife, Josephine Corston, July 14, 1963.

Education: "Low English."

Career: Civil servant.

First Professional Sale: *Aftermath*, Robert Hale, 1968.

* * * * *

JULIO CORTAZAR

Full Name: Julio Cortazar.
Born August 26, 1914, at Brussels, Belgium. Son of Julio José Cortazar and Maria Herminia Descotte. Married Aurora Bernardez, August 23, 1953.

Education: Received literature degree from the teachers college, Buenos Aires, 1935.

Career: Writer.
Lives in Paris, where he is a free-lance translator of French and English into Spanish; has also been an amateur jazz trumpeter; Member of Jury, Casa de las Americas Award.

* * * * *

NORMAN CORWIN

Full Name: Norman Lewis Corwin.
Born May 3, 1910, at Boston, Massachusetts. Son of Samuel Haskell Corwin and Rose Ober. Married Katherine Locke, March 17, 1947. Two children: Anthony, Diane.

Career: Screen writer.
Radio Editor, *Springfield Daily Republican*, 1929-36; Writer, director, producer, CBS, 1938-47; Chief of Special Projects, U.N. Radio, 1949-52; Screen

writer for Metro-Goldwyn-Mayer, at various periods, 1945-DATE; Director of Theater Group, UCLA, 1960-DATE; Chairman of Documentary Awards Committee, Academy of Motion Picture Arts and Sciences, 1963-DATE.

Agent: Leah Salisbury, 790 Madison Avenue, New York, NY 10021.

Awards:
Numerous awards from American Academy of Arts and Letters, Metropolitan Opera, Freedoms Foundation, and National Conference of Christians and Jews; Peabody Medals; Fellowship in Radio Hall of Fame.

Member:
Screen Writers Guild; Dramatists League; American Society of Composers, Authors & Publishers.

* * * * *

THOMAS B. COSTAIN

Full Name: Thomas Bertram Costain.
Born May 8, 1885, at Brantford, Ontario, Canada. Son of John Herbert Costain and Mary Schultz. Married Ida Randolph Spragg, January 12, 1910. Two children: Molly, Dora.

Career: Editor.
Reporter, *Brantford Courier*, till 1908; Editor, *Guelph Daily Mercury*, 1908-10; Editor, *Maclean's*, 1910-12; Chief Associate Editor, *Saturday Evening Post*, 1920-34; Story Editor, Twentieth Century-Fox, 1934-36; Editor, *American Cavalcade*, 1937; Advisory Editor, Doubleday, Doran, & Co., 1939-46; full-time writer, 1946-65. Died October 8, 1965.

Awards:
D.Litt., University of Western Ontario; Medal of the Canadian Club of New York; a school in Brantford, Ontario, has been named after him.

* * * * *

JONATHAN COTT

Full Name: Jonathan Cott.
Born December 24, 1942, at New York, New York. Son of Ted Cott (a television executive) and Jean Cahan.

Education: B.A., Columbia University, 1964; M.A., University of California, Berkeley, 1966.

Career: Editor.
Fulbright Fellow, University of Essex, England, 1967-69; Production Deviser, Granada Television, 1969-70; Contributing Editor, *Rolling Stone*, 1970-75; Executive Editor, Stonehill Publishing Co., 1974-DATE.

* * * * *

JUANITA COULSON

Full Name: Juanita Ruth Coulson.
Born February 12, 1933, at Anderson, Indiana. Daughter of Grant Elmer Wellons (a tool and die maker) and Ruth Margaret Oemler. Married Robert Stratton Coulson, August 22, 1954. One son, Bruce Edward (born 1957).

Education: B.S., Ball State University, 1954; M.A., 1961.

JUANITA COULSON (cont.)

Career: Writer.
Elementary school teacher, 1954-55; collator, Heckman's Bindery, 1955-57; operated a home mimeograph business for ten years; now a full-time writer.

First Professional Sale:
"Another Rib," in *The Magazine of Fantasy and Science Fiction*, June, 1963 (under the pseudonym of John Jay Wells, co-authored with Marion Zimmer Bradley).

Agent: Virginia Kidd, Box 278, Milford PA 18337.

Awards:
Co-Fan Guest of Honor, 30th World Science Fiction Convention (L.A.Con), Los Angeles, 1972; Hugo Award, Best Amateur Publication, 1964 (1965), *Yandro* (with Robert Coulson).

Member: Science Fiction Writers of America (edited *SFWA Forum* for two years); various fan groups.

Interests:
"Semi-pro folk singing (have occasionally been paid, but mostly for free); contributor and entrant in local art societies and shows; rock music--column writing and record collecting; original clothes design and manufacture; trivia. The Coulsons have edited and published the award-winning fanzine *Yandro* since 1953.

Coulson writes:
"I suffer from that fannish syndrome--the trash-heap mind--meaning almost any subject or activity is grist for my mill, and it would be impossible to single out a prominence. I like to write. I wrote when there was no chance of sale, for my own pleasure. I still do. But sometimes a commercially viable idea occurs, and.... It's like getting paid for breathing."

* * * * *

S. H. COURTIER

Full Name: Sidney Hobson Courtier.
Born January 28, 1904, at Kangaroo Flat, Victoria, Australia. Son of Sidney Ernest Courtier and Maud McKenzie Hobson. Married Audrey Jennie George, December 28, 1932. Three children: Colin, Brian, Lynne.

Education: Certificate in Education, University of Melbourne.

Career: Teacher.
Teacher and principal in schools in Victoria and Melbourne; lecturer on literary subjects. Died 1974.

Agent: Laurence Pollinger, 18 Maddox St., Mayfair, London W.1, England. Member: P.E.N.

* * * * *

ARTHUR BYRON COVER

Full Name: Arthur Byron Cover.
Born January 14, 1950, at Grundy, Virginia. Son of William A. Cover (a doctor) and Margaret Peery (a politician).

Education: B.A., Virginia Polytechnic Institute, 1971.

Career: Writer.

First Professional Sale: "Various Kinds of Conceits," a story in the anthology, *Last Dangerous Visions*, edited by Harlan Ellison (forthcoming).

Agent: Jane Rotrosen, 212 E. 48th St., New York, NY 10017.

Member: Science Fiction Writers of America.

Interests: Listening to rock & roll music and classical music, reading comic books, movies.

* * * * *

RICHARD COWPER

Full Name: John Middleton Murry, Jr.
Born May 9, 1926, at Abbotsbury, Dorset, England. Son of John Middleton Murry (the author and critic) and Violet le Maistre. Married Ruth Jezierski, July 28, 1950. Two children: Jacqueline, Helen.

Education: B.A., Oxford University, 1950.

Career: Teacher and author.
Senior Master, Whittingehame College, 1952-67; Head, English Dept., Atlantic College, South Wales, 1967-70?; now a full-time author.

First Professional Sale: *The Golden Valley*, Hutchinson, 1958 (as Colin Murry).

Agent: A. D. Peters & Co., 10 Buckingham St., London W.C.2, England; Harold Matson Co., 22 E. 40th St., New York, NY 10016.

Member: Science Fiction Writers of America; British Science Fiction Association; Authors Society.

Cowper writes:
"You ask why I adopted the pseudonym 'Richard Cowper' for my science fiction novels, and, scratching my head for an answer, I can only say that I *believe* it was an effort to change my luck--Murrys, Middleton and otherwise, have all been dogged with misfortune of one kind or another. A secondary reason was that poet William Cowper was an ancestor of my mother's, and I rather liked the idea of touching my forelock to him down the centuries. He went mad, incidentally!
"I have always been fascinated by SF. (Though I hate the term 'SF' in itself.) I read all H. G. Wells' short stories and novels as a schoolboy, and still regard *The War of the Worlds* as one of the 'all-time greats.' I never lost touch, and read such as came my way--Bradbury, Walter Miller, Clarke, Stapledon, Capek, and so on.
"My chief concern is to *write* as well as I can while allowing my imagination free range; my field of action is really *people*. I was once moved to describe myself as 'a writer of fairy stories for grown-ups'--it didn't go down very well with the serious-minded SF fans I was addressing, but I still think it's me."

* * * * *

JAMES GOULD COZZENS

Full Name: James Gould Cozzens.
Born August 19, 1903, at Chicago, Illinois. Son of Henry William Cozzens and Bertha Wood. Married Bernice Baumgarten, December 31, 1927.

JAMES GOULD COZZENS (cont.)

Education: Attended Harvard University, 1922-24.

Career: Writer.
  Taught children of American engineers in Santa Clara, Cuba, 1925; spent a year in Europe, 1926-27; Associate Editor, *Fortune*, 1938; farmer and writer. Died August 9, 1978.

Agent: Brandt & Brandt, 101 Park Avenue, New York, NY 10017.

Awards:
  O. Henry Award, 1936; Pulitzer Prize, 1949, for *Guard of Honor*; Litt.D., Harvard University, 1952; William Dean Howells Medal, American Academy of Arts and Letters, 1960, for *By Love Possessed*. Member: National Institute of Arts and Letters.

* * * * *

DAVID CRAIG

Full Name: Allan James Tucker.
  Born August 15, 1929, at Cardiff, Wales. Son of William Arthur Tucker (a company director) and Irene Bushen. Married Marian Craig, July 17, 1954. Four children: Patrick, Catherine, Guy, David.

Education: B.A., University College of South Wales and Monmouthshire.

Career: Reporter.
  Leader writer, *Cardiff Western Mail*, 1954-56; reporter, *London Daily Mirror*, 1956-58; reporter and editor for various Welsh newspapers, 1958-DATE. Member: P.E.N.

Agent: Peter Janson-Smith, 42 Great Russell St., London W.C.1, England.

* * * * *

MILDRED CRAM

Full Name: Mildred Cram.
  Born October 17, 1889, at Washington, D.C. Daughter of Nathan Dow Cram (an editor) and Mary Queen. Married Clyde S. McDowell (a naval officer), 1925 (dead).

Career: Author, 1917-DATE.

* * * * *

WILLIAM L. CRAWFORD

Full Name: William Levi Crawford.
  Born September 10, 1911, at Trafford, Pennsylvania. Son of Fred Crawford and Cora Rinard. Married Margaret Finn, July 1, 1941.

Career: Bookseller and publisher.
  Started *Marvel Tales* in 1932 with a hand press; later published Lovecraft's first book, *Shadow over Innsmouth*. In 1946, Fantasy Publishing Company Inc. was formally organized, and Crawford issued books until 1953, and published the professional magazines *Spaceway* (Publisher & Editor, Dec. 1953-June 1955) and *Fantasy Book* (Publisher & Editor, #1-8, 1947-51).

Operations were resumed briefly in 1972 and 1973, and *Spaceway* was revived for four issues (January, 1969-June, 1970); Crawford bought out another magazine, *Coven 13*, changed its title to *Witchcraft and Sorcery*, and published five issues (January, 1971-1973). Since 1973, Crawford has organized the annual Witchcraft and Sorcery convention in Los Angeles, and sells and distributes books from his Alhambra address.

Agent: Fantasy Publishing Company, Inc., 1855 W. Main St., Alhambra, CA 91801.

Margaret Crawford writes:
  "In the late 1940s, FPCI published a magazine called *Fantasy Book*; the editor was listed as Garret Ford. This name came from my name, Margaret Crawford. I never acted as editor; Bill selected all the material used, and therefore 'Garret Ford' should be listed as a pen-name for him. I do not believe Forry Ackerman ever used the name Garret Ford for any reason, but I think he originated the 'Garret' part of the name, perhaps because Bill and I, along with Russ Hodgkins and Fred Schroyer, had published Garrett P. Serviss' novel, *Edison's Conquest of Mars*, under the Carcosa House imprint."

* * * * *

JOHN CREASEY

Full Name: John Creasey.
  Born September 17, 1908, at Southfields, Surrey, England. Son of Joseph Creasey and Ruth Creasey. Married Margaret Cooke (divorced, 1939); married Evelyn Jean Fudge (divorced); married Jeanne Williams (divorced, 1973). Three children: Colin, Martin John, Richard John.

Career: Author.
  Various clerical jobs, 1926-35; full-time author, 1935-73; Member, Governing Body, Liberal Party, 1945-50. Creasey wrote over 565 books under 25 pseudonyms, thereby establishing himself as one of the most prolific authors of modern times. Died June 9, 1973.

First Professional Sale: *Seven Times Seven*, Andrew Melrose, 1932.

Agents:
  Lynette Howis, New Hall, Bodenham, Salisbury, England; Harold Ober Associates, 40 E. 49th St., New York, NY 10017.

Honors & Awards: Order of the British Empire; Edgar Award, Best Novel, 1961. Member: Mystery Writers of America; Crime Writers Association; P.E.N.

* * * * *

HELEN CRESSWELL

Full Name: Helen Cresswell.
  Born July 11, 1936, in Nottinghamshire, England. Daughter of J. E. Cresswell (an electrical engineer) and A. E. Clarke. Married Brian Rowe (in textiles), April 14, 1962. One daughter, Caroline Jane.

Education: B.A., University of London, 1955.

Career: Writer.
  Has been a literary assistant to a foreign author,

HELEN CRESSWELL (cont.)

a fashion buyer, and a teacher, and has also done television work for the BBC; writer, 1961-DATE.

Agent: A. M. Heath, 35 Dover St., London W.1.

Award:
Nottingham Poetry Society Award for best poem submitted in annual competition, 1950. Member: Society of Authors.

* * * * *

MICHAEL CRICHTON

Full Name: John Michael Crichton [pronounced cry-ton]. Born October 23, 1942, at Chicago, Illinois. Son of John Henderson Crichton (a corporate executive) and Zula Miller. Married Joan Radam, January 1, 1965 (divorced, 1971).

Education: A.B., Harvard College, 1964; M.D., Harvard Medical School, 1969.

Career: Author and director.
Full-time author and motion picture director, 1969-DATE.

First Professional Sale: "Sunset Crater," in *New York Times*, 1958.

Agent: Lynn Nesbit, c/o IFA, 1301 Avenue of the Americas, New York, NY 10019.

Member:
Aesculaepian Club; Authors Guild; Mystery Writers of America; Science Fiction Writers of America; Writers Guild of America, West; Directors Guild.

Interests: Tennis, scuba diving. Crichton wrote thrillers during his college years as "John Lange."

* * * * *

FRANK CRISP

Full Name: Frank Robson Crisp.
Born November 30, 1915, at Durham, England. Son of Frank Robson Crisp and Sarah Sinton. Married Margaret Diston, December 6, 1941. Three children: Judith, Sally Ann, Kathleen.

Career: Writer.
Served in the British Merchant Navy, spent several years as bosun aboard an inter-island steamer in Indonesia, pearled in Western Australia, made two whaling trips to the Antarctic; currently director of a catering service, and a part-time writer.

* * * * *

EDMUND CRISPIN

Full Name: (Robert) Bruce Montgomery.
Born October 2, 1921, at Chesham Bois, England. Son of Robert Ernest Montgomery and Marion Blackwood.

Education: Attended Merchant Taylors' School, and St. John's College, Oxford (B.A., 1943).

Career: Writer and editor.
Was a school teacher for three years; under his own name, was a composer and conductor, chiefly of film music; crime fiction critic, *London Sunday Times*; full-time author and editor (his work includes 10 novels, 50 short stories, 4 radio plays, 2 film scripts, etc.). Died 1978.

First Professional Sale: *The Case of the Gilded Fly*, Victor Gollancz, 1944.

Member: British Science Fiction Association (Past Chairman).

* * * * *

CRISTABEL

Full Name: Christine Elizabeth Abrahamsen.
Born September 6, 1916, at Oak Hill, West Virginia. Daughter of Charles Earl Campbell (an auto mechanic) and Macie Boothe. Married Harry Abrahamsen, October 11, 1943 (divorced, 1945). One daughter, Cherri (born 1944).

Education:
R.N. Diploma, Somerset Hospital, New York, 1938; B.S., Hunter College, 1954; M.A., Columbia University, 1959; Professional Diploma, Columbia University, 1961.

Career: Nurse and nursing instructor.
Nurse at various hospitals, 1939-71; Associate Professor of Nursing, West Virginia Institute of Technology, 1971-DATE.

First Professional Sale: *Manalacor of Veltakin*, Curtis Books, 1970.

Agent: Jay Garon-Brooke, New York, NY.

Awards: Several nursing fellowships.

Member:
American Nurses Association; National League for Nursing; Science Fiction Writers of America; American Public Health Association; Public Health Association of New York City; American National Council for Health Education of the Public and International Health Union; American Educational Research Association; New York Academy of Sciences; Aerospace Medical Association; Teachers College Nurses Alumni Association; Hunter College Alumni Association; American National Red Cross Nurse.

Cristabel writes:
"*The Cruachan and the Killane* picks up the heroes of *Manalacor of Veltakin* about a third of the way through the book. I have another novel which has not sold that is a part of the same series. When I started writing, I wanted to divorce myself from my professional life; and I also found that I could write more freely that way, by using the pseudonym. It really doesn't matter, but I find it fun to be more people than just one! I'm also Kathleen Westcott, gothic writer (one book to date). I made up "Cristabel" with the aid of a fortune telling book, and with the use of all of my real names. It means "good luck" and success. I'm still hoping!"

Cristabel is now compiling a collection of letters from the "dean of muzzle-loading long rifles," to include biographical sketches of writer and recipient, who is also a gunsmith.

RICHMAL CROMPTON

Full Name: Richmal Crompton Lamburn.
   Born November 15, 1890, at Bury, Lancashire, England. Daughter of Edward John Sewell Crompton (a clerk in Holy Orders) and Clara Crompton.

Education: B.A., Royal Holloway College, 1914.

Career: Writer.
   Classical Mistress, St. Elphin's School, Darley Dale, England, 1914-17, and at Bromley High School, 1917-24; writer, 1922-69. Died January 11, 1969.

Agent: A. P. Watt & Sons, Hastings House, 10 Norfolk St., London W.C.2, England.

Member: Authors Society; National Book League.

* * * * *

KENDELL FOSTER CROSSEN

Full Name: Kendell Foster Crossen.
   Born July 25, 1910, at Albany, Ohio. Son of Samuel Richard Crossen and Clo Foster. Married Lisa Palmieri Magazu, 1958.

Education: Attended Rio Grande College.

Career: Writer.
   Has been a director and producer of stage revues, an editor of Detective Fiction Weekly and Spark and Play; full-time writer, 1940-DATE.

Crossen has written books under the names Bennett Barley, M. E. Chaber, Richard Foster, Christopher Monig, and Clay Richards.

* * * * *

JANE LOUISE CURRY

Full Name: Jane Louise Curry.
   Born September 24, 1932, at East Liverpool, Ohio. Daughter of William Jack Curry, Jr. and Helen Willis.

Education: B.S., Indiana State College, 1954; M.A., Stanford University, 1962; Ph.D., 1969.

Career: Writer and artist.
   Art teacher in the Los Angeles city schools, 1955-59; teaching assistant and instructor, Stanford University, 1964-65, 1967-68; painter, with showings at exhibitions of Royal Society of British Artists and other groups; full-time writer.

Awards:
   Fulbright grant, 1961-62, at the University of London; Stanford-Leverhulme Fellowship, 1965-66, also at the University of London; Book World Spring Children's Book Festival honor book award, for The Daybreakers; Southern California Council on Literature for Children and Young People, Outstanding Book by a Southern California Author Award, 1970, also for The Daybreakers.

Member:
   Mediaeval Academy of America; International Arthurian Society; London Mediaeval Association; Authors Guild; Medieval Association of the Pacific.

RICHARD A. CURTIS

Full Name: Richard Alan Curtis.
   Born June 23, 1937, at Bronx, New York. Son of Charles and Betty Curtis. Married Joanne Stone, August 17, 1966.

Education: B.A., Syracuse University; M.A., University of Wyoming.

Career: Writer.
   "I've had articles in Esquire, Escapade, Diners Club, News Front, American Legion, Gentleman's Quarterly, among others, crime fiction in all the mystery magazines, and books published by Putnam, Macmillan, and Doubleday."

First Professional Sale: A crime story to Ellery Queen's Mystery Magazine in the early 1960s.

Curtis writes:
   "I had a story in the April 1968 issue of Cavalier called 'Introduction to "The Saint."' Written before the first heart transplant, it dealt with a writer who has heart disease, yet desperately needs time to finish The Saint, the last book of a stupendous five-book cycle establishing him as one of the world's leading authors. When he is offered the privilege of having his heart replaced, however, he turns it down. All great works of art have been produced because the creators were working against the deadline of mortality. Take that deadline away, and anyone can be an artist, having all the time in the world. Thus our author is one of the last of his kind."

* * * * *

ROALD DAHL

Full Name: Roald Dahl.
   Born September 13, 1916, at Llandaff, South Wales. Son of Harald Dahl (a shipbuilder) and Sofie Hesselberg. Married Patricia Neal (the actress), July, 1953. Five children: Olivia (born 1955, and deceased), Tessa (born 1957), Theo (born 1960), Ophelia (born 1964), Lucy (born 1965).

Education: Attended Repton, 1929-32.

Career: Writer.

First Professional Sale: "A Piece of Cake," in Saturday Evening Post, 1943.

Agent: Ann Watkins, 77 Park Avenue, New York, NY.

Awards: Has won an Edgar award twice. Interests: orchid growing and breeding, wine, pictures, furniture.

* * * * *

MARY DANBY

Full Name: Mary Heather Danby.
   Born May 26, 1941, at Dorking, Surrey, England. Daughter of Denys Danby (a veterinary surgeon) and Doris Dickens (a teacher). Married Brian Calvert, April 15, 1972.

Education: Attended Ursuline Convent School, 1948-58, and Kingston Technical College, 1958-59.

MARY DANBY (cont.)

Career: Writer and editor.
Secretary, 1959-62; TV production assistant, 1962-69; Fiction Editor, Fontana Books, 1969-72; Consultant Editor, Armada Books, London, 1973-DATE; freelance writer and editor.

First Professional Sale:
"Quid Pro Quo," in the anthology *The Fifth Fontana Book of Great Horror Stories*, Fontana, 1970.

Interests: Riding horses, film-making, mending things.

Danby writes:
"I have never written any science fiction per se, nor do I have any ambitions to do so. The hard core of my work is novel-writing, and I've had two published thus far: *A Single Girl*, and *The Best of Friends*.
"With regards to my anthologies, I have a large number of writers who send me stories regularly, and I collect as many suitable books of short stories (old and new) as I can find. Compiling several series, as I do, means keeping a constant eye open for material."

She adds: "My great-great-grandfather was Charles Dickens."

* * * * *

JERRY C. DANIEL

Full Name: Jerry Clayton Daniel.
Born June 30, 1937, at Mount Vernon, Missouri. Son of Thomas C. Daniel (a railroad engineer) and Frances Smith. Married Mary G. Columbus, March 15, 1957. Four children: Stormy Amber, Jerry Clayton II, Dane Thor, Susan Constance.

Education: B.S.B.A., University of Denver, 1958; J.D., 1960.

Career: Attorney.
Admitted to the Bar of the State of Colorado, 1963; Special Agent, Federal Bureau of Investigation, 1963-66; Attorney with various firms, 1967-DATE.

Member: American Bar Association; Arapahoe County Bar Association; Phi Kappa Sigma.

* * * * *

JONATHAN DANIELS

Full Name: Jonathan Daniels.
Born April 26, 1902, at Raleigh, North Carolina. Son of Josephus Daniels (an editor and stateman) and Addie Bagley. Married Elizabeth Bridgers, Sept. 7, 1923 (died 1929); married Lucy Billing Cathcart (an editorial researcher), April 30, 1932. Four children: Elizabeth, Lucy, Adelaide, Mary Cleves.

Education: A.B., University of North Carolina, 1921; M.A., 1922.

Career: Editor.
Reporter for various newspapers, 1922-25; Washington correspondent, *Raleigh News and Observer*, 1925-28;

Staff writer, *Fortune*, 1930-31; Editor, *Raleigh News and Observer*, 1932-42; Associate Director, Office of Civilian Defense, 1942; Administrative Assistant and Press Secretary to President Franklin D. Roosevelt, 1943-45; Editor, *Raleigh News and Observer*, 1947-69; Editor Emeritus, 1969-DATE; U.S. Representative on the United Nations Subcommission on Prevention of Discrimination and Protection of Minorities, 1947-53; Member, Federal Hospital Council of U.S. Public Health Service, 1950-53; Democratic National Committeeman from North Carolina, 1949-52; active in the presidential campaigns of Harry S. Truman in 1948, and Adlai Stevenson in 1952.

Agent: Brandt & Brandt, 101 Park Avenue, New York, NY 10017.

Awards: Guggenheim Fellowship for study in France, Italy, and Switzerland, 1930.

* * * * *

JACK DANN

Full Name: Jack Mayo Dann.
Born February 15, 1945, at Johnson City, New York. Son of Murray I. Dann (a lawyer) and Edith Nash.

Education: B.A., State University of New York, Binghamton, 1968; has also attended St. John's Law School.

Career: Writer.
Instructor, Dept. of Continuing Education, Broome Community College, 1972; Asst. Professor, Cornell University, Summer, 1973. Managing Editor, *SFWA Bulletin*.

First Professional Sale:
"Traps," in *Worlds of If*, March, 1970 (with George Zebrowski).

Honors: Nebula Award finalist, novella category, 1973, for "Junction."

Member:
Science Fiction Writers of America; World Future Society; Mark Twain Society (Esteemed Knight).

Interests:
Print collecting, sketching, poetry, future studies.
"I attended the Manlius Military Academy, studied drama at Hofstra University, received a B.A. in political science from SUNY Binghamton, dropped out of law school to become a 'full-time writer,' and am now selling to a wide variety of markets. I've appeared on WOR radio in New York, and on educational television, as well as panels at the Center for Integrative Studies. At one time or another, I've worked as a law investigator, ghost-writer, rug-layer, soup distributor, motel clerk, window washer, beer hall piano player, cafe barker, artist, promo-man for a recording artist."

* * * * *

JACK DANVERS

Full Name: Camille Auguste Marie Caseleyr.
Born September 22, 1909, at Antwerp, Belgium. Became an Australian citizen. Son of Gustave Pierre Caseleyr and Alice de Staepeleere. Married Doreen Felice Nicholson (a bursar), September 12, 1941. Two children: Alice, Veronique.

JACK DANVERS (cont.)

Education:
   Licencie en Sciences Commerciales, Institut Supér-
ieur de Commerce d'Anvers, University of Antwerp, 1930.

Career: Teacher.
   Foreign Language Specialist, BBC, 1941-43; Principal
Territorial Agent, Government of Belgian Congo, 1943-
49; Accounting Officer, Victorian State Rivers Com-
mission, Victoria, Australia, 1951-53; secondary
school teacher in South Australia, 1954-58; Senior
English and French Master, All Souls' School, Charters
Towers, Queensland, Australia, 1959-DATE.

Agent: A. P. Watt & Son, 10 Norfolk St., Strand,
   London W.C.2, England.

* * * * *

W. A. DARLINGTON

Full Name: William Aubrey Cecil Darlington.
   Born February 20, 1890, at Taunton, Somersetshire,
England. Son of Thomas Darlington (an inspector of
schools) and Edith Bainbridge. Married Marjorie
Sheppard, October 3, 1918 (died 1973). Two children:
Anne (deceased), Phoebe Joanna.

Education: B.A., Cambridge University, 1912; M.A.,
   Cambridge University.

Career: Critic.
   Schoolmaster, 1913-14; Editor, *London World*, 1919;
Chief Dramatic Critic, *London Daily Telegraph*, 1920-
68; London Drama Correspondent, *New York Times*, 1939-
60.

Agent: Curtis Brown Ltd., 13 King St., Covent Garden, London W.C.2, England.

Awards: Commander of the British Empire, 1967.

Member: Institute of Journalists; Guild of Adjudi-
   cators; Society of Authors; League of Dramatists.

* * * * *

HUGH DARRINGTON

Full Name: Hugh Darrington.
   Born September 30, 1940, at Bisitor Stortford, Essex, England. Son of Richard Darrington (a headmaster) and Vera De Wilde (a school teacher). Married Ann Gordon, 1962. One son, James (born 1968).

Career: Editor.
   Reporter for various trade papers, 1961-65; Features
Editor, *Self Service & Supermarket*, 1965-69; Editor,
RHM house journal, 1969-70; Editor, *Brewers' Guardian
Magazine*, 1970-DATE. Interests: cinematography.

* * * * *

LEONARD DAVENTRY

Full Name: Leonard John Daventry.
   Born March 7, 1915, at Brixton, London, England.
Son of Leonard Daventry (Capt., British Army) and
Dora Davies. Married Margaret Alexander, 1941. Two
children: Anna Betsy (born 1942); Martin Leonard

(born 1946, died 1967).

Career: Busker.
   Has been a soldier, lorry driver, hearse driver,
clerk, vegetable merchant. "You will note that my
latest occupation is that of a 'busker.' In case you
are not familiar with the word, it means itinerant
street musician or actor. These still exist in England,
but are dying out fast."

First Professional Sale: *A Man of Double Deed*,
   Victor Gollancz, 1965.

Interests:
   Painting, sculpture, photography, music (accordion).
"I've never gone in for 'gimmicks' or avant-garde stuff,
for I believe that the definition of a story-teller is
as it was in the beginning, and will continue to the
end: i.e., one who spins a tale with a fair opening,
a good middle, and a strong ending. *Degree XII* was
my best SF literary effort, and is probably my last,
as, since the long and slow death of my son in 1967,
my personality has undergone a change. I no longer
have the inclination to write for money or notoriety,
and certainly feel unable to spin fantasies of any
sort. I am engaged upon a literary work of another
kind, an autobiographical novel entitled *Happy Days
Are Definitely Here Again*."

* * * * *

AVRAM DAVIDSON

Full Name: Avram Davidson.
   Born April 23, 1923, at Yonkers, New York. Son of
Harry Jonas Davidson and Lillian Adler. Married Grania
Kaiman (divorced). One son, Ethan Michael Anders.

Education: Attended New York University, 1940-42,
   1947-48, and Pierce College, 1950-51.

Career: Writer.
   Executive Editor, *The Magazine of Fantasy and Science Fiction*, April, 1962-November, 1964; free-lance
writer.

First Professional Sale: To *Orthodox Jewish
   Life Magazine*, 1946.

Awards:
   Hugo Award, Best Short Story, 1957 (1958), "Or All
the Seas with Oysters"; Hugo Award, Best Professional
Magazine, 1962 (1963), *The Magazine of Fantasy and
Science Fiction*; World Fantasy Award, Best Collection,
1975 (1976), *The Enquiries of Dr. Esterhazy*; Edgar
Award, Best Short Story, 1962, "The Affair at the La-
hore Cantonment"; Ellery Queen Award, 1958, "The Necessity of His Condition."

"I don't know where science fiction, mankind, or, for
that matter, me is going. I can no longer read SF,
and consider my present and recent work to be fantasy."

* * * * *

L. P. DAVIES

Full Name: Leslie Purnell Davies.
   Born October 20, 1914, at Crewe, Cheshire, England.
Son of Arthur Davies (a gardener) and Annie Sutton.
Married Winifred Tench, November 13, 1940.

L. P. DAVIES (cont.)

Education: Degree in Ophthalmic Optics, Manchester
  University, 1939.

Career: Writer and optician.
  Dispenser (pharmacist), Galloway, Crewe, 1928-33;
Dispersen, McCutcheon, 1933-39; Sergeant, British
Army, in North Africa and Italy, 1939-45; Sub-Post-
master, Birmingham, 1946-57; Optician, various cities,
1960-DATE; writer, 1960-DATE.

First Professional Sale: "Because Susie Didn't
  Go Straight Home!," in *Family Star*, 1960.

Agent: Carl Routledge, 176 Wardour Street, London.

Honors: Knight of Mark Twain, for *The Shadow Before*.

Interests: Painting, Travelling, filling up ques-
  tionaires.

Davies writes:
  "My first novel, *The Paper Dolls*, was rejected by
five publishers because it didn't fit into any of
their categories. This hybrid state of affairs has
been the bane of my writing career, it being an un-
pardonable thing to mix SF with whodunit. People in
trains ask, 'What sort of books do you write?' and
I say, 'I don't know,' and they think I'm made. I
call it psychofiction. Doubleday calls it 'Tomorrow
Fiction.'
  "I started off with shorts, and had something over
350 stories published, under ten different pen-names,
and covering every subject from rawish sex in *Mayfair*
to Welsh country life in *Blackwood's*. But my main
buyer was *The London Mystery Magazine*, who once, in
one of their issues, published ten of my stories,
each under a different name. And I think it was for
that mag that I first tried mixing everything within
sight--because they bought everything of that nature
I produced. So I suppose it was natural in a way
that when my agent said I should have a bash at a
novel, I should stick with the same genre. Which
was *The Paper Dolls*, which is still selling well,
bless it, and my American readers. For every copy of
one of my books in either hard or paperback that is
sold here in the U.K., 115 are sold in other coun-
tries--the U.S. being the main one. I do particularly
well in Brazil and Japan. Much better than in my own
country.
  "My first professional sale in general fiction was
a short story called (retitled by the editor, I beg
to add!), "Because Susie Didn't Go Straight Home."
It was sold on July 17, 1959, and appeared in 1960
in a terrible magazine with a very large circulation
called *Family Star*. It was the only romance that I
have ever written. That I ever will write!. And
my first sale of a science fiction story was a year
later, on June 6, 1960--26 mystery and horror stories
later. It was called "The Wall of Time," and it
appeared in *The London Mystery Magazine*."

* * * * *

GWEN DAVIS

Full Name: Gwen Davis.
  Born May 11, 1936, at Pittsburgh, Pennsylvania.
Daughter of Lewis W. Davis and Helen Fink.

Education: A.B., Bryn Mawr College, 1954; studied
  at Stanford University, 1959-60.

Career: Writer.
  Comedy writer, New York, 1955; novelist, 1956-60;
screenplay writer, 1960-61; musical comedy bookwriter
and lyricist, 1961-62; free-lance writer, 1962-DATE.
Member: Bryn Mawr Club; Mars Club, Paris.

Agent: William Morris Agency, 151 El Camino, Beverly
  Hills, CA 90212.

* * * * *

RICHARD DAVIS

Full Name: Richard Davis.
  Born at London, England. Educated in England.

Agent: Michael Bakewell Associates, 118 Tottenham
  Court Rd., London W.1, England.

Career: Writer, film producer, editor.

* * * * *

BRADFORD M. DAY

Full Name: Bradford Marshall Day.
  Born September 20, 1916, at Marblehead, Massachusetts.
Son of Bradford Marshall Day (a secretary) and Bertha
Edna Montgomery. Married Rita Jezewska, October 6,
1945. Six children: Bradford (born 1946), Sharon
(born 1947), Irene (born 1954), Diana (born 1957),
Richard (born 1959), Janet (born 1960).

Career: Highway landscape maintenance worker.
  Served in the Civilian Conservation Corps, 1934;
miscellaneous jobs, 1934-39; merchant seaman, 1939-44;
machine shop worker, 1944-45; biochemical lab work,
1945-62; bookseller, 1962-70; restauranteur, 1970;
highway landscape maintenance worker, 1970-DATE.

First Professional Sale: *A Checklist of Fantastic
  Magazines*, Bradford M. Day, 1951.

Member: Mensa.

Interests: "Inventing and ratiocinating a consistent
  system of cosmogony."

* * * * *

CATHERINE CROOK de CAMP

Full Name: Catherine Adelaide Crook de Camp.
  Born November 6, 1907, at New York, New York. Daughter of Samuel Crook (a lawyer) and Mary Eliza Beekman.
Married Lyon Sprague de Camp, August 12, 1939. Two
children: Lyman Sprague (born 1941), Gerard Beekman
(born 1951).

Education: A.B., Columbia University, 1933.

Career: Writer, lecturer, editor.
  Teacher of English and history, Oxford School, Hartford, Conn., 1934-35, at Laurel School, Shaker Heights,
Ohio, 1935-37, at Calhoun School, New York, 1937-39;
Instructor, Temple University, 1949-50; free-lance
writer, 1950-DATE; also manages business affairs of her
husband, and edits his works.

First Professional Sale: "Windfall," in *Astoun-*

CATHERINE CROOK de CAMP (cont.)

ding Science Fiction, July, 1951.

Member:
    Phi Beta Kappa; Cum Laude Society (Honorary Member);
Authors League of America; Barnard College Club of
Philadelphia; Fellows in American Studies; University
Museum of the University of Pennsylvania. Listed in
*Who's Who of American Women, Who's Who in the East,
Dictionary of International Biography*.

Interests:
    Travel, gardening, theater, Philadelphia Orchestra,
interior decorating, education in money-management
skills.

Mrs. de Camp writes:
    "No two collaborators work the same way, and no
pair of collaborators always work the same way. Sometimes Sprague does the rough draft; sometimes we
share the research; sometimes (as with *Tales Beyond
Time*) the project was 99 1/2% my idea and editorial
work and the retelling of the Daedalus myth all mine;
sometimes Sprague's is the larger share by far.
    "Although our style of writing and way of thinking
are quite different, we have developed a joint style
for the collaborating, and pride ourselves that readers rarely can tell which parts are his and which
parts are mine. But then, I've served as Sprague's
editor for years, and always try to add some milk of
human kindness to his meticulous research and learned
language. People seem to like the amalgam; the books
sell.
    "Regarding editorial disputes, we discuss places
where our points-of-view continue to diverge. Our
son says it sounds as if we were having a battle royal on the rare occasions when he comes home during
a discussion. When it comes to how much learning
people can take, I usually win, and chop some out.
Once I chopped too much. In our book on dinosaurs,
I got bored with the long chapter on the ancestors
of aquatic dinosaurs, and deleted a whole section.
When he said, "What have you done to my fishes?" I
knew I'd erred. So I tidied up the text, streamlined
several species, and put them back in the prehistoric
seas, in a somewhat more readable environment.
    "May I add that we've been married over 35 years,
and still enjoy every bit of each other's company,
and are fiercely proud of each other and of our several and joint successes. No Gilbert and Sullivan
we. We just wish our collaborations might last as
long as theirs!"

* * * * *

L. SPRAGUE de CAMP

Full Name: Lyon Sprague de Camp.
    Born November 27, 1907, at New York, New York. Son
of Lyon de Camp (in real estate and lumber) and Emma
Beatrice Sprague. Married Catherine Adelaide Crook,
August 12, 1939. Two Sons: Lyman Sprague (born 1941)
and Gerard Beekman (born 1951).

Education:
    B.S., California Institute of Technology, 1930;
M.S., Stevens Institute of Technology, 1933.

Career: Writer.
    Instructor, Inventors Foundation, Hoboken, NJ, 1933-
36; Principal, School of Inventing and Patenting,

International Correspondence Schools, Scranton, Penn.,
1936-37; Editor, Fowler-Becker Publishing Co., 1937-
38; Asst. Editor, American Society of Mechanical Engineers, 1938; free-lance writer, 1938-42; Assistant
Mechanical Engineer, Naval Aircraft Factory, Philadelphia, 1942; Lieut. and Lieut. Commander, U.S. Naval
Reserve, 1942-46; free-lance writer, 1946-56; Publicity
Writer, Gray & Rogers (an advertising agency), Philadelphia, 1956; free-lance writer, 1956-DATE.

First Professional Sale: "The Isolinguals," in
    Astounding Stories, September, 1937.

Awards:
    Guest of Honor, 24th World Science Fiction Convention
(Tricon), Cleveland, 1966; International Fantasy Award,
Nonfiction, 1953, *Lands Beyond* (with Willy Ley); Gan-
dalf Award, 1976; Cleveland Science Fiction Award, 1953,
for *Tales from Gavagan's Bar* (with Fletcher Pratt);
Fiction Award of the Athenaeum of Philadelphia, 1959,
for *An Elephant for Aristotle*; Invisible Little Man
Award, 1965; Pat Terry Award, 1973; Guest of Honor,
Boskone IX, 1972.

Member:
    History of Science Society; American Historical As-
sociation; Society for the History of Technology; As-
sociation Phonétique Internationale; Science Fiction
Writers of America; Authors Guild; Hyborian Legion;
Dark Brotherhood; Swordsmen and Sorcerers Guild of
America; University of Pennsylvania Museum; Academy of
Natural Sciences; Fellows in American Studies; Athen-
aeum of Philadelphia.

Interests: Reading, gardening, classical recordings,
    sailing, riding, archery, model ship building. He
    adds: "I've been lucky."

* * * * *

MIRIAM ALLEN deFORD

Full Name: Miriam Allen deFord.
    Born August 21, 1888, at Philadelphia, Pennsylvania.
Daughter of Moise deFord (a physician and surgeon) and
Frances Allen (a physician and surgeon). Married
Armistead Collier, February 14, 1916 (divorced, 1920);
married Maynard Shipley, April 16, 1921 (died 1934).

Education: A.B., Temple University, 1911; attended
    University of Pennsylvania, 1911-12.

Career:
    "Utterly impossible to give in detail. Labor jour-
nalist (*Federated Press, Labor's Daily*) for 36 years;
insurance claim adjuster, 1918-23; feature writer for
Philadelphia North American and *Boston Post*; public
stenographer in San Diego, 1915; on staff of Associated
Advertising; reporter, Ford Hall Open Forum, Boston,
1913-15; editor of a house organ, Baltimore, 1917-18;
editor (non-relief), WPA Writers' Project, 1936-39;
have also been a medical secretary, theater program
writer, etc.; now review books for *San Francisco Chronicle* and *Pacific Sun*." Died February 22, 1975.

First Professional Sale: Series of articles, 1906,
    to a church magazine.

Awards:
    Edgar Award, Best Nonfiction, 1961, *The Overbury
Affair*; Edgar Award, Best Nonfiction, 1965, *Murderers
Sane and Mad*; $500 Award for Essay Competition of

MIRIAM ALLEN deFORD (cont.)

Committee for Economic Development, 1958; Watts Essay Competition, R.P.A., 1964; numerous poetry awards.

Member:
   Authors Guild; Mystery Writers of America; Science Fiction Writers of America; Poetry Society of America.

deFord writes:
   "I'm active as a feminist and secularist; my only hobby is answering questionnaires!
   "Failing eyesight (cataracts) and my present disability make it too difficult to write much about my work. A list of my published books is in *Who's Who in America*. My work is included in at least 100 anthologies, and countless magazines. My latest book is *Elsewhere, Elsewhen, Elsehow* (Walker, 1972). You ask how I became involved in writing science fiction. (It had nothing to do with World War II.) My husband was a writer and lecturer on science, and I have always read much in the field, especially in biology and psychology. I've written fantasy for at least 50 years, and just gradually began writing straight SF as well. If I have a predominant field, it is fact crime, with which five of my books deal.
   "As you can observe, I can scarcely see."

* * * * *

ALLEN DeGRAEFF

Full Name: Albert Paul Blaustein.
   Born October 12, 1921, at New York, New York. Son of Karl Allen Blaustein (a lawyer) and Rose Brickman. Married Phyllis Migden, December 21, 1948. Three children: Mark Allen (born 1950), Eric Barry (born 1951), Dana Beth (born 1957).

Education: A.B., University of Michigan, 1941; J.D., Columbia University, 1948.

Career: Professor of Law.
   Admitted to the New York Bar, 1948. Reporter, City News Bureau, Chicago, 1941-42; Major, U.S. Army, 1942-46, 1950-52; private law practice, New York, 1948-50, 1952-55; Professor of Law, Rutgers University, 1955-DATE; Adviser and Consultant to many foreign governmental and judicial bodies.

Member: Numerous legal associations, and Anti-Slavery Society, International League for Rights of Man.

DeGraeff/Blaustein writes:
   "The late Basil Davenport was my very good friend. He was for many years an editor of the Book-of-the-Month Club. And he *knew* his short stories. Alas--he was not a self-starter. In our many meetings, he always asked me what he should do with his knowledge and spare time (he was a bachelor).
   "Anyway, it was my idea to do *Deals with the Devil* and *Invisible Men* (the first was published by Dodd, Mead in 1958, and reprinted by Ballantine Books in paperback in 1959 and 1966; the second was issued by Ballantine as an original paperback in 1960). We split all royalties, etc., 50-50, but, as a law person, I didn't want my name used. *Famous Monster Tales*, published posthumously by Van Nostrand (1967), was only about 25% mine. So--let's not give me credit on that one!"

MAURICE DEKOBRA

Full Name: Ernst-Maurice Tessier.
   Born May 28, 1885, at Paris, France. Education: B.A., University of Paris.

Career: Writer.
   Writer for newspapers and magazines in Europe, 1920-45; free-lance writer, 1945-DATE.

Awards:
   Literary Gold Model of City of Paris for Literature, 1954; Grand Cross of Temple of Jerusalem; Grand Cross of St. John the Baptist; Doctor of Letters, Andrah University, India.

Member:
   National Union of French Writers and Composers; International Academy, Washington, DC.

* * * * *

SAMUEL R. DELANY

Full Name: Samuel Ray Delany, Jr.
   Born April 1, 1942, at New York, New York. Son of Samuel Ray Delany and Margaret Carey Boyd. Married Marilyn Terry Hacker, August 24, 1961.

Education: Attended City College of New York for two years.

Career: Writer.
   "Youth spent between city house in New York's Harlem and country home in Hopewell Junction, New York. Spent a year in Europe. Primary interest is the speculative novel. I have only been able to support myself solely through writing since 1967. Speculative fiction, for the writer, provides a fascinating internal adventure."

First Professional Sale: An article on folk music to *Seventeen Magazine*, 1960.

Awards:
   Nebula Award, Best Novel, 1966 (1967), *Babel-17*; Nebula Award, Best Novel, 1967 (1968), *The Einstein Intersection*; Nebula Award, Best Short Story, 1967 (1968), "Aye, and Gomorrah"; Nebula Award, Best Novelette, 1969 (1970), "Time Considered as a Helix of Semi-Precious Stones"; Hugo Award, Best Short Story, 1969 (1970), "Time Considered as a Helix of Semi-Precious Stones."

Delany writes:
   "Recently, I've been terribly aware of a conflict between bibliographical good intentions and the realities of publishing. Bibliographers (and conscientious readers) are interested in first editions because (after the objective fact of *when* the work appeared) there is a tacit assumption that the first edition is the most accurate: editor and author worked together, galleys were corrected, etc. Subsequent editions, it is assumed, are simply copies, and editions after that, copies of copies; naturally, mistakes creep in, as well as unapproved editorial tampering.
   "In the SF field, or in any popular genre field, nothing could be further from the truth. SF publishing, both hard and softcover, is essentially mechanical. Even in hardcover houses, authors get galleys only on *insistent* request. If an editor should see a problem in a book, he cuts, re-writes, or what have you, freely.

SAMUEL R. DELANY (cont.)

"Copy editors and proof readers, in paperback houses at any rate, do the same. Magazine publishing is the same, only more so. The first edition of any SF work in this country is, *a priori*, atrocious. It is only if a work gains enough popularity to go into second or third editions that--if the author himself is willing to put himself to an awful lot of effort--you are likely to get "authentic" versions.

"One has the bibliographic dream of seeing "author approved" editions noted in listings along with the first appearance of each book. I note this, because it is a situation I have heard in one form or another deplored by just about every SF author I've ever talked to."

* * * * *

ANTHONY DELIUS

Full Name: Anthony Ronald St. Martin Delius.
  Born June 11, 1916, at Simonstown, South Africa. Son of Edwin St. Martin Delius (an officer in the Royal Navy) and Mignonne Elliott. Married Christina Truter, August, 1941. Two children: Christonie, Peter Nicholas.

Education: B.A., Rhodes University, 1938.

Career: Political writer.
  Co-founder, Editor, and Political Correspondent, *Port Elizabeth Saturday Post*, South Africa, 1947-50; Parliamentary Note- and Leader-Writer, *Cape Times*, South Africa, 1951-54, 1958-DATE.

Awards: South African Poetry Prize, 1960.

* * * * *

LESTER del REY

Full Name: Ramon Felipe San Juan Mario Silvio Enrico Smith Heathcourt-Brace Sierra y Alvarez-del Rey y de los Verdes. Born June 2, 1915, at Clydesdale, Minnesota. Son of Franc del Rey (a carpenter and farmer) and Jane Sidway. Married Evelyn Harrison (died, 1970); married Judy-Lynn Benjamin (an editor), March 21, 1971.

Education: Attended George Washington University, 1931-33.

Career: Writer and editor.
  Sheet metal worker, McDonnell Aircraft Corporation, St. Louis, 1942-44; Author's Agent, Scott Meredith Literary Agency, 1947-50; Editor, *Space Science Fiction*, May 1952-Sept. 1953; Publisher, *Science Fiction Adventures*, November, 1952 (as R. Alvarez); Editor, *Science Fiction Adventures*, Nov. 1952-Sept. 1953 (as Philip St. John); Editor, *Fantasy Fiction*, Feb./Mar. 1953-Aug. 1953 (also listed as Associate Editor for Feb./Mar. 1953 as Marion Henry); Editor, *Fantasy Fiction*, November, 1953 (with Harry Harrison under the joint pseudonym Cameron Hall); Editor, *Rocket Stories*, Apr. 1953-Sept. 1953 (as Wade Kaempfert); Managing Editor, *Galaxy*, June 1968-May 1969; Feature Editor, *Galaxy*, July 1969-Dec. 1974; Managing Editor, *Worlds of If*, June 1968-May 1969; Feature Editor, *Worlds of If*, July 1969-Nov./Dec. 1974 (last issue); Managing Editor, *International Science Fiction*, June 1968;

Editor, *Worlds of Fantasy*, #1-2, 1968-70; Associate Editor, *Worlds of Fantasy*, #3-4, Winter 1970/71-Spring 1971 (last issue); Teacher of fantasy fiction, New York University, 1972-73; Fantasy Editor, Ballantine Books, 1975-DATE; free-lance writer, 1937-DATE.

First Professional Sale: "The Faithful," in *Astounding Stories*, April, 1938.

Agent: Scott Meredith Literary Agency, 845 Third Avenue, New York, NY 10022.

Honors & Awards:
  Guest of Honor, 25th World Science Fiction Convention (NyCon 3), New York, 1967; Boys' Clubs of America Science Fiction Award, 1953, for *Marooned on Mars*.

Member: Authors Guild; Trap Door Spiders.

Interests: Cooking, typewriters.

* * * * *

RICHARD de MILLE

Full Name: Richard de Mille.
  Born February 12, 1922, at Monrovia, California. Son of Cecil Blount de Mille (a motion picture director) and Constance Adams. Married Margaret Belgrano, August 7, 1955. Two children: Anthony B. van Fossen; Cecil Belgrano de Mille.

Education: B.A., Pepperdine College, 1955; Ph.D., University of Southern California, 1961.

Career: Technical Researcher.
  Director, KTLA-TV, Hollywood, 1946-50; Research Associate, University of Southern California, 1961-62; Lecturer in Psychology, University of California, Santa Barbara, 1962-65; Member of technical staff, General Research Corporation, Santa Barbara, 1967-DATE.

Member: American Psychological Association; California State Psychological Association.

* * * * *

ALICE DENHAM

Full Name: Alice Denham.
  Born January 21, 1933, at Jacksonville, Florida. Daughter of T. B. Simkins Denham (a Federal Housing Administration official) and Leila Meggs. Married S. Lee Kutz, 1953 (divorced, 1954).

Education: B.A., University of North Carolina, 1953; M.A., University of Rochester, 1954.

Career: Actress and writer.
  Professional model (*Playboy's* Playmate-of-the-Month, 1956) and actress in films and TV commercials, 1955-64; full-time writer, 1964-DATE, with occasional jobs as as model and television actress. Teacher of fiction at Writers Conference of Georgetown University, 1966, and Ryerson Institute, Toronto, 1968.

Agent: James Brown Associates, 22 E. 60th St., New York, NY 10022.

Member:
  Phi Beta Kappa.

AUGUST DERLETH

Full Name: August William Derleth.
Born February 24, 1909, at Sauk City, Wisconsin. Son of William Julius Derleth and Rose Louise Volk. Married Sandra Evelyn Winters, 1953 (divorced 1959). Two children: April Rose (born 1954), Walden William (born 1956).

Education: B.A., University of Wisconsin, 1930.

Career: Author, Publisher, Editor.
Free-lance author, 1926-30; Associate Editor, Fawcett Publications, Minneapolis, 1930-31; free-lance author, 1931-71; Director and Editor, Arkham House, Sauk City, Wisconsin, 1939-71; weekly columnist and Literary Editor, *Madison Capital Times*, 1941; Director, Sauk City Board of Education, 1937-43. Died July 4, 1971, at Sauk City, Wisconsin.

Honors & Awards: Guggenheim Fellowship, 1938; Governor's Award of Service to Creative Arts, 1966.

Member:
Authors Guild; Midland Authors; Milwaukee Press Club; Wisconsin State Historical Society; Baker Street Irregulars; Cliff Dwellers Club, Chicago.

First Professional Sale: "Bat's Belfry," in *Weird Tales*, May, 1926.

* * * * *

DIANE DETZER

Full Name: Diane Detzer de Reyna.
Born May 13, 1930, at Ridgefield, Connecticut. Daughter of August J. Detzer (Captain, U.S.N., retired) and Dorothy Allée. Two children: Peter, Margaret.

Education: Attended Barnard College and Penn State.

Career: Writer.
"Wrote personal articles at 9, newspaper reviews for a New England newspaper at 16; plus outside secretarial jobs, and a position with Silvermine Publishing in Norwalk, Conn. in between books. Wrote my first science fiction story in 1958."

First Professional Sale: "Follow the Fleet," in *Ridgefield Press*, Fall, 1939.

* * * * *

CHARLES V. DE VET

Full Name: Charles Vincent De Vet.
Born October 28, 1911, at Fayette, Michigan. Son of John De Vet (a chief engineer on a United Fruit Company steamer) and Lucille Feastre. Married Elenore Derwin, November 10, 1935. Two children: Annette (born 1938), Charles F. (born 1941).

Education: B.S., Ferris State Teachers, 1938; attended University of Michigan, 1938-40.

Career: Postal worker.
Teacher, Brampton, Michigan, 1934-38; Teacher, Ida, Michigan, 1938-39; Teacher, Manistee, Michigan, 1939-40; Postal Transport Worker, U.S. Postal Service, 1940-1968; currently retired.

First Professional Sale: "The Unexpected Weapon," in *Amazing Stories*, September, 1950.

Agent: Robert P. Mills Ltd., 156 E. 52nd St., New York, NY 10022.

Member: Science Fiction Writers of America.

* * * * *

PHILIP K. DICK

Full Name: Philip Kindred Dick.
Born December 16, 1928, at Chicago, Illinois. Son of Joseph Edgar Dick and Dorothy Kindred Hudner. Married 1st wife, Jeanette, 1949; married 2nd wife, Kleo, 1951; married 3rd wife, Ann, 1958; married 4th wife, Nancy, 1967 (divorced, 1972); married 5th wife, Tessa, 1973. Three children: Laura (born 1960), Isolde (born 1967), Christopher (born 1973).

Education: Attended University of California, Berkeley, for one term.

Career: Writer.
In the retail record business through 1951; full-time writer, 1951-DATE.

First Professional Sale: "Beyond Lies the Wub," in *Planet Stories*, July, 1952.

Agent: Scott Meredith Literary Agency, 580 Fifth Avenue, New York, NY 10036.

Awards:
Hugo Award, Best Novel, 1962 (1963), *The Man in the High Castle*; John W. Campbell Memorial Award for Best Science Fiction Novel of the Year, 1974 (1975), *Flow My Tears, the Policeman Said*.

Member: Science Fiction Writers of America.

Interests:
Drug rehabilitation. "I have been married five times, and every one of my marriages ends in disaster." He adds: "I've never made much money writing, but I've sure had a hell of a good time doing it."

* * * * *

GEORGE DICK-LAUDER

Full Name: Sir George Andrew Dick-Lauder, 12th Bart.
Born November 17, 1917, at Poona, India. Son of Sir John North Dalrymple Dick-Lauder (an Army officer) and Phyllis Mary Iggulden. Married Hester Marguerite Sorel-Cameron, 1945. Four children: Piers Robert (born 1947), Georgina Jane (born 1949), Mark Andrew (born 1951), Selina Rose (born 1955).

Education: STOWE; Royal Military College, Sandhurst.

Career: British Army officer.
Has been an Army officer all of his life; part-time writer, 1960-DATE.

First Professional Sale: "Missionary Stew," in *Blackwood's*, 1960.

Agent: John Farquharson Ltd., 15 Red Lion Square, London WC1R 4QW, England.

GEORGE DICK-LAUDER (cont.)

Honors: Knight of Grace, Military and Hospitaller
   Order of St. Lazarus of Jerusalem.

Sir George writes:
   "If being the only Nova Scotian Baronet who is
writing science fiction earns distinction, then I
suppose I have it! On the other hand, I was an officer of the Black Watch, a Highland Regiment which in
one generation has produced five writers: Lord Wavel,
Lord Ballantrae (Bernard Fergusson), Eric Linklater,
David Walker, and, last and least, myself.
   "I took up writing at the instigation of my wife
when I retired from the Army, she then reminding me
that my great-great-grandfather, Sir Thomas Dick-
Lauder, had been a distinguished Scots author, who is
still known and admired among Scots scholars (he was
a friend and contemporary of Sir Walter Scott, and
though not so prolific perhaps the better writer of
the two). I published some short stories and a novel
about soldiering in British Guiana, then turned to
SF, somewhat against the advice of my agent (the cult
of SF had not then reached this country to the extent
it has now). It never occurred to me to consider
whether SF was respectable, or not. I had been reading it since I was a child, and in my opinion there
were some sincere authors of the first rank writing
it, whatever the critics might say. If it has achieved
some added 'respectability,' then it is in some horrible current sense, judging by the incursion of pornography and violence--there are some truly terrible
books disguised as SF which lurk on the shelves to
trap the unwary. Nevertheless, people no longer scoff
at SF as once they did (in this country at least),
and many more read it with enjoyment. Perhaps this
is because they have found that good SF offers a
story, wonder, imagination, and an idea or two (but
preserve us from any more 'satires' if you can!).
There is also the element of prophecy, but I don't
think people read it for that, not in this country.
It is too often unpleasant. For myself, I have always
loved the marvellous; the landing of your astronauts
on the Moon was a supreme moment."

* * * * *

JAMES DICKIE

Full Name: James Dickie.
   Born September 3, 1934, at Greenock, Scotland. Son
of Arthur Dickie (a marine engineer) and Margaret
Dink.

Education: M.A., Glasgow University, 1959; L. en L.,
   Barcelona University, 1962; Ph.D., Granada, 1967.

Career: Lecturer in Islamic Studies.
   Lecturer in Islamic Studies, Lancaster University,
1969-74; Senior Lecturer, 1974-DATE; Special Research
Adviser, World of Islam Festival, London, 1974-DATE.

First Professional Sale:
   The Undead, an anthology published by Neville Spear-
man, 1971.

Dickie is known primarily as an expert in Arabic
languages and literature, and has authored two books
on the poetry of the Spanish Arabs. His recreations
include "flagellation and ecclesiology," and he enjoys travelling in the Middle East.

PETER DICKINSON

Full Name: Peter Malcolm Dickinson.
   Born December 16, 1927, at Livingstone, Northern
Rhodesia (now Zambia). Son of Richard Sebastian Wil-
loughby Dickinson (a colonial officer) and May Southey
Lovemore (a tomb restorer ["true"]). Married Mary
Rose Barnard, April 20, 1953. Four children: Philippa
Lucy Anne (born 1955), Dorothy Louise (born 1956), John
Geoffrey Hyett (born 1962), James Christopher Meade
(born 1963).

Education: B.A., Kings College, Cambridge, 1951.

Career: Writer and editor.
   Assistant Editor, Punch, 1952-69; full-time writer,
1969-DATE.

First Professional Sale: An article to Punch, 1952.

Agent: A. P. Watt & Son, 26/28 Bedford Row, London
   WC1R 4HL, England.

Awards: Two Crime Writers Association Golden Daggers,
   for Best Crime Novels of 1968 and 1969. Member:
   Crime Writers Association.

Interests:
   "Care and after care of prisoners; gardening. What's
done is done, and what's not yet done it's tempting
fate to talk about. Most of my books, though not SF,
use the common SF technique of imagining an alien society as their setting. A religion, a tribe, even an
historical period."

* * * * *

SUSAN DICKINSON

Full Name: Susan Margery Dickinson.
   Born December 26, 1931, in Surrey, England. Daughter
of William Croft Dickinson (a university professor)
and Margery Tomlinson. Married Arnold Gibson (an insurance consultant), February 11, 1961. Two children:
Sophie Elizabeth, Emily Jane.

Education: M.A., University of Edinburgh, 1953.

Career: Editor and writer.
   Editorial Assistant, Thomas Nelson & Sons, Edinburgh,
1954-56; Asst. Editor of Children's Books, London, 1956-
59; Children's Books Editor, William Collins Sons, 1960-
DATE.

* * * * *

W. CROFT DICKINSON

Full Name: William Croft Dickinson.
   Born August 28, 1897, at Leicester, England. Son of
William Dickinson (a minister) and Elizabeth Croft.
Married Florence Margery Tomlinson, 1930. Two children:
Susan Margery (born 1931); Jane Elizabeth.

Education: M.A., University of St. Andrews, 1921;
   D.Litt., University of London, 1928.

Career: Professor of Scottish History.
   Librarian, London School of Economics, 1933-44; Professor of Scottish History, University of Edinburgh,
1944-63. Died May, 1963.

GORDON R. DICKSON

Full Name: Gordon Rupert Dickson.
   Born November 1, 1923, at Edmonton, Alberta, Canada.
Son of Gordon Fraser Dickson (a mining engineer) and
Maude Leola Ford.

Education: B.A., University of Minnesota, 1948;
   graduate student, University of Minnesota, 1948-50.

Career: Writer.
   Full-time writer, 1950-DATE.

First Professional Sale: "Trespass!" in *Fantastic Story Quarterly*, Spring, 1950 (with Poul Anderson).

Awards:
   Nebula Award, Best Novelette, 1966 (1967), "Call
Him Lord"; Hugo Award, Best Short Fiction, 1964 (1965),
"Soldier, Ask Not."

Member: Science Fiction Writers of America (President, 1969-71); Mystery Writers of America; Authors
   League.

Dickson writes:
   "The "Dorsai" Cycle was originally intended to con-
sist of nine volumes, three historical novels, three
contemporary novels, and three science fiction novels
of the future, so that the whole Cycle spans a stretch
of time from the early fourteenth century to the late
twenty-fourth century--or roughly a thousand years.
   "The science fiction end of it, as you may know,
has grown. Already published are *Dorsai*, *Necromancer*,
Soldier, Ask Not, and *Tactics of Mistake*.
   "In addition to these titles, the final act of the
Cycle--which, by the way, is correctly named the
Childe Cycle--are to be *Armageddon* and *Childe*.
   "Of the three contemporary, and three historical
novels, none are finished at the present time, and
only two have prospective titles. The first histori-
cal--the one that starts the cycle--is to be titled
Hawkwood, being a fictionalized biography of Sir John
Hawkwood, a painting of whom can still be seen in the
Duomo in Florence--unless the flood there managed to
damage it, along with many other art treasures in
that city.
   "The first book, or perhaps the second, of the
three contemporary novels, is currently titled *Stone-
man's Walk*. While the Hawkwood title is firm, the
other title may be changed around.
   "I expect it may take me fifteen years before the
Cycle is finally finished. But it is a project very
dear to my heart, and if I keep writing long enough,
it most assuredly will be done."

* * * * *

T. E. DIKTY

Full Name: Thaddeus Eugene Dikty.
   Born June 16, 1920, at Port Clinton, Ohio. Son of
Ignatius and Eleanor Dikty. Married his wife, Julian
May Dikty, January 10, 1953. Three children: Sam,
David, Barbara.

Career: Editor.
   Editor, *Best Science Fiction Stories (Year's Best
Science Fiction Stories [and Novels]* series, 1949-58;
currently Publisher and Editor of Fax Editions, West
Linn, Oregon.

First Professional Sale: *Best Science Fiction
Stories*, Frederick Fell, 1949 (anthology).

* * * * *

ISAK DINESEN

Full Name: Baroness Karen Christentze Blixen-Finecke.
   Born April 17, 1885, at Rungsted, Denmark. Daughter
of Wilhelm Dinesen (a naval officer and writer) and
Ingeborg Westenholz. Married Baron Bror Blixen-Finecke
(a big-game hunter and writer), January 14, 1914 (divorced, 1921).

Education: Studied English at Oxford University,
   1904, and painting at Royal Academy in Copenhagen.

Career: Writer.
   With her husband, managed a coffee plantation in
Nairobi, British East Africa (now Kenya), 1913-21,
and was sole manager from 1921-31; commissioned by
three Scandinavian newspapers to write a series of
twelve articles on wartime Berlin, Paris and London,
1940; writer, 1907-62. Died September 7, 1962.

Awards:
   Ingenio e Arti Medal from King Frederik IX of Denmark, 1950; Henri Nathansen Memorial Fund, 1951; The
Golden Laurels, 1952; Hans Christian Andersen Prize,
1955; Danish Critics' Prize, 1957.

Member:
   American Academy of Arts and Letters and National
Institute of Arts and Letters (honorary); Bayerische
Akademe der Schoenen Kuenste; Danish Academy; Cosmo-
politan Club, New York.

* * * * *

ALAN DIPPER

Full Name: Alan Dipper.
   Born May 1, 1922, at Sheerness, Isle of Sheppy, Kent,
England. Son of Cecil Dipper (a civil servant) and
Dora Warner. Married Elspeth Eliot Lloyd, March 24,
1948. Five children: Simon Fraser Lloyd, Frances
Anne, Nigel Harvey, Giles, Roger Martin.

Education: Attended Royal Academy of Dramatic Art,
   1937-38.

Career: Actor and businessman.
   Actor in England, 1938-40, 1945-48; farmer, Stratford,
England, 1948-63; Owner, Brompton Company (office
maintenance firm), London, 1963-DATE.

Agent: Brandt & Brandt, 101 Park Avenue, New York,
   NY 10017. Member: Crime Writers Association.

* * * * *

THOMAS M. DISCH

Full Name: Thomas Michael Disch.
   Born February 2, 1940, at Des Moines, Iowa. Son of
Felix Henry Disch and Helen Margaret Gilbertson.

Education: Attended New York University, and Washington Square College.

THOMAS M. DISCH (cont.)

Career: Writer.
Copywriter, Doyle Dane Bernbach (an advertising agency), 1963-64; full-time writer, 1964-DATE.

First Professional Sale: "The Double Timer," in *Fantastic Stories*, October, 1962.

Agent: Marie Rodell Agency, 141 E. 55th St., New York, NY 10022.

Disch writes:
"No one can judge their own 'significance.' The two books in which I feel I've exerted myself most are *334* and the stories in *Getting into Death*. Ideally, I would like to publish everything without a label. I think it's ridiculous to limit a bibliography to works with SF or fantasy content. As if a doctor were to examine my liver, but not my pancreas."

* * * * *

ROGER DIXON

Full Name: Roger Dixon.
Born January 6, 1930, at Portsmouth, England. Son of Robert George Dixon (a sales director) and Florence Gladys Dixon (an opera soprano). Married Carolyn Anne Shephard, June 28, 1966. Six children: Louise (born 1956), Sally (born 1959), Oliver George (born 1969), Lucy (born 1970), Robert Henry (born 1972), Sophia (born 1974).

Education: Associate, Institute of Chartered Accountants (equivalent to C.P.A.), 1955.

Career: Writer and accountant.
Chartered accountant, 1955-64· full-time writer, 1964-DATE.

First Professional Sale: *Noah II*, Ace Books, 1970.

Agent: Basil Bova, 1733 Broadway, New York, NY 10019.

Member: Institute of Chartered Accountants (Fellow); British Astronomical Association; Sussex County Cricket Club.

Interests: Travel, music, comparative religions, the Middle East, science generally.

* * * * *

TERRY DIXON

Full Name: Terrence Eugene Dixon.
Born February 14, 1950, at Seaside, Oregon. Son of Walter John Dixon and Sara Louise Jenkins. Has been living together with Goldie Nillsen since 1972. One son, Toussaint Nillsen-Dixon (born 1973).

Education: "Forget it."

Career: Free-lance writer.

First Professional Sale:
"Hate Is a Sandpaper Ice Cube with Polka Dots of Love on It," in *The Future Is Now*, an anthology edited by William F. Nolan, Sherbourne Press, 1970.

Awards:
Thorne Kenneth Nupton Memorial Award, Best First Novel by a Black Writer, 1973, for *No Fart for Glory*; Grand Prix de Fantaisie (France), 1974, for *La Liberté Noire [Black Liberty]*.

Member: Black Bottoms (Secretary-Treasurer, 1970-71, Top Jock, 1971-72).

Interests: Karate (Black Belt), archery, fencing, boxing, hypnotism.

Dixon writes:
"My strongest antipathy is toward the fakery and pomposity that marks much of the 'New Wave.' And because I'm still in my mid-twenties, I can't be called an old fogey for holding this opinion. Olaf Stapledon, a science fiction writer greater than any of us living today, said: 'Visions, if they are to be permanently helpful, must not be crude, extravagant, lop-sided. They must be conceived not only with originality, but with sanity.' New Wave 'visions' are too often either crude, extravagant, lop-sided, or so irresponsibly paranoid that they verge on insanity. As such, they can't be 'permanently helpful,' or even fleetingly helpful, despite bloated and bombastic claims to being Cautionary Tales and the like. 'The merely fantastic has only minor power,' said Stapledon. 'We must achieve myth. A true myth is one which, within the universe of a certain culture (living or dead), expresses richly, and often perhaps tragically, the highest admirations possible within that culture. A false myth is one which either violently transgresses the limits of credibility set by its own cultural matrix, or expresses admirations less developed than those of its culture's best visions.' *False Myths* might, therefore, be an appropriate title for the allegedly dangerous so-called visions of the New Wave."

* * * * *

E. L. DOCTOROW

Full Name: Edgar Laurence Doctorow.
Born January 6, 1931, at New York, New York. Son of David R. Doctorow and Rose Doctorow Buck. Married Helen Setzer, August 20, 1954. Three children: Jenny, Caroline, Richard.

Education: A.B., Kenyon College, 1952; graduate student, Columbia University, 1952-53.

Career: Writer and editor.
Senior Editor, New American Library, 1959-64; Editor-in-Chief, Dial Press, 1964-69, and Vice-President, 1968-69; Writer-in-Residence, University of California, Irvine, 1969-70; Member of Faculty, Sarah Lawrence College, 1971-DATE. Award: Guggenheim Fellowship, 1972.

Agent: International Famous Agency, 1301 Avenue of the Americas, New York, NY 10019.

* * * * *

G. D. DOHERTY

Full Name: Geoffrey Donald Cosford Doherty.
Born February 17, 1927, at Sheffield, Yorkshire, England. Son of Michael John Doherty (a civil servant) and Ethel Cosford. Married Helen Margaret Jessop, Feb. 18, 1950. Two children: Elizabeth Jane (born 1954), Michael John (born 1956).

G. D. DOHERTY (cont.)

Education: B.A., University of Sheffield, 1948.

Career: Instructor.
In the Royal Air Force, 1948-50; Head of English Dept. at various English grammar schools, 1950-62; Head of Drama, Crewe and Alsager College of Education, Cheshire, England, 1962-65; Head of Department of Drama, 1965-73; Director of Studies, 1973-DATE.

First Professional Sale: *Aspects of Science Fiction*, John Murray, 1959 (anthology).

Interests: Experimental theatre production, photography, golf.

* * * * *

ROY DOLINER

Full Name: Roy Doliner.
Born April 9, 1932, at New York, New York. Son of George Doliner and Sylvia Seigel.

Education: B.A., New York University, 1954.

Career: Novelist. Member: Authors Guild.

* * * * *

MIKE DOLINSKY

Full Name: Meyer "Mike" Dolinsky.
Born October 13, 1923, at Chicago, Illinois. Son of Hyman Dolinsky (a house painter) and Lillian Milchman.

Education:
B.A., University of California, Los Angeles, 1949; Secondary Credential, University of Southern California, 1950.

Career: Screenwriter.
Full-time writer, primarily of television and movie screenplays, 1947-DATE; has also been an instructor at West Los Angeles College.

First Professional Sale: *There Is No Silence*, Robert Hale, 1959.

Agent: (East) Theron Raines, 244 Madison Avenue, New York, NY 10016; (West) Frank Cooper Agency, 9000 Sunset Blvd., Los Angeles, CA.

Member: TV Academy; Writers Guild of America.

Interests:
Photography, psychology, chess, sailing, poker, the commodities market.

* * * * *

MILES DONIS

Full Name: Miles Donis.
Born December 6, 1937, at Scranton, Pennsylvania.
Education: B.A., Dartmouth College, 1958.

Career: Writer.
Worked for Columbia Pictures; now a full time writer, 1969-DATE. Member: Authors Guild.

CYRIL DONSON

Full Name: Cyril Donson.
Born May 26, 1919, at Mexborough, Yorkshire, England. Son of Ernest Donson (a coal miner) and Ada Wagstaffe. Married Dorothy Denham (a school teacher), May 23, 1956.

Education: D.L.C., Loughborough College, Nottingham University, 1950.

Career: Author and journalist.
Served in the Royal Air Force for six years; has been a newspaper journalist (four years), schoolmaster (20 years), a county magazine editor (one year); currently a free-lance writer.

First Professional Sale: "Mouse into Man," in *Titbits Magazine*, 1940.

Honors: Recommended for Tom Gallon Trust Award as Best Short Story Writer.

Member: Crime Writers Association; Western Writers.

Interests:
Caravanning, shooting, travel, motoring. "My list of published short stories now numbers over 2000, and features over 6000, in all genres. Some of my pennames are: Russ Kidd, Lonny Cordis, Anita Mackin, Via Hartford."

* * * * *

KURT DREIFUSS

Full Name: Kurt Dreifuss.
Born September 18, 1897, at Offenburg, Baden, Germany. Son of Adolph Simon Dreifuss and Augusta Spitzer. Married Bessie Barth. Two children: Pauline, Frank.

Education: Ph.B., University of Chicago, 1924.

Career: Industrial development specialist.
Vocational Supervisor, Jewish Vocational Service, Chicago, 1940-45; Organization Committee and Director, Chicago Consumers Cooperative, 1945-47; Director of Rehabilitation, Chicago Dept. of Welfare, 1947-52; Industrial Development Specialist, Bureau of Indian Affairs, Chicago, 1952-DATE; Founder & President, Northside Symphony Orchestra, Chicago; Founder & President, Society for a World Service Federation, 1964-DATE.

* * * * *

NAT DRING

Full Name: R. Curtis McBroom.
Born September 8, 1910, at Lowpoint, Illinois. Son of Elam Rowland McBroom (a country doctor) and Clara Curtis (a speech teacher). Married Esther Adams, Aug. 28, 1931. Three sons: Robert (born 1935), Paul (born 1936), William (born 1939).

Education: A.B., University of Illinois, 1932; graduate student, Southern Methodist University, 1950.

Career: Attorney and oil executive.
Attorney and oil executive, Fort Worth, Texas, 1934-73; now retired.

Member: American Bar Association; American Institute of Mining Engineers; American Petroleum Landmen.

MAURICE DRUON

Full Name: Maurice Samuel Roger Charles Druon.
Born April 23, 1918, at Paris, France. Married
Madeline Marignac, September 25, 1968. Education:
attended Lycée Michelet and Faculté des Lettres,
École des Science Politiques.

Career: Author and government official.
Author, 1945-DATE; Minister of Cultural Affairs,
France, 1973-DATE.

Agent: André Berheim, 55 avenue George V, Paris.

Awards:
Prix Goncourt, 1948, for *Les Grandes Familles*; Mon-
aco Literary Council Prize for his literary work, 1966;
Knight of the Legion of Honor.

Member:
French Academy; Societé des Gens de Lettres; Societé
des Auteurs et Compositeurs Dramatiques; Societé des
Auteurs, Compositeurs et Éditeurs de Musique; Savile
Club, London.

* * * * *

ALLEN DRURY

Full Name: Allen Stuart Drury.
Born September 2, 1918, at Houston, Texas. Son of
Alden Monteith Drury and Flora Allen.

Education: B.A., Stanford University, 1939.

Career: Journalist and writer.
Editor of several California newspapers, 1940-42;
U.S. Senate Staff, United Press International, 1943-
45; free-lance correspondent, 1946; National Editor,
Pathfinder, 1947-53; national staff, *Washington Evening
Star*, 1953-54; Senate Staff, *New York Times*, 1954-59;
Political Contributor, *Reader's Digest*, 1959-62; free-
lance writer and correspondent, 1962-DATE.

Awards:
Sigma Delta Chi Award for Editorial Writing, 1942;
Pulitzer Prize in Fiction, 1960, for *Advise and Con-
sent*; Litt.D., Rollins College, 1961.

Member:
National Press Club; Sigma Delta Chi; Alpha Kappa
Lambda; Cosmos Club and University Club, Washington;
Bohemian Club, San Francisco.

* * * * *

WILLIAM PÈNE du BOIS

Full Name: William Sherman Pène du Bois.
Born May 9, 1916, at Nutley, New Jersey. Son of
Guy Pène du Bois (an artist) and Florence Sherman.
Married Willa Kim (a theatrical designer), March 26,
1955.

Education: Attended Lycée Hoche, Versailles, 1924-
28, and Lycée de Nice, 1928-29.

Career: Author and illustrator.
Art Editor, *Paris Review*; full-time author & artist.

Agent: Ann Watkins, 77 Park Avenue, New York 10016.

Awards:
New York Herald Tribune Spring Book Prize, 1946, for
The Twenty-One Balloons; and 1955, for *Lion*; Newbery
Medal, 1946, for *The Twenty-One Balloons*.

* * * * *

LINDA DuBREUIL

Full Name: Elizabeth Lorinda DuBreuil.
Born October 20, 1924, at Le Roy, Illinois. Daughter
of Frank Hagen (a carpenter) and Eva May Emmons. Married her third husband, Frank DuBreuil, ?1960 (died
1974).

Education: Attended University of Cincinnati, 1940.

Career: Writer.
"Was a professional photographer and dancer in my
youth. I've had so many different occupations and
owned so many different businesses that I couldn't
possibly remember." Now a full-time writer. "Altogether, I've sold over 300 paperback books, about half
of which fall into the adult fiction category, or pornography, if you want to call it that. The rest of
my books have to do with occult themes mostly, although
I've sold some murder mysteries and many historical
novels. Right now I'm in the process of writing a
novel about the town where I live (French Lick, Indiana).
I've used thirty or so pennames, including L. J. Brown,
L. J. Browning, D. Berry Lindner, Catherine Marshall,
Seattle Frank, Ellen Evans, Emerald Evans, Carolyn Dragon, Eric Todd, S. C. Carewe, D. Royal, and Kate Cameron."

First Professional Sale: A story to *Mr. Magazine*,
1964.

Interests: Gourmet cooking, antique collecting.

DuBreuil writes:
"Mostly men write porn. This is probably because women are not supposed to know so much about sex, and
also because they're not considered good in the fanta-
cizing department (sexual). Most of the women porno-
graphers do two or three books at the most. A girl
named Betty has written about twenty, and another named
Suzy has done ten. I think I know most of the lady smut
writers, or at least know of them. Betty is an alcoho-
lic broad without much smarts. Suzy is a delightfully
beautiful girl with great talent, and a weakness for
no-good men. My weakness is my family. I think the
reason I'm such a successful writer of dirty books is
because of my masculine outlook on life. At least, my
personality has an aggressive drive, and the kind of
toughness usually associated with men. Also, I'm logical and reasonable, traits not usually considered feminine. I like people who are intelligent and open-minded. Those who converse about ideals and ideas instead
of petty personal problems. Idiot women bore me in
the same way they bore men; but I'm a skillful actress,
and the dumb-broad types don't know how they turn me
off any more than the dumb jocks do. My small, rather
fragile build, and delicate-looking face are a real
paradox to a lot of people, because I don't behave the
way my looks tell most people I should.
"I've done a number of fantasy and science fiction
books in the adult field, yes. *Getting It Together*
was about the need for a meat substitute, year 2010,
probably when the people sat around and talked about
how great it was back in the good old days when there
was real meat to eat. Two scientists went somewhere

LINDA DuBREUIL (cont.)

"in the tropics, and found a white flower that was an excellent substitute for meat, brought it back to the States, and grew it for mass consumption. While they were there, they experimented with a red flower, which proved to be an aphrodisiac. Naturally, the scientists enjoyed their find. One was young and handsome and horny, and the other older, about over the hill sexually, with a frigid wife.

"*Libido 23* had to do with a blue capsule two young scientists discovered in their attempt to find a substitute for marijuana. The capsules weren't a substitute for pot, but when they tried it out on their pig (who was named Mayor Daley), he became sexually aroused. These young men enjoyed a wide variety of unusual circumstances with their marvelous blue capsules (Libido 23). Both of these books were humorous.

"*Pandora Descending* was about a lovely young high school girl who loved to fantasize. She found out she was tuned in to the psychic world. Her lover decided to cash in on this bonanza. It didn't work.

"*Silver Bells and Cockle Shells* was a kind of gothic/science fiction/adult book. A girl answered an ad in the newspaper, and was given a job on a desert island where the gentleman grew exotic flowers. She went to work there, and found out the job included being his mistress. Worse, when he was tired of the girls, he put them on the assembly line. They were fed dog food in common feeding troughs, reacted to bells that ordered them to work, eat, or sleep, and underwent an operation that removed the part of their brains that governs reason.

"*Doctor Procter* was a hideous horror book about this mad doctor who killed the real scientist, and took over his identity. He then went about accomplishing his mission in life, which was to create the perfect woman. To do this, he had to transplant the brain of a dog (for faithfulness) into the head of a woman. Naturally, all the operations failed, but a few of the patients did live for a few days. That is, the test-cases that he kept trying to perfect until that Big Day when he would do the trip with his wife.

"*The Hat* was the story of a hat that had magical powers, and had lasted from shortly after the Civil War until present times.

"Aside from being a compulsive writer, I also believe a writer owes the reading public a reason for reading his book. It's also my belief that writers must use their talents in order to help make a better world. My erotic literature is not just meaningful from a sexual point-of-view. It pleases me to be able to get across my own philosophy through my characters. At one point, my editors wrote me many letters in which they ordered me to get off my soap box, but I kept on writing the way I felt I must, and they kept on buying them, and my books kept on selling. They don't ever tell me how to write anything anymore.

"Gothics bore me, so I put in a good bit of occult science when I write them. It was my good fortune to have been brought up by a woman of uncommon sense, who didn't care if I went to different churches from the more socially acceptable ones. Because of this, I received a good solid background in psychic lore. My mother also refused to censor what I read. The Whispering Hills Series, and the Holderly Hall Series, each consisting of six novels, both have a good bit of the occult.

"On the personal level, I'm rather conventional in spite of my past divorces (two), and the fact I write erotica. There is no similarity between my own behavior and that of any of my characters. Just as I'm not like the crazy ladies who go around committing murders in some of my novels. I resent it when men offer to help me out on my research with an accompanying leer, when people ask me unpolitely how I can know so much about so many areas of sex. Don't they ever wonder how I know so much about how it feels to be, for example, a male bent on murder? This kind of talk implies that I have a good imagination, and some writing talent, when it comes to crime fiction, but not sex books. Because I write erotica, people think I must be a real swinger.

"If I could have a perfect writing situation, it would be an office complete with food, restroom facilities, water, cigarettes, and coffee, all somehow built-in to office chair and typewriter. No telephone would ever ring, no voice would ever be heard. I would write without getting an ache in my shoulders, or requiring sleep. It would be possible for me to start a book and finish it without a single interruption. As it is, I often start and finish the first draft of a novel within ten days. Which explains why letters go unanswered, and why I sometimes answer the telephone and say, 'What grandson?' Sometimes I think I should have been a writer of stories and articles, but I've tried that, and like books much the best."

* * * * *

IVO DUKA

Full Name: Ivo Duka Duchacek.
  Born February 27, 1913, in Prostejov, Czechoslovakia. Son of Francis Duchacek and Irena Cermak. Married Helena Kolda, 1956. Two children: Ivo-Jan, Sylvia.

Education: JuDr., Masaryk University, 1935.

Career: Professor.
  With the Czechoslovakian Diplomatic Service in Paris and London, 1939-45; Member of Parliament, Prague, 1945-48; Visiting Lecturer, Yale University, 1949-51; Professor, City University of New York, 1949-DATE; Editor-in-Chief, U.S. Department of State and U.S. Information Agency, 1949-54.

Awards: Junior Book Award, Boys' Clubs of America.

Member:
  American Political Science Association; American Association of University Professors; Association for Asian Studies; Conference on Slavic and East European Studies; American Association for the Advancement of Slavic Studies.

* * * * *

MADELAINE DUKE

Full Name: Madelaine Elizabeth Duke.
  Born August 21, 1925, at Geneva, Switzerland. Daughter of Richard and Federica Duke (killed in a concentration camp at Minsk, 1942). Married Dr. Alexander Macfarlane, August, 1946.

Education: Attended University of St. Andrews, and University of Edinburgh; qualified in medicine and science.

Career: Writer. First Professional Sale: A short story published in 1945; first book: *Top Secret Mission*, Evans Bros., 1954.

MADELAINE DUKE (cont.)

Agent: Murray Pollinger, 11 Long Acre, London WC2E 9LH, England.

Awards: Book Society Choice, 1958, for *Azael and the Children*; Fellow, Huntington Hartford Foundation, 1962. Member: P.E.N.; Society of Authors.

Interests: Geology, silversmithing, world travel.
"Why are so few women involved in the science fiction field? I guess it's because few women, until recently, went for science degress at universities. Science is still largely a man's world and--traditionally--women aren't supposed to be interested in such subjects as physics, chemistry, and aeronautics. I don't think this situation will change within the next quarter century, despite women's lib. I am not a women's libber. I am a trained scientist, but I've never felt frustrated in a man's world. I'm now engaged in a series of medical science novels."

* * * * *

DAPHNE du MAURIER

Full Name: Daphne du Maurier.
Born May 13, 1907, in London, England. Daughter of Gerald du Maurier (an actor) and Muriel Beaumont. Married Sir Frederick Arthur Montague Browning (a Lt. General, and former treasurer to the Duke of Edinburgh) July 19, 1932 (died 1965). Three children: Tessa, Flavia, Christian.

Career: Writer, 1931-DATE. Agent: Curtis Brown Ltd., 60 E. 56th St., New York, NY 10022.

Awards: National Book Award, 1938, for *Rebecca*. Member: Bronte Society; Royal Society of Literature.

* * * * *

DAVID DUNCAN

Full Name: David Duncan.
Born February 17, 1913, at Billings, Montana. Son of Robert Llewellyn Duncan (a livestock broker) and Lela Davis. Married Elaine Sulliger (a teacher), May 5, 1940. Two children: Emily, Margaret.

Education: B.A., University of Montana, 1935.

Career: Writer.
Personnel Examiner, U.S. Department of Agriculture, Washington, 1936; Social Worker, California State Relief Administration, Fresno, 1936-40; free-lance writer in Mexico, 1940; Manager of housing project in California, U.S. Farm Security Administration, 1941-43; Field Director, in California and Nevada, American Red Cross, 1943-44; Labor Economist, National Labor Bureau, San Francisco, 1944-46; Free-lance writer, 1946-DATE.

Agent:
H. N. Swanson, Inc., 8523 Sunset Boulevard, Hollywood, California 90046.

Member:
Writers Guild of America, West.

Duncan wrote the screenplays of "Fantastic Voyage" and H. G. Wells' "The Time Machine."

LOIS DUNCAN

Full Name: Lois Duncan Arquette.
Born April 28, 1934, at Philadelphia, Pennsylvania. Daughter of Joseph Janney Steinmetz (a photographer) and Lois Foley (a photographer). Married Donald Wayne Arquette. Five children: Robin (born 1954), Kerry (born 1956), Brett (born 1960), Donald Wayne Jr. (born 1967), Katlyn (born 1970).

Education: Attended Duke University, 1952-53, and University of New Mexico, 1972-DATE.

Career: Writer, lecturer, photographer.
"I lecture at writers' conferences during the summer months. These include the conferences at Temple Buell College in Denver (where I was writer-in-residence), Cape Cod, St. Simon's Island, Southwest Writers Conference, Pacific Northwest, University of California, San Diego, and many others. I also lecture on writing at the University of New Mexico."

First Professional Sale: "P.S. We Are Fine," in *Calling All Girls*, ca. 1947.

Awards:
Zia Award; Seventeenth Summer Literary Award; two times runner-up for Mystery Writers of America Edgar Award; National Press Women Award; Winner, *Writers Digest* Creative Writing Contest; Dorothy Canfield Fisher Award; miscellaneous poetry awards in contests sponsored by the National Federation of State Poetry Societies.

Interests: Photography, travel, reading (of course), going to college, horseback riding, enjoying my family.

Duncan writes:
"I started writing professionally at 13, sold to national magazines all through my teen years, and published my first novel at 21. I've tried my hand at most areas of writing--magazine slick fiction, confessions, religious articles, humor, novels for adults and teens, mysteries, biography, a historical novel, romances, three books for pre-schoolers. My last three books have been fantasy/supernatural/ESP sorts of novels for teenagers--and at this point I am enjoying this challenge of making the impossible seem possible more than anything else I have done."

* * * * *

RONALD DUNCAN

Full Name: Ronald Frederick Henry Duncan.
Born August 6, 1914. Son of Reginald John Dunkelsbuhler and Ethel Cannon. Married Rose Marie Hansom. Two children: Briony, Roger Jeremy.

Education: M.A., Cambridge University, 1936.

Career: Poet and playwright. Member: English Stage Company; Garrick Club.

* * * * *

ALAN DUNN

Full Name: Alan Cantwell Dunn.
Born August 11, 1900, at Belmar, New Jersey. Son of George Warren Dunn (a lawyer) and Sarah Benton Brown. Married Mary Petty (an artist), December 8, 1927. Education: Attended various art schools here and abroad.

ALAN DUNN (cont.)

Career: Artist and writer.
Staff contributor, *New Yorker*, 1926-1974; Editorial Cartoonist, *Architectural Record*, 1936-1974; has exhibited paintings and cartoons throughout the world, and is represented in such museums as the Metropolitan Museum, New York. Died May 20, 1974.

Member: Authors Guild; Century Association; Phi Gamma Delta.

* * * * *

ROBERT DURAND

Full Name: Robert Durand.
Born August 10, 1944, at St. Louis, Missouri. Son of Robert Louis Durand (a physician) and Florence Snyder. One son, Christian James.

Education: B.A., University of Portland, 1966; M.A. San Francisco State College, 1969.

Career: Editor and writer.
Inventory Control Manager, Richard Abel & Co., Portland, 1967-71; Editor, Capra Press Chapbook Series, 1972-DATE; Publisher and editor of Yes! Press, 1970-72; Publisher and Editor, Pleiade Press, 1974-DATE; Poetry and Drama Book Buyer, Cody's Books, Berkeley, CA, 1973-74.

* * * * *

GERALD DURRELL

Full Name: Gerald Malcolm Durrell.
Born January 7, 1925, at Jamshedpur, India. Son of Lawrence Samuel Durrell (a civil engineer) and Louise Florence Dixie. Married Jacqueline Sonia Rasen, 1951. Durrell is the younger brother of novelist Lawrence Durrell.

Education: Educated by private tutors in France, Italy, Switzerland, and Greece.

Career: Zoologist.
Student Keeper, Whipsnade Zoological Park, England, 1945-46; Founder, Jersey Zoological Park, Channel Islands, 1958; leader and underwriter of zoological collecting expeditions to remote parts of Africa, South America, Australia, and Southeast Asia, 1946-DATE.

Awards: National Association of Independent Schools Award, 1956, for *Three Tickets to Adventure*.

Member:
Zoological Society of London (Fellow); Bombay Natural History Society; Nigerian Field Society; Fauna Preservation Society; British Ornothologists Union; Australian Mammal Society; Malayan Nature Society; American Zooparks Association, International Institute of Arts and Letters (Fellow).

Agent: Curtis Brown Ltd., 60 E. 56th St., New York, NY 10022.

Interests: Reading, photography, drawing, swimming. Speaks French, Greek, and some Spanish.

LAWRENCE DURRELL

Full Name: Lawrence George Durrell.
Born February 27, 1912, in Julundur, India. Son of Lawrence Samuel Durrell (a civil engineer) and Louise Florence Dixie. Married Nancy Myers, 1935 (divorced, 1947); married Yvette Cohen, 1947 (divorced); married Claude Marie Vineeden, March 27, 1961 (died 1967). Two children: Penelope Berengaria, Sappho-Jane.

Education: Attended College of St. Joseph, Darjiling India, and St. Edmund's College, Canterbury, England.

Career: Writer.
Has been a jazz pianist, automobile racer, composer, real estate agent, photographer; taught at the British Institute in Athens, 1940; Foreign Press Service Officer, British Information Office, Cairo, 1941-44; Press Attache, Alexandria, 1944-45; Public Relations Director, Dodecanese Island, Greece, 1946-47; Director of Institute, British Council in Cordoba, Argentina, 1947-48; Press Attache at British Legation, Belgrade, 1949-52; schoolteacher, 1951; teacher of English, then director of public relations for British government in Cyprus during the 1950s; moved to France and became full-time writer, 1957-DATE.

Awards:
Duff Cooper Memorial Prize, 1957, for *Bitter Lemons*; Prix du Meilleur Livre Étranger, 1959, for *Justine* and *Balthazar*.

* * * * *

GEORGE W. EARLEY

Full Name: George Whiteford Earley.
Born February 15, 1927, at Warrenton, Virginia. Son of Guy B. Earley and Carol B. Whiteford. Married Margaret Griffith, September 8, 1951. Four children: David (born 1952), Stephen (born 1957), Kathryn (born 1961), Christine (born 1969).

Education: B.S., Miami University (Ohio), 1951; M.A. Trinity College, 1973.

Career: Engineer and administrator.
Adjutant and Personnel Officer, U.S. Air Force, 1951-53; Technical Writer, Martin Aircraft, 1953-54; Aerospace Administrative Engineer, United Aircraft, 1954-71; Church business administrator, 1971-DATE.

First Professional Sale: "Moon Gun," in *Journal of the Interplanetary Exploration Society*, Dec. 1960.

Interests:
Fortean Research, specifically UFOs, mystery monsters, ancient astronauts, and pre-Columbian artifacts; backpacking; photography. "I have gradually come to feel that nonfiction is much more fascinating than fiction--too many real anomalies needing a solution. SF is now relegated to 'relaxation reading' when I need a few laughs."

Earley is a strong supporter of manned space exploration, having protested editorially the death of the Apollo program in *The Hartford Courant* (January 1, 1973). He wrote: "I would merely say that the recent Skylab experiments prove, to me at least, that men can make a Mars trip and that we should go there, and to hell with this joint US-USSR business!"

ANTHONY EARNSHAW

Full Name: Anthony Earnshaw.
   Born September 10, 1924, at Ilkley, Yorkshire, England. Son of Ernest Earnshaw and Dorothy Myers. Married Monica Simpson, 1957 (divorced, 1969). Two children: Ruth (born 1957), Frances (born 1959).

Education: "Somewhat limited; left school at the
   age of 14 years."

Career: Writer and lecturer.
   Worked for 26 years at various factories in and around Leeds, England; from 1966, a lecturer at the Bradford College of Art.

First Professional Sale: *Musrum*, Jonathan Cape,
   1968 (with Eric Thacker).

Earnshaw writes:
   "In the 1940s an interest in surrealism led me to take up painting. In recent years, I have exhibited work in various shows in Britain, e.g., C.E.M.A., Belfast, 1962 (prize winner), The Enchanted Domain, Exeter, 1967, Homage to Apollinaire, I.C.A., London, 1968.
   "My friendship with my co-author/co-illustrator Eric Thacker dates from 1942. In 1967, we wrote and drew and produced *Musrum* 'to keep ourselves amused.'
   "*Musrum* is not SF; the book can best be described as an 'astounding novel.' Reality contains every possible and every impossible thing. It is the role of SF, as with all imaginative art and literature, to explore and illuminate the frontiers of experience, and thereby pave the way for the fulfillment of desires.
   "'Mind can only triumph in its most perilous activities. No daring is fatal.'--Paul Eluard."

* * * * *

BRIAN EARNSHAW

Full Name: Brian Earnshaw.
   Born December 26, 1929, at Wrexham, Wales. Son of Eric Earnshaw and Annie Barker.

Education:
   B.A., Cambridge University, 1952; M.A., 1955; Certificate in Education, University of Bristol, 1957.

Career: School teacher.
   Teacher at various English schools, 1952-65; currently Teacher of Creative Writing, St. Paul's College, England.

Agent: Jonathan Clowes, 20 New Cavendish St., London
   WlA 3AH, England.

* * * * *

ROBERT EASSON

Full Name: Robert Watson Easson.
   Born April 10, 1941, at Aberdeen, Scotland. Son of Alexander Easson and Anne Watson. Education: Attended Washburn University.

Career: "Undecided."

Easson resides in Topeka, Kansas.

EVELYN EATON

Full Name: Evelyn Sybil Mary Eaton.
   Born December 22, 1902, at Montreux, Switzerland. Daughter of Daniel Isaac Vernon Eaton (a colonel in the Royal Canadian Horse Artillery) and Myra Randolph. Became a naturalized U.S. citizen, 1944. Married Ernst Paul Richard Viedt, October 28, 1928 (died 1942). One daughter, Theresa Neyana.

Education: Attended the Sorbonne, University of Paris, 1920-21.

Career: Poet and novelist.
   Free-lance writer, 1925-DATE; has also served as a war correspondent in Burma, 1945, and a lecturer at numerous colleges and universities.

Agent: McIntosh & Otis, 475 Fifth Avenue, New York,
   NY 10017.

Awards: John Masefield Award, 1923, for short lyrics
   later published in *Stolen Hours*.

Member:
   Authors Guild; P.E.N.; Poetry Society of America; Canadian Authors Association; International Platform Association; Pen and Brush Club; Poetry Society of Virginia.

* * * * *

EDWARD EDELSON

Full Name: Edward Edelson.
   Born September 19, 1932, at New York, New York. Son of Saul Edelson (a restaurateur) and Sarah Sunshine. Married Phyllis Kaplan, October 26, 1957. Three children: Noah, Daniel, Anne.

Education: B.S., New York University, 1953; graduate
   student, Columbia Universtiy, 1963-64.

Career: Editor and author.
   Telegraph Editor and City Editor, *Middletown Times-Herald Record*, 1959-62; Reporter and Science Editor, *New York World Telegram*, 1962-66; Science Editor, *New York World Journal Tribune*, 1966-67; Science Editor, WNDT-TV, New York, 1968-70; Senior Staff Writer, *Family Health*, 1968-71; Contributing Editor, 1971-DATE; Science Writer, *New York News*, 1971-DATE.

Awards:
   New York Citizens for Clean Air Award, 1966; Writing Award Certificate of Merit, American Medical Association, 1970; Science Writing Award, American Dental Association, 1970. Member: National Association of Science Writers.

* * * * *

KEN EDGAR

Full Name: Ken Edgar.
   Born May 23, 1925. Son of Frank O. Edgar (a businessman) and Eileen Davis. Married Aggie Sechler. Two sons: Mark, Mike.

Education: B.A., Pennsylvania State University, 1947;
   M.A. and Ph.D., University of Pittsburgh.

KEN EDGAR (cont.)

Career: Professor of Psychology.
  Director of Counseling Center, Slippery Rock State
College, Pennsylvania, 1961-66; Professor of Psycho-
gy, Indiana University, 1966-DATE; clinical psychologist at Indiana County Guidance Center (part-time),
1966-71. Member: American Psychological Association.

Agent: Alex Jackinson Agency, 55 W. 42nd St., New
  York, NY 10036.

* * * * *

G. C. EDMONDSON

Full Name: José Mario Garry Ordoñez Edmondson y
  Cotton. Born October 11, 1922, either in Washington
State or Rascuachitlán, Tabasco, Mexico. Son of
William J. Edmondson and Edith Cotton. Thrice mar-
ried. Four children, two sons and two daughters, all
grown.

Education: "Percussion University." Cited by some
  authorities as having an M.D. from an Austrian
  school.

Career: Writer; "blacksmith."
  One of the few remaining practicing blacksmiths in
the U.S.; free-lance writer.

First Professional Sale:
  Either a short story to McCall's, 1954?; or "Bles-
sed Are the Meek," in Astounding Science Fiction,
September, 1955.

Agent: Robert P. Mills Ltd., 156 E. 52nd St., New
  York, NY 10022.

Interests: "Addicted to eating, drinking, breathing."

Edmondson is reticent about much of his life and
career. When questioned about his writing, he had
this to say:

"I only do it for money. The way to create a believable alien is, quite simply, to extrapolate from
the problems in communication between two human cultures. Once a thorough knowledge of a new language
has been achieved, then one must spend years acquiring all the semantic and cultural background. Often
one discovers only years later that what was intended
as a compliment came out as a not too deft insult."

Regarding his career, he said:
"I shod Pancho Villa's horse. At the time, the
horse was doing what they usually do when one lifts
the off-hind foot. And on that particular day, the
horse had diarrhea.
"I became addicted to eating one morning when I
was 14 years old, and made the novel discovery that
oatmeal and breakfast were not synonyms. Just after
the Japanese war I spent some time in Los Angeles,
and am still trying to catch up on the breathing I
missed there.
"During the same war, I revolutionized science
with the discovery that flies spread disease. I won
the good conduct medal by keeping mine buttoned.
"My parent's names were Pop and Mom.
"My eldest daughter, named after a first century
BC Roman reformer, has just produced a child named

"in highly original fashion from Old Testament sources.
In English, her name is 'bee.'
"#1 boy is named after a famous loser in the Trojan
campaign; he spent some time losing another war in
Vietnam.
"#2 boy bears the name of one of history's famous
bastards.
"#2 girl was immortalized by the late Chas. Lutwidge
Dodgson.
"My spouse was done the same honor by Georges Bizet.
"There is a tiny verse about my natal village, Villa
Hermosa de Rascuachitlán, which might be helpful in
visualizing the terrain:

> Un pinche petate fué mi cuna
> en tristes pañales me envolvieron.
> Tan rechingada fué mi fortuna
> que pura verga a mamar me dieron.

Though he's eager to disclaim it, I believe the author
was Antonio Plazas.
"If you ever get to San Diego, and run into a handsome, extremely virile type with large amounts of char-
isma, rest assured, it isn't me."

* * * * *

GEO. ALEC EFFINGER

Full Name: George Alec Effinger.
  Born January 10, 1947, at Cleveland, Ohio. Son of
George Paul Effinger and Ruth Uray. Married Diana
Smith (a program analyst), November 15, 1969.

Education: Attended Yale University, 1965, 1969;
  and New York University, 1968.

Career: Writer.
  Writer, Marvel Comic Books, 1971-DATE; free-lance
author. Member: Science Fiction Writers of America.

Agent: Virginia Kidd, Box 278, Milford, PA 18337.

* * * * *

IVAN EFREMOV

Full Name: Ivan Antonovich Efremov [spelled variously, Yefremov]. Born April 22, 1907, at Vyretsa,
Tsarskosel'skogo (now Peterburgskoi) Province, Russia.
Son of Anton Kharitonovich Efremov and Varvara Alek-
sandrovna Anan'eva. Married Taisiia Iosifovna IUkh-
nevskaia. One son, Allan Ivanovich (born 1936).

Education:
  Attended Leningrad State University, 1924-27, and
Leningrad Mining Institute, 1932-35; Candidate of
Geological Science, 1935; Doctor of Biological Science,
1940.

Career: Paleontologist and geologist.
  Unskilled laborer (driver), on the farm Krasnaia
Bovariia, Petrograd, 1921-23; sailor on the Pacific
Ocean and Caspian Sea, 1923-25; laboratory assistant,
Geological Museum, Leningrad, 1925-27; Professor of
Paleontology, and Director, Laboratory of Lowest
Vertebrates, Paleontological Institute, Academy of
Science, USSR, 1941-72; also worked as a geologist for
Lenzoloto in Eastern Siberia, Yakut, Middle Asia, Altai,
and Ural. Died October 5, 1972.

IVAN EFREMOV (cont.)

Awards:
State Prize, USSR, 1952, for *Tofonomiia i Geologich-eskaia Letopis' Zemli*; First Prize, Ministry of Education, 1959, for *Tumannost' Andromedy* (published in English as *Andromeda*).

Member:
Royal Linnaean Society, England; Geographical Society, United States; P.E.N.

Agent:
Vsesojuznoje Agentstvo po Avtorskim Pravam (VAAP), K-104, B. Bronnaja, 6a, 103104 Moskva, USSR.

* * * * *

CLIVE EGLETON

Full Name: Clive Frederick Egleton.
Born November 25, 1927, at South Harrow, Middlesex, England. Married Joan Evelyn Lane, April 9, 1949. Two sons: Charles (born 1953), Richard (born 1958).

Education: Attended Haberdashers' Aske's, 1938-44.

Career: British Army Officer.
Lt. Colonel, Staffordshire Regiment, British Army; free-lance writer.

First Professional Sale: *A Piece of Resistance*, Hodder & Stoughton, 1970.

Agent: Paul Reynolds, 599 Fifth Avenue, New York, NY 10017.

Interests: Politics.

* * * * *

MAX EHRLICH

Full Name: Max Simon Ehrlich.
Born October 10, 1909, at Springfield, Massachusetts. Son of Simon Ehrlich and Sarah Siegel. Married Doris Rubinstein, 1940. Two children: Amy, Jane.

Education: B.A., University of Michigan.

Career: Author. Member: Authors Guild; Authors League of America; Writers Guild of America.

Agent: Annie Laurie Williams, 18 E. 41st St., New York, NY 10017.

* * * * *

HENRY M. EICHNER

Full Name: Henry M. Eichner.
Born 1909, at Cleveland, Ohio. Married Gertrude Eichner. One daughter, Barbara.

Career: Medical artist. Died November 24, 1971.

Awards: Tenth Annual Ann Radcliffe Award for Literature, Count Dracula Society. Member: Count Dracula Society. The Henry M. Eichner Medal for Service is now presented annually by the Count Dracula Society.

CHARLES EINSTEIN

Full Name: Charles Einstein.
Born August 2, 1926, at Boston, Massachusetts. Son of Harry and Lillian Einstein. Married and divorced. One daughter, three sons.

Education: Ph.B., University of Chicago.

Career: Writer. Member: Authors League; Writers Guild of America.

First Professional Sale: "Tunnel 1971," in *Saturn*, May, 1957.

* * * * *

LARRY EISENBERG

Full Name: Lawrence Eisenberg.
Born December 21, 1919, at New York, New York. Son of Sidney Eisenberg (a furniture salesman) and Yetta Yellen. Married Frances Brenner, October 27, 1950. Two children: Beth Lee (born 1954), Michael Allen (born 1956).

Education:
B.S., City College of New York, 1940; B.E.E., 1944; Ph.D., Polytechnic Institute of Brooklyn, 1966.

Career: Electronic engineer.
Co-head, Electronic and Computer Laboratories, Rockefeller University, 1958-DATE.

First Professional Sale: "The Mynah Matter," in *Fantastic Stories*, August, 1962 (as Lawrence Eisenberg).

Member: Science Fiction Writers of America; Authors Guild.

Interests:
Classical Music, opera, theatre, reading. "I enjoy wedding humor with science fiction, particularly where some unsavory aspect of our society can be pricked."

* * * * *

GORDON EKLUND

Full Name: Gordon Stewart Eklund.
Born July 24, 1945, at Seattle, Washington. Son of Alfred J. Eklund (a dental technician) and DeLois Stewart. Married Dianna Mylarski, March, 1969. One son, Jeremy Clark (born 1969).

Education: Attended Contra Costa College, 1973-74.

Career: Writer, 1968-DATE. Member: Science Fiction Writers of America; Lilapa. First Professional Sale: "Dear Aunt Annie," in *Fantastic Stories*, April, 1970.

* * * * *

RICHARD M. ELAM

Full Name: Richard Mace Elam, Jr.
Born July 16, 1920, at Richmond, Virginia. Son of Richard Mace Elam (an accountant) and Louise S. Elam.

Education: Studied at Arizona State University.

RICHARD M. ELAM (cont.)

Career: Corporation executive.
Started as a bank teller at age seventeen; later became a show card writer and photographer; Secretary-Treasurer, Precision Silkscreen, Inc., Dallas, 1970-DATE.

* * * * *

MICHAEL ELDER

Full Name: Michael Aiken Elder.
Born April 30, 1931, at London, England. Son of Howard Hugh Elder (a medical practicioner) and Marjorie Eileen Adams. Married Sheila Mary Donald (an actress), April 2, 1953. Two sons: Simon Donald (born 1955), David John (born 1958).

Education: Diploma, Royal Academy of Dramatic Art, 1951.

Career: Actor.
Actor, having appeared with every Scottish repertory theatre, and in over 1000 radio broadcasts, 1951-DATE; Elder has also appeared frequently on British television; Director, Edinburgh Film Festival, 1961-63.

First Professional Sale: *The Affair at Invergarroch*, A. & C. Black, 1951.

Member: Science Fiction Writers of America.

Interests: Philately, ornithology, Scottish history.

* * * * *

PAUL ELDRIDGE

Full Name: Paul Eldridge.
Born May 5, 1888, at Philadelphia, Pennsylvania. Son of Leon Eldridge and Jeanette Lefleur. Married Sylvette De Lamar (a writer).

Education:
B.S., Temple University, 1909; M.A., University of Pennsylvania, 1911; Docteur de l'Université, University of Paris, 1913.

Career: Writer and teacher.
High school teacher of romance languages in New York, 1914-45; free-lance writer, 1911-DATE.

Member: Authors League; Dramatists League.

* * * * *

SUZETTE HADEN ELGIN

Full Name: Suzette Haden Elgin.
Born November 18, 1936, at Louisiana, Missouri. Daughter of Gaylord Wilkins (a lawyer) and Hazel Lewis (a teacher). Married Peter Haden (deceased); married George Elgin. Four children: Michael Haden (born 1956), Rebecca Haden (born 1958), Patricia Haden (born 1961), Benjamin Elgin (born 1966).

Education: B.A., Chico State College, 1968; M.A., University of California, San Diego, 1970; Ph.D., 1973.

Career: Professor of Linguistics.
Assistant Professor, Dept. of Linguistics, San Diego State University, 1972-DATE.

First Professional Sale: "For the Sake of Grace," in *The Magazine of Fantasy and Science Fiction*, May, 1969.

Agent: James Byron, Hollywood, CA.

Awards:
Academy of American Poets Award, University of Chicago, 1956; Sexton Fellowship (now Harper's) in Poetry, 1957-58.

Member: Linguistic Society of America; Science Fiction Writers of America. Interests: Guitar; singing.

* * * * *

GEORGE ELLIOTT

Full Name: George Paul Elliott.
Born June 16, 1918, at Knightstown, Indiana. Son of Paul Revere Elliott and Nita Gregory. Married Mary Emma Jeffress (editor of *Hudson Review*), Jan. 18, 1941. One daughter, Nora Catherine.

Education: A.B., University of California, Berkeley, 1939; M.A., 1941.

Career: Professor of English.
Asst. Professor of English, St. Mary's College, Cal., 1947-55; Asst. Professor of English, Cornell University, 1955-56; Asst. Professor, Barnard College, 1957-60; Lecturer, Writers Workshop, University of Iowa, 1960-61, at University of California, Berkeley, 1962, and at St. Mary's College, 1962-63; Professor of English, Syracuse University, 1963-DATE.

Awards:
Hudson Review Fellowship in Fiction, 1956-57; Guggenheim Fellowship, 1961-62; Indiana Authors' Day Award, 1962, for *Among the Dangs*; D. H. Lawrence Fellowship, University of New Mexico, 1962; Ford Foundation Fellowship, 1965-66. Member: P.E.N.; American Association of University Professors.

* * * * *

HARLAN ELLISON

Full Name: Harlan Jay Ellison.
Born May 27, 1934, at Cleveland, Ohio. Son of Louis Laverne Ellison (a dentist and jeweler) and Serita Rosenthal. Married Charlotte B. Stein, February 19, 1956 (divorced, 1960); married Billie Joyce Sanders, November 13, 1960 (divorced, 1963); married Lory Pastick Patrick, January 30, 1966 (divorced, 1966); married Lori Horowitz, June 5, 1976.

Education: Attended Ohio State University, 1953-54.

Career: Writer.
Free-lance author, 1954-DATE; Ellison's credits include short stories, articles, numerous teleplays, screenplays, editing anthologies, etc.; Editor, *Rogue Magazine*, 1959-60; Founder and Editor, Regency Books, 1961-62; Editor, *Dangerous Visions*; *Again, Dangerous Visions*; and *The Last Dangerous Visions*; author, "The Glass Teat," a series of weekly columns in the *Los Angeles Free Press* on television (collected in *The*

HARLAN ELLISON (cont.)

Glass Teat and *The Other Glass Teat*; Editor, Pyramid Books Harlan Ellison Discovery Series, 1975-DATE.

First Professional Sale:
  "My *first* sale (I was paid with tickets to a Cleveland Indians game) was a five-part serial titled, "The Sword of Parmegon," to the "Rangers," a kiddie column of the now-defunct *Cleveland News*, 1947, when I was 13 years old. Second sale, another serial to the same newspaper (payment in World Series tickets), titled "Trail of the Gloconda." Both were heroic fantasy. Third sale was to Wm. Gaines's EC magazine, *Weird Science-Fantasy*, June, 1954, the script of a story which appeared as "Upheaval," illustrated by Al Williamson (I subsequently sold this story to *Imagination* in the middle fifties under its original title, "Mealtime"). The fourth sale was a cartoon to *Imagination*, July, 1952." Ellison's first full-length story for which he was paid was "I Ran With a Kid Gang!" in *Lowdown*, October, 1955.

Agent: Robert P. Mills Ltd., 156 E. 52nd Street, New York, NY 10022.

Awards:
  Nebula Award, Best Short Story, 1965 (1966), "'Repent, Harlequin!' Said the Ticktockman"; Nebula Award, Best Novella, 1969 (1970), "A Boy and His Dog"; Jupiter Award, Best Novelette, 1973 (1974), "The Deathbird"; Hugo Award, Best Short Fiction, 1965 (1966), "'Repent, Harlequin!' Said the Ticktockman"; Hugo Award, Best Short Story, 1967 (1968), "I Have No Mouth, and I Must Scream"; Hugo Award, Best Dramatic Presentation, 1967 (1968), "City at the Edge of Forever" (*Star Trek*); Special Plaque, 26th World Science Fiction Convention (Baycon), 1968, for *Dangerous Visions* (anthology); Hugo Award, Best Short Story, 1968 (1969), "The Beast That Shouted Love at the Heart of the World"; Special Plaque, 30th World Science Fiction Convention (L.A.Con), 1972, for *Again, Dangerous Visions* (anthology); Hugo Award, Best Novelette, 1973 (1974), "The Deathbird"; Hugo Award, Best Novelette, 1974 (1975), "Adrift Just Off the Islets of Langerhans"; Hugo Award, Best Dramatic Presentation, 1975 (1976), "A Boy and His Dog"; Edgar Award, Best Mystery Story, 1973 (1974), "The Whimper of Whipped Dogs"; Writers Guild of America Award, Best Anthology Script, 1964-65 Season, "Demon with a Glass Hand" (*The Outer Limits*); Writers Guild of America Award, Best Dramatic-Episodic Script, 1966-67 Season, "The City on the Edge of Forever" (*Star Trek*); Writers Guild of America Award, Best Dramatic-Episodic Script, 1973-74 Season, "Phoenix Without Ashes" (pilot for *The Starlost*, but never shown as written); selected by *Cosmopolitan* as one of the four most eligible bachelors in Hollywood, 1967; Certificate of Honor, XIII International Film Festival of Fantasy, Trieste, 1970, for "Demon with a Glass Hand"; Nova Award, 1968.

Member:
  Science Fiction Writers of America (Vice-President, 1965-66); Writers Guild of America, West (past Member, Board of Directors).

Ellison writes:
  "Why do I write? Over the years, I find my responses to that question have been pretty uniform. From time to time, I grow more or less analytical about it (depending on the pompousness of the interviewer), but the most truthful answer, the most honest answer, is quite simply that I simply *do it*. I can

"do no other. I feel unfulfilled when I'm not working, and, with what I take to be my share of 2000 years retroactive guilt (as a proud and card-carrying Jew), I feel as if I'm wasting time. I genuinely *enjoy* writing. It is a hobby, a craft, a solace, an ego-trip, the centerpost of my existence. Writing for me is what having a son and heir is to most other people. My secret desire is that my stories will live on long after I've been planted. But when people ask me why do I write, I usually answer with this story: in the film *The Red Shoes*, a Diaghilev-style ballet empresario, trying to establish the degree of commitment to the grueling art of an aspiring young ballerina, says to the young woman, "Why do you dance?" She thinks on it for a long moment, then smiles and replies, "Why do you breathe?" The *balletomane* seems amused for an instant, then shrugs and says with obviousness, "Because I must." The ballerina gives him a loving smile of triumph far beyond her years, and walks away. That is my answer."

* * * * *

GRACIA FAY ELLWOOD

Full Name: Gracia Fay Ellwood.
  Born July 17, 1938, at Lynden, Washington. Daughter of George Lambert Bouwman and Alice Martha Kok. Married Robert Scott Ellwood Jr., August 28, 1965. One son, Richard Scott (born 1974).

Education: A.B., Calvin College, 1961; M.A., University of Chicago Divinity School, 1964.

Career: Writer.
  Instructor in English, Evansville College, 1964-66; Associate Editor, *Mythlore*, 1974-DATE.

First Professional Sale: "The Soal-Cooper-Davis Communal 'I'", in *International Journal of Parapsychology*, Winter, 1968.

Member: Mythopoeic Society (Member, Board of Advisers).

Interests: Music, parapsychology; suicide prevention volunteer.

* * * * *

ROGER ELWOOD

Full Name: Roger Elwood.
  Born January 13, 1943, at Atlantic City, New Jersey. Son of Raymond C. Elwood (an accountant) and Dorothy F. Elwood. Education: Attended high school in N.J.

Career: Writer and editor, 1965-DATE.

* * * * *

GUY ENDORE

Full Name: Samuel Guy Endore.
  Born July 4, 1900, at New York, New York. Married Henrietta Portugal, 1927. Two children: Marcia, Gita. Education: A.B., Columbia University, 1923; M.A., 1925.

Career: Writer and novelist. Died 1970. Member: Academy of Motion Pictures; Screen Writers Guild; Authors League of America.

DICK ENEY

Full Name: Richard Harris Eney.
   Born September 13, 1937, at New London, Connecticut. Son of Harry E. Eney (a naval officer) and Dora F. Harris (a nurse).

Education: M.A., George Washington University, 1964.

Career: Evaluation Officer.
   Project/Program Management, Agency for International Development, 1964-DATE (currently an evaluation officer).

First Professional Sale: "Mix a Little Magic," to John Brunner.

Agent: Sr. E. Lindsay, 6 Langley Avenue, Surbiton, Surrey, England.

Interests:
   "Amateur journalism, photography, futurology. At various times, I've worked as a college teacher (sociology), a medical laboratory technician, and a wardmaster in a MASH hospital. I also worked in or on Vietnam for seven years, got refused security clearance by NSA due to my SF affiliations, funded a covert intelligence-gathering operation, was denounced by right-wingers as a Marxist, and by left-wingers as an Imperialist, got on the spit list of an influential religious group, encouraged the Union movement, debunked some propaganda, and shuffled a ridiculous quantity of papers, with what effect on the total of human happiness I still can't say."

* * * * *

HUGH ENFIELD

Full Name: Fielden Hughes.
   Attended University of Southampton, 1919-21; obtained a Teaching Certificate, Ministry of Education, London.

Career: Teacher.
   Headmaster at various English schools, 1921-63; has been a lecturer in education at College of St. Mark and St. John, a member of the Advisory Council, Educational Television, a regular broadcaster on BBC for ten years on English language and literature, and a special correspondent for the *London Daily Express* in education; currently a consultant to P & O Shipping Line in education and public relations.

First Professional Sale: *The Splendid Eli*, Chapman and Hall, 1943.

Agent: London Management, 235-241 Regent St., London, W.1, England.

Member: Institute of Directors; Savage Club.

* * * * *

SYLVIA LOUISE ENGDAHL

Full Name: Sylvia Louise Engdahl.
   Born November 24, 1933, at Los Angeles, California. Daughter of Amandus J. Engdahl and Mildred Allen Butler. Education: A.B., University of California, Santa Barbara, 1955.

Career: Writer.
   Elementary school teacher near Portland, Oregon, 1955-56; Computer Programmer, then Computer Systems Specialist, working on the SAGE Air Defense System, 1957-67; full-time writer, 1967-DATE.

First Professional Sale: *Enchantress from the Stars*, Atheneum, 1970.

Awards: Newbery Honor Book Award, 1971, for *Enchantress from the Stars*; Christopher Award, 1973, for *This Star Shall Abide*.

Interests: Collecting commemorative stamps and medals pertaining to space exploration.

Engdahl writes:
   "Though my novels have been published as young people's books, and are enjoyed by children of advanced reading ability, they are directed more specifically to older adolescents and young adults. Also, they are directed to a general audience rather than to readers with background in science fiction, and are intended to appeal to people without such background as well as to fans. I believe that today's young people are seriously concerned about questions of man's place in the universe; my aim is to bring these questions into perspective through speculation about the future as related to the past, with particular emphasis on space exploration, which I consider of vital importance to human progress.
   "Almost all the distinctions between modern novels for teenagers and adult novels arise from the structure of the publishing business. Hardbound novels for young people are sold almost exclusively to libraries; little or no attempt is made to market them to the general public. The field is thus less subject to the dictates of fashion than the adult market, and somewhat more emphasis is placed on the enduring quality of a book, since librarians won't buy books that can't be expected to be of continuing interest. Many authors, like myself, have chosen to direct our books to young people because at present there is no adult market for the type of novels we wish to write. The books appearing as "young adult" today would have been issued as adult ten or fifteen years ago--I'm speaking in general terms, not specifically of science fiction-- and many adults prefer them to the more sensational types of material the adult market now demands. There are few if any taboos left in the junior book field. The only limitations on an author, apart from the use of adolescent protagonists, are those imposed by good taste, plus the fact that one cannot put in quite as much abstract discussion of philosophical issues as one would if writing for adults exclusively."

* * * * *

ELOISE ENGLE

Full Name: Eloise Engle.
   Born April 12, 1923, at Seattle, Washington. Daughter of Floyd C. Hopper and Lois Best. Married Paul Raymond Engle, 1943. Three children: Paula, David, Margaret. Education: Attended George Washington University, 1944-47.

Career: Writer.
   Various clerical positions, 1940-48; now a full-time author. Member: Authors League; Air Force Association; U.S. Naval Institute; Aviation/Space Writers Assoc.

SUSAN ERTZ

Full Name; Susan Ertz.
Born in Walton-on-Thames, Surrey, England. Daughter of Charles Edward Ertz and Mary Leviness. Married John Ronald McCrindle (a British Army officer), 1932.

Career: Novelist, 1922-DATE.
Has also been a lecturer on country-wide tour in the United States, 1937. Member: Royal Society of Literature (Fellow); P.E.N.; Authors Society.

Agent: Brandt & Brandt, 101 Park Avenue, New York, NY 10017.

* * * * *

GABE ESSOE

Full Name: Gabor Attila Essoe.
Born August 16, 1944, at Budapest, Hungary. Son of Ira Essoe (production control supervisor) and Gabriella Nagy (a piano teacher). Married Donna Hyatt, Sept. 3, 1967 (divorced); married Kelley Frances Miles (an actress), February 14, 1974.

Education: B.A., University of California, Los Angeles, 1966; graduate study at UCLA and Loyola Univ.

Career: Screen writer.
Shoe salesman, 1959-66; errand boy and Publicist Trainee, MGM, 1964-66; Publicist, Walt Disney Productions, 1967-73; Staff Writer, 1973-74; free-lance screen writer, 1974-DATE; was a frequent contributor to *Los Angeles Times*, 1967-72.

First Professional Sale: "Gable Cult Flexes Its Muscles," in *Los Angeles Times Calendar*, June, 1967.

Member: Writers Guild of America, West.

Interests: Painting, collecting comic books, plants, woodworking, guitar.

Essoe notes:
"I've contributed to dozens of major publications, including *TV Guide*, *Adam*, *Films in Review*, etc. I've also written scripts for Mickey Mouse and Donald Duck comic books. One of my longest ambitions has been to write and draw children's books, an ambition I will soon actualize, with a book called *Pepper, the Magic Cat*."

* * * * *

ELEANOR ESTES

Full Name: Eleanor Estes.
Born May 9, 1906, at West Haven, Connecticut. Daughter of Louis Rosenfeld and Caroline Gewecke. Married Rice Estes, December 8, 1932. One daughter: Helena.

Education:
Attended Pratt Institute Library School, 1931-32.

Career: Librarian and writer.
Children's Librarian, 1924-40; writer, 1940-DATE.

Awards: *New York Herald-Tribune* Spring Book Festival Award, 1951, Newbery Medal, 1952, for *Ginger Pye*.

ELAINE EVAIN

Full Name: Elaine Evain.
Born January 14, 1931, at Indianapolis, Indiana. Daughter of James Orville Newell (a purchasing agent) and Winifred Whitehead. Married Jean André Evain, September 14, 1957. Four children: Peggy Ann, Leslye Carole, Michael Gerard, Eric James.

Education: Attended Butler University.

Career: Writer, 1971-DATE.
Dancer with USO, 1945-47; has also travelled with a road company, and appeared in little theatre and summer stock. Member: Authors Guild; Authors League.

* * * * *

BILL EVANS

Full Name: William Harrington Evans.
Born February 26, 1921, at Salem, Oregon. Son of William D. Evans (a salesman) and Sibyl Harrington. Married Buddie Jacoby, April 2, 1965. Two step-children: Toni, Peggy Rae.

Education: B.A., Willamette University, 1942; Ph.D., Oregon State College, 1947.

Career: Chemist.
Thermochemist, National Bureau of Standards, Washington, DC, 1947-DATE.

First Professional Sale: *Selected Values of Chemical Thermodynamic Properties*, Government Printing Office, 1952.

Member:
American Chemical Society; American Physical Society; Fantasy Amateur Press Association (has been President, Vice-President, Secretary/Treasurer); served on the organizing committees of Discon I and Discon II.

Interests: Philately, numismatics, collecting detective stories, collecting prints.

* * * * *

CHRISTOPHER EVANS

Full Name: Christopher Riche Evans.
Born May 29, 1931, at Aberdovey, Merionethshire, Wales. Son of Herbert Riche Evans (a civil engineer) and Kathleen Gorst. Married Nancy Jane Fulmer, August 18, 1963. Two children: Victoria Amelia (born 1966), Christopher Samuel (born 1968).

Education: B.A., University College, London, 1960; Ph.D., University of Reading, 1963.

Career: Research Psychologist.
Head, Man-Computer Interaction Section, Computer Science Division, National Physical Laboratory, England, 1963-DATE.

Agent: Patrick Seale & Associates, 2 Motcomb St., London SW1X 8JU, England.

Member: British Psychological Society; Ergonomics Research Society; British Association of Behavioural Psychology; Brain Research Association.

CHRISTOPHER EVANS (cont.)

Interests: Flying light aircraft, lecturing, making TV and radio programmes.

Evans writes:
"I think science fiction passed out of its golden age in the 1950s, and while I think the SF of the type promoted by Moorcock in the mid-sixties version of *New Worlds* was very innovative, I think it was more symptomatic of the realisation that mainstream SF had shot its bolt rather than anything else. For what it's worth, I agree absolutely with Jim Ballard, who's been a close friend of mine for some years, that SF really needs to make the kind of adventurous excursions into psychology that the old SF did into technology a quarter of a century ago. It's for this reason that I consider *The Drowned World*, which very subtly blends technology-type SF with psychology-type SF, as being one of the really significant books of this genre."

* * * * *

I. O. EVANS

Full Name: Idrisyn Oliver Evans.
Born November 11, 1894, at Bloemfontein, Orange Free State, South Africa. Son of Harry Evans (a stationer) and Sarah Winifred Sutton (a state registered nurse). Married Marie Elizabeth Mumford, March 6, 1937.

Education: Attended Brynmill Council School, and Swansea Grammar School, both in Glamorganshire.

Career: British civil servant, author.
Executive Officer, Ministry of Public Buildings and Works, England, 1913-56; Editor, Fitzroy Edition of the works of Jules Verne for Arco Publications, London, 1956-66. Died February 13, 1977.

First Professional Sale: *Woodcraft and World Service*, Noel Douglas, 1930.

Member:
Royal Geographical Society (Fellow); Heraldic Society; Society of Civil Service Authors (Founder); British Science Fiction Association; Geologists' Association; Société Jules Verne.

Interests:
"Until my health failed, I was a keen hiker, and a field geologist; general writer on a variety of nonfiction topics, with special interest in geology and flags."

Evans talks about science fiction:
"I became a science fiction addict in my boyhood, through reading Jules Verne's *Journey to the Centre of the Earth*, which I re-read many times (and enjoyed re-translating for the Fitzroy edition). From Verne, I progressed to Wells and then to contemporary SF authors, and I became deeply interested in the early development of this age-old art form. Around 1950, I wrote a critical biography of H. G. Wells, whom I had been in touch with, and who very kindly allowed me to write a Junior Edition of his magnificent *Outline of History*. The publisher to whom I submitted it, Sidgwick & Jackson, said that it didn't interest them, but suggested something along the same lines

"on Jules Verne. The result was *Jules Verne: Master of Science Fiction*, which led to my being invited to compile the Fitzroy Edition.
"Denis Archer, the enterprising little house which published *The Junior Outline of History*, invited me to compile a book on possible future inventions, which was published in 1933 as *The World of Tomorrow*. Shortly thereafter, the house went out of business, but it did lead me to give some lectures. I became what Wells' character Kipps called 'a Nauthor,' simply because there was 'ink in my veins,' and even in my schooldays it started to unclot. I wrote on a wide variety of subjects, including popularisations of geology and other branches of science for adults and young people. On the whole, my work has not been particularly remunerative, but I'm not writing for money--not, needless to say, that I have any objections to earning something to eke out our somewhat exiguous pensions!
"Nor do I write merely as a 'hobby.' I take my work very seriously, apart from a few occasional light trifles. My aim is to give modern readers, especially young readers, material that may be helpful in trying to counteract, in however small a degree, the evil tendencies of modern times. If this sounds priggish, I don't care--it's me, and I'm not ashamed of it.
"I think Jules Verne will be regarded, as long as SF lasts, as one of its pioneers and masters; and as long as French is read, he will be regarded as a great figure among the authors and men of genius which France has given to the world."

* * * * *

ROBLEY EVANS

Full Name: Robley J. Evans.
Born November 28, 1933, at Portland, Oregon. Son of Robley Evans (a publisher) and Inez Lacey. Married and divorced. One daughter, Jennifer (born 1965).

Education: B.A., Reed College, 1956; M.A., Ph.D. (1964), University of Washington.

Career: Professor of English.
Professor of English, Connecticut College, 1964-DATE. Asst. Editor, *Poetry Northwest*, 1961-63.

First Professional Sale: *J. R. R. Tolkien*, Warner Books, 1972.

Interests: Writing poetry, travelling, birds, antiques, cooking.

Robley Evans comments on Tolkien:
"I'd say Tolkien is still popular because he writes very well, he really makes us *believe* in his imaginary world; and therefore, we care about what happens to his fantastic characters, as we do with characters created by the greatest novelists. I think we also see a very positive affirmation of life and action that seems impossible in our own lives. And so I have to add that I do *not* think his popularity will fade. But *that* only time can prove or contradict."

* * * * *

WILLIAM K. EVERSON

Full Name: William Keith Everson.
Born April 8, 1929, at Yeovil, Somerset, England. Son of Percival Wilfred Everson and Catherine Ward. Married 1958; one daughter, Bambi Elizabeth.

WILLIAM K. EVERSON (cont.)

Career: Writer, editor, film producer.
  Publicity Director, Renown Pictures, London, 1944-47; Publicist and Theatre Manager, Monseigneur News Theatres, London, 1950; Foreign Publicity Manager, Allied Artists Productions, 1951-56; Writer, editor, and film producer, Sterling Television, New York, 1956-DATE; lecturer, Museum of City of New York, 1962; guest on radio and TV programs.

* * * * *

CLIFTON FADIMAN

Full Name: Clifton Paul Fadiman.
  Born May 15, 1904, at Brooklyn, New York. Son of Isidore Michael Fadiman (a pharmacist) and Grace Elizabeth Fadiman (a nurse). Married Pauline Elizabeth Rush, 1927 (divorced, 1949); married Annalee Whitmore Jacoby (a writer), 1950. Three children: Jonathan, Kim, Anne.

Education: A.B., Columbia University, 1925.

Career: Writer and lecturer.
  Teacher of English, Ethical Culture High School, New York, 1925-27; Lecturer, People's Institute, 1925-33; Asst. Editor, Simon & Schuster, 1927-29, and General Editor, 1929-35; Book Editor, New Yorker, 1933-43; Master of Ceremonies and host of a number of radio and TV programs, including "Information, Please!," 1938-48, "Conversation," 1954-57; free-lance writer and lecturer, 1957-DATE; Consultant in Humanities, and Writer and General Editor, Encyclopaedia Britannica Educational Corp., 1963-DATE; Member, Board of Judges, Book-of-the-Month Club, 1944-DATE, and National Book Award for Children's Books, 1974.

Awards:
  Saturday Review of Literature Award for Distinguished Service to American Literature, 1940, for "Information, Please!"; American Library Association Clarence Day Award, 1969. Member: California Citizens for Better Libraries; Phi Beta Kappa.

* * * * *

JOHN FAIRFAX

Full Name: John Fairfax.
  Born November 9, 1930, at London England. Married Esther Fairfax, 1952. Two children: Michael Lee (born 1953), Jonathan Grant (born 1957).

Education: Attended Plymouth College, 1940-46.

Career: Writer and poet.
  Has also served as Editor of Nimbus: Panache.

First Professional Sale: A poem to Poetry Quarterly, 1942.

Awards: Gregory Poetry Award (twice); Arts Council of Great Britain Writers Award.

Fairfax edited one of the first anthologies of SF poetry, The Frontier of Going (Panther Books, 1969). He has also written a great deal of science fiction verse himself. In commenting on the field, he had this to say:

"Much science fiction poetry has been written, but publishers are very backward in publishing it. I know many poets writing such work. The exploration of inner and outer space is something I'd suggest poets have been concerned with for a good long time.
  "Last autumn, I attended and read poems at a Science Fiction and Science Fact Festival held in Sunderland, England. It was widely attended. The Festival produced an anthology called Beyond This Horizon, which I recommend.
  "Personally, I'm most interested in the continuing imaginative spur that urges man to explore himself and for himself in the blackness that spread out in front of him more and more demanding, more and more tantalizing with every step he takes either in fact or in imagination.
  "I could go on with my theories and themes for page after volume about the compatibility of poetry with exploration of whatever nature. The introduction to Frontier of Going says a bit in this field; however, I hope these few words will show you that I'm convinced (with other poets I know) that Science Fiction and Science Fact is a theme easily harnessed by contemporary poets."

He adds: "I co-founded a creative-writing centre called The Arvon Foundation; I'm concerned that creative writers should be able to work with students and others interested in imaginative expression outside formal establishments."

* * * * *

R. LIONEL FANTHORPE

Full Name: Robert Lionel Fanthorpe.
  Born February 9, 1935, at Dereham, Norfolk, England. Son of Robert Fanthorpe (a shop keeper) and Greta Christine Garbutt (a teacher). Married Patricia Alice Tooke, September 7, 1957. Two children: Stephanie Dawn Patricia (born 1964), Fiona Mary Patricia Alcibiadette (born 1966).

Education: Teacher's Certificate, Norwich Teachers' Training College, England, 1963.

Career: Teacher.
  Schoolmaster, Dereham Secondary Modern School, 1958-61, 1963-67; Further Education Tutor, Gamlingay Village College, 1966-69; Industrial Training Officer, Phoenix Timber Company, Rainham, Essex, 1969-71; Director of Studies and Second Master, Hellesdon School and Norfolk County Council, England, 1972-DATE; Extra-mural Tutor (part-time), for Cambridge University; Examiner for C.S.E., English; writer, 1952-67.

First Professional Sale: "Worlds Without End," in Futuristic Science Stories, #6, 1952.

Agent: Gerald Bishop, Aardvark House, 10 Marlborough Road, Exeter EX2 4TJ, England.

Member: Mensa; British Institute of Management; Society for Psychical Research.

Interests:
  "Having a grasshopper mind, I'm interested in almost everything. I'm basically pro-liberal, pro-permissive, anti-puritan, and anti-authoritarian; I toe the line like Machiavelli because I have to eat! I like people and believe individuals to be more important than abstract ideals. A friend is worth dying for—a country

R. LIONEL FANTHORPE (cont.)

"isn't. A woman is worth living for--a philosophy isn't. I love my own kids, and I enjoy teaching because I try to treat other parents' children the way I hope some other teacher will treat mine.

"One day, when I get my work schedule properly organised, I shall try to write something worthwhile to make up for all the corn I've showered on an innocent reading public. My early SF was written for bread, under pressure and at speed. Reading it again after twenty-odd years gives me the strange sensation that someone else must have written it. Maybe one or two of the ideas could be used again, if...?"

* * * * *

DANA FARALLA

Full Name: Dana Faralla.
Born August 4, 1909, at Renville, Minnesota. Daughter of John Frederick Wein (a merchant) and Estella Gilger. Married Dario Faralla (a film executive and producer), August 6, 1935 (died 1944).

Education: Attended University of Minnesota, 1927-28.

Career: Author.
Has worked as an actress, private secretary, screen story analyst in Hollywood, in a rare book shop in New York; Associate Editor, Poets Magazine, 1930-31; free-lance novelist and author. Member: Poetry Society of America.

Agent: Curtis Brown Ltd., 60 E. 56th St., New York, NY 10022.

* * * * *

MARIE C. FARCA

Full Name: Marie C. Farca.
Born June 6, 1935, at Philadelphia, Pennsylvania. Daughter of George Farca (a quality control manager) and Catherine Candea.

Education: B.S.Ed., University of Pennsylvania, 1957.

Career: School Teacher.
Demonstration Teacher, Trenton State College, 1963-69; public school teacher, Trenton Public Schools; free-lance photographer and writer. Member: National Education Association; New Jersey Education Assoc.

Agent: Scott Meredith, 580 Fifth Avenue, New York, NY 10036.

* * * * *

ELEANOR FARJEON

Full Name: Eleanor Farjeon.
Born February 13, 1881, at London, England. Daughter of Benjamin Leopold Farjeon (a novelist) and Margaret Jane Jefferson.

Career: Writer.
Was a full-time writer for more than 70 years; died

June 5, 1965. Member: P.E.N.; Society of Authors.

Agent: David Higham Associates, 76 Dean St., London.

Awards:
International Hans Christian Andersen Award, 1956, for The Little Bookroom; Carnegie Medal of the Library Association, 1956, for the same book; Regina Medal, Catholic Library Association, 1959.

* * * * *

WALTER FARLEY

Full Name: Walter Farley.
Born June 26, 1915, at Syracuse, New York. Son of Walter Farley and Isabelle Vermilyea. Married Rosemary Lutz, 1945. Four children: Pamela, Alice, Steve, Tim.

Education: Attended Mercersburg Academy and Columbia University.

Career: Horse breeder and writer.
Copywriter for a New York advertising agency, 1941; breeds and races trotters; now a full-time writer.

* * * * *

PENELOPE FARMER

Full Name: Penelope Jane Farmer.
Born June 14, 1939, at Westerham, Kent, England. Daughter of Hugh Farmer and Penelope Boothby. Married Michael Mockridge, 1962. Two children: Clare (born 1964), Thomas (born 1964).

Education: B.A., Oxford University, 1960.

Career: Writer.
"All kinds of odd jobs: cleaning, waiting, child minding, some teaching."

First Professional Sale: The China People, Hutchinson, 1960.

Agent: Deborah Owen, 78 Narrow St., London E.14.

Member: P.E.N.; Society of Authors; Writers Action Group. Interests: William Blake, poetry.

"Once I was happy to write for hours on 'myself as writer.' No more: it's enough effort to write the real stuff: fiction--poetry. The energy goes there."

* * * * *

PHILIP JOSÉ FARMER

Full Name: Philip José Farmer.
Born January 26, 1918, at North Terre Haute, Indiana. Son of George Farmer (a civil and electrical engineer) and Lucile Theodora Jackson. Married Elizabeth Virginia André, May 10, 1941. Two children: Philip Laird (born 1941), Kristen (born 1945).

Education: B.A., University of Bradley, 1950.

Career: Writer.
Billet Inspector and Crane Operator, Keystone Steel,

PHILIP JOSE FARMER (cont.)

1942-53; Parts Order Clerk, LeTourneau-Westinghouse, 1954-56; Electromechanical Technical Writer, General Electric, 1956-58, for Motorola, 1958-65, for MacDonnel-Douglas, 1967-69; free-lance author, 1965-67, 1969-DATE.

First Professional Sale: "O'Brien and Obrenov," in *Adventure Magazine*, March, 1946.

Agent: Scott Meredith, 580 Fifth Avenue, New York, NY 10036.

Awards & Honors:
Guest of Honor, 26th World Science Fiction Convention (Baycon), Oakland, 1968; Hugo Award, Best New Science Fiction Author or Artist, 1952 (1953); Hugo Award, Best Novella, 1967 (1968), "Riders of the Purple Wage"; Hugo Award, Best Novel, 1971 (1972), *To Your Scattered Bodies Go*; guest of honor at various other science fiction conventions.

Member:
Science Fiction Writers of America; Southern California Professional Engineers; Society for Prevention of Cruelty to Writers and Extra-Terrestrials.

Interests: Linguistics, airships, Esperanto, pop-lit, Homo sapiens, Sufism, Homer and the Mycenaean world.

Farmer writes:
"I belong to a species which has never been able to figure out what it's doing or where in hell it's going. Aside from that, I believe that we live in the midst of a raging chaos, but that our peculiar psychosomatic prisms (or filters) have imposed a seeming order. Heraclitus long ago gave writers two of the only three guides they need. 'Character determines destiny,' and 'You can't step in the same river twice.' The Preacher provided the third: 'My son, consider thy end and be wise.'
"I am the perpretator of twelve series, none of which I have so far finished. Those that have appeared in print are the Wolff-Kicka series (first book is *The Maker of Universes*), the Riverworld series (*To Your Scattered Bodies Go*, etc.), the Father John Carmody series (*Night of Light* and some novelets), the Doc Caliban-Lord Grandrith series (*A Feast Unknown*, etc.), the Herald Childe series (*The Image of the Beast*, etc.), the Hadon of Opar books (*Hadon of Ancient Opar* and *Flight to Opar*), the fictional biography series (*Tarzan Alive*, etc.), the Polytropical Paramyth series (*Totem and Tabu*), the Kent Lane series (a short story called "Skinburn," a novel coming up called *Why Everybody Hates Me*; I hope to switch Lane from SF to the mystery field eventually).
"I got permission from 'Kilgore Trout' (author of *Venus on the Half-Shell* [which Farmer wrote]) to write a series about Ralph von Wau Wau, the German police dog turned private eye. A number of these tales have appeared in *The Magazine of Fantasy and Science Fiction*.
"I am writing (and have sold) some stories in my fictional-author series. These are stories supposedly by authors who are characters in fiction. Some of these I've farmed out; Gene Wolfe, for instance, has written a story by David Copperfield. I plan to write one by him also.
"I am planning a series about the Sufi poet, Hadji Abdu. He is the supposed creator of *The Kasidah*, which was actually written by Sir Richard Francis

"Burton. Abdu will be the first-person narrator of a series of adventures which will reflect my interest in Sufism.
"My main ambition is to write a massive mainstream novel about the science fiction world. Tentative title: *A Wild Weird Clime*."

* * * * *

HOWARD FAST

Full Name: Howard Melvin Fast.
Born November 11, 1914, at New York, New York. Son of Barney Fast (a designer) and Ida Miller. Married Bette Cohen, June 6, 1937. Two children: Rachel (born 1944), Jonathan (born 1948).

Education: Attended National Academy of Design.

Career: Writer.
Foreign Correspondent for *Esquire* and *Coronet*, 1945; full-time writer and lecturer.

Awards:
Breadloaf Literary Award, 1937; Schomburg Award for Race Relations, 1944; Newspaper Guild Award, 1947; Jewish Book Council of America Annual Award, 1947; International Peace Prize of the Soviet Union, 1954; Screen Writers Annual Award, 1960; Secondary Education Board Annual Book Award, 1962.

First Professional Sale: "Wrath of the Purple," in *Amazing Stories*, October, 1932.

Fast writes:
"If one could make a living out of it, I would write nothing but the type of stories included in the four books you list for the rest of my life. Whether or not they are science fiction, I don't know. The fiction is heavy, and the science is rather light. But at least they allow me to express my attitude toward the world and the universe, which I find fascinating, mystifying, and often ridiculous. They constitute an art form which I think is one of the most original to be devised in the United States, and certainly we can take the credit for that; and also they allow me an expression for whatever philosophy I have worked out in my lifetime.
"I find these stories fascinating to write, intriguing to devise, and enormously satisfying in their execution. As a kid a long, long time ago, I was utterly enthralled by the original *Amazing Stories*. It became a very unique part of my life. I never missed an issue, and to me it was absolutely the most wonderful manifestation of the late 1920s and the 1930s.
"Good science fiction is social commentary, and thoughtful social commentary—something that cannot be said of most of the fiction written today. While it appears to anticipate the future, for the most part the good stuff comments on the situation today.
"Interestingly enough, the very first story I sold, in 1932 if I am not mistaken, was science fiction, and it appeared in *Amazing Stories* under the title, "Wrath of the Purple." Now history repeats itself, and my son's first sold story has appeared in *The Magazine of Fantasy and Science Fiction*. His name is Jonathan Fast, and he has already sold a second science fiction story to an anthology of original pieces, and is on his way down the line.
"As to my future—of course I will go on. I am just wetting my toes in the field, and I love it. More power to all who practice it!"

JULIUS FAST

Full Name: Julius Fast.
    Born April 17, 1919, at New York, New York. Son of Barnett A. Fast (a pattern maker) and Ida Miller. Married Barbara Hewitt Sher (a novelist), June 8, 1946. Three children: Jennifer, Melissa, Timothy.

Education: B.A., New York University, 1942.

Career: Writer and editor.
    Writer, Smith, Kline & French (drugs), 1952-54; Research Associate, Purdue Frederick (drugs), 1954-61; Feature Editor, *Medical News*, 1961-62; Editor and writer, *Medical World News, 1962-63*; Editor, *Ob-Gyn Observer*, 1963-DATE; free-lance writer.

Agent: Robert P. Mills Ltd., 156 E. 52nd St., New York, NY 10022.

Awards: Edgar Award, Best First Mystery Novel, 1946, *Watchful at Night*.

* * * * *

JOHN M. FAUCETTE

Full Name: John Matthew Faucette, Jr.
    Born September 15, 1943, at New York, New York. Son of John Matthew and Dorothy Faucette. Education: attended Polytechnic Institute of Brooklyn for one year.

Career: Writer.

Member: United States Chess Federation [won 3rd place, Nassau Open Chess Championship, 1967].

* * * * *

JOHN RUSSELL FEARN

Full Name: John Francis Russell Fearn.
    Born June 8, 1908, at Worsley, near Manchester, Lancashire, England. Son of John Slate Fearn (a cotton salesman) and Florence Rose Armstrong (a secretary). Married Carrie Fearn, August, 1957.

Education: Attended Chorlton Grammar School, 1919-24.

Career: Writer.
    Cotton salesman for his father's firm, 1925-29; Solicitor's Clerk, 1929-30; Fairground Assistant, Blackpool Pleasure Beach, 1931; full-time writer, 1931-42; worked in a munitions factory, and as a cinema projectionist, 1942-45; full-time writer, 1945-60; Editor, *Vargo Statten Science Fiction Magazine/British Science Fiction Magazine/British Space Fiction Magazine*, January, 1954-1956 (all issues published). Died at Blackpool, Lancashire, September 18, 1960.

First Professional Sale: "Hands That Speak," in *Film Weekly*, 1931.

Agent: Philip Harbottle, Cosmos Literary Agency, 32 Tynedale Avenue, Wallsend, Tyne & Wear, England.

Member: Fylde Writers Society (Chairman); Fylde Cine Society (Chairman); National Writers' Club (Honorary Life Member).

Interests: Film making, play writing, stage acting.

Philip Harbottle, Fearn's agent, had these additional comments:
    "Fearn lived most of his life in Blackpool, apart from a short spell in Brighton in 1937. He was very active as Secretary and Chairman of a number of writing societies, and an extraordinary number of writers enjoyed wide and varied success from their ranks. Many of these authors freely acknowledged the tremendous and unselfish help Fearn gave them, including collaborations and unpaid agenting. In his later life, he wrote and acted in plays in his locality, often for charity; his wife was herself an actress with a theatrical background. Unpublished work is still being discovered amongst his papers (à la Howard and Burroughs), including at least one Golden Amazon novel, and it is hoped some may be published later."

* * * * *

CAMILLA FEGAN

Full Name: Camilla Fegan.
    Born August 14, 1939, at Belfast, Northern Ireland. Daughter of B. T. O. Fegan (a colonel in the British Army) and Merrill C. Gotto. Education: Studied at various schools in England, Ireland, and Germany.

Career: Writer. Member: Museums Association of Great Britain; Surrey Archaeological Society.

* * * * *

HENRY GREGOR FELSEN

Full Name: Henry Gregor Felsen.
    Born August 16, 1916, at Brooklyn, New York. Son of Harry Felsen and Sabina Bedrick. Married Isabel Marie Vincent, 1937. Two children: Daniel, Holly.

Education: Attended State University of Iowa for two years.

Career: Free-lance writer. Member: Des Moines Warriors Professional Football Club (Secretary); Future Professional Drivers Association (President).

* * * * *

PHYLLIS R. FENNER

Full Name: Phyllis Reid Fenner.
    Born October 24, 1899, at Almond, New York. Daughter of William LaVern Fenner (a merchant) and Viola V. Van Orman. Education: A.B., Mount Holyoke College, 1921; B.L.S., Columbia University, 1934.

Career: Librarian, 1923-55; Author, 1940-DATE. Member: Woman's National Book Association; Pen & Brush; American Library Association.

* * * * *

BETTY FERM

Full Name: Betty Ferm.
    Born December 4, 1926, at New York, New York. Daughter of Jack Chefetz and Libby Wetsky. Married Max Ferm July 3, 1957. Two children: Matthew, Stephanie.

BETTY FERM (cont.)

Education: Attended New York University.

Career: Writer.
  Owner, House of Alexander (interior decoration), Brooklyn, 1951-55; worked in advertising posts with Revlon, 1955, and Swirl, Inc., 1955-57; full-time writer. Member: Women's National Book Association.

Agent: McIntosh & Otis, 475 Fifth Avenue, New York, NY 10017

* * * * *

EDWARD L. FERMAN

Full Name: Edward Lewis Ferman.
  Born March 6, 1937, at New York, New York. Son of Joseph Wolfe Ferman (a publisher) and Ruth Eisen. Married Audrey Bonchak, May, 1964. One daughter, Emily Allison (born 1965).

Education: B.A., Middlebury College, 1958.

Career: Editor and publisher.
  Editorial Assistant, *The Magazine of Fantasy and Science Fiction*, November, 1958-January, 1959; Managing Editor, April, 1962-December, 1965; Editor, January, 1966-DATE; Publisher, November, 1970-DATE; Editor, *Venture Science Fiction*, May, 1969-August, 1970.

Awards:
  Hugo Award, Best Professional Magazine, 1968 (1969), 1969 (1970), 1970 (1971), 1971 (1972), *The Magazine of Fantasy and Science Fiction*.

Member:
  Housatonic Valley Association (Secretary, Director); National Audobon Society; Common Cause. Interests: municipal politics; conservation.

* * * * *

JOSEPH W. FERMAN

Full Name: Joseph Wolfe Ferman.
  Born June 8, 1906, at Lida, Lithuania. Son of Wolfe Ferman and Esther Little. Married Ruth Eisen, January 29, 1931. One son, Edward Lewis (born 1937).

Education: B.C.S., New York University, 1927.

Career: Publisher.
  Ferman joined Alfred A. Knopf as a bookkeeper after graduating from high school, and was named Circulation Manager of *The American Mercury* shortly after it was founded. He then became Vice President and General Manager of Mercury Publications, when Lawrence Spivak bought the magazine from Knopf. He purchased Mercury Publications in 1954. His posts included: General Manager, *The Magazine of Fantasy and Science Fiction*, Fall, 1949-July, 1954; Publisher, August, 1954-October, 1970; Editor, December, 1964-December, 1965; Chairman of the Board, November, 1970-May, 1975; Publisher, *Venture Science Fiction*, January, 1957-July, 1958, May, 1969-August, 1970 (all issues published). Ferman was also publisher for a time of *Ellery Queen's Mystery Magazine*, and three paperback lines: Mercury Mysteries, Bestseller Mysteries, and Jonathan Press. Ferman

died December 29, 1974.

Awards:
  Hugo Award, Best Professional Magazine, 1957 (1958), 1958 (1959), 1959 (1960), 1962 (1963), 1968 (1969), 1969 (1970), 1970 (1971), 1971 (1972), *The Magazine of Fantasy and Science Fiction*.

Member: Hundred Million Club; Unity Club of Nassau County; Committee for World Human Rights (Charter Member).

Commenting on the place of the speciality magazine, Ferman had this to say: "Yes, I think the specialty magazine will survive--science fiction perhaps even more than mysteries or westerns. They were never big money makers, and the people who edit and publish SF enjoy their work, and are willing to settle for less financially. The problems today are especially difficult, because of sharp increases in the cost of paper and postage. But most will survive."

* * * * *

PAUL FERRIS

Full Name: Paul Frederick Ferris.
  Born February 15, 1929, in Swansea, Wales. Son of Frederick Morgan Ferris (an engineer) and Olga Boulton. Married Gloria Moreton, December 29, 1953. Two children: Jonathan Moreton, Virginia Ann.

Career: Editor and columnist.
  Member of editorial staff, *South Wales Evening Post*, 1949-52, and the *Women's Own*, 1953; Radio Columnist, *London Observer*, 1954-DATE; free-lance writer.

Agent: Curtis Brown Ltd., 60 E. 56th St., New York, NY 10022.

* * * * *

LESLIE A. FIEDLER

Full Name: Leslie Aaron Fiedler.
  Born March 8, 1917, at Newark, New Jersey. Son of Jacob J. Fiedler (a pharmacist) and Lillian Rosenstrauch. Married Margaret Ann Shipley, October 6, 1939 (divorced); married Sally Andersen, February, 1973. Six children: Kurt, Eric, Michael, Deborah, Jenny, Miriam; two stepchildren: Soren Andersen, Eric Andersen.

Education:
  B.A., New York University, 1938; M.A, University of Wisconsin, 1939; Ph.D., 1941; post-doctoral study as a Rockefeller fellow, Harvard University, 1946-47.

Career: Professor of English.
  Asst. Professor, Montana State University, 1948-52; Professor of English, 1956-64; Professor of English, State University of New York, Buffalo, 1964-DATE; Fulbright Fellow and lecturer, Universities of Rome and Bologna, 1951-53, and University of Athens, 1961-62; Resident Fellow in Creative Writing and Gauss Lecturer, Princeton University, 1956-57; Visiting Professor, University of Sussex, 1967-68, and University of Vincennes, 1971.

Honors & Awards:
  Junior Fellow, School of Letters, Indiana University,

LESLIE A. FIEDLER (cont.)

1953; *Kenyon Review* Fellow in Literary Criticism, 1956-57; National Book Awards Judge, 1956, 1972; American Council of Learned Societies Grants-in-Aid, 1960, 1961; Furioso Prize for Poetry; National Institute of Arts and Letters Prize for Excellence in Creative Writing, 1957; Guggenheim Fellowship, 1970-71.

Member:
American Association of University Professors; Modern Language Association of America; English Institute; Dante Society of America; P.E.N.; Phi Beta Kappa.

* * * * *

WILLIAM FIFIELD

Full Name: William Fifield.
Born April 5, 1916, at Chicago, Illinois. Son of Lawrence Wendell Fifield (a Congregational Minister) and Juanita Sloan. Married Donna Hamilton (an actress). Three children: John Lawrence, Donna Lee, Brian Robert.

Education: A.B., Whitman College, 1937.

Career: Writer.
Radio announcer, writer, actor, producer-director, for CBS and NBC, 1937-60; onetime bullfighter; full-time writer, 1957-DATE.

Agent: Brandt & Brandt, 101 Park Avenue, New York, NY 10017.

Awards:
O. Henry Memorial Award for "Fishermen of Patzcuaro"; Huntington Hartford Foundation Award for creative writing. Member: Phi Beta Kappa.

* * * * *

RALPH ADAM FINE

Full Name: Ralph Adam Fine.
Born February 14, 1941, at New York, New York. Son of Sidney Fine (a New York Supreme Court justice) and Libby Poresky. Married Kay Prange (a teacher), July, 1971.

Education: A.B., Tufts University, 1962; LL.B., Columbia University, 1965.

Career: Attorney and writer.
Admitted to New York Bar, 1965; became a law clerk for the U.S. district court judge, Brooklyn; joined U.S. Dept. of Justice, Washington, and prepared briefs for U.S. Supreme Court cases, 1967-70; full-time writer, 1970-DATE.

Agent: Philip Spitzer, 111-25 76th Avenue, Forest Hills, NY 11375.

* * * * *

R. L. FINN

Full Name: Ralph Leslie Finn.
Born January 17, 1912, at London, England. Son of Alec Finerman (an architect) and Leah Lev (a school teacher). Married Freda Nathanson, June 15, 1937. Two children: Alan Hugh (born 1941), Andrea Anne (born 1948).

Education: A.B., Oxford University, 1933; Diploma in Modern Literature, University Extension, 1945.

Career: Writer and advertising consultant.
Served with various advertising agencies in England, 1941-196?; free-lance writer, 1941-DATE; free-lance consultant in advertising and finance.

First Professional Sale: *Out of the Depths*, RAF Benevolent Fund, 1941.

Member:
Institute of Arts and Letters (Fellow); Institute of Practitioners in Advertising; Institute of Journalists.

Interests: Chess, music, soccer ("more books on soccer than anyone else in the world").

Finn adds: "I'm one of Britain's 'best borrowed authors' at Britain's free libraries."

* * * * *

CHARLES G. FINNEY

Full Name: Charles Grandison Finney.
Born December 1, 1905, at Sedalia, Missouri. Son of Norton Jamison Finney (a railroad superintendent) and Florence Bell. Married Marie Lucy Doyle, September 12, 1939. Two children: Sheila (born 1942); Felice (born 1947).

Education: Attended Missouri University, 1925.

Career: Newspaper editor.
With U.S. Army, Tientsin, China, 1927-29; joined *Arizona Daily Star*, Tucson, and served successively as proofreader, night wire editor, copy reader, and Financial Editor; retired in 1970.

First Professional Sale: *The Circus of Dr. Lao*, Viking Press, 1935.

Awards: American Booksellers Association Award, Most Original Novel of the Year, 1935, *The Circus of Dr. Lao*.

Finney notes: "Six books. Numerous short stories in *New Yorker, Harper's, Paris Review*, etc. Satisfactory life. Enjoyed writing, but ran out of ideas and gave it up. Suffered stroke 1972. Only interest now is doubtful hope of spontaneous remission."

* * * * *

VARDIS FISHER

Full Name: Vardis Alvero Fisher.
Born March 31, 1895, at Annis, Idaho. Son of Joseph Oliver Fisher and Temperance Thornton. Married Leona McMurtrey, September 10, 1918 (died 1924); married Margaret Trusler, 1928 (divorced, 1929); married Opal Laurel Holmes, April 16, 1940. Three children: Grant, Wayne, Thornton Roberts. Education: A.B., University of Utah, 1920; A.M., University of Chicago, 1922; Ph.D., 1925.

VARDIS FISHER (cont.)

Career: Writer.
Asst. Professor of English, at University of Utah, and New York University, 1925-31; Idaho State Director, Federal Writers Project, 1935-39; General Editor for Rocky Mountain states, 1938-39; newspaper columnist, 1941-68; free-lance writer, 1927-68. Died July 9, 1968.

Awards: Harper Prize Novel Award, 1939, for *Children of God*.

* * * * *

NICHOLAS FISK

Full Name: unknown.
Born October 18, 1923, at London, England. Fisk is married, and has three children. Education: studied at Ardingly College, Sussex.

Career: Writer and editor.
Served in the RAF during World War II; writer since age 16; has also been an illustrator, musician, publisher, Director of Icon Books Ltd., and a photographer.

First Professional Sale: A story to *Strand Magazine*, 1939. Member: Savile Club, London.

* * * * *

GREGORY FITZ GERALD

Full Name: Gregory Fitz Gerald.
Born April 23, 1923, at New York, New York. Son of Benedict J. Fitz Gerald (a composer) and Erna von Schueller (a poet). Married Barbara Farquhar, Nov. 26, 1957 (divorced, 1973). One daughter, Geraldine Adare.

Education: A.B., Boston University, 1946; M.A., Middlebury College, 1953; Ph.D., University of Iowa, 1967.

Career: Professor of English.
Instructor in English, University of Iowa, 1954-55, 1956-61; Instructor in English, Jackson Junior College, 1961-62; Asst. Professor of English, Indiana State University, 1962-65; Associate Professor of English, Ithaca College, 1965-67; Professor of English, State University of New York, Brockport, 1967-DATE.

Awards:
Smith-Mundt Fellowship to Damascus, 1955-56; SUNY Research Foundation grant-in-aid in satire, 1968-70; Fellowship in Criticism, 1969; Fellowships in Fiction, 1970, 1974.

Member: Authors Guild; Modern Language Association; American Association of University Professors.

* * * * *

CONSTANTINE FitzGIBBON

Full Name: Robert Louis Constantine Dillon FitzGibbon. Born June 8, 1919, at Lenox, Massachusetts. Son of Francis Lee-Dillon FitzGibbon (a Commander in the Royal Navy) and Georgette Folsom. Married Marion Gutmann, 1960. One son, Francis.

Education:
Attended Wellington College, 1933-35, University of Munich and Sorbonne, 1935-37, Exeter College, Oxford University, 1937-39.

Career: Writer.
Schoolmaster, Saltus Grammar School, Bermuda, 1946-47; full-time writer, 1947-DATE. Member: Irish Academy of Letters.

Agent: Harold Ober Associates, 40 E. 49th St., New York, NY 10017.

* * * * *

BERRY FLEMING

Full Name: Berry Fleming.
Born March 19, 1899, at Augusta, Georgia. Son of Porter Fleming and Daisy Berry. Married Anne Shirley Molloy, 1925. One daughter, Shirley Moragne.

Education: B.S., Harvard College, 1922.

Career: Writer.

* * * * *

BARTHOLD FLES

Full Name: Barthold Fles.
Born February 7, 1902, at Amsterdam, Holland. Son of Louis Fles and Celine van Straaten. Fles has been married and divorced.

Education: Attended junior high school in Amsterdam.

Career: Editor and agent.
Fles started his publishing career as a Receiving Clerk for Harper & Bros. in 1923, and has worked as an editor and buyer for various publishers and bookstores in the U.S., England, Germany, and Holland; he also runs his own literary agency in New York.

Agent: Barthold Fles, 507 Fifth Avenue, New York, NY 10017.

Interests: Reading, string quartet, playing and listening to music, travel.

* * * * *

CHARLES BRACELEN FLOOD

Full Name: Charles Bracelen Flood.
Born November 14, 1929, at New York, New York. Son of John L. Flood and Ellen Bracelen. Education: B.A., Harvard University, 1951.

Career: Writer.
Instructor in Creative Writing and World Literature, Sophia University, Tokyo, 1963-65; has also worked as a reporter.

Agent: Sterling Lord Agency, 660 Madison Avenue, New York, NY 10021.

Member: Authors Guild; Authors League, P.E.N.; National Book Committee.

ANTHONY FON EISEN

Full Name: Anthony T. Fon Eisen.
Born May 20, 1917, at Avon, Connecticut. Married Marjorie Domick, October 15, 1951. Two sons: David, Michael.

Career: Product analyst.
Product analyst, G. C. Heublein, Inc. (food and liquor manufacturer), Hartford, Conn., 1945-DATE.

* * * * *

CHARLES L. FONTENAY

Full Name: Charles Louis Fontenay.
Born March 17, 1917, at Sao Paulo, Brazil. Son of Charles Robert Fontenay (a steel company executive) and Miriam Steel (a missionary). Married Glenda Lucille Miller, October 25, 1943 (divorced, 1960); married Martha Mae Howard, December 13, 1962. Two children: Margarethe Louise [Gretchen] (born 1963), Charles Howard Blake [Blake] (born 1966).

Education: Attended Vanderbilt University, 1967-71.

Career: Reporter.
Reporter and Sports Editor, *Union City Daily Messenger*, 1936-40; Editor, Associated Press Tennessee Bureau, 1940-42; Captain, U.S. Army, 1942-46 (served in South Pacific); Sports Editor, *Johnson City Press-Chronicle*, 1946; successively reporter, political writer, City Editor, and now Rewrite Editor, *Nashville Tennessean*, 1946-DATE.

First Professional Sale: "Disqualified," in *Worlds of If*, September, 1954.

Agent: Scott Meredith, 580 Fifth Avenue, New York, NY 10036.

Honors & Awards:
Southern Regional Education Board Fellowship, Vanderbilt University, 1967-68; Ted V. Rodgers Journalism Award (2nd place), 1961; First Prize, self-taught artist's work, Tennessee State Fair, 1957; First Place, North American Correspondence Chess Tournament, Class C, 1950; Tennessee State Senate Resolution No. 21, 1969, "commending Mr. Charles L. Fontenay for his contributions to literature"; Commendation Award, Korea Tae Kwon Do Moo Duk Kwan Association, 1973, "for his great achievements to the...spread of Taekwondo"; Second Place, Senior Free Fighting, 6th Annual National Karate Championships, Atlanta, 1972; Second Place, Senior Forms, and Third Place, Senior Free Fighting, 7th Annual National Karate Championships, Atlanta, 1973; Second Place, Senior Forms, and Third Place, Senior Free Fighting, Bluegrass Invitational Karate Tournament, Louisville, 1973.

Member: Korean Tae Kwon Do Association.

Interests:
Korean karate, chess, flower and vegetable gardening, Chinese cooking, golf, oil painting, water colour painting, sumi-e painting, astrology, German and Chinese languages, extra-sensory perception, sex.

Fontenay writes:
"I read my first science fiction about 1929, when I picked up a copy of the old *Amazing Stories*, with the first part of Jack Williamson's "The Green Girl";

"almost from that time on I wanted to write the stuff successfully. All my efforts at it and other fiction were abortive, however, until I decided to approach it on a rationally organized basis in 1953. I wrote SF with considerable regularity from then until publication of my second novel in 1961. During this period, I had about three dozen stories published in various science fiction magazines. Due to developments in my personal life, I became interested then in writing other kinds of fiction, and did three psychological novels, but failed to sell any of them. I did, however, write a philosophical work, *Epistle to the Babylonians*, which was published in 1969 by the University of Tennessee Press, and won some academic praise. In 1951-52, I tried my hand at a biography of Estes Kefauver, whom I knew and liked, but was unable to find a publisher, and sold the manuscript to Jack Anderson, who rewrote it, and had it published as *The Kefauver Story*. Several years ago, I contracted with Atheneum to write a definitive Kefauver biography, which was written as *The Last Populist*, but during the writing the publishers changed their minds, and the manuscript is still on the market. My latest effort, *The Keyen of Fu Tze*, is a somewhat more personal commentary on my explorations into mysticism.

"My bread-and-butter work since age 19 has been the newspaper business, except for service in World War II. My outside interests at various periods have been intense; when I was immersed in correspondence chess and oil painting, I won several ribbons and medals other than those listed. At the age of 53, I took up Korean karate, and have attained the grade of red belt, and am working toward my black belt, possibly this year. My interest in experimental magic and ESP has been an outgrowth of my personal work in mysticism in recent years, and I am currently taking the ESP development course of Dr. Milan Ryzl, the Czech parapsychologist.

"In view of the variety of ingredients in the above potpourri, it may sound peculiar to call my interest in science fiction one of the major brands of cement holding it all together, but I think that is true (it has even been involved importantly in my love life, of which the less said the better, perhaps). But it did constitute my basic reason for writing in the first place, and I enjoyed writing SF very much during the period I was doing it. It also contributed to the development of my philosophy, and a number of my other activities were initiated as offshoots from it."

* * * * *

ESTHER FORBES

Full Name: Esther Forbes.
Born June 28, 1891, at Westborough, Massachusetts. Daughter of William Trowbridge Forbes (a judge) and Harriette Marrifield. Married Albert Learned Hoskins, 1926 (divorced, 1933). Education: Attended Bradford Junior College, 1912, and University of Wisconsin, 1916-18.

Career: Writer.
Also served a member of editorial staff, Houghton Mifflin Company, Boston, 1920-26, 1942-46. Died August 12, 1967.

Awards:
Pulitzer Prize in History, 1942, *Paul Revere and the World He Lived In*; Newbery Medal, 1944, *Johnny Tremain*; Metro-Goldwyn-Mayer Novel Award, 1948; Litt.D., Clark University, 1943, Univ. of Maine, 1949, Northwestern Univ., 1949, Wellesley College, 1959; LL.D., Tufts Univ.

CHARLES HENRI FORD

Full Name: Charles Henri Ford.
  Born 1913, at Hazlehurst, Mississippi. Son of
Charles Lloyd Ford and Gertrude Cato.

Career: Artist, writer, film-maker.
  Editor, *Blues*, 1930; Editor, *View*, 1942-47; photo-
graphs exhibited at London, 1955, and paintings and
drawings exhibited in Paris during the late 1950s;
poem posters exhibited in New York, Mexico City, and
at Southern Illinois University.

Agent: Oscar Collier, 280 Madison Avenue, New York.

* * * * *

ROBERT FORREST-WEBB

Full Name: Robert Forrest-Webb.
  Born April 9, 1929, at Nottingham, England. Son of
Cecil Frederik Forrest-Webb and Constance Ella Wynne.
Married Wendy Patricia Waterson (a secretary), Dec.
8, 1972. One daughter, Anne.

Career: Writer and editor.
  Journalist and editor of various British magazines
and newspapers; Executive Editor, Haymarket Press,
London, 1965-69; writer, 1969-DATE; Chairman, Hemarvine
Productions (film company).

Award: Salone Internazionale Umorismo Award, Most
  Humorous Book Published in Italy, 1973, for *After
  Me, the Deluge*.

Agent: Desmond Elliot, 38 Bury St., St. James's,
  London S.W.1, England.

* * * * *

ALAN DEAN FOSTER

Full Name: Alan Dean Foster.
  Born November 18, 1946, at New York, New York. Son
of Maxwell Feinberg [Foster] (a salesman) and Helen
Smith. Married Jo Ann Oxley, 1975.

Education: B.A., University of California, Los Angeles, 1968; M.F.A. (cinema), 1969.

Career: Writer.
  Has been an Instructor in Cinema, Los Angeles City
College; full-time writer.

First Professional Sale: "Some Notes Concerning
  a Green Box," in *Arkham Collector*, Summer, 1971.

Agents: (Prose) Virginia Kidd, Box 278, Milford, PA
  18337; (cinema/TV) Paul Kohner, 9169 Sunset Blvd.,
  Los Angeles CA 90069.

Member: Science Fiction Writers of America (past
  chairman, Nebula Awards Committee).

Interests:
  Tang Soo Do (Korean karate; now 2nd degree Red Belt);
SF 1st editions and art; basketball; classical music;
history of motion pictures; body surfing; backpacking.
  "*Bloodhype, The Tar-Aiym Krang,* and *Icerigger* are set
in the same universe (no series name), based upon the
semi-symbiotic relationship between man and a race of
insects known as the Thranx."

GARDNER F. FOX

Full Name: Gardner Francis Fox.
  Born May 20, 1911, at Brooklyn, New York. Son of
Leon Francis Fox (an engineer) and Julia V. Gardner.
Married Lynda Julia Negrini, November 14, 1937. Two
children: Jeffrey Francis (born 1940), Lynda Anne
(born 1943).

Education: B.A., St. John's University, 1932; LL.B.,
  1935.

Career: Writer.
  Practiced law, 1935-38; full-time writer, 1938-DATE.

First Professional Sale: "The Weirds of the Wood-
  carver," in *Weird Tales*, September, 1944.

Agent: Scott Meredith, 580 Fifth Avenue, New York,
  NY 10036.

Awards: Alley Award, 1963. Member: Science Fiction
  Writers of America; Academy of Comic Book Arts.

Interests: Bridge, collecting and painting miniature
  soldiers, reading, doing historical research.

Fox writes:
  "I've had over 110 novels published, using about a
dozen different pennames: historical, spy, mystery,
science fiction, western, etc. Wrote comics for about
32 years for National and Marvel. Don't do it anymore.
Created such characters as Flash and Hawkman. Did
Superman and Batman scripts, among a host of others.
  "Strictly speaking, I suppose, I don't really consider myself much of a science fiction writer, certainly
as far as output goes. I've written far more histori-
cals, together with adventure and other branches of
the writing trade.
  "As far as series characters go, I do enjoy doing
them, since I feel I get to know my characters better
with each book. The main problem comes with getting
plots that will interest the reader, especially after
you've done a number of them. One series I've done
(not science fiction or fantasy) has included eighteen
books about one character. You can begin to see the
plot problems. However, it's fun, and I wouldn't do
anything else in the world but write. It's a kind of
compulsion with me, aside from the more practical aspects of making a living at it.
  "I've done an awful lot of comic book writing in the
past. I was guest of honor, along with Jim Steranko,
at the Comic Book Convention in New York in 1971. I've
pretty well retired from this branch of writing, however,
preferring to concentrate on writing novels."

* * * * *

GEORGE FOX

Full Name: George Richard Fox.
  Born September 8, 1934, at Camden, New Jersey. Son
of George Julius Fox (an engineer) and Lillian Geist.
Married Helen Gray, March 26, 1960. Two children:
Stephen, Karen.

Education: B.A., University of Missouri, 1958.

Career: Author and editor.
  Reporter, *Perth Amboy Evening News*, 1959-61; Editorial
Director, Magazine Management Company, 1962-68. Member:
Writers Guild of America.

JANET FRAME

Full Name: Janet Paterson Frame.
Born August 28, 1924. Daughter of George Samuel Frame (a train engineer) and Lottie Clarice Godfrey. Married and divorced.

Education: Attended Dunedin Teachers Training College, and Otago University, New Zealand.

Career: Writer.

Agent: Brandt & Brandt, 101 Park Avenue, New York, NY 10017.

Awards:
Hubert Church Memorial Awards, for *The Lagoon* and *Scented Gardens for the Blind*; Literary Fund Award, New Zealand, for *Owls Do Cry*; New Zealand Scholarship in Letters, 1964; Robert Burns Fellowship, Otago University, 1965.

* * * * *

JOSEPH FRANK

Full Name: Joseph Frank.
Born December 20, 1916, at Chicago, Illinois. Son of A. Richard Frank and Gertrude Greenbaum. Married Margery Goodkind, 1941. Three children: Thomas, Peter, Andrew.

Education: B.A., Harvard University, 1939; M.A., 1948; Ph.D., 1953.

Career: Professor of English.
Professor of English, University of Rochester, 1948-67; Chairman, Dept. of English, University of New Mexico, Albuquerque, 1967-DATE.

Awards: Huntington Library Fellow, 1955-56; Guggenheim Fellowship, 1957-58, 1961; Folger Shakespeare Library Fellow, 1961-62.

Member: Modern Language Association; American Association of University Professors.

* * * * *

PAT FRANK

Full Name: Pat Harry Hart Frank.
Born May 5, 1907, at Chicago, Illinois. Son of Harry Hart Frank and Doris Aileen Cohen. Married and divorced. Two children: Perry Patrick, Anina (adopted). Education: Attended University of Florida, 1925-26.

Career: Correspondent and consultant.
Reporter, *Jacksonville Journal*, 1927-29; Reporter, *New York Journal*, 1929-32; Reporter, *Washington Herald*, 1933-38; Chief, Washington Bureau, Overseas News Agency, 1938-41; Assistant Chief of Mission, Office of War Information, Washington, 1941-44; war correspondent in Italy, Austria, Germany, Turkey and Hungary, 1944-46; Chief of Staff Emeritus, Atlantic Beach Navy, 1949-64; Member of mission to Korea, United Nations, 1952-53; Member of Staff, Democratic Central Committee, 1960; Consultant, NASA, 1961; Consultant, Dept. of Defense, 1963-64. Died October 12, 1964.

Agent: Littauer & Wilkinson, 500 Fifth Avenue, New York, NY 10036.

Awards:
War Dept. special commendation, 1945; distinguished service citation, Reserve Officers Association, 1957; American Heritage Foundation Award, 1961. Member: Overseas Press Club; National Press Club.

* * * * *

H. BRUCE FRANKLIN

Full Name: Howard Bruce Franklin.
Born February 28, 1934, at Brooklyn, New York. Son of Robert Franklin and Florence Cohen. Married Jane Morgan, February 11, 1956. Three children: Karen (born 1956), Gretchen (born 1958), Robert (born 1963).

Education: B.A., Amherst College, 1956; Ph.D., Stanford University, 1961.

Career: Professor of English.
Batch worker, Mayfair Photofinishing Company, Brooklyn, 1951-52; Upholsterer, Carb Manufacturing Company, 1953; Foreman, Shipping Dept., Carb, 1954; tugboat deckhand and mate, Jersey City, NJ, 1955-56; navigator and intelligence officer, Strategic Air Command, 1956-59; scientific writing consultant, Stanford Research Institute, 1962-64; Asst. Professor of English, Johns Hopkins University, 1964-65; Associate Professor of English, Stanford University, 1965-72; Commentator, radio station KPFA, Berkeley, 1970-74; on editorial board, *Science-Fiction Studies*, 1973-DATE; Visiting Fellow, Center for the Humanities, 1974; Professor of English, Rutgers University, 1975-DATE.

Franklin writes:
"Back in 1961, Mark Hillegas (at Colgate) and I (at Stanford) taught the first courses in science fiction ever offered at American colleges and universities. Although I had tenure at Stanford, I was fired in 1972 for giving speeches opposing Stanford's participation in the Indochina War."

* * * * *

DONALD FRANSON

Full Name: Donald Lewis Franson.
Born November 11, 1916, at Chicago, Illinois. Son of Robert Franson (a superintendent of an ice manufacturing plant) and Edith Rose. Education: attended business college.

Career: Material Control Clerk.
Material Control Clerk, General Motors, 1947-74; now retired.

First Professional Sale: "Comes the Revolution," in *Science Fiction Stories*, March, 1956.

Member: Science Fiction Writers of America; National Fantasy Fan Federation; Los Angeles Science Fantasy Society; First Fandom; Mensa.

Interests:
Collecting SF magazines, books, fanzines; automobile pictures; stamps; science fiction fan since 1930. "My writing career is still ahead of me, I feel; I'm going to write more, and, hopefully, sell more of what I write."

MICHAEL FRAYN

Full Name: Michael Frayn.
   Born September 8, 1933, at London, England.
Son of Thomas Allen Frayn (a manufacturer's representative) and Violet Alice Lawson. Married Gillian Palmer, February 18, 1960. Three daughters.

Education: B.A., Emmanuel College, Cambridge University, 1957.

Career: Writer.
   Reporter, 1957-59; Columnist, *The Guardian*, Manchester, 1959-62; Columnist, *London Observer*, 1962-68;
full-time writer, 1968-DATE.

Agent: Elaine Greene, 31 Newington Green, London
   N16 9PU, England.

Awards:
   Somerset Maugham Award, 1966, for *The Tin Men*; Hawthornden Prize, 1967, for *The Russian Interpreter*;
National Press Club Award, 1970, for a series of articles in the *Observer* on Cuba.

* * * * *

STEVE FRAZEE

Full Name: Charles Steve Frazee.
   Born September 28, 1909, at Salida, Colorado. Son
of Charles William Frazee and Laura Belle Blevins.
Married Patricia Thomass, September 2, 1937. Two
children: Eric, Linda.

Education: A.B., Western State College, 1937.

Career: Writer.
   Heavy construction and mining worker, La Junta, Colo-
rado, 1926-36, 1941-43; Instructor in Journalism,
La Junta High School, 1937-41; full-time writer, 1946-
DATE; Director, Salida Building and Loan Association;
Building Inspector, City of Salida, 1950-63; on advi-
sory council, San Isabel National Forest, 1959-DATE.

Awards: Western Heritage Award, 1960, for "Legal and
   Proper"; 1st annual short story award, Cowboy Hall
   of Fame, 1961.

Member: Western Writers of America; Colorado Authors
   League; FibArk; American Canoe Association; American
   White Water Association.

* * * * *

NANCY FREEDMAN

Full Name: Nancy Freedman.
   Born July 4, 1920, at Chicago, Illinois. Daughter
of Hartley Farnham Mars (a surgeon) and Brillianna
Hintermeister (a reporter). Married Benedict Freedman (a philosopher and novelist), June 29, 1940.
Three children: Johanna (born 1949), Michael Hartley
(born 1951), Deborah Benedict (born 1953).

Education:
   "Dropout from every university in Southern California; worked in theatre with Max Reinhardt; attended
the Art Institute, Chicago, for two summers."

Career: Writer and sometime actress.

First Professional Sale: *Mrs. Mike*, Coward-McCann,
   1947 (with Benedict Freedman).

Agent: Scott Meredith, 580 Fifth Avenue, New York,
   NY 10036.

Honors: "Boston University has set up a Benedict and
   Nancy Freedman Collection, Mugar Library."

Interests:
   Art, theater, climbing waterfalls, sailing. "I have
lived, worked, brought up three children on the island
of Mallorca, on Barbados, in Italy and Switzerland,
and North Africa. Much of my work has been in collaboration with my husband, Benedict, who is Chairman of
the Mathematics Dept. at Occidental College. He is
now engaged on an *Ethics* based on modal logic, on which
I am assisting.
   "It is my belief that the future must be constantly
striven for, that man himself must take a role in the
development of man. I consider the artist, the novel-
list, those who work in the creative and philosophic
fields to be fighters for the future. They set forth
the possibilities, give the vision which later generations implement."

* * * * *

RUSSELL FREEDMAN

Full Name: Russell Bruce Freedman.
   Born October 11, 1929, at San Francisco, California.
Son of Louis N. Freedman (a publishers' representative)
and Irene Gordon. Education: B.A., University of
California, Berkeley, 1951.

Career: Writer and editor.
   Newsman, Associate Press, San Francisco, 1953-56;
television publicity writer, J. Walter Thompson Co.
(advertising agency), 1956-60; associate staff member,
Columbia Encyclopedia, 1961-63; Editor, Crowell-Collier
Educational Corp., 1964-65; Instructor of writing work-
ships, New School for Social Research, 1969-DATE; free-
lance writer. Member: Authors League; American Civil
Liberties Union.

* * * * *

CELIA FREMLIN

Full Name: Celia Fremlin Goller.
   Born June 20, 1914, at London, England. Daughter of
Heaver Stuart Fremlin (a bacteriologist) and Margaret
Addiscott. Married Elia Goller (a school teacher),
July 6, 1942. Three children: Nicholas, Geraldine,
Sylvia.

Education: B.A., Oxford University, 1937; B.Litt.,
   1937.

Career: Writer. Award: Edgar Award, Best Novel,
   1959, *The Hours Before Dawn*.

* * * * *

GLYN FREWER

Full Name: Glyn Frewer.
   Born September 4, 1931, at Oxford, England. Son of
Louis Frewer (a library superintendent) and Dorothy
Poulter. Married Lorna Townsend, August 11, 1956.
Three children: Neil, Sean, Claire.

GLYN FREWER (cont.)

Education: B.A., St. Catherine's College, Oxford University, 1955; M.A., 1959.

Career: Copywriter.
Student Officer, British Council, London, 1955; Trainee Copywriter, Spottiswoode Ltd. (advertising agency), London, 1955-57; Creative Controller, Masius, Wynne-Williams & D'Arcy MacManus (advertising agency), London, 1961-DATE. Member: Society of Authors.

Agent: Bolt & Watson, 8 Storey's Gate, London S.W.1, England.

* * * * *

GERTRUDE FRIEDBERG

Full Name: Gertrude Friedberg.
Born March 17, 1908, at New York, New York. Daughter of George and Sylvia Tonkonogy. Married Charles K. Friedberg (a medical doctor; died 1972). Two children: Richard, Barbara.

Education: B.A., Barnard College, 1929.

Career: Writer and teacher.
Substitute teacher of mathematics, New York Public School System, 1964-DATE; writer.

First Professional Sale: "Three-Cornered Moon," a play produced on Broadway, 1933.

* * * * *

OSCAR J. FRIEND

Full Name: Oscar Jerome Friend.
Born January 9, 1898, at Saint Louis, Missouri. Son of Joseph Friend (a pharmacist) and Virginia Lillian Dooley. Married Irene Marquess Ozment, Jan. 24, 1917. Two children: Kittie Sue (born 1920), Janice Adair (born 1925).

Education: Two years of pharmacy school; became a licensed pharmacist.

Career: Pharmacist and author.
Pharmacist , Friend Drug Co., 1916-36; Editor and writer, Popular Publications, 1936-44; screenwriter, Monogram Studios (and others), Hollywood, 1944-48; full-time author, 1944-63. Died at Levittown, New York, January 19, 1963.

First Professional Sale: A story to *Saturday Evening Post*, 1919.

Agent: Kittie West, Otis Kline Associates, 39 Andover Road, Roslyn Heights, NY 11577.

Interests:
Cooking, amateur art, card games (especially poker), inventing gadgets, music, literature.

Kittie West, Oscar Friend's daughter, provided the following reminiscences of her father:
"My grandfather's drugstore, in Fort Smith, Arkansas, was on the main street, Garrison Avenue, about three blocks up from the Poteau River, which bordered on Oklahoma. Granddad was what then was called a "registered pharmacist and minor surgeon. He was quite a character himself. He played mandolin and sang, was a terrific amateur chef, loved every sort of game-- especially poker--and had a wonderful sense of humor. In the back of the drugstore there was a long room, as big as the front of the store. There you could find the counter with all the weights and measures (for there was very little patent medicine then, and he made up all his liquid doses as well as rolled pills), an ice box, a huge old stove, and a long table with benches and chairs pulled up to it. This back room was the gathering place for many an old-timer, plus the town's one rabbi, Father Horn, and any drummer who happened by. There they could find food and drink and friendly conversation. On Saturdays, the dirt farmers, blacks, a few cowboys, and the Indians from across the river came to town and to the drugstore for goods, a little doctoring, sympathy, or just to exchange wild yarns about the old days. Dad grew up on all this, and it was natural for him to write of it.
"Then, one night Dad had a terrible nightmare. He tried to shake it off and go back to sleep, but soon realized it was useless. So he got up and wrote about it until dawn. He spent two weeks more making a horror novel out of it. After that, he wrote one or two more of this genre. Then he wrote detective stories, one of which blackened the name of Friend in our home town for many years to follow. Many of these tales were written under the pseudonym Owen Fox Jerome. When my grandfather died, Dad took over the drugstore, and didn't write much for a few years until his younger sister finished college. Then, through his agent, Leo Margulies, he had the opportunity to join the Ned Pines outfit [Popular Publications] in New York.
"They put him to work editing and writing--westerns and mysteries, of course. One day a fellow rushed in to his office waving the current cover of *Thrilling Wonder Stories*, and demanded a story to fit the cover as soon as possible. The picture was the typical one of that era--the swooning, lightly-clad maiden being carried off by a bug-eyed monster. Being a veteran 'hack' by then, Dad wrote it. And that started him off in the science fiction field.
"My sister and I have always been avid readers of science fiction, and we delightedly encouraged him to write more. When we were very young--I about seven and she about two or so--Dad would tell us stories every night. We made him keep one cast of characters going for six weeks. His fairy tales--or fantasy-- were always delightful. And aren't science fiction tales fairy stories for adults?
"On the other hand, Dad always said anything man can imagine he can accomplish sooner or later. Another thing he said not too long before his death was that it seemed the world was catching up with the science fiction field. I don't believe he really thought that, though."

* * * * *

MEADE FRIERSON

Full Name: Meade Frierson III.
Born August 14, 1940, at Nashville, Tennessee. Son of William Coleman Frierson (an English professor) and Jane Davis Smith. Married Penelope Miller, June 11, 1964. Three sons: K. William (born 1966), Meade IV (born 1967), Eric Sean (born 1973).

Education: B.A., University of Alabama, 1963; LL.B., University of Virginia, 1966.

MEADE FRIERSON (cont.)

Career: Attorney.
Partner in the law firm of Cabaniss, Johnston, Gardner, Dumas, and Oneal, Birmingham, Alabama.

First Professional Sale: Verse published in the *Arkham Collector*, #6.

Honors: Fan Guest of Honor, Deep South Con '73, New Orleans. Member: Southern Fandom Confederation (President).

Interests: SF research, writing pastiches and parodies, poetry.

* * * * *

ARTHUR FRIGGENS

Full Name: Arthur Henry Friggens.
Born March 2, 1920, at Penzance, Cornwall, England. Son of James Ede Friggens (Manager, Penzance Gas Co.) and Mary Strick. Married Elsa Duthie, March 31, 1955. One step-daughter, Christine Simpson (born 1942).

Education: Certificate, Oxford University, 1937; Matriculation, London University, 1937.

Career: Customs officer.
Captain, Royal Artillery, 1940-47; Officer of Customs and Excise, H.M. Government, England, 1948-DATE; author.

First Professional Sale: *Mortorio*, Robert Hale, 1973 (with Eric Burgess).

Agent: Elspeth Gordon, Manor House, Popes Avenue, Twickenham, Middlesex, England.

Member: Royal Overseas League; Folio Society.

Interests: Reading, modern languages (especially German), travel, cooking.

Friggens discusses the art of collaboration:
"Eric Burgess and I are now engaged in writing our fifth SF novel together, and our period of collaboration has lasted since 1970. We try to complete two books every eighteen months, so have no real time to engage in 'prima-donna' attitudes. But obviously, difficulties do arise. Before they get too serious, we down pens and adjourn to a conveniently placed local 'pub,' where a few pints of real English draught ale do much to mollify--and probably help to produce other ideas better than the ones in dispute. So differences of opinion have their good points too!"

* * * * *

LOIS HAMILTON FULLER

Full Name: Lois Hamilton Fuller.
Born August 13, 1915, at Bayonne, New Jersey. Daughter of Emmett S. Hamilton (a banker) and Mabel Havens. Married Donald L. Fuller (a scientist), October 15, 1938. Two children: Margaret, John.

Education: A.B., Smith College, 1937; attended graduate school at University of California, Berkeley, and University of Maryland.

Career: English teacher.
English teacher, Briarcliff Junior College, 1937-38; English and shorthand teacher, Churchman Business College, 1945-46; substitute teacher, Ridgewood, New Jersey public schools, 1958-DATE.

Member: Authors Guild; Mystery Writers of America; Children's Book Guild; Smith College Club.

* * * * *

H. B. FYFE

Full Name: Horace Bowne Fyfe, Jr.
Born September 30, 1918, at Jersey City, New Jersey. Son of Horace Bowne Fyfe and Lillian Lewis. Married Adeline Marie Dougherty, September 8, 1946.

Education: B.S., Columbia University.

Career: Author. Member: Science Fiction Writers of America.

First Professional Sale: "Locked Out," in *Astounding Science Fiction*, February, 1940.

* * * * *

JOHN KENNETH GALBRAITH

Full Name: John Kenneth Galbraith.
Born October 15, 1908, at Iona Station, Ontario, Canada. Son of William Archibald Galbraith (a politician and farmer) and Catherine Kendall. Married Catherine Atwater, September 17, 1937. Three sons: John Alan, Peter, James.

Education: B.S., University of Toronto, 1931; M.S., University of California, 1933; Ph.D., 1934.

Career: Professor of Economics; diplomat & advisor.
Professor of Economics, Harvard University, 1934-39, 1948-DATE; Asst. Professor of Economics, Princeton University, 1939-42; Member, Board of Editors, *Fortune*, 1943-48; economic advisor, National Defense Advisory Committee, 1940-41; administrator in charge of Price Division, U.S. Office of Price Administration, 1941-42; Department Administrator, 1942-43; Director, U.S. Strategic Bombing Survey, 1945; Director, Office of Economic Security Policy, 1946; presidential advisor to Presidents John F. Kennedy and Lyndon B. Johnson; American Ambassador Extraordinary and Plenipotentiary in India, 1961-63; National Chairman, Americans for Democratic Action, 1967-DATE.

Awards:
Research Fellow, University of California, 1931-34; Fellow, Social Science Research Council, 1937-38; Medal of Freedom, 1946; LL.D., Bard College, 1958, Miami University (Ohio), 1959, University of Toronto, 1963, University of Guelph, 1965, University of Saskatchewan, 1965; Sarah Josepha Hale Award, Friends of the Richards Free Library, 1967.

Member:
National Institute of Arts and Letters; American Academy of Arts and Sciences (Fellow); Twentieth Century Fund (Trustee); American Economic Association; American Farm Economists Association; Century Club; Harvard Club, New York.

PAUL GALLICO

Full Name: Paul William Gallico.
    Born July 26, 1897, at New York, New York. Son of
Paolo Gallico (a concert pianist) and Hortense Erlich.
Married Alva Thoits Taylor, 1921 (divorced, 1934);
married Elaine St. Johns, 1935 (divorced, 1936); married Baroness Pauline Gariboldi, 1939 (divorced);
married Baroness Virginia von Falz-Fein, 1963. Children: William Taylor, Robert Leston.

Education: B.A., Columbia University, 1921.

Career: Writer.
    Worked as a gym instructor, translator, longshore-
man; Review Secretary, National Board of Motion Picture Review, 1921; Assistant Managing Editor, *New York
Daily News*, 1922-36; free-lance author, 1936-76. Died
July 15, 1976.

Agent: Harold Ober Associates, 40 E. 49th St., New
    York, NY 10017.

Member: Quiet Birdman; Fencer's Club; London Fencing
    Club; Buck's Club; Epee Club.

* * * * *

RAYMOND Z. GALLUN

Full Name: Raymond Zinke Gallun.
    Born March 22, 1910, at Beaver Dam, Wisconsin. Son
of Adolph Gallun (a farmer) and Martha Emmalina Louisa
Zinke. Married Frieda Ernestine Talmey, December 26,
1959 (died 1974).

Education: Attended University of Wisconsin, 1929-30,
    Alliance Française, 1938-39, San Marcos Univer-
    sity, Peru, 1960.

Career: Technical writer.
    Employed at Edo Corporation (manufacturer of sonar
equipment), Publications Division, 1964-DATE; "otherwise a long and various history of occupational--and
other--vagabondage, generally quite pleasant, if lowly."

First Professional Sales:
    "The Crystal Ray," in *Air Wonder Stories*, November,
1929; "The Space Dwellers," in *Science Wonder Stories*,
November, 1929 (simultaneous).

Agent: Robert P. Mills Ltd., 156 E. 52nd St., New
    York, NY 10022.

Member: Science Fiction Writers of America.

Gallun writes:
    "*Amazing, Astounding, Wonder, Startling, Marvel*--
there was a magical innocence even in the old names
of the mags, and a Charm of the Improbable, much of
it lost now, it seems to me, though there is, of
course, also a vast gain in sophistication.
    "To me, being of a generation that can look back to
when they were only wild dreams to most folks, Moon
journeys, atomic power, etc., remain rather miracu-
lous to this day. I hope that those born nearer to
such accomplishments can still feel some of that, instead of merely accepting them.
    "In the old days we dreamed free, with few guide-
lines. Relatively little speculative fiction was yet

written. So the field was wide open for our own grop-
ings and yearnings to know about the hidden things in
time and space. Literary quality wasn't of very great
importance. We couldn't profit so much from what others
had done. But we could get a new idea a lot more easily.
    "Science fiction didn't have much recognition. If
you read it or wrote it, quite a few people thought
you were nuts. And you could feel sort of guilty and
ashamed.
    "Myths that we loved as substitutes for unreachable
realities have since sadly been smashed. We are now
told that Percival Lowell was mistaken--that there
are no canals on Mars. Nor is there any Barsoom or
Pellucidar.
    "But maybe the reality, or the dreams nearer the
reality, have an improved romanticism. And the job
of writing isn't so very much changed.
    "I still opt for a positive approach to the future.
I still think that advancing science and technology--
under control by good and broad judgment--offer the
best means for making the centuries to come good ones.
Though there are many incomplete areas to be filled.
Even in just our own solar system, there is surely not
yet any shortage of energy or materials, if we can
find ways to reach and handle them, and the spiritual
acumen to keep ourselves and whatever we touch in balance. I like simple living, with no over-emphasis on
material possessions. But I do like to think that, before so very long, Mars and Venus will be made habi-
table, and that a two century life-span will be the
regular thing. I even hope that somebody will actually set off for the stars.
    "I suspect that--granting the application of good
sense as much as possible--there is no need to retreat,
and close doors, either externally or inside ourselves.'

* * * * *

DANIEL F. GALOUYE

Full Name: Daniel Francis Galouye [ga-loúie].
    Born February 11, 1920, at New Orleans, Louisiana.
Son of Jean Baptiste Galouye (a businessman) and Hilda
Jeanne Mouney. Married Carmel Barbara Jordan, Dec.
26, 1945. Two children: Denise Marie (born 1946),
Jeanne Arlene (born 1948).

Education: B.A., Louisiana State University, 1941.

Career: Journalist and writer.
    Naval pilot during World War II; successively repor-
ter, rewrite, assistant news editor, editorial writer,
chief editorial writer, and associate editor, *New Orleans States-Item*, 1946-65; writer, 1965-76. Died
September 7, 1976.

First Professional Sale:
    "Tonight the Sky Will Fall," in *Imagination*, May,
1952 ("Rebirth," purchased later, was published by
Imagination in March, 1952).

Agent: Lurton Blassingame, 60 E. 42nd St., New York,
    NY 10017.

Awards: *Dark Universe* was cited by *Books and Bookmen*
    as the best SF novel published in England in 1962.

Member: Science Fiction Writers of America; United
    States Retired Officers Association. Interests:
    telescopy, astronomy, clock building, air flight.

DANIEL F. GALOUYE (cont.)

Galouye writes:

"Science fiction, I find, is currently in its heal-thiest state thus far, although the medium appears to be undergoing revolutionary change in at least two directions.

"First, there is the ascendancy of nonperiodical publications, to the apparent detriment of our pro-fessional magazines. Hardbound and/or paperback prin-tings are claiming more and more attention--with the end result that periodicals, although probably 'hol-ding their own' circulationwise, are not realizing growth commensurate with expanding population. Hard-and soft-covers have not only walked off with all the benefits accruing from both a growing readership and increased interest in science, but have also rendered magazine submissions more unprofitable to authors in the field. A single book, written over a three- or four-(with sub-month period, will fetch more income (with sub-sidiary and foreign-rights earnings taken into con-sideration) than a whole year's worth of submissions to the periodicals. Unless the magazines can manage a breakthrough in the area of circulation, and become competitive with paperbacks, we may well witness the demise of the periodical format. (This would indeed be unfortunate for, oddly enough, successful and re-peated publication in SF magazines is a credential that is still generally expected of new novelists by book publishers. In other words: from where are our new writers going to come if opportunity for publica-tion in the magazines becomes increasingly restricted, or perhaps eliminated entirely?)

"Second, revolutionary change involving the so-called 'new wave,' although having profound impact on the field at present, will nevertheless prove to be of ephemeral consequences. Throughout the history of literature, there have been various deviationist schools--flashy stylistic efforts striking off in new directions, and demanding attention on the strength of their very bold and unorthodox nature. But, always, these movements have ended up on spur tracks, while literature in general has adhered to the basics of 'story-telling' in the classic sense, as epitomized in the epic narrative. Only when the 'tools of car-pentry' become more important than the finished pro-ducts for which they were designed to construct--only then will 'cute and unorthodox' styles of prose-design-ing become more important than the fundamental purpose underlying literary effort, i.e.: conveying to the reader a precise and clearly-understandable 'idea,' 'intriguing plot,' or 'fascinating concept.' When a story is intended only as a showcase for manipulation of words in bizarre arrangement, it may gain the author momentary recognition as a phraseologist, but the story itself is soon forgotten. When the story's ul-timate aim is to present a straightforward account of situation-complication-resolution, however, it stands on its own merit, and, if sufficiently worthy, will be long and clearly remembered. Phraseologists we'll always have (at present, too many of them--all riding the 'new wave' crest). But there'll always be a much greater demand for down-to-earth story-telling. The nonliterati will stay in the majority.

"It's interesting to note that (in my opinion, at least, and in the opinion of many SF writers whom I know) SF is enjoying an ever greater upsurge else-where than in the U.S. This phenomenon no doubt re-sults from admiration of and fascination over America's scientific achievements. And we find that, here a-gain, the works most in demand--or, at least, those considered most presentable by foreign publishers--are the ones which were first published in the U.S.

"long before the 'new wave' was a gleam in Michael Moorcock's eyes.

"What have my own contributions been to the develop-ment of the SF genre? Insignificant indeed, relative to the benefits I have derived from association with the field and its personalities."

He adds: "I have no works in progress at the moment, although I hope for improved medical circumstances to permit resumption of literary output. Belated neuro-logical injury from WWII head wounds as a Naval pilot forced resignation from a journalistic career in 1965, and has, over the past few years, damped initiative in the field of fiction writing. But, like MacArthur, I hope to return."

* * * * *

NORMAN GARBO

Full Name: Norman Garbo.
    Born February 15, 1919, at New York, New York. Son of Maximillian W. Garbo and Fannie Deitz. Married Rhoda Locke, April 15, 1942. One son, Mickey.

Education: Studied at City College of New York, 1935-37, and at New York Academy of Fine Art, 1937-41.

Career: Artist and writer.
    Portrait painter, 1941-DATE; also a free-lance writer and lecturer.

* * * * *

GABRIEL GARCIA MARQUEZ

Full Name: Gabriel Garcia Marquez.
    Born March 6, 1928, at Aracataca, Colombia. Married Mercedes Barcha. Two children: Rodrigo, Gonzalo.

Education: Attended Liceo Nacional de Zipaquira, Colombia, and Universidad Nacional de Colombia.

Career: Writer. Awards: Colombia Association of Writers and Artists Award, 1954, for "Un Dia Despues del Sabado."

Agent: Carmen Balcells, Urgel 241, Barcelona 11, Spain.

* * * * *

MAURICE B. GARDNER

Full Name: Maurice Benjamin Gardner.
    Born July 15, 1905, at Portland, Maine. Education: attended Deering High School.

Career: Railroad machinist, Portland Terminal Co., 1923-69; now retired.

* * * * *

LEON GARFIELD

Full Name: Leon Garfield.
    Born July 14, 1921, at Brighton, Sussex, England. Son of David Kalman Garfield (a businessman) and Rose Blaustein. Married Vivien Dolores Alcock, Oct. 23, 1948. One daughter, Jane Angela.

LEON GARFIELD (cont.)

Career: Writer.
Biochemical Technician, Whittington Hospital, London, 1946-66; part-time biochemical technician in various hospital laboratories in London, 1966-69; full-time writer, 1969-DATE.

Agent: Monica McCall, 667 Madison Avenue, New York, NY 10021.

Awards: Gold Medal, Boys Clubs of America. Member: P.E.N.

* * * * *

WILLIAM GARNER

Full Name: William Garner.
Born at Grimsby, Lincolnshire, England. Married Gwen Owen, 1944. Education: B.Sc., University of Birmingham, 1941.

Career: Writer.
Free-lance writer, 1947-49; did public relations work for Monsanto Co., London, 1949-64, and for Massey-Ferguson Ltd., London, 1964-66; full-time novelist, 1966-DATE.

Agent: Jonathan Clowes, 20 New Cavendish St., London W.1, England.

* * * * *

DAVID GARNETT

Full Name: David Garnett.
Born March 9, 1892, at Brighton, Sussex, England. Son of Edward Garnett (a literary critic) and Constance Black (a translator). Married Rachel Alice Marshall, 1921 (died 1940); married Angelica Bell, May, 1942. Six children: Richard Duncan (born 1923), William Tomlin Kasper (born 1925), Amaryllis Virginia (born 1943), Henrietta Catherine Vanessa (born 1945), Frances Olivia (born 1946), Nerissa Stephen (born 1946).

Education:
A.R.C.S., Imperial College of Science and Technology, 1913; D.I.C., 1915; Fellow, Imperial College of Sciences. Interests: Fishing, travel.

Career: Author.
Publisher, Nonesuch Press, 1923-32; Literary Editor, New Statesman, 1932-34; with British Foreign Office, 1941-46; has also been a bookseller.

Agent: A. P. Watt & Son, 26/28 Bedford Row, London WC1R 4HL, England.

Awards: Hawthornden Prize; James Tait-Black Prize, for Lady into Fox; Commander of the British Empire.

* * * * *

DAVID S. GARNETT

Full Name: David S. Garnett.
Born June 15, 1947, in Cheshire, England. Education: B.Sc., University of London, 1968.

Career: Writer.
Has been a transport executive in a department store, a wine taster and bottler, and many others "too numerous to mention."

First Professional Sale: Mirror in the Sky, Berkley, 1969.

* * * * *

PAUL GARSON

Full Name: Gary Paul Garson.
Born March 7, 1946, at Washington, D.C. Son of Harry Garson and Rae Goldfaden.

Education: B.A., Tulane University, 1968; M.A., Johns Hopkins University, 1970.

Career: School teacher.
Teacher, private progressive school, secondary level.

First Professional Sale: The Great Quill, Doubleday, 1973.

Agent: Elaine Markson, 44 Greenwich Avenue, New York NY 10011.

Awards: First Prize, Young Writers Fiction Contest, Carolina Quarterly, 1970.

Interests:
Karate (1st degree black belt), archery, astronomy, travel (20-odd countries, including USSR), sports cars, film making. "When I was young I was constantly told (1) that you can't do more than one thing at a time, (2) writing was nice but not something you would want to do with your life, (3) that one should settle down to earth, and (4) that Man would never land on the Moon. I didn't believe them."

* * * * *

RICHARD M. GARVIN

Full Name: Richard McClellan Garvin.
Born August 4, 1934, at Hollywood, California. Son of John N. Garvin (a publisher's representative) and Elizabeth Nolte. Married Carolyn Mathis, April 29, 1962. Two children: Elizabeth Ann (born 1966), Jessica (born 1970).

Education: B.A., San Jose State College, 1956.

Career: Creative Director, Bozell & Jacobs (advertising agency), 1961-DATE. Agent: Curtis Brown Ltd., 60 E. 56th St., New York, NY 10022.

* * * * *

JANE GASKELL

Full Name: Jane Gaskell Lynch.
Born July 7, 1941, at Grange-over-Sands, Lancaster, England. Daughter of Andrew Gaskell Denvil (a watercolour painter) and Edith Hackett (a teacher). Married Gerald Lynch, May 10, 1963 (divorced 1968). One daughter, Lucy Emma Lynch (born 1965). Education: Educated at home by parents.

JANE GASKELL (cont.)

Career: Journalist.
Has been an usherette for a London theatre, and a
reader for *Argosy*; Feature Writer, *London Daily Mail*,
1965-DATE.

Agent: Robin Dalton, IFA, 11 Hanover Street, London
W.1, England.

Awards:
Runner-up, Llewellyn Rhys Award, 1961, for *Attic
Summer*; Somerset Maugham Award, 1970, for *A Sweet,
Sweet Summer*.

Gaskell writes:
"I haven't yet worked out a smooth definition of
fantasy--though I know why science fiction makes me
unhappy. SF seems to be used as a vehicle by so many
pamphleteers whose interest is in lecturing us: telling us how we should achieve utopia, or how naughty
we are to contaminate our earth, or how essentially
we should vote. SF is so often political or satiri-
cal--concerned with here and now while it's pretending
to be concerned with space and time and miracle.
"The SF man with the axe to grind so often seems to
use the old detective-story formula of shutting his
dozen characters away (it used to be on a desert island, or in a drawing-room after a murder--now it's
in a spaceship or on an all-too-familiar star or planet or in some arid future) so that the author can
slap them around a bit, pull their strings, and 'demonstrate' how human nature reacts to the situation--
to the author's recipe, depending on this author's
social blueprint.
"Fantasy perhaps has more juice in it--more excess,
more 'let's go....' Fantasy is packed with nuance,
flavour, weather, quest, far-off horizons. Fantasy
revels in the setting-out on the journey. SF seems
to be providing all the answers, and while this may
make some readers feel safe, and reassured that they
really aren't adventuring into anything strange after all, it makes me feel boxed-in."

* * * * *

DIMITRI V. GAT

Full Name: Dimitri Vsevolod Gat.
Born October 5, 1936, at Pittsburgh, Pennsylvania.
Son of John Dimitri Gat and Anne Prunte. Married
Margaret Ann Moses, June 24, 1967. Two children:
Christine (born 1968), Alexandra (born 1970).

Education: B.A., University of Pittsburgh, 1960;
M.A. in L.S., University of Pittsburgh.

Career: Professor of Technical Communications.
Advertising Assistant, Calgon Corporation, 1960-62;
Asst. Librarian, Harvard University Library, 1963-69;
Editor, *Harvard Librarian*, 1965-67; Librarian, Mount
Holyoke College, 1969-71; Professor of Technical Com-
munications, University of Massachusetts, 1971-DATE.

First Professional Sale: *The Shepherd Is My
Lord*, Doubleday, 1971.

Agent: Curtis Brown Ltd., 60 E. 56th St., New York,
NY 10022.

Awards: Honorable Mention, *Atlantic* short story contest for college students, 1959, for "Queen's Gambit

Declined"; Fourth Prize, *Atlantic* Short Story Contest
for College Students, 1960, for "Nancynancynancynancy."

Member: Science Fiction Writers of America.

Interests: Vegetable gardening, golf, squash rackets,
softball, poker, films.

Gat comments: "Stay out of the hands of doctors."

* * * * *

JACK GAUGHAN

Full Name: John Brian Francis Gaughan.
Born September 24, 1930, at Springfield, Ohio. Son
of James J. and Elizabeth Gaughan. Gaughan is married,
and has two children: Brian, Norah.

Education: Attended Dayton Art Institute.

Career: Professional artist.

First Professional Sale: The dustjacket for Austin Hall's *People of the Comet*, Griffin Publishing
House, 1948.

Awards:
Guest of Honor, 27th World Science Fiction Convention
(St. Louiscon), St. Louis, 1969; Hugo Award, Best Pro-
fessional Artist, 1966 (1967), 1967 (1968), 1968 (1969).

Gaughan notes:
"SF in now *large enough* to accommodate Conan, Cummings,
Bradbury, Aldiss, Delany, Spinrad, etc. Why favor one
while trying to exclude the other?"

* * * * *

VANCE A. GEIGLEY

Full Name: Vance Acton Geigley.
Born October 10, 1907, at Webb City, Missouri. Son
of Joseph D. and Ella Mae Geigley. Married Mary Catherine Snyder, October 30, 1937.

Career: Businessman.
Has been a mining and general building contractor,
and a real estate investor. Member: Elks Lodge,
American Legion, Veterans of Foreign Wars.

* * * * *

RICHARD E. GEIS

Full Name: Richard Erwin Geis.
Born July 19, 1927, at Portland, Oregon. Son of
Walter Erwin Geis and Delores Petke. Education: Attended Vanport College (now Portland State University)
1942-43.

Career: Writer and editor.
Has been a stockman, dishwasher, TV repairman, apartment house manager, auto painter; Publisher and Editor
of *Science Fiction Review* (formerly *The Alien Critic*),
1972-DATE; free-lance author.

First Professional Sale: "Fight Game," in *Adam*,
January, 1959.

RICHARD E. GEIS (cont.)

Agent: Virginia Kidd, Box 278, Milford, PA 18337.

Awards:
Hugo Award, Best Amateur Publication, 1968 (1969), *Psychotic*; Hugo Award, Best Amateur Publication, 1969 (1970), *Science Fiction Review*; Hugo Award, Best Fanzine, 1973 (1974), *The Alien Critic*; Hugo Award, Best Fanzine, 1974 (1975), *The Alien Critic*; Hugo Award, Best Fan Writer, 1970 (1971), 1974 (1975), 1975 (1976).

Interests: Collection of porno films; conspiracy theories.

Geis writes:
"Neurotic, introverted. Talent for editing and writing. Dropped by doctor when infant--result was spine injury; faulty coordination, psychological tension, extreme self-consciousness. Security oriented. High degree of self-awareness, sophistication, insight, empathy, tolerance."

Member: Science Fiction Writers of America; Fantasy Amateur Press Association.

* * * * *

CURT GENTRY

Full Name: Curt Gentry.
Born June 13, 1931, at Lamar, Colorado. Son of Curtis Herman Gentry (a city clerk) and Coral McMillin. Married Laura Wilson Spence (a professional librarian) October 30, 1954.

Education: B.A., San Francisco State College, 1957.

Career: Writer.
Part-time reporter for various Colorado newspapers, 1947-50; Head of Mail Order Department, Paul Elder Books, San Francisco, 1954-57; Manager, Tro Harper Books, San Francisco, 1957-61; full-time writer, 1961-DATE.

Agent: Paul R. Reynolds, 599 Fifth Avenue, New York NY 10017.

Awards:
Command prizes in Air Force short story contests, 1953, 1954; honorable mention for novel in progress, first annual Joseph Henry Jackson Competition, 1957; Edgar Award, Special Award, 1967, for *Frame-Up: The Incredible Case of Tom Mooney and Warren Billings*.
Member: Authors Guild; California Historical Society.

* * * * *

S. C. GEORGE

Full Name: Sidney Charles George.
Born June 2, 1898, at Grimsby, England. Education: educated in England.

Career: Air Force officer.
Served in the Royal Garrison Artillery of the British Army, 1917-20; career officer, Royal Air Force, 1924-53, serving in India, Palestine, Transjordan, Egypt, Sudan, Malaya, Australia; retired as Group Captain; full-time author, 1953-DATE.

Honors: Member, Order of the British Empire, 1948; Member, Royal Victorian Order, 4th Class, 1953.

Member:
Society of Authors; Institute of Chartered Accountants (Fellow); Chartered Institute of Secretaries (Fellow).

* * * * *

WILLIAM GERHARDI

Full Name: William Alexander Gerhardie.
Born November 21, 1895, at St. Petersburg, Russia. Son of Charles Alfred Gerhardi and Clara Wadsworth.

Education: B.Litt., Worcester College, Oxford University; M.A., Worcester College, Oxford.

Career: Writer.
First Editor of "English by Radio," BBC, 1942-45; Director, DeJersey & Co. Ltd.; free-lance author. Died July 15, 1977.

Awards & Honors:
Phoenix Award, 1965; Arts Council of Great Britain Bursary, 1966; Order of the British Empire; Order of St. Stanislaus of Russia; War Cross of Czechoslovakia.

* * * * *

DAVID GERROLD

Full Name: Jerrold David Friedman.
Born January 24, 1944, at Chicago, Illinois. Son of Louis Friedman and Johanna Fleischer.

Education: B.A., San Fernando Valley State College, 1967.

Career: Writer.
Has also been an assistant manager of a toy department, clerk in a dirty book store, and a television producer; currently a full-time writer.

First Professional Sale: "The Trouble with Tribbles," an episode on the TV series *Star Trek*, aired December 29, 1967.

Agent: Henry Morrison, 58 W. 10th St., New York, NY 10011.

Member: Science Fiction Writers of America; Writers Guild of America, West.

Gerrold writes:
"My *main* concern is that my writing should justify the kind of praise that has been bestowed on me so lavishly. Some of the praise--as well as some of the criticism--is undeserved. (I know what my faults are better than anyone else; after all, I am exposed to them more often.)
"To be quite blunt about fans and fandom, now that I have sampled fame, I find (just like many others before me) that it is only a temporary high. After a while, it is only a bore. My ideal now is to be a nonentity and find my fulfillment on more personal levels. Part of the fulfillment (but not all) involves writing the very best possible stories that I can.
"It is not as important to me as it once was that my

DAVID GERROLD (cont.)

"books win awards and fame, although that would be
nice. It is of much more importance that they be as
good as I can write them, and that they entertain the
readers. I don't believe that a book, no matter how
good or important it is, should have to carry around
the baggage of its author. A book should be able to
stand on its own, without salesmanship or apologists
or explanations, just as a human being should stand
on his own.

"Therefore, more and more I am divorcing myself
from my books--or at least from the cult of 'writer-
hood.' Once I am finished with a work, I want to be
completely finished with it, and move on to the next.
My favorite book is always the one currently in the
typewriter. (My next one.) Or, as my mother says,
'My children are going to have enough aggravation;
they don't need me following them around.'"

* * * * *

MARK S. GESTON

Full Name: Mark Symington Geston.
   Born June 20, 1946, at Atlantic City, New Jersey.
Son of John C. Geston (a teacher) and Mary Symington
(a teacher and lecturer). Married Gayle Howard,
June 12, 1971 (divorced 1972).

Education: A.B., Kenyon College, 1968; J.D., New
   York University Law School, 1971.

Career: Attorney.
   Attorney with the firm of Eberle, Berlin, Kading,
Turnbow & Gillespie, Boise, Idaho, 1971-DATE; free-
lance author (part-time), 1967-DATE.

First Professional Sale: *Lords of the Starship*,
   Ace, 1967.

Agent: Paul R. Reynolds, 599 Fifth Avenue, New York,
   NY 10017.

Honors & Awards:
   Root-Tilden Scholar, New York University; Kenyon
Review Prize for Achievement in Fiction, 1968.

Member: Science Fiction Writers of America; American Bar Association; Phi Beta Kappa.

Interests: Skiing, history, sick humor, and Coors.

Geston writes:
   "I suppose my main interest or inclination remains
history, my major in undergraduate school. Thus, the
first novel was virtually a fabricated history paper
concerning a distinct historical event. That is also
one of the main reasons for the multiple references
in the second book, *Out of the Mouth of the Dragon*,
to the first. Even though time is largely irrelevant,
because my imagination seems to prefer myth as its
natural environment, it still felt right to have some
thread of commonality running through the first efforts. Later works seem to be standing more on their
own. I must say, however, that this earning-a-living
business gets in the way of one's writing."

He adds: "The most fantastic of all novels, those
whose substance thrived on magic, were written by Thomas Wolfe, the inspiration but too much a genius to be
a guide for my own writing."

VIC GHIDALIA

Full Name: Victor Simon Ghidalia.
   Born January 30, 1926, at New York, New York. Son
of David Ghidalia (an importer) and Hollande Josephat.
Married Roberta Carolyn Epstein, March 30, 1952. One
daughter, Laurie Jill (born 1956).

Education: Attended Pace College, 1945-49.

Career: Public relations expert.
   Ghidalia has handled magazine publicity for the American Broadcasting Company, 1956-DATE.

First Professional Sale: *The Little Monsters*,
   Macfadden, 1969 (anthology).

Member: Sons of the Desert (Board of Governors).

Interests: Collecting SF books, books on movies, movie soundtrack recordings, screen horror movies.

Ghidalia notes:
   "I began this interest by collecting books of imaginative stories. By the time I completed my Arkham
House collection, plus the pulps of the '30s and '40s,
I decided I'd like to share some of the better material
with new readers who probably did not have access to
these yarns. I approached Roger Elwood to act as my
agent, and acting as co-editor, he sold a number of
titles for publication. This collaboration has since
concluded. My goals in this field are to produce anthologies with themes which have never before been published. I have been successful, but there is much more
to do, since not all publishers are as far-sighted as
those who accepted my innovative collections. I've
also had the pleasure of starting my wife (by day a
housewife and mother) as an SF writer; she's just now
beginning to accumulate professional credits."

* * * * *

ANTHONY GIBBS

Full Name: Anthony Gibbs.
   Born March 9, 1902, at Bolton, England. Son of Sir
Philip Gibbs (a journalist and novelist) and Agnes Row-
land. Married Ysobel Maisie Martin, September 15, 1928.
Two children: Philip Martin, Frances Joscelin.

Education: Attended Stonyhurst College, 1918, Royal
   Academy of Music, 1919, Oxford University, 1920.

Career: Author and publisher.
   Free-lance writer, 1925-DATE; London correspondent,
New Yorker, 1929; script writer for Twentieth Century-
Fox, in the 1930s; war correspondent, 1939; parliamentary candidate, 1945; Director, Allan Wingate Ltd. (a
publishing firm), 1948-57, and of Anthony Gibbs and
Phillips Ltd., during the 1960s; founded Tandem Books
(a British paperback line) in 1965, and later sold it
to UPD; currently Chairman, Publishing Investments Inc.

* * * * *

HENRY GIBBS

Full Name: Henry St. John Clair Gibbs.
   Born at Salisbury, Wiltshire, England. Son of Henry
John Gibbs (a farmer and brewer) and Beatrice Evelyn
Rumbold (a concert pianist). Married Mary Elizabeth
Hutchings.

HENRY GIBBS (cont.)

Education: Attended Marlborough College.

Career: Painter and writer.
Has worked as a portrait-painter, industrial reporter, film critic, publisher's reader, foreign and war correspondent, chicken farmer, political analyst, etc.

Awards: Anisfield-Wolf Award for improving racial understanding, 1950, for *Twilight in South Africa*.

Member: Society of Authors; P.E.N.; Mystery Writers of America; Authors Guild; Paternosters.

* * * * *

DENIS GIFFORD

Full Name: Denis Gifford.
Born December 26, 1927, at London, England. Son of William Gifford (a printer) and Amelia Hutchings. Married Angela Kalagias (divorced). One daughter, Pandora Jane (born 1965).

Education: Attended Dulwich College, 1939-44.

Career: Creator/Compiler of TV game shows.
Cartoonist, *Reynolds News*, 1944-45; served in the Royal Air Force, 1946-48; free-lance cartoonist, editor, and writer, 1948-60; creator of the daily newspaper comic strip "Telestrip Evening News"; from late 1950s went increasingly into comedy writing for TV and radio; creator, radio panel game *Sounds Familiar*, 1964; creator of the television version called *Looks Familiar*, 1972; creator, TV original panel game show, *Quick on the Draw*, 1974; writer/producer of compilation films, including "Highlight," a history of musicals, 1963; editor/writer, *Ray Regan Comics*, *Fizz Comics*, etc., 1949; free-lance writer and artist.

First Professional Sale: "Magical Monty," in *All Fun*, 1942.

Member:
British Film Institute; Cartoonists Club of Great Britain; Gothique Film Society; Old Boys Book Collections Club; Sherlock Holmes Society.

Interests: Collecting comics, films, records; video cassette recording.

"I have a determination to establish the British comic paper as a valuable artform and a source of history."

* * * * *

STEPHEN GILBERT

Full Name: Stephen Gilbert.
Born July 22, 1912, at Newcastle, Northern Ireland. Son of William Gilbert and Evelyn Helen Haig. Married Kathleen Ferguson Stevenson, September 21, 1945. Four children: Kathleen, Sally, John, Tom.

Education: Attended private schools in Northern Ireland and Scotland, 1922-30.

Career: Writer and businessman.
Chairman, Samuel McCausland Ltd., Belfast, 1953-DATE; free-lance writer. Member: Farmers Club; National Institute of Agricultural Botany (Fellow).

RAYMOND GILES

Full Name: John Robert Holt.
Born September 24, 1926. Son of Harold Griffith Holt (an Episcopal priest) and Helen Ritter. Married Margaret Stone, May 7, 1955. Two children: Helen Margaret, Carol Elizabeth.

Education: B.A., University of Illinois, 1951.

Career: Literary agent.
Has served as manager of National Association of Educational Broadcasters Network; Manager of Foreign Department, Scott Meredith Literary Agency, 1960-DATE.

Agent: Scott Meredith, 580 Fifth Avenue, New York, NY 10036.

* * * * *

C. B. GILFORD

Full Name: Charles Bernard Gilford.
Born November 10, 1920, at Kansas City, Missouri. Son of Harry A. Gilford and Frances Meehan. Married Martha Patricia Campbell (a teacher), August 16, 1947. Four children: Pamela, Robb, Stasia, Kevin.

Education:
B.S., Rockhurst College, 1942; M.A., Catholic University, 1947; Ph.D., University of Denver, 1952.

Career: Instructor in Creative Writing.
Instructor in Speech and English, Rockhurst College, 1947-51; Associate Professor of Drama, St. Louis University, 1952-59; Lecturer in Theatre, University of Missouri, 1959-69; Instructor in Creative Writing, Johnson County Community College, 1970-DATE.

Agent: Scott Meredith, 580 Fifth Avenue, New York, NY 10036.

* * * * *

PENELOPE GILLIATT

Full Name: Penelope Ann Douglass Gilliatt.
Born March 25, 1932, at London, England. Daughter of Cyril Conner (a barrister) and Mary Douglass. Married Roger William Gilliatt (a professor), December, 1954 (divorced); married John Osborne (a playwright), May 25, 1963 (divorced). Children: Nolan Kate Osborne.

Education: Attended Bennington College, 1948.

Career: Film critic and writer.
Worked at the Institute of Pacific Relations, New York, and for magazines in London, including *Vogue*, where she became Feature Editor; Film Critic, *London Observer*, 1961-64; Drama Critic, 1964-67; Guest Film Critic, *New Yorker*, 1967, and regular Film Critic, 1968-DATE; novelist, short story writer, screen writer.

Agent: David Higham Associates, 76 Dean St., London W.1, England.

Awards:
Prizes for best screenplay from National Society of Film Critics and New York Film Critics, 1971, and Writers Guild of Britain, 1972, all for "Sunday Bloody Sunday"; American Academy of Arts and Letters Award for Literature, 1972.

DIANA GILLON

Full Name: Diana Pleasance Gillon.
   Born September 1, 1915, at London, England. Daughter of Thomas Henry Towler Case and Evelyn Beatrice White. Married Meir Selig Gillon, June, 1937. Three children: Evelyn Zvi Raanan (son, born 1941), Richard Benedict (born 1944), Dikla Lalage (daughter, born 1945).

Education: Diploma in Librarianship, University of London, 1935.

Career: Critic and author.
   Archivist, Imperial Chemical Industries, 1935-38; Film Critic and member of editorial staff, *Palestine Post*, 1941-47; Film Critic, Palestine Broadcasting Service, 1944-45; free-lance journalist and author; has also appeared on BBC radio, talking about films and books.

Member: Society of Authors.

Diana Gillon writes:
   "As to our views on SF--for what they are worth. We feel that with truth so rapidly catching up with fiction at the moment, there may well be a slight temporary falling-off in new ideas. But as imaginative writers get used to the new set-up of truth, they will certainly come up with a new crop. SF remains the one really effective way of getting revolutionary ideas across to the reader."

* * * * *

MEIR GILLON

Full Name: Meir Selig Gillon.
   Born August 11, 1907, at Sibiu, Transylvania. Son of Josef Hirsch Goldstein and Sara Weinberger. Married Diana Pleasance Case, June, 1937. Three children: Evelyn Zvi Raanan (son, born 1941), Richard Benedict (born 1944), Dikla Lalage (daughter, born 1945).

Education: LL.B., University of London, 1943.

Career: Author.
   Civil servant, Government of Palestine, 1941-46; writer and editor with BBC, 1949-50; free-lance journalist and author, often in collaboration with his wife, 1950-DATE.

Member: Society of Authors; Muswell Hill Bridge Club, London.

Meir Gillon writes:
   "Our own *Unsleep* is, of course, satire of the present (as it was in 1961), told in terms of the future. Successful? Well, the topless dresses didn't really catch on, did they? But apart from that, almost everything we visualized has come true--so perhaps it's been more successful as prophecy than satire."

The Gillons add:
   "Regarding SF and satire, the story must not be so far from present conditions that the parallel is not clear. But given this proviso, the Unnamed Future setting gives the writer freedom to express ideas which, if set in present conditions, might bring him into conflict with the Law of Libel or even, in some places, involve him in political persecution."

MIRRA GINSBURG

Full Name: Mirra Ginsburg.
   Born June 10, 19--, at Bobruisk, Minsk, Russia. Daughter of Iosif Ginsburg and Bronia Geier.

Education: Educated in Russia, Latvia, Canada, U.S.

Career: Translator and editor.
   Translates from the Russian and Yiddish.

First Professional Sale: A translation of Mikhail Bulgakov's story, "The Fatal Eggs," in *The Magazine of Fantasy and Science Fiction*, December, 1964.

Member: P.E.N. Interests: Early art, early music, folklore, cats (big and little).

Ginsburg notes:
   "I hate machines, big cities, new houses (alas, live in one and the other--not in a machine, though, thank heaven). I like SF because and when it is close to myth and folk tale, when it has wit and imagination, not gimmicks. I have also translated such marvelous fantastic and satirical books as Bulgakov's *The Master and Margarita*, *Heart of a Dog*, and "The Fatal Eggs," title story in my anthology of Soviet satire; also, Isaac Bashevis Singer's stories, and folk tales.
   "Regarding Russian science fiction, the Soviet government has cracked down during the last two or three years. Much less is published, and most of it translations from other languages, on both sides of the curtain. In the past several years, collections have been equipped, as a rule, with hortatory articles, laying down the line--overtly or covertly, but effectively nonetheless."

* * * * *

JOHN GLASBY

Full Name: John Stephen Glasby.
   Born September 23, 1928, at East Retford, Nottinghamshire, England. Son of Edgar Stuart Glasby (a locomotive engineer) and Elizabeth Alice Hempsall. Married Janet Beattie Hannah, July 10, 1954. Six children: John Stuart (born 1955), Anne Marie (born 1957), Raymond Vincent (born 1962), Edmund Patrick (born 1970), Jennifer Frances (born 1972).

Education: B.Sc., Nottingham University, 1952.

Career: Chemist.
   Research Chemist, ICI Ltd., 1952-DATE; free-lance author, 1952-DATE; lecturer in astronomy, Glasgow University.

First Professional Sale: *Satellite B.C.*, Curtis Warren, 1952 (with Arthur Roberts as Rand Le Page).

Member: British Astronomical Association; Royal Astronomical Society (Fellow); Authors Guild.

* * * * *

GERALD M. GLASKIN

Full Name: Gerald Marcus Glaskin.
   Born December 16, 1923, at Perth, Western Australia. Son of Gilbert Henry Glaskin (a clerk) and Delia Mary Gugeri. Education: Attended schools in Australia.

GERALD M. GLASKIN (cont.)

Career: Writer.
Auditor, Coulton & Meagher, Perth, 1939-40; Clerk, Soap Distributors Ltd., W. Australia, 1940-41; Sales Clerk, J. Kitchen & Sons, Sydney, 1943; Acting Manager, Fremantle Sports Depot, Fremantle, W. Australia, 1946; Sales Statistician, Ford Motor Co. of Australia, 1947-48; Executive, Warne Brothers, Singapore, 1949; Acting Manager, McMullan & Co., Singapore, 1949-50; partner, Lyall and Evatt (stockbrockers), Singapore, 1950-59; full-time writer, 1959-DATE.

Agent: Georges Bouchardt, 145 E. 52nd St., New York, NY 10022.

Awards:
Commonwealth of Australia Literary Fund Fellow, 1957, 1972, for research in the Netherlands; Australian Council for the Arts grant, 1974; Western Australia Arts Council Bursary, 1975.

Member: Society of Authors; Australian Society of Authors; Fellowship of Australian Writers.

* * * * *

DONALD F. GLUT

Full Name: Donald Frank Glut.
Born February 19, 1944. Son of Frank C. Glut (a baker) and Julia Blasovits.

Education: B.A., University of Southern California, 1967.

Career: Writer.
Has worked as an assistant copywriter for a Van Nuys advertising agency, as a bookstore clerk in Hollywood, an actor, professional musician, and singer in California, 1965-71; writer, 1966-DATE.

Agent: Forrest J Ackerman, 2495 Glendower Avenue, Hollywood CA 90027.

Member:
International Tom Steele Fan Club; Academy of Comic Book Artists; American Federation of Musicians; American Federation of Television and Radio Artists; Alpha Chi.

* * * * *

NEIL GOBLE

Full Name: Lloyd Neil Goble.
Born August 21, 1933, at Oklahoma City, Oklahoma. Son of Lloyd Earl Goble (a businessman) and Thena Felts. Married Ann Broadhurst (a teacher), November 22, 1954. Three children: Thena, Tana, Sara.

Education: B.S., Oklahoma State University, 1955.

Career: U.S. Air Force Officer.
Reporter, Oklahoma City, 1955-56; Officer, U.S. Air Force, 1956-DATE, currently with rank of Major; stationed in Tokyo, Japan, as electronic warfare officer, 1958-61, and as developmental engineer and electronic test officer, 1963-67; Assistant Professor of Aerospace Studies, Air Force Reserve Officers Training Corps at Rensselaer Polytechnic Institute, 1967-DATE.

Agent: Nicholas Literary Agency, 161 Madison Avenue, New York, NY 10016.

Awards: Air Force Commendation Medal (twice); All-Pacific winner in USAF Short Story Contest, 1958.

Member: Armed Forces Writers League; Sigma Delta Chi; Kappa Sigma.

* * * * *

RUMER GODDEN

Full Name: Margaret Rumer Godden.
Born December 10, 1907, in Sussex, England. Daughter of Arthur Leigh Godden and Katherine Hingley. Sister of Jon Godden, the novelist and painter. Raised in India. Married Laurence S. Foster, 1934; married James Haynes Dixon, November 11, 1949. Two children: Jane, Paula.

Education: Attended Moira House Eastbourne; studied dancing.

Career: Writer.
During the 1930s, founded and operated a children's dancing school in Calcutta; during the 1940s, trained as an auxiliary nurse in case India should become actively involved in World War II; novelist, poet, playwright, scriptwriter.

Agent: Curtis Brown Ltd., 60 E. 56th St., New York, NY 10022.

* * * * *

H. L. GOLD

Full Name: Horace Leonard Gold.
Born April 26, 1914, at Montreal, Quebec, Canada. Son of Henry Gold and Regina Goldenberg. Married Evelyn Stein, September 3, 1939 (divorced, 1957); married Muriel Nicholson, August 21, 1965. One son, Eugene Gold (born 1941); three stepchildren: Linda Anderson (born 1942), Christopher Conley (born 1943), Sherill Conley (born 1957).

Career: Writer and editor.
Free-lance writer, 1934-39; Associate Editor, Standard Magazines (including such publications as *Thrilling Wonder Stories*, *Startling Stories*, *Capt. Future*), 1939-41; Managing Editor, *Scoop* and *Special Detective*, 1941-43; Editor, *Galaxy*, October, 1950-October, 1961; Editor, Galaxy Novels, 1951-61; Editor, *Beyond Fantasy Fiction*, July, 1953-#10, 1955 (all issues published); Editor, *Worlds of If*, July, 1959-September, 1961; has also written magazine comics, radio scripts, and has been a TV executive story editor; now retired.

First Professional Sale: "Inflexure," in *Astounding Stories*, October, 1934 (as Clyde Crane Campbell).

Awards: Hugo Award, Best Professional Magazine, 1952 (1953), *Galaxy*; Eastern Science Fiction Plaque, 1965.

Member: Science Fiction Writers of America; Disabled American Veterans. Interests: Classical music, reading, being read to, TV, cat and dog rearing.

"I set out to be a writer; I became one. I set out to become a magazine editor; I became one. In fact, I

H. L. GOLD (cont.)

"have accomplished everything I wanted to do. I deserve retirement, and I intend to put that ahead of any goals that might rear up in my way, including money, fame, and such. But I might become ambitious again, though it seems unlikely right now."

* * * * *

STEPHEN GOLDIN

Full Name: Stephen Charles Goldin.
   Born February 28, 1947, at Philadelphia, Pennsylvania. Son of David Goldin (a salesman) and Frances Cohen (a bookkeeper). Married Kathleen Ellan Sky, September 2, 1972.

Education: B.A., University of California, Los Angeles, 1968.

Career: Writer.
   Space scientist, U.S. Navy space systems activity, 1968-71; grocery store manager, Circle K Inc., 1972; Editor, Jaundice Press, 1973-74 (edited the magazine *National Ball*, March, 1973-June, 1974); free-lance writer, 1974-DATE.

First Professional Sale: "The Girls on USSF 193," in *Worlds of If*, December, 1965.

Awards:
   First runner-up in Nebula Awards, 1971, for best short story; received citation from Science Fiction Writers of America as editor of *The Alien Condition*, which included James Tiptree's award-winning story, "Love Is the Plan, the Plan Is Death," 1973.

Member:
   Science Fiction Writers of America; World Future Society; Astronomical Society of the Pacific; Society for Creative Anachronism, Inc.; Los Angeles Science Fantasy Society.

Goldin notes: "I believe that something can only hurt you to the extent that you take it seriously--so I try not to take anything to me. My villains are usually the ones without a sense of humor."

* * * * *

MORTON J. GOLDING

Full Name: Morton Jay Golding.
   Born July 24, 1925, at New York, New York. Son of Samuel H. Golding (a businessman) and Sue Feldman. Married Patricia E. Gibbons, 1953. Two sons: Geoffrey E. (born 1954), Gower Edward (born 1960).

Education: B.A., University of Denver, 1949; M.A., 1950.

Career: Writer.
   Copywriter, Barkas & Shalit (a public relations firm), 1953-54; Associate Editor, *Enterprise Magazine Management*, 1954-56; Features Editor, J.B. Publications, 1956-57; free-lance writer, 1957-DATE.

First Professional Sale: An article written in the summer of 1956 ("it was terrible").

Agent: Henry Morrison, 311 1/2 W. 20th St., New York

NY 10011.

Member: Authors Guild.

"In addition to general reading, which I do incessantly, I enjoy mythology, opera (in my next incarnation, I would like to be the world's greatest Boris Godunov, please), and travel."

* * * * *

WILLIAM GOLDING

Full Name: William Gerald Golding.
   Born September 19, 1911, at St. Columb Minor, Cornwall, England. Son of Alec A. Golding and Mildred Golding. Married Ann Brookfield (an analytical chemist) 1939. Two children: David, Judith.

Education: B.A., Brasenose College, Oxford University, 1935.

Career: Writer and teacher.
   Was a settlement house worker after graduation from Oxford; teacher of English and philosophy, Bishop Wordsworth's School, Salisbury, England, 1939-61; playwright, producer, and actor, 1934-40, 1945-54; writer in residence, Hollins College, 1961-62; writer, 1954-DATE.

Honors: Commander of the British Empire, 1965. Member: Royal Society of Literature (Fellow); Savile Club; Royal Southampton Yacht Club.

* * * * *

WILLIAM GOLDMAN

Full Name: William W. Goldman.
   Born August 12, 1931, at Chicago, Illinois. Son of Maurice Clarence Goldman and Marion Weil. Married Ilene Jones, April 15, 1961. Two children: Jenny Rebecca, Susanna.

Education: B.A., Oberlin College, 1952; M.A., Columbia University, 1956.

Career: Writer, 1956-DATE.

Awards: Oscar, 1970, Best Original Screenplay, "Butch Cassidy and the Sundance Kid."

Agent: International Famous Agency, 1301 Avenue of the Americas, New York, NY 10019.

* * * * *

ROBERT C. GOLDSTON

Full Name: Robert Conroy Goldston.
   Born July 9, 1927, at New York, New York. Son of Philip Henry Goldston (a salesman) and Josephine Conroy. Married Marguerite Garvey, January 3, 1956. Six Children: Rebecca, Gabrielle, Sarah, Francesca, Maximilian, Theresa.

Education: Attended Columbia University, 1946-53.

Career: Writer, 1953-DATE. Awards: Guggenheim Fellow in fiction, 1957-58. Agent: Collins-Knowlton-Wing, 60 E. 56th St., New York, NY 10022.

REINHOLD W. GOLL

Full Name: Reinhold Weimar Goll.
   Born March 20, 1897, at Philadelphia, Pennsylvania.
Son of Christian W. Goll and Catherine Seiz. Married
Florence M. Leipe, September 30, 1919. Three child-
ren: Robert R., Florence, Richard Eugene.

Education: B.S, Temple University, 1921; M.S.,
   1923; Ph.D., University of Pennsylvania, 1930.

Career: Teacher.
   Teacher, supervisor, and principal, Philadelphia
public schools, 1919-DATE. Member: National Education Association.

* * * * *

JOHN GORDON

Full Name: John Gordon.
   Born November 19, 1925. Son of Norman Gordon (a
teacher) and Margaret Revely. Married Sylvia Young,
January 9, 1954. Two children: Sally, Robert.
Education: Educated in Jarrow and Wisbech, England.

Career: Reporter and editor.
   Reporter, *Isle of Ely and Wisbech Advertiser*,
England, 1947-51; Chief Reporter and Sub-Editor, *Bury
Free Press*, Bury St. Edmunds, England, 1951-58; Sub-
Editor, *Western Evening Herald*, Plymouth, England,
1958-62; Columnist and Sub-Editor, *Eastern Evening
News*, Norwich, England, 1962-DATE.

* * * * *

REX GORDON

Full Name: Stanley Bennett Hough.
   Born February 25, 1917, at Preston, Lancashire,
England. Son of Simeon Hough (a business manager)
and Eva Bennett (a teacher). Married Justa Elisabeth
Cecilia Wodschow, June 25, 1938.

Education: PMG Certificate, Northern Counties
   Radio College (qualified as ship's radio officer).

Career: Writer.
   Radio operator on a merchant ship, 1936-45; Professional yachtsman, 1946-51; writer, 1951-DATE; Creative
Writing Tutor, Workers Educational Association, Cornwall, England.

First Professional Sale: A short story to *Cycling* magazine, 1935.

Agent: A. M. Heath, 40 William IV St., London.

Awards: Infinity Award for Best Science Fiction Novel of the Year, 1957, *First on Mars [No Man Friday]*.

Member: Royal Cornwall Polytechnic Society (Hon.
   Editor); Workers Educational Association.

Interests: Sailing, hi-fi, radio technology, organ-
   ising literary (writers') week-ends, making beer
   and wine, talking to women in pubs.

Gordon writes:
   "My work falls into four categories: (1) science
fiction under the name of Rex Gordon, most successful
"in world sales, the early books being reprinted in
Britain and the U.S.; (2) more literary works under
the name S. B. Hough, usually reviewed in the 'better'
papers; (3) travel books as S. B. Hough; (4) thrillers
or adventure stories under the name of Bennett Stanley.

   "In my own work, I try to stick to the classical tradition of writing science fiction, not fantasy or horror stories or disguised sex-dreams or sadism. The
story has to have a point that is connected with scientific developments that we can envisage. These developments must not contradict the laws of nature as
we now know them unless some likely error in our present knowledge can be demonstrated. Science fiction
is for intelligent people, not morons. Supermen are
no more acceptable than bug-eyed monsters. Any game
is the better for being played according to known
rules, and the unexpected should be produced by thinking out new moves in the game, not by making up new
rules in order to cheat.

   "Science fiction written in this way performs a definite service to the community, demonstrating the
real consequences to human life of social tendencies
and scientific possibilities that scientists themselves
are liable to view only theoretically. It is also a
vehicle for philosophic wit, whether about the actual
nature of the universe, or Joe Doakes' probable actual
reactions to situations that the theorist would tend
to regard as ideal, but which might go wrong in practice. In this sense, SF is our modern version of philosophy: a philosophy tied to possible actual events
and sense-impressions which not only gives speculation
a new force and realism, but also demands that we look
at our ideas realistically, and make sure that they
actually work--or enables us to demonstrate that other
people's ideas don't.

   "SF is not only philosophy for the multitude, invented by the genius of the American people (it came up
from the grass roots of popular demand, and was not
imposed from above), but it is *better* philosophy because the narrative form demands that all speculations
be envisaged and presented in terms of precise events.
It is an offshoot of American pragmatism. It is a vehicle for true scientific speculation, and its social
consequences are liable to be enormous.

   "Definitions: SCIENCE FICTION: works dependent for
location or plot on extrapolation (preferably logical
and knowledgeable) from existing scientific knowledge.

   "FANTASY: works of free imagination, irrelevant
to, or contradicting, man's present knowledge of the
universe.

   "As a 'true' science fiction writer, I greatly regret the fortuitous conjunction of two quite different
genres, but I see the difficulty. Under my definitions,
John Wyndham's *The Day of the Triffids* would have to
be counted fantasy, not SF, while stories which merely
rely on the application of existing scientific knowledge, with such improvements of technology as anyone
can anticipate, would not be in either category. Obviously, I am being narrow and pedantic, but it makes
a talking point!"

* * * * *

THEODORE J. GORDON

Full Name: Theodore J. Gordon.
   Born June 30, 1930, at New York, New York. Son of
Robert L. Gordon. Married Ann Jason. Four children:
Katherine, Tom, Lisa, Michael.

Education: B.S.A.E., Louisiana State University,
   1950; M.S.A.E., Georgia Institute of Technology, 1951.

THEODORE J. GORDON (cont.)

Career: Businessman.
   Director of Advanced Saturn Project, Douglas Aircraft Co., Huntington Beach, Calif., 1964-68; Vice-
President, Institute for the Future, Menlo Park, 1968-
71; President, The Futures Group, Glastonbury, Conn.,
1971-DATE; Consultant, Regent's Professor, University
of California, Los Angeles, 1968; Lecturer, Columbia
University. Member: World Future Society.

* * * * *

EDWARD GOREY

Full Name: Edward St. John Gorey.
   Born February 22, 1925, at Chicago, Illinois. Son
of Edward Leo Gorey and Helen Garvey. Education:
A.B., Harvard University, 1950.

Career: Designer, illustrator, writer, editor.

* * * * *

PHYLLIS GOTLIEB

Full Name: Phyllis Fay Gotlieb.
   Born May 25, 1926, at Toronto, Ontario, Canada.
Daughter of Leo Bloom (a movie theater manager) and
Mary Kates. Married Calvin Carl Gotlieb, June 12,
1949. Three children: Leo (born 1950), Margaret (born
1952), Jane (born 1956).

Education: B.A., University of Toronto, 1948; M.A.,
   1950.

Career: Writer and housewife.

First Professional Sale: A group of poems to
   the Canadian Broadcasting Company program Anthology
   in November, 1955.

Member: Science Fiction Writers of America; League
   of Canadian Poets.

Gotlieb writes:
   "I started writing at the age of eleven, mainly
poetry, till the source seemed to dry up at the age
of twenty. After I got married, my husband suggested
I try writing science fiction to break the writer's
block. It took me nine years to make the first sale,
but by then the poetry had come back; and since that
time, I have had a dual career (very modest in both
divisions) as a Canadian poet and American science
fiction writer. So far the two have not meshed.
   "Since I write very slowly, and my output is small,
I have gotten far more than I have been able to give
to SF; it taught me to write in a quick clean style
that has helped my poetry and mainstream writing as
well. To science fiction I have tried to bring an
unsentimental sense of humanity and depth of character,
a feeling that whatever happens out in the depths of
space, it depends ultimately on people of one sort
or another, whatever their form or planetary origin.
I do my best to understand and present them as completely as I can."

She adds:
   "I want to know everything about humanity (and the
cosmos) and use it in my writing."

ELIZABETH GOUDGE

Full Name: Elizabeth Goudge.
   Born April 24, 1900, at Wells, Somerset, England.
Daughter of Henry Leighton Goudge and Ida de Beauchamp
Collenette. Education: Attended Reading University
for two years.

Career: Writer.
   Taught design and applied art in her home, 1922-32;
part-time writer, 1932-38; full-time writer, 1938-DATE.
Member: Royal Society of Literature (Fellow).

Agent: David Higham Associates, 76 Dean St., Soho,
   London W.1, England.

Awards:
   Metro-Goldwyn-Mayer $125,000 Literary Award, 1944,
for Green Dolphin Street; Carnegie Medal, 1947, for
Little White Horse.

* * * * *

RON GOULART

Full Name: Ronald Joseph Goulart.
   Born January 13, 1933, at Berkeley, California. Son
of Joseph Silveira Goulart (a factory worker) and Josephine Macri (a cafeteria cook). Married Frances Sheridan, June 13, 1964. Two sons: Sean (born 1962), Stef-
fan (born 1970).

Education: B.A., University of California, Berkeley,
   1955.

Career: Writer.
   "Graduated from Cal in 1955, and went to work in San
Francisco for an advertising agency. I'd taken a short
story course from Anthony Boucher while in high school
(a private course he taught in his home), and made my
first sales to him in 1952. After working at several
agencies, I returned to free-lancing in 1960, and have
been doing it ever since."

First Professional Sale:
   "My first SF sale (and my first professional sale of
any kind) was actually a parody called "Letters to the
Editor," and it appeared in the April, 1952, of The
Magazine of Fantasy and Science Fiction. It was a
reprint from the University of California Pelican, a
humor magazine with which I was connected in my undergraduate days. "Conroy's Public" was my first short
story to get into print, in the December, 1952 issue.
I had a lapse of six years during which I completed
college, and wrote commercials for Skippy Peanut Butter.
After the big sci-fi boom ended, I returned to the
field in 1958."

Awards: Edgar Award, Best Mystery Novel, 1970 (1971),
   After Things Fell Apart.

Member: Science Fiction Writers of America (Vice-
   President, 1969-70); Mystery Writers of America (ex-
   member, Board of Directors).

Interests: Cartooning, blues guitar, jogging.

Goulart talks about his early days in advertising:
   "I met my wife while she was working in San Francisco
as a copywriter for Guild, Bascom & Bonfigli, an advertising agency that at the time specialized in humorous

RON GOULART (cont.)

"commercials. This was the same outfit I'd worked for a few years before, in the middle 1950s. When I was at GBB, I wrote ads and commercials for Skippy Peanut Butter (which at that dim period in time sponsored a show called "You Asked for It"), Regal Pale Beer, Foremost Dairies, Mother's Cookies, Chicken of the Sea Tuna, etc. One of the Skippy ads I did showed Casey Stengel eating a cracker. This won several awards at the time, and I think eventually was even included in a book with the lovely title of *The Hundred Best Ads from the Reader's Digest*. The ad also ran in *Life*, and I recall it cost them more to have the dab of peanut butter run in color than they paid me in a whole year. GBB also had the Ralston account. I did some TV commercials for the cereals, and then did *The Chex Press*, which ran on the backs of all the Chex boxes. There were 55 different ones, and the series folded when GBB lost the account.

"My mother is Italian; her father, Giacomo Macri, came over from the Calabria region of Italy. There have been a couple of famous bandits with this name over there. My father, by the way, is Portuguese, and was born in the Azores."

Regarding his work, Goulart had this to say:

"All of the planet stories I've done in the last dozen years of so use the Barnum System [named after PTBarnum] of planets. I haven't kept track of the system too well, nor do I have a chart or plan of the whole thing drawn up. I'm not even sure how many planets there are in the system, since I make up a new one when I get tired of the old ones. Barnum itself dominates the whole system [much the way America dominates the Earth]. Murdstone [named after David Copperfield's stepfather] seems to figure more than most, but I'm not sure why.

"Jolson of the Chameleon Corps operates in the system. *The Sword Swallower, The Chameleon Corps,* and *Flux* all deal with him. Jack Summer, and his partner Palma, figure in *Death Cell* and *Plunder*. Palma has made a comeback, and appears, without Summer and as second banana to somebody else, in *Spacehawk, Inc.* John Wesley Sand, a mercenary, figures in *Clockwork's Pirates* and in one short story, "Dingbat [named after Herriman's comic strip and not Archie Bunker], which is included in the collection *Nutzenbolts*. He worked on the Barnum planet Esmeralda in the novel, which is the same planet where Raker worked in *The Fire Eater*. Peter Torres, the hero in *Shaggy Planet*, is more or less Raker under another name. José Silveira, the free-lance writer, also works the Barnum system. He's been in short stories only so far; three or four of them are included in my collection, *Odd Job #101*, published by Scribner's.

"I've done a number of books under pseudonyms. As Frank S. Shawn, I wrote six novels in Avon's Phantom series. As Con Steffanson, I did the first three Flash Gordon paperbacks for Avon's series. As Howard Lee, I did #s two and three in the Kung Fu series from Warner Paperback Library. And I also wrote 12 Avenger novels for Warner under the name Kenneth Robeson (#s 25-36)."

* * * * *

PHILIP BABCOCK GOVE

Full Name: Philip Babcock Gove.
Born June 27, 1902, at Concord, New Hampshire. Son of John McClure Gove (a physician) and Florence Babcock. Married Grace Potter, August 17, 1929. Three

children: Norwood B., Susan, Doris.

Education:
A.B., Dartmouth College, 1922; A.M., Harvard University, 1925; Ph.D., Columbia University, 1941.

Career: Editor.
Instructor in English, Rice Institute, 1924-27, and at New York University, 1927-42; Asst. Editor, G. & C. Merriam Co., 1946-51; Managing Editor, 1951-52; General Editor, 1952-60; Editor-in-Chief, supervising production of *Webster's Third New International Dictionary*, 1961-67; Consultant, 1967-72; Member of Advisory Board, Center for Documentation and Communication Research, Case Western Reserve University; Member, Board of Directors, Warren Library; Member, Board of Editors, *Encyclopaedia Britannica*. Died Nov. 16, 1972.

Awards: Litt.D., Dartmouth College, 1963.

Member:
National Council of Teachers of English; Linguistic Society of America; American Standards Association; Modern Language Association; International Society of General Semantics; College English Association; Johnson Society of London; North Carolina English Teachers Association; English Graduate Union; Phi Gamma Delta.

* * * * *

MICHAEL GRAINEY
[contributor]

Full Name: Michael William Grainey.
Born May 29, 1947, at Washington, D.C. Son of John J. Grainey and Margaret Hogue.

Education: A.B., Gonzaga University, 1969; J.D., New York University, 1972.

Career: Attorney.
Trial Attorney, U.S. Atomic Energy Commission, Washington, DC, 1972-DATE; Asst. Editor, *Charter*, 1968-69.

Awards: Root-Tilden Fellowship, NYU Law School, 1969-72.

Member: American Bar Association; Spokane County Bar Association; Washington State Bar Association.

Interests: Touch football, stain glass, hiking.

* * * * *

JOAN GRANT

Full Name: Joan Grant Kelsey.
Born April 12, 1907, at London, England. Daughter of John Frederick Marshall and Blanche Emily Hughes. Married Leslie Grant, November 30, 1927; married Charles Beatty, March 14, 1940; married Dr. Denys Kelsey, September 1, 1960. One daughter, Gillian Grant Wynne.

Education: Privately educated by governesses and tutors.

Career: Writer, 1937-DATE.

Agent: A. P. Watt & Son, 26/28 Bedford Row, London WC1R 4HL, England.

ROBERT GRAVES

Full Name: Robert von Ranke Graves.
   Born July 24, 1895, at London, England. Son of Alfred Perceval Graves (an Irish poet and ballad writer)
and Amalia von Ranke. Married Beryl Pritchard. Children: Jenny, David, Catherine, Samuel, William,
Lucia, Juan, Thomas.

Education: B.Litt., Oxford University, 1926.

Career: Writer and teacher.
   Professor of English Literature, Egyptian University,
Cairo, 1926; Professor of Poetry, Oxford University,
1961-DATE; Clarke Lecturer, Cambridge, 1954; lectured
in the United States, 1958, 1966-67, and at Mediterranean Summer Institute, 1967; appeared in "Deadfall,"
a film set in Majorca, 1968; owns the Majorcan jazz
club, The Indigo; free-lance author, 1916-DATE.

Awards:
   James Tait Black Memorial Prize, 1935, for *I, Clau-
dius* and *Claudius the God*; Hawthornden Prize, 1935,
for *I, Claudius*; Femina-Vie Heureuse Prize and the
Stock Prize, 1939, for *Count Belisarius*; Russell Loines
Memorial Fund Award of $1000, 1958; Gold Medal of
Poetry Society of America, 1959; M.A., Oxford Univer-
sity, 1961.

Agent: A. P. Watt & Son, 26/28 Bedford Row, London
   WC14 4HL, England.

* * * * *

NICHOLAS STUART GRAY

Full Name: Nicholas Stuart Gray.
   Born October 23, 1922, in Scotland. Son of William
Stuart Gray and Lenore May Johnson. Education: At-
tended various private grammar schools in England.

Career: Writer and actor.
   Gray's first play was produced at age 17; he has
also acted in and directed many British productions,
playing such roles as Hamlet, Richard II, and Iago;
also a novelist and illustrator.

Agent: Samuel French, 25 W. 45th St., New York, NY
   10036. Member: P.E.N.; Société des Auteurs.

* * * * *

JOSEPH L. GREEN

Full Name: Joseph Lee Green.
   Born January 14, 1931, at Compass Lake, Florida.
Son of Francis Marion Green and Mattie Carlisle. Mar-
ried Juanita Henderson, March 3, 1951. Two children:
William Merritt (born 1952), Rose-Marie (born 1955).

Career: Technical writer.
   Laboratory technician, International Paper Company,
1949-51; shop worker & welder, 1952-54; construction
millwright, 1955-58; Senior Supervisor, Boeing, 1959-
63; engineering writer, Kennedy Space Center, 1965-66;
Lead Technical Writer, Boeing, 1966-DATE.

First Professional Sale:
   "Once Around Arcturus," in *Worlds of If*, Sept. 1962.

Agent: Lurton Blassingame, 60 E. 42nd St., New York,
   NY 10017.

Member: Science Fiction Writers of America; American
   Civil Liberties Union; Authors Guild.

Interests:
   Travel, music, exotic foods. "My life is of interest
mostly to me. As for my work--writing is addictive.
Stay away from it! More and easier money is to be
made in other fields."

Regarded space exploration, Green had this to say:
   "Manned space exploration will proceed, slowly but
surely. The big push through the end of *this* decade,
though, will be on practical applications and *unmanned*
scientific exploration. Manned spaceflight will become
important (but routine) in the 1980s."

* * * * *

JULIEN GREEN

Full Name: Julian Hartridge Green.
   Born September 6, 1900, at Paris, France. Has used
the French spelling of his given name since the late
1920s. Son of Edward Moon Green (a business agent)
and Mary Adelaide Hartridge. Brother of novelist Anne
Green.

Education:
   Attended the Lycée Janson-de-Sailly, Paris, University of Virginia, 1919-22; La Grande Chaumiere, Paris,
1922-23, where he studied drawing.

Career: Writer.
   Asst. Professor of French, University of Virginia,
1921-22; returned to France, 1922, where he embarked
upon a full-time literary career; lectured at various
American colleges, 1940-42; returned to Paris, 1945.

Awards:
   Prix Paul Flat, and Femina-Bookman Prize, 1928,
for *Adrienne Mesurat*; Harper Prize, 1929, for *Leviathan*;
Harper 125th Anniversary Award, 1942, for *Memory of
Happy Days*; Officier de la Legion d'Honneur; Grand Prix
Litteraire de Monaco, 1951, for the whole of his work;
Grand Prix National de Lettres, 1966; Prix Ibico Reg-
gino, 1968. Member: Académie de Bairere; L'Académie
Royale de Belgique (Honorary).

* * * * *

ROGER LANCELYN GREEN

Full Name: Roger Gilbert Lancelyn Green.
   Born November 2, 1918, at Norwich, Norfolk, England.
Son of Gilbert Arthur Lancelyn Green (a retired British
Army major and a landowner) and Helena Mary Phyllis
Sealy. Married June Burdett, March 31, 1948. Three
children: Scirard Roger Lancelyn (born 1949), Priscilla
June Lancelyn (born 1951), Richard Gordon Lancelyn
(born 1953).

Education: B.A., Merton College, Oxford, 1940; M.A.,
   1944.

Career: Author.
   Professional actor, at the Oxford Repertory Theatre
and others, 1942-44; Deputy Librarian, Merton College,
Oxford, 1945-50; William Noble Research Fellow in English Literature, Liverpool University, 1950-52; free-
lance author, 1952-DATE. Editor, *Kipling Journal*,
1957-DATE; Andrew Lang Lecturer, St. Andrew's University, 1963.

ROGER LANCELYN GREEN (cont.)

First Professional Sale: *Tellers of Tales*, Edmund Ward, 1946.

Member:
  Oxford University Dramatic Society (Secretary); Kipling Society (Editor); Sherlock Holmes Society of London; William Morris Society; Dickens Fellowship; Lewis Carroll Society; Hellenic Society; Hellenic Travellers Club.

Interests:
  Travel, ancient Greece, the Greek theatre and its drama. Green is the Hereditary Lord of the Manors of Poulton-Lancelyn and Lower Bebington.

Green writes:
  "*From the World's End* grew from finding the old house of Echursey in a valley called The World's End in North Wales. Some of an unfinished morality play was incorporated. The Phoenix was there because I had just been doing a lot of research on the legend, and had written a book (never published) on it. My other two fantasies, *The Wood That Time Forgot* and *The Castle in Lyonesse*, written at much the same time, still remain unpublished."

* * * * *

ROLAND GREEN

Full Name: Roland James Green.
  Born September 2, 1944, at Bradford, Pennsylvania. Son of James Ernest Green (a professor of history) and Bertha Mariasha Cohen (a public school library administrator). Married Frieda Green, November, 1975.

Education: B.A., Oberlin College, 1966; M.A., University of Chicago, 1966; Ph.D. pending.

Career: Writer, 1969-DATE.

First Professional Sale: *Wandor's Ride*, Avon, 1973.

Agent: Lurton Blassingame, 60 E. 42nd St., New York, NY 10017.

Member: Science Fiction Writers of America; Windy Writers' Conference; Society for Creative Anachronism, Inc.

Interests: Naval and military history.

Roland Green writes:
  "I was originally intended for an academic career (as a professor of political science), and stuck to that direction as long as I had no notion I was good at anything else, or ever could be. However, Mr. Michael Bradley (all honor to his name) convinced me in September of 1969 that we should sit down and collaborate on a science fiction novel. We did. It is still unsold as of this date, but we did get ourselves an agent on the strength of the first eight chapters. Then we wrote a novella, also still unsold.
  "In the summer of 1970, I noticed that sword-and-sorcery seemed to be popular, and that the standards in the genre were--let us say, elastic. So I sat down to write *Wandor's Ride* in the venerable if unglorious spirit of "My God, if *that* crap is selling, why don't I grab myself a piece of the action!" I sat

down, I wrote it, I sent it off, and at the beginning of June, 1971, Avon took it. Then they took two years to bring it out, while I worked on other projects, helped edit a geographical dictionary, clerked in Mike Bradley's newly-acquired bookstore, pushed ahead on my dissertation, etc.
  "Came June of 1973, and *Wandor's Ride* came out. *Six weeks later*, on the strength of that one book, I was able to move into full-time writing (adventure series of novels on contract); I have been writing full-time ever since. In that time, I have written ten adventure novels, the second book (out of a projected five) of the Wandor series, a novella, a short-short, and part of a work in collaboration with Bradley, *And All the Trumpets Sounded*. Full-time writing is admittedly a little like a foot race in Wonderland--'It takes all the running you can do to stay in the same place'--but at the moment I cannot imagine myself willingly changing it for any other career. (Not the least of its virtues is that currently I am making more money than I could at college teaching or any other position for which I would have *any* chance of being hired. I am *not* a starving writer, even if I am trying to take off weight!)
  "Generally speaking, I prefer to describe myself as a professional writer rather than an author. The difference between the two is that the former doesn't stop when his soul is bared in the words on the paper (assuming that he bares his soul in the first place, at least until he's been selling steadily for about five years), but keeps watch over those words every step of the way (with or without the cooperation of his agent) until they appear in the bookstores, and even beyond *that*.
  "The writer facing an editor/publisher should picture himself as a hog farmer trying to sell his hogs to a meat packer. The farmer wants to sell as high as possible; the packer wants to buy as low as possible. *Both* want and need to be able to make the grocery shopper prefer ham, pork chops, or sausage, to chicken, liver, or lamb. If they cannot do that, *neither* of them is going to make very much money. It is a straight business deal all along the line, and the farmer's emotional attachment to the hogs or their gentle and loving disposition isn't going to help his position if they won't make good bacon!
  "The whole Wandor cycle and much of my other writing is going to owe an immense debt to the Society for Creative Anachronism, particularly the people of its Middle Kingdom. In fact, I owe more to the SCA both personally and professionally than I can express in any words that I would right now care to see appear in print. So all of you in the SCA who helped, whether you intended it or not (and some of you certainly didn't)--*thank you*.
  "I believe in a well-filled notebook, so currently it's running about five years ahead of my typewriter. I cannot, honestly, list any of the material there as works in progress, and if I tried, the section would run five pages. I just plough onwards, hoping in vain to reduce the gap."

How to create a civilization:
  "(1) Look for historical analogues wherever you can. Benzos, for example, is the Wandorian equivalent of 15th-century France--*but* there have been some changes made. A more centralized national monarchy, which beat down the feudal nobility and elevated the merchants, no Black Plague, and no Hundred Years' War, are just a few of the differences. Using historical analogues is a great time-saver, since you can borrow economic systems, legal systems, educational systems, etc., more or less ready-made. However, don't do it too slavishly.

ROLAND GREEN (cont.)

"The goal of researching an analogue is to be able to make an intelligent choice of the things you want to *change*. The most nearly perfect example of an intelligently-used analogue that comes readily to mind is Katherine Kurtz's Deryni novels.

"(2) Pick your technology carefully. You can use any level that the story requires (although pre-gunpowder is usually best for fantasy), but be reasonably consistent. If one has too wide a gap in the same world, one usually winds up with the more advanced technology absorbing the other, peacefully or otherwise. If the scene of the action is a whole world, and communications are poor, one can have widely varying styles of technology (in the 13th century, for example, Earth accomodated the Mayas, the Chinese, and Western Europe--all different, none much in touch with the others, if at all). But in the Wandor world, communications are reasonable good, at least among the various peoples and nations bordering on the Ocean.

"(3) Avoid conventionalizations. This is my term for what other critics/authors/etc. may call by other names--simply sticking in a word ("castle," "peasant," "sorcerer," etc.), and expecting the word alone to do all the work of conjuring up in the reader's mind all the details you need to keep the story alive and moving. This is a particularly easy trap to fall into when handling the supernatural--that is why I take what might be called the "hardware" approach to my magicians--showing them at work, instead of just the results (Tolkien does the second). One's castles should be damp and smelly underground (I've been in enough of them in Europe to know that they are), one's peasants should be lice-ridden, smelly, and usually hungry, one's sorcerers should have their little vanities, their favorite dishes, and so on. This is one thing that good historical novelists know and do."

* * * * *

MARTIN HARRY GREENBERG

Full Name: Martin Harry Greenberg.
    Born March 1, 1941, at Miami Beach, Florida. Son of Max Isidor Greenberg (a merchant) and Mollie Cohen. Married Sally Shannon, June 3, 1972. Two children: Kari, Kathleen.

Education: B.B.A., University of Miami (FL), 1962; M.A., University of Connecticut, 1965; Ph.D., 1969.

Career: Professor of Political Science.
    Lecturer in political science, University of Connecticut, 1966; Asst. Professor of Political Science, University of Wisconsin, Green Bay, 1969-72; Assoc. Professor of Political Science, Florida International University, 1972-DATE; co-founder of the H. G. Wells Award for science fiction.

Member:
    International Political Science Association; American Political Science Association; American Society for Public Administration; Latin American Development Administration Committee; Comparative Administration Group; Society for International Development; Science Fiction Research Association; Science Fiction Writers of America (associate); Southern Political Science Association; South Florida Jewish Historical Society; Pi Sigma Alpha.

Agent: Del Walker, 520 Fifth Avenue, New York, NY 10036.

GRAHAM GREENE

Full Name: Henry Graham Greene.
    Born October 2, 1904, at Berkhamsted, Hertfordshire, England. Son of Charles Henry Greene (a headmaster) and Marion Raymond Greene (her maiden name). Married Vivien Dayrell Browning, 1927. One son, one daughter.

Education: Attended Balliol College, Oxford, 1922-25.

Career: Writer and editor.
    Writer, 1925-DATE; Sub-Editor, *London Times*, 1926-30; Film critic for *Night and Day* during the 1930s, and for the *Spectator*, 1935-39; Literary Editor, 1940-41; with the Foreign Office in Africa, 1941-44; Director, Eyre & Spottiswoode, 1944-48; Indo-China correspondent for the *New Republic*, 1954; Director, Bodley Head, 1958-68.

Awards:
    Hawthornden Prize, 1940, for *The Labyrinthine Ways (The Power and the Glory)*; James Tait Black Memorial Prize, 1949, for *The Heart of the Matter*; Catholic Literary Award, 1952, for *The End of the Affair*; Boys' Clubs of America Junior Book Award, 1955, for *The Little Horse Bus*; Pietzak Award, Poland, 1960; Litt.D., Cambridge University, 1962; Honorary Fellow, Balliol College, Oxford University, 1963; Royal Society of Literature Prize; Companion of Honour, 1966; D.Litt., University of Edinburgh, 1967; Legion d'Honneur, Chevalier, 1969.

* * * * *

JAY E. GREENE

Full Name: Jay E. Greene.
    Born April 4, 1914, at Brooklyn, New York. Son of Solomon Greene (a tailor) and Esther Yagod. Married Natalie Schumer (a teacher), January 25, 1941. Three children: Robert, Howard, Marjorie.

Education:
    B.A., Brooklyn College, 1932; M.S. in Education, City College of New York, 1934; Ed.D., New York University, 1953.

Career: Teacher.
    High school teacher of English, New York, 1936-45; chairman of the department, 1945-50; member, Board of Examiners, 1950-DATE. Member: American Association of School Personnel Administrators; New York State Teachers Association; New York State Association of School Personnel Administrators; Council of Supervisory Associations of New York City; American Legion.

* * * * *

LESLIE GREENER

Full Name: Leslie Greener.
    Born February 13, 1900, at Cape Town, South Africa. Son of Herbert Greener (a military officer) and Helen Bennett. Married Rhona Haszard, December 20, 1925 (deceased); married Margaret Edmunds, April 20, 1934 (deceased). One son, Guy.

Education: Graduate, Royal Military College at Sandhurst, 1919; studied art at Académie Julien, Paris, 1927-28, and did external work at the University of London, 1930.

LESLIE GREENER (cont.)

Career: Writer and archaeological artist.
  Career officer, British Indian Army, 1919-24; teacher of art and French, Victoria College, Alexandria, Egypt, 1928-31; archaeological artist, Oriental Institute Expedition of University of Chicago, Luxor, Egypt, 1931-36, 1958-67; journalist, Associated Newspapers, Sydney, Australia, 1937-41, 1945-49; in the Australian Army, 1941-45; taken prisoner in Malaya and held by the Japanese for three and one-half years; Director of Adult Education, Tasmania, 1949-54; author. Died 1974.

Awards: Commonwealth of Australia Literary Fellowship, 1957. Member: Society of Australian Writers.

Agent: A. Watkins, 77 Park Avenue, New York NY 10016.

* * * * *

IRVING A. GREENFIELD

Full Name: Irving A. Greenfield.
  Born February 22, 1928, at Brooklyn, New York. Son of Samuel Greenfield (a jeweler) and Anna Berkowitz. Married Anita Mittag, September 2, 1950. Two sons: Richard (born 1955), Nathan (born 1959).

Education: B.A., Brooklyn College, 1950.

Career: Writer.
  Spent several years as a technical writer, and several years as Vice-President, Groody Advertising Co. 1957-65; free-lance writer, 1962-DATE.

First Professional Sale: *The Schemers*, Soft Cover Library, 1962.

Agent: Henry Morrison, 311 1/2 W. 20th St., New York, NY 10011.

Member: Authors Guild. Interests: painting, photography, music, travel.

Greenfield notes: "I find all writing difficult. Each particular book has its own problems. Some are faster than others, and some slower, but all have their own difficulties."

* * * * *

HARMAN GRISEWOOD

Full Name: Harman Joseph Gerard Grisewood.
  Born February 8, 1906, at Broxbourne, England. Son of Harman Grisewood (a Lt. Col. in the British Army) and Lucille Cardozo. Married Margaret Bailey, Sept. 14, 1940. One daughter, Sabina.

Education: Attended Ampleforth College, 1916-24, and Worcester College, Oxford, 1924-27.

Career: Broadcaster.
  Member of repertory company, British Broadcasting Company, London, 1929-33; announcer, 1933-36; assistant to program organizer, 1936-39; Assistant Director of Program Planning, 1939-41; Assistant Controller of European Division, 1941-45; Acting Controller, 1945-46; Director of Talks, 1946-47; Planner of Third Programme, 1947-48; Controller of Third Programme, 1948-

52; Director of the Spoken Word, 1952-55; Chief Assistant to the Director-General, 1955-64; Vice-President, European Broadcasting Union, 1953-54; now retired.

Awards:
  Christian X Freedom Medal, 1946; Commander of the Order of the British Empire, 1960; Knight of the Order of Malta, 1960. Member: Royal Society of Arts (Fellow).

* * * * *

ARTHUR GROOM

Full Name: Arthur William Groom.
  Born 1898, at Hove, Sussex, England. Son of William Samuel Groom and Emily Ann Short. Married Marjorie Helen Grimsley, 1928. One daughter, Susan.

Education: Attended Montrose College, 1908-12, and Whitgift School, 1912-16.

Career: Writer.
  Clerk, Bank of Scotland, England, 1916-19; Sub-Manager, Barclay's Bank, British West Indies and British Guiana, 1919-22; Editor of staff magazine, London's Underground Railways, 1922-28; writer, 1928-DATE. Member: P.E.N.; Society of Authors; Savage Club, London. Died 1964.

Agent: A. M. Heath & Co., London.

* * * * *

RICHARD GROSSINGER

Full Name: Richard Selig Grossinger.
  Born November 3, 1944, at New York, New York. Son of Paul Grossinger (in the hotel business) and Martha Rothkrug. Married Lindy Hough, June 21, 1974. Two children: Robin (boy, born 1969), Miranda (born 1974).

Education: B.A., Amherst College, 1966; M.A., University of Michigan, 1968; Ph.D. candidate.

Career: College instructor, writer, editor.
  College instructor, University of Maine at Portland, 1970-72; Instructor, Goddard College, 1972-DATE; Editor, *Io* magazine, 1964-DATE; Editor, North Atlantic Books, 1973-DATE.

First Professional Sale: *Solar Journal: Oecological Sections*, Black Sparrow Press, 1970.

Honors: NSF Fellowship; NIH Research Grant to study lobster fishing in Maine.

Grossinger notes:
  "I am not a science fiction writer in any pure sense of the word, but science fiction is a major theme in every piece of writing I have done. Since I read science fiction as a child and teen-ager, it is one of the original proposals on which I continue to work. But, insofar as science fiction poses a series of riddles, I try to integrate those riddles into other structures. Each of the planets has a particular place in my work, based more on its science fiction referent than on any occult or astrological signification. Every science fiction plot that has interested me or that I have made up, I have integrated into a book, not as a plot for a story, but an unsolved tension in the fabric of it."

THOMAS E. GROULING

Full Name: Thomas Edward Grouling.
   Born June 9, 1940, at Baltimore, Maryland. Son of Charles and Anna Grouling. Education: B.A., University of Baltimore, 1965; M.A., University of Kansas, 1967.

Career: Instructor in English.
   Credits and Adjustments, Best Foods-Corn Products Co., Baltimore, 1957-61; Customer Service Dept., Sears Roebuck, Baltimore, 1964-66; Instructor in English, St. Benedict's College, Atchison, Kansas, 1967-DATE.

Member: Modern Language Association.

* * * * *

J. W. GROVES

Full Name: John William Groves.
   Born November 6, 1910, at Catford, London, England. Son of John William Groves and Edith Rose Winterbourne. Married Ada May Groves, December 14, 1935.

Career: Writer, 1967-DATE.
   "I've had no career. Just jobs. And, occasionally, short story sales to the magazines. I switched to novels about the end of '67."

First Professional Sale: "The Sphere of Death," in *Amazing Stories*, October, 1931.

* * * * *

JAY GROVES

Full Name: Jay Voelker Groves.
   Born August 4, 1922, at Minneapolis, Minnesota. Son of Jay N. and Vivian Groves. Married Martha Gould. Three children: Lester (born 1951), Sarah (born 1954), Catherine (born 1956).

Education: B.S.Ed., University of Minnesota, 1943; M.A., 1946; M.A., West Virginia University, 1967.

Career: Instructor in Economics.
   College teacher, 1947-DATE; Instructor in Economics, West Virginia Wesleyan College, 1958-DATE. Member: American Economic Association; American Association of University Professors; Civil Air Patrol.

* * * * *

DAVIS GRUBB

Full Name: Davis Alexander Grubb.
   Born July 23, 1919, at Moundsville, West Virginia. Son of Louis Delaplain Grubb and Eleanor Louise Alexander. Education: Student, Carnegie Institute, 1938-39.

Career: Writer, 1944-DATE. Agent: Harold Matson, 22 E. 40th St., New York, NY 10016.

* * * * *

CARRIE E. GRUHN

Full Name: Carrie E. Gruhn.
   Born April 3, 1907, at Clarinda, Iowa. Daughter of Frank R. Myers (a researcher) and Clara DeVoe. Married

Stanley G. Gruhn (a printer), May 18, 1929. Two sons: Edward L., Gerald L. Education: Attended Iowa State Teacher's College, one year.

Career: Writer. Member: Women's Christian Temperance Union.

* * * * *

ALBERT JOSEPH GUERARD

Full Name: Albert Joseph Guerard.
   Born November 2, 1914, at Houston, Texas. Son of Albert Leon Guerard and Wilhelmina McCartney. Married Mary M. Bocock, 1941. Three children: Catherine Collot, Mary Maclin, Lucy Lundie.

Education: B.A., Stanford University, 1934; Ph.D., 1938; M.A., Harvard University, 1936.

Career: Professor of English.
   Instructor in English, Amherst College, 1935-36: Professor of English, Harvard University, 1938-61; Professor of English, Stanford University, 1961-DATE.

Agent: Curtis Brown, 60 E. 56th St., New York, NY 10022.

Awards:
   Rockefeller Fellowship, 1946-47; Fulbright Fellowship, 1949-50; Guggenheim Fellowship, 1955-56; Ford Fellowship, 1959-60; *Paris Review* Fiction Prize, for *The Exiles*; National Foundation of Arts Fellowship, 1967-68. Member: Phi Beta Kappa; Modern Language Association; American Academy of Arts and Sciences.

* * * * *

RENE GUILLOT

Full Name: René Guillot.
   Born January 24, 1900, at Courcoury, Charente-Maritime, France. Son of Arsène Guillot and Marie-Louise Drouard. Married Gisele Mervaud (a writer). One son, Jean-Marie.

Education: Licence és Sciences Mathématiques, Sorbonne, University of Paris, 1922.

Career: Professor of Mathematics.
   Teacher of mathematics in French West Africa, principally in Dakar, 1923-50; Professor of Mathematicz, Lycée Concorcet, Paris, 1950-60; writer. Died 3/28/69.

Member: Société des Gens de Lettres; Société des Auteurs Dramatiques; Société des Écrivains Combattants; Société des Écrivains de La Mer et de l'Outre Mer.

* * * * *

WYMAN GUIN

Full Name: Wyman Woods Guin.
   Born March 1, 1915, at Wanette, Oklahoma. Son of Joel Guin and Marie Menasco. Married Jean Adolph, 1939 (deceased 1955); married Valerie Carlson, 1956. Five children: Joel, Jennifer, Cynthia, Kevin, Kristen.

Career: Advertising Executive.
   Employed successively as a technician in pharmacology, advertising writer, advertising manager, Vice-President,

WYMAN GUIN (cont.)

Marketing, for Lakeside Laboratories, Milwaukee, 1938-62; Vice-President, Medical Television Communications, Chicago, 1962-64; Planning Administrator, L. W. Frohlich and Company/Intercon International Inc. (an advertising agency), 1964-DATE.

First Professional Sale: "Trigger Tide," in *Astounding Science Fiction*, October, 1950 (as Norman Menasco).

* * * * *

JAMES E. GUNN

Full Name: James Edwin Gunn.
Born July 12, 1923, at Kansas City, Missouri. Son of J. Wayne Gunn (a printer) and Elsie Mae Hutchison. Married Jane Anderson, February 6, 1947. Two sons: Christopher Wayne (born 1949), Kevin Robert (born 1954).

Education: B.S., University of Kansas, 1947; M.A., 1951.

Career: Professor of English.
Free-lance author, 1948-49, 1952-55; Editor, Western Printing & Lithographing Co., Racine, Wisconsin, 1951-52; Managing Editor, Alumni Publications, University of Kansas Alumni Association, 1955-58; Professor of English, University of Kansas, 1958-DATE; Administrative Assistant to the Chancellor, University of Kansas, 1958-70.

First Professional Sale:
"Paradox," in *Thrilling Wonder Stories*, October, 1949 ("Communications," in *Startling Stories*, Sept., 1949, was sold later, but published first).

Agent: Robert P. Mills Ltd., 156 E. 52nd St., New York, NY 10022.

Awards: Byron Caldwell Smith Award (given to a Kansas or Midwest author in recognition of literary achievement in the area of the humanities; awarded every seven years).

Member: Science Fiction Writers of America (President, 1971-72); Science Fiction Research Association (Member, Executive Committee, 1973-DATE).

Interests: Golf, bridge.

Gunn writes:
"Lately, I have been devoting a considerable amount of my time to the teaching of science fiction, and working toward better teaching of science fiction, and the writing of critical materials to assist the teaching of science fiction, which have appeared (or will appear) in various books and publications. I have also developed a series of lecture films using prominent figures in science fiction to talk about an aspect of SF they know best, to be used in teaching; and I have accepted the editorship of the Harper & Row Basic Science Fiction Library, to keep contemporary classics available for teaching.

"I have the feeling that science fiction is about ready to expand into broader areas of appeal, if the right things happen or are made to happen. It once had a broad, general readership. Then Hugo Gernsback focused it and nourished it with *Amazing Stories* and "its successors and competitors. Now, after a period of inbreeding, it seems ready to burst forth again. My hope is that it does not forget its past and its strengths. The period of the magazines was the period when I came to know and love science fiction. That love was the reason I turned to writing science fiction back in 1948, when the idea I had been working on-- writing a series of radio plays based on Kansas City history--found no one interested.

"My part in science fiction has been a minor one. I was neither a trail blazer nor a definer. Perhaps I might have done more if I had continued to write full-time, as I did between 1953 and 1955, but offers came along to lead me in other directions. If I have stood for anything, perhaps it was for craftsmanship in writing, for a concern about knowing the techniques of writing and applying them to science fiction. But I have never overdone it: I think technique without content is a meaningless exercise, and I think there is a basic strength that science fiction developed, a way of looking at the universe, that should be retained and developed. Those writers who are bursting out of the field in coruscations of scintillating prose and invention may be leaving their source of strength behind: science fiction's philosophy of rationalism, pragmatism, existentialism....

"But where science fiction is going, and how far it goes, depends on all of us. I think it has something to give the world, particularly young people, in the way of mind liberation without lawlessness. I hope it has that opportunity."

* * * * *

JOHN GUNTHER

Full Name: John Gunther.
Born August 30, 1901, at Chicago, Illinois. Son of Eugene McClellan Gunther and Lisette Schoeninger. Married Frances Fineman, 1927 (divorced, 1944); married Jane Perry Vandercook, 1948. Two children: John (deceased), Nicholas.

Education: Ph.B., University of Chicago, 1922.

Career: Correspondent and author.
Reporter, *Chicago Daily News*, 1922; correspondent in London, 1924-26, and in other capitals of Europe, 1926-29, in Vienna, 1930-35, and again in London, 1935-36; special correspondent for North American Newspaper Alliance in Persia, India, China, and Japan, 1937-39; roving correspondent in Europe, 1939, for NBC; war correspondent, 1939-44; travelled throughout the United States, 1944-45; covered Summit Conference, Paris, 1960; author, network radio commentator, lecturer. Died May 29, 1970.

Agent: Harold Ober Associates, 40 E. 49th St., New York, NY 10017. Award: D.Litt., Gettysburg College, 1955. Member: New York Council on Foreign Relations; Association of Radio News Analysts; Century Club.

* * * * *

LINDSAY GUTTERIDGE

Full Name: Lindsay Gutteridge.
Born May 20, 1923, at Easington, Durham, England. Son of Thomas Gutteridge (a tailor) and Alice Lindsay. Married Marjorie Kathleen Carpenter. One daughter, Susan Jane. Education: Attended art school in Newcastle, England.

LINDSAY GUTTERIDGE (cont.)

Career: Artist and writer.
    Commercial artist for various London firms, 1939-46, 1950-68; Art Teacher, King Edward School of Art, Newcastle, England, 1941-43; stockman on Australian sheep and cattle stations, 1946-48; self-employed photographer, 1958-60; Art Director, Robert Sharp & Partners (an advertising agency), London.

* * * * *

WILLIAM HAGGARD

Full Name: Richard Henry Michael Clayton.
    Born August 11, 1907, at Croydon, Surrey, England. Son of Henry James Clayton and Mabel Sarah Haggard. Married Barbara Myfanwy Sant, 1939. Two children: Michael Edward, Julia Katharine.

Education: B.A., Christ Church, Oxford University, 1929; M.A., 1947.

Career: British civil servant.
    Magistrate, Indian Civil Service, 1931; Sessions Judge, 1937; Controller, Enemy Property Branch of Board of Trade, British Civil Service, 1957-DATE. Member: Travellers' Club, London.

Agent: Paul Reynolds, 599 Fifth Avenue, New York, NY 10017.

* * * * *

ISIDORE HAIBLUM

Full Name: Isidore Haiblum.
    Born May 23, 1935, at Brooklyn, New York. Son of Alex Haiblum (in fancy leather goods) and Sara Jijmerskaia.

Education: B.A., City College of New York, 1958.

Career: Writer.
    Served a hitch in the U.S. Army; conducted a door-to-door survey on health, happiness, and mental stability; wrote scripts for a radio series on the educational network; was an agent for folk-singers; now a full-time writer.

First Professional Sale: *The Return*, Dell, 1973 (sold in 1970, but not published until 1973; a second novel, *The Tsaddik of the Seven Wonders*, was published by Ballantine in 1971).

Agent: Henry Morrison, 311 1/2 W. 20th St., New York, NY 10011.

Member: Science Fiction Writers of America.

Interests:
    Yiddish language, literature and culture; painting, drawing, cartooning; slang and idioms.

The Tsaddik of the Seven Wonders was billed by its publishers as "the world's first Yiddish science fantasy novel." When asked why so few writers have used the rich world of Jewish and Yiddish mythology as a basis for their stories, Haiblum had this to say:
    "(1) A good deal of Yiddish mythology is anti-heroic. (2) Not all writers of Jewish descent are interested

"in their cultural origins. (3) Until recently, few publishers would buy Jewish science fiction. Some still consider it 'too ethnic.' (4) Science fiction readers seeking escape in space ships, or, if you wish, Welsh mythology, might very well find Jewish mythology too close to home."

* * * * *

PETER HAINING

Full Name: Peter Alexander Haining.
    Born April 2, 1940, at Enfield, Middlesex, England. Son of William Haining (a building society manager) and Margaret Joan Pattrick. Married Philippa June Waring, October 2, 1965. Two sons: Richard Alexander (born 1967), Sean Peter (born 1969).

Education: Attended Buckhurst Hill County High School, Essex, 1951-57.

Career: Author and anthologist.
    Journalist for several Essex newspapers, 1957-62; Feature Writer for a London magazine, 1962-65; successively Editor, Senior Editor, and Editorial Director, New English Library, London, 1965-72; free-lance author, 1972-DATE.

First Professional Sale: *Devil Worship in Britain*, Corgi Books, 1964.

Honors: "Man of Distinction" Award, 1974. Member: P.E.N.

Interests: Sport, book collecting, traction engines, sailing barges.

Haining writes:
    "My major work in this field has been as an anthologist. My primary purpose has been to return to print stories of merit in the ghost and horror categories, with particular emphasis on early work by now famous writers. My collections are mainly thematic, usually presented in chronological order, and with great emphasis placed on one story leading naturally to the next, so the book can be read with the same sense of development as a novel.
    "A good horror story must consist of an imaginative plot, atmospheric build-up, and a strong denoument. I am strongly opposed to 'butcher shop' tales describing violence and unpleasant topics in a way which might cause offense to some readers. While stories of this kind demand a certain suspension of disbelief, they are primarily an entertainment, and as such should not encroach on the sensibilities of the audience. The obvious, too, should be avoided--it is what the reader himself conjures up in his mind which makes for the most successful stories."

* * * * *

D. S. HALACY

Full Name: Daniel Stephen Halacy, Jr.
    Born May 16, 1919, at Charleston, South Carolina. Son of Daniel Stephen Halacy and Pearl Edwards. Married Beth Ann Debolt, June 2, 1946. Two children: Jessie Ann, Deirdre Jean.

Education: A.A., Phoenix College, 1956; B.A., Arizona State University, 1957.

D. S. HALACY (cont.)

Career: Writer.
Foreman, Convair Corp., San Diego, 1952-54; Engineering Writer, AiResearch Manufacturing Co., Phoenix, 1957-58; Chief Editor, Goodyear Aircraft, Litchfield Park, AZ, 1958-60; Manager, Technical Information Center, Motorola Corp., Phoenix, 1961-62; full-time writer, 1962-DATE; also part-time teacher of creative writing.

Agent: Curtis Brown Ltd., 60 E. 56th St., New York, NY 10022.

Member:
Association for Applied Solar Energy; Adult Education Association; Authors League of America; Toastmasters International; Arizona Soaring Association.

* * * * *

JOE HALDEMAN

Full Name: Joe William Haldeman.
Born June 9, 1943, in Oklahoma. Son of Jack Carroll Haldeman (a hospital administrator) and Lorena Spivey. Married Mary Gay Potter (a teacher), August 21, 1965.

Education: B.S., University of Maryland, 1967; has also attended American University, University of Oklahoma, University of Iowa.

Career: Writer.

Agent: Robert P. Mills Ltd., 156 E. 52nd St., New York, NY 10022.

Awards:
Nebula Award, Best Novel, 1975 (1976), *The Forever War*; Hugo Award, Best Novel, 1975 (1976), *The Forever War*.

Member: Science Fiction Writers of America (Treasurer, 1970-73).

In addition to his award-winning novel, Haldeman has also written two books in the Attar series, *Attar's Revenge* and *War of Nerves*, published by Pocket Books in 1975 under the pseudonym Robert Graham.

* * * * *

ANGUS HALL

Full Name: Angus Hall.
Born March 24, 1932, at Newcastle-on-Tyne, England. Son of Angus Henry Hall (a timber merchant) and Ann Calvert. Married Theresa Geraldine Garcia (a painter) July 12, 1963. One son, Andrew Henry (born 1965).

Education: Attended Sherries Technical College, Newcastle-on-Tyne, 1942-50, receiving a General Education Certificate.

Career: Author.
Reporter, *Newcastle Evening Chronicle*, 1952-53; Feature Writer, *London Daily Mirror*, 1953-55; Film and Theatre Critic, *London Daily Sketch*, 1955-61; full-time writer, 1961-DATE; Editor, *Headlines*, Sept. 1972-DATE; Editor, *Crimes & Punishment*, Feb. 1973-DATE.

First Professional Sale: *Love in Smoky Regions*, Constable, 1962.

Agent: Harvey Unna, 14 Beaumont Mews, London W.1, England.

Member: National Union of Journalists; Writers Guild.

Interests:
Reading, writing, travel, most sports, chess, classical music, cinema, TV. "I desire to write better, write truer."

* * * * *

H. W. HALL

Full Name: Halbert Weldon Hall.
Born October 29, 1941, at Waco, Texas. Son of Halbert Theon Hall (a farmer) and Edna Mae Faris. Married Betty Ann Gloff, December, 1963. One daughter, Julia (born 1968).

Education: B.A., University of Texas, Austin, 1964; M.L.S., North Texas State University, 1968.

Career: Librarian.
Serials Librarian, Sam Houston State College, 1967-70; Serials Librarian, Texas A&M University, 1970-DATE.

First Professional Sale: *Science Fiction Book Review Index, 1923-1973*, Gale Research Company, 1975.

Member: Science Fiction Research Association (Member, Executive Committee; Editor, SFRA Miscellaneous Publications, 1972-DATE).

Interests: SF bibliography; woodcarving; handball.

Hall writes:
"After receiving my degrees in biology, I decided to take a stab at high school teaching. I loved the kids, but hated the extra duties, and also needed a source of income, so off to library school. Since I received my library degree, I've been fortunate to mix my vocation with the SF avocation fairly regularly, first with SFBRI, and second by beginning and building a major SF collection at Texas A&M University. That collection now has about 90% of the SF magazines in English since 1923, 5000 monograph titles, and a sample collection of 2000 fanzine issues, and is still being actively developed.
"I've been very interested in watching the development of the academic interest in science fiction over the past few years. All in all, I view it as a healthy trend, providing the writers and would-be critics don't try to take themselves too seriously, and let concern for criticism get in the way of writing good stories, or, in the case of the critics, let attempts at criticism carry them so far afield as to be meaningless. One of the things that has particularly interested me as a librarian has been the bibliography of science fiction. Obviously, it leaves a lot to be desired as it currently exists, although many bibliographic works are available. Perhaps science fiction is the most thoroughly indexed and referenced literary field which exists, but even so, a number of other things do need to be done. The simplest and most likely to be done quickly, is a cumulative bibliography including all the material in Bleiler's *Checklist of Fantastic Literature*, Day's *Supplemental Checklist of Fantastic Literature*,

H. W. HALL (cont.)

"and Day's *Checklist of Fantastic Literature in Paper-bound Books*, plus a number of other works of a similar nature. All this material needs to be brought together under one cover using a standard bibliographic format which provides all the necessary data for scholars and bibliographers in the field. In addition, there are many other bibliographic works which need to be done. Rather than repeat all of those here in this note, however, I will simply refer the reader to my article "The Bibliographic Control of Science Fiction, Current State and Future Needs," which appeared in *Extrapolation*, December, 1973 issue."

* * * * *

ATLANTIS HALLAM

Full Name: Samuel Benoni Atlantis Hallam.
   Born September 12, 1915, at Ortega, Florida. Son of Arthur Atlantis Hallam and Hilda Eudora Lazaros. Education: Attended schools in New York State.

Career: Novelist. Member: Authors League of America.

* * * * *

LOUIS J. HALLE

Full Name: Louis Joseph Halle.
   Born November 17, 1910, at New York, New York. Son of Louis Joseph Halle and Rita Sulzbacher. Married Barbara Mark, March 16, 1946. Five children: John Joseph, Julia, Mark, Robin, Anne.

Education: B.S., Harvard University, 1932; student, National War College, 1951-52.

Career: Professor.
   With International Railways of Central America, Guatemala, 1934-35; Assistant to the Editor, Longmans, Green, New York, 1935-36; with the Department of State, as an adviser for Inter-American affairs, 1941-54; Research Professor, University of Virginia, 1954-58; Professor, Graduate Institute of International Studies, Geneva, 1956-DATE.

Awards: John Burroughs Award, 1941, for *Birds Against Man*.

* * * * *

ALEX HAMILTON

Full Name: Alex John Hamilton.
   Married Stephanie Nettell. Two sons. Education: B.A., Oxford University.

Career: Journalist and writer.

* * * * *

EDMOND HAMILTON

Full Name: Edmond Moore Hamilton.
   Born October 21, 1904, at Youngstown, Ohio. Son of Scott B. Hamilton (a cartoonist) and Maude Whinery (a school teacher). Married Leigh Douglass Brackett, December 31, 1946.

Education: Attended Westminster College, 1919-22.

Career: Writer.
   Yard Clerk, Pennsylvania Railroad, 1922-25; full-time writer, 1925-1977. Died February 1, 1977.

First Professional Sale: "The Monster-God of Mamurth," in *Weird Tales*, August, 1926.

Agent: Scott Meredith, 580 Fifth Avenue, New York, NY 10036.

Honors & Awards:
   Co-Guest of Honor, 22nd World Science Fiction Convention (Pacificon II), Oakland, 1964; Jules Verne Award, 1933; elected to First Fandom Hall of Fame, 1967.

Interests: Photography, gardening.

Hamilton writes:
   "I consider it a piece of lunacy to have decided to make a lifetime career of writing SF...but it has worked. Since 1925, when I wrote my first story, I have done nothing else. And on the whole it has been a richly rewarded career, not in money, but in friends, and in satisfying and fulfilling old dreams.
   "What is my opinion of the present state of science fiction? In the first place, I must say that I protest against all attempts to lay down dogmatic rules about SF. It can be many things, and all can be good. But having said that, I record my belief that SF has got far away from the literature of anticipation to a mixed bag of psychological fiction and fantasy. There is, I think, too much coterie writing in SF these days. The thing that troubles me most is that comparatively few science-fictionists seem to have much real interest in the continuation of the space program. After decades of writing about these things, they are beginning to come true before our eyes, but few seem to care much. If this is true, it would seem to indicate that SF has changed from a broad and often lurid literature dreaming of the future, into a small field in which the desire to shine as a 'literary' writer has completely replaced the old burning interest in possible things to come.
   "What advice would I give to an aspiring writer? I can do no better than repeat the advice which A. Merritt gave me when I was just starting. He wrote me, 'Do not read too much of other peoples' science fiction. Read books of a scientific nature, and let your imagination play around the facts therein.'
   "What do I think I've contributed to science fiction? That's hard to answer. While I've never confined my-self solely to space adventure stories, I've written a great many of them, and perhaps in them indicated my belief that the conquest of space would be the great adventure. And if what Borman and McDivitt and the others have done is not adventure...what is?
   "As to whether it's more or less difficult to write novels in a series as against single stories, I would say it is harder when you *begin* a series. One is very conscious that you are establishing a framework, and apprehensive of saying things that will make trouble for you in later stories. But, once again, a series is easier because you begin to know your own characters better.
   "My favorite among my own stories is *The Star Kings*. The reason: it embodies an old juvenile day-dream of 'days of glory.' Who wouldn't like to be transformed suddenly from an insurance clerk into a king of the stars? It seems a universal wish, for this has been my most popular story, translated into many languages. As G. K. Chesterton said in his *Charles Dickens*, 'In obscure shops and furtive publications, mankind still drives its dark trade in heroes.'"

WILLIAM HANSMAN

Full Name: William Donald Hansman.
Born February 13, 1913, at Smiths' Falls, Ontario, Canada. Married, with two children.

Career: Engineer.

* * * * *

PHILIP J. HARBOTTLE

Full Name: Philip James Harbottle.
Born October 2, 1941, at Wallsend-on-Tyne, Northumberland, England. Son of James Pringle Harbottle (a draughtsman) and Agnes Talbot Hardwick (a domestic servant). Married Maureen Doyle (a secretary), Sept. 27, 1969. One daughter, Claire Jane (born 1972).

Education: Attended Wallsend Grammar School, 1953-60, attaining a GCE 'A' Level.

Career: Government officer.
Audit Clerk, Newcastle City Treasurer, 1960-63; Chief Clerk, Northumberland County Council, 1963-69; Manager and Editor, *Vision of Tomorrow*, August, 1969-Sept., 1970 (all issues published); Administrative Assistant, Tynemouth Education Authority, 1970-74, and North Tyneside Education Authority, 1974-75; Administrative Assistant, Blyth Valley District Council, 1975-DATE.

First Professional Sale: "Purge," in *Con*, 1965.

Agent: Cosmos Literary Agency, 32 Tynedale Avenue, Wallsend-on-Tyne, England.

Interests: Drawing, painting, strip cartoons, lawn tennis, agenting.

Harbottle writes:
"I've always been interested in science fictional matters, since childhood, first in comics, then in films. My first realisation that SF existed as a literary genre came with the discovery on a 1953 paperback by John Russell Fearn (published under one of his many pseudonyms). Intense searching thereafter turned up dozens of SF novels, all eagerly devoured, 75% of which were written by Fearn under various names, and about 20% by E. C. Tubb, again under various names. I formed an intense regard for both writers as a consequence. The real identities of these authors were unknown to me at the time. My later discovery that my ten favorite writers were all in fact Fearn or Tubb triggered my interest in bibliographical research to uncover more names of my favourites. This led/introduced me to the entire SF canon in due course. My bibliographical pamphlets led to my being offered editorship of the professional magazine, *Vision of Tomorrow*, since, in their compilation, I had contacted and become acquainted with most of the British SF writers."

* * * * *

GARRETT HARDIN

Full Name: Garrett James Hardin.
Born April 21, 1915, at Dallas, Texas. Son of Hugh Hardin (a businessman) and Agnes Garrett. Married Jane Swanson, September 7, 1941. Four children: Hyla, Peter, Sharon, David.

Education: Sc.B., University of Chicago, 1936; Ph.D., Stanford University, 1941.

Career: Professor of Human Ecology.
Staff member, Division of Plant Biology, Carnegie Institute of Washington, 1942-46; Asst. Professor of Biology, University of California, Santa Barbara, 1946-50; Associate Professor, 1950-56; Professor of Human Ecology, 1956-DATE.

Member:
American Association for the Advancement of Science; American Philosophical Society; American Academy of Arts and Sciences; Sigma Xi.

* * * * *

W. G. HARDY

Full Name: William George Hardy.
Born February 3, 1895, at Oakwood, Ontario, Canada. Son of George William Hardy (a farmer) and Anne White. Married Llewella May Sonley, September 9, 1919 (deceased). Three children: Helen Elizabeth Dickinson; George Evan; Margaret Ann Simpson.

Education: B.A., University of Toronto, 1917; M.A., 1920; Ph.D., University of Chicago, 1922.

Career: Professor of Classics.
Lecturer in Classics, University of Toronto, 1918-20; Classics Lecturer, University of Alberta, 1920-22; Assistant Professor, 1922-28; Associate Professor, 1928-33; Professor, 1933-DATE; President, Alberta Amateur Hockey Association, 1932-33, and Canadian Amateur Hockey Association, 1938-40, and Ligue Internationale de Hockey sur Glace, 1948-51; speaker or lecturer on about 1000 radio and TV programs in Canada.

Awards: National Award in Letters, University of Alberta, 1962. Member: Canadian Authors Association; Classical Association of Canada.

* * * * *

DONALD HARINGTON

Full Name: Donald Harington.
Born December 22, 1935, at Little Rock, Arkansas. Son of Conrad Fred Harrington and Jimmie Walker. Married Nita Harrison, July 20, 1957. Three children: Jennifer, Calico, Katy.

Education: B.A., University of Arkansas, 1956; M.F.A., 1958; M.A., Boston University, 1959.

Career: Professor of Art History.
Instructor, Bennett College, 1960-62; Assoc. Professor of Art History, Windham College, 1964-DATE. Award: Rockefeller Foundation Fellowship, 1966-67.

* * * * *

KENNETH HARKER

Full Name: Kenneth Harker.
Born April 2, 1927, at Darlington, Durham, England. Son of John William Harker (a station master) and Ella Pallister. Education: B.Sc., University College, Durham, 1947.

KENNETH HARKER (cont.)

Career: Technical officer.
   National Service, R.E.M.E. (radar), 1947-49; health physics, Ministry of Supply, 1949-51; ceramic research, British Ceramic Research Association, 1951-55; chemical engineering and instrumentation, I.C.I. Ltd., 1955-62; free-lance author, 1962-66; Technical Officer in thermal and acoustical insulation, Newalls Insulation Co., 1966-DATE.

First Professional Sale: "The Raid," in *Reveille*, 1950.

Awards: Certificate of Merit, for short story "Colossus of Roads," in August, 1961 issue of *Storyteller*.

Member: Society of Authors; Middlesbrough Writers Group.

Interests: Electronics (mainly TV construction), bird-watching, countryside flora and fauna, photography, motoring.

"I tried full-time writing between 1962 and 1966, but found difficulty in making it pay sufficiently, although my two science fiction novels were written then."

* * * * *

PHILIP HARKINS

Full Name: Philip Harkins.
   Born September 29, 1912, at Boston, Massachusetts. Son of E. F. Harkins. Married Anita Nash, 1953. Three children: Joan, Arthur Dodge, Abbie Dodge.

Education: Attended University of Grenoble, 1931-32, and School of Political Science, Paris, 1932-33.

Career: Writer.
   Travelled in North Africa and Europe after finishing high school; has been a reporter and semi-pro hockey player; now a full-time writer.

* * * * *

JIM HARMON

Full Name: James Judson Harmon.
   Born April 21, 1933, at Mount Carmel, Illinois. Son of John Russell Harmon and Valeria Irene Odom. Education: Attended Los Angeles City College for a year.

Career: Writer.
   Has been a radio, TV, and motion picture performer, consultant to NBC, and Canadian Broadcasting Corp., and Hollywood Museum on Broadcasting.

* * * * *

CHARLES L. HARNESS

Full Name: Charles Leonard Harness.
   Born December 29, 1915, at Colorado City, Texas. Son of Conrad T. and Lillian B. Harness. Married Nell W. Harness, July 27, 1938. Two children: Mollie Shan, Charles Bryan. Education: B.S., George Washington University, 1942; LL.B., 1946.

Career; Attorney. Member: American Patent Law Association.

First Professional Sale: "Time Trap," in *Astounding Science Fiction*, August, 1948.

* * * * *

ALF HARRIS

Full Name: Alfred Harris.
   Born February 2, 1928, at Toronto, Ontario, Canada. Son of Samuel Henry Harris (vaudevillian and chef) and Annabelle Golden. Married Maria Justina Wittig (a high school teacher of German), May 30, 1967. Stepchildren: Peter B. Ruehl, Bettina E. Ruehl.

Education: Attended Academy of Radio Arts, Toronto.

Career: Writer.
   Reporter, *Kingston Whip-Standard*, 1948; with Keston Enterprises (an advertising and public relations firm), 1949-52; News Editor, CKEY-Radio, Toronto, 1952-57; full-time writer, 1957-DATE.

* * * * *

BARBARA S. HARRIS

Full Name: Barbara Harris.
   Born November 15, 1927, at Earlville, Iowa. Daughter of Cecil Sigsbee Seger (a businessman) and Gladys B. Bancroft (a teacher). Married Dale Harris, February 13, 1949. One son, Michael Robert (born 1950).

Education: Attended Coe College, 1945-46, and Goodman School of the Theatre, 1947-48, 1949-50.

Career: High rise office building manager. Member: P.E.N.

First Professional Sale: *Who Is Julia?*, David McKay, 1972.

Agent: James Brown Associates, 22 E. 60th St., New York, NY 10022.

Interests: Travel.

* * * * *

CHRISTIE HARRIS

Full Name: Christie Lucy Harris.
   Born November 21, 1907, at Newark, New Jersey. Daughter of Edward Irwin (a farmer) and Matilda Christie. Married Thomas Arthur Harris (an immigrations officer), February 13, 1932. Five children: Michael, Moira, Sheilagh, Brian, Gerald.

Education: Teachers' Certificate, Provincial Normal School, British Columbia, 1925.

Career: Writer.
   Teacher in British Columbian Schools, 1926-32; free-lance writer, 1936-DATE, mainly for Canadian Broadcasting Corp. Radio. Member: Authors League of America.

Agent: McIntosh & Otis, 475 Fifth Avenue, New York, NY 10017.

MARILYN HARRIS

Full Name: Marilyn Harris Springer.
  Born June 4, 1931, at Oklahoma City, Oklahoma.
Daughter of John P. Harris (an oil man) and Dora Veal.
Married Edgar V. Springer, Jr. (a professor at the
University of Oklahoma), February 21, 1953. Two
children: John P., Karen Louise.

Education: B.A., University of Oklahoma, 1953; M.A.,
  1955.

Career: Writer.

* * * * *

ROSEMARY HARRIS

Full Name: Rosemary Jeanne Harris.
  Born at London, England. Daughter of Arthur Travers
Harris (in the Royal Air Force) and Barbara D. K.
Money. Education: Studied at the Chelsea School of
Art, and the Courtauld Institute, London.

Career: Writer.
  Has also been a picture restorer, and a reader for
Metro-Goldwyn-Mayer. Member: Society of Authors.

Agent: A. P. Watt & Son, 26/28 Bedford Row, London
  WC1R 4HL, England.

Awards:
  Carnegie Medal, 1968, for The Moon in the Cloud;
Arts Council Grant for research, 1971.

* * * * *

G. B. HARRISON

Full Name: George Bagshawe Harrison.
  Born July 14, 1894, at Hove, Sussex, England. Son
of Walter Harrison and Ada Bagshaw. Married Dorothy
Agnes Barker, 1919. Two children: Leslie Michael,
Joan Cicely McIntosh.

Education: B.A., Queen's College, Cambridge, 1919;
  M.A., 1922; Ph.D., King's College, University of
  London, 1928.

Career: Professor of English.
  Assistant, lecturer, reader, University of London,
1924-43; Professor of English, Queen's University,
Canada, 1943-49; Professor of English, University of
Michigan, Ann Arbor, 1949-64; now retired.

Awards & Honors:
  Litt.D., Villanova University, 1960, and Holy Cross
College, 1961; LL.D., Assumption College, 1962; L.H.D.,
Fairfield University, 1964. Member: Modern Language
Association; American Assoc. of University Professors.

* * * * *

HARRY HARRISON

Full Name: Harry Maxwell Harrison [name originally
  Henry Dempsey]. Born March 12, 1925, at Stamford,
Connecticut. Son of Leo Harrison [Dempsey] and Ria
Kirjassoff. Married Joan Merkler, June 4, 1954. Two
children: Todd (born 1955), Moira (born 1959).

Career: Writer and editor.
  Free-lance commercial artist, 1946-55; Editor, Science Fiction Adventures, December, 1953-May, 1954;
Editor, under the pseudonym Cameron Hall, Fantasy Fiction, November, 1953; Editor, SF Impulse, October, 1966-
February, 1967; Editor, Fantastic Stories, November,
1967-October, 1968; Assoc. Editor, December, 1968;
Editor, Amazing Stories, December, 1967-September,
1968; Associate Editor, November, 1968; free-lance
writer, 1955-DATE.

First Professional Sale: "Rock Diver," in Worlds
  Beyond, February, 1951.

Agent: Robert P. Mills Ltd., 156 E. 52nd St., New
  York, NY 10022.

Member: Science Fiction Writers of America (Vice-
  President, 1968-69); British Science Fiction Association; Knight of St. Fantony.

Awards: Nebula Award, Best Dramatic Presentation,
  1973 (1974), "Soylent Green" (from the novel, Make
  Room! Make Room!).

Harrison notes:
  "Regarding my name, it all sounds complicated but
isn't. I was raised and went to school and the army,
etc., as Harry Maxwell Harrison. When I went to get
a passport, I discovered my birth certificate was in
the name Henry Dempsey. After I was born, my father
changed his name to that of his stepfather, Harrison.
So I really am the only author who uses his birth name
for a yen name. Since the thing was so cocked up anyway, and I hated Maxwell, I dropped the 'well' back
to Max, a favorite uncle of mine in the Consular Dept.,
killed in the Yokohama Earthquake."

  "I think that science fiction is a natural field for
humor. There are very few humorous stories and books
in SF only because it is so hard to write well. It is
easy to be light in SF, it is very hard to be funny.
I depress myself when I write gloomy stories of the
future, so I write humor to cheer myself up and--hope-
fully--others. I want readers to relax and enjoy, to
escape reality a bit, and aid their digestion and tem-
per by a chuckle and, occasionally, a loud belly laugh.
That is success indeed, and makes all the effort worthwhile.
  "I wrote Deathworld (among other reasons) because I
thought SF at that time was getting too cerebral, and
too much of the action and entertainment had gone out
of it. The reader reaction to the book seems to have
proven I was right. It has been reprinted four times,
and translated into seven languages. My feelings have
changed during the years, and now I see more than
enough color and action--at times little else--so I am
plugging for better writing, better thinking, more
attention to our specialized craft. With this in mind,
I published and edited (with Brian Aldiss) SF Horizons,
the first magazine of SF criticism. We only did two
issues, but the impact was enough to start other people
thinking and working along the same lines."

* * * * *

M. JOHN HARRISON

Full Name: Michael John Harrison.
  Born July 26, 1945, in Great Britain. Son of Alan
Spencer Harrison (an engineer) and Dorothy Lee (a clerk).
Education: Educated in England.

M. JOHN HARRISON (cont.)

Career: Writer.
Groom, Atherstone Hunt, Atherstone, England, 1963; student teacher in Warwickshire, 1963-65; Clerk, Royal Masonic Charity Institute, London, 1966; writer, 1966-DATE.

Agent: Kirby McCauley, 220 E. 26th St., New York, NY 10010.

* * * * *

WILLIAM HARRISON

Full Name: William Harrison.
Born October 29, 1933, at Dallas, Texas. Son of Samuel Scott Harrison and Mary Etta Cook. Married Merlee Kimsey, February 2, 1957. Three children: Laurie, Sean, Quentin.

Education: B.A., Texas Christian University, 1955; M.A., Vanderbilt University, 1959.

Career: Instructor in English.
Instructor in English, University of Arkansas, Fayetteville, 1964-DATE; writer. Member: American Association of University Professors.

Agent: William Morris Agency, 151 El Camino, Beverly Hills, CA 90212.

Awards: Guggenheim Fellowship, 1973-74; Pulitzer Prize nomination, 1974.

* * * * *

L. P. HARTLEY

Full Name: Leslie Poles Hartley.
Born December 30, 1895, at Whittlesey, Cambridgeshire, England. Son of Harry Bark Hartley (a solicitor) and Mary Elizabeth Thompson.

Education: B.A., Balliol College, Oxford University, 1922.

Career: Reviewer and author.
Tutor, Preparatory School, Northdown, Margate, England, in the early 1920s; full-time author, 1923-72; Clark Lecturer, Trinity College, Cambridge University, 1964. Died December 13, 1972, at London, England.

First Professional Sale: *Night Fears*, G. P. Putnam's Sons, 1924.

Awards:
Companion of the British Empire, 1956; Companion of Literature, 1972; Book Society Choice, and *Daily Mail* Book of the Year, 1953, for *The Go-Between*; James Tait Black Memorial Prize, 1947, for *Eustace and Hilda*; Catholic Book of the Year, and *Daily Mail* Book of the Month, 1951, for *My Fellow Devils*.

Member:
P.E.N. (former President); Royal Society of Literature (Council member); Society of Authors (on Management Committee, 1955-58).

Interests: Sculling, swimming, walking, music.
[Courtesy of Miss A. N. Hartley].

LIVINGSTON HARTLEY

Full Name: Harry Livingston Hartley.
Born December 2, 1900, at Brookline, Massachusetts. Son of Harry Hartley (a manufacturer) and Jane Elizabeth Fletcher. Married Louise Harris Randolph, March 7, 1931. Three children: Charles Randolph, Robert Fletcher, Bettina Rathbone.

Education: B.A., Harvard University, 1923.

Career: Diplomat.
Member, U.S. Delegation, League of Nations Association, Geneva, 1925-27; with the U.S. Foreign Service, as Vice-Consul in London, Brazil, and Buenos Aires, 1928-33; Author, 1933-40, and 1945-49; Naval officer, 1942-45; Member, Board of Directors, Atlantic Union Committee, 1949-61; Consultant, U.S. Citizens Commission on NATO, 1961-62; Member, Board of Directors, Atlantic Council of the United States, Washington, DC, 1963-DATE; Member, Board of Directors, Committee to Defend America by Aiding the Allies, 1940-42.

Member: English-Speaking Union; Metropolitan Club, Washington; Harvard Club; New Bedford Yacht Club.

* * * * *

FRANK HARVEY

Full Name: Frank Laird Harvey.
Born February 15, 1913, at Pittsburgh, Pennsylvania. Son of Frank Laird Harvey (a judge) and Helen Price. Married Alma Christine Holzer (a pianist), July 24, 1937. Three children: Frank L., Emilie, Henry Richard.

Education: B.S., Columbia University, 1937.

Career: Writer.
Copywriter, Bethlehem Steel Co., 1937-43; Publicity Director, Chamber of Commerce, Daytona Beach, FL, 1946; copy account contact, William Esty & Co., New York, 1946-50; Contributing Editor, *Argosy*, 1950-54; full-time writer, 1954-DATE; also a magazine photographer and a private pilot; member, Hackettstown First Aid and Rescue Squad, 1958-DATE.

Agent: H. N. Swanson, 8523 Sunset Blvd., Los Angeles, CA 90069.

Awards: William Strebig Award, Best Aviation Article of the Year, 1954.

Member: Aviation/Space Writers Association; American Institute of Aeronautics and Astronautics; Society of Magazine Writers; Authors League; Writers Guild of America, West.

* * * * *

KENNETH W. HASSLER

Full Name: Kenneth Wayne Hassler.
Born March 8, 1932, at Wernersville, Pennsylvania. Son of Earl W. Hassler and S. Ellen Keehn. Married Ethel L. Matthew, January 24, 1953. Two children: Sharon L. (born 1955), Mary Beth (born 1960). Education: Attended Muhlenberg College, 1950-53.

Career: Personnel specialist.
U.S. Army, 1953-55; personnel specialist, 1955-DATE.

KENNETH W. HASSLER (cont.)

First Professional Sale: An article to *Field and Stream*, 1968.

Interests: Hunting, fishing, jogging, weight lifting, reading other people's science fiction.

* * * * *

MACDONALD HASTINGS

Full Name: Macdonald Hastings.
  Born October 6, 1909, at London, England. Son of Basil Macdonald Hastings (a playwright, author, and essayist) and Wilhelmina Harriet White. Married Anne Scott-James (an author), 1944 (divorced); married Anthea Hodson Joseph (an editor), 1963. Three children: Max Hugh Macdonald, Clare Selina, Susan Harriet Selina.

Education: Attended Stonyhurst College, 1917-27.

Career: Writer.
  War correspondent and feature writer, *London Picture Post*, 1939-45; Editor, *Strand Magazine*, 1946-49; Founder and Editor, *Country Fair*, 1951-58; free-lance writer, 1951-DATE; also a radio broadcaster and television commentator for the BBC.

Agent: John Cushman Associates, 25 W. 43rd St., New York, NY 10036.

Member: Detection Club; Savage Club; Beefsteak Club; Saintsbury Club; Thursday Club, all in London.

* * * * *

HECTOR HAWTON

Full Name: Hector Hawton.
  Born February 7, 1901, at Plymouth, Devonshire, England. Son of James Hawton and Harriet Goddard. Married his second wife, Mary Bishop, 1958. Two sons.

Education: Attended Plymouth College.

Career: Journalist.
  Reporter, *Western Morning News*, 1919-23; Parliamentary Correspondent, National Press Agency, 1923-27; Sub-Editor, *Empire News*, 1927-29; free-lance writer, 1929-39; with Rationalist Press Association, 1946-49; Managing Director, 1952-71; former Editor of *Humanist*, and *Rationalist* annual; Director, Pemberton Publishing Co. Member: National Liberal Club.

Agent: International Literary Management, 2 Ellis St., Sloane St., London, S.W.1, England.

* * * * *

JACOB HAY

Full Name: Jacob Hay.
  Born October 2, 1920, at York, Pennsylvania. Son of Jacob Hay and Sylvia Young. Married Joy D. Ryan, April 7, 1946.

Education: B.A., Pennsylvania State University, 1941.

Career: Editor.
  Assistant Director of Public Relations, Baltimore & Ohio Railroad; Assistant Editor, *National Geographic*, 1959-61; Editorial Consultant to Applied Physics Laboratory of Johns Hopkins University, to World Book Encyclopedia Science Service, and to Maryland Port Authority, 1961-DATE; Member, Board of Directors, York Academy of Arts, Carroll County Humane Society, and Shriver Home Museum.

Agent: Harold Matson Co., 22 E. 40th St., New York, NY 10016.

Member: Society of American Travel Writers; Authors League; National Press Club; Carroll County Historical Society.

* * * * *

JOHN HAY

Full Name: John Warwick Dalrymple-Hay.
  Born August 16, 1928, at Sydney, Australia. Son of Charles Stewart Dalrymple-Hay and Barbara Charlotte Chambers. Married Barbara Deirdre Moir, October 31, 1953. Two children: Heather Nancy (born 1954), Ann Louise (born 1956).

Education: Graduate, Australian School of Pacific Administration, Mosman, New South Wales.

Career: Journalist and author.
  Patrol Officer, Territory of Papua and New Guinea, 1949-50; Farmer, cattle breeder, wool classer, 1952-68; agricultural journalist, 1956-DATE; television critic, 1965-69; columnist, *Canberra Times*, 1965-68; free-lance writer.

First Professional Sale: An article to *Australian Country Magazine*, 1956.

Member: Australian Society of Authors.

* * * * *

RALPH HAYES

Full Name: Ralph Eugene Hayes.
  Born September 3, 1927, at Columbus, Indiana. Son of Ralph Emmons Hayes and Ruth Lister. Married Donna Ford (an artist), July 21, 1951.

Education: J.D., University of Michigan, 1954.

Career: Attorney.
  Admitted to Michigan Bar, 1954; attorney, 1954-DATE; writer, 1966-DATE. Member: Grand Rapids Bar Association; State Bar of Michigan.

* * * * *

HENRY HAZLITT

Full Name: Henry Hazlitt.
  Born November 28, 1894, at Philadelphia, Pennsylvania. Son of Stuart Clark Hazlitt and Bertha Zauner. Married Frances S. Kanes, 1936. Education: Attended City College of New York, 1912.

HENRY HAZLITT (cont.)

Career: Editor and writer.
   Staff member, *Wall Street Journal*, 1913-16; on financial staff, *New York Evening Post*, 1916-18; writer of
monthly financial letter, Mechanics and Metals National
Bank, 1919-20; Financial Editor, *New York Evening
Mail*, 1921-23; editorial writer, *New York Herald*, 1923-
24; editorial writer, *New York Sun*, 1924-25, and Literary Editor, 1925-29; Literary Editor, *Nation*, 1930-
33; Editor, *American Mercury*, 1933-34; on editorial
staff, *New York Times*, 1934-46; co-founder and Editor,
Freeman, 1950-53; columnist, *Newsweek*, 1946-DATE; also
lecturer at colleges and universities, and television
and radio commentator.

Honors: Litt.D., Grove City College, 1958; LL.D.,
   Bethany College, 1961. Member: Authors Club; Century Association; Dutch Treat Club.

* * * * *

H. F. HEARD

Full Name: Henry FitzGerald Heard.
   Born October 6, 1889, at London, England. Son of
Henry James Heard (a priest of the Church of England)
and Maude Bannatyne.

Education: B.A., Gonville & Caius College, Cambridge University, 1914.

Career: Author.
   Writer, lecturer, science commentator for BBC, TV
commentator for CBS; Editor, *The Realist*, 1929. Died
August 14, 1971, at Santa Monica, California.

First Professional Sale: "The Great Fog," in
   Harper's, 1943.

Awards: Bollingen Foundation Grant, 1955-56; Henrietta Hertz Award of the British Academy, for *The
   Ascent of Humanity*.

* * * * *

ROBERT A. HEINLEIN

Full Name: Robert Anson Heinlein.
   Born July 7, 1907, at Butler, Missouri. Son of Rex
Ivar Heinlein and Bam Lyle. Married Virginia Gersten-
feld, 1948.

Education: Graduate, U.S. Naval Academy, Annapolis,
   1929; attended University of California, Los Angeles,
   1934.

Career: Writer.
   U.S. Naval Officer, 1929-34 (disabled and retired
as Lieut.); writer, 1934-DATE.

First Professional Sale: "Life-Line," in *Astounding Science Fiction*, August, 1939.

Honors & Awards:
   Guest of Honor, 3rd World Science Fiction Convention
(Denvention), Denver, 1941; Guest of Honor, 19th World
Science Fiction Convention (Seacon), Seattle, 1961;
Guest of Honor, 34th World Science Fiction Convention
(Midamericon), Kansas City, 1976; Nebula Grand Master
Award, 1975; Hugo Award, Best Novel, 1955 (1956),

Double Star; Hugo Award, Best Novel, 1959 (1960), *Starship Troopers*; Hugo Award, Best Novel, 1961 (1962),
Stranger in a Strange Land; Hugo Award, Best Novel,
1966 (1967), *The Moon Is a Harsh Mistress*; Sequoyah
Book Award, 1961; Boys' Clubs of America Award, 1959.

Member:
   Science Fiction Writers of America; Authors League;
American Association for the Advancement of Science;
American Institute of Aeronautics and Astronautics;
World Future Society.

Heinlein notes:
   "My papers, correspondence, mss., and file copies
of editions are being collected by the University of
California, Santa Cruz. Eventually, someone with a
taste for this sort of work may make a complete list.
But, I shan't, as I have trouble enough keeping my
contracts straight, and finding time to write.
   "I never answer personal questions, nor comment on
my own work, nor on that of my colleagues. So I have
nothing to say on the 'state of the art.' I never
look back."

* * * * *

RANDEL HELMS

Full Name: Randel Helms.
   Born November 6, 1942, at Montgomery, Alabama. Son
of Loyce Virgil Helms (a contractor) and Vernell Helms
Married Penelope Palmer, August 1, 1964. One daughter,
Katherine.

Education: B.A., University of California, Riverside,
   1964; Ph.D., University of Washington, 1968.

Career: Professor of English.
   Asst. Professor of English, University of California,
Los Angeles, 1968-DATE. Member: Modern Language As-
sociation.

* * * * *

PHILIP HENDERSON

Full Name: Philip Prichard Henderson.
   Born February 17, 1906, at Barnes, Surrey, England.
Married Millicent Rose, 1938 (divorced, 1947); married
Belinda Hamilton (a painter), 1948. Two children:
John Sebastian, Julian Urskwick. Education: Attended
Bradfield College.

Career: Editor.
   Assistant Editor, Everyman's Library, 1929-32; Fire-
man, National Fire Service, 1939-43; Co-Editor, *British
Book News*, 1943-46; Editor of Feature Articles, British
Council, 1959-64; Editor, Chatto & Windus, 1964-66;
free-lance author and editor, 1929-DATE. Award: Arts
Council Award, 1967.

Agent: A. M. Heath, 35 Dover St., London W.1, England.

* * * * *

ZENNA HENDERSON

Full Name: Zenna Henderson.
   Born November 1, 1917, at Tucson, Arizona. Daughter
of Louis Rudolph Chlarson and Emily Vernell Rowley.
Education: B.A., Arizona State College, 1940; M.A.,
Arizona State University, 1954.

ZENNA HENDERSON (cont.)

Career: School teacher.
"I have taught since 1940, all but one year, all over America, at the Japanese Relocation Camp, Rivers, Arizona, in 1942-43, in France, 1956-58, and in Conn., 1958-59; since 1961, I have taught in the Eloy, AZ, public schools."

First Professional Sale: "Come on, Wagon!", in *The Magazine of Fantasy and Science Fiction*, Dec., 1951.

Agent: Collins-Knowlton-Wing, 60 E. 56th St., New York, NY 10022.

Member:
Science Fiction Writers of America; Catalina United Methodist Church, Tucson; Arizona State Poetry Society; Society of Southwestern Authors; National Education Association; Arizona Education Association.

Interests: Collecting ephemera, travelling, reading, knitting and most forms of needlework.

Henderson is best known for her series of short stories about The People, concerning which she said:
"The People series developed story by story in *Fantasy and Science Fiction* when McComas and Boucher were editors--way back. It started as a sort of one-up-manship of children over teacher/teacher over children bit. It's been fun, and I hope to continue with the theme."

Regarding science fiction, she had this to say:
"I am afraid I'm not qualified to comment on the present state of SF--I have read very little of it in the past 15 years, mainly because, as in American history, my interest dies quickly after the exploratory period [individuals against environment] turns into political or economic history [masses manipulated]. From the little I have read, it has lost spontaneity and the light touch. It has fallen in with the contemporary scene--violence, sex, and the erasing of individuality. It tends to be ponderous with theses that aren't that weighty, or that worth wading through. These are the points on which I 'bias' my opinions. I reiterate: I'm not qualified to judge.
"I began writing about the time I began reading, but began with SF when I decided I should write in the field in which I read the most. Lacking a technical background, I turned to people functioning in SF surroundings, but most of my stories are mostly fantasy, adult wishful thinking.
"As to my contribution--well, from the fan letters I receive (which cover an amazing range of ages, occupations, and geographical locations), the consensus seems to be that I depict the sort of ordinary people who so often get trampled in a technological society, and also the 'goodness' and orderliness of a life that is functioning according to a plan no matter how much we hack it up. In other words, man is *not* the measure of life--God is. I might add that the interpretations of God that I receive are also amazing divergent. Most of my correspondents seem to draw comfort from my stories, which is pleasant, because comfort is what you cain't hardly get none of no more!"

The People stories have been collected in two volumes, *Pilgrimage: The Book of the People*, and *The People: No Different Flesh*, both published by Doubleday.

FRANK HERBERT

Full Name: Frank Patrick Herbert.
Born October 8, 1920, at Tacoma, Washington. Son of Frank Herbert and Eileen Marie McCarthy. Married Flora Parkinson, March, 1941 (divorced, 1945); married Beverly Ann Stuart, June, 1946. Three children: Penny (born 1942), Brian Patrick (born 1947), Bruce Calvin (born 1951).

Education: Attended the University of Washington.

Career: Writer.
Has worked as a newspaper reporter, newspaper editor, photographer, analyst, oyster diver, and oenologist; full-time writer, 1970-DATE.

First Professional Sale: "Survival of the Cunning," in *Esquire*, March, 1945.

Agent: Lurton Blassingame, 60 E. 42nd St., New York, New York 10017.

Awards: Nebula Award, Best Novel, 1965 (1966), *Dune*; Hugo Award, Best Novel, 1965 (1966), *Dune*.

Herbert is best known for his Dune Trilogy (*Dune, Dune Messiah, Children of Dune*), the idea for which originated in 1958, when reporter Herbert was dispatched to an Oregon coast research station to write about an experiment in the control of shifting sand dunes.

* * * * *

DAN HERR

Full Name: Daniel J. Herr.
Born February 11, 1917, at Huron, Ohio. Son of William Patrick Herr and Wilhelmina Slyker.

Education: A.B., Fordham University, 1938.

Career: Executive.
Taught magazine writing at Loyola University; served for several years as a staff member on the *New York Daily News*; President, Thomas More Association, 1948-DATE. Member: Catholic Press Association.

Award: Pere Marquette Medal for Outstanding Laymen, Marquette University, 1958.

* * * * *

JOHN HERSEY

Full Name: John Richard Hersey.
Born June 17, 1914, at Tientsin, China, the son of missionary parents. Married Frances Ann Cannon, 1940 (divorced); married Barbara Day Kaufman, 1958. Four children: Martin, John Richard Jr., Ann, Brook.

Education:
Attended Tientsin Grammar School, and Tientsin American School. B.A., Yale College, 1936; attended Clare College, Cambridge, 1936-37.

Career: Writer.
Hersey's first job was as secretary, driver, and factotum to Sinclair Lewis; writer and editor for *Time*, 1937-44, covering China, Japan, and the war in the South

JOHN HERSEY (cont.)

Pacific; correspondent in Moscow, 1944-45; editor for *Life*, 1944-45, and for *New Yorker*, 1945-46; free-lance author, 1947-DATE; lecturer at many colleges and universities in the United States and England.

Awards:
Pulitzer Prize for Literature, 1945; Anisfield-Wolf Award, 1950; Jewish Book Council of America's Daroff Award, 1950; Sidney Hillman Foundation Award, 1951; elected to National Institute of Arts and Letters, 1950; Howland Medal, Yale University, 1952; elected to American Academy of Arts and Letters, 1953; National Association of Independent Schools Award, 1957; Tuition Plan Award, 1961; Sarah Josepha Hale Award, 1963.

Member:
Authors League of America; Authors Guild; P.E.N.

* * * * *

MORRIS HERSHMAN

Full Name: Morris Hershman.
Born January 31, 1920. Son of Benjamin Hershman (a pharmacist) and Ida Macinski. Married Florence Verbell (a writer and editor), September 6, 1969. One stepdaughter, Janet Brown.

Education: Attended New York University.

Career: Writer and editor.
Editorial Assistant, Topics Publications, 1955-58; Editorial Assistant, HMH Publications; free-lance author, 1964-DATE; lecturer at New York University.

Member: Mystery Writers of America.

* * * * *

MICHAEL HERVEY

Full Name: Michael Hervey.
Born October 11, 1920, at London, England. Settled in Australia, 1951. Married Lilyan Stella (a secretary), October 27, 1951. One son, Gordon Selwyn. Education: Attended Coopers Foundation College.

Career: Author.
Has been a commercial artist, ship's interpreter, Editor of Everybody's Publications, Drama Critic for the *London Observer*, editorial assistant for the secret publications department of the British War Office; author of "Smoke Rings," a syndicated column, 1953-DATE; free-lance author, 1943-DATE; Managing Director, Hampton Press, Henley, New South Wales; justice of the peace. Member: Australian Journalist Association; Institute of Journalists; Writers Guild.

Awards: B.E.M., for services to literature.

* * * * *

ARTHUR HERZOG

Full Name: Arthur Herzog III.
Born April 6, 1927, at New York, New York. Son of Arthur Herzog, Jr. and Elizabeth Dayton. Married and divorced. One son, Matthew.

Education: B.A., Stanford University, 1950; M.A., Columbia University, 1956.

Career: Writer.
Editor, Fawcett Publications, Greenwich, Conn., 1954-57; full-time author, 1957-DATE.

Agent: Candid Donadio, 111 W. 57th St., New York, NY 10017.

* * * * *

OLGA HESKY

Full Name: Olga L. Hesky.
Born at London, England. Daughter of Lewis Cowen and Rachel Franks. Married Mark Lynford; married George Hesky, 1954. Two children: Adam Lynford, Gabrielle Lynford. Education: Attended University of London, 1930-31.

Career: Writer.
Prior to 1949, was a sub-editor, reporter, and film/theatre critic for various newspapers in England and South Africa; Editor, *Wizo in Israel*, Tel Aviv, 1949-59; full-time writer, 1959-74. Died October 7, 1974.

Agent: Curtis Brown Ltd., 13 King St., London W.1.

* * * * *

CLIFFORD B. HICKS

Full Name: Clifford B. Hicks.
Born August 10, 1920, at Marshalltown, Iowa. Son of Nathan L. Hicks and Kathryn Marie Carson. Married Rachel G. Reimer. Three sons: David, Douglas, Gary.

Education: B.A., Northwestern University, 1942.

Career: Editor.
Member, editorial staff, *Popular Mechanics*, 1945-DATE.

Awards: Friends of American Writers Prize, Best Juvenile Book of the Year, 1960, for *First Boy on the Moon*.

Member: Society of Midland Authors; Chicago Press Club; Chicago Headline Club.

* * * * *

HAL HIGDON

Full Name: Hal Higdon.
Born June 17, 1931, at Chicago, Illinois. Son of H. H. Higdon (an editor) and Mae O'Leary. Married Rose Musacchio, April 12, 1958. Three children: Kevin, David, Laura. Education: B.A., Carleton College, 1953.

Career: Writer.
Asst. Editor, *Kiwanis Magazine*, 1957-59; free-lance writer, primarily for magazines, 1959-DATE; served in the U.S. Army, 1954-56.

Agent: Max Siegel, 154 E. Erie, Chicago, Illinois 60611.

Member: Society of Magazine Writers; National Road Runners Club.

PHILIP E. HIGH

Full Name: Philip Empson High.
   Born April 28, 1914, at Biggleswade, Bedfordshire, England. Son of William High (a bank clerk) and Muriel High. Married Pamela Baker, July 17, 1950. Two daughters: Jacqueline (born 1957), Beverley (born 1963).

Education: Attended Kent College, Canterbury, 1924-30.

Career: Bus driver.
   Bus driver, East Kent Road Car Company Ltd., 1950-DATE; part-time writer, 1956-DATE.

First Professional Sale: "The Statics," in Authentic Science Fiction, September, 1955.

Agent: E. J. Carnell Literary Agency, 17 Burwash Road, Plumstead, London S.E.18, England.

Interests: Languages (speaks some German and French, learning Spanish and Italian); verse, ESP, psychology, mysticism.

High comments:
   "I'm a seeker after truth (yet to find it), and have translated much of what I have read as regards mysticism, psychology, philosophy, etc., into fiction, where (in my opinion only) 98% of it belongs."

* * * * *

CHARLES HIGHAM

Full Name: Charles Higham.
   Born February 18, 1931, at London, England. Son of Sir Charles Frederick Higham (a publicist and author) and Josephine Webb. Education: Studied privately.

Career: Film critic.
   Literary and film critic in London and Sydney, 1954-69; Film Critic, KPFK Radio, Los Angeles, 1969-DATE; Regents Professor, University of California, Santa Cruz, 1969.

Agent: John Cushman Associates, 25 W. 43rd St., New York, NY 10036.

* * * * *

DOUGLAS HILL

Full Name: Douglas Arthur Hill.
   Born April 6, 1935, at Brandon, Manitoba, Canada. Son of William Hill (an engineer) and Cora Alexandra Smith (a nurse). Married Gail Robinson (a poet), 1958. One son, Michael Julian (born 1963).

Education: B.A., University of Saskatchewan, 1957; graduate study, University of Toronto, 1957-59.

Career: Writer and editor.
   Writer, 1959-62; Editor, Aldus Books, 1962-64; freelance author, 1964-71; Literary Editor, London Tribune, 1971-DATE; science fiction consultant to Rupert Hart-Davis, Mayflower Books, J. M. Dent & Sons Ltd.

First Professional Sale: A poem to an English publication, 1961.

Agent: Bolt & Watson, 8 Storeys Gate, London S.W.1, England.

Awards: Canada Council short-term arts grant, 1968, for poetry.

Hill has resided in Britain since 1959. He served briefly as Associate Editor of New Worlds from 1967-68. Concerning his career and science fiction, he commented:

   "Science fiction is only a small part of my professional writing life. I have written books on North American history, London history, popular folklore, occultism, and even popular science. I have also published a good deal of poetry, and, of course, journalism. Also, I review SF pseudonymously, and write some as well, though only stories so far.
   "SF has changed over the past decade, as if the temporary schism of the Moorcock-Ballard "New Wave" broke it free of its comfortable Fifties groove. So now in the Seventies, it is much more sophisticated, mature, self-reliant, able to hold its head up (when at its best) in the finest fictional company."

* * * * *

ELIZABETH STARR HILL

Full Name: Elizabeth Starr Hill.
   Born November 4, 1925, at Lynn Haven, Florida. Daughter of Raymond King Cummings (the science fiction writer) and Gabrielle Wilson. Married Russell Gibson Hill (a chemical engineer), May 28, 1949. Two children: Andrea van Waldron, Bradford Wray.

Education: Attended Finch Junior College, and Columbia University.

Career: Writer.
   Has been a free-lance author since her early years; has also been an actress in radio and summer stock productions.

Agent: Brandt & Brandt, 101 Park Avenue, New York, NY 10017.

* * * * *

ERNEST HILL

Full Name: Ernest Hill.
   Born July 14, 1914, at Stourbridge, England. Son of Ernest (a farmer) and Agnes Hill. Married Marjorie Potter, April 1, 1950. Two children: Kenneth (born 1937), Raymond (born 1939).

Education: Attended Warwick School, 1927-31.

Career: Advertisement manager.
   Has been a farmer, policeman, soldier, civil servant; Advertisement Manager, Consulting Engineer (a technical journal in the Thomson Group), 1955-DATE; script writer, Zeta, 1963-64.

First Professional Sale: A poem in a magazine called New Helios, date unknown (prior to 1964).

Agent: E. J. Carnell Literary Agency, 17 Burwash Rd., Plumstead, London SE18, England. Member: British Science Fiction Association.

ERNEST HILL (cont.)

Awards: First Prize, Beckenham Drama Festival, 1958, for his play, "Gods in Retirement."

Hill writes:
I was brought up in Stratford-upon-Avon, moved around the continent during and between wars, and came to rest in an ancient mill-house where the original water wheel ground the charcoal for some of the first gunpowder used for lethal purposes in Europe. More recently, I've settled in London.
"I'm interested in verse plays acted by a number of amateur companies; played a great deal of sport when younger (but not now interested in watching); write poetry for·a hobby; am very much interested in new developments in theatre and literature; like Bohl, Nabokov, and Asimov; hate pornography; speak and translate German."

* * * * *

MARK HILLEGAS

Full Name: Mark Robert Hillegas.
Born December 26, 1926, at Glendale, California. Son of Elwyn Guy Hillegas and Louise Ruth Westervelt. Married Elizabeth Jane Connolly, August 12, 1951. Two children: Jane Carr (born 1956), Richard Newton (born 1957).

Education: A.B., Columbia University, 1949; M.A., 1950; Ph.D., 1957.

Career: Professor of English.
Lecturer and Instructor, Columbia University, 1950-58; Instructor, University of Michigan, 1958-61; Instructor, Colgate University, 1961-65; Associate Professor, Southern Illinois University, 1965-70; Professor of English, 1970-DATE.

First Professional Sale: "Dystopian Science Fiction," in New Mexican Quarterly, Autumn, 1961.

Honors & Awards:
Lucius N. Littauer Foundation/Alfred P. Sloan Foundation/Research Corporation Fellowship, 1963; Shadows of Imagination was selected for inclusion by the Modern Language Association for their Scholar's Library.

* * * * *

AL HINE

Full Name: Alfred Blakelee Hine.
Born December 11, 1915, at Pittsburgh, Pennsylvania. Son of Alfred Blakelee Hine and Marguerite Gibson. Married Sesyle Joslin, 1949. Three children: Victoria, Alexandra, Julia.

Education: Attended Shady Side Academy, 1926-34; B.A., Princeton University, 1938.

Career: Writer.
Copywriter, Ketchum, McLeod, and Grove, Pittsburgh, 1939-41; Associate Editor, Holiday, 1945-52; freelance writer, 1952-DATE; has also been involved in film production work, serving as Executive Producer of the film, "Lord of the Flies"; during World War II, served as Managing Editor of Yank.

RONALD HINGLEY

Full Name: Ronald Francis Hingley.
Born April 26, 1920, at Edinburgh, Scotland. Son of Robert Henry Hingley and Ruth Esther Dye. Married his wife, August 30, 1953. Seven children: Peter James, Richard Charles, Joseph Martin, Andrew John, Victoria Frances, Helen Ann, Thomas William.

Education: B.A., Corpus Christi College, Oxford University; M.A., 1946; Ph.D., University of London, 1951.

Career: Lecturer in Russian.
Lecturer, School of Slavonic and East European Studies, University of London, 1947-55; Director of Studies, 1951-55; University Lecturer in Russian, Oxford University, 1955-DATE; Fellow, St. Antony's College, 1961-DATE.

Agent: A. D. Peters Ltd., 10 Buckingham St., London W.C.2, England.

* * * * *

NAOMI HINTZE

Full Name: Naomi Hintze.
Born July 8, 1909, at Camden, Illinois. Daughter of Jesse Estes Agans and Estella Rang. Married Harold Sanborn Hintze (a fund-raiser), April 19, 1930. Three children: Douglas, Jonathan, Elizabeth.

Education: Studied at Maryville College, 1927-29, and Ball State Teachers College, 1929-30.

Career: Writer.
Also Member of Advisory Board, Virginia Center for the Creative Arts. Member: Authors Guild; Authors League; American Society for Psychical Research; Spiritual Frontiers Fellowship.

Agent: McIntosh & Otis, 475 Fifth Avenue, New York, NY 10017.

Awards: Edgar Award, 1970, for You'll Like My Mother.

* * * * *

RAYMOND HITCHCOCK

Full Name: Raymond John Hitchcock.
Born February 9, 1922, at Calcutta, India. Son of John Henry Frederick Hitchcock (a British Army officer) and Ruby Hilda Rogers. Married Elizabeth Joyce Watts, August 27, 1949. Three children: Robyn Rowan (born 1953), Lalage Freya (born 1956), Fleur Rowena (born 1963).

Education: B.A., Emmanuel College, Cambridge University, 1948; M.A., 1955.

Career: Writer, artist, cartoonist.
With the Royal Engineers, 1940-45; Electrical Engineer, Cable & Wireless Ltd. (working on radio frequency allocations, ionospheric propagation, antenna design, and communication satellite projects), 1949-60; Cartoonist for Punch, Tatler, and other magazines during the early 1950s; painter, 1959-65, with six one-man exhibitions in London and others; writer, 1969-DATE.

First Professional Sale: Percy, W. H. Allen, 1969.

RAYMOND HITCHCOCK (cont.)

Agent: Curtis Brown Ltd., 60 E. 56th St., New York, NY 10022.

Member: Institution of Electrical Engineers.

Interests: Folk music, archaeology, military history, lost causes.

* * * * *

WILLIAM HJORTSBERG

Full Name: William Reinhold Hjortsberg [yórtsberg].
Born February 23, 1941, at New York, New York. Son of Helge Hjortsberg (a restaurateur) and Ida Anna Welti. Married Marian Souidee Renken, June 2, 1962. Two children: Lorca Isabel (born 1966), Max William (born 1974).

Education: B.A., Dartmouth College, 1962; attended Yale School of Drama, 1962-63, and Stanford University, 1967-68.

Career: Writer.
Teacher in St. Croix, Virgin Islands, 1963-64, 1966-67; has also been a dishwasher, pizza cook, graphic design assistant; currently a full-time novelist and writer.

First Professional Sale: Sometimes Horses Don't Come Back, Random House, 1963.

Agent: Phoenix Literary Agency, 225 E. 49th St., New York, NY 10017.

Awards:
Wallace Stegner Creative Writing Fellowship, Stanford University, 1967-68; Playboy Editorial Award, Best New Fiction Contributor, for shorter version of Gray Matters, 1971. Interests: Fly fishing, backpacking, skiing, gardening.

* * * * *

RUSSELL HOBAN

Full Name: Russell Conwell Hoban.
Born February 4, 1925, at Lansdale, Pennsylvania. Son of Abram T. Hoban and Jeanette Dimmerman. Married Lillian Aberman (an illustrator), January 31, 1944. Four children: Phoebe, Abrom, Esme, Julia.

Education: Attended Philadelphia Museum School of Industrial Art, 1941-43.

Career: Writer and artist.
Artist and illustrator for various magazines and advertising studios, 1945-51; Television Art Director, Batten, Barton, Durstine & Osborn, New York, 1951-56; free-lance writer, 1959-DATE; also copywriter, Doyle, Dane, Bernbach (an advertising agency), New York.

Member: Authors Guild.

Hoban was a free-lance artist from 1956 through the early 1960s, when he began turning his attention to book writing; his illustrations appeared in Time, Life, Fortune, Saturday Evening Post, True, and others.

EDWARD D. HOCH

Full Name: Edward Dentinger Hoch.
Born February 22, 1930, at Rochester, New York. Son of Earl G. Hoch (a banker) and Alice Dentinger. Married Patricia McMahon, June 5, 1957.

Education: Attended University of Rochester, 1947-49.

Career: Writer.
Research Assistant, Rochester Public Library, 1949-50; Distribution Assistant, Pocket Books Inc., 1952-54; Public Relations Writer, Hutchins/Darcy Inc., 1954-68; full-time writer, 1968-DATE.

First Professional Sale: "Village of the Dead," in Famous Detective Stories, December, 1955.

Agent: Larry Sternig, 2407 N. 44th St., Milwaukee, Wisconsin 53510.

Awards: Edgar Award, Best Mystery Short Story, 1967 (1968), "The Oblong Room."

Member: Science Fiction Writers of America; Authors Guild; Mystery Writers of America (past Director).

* * * * *

CHRISTOPHER HODDER-WILLIAMS

Full Name: John Christopher Glazebrook Hodder-Williams. Born August 25, 1926, at London, England. Son of Ralph Hodder-Williams (publisher of Hodder & Stoughton Ltd.) and Marjorie Hodder-Williams. Married Deirdre Matthew. Two children: Simon Glazebrook (born 1968), Petra Louise (born 1970).

Education: Attended Eton, 1939-44.

Career: Copy Controller; writer.
Has been a song writer, jazz pianist, night-club performer, propsman, television writer; currently a Copy Controller and electronics engineer, International Computers Ltd.

First Professional Sale: The Cummings Report, Hodder & Stoughton, 1957.

Agent: A. P. Watt & Son, 26/28 Bedford Row, London W.C.1, England.

Member: Writers Action Group; Institution of Computer Sciences.

Interests:
"Watching top class tennis on TV, annoying Authority, inventing electronic gear, smoking, drinking coffee, infuriating publishers, getting thrown from horses, playing pianos (Steinways only), commuting 400 yards by car to the office, flying small aircraft, experimenting with recording techniques, listening to Beethoven/Brahms/Brubeck/Bach/Gershwin/Coleman Hawkins/Ellington/Basie, confusing people generally."

Hodder-Williams writes:
"I studied various electronic systems as a boy at Eton, and pre-empted serial pulse modulation speech transmission systems. Joined the Royal Signals, British Army, and in Cairo was nicknamed 'Nuts & Bolts' when Personal Assistant to Major General C. M. F. White

CHRISTOPHER HODDER-WILLIAMS (cont.)

"(Chief Signal Officer, Middle East, British Army). Lost an entire set of secret documents in a Cairo tram, causing a major change in British policy in the Middle East. Wrote the signature tune of the Forces Dance Orchestra in Cairo, in the tradition of Duke Ellington.

"I built an entire recording studio, with amplifiers of my own design, while trying to think what on earth to do after leaving the army in 1948. Tried publishing, but started writing books under a pseudonym, eventually getting accepted as an Unknown by my own family's firm!

"Long before that, I went to Kenya in 1950, to become props and wardrobe for a Tarzan picture; erroneously signed a cheque on behalf of RKO Pictures which nearly froze the dollar throughout Africa.

"I returned to England and studied music feverishly by ear so as to write my first musical, based on Richard Mason's "The Wind Cannot Read." The show was accepted by a prominent producer, but British Lion bought the film rights between the night of the celebration party and the following day's signature on the contract—after eighteen months work on the score.

"Fled to America and met the fabulous Doc Surmay, legend of Chappell's and Broadway. Chappell's published a song, as I was starving in New York, and couldn't pay my hotel bill. Staged a major audition for Arnold Weissberger, who clapped. Did the town in a very big way, but forgot the limit on my visa, and nearly lost my reputation with the U.S. Immigration (but not quite).

"Wrote flat out for commercial TV when it opened in the UK in 1955, both music and lyrics. At one time, I was writing for three weekly shows simultaneously—once sang a number written on a remote beach, and had it taken down on the phone, just one day before transmission.

"Got het up about computer intrusions around 1964, and started the long business of researching *A Fistful of Digits*, doing work—among other places—at the University College of Swansea. (This after a series of novels, including a threesome on aviation.) Fought for controls on computer privacy along with Lord Taylor of Gryfe and Professor Banesh Hoffmann of the City University of New York, author of recent books on Einstein, and a scathing attack on computerized examinations which he called *The Tyranny of Testing*.

"Studied computer technology informally at Swansea, 1972-73, and prior to that lectured throughout Somerset and talked on TV about computer abuses.

"Currently engaged in a campaign to provide authors with royalties, paid from central government funds, with the Writers Action Group, under the leadership of Brigid Brophy and Maureen Duffy.

"Concerned with several different aspects of 'Freedom of Opinion and Speech,' which is, of course, what the WAG is all about. Public Lending Right is significant for the following reasons:

"(1) No writer can express an opinion very lucidly if he has been starved to death.

"(2) No writer should be prone to unofficial censorship (in the big bookstore chains), and must therefore gain revenue from the libraries so that he (or she) may eat.

"(3) No writer should rely solely on retail sales figures as proof that his work is being read and is worth publishing.

"(4) No writer's opinion or work of art should be truncated through the fact that a publisher has allowed a book to go out of print. The archive and register value of PLR is of social significance, and it is therefore necessary that a feedback path should extend "back from the libraries to the overall book production system.

"(5) No writer's work should be judged, either one way or the other, by its commercial viability. PLR (in the form proposed by WAG) does not discriminate between popular and esoteric literature."

* * * * *

MATTHEW HODGART

Full Name: Matthew John Caldwell Hodgart.
  Born September 1, 1916, at Paisley, Scotland. Son of Matthew Hodgart (an engineer) and Katherine Gardner. Married Margaret Patricia Elliott (tutor and author), August 3, 1949. Three children: Matthew Stephen, Suzanne Louise, Jane Katherine.

Education: B.A., Pembroke College, Cambridge University, 1938; M.A., 1945.

Career: Professor of English.
  Lecturer, University of Cambridge, 1945-64; Fellow of Pembroke College, 1949-64; Professor of English, University of Sussex, 1964-DATE. Member: Oxford and Cambridge Club, London.

* * * * *

LEE HOFFMAN

Full Name: Shirley Bell Hoffman.
  Born August 14, 1932, at Chicago, Illinois. Daughter of William E. Hoffman (a radio and TV salesman) and Vera L. Ray.

Education: A.A., Armstrong Junior College, Savannah, Georgia, 1951.

Career: Writer.
  Has worked as a printer's devil, girl Friday, clerk in the claims department of Hoffman Motors (no relation), and in printing production; Assistant Editor, *Infinity Science Fiction*, October, 1956-November, 1958; Asst. Editor, *Science Fiction Adventures*, December, 1956-June 1958 (all issues published); full-time writer, 1965-DATE.

First Professional Sale: A column and interview to *Savannah All-Amusement Monthly*, May, 1948.

Agent: Henry Morrison, 58 W. 10th St., New York, NY 10011.

Awards: Spur Award, Best Western Novel, 1967, for *The Valdez Horses*. Member: Authors Guild; Western Writers of America.

* * * * *

BERNARD C. HOLLISTER

Full Name: Bernard Claiborne Hollister.
  Born March 17, 1938, at Chicago, Illinois. Son of Joseph Hollister (a printer) and Mildred Pillinger. Married Edna Rozanski, August 10, 1963. One child, Suzanne (born 1969).

Education: B.A., Roosevelt University, 1962; M.A., Northern Illinois University, 1968; M.S.T., Illinois Institute of Technology, 1971.

BERNARD C. HOLLISTER (cont.)

Career: Teacher of social studies.
Has been a case worker with the Cook County, Illinois Dept. of Public Aid; currently a teacher of social studies in Villa Park, Illinois; also Contributing Editor, *Media and Methods*.

First Professional Sale: "Violence: A Selective Bibliography," in *Media and Methods*, October, 1972.

Awards: John Hay Fellowship.

Interests: Collecting old radio programs, drinking beer, eating sea food.

* * * * *

J. HUNTER HOLLY

Full Name: Joan Carol Holly.
Born September 25, 1932, at Lansing, Michigan. Daughter of Arthur Hunter Holly (an engineer) and Hazel Belle Trumbo (an artist).

Education: B.A., Michigan State University, 1954.

Career: Writer.
Has been a photographer, clerk, receptionist, ballet teacher; currently a full-time writer.

First Professional Sale:
"First sale was in 1952, and again in 1953; these were not SF; my first science fiction sale was *Encounter*, Avalon Books, 1959."

Awards: Sarah Hinmon Scholarship Award.

Member: Science Fiction Writers of America (Treasurer, 1976-DATE).

Interests:
Cat fancier extraordinaire, American Indian culture and crafts, music (*all* varieties), SF, ballet, gardening, natural science, astronomy, film & TV sciences, some politics.

Holly writes:
"How did I first get started as a writer? I didn't! Writing got started with *me*! It actually happened when I was about five years old, and I dictated a short piece to my Mother--an imaginative story concerning the possible past life of an American Indian doll I owned as part of a collection of 'character dolls.' From that day on, it was fairy tales, nature stories, and poetry. I changed to writing plays in grammar school, and my Brownie troop put them on; and finally my sixth grade graduating class staged a three-act fantasy I wrote as our commencement program, instead of just doing the usual 'singing' bit.
"I've never stopped writing since. I believe it's a *disease*. I was accepted into, and about to start graduate school in 1955 when an idea hit me for my first attempt at a book, and there went grad school.
"Now--why did I choose SF? For two reasons. First of all, I was an avid SF reader, thoroughly intrigued and 'mind-stretched' by it. Secondly, I feel that it offers me more freedom than any other genre. SF lets me dream, to set my imagination loose to speculate, to extrapolate present-day trends to their possible future effects on human beings and life in general. Then, by investigating (within the bounds of the story

"I'm doing), I can examine how these trends will possibly help humanity, or even sound a warning about their danger. In the third place, SF allows an arena for putting forward my own particular philosophies, if I'm careful to do it without boring the reader or lecturing him. It's even good for easing my own frustrations. About 1960, I was infuriated when my previously peaceful neighborhood suddenly sprouted ten power mowers, all un-muffled, and I wrote a story called "Silence" which pointed out the dangers of noise pollution, and threatened the world with deafness if something wasn't done about it.
"If I have a recurrent theme, I suppose it's the Unity of Life--Man, Animal, and Earth. As I moved through my novels, I discovered that I was continuing to develop one particular idea which began in *Encounter*, went further in *The Green Planet*, and (I think) reached its culmination in *The Grey Aliens*. Yet, I don't know. It may turn up again with an even further extension.
"*The Mind Traders* was an attempt to present an 'alien' alien, and perhaps, even more, to take the alien character who appeared in *Encounter*, and put him on his home planet, depicting the culture of a race which was able to accomplish the things he accomplished while he was alive on Earth. I never thought that character in *Encounter* was villainous, you see, although the readers of the book definitely saw him that way. I saw him as a lost being, alone on a hostile world, making his own way with the abilities he had within himself. He was ruthless because he had to be, but his potential was such that in the end he had to die. To justify him for myself, I wrote *The Mind Traders*, which so hung me up on that character that I'm even now writing a sequel.
"The majority of my stories have up-beat endings, and this, I suppose, is my reaction to the world, wanting to hope, having been saved from a terrible death myself [between 1966 and 1971 I suffered from a brain tumor; it caused so much pain, and finally blindness (cured, now), that I was unable to work; surgery in late 1970 put me back at the typewriter again], and believing that human beings have a strength they seldom use but which is there to *be* used when they need to call on it. Besides, I think down-beat endings are easier to write. I often do my short stories both ways, and then choose the one I think best. The up-beat conclusion must be plausible and possible, and this requires a great deal of working-out, so I feel it's more difficult. I like to pull things together, and through the development of the protagonist's character, capabilities, and insights, allow him to overcome his crisis. The 'shocker' ending is gratifying at times, though, especially when I'm angry about my subject, and want to make a harsh point."

* * * * *

SVEN HOLM

Full Name: Sven Holm.
Born April 13, 1940, at Copenhagen, Denmark. Son of Vagn Holm (a colonel in the Danish Army) and Else Schalburg Knudsen. Married Sandra Margaretha Eriksson, June 3, 1964 (divorced 1972).

Education: Attended University of Copenhagen, 1960-62.

Career: Author.
Has been a private tutor, magazine editor, and a broadcaster for Danmarks Radio; currently a full-time writer.

SVEN HOLM (cont.)

First Professional Sale: *Den Store Fjende*, Gyldendal, 1961.

Agent: Gyldendal, Klareboderne 3, DK 1115, Copenhagen, Denmark.

Awards: Henrik Pontoppidans Mindelegat, 1973; Det Danske Akademis Store Pris, 1974, both for the entire body of his work.

Member: P.E.N. Interests: music.

* * * * *

HANS HOLZER

Full Name: Hans Holzer.
   Born January 26, 1920, at Vienna, Austria. Son of Leo Holzer (a businessman) and Martha Stransky. Married Countess Catherine de Buxhoeveden, September 29, 1962. One daughter, Nadine Joan de Buxhoeveden.

Education: Attended University of Vienna; B.A., Columbia University; M.A., College of Applied Science, London.

Career: Author and parapsychologist.
   Has been a writer and producer of off-Broadway musical revues, a composer and lyricist, and columnist; Editor-in-Chief, EPS News Syndicate, 1948-53; currently an author, lecturer, parapsychologist, television and radio personality, Assistant Professor at the New York Institute of Technology, and Director of the New York Committee for the Investigation of Paranormal Occurrences, and the American Society for the Occult Sciences.

Member: Dramatists Guild; Writers Guild; Authors Guild; American Society of Composers, Authors & Publishers; Kit Kat Club; College of Psychic Studies, London (Fellow); Austrian Numismatic Society; Archeological Institute of America (Fellow); New York Historical Society.

Honors: Presidential Citation, West Los Angeles College; several study grants in parapsychology from Parapsychology Foundation, New York.

* * * * *

NED E. HOOPES

Full Name: Ned Edward Hoopes.
   Born May 22, 1932, at Safford, Arizona. Son of Cloyde M. Hoopes and Pearl Greenhalgh.

Education: B.A., Brigham Young University, 1956; M.A., 1957; M.A., Northwestern University, 1958; Ph.D., 1967.

Career: Professor of English.
   Special Lecturer, Evanston Township High School, 1959-62; Instructor, Hofstra University, 1962-63; Lecturer in School of General Studies, and Instructor, Hunter College High School, 1963-68; Associate Professor of English, Pace University, 1968-DATE; TV host for "The Reading Room," a CBS show for children; narrator of records; former member of editorial board, Laurel Leaf Editions, Dell Publishing Co.

PAUL HORGAN

Full Name: Paul Horgan.
   Born August 1, 1903, at Buffalo, New York. Son of Edward Daniel Horgan and Rose Marie Rohr. Education: Attended New Mexico Military Institute, 1920-23.

Career: Writer and instructor.
   On production staff, Eastman Theatre, Rochester, NY, 1923-26; Librarian, New Mexico Military Institute, 1926-42; Assistant to President, 1947-49; Fellow of the Center for Advanced Studies, Wesleyan University, 1959, 1961; Director of the Center, 1962-67, and Adjunct Professor of English, 1967-71; Author-in-Residence, 1971-DATE; Member of Board of Roswell Museum, 1948-55; Santa Fe Opera, 1958-71; Roswell Public Library, 1958-62; Trustee, St. Joseph's College, 1964-68; Member of Advisory Board, J. S. Guggenheim Foundation, 1961-67; Member of Board of Judges, Book-of-the-Month Club, 1969-72, and associate, 1972-DATE; Scholar in Residence, Aspen Institute for Humanistic Studies, 1973-DATE.

Awards & Honors:
   Harper Prize Novel Award, 1933, for *The Fault of Angels*; Guggenheim Fellowship, 1945, 1959; Pulitzer Prize in History, 1955, and Bancroft Prize, 1955, both for *Great River: The Rio Grande in North American History*; Campion Award, 1957; Knight of St. Gregory, 1957; honorary doctorates from at least 16 colleges and universities.

Member:
   National Institute of Arts and Letters; American Catholic Historical Association; National Council of the Humanities; Phi Beta Kappa; Athenaeum Club, London; Century Club, New York; University Club, New York; Army-Navy Club, and Cosmos Club, both in Washington, DC.

* * * * *

ELAINE HORSEMAN

Full Name: Elaine Horseman.
   Born November 23, 1925, at Lichfield, Staffordshire, England. Daughter of Harold Hall (a vicar choral) and Olive E. Bowey. Married Leslie A. Horseman (a computer applications engineer), 1950. Two sons: Stephen Thomas, Christopher Michael. Education: Qualified as a teacher, University of Birmingham.

Career: Writer and teacher.
   Primary school teacher in England, 1944-62; writer.

* * * * *

ROBERT HOSKINS

Full Name: Robert Hoskins.
   Born May 26, 1933. Son of Frederic M. Hoskins (a builder) and Irene Clune. Education: Attended Albany State College for Teachers, 1951-52.

Career: Writer and editor.
   Employed in his family's business, 1952-64; Child Care Worker, New York State Dept. of Mental Hygiene, 1964-66; Child Care Worker, Brooklyn Home for Children, 1966-68; Sub-Agent, Scott Meredith Literary Agency, 1967-68; Senior Editor, Lancer Books, 1969-73; freelance author, 1973-DATE.

Agent: Scott Meredith, 580 Fifth Avenue, New York, NY 10036.

ROBERT HOSKINS (cont.)

Member:
Science Fiction Writers of America; American Numismatic Society; American Numismatic Association; Canadian Numismatic Association.

Hoskins also writes gothics under the name Grace Corren.

* * * * *

ELIZABETH JANE HOWARD

Full Name: Elizabeth Jane Howard.
Born March 26, 1923, at London, England. Daughter of David Liddon Howard and Katharine Margaret Somervell. Married Peter Scott, 1942 (divorced); married James Douglas Henry, 1960 (divorced); married Kingsley Amis (the author), 1965. One daughter, Nicola Scott.

Career: Editor and writer.
Actress at Stratford-on-Avon, and in repertory theatre in Devon; model and broadcaster, BBC, 1939-46; Editor for various publishers, including Chatto & Windus, Weidenfeld & Nicolson; free-lance writer; member of awards committees for John Llewellyn Rhys Memorial Prize, Somerset Maugham Award; Artistic Director, Cheltenham Literary Festival, 1962.

Agent: A. D. Peters, 10 Buckingham St., London W.C. 2, England.

Award: John Llewellyn Rhys Memorial Prize, 1951, for *The Beautiful Visit*.

* * * * *

SUSAN HOWATCH

Full Name: Susan Howatch.
Born July 14, 1940, at Leatherhead, Surrey, England. Daughter of George Sturt (a stockbroker) and Ann Watney. Came to the U.S. in 1964. Married Joseph Howatch (a sculptor), August 15, 1964. One daughter, Antonia.

Education: Bachelor of Laws, Kings College, London, 1961.

Career: Writer.
Law Clerk, Masons of London, 1961-62; Secretary, RCA Victor Record Corp., 1964-65; writer, 1965-DATE.

Member: Authors Guild; Mystery Writers of America.

Agent: Harold Ober, 40 E. 49th St., New York, NY 10017.

* * * * *

MURIEL HOWORTH

Full Name: Muriel Howorth.
Born at Bishop Auckland, Durham, England. Daughter of Charles Smith Edgar (a lawyer) and Mary Dunn. Married Sheldon Wilkinson; married Humphrey Howorth (an army officer). One son, Darrell Sheldon Wilkinson.

Education: L.R.A.M., Royal Academy of Music.

Career: Writer and lecturer.
President, Layman's Institute of Atomic Information; Director, Seed Mutation Research Laboratories, and World's International Film Association; Chairman, Soddy Memorial Trust; holder of recording patents; writer, 1939-DATE.

Member:
Royal Academy of Music; Royal Astronomical Society (Fellow); Royal Horticultural Society (Fellow); Royal Society of Art (Fellow); British Nuclear Energy Society; British Society for the History of Science; Physical Society.

* * * * *

FRED HOYLE

Full Name: Sir Fred Hoyle.
Born June 24, 1915, at Bingley, Yorkshire, England. Son of Ben and Mable Hoyle. Married Barbara Clark, December 28, 1939. Two children: Geoffrey (born 1941), Elizabeth Jeanne.

Education:
Mathematical Tripos, Emmanuel College, Cambridge University, 1936; M.A., St. John's College, Cambridge, 1939; D.Sc., University of Norwich, 1967; D.Sc., University of Leeds, 1969.

Career: Astronomer, teacher, writer.
Fellow, St. John's College, Cambridge University, 1939-72; War service for the British Admiralty, 1939-45; University Lecturer in Mathematics, Cambridge, 1945-58; Visiting Professor of Astrophysics, California Institute of Technology, 1953-54, and Visiting Professor of Astronomy, 1956; staff member, Mount Wilson and Palomar Observatories, 1957-62; Plumian Professor of Astronomy and Experimental Philosophy, Cambridge, 1958-72; Director, Institute of Theoretical Astronomy, Cambridge University, 1966-72; Visiting Associate, California Institute of Technology, 1963-DATE; Professor of Astronomy, Royal Institution, London, 1969-DATE; Andrew D. White Professor-at-Large, Cornell University, 1972-DATE; Honorary Research Professor, University of Manchester, 1972-DATE.

Honors & Awards:
Mayhew Prize, Cambridge, 1936; Smith Prize and Senior Exhibitioner, Royal Commission of the Exhibition of 1851, 1939; Gold Medal, Royal Astronomical Society, 1968; Kalinga Prize, 1968; Bruce Medal, Astronomical Society of the Pacific, 1970; Knighted by Queen Elizabeth II, in the New Year's Honours list, 1972; Royal Medal, Royal Society, 1974.

Member:
American Academy of Arts and Sciences; Royal Society (Fellow); National Academy of Sciences; Royal Astronomical Society (President, 1971-73); Science Research Council (Member, 1967-72).

* * * * *

GEOFFREY HOYLE

Full Name: Geoffrey Hoyle.
Born January 1, 1941, at Scunthorpe, Lincolnshire, England. Son of Fred Hoyle (the writer and astronomer) and Barbara Clark. Married Valerie Jane Coope (an accountant), April 21, 1971. Education: Attended St. John's College, Cambridge, 1961-62.

GEOFFREY HOYLE (cont.)

Career: Writer.
   Maker of film documentaries, 1963-66; full-time writer, 1966-DATE.

First Professional Sale: *Fifth Planet*, Heinemann, 1963.

Interests: Target shooting, skiing, motor racing.

* * * * *

CLEDWYN HUGHES

Full Name: John Cledwyn Hughes.
   Born May 21, 1920, at Llansantffraid, Montgomeryshire, Wales. Son of John Watkin Hughes (a gentleman farmer) and Janet Bynner. Married Alyna Jones-Davies, 1947. Two children: Janet, Rebecca.

Education: Registered Pharmacist, Pharmaceutical Chemist Diploma, University of Liverpool, 1945.

Career: Writer.
   Hospital Pharmacist, Liverpool Cancer Hospital, and Maelor General Hospital, Wrexham, Wales, 1945-47; full-time writer, 1947-DATE. Member: Pharmaceutical Society of Great Britain.

Award: Short story awards from the *New York Herald Tribune*.

* * * * *

RICHARD HUGHES

Full Name: Richard Arthur Warren Hughes.
   Born April 19, 1900, at Weybridge, Surrey, England. Son of Arthur Hughes and Louisa Grace Warren. Married Frances Catharine Rutn Bazley, January 8, 1932. Five children: Robert Elystan-Glodrydd, Penelope, Lleky Susanna, Catharine Phyllida, Owain Gardner Collingwood.

Education: B.A., Oriel College, Oxford, 1922.

Career: Writer.
   Has been a tramp, beggar, pavement artist; Gresham Professor of Rhetoric, University of London, in the 1920s; co-founder, Portmadoc Players, a Welsh theatrical company, 1923; First Vice-President, Welsh National Theatre, 1924-36; screenwriter, Ealing Studios, 1940s-1955.

Awards:
   Femina-Vic Heureuse Prize, for *A High Wind in Jamaica*; Member, Order of the British Empire, 1946, for wartime service; D.Litt., University of Wales, 1956; Arts Council Award, 1961, for *The Fox in the Attic*. Member: Royal Society of Literature (Fellow).

* * * * *

ZACH HUGHES

Full Name: Hugh Zachary.
   Born January 12, 1928, at Holdenville, Oklahoma. Son of John F. Zachary (construction worker) and Ida Duckworth. Married Elizabeth Wiggs, January 10, 1948. Two children: Leigh (born 1949); Beth (born 1954).

Education: B.A., University of North Carolina, Chapel Hill, 1951.

Career: Writer.
   Announcer and newsman for various radio and TV stations, 1948-61; full-time writer, 1961-DATE, with over 85 book credits under various pseudonyms.

Agent: Virginia Kidd, Box 278, Milford, PA 18337.

Member: Science Fiction Writers of America.

Interests: Kitchen design and installation, plants and flowers.

* * * * *

MALCOLM HULKE

Full Name: Malcolm Hulke.
   Born November 24, 1924, at Hampstead, London, England. Son of Elsie Marian Ainsworth (a hotelier).

Career: Writer.
   "Many jobs in offices, in a factory, in the Royal Navy during World War II; Appeals Organiser, National Union of Students, 1956; Advertising Manager, Leighton, Baldwin & Cox, 1957; Advertisement Manager, Educational Publicity Ltd., 1957-58; writer, 1958-DATE."

First Professional Sale: "The Dead Don't Cry," in *Modern Fiction*, 1956.

Agent: Harvey Unna Ltd., 14 Beaumont Mews, Marylebone High Street, London W1N 4HE, England.

Member:
   Writers Guild of Great Britain; Australian Writers Guild; National Council for One Parent Families; Society of Authors; Crime Writers Association; After Eight Society.

Interests:
   Foreign travel, history and futurology, social/racial/sexual equality of opportunity, lecturing on writing, other peoples' customs, languages "(at which I'm miserably inept but do try)".

Hulke notes:
   "For fifteen years, I've been a TV writer, but over the past few years have started to move over, partly by design, and partly by serendipity, to prose--and much prefer it. I want to emigrate from the UK before it finally goes broke, and reckon as a novelist/journalist I can work anywhere where there's a flat surface for a typewriter (can't think without one)."

* * * * *

E. MAYNE HULL

Full Name: Edna Mayne Hull.
   Born May 1, 1905, at Brandon, Manitoba, Canada. Daughter of John Thomas Hull and Jane Moss. Married A. E. van Vogt (the science fiction writer), May 9, 1939.

Education: Some college courses.

Career: Writer, Dianetics auditor.
   Was a secretary to Henry Wise Wood, "the uncrowned

E. MAYNE HULL (cont.)

King of Alberta," for three years, an editor for a nursing magazine, newspaper correspondent, short story writer; practiced dianetics as an auditor from 1950-75. Died January 20, 1975, in Hollywood, California.

Honors: Co-Guest of Honor, 4th World Science Fiction Convention (Pacificon I), Los Angeles, 1946.

* * * * *

ROLFE HUMPHRIES

Full Name: George Rolfe Humphries.
  Born November 20, 1894, at Philadelphia, Pennsylvania. Son of John Henry Humphries and Florence L. Yost. Married Helen W. Spencer, June 26, 1925. One son, John Henry III (died 1965).

Education: A.B., Amherst College, 1915.

Career: Teacher.
  Teacher and coach at Potter School for Boys, San Francisco, 1914-23; at Browning School for Boys, New York, 1923-24; at Woodmere Academy, 1925-56; Professor of Latin, Hunter College, 1957; Lecturer in English, Amherst College, 1957-65. Died April 22, 1969.

Awards:
  Guggenheim Fellow in Poetry, 1938-39; Shelley Memorial Award for Poetry, 1947; A.M., Amherst College, 1950; Borestone Mountain Poetry Award, 1951, for *The Wind of Time*, and 1956, for *Poems, Collected and New*; Academy of American Poets $5000 Fellowship, 1955; Winterfest Poetry Award ($500), 1966.

Member: National Institute of Arts and Letters; American Association of University Professors.

* * * * *

BARBARA HUNT

Full Name: Barbara Hunt.
  Born October 17, 1907, at Chicago, Illinois. Daughter of Anthony Charles Hunt (a broker) and Margaret Paddock. Married James William Watters (a research chemist), December 28, 1940. Education: Attended University of Chicago, 1923-25; Art Institute of Chicago, 1925-27; Brown University, 1954-57.

Career: Writer.
  Has also run a knitting shop, raised chickens in Florida, worked in an art gallery and as a comparison shopper, and told fortunes. Member: Authors Guild.

Agent: Curtis Brown Ltd., 60 E. 56th St., New York, NY 10022.

* * * * *

EVAN HUNTER

Full Name: Evan Hunter [originally S. A. Lombino].
  Born October 15, 1926, at New York, New York. Son of Charles Lombino and Marie Coppola. Legally changed his name. Married Anita Melnick, October 17, 1949. Three children: Ted, Mark, Richard.

Education: B.A., Hunter College, 1950.

Career: Writer.
  Taught at two vocational high schools in New York about 1950; has held various jobs, including answering the night phone of the American Automobile Association, and selling lobsters for a wholesale lobster firm; worked for Scott Meredith Literary Agency for six months; now a full-time writer. Member: Phi Beta Kappa.

Agent: Scott Meredith, 580 Fifth Avenue, New York, NY 10036.

Awards: Edgar Award, Best Short Mystery Story, 1957, "The Last Spin."

* * * * *

JIM HUNTER

Full Name: Jim Hunter.
  Born June 24, 1939, in Stafford, England. Son of David Hunter (a teacher) and Gwendolyn Castell-Evans. Education: M.A., Gonville & Caius College, Cambridge University, 1960; Certificate of Education, Bristol University, 1962.

Career: English teacher.
  English Master, Bradford Grammar School, England, 1962-66; English Master, Bristol Grammar School, 1966-DATE.

Agent: Harold Matson Co., 22 E. 40th St., New York, NY 10016.

Awards: Authors Club Award for Best First Novel of 1961, for *The Sun in the Morning*.

* * * * *

MOLLIE HUNTER

Full Name: Maureen Mollie McIlwraith.
  Born June 30, 1922, at Longniddry, East Lothian, Scotland. Daughter of William George McVeigh and Helen Eliza Smeaton Waitt. Married Thomas McIlwraith (a hospital catering manager), December 23, 1940. Two sons: Quentin Wright, Brian George.

Career: Writer. Agent: McIntosh & Otis, 475 Fifth Avenue, New York, NY 10017.

* * * * *

DOUGLAS HURD

Full Name: Douglas Richard Hurd.
  Born April 8, 1930, at Marlborough, Wiltshire, England. Son of Sir Anthony Richard Hurd (a Member of Parliament) and Lady Stephanie Corner. Married Tatiana Eyre, November 10, 1960. Three children: Nicholas (born 1962), Thomas (born 1964), Alexander (born 1969).

Education: B.A., Trinity College, Cambridge, 1952.

Career: Member of Parliament.
  Diplomat, with H.M. Foreign Service, in Peking, New York, Rome, and London, 1952-66; Member of Parliament,

DOUGLAS HURD (cont.)

First Professional Sale: *Arrow War*, Collins, 1967.

Honors: Commander of the British Empire.

Hurd notes: "The career of a politician and of a novelist is hard to mix--but each job gives fascinating insights into the other."

* * * * *

FANNIE HURST

Full Name: Fannie Hurst.
   Born October 18, 1889, at Hamilton, Ohio. Daughter of Samuel Hurst (owner of a shoe factory) and Rose Koppel. Married Jacques S. Danielson (a pianist), 1915 (died, 1952).

Education: B.A., Washington University, St. Louis, 1909; studied at Columbia University, 1910-12.

Career: Writer.
   Worked as an actor, in department stories and restaurants, in factories and tenements; wrote for two years before her first story was sold; full-time writer, 1914-1968. Chairman, National Housing Commission, 1936-37; Member, National Advisory Committee to Works Progress Administration, 1940-41; Delegate, World Health Organization Assembly, Geneva, 1952; Trustee of Heckscher Foundation, 1949-60. Died 1968.

Honors: D.Litt., Washington University, St. Louis, 1953; D.Litt., Fairleigh Dickinson University. Member: Authors Guild (former President and Vice-President).

* * * * *

BERNHARDT J. HURWOOD

Full Name: Bernhardt Jackson Hurwood.
   Born July 22, 1926, at New York, New York. Son of Abraham Hurwood (an accountant) and Jeannette Jackson. Married Laura Fenga, April 26, 1958.

Education: B.S., Northwestern University, 1949.

Career: Author.
   Merchant Marine seaman, 1945-47; Film Editor, TV Arts Productions, 1949; Film Editor, Chicago Film Lab, 1949-50; Film Editor, NBC News (an original staff member of the "Today" show), 1950-51; Agent, National Airlines, 1951-55; free-lance film editor, 1955-61; free-lance author, 1961-DATE; Entertainment Editor of *Gallery* and *Genesis* during their first year of publication.

Agent: John Cushman Associates, 25 W. 43rd St., New York, NY 10036.

First Professional Sale: A Dracula comic book to Dell Comics, 1962.

Member: Authors Guild; Writers Guild of America, East; Society of Magazine Writers.

Interests: Photography, art, conversation.

Hurwood comments: "I wrote one feature film--a Japanese sci-fi epic called "The Creatures from the Negative." I do not know whether it was ever produced. At least, I was paid WGA scale. I also wrote one short fantasy film, "The Mummynappers." It was produced but never released."

* * * * *

ROY HUSS

Full Name: Roy Gerard Huss.
   Born June 26, 1927, at New Orleans, Louisiana. Son of Joseph J. Huss (a salesman) and Adeline Guerchoux.

Education: B.A., Tulane University, 1947; M.A., 1949; Ph.D., University of Chicago, 1959.

Career: Professor of English.
   Instructor, Wayne State University, 1957-62; Assoc. Professor of English, Queens College, 1962-DATE. Also serves on editorial staff of *Psychoanalytic Review*, *Quarterly Review of Film Studies*, and *Psychology and the Humanities* (Founder & Editor-in-Chief).

First Professional Sale: *The Film Experience*, Harper & Row, 1968.

Member: Phi Beta Kappa; Association for Applied Psychoanalysis; American Federation of Film Societies.

Interests: Psychotherapy.

* * * * *

R. C. HUTCHINSON

Full Name: Ray Coryton Hutchinson.
   Born January 23, 1907, at London, England. Son of Harry Hutchinson and Lucy Mabel Coryton. Married Margaret Owen Jones, 1929. Four children: Ann Coryton, Jeremy Olpherts, Elspeth Owen, Piers Evelyn.

Education: M.A., Oxford University, 1927.

Career: Writer.
   Assistant Advertising Manager, Colman Ltd., Norwich, England, 1927-35; novelist, 1935-1975. Member: Royal Society of Literature (Fellow). Died August, 1975.

Agent: Curtis Brown Ltd., 60 E. 56th St., New York, NY 10022.

Award: Gold Medal Award, *London Sunday Times*, for *Testament*.

* * * * *

EDWARD HYAMS

Full Name: Edward Solomon Hyams.
   Born September 30, 1910, at London, England. Married Hilda Mary Aylett, 1933. Education: Attended University College School, London, and Lycée Jacquard, Lausanne, Switzerland; License és Lettres, University of Lausanne. Died November 25, 1975.

Career: Writer & translator. Agent: Harold Ober Associates, 40 E. 49th St., New York, NY 10017.

JOHN IGGULDEN

Full Name: John Manners Iggulden.
  Born February 12, 1917, at Brighton, Victoria, Australia. Son of William Alfred Iggulden (a manufacturer) and Jessie Lang Manners. Married Helen Carroll Schapper. Two children: Roberta (born 1948), Kari Helen (born 1960).

Career: Managing Director, manufacturer, author.
  "I've been involved since my school days with a number of family concerns in engineering and business, which I now manage."

First Professional Sale: Breakthrough, Chapman & Hall, London, 1960.

Agent: Fox Chase Agency, 60 E. 42nd St., New York, NY 10017.

Member: Gliding Federation of Australia (Life Governor); Port Phillip Conservation Council (Life Governor).

Interests:
  "In a sense, all of my activities--business management, writing, conservation, landscape gardening, farming, to name the main ones, are hobbies or avocations (though with an element of compulsion). I read a great deal, and was an active glider pilot, though now retired (perhaps temporarily).
  "My main present concern is a project by which the business concerns I manage will be decentralised to a rural site a thousand miles from their present location. Thereafter, I hope to explore the requirements for operating these concerns on a zero growth-rate basis, and for providing a particular kind of 'life-mix' for those involved--this will, perhaps, eventually result in the development of a community, sophisticated yet close to the realities of life, better able to survive the crises now approaching."

* * * * *

DORIS ILLES
[contributor]

Full Name: Theodora Illes.
  Born January 28, 1946, at Brannenburg, West Germany. Daughter of Alexander Illes (a scale technician) and Ethel Rozova (Asst. Manager, House of Fabrics). Married Rex Allison.

Education: B.A., University of California, Riverside, 1969; currently working on her M.S. in library science at California State University, Fullerton.

Career: Library Assistant.
  Currently a Library Assistant at the University of California, Riverside Library; SF bibliographer for the J. Lloyd Eaton Special Collection.

* * * * *

ANNE BOWER INGRAM

Full Name: Anne Whitten Ingram.
  Born October 18, 1937, at Manilla, New South Wales, Australia. Daughter of John Bower (a watchmaker and jeweler) and Mary Rowland (a bookseller). Married Clark Morris Ingram, March 30, 1964. One son, Nicholas Morris Bower (born 1967).

Education: Attended St. Aidans Girls School, Brisbane, Australia, 1950-52.

Career: Editor and author.
  Bookseller, Thomsons Bookstore, Brisbane, 1953-58, 1960-64, 1966-69; Bookseller, Times Bookshop, London, 1959; Bookseller, Children's Bookcentre, London, 1964-65; Editor, Children's Book News, 1964-65; Editor, Wentworth Books, 1969-71; Editor, Reading Time, 1969-DATE; Children's Book Editor, William Collins (Australia), Sydney, 1971-DATE.

First Professional Sale: It's Reading Time, Hodder & Stoughton, 1972.

Member: Children's Book Council of Australia.

Interests: Reading, theatre, music, art, swimming, boating.

Ingram notes:
  "I come from a family of booksellers, three generations. Have worked with children's books for 21 years now. Am a member of the Literature Board of the Australian Council for the Arts, working for children's literature and aboriginal literature. Also review children's books for The Sydney Morning Herald."

* * * * *

KENNETH INGRAM

Full Name: Archibald Kenneth Ingram.
  Born June 7, 1882, at London, England. Son of Archibald Brown Ingram and Kate Francis. Education: Attended Charterhouse School.

Career: Barrister.
  Called to the bar, 1909; Barrister-at-Law, Inner Temple, London; Secretary of Grants Committee, Appointments Dept., British Ministry of Labour, 1919-23. Member: Reform Club. Died 1965.

* * * * *

EUGENE IONESCO

Full Name: Eugene Ionesco.
  Born November 26, 1912, at Slatina, Rumania. Son of Eugene Ionesco (a lawyer) and Marie-Therese Icard. Married Rodika Burileano, July 12, 1936. Children: Marie-France. Now a French citizen.

Education: Attended University of Bucharest; Licencie és Lettres, University of Paris.

Career: Writer.
  Was a Professor of French in Rumania, 1936-39; worked for a publisher in France; now a full-time writer.

Awards:
  Prix de la Critique, Tours Festival, 1959, for film "Monsieur Tête"; Chevalier des Arts et Lettres, 1961; Grand Prix Italia, 1963, for ballet version of "La Leçon," as shown on Eurovision; Grand Prix du Théâtre de la Société des Auteurs, 1966, for the total body of his work; Le Prix National du Théâtre, 1969; Prix Littéraire de Monaco, 1969; Austrian Prize for European Literature, 1971; Jerusalem Prize (Israel), 1973, for the total body of his work, with special mention of "Rhinoceros." Member: Académie Francaise.

DAHLOV IPCAR

Full Name: Dahlov Ipcar.
    Born November 12, 1917, at Windsor, Vermont. Daughter of William Zorach (a sculptor) and Marguerite Thompson (a painter). Married Adolph Ipcar, September 29, 1936. Two sons: Robert William (born 1939), Charles (born 1942).

Education: Attended Oberlin College, 1934-35.

Career: Artist, author, illustrator.
    Had a number of one-person art shows from 1939 on; author and illustrator, mainly of children's books.

Agent: McIntosh & Otis, 475 Fifth Avenue, New York, NY 10017.

Awards:
    Maine State Award, Commission of Arts and Humanities, 1972, for "contributions to the arts"; Clara A. Haas Award of the Silvermine Guild, 1957.

Member:
    Citizens for Safe Power (Director); American Civil Liberties Union; Bath-Brunswick Regional Arts Council (Director, 1971-73).

Interests: Old folk songs, chess, gardening.

Ipcar writes:
    "I have written stories and poems, and painted pictures, since earliest childhood. I've always had an overpowering imagination. I wrote a dragon dream story when I was seven, and at the same age painted a frieze of dragons and imaginery prehistoric monsters around my room. That was just the beginning.
    "I started illustrating children's books in 1945, with *The Little Fisherman*, by Margaret Wise Brown (published by William R. Scott). In 1947, I sold a children's book of my own to Scott, *Animal Hide and Seek*. Since then I have written, illustrated, and had published 26 children's picture books, illustrated three others, and have written three teen-age novels. In 1958, I started writing adult short stories, and have sold three. I had one in *Argosy* in June, 1964, which was a fantastic tale about a man who was haunted by cats. Some of my unsold stories also fall into the fantasy category, as do two of my novels.
    "In the 1950s, when my two sons were teenagers, we discovered *Galaxy Magazine*, and were avid readers for some years. I finally lost interest because there seemed to be a limited number of ideas that were being explored, although some of the ideas still hold tremendous appeal to me. I think pure fantasy is really more interesting. In my own fantasy writing, I like to try to make a story work on two levels. It can be accepted just as fantasy, or it can have a 'logical' explanation. In my novel *The Warlock of Night*, there is no actual 'magic' (except for an omniscient raven). My novel *The Queen of Spells* is based on an ancient Scottish ballad, "Tam Lin." I've also handled this one on two levels, real and unreal. There is, in addition, a science fictional use of time changes between the real and unreal worlds of the story (a tradition of tales dealing with Faerieland).
    "It's been noted that *The Warlock of Night* is one of only three full-length fantasies on chess. I was planning a medieval tale, and happened to be reading *The Annotated Alice*. I was struck by Martin Gardner's comment on the chess game in *Through the Looking Glass*. He writes: 'Considering the staggering difficulties "involved in dovetailing a chess game with an amusing nonsense fantasy, Carroll does a remarkable job.' This was sort of a challenge to me. I love both Alices, but as chess, Carroll's game is really a mess. I thought the way to go about writing such a story was to start with the chess game. So I picked a Grandmasters' game in which a pawn captures a rook at the end, and let the game dictate the story line.
    "My interest in chess came rather late in life, too late to learn much! Although I learned the moves at age 12, I was a hopeless dud, and after marrying my husband, a rather sharp player, I dropped chess entirely. We only picked it up again about six years ago. We've entered a few tournaments and played steadily at a local club. It's the most exciting of all games to me. I did win one trophy as 'first lady' in the Maine Championship Tourney in 1969, but my rating is laughable. As to why more women don't play or play well, I think it's a matter of having talent, and starting very young, and being continually encouraged. Also, most small chess clubs are so completely male that a woman feels very out of place. It doesn't bother me, but when other women come to our club, they show up once, and never come back. Maybe things will change in the future. I heard of one nine year old girl who seems a potential prodigy.
    "My main career is as an artist, painting mostly in oils, mostly of animals, fanciful jungle scenes, etc. Everything I do is from my imagination. There is a good article with lots of pictures on me and my art in the April, 1974 *Down East Magazine*. Also more biographical data in *Books Are by People*, by Lee Bennett Hopkins (Citation Press). We have lived year round in Maine for 37 years now. For 30 years we ran a small dairy. Now the cows are gone, but we still garden, and it's a beautiful place to live: one hundred acres of fields, woods, and shore all to ourselves. We never travel anywhere. Our own land is too beautiful to leave."

* * * * *

BARBARA IRESON

Full Name: Barbara Ireson.
    Born April 2, 1927, at Eastbourne, Sussex, England. Daughter of Thomas Francis and Amy Page. Married John Clifford Ireson (a professor of French), December 10, 1949. Three children: Jane, Richard, Nicholas.

Education: B.Sc., University of Nottingham, 1949.

Career: Free-lance writer.

* * * * *

NEIL D. ISAACS

Full Name: Neil David Isaacs.
    Born August 21, 1931, at New York, New York. Son of Maurice B. Isaacs and Florence Braun. Married Esther Reece Karmazine, December 21, 1953. Four children: Ian Mark, Jonathan Dean, Daniel Reece, Amy Braun.

Education: A.B., Dartmouth College, 1953; A.M., University of California, Berkeley, 1956; Ph.D., Brown University, 1959.

Career: Professor of English.
    Instructor, City College of New York, 1959-63; Asst.

NEIL D. ISAACS (cont.)

Professor of English, University of Tennessee, 1963-65; Associate Professor, 1965-DATE.

Awards: National Endowment for the Humanities Fellowship, 1969-70.

Member: Modern Language Association; American Association of University Professors; Mediaeval Academy of America; Kyushu American Literature Society.

* * * * *

SHIRLEY JACKSON

Full Name: Shirley Jackson.
   Born December 14, 1919, at San Francisco, California. Daughter of Leslie Hardie Jackson and Geraldine Bugbee. Married Stanley Edgar Hyman (author and critic), 1940. Four children: Laurence Jackson, Joanne Leslie, Sarah Geraldine, Barry Edgar.

Education: B.A., Syracuse University, 1940.

Career: Novelist and writer.   Award: Edgar Award, 1961.   Died August 8, 1965.

Agent: Brandt & Brandt, 101 Park Avenue, New York, NY 10017.

* * * * *

CARL JACOBI

Full Name: Carl Richard Jacobi.
   Born July 10, 1908, at Minneapolis, Minnesota. Son of Richard Cleveland Jacobi and Matie Hoffman.

Education: B.A., University of Minnesota, 1931.

Career: Reporter and writer.
   Formerly a reporter for *Minneapolis Star*; has also been an editor of *Midwest Media* (an advertising trade journal), and a public relations man with Key Center of War Information; currently a full-time writer.

Agent: Scott Meredith, 580 Fifth Avenue, New York, NY 10036.

* * * * *

HARVEY JACOBS

Full Name: Harvey Jay Jacobs.
   Born January 7, 1930, at New York, New York. Son of Louis Jacobs (a dentist) and Laura Jacobs. Married Estelle Rose (a textile designer), October 18, 1956. One son, Adam (born 1963).

Education: A.B., Syracuse University, 1950; attended Columbia University, 1950-51.

Career: Writer.
   In public relations, Weizman Institute of Science, 1954-55; staff member, *Village Voice*, 1955-56; Publisher, *East*, 1956-57; Director, Audience and Industry Relations, American Broadcasting Company, 1959-73; full-time writer, 1973-DATE.

First Professional Sale: "A Wind Age," in *Tomorrow Magazine*, 1951.

Agent: Bernard Sezigman, Parc Vendome, 333 W. 56th St., New York, NY.

Awards:
   Playboy magazine fiction award, 1961, for "The Lion's Share"; Earplay-University of Wisconsin Award, 1973, for his radio drama, "Tweet."

Member: Writers Guild of America, East; TV Academy; Science Fiction Writers of America.

Jacobs notes: "Judith Merril introduced me to the SF community through her "Best of..." anthologies."

* * * * *

T. C. H. JACOBS

Full Name: Jacques Pendower.
   Born December 30, 1899, at Plymouth, Devonshire, England.   Son of Robert Pendower (an artist) and Mary Pendower. Married Muriel Newbury, June 1, 1925.   One son.

Career: Author.
   Former investigating officer for the British revenue service; full-time author, 1950-DATE.

Member:
   Crime Writers Association (founding member; Chairman, 1960-61); Press Club; Radio and Television Guild; Society of Authors; Bexley Rotary Club.

* * * * *

DAN JACOBSON

Full Name: Dan Jacobson.
   Born March 7, 1929, at Johannesburg, South Africa. Son of Hyman Michael Jacobson and Liebe Melamed.   Married Margaret Pye, 1954.   Two sons: Simon Orde, Matthew Lindsay.

Education: B.A., University of the Witwatersrand, 1949; attended Stanford University, 1956-57.

Career: Writer.
   Public relations assistant, South African Jewish Board of Deputies, Johannesburg, 1951-52; correspondence secretary, 1952-54; full-time writer, 1954-DATE; Visiting Professor, Syracuse University, 1965-66.

Awards: John Llewellyn Rhys Award, 1959; W. Somerset Maugham Award, 1964.   Agent: Russell & Volkening, 551 Fifth Avenue, New York, NY 10017.

* * * * *

C. K. JAEGER

Full Name: Cyril Karel Stuart Jaeger.
   Born at Bradford, Yorkshire, England. Son of Albert Stuart Jaeger and Mary Ellen Stuart. Married Nancy Lydia Nicholls, 1935.   Two children: Karel Lydia Alexandra Stuart; Nicholas Stuart. Education: Attended King's College, Montpellier University, 1930-38.

C. K. JAEGER (cont.)

Career: Scenario writer, journalist, naval librarian.
Member: Sussex Cricket Club.

Agent: David Higham Associates, 76 Dean St., London,
England.

* * * * *

MARY JAFFEE

Full Name: Mary Flora Jaffee.
Born at New York, New York. Daughter of Guy Robert
Lindsley (an actor) and Florence Everett. Married
Irving Lincoln Jaffee (a writer), January 26, 1963.

Education: A.B., Hunter College, 1929; M.A., Columbia University, 1932.

Career: Professor of English.
Associate Professor of English Literature and Crea-
tive Writing, Hunter College (now City University of
New York), 1930-71; writer, 1971-DATE.

Awards:
Bronze Medal from Accademia Leonardo da Vinci, 1965,
and Silver Medal, 1966; President Marcos Medal from
the Philippines, 1968; Golden Laurel Crown, United
Poets Laureate International, 1968, 1969, 1973, 1975;
D.H.L., Free University of Asia, 1969; trophy from
the California Olympiad of the Arts, 1972; medal from
the Chinese Poetry Society, 1973; Order of Merit of
Eight Chinese Virtues, World University, Hong Kong,
1973; Order of Merit of Six Chinese Arts, 1974; D.L.A.,
Great China Arts College, World University, 1973.

Member:
International Biographical Society (Fellow); International Institute of Community Service (Fellow); United Poets Laureate International; World Poetry Society;
Poetry Society of America; American Association of
University Women; Accademia Leonardo da Vinci (honorary representative); Australian Society; Dickens Fellowship; New York Poetry Forum; California Federation
of Chaparral Poets; Praed Street Irregulars; Sherlock
Holmes Society of Los Angeles.

* * * * *

JOHN JAKES

Full Name: John William Jakes.
Born March 31, 1932, at Chicago, Illinois. Son of
John A. Jakes (a corporate general manager) and Bertha
Retz. Married Rachel Ann Payne, June 6, 1951. Four
children: Andrea (born 1953), Ellen (born 1955),
John Michael (born 1957), Victoria (born 1960).

Education: A.B., DePauw University, 1953; M.A.,
Ohio State University, 1954.

Career: Writer.
"Formerly held a variety of creative posts with advertising agencies, including a stint as a creative
director for one of America's ten largest agencies";
free-lance writer, 1950-DATE.

First Professional Sale: "Machine," in *The Magazine of Fantasy and Science Fiction*, April, 1952.

Agent: Richard Curtis, 1215 Fifth Avenue, New York,
NY 10029.

Member: Science Fiction Writers of America; Authors
Guild; Dramatists Guild.

Interests:
"I originally studied acting, and return to it in
community theatre as time permits. Also active as a
playwright/librettist for stock play market (for example, the book and lyrics, *Pardon Me, Is This Planet
Taken?*, published by Dramatic Publishing Company, Chicago, 1973)."

Jakes is the author of the best-selling American Bicen-
tennial Series. He is best-known in the SF field for
his sword-and-sorcery stories about Brak the Barbarian.
He commented:
"I think the appeal of the sword-and-sorcery genre
is two-fold:
"First, the myth-hero has always exerted universal
appeal. And very few 'live' heroes remain in the contemporary world for us to admire; hence, as child-like
as the s-&-s hero may be, I feel he (or she!) fills
a basic emotional need for readers everywhere.
"Another key may lie in the quote (whose source or
exact wording I can't recall)--'People remember characters, never plots.' Larger-than-life s-&-s protagonists
are certainly memorable, if seldom wholly believable!
This ties in with the first point, and offers the best
explanation I can give you."

* * * * *

JOHN JAMES

Full Name: David John James.
Born in Wales. Married Helen Mary Norman. Two children: Helen Sarah, David Owen.

Education: M.A., Selwyn College, Cambridge, 1950.

Career: Civil servant.
British civil servant, 1949-DATE. Member: British
Psychological Society; P.E.N.; East Anglia Writers As-
sociation.

Agent: Hope Leresche & Steele, 11 Jubilee Place, Chelsea, London SW3 3TE, England.

* * * * *

LAURENCE M. JANIFER

Full Name: Laurence Mark Harris.
Born March 17, 1933, at Brooklyn, New York. Son of
Bernard N. Harris (a photographer for the Associated
Press) and Hilda Warshauer (an editorial researcher).
Married Sylvia Siegel, 1955 (divorced, 1959); married
Sue Blugerman, 1960 (divorced, 1961); married Rae Mon-
tor, 1966 (divorced 1967); married Beverly Goldberg,
1969. Two children: Mary Elizabeth (born 1970); Ber-
nard Laurence (born and died 1973).

Education: Attended City College of New York, 1950-
53.

Career: Writer.
Literary agent, Scott Meredith Literary Agency, 1952-
57; editor for various publications, 1954-57; occasional

LAURENCE M. JANIFER (cont.)

pianist, accompanist, arranger, band musician, performance coach for singers, MC, off-off-Broadway producer, actor, monologist, 1953-64; full-time writer, 1964-DATE.

First Professional Sale: A true war story to a short-lived magazine in 1953.

Agent: Virginia Kidd, Box 278, Milford, PA 18337.

Member: Hydra Club, New York.

Interests:
  "Music, mathematics, mathematical physics, history (especially American and Roman), language and languages, detective stories, movies, politics, people. Not necessarily in that, or any, order. I also seem to write a great many letters.
  "Ambition: to make enough money writing to keep writing. It's a craft as well as an art, and the craft consists of conveying a world in my head to your head. I'm not in the propaganda business, and I'm not in the art-for-my-sake business: communication is the requirement, and if you don't understand a story, the fault is mine, not yours; you have no obligation in the matter. This is a small and unimportant trade, not necessary to anyone, but I am stuck with it and can't stop. The basic rule seems to be clarity: work one word at a time, purify the language, say what you mean as clearly, and as briefly, as possible, and quit. It is also nice if the writer knows something beside the inside of his own head--unless he does, he will be wrong about the inside of his head, too."

Janifer notes:
  "'Harris' was a name given to my paternal grandfather when he got off the boat (from Poland), since the poor man spoke no English, and had no idea what was going forward. The story of our christening, so to call it, has been a family joke throughout the generations. I determined, though, to be named for my line, rather than by an immigration inspector, and began digging round for the original name. Most of the people who knew it were dead or senile. After six years of search, in the summer of 1962, my brother found the name for me, and I immediately resumed it-- or changed it, if you like the phrasing. My brother and mother (the only other people concerned) have not changed, and remain Harrises. 'Janifer' is the simplest spelling of a Polish name meaning, simply, 'inhabitant of, or person from, Janov,' a town in what is sometimes Poland and sometimes Russia, depending on how things go. The switch from H. to J. was advised against by several editors, many friends, two agents, and very nearly everyone else. It doesn't seem to have done any public harm or good; it has done me good. It has made for no strain between my Harris family and me. I have never changed the name legally, and have no intent of doing so--it's an unnecessary complication. I may, of course, use any name I wish as long as there is no intent to defraud involved; very well, I use Janifer. 'Laurence' for the previous Larry was a matter entirely of euphony. It's surprising, when you get to digging, how many Harrises (this by the way) turn out to be remote results of immigration-christening. There are lots of other Janifers-- at least one other with my spelling in Manhattan alone, and many others all over spelling the name Janover, Jannifer, Janiver, Janoffer, and other variants; also counted in this confusing tribe are all the people named Janov, Janoff, and their variants. I went to high school with a boy named David Janov, and now buy "my paper and typewriter ribbons from a store-owner named Janoff; the world is much too small."

Janifer has written many of his books in collaboration with other writers, and he had these comments about the art of writing fiction in tandem:
  "About collaboration: I've done a fair amount of it, one way and another. There seems to be a worry that collaboration somehow destroys the integrity of the finished work, or that it leads to a loss of the writer's control over the work. It can. The only safe rule for collaboration is the one I wrote in a piece on the subject for *Variety* some years back: if the collaboration is not necessary, it should be avoided. But there are a couple of ways in which it becomes necessary.
  "If you need technical aid to such a degree that without it the book simply isn't a book at all (of course, this can also happen with a magazine story), then you need a collaborator, not just an advisor. *The Wonder War* should have carried a double byline--the money splits that way, and the only excuse I have is that neither Mike Kurland nor I thought of it at the time-- because the whole book is about the war, which Mike kindly plotted for me and explained for me. There is an acknowledgement to him in the book; but the book is really a collaboration of that sort.
  "What happens just as often, it seems to me, is the situation in which two writers come together to make a third writer. This may happen if the writers are male and female, the result of the collaboration then being a son or daughter; but it also happens with such new writers as Mark Phillips, or the compound Janifer-&-Treibich. Mark Phillips isn't Randall Garrett, and he isn't me, and he isn't the two of us: he's a whole new being in his own right, and the stuff he writes is stuff neither Garrett nor I can write on our own. (I know: I tried to do a Mark Phillips novel, and found a) I needed technical aid--the book was *The Wonder War*-- and b) the result wasn't really very good.) The way it worked was that Garrett sat in one room and typed away at a long, extended plot outline, about half the length of the finished book. I sat in another room and worked from his pages, expanding them by adding dialogue, people, lines, timing, anything wanted to set scenes, and so forth. The feedback was very fast: about every four or five of my pages Garrett would come in, grab the new sheaf and read it through. Anything I had thought of adding in, any new emphasis or direction the thing was getting, could immediately influence the ongoing plot line as he went on typing it out. (There is, by the way, one scene in each of the Mark Phillips books that is entirely plotted and written by me, and one entirely written and plotted by Garrett. It is hard to remember which they are.) I have now no idea who thought of anything in the books, and I don't think Garrett does. I have no idea who thought of collaborating, either; in my recollection nobody thought of it, exactly, it happened. We were visiting John Campbell one afternoon and he was lamenting that there were not many laughs in SF any more, and somebody (not Campbell) dreamed up our Little Old Lady on the spot, and Campbell, I think, posed the question: How do you catch a telepathic spy? He didn't have an answer. Neither did we when we left. We were rooming together then. We went home and kept talking about the notions involved, and sat down (it was Friday, early evening) and started. The method simply happened; it was what we discovered we were doing. The first book was finished by 7AM Monday morning. (Incidentally again: Randall and I wrote ourselves into the book to see if we would get illustrations. My character did get one small inside spot. His, because I turned him into a major character--not out of any feeling toward Randall, but because the character worked

LAURENCE M. JANIFER (cont.)

"out that way--got the first-issue cover.) We put the Mark Phillips byline on because John didn't much like long double bylines, and anyhow the book did feel like a new thing, a new author.

"We could deliberately get together and turn into Mark Phillips from then on, and we did. It was a great deal of fun. (One of the great advantages of this form of collaboration is that each writer is convinced that the other is doing all the work. I would a lot rather write than plot, and Randall, whose gifts as a pure maker of Story I have seen equalled only once, is like most Story people, impatient of the fussy job of lining up the exact words, the exact timing, and so forth.) We wrote the second book before the first had appeared, because we wanted to have some more fun; and we wrote the third because there was still more fun to be had. (The third exists in two quite different versions, by the way. Our original title for it has never been on any version. We called it *They're Coming Through the Windows*, and John's reaction to it was that it was the funniest thing he had ever read-- I'm quoting--but that it had no real plot at all. We said we knew that; did it need one? [A story is not a plot.] John said yes, so we rewrote the last three-quarters of the book and put in a plot. The magazine version is the rewritten one. When Pyramid bought the series for book publication, Randall came up with a copy of our original version, which I'd thought was lost forever, and Pyramid was willing to use that. I think it's the best Mark Phillips there is [Randall, last I heard, prefers our first job.] But that is, really, the amount and kind of rewriting we did for *Analog* on the books. I have heard people say that John insisted on all sorts of things to go along with his philosophy, or his notions, or something. Nope. John wanted a plot. He also wanted one very bad pun excised from the last part of that third book. We excised it. [It was bad, too: we took it out of the Pyramid version, when that was going in for publication.])

"Now, there is no loss of control or loss of integrity in all this--quite beyond the question of John dictating the series to us, which people apparently do think occurred--because the control and the integrity belong to Mark Phillips. Randall and I could *become* Mark Phillips; but when we did we were a single thing, not two writers struggling for control of a manuscript.

"About the same thing happened with Steve Treibich when we began to write the three novels we did for Ace. I forget who had the original notion for the books, but it was probably Steve. The same collaborative method occurred, because it was most natural for both of us--Steve was the only other person I've known with a head for pure Story that matched Randall's, and he was just as impatient with the finicky sort of thing I like doing. I think that Steve did even more of the story work, less of the final writing. But here is the test: neither Mark Phillips nor Janifer&Treibich sound, noticeably, like me, though I did the final drafts (exclusive of arguments, polishing, and the one scene per book in the Phillips novels that Randall took over) on all of them. They're themselves, their own persons.

"Most of my short-story collaborations are the result of someone tossing me an idea which I then write down. This is the way most of the short collaborations with Mike Kurland went. We were kicking things around, and sometimes we kicked them around in print. One story I remember was being written by both of us at the same time; I did the actual typing, since at the

"time, I think, I typed faster, but Mike hung over my shoulder and dictated, or said Wait a minute, or suggested another phrasing or another notion. This sort of thing is not 'serious' writing, as people want to think of it, at all: it is just having fun. The same thing as a couple of musicians getting together to jam.

"The exception is the short collaboration with Don Westlake. I described that one when I dropped the story into a collection. I had had the first half of that story in my head for eight years. I knew it went somewhere, but had no notion where. I kept going up to people and saying Finish this; finally I asked Don, and he said, instantly: 'It goes like this,' and told me, and it did, and I wrote it and sent it out with a double byline. It was a great relief. I have another one of those first-half things in my head now, have had for a number of years. Eventually I'll either finish it or I'll run into the person who owns the other half.

"Anyhow--aside from collaboration--I'm not much on control, if I understand the way the word is used. I don't write my stories (or rather, when I do they're lousy); I'm the means by which they are written. I sit here and do my best to get down exactly right the world, and the events and people, that are in my head; and I do the necessary formal arranging. But I didn't put the things there. I would be much bothered about control if someone else did the final draft; I am insistent, as a few editors know after a fight or two, on the exact words and the exact punctuation I finally do decide on. It is the actual words themselves and their look on the page, the punctuation, and all the things of that sort that make the greatest difference to me. What I'm writing *about* is something I have little control over, and want little control over. I'm a microphone, a conduit whose job it is to make sure I transmit, with as much care and as much knowledge as I can, what has come to me. I arrange and juggle the things in my head; but I don't put them there."

* * * * *

JULIE JARDINE

Full Name: Julie Ann Jardine.
    Born February 6, 1926, at Harbin, Manchuria. Daughter of Mr. and Mrs. Hariton Shohor. Married Jack Jardine (a science fiction writer), 1956 (divorced, 1968). One daughter, Sabra Fiona Elgin.

Career: Dancer and writer.
    "Travel abroad, theater work for 30 years; dancer and writer." Member: Temple Beth Sholem.

First Professional Sale: "The Party," in *Fling*, 1958 (with Jack Jardine as Corrie Howard).

Interests: Sewing, reading, cooking, "my daughter."

* * * * *

RANDALL JARRELL

Full Name: Randall Jarrell.
    Born May 6, 1914, at Nashville, Tennessee. Son of Owen Jarrell and Anna Campbell. Married Mary Eloise von Schrader, November 8, 1952.

Education: A.B., Vanderbilt University, 1935; A.M., 1938. Member: Academy of American Poets (Chancellor); National Institute of Arts and Letters; Phi Beta Kappa.

RANDALL JARRELL (cont.)

Career: Professor of English; poet.
   Instructor, Kenyon College, 1937-39; Instructor in English, University of Texas, Austin, 1939-42; Instructor in English, Sarah Lawrence College, 1946-47; Visiting Fellow in Creative Writing, Princeton University, 1951-52; Associate Professor, Woman's College of the University of North Carolina, 1947-51, 1953-54; Professor of English, 1958-65. Lecturer and visiting instructor at numerous colleges and universities. Died October 14, 1965.

Awards:
   Guggenheim Fellowship in Poetry, 1946; Levinson Prize, 1948; Oscar Blumenthal Prize, 1951; National Institute of Arts and Letters Grant, 1951; National Book Award, 1961, for *The Woman at the Washington Zoo*; O. Max Gardner Award, 1962; D.H.L., Bard College, 1962; Ingram-Merrill Literary Award, 1965; Fellow, Indiana University School of Letters.

* * * * *

FRED G. JARVIS

Full Name: Frederick Gordon Jarvis, Jr.
   Born July 25, 1930. Son of Frederick Gordon Jarvis (an insurance consultant) and Ruth Bisbee. Married Helen Norris Smith, September 2, 1967. One child: Emily Ruth.

Education: B.A., Yale University, 1952; attended Manhattan School of Music, 1953.

Career: Editor and writer.
   Restaurant Reviewer, *Metropolitan Host*, 1956-61; Editor, *Winged Foot* (publication of the New York Athletic Club), 1961-70; President, F. J. Corporation (magazine publishing), 1970-DATE.

* * * * *

GEOFFREY JENKINS

Full Name: Geoffrey Jenkins.
   Born June 16, 1920, at Port Elizabeth, Cape Province, South Africa. Son of Ernest Henry Jenkins (an editor) and Daisy Gardiner. Married Eve Palmer (an author), March 17, 1950. One son, David.

Career: Writer.
   Journalist in Salisbury, Rhodesia, 1940-46, and in London, 1947-48; chief representative of the *Star* in Pretoria, South Africa, 1949-62; full-time author and screenwriter, 1962-DATE.

Awards: Lord Kemsley's Commonwealth scholarship for journalists. Member: British Screen Writers Guild; Authors Guild (U.S.); Arts Club.

* * * * *

J. O. JEPPSON

Full Name: Janet Opal Jeppson.
   Born August 6, 1926, at Ashland, Pennsylvania. Daughter of John Rufus Jeppson (a physician) and Rae Knudson. Married Isaac Asimov (the science fiction author), November 30, 1973.

Education: B.A., Stanford University, 1948; M.D., New York University, 1952; attended William A. White Psychoanalytic Institute, 1955-60.

Career: Doctor and psychiatrist.
   Licensed to practice medicine in New York; Intern, Philadelphia General Hospital, 1952-53; Psychiatric Resident, Bellevue Hospital, New York, 1953-56; private practice of medicine in New York, 1953-DATE; Training and Supervisory Analyst, William A. White Psychoanalytic Institute, New York, 1969-DATE; Director of Training, 1974-DATE; writer.

Member:
   American Psychiatric Association; American Academy of Psychoanalysis; William Alanson White Society; New York State Medical Society; New York County Medical Society; Phi Beta Kappa.

* * * * *

OLOF JOHANNESSON

Full Name: Hannes Olof Goesta Alfven.
   Born May 30, 1908, at Norrkoeping, Sweden. Son of Johannes Alfven (a physician) and Anna-Clara Romanus (a physician). Married Kerstin Erikson (a teacher of social science), June 18, 1935. Five children: Cecilia, Inger, Goesta, Reidun, Berenike.

Education: Ph.D., University of Uppsala, 1934.

Career: Professor of Physics.
   Professor of Physics, Royal Institute of Technology, Stockholm, Sweden, 1940-DATE; member, Swedish Atomic Energy Commission, 1946-47.

Member: National Academy of Sciences-National Research Council; Akademiia Nauk SSSR (Russia).

* * * * *

EDGAR JOHNSON

Full Name: Edgar Johnson.
   Born December 1, 1901, at Brooklyn, New York. Son of Walter Conover Johnson (a sales manager) and Emily Haas. Married Eleanor Kraus (an editor and teacher), June 21, 1933. Two children: Judith Evelyn, Laurence Michael.

Education: A.B., Columbia University, 1922; graduate student, 1922-24, 1926-27.

Career: Professsor of English.
   Instructor, Columbia University, 1922-24, at Washington University, St. Louis, 1924-26, and at Hunter College, 1926-27; Professor of English, City College of New York, 1927-71. Died 1972.

Awards:
   Fulbright Senior Scholar, University of Edinburgh, 1956-57; Guggenheim Fellow in England and Scotland, 1966-67; Officier de l'Ordre des Palines Académiques (France), 1966; Fellow, Royal Society of Arts, England, 1968; American Heritage Biography Prize, 1969, for *Walter Scott: The Great Unknown*.

Member: Modern Language Association; Council for Basic Education; P.E.N.; Dickens Fellowship; Phi Beta Kappa; Century Association; Lotos Club.

GORDON JOHNSON
[contributor]

Full Name: Gordon Johnson.
   Born July 28, 1943, at Greenock, Renfrewshire, Scot-
land. Son of William T. W. Johnson (an engineer) and
Jessie Bennet Pert. Married Kay R. Young, February
21, 1968. Two children: Alexandra Young (born 1970),
Thomas Pert (born 1972).

Education: Attended Scottish School of Librarianship, 1962-63; Associate of the Library Association,
   1966.

Career: Chartered librarian.
   Various posts with the Renfrewshire County Council,
1961-67; Senior Assistant and Reader's Advisor, Scar-
borough Town Council, 1967-70; Stock Editor, Clyde-
bank Town Council, 1970-71; Deputy Burgh Librarian,
1971-73; Deputy County Librarian, Aberdeen County Council, 1973-DATE.

Member: British Science Fiction Association.

Interests:
   Gardening, tropical fish, agates, local history,
general science, ancient history (and archaeology),
cine filming, the countryside, UK politics. "I'm a
jack of all trades, master of one. Religious and tolerant, lazy and overworked, family man who loves his
own company, nonconformist who dislikes extremists.
Hopeless optimist."

* * * * *

STANLEY JOHNSON

Full Name: Stanley Patrick Johnson.
   Born August 18, 1940, at Penzance, Cornwall, England.
Son of Wilfred Johnson (a farmer) and Irene Williams.
Married Charlotte Fawcett, July 20, 1963. Three child-
ren: Alexander, Rachel, Leo.

Education: B.A., Oxford University, 1963; Diploma
   in Agricultural Economics, 1965.

Career: Writer.
   Writer and economist, World Bank, Washington, 1966-
68; Writer, 1968-DATE. Awards: Sir Roger Newdigate
Prize for English Verse, 1962, for "May Morning."

Agent: John Cushman Associates, 24 E. 38th St., New
   York, NY 10016.

* * * * *

ADRIENNE JONES

Full Name: Adrienne Jones.
   Born July 28, 1915, at Atlanta, Georgia. Daughter
of Arthur Washington Applewhite and Orianna Mason.
Married Richard Morris Jones, 1939. Two children:
Gregory, Gwen.

Education:
   Attended Theosophical School of the Open Gate; also
studied at University of California, Los Angeles,
1958-59, and University of California, Irvine, 1972.

Career: Writer.
   Professional free-lance writer and novelist; has

also worked as an office and managerial worker, cattle
rancher, and with youth groups; speaker at conferences,
schools, and libraries.

Member:
   P.E.N.; American Civil Liberties Union; National
Association for the Advancement of Colored People;
Audobon Society; Southern California Council on Litera-
ture for Children and Young People; California Writers
Guild; Southern Christian Leadership Conference.

* * * * *

MERVYN JONES

Full Name: Mervyn Jones.
   Born February 27, 1922, at London, England. Son of
Ernest Jones (a psychoanalyst) and Katharine Jokl. Mar-
ried Jeanne Urquhart, April 2, 1948. Three children:
Jacqueline, Marian, Conrad.

Education: Attended New York University, 1939-41.

Career: Journalist.
   Free-lance journalist, 1947-DATE; Asst. Editor, *London Tribune*, 1955-60; Drama Critic, 1958-67; Asst. Editor, *New Statesman*, 1966-68; novelist, 1952-DATE.

Agent: Richard Scott Simon, 36 Wellington St., London
   W.C.2, England.

* * * * *

NEIL R. JONES

Full Name: Neil Ronald Jones.
   Born May 29, 1909, at Fulton, New York. Son of
Clarence E. Jones and Etta Davis. Married Rita Gwen-
doline Rees, June 19, 1945 (died 1964).

Career: Insurance claims examiner.
   Unemployment insurance claims examiner for New York
State, now retired; served in the U.S. Army, 1942-45,
and was among the first American troops in Berlin on
July 4, 1945.

First Professional Sale: "The Death's Head Meteor,"
   in *Air Wonder Stories*, January, 1930.

Member: Hiram Lodge.

Jones writes:
   "Most of my works come under one of three categories:
the Professor Jameson series, tales of the 24th century,
and tales of the 26th century.
   "The two latter are historical in nature, as characters and events from one story often tie in with another one. "The Citadel in Space" is from Tales of the
26th Century. "The Death's Head Meteor," my first published story, is also from this series.
   "On the other hand, "Hermit of Saturn's Ring," which
appeared in *Planet Stories*, is from Tales of the 24th
Century, and was also used by Donald Wollheim in his
Flight into Space anthology.
   "A good many readers mention my Durna Rangue Stories
as a definite series. Possibly, but these stories in-
terwork into both the 24th and 26th century series.
Two hundred years after the 24th century, we find that
the cult has banded with the space pirates, and conquered the Earth. That is what "The Citadel in Space"
is all about. I called this story "The Outlawed World"

NEIL R. JONES (cont.)

"when I wrote it.

"Incidentally, there are 30 written Professor Jameson stories, of which 23 have now seen publication. Donald Wollheim terms the series the longest-lived series in science fiction history, from the first publication date of the earliest story to the most recent. Reprints do not count. "The Jameson Satellite" first appeared in 1931. Numbers 22 and 23 were published early in 1968 for the first time ("In the Meteoric Cloud" and "The Accelerated World"). The current span of years is 37. Any future publication of the remaining seven stories will extend it.

"There are enough of the stories to make up three more books like the ones Ace published. The professor has been discontinued several times during the past 37 years, but always bobs back to the top again, eventually. I wrote the last three, "The Satellite Sun," "Hidden World," and "The Metal Menace" in 1967-68, when Ace started running the earlier ones, and I started one called "The Sun Dwellers," which would have been the 31st. It is too bad they couldn't have finished all eight or nine volumes, as two of the best ones were never published: "The Voice Across Space," and "Battle Moon." The latter story was planned in an editorial office in New York by Ejler Jakobsson and myself, and I was even paid for it, when *Super Science Stories* discontinued. The series is just what it is, and can be nothing more. There are no human characteristics or situations, only novel phenomena, plenty of adventure and action on strange worlds. There is no final conclusion to the series. Why should there be when the entire theme deals with infinity?"

* * * * *

ROBERT F. JONES

Full Name: Robert Francis Jones.
Born May 26, 1934, at Milwaukee, Wisconsin. Son of Charles F. Jones (a banker) and Rose Mary Pueringer. Married Louise Tyor (a writer), October 21, 1956. Two children: Leslie Ellen, Benno Francis.

Education: B.A., University of Michigan, 1956.

Career: Magazine writer.
Associate Editor, *Time*, 1960-68; writer for *Sports Illustrated*, 1968-DATE. Member: Hudson River Fishermen's Association; Kappa Tau Alpha.

Agent: Robert D'Attilla, 225 W. 49th St., New York.

* * * * *

M. K. JOSEPH

Full Name: Michael Kennedy Joseph.
Born July 9, 1914, at Chingford, Essex, England. Son of George Frederick Joseph and Ernestine Kennedy. Married Mary Julia Antonovich, August 23, 1947. Five children: Anthony George (born 1948), Charles Edward (born 1951), Barbara Anne (born 1953), Peter Robert (born 1954), Nicholas Patrick (born 1956).

Education:
B.A., Auckland University College, New Zealand, 1933; M.A., 1934; B.A., Merton College, Oxford University, 1938; B.Litt., 1939; M.A., 1946.

Career: Professor of English.
Lecturer in English, Auckland University College, 1946-49; Senior Lecturer, 1950-59; Associate Professor, University of Auckland, 1960-69; Professor of English, 1970-DATE.

First Professional Sale: *I'll Soldier No More*, Victor Gollancz, London, 1958.

Awards: Hubert Church Prose Award, 1958, for *I'll Soldier No More*; Jessie Mackay Poetry Award, 1959, for *The Living Countries*.

Member: Oxford Society; Merton Society; English Association; British Film Institute.

Interests: Travel, film-going, modelling (military and railway).

Joseph writes:
"*The Hole in the Zero* originated from a conversation with Hilary Rubinstein, who had been my main contact at Victor Gollancz Ltd. when they published two novels of mine, *I'll Soldier No More* and *A Pound of Saffron*. Gollancz publishes a good deal of SF in Britain, and Hilary Rubinstein asked me why I didn't try an SF novel. I explained that, though I'd been an avid reader of SF since about the age of seven, I didn't really know much science. 'That's all right,' he said, 'just make it up as you go along.'

"I remembered this a few years later when I was lecturing on *Paradise Lost*, and especially when I came to Satan's journey through Chaos in Book II. The thought occurred that it would be fun to do a sort of SF equivalent--with 'made up' science--and the result was *The Hole in the Zero*. In spite of this, I still really prefer 'hard' SF, like Arthur C. Clarke."

* * * * *

NORTON JUSTER

Full Name: Norton Juster.
Born June 2, 1929, at New York, New York. Son of Samuel H. Juster (an architect) and Minnie Silberman. Married Jeanne Ray (a book designer), August 15, 1964. Education: B. of Arch., University of Pennsylvania, 1952; studied at University of Liverpool, 1952-53.

Career: Architect.
Architect, Juster & Gugliotta, New York, 1960-68; Instructor in Interior Design, Pratt Institute, 1960-70; Director, Norton Juster Architect, 1969-DATE; Adjunct Professor of Design, Hampshire College, 1970-DATE.

Award: George G. Stone Center for Children's Books Seventh Recognition of Merit, 1971. Agent: Sterling Lord, 75 E. 55th St., New York, NY 10022.

* * * * *

NICK KAMIN

Full Name: Robert J. Antonick.
Born October 9, 1939, at Chicago, Illinois. Son of Nicholas Antonick (an engineer) and Anne Kaminski. Married Martha Hunter, June 19, 1965.

Education: B.F.A., University of Dayton, 1961.

NICK KAMIN (cont.)

Career: Graphic artist.
   Instructor in Graphic Communications, School of the Dayton Art Institute, 1965-68; Creative Director, Sabatino Advertising, Dayton, 1968-72; Partner, Darqram (imports), Dayton, 1970-72; with Bergen Advertising Art, Dayton, 1972-DATE; product and graphic design consultant. Associate Editor, *Exponent*, 1959-64, and *Rap*, 1970-71.

* * * * *

MacKINLAY KANTOR

Full Name: MacKinlay Kantor.
   Born February 4, 1904, at Webster City, Iowa. Son of John Martin Kantor and Effie Rachel McKinlay (a newspaper editor). Married Florence Irene Layne, July 2, 1926. Two children: Layne (daughter), Thomas (Tim) MacKinlay.

Career: Writer.
   Reporter, *Webster City Daily News*, 1921-25; worked as an advertiser and claims correspondent, Chicago, 1925-26; reporter, *Cedar Rapids Republican*, 1927; Columnist, *Des Moines Tribune*, 1930-31; worked as scenario writer for various Hollywood studios during the 1930s; member of uniformed division, New York City Police, 1948-50; war correspondent in World War II and the Korean conflict; technical consultant to the Air Force, 1951-DATE; Trustee, Lincoln College, 1960-68; writer, 1928-DATE.

Awards:
   O. Henry Award, 1935, for "Silent Grow the Guns"; Pulitzer Prize, 1956, for *Andersonville*; Medal of Freedom; D.Litt., Grinnell College, 1957, and from Drake University, 1958, Lincoln College, 1959, and Ripon College, 1961; LL.D., Iowa Wesleyan College, 1961.

Member:
   Society of American Historians (Fellow); American Society for Psychical Research; National Association of Civil War Musicians; Sons of Union Veterans of the Civil War; Military Order of the Loyal Legion of the United States.

* * * * *

MARVIN KARLINS

Full Name: Marvin Karlins.
   Born October 4, 1941, at Minneapolis, Minnesota. Son of Arnold A. Karlins (a lawyer) and Miriam Karlins. Married Nancy Flaun Green, July 27, 1968.

Education:
   B.A., University of Minnesota, 1963; M.A., Princeton University, 1965; Ph.D., 1966.

Career: Professor of Psychology.
   Instructor in Psychology, Princeton University, 1966-67; Lecturer, 1967-68; Asst. Professor of Psychology, University of Pittsburgh, 1968-69; Asst. Professor of Psychology, City University of New York, 1969-DATE.
Member: American Psychological Assoc.; Authors Guild.

Agent: Paul R. Reynolds, 599 Fifth Avenue, New York, NY 10017.

DAVID KARP

Full Name: David Karp.
   Born May 5, 1922, at New York, New York. Son of Abraham Karp (a butcher) and Rebecca Levin. Married Lillian Klass, December 25, 1944. Two sons: Ethan Ross (born 1952), Andrew Gabriel (born 1956).

Education: B.S.S., City College of New York, 1948.

Career: Writer.
   "It is always a puzzler for a writer to sit and discuss his 'career.' My favorite fantasy is the one in which a gentleman, having reached some repute, is asked to discuss his 'career' as a writer. He sits and thinks and scratches his beard and writes: 'Failed in politics. Failed in business. Failed in law. Got elected president.' And signs it, of course, A. Lincoln. How many writers can duplicate that 'career'? Failed at one thing or another, fragmentary work. My own 'career' amounts to nothing more than having graduated from college. I worked as a continuity writer for a radio station in New York (WNYC) for about a year and a half, and then quit to write a television show for Wendy Barrie (in 1949), and then lost that show early in the summer of 1949, and was unemployed at the age of 27, without any skills or prospects. I worked for Scott Meredith for three memorable weeks as one of his 'readers' for fee-client material, and met a lot of the elves and gnomes who write sci-fi--Lester del Rey among them. I like them but didn't understand them. Scott fired me as an employee, and then took me on as a client, and managed not to sell anything at all for me. I owe the job to a classmate, Evan Lee Heyman, who later did reprint a lot of my old paperback books when he became an editor to a line of paperbacks put out by the Hearst Corporation.
   "Somehow or other I drifted into the arms of Frederik Pohl, who was then running an agency called the Dirk Wylie Literary Agency, and Fred Pohl sold my first short story to a magazine (1950). The title escapes me, but I remember I made $400 and I was most impressed. I think it was called *Argosy All-American* or something like that.
   "My career as a writer was launched really in 1950 when I sold a radio script to a soap opera in New York called "Aunt Jenny's Real Life Stories." For the next five years I managed, on a free-lance basis, to come to some affluence writing for this show. All told I wrote about 600 episodes of that soap opera--and extracted from the up-dated versions of *King Lear, Romeo and Juliet, Macbeth* (and I am not kidding--I retold all of those plays, in soap form) enough money to move to the suburbs, buy a house, have my children, buy a car, and never really hold down a 'job' again.
   "How's that for a career? I never really held any editorial posts except for being a member of the editorial board of *Television Quarterly*, the house organ for the National Academy of Television Arts and Sciences from 1966 to date."

Agent: Frank Cooper, 9000 Sunset Boulevard, Los Angeles, CA 90069.

Awards:
   "I did a television adaptation of *One* for the *Kraft Television Theatre* which won a First Award for NBC in the Ohio State University Competition in 1956; the same show won an honorable mention in the Robert E. Sherwood Awards made by The Fund for the Republic in 1956. Other awards include: a Guggenheim Fellowship for Creative Writing, 1966; *Look Magazine* Award for "Best Television Program of 1958," for "The Plot to Kill Stalin"; "Emmy"

DAVID KARP (cont.)

Award from the National Academy of Television Arts and Sciences, 1964, for "The Seven Hundred Year Old Gang"; Edgar Award, Best Crime Television Program, 1960, for "The Empty Chair"; Gavel Award, American Bar Association, 1963, for "Charles Evans Hughes" (*Profiles in Courage* TV series); Honorable Mention, American Library Association's Competition, 1957, for *All Honorable Men.*"

Member:
 Writers Guild of America, East (Member, Board of Directors, 1964-66); Writers Guild of America, West (Member, Board of Directors, 1967-74; President of Television Branch, 1969-71); P.E.N.; Academy of Motion Picture Arts and Sciences; National Academy of Television Arts and Sciences; Dramatists Guild.

Interests: Photography, getting rich.

Karp writes:
 "I wrote my first novel in college, and when my teacher of English lit asked me what I had written, I gave him a four hundred page manuscript. I think he was sorry he asked, but he was not unimpressed. He gave me an 'A' for the course, and suggested that I might be able to sell it to some avant-garde publishing house. I never sold it."
 "I wanted to be a novelist when I was very young. I wanted my books to be on the shelves of a public library, and today when I walk into the Santa Monica Public Library--there, sure enough, they are. So, in a sense, I have fulfilled a boy's dream. But boys become men, and dreams somehow manage to come true, but not in precisely the terms in which they were dreamed. Some one observed that it was a curse to live long enough to realize your dreams. The implication, of course, is that one cannot dream further. It's nonsense, of course. The curse is that realized dreams are never realized *in detail*. It is the detail which makes dreams worth having. I recall the punch line for a recent *New Yorker* cartoon in which one tycoon says to another, 'Of course I'm rich, but I'm not rich beyond my wildest dreams.'
 "So I was a novelist. I am a novelist. But few people have ever heard of my novels, and all of my novels put together have not earned me the kind of money I made last year from one television series. It's nice to be on the shelves of a public library. It is even nicer to be read. But nicest of all, I think, is to be rich.
 "I am devoting my declining years to becoming rich, and it has nothing to do with writing novels, and it sure has nothing to do with writing things like this."
 "I had a hunch that I knew what a dystopia was--and when I went to the dictionary I was pleased to discover I was right, and a little startled to discover that there was such a word.
 "There is no question in my mind that we will, one day, be living in a fully adjusted society in which psychiatric 'norms' will adjust all social behavior. The Russians, who are really human obscenities, have made a bear-like pass at the problem. My hunch is that it will be perfected in the sterile societies of Scandinavia, and that it will seep down to Great Britain, and that it will have its final, perfect flowering in our own country--short of outright slaughter of the undesirables among us, the only 'humane' solution will be the psychiatric adjustment of the sociopaths in our society. Wait until the liberals get their hands on blacks and do 'good' on them. It will chill the blood. Like to read a book based on that

"projection? I have a feeling I'd be lynched for writing it.
 "Nonetheless--and thank god for that compound word--nonetheless, I believe still what I believed when I wrote *One*: man's ego is really indestructible. It is like the commonest weed put on earth--scorched by fire, poisoned by chemicals, covered with asphalt or concrete, it manages still to come through a tiny crack and to grow green and expand. The earth is dark, but I see the faint greenness of renewed life."

* * * * *

HERBERT D. KASTLE

Full Name: Herbert David Kastle.
 Born July 11, 1924, at Brooklyn, New York. Son of Meyer Kastle (a salesman) and Eva Katz (a wigmaker). Married and divorced. Two children: Rhona Deborah (born 1958), Matthew Lloyd (born 1953).

Education: B.A., Washington Square College, New York University, 1949; M.A., 1950.

Career: Novelist.
 Has been an advertising copywriter; now a full-time writer; Editor, *Startling Stories*, 1955 ("I officiated over its death"); Associate Editor, *Front Page Detective* and *Inside Detective*, 1959-61.

First Professional Sale: "The Slow Draw," in *Thrilling Western Stories*, 1955.

Agents:
 (Fiction) Theron Raines, Raines & Raines, 244 Madison Avenue, New York, NY 10016; (Films) Marty Shapiro, Shapiro-Lichtman, 9200 Sunset Boulevard, Los Angeles, CA 90069.

Member: Writers Guild of America, West; Disabled American Veterans.

Interests: Jogging, bicycle riding, travelling, reading.

Kastle notes:
 "I have published 14 novels and one nonfiction book to date, with 123 short stories and articles in my background (I no longer do short pieces). Seven, to the best of my recollection, of the short stories were science fiction, and two of the novels. However, I have always been relaxed by reading SF, fantasy and horror, when not ridiculous, as so much of the film material is."

* * * * *

STEVE KATZ

Full Name: Steven Katz.
 Born May 14, 1935, at Bronx, New York. Son of Alexander Katz (a salesman) and Sally Goldstein. Married Patricia Bell, June 7, 1956. Three children: Avrum, Nikolai, Rafael.

Education: B.A., Cornell University, 1956; M.A., University of Oregon, 1959.

Career: Professor of English, Cornell University, 1962-DATE.

Agent: Georges Borchardt, 145 E. 52nd St., New York, NY 10022.

ANNA KAVAN

Full Name: Helen Edmonds.
   Born 1904, at Cannes, France. Daughter of C. C. E.
Woods and Helen Bright. Married Donald Ferguson;
married Stuart Edmonds. Education: Privately educated.

Career: Writer, 1940-68. Died December 5, 1968.
   Kavan was raised in California, and lived in Burma,
Europe, Australia, and New Zealand.

* * * * *

JOSEPH E. KELLEAM

Full Name: Joseph Everidge Kelleam.
   Born February 11, 1913, at Boswell, Oklahoma. Son
of Edwin A. Kelleam (a physician) and Ophelia Everidge.
Married Alta Tolle, October 6, 1934. Two children:
Aljo, Edwina.

Education:
   "I went to three colleges. My father opened up
quite a number of hospitals and clinics for the government and Indian Service during the Depression, and we
moved around quite a bit. I went to Oklahoma University, Southwestern Tech at Weatherford, Oklahoma, and
Central State College at Edmond, Oklahoma. I received
a B.S. degree in English from the latter in 1936.
Then another half-year toward a Master's, but by then
the Depression was just too rough, and I had to leave
the halls of ivy."

Career: Civil servant.
   Contract officer (civilian) with the U.S. Army Engineers and the U.S. Air Force; now retired.

First Professional Sale: "Rust," in *Astounding
Science Fiction*, October, 1939.

Member: Sigma Tau Delta; Pi Kappa Phi; Oklahoma Poetry Writers; Science Fiction Writers of America.

Kelleam writes:
   "My family was one of the first five or six to settle
in SE Oklahoma. They were chased out of Mississippi
for taking up for the Five Civilized Tribes who were
also being chased out at the time.
   "The name Kelleam came from the Scotch Irish border,
and I have been told it is Gaelic for 'church-man,'
though I'm not much of a church man. A friend of mine
who once introduced me on radio and TV (later), pre-
faced his remarks by saying the name rhymed with 'tell
'em' and 'sell 'em'--but I *shore* haven't been able to
tell 'em or sell 'em very much!"

* * * * *

LEO P. KELLEY

Full Name: Leo Patrick Kelley.
   Born September 10, 1928, at Wilkes Barre, Pennsylvania. Son of Leo A. Kelley and Regina Caffrey.

Education: B.A., New School for Social Research,
   1957.

Career: Writer.
   Advertising copywriter and manager, McGraw-Hill Book
Co., 1959-69; full-time writer, 1969-DATE.

First Professional Sale: "Dreamtown, U.S.A.," in
   Worlds of If, February, 1955.

Member: Mensa; Mystery Writers of America; Science
   Fiction Writers of America.

* * * * *

ROBERT KELLY

Full Name: Robert Kelly.
   Born September 24, 1935, at Brooklyn, New York. Son
of Samuel Jason Kelly and Margaret Kane. Married Joan
Lasker, August 27, 1955 (divorced); married Helen Bel-
inkaya, April 17, 1969.

Education: A.B., City College of New York, 1955;
   attended Columbia University, 1955-58.

Career: Professor of English.
   Treasurer, Continental Translation Service, 1955-58;
Lecturer in English, Wagner College, 1960-61; Asst.
Professor of English, Bard College, 1961-69; Associate
Professor, 1969-74; Professor of English, 1974-DATE;
Poet-in-Residence, California Institute of Technology,
1971-72.

Member: Phi Beta Kappa.

Kelly notes: "My arms are: gules, a triple-towered
tower argent, a star of seven rays, or, in chief."

* * * * *

EARL KEMP

Full Name: Earl Kemp.
   Born November 24, 1929, at Crossett, Arkansas. Son
of F. W. Kemp (a papermaker) and Ruth Underwood. Married Nancy Neumann, September 12, 1949. Five children:
Edith (born 1950), Elaine (born 1952), Earl Terry (born
1955), Erik James (born 1963), Erina Leah (born 1967).

Education: Attended Wright Junior College in the
   1940s; also attended University of Chicago.

Career: Editor.
   Has been Editor of Regency Books, and Editorial Direc-
tor of Greenleaf Classics during the 1960s; currently
Editorial Director, Surrey House; sometime lecturer at
the University of Paris, San Diego State University,
California Western University; Chairman, 1962 World
Science Fiction Convention (Chicon III), Chicago.

Awards: Hugo Award, Best Amateur Publication, 1960
   (1961), *Who Killed Science Fiction?*

Interests:
   Travel, foreign living, swimming, food and sex, con-
sciousness-expanding (augmented). "I travel extensively
and commune with science fiction people in remote places."

* * * * *

CAROL KENDALL

Full Name: Carol Kendall.
   Born September 13, 1917, at Bucyrus, Ohio. Daughter
of John Adam Seeger (a cabinetmaker) and Laura Price.
Married Paul Murray Kendall (a college professor), June
15, 1939. Two children: Carol Seeger, Gillian Murray.

CAROL KENDALL (cont.)

Education: A.B., Ohio University, 1939.

Career: Writer, 1946-DATE. Member: Phi Beta Kappa; Phi Mu.

Awards: Ohioana Award, and runner-up for Newbery Award, both for *The Gammage Cup*, 1960.

* * * * *

JAMES KENNAWAY

Full Name: James Ewing Peebles Kennaway.
Born June 5, 1928, in Perthshire, Scotland. Son of Charles Gray Kennaway and Marjory Helen Kennaway. Married Susan Kennaway, 1951. Four children: Emma, Jane, Guy, David.

Education: Attended Glenalmond, Scotland, and Trinity College, Oxford University.

Career: Writer.
Editor at Longmans, London, 1951-57; full-time writer, 1957-68. Died in an automobile accident, December 21, 1968.

Member: Royal Institution; Chelsea Arts Club; Raffles Club.

* * * * *

JAMES KENWARD

Full Name: James Macara Kenward.
Born January 1, 1908, at New Eltham, Kent, England. Son of Frederick Montague Kenward (an insurance agent) and Dora Ethel Symons. Married Rubina Rose Grunig, December 17, 1938. Four children: Richard Francis Edward, Peter John, David Macara, Margaret Jean.

Education: Attended Brighton College.

Career: Writer.
Insurance agent, Lloyd's of London, 1925-28; full-time writer, 1928-DATE. Member: Peace Pledge Union.

* * * * *

JOHN M. KESHISHIAN

Full Name: John M. Keshishian.
Born August 15, 1923, at Corfu, Greece. Son of Margos Hagop Keshishian (a businessman) and Margaret Devletian. Married Catherine Morgan Wrather, April 2, 1949. Four children: Caren, Peggy, Alicia, Billy.

Education: M.D., George Washington University, 1950.

Career: Medical doctor.
Intern and resident at various hospitals, 1950-55; surgeon in private practice (thoracic and vascular surgery), Washington, 1956-DATE; Assistant Clinical Professor of Surgery, George Washington University, 1960-DATE.

Member: American Medical Association; Association of Thoracic Surgeons; Explorers Club; American College of Surgeons; American College of Chest Physicians.

DAVID KETTERER

Full Name: David Anthony Theodor Ketterer.
Born June 13, 1942, at Leigh-on-Sea, Essex, England. Son of Joseph Theodor Ketterer (a chartered accountant) and Eileen Philp. Married Jacqueline Ruth Langsner (a librarian), March 17, 1972.

Education:
B.A., University of Wales, 1964; M.A., Carleton University, 1965; D.Phil., University of Sussex, 1969.

Career: Professor of English.
Lecturer in English, McGill University, 1965-66; Assoc. Professor of English, Concordia University, Sir George Williams Campus, Montreal, 1967-DATE.

Awards: Canada Council Fellowship, 1973-74.

* * * * *

ALEXANDER KEY

Full Name: Alexander Hill Key.
Born September 21, 1904, at LaPlata, Maryland. Son of Alexander Hill Key (a cotton and lumber dealer) and Charlotte Ryder. Married Alice Towle, December 21, 1945. One son, Alexander Towle (born 1953).

Education: Attended Chicago Art Institute, 1922-24.

Career: Illustrator and writer.
"Have always been a free-lance; the only job I ever held was that of Intelligence Officer in the Navy during World War II"; started his career in Chicago as a book illustrator at age 19.

First Professional Sale: *The Red Eagle*, P. F. Volland, 1930.

Agent: McIntosh & Otis, 475 Fifth Avenue, New York, New York 10017.

Awards: American Association of University Women Award, 1965, and Lewis Carroll Shelf Award, 1972, both for *The Forgotten Door*. Member: Authors Guild.

Interests:
"Have long been a professional designer and landscape painter. In the past, I have written for *Saturday Evening Post*, *Cosmopolitan*, *Argosy*, *Elks*, *American Mercury* and others, but now I write only for young people, about one book a year, and take it far more seriously than any of my other work."

* * * * *

DANIEL KEYES

Full Name: Daniel Keyes.
Born August 9, 1927, at New York, New York. Son of William Keyes and Betty Alicke. Married Aurea Georginia Vazquez, October 14, 1952. Two children: Hillary Ann (born 1959), Leslie Joan (born 1964).

Education: B.A., Brooklyn College, 1950; M.A., 1961.

Career: Professor of English.
Editorial Associate, *Marvel Science Stories*, February-November, 1951; English teacher, New York City, 1955-61; Instructor in English, Wayne State University, 1962-

DANIEL KEYES (cont.)

66; Lecturer in English, Ohio University, Athens, Ohio, 1966-72; Professor of English, 1972-DATE.

First Professional Sale: "Robot Unwanted," in *Other Worlds*, June, 1952 ("Precedent," in *Marvel Science Fiction*, May, 1952, was published one month earlier).

Agent: Robert P. Mills Ltd., 156 E. 52nd St., New York, NY 10022.

Awards:
Nebula Award, Best Novel, 1966 (1967), *Flowers for Algernon* [novel version]; Hugo Award, Best Short Fiction, 1959 (1960), "Flowers for Algernon" [novella version].

Member: P.E.N.; Science Fiction Writers of America.

Flowers for Algernon was made into the film "Charly," starring Cliff Robertson and Claire Bloom. Robertson received an Oscar for Best Actor of 1969 for his title role in the movie.

* * * * *

NOEL KEYES

Full Name: David Noel Keightley.
Born October 25, 1932, at London, England. Son of Walter A. Keightley (a petroleum engineer) and Jeanne G. Desoutter. Married Vannie Louise Traylor, August 20, 1965. Two children: Steven Traylor (born 1967), Richard Duret (born 1970).

Education:
B.A., Amherst College, 1953; M.A., New York University, 1956; Ph.D., Columbia University, 1969.

Career: Professor of History.
Free-lance writer, 1960-62; graduate student in Chinese history, 1962-69; Assistant Professor of History, University of California, Berkeley, 1969-DATE. Also served as an associate editor for World Publishing Company, 1957-60.

First Professional Sale: "Black Eyes and Truculence," in *Cavalier*, September, 1961.

Agent: Sterling Lord, 660 Madison Avenue, New York.

Interests: Shang history and religion.

* * * * *

VIRGINIA KIDD

Full Name: Mildred Virginia Kidd.
Born June 2, 1921, at Germantown, Pennsylvania. Daughter of Charles Lemuel Kidd (a printer) and Zetta Daisy Whorley. Married Jack Emden, April 17, 1942 (divorced, 1947); married James Benjamin Blish (the science fiction writer), May 17, 1947 (divorced 1963). Four children: Karen Anne Emden (born 1944), Asa Benjamin Blish (born & died 1947), Dorothea Elisabeth Blish (born 1954), Charles Benjamin Blish (born 1956).

Education: "No college, because I couldn't go to the University of Chicago, and I wouldn't go to any other."

Career: Literary Agent.
Has been a music librarian in South Carolina, a proof reader for Waverly Press in Baltimore, a secretary in New York City, a ghost writer's ghost writer, a freelance author; director, Virginia Kidd--Literary Agent, January, 1965-DATE; free-lance editor.

First Professional Sale: A poem to *Accent* in 1951 or 1952.

Agent: Virginia Kidd--Literary Agent, Box 278, Milford, PA 18337.

Member: Science Fiction Writers of America.

Interests:
"Music--all kinds except over-arranged schmaltz. I love classical music, most particularly the operas of Richard Strauss; and I am also a devoted listener to rock, the harder the better."

Virginia Kidd writes:
"I have been held (held myself) silent for the most part for many years, because (although I was assured that I had the ability to write by judges I trusted) I could not feel that I had anything to say that really HAD to be said. I firmly believe there are too many books published, especially lately, when the forests are running out (and the publishing emphasis is increasingly on what will make money rather than what should see print).

"Belatedly, a personal understanding of feminism and a renaissance of excitement about SF is moving me to want to have some things see print, both other people's work edited by me, and my own work.

"Regarding science fiction, I think the genre has gone from a state of generally better health into what looks very like a high fever. Though it might seem inimical to my trade to say so, I think far too much run-of-the-mill science fiction is being published; and far too high a proportion is also being published that seems to me to be not much better than floor sweepings. SF has had periods of overproduction before; the last time, magazine titles proliferated beyond what the market could bear. At present, I think there is a good probability that there are more books being published than the market can absorb, in the areas of college texts (specialised readers), original anthologies, and paperback titles, in general. What looks like the bloom of health this year may shortly turn out to have been a pretty hectic flush, with a consequent period of invalidism dead ahead. Boom and bust is a phenomenon we're all familiar with. And it does seem to me that, if bad books do not quite succeed in driving out the good, they do somewhat imperil the chances of the occasional outstanding titles being noticed.

"The obvious drawback of this situation is likely to be not only severe underproduction after the sales figures are in on the current glut of titles, but an unwillingness to purchase anything other than proven mass market items. It seems to me to be a situation analogous to what happened to films in general, and somewhat like what's happening on television. Sure-thingism, bandwagonitis, the inexorable operation of Sturgeon's Law on a bigger and bigger 100%.

"I don't think the bust part of the cycle will affect me very much. I have a built-in remedy in my motto, 'Nothing but the best, and not much of that.' I do think it will affect the genre *qua* genre.

"The foregoing is a sad and negative view, and I would not be unhappy to be proven wrong--even if only by a prolonged period of what I can only regard as overproduction: non-books, near-books, and instant

VIRGINIA KIDD (cont.)

"books by the galore.

"At the other end of the scale from the stupefyingly bad, the good 10% seems to me to get better and better. At the same time (still speaking only of the excellent few), the outstanding practitioners transmute the genre into a form which is not exactly mainstream--it demands a degree of sophistication, after all--but which is no longer oldfashioned science fiction. Its appeal is to the general reader, and I am glad to see this happening; it seems to me to take us full circle, back to Wells, for instance. From Wells and Verne, in a sense, to Le Guin and Crichton--none of whom addresses him- or herself to an in-group, but to the *reading* audience, wherever it may be found.

"You ask why I think so few women seem to be involved in SF, either from a reading or writing point of view. A straightforward answer would involve me in what might seem (but would only seem) to be anti-feminism, and I think neither of us has the time to wade through the necessary disclaimers. Science fiction as a way of thought involves a willingness to ask unanswerable questions. I think this is why its appeal has been limited--and why hardcore science fiction will continue to be of interest only to a small proportion of the vast audience that reads books: both hardcover and paperback, both fiction and (oh, ever more so) nonfiction.

"However, the proportion of women involved in SF seems to me to have been steadily rising in recent years. I am judging from the tip of the iceberg, of course, if an iceberg can be thought of as vocal! When I attended my first Science Fiction League meeting, I was the only girl present, among an approximate dozen--all but one of us in our teens. Nowadays, convention attendance is closer fifty-fifty division by sexes; and I am told that the subscription list for fanzines shows a steadily--and rapidly--rising number of female names. I don't know about the fanzines readers' ages, but convention attendance is not limited to teenagers.

"SF is fathering and mothering half a dozen tremendously fine books a year. I am not entirely pessimistic!"

* * * * *

JOHN KING

Full Name: Ernest Lionel McKeag.
  Born September 19, 1896, at Newcastle-upon-Tyne, England. Son of John McKeag and Alice Ingledew. Married Constance Hibbs, October 3, 1928. Two sons: Michael, Roderick.

Education: Master Mariner's Certificate, South
  Shields Marine School, 1919; also studied at Armstrong College, University of Durham.

Career: Writer and editor.
  Apprentice Officer, British Merchant Marine, 1913-15; in the Royal Navy, 1915-19; began his career as a journalist in England, 1919, working for various newspapers, and for Newspaper Features Ltd., 1919-22; Editor, *Northern Weekly Review* and Amalgamated Press Juvenile Publications, 1923-28; in the Royal Navy, 1939-43; Reporter and Feature Writer for *London Daily Mirror* and *London Sunday Pictorial*, 1943; Editor, Fleetway Publications, 1951-61; free-lance writer, primarily of paperbacks, 1928-DATE; parliamentary candidate (Labour), 1929 and 1931. Member: Royal Press Club.

STEPHEN KING

Full Name: Stephen King.
  Born September 21, 1947, at Portland, Maine. Son of Donald King (a sailor) and Ruth Pillsbury. Married Tabitha Spruce (a poet), January 2, 1971. Two children: Naomi, Joseph Hill.

Education: B.Sc., University of Maine, 1970.

Career: Writer.
  Has been a janitor, mill worker, laundry worker, and a high school teacher of English in Hampden, Maine; now a full-time writer. Member: Authors Guild.

* * * * *

VINCENT KING

Full Name: Rex Thomas Vinson.
  Born October 22, 1935, at Falmouth, Cornwall, England. Son of Earnest Leonard Vinson (a builder) and Irene Verran. Married Jean Blackler, 1961. Two children: Mark (born 1965), Kay (born 1966).

Education:
  Attended Falmouth College of Art, West of England College of Art, London University; National Diploma of Design (Painting, Special Level), 1959; Art Teacher's Diploma, 1961.

Career: Art teacher.
  Lecturer in Drawing, Painting and Print Making, College of Art, Newcastle-upon-Tyne, England, 1963-68; Head of Art Dept., Redruth County Grammar School, 1968-DATE; free-lance writer and illustrator.

First Professional Sale: "Defence Mechanism," in *New Writings in S.F.-9*, Dennis Dobson, 1966.

Agent: E. J. Carnell Literary Agency, 17 Burwash Road, Plumstead, London SE18 7QY, England.

Member: Artist's International Association.

Interests:
  Gliding, toys, painting and etching, chess, fishing, blues music and jazz, most things except sport. "I'd very much like the opportunity to illustrate, design covers and what have you for SF books. I began using a pseudonym in the first place because at the time I was exhibiting and selling paintings/prints under my own name."

* * * * *

MAGDALEN KING-HALL

Full Name: Magdalen King-Hall.
  Born July 22, 1904, at London, England. Daughter of Sir George Fowler King-Hall (an admiral in the Royal Navy) and Olga Kerr. Married Patrick Perceval Maxwell (a landowner), January 19, 1929. Three children: Richard Stephen, Alastair Patrick, Brigid Louise.

Education: Attended Downe House and St. Leonards
  School, St. Andrews, Scotland.

Career: Writer, 1925-71. Died March 1, 1971. Agent:
  A. P. Watt & Son, 26/28 Bedford Row, London WC1R 4HL.

STEPHEN KING-HALL

Full Name: William Stephen Richard King-Hall.
    Born January 21, 1893, at London, England. Son of
Sir George Fowler King-Hall (an admiral in the Royal
Navy) and Olga Kerr. Married Kathleen Spencer, April
15, 1919. Three children: Ann, Susan, Jane.

Education: Attended Royal Naval College, Military
    Staff College, and Naval Staff College.

Career: Writer.
    Officer in the Royal Navy, 1914-29, retiring as Com-
mander; served on *H.M.S. Southampton* with the Grand
Fleet, 1914-17; with the China Squadron, 1921-23;
Intelligence Officer, Mediterranean Fleet, 1925-26;
with Atlantic Fleet, 1927-28; Founder, 1936, and Editor of a newsletter service on public affairs, variously titled *K-H News Service, King-Hall News Letter,
National News Letter*, 1936-66; Member of Parliament,
Ormskirk Division of Lancashire, 1939-44; served in
Ministry of Aircraft Production and Ministry of Fuel
and Power, 1939-45; writer, radio and TV commentator,
1917-66. Died June 2, 1966.

Honors: Gold Medal of Royal United Service Institu-
    tion, 1919; made a life peer by Queen Elizabeth II
    in 1966 as Baron King-Hall.

Member: Hansard Society for Parliamentary Government
    (Founder, 1944); Athenaeum Club.

* * * * *

JOHN KIPPAX

Full Name: John Charles Hynam.
    Born June 10, 1915, at Alwalton, Huntingdonshire,
England. Son of Percy Charles Hynam (a transport man-
ager) and Elizabeth Jane Kippax. Married Phyllis Mary
Manning (a teacher), November 8, 1941. One child:
Jennifer Margaret (born 1944).

Education: Attended Trinity College, Carmarthen,
    South Wales, 1934-36.

Career: Writer.
    Has been an artist, club comedian, teacher, ditch
digger, dance band musician, teacher, soldier. "Some
of 'em didn't even know I was on the payroll! As I
am now a writer, dates don't mean a damn thing. Sometimes I feel I've had all the cares in the world, sometimes like if I fell down a latrine I'd come up smel-
ling roses. My official answer to 'how old are you?'
is that I've been forty-five for a number of years."
He notes: "I was a chucker out at a dump called 'Mom-
ma's Knee.' Lowest joint I ever saw."

First Professional Sale: "Two Guitars," in *Pit-
    man's Pick of the Year's Short Stories*, 1954.

Agent: G. J. Pollinger, 18 Maddox Street, Mayfair,
    London W1R OEU, England.

Awards: "In these, I am strictly one of the ap-
    plauding mob."

Member: "I am a gregarious non-joiner. Belong to
    the town's Chamber of trade; many old school contem-
    poraries there."

Interests: "Hi-fi kit as a means of giving me great

"sound--Duke or Bach or anywhere in between. Sometimes
I look back with a touch of regret to the days when I
was number five on the saxophone team, playing a beautiful (borrowed) Selmer baritone sax, which was the
ultimate in ease and balance. Any clinkers were all
my own, with that instrument."

Kippax writes:
    "I did number four of the "Venturer Twelve" series
(*Where No Stars Guide*) as a solo effort. So many shorts
that I'd not be able to find a complete list. Also have
done thirty radio plays (radio is still big in Britain),
a documentary film script, and have also been a ghost,
which is odd; I'm built on similar lines to William Conrad, very much more for comfort than speed. Have to
limit my intake of Chinese food, otherwise I'd be eight
stones overweight instead of a mere five. Being a non-
smoker, English beer comes to me in all its real (55
deg) freshness. I'm an idle sod. Work best to dead-
lines; for the rest, see the lyrics of 'I Haven't Time
to Be a Millionaire.' An odd coincidence: Dan Morgan
and I were preparing a TV series "Venturer Twelve" at
the same time that they were on the first scripts of
Star Trek. We turned ours in because of a certain third
party with whom we found we just couldn't work. But
all was not lost. We still have all that material we
sweated out in six and seven hour conferences. *Strong
belief*: that Britain and the USA should shoot all their
lousy public relations men, and start again with a fresh
lot, these being told 'succeed in presenting the one
country to the other with some tact and balance, or
you get the chop.'"

Kippax was killed in an automobile accident near
Werrington, England, on July 17, 1974.

* * * * *

RUSSELL KIRK

Full Name: Russell Amos Kirk.
    Born October 19, 1918, at Plymouth, Michigan. Son
of Russell Andrew Kirk and Marjorie Pierce. Married
Annette Yvonne Courtemanche, September, 1964.

Education:
    B.A., Michigan State College, 1940; M.A., Duke Univer-
sity, 1941; D.Litt., St. Andrews University, 1952 (the
only American to hold this earned degree).

Career: Professor of Politics.
    Worked for Ford Motor Company, 1941; Asst. Professor
of the History of Civilization, Michigan State College,
East Lansing, 1946-53; Research Professor of Politics,
C. W. Post College, 1957-DATE; Founder and Editor, *Mo-
dern Age*, 1957-60; Editor, *University Bookman*, 1961-
DATE; writer and lecturer; Justice of the Peace, Morton
Township, Mecosta County, Michigan, 1961-64.

Awards: Senior Fellow, American Council of Learned
    Societies, 1950-51; Guggenheim Fellow, 1956; Litt.D.
    from Boston College, St. John's University, Le Moyne
    College; LL.D., Park College, 1961.

* * * * *

GERARD KLEIN

Full Name: Gérard Klein.
    Born May 27, 1937, at Neuilly, France. Son of Paul
Klein (an executive) and Antoinette Lahure. Member:
Société Française de Psychologie.

GÉRARD KLEIN (cont.)

Education: Diplôme, Institut d'Études Politiques, 1957; Diplôme, Institut de Psychologie, 1959.

Career: Economist.
Consultant Economist, specializing in the savings field, Société d'Études pour le Développement Économique et Social, 1963-DATE; free-lance writer, 1958-DATE; Editor, *Ailleurs et Demain*, 1969-DATE.

* * * * *

JAY KAY KLEIN

Full Name: Jay Kay Klein.
Born July 28, 1931, at Philadelphia, Pennsylvania. Son of Louis and Florence Klein.

Education: B.A., Syracuse University, 1953; graduate study, 1956-59.

Career: Editor.
Has been Assistant Editor, *Journal of the American Water Works Association*, a teaching assistant at Syracuse University English Dept., a technical writer of U.S. military handbooks on radar systems and missile complexes; Promotions and Communications Specialist, General Electric Company, 1964-71; Editor, *Carrier World* and *Carrier Family*, 1971-DATE; writer, editor, and photographer.

First Professional Sale: "The Towering Problem," in *QST*, October, 1962.

Honors: Fan Guest of Honor, 32nd World Science Fiction Convention (Discon 2), Washington, D.C., 1974.

Member:
Science Fiction Writers of America.

Interests:
Photography, chess, folksinging and guitar, amateur radio, hi fi and electronics, science fiction. "I have combined my knowledge of photography with my interest in science fiction to document activities and persons in science fiction. The result is an archive of more than 17,000 negatives of many of the science fiction notables, professionals, and fans."

* * * * *

FLETCHER KNEBEL

Full Name: Fletcher Knebel.
Born October 1, 1911, at Dayton, Ohio. Son of A. G. Knebel and Mary Lewis. Married his second wife, Marian Park, 1953. Two children: Jack G., Mary; one step-daughter: Judith Hatch.

Education: B.A., Miami University (Ohio), 1934.

Career: Writer.
Reporter for newspapers in Coatesville, PA, 1934, Chattanooga, Tenn., 1934-35, and Toledo, Ohio, 1935-36; Reporter, *Cleveland Plain Dealer*, 1937-50; Washington Correspondent, Cowles Publications, 1950-64, writing the political column "Washington Fever"; free-lance writer, 1964-DATE. Award: Sigma Delta Chi Award, for Best Magazine Reporting of 1955. Member: Authors Guild; National Press Club; Phi Beta Kappa; Sigma Chi.

DAMON KNIGHT

Full Name: Damon Francis Knight.
Born September 19, 1922, at Baker, Oregon. Son of Frederick Stuart Knight (a high school principal) and Leola LaDorie Damon (a teacher). Married Gertrud Werndl (divorced); married Helen Schlaz (divorced); married Kate Wilhelm (the science fiction writer), February, 1963. Four children: Valerie, Christopher, Leslie, Jonathan.

Education: Graduated from Hood River High School, Hood River, Oregon, 1940; attended Salem WPA Art Center, Salem, Oregon, 1940-41.

Career: Writer and editor.
Free-lance writer, 1941-DATE; Assistant Editor, Popular Publications, 1943-44, 1949-50; Editor, *Worlds Beyond*, December, 1950-February, 1951 (all issues published); Book Editor, *Science Fiction Adventures*, Feb. 1953-May, 1954; Editor, *Worlds of If*, October, 1958-February, 1959; Book Editor, *The Magazine of Fantasy and Science Fiction*, April, 1959-September, 1960; past Director of the annual Milford Writers Conferences.

First Professional Sale: "Resilience," in *Stirring Science Stories*, February, 1941.

Agent: Robert P. Mills Ltd., 156 E. 52nd St., New York, NY 10022.

Awards: Hugo Award, Best Critic, 1955 (1956); Pilgrim Award, 1975.

Member: Science Fiction Writers of America (Founder and President, 1965-67).

Interests:
Cooking, travel. "I was the founder (with Judith Merril) and director of the Milford Science Fiction Writers' Conferences, 1956-DATE. Lecturer, Clarion Workshop in Science Fiction and Fantasy, 1967-DATE. Have done or tried to do everything there is to be done in science fiction except publish. Illustration was the hardest and least paid, anthologies the easiest and pays best." Knight has edited the award-winning series of anthologies, *Orbit* (Putnam and Harper & Row), since 1966.

* * * * *

NORMAN L. KNIGHT

Full Name: Norman Louis Knight.
Born September 21, 1895, at St. Joseph, Missouri. Son of Louis Ruthven Knight and Mary Elizabeth Stauber. Married Marie Sarah Yenn, June 4, 1921. One child: Paula Marie.

Education: B.S., George Washington University, 1925.

Career: Chemist.
Served with the U.S. Army in France during World War I; Observer and Code Translator, U.S. Weather Bureau, 1919-25; Pesticide Chemist, U.S. Food and Drug Administration, and also with Pesticide Regulation Division, U.S. Dept. of Agriculture, 1925-64. Died 1970?

First Professional Sale: "Frontier of the Unknown," in *Astounding Stories*, July, 1937 and August, 1937 (serialized).

NORMAN L. KNIGHT (cont.)

Honors: Achievement Award, U.S. Department of Agriculture, 1962.

Member:　Science Fiction Writers of America.

Knight wrote the novel *A Torrent of Faces* in collaboration with James Blish. He had these comments about the book:
"I wrote the parts of *Torrent* pertaining to the Tritons, at Jim's request, since I invented them. Also the chapter, "A Walk in the Paradise Garden." The rest is Jim's handiwork, plus some editing of mine by Jim, which improved it."

* * * * *

WILLIAM C. KNOTT

Full Name:　William Cecil Knott.
Born August 7, 1927, at Boston, Massachusetts. Son of William Cecil Knott (a salesman) and Madeline Guay. Married Elizabeth Ann Knott, September 20, 1950 (divorced); married Constance Seifert, December 30, 1971. Three children:　Carolyn, William, Judith.

Education:
A.A., Boston University General College, 1949; B.S., Boston University School of Education, 1951; M.S., State University of New York, Oswego, 1967.

Career:　Professor of English.
School teacher in public schools in Connecticut, New Jersey, West Virginia, and New York, 1951-67; Assistant Professor of English, State University of New York, Potsdam, 1967-DATE.

First Professional Sale:　*Junk Pitcher*, Follett Publishers, 1963.

Agent:　Ruth Cantor, 156 Fifth Avenue, New York, NY.

Interests:
"Classical music, history, general science, science fiction, sports--everything! I have come to science fiction as a writer late in my writing career, having already published about thirty books for young readers with a sports background (as "Bill J. Carol"), and also a few mysteries. *Journey Across the Third Planet* was my first sci-fi, and I hope my next one will be finished soon."

* * * * *

HUGH KNOX

Full Name:　Hugh Randolph Knox.
Born August 12, 1942, at Artesia, New Mexico. Son of Hugh Knox (body and fender repair) and Bethel Swisher. Married Elena Segal. One daughter, Nicole Kyner (born 1963).

Education:　"Self-educated."

Career:　Free-lance writer. First Professional Sale: *A Place in Hell*, Holloway House, 196?.

Agent:　Alex Jackinson, 55 W. 42nd St., New York, New York.

Interests:　Kite flying.

"Having been influenced by the ideas of Jung and Norman O. Brown, I consider myself a prose symbolist, and use the term as it was used by the French symbolist poets."

* * * * *

MANUEL KOMROFF

Full Name:　Manuel Komroff.
Born September 7, 1890, at New York, New York. Son of Samuel Komroff (a businessman) and Belle Bronson. Married Odette Steele, October 19, 1938.

Career:　Writer and editor.
Newspaper reporter in New York, 1917-19; Motion Picture Critic, *Film Daily*, 1919-21; Editor, Boni & Liveright Publishing Corp., and Modern Library, 1921-28; Founder and Editor, Black and Gold Library, 1928; Founder and Editor, Library of Living Classics, Dial Press, 1929-30; Instructor and Editor, Columbia University, 1929-30, and Instructor in Novel Technique, 1944-46; Writer's War Board advisor, 1941-45; free-lance author, 1925-74. Died December 10, 1974.

Agent:　Barthold Fles, 507 Fifth Avenue, New York, NY 10017.

Member:
Authors Guild (Vice-President, 1941-43, 1946-47); Overseas Press Club of America; P.E.N.; Circle of Confusion.

* * * * *

JEFFREY KONVITZ

Full Name:　Jeffrey Konvitz.
Born July 22, 1944, at Brooklyn, New York. Son of Arthur Harry Konvitz (a public relations executive) and Florence Karp.

Education:　A.B., Cornell University, 1966; J.D., Columbia University, 1969.

Career:　Attorney.
Admitted to the Bar of New York, 1969; attorney and agent, Creative Management Associates, 1969-70; private law practice in New York, 1970-72; motion picture executive, Metro-Goldwyn-Mayer, 1972-73; full-time writer and producer, 1973-DATE; General Counsel, Jerry Lewis Theatre Chain, 1971-72; Co-Producer of movie "Silent Night, Bloody Night," and Producer of "The Sentinel."

Agent:　William Morris Agency, 151 El Camino, Beverly Hills, CA 90212.

* * * * *

DEAN R. KOONTZ

Full Name:　Dean Ray Koontz.
Born July 9, 1945, at Everett, Pennsylvania. Son of Ray and Florence Koontz. Married Gerda Koontz, Oct. 15, 1966. Education: Has a bachelor's degree in English.

Career:　Writer.
Has been a school teacher in Appalachia; full-time writer, 1969-DATE.

DEAN R. KOONTZ (cont.)

First Professional Sale: "The Kittens," in *Readers and Writers*, 196?.

Awards: *Atlantic Monthly* Creative Writing Award.

* * * * *

E. KIRKER KRANZ

Full Name: Edwin Kirker Kranz.
  Born January 12, 1949, at Flint, Michigan. Son of Edwin Earl Kranz (assembles automotive guidance components) and Mary Lucille Kirker.

Education: A.A., Delta College, 1969; B.A., Saginaw Valley College, 1971.

Career:
  "Currently, I'm Resident Tinker (not their name for the job) at Saginaw Valley College. The post developed from the work-study activities while getting my B.A. (major: English; minors: math and Russian), and is based partially on an AAS from Delta College.
  "I write a regular column of semi-literate madness for SVC's *Valley Vanguard*, which seems to be appreciated primarily by the editor.
  "For years I've been an unemployed rhythm guitar-player/vocalist, a sometime songwriter and poet, an insular extrovert, and a Known Strange Person."

Interests: "My hobby is growing moustaches and
  other hair."

* * * * *

LLOYD KROPP

Full Name: Lloyd Edward Kropp.
  Born July 16, 193?, at Grand Rapids, Michigan. Son of Willis Ahlborn Kropp (an engineer) and Cornelia Trapp (an artist). Married Carolyn Steine, 1957. Two sons: Stephen Jeremy (born 1968), Alexander Nathan (born 1970).

Education:
  B.A., University of Pittsburgh, 1957; M.A., University of Pittsburgh, 1961; A.B.D., Ohio State University, 1969.

Career: Writer and instructor.
  Medical examiner, U.S. Army, 1956-58; graduate assistant, University of Pittsburgh, 1959-61; Instructor, Otterbein College, 1961-63; graduate assistant, Ohio State University, 1963-70; Lecturer and Writer-in-Residence, University of North Carolina at Greensboro, 1970-DATE; has been a composer, nightclub pianist, ballroom dance teacher, attendant in a mental hospital.

First Professional Sale: *The Drift*, Doubleday &
  Company, 1969.

Awards:
  "I won a series of first and second prizes for poetry in the Ohio Poetry Day contests between 1963 and 1965. Other awards in high school and college seem too minor to mention."

Member: Science Fiction Writers of America; American
  Association of University Professors; Modern Language
  Association.

Interests:
  "I have an enduring interest in music; several of my compositions have been performed in concert, and one was done on TV. I have also done short professional gigs in nightclubs. Apart from this, I have a love of anything ancient or far away. Thus my active interest in astonomy, ancient history, archeology, and geology."

Kropp comments:
  "I have a talented wife and two beautiful children. During the school year I teach Fiction Writing, Victorian Literature, a survey in American Literature, Science Fiction, and various experimental courses. During the summer I write. I love parties. I am subject to visionary romantic longings. My outsides are quite conventional, but my insides are weird. I live with my family in a nice house in a manicured and tamed pseudo-forest."

* * * * *

ERIK von KUEHNELT-LEDDIHN

Full Name: Erik Maria, *Ritter* von Kuehnelt-Leddihn.
  Born July 31, 1909, at Tobelbad, Austria. Son of Erik, Ritter von Kuehnelt-Leddihn and Isabella von Leddihn. Married Countess Marie-Christiane Goess, July 3, 1937. Three children: Erik, Isabel, Gottfried.

Education: B.A., Theresianic Academy, Vienna, 1927;
  M.A., University of Budapest, 1934; Dr.Pol.Sc., 1937.

Career: Instructor and writer.
  Free-lance writer, 1931-DATE; Master, Beaumont College, England, 1935-36; Asst. Professor of Political Geography, Georgetown University, 1937-38; Chairman of History Department, St. Peter's College, 1938-43; Lecturer on Japanese, Fordham University, 1942-43; Professor of History and Sociology, Chestnut Hill College, 1943-47.

Awards: Literary Prize, Entr'aide Sociale, Paris,
  1936. Member: Sovereign Order of Knights of Malta.

* * * * *

MICHAEL KURLAND

Full Name: Michael Joseph Kurland.
  Born March 1, 1938, at New York, New York. Son of Jack Kurland (a manufacturer) and Stephanie Yacht (a dress designer). Married Rebecca Jacobson, May 29, 1976.

Education: Attended Hiram College, 1955-56; University of Maryland, 1959-60; Columbia University, 1963-64.

Career: Writer.
  Editorial Writer, *National Examiner*, 1966; Managing Editor, *Crawdaddy* (a periodical devoted to rock and popular music), 1968; free-lance writer, 1965-DATE.

First Professional Sale: "Bond of Brothers," in
  Worlds of Tomorrow, May, 1965 (*Ten Years to Doomsday*, a novel written with Chester Anderson, was published by Pyramid in 1964).

Agent: Richard Curtis, 1215 Fifth Avenue, New York,
  NY 10029. Member: Science Fiction Writers of America; Mystery Writers of America.

Awards: Edgar Award, Best Novel, 1969, *A Plague of
  Spies*.

MICHAEL KURLAND (cont.)

Interests: National politics, bear baiting, barn
   storming, lighter-than-air craft, carnivals, vaudeville, science fiction incunabula.

Kurland notes:
   "*The Unicorn Girl* (Pyramid, 1969), is part of a u-
nique trilogy, the middlework of a linked three-book
opus with three different authors. The first was *The
Butterfly Kid* by Chester Anderson, and the third was
The Probability Pad by T. A. Waters."

* * * * *

KATHERINE KURTZ

Full Name: Katherine Irene Kurtz.
   Born October 18, 1944, at Coral Gables, Florida.
Daughter of Fredrick Harry Kurtz (an electronics
technician) and Margaret Frances Carter (a teacher).

Education: B.S., University of Miami, 1966; M.A.,
   University of California, Los Angeles, 1971.

Career: Technician.
   Senior Training Technician, Los Angeles Police Academy, 1969-DATE.

First Professional Sale: *Deryni Rising*, Ballantine Books, 1970.

Member:
   Science Fiction Writers of America; Swords and Sorcery Guild of America; Society for Creative Anachronism, Inc.; Pi Kappa Phi; Alpha Epsilon Delta.

* * * * *

KARLA KUSKIN

Full Name: Karla Kuskin.
   Born July 17, 1932, at New York, New York. Daughter
of Sidney T. Seidman and Mitzi Salzman. Married
Charles M. Kuskin (a musician), 1955. Two children:
Nicholas, Julia.

Education: B.F.A., Yale University, 1955.

Career: Writer and illustrator of books.

Awards:
   American Institute of Graphic Arts awards for *Roar
and More*, *Square as a House*, *In the Middle of the
Trees*.

* * * * *

HENRY KUTTNER

Full Name: Henry Kuttner.
   Born April 7, 1915, at Los Angeles, California.
Son of Henry Kuttner (a book dealer and seller) and
Anne Lewis. Married Catherine Lucile Moore (the
science fiction writer), June 7, 1940.

Education: B.A., University of Southern California,
   1957; had completed all of his course work for his
   M.A. at the time of his death.

Career: Writer.
   Except for a brief stint as a reader for a Los Angeles
literary agency in the late 1930s, Kuttner was a full-
time professional author all of his adult life. Died
at Santa Monica, California, February 13, 1958.

Agent: Harold Matson Company, 22 E. 40th St., New
   York, NY 10016.

* * * * *

R. A. LAFFERTY

Full Name: Raphael Aloysius Lafferty.
   Born November 7, 1914, at Neola, Iowa. Son of Hugh
David Lafferty (a broker, in oil leases and royalties)
and Julia Mary Burke (a school teacher).

Education: Attended the University of Tulsa, 1933-
   34.

Career: Writer.
   With the U.S. Civil Service, Washington, 1934-35;
billing clerk, inventory clerk, buyer, Clark Electrical
Supply Company, Tusla, 1936-42, 1946-50, 1952-71; soldier, U.S. Army, 1942-46; warehouseman, Emsco Supply
Company, Oklahoma City, 1950-51; free-lance author,
1971-DATE.

First Professional Sale: "The Wagons," in *New Mexico Quarterly Review*, Spring, 1959.

Agent: Virginia Kidd, Box 278, Milford, PA 18337.

Awards: Hugo Award, Best Short Story, 1972 (1973),
   "Eurema's Dam"; Invisible Little Man Award, 1972;
   Phoenix Award, 1971; Smith Award, 1973.

Member: Science Fiction Writers of America; Authors
   Guild.

Interests: History, languages, geology, travel.

"My favorite book of my own work is *Okla Hannali*,
Doubleday, 1972, but it is an historical novel, and
not science fiction. My favorite of the science fic-
tion/fantasy is *Past Master*, Ace, 1968. My favorite
of the SF/fantasy short stories is "Continued on Next
Rock," first published in *Orbit* 7, Putnam, 1970, and
often reprinted."

* * * * *

ALEXANDER LAING

Full Name: Alexander Kinnan Laing.
   Born August 7, 1903, at Great Neck, Long Island, New
York. Son of Edgar Hall Laing and Mary Adeline Pray.
Married Isabel Lattimore Frost, June 10, 1930 (divorced);
married Dilys Bennett, May 30, 1936 (died 1960); mar-
ried Veronica Ruzicka, March 22, 1961. One son, David.

Education: A.B., Dartmouth College, 1933; A.M.,
   1947.

Career: Professor of Belles Lettres.
   Technical Editor, *Radio News*, 1925-26; Editor, *Power
Specialist*, 1927-28; copywriter, Erwin, Wasey Co., 1929;
Tutorial adviser, Dartmouth College English Dept., 1930;
adviser to the arts, 1930-34; Assistant Librarian, 1937-

ALEXANDER LAING (cont.)

50; Director of Public Affairs Laboratory, 1947-52; Educational Services Adviser for the Library, 1952; Professor of Belles Lettres, 1952-DATE.

Agent: Harold Matson, 22 E. 40th St., New York, NY 10016.

Member: American Civil Liberties Union; Authors Guild; American Association of University Professors; Dartmouth Sailing Club.

Awards: Guggenheim Fellowshop for Creative Writing Abroad, 1934-35.

* * * * *

HUGH LAMB

Full Name: Hugh Lamb.
Born February 4, 1946, at Sutton, Surrey, England. Son of Charles Lamb (a plumber) and Joyce Russell. Married Susan Tadgell, September 30, 1967. Two sons: Richard, Andrew.

Career: Journalist and editor.
Free-lance editor, 1972-DATE.

* * * * *

JOHN LAMBOURNE

Full Name: John Battersby Crompton Lamburn.
Born April 3, 1893, in England. Son of Edward John Sewell Lamburn (a clerk in Holy Orders) and Clara Crompton. Married Doris Joan Mariott, 1932. One son, David John Crompton; one daughter, Sarah Crompton.

Education: Attended University of Manchester.

Career: Writer.
Policeman, British South Africa Police, 1913-19; employee, Butterfield & Swire (a shipping firm), China, 1919-32; full-time writer, 1932-DATE.

* * * * *

GIL LAMONT

Full Name: Gilvan Derwent Lamont.
Born April 28, 1947, at London, England. Son of John McIntyre Lamont (a drafting engineer) and Kathleen Winifred York (a dress maker and designer). Married Karen Ann Smith, December 22, 1966 (divorced 1969); married Dena Leslie Ramras, May 8, 1971 (divorced 1973). One daughter, Charlotte Heather Ort (born 1967, and re-adopted).

Education: Attended University of Wisconsin, Madison, 1964-65.

Career: Writer.
Editorial Assistant, *San Gabriel Sun*, 1966; clarinetist, U.S. Army, 1966-68; bank teller, State Mutual Savings and Loan, Los Angeles, 1968-69; Contributing Editor, *Tuesday's Child*, 1969; Editorial Assistant, American Art Agency, Chatsworth, CA, 1970; flea market and store salesman and warehouse helper, Liquidators Unlimited, Phoenix, 1970-73; writer, 1973-DATE.

First Professional Sale: *Roach*, Essex House, 1969.

Member: Los Angeles Science Fantasy Society.

Interests:
  "Collecting SF, 20th century classical music, rock music, orchestral scores; play clarinet and sax; Laurel & Hardy; sex and drugs; alcohol; progressive country music and jazz. I dislike nearly everything I write. I'm still a British subject. I've published 7 porn books (6 novels) and 3 or 4 articles in the porn field. I have one brother (fraternal twin)."

* * * * *

LOIS LAMPLUGH

Full Name: Lois Lamplugh [pronounced Lamploo].
  Born June 9, 1921, at Barnstaple, Devonshire, England. Daughter of Aubrey Penfound Lamplugh and Ruth Lister. Married Lawrence Carlile Davis (a sales representative) September 24, 1955. Two children: Susan Ruth, Hugh Lawrence.

Career: Writer and editor.
  Has served on the editorial staff of Jonathan Cape; author, 1949-DATE. Member: P.E.N.; West Country Writers' Association.

Agent: A. P. Watt & Son, 26/28 Bedford Row, London WC1R 4HL, England.

* * * * *

EVELYN LAMPMAN

Full Name: Evelyn Lampman.
  Born April 18, 1907, at The Dalles, Oregon. Daughter of Joseph E. Sibley and Harriet Bronson. Married Herbert Sheldon Lampman, May 12, 1934 (died 1943). Two children: Linda Sibley, Anne Hathaway.

Education: B.S., Oregon State University, 1929.

Career: Writer.
  Continuity writer, Radio Station KEX, Portland, OR, 1929-34; continuity chief, 1937-45; Educational Director, Radio Station KGW, Portland, 1945-52; full-time writer, 1952-DATE. Member: Delta Delta Delta.

Awards:
  Committee on the Art of Democratic Living Award, 1949, for *Treasure Mountain*; Dorothy Canfield Fisher Memorial Children's Book Award, 1962, for *City Under the Back Steps*; Western Writers of America Spur Award, 1970, for *Cayuse Courage*.

* * * * *

ALLEN KIM LANG

Full Name: Allen Kim Lang.
  Born July 31, 1928, at Fort Wayne, Indiana. Son of Frank J. Lang and Ona J. Allen. Married Alberta R. Miller. Education: Attended Indiana University and Roosevelt University.

Career: Blood Bank Supervisor, Michael Reese Research Foundation, Blood Center, Chicago, Illinois. Member: Mystery Writers of America.

GREGOR LANG

Full Name: Faber Birren.
   Born September 21, 1900, at Chicago, Illinois. Son of Joseph P. Birren and Crescentia Lang. Married Wanda Martin, April 25, 1934. Two children: Zoe, Fay.

Education: Attended Art Institute of Chicago, 1918-20, and University of Chicago, 1920-21.

Career: Color consultant.
   Self-employed color consultant, 1934-DATE, currently with headquarters in Stamford, Conn., and an office in Montreal; developer of manuals of color practice for U.S. Navy, U.S. Army, U.S. Coast Guard. Member: Optical Society of America; American Institute of Architects; American Society for Photobiology.

Honors: M.S., Arnold College, 1941.

* * * * *

SIMON LANG

Full Name: Darlene Hartman.
   Born December 23, 1934, at Melville, Louisiana. Daughter of Joseph Paul Artell (State Tax Collector for Jefferson Parish, Louisiana) and Anna-Helena Lange-Bunt. Married Alfred Anthony Hartman, April 16, 1955. Six children: Mark Anthony (born 1956), Christopher Paul (born 1957), Theresa Lynn (born 1958), Elizabeth Anne (born 1960), Marguerite Germaine (born 1961), Hansel Martin (born 1962); two adopted children: Katherine Grace (born 1966), Peter Damian (born 1969).

Education: Attended Loyola University, South, 1952-54, Saddleback Community College, 1972-73.

Career: Writer.
   "All the Gods of Eisernon was my first attempt at a novel. Heretofore I had always worked in film. 'Victory' was followed by a second film, for which they doubled my price; my first network sale was to Star Trek; I have since done teaching films and Tele-SPOTs for the Franciscan Community Center."

First Professional Sale: "Victory," a film appearing on the syndicated television program, The Hour of St. Francis, 1965.

Agent: Polly Connell, 20th Century Artists, 4747 Vineland, Hollywood, CA 90028.

Awards: CBA "Gabriel" Award for general excellence, 1965.

Member: Writers Guild of America, West.

Interests:
   Carving miniature wooden figurines; rug-making; gardening; swimming; reading, especially medicine, history, archaeology; making "little" films; horseback riding.

Lang writes:
   "Having been in and out of crippled children's wards much of my young life, I was fascinated to find out how resourceful the human spirit can be; from the born-blind friend who used power tools for his woodworking, to the deaf girl who loved poetry, they were gutsy, funny, tough kids who are a credit to the race. Not much wonder I'm an ardent Right-to-Lifer. All the

"Gods of Eisernon was written as a stopgap, an alternative to the 'if it's not perfect, kill it' syndrome that looms frighteningly over our world today. It's a nice thought: a stockpile of humanity, a genetic pool from which to draw for prenatal adoptions, a reserve of true humanity in case some nut pushes the wrong button and leaves us nothing but sour mutations. Great way to transport colonists someday, too. Of course, you understand that my prime interest is in preserving the children rather than having them slaughtered at the rate of one million a year, current count for America alone. Suspension is a poor second to wombness, but it beats the incinerator by helluva long shot. Anyway--
   "All the Gods of Eisernon is the 'pilot' book for a series, hopefully. The second and third books are fleshing out, and ATGOE lends itself well, I find, to film. Nothing definite yet. Just nibbles. I'm hoping. Paige deserves a book all to himself, I've been told. Maybe.
   "My philosophy? Oh--love life, enjoy to the hilt, laughter, pasta, tumbling children, Beagles, kitten-litters, Socrates, Aquinas, Buchwald, and Walt Kelly, chuckling babies, sycamore trees, grumpy neighbors, sudden storms, tall clouds, and the Louisiana Gulf coast. That's in the first breath. Not to mention bayou fishing, shrimp-boilings, the Dorothy Chandler Pavilion, rosaries, stockholders' meetings, Hawaii, and preying mantises.
   "So much for me; too much to tell. Maybe we keep trying. Maybe that's why we write."

* * * * *

A. J. LANGGUTH

Full Name: Arthur John Langguth.
   Born July 11, 1933, at Minneapolis, Minnesota. Son of Arthur J. Langguth and Doris Turnquist. Education: A.B., Harvard University, 1955.

Career: Writer.
   Reporter in Washington, Look, 1959; reporter, North Hollywood Valley Times, 1960-63; reporter, New York Times, 1963-65; writer, 1965-DATE. Agent: International Creative Management, 40 W. 57th St., New York, NY 10019.

* * * * *

NOEL LANGLEY

Full Name: Noel Langley.
   Born December 25, 1911, at Durban, South Africa. Became U.S. citizen, 1961. Married Naomi Mary Legate, 1937 (divorced 1954); marrried Pamela Deeming, 1959. Three sons, two daughters. Education: B.A., University of Natal. Member: Writers Guild of America.

Career: Author, playwright, director of films. Award: Donaldson Award, 1948, for "Edward My Son."

* * * * *

STERLING E. LANIER

Full Name: Sterling Edmund Lanier [Lanéer]
   Born December 18, 1927, at New York, New York. Son of Berwick Bruce Lanier (a naval officer and attorney) and Priscilla Thorne Taylor. Married Martha Hanna Pelton, Sept. 3, 1961. Children: Berwick Bruce (born 1965); Kate Williams (born 1967).

STERLING E. LANIER (cont.)

Education: A.B., Harvard University, 1951; graduate study at University of Pennsylvania, 1953-58.

Career: Author and sculptor.
Research historian, Winterthur Museum, 1958-60; Editor, John C. Winston Company, 1961; Editor, Chilton Books, 1961-63; Editor, Macrae-Smith Company, 1963-64; Editor, Chilton Books, 1965-67; full-time author and sculptor, 1967-DATE.

First Professional Sale: "Join Our Gang?" in *Analog Science Fact and Fiction*, May, 1961.

Agent: Curtis Brown Ltd., 60 E. 56th St., New York, NY 10022.

Awards: Follett Gold Medal, for *The War in the Lot*.

Member: Science Fiction Writers of America; Save Our Bays; Sierra Club; National Audobon Society.

Interests: Skin-diving, reading, bird-watching, conservation, military & naval history, sailing, working with migrants.

Lanier writes:
"In re Brigadier Ffellowes: the direct inspirations were Doyle's Brigadier Gerard and Holmes stories, also Hodgson's Carnacki, the Ghost Finder. I like stories with one central character, and I prefer the leisurely pace of M. R. James, Dunsany, and Blackwood's John Silence, which does indeed seem to date the stories. The idea of making the main character British, and hewing to the correct dialogue is an exercise. It fooled Arthur C. Clarke, who thought I *was* British. Pure fun.
"My main source of income is from miniature sculpture, mostly though not entirely using animal motifs. Some of my pieces are in a permanent collection at the Smithsonian. Self-taught, no art schools or courses."

* * * * *

GEORGE LANNING

Full Name: George William Lanning, Jr.
Born July 3, 1925, at Lakewood, Ohio. Son of George William Lanning and Helen Cravatt.

Education: A.B., Kenyon College, 1952.

Career: Writer.
Assistant Editor, World Publishing Company; Assoc. Editor, *Kenyon Review*, 1960-67; Editor, 1967-71; freelance author, 1971-DATE.

First Professional Sale: "Old Turkey Neck," in *Tomorrow Magazine*, 1950.

Agent: McIntosh & Otis, 475 Fifth Avenue, New York, NY 10017.

Awards:
Kenyon Review Fellowship in Fiction, 1954-55; Yaddo Fellowship; Special Award, Mystery Writers of America, 1967, for *The Pedestal*.

Member: Phi Beta Kappa; Authors Guild; Rowfant Club, Cleveland. Interests: Travel, walking, gardening, houses.

EGON LARSEN

Full Name: Egon Larsen [originally Lehrburger].
Born July 13, 1904, at Munich, Germany. Son of Albert David Lehrburger (a manufacturer) and Beatrice Koenigsberger. Married his second wife, Ursula Lippmann (a translator), July 3, 1940. One son, Peter.

Career: Author and journalist, 1928-DATE.
On civilian staff, U.S. Office of Strategic Services, London, 1944-45; London Correspondent, Radio Munich, 1954-DATE; correspondent for various European newspapers.

Awards: Dissel Silver Medal, 1963. Member: P.E.N.

Agent: Robert Harben, 3 Church Vale, London N.2.

* * * * *

GREYE LA SPINA

Full Name: Fanny Greye La Spina.
Born July 10, 1880, at Wakefield, Massachusetts. Daughter of Alonzo Dow Bragg (a Methodist minister) and Ella Celia Perkins. Married Ralph Geissler, 1898 (died 1900); married Robert Rosario La Spina, 1910. One daughter, Celia Geissler (born 1900).

Career: Writer and farmer.
Was a proofreader, photographer, and farmer (raised pheasants, goats, hens, kept a peach orchard, etc.); in her later years became a master weaver in Quakertown, Pennsylvania; writer during the 1920s and 1930s. Died July 9, 1969.

First Professional Sale: "Wolf of the Steppes," in *Thrill Book*, March 1, 1919.

* * * * *

JACQUELINE LA TOURRETTE

Full Name: Jacqueline La Tourrette.
Born May 5, 1926, at Denver, Colorado. Daughter of Charles O. La Tourrette and Stella Bobb. Married David Gibeson, November, 1948 (divorced, 1970). Three children: Noel, Shane, Brian.

Education: Attended San Jose State College, 1948-51.

Career: Medical Secretary.
Teletype operator, Alaska Communications System, 1954-55; Medical Secretary, MIT, 1961-69; Medical Secretary, Kaiser Permanente Medical Center, Santa Clara, 1969-DATE.

Agent: Theron Raines, 244 Madison Avenue, New York, NY 10016.

* * * * *

SANDERS ANNE LAUBENTHAL

Full Name: Sanders Anne Laubenthal.
Born December 25, 1943, at Mobile, Alabama. Daughter of Wilbert Joseph Laubenthal (an accountant) and Mabel Eloise Sanders (a registered nurse).

Education: B.A., Spring Hill College, 1965; M.A., University of Alabama, 1967; Ph.D., 1970.

SANDERS ANNE LAUBENTHAL (cont.)

Career: Training officer.
  Instructor in English, University of Alabama, 1968;
Assistant Professor of English, Troy State University,
1969-72; Education and Training Officer, U.S. Air
Force, 1972-DATE.

First Professional Sale: *Songs of Mobile*, Spring
  Hill College Press, 1962.

Awards: Merilh Medal, Spring Hill College, 1962, for
  verse play, "Stella"; Alabama State Poetry Day A-
  ward, 1969, for *Interlude and Other Poems*.

Member: Modern Language Association; South Atlantic
  Modern Language Association.

Interests: Art, travel.

Laubenthal's fantasy novel, *Excalibur*, was based on
an ancient legend of the Welsh discovering America.
The author comments: "As for the Madoc legend, historians have debated it for a long time. The most
recent book, as far as I know, is Richard Deacon's
Madoc and the Discovery of America. Deacon believes
the story to have a historical basis."

* * * * *

KEITH LAUMER

Full Name: John Keith Laumer.
  Born June 9, 1925, at Syracuse, New York. Son of
William F. Laumer, Jr. (Colonel, U.S. Air Force, ret.)
and Virginia Laumer. Married Janice K. Derkinson,
February, 1949 (divorced, 1968). Three children:
Virginia Kathleen (born 1949), Janice Antoinette (born
1951), Sabrina Dian (born 1957).

Education: B.Sc., University of Illinois, 1949; B.
  Arch., 1951; Certificate, University of Stockholm,
  1948.

Career: Writer.
  Captain, U.S. Air Force, 1952-57, 1960-65; Third
Secretary, Embassy of the United States of America,
Rangoon, Burma, 1957-59; full-time writer, 1965-DATE.

First Professional Sale: "Greylorn," in *Amazing
  Stories*, April, 1959.

Agent: Robert P. Mills Ltd., 156 E. 52nd St., New
  York, NY 10022.

Awards: First in sculpture, Decatur Art Show, 1949.

Member:
  National Association for the Advancement of Colored
People; White Citizens Council of Biloxi; Black Pan-
thers; John Birch Society; Science Fiction Writers of
America; American Air Racing Association.

Interests:
  Swedish girls, French wine, German beer, classic
cars and airplanes, airplane models, travel, music
(especially Puccini), woodworking (fine furniture),
painting (à la Van Gogh), aerobics.

Laumer writes:
  "As to the current state of SF, it is enjoying
unprecedented economic prosperity, with many major
"publishers getting into the act. Its scope is broad-
ening, at the same time that the limitations of 'main-
steam' fiction are disappearing; thus, SF is merging
with the mainstream--or possibly the mainstream is
merging with so-called SF. 'Science Fiction' is, of
course, a terrible piece of nomenclature. It reflects
the primitive preoccupation with technological developments that were the chief evidence that the future was
happening back in the 1920s. Remember, people like
Hugo Gernsback grew up in a world without airplanes,
radio, etc.; phones, phonographs, automobiles were rare.
As for jets, TV, space technology, they were assumed
to be five hundred years ahead. Naturally, they were
awed and fascinated by the transformation.
  "Today we've gotten into the rhythm of change. We
are no longer hung up on the idea that some ICS educated dropout is going to invent a time machine in his
basement. We are exploring the new horizons of human
experience opened up, or to be opened up, by the changes that have come or are coming. The emphasis on the
human condition, human accomodation to a widening universe, is the concern of modern SF. The "New Wave"
seems to be a term that can be applied to (a) any story
you like, or (b) any story you don't like, depending
on whether you consider yourself a New Wave fan. The
only actual earmark I can sometimes detect in a group
of alleged New Wave stories is a preoccupation with
stylistic devices, as opposed to story values.
  "I began writing by sitting down at the typewriter
one day, while in Rangoon, Burma (and suffering from
amoebic dysentery), and typing out the kind of story
I wanted to read ("Greylorn"). As for my contribution
to the development of the genre, I doubt if I have made
one. I am probably too 'reactionary' to have influenced its course; by reactionary, I mean that I have
been well content to accept the conventions of literature as I found them, and work within the framework,
devoting my ingenuity to devising stories and characters and dialogue, and getting across (I hope) a few
ideas which I consider important.
  "Retief originated in my experience as a U.S. diplomat in the Foreign Service. I attribute his long life
to his excellence, plus my interest in detailing the
iniquities of one State Department. Sorry, the Retief
stories are true, only toned down somewhat.
  "All my best books are still to be written. Four
years ago, they tried to kill me (the first quack said
it was a stroke, another disagreed), but I'm recovering
and will soon be myself again, if not several additional
people."

* * * * *

FRANK LAURIA

Full Name: Frank Jonathan Lauria.
  Born October 26, 1935, at Brooklyn, New York. Son of
Melchiorre Lauria (a structural engineer) and Vittoria
Agneta (a teacher). Married E. Margareta Prins (a
fashion designer), June 3, 1965.

Education: B.S., Manhattan College, 1958.

Career: Writer.
  Has been an actor (appearing on Broadway, television
programs, and in the films), model, photographer, social
worker, songwriter; Asst. Copy Chief, Bantam Books,
1967-68; Special Projects Editor, Pyramid Books, 1968;
Senior Editor, Paperback Library, 1969-70; Account Executive, Wunderman Ricattasklien, 1972; full-time writer,
1972-DATE. Member: Actor's Equity; Screen Actors
Guild; P.E.N.; N.O.R.M.L.

FRANK LAURIA (cont.)

First Professional Sale: "Crazyface" (poem), in *Arkangel*, 1962.

Agent: William Morris Agency, 151 El Camino, Beverly Hills, CA 90212.

Award: First Prize (Poetry), Valley Writers Conference, San Jose, California, 1963.

Interests:
Collecting SF and comic art; pig collector; modern jazz enthusiast; outdoor running; yoga; telepathy; herb therapy; pyramidology; collecting modern sculpture. "I've been working on the Doctor Orient series since 1967--all the books are based on authentic records and phenomena, and personal investigation."

* * * * *

JAMES LAVER

Full Name: James Laver.
Born March 14, 1899, at Liverpool, England. Son of Arthur James Laver and Florence M. Barker. Married Veronica Turleigh, 1928. Two children: Patrick Martin, Brigid Cecilia.

Education: B.A. and B.Litt., New College, Oxford University.

Career: Museum director and writer.
Deputy Director, Victoria and Albert Museum, 1922-59; writer, 1921-75. Died 1975.

Awards: Newdigate Prize, for *Cervantes*; Commander of the British Empire.

Member:
Art Worker's Guild; P.E.N.; Authors Society; International Faculty of Arts; Society of Civil Service Authors; Society of International Artists; Society for Theatre Research; Royal Academy of Dramatic Arts; Beefsteak Club; Chelsea Arts Club; Saintsbury Club; Dilettanti Club.

* * * * *

H. L. LAWRENCE

Full Name: Henry Lionel Lawrence.
Born April 22, 1908, at London, England.

Career: Advertising copywriter.
Copywriter in various advertising agencies in London (and formerly at Sydney, Australia), 1933-DATE. Member: Crime Writers Association; P.E.N.; Television and Screen Writers Guild; Institute of Practitioners of Advertising. Agent: Winant Towers Ltd., 1 Furnival St., London E.C.4, England.

* * * * *

LOUISE LAWRENCE

Full Name: Elizabeth Rhoda Wintle.
Born June 5, 1943, at Leatherhead, Surrey, England. Daughter of Fred Holden (a bricklayer) and Rhoda Edith Cowles. Married and divorced. Three children: Rachel Louise (born 1964); Ralph Lawrence (born 1966); Rebecca Jane (born 1967).

Education: Attended Lydney Grammar School, Gloucestershire, 1954-61.

Career: Writer.
"Either unemployed or in casual labour; spent a few years as a junior assistant in a local library."

First Professional Sale: *Andra*, Collins, 1971.

Agent: A. M. Heath & Co., 40-42 William IV Street, London WC2N 4DD, England.

Interests: Painting, sewing, interior decorating, rambling, reading, spiritualism.

"I write: for personal reasons and: as an escape--from a social system I don't wish to belong to--from environmental changes I don't wish to be engulfed by--and from moral and political influences which seem to grow more and more degenerate."

* * * * *

KEO FELKER LAZARUS

Full Name: Keo Felker Lazarus.
Born October 22, 1913, at Callaway, Nebraska. Daughter of John Edwin Felker (a jeweler and rancher) and Penola Smith (a musician). Married Arnold Leslie Lazarus, July 24, 1938. Four children: Kearvelle (daughter, born 1940), Dianne (born 1943), Jonathan David (born 1944), Peter Darrell (born 1947).

Education: B.E., University of California, Los Angeles, 1938; attended Purdue University, 1966.

Career: Writer.
Teacher of physical education and dance, Los Angeles City Schools, 1939-40, 1952-60; writer, 1968-DATE.

First Professional Sale: *Rattlesnake Run*, Follett, 1968.

Agent: Ruth Cantor, R 1005, 156 Fifth Avenue, New York, NY 10010.

Member: Authors Guild of America; Children's Reading Round Table, Chicago.

Interests: House designing, swimming, tennis, gardening, archeology, field work, UFO investigations.

Lazarus notes: "Research and imagination form the springboard that catapults ideas into the Sci-Fi world. Youngsters latch onto these ideas with ease, and for this reasons I enjoy writing for them. History that comes out of the ground fires thought with the same intensity as glowing lights in the sky, so I find writing about the past equally as exciting as writing about the future. After all, it's only a matter of stretching the mind either way, isn't it?"

* * * * *

HECTOR LAZO

Full Name: Hector Lazo.
Born October 9, 1899, at Guatemala City, Guatemala. Son of Luis Lazo (a physician) and Emilia Pena. Married Susan Bullock, December, 1920 (died 1939); married Edith Pack (an artist), 1941. Two children: Charles R., Susan Belle.

HECTOR LAZO (cont.)

Education: A.B., Harvard University, 1921; M.B.A., New York University, 1946; Ph.D., 1948.

Career: Professor of Marketing.
Special agent, U.S. Dept. of Commerce, 1923-27; Director of Foreign Advertising, Dodge Brothers, Detroit, 1927-28; Director of Foreign Advertising, General Motors, 1928-31; Executive Vice-President, Cooperative Food Distributors, Washington, 1931-43; Assistant Director, Board of Economic Warfare, 1943-44; Assistant to the President and Director of Public Relations, Sunshine Biscuits; Professor of Marketing, New York University; Chairman of School Committee, Town of Pound Ridge.

Awards: Médaille France Amérique; *American Heritage* Award; named marketing educator of the year, 1964.

Member:
American Marketing Association; American Management Association; Industrial Conference Board; New York University Club; Phi Beta Kappa.

* * * * *

ROBERT C. LEE

Full Name: Robert Corwin Lee, Jr.
Born December 21, 1931, at Brooklyn, New York. Son of Robert Corwin Lee (a business executive) and Elsie Calder. Married Marilyn Superak (a trainer of horses) March 27, 1951. Children: Robert III, Christopher, Scott.

Education: A.B., Stanford University, 1956; M.A., San Jose State College, 1962.

Career: Teacher.
Teacher, Aptos Unified School District, 1956-60; Teacher, Corralitos Unified School District, 1960-65; Teacher, Pajaro Valley Unified School District, 1965-67; Teacher, Buffalo High School, Buffalo, Mo., 1967-DATE. Member: National Education Association; Missouri State Teachers Association.

* * * * *

WALT LEE

Full Name: Walter William Lee.
Born August 16, 1931, at Eugene, Oregon. Son of Walter William Lee and Okria Mooney. Married Eve Olveda, May 9, 1959. Two children: Cindy (born 1960), Steven Marco (born 1965).

Education: B.S., California Institute of Technology, 1954; graduate study at University of California, 1954-55.

Career: Writer and film coordinator.
Member, technical staff, Hughes Aircraft Company, 1955-59; Vice President, Technical Communications, Inc., 1959-62; on technical staff, Hughes Aircraft, 1962-DATE.

Awards: Special Plaque, 33rd World Science Fiction Convention (Aussiecon), Sydney, 1975, for *Reference Guide to Fantastic Films*. Interests: Mass media, philosophy.

SYBIL LEEK

Full Name: Sybil Leek.
Born February 22, 1923, in England. Two children: Stephen B. Leek (born 1950), Julian Leek (born 1951).

Career: Author and columnist.
Publisher and Editor, Twin World Publications, Inc., 1969-72; full-time writer and columnist.

First Professional Sale: Several poems in 1939.

Agent: Mrs. Carlton Cole, Waldorf Towers, Park Avenue, New York, NY 10022.

Interests:
Writing, experimenting in writing styles; astrology; collecting antiques; space travel. "I am a disciplined writer who enjoys research of any kind, but particularly anything to do with space travel and the inter-planetary system."

* * * * *

JOHN F. LEEMING

Full Name: John Fishwick Leeming.
Born January 8, 1900, at Chorlton, England. Son of Henry Heatley Leeming and Edith Lowe. Married Gladys Birch, June 25, 1920. Two children: John Birch, David Christopher.

Career: Writer.
Full-time writer, 1923-DATE. Member: Royal Aero Club; Lancastershire Aero Club; Manchester Chamber of Commerce.

* * * * *

URSULA K. LE GUIN

Full Name: Ursula Kroeber Le Guin.
Born October 21, 1929, at Berkeley, California. Daughter of Alfred L. Kroeber (the noted anthropologist) and Theodora Kracaw (who writes under the name Theodora Kroeber). Married Charles A. Le Guin (a historian), December 22, 1953. Three children: Elisabeth (born 1957), Caroline (born 1959), Theodore (born 1964).

Education: A.B., Radcliffe College, 1951; A.M., Columbia University, 1952.

Career: Writer.
Writer, 1962-DATE; occasional teacher at the Clarion Science Fiction Workshops, and Portland State University.

First Professional Sale: "April in Paris," in *Fantastic Stories*, September, 1962.

Agent: Virginia Kidd, Box 278, Milford, PA 18337.

Awards:
Guest of Honor, 33rd World Science Fiction Convention (Aussiecon), Sydney, 1975; Nebula Award, Best Novel, 1969 (1970), *The Left Hand of Darkness*; Nebula Award, Best Novel, 1974 (1975), *The Dispossessed*; Nebula Award, Best Short Story, 1974 (1975), "The Day Before the Revolution"; Jupiter Award, Best Novel, 1974 (1975), *The Dispossessed*; Jupiter Award, Best Short Story, 1974 (1975), "The Day Before the Revolution"; Hugo Award,

URSULA K. LE GUIN (cont.)

Best Novel, 1969 (1970), *The Left Hand of Darkness*; Hugo Award, Best Novella, 1972 (1973), "The Word for World Is Forest"; Hugo Award, Best Short Story, 1973 (1974), "The Ones Who Walk Away from Omelas"; Hugo Award, Best Novel, 1974 (1975), *The Dispossessed*; Newbery Silver Medal, 1972, for *The Tombs of Atuan*; National Book Award, 1973, for *The Farthest Shore*.

Member: Science Fiction Writers of America; Phi Beta Kappa.

Le Guin writes:
"Most of my science fiction novels and some of the short stories are set against the same general background; pseudo-chronologically, the novels and major stories run: [*The Lathe of Heaven*?], *The Dispossessed*, "Vaster Than Empires and More Slow," "The Word for World Is Forest," *Rocannon's World*, *Planet of Exile*, *City of Illusions*, *The Left Hand of Darkness*.
"The three Earthsea books, *A Wizard of Earthsea*, *The Tombs of Atuan*, *The Farthest Shore*, are set in an entirely different (fantasy) secondary universe, run chronologically, and form a trilogy.
"I cannot tell you where I got the idea for *The Left Hand of Darkness*. When I write a book, every idea I ever had, and a good many I never had before, come together and make sense; which makes the novel.
"I write science fiction in part because my gift and inclination is for what comes out of profound fantasy when it is controlled by disciplined intelligence. I think that the imagination is as singularly human a faculty as rational intelligence, and that its uses are as various, and as necessary to our happiness as individuals and our viability as a species. I think that the imaginative faculty should be developed and trained just as intelligence is. The best and pleasantest school for such an education of the imagination is probably the practice, or the appreciation, of an imaginative art."

* * * * *

FRITZ LEIBER

Full Name: Fritz Reuter Leiber.
Born December 24, 1910, at Chicago, Illinois. Son of Fritz Leiber and Virginia Bronson. Married Jonquil Stephens, January 16, 1936 (died 1969). One son, Justin (born 1938).

Education: Ph.B., University of Chicago, 1932.

Career: Writer, 1939-DATE; has also been a stage actor.

First Professional Sale: "Two Sought Adventure," in *Unknown*, August, 1939.

Awards:
Guest of Honor, 9th World Science Fiction Convention (Nolacon), New Orleans, 1951; Nebula Award, Best Novelette, 1967 (1968), "Gonna Roll the Bones"; Nebula Award, Best Novella, 1970 (1971), "Ill Met in Lankhmar"; Nebula Award, Best Short Story, 1975 (1976), "Catch That Zeppelin"; Hugo Award, Best Novel, 1957 (1958), *The Big Time*; Hugo Award, Best Novel, 1964 (1965), *The Wanderer*; Hugo Award, Best Novelette, 1967 (1968), "Gonna Roll the Bones"; Hugo Award, Best Novella, 1969 (1970), "Ship of Shadows"; Hugo Award, Best Novella, 1970 (1971), "Ill Met in Lankhmar"; Hugo Award, Best Short Story, 1975 (1976), "Catch That Zeppelin"; Gandalf Award, 1975; World Fantasy Award, Best Short Fiction, 1975 (1976), "Belsen Express"; World Fantasy Award, 1976, Life Award.

Member: Science Fiction Writers of America.

* * * * *

MURRAY LEINSTER

Full Name: William Fitzgerald Jenkins.
Born June 16, 1896, at Norfolk, Virginia. Son of George Briggs Jenkins and Mary Louise Murry. Married Mary Mandola, August 9, 1921. Four children: Mary, Elizabeth, Wenllian, Joan.

Career: Writer.
Writer and inventor, 1915-75. Died in Virginia June 8, 1975.

First Professional Sale:
"The very first one of all was six epigrams--no, twelve--to *Smart Set* magazine, then edited by H. L. Mencken and George Jean Nathan. This was in 1915, but I can't give you a publication date. As epigrams, they were unsigned and used as fillers, and were undoubtedly scattered through several issues. Groff Conklin once observed that at least eight thousand people went around at cocktail parties, saying negligently that they used to write half the epigrams in *Smart Set*, and Mencken the other half. I was the one person who did *not* say that at cocktail parties. I was rarely invited. But I could have said it and proved it.
"My first science fiction sale was "Oh, Aladdin!" It was published in the January 11th issue of *Argosy* in 1919. Sam Moskowitz gave me a copy of that issue as a present in March of 1968, when the Newark Club presented me with a plaque in celebration of my fifty years (count 'em) writing science fiction."

Awards:
Guest of Honor, 21st World Science Fiction Convention (DisCon I), Washington, 1963; Hugo Award, Best Short Story, 1955 (1956), "Exploration Team."

Leinster writes:
"I had a book titled *Time Tunnel* on the stands when the TV series *Time Tunnel* was started. Naturally assuming that the same title meant the same story as the TV series, people bought four printings of the original book. The producers asked me to do a story using their characters. I did. Hence, there are two different books (one TV) with the same title."
He adds: "I invented 'Front Projection,' got two patents out on it, and still collect occasional sums from the Front Projection Corporation."

* * * * *

MADELEINE 1'ENGLE

Full Name: Madeleine 1'Engle.
Born November 29, 1918, at New York, New York. Daughter of Charles Wadsworth Camp (a foreign correspondent) and Madeleine Barnett (a pianist). Married Hugh Franklin (an actor), January 26, 1946. Three children: Josephine (born 1947), Maria (born 1947), Bion (born 1952).

Education: A.B., Smith College, 1941.

MADELEINE l'ENGLE (cont.)

Career: Writer.
Actress on Broadway and summer stock, 1941-47 ("wrote my first novel on tour with my first play"); has also been a teacher at the elementary level; writer, 1945-DATE.

First Professional Sale: *The Small Rain*, Vanguard Press, 1945.

Agent: Theron Raines, 244 Madison Avenue, New York, NY 10016.

Awards:
Newbery Medal, 1963, for *A Wrinkle in Time*; Lewis Carroll Shelf, 1965, for *A Wrinkle in Time*; Sequoia Award, 1965, for *A Wrinkle in Time*; Austrian State Literary Prize, for *The Moon by Night*.

Member:
Order of St. John of Jerusalem; Authors Guild (member of Council, Membership Committee, Authors Guild Foundation, and Children's Book Committee).

Interests: Playing Bach and Mozart on the piano; walking; travelling; cooking for family and friends.

* * * * *

JOHN LEONARD

Full Name: John Leonard.
Born February 25, 1939, at Washington, D.C. Son of Daniel D. Leonard and Ruth Woods. Married Christiana Morison, June 13, 1959. One son, Andrew Warren.

Education: B.A., University of California, Berkeley, 1962.

Career: Newspaper writer.
Editorial Apprentice, *National Review*, 1959-60; book reviewer, and drama and literature program producer, Radio Station KPFA, 1963-64; publicity writer in Boston, 1964-67; book reviewer, *New York Times*, 1969-70; Book Review Editor, 1971-DATE; writer.

* * * * *

RHODA LERMAN

Full Name: Rhoda Lerman.
Born January 18, 1936, at Far Rockaway, New York. Daughter of Jacob Sniderman (an accountant) and Gertrude Langfur. Married Robert Rudolph Lerman (a carpet distributor), September 15, 1957. Three children: Jill, Julia, Matthew.

Education: B.A., University of Miami, Coral Gables, Florida, 1957.

Career: English teacher.
Instructor in English and parapsychology, Syracuse University, Syracuse, New York; has also been the manager of a rock band.

Agent: Helen Brann Agency, 14 Sutton Place, New York, New York.

Politics: "Traditional Democrat, becoming conservative."

DESMOND LESLIE

Full Name: Desmond Arthur Peter Leslie.
Born June 29, 1921, at London, England. Son of Sir Shane Leslie (the author and biographer) and Marjorie Ide. Married Agnes Bernauer (divorced); married Helen Jennifer Strong. Children: Shaun, Mark, Antonia, Samantha, Camilla.

Career: Businessman.
Was director of several film companies before establishing Leslie & Leslie Ltd., makers of electronic music for films, plays, radio, television, and commercial records; writer, 1945-DATE. Member: White Eagle Lodge.

* * * * *

PETER LESLIE

Full Name: Peter Leslie.
Born February 5, 1922, at Launceston, Cornwall, England. Son of Kenneth Chapelow and Doris Ellen Leslie. Married Helene Bond, November 27, 1954 (deceased). One daughter, Tanya Karen (born 1956).

Education: Attended The Queen's University, Belfast, Northern Ireland.

Career: Writer.
Has been a journalist, publicist, jazz musician, draughtsman, actor, dancer, press censor, designer of record covers, typographer, magazine editor, interior decorator, columnist on showbiz, designer of film titles, radio and television broadcaster and interviewer; worked at various times for Reuters, *Daily Mirror*, *Daily Express*, *Daily Herald*, Odhams Press, BBC; now a full-time writer.

First Professional Sale: *The Book of Bilk*, MacGibbon & Kee, 1962.

Awards: "A hack professional should be so lucky!"

Member: Vintage Sports Car Club; Lancia Motor Club; Capricorn Club.

* * * * *

MILTON LESSER

Full Name: Milton Lesser.
Born August 7, 1928, at New York, New York. Son of Norman Lesser (a broker) and Sylvia Price. Married his second wife, Ann Humbert. Two children: Deirdre, Robin.

Education: B.A., College of William and Mary, 1949.

Career: Full-time Writer, 1954-DATE. Member: Mystery Writers of America. Agent: Scott Meredith, 580 Fifth Avenue, New York, NY 10036.

* * * * *

DORIS LESSING

Full Name: Doris May Lessing.
Born October 22, 1919, in Persia. Daughter of Alfred Cook Tayler (a farmer) and Emily Maude McVeagh. Married Frank Charles Wisdom, 1939 (divorced 1943); married Gottfried Anton Lessing, 1945 (divorced, 1949). Three children: John, Jean, Peter.

DORIS LESSING (cont.)

Education: Attended high school in Southern Rhodesia.

Career: Writer.
Lived in Southern Rhodesia, 1924-49, then moved to England; has been a nursemaid, lawyer's secretary, Hansard typist, and a Parliamentary Commissioner's typist; now a full-time writer.

Awards: Somerset Maugham Award, 1954, for *Five Short Novels*.

Agent: Greyson & Wigan, 58 Old Compton St., London, England.

* * * * *

MALCOLM LEVENE

Full Name: Malcolm Levene.
Born June 24, 1937, at London, England. Son of David Levene and Rayna Lewis. Married Ruth Levi (a psychologist), July 1, 1960. Children: Caitlin.

Education: B.A., University of Western Australia, 1957; M.A., 1967.

Career: Psychologist.
Psychologist, Department of Labour, Perth, Western Australia, 1959-62, 1963-65; Psychologist, Child Welfare Department and Children's Hospital, both in Perth, 1962; Psychologist, Immigration Department, Perth, 1965-67; Psychologist, Vocational Guidance Organization, London, 1967-DATE. Member: Poet's Workshop.

Agent: David Higham Associates, 76 Dean St., Soho, London, England.

* * * * *

BARRY R. LEVIN
[contributor]

Full Name: Barry Raymond Levin.
Born June 11, 1946, at Philadelphia, Pennsylvania. Son of Sidney Levin (self-employed inventory service) and Bertha Zwerman.

Education: Attended Santa Monica City College, 1964-65.

Career: Book dealer.
Soldier, U.S. Army, 1965-67; Production Control Dispatcher, McDonnell Douglas, 1967-69; Shot Peener, Astro Peen Inc., 1969-72; Book Dealer, Barry R. Levin Science Fiction & Fantasy Literature, Los Angeles, 1973-DATE.

* * * * *

IRA LEVIN

Full Name: Ira Levin.
Born August 27, 1929, at New York, New York. Son of Charles Levin (a toy importer) and Beatrice Schlansky. Married Gabrielle Aronsohn, August 20, 1960 (divorced 1968). Three children: Adam, Jared, Nicholas.

Education: B.A., New York University, 1950.

Career: Writer, primarily of plays.

Awards: Edgar Award, 1953, for *A Kiss Before Dying*.

Member: Dramatists Guild; American Society of Composers, Authors and Publishers.

* * * * *

MEYER LEVIN

Full Name: Meyer Levin.
Born October 8, 1905, at Chicago, Illinois. Son of Joseph Levin (a tailor) and Goldie Basiste. Married Mabel Schamp Foy, 1934 (divorced 1944); married Tereska Szwarc (a French novelist under the name Tereska Torres) March 25, 1948. Three children: Eli, Gabriel, Mikael; one step-daughter: Dominique.

Education: Ph.B., University of Chicago, 1924; attended Académie Moderne Art School, Paris, 1925.

Career: Film producer and writer.
Reporter, *Chicago Daily News*, 1923-29; one-time member of a collective farm community in Palestine; producer of marionette plays at New School for Social Research; Associate Editor, *Esquire*, 1933-38, and Film Critic, 1933-39; writer and producer for U.S. Office of War Information, 1942-43; war correspondent for Overseas News Agency and Jewish Telegraphic Agency; now a film producer and writer.

Awards:
Harry and Ethel Daroff Fiction Award, 1966, for *The Stronghold*; Isaac Siegel Memorial Juvenile Award of Jewish Book Council of America, 1967, for *The Story of Israel*; Special Citation, World Federation of Bergen/Belsen Associations, 1969, for "excellence and distinction in literature of the Holocaust and Jewish destiny."

Member: American War Correspondents Association; Authors League; Dramatists Guild.

Agent: Georges Borchardt, 145 E. 52nd St., New York, NY 10022.

* * * * *

DAVID LEVY

Full Name: David Levy.
Born January 2, 1913, at Philadelphia, Pennsylvania. Son of Benjamin Levy and Lillian Potash. Married Lucille Alva Wilds (an executive assistant), July 25, 1941. Two children: Lance, Linda.

Education: B.S., University of Pennsylvania, 1934; M.B.A., 1935.

Career: Film executive.
With Young & Rubicam (an advertising agency), 1938-59, becoming Associate Director of the Radio and Television Department; Vice-President in Charge of Network Programs and Talent, NBC, 1959-61; Executive Producer, Filmways Television Productions, 1964; Executive Vice President in Charge of Television Activities, Four Star International, 1970-72; Producer, Paramount Television, 1972-73; President, Wilshire Productions; Executive Producer, Universal Studios, 1971-72; member of faculty, California State University, Northridge, 1973-74. Member: ASCAP; National Academy of Television Arts & Sciences; Authors Guild; Dramatists Guild; Producers Guild.

ARTHUR O. LEWIS JR.

Full Name: Arthur Orcutt Lewis, Jr.
   Born October 8, 1920, at Wellsville, Pennsylvania.
Son of Arthur Orcutt Lewis (a manufacturer) and Janet
Morrison Sanderson (a secretary). Married Céleste
Cécile Juneau, March 1, 1945. Three children: Janet
Rebecca (born 1946), Arthur Orcutt III (born 1948),
Mary Jameson (born 1956).

Education: A.B., Harvard University, 1940; A.M.,
   1942; Ph.D., Pennsylvania State University, 1951.

Career: Professor of English.
   Instructor in English, Rice Institute, 1946-48;
Graduate Assistant in English, Pennsylvania State
University, 1948-50; Instructor, 1950-52; Asst. Pro-
fessor, 1952-56; Associate Professor, 1956-60; Profes-
sor of English, 1960-DATE; Associate Dean, College of
the Liberal Arts, 1965-DATE. Advisory Editor, Arno
Press Utopian Literature Series (41 volumes), 1971.

First Professional Sale: 1950.

Member:
   Modern Language Association; American Studies Assoc-
iation; College English Association; Society for the
History of Technology; American Association for Higher
Education; Science Fiction Research Association; World
Future Society.

Lewis notes: "I have been involved in science fiction research and teaching for some thirty years."

* * * * *

IRWIN LEWIS

Full Name: Irwin Lewis.
   Born November 17, 1916, at New York, New York. Son
of David Levenson (an actor) and Anna Meltzer (an actress). Married Sidney Kulkin, 1946. Two sons:
David (born 1948), Mitchell (born 1951).

Education: B.A., University of Pennsylvania, 1938.

Career: Radio & TV Director, American Heart Association.

First Professional Sale: An article to *This Week
   Magazine*, 1951.

Agent: Jay Garon, 100 Central Park West, New York.

Member:
   Writers Guild of America; National Academy of Tele-
vision Arts and Sciences; Science Fiction Writers of
America; Health, Education, Science Communications of
America.

* * * * *

OSCAR LEWIS

Full Name: Oscar Lewis.
   Born May 5, 1893, at San Francisco, California. Son
of William Francis Lewis and Anna Amanda Walter. Married Betty Mooney, June, 1925.

Career: Writer.
   Has been a free-lance author most of his life, starting with boys stories; wrote for young people's maga-

zines, 1914-20, for general magazines, 1920-35; author
and editor of books, primarily on West Coast history
and biography, 1930-DATE; Member, San Francisco Art
Commission, 1948-60.

Member: P.E.N.; Book Club of California; Roxburgh
   Club and Bohemian Club, both in San Francisco.

* * * * *

ROY LEWIS

Full Name: Ernest Michael Roy Lewis.
   Born November 6, 1913, at Felixstowe, England. Son
of Ernest I. Lewis (a teacher) and Susannah Edmonds.
Married Christine Tew, June 6, 1939. Two children:
Christine Miranda, Elizabeth Rachel.

Education: B.A., University College, Oxford University, 1934; graduate study at the London School of
   Economics and Political Science, University of London,
   1935-36.

Career: Writer.
   Economist, Royal Institute of International Affairs,
London, 1935-36; Assistant Editor, *Statist*, 1936-39;
Manager, Pekin Syndicate, 1943-46; Feature Writer, *Scope*,
1946-48; Assistant Editor and Washington Correspondent,
Economist, 1952-61; Assistant Foreign Editor, *London
Times*, 1961-DATE.

Agent: David Higham Associates, 76 Dean St., Soho,
   London W.1, England.

Member: Institute of International Affairs; London
   Library; Savile Club.

First Professional Sale:
   "I earned my first free-lance fee with an article in
the *Birmingham Post* on "Birmingham in 1975," in 1933,
as a boy of 16, in which I correctly forecast closed
circuit television in business offices! But I have no
other record. I got an SF short story into *The Adelphi*
in 1936, I think, and have no record of that either. I
think these must be the first.
   "But I published a fantasy, "An Un-natural History of
Monsters" from my own private press in 1931. It was
in verse and rather spottily printed on a hand press,
and a few copies were sold; H. G. Wells got a complimentary copy, and sent a friendly postcard, which is
also lost, alas. War and death has rolled over one's
youth. I only began to earn money as a journalist in
1936."

Lewis writes:
   "I don't think I am a writer in the science fiction
field, my book *The Evolution Man* being something between a parable and a fantasy; though it was, I admit,
published as SF, which may have indeed disappointed
some readers.
   "However, I enjoy a measure of science fiction in my
reading, and I might try to write some, one day. (I
am aging, and having to earn a living by journalism,
you will understand.) My feeling is that science fiction should try to explore the effect of technological
development, or scientific discovery, on human personality, and/or human institutions as we know them; I am
not very interested in 'Far Future' galaxy empire building, much of which extends into spacemanship (I think)
the American idea of life and politics as a perpetual
cops v. robbers story--which we effete Europeans think
a bit simple. Please don't take offence!

ROY LEWIS (cont.)

"It seems to me there is a case for setting up fictional 'models' of people and institutions under extraordinary impacts--i.e., you feed into a given known situation one strange event, which enables you to study reactions, or illuminate our limitations; and this is a kind of simplified drawing of what is happening to us, as the result of inventions and discoveries, all the time. I like this--but not apocalyptic visions, like Ray Bradbury's, which do not have, for me, any frame of reference to present human society. I feel, with Renaissance man, that Man is the measure of All Things--so I must have present-day society, and the personalities within it, as my module.

"Actually, this is asking a terrific lot, if you want to write SF credibly. What author now living can portray an American group of people, a Russian group, a Chinese group, a European group (mixed; e.g., English, French and German), and an African group, for example, to test the impact of a visitor from Mars, to take a simple case--and why should a visitor from Mars, as usually happens in these stories, spend his time in New York or London? I have travelled all over the world, except South America, and I affirm, as an Earthling, that he just would NOT. But so much science fiction, which should be global, in its scenery and characterisation, is parochial.

"Of course, the other thing you can do, either for imagination's sake, or satirically, is to destroy the world with the Bomb, and construct a new society--but this is either to create a Utopia or an Erewhon, which isn't really new, or to produce a kind of bastard anthropology. Either way, you don't really deal in human emotions.

"I think imaginative writing does deal in human emotions; that's what it's for. We can read up on sociological reports, case-histories, or marketing reports for the other measurements of life. What we want in novels is people, real people, and a sort of story--something a little more of a pattern, more complete, than our own lives are....I don't, as you see, believe in fiction producing Truth about humanity directly, but only by interpretation, for which I find both plot and character vital to each other.

"When a man like Williamson writes a fantasy about animals, like Tarka the Otter, in fact he is writing about trans-bodied humanity--the virtues of effort and survival, love and sacrifice--not about animals at all, about whose consciousness we know nothing. And so it goes with the rest of fantasy, in my opinion; it is simply a way of studying human beings in an unfamiliar framework--but they must be human, very deeply so. This is where so much science fiction gives us only cardboard figurines, and rather bogus 'miracle' type science, and very inexact technology.

"The experts may not agree with any of this; I have friends devoted to SF who would not do so. But this is how I, as one reader, react; and I first read *The War of the Worlds*, and was bemused by it, in 1925, aetat. 12 or so. The people were real Victorians--my great aunt who lived with us, was a Wellsian character, of 1898 vintage. So it *was* distressingly real."

* * * * *

ROSALIE LIEBERMAN

Full Name: Rosalie Lieberman.
   Born at Louisville, Kentucky. Daughter of Ignace Lieberman and Dollie Meyer. Education: Studied at Columbia University, 1930-35, and 1949-53.

Career: Writer.
   Script reader, Warner Brothers Pictures, 1932-36, and Twentieth Century-Fox, 1936-39; writer.

* * * * *

A. M. LIGHTNER

Full Name: Alice Martha Hopf.
   Born October 14, 1904, at Detroit, Michigan. Daughter of Clarence Ashley Lightner (a lawyer) and Frances McGraw (a playwright). Married Ernst Joachim Hopf, April 29, 1935. One son, Christopher (born 1942).

Education: B.A., Vassar College, 1927.

Career: Writer.
   "I have a kind of amateur secondary career as a lepidopterist and ecologist/conservationist. Hobby of tagging monarch butterflies. Have published a children's book on the monarch (*Monarch Butterflies*, Crowell), and a number of natural history books from various publishers, under the name Alice L. Hopf."

First Professional Sale: "A New Game," in *Boys' Life*, 1959.

Awards: Two awards from the National Science Teachers Association, for *Biography of a Rhino* (1972), and *Misunderstood Animals* (1973).

Member: Authors Guild; Science Fiction Writers of America; Museum of Natural History; Xerxes Society.

Interests: Nature.

Lightner writes:
   "I should say a juvenile novel should not have a lot of long-winded philosophizing and not too much description. Kids like to have action, and to see a lot of dialogue. Also, I should say, no anti-heroes. There should be a sense of idealism. The hero is trying to accomplish some difficult and worthwhile mission; to get out of some predicament. He may have gotten into it from his own foolishness...but not because he's a completely rotten individual, as in many adult novels today. But mostly, I guess it should have action, preferably at the start, and building to a climax.

"I recently had some argument with my editor about this. She said my newest novel did not start fast enough, and I thought the end of the first chapter carried a punch, and that was enough. Well, eventually I wrote in a bomb in the first scene, which satisfied her, and I have since decided that she was right. I got a letter from a boy in Canada about *The Thursday Toads*, in which he said it was so much better than most books, because it began with great excitement--and kept on that way till the end. (God knows how I achieved all this!) Well, as soon as one says a novel (or play or what-not) should be thus and so, somebody comes along and breaks all the rules, and achieves a great effect. So one can't be too dogmatic about it. As far as pleasing editors (and selling) goes--juveniles are aimed at different age levels. I have mostly written for the older group (teens and subteens), because I don't want to be thinking about making it simple. But there is a demand right now for SF at the early-reader level. I've been unable to come up with anything, unfortunately. I write nature books for that level with no trouble. (See *The Space Ship Under the Apple Tree*, by Slobodkin, for a good job!)"

LIN YUTANG

Full Name: Yü-t'ang Lin.
  Born October 10, 1895, at Changchow, China. Son of
Chi-seng Lin (a minister) and Sun-meng Yang. Married
Tsui-feng Liao, July 9, 1919. Three children: Adet,
Anor, Hsiang-ju. Died March 26, 1976.

Education:
  B.A., St. John's College, 1916; M.A., Harvard University, 1920; Ph.D., University of Leipzig, 1923.

Career: Writer.
  Professor of English Philology, Peking National Uni-
versity, 1923-26; Professor of English and Dean of the
College of Arts, National Amoy University, China, 1926-
27; Secretary, Revolutionary Government of China Minis-
try of Foreign Affairs, 1927; Head of Arts and Letters
Division, UNESCO, Paris, 1948-49; Chancellor, Nanyang
University, Singapore, 1954-55; writer, 1931-DATE.

* * * * *

RICHARD R. LINGEMAN

Full Name: Richard Roberts Lingeman.
  Born January 2, 1931, at Crawfordsville, Indiana.
Son of Byron Newton Lingeman and Vera Spencer. Married
Anthea Nicholson (a graphic designer), April 3, 1965.

Education: B.A., Harverford College, 1953; studied
  law at Yale University.

Career: Editor.
  Co-founder and Executive Editor, *Monocle*, 1962-DATE;
free-lance author; public relations consultant to the
Peace Corps.

* * * * *

DAVID LIPPINCOTT

Full Name: David McCord Lippincott.
  Born June 17, 1925, at New York, New York. Son of
William Jackson Lippincott (a banker) and Dorothy Mc-
Cord. Married Joan Bentley, October 16, 1959. One
son, Christopher Bentley.

Education: B.A., Yale University, 1949.

Career: Advertising copywriter and writer.
  Copywriter, McCann-Erickson Inc. (an advertising
firm), New York, 1950-53; Television Head, 1953-58;
Vice-President and Associate Creative Director, 1958-
63; Senior Vice-President, 1963-69, 1969-70; Vice-
Chairman, Board of Directors, Erwin-Wasey, Ruthrauf
& Ryan, Los Angeles, 1967-68; novelist, composer-lyri-
cist, and television writer, 1950-DATE.

Agent: Wallace, Aitken & Sheil, 118 E. 61st St.,
  New York, NY 10021.

Member:
  American Society of Composers, Authors, and Publi-
shers; American Guild of Authors and Composers; The
Players, New York City.

Lippincott has written scripts for the television programs *Studio One* and *Captain Kangaroo*, and is the composer of 28 published songs, including the record album, "The Body in the Seine."

FREYA LITTLEDALE

Full Name: Freya Lota Littledale.
  Born at New York, New York. Daughter of David Milton
(a pianist). Married Harold Littledale (an editor and
author). One son, Glenn David.

Education: B.S., Ithaca College, 1951; studied at
  New York University, 1952.

Career: Writer and editor.
  English teacher, Willsboro, New York, public schools,
1952-53; Editor, *South Shore Record*, Woodmere, NY, 1953-
55; Associate Editor, Maco Magazine Corp., 1960-61;
Associate Editor, Rutledge Books and Ridge Press, 1961-
62; Juvenile Book Editor, Parents Magazine Press, 1962-
65; free-lance writer and editor, 1965-DATE.

Agent,: Curtis Brown Ltd., 60 E. 56th St., New York,
  NY 10022.

* * * * *

PENELOPE LIVELY

Full Name: Penelope Lively.
  Born March 17, 1933, at Cairo, Egypt. Married Jack
Lively (a university teacher), June 27, 1957. Two
children: Josephine, Adam.

Education: B.A., St. Anne's College, 1956.

Career: Free-lance author. Member: Society of Authors.

Agent: Murray Pollinger, 11 Long Acre, London WC2E
  9LH, England.

* * * * *

HAROLD LIVINGSTON

Full Name: Harold Livingston.
  Born September 4, 1924, at Haverhill, Massachusetts.
Son of Myron Livingston and Betty Segal. Married Lois
Leavitt, 1958. Three children: Myra, Leah, Eve.

Education: Attended Harvard University, 1951, and
  Brandeis University, 1951-53.

Career: Writer.
  Has worked as a communications supervisor for Trans
World Airlines in Cairo, a copywriter for an advertising
agency, a flight communications officer for Flying Tiger Airlines, a sportswriter for the *Boston Globe* and
the Associated Press; now a full-time writer.

Awards: Literary Fellowship, Houghton Mifflin Co.,
  1954. Agent: Sterling Lord, 75 E. 55th St., New
  York, NY 10022.

* * * * *

DAN LJOKA

Full Name: Daniel John Ljoka.
  Born August 16, 1935, at Philadelphia, Pennsylvania.
Son of Marian Ljoka (a longshoreman) and Marie Leeman.
Married Jane Ryan, April, 1958. Two children: Daniel
(born 1959), Linda (born 1961).

DAN LJOKA (cont.)

Career: President, Continental Land Corporation.

First Professional Sale: *Shelter*, Manor Books, 1973.

* * * * *

GEORGE LOCKE

Full Name: George Walter Locke.
   Born February 9, 1936, at London, England. Son of George Edward Locke and Marie Spacil. Married Rita Mary Winward, 1969. One son, Brian George Winward (born 1969).

Education: B.Pharm., Chelsea College of Science and Technology, 1958.

Career: Bookseller, publisher, journalist.
   Pharmacist, 1959-67; Sub-Editor, *Pharmaceutical Journal*, 1967-70; Editor, *Sailplane & Gliding*, 1970-72; Director, Ferret Fantasy (book dealer and publishing house), 1972-DATE.

First Professional Sale: "The Human Seed," in *Authentic Science Fiction*, October, 1957 (as G. W. Locke).

Agent: E. J. Carnell Literary Agency, 17 Burwash Rd., Plumstead, London SE18 7QY, England.

Member: Pharmaceutical Society of Great Britain.

Interests:
   "Gliding (inactive at present, have hopes of taking up again); research into early SF, fantasy, and weird fiction--now increasingly my business; collecting same, especially early interplanetary fiction."

Locke writes:
   "I spent a good many years in the '50s and early '60s writing SF, and began to sell more or less regularly by about 1963-65. This while doing various locum jobs in pharmacy, not liking it very much, and in fact only working when it didn't interfere too much with other things like gliding. By 1967 decided that I'd come to the end of the road where pharmacy was concerned--no interest. At that time I was in the middle of writing a novel (a previous novel, SF, had remained unsold). A job as Sub-Editor of the *Pharmaceutical Journal* came up, and I produced my finest piece of science fiction in response--my letter of application. It stunned the Editor of the journal, and I took the job, much against the advice of SF writer and close friend Arthur Sellings, who declared I wouldn't write any more fiction while working on the PJ. I scoffed--and didn't write any more fiction. And didn't finish the novel.
   "I worked for the PJ for three years, then took a job as Editor of *Sailplane and Gliding*, combining sport with my new vocation as a journalist. Should have been perfect, were it not for the thoroughly unprofessional attitudes of a (hopefully untypical) small British sporting organisation. Packed it in after two years, and took up full-time dealing in old SF and fantasy books. I'd been collecting the stuff since the '50s, and had been dealing part-time for several years. But the journalistic bug didn't die, and I kept it down by doing some specialty publishing for collectors of SF, fantasy, and mystery fiction.

"The publishing activity isn't too unsuccessful--overall, I haven't lost money, though it tends to get subsidised from time to time by the bookselling activity when the printer's bills come in. By the end of my second year on S&G, I felt the writing (fiction; hell, I was writing all the time) bug biting again, and took the opportunity afforded by the British Milford Conference to write a piece of SF. It was the first chapter of a novel, since completed and awaiting the kindly eye of a well-disposed editor. Achieved a major ambition at the end of 1973 by selling the *Pharmaceutical Journal*, for whom I still do some reporting, a short SF story. The PJ was a very staid professional organ, and the only time it would ever consider something in the least escapist would be the Christmas issue. I wrote the piece in longhand while watching television one Sunday evening, and took it into the PJ on the Monday morning. *They* typed it out for me, I revised it lightly (taking out one or two of the nastier cracks), and it duly appeared. So did the cheque. I intend to do the same this year, except that it will be a somewhat longer piece with a stronger plot, and I'll probably type it out for them."

* * * * *

RONALD LOCKLEY

Full Name: Ronald Mathias Lockley.
   Born November 8, 1903, at Cardiff, Wales. Son of Harry Lockley and Emily Mathias. Three children: Ann, Martin, Stephen.

Career: Author and naturalist, 1921-DATE.
   Lived on Skokholm, a remote Welsh island, 1927-39, establishing the first British bird observatory there in 1933; part-time duty with Naval Intelligence, 1940-41; Flax Field Officer, Ministry of Supply, Britain, 1941-46; Research Naturalist with Nature Conservancy, 1955-58; founder, West Wales Naturalists' Trust.

Agent: E. P. S. Lewin & Partners, 7 Chelsea Embankment, London SW3, England.

* * * * *

NORAH LOFTS

Full Name: Norah Lofts.
   Born August 27, 1904, in England. Daughter of Isaac Robinson and Ethel Garner. Married Geoffrey Lofts (deceased); married Robert Jorisch, 1949. One son, Geoffrey St. Edmund Clive Lofts.

Education: Teaching Diploma, Norwich Training College, 1925.

Career: Writer.
   English teacher, 1925-36; writer, 1936-DATE. Member: Family Planning Association. Agent: Curtis Brown Ltd., 60 E. 56th St., New York, NY 10022.

* * * * *

CHARLES R. LONG

Full Name: Charles Russell Long.
   Born June 25, 1904, at Paragould, Arkansas. Son of Charles Alvin Long and Alice Van Tassel.

Career: Morse Code Operator, Western Union, 1921-53.

FRANK BELKNAP LONG

Full Name: Frank Belknap Long.
  Born April 27, 1903, at New York, New York. Son of Frank Long (a surgeon dentist) and May Doty. Married Lyda Arco, August 9, 1959.

Education: Attended New York University.

Career: Writer.
  Associate Editor, *Satellite Science Fiction*, Feb.-May, 1959; Associate Editor, *Short Stories*, 1959-60; Associate Editor, *Mike Shayne Mystery Magazine*, until 1966; uncredited Associate Editor of *The Saint Mystery Magazine* and *Fantastic Universe* during the 1950s; free-lance author.

First Professional Sale: "The Desert Lich," in *Weird Tales*, November, 1924.

Member: Science Fiction Writers of America.

Interests:
  "Classical music, particularly Bach; summer vacations in New England, particularly the coastal regions; meeting new and interesting people; discussing literature, painting, sociology, even politics occasionally; bird watching and natural history in general; long walks in the country; fishing; week-end parties; quiet hours of reading; museums; art gallery openings; tragically grim, psychologically-insightful plays and movies (do not care for comedies). Hate TV and 'beautiful people' programs."

Long writes:
  "A direct maternal ancestor, Edward Doty, was the only non-Puritanic rebel on the *Mayflower*, a young lad who was indentured to an English family. He was the first man to fight a duel on the American continent, was put in the stocks, and had, I believe, about thirteen children. My paternal grandfather, a building contractor, erected the pedestal of the Statue of Liberty, and was superintendent of the Statue for a number of years. I still have an obituary cutting from the *New York Times*--"Liberty's Guardian Dead," etc. I'm of New England ancestry on my mother's side, English and Pennsylvanian Dutch on my father's.
  "I was H. P. Lovecraft's closest friend for a number of years--certainly one of his two or three closest friends. He was frequently a guest at our home, and I visited him several times in Providence. The correspondence I exchanged with him would fill several large volumes.
  "As for the current state of the supernatural tale in America, I agree that although the occult intrigues a vast number of people, the classic horror story is in a distinctly separate category. When a wave of interest in the occult sweeps the country to the extent that it has today, writers of supernatural horror naturally benefit. Not to be grateful would be the equivalent of looking a gift horse in the mouth. But though I'm a firm believer in extrasensory perception, and the possibility of paranormal occurrences of a very specialized nature, I place no credence in the occult as that term is commonly defined. To me the classic horror story has always been an important branch of literature, quite as important as science fiction. Critics in general make a great mistake, I've always felt, in drawing any kind of distinction between the best writing in both genres and mainstream writing. A horror story as magnificent as Henry James's "The Turn of the Screw" *is* mainstream writing, and so are the ghost stories of M. R. James, much of

"Lovecraft, and three dozen other horror-realm masterpieces I could mention. And that is true, also, of the mystery story at its very best, for the actual medium is of far less importance than the quality of the writing. In maturity, subtlety, atmospheric splendor, not even Poe, at his best, could have equalled or surpasssed the finest supernatural horror stories of today, in both America and England."

* * * * *

NORMAN LONGMATE

Full Name: Norman Richard Longmate.
  Born December 15, 1925, at Newbury, Berkshire, England. Son of Ernest Longmate (a photographer) and Margaret Rowden. Married Elizabeth Taylor (a teacher), August 8, 1953. One daughter, Jill.

Education: B.A., Worcester College, Oxford University, 1950; M.A., 1954.

Career: Radio executive.
  Feature Writer, *London Daily Mirror*, 1953-57; Administrator in Industrial Relations Dept., Electricity Council, London, 1957-63; Radio Producer, BBC, 1963-65; Administrator in Secretariat, 1965-DATE. Member: Association of Broadcasting Staff; Oxford Society; Society of Sussex Downsmen.

Agent: Bolt & Watson Ltd., Chandos House, Buckingham Gate, London SW1, England.

* * * * *

T. MORRIS LONGSTRETH

Full Name: Thomas Morris Longstreth.
  Born February 17, 1886, at Philadelphia, Pennsylvania. Son of Benjamin Taylor Longstreth and Frances Haldeman.
Education: B.A., Haverford College, 1908.

Career: Writer.
  Traveling tutor, 1908-12; teacher, De Lancey School, Philadelphia, 1912-13; teacher, Montgomery Country Day School, Wynnewood, PA, 1917; free-lance author, 1917-DATE. Member: Authors League; Phi Beta Kappa.

* * * * *

NOEL LOOMIS

Full Name: Noel Miller Loomis.
  Born April 3, 1905, at Wakita, Oklahoma. Son of LeRoy Parker Loomis and Florida Bess Miller. Married Dorothy Moore Green, 1945. Two children: James LeRoy, Mary Nell.

Education: Attended Clarendon College, 1921, and University of Oklahoma, 1930.

Career: Writer and instructor.
  Worked as a printer, editor, and newspaper writer all over the west; free-lance author, 1929-69; Instructor in England, San Diego State University, 1958-69; Director of Writers' Workshop, 1963-69; President, Hulburd Grove Improvement Association. Died Sept. 7, 1969.

Member: California Writers Guild; P.E.N.; American Historical Association; Westerners Club; Longhorn

NOEL LOOMIS (cont.)

Cowboy Club, Duesseldorf, Germany; American Academy of Political and Social Science; American Association of University Professors.

Awards:
  Spur Award, Best Western Novel, 1958, for *Short Cut to Red River*; Spur Award, Best Western Story, 1959, for "Grandfather Out of the Past."

* * * * *

BEMAN LORD

Full Name: Beman Lord.
  Born November 22, 1924, in Delaware County, New York. Son of Harold Beman Lord (a printer) and Eloisae Judd. Married Patricia Cummings (an editor), September 26, 1959. Two children: Edwin, Patricia Duffy.

Career: Writer and publisher's representative.
  Has been employed by Library Services Associates, Lord Associates, Lord Book Representatives, Inc.; presently with Charles Scribner's Sons; writer, 1958-DATE. Member: Library Public Relations Council; American Library Association.

* * * * *

ROBERT LORY

Full Name: Robert Edward Lory.
  Born December 29, 1936, at Troy, New York. Son of Edward Lory and Dorothy Doughty. Married Barbara Banner, June 9, 1968. Four children: Dominique Lynn (born 1958), Robert Edward Jr. (born 1961), Shana Erin (born 1972), Joshua Jared (born 1973).

Education: B.A., Harpur College, 1961; Diploma, Famous Writers Course, 1964; Diploma, Washington School of Art, 1973.

Career: Public relations advisor.
  Has been a guitar-playing folk-rock singer, free-lance industrial photographer, PR and advertising copywriter for an electric and gas utility company, sales promotion coordinator for a business supply firm, and manager of publications for Reynolds Metals Company; joined The Exxon Corporation in 1967, serving as Editor of *Esso Manhattan*, *Exxon Manhattan*, and *Esso Eastern Review*; Public Relations Advisor, Esso Eastern Inc., 1971-DATE.

Member: Science Fiction Writers of America.

Lory notes:
  "A series with common characters (or a common protagonist) allows you to really get to know the people about whom you're writing. From the non-writing but more business-like viewpoint, it gives your readers a chance to identify with your people over a period of several adventures. If the readers like your first couple of entries, you've got a loyal following--until you start boring them. But that, of course, is just as fatal to the non-series writer.
  "Liabilities? None--if you've done your planning right *before* the first book in the series hits the stands. Not necessarily plot-progression planning. More in the way of character-development planning. The protagonists of a series have got to be people the wri-

"ter, for whatever reason, *likes*. If he doesn't, it's tough to keep on writing about a bunch of dullards."

First Professional Sale: "Rundown," in *Worlds of If*, May, 1963.

* * * * *

RICHARD L. LOUGHLIN

Full Name: Richard Lawrence Loughlin.
  Born October 29, 1907, at Brooklyn, New York. Son of Richard Lawrence Loughlin and Annie Cannon. Married Laura Brennan, July 15, 1950. One daughter, Laurie Bernadette (born 1951).

Education:
  B.S., St. John's College, 1929; M.A., Columbia University, 1931; Ph.D., New York University, 1947.

Career: Professor of English.
  Teacher of English and speech in private and public high schools in New York City, 1929-60; Professor of English, Bronx Community College, 1960-73; now retired; co-Editor, *English Review*, 1962-66.

Member: Doctorate Association of New York Educators; Kappa Delta Pi; New York State English Council.

Interests: Swimming, golf, and bridge.

* * * * *

EDMUND G. LOVE

Full Name: Edmund George Love.
  Born February 14, 1912, at Flushing, Michigan. Son of Earl Dalzell Love (a merchant) and Muda Perry. Married Anna Virginia Wurts (a librarian), April 2, 1959. Two children: Shannon Gay, Nicholas Gregory.

Education: A.B., University of Michigan, 1936; M.A., 1940.

Career: Writer.
  Teacher, Board of Education, Flint, Michigan, 1935-42; Historian, U.S. War Department, Historical Division, 1946-49; free-lance writer, 1949-DATE. Member: Authors League; Dramatists Guild.

Agent: Sterling Lord, 75 E. 55th St., New York, NY 10022.

* * * * *

DELOS W. LOVELACE

Full Name: Delos Wheeler Lovelace.
  Born December 2, 1894, at Brainerd, Minnesota. Son of Mortimer Lovelace and Josephine Wheeler. Married Maud Palmer Hart (a writer), November 29, 1917. One daughter, Merian. Education: Attended University of Minnesota, 1916-17, Cambridge University, 1919, and Columbia University, 1921.

Career: Writer and reporter.
  Reporter, *Fargo Courier News*, 1913-14; Reporter, *Minneapolis Daily News*, 1914-15; Reporter and Night Editor, *Minneapolis Tribune*, 1915-17, 1919-20; Reporter, *New York Daily News*, 1920-31; Assistant City Editor, *New*

DELOS W. LOVELACE (cont.)

York Sun, 1928-50; Staff Writer, *New York World-Telegram and Sun*, 1950-52. Member: University Club, Claremont, CA. Died January 17, 1967.

Agent: Nannine Joseph, 200 W. 54th St., New York, NY 10019.

* * * * *

MARC LOVELL

Full Name: Mark McShane.
  Born November 28, 1930, at Sydney, Australia. Son of Mark McShane (a merchant) and Albereda Fowler. Married Rosemarie Armstrong, October 5, 1963. Four children: Rebecca, Marcus Aurelius, Damon, Todd. Education: Attended Technical College, Blackpool, England.

Career: Writer, 1960-DATE.

Agent: Paul R. Reynolds, 599 Fifth Avenue, New York, NY 10017.

* * * * *

ROBERT A. W. LOWNDES

Full Name: Robert Augustine Ward Lowndes.
  Born September 4, 1916, at Bridgeport, Connecticut. Son of Henry Irving Lowndes (in electronics) and Fanny Raymond Stevens. Married Dorothy Sedor Rogalin, August 14, 1948 (divorced, 1974). One stepson, Peter Michael Rogalin (born 1942).

Education: Attended Stamford Community College, 1936.

Career: Editor.
  Editor, *Future Science Fiction*, April, 1941-April, 1960; Editor, *Science Fiction Quarterly*, Winter, 1941/42-February, 1958; Editor, *Science Fiction Stories*, April, 1943-May, 1960; Editor, *Dynamic Science Fiction*, December, 1952-January, 1954 (all issues published); Editor, *The Magazine of Horror*, August, 1963-April, 1974 (all issues published); Editor, *Startling Mystery Stories*, Summer, 1966-March, 1971 (all issues published); Editor, *Famous Science Fiction*, Winter, 1967/67-Spring, 1969 (all issues published); Editor, *Weird Terror Tales*, Winter, 1969-Fall, 1970 (all issues published); Editor, *Bizarre Fantasy Tales*, Fall, 1970-March, 1971 (all issues published); Editor, Avalon Books science fiction line, 1956-58, 1958-68 (edited the entire series save for four books published in 1958); Associate Editor and Producer, *Sexology* and *Luz* magazines, 1971-DATE.

First Professional Sale:
  "A Green Cloud Came," in *Comet Stories*, January, 1941 ("To Edgar Allan Poe," a poem, appeared in *Fantastic Novels*, September, 1940; "The Outpost at Altark" which appeared in *Super Science Stories*, November, 1940, was actually written by Donald A. Wollheim, and revised by Lowndes).

Agent: Scott Meredith, 580 Fifth Avenue, New York, NY 10036.

Honors: Guest of Honor, Lunacon, 1969, and Boskone, 1973.

Member: Science Fiction Writers of America.

Interests:
  "Sherlockiana--investitured member of the Baker Street Irregulars, Scandalous Bohemians of New Jersey, and Praed Street Irregulars; love classical music and records; have acted in community theater."

Lowndes writes:
  "My editorials for the Health Knowledge Publications quite naturally dealt with older fantasy and science fiction, since these were mainly revivals. However, it is true that when I read science fiction and fantasy these days (not a lot), I generally prefer either to re-read the old stories or something new by an old-timer, such as Heinlein or Jim Blish. The most important element, however, is that fantasy and science fiction have become fringe interests for me; such time as I have for reading I generally prefer to expend in different fields.
  "It's true that I do not find the present magazines particularly interesting, aside from the departments. But that is strictly a subjective matter, and it hasn't prevented me from seeing that some of the new material is very good. Most of it is, at best, forgettable--but that's true of every other kind of fiction produced in quantity too. However, I do not have the time (and/or energy) to read *any* of the magazines at the present time, and have let my subscriptions lapse."

* * * * *

EDWARD W. LUDWIG

Full Name: Edward William Ludwig.
  Born July 10, 1920, at Tracy, California. Son of Edward May Ludwig (a bartender) and Ethel Adelia Harris (a truck driver). Married Cris Marjorie Story (divorced 1972). Two children: Adrienne Gail (born 1954); Felicia Harriet (born 1957).

Education: B.A., University of the Pacific, 1942; graduate study, 1946-47.

Career: Book store manager.
  Sailor, gunnery officer, ship captain, U.S. Navy, 1942-46; English teacher and journalist, California, 1946-47; free-lance writer and musician, 1947-50; law clerk and Assistant County Clerk, San Joaquin County, California, 1950-65; Manager, General Book Dept., Spartan Bookstore, San Jose State University, 1965-DATE; Editor and Publisher, Polaris Press, 1973-DATE.

First Professional Sale: "Inheritance," in *Imagination*, October, 1950.

Member: Science Fiction Writers of America; National Fantasy Fan Federation.

Interests: Organic gardening, archeology, music (jazz and dixieland), foreign literature, publishing, minority groups, cigarettes, and booze.

* * * * *

I. LUKODYANOV

Full Name: Isai Borisovich Lukodianov.
  Born June 8, 1913, at Baku, in what is now the Azerbaijan Republic of the USSR. Son of Boris Lukodianov (a bookkeeper) and Vera Rozengauza (a stenographer). Married Olga Lukodianova, 1953. One son, Vladimir.

I. LUKODYANOV (cont.)

Education: Attended Central Institute of Leningrad, 1932-36, obtaining a degree as a mechanical engineer.

Career: Engineer.
Designer of oil-field equipment; Chief Engineer of Project, The Design Institute of "Gipromorneft," 1947-DATE; writer, 1960-DATE.

First Professional Sale: "Fifty Feet Through a Shot," in IUny Tekhnik magazine, 1960.

Agent: VAAP, Bol'shaia Bronnaia 6a, K-104, 103104 Moskva, USSR.

Honors and Awards:
USSR government award for participating in World War II; Second National Prize, International Science Fiction Competition.

Member: Science Fiction Section, Azerbaijan Writers Union; various scientific research societies.

Interests:
Engineering history, sailing, science fiction. "I am preparing a series of science fiction stories on the topic 'It should have been done earlier' (for instance, the electric motor could have been invented before the steam engine, etc.)."

* * * * *

SAM J. LUNDWALL

Full Name: Sam Jerrie Lundwall.
Born February 24, 1941, at Stockholm, Sweden. Son of Thore Lundwall (a master mechanic) and Sissi Kühn. Married Ingrid Christine Olofsdotter, June 16, 1972.

Education: E.E., University of Stockholm, 1967.

Career: Author and publisher.
Electronics engineer, Stockholm, 1956-60; professional photographer, University of Stockholm, 1967-67; professional photographer, Christer Christian Photographic School, Fox Amphoux, France, 1968-69; Editor of Science Fiction and Occult Books, Askild & Kaernekull Foerlag AB, Stockholm, 1970-73; President, Delta Foerlags AB (publishers), Bromma, Sweden, 1973-DATE; Editor-in-Chief, Jules Verne-Magasinet, 1972-DATE; Editor, Science Fiction-Serien, 1973-DATE; has also directed television films, made a short animated film based on his song "Waltz with Karin," has recorded his own songs for Philips and Knaeppupp recording companies, has appeared on radio, television, and film as a singer and artist.

First Professional Sale: A radio play to the Swedish Broadcasting Company in 1952.

Agent: Gösta Dahl & Son AB, Aladdinsvägen 14, S-161 38, Bromma, Sweden.

Awards:
"Waltz with Karin" was named Sweden's Best Short Film by the Swedish Film Institute, 1967; Alvar Award, from the Futura Science Fiction Organization, 1971, as Scandinavia's leading science fiction author.

Member: Science Fiction Writers of America; Ted Carnell Society; Par Bricole.

Interests: Model railroads.

Lundwall writes:
"I do, as a matter of fact, write all fiction in English these days, afterwards translating to Swedish for the Swedish editions of the novels. This means difficulties, of course, since English is not my native language, and there are certainly many works that I would not dare to attempt to write in English....One can never hope to master a foreign language as well as one's own. I do find, however, that science fiction generally is easier to write in English than in Swedish. This is somewhat hard to explain, but the English phrasing is at times more straight and to the point than Swedish, making it easier to describe complicated events. (I find this when I translate back to Swedish, and often have lots of trouble doing so.) I am the first to admit that my English is far from perfect, but I find it a good and trustworthy tool, the use of which does not present me with any grave problems.
"Originally, of course, I started writing in English because I could not make a living publishing my novels in Sweden alone. Now, I write in English mainly because of the many readers I can hope to get with a work written in a truly international language. As far as I know, I'm the only Swedish author writing in a foreign language--and also the only science fiction writer here. This means a certain feeling of loneliness. I do visit conventions and personal friends in the field outside of Scandinavia regularly, though."

* * * * *

RICHARD A. LUPOFF

Full Name: Richard Allen Lupoff.
Born February 21, 1935, at Brooklyn, New York. Son of Sol J. Lupoff (an accountant) and Sylvia Feldman. Married Patricia Loring, August 27, 1958. Three children: Kenneth Bruce (born 1961), Katherine Eve (born 1964), Thomas Daniel (born 1968).

Education: B.A., University of Miami (FL), 1956.

Career: Writer.
Computer programmer, Sperry Rand, 1958-63; writer, speech writer, film script writer, and director, IBM, 1963-70; Editor, Canaveral Press, 1963-65; West Coast Editor, Crawdaddy, 1970-71; West Coast Editor, Changes, 1971-72; Contributing Editor, Organ, 1972; free-lance author; Book Editor, Algol, 1963-DATE.

First Professional Sale: "What's Left of the Science Fiction Scene," in The Writer, 1952.

Agent: Henry Morrison, 58 W. 10th St., New York NY 10010.

Awards: Hugo Award, Best Amateur Magazine, 1962 (1963), Xero.

Member: Science Fiction Writers of America.

Interests: "Music--I listen well and play badly."

Lupoff writes:
"Regarding the influence of comics--particularly comic books--on science fiction, I think there has been a great deal of influence, but it has almost all been the other way around. Both the newspaper adventure comic à la Dick Tracy, Flash Gordon, Buck Rogers, and the comic book, were offspring of the pulps. (The

RICHARD A. LUPOFF (cont.)

"family sitcom newspaper comic is another matter.)
    "At any rate, many editors, writer, and artists moved from the pulps, particularly the science fiction pulps, to the comic books. Even off the top of my head, let me give you a few names: Julius Schwartz, Mort Weisinger, Otto Binder, Jack Binder, Horace Gold, Virgil Finlay, Edmond Hamilton, Jack Williamson, Alfred Bester, Henry Kuttner.
    "Most of the science fiction in the comics is a watered-down version of what appeared earlier in the 'legitimate' SF media.
    "In recent years, a few people have moved over the other way. I think of Gerry Conway and Dennie O'Neil. But the significant flow of talent and ideas has been almost entirely *from* science fiction *to* the comics."

* * * * *

JOHN LYMINGTON

Full Name: John Newton Chance.
    Born 1911, at Streatham Hill, England. Married Shirley Savill. Three sons.

Education: Attended Streatham Hill College, England.

Career: Full-time writer most of his life.

Lymington comments: "In my own name, I have been writing thrillers and novels for forty years, published by Victor Gollancz, Macdonald, Robert Hale, and a lot of unpronounceable Continental verlaggers, etc. I think John Lymington's SF is classy!"

* * * * *

ANDREW LYTLE

Full Name: Andrew Nelson Lytle.
    Born December 26, 1902, at Murfreesboro, Tennessee. Son of Robert Logan Lytle (a farmer and lumberman) and Lillie Belle Nelson. Married Edna Langdon Barker, June 20, 1938 (deceased). Three children: Pamela, Katherine Anne, Lillie Langdon.

Education: Graduate, Sewanee Military Academy; B.A., Vanderbilt University, 1925; student, Yale University School of Drama, 1927-29.

Career: Professor of English.
    Lecturer in American History, Southwestern College, 1936; Lecturer in History, and Managing Editor of the *Sewanee Review*, University of the South, 1942-43; Lecturer in Creative Writing, 1961-68; Professor of English, 1968-DATE; Lecturer, University of Florida, 1948-61.

Awards:
    Guggenheim Fellowship for Creative Work in Fiction, 1940-41, 1941-42, 1960-61; Kenyon Review Fellowship for Fiction, 1956; National Foundation on Arts and Letters Grant, 1966-67; Litt.D., Kenyon College, 1965; Litt.D., University of Florida, 1970.

Member:
    Association of Literary Magazines of America; South Atlantic Modern Language Association.

Lytle is a well-known lecturer on the college circuit.

JOHN D. MacDONALD

Full Name: John Dann MacDonald.
    Born July 24, 1916, at Sharon, Pennsylvania. Married Dorothy M. Prentiss, 1937. One son, John Prentiss.

Education: B.S., Syracuse University, 1938; M.B.A., Harvard University, 1939.

Career: Writer, 1946-DATE. Served in the Army from 1940-46, becoming a Lieutenant Colonel.

Agent: Littauer & Wilkinson, 500 Fifth Avenue, New York, NY 10036.

Awards: Ben Franklin Award, Best American Short Story, 1955; Gran Prix de Littérature Policière, 1964.

Member: Mystery Writers of America (President, 1962).

* * * * *

GWENDOLYN MacEWEN

Full Name: Gwendolyn MacEwen.
    Born September 1, 1941, at Toronto, Ontario, Canada. Daughter of Alick James MacEwen and Elsie Mitchell.

Career: Librarian.
    Part-time Assistant Librarian, Children's Public Library, Toronto, 1960-DATE; writer, 1960-DATE. Awards: Governor General's Award, 1970, for *The Shadow-Maker*.

* * * * *

GEDDES MacGREGOR

Full Name: John Geddes MacGregor.
    Born November 13, 1909, at Glasgow, Scotland. Son of Thomas MacGregor and Blanche Geddes. Married Elizabeth Sutherland McAllister, August 14, 1941. Two children: Marie Geddes (born 1944), Martin Gregor Geddes (Born 1946). Naturalized U.S. citizen, 1957.

Education:
    B.D., Universities of Oxford and Edinburgh, 1939; LL.B., University of Edinburgh, 1943; D.Phil., Oxford University, 1945.

Career: Professor of Philosophy.
    Senior Assistant to the Dean of the Chapel Royal in Scotland, at St. Giles' Cathedral, Edinburgh, 1939-41; served in the British Civil Defence, World War II; Assistant to the Professor of Logic and Metaphysics, University of Edinburgh, 1947-49; First Holder, Rufus Jones Chair of Philosophy and Religion, Bryn Mawr College, 1949-60; Dean, Graduate School of Religion, University of Southern California, 1960-66; Distinguished Professor of Philosophy, 1966-DATE; sometime lecturer and visiting fellow and professor at numerous colleges and universities; Canon Theologian, St. Paul's Cathedral, Los Angeles, 1968-74; writer and critic.

First Professional Sale: *Aesthetic Experience in Religion*, Macmillan, 1947.

Honors and Awards:
    Doctor és Lettres, University of Paris, 1951; D.D., Oxford University, 1959; Gold Medal, Commonwealth Club, for Best Non-Fiction Work by a California Author in 1963, for *The Hemlock and The Cross*.

GEDDES MacGREGOR (cont.)

Member:
Royal Society of Literature (Fellow); American Philosophical Association; Phi Kappa Phi; American-Scottish Foundation; Royal Commonwealth Society; English-Speaking Union; Royal Zoological Society of Scotland; National Trust for Scotland; Speculative Society; Dialectic Society of Edinburgh; Union Society, Oxford; Oxford Society.

Interests: Manual labor, walking, music, travel.

MacGregor notes: "I have travelled extensively in Europe; also in the Middle East and the Orient. My only speculative novel was written while I was the first holder of the Rufus Jones Chair at Bryn Mawr College in Pennsylvania, the appointment that brought me to the U.S. Much as I like women, after ten years there with 1,000 of them, I felt that was enough in the life of any one mere man."

* * * * *

R. W. MACKELWORTH

Full Name: Ronald Walter Mackélworth.
Born April 7, 1930, at London, England. Son of William James Mackelworth (a company director) and Lillian Andrews. Married Sheila Elizabeth Scotland, June 1, 1957. Three children: David William (born 1960), Siona Elizabeth (born 1963), Mhairi Elizabeth (born 1970).

Education: Attended Raynes Park Grammar School, 1941-48.

Career: Sales manager.
Intelligence officer in the British Army, 1948-50; with Thomas Cook & Sons (a travel agency), 1950; with Norwich Union Assurance, 1950-53; Sales Manager, Legal and General Assurance Society, 1953-DATE.

First Professional Sale: "The Statue," in *New Worlds*, January, 1963.

Agent: E. J. Carnell Literary Agency, 17 Burwash Road, Plumstead, London SE18 7QY, England.

Member: Institute of Professional Salesmen (Founder and Fellow).

Interests: Golf, bridge, reading, music, research into management and sales development.

Mackelworth writes:
"I started writing short stories in 1962, but wish I had started sooner, since I've always loved description. Eventually, I began when I found I had some time free from the necessity of earning a living from insurance. I wrote at six in the morning, or twelve at night when I was short of time. Writing is something of a vice with me, and I do not think I will ever be able to stop.
"I chose SF because it has the greatest potential for the imaginative plot and freedom of style. It can combine poetry with the pace of a thriller, and it has the whole future in which to expand. Indeed, its possibilites are infinite. At the present time, it is breaking free from its old problems, and discarding the 'cardboard' characterisations and scientific 'mumbo jumbo' which spoiled the earlier stories.

"We even write about women as well as space heroes now!
"I admire authors such as Ballard and Wyndham, as well as the younger authors. There are a whole list of others from Bradley to Pohl I have read with relish, and I think the numbers indicate the strength of SF.
"My one hate in modern SF is the attempt, in a few short stories, to anticipate the pornography of the future--they will have enough to contend with!
"My main professional interest at the present time outside writing is in new forms of cooperation--management by objectives, etc. I have a strong belief in 'humanising' working and social relationships. My writing objectives are to entertain and improve my style, to popularise potential life styles and new ideas in science, and to help people face future changes."

* * * * *

COMPTON MACKENZIE

Full Name: Edward Montague Compton Mackenzie.
Born January 17, 1883, in West Hartlepool County, Durham, England. Son of Edward Compton Mackenzie (an actor, as Edward Compton) and Virginia Frances Bateman. Married Faith Stone, November 30, 1905 (died 1960); married Christina MacSween, January 23, 1962 (died 1963); married Lilian MacSween, March 4, 1965.

Education: B.A., Magdalen College, Oxford University.

Career: Writer and editor.
Settled on the island of Barra in the Outer Hebrides, Scotland, and helped found the Scottish Nationalist Party; Rector, Glasgow University, 1913-34; Literary Critic, *Daily Mail*, London, 1931-35; was reputedly the first disc jockey on the BBC; President, Dickens Fellowship, 1939-46; Founder and Editor of *Gramophone*, 1923-62; Writer, 1907-72. Died November 30, 1972.

Awards:
Officer of the Order of the British Empire, 1919; knighted in 1952; LL.D., University of Glasgow; LL.D., St. Francis Xavier University, Canada; Legion of Honor, France; Knight Commander of the Phoenix, Greece.

Member:
Croquet Association; Songwriters Guild; Poetry Society; Greek League of Democracy; Dickens Fellowship; Royal Stuart Society; Royal Society of Literature (Fellow); Royal Scottish Academician; Savile Club; Pratt's Club; Authors Club; New Club; Scottish Arts; Siamese Cat Club of Great Britain.

* * * * *

KATHERINE MacLEAN

Full Name: Katherine Anne MacLean.
Born January 22, 1925, at Glen Ridge, New Jersey. Daughter of Gordon MacLean (a chemical engineer) and Ruth Crawford. Married Charles Dye, 1951 (divorced 1952, died 1955); married David Mason, February 15, 1956 (divorced 1962, died 1974). One son, Christopher Dennis Mason (born 1957).

Education: B.A., Barnard College, 1950.

Career: Writer and lecturer.
Has been a nurse's aide, store detective, pollster, econ graph-analyst, antibiotic lab researcher, EKG and

KATHERINE MacLEAN (cont.)

laboratory quality control technician, food analyst; alternates lab work with writing and lecturing.

First Professional Sale: "Adding Molasses to the Table," an article to a small business magazine in 1946.

Agent: Virginia Kidd, Box 278, Milford, PA 18337.

Awards: Nebula Award, Best Novella, 1971 (1972), for "The Missing Man."

Member:
Science Fiction Writers of America; Science Fiction Research Association; Teilhard de Chardin Center, Canada; Society for Research in General Systems; World Future Society; Mensa; Audobon Society; American Association for the Advancement of Science.

Interests:
Science, history, ESP, carpentry, medicine, health, encounter groups, the real future, ecology, psychotherapy, dianetics, and attempts to figure out a way for the Earth to survive.

MacLean writes:
"I try to read everything. Eyestrain. This century is increasingly exciting, dangerous, and involved in threats to the entire planet, like a very wild early science fiction plot. Perhaps I should write realistic contemporary novels to try to deal with it, but the respectable literary realism usually deals totally with characters, rather than the big background picture. To me, science fiction makes alternative histories the hero of the story, and the great events are characterized. I've always liked it that way."

* * * * *

ANGUS MacLEOD

Full Name: Angus MacLeod.
Born September 13, 1906, at Wester Ross, Scotland. Son of Colin MacLeod and Katherine MacRae. Married Odwen Peat, July 26, 1947.

Education: Attended Edinburgh College of Art, 1924-29; attended University of Aberdeen, 1935-37.

Career: Writer.
Was an art teacher at Kendal Grammar School, and then at Hove County School for Boys, England, before becoming a full-time writer.

First Professional Sale: Short stories in 1935.

Member: Society of Authors; P.E.N.

* * * * *

ANGUS MacVICAR

Full Name: Angus MacVicar.
Born October 28, 1908, at Duror, Argyll, Scotland. Son of Angus John MacVicar (a clergyman) and Marsali Mackenzie. Married Jean Smith McKerral, June 24, 1936. One son, Angus John.

Education: M.A., Glasgow University, 1930.

Career; Author.
Reporter for a newspaper in Campbeltown, Scotland, 1931-33; free-lance author, 1933-DATE.

First Professional Sale: *The Purple Rock*, Stanley Paul & Co., 1933.

Agent: A. M. Heath & Co., 40-42 William IV Street, London WC2N 4DD, England.

Honors: Made honorary sheriff, Argyll County, 1967.

Member: Society of Authors; Dunauerty Golf Club; Dunauerty Players Drama Club.

Interests: Golf, amateur drama.

"I am mad keen on history, religion and golf, not necessarily in that order! My science fiction has always had a moral--human love is the answer to most problems. I live and work in the country, which, in my opinion, affords perspective."

* * * * *

SALVADOR MADARIAGA

Full Name: Salvador de Madariaga y Rojo.
Born July 23, 1886, at La Coruna, Spain. Son of José de Madariaga (a colonel) and Ascension Rojo. Married Constance Helen Margaret Archibald, October 10, 1912 (died 1970); married Emilie Szekely Rauman, November 18, 1970. Two daughters: Nieves, Isabel.

Education: Attended various schools in Paris, 1906-11.

Career: Writer.
Employed by Railway Company of Northern Spain, 1911-16, simultaneously writing political articles for a newspaper under a pseudonym; spent 1916-21 in London, working as a journalist and critic; worked for the Secretariat of the League of Nations, 1921-27; first occupant of the King Alfonso XIII Chair of Spanish Studies at Oxford University, 1927-30; Spanish Ambassador to the United States, 1931, and to France, 1932-34; Spain's permanent delegate to the League of Nations, 1931-36; served as Spain's Minister of Education, 1934, then as Minister of Justice; declined to take sides in the Spanish Civil War, and returned to Oxford in 1936.

Member:
Spanish Academy of Letters; Spanish Academy of Moral and Political Sciences; French Academy of Moral and Political Sciences; Academy of History of Caracas; Reform Club, London; Ateneo, Madrid.

Awards and Honors:
M.A., Oxford University, 1928; Gold Medalist, Yale University; Fellow, Exeter College, University of Pavia; Honorary Doctor of the Universities of Arequipa, Lima, Poitiers, Liege, Lille, Oxford, Princeton; Ere Nouvelle Prize; Knight Grand Cross of the Order of the Republic of Spain; White Lion, Czechoslovakia; Order of Merit, Chile; Order of Jade in Gold, China; Order of the White Rose, Finland; Grand Cross of Legion d'Honneur, France; Aztec Eagle, Mexico; Order of the Sun, Peru; Europa Prize, Hans Deutsch Foundation, Bern University, 1963; Hanseatic Goethe Prize, 1967.

Madariaga currently resides in Switzerland.

LARRY MADDOCK

Full Name: Jack Owen Jardine.
Born October 10, 1931, at Eaton Rapids, Michigan. Son of John W. and Blanche M. Jardine. Married Julie Anne Harihor, 1958 (divorced, 1967); married Marilyn Jardine, January 9, 1968. One Daughter, Sabra.

Education: Attended college for two years.

Career: Writer.
Has been a newspaper reporter, radio announcer, men's magazine editor, TV troubleshoot technician, salesman, and Creative Director of two Arizona radio stations.

First Professional Sale: "The Disembodied Man," in *Imagination*, April, 1954.

* * * * *

RACHEL MADDUX

Full Name: Rachel Maddux.
Born December 15, 1912, at Wichita, Kansas. Daughter of Harry A. Maddux and Malisa Morison. Married King Baker, 1941.

Education: B.A., University of Kansas, 1934.

Career: Writer. Awards: Honorable mention, Friends of American Writers.

Agent: A. Watkins, 77 Park Avenue, New York, NY 10016.

* * * * *

ROBERT MAGIDOFF

Full Name: Robert Magidoff.
Born December 26, 1905, at Kiev, Russia. Son of Charles and Jennie Magidoff. Married Nila Shevko, October 14, 1937.

Education: B.A., University of Wisconsin, 1932; Ph.D., University of Michigan, 1963.

Career: Professor of Russian Literature.
Foreign correspondent for the Associated Press and NBC, 1935-49; free-lance writer and lecturer, 1949-58; Lecturer in Russian, University of Michigan, 1958-61; Professor of Russian Literature, New York University, 1961-70; conducted full-length course on Russian literature over CBS Network, 1964-65. Died February, 1970.

Agent: Harold Matson Co., 22 E. 40th St., New York, NY 10016.

* * * * *

CHARLES ERIC MAINE

Full Name: David McIlwain.
Born January 21, 1921, at Liverpool, Lancashire, England. Son of David McIlwain (an engineer) and Caroline Jones. Married Joan Lilian Hardy, 1947 (divorced 1960); married Clare Mary Came, 1961. Four daughters, two sons.

Career: Editorial consultant, journalist, author.
Editor of various monthly and weekly publications in electronics, computers, mining, and metallurgy; industrial journalist; contributor to British newspapers and periodicals; author of SF and crime novels, radio plays, television plays, and motion picture screenplays. Journalist since 1948.

First Professional Sale: "Spaceways," a radio play to the BBC, 1952 (later novelized by Maine).

Agent: Scott Meredith Literary Agency, 580 Fifth Avenue, New York, NY 10036.

Member: Crime Writers Association; National Union of Journalists.

Interests: Physics, photography, music.

McIlwain writes science fiction under the name Charles Eric Maine, crime novels as Richard Rayner, and general fiction as Robert Wade. His factual journalism appears under his real name, David McIlwain. He commented:

"Although I started as a SF fan along with Clarke, Temple, Carnell, and the rest in the late thirties, I seldom read SF at all now. It is too remote from reality. I still write it, though, when I can find time and a subject that amuses me. All I ask for is a faint ring of truth, whatever that might be.
"Very few of my books have dealt with disaster on a global scale. Personally, I like to explore the economic and political effects on society of technology 'gone wrong.' I always seem to reach the same conclusion, that whatever happens the top dogs will try to remain top dogs, and if they fail then the underdogs who take over will generally be just as brutal and ruthless as the top dogs they ousted. The technology is not important; it merely provides the disaster environment.
"As to why other British SF writers may be disaster-oriented, your guess is as good as mine. Certainly, Britain is not a pessimistic place to live in, although we seem to be sliding at a quickening pace into a Swedish style welfare state, which I personally find depressing. It may be that this increasing drive to social security in a small country impels our writers (or some of them) to devise situations of insecurity on a planetary basis.
"Also, people are actually questioning the validity and usefulness of today's science and technology--space flight, genetic engineering, and so on--so that it is not difficult for a writer to show how a simple scientific error or misjudgment could reduce the orderly (?) society we know to a shambles. At present. It won't be long before the computers, the mind-benders, and the genetic engineers will have solved all our social problems for all time--and that's one imminent disaster that is not science fiction."

* * * * *

BARRY N. MALZBERG

Full Name: Barry Norman Malzberg.
Born July 24, 1939, at New York, New York. Married Joyce Z. Malzberg, May 31, 1964. Two children: Stephanie Jill (born 1966), Erika Cornell (born 1970).

Education: B.A., Syracuse University, 1960; Schubert Playwriting Fellow, Syracuse University, 1964-65.

BARRY N. MALZBERG (cont.)

Career: Novelist.
  Managing Editor, *Escapade*, 1968; Associate Editor,
Amazing Stories, September, 1968; Editor, November,
1968-January, 1969; Associate Editor, *Fantastic Stories*, October, 1968; Editor, December, 1968-February,
1969; free-lance author, 1967-DATE.

First Professional Sale: "We're Coming Through
  the Window," in *Galaxy*, August, 1967 (as K. M. O'Donnell).

Awards: John W. Campbell Memorial Award for Best
  Science Fiction Novel of the Year, 1972 (1973), for
  Beyond Apollo.

Malzberg writes:
  "I consider my collected works to be essentially
optimistic, as they express a view of the range of
human consciousness and response which exceeds that
to be suggested in most science fiction. I have also
written a great deal of comic work, and resent being
stereotyped as a pessimistic writer. I also resent
being thought of as an SF writer."

* * * * *

FRANK MANCHEL

Full Name: Frank Manchel.
  Born July 22, 1935, at Detroit, Michigan. Son of
Lee Manchel and Olga Fluhr. Married Sheila Wachtel,
1958. Two sons: Steven Lloyd, Gary Howard.

Education: A.B., Ohio State University, 1957; M.A.,
  Hunter College, 1960; Ed.D., Columbia University,
  1966.

Career: Professor of Communications & Theatre.
  High school instructor in English, New Rochelle,
New York, 1958-64; Asst. Professor of English, Southern Connecticut State College, 1964-67; Associate
Professor of English and Speech, University of Vermont, 1967-71; Professor of Communications and Theatre, 1971-DATE.

Awards: Simmonds Foundation Grant for research into
  English, 1970.

Member: National Council of Teachers of English;
  American Federation of Film Societies; Society for
  Cinema Studies; American Film Institute; British
  Film Institute.

* * * * *

ALEXANDRA MANNERS

Full Name: Anne Rundle.
  Born at Berwick-on-Tweed, England. Daughter of
George Manners Lamb (a soldier) and Annie Sanderson.
Married Edwin Charles Rundle (a civil servant), Oct.
1, 1949. Three children: Anne, James, Iain.

Education: Attended schools in England.

Career: Writer.
  Civil servant, British Civil Service, Berwick-on-
Tweed and Newcastle-on-Tyne, 1942-50; full-time writer,
1967-DATE.

Agent: John McLaughlin, 31 Newington Green, London
  N16 9PU, England.

Awards:
  Netta Muskett Award of Romantic Novelists Association,
1967; Romantic Novelists Association major awards, 1970
and 1971; named Daughter of Mark Twain, 1974, in recognition of her work as a romantic novelist.

* * * * *

MARYA MANNES

Full Name: Marya Mannes.
  Born November 14, 1904, at New York, New York. Daughter of David Mannes and Clara Damrosch. Married Christopher Clarkson (divorced). One son, David J. Blow.

Career: Writer and broadcaster.
  Was an editor of several women's magazines in the
1930s and 1940s; staff writer, *Reporter*, 1952-63; free-
lance author and lecturer.

Awards:
  L.H.D., Hood College, 1960; George Polk Memorial A-
ward for magazine reporting, 1958; Achievement Award,
Federation of Jewish Women's Organizations, 1961;
Award of Honor, Theta Sigma Phi, 1962; American Jewish
Congress National Women's Division Award, 1969; L.H.D.,
Williams College, 1971.

* * * * *

ETHEL MANNIN

Full Name: Ethel Edith Mannin.
  Born October 11, 1900, at London, England. Daughter
of Robert Mannin (a post office sorter) and Edith Gray.
Married John A. Porteous, 1919 (deceased); married
Reginald Reynolds (an author), 1937 (deceased). One
daughter, Jean.

Career: Writer.
  Stenographer for an advertising firm, 1915; copywriter, 1916-19; full-time author, 1919-DATE.

* * * * *

WARWICK MANNON

Full Name: Kenneth Hopkins.
  Born December 7, 1914, at Bournemouth, Hampshire,
England. Son of Reginald Marshall Hopkins and Elsa
Adams. Married Elizabeth Coward, 1939. One son, Ed-
mund Marshall.

Career: Writer and teacher.
  Professional writer, 1945-DATE; Associate Professor
of English, Southern Illinois University, 1964-DATE.
Member: Royal Society of Literature (Fellow).

* * * * *

D. KEITH MANO

Full Name: D. Keith Mano.
  Born February 12, 1942, at New York, New York. Son
of William Franz Mano (a manufacturer) and Marion Elizabeth Minor. Married Jo Margaret McArthur, August 3,
1964. Two sons: Roderick Keith (born 1965); Christopher Carey (born 1970).

D. KEITH MANO (cont.)

Education:
  B.A., Columbia College, 1963; Kellett Fellow, Clare College, Cambridge University, 1963-64; Woodrow Wilson Fellow, Columbia College, 1964.

Career: Writer and businessman.
  Actor in various off-Broadway productions, 1964-65; toured with the National Shakespeare Company; Vice-President, X-Pando Corporation (a cement company), 1965-DATE; writer, 1968-DATE.

First Professional Sale: *Bishop's Progress*, Houghton Mifflin Company, 1968.

Agent: Harold Matson Company, 22 E. 40th St., New York, NY 10016.

Awards: International Feetball Champion, 1974.

Interests: Cats, poker.

Mano notes: "I don't properly call myself a science fiction writer, though my reluctance is not the product of snobbishness. I am rather a writer of transcendences, and occasionally these have to do with time and an imaginative restructuring of the known world."

* * * * *

ROGER MANSFIELD

Full Name: Roger Ernest Mansfield.
  Born November 27, 1939, at Cambridge, England. Son of Ernest Walter Mansfield and Ruby May Welch. Married his wife, 1962. Three children: Kim, Kerry, Conrad.

Education: Attended City of Worcester Training College, 1958-60.

Career: English teacher.
  Teacher of English for the inner London Education Authority, 1960-DATE; free-lance editor.

First Professional Sale: *Every Man Will Shout*, Oxford University Press, 1964 (an anthology).

* * * * *

ROGER MANVELL

Full Name: Arnold Roger Manvell.
  Born October 10, 1909, at Leicester, England. Son of Arnold Edward William Manvell (a Canon of the Church of England) and Mary Theresa Manvell. Married Louise Adams, February 8, 1956. Two stepchildren: Anthony Adams, Susan Adams.

Education: B.A., University of London, 1930; Ph.D., 1936.

Career: Author and lecturer.
  Lecturer in Literature and Drama, University of Bristol, 1938-40; with the Films Division, Ministry of Information, 1940-45; Lecturer and Research Officer, British Film Institute, 1945-47; Director, British Film Academy, 1947-59; currently Visiting Fellow, University of Sussex, and Head of the Department of Film History, London Film School; also has served as

Editor of several film journals.

First Professional Sale: *Film*, Penguin Books, 1944.

Agent: John & Charlotte Wolfers, 3 Regent Square, Bloomsbury, London, WC1, England.

Awards:
  Commander of the Order of Merit of the Italian Republic, for services to the film, 1970; Order of Merit, First Class, German Federal Republic, for services in research and authorship of books on the Nazi period, 1971; D.Litt., University of Sussex, 1971; D.F.A., New England College, 1972; D.Litt., University of Leicester, 1974.

Member: Society of Authors; Authors Club; Radiowriters Association; American Screen Directors Guild; Consultant to the Society of Film and Television Arts, and Editor of their Journal since 1948.

Manvell's scary novel of the supernatural, *The Dreamers*, deals with native witchcraft. He had these comments about the book:

"The African witchcraft is, of course, wholly invented. I wrote the whole novel in 21 days as a kind of exercise, and partly with a view to it becoming a film. (It was, indeed, bought by the then Hecht-Hill-Lancaster Company, but they broke up shortly afterwards, and the film was never made, though I prepared a treatment for them, and the script was completed by Ray Bradbury.) I place no real-life credence in the supernatural myself; indeed, I am a rationalist, and Associate Editor of the British rationalist journal, *The New Humanist*. But as long as there are human beings who accept the supernatural, human beings will remain affected by it psychologically and irrationally."

* * * * *

WILLIAM MARDEN

Full Name: William Edward Marden.
  Born March 24, 1947, at Palatka, Florida. Son of Roy Foster Marden (a prison counselor) and Elena Polverino).

Education: A.A., St. Johns River Junior College, 1967; B.S., University of Florida, 1969.

Career: Reporter.
  Reporter for various Florida newspapers, 1969-72; with the *Florida Times-Union*, 1972-DATE. Member: Authors League of America; Sigma Delta Chi.

* * * * *

ROBERT E. MARGROFF

Full Name: Robert Ervien Margroff.
  Born March 5, 1930, in Fayette County, Iowa. Son of Ervie Margroff (a farmer) and Lulu Timmons.

Career: Farmer and writer.
  Has been a linotype operator for various Iowa newspapers; still lives on the farm owned by his parents at the time of his birth.

First Professional Sale: "Monster Tracks," in *Worlds of If*, October, 1964.

ROBERT E. MARGROFF (cont.)

Agent: Jay Garon, 415 Central Park West, 17D, New York, NY 10025.

Awards: "My first story was 2nd prize winner in the N3F contest."

Member: Science Fiction Writers of America.

Interests:
"I've always loved fishing and hunting and assorted outdoor activities. The older I get, the more I appreciate the positive sides of country living, and the better I cope with the negative.
"I've always felt more handicapped with my rural background than blessed. In a city or even a large town there might have been opportunities for typewriter employment that might have helped. In a city or large town there might have been educational opportunities. At age 44, I look back and wonder. But then there's the other side--with a different background would I have been dissatisfied and unhappy enough to have had to write?"

* * * * *

LEO MARGULIES

Full Name: Leo Margulies.
Born 1900, at Brooklyn, New York. Son of Jacob Margulies and Esther Goldberg. Married Cylvia Kleinman, December, 1937.

Education: Attended Columbia University.

Career: Editor.
Editorial Director, Thrilling Publications (some 50 magazine titles, including *Captain Future*, *Thrilling Wonder Stories*, *Startling Stories*, *Fantastic Stories*), circa 1932-circa 1952; Publisher, *Fantastic Universe*, June/July, 1953-August, 1956; Editorial Director, May, 1954-August, 1956; Publisher, *Mike Shayne Mystery Magazine*, September, 1956-1975; Publisher of various associated titles, including *Satellite*, October, 1956-May, 1959 (all issues published); free-lance editor. Died in Los Angeles December 26, 1975.

* * * * *

DAVID MARINER

Full Name: David MacLeod Smith.
Born July 15, 1920, at Strathpeffer, Ross & Cromarty, Scotland. Son of A. E. D. Smith (an army and excise officer) and Margaret MacLeod. Married Jean Armour Macinnes (a teacher), July 11, 1952.

Education: Attended St. Andrews University, 1946-48, Ealing Technical College, 1951, and Manchester School of Technology, 1954.

Career: Writer.
Served in the Royal Navy, 1937-46, becoming a Chief Petty Officer, and participating in numerous commando raids on the French coast; free-lance journalist, 1947-64; has also been a salesman, export executive, sales manager, and marketing adviser; novelist, 1964-DATE. Member: Institute of Packaging (founding member, 1955).

JOHN MARSH

Full Name: John Marsh.
Born August 8, 1907, at Halifax, Yorkshire, England. Son of Thomas William Marsh (a caterer) and Lilian Woodward. Married Irene Andrew, June 1, 1938.

Education: Attended Giggleswick School, 1922-24.

Career: Public relations officer.
Press and Public Relations Officer, King George's Fund for Sailors (maritime charitable trust), 1949-DATE; free-lance author, 1932-DATE.

Agent: J. F. Gibson's Literary Agent, 17 Southampton Place, London WC1, England.

Member: P.E.N. (fellow); Society of Authors; Crime Writers Association; Press Club, London.

* * * * *

BRUCE MARSHALL

Full Name: Bruce Marshall.
Born June 24, 1899, at Edinburgh, Scotland. Son of Claude Niven Marshall and Annie Margaret Bruce. Married Mary Pearson Clark, 1928. One daughter, Sheila.

Education: B.Com., and M.A., Edinburgh University.

Career: Writer.
Scottish chartered accountant in Paris, 1926-40; writer, 1931-DATE; lecturer in Britain, Germany, Italy, and the United States. Member: Institute of Chartered Accountants; Bath Club, London.

Agent: Peter Janson-Smith, 2 Caxton St., London SW1, England.

Awards: Wlodimierz Petrzak Prize, Warsaw, 1959.

* * * * *

EDISON MARSHALL

Full Name: Edison Telsa Marshall.
Born August 29, 1894, at Rensselaer, Indiana. Son of George Edward Marshall and Lille Bartoo. Married Agnes Sharp Flythe, January 4, 1920. Two children: Edison Telsa Jr., Nancy Silence.

Education: Attended University of Oregon, 1913-16.

Career: Writer.
Magazine writer, 1916-17; free-lance author, 1919-67; hunter and explorer in East Africa, Alaska, Siam, China, Japan, Nepal, and other countries. Died Oct. 29, 1967.

Awards:
O. Henry Memorial Award, 1921, for "The Heart of Little Shikara"; M.A., University of Oregon, 1941; Gold Cross, Order of Merit, University of Miami.

Member:
Georgia Authors Association (Trustee); Delta Tau Delta; Sigma Upsilon; Attic Club, Augusta.

Agent: Paul R. Reynolds, 599 Fifth Avenue, New York, NY 10017.

DAVID S. MARTIN

Full Name: David Stephen Martin.
  Born October 24, 1913, at Gravesend, Kent, England.
Son of Edward Martin and Nellie Slingsby. Married
June Horden, October 4, 1947. One son, Raymond Martin
(born 1950).

Education: Attended Gravesend County School, 1924-
  29.

Career: Self-employed news agent, confectionery,
  tobacconist.

First Professional Sale: *No Lack of Space*, Arthur H. Stockwell, 1967.

Interests: Fishing, cage-birds, cats, football
  [soccer], reading science fiction.

  "I wrote my original book of short stories because
I thought I could do better than some I had read,
and to give possible pleasure to those with the same
story tastes as myself.
  "On leaving school, I emigrated to Australia, where
I spent ten years in varied occupations, a lot of them
in the outback.
  "I returned to England in 1939 when my mother was
dying (she lived a further 18 months), and walked
into the war years, serving in the British Army. After discharge, I tried one or two occupations, including self-employed milk retailer on a country milk
round, but felt the urge for the varied army life
again; I spent another twenty years at this, including
twelve years as a parachutist.
  "At the age of 60, I am still fit and active, but
time marches on. I hope to see many more science fiction wonders come true, as I have quite a few of them
already. Cook and bottle-washer on the first Mars
expedition would suit me fine! If they couldn't offer
me anything better, of course."

* * * * *

JOHN S. MARTIN

Full Name: John Stuart Martin.
  Born November 9, 1900, at Winnetka, Illinois. Son
of William Hoffman Martin (a grain broker) and Emily
Busch. Married his third wife, Mary Mitchell Gilbert.
Four children: David, Jill, Barry (daughter), Susan.

Education: A.B., Princeton University, 1923.

Career: Writer.
  Member of editorial staff, *Time*, 1922-41; free-lance
writer, 1941-DATE. Member: Princeton Club.

Awards: Oscar Award, 1944, for narration of "The
  Fighting Lady."

* * * * *

VIRGILIO MARTINI

Full Name: Virgilio Martini.
  Born May 3, 1903, at Fiesole, Firenze, Italy. Son
of Luigi Martini (a mason) and Annunziata Manzani.
Married Tina Volpi (a schoolteacher), July 16, 1955.
One daughter, Sandra. Education: Attended techni-
cal school in Firenze (Florence).

Career: Writer and publisher.
  Has been a hod carrier, cowboy, teacher of Italian
and French, translator, bank clerk, advertising writer,
caricaturist, playwright assistant, salesman for a ver-
mouth company, reporter, book publisher; writer, 1922-
DATE; Founder, owner, and manager, *Voce di Jesolo*, Lido
di Jesolo, Italy, 1965-DATE.

* * * * *

DAVID MASON

Full Name: David Mason.
  Married Katherine MacLean, February 15, 1956 (divorced 1962). One son, Christopher Dennis (born 1957).

Career: Writer.

Mason's response to the CSFA questionnaire was dated
May 13, 1974: "There must be some advantage to being
a mystery name in the sword and sorcery field. I am
in transit between agents. Can't name her. At any
rate, I am temporarily ill, and unable to pull myself
together to do my own typing. I'm shuttling in and
out of the Hospital, and living at times at 2425 Market Street, San Francisco. This letter is being typed
from there [by Katherine MacLean, his former wife].
On reading this back, it sounds too cold, but I'm too
sleepy to say exactly what I mean. Might as well mail
it." Mason never recovered from his illness, dying
six weeks later, on June 28, 1974.

* * * * *

DOUGLAS R. MASON

Full Name: Douglas Rankine Mason.
  Born September 26, 1918, at Hawarden, Flintshire,
England. Son of Russell Mason (an engineer) and Bertha
Greenwood. Married Mary Norma Eveline Cooper (a social
worker), May 26, 1944. Four children: Keith Rankine
(born 1947), Norma Patricia (born 1950), John Rodney
(born 1957), Elaine Rosemary (born 1961).

Education: B.A., Manchester University, 1947; Teachers Diploma, 1948.

Career: Teacher.
  With the British Army, 1939-46; Headmaster, Somerville
Junior School, 1954-66; Headmaster, St. Georges Primary
School, Wirral County Borough, England, 1966-DATE; free-
lance writer, 1964-DATE.

First Professional Sale: "Two's Company," in *New
  Writings in SF 1* (an anthology edited by John Carnell), Dobson, 1964 (as John Rankine).

Agent: E. J. Carnell Literary Agency, 17 Burwash Rd.,
  Plumstead, London SE18 7QY, England.

Awards: "Virtue must be its own reward."

Member: Society of Authors; National Association of
  Headmasters.

Interests: "No time as of now for anything but survival."

A number of Mason's books contain the series character
Dag Fletcher, concerning whom Mason writes: "On the

DOUGLAS R. MASON (cont.)

"Fletcher Series. I was a C. S. Forester fan, and conceived Fletcher as a galactic Hornblower. There are five novels, and from the point of view of Fletcher's progress through the organisation, the order is: 1) *The Ring of Garamas*, 2) *Interstellar Two-Five*, 3) *The Plantos Illusion*, 4) *The Bromius Phenomenon*, 5) *One Is One*.

"He also figures in a number of short stories in various editions of *New Writings in SF*. Series writing is harder in my view, and I haven't added to the saga for some years. But I have always had in mind that sometime there will be a 'last mission' for Dag Fletcher!"

* * * * *

DAVID I. MASSON

Full Name: David Irvine Masson.
    Born 1915, at Edinburgh, Scotland. Education: Attended Oxford University. Masson is married and has children.

Career: Rare book librarian in Leeds, England.

First Professional Sale: "Traveller's Rest," in *New Worlds*, September, 1965.

* * * * *

RICHARD MATHESON

Full Name: Richard Burton Matheson.
    Born February 20, 1926, at Allendale, New Jersey. Son of Bertolf Matheson and Fanny Mathiesen. Married Ruth Ann Woodson, July 1, 1952. Four children: Richard, Alison, Christian, Bettina (adopted).

Education: Bachelor of Journalism, University of Missouri, 1949.

Career: Writer.
    "Since 1955, I have been primarily a television and screen writer, although I have attempted to produce some short stories and novels at the same time."

First Professional Sale: "Born of Man and Woman," in *The Magazine of Fantasy and Science Fiction*, Summer, 1950.

Awards and Honors:
    Guest of Honor, 16th World Science Fiction Convention (Solacon), Los Angeles, 1958; Hugo Award, Best Motion Picture, 1957 (1958), "The Incredible Shrinking Man"; World Fantasy Award, Best Novel, 1975 (1976), *Bid Time Return*. Member: Writers Guild of America, West.

* * * * *

RICHARD MATHEWS

Full Name: Richard Barrett Mathews.
    Born November 16, 1944, at Washington, D.C. Son of James Thomas Mathews (in public relations) and Martha Anne Moss (a furniture salesperson). Married Julienne Helen Empric, August 19, 1975.

Education: B.A., University of Florida, 1966; Ph.D.,

University of Virginia, 1973; also studied at University of Heidelberg, 1968-69.

Career: Professor of Literature.
    Associate Professor of Literature, and Poet-in-Residence, Eckerd College, St. Petersburg, Florida, 1970-DATE; Editor, *Florida Quarterly*, 1966-67; Founder, Editor, Publisher, and Printer, Konglomerati Press, Gulfport, Florida, 1971-DATE; poet and critic.

First Professional Sale: "O Do You Know the Muffin Man," in *Lyric* magazine, 1967.

Awards and Honors:
    Academy of American Poets Prize, University of Virginia, 1968, for *Pear Honey and Other Poems*; Rotary International Foreign Study Fellowship; Honorary Woodrow Wilson Fellow; NDEA Fellow; First Visiting Research Fellow, William Morris Centre at Kemscott House, London.

Member:
    Modern Language Association; COSMEP (founder of COSMEP South); International Poetry Society; Phi Beta Kappa; William Morris Society.

Interests: Printing, gardening, reading.

Mathews notes: "My poetry has appeared widely in magazines and anthologies, mostly from small presses. I look upon myself as an experimental poet and craftsman. I taught myself the techniques of letterpress printing."

* * * * *

ARTHUR S. MATTES

Full Name: Arthur S. Mattes [no middle name].
    Born July 11, 1901, at Creamery, Pennsylvania. Son of A. B. Mattes and Kate H. Scholl. Married Edna Irene Corson, July 1, 1930.

Career: Telegraph operator.
    Commercial wireless telegraph operator, 1926-66; now retired. Ham radio operator since 1947, with the call letters W5JE.

* * * * *

ROBIN MAUGHAM

Full Name: Robert Cecil Romer Maugham.
    Born May 17, 1916, at London, England. Son of Frederic Herbert Maugham, First Viscount Maugham (a judge and Lord Chancellor of England) and Helen Mary Romer. Education: Attended Eton and Trinity Hall, Cambridge.

Career: Barrister and writer.
    Maugham was trained as a barrister, and took up writing in 1943 while hospitalized with war injuries; when his health made it impossible for him to resume his law practice, he became a full-time writer in 1945; succeeded his father as second Viscount Maugham of Hartfield in 1958, and took his seat in the House of Lords, 1960; free-lance writer and lecturer. Maugham is a nephew of W. Somerset Maugham.

Agent: Julian Bach, Jr., 3 E. 48th St., New York, NY 10017.

Member: Garrick Club, London.

W. SOMERSET MAUGHAM

Full Name: William Somerset Maugham.
Born January 25, 1874, at Paris, France. Son of Robert Ormond Maugham (a solicitor to the British Embassy) and Edith Mary Snell. Married Syrie Barnardo Wellcome, 1915 (divorced, 1927; died, 1955). One daughter, Liza, now Lady Glendevon.

Education: Attended the University of Heidelberg.

Career: Writer.
After completing his M.R.C.S. at St. Thomas Hospital (medical degree), he left for Spain to write full time (1897-1965), and lived in Spain, London, and Paris. Died 1965.

Awards:
D.Litt., Oxford University; D.Litt., University of Toulousse; Fellow, Library of Congress; Commander, Legion of Honour; Companion of Honour, 1954; Honorary Senator of Heidelberg University, 1961. Member: Garrick Club.

* * * * *

ANDRÉ MAUROIS

Full Name: André Maurois [original name: Émile Salomon Wilhelm Herzog; legally changed 1947]. Born July 26, 1885, at Elbeuf, France. Son of Ernest Herzog (a textile manufacturer) and Alice-Hélène Levy. Married Jeanne-Marie Wande de Szymkievicz, October 30, 1912 (died 1924); married Simone de Caillavet, Sept. 6, 1926. Three children: Michelle, Gérald, Oliver; one stepdaughter, Françoise (died 1930).

Education: Prix d'Honneur de Philosophie, Lycée Corneille, 1902; Diplôme, l'Université de Caen, Licence és Philosophie, 1902.

Career: Writer and lecturer.
Industrial manager in family textile factory, 1904-14, 1919-26; made a lecture tour in the U.S., 1927-32; elected to French Academy, 1938; writer, 1918-67. Died 1967.

Awards:
Honorary doctorates from Edinburgh University, 1928; Princeton University, 1933; Oxford University, 1934; University of Saint Andrews, 1934; University of Louisiana, and others; Grand Officer of the Legion of Honor, 1937; Knight of the Order of the British Empire, 1938; Commandeur des Arts et des Lettres; Commandeur du Mérite Sportif; Prix des Ambassadeurs.

Member: Association France-États-Unis; Société des Gens de Lettres; Comité de Lecture de la Comédie-Française; Portuguese Academy; Brazilian Academy.

* * * * *

NICHOLAS MAX

Full Name: Bernard Asbell.
Born May 8, 1923, at Brooklyn, New York. Son of Samuel Asbell and Minnie Zevin. Married Mildred Sacarny, January 2, 1944 (divorced 1971); married Marjorie Baldwin, June 11, 1971. Four children: Paul, Lawrence, Jonathan, Jody.

Education: Attended Univ. of Connecticut, 1943-44.

Career: Writer.
Reporter for a Virginia newspaper, 1945-47; public relations agent in Chicago, 1947-55; Managing Editor, *Chicago*, 1955-56; Lecturer in Nonfiction Writing, University of Chicago, 1956-60; Lecturer in Nonfiction Writing at Breadloaf Writers Conference, Middlebury College, 1960-61; Lecturer in Journalism, University of Bridgeport, 1961-63; full-time writer, 1963-DATE; consultant to Educational Facilities Laboratories, 1963 & 1970, to the Ford Foundation, 1963 & 1968-69, to the Secretary of Health, Education & Welfare, 1965-68, to the Carnegie Corporation and IBM; Justice of the Peace, Wilton, Conn., 1966-67.

Awards:
Educational Writers Association First Prize, 1956, for magazine coverage of education; citation, 1966; National Education Association School Bell Award, 1965; Second Place Award from National Council for the Advancement of Educational Writing, 1968, for best educational writing in magazines. Member: Society of Magazine Writers; Coffee House, New York.

* * * * *

WILLIAM MAYNE

Full Name: William James Carter Mayne.
Born March 16, 1928, at Kingston-upon-Hull, Yorkshire, England. Son of William Mayne and Dorothy Fea.

Career: Writer, 1953-DATE. Awards: Carnegie Medal, 1957, for *A Grass Rope*.

Agent: David Higham Associates, 3 Lower John Street, London WlR 3PE, England.

* * * * *

BRUCE McALLISTER

Full Name: Bruce Hugh McAllister.
Born October 17, 1946, at Baltimore, Maryland. Son of James Addams McAllister (a professor of physics and electronics) and Bernice Lyons (a professor of social sciences). Married Caroline Reid (a photographer), September 5, 1970.

Education: B.A., Claremont Men's College, 1969; M.F.A., University of California, Irvine, 1971.

Career: Professor of English.
Has been a sports department rewriter, United Press International in New York; an advertising consultant for Three's Company, Newport Beach, Calif.; a film-guide, learning-program, and sale-product information writer for Doubleday Multimedia, Santa Ana, Calif.; Instructor in English, Long Beach City College, 1971-73; Instructor in English, California State University, Fullerton, 1973-74; Visiting Instructor of English, University of Redlands, 1971-74; Assistant Professor of English and Director of the Writing Program, 1974-DATE; Overseas Editor, *Cave*, 1971-72; Contributing Editor, *Edge*, 1972; Editor, *SF Directions*, 1972; Editor, *Dictics*, 1973-74; Associate Editor, *West Coast Poetry Review* and West Coast Poetry Press, 1972-DATE; Managing Editor, *Year's Best SF* (edited by Aldiss & Harrison), 1973-DATE.

First Professional Sale: "The Faces Outside," in *Worlds of If*, July, 1963.

BRUCE McALLISTER (Cont.)

Honors: Fellow in Fiction, Squaw Valley Community of
Writers, 1973; Scholar in Poetry, Bread Loaf Writers
Conference, 1972.

Member:
Science Fiction Writers of America; International
Society for the Study of Symbols; Coordinating Council
of Literary Magazines; Committee of Small Magazine
Editors and Publishers.

Interests: Languages, marine sciences, anthropology, archaeology, astronomy, the plastic arts, film
and TV writing.

* * * * *

ANNE McCAFFREY

Full Name: Anne Inez McCaffrey.
Born April 1, 1926, at Cambridge, Massachusetts.
Daughter of George Herbert McCaffrey (a city administration expert) and Anne Dorothy McElroy (a real estate agent). Married H. Wright Johnson, January 14,
1950 (divorced, 1970). Three children: Alec Anthony
(born 1952), Todd (born 1956), Georgeanne (born 1959).

Education: B.A., Radcliffe College, 1947.

Career: Writer.
Worked as a copywriter and layout artist for Liberty
Music Shops, New York, 1948-50; copywriter, Helena
Rubinstein, New York, 1950-52; summer stock with Lam-
bertville Music Circus, 1949; studied voice and drama
for nine years, in the U.S. and Germany; directed o-
pera and operetta in Wilmington, Delaware; staged and
directed the American Premier of Carl Orff's "Ludus
de Nato Infante Mirificus," 1963, Delaware; free-lance
author, 1954-DATE.

First Professional Sale: "Freedom of the Race,"
in Science Fiction +, October, 1953.

Agent: Virginia Kidd, Box 278, Milford, PA 18337.

Awards:
Nebula Award, Best Novella, 1968 (1969), "Dragon
Rider"; Hugo Award, Best Novella, 1967 (1968), "Weyr
Search."

Member:
Science Fiction Writers of America (Secretary-Trea-
surer, 1968-70); P.E.N.; Mystery Writers of America;
Authors Guild.

Interests: Singing, opera directing, riding and
horse care.

McCaffrey is best known for her Dragon series, concerning which she writes:

"The true genesis of the Dragon series was a conversation I had with an underground film director, a
young friend of Ed Emshwiller's, Dick Adams. We'd
seen his excellent film on the tribulations of American teachers of English in a Polish university summer
course. Dick mentioned that he wanted to do a film
on the 'aloneness' of man. I suggested that that had
been done to death, but had he ever considered filming
those times when man/woman/child are united in a common emotion?

"This must have been at the back of my mind when I
started casting about my brains for a story idea. That's
why the dragons are telepathic: their riders are never
alone. Further, the dragon never criticizes: he adores
his rider no matter what he does or is. This is the
facet of the dragon stories which, I feel, has captured
the attention of readers. And so much of modern literature is keyed to the statement of aloneness or sharing:
the great togetherness urge.
"My idea, then, of the dragons is scarcely original:
the application is.
"There are two more Pern novels in work: one the
third of the main theme, White Dragon, in which I will
attempt to answer some of the questions left burning
in the background around the Threads. The other is a
juvenile, set in the Hold culture of Pern, using the
same background as Dragonquest--historically speaking.
"It's pure blind luck to hit a subject that draws
attention: absolutely difficult to sustain that attention in a sequel, and really begging problems to go
for Broke Third. We'll see, but patience, good readers,
patience! The impossible takes a little time."

* * * * *

PHILIP McCUTCHAN

Full Name: Philip Donald McCutchan.
Born October 13, 1920, at Cambridge, Cambridgeshire,
England. Son of Donald Robert McCutchan (a master mariner, trained in sail on the old Cape Horners) and Margaret Frances Gardner. Married Elizabeth May Ryan,
June 30, 1951. Two children: James Donald Shaw (born
1957), Rosemary Elizabeth Deno (born 1961).

Education: Attended Royal Military College, Sandhurst, 1939 (resigned to go to sea).

Career: Writer.
Lieutenant, Royal Navy, 1939-46; Assistant Purser,
Orient Steam Navigation Company, 1946-49; Assistant
Master, various preparatory schools, 1952-54; full-
time writer, 1954-DATE.

First Professional Sale: "Cats on the Files," in
London Opinion, 1951.

Member: Crime Writers Association (Chairman, 1965-66);
Authors Guild.

Interests:
"Naval and military affairs, chiefly prior to 1946;
motoring; brewing beer. My work now is not really
classifiable as SF or fantasy. I write three books
per year, for Hodder & Stoughton and Arthur Barker.
One is an adventure-thriller series featuring Det. Ch.
Supt. Simon Shard of the Special Branch; one is set in
the Royal Navy of the 1890s, also a series, featuring
Lt. St. Vincent Halfhyde, R.N.; the third is published
under the pseudonym Duncan MacNeil, and features James
Ogilvie of the 114th Highlanders, a Scots regiment on
the old NW Frontier of India in the 1890s."

* * * * *

DAVID McDANIEL

Full Name: David Edward McDaniel.
Born June 16, 1939, at Toledo, Ohio. Son of Calvin
Dale McDaniel (a teacher) and Margaret Allis. Married
Joyce Potter (a computer programmer), December 21, 1963.

DAVID McDANIEL (Cont.)

Education: A.A., Pasadena City College, 1960; B.S., San Diego State College, 1963; graduate study at University of California, Los Angeles, 1963.

Career: Writer.
Classical and pop disc jockey and TV actor and director, station KEBS (FM radio and television), San Diego, 1961-63; free-lance writer and still and motion picture photographer. Died October 31, 1977.

Member:
Baker Street Irregulars; Los Angeles Science Fantasy Society; Spectator Amateur Press Society; Fellowship of the Ring (founder).

* * * * *

BARRY McGHAN

Full Name: Barry Robert McGhan.
Born November 30, 1939, at Flint, Michigan. Son of Lawrence Oliver McGhan (a high school teacher) and Lois Ellen Resseguie (a secretary). Married Barbara Alice Durell, June 23, 1962. Two children: Meredith Ellen (born 1967), Pegeen Allissa (born 1969).

Education: B.A., Michigan State University, 1961; M.S., Syracuse University, 1964.

Career: High school teacher.
Secondary school mathematics teacher, Flint Public Schools, 1961-DATE.

First Professional Sale: *Teaching Tomorrow*, Pflaum/Standard, 1972.

Member:
National Education Association and its affiliates; American Federation of Teachers and affiliates; American Civil Liberties Union; American Forestry Association.

Interests: Photography, collecting and reading science fiction, working on my doctoral dissertation in educational sociology.

McGhan writes:
"To one who is both an academic and an SF fan--and the latter first--the recent growth of academic interest in SF seems to be a largely unmixed blessing. What could be more gratifying than to be able to add the respectability that academic interest brings to the other values one has always found in science fiction? While academia may or may not enhance the special kind of creativity found in SF , it can certainly examine that creativity, and provide economic and professional opportunities for both writers and academics. Especially important to this examination is the development of reference materials which can aid research--a task which is never-ending since old materials can always be improved, revised, and expanded."

* * * * *

TOM McGOWEN

Full Name: Thomas McGowen.
Born May 6, 1927, at Evanston, Illinois. Son of William Robert McGowen (a salesman) and Helene Nelson. Married Loretta Swok. Four children: Alan, Gayle, Maureen, Kathleen.

Education: Studied at Roosevelt University, 1947-48, and American Academy of Art, 1948-49.

Career: Advertising manager.
Production Manager, Sidney Clayton & Associates (advertising), Chicago, 1949-53; Advertising Manager, Justrite Manufacturing Co., 1953-54; Sales Promotion Director, National Safety Council, Chicago, 1954-59; Creative Director, Hensley Co. (advertising), 1959-DATE.

Member: Artists Guild of Chicago; Die Schlachtenbummler (group of military history buffs).

* * * * *

GEORGESS McHARGUE

Full Name: Georgess McHargue.
Born at Norwalk, Connecticut. Daughter of W. R. McHargue (in advertising) and Georgess Boomhower.

Education: B.A., Radcliffe College, 1963.

Career: Writer.
Staff member, Golden Press, 1963-65; Associate Editor, Doubleday & Co., 1965-68; Editor, 1968-70; free-lance author, 1970-DATE. Member: American Civil Liberties Union; Wilderness Society; Phi Beta Kappa; Lexington Democratic Club.

Agent: Paul R. Reynolds, 599 Fifth Avenue, New York, NY 10017.

* * * * *

GRAHAM McINNES

Full Name: Graham Campbell McInnes.
Born February 18, 1912, at London, England. Son of James Campbell McInnes (a concert singer) and Angela Mackail. Married Joan Burke. Two sons, one daughter.

Education: B.A., University of Melbourne, 1933; M.A., 1940.

Career: Diplomat.
Emigrated from Melbourne to Canada in 1934, spent a year studying fine arts in Europe, and became Art Editor of *Saturday Night*, 1935-40; Lecturer in Fine Arts, University of Toronto Extension, 1938-41; Senior Producer of Industrial and Art Films and Coordinator of Graphic Projects, National Film Board of Canada, 1942-48; with the Canadian Department of External Affairs since 1948, serving as a diplomat in New Delhi, India, Wellington, New Zealand, Head of Commonwealth Division in Ottawa, Minister in London, high commissioner in Jamaica, and Canada's Minister and Delegate to the United Nations.

* * * * *

J. T. McINTOSH

Full Name: James Murdoch Macgregor.
Born February 14, 1925, at Paisley, Renfrewshire, Scotland. Son of Murdoch Macgregor (a civil servant) and Marion Dracup. Married Margaret Murray, July 28, 1960.

Education: Attended Robert Gordon's College, Aberdeen, 1936-41; M.A., University of Aberdeen, 1947.

J. T. McINTOSH (Cont.)

Career: Writer.
  Has been a musician, teacher, photographer, free-lance journalist; Sub-Editor of several Aberdeen journals; free-lance author, 1954-DATE.

First Professional Sale: "The Curfew Tolls," in *Astounding*, December, 1950.

Agent: Lurton Blassingame, 60 E. 42nd St., New York, NY 10017.

McIntosh writes:
  "It is disappointing that editors and publishers continue to exclude more humanistic works by labelling them 'not science fiction.' In theory, SF should be the freest of all fields, in that in SF anything is possible. But if an author who has set his story in a science fiction framework becomes particularly interested in the characters, and works the story out in terms of human relationships rather than pseudo-science, he is liable to find the story unpublishable.
  "I have run several times up against this barrier. While we all agree that there is no point in writing stories in which SF gimmicks are merely stuck onto a story which doesn't need them, I find it sad that it's so often not possible (if the book is to be published, that is) to leave out the trappings of SF in concentrating on the people, the story, the solution, the moral. It's even sadder to have to record that several times when a story has been rejected as 'not SF,' I've been able, merely by sticking in a few paragraphs of pseudo-scientific gobbledegook, to turn the story miraculously into SF, and sell it."

* * * * *

RICHARD McKENNA

Full Name: Richard Milton McKenna.
  Born May 9, 1913, at Mountain Home, Idaho. Son of Milton Lewis McKenna and Lucy Ertz. Married Eve Mae Grice (a librarian), January 28, 1956.

Education: B.A., University of North Carolina, 1956.

Career: Writer.
  With the U.S. Navy, 1931-53, retiring as a chief machinist's mate; free-lance writer, 1956-64. Died November 1, 1964.

Awards:
  Harper Prize Novel of 1963, $10,000 for *The Sand Pebbles*; Nebula Award, Best Short Story, 1966 (1967), for "The Secret Place" (posthumously published).

* * * * *

STEPHEN McKENNA

Full Name: Stephen McKenna.
  Born February 27, 1888, at Breckenham, Kent, England. Son of Leopold McKenna and Ellen Gethen.

Education: B.A., Christ Church, Oxford, 1909; M.A., 1913.

Career: Writer.
  Director of a private liability company, London, 1910-14; temporary staff member, Westminster School,

London, 1914-15; full-time writer, 1915-67; served in British War Trade Intelligence Department, 1915-18; member of Balfour Mission to U.S., 1917; served as Secretary of Enemy Exports Committee of Ministry of Economic Warfare, 1939-40. Died September 26, 1967.

Agent: A. M. Heath, 35 Dover St., London, W1X 4EB, England.

* * * * *

PATRICIA A. McKILLIP

Full Name: Patricia Anne McKillip.
  Born February 29, 1948, at Salem, Oregon. Daughter of Wayne T. McKillip and Helen Roth.

Education: B.A., San Jose State University, 1971; M.A., 1973.

Career: Writer, 1973-DATE. Award: World Fantasy Award, Best Novel, 1973/74 (1975), *The Forgotten Beasts of Eld*.

* * * * *

DEAN McLAUGHLIN

Full Name: Dean Benjamin McLaughlin, Jr.
  Born July 22, 1931, at Ann Arbor, Michigan. Son of Dean Benjamin McLaughlin and Laura Hill.

Education: B.A., University of Michigan, 1953.

Career: Writer. Member: Science Fiction Writers of America.

First Professional Sale: "For Those Who Follow After," in *Astounding*, July, 1951.

* * * * *

RAYMOND T. McNALLY

Full Name: Raymond T. McNally.
  Born May 15, 1931, at Cleveland, Ohio. Son of Joseph Michael McNally (a meat cutter) and Marie Kinkoff. Married Rita Keane (a teacher), June 10, 1957. Four children: Michael, Catherine, Brigit, Tara.

Education: A.B., Fordham University, 1953; Ph.D., Free University of Berlin, 1956; studied at University of Leningrad, 1961.

Career: Professor of Slavic Studies.
  Instructor, John Carroll University, 1956-58; Professor, Boston College, 1958-DATE; Director of Slavic and East European Center, 1964-DATE.

* * * * *

MAY McNEER

Full Name: May McNeer.
  Born at Tampa, Florida. Daughter of Hampton Chilton McNeer and Isabel Weedon. Married Lynd Ward (an artist) June 11, 1926. Two children: Nanda, Robin.

Education: B.Litt., Columbia University, 1926.

MAY McNEER (Cont.)

Career: Writer.
Served as society page editor for a Tampa, Florida, newspaper, for one year; full-time writer, 1929-DATE. Member: P.E.N.

Awards: Honorary Member, Boys' Clubs of America; Thomas Alva Edison Award for special excellence in contributing to character development of children, 1958.

* * * * *

WILLIS E. McNELLY

Full Name: Willis Everett McNelly.
Born December 16, 1920, at Waupun, Wisconsin. Son of Willis Everett McNelly (a salesman) and Mary Creighton. Married Genevieve Skilondz, January 22, 1944. Five children: Peter (born 1945), Patrick (born 1946), Margaret (born 1949), James (born 1950), Jean (born 1955).

Education:
B.A., Central YMCA College, 1942; M.A., Loyola University, 1948; Ph.D., Northwestern University, 1957.

Career: Professor of English.
Served in the U.S. Army, 1942-46, 1950-51; college teacher, Loyola University, 1948-50, 1951-52; high school teacher, Rich Township High School, Park Forest, Illinois, 1952-58; college teacher, Santa Ana College, 1958-61; Professor of English, California State University, Fullerton, 1961-DATE.

First Professional Sale: *Mars, We Love You*, Doubleday & Co., 1971 (an anthology edited with Jane Hipolito).

Member:
Science Fiction Writers of America; American Association of University Professors; College English Association.

Interests: Works of James Joyce and William Butler Yeats.

"SF criticism is still in exploratory form; I have much to say about it in "SF: The Academic Awakening." In general, I feel that the more we get out of the ghetto and let SF stand on its own merits, without the mutual admiration society we provide for each other, the better off SF will be. Let's stop being either sycophantic or paranoic about SF, and simply enjoy it."

* * * * *

HAROLD MEAD

Full Name: Harold Charles Hugh Mead.
Born September 25, 1910, at Ootacamund, Travancore, India. Son of Alfred Hugh Mead (a tea planter) and Winifred Ada Whitby. Married Kathleen Richards, Apr. 26, 1936. Two sons: Arthur Hugh (born 1939), Henry Charles Harold (born 1948).

Education: Attended Royal Military College, Sandhurst, 1929-30; P.S.C., Staff College, Camberley, 1941; M.A., St. Catherines College, Cambridge, 1950.

Career: Writer.
Soldier, Dorsetshire Regiment, British Army, 1930-48, including four years in a Japanese P.O.W. camp in Siam; Warden, Hall of Residence, Southampton University, 1952-63; now retired.

First Professional Sale: A story to *Blackwood's* in 1945.

Agent: Curtis Brown Ltd., 60 E. 56th St., New York, NY 10022.

* * * * *

SHEPHERD MEAD

Full Name: Edward Shepherd Mead.
Born April 26, 1914, at St. Louis, Missouri. Son of Edward Mead (a salesman) and Sarah Woodward. Married Annabelle Pettibone, September 18, 1943. Three children: Sally Ann, Shepherd, Edward.

Education: B.A., Washington University, 1936.

Career: Writer.
With Benton & Bowles, New York, 1936-56, becoming Vice-President; Consultant, S. H. Benson Ltd., London, 1958-62; full-time writer, 1956-DATE.

First Professional Sale: *The Magnificent MacInnes*, Farrar, Straus, 1949.

Agent: Scott Meredith, 580 Fifth Avenue, New York, NY 10036.

Member: P.E.N.; Phi Beta Kappa; Montchoisi Tennis Club. Interests: Tennis, skiing.

"I'm a satirist, and SF can be a powerful vehicle for satire, saying things about our own civilization and our own time more strongly--in certain cases--than they can be said otherwise.

* * * * *

RICHARD MEADE

Full Name: Benjamin Leopold Haas.
Born July 21, 1926, at Charlotte, North Carolina. Son of Otto Haas (a motion picture exhibitor) and Lorena Jo Michael. Married Douglas Thornton Taylor, March 31, 1950. Three sons: Joseph Elliott (born 1951), Benjamin Michael (born 1954), John Douglas (born 1957).

Career: Writer.
Clerk, estimator and sales manager in structural steel and petroleum industries, through 1961; full-time writer, 1961-77. Died October 29, 1977.

First Professional Sale: A story to a Western pulp magazine in 1944.

Agent: Paul R. Reynolds, 599 Fifth Avenue, New York, NY 10017.

Member: Authors Guild; Western Writers of America.

Interests: Travel, camping, all facets of outdoor life, including amateur archeology

Awards: "Nothing particular."

RICHARD MEADE (Cont.)

Meade writes:

"I write serious and as carefully wrought as possible hardcover novels under my own name, and under various pennames Western, fantasy, and suspense, for both hardcover and paperback publication. Have been a professional writer, living solely from writing novels and a few short stories, since March, 1961.

"I find fantasy writing easier than writing in other fields because in a sense it requires much less research. All my other books have a hard core in fact, and are researched; the two fantasies I have done simply sprang out of a period of time living in Central Europe, and exploring the remnants of the medieval period, and searching for a way to translate the atmosphere of that time into a kind of writing which would not require extensive research.

"I thoroughly enjoy writing fantasy, and in my youth was an avid reader of the fantasy pulps, and still enjoy L. Sprague de Camp and Theodore Sturgeon, plus Fritz Leiber; they are fine writers. Unfortunately, insofar as I can ascertain, the first two books in the Gray Lands Series for Signet did not attain success enough to justify my spending time continuing the series, since I have other heavy commitments. I would like to do more books in the series, but neither the necessary rewards nor demand has been there.

"On the other hand, curiously, I have no interest whatsoever in science fiction, though I used to read it also in my younger days; and it is about the only genre in which I have published no work. My chief interest is in people; and I find the average science fiction work, including major ones, long on technology and deplorably short on style and characterization."

* * * * *

S. P. MEEK

Full Name: Sterner St. Paul Meek.
Born April 8, 1894, at Chicago, Illinois. Son of John Washington Meek and Ella Sterner. Married Edna Brundage Noble, July 12, 1927. One son, Noble Stafford.

Education:
Sc.A., University of Chicago, 1914; S.B., University of Alabama, 1915; attended University of Wisconsin, 1916, and MIT, 1921-23.

Career: Army officer and writer.
Chemist with U.S. Army (attained rank of Colonel), 1917-47; writer, 1947-72. Died June 10, 1972.

First Professional Sale: "Taming Poachers," in Field & Stream, September, 1928.

Member: Phi Beta Kappa; Pi Tau Phi; North American Committee, Christian Children's League.

* * * * *

DAVID MELTZER

Full Name: David Meltzer.
Born February 17, 1937, at Rochester, New York. Son of Louis Meltzer (a cellist) and Roseamunde Lovelace (a harpist). Married Christina Meyer (a teacher), April 1, 1959. Three children: Jennifer Love (born 1963), Margaret Joy (born 1965), Amanda Rose (born 1967).

Education: Attended University of California, Los Angeles, and Los Angeles City College.

Career: Writer and poet.
Has been a musician and book store clerk; Co-Editor and Publisher, Maya Quartos, 1967-68; Editor and Publisher, Tree Books, 1969-DATE; free-lance writer, 1956-DATE.

First Professional Sale: "Kick Me Deadly," in Dazzle, 1956.

Member: Coordinating Council of Literary Magazines.

Meltzer notes: "I have always been deeply interested in science fiction, and felt it to be the correct mode for moral and angry tracts during that period. In the back of my mind, I am always planning to write some more science fiction. Perhaps again. All my first published stories were fantasy-prone. Used to have F. J. Ackerman as an agent due to the kind encouragement of Kris Neville and Jerome Bixby."

* * * * *

FELIX MENDELSOHN, JR.

Full Name: Felix Mendelsohn, Jr.
Born August 20, 1906, at Chicago, Illinois. Son of Felix Mendelsohn (an expositions manager) and Rose D. Despres. Education: Attended University of Chicago, 1923-24.

Career: Writer.
Advertising copywriter, Meyer Both Co., Chicago, 1926-30; free-lance writer, 1930-42; cryptanalyst, U.S. Army Signal Corps, 1942-45; Foreign News Rewrite, Chicago Sun, 1945-46; Editorial Writer, Journal of Commerce, 1946-51; publicist, Southern California Gas Co., Rand Corporation, Twentieth Century-Fox, and others, 1952-66; free-lance writer, 1966-DATE.

First Professional Sale: "What's the Chance?", in Esquire, March, 1942.

* * * * *

AUBREY MENEN

Full Name: Salvator Aubrey Clarence Menen.
Born April 22, 1912, at London, England. Changed name from Menon to Menen. Son of Kali Narain Menon and Alice Everett. Education: Attended University College, London, 1930-32.

Career: Writer.
Has been a dramatic critic, theater director, war propagandist on radio, script editor; free-lance author, 1947-DATE. Agent: William Morris Agency, 151 El Camino, Beverly Hills, CA 90212.

* * * * *

DOUGLAS MENVILLE

Full Name: Douglas Alver Menville.
Born August 16, 1935, at Baton Rouge, Louisiana. Son of Raoul Louis Menville, Jr. (a chemist) and Nevalee Bradsher. Education: B.A., University of Southern California, 1958; M.A., 1959.

DOUGLAS MENVILLE (Cont.)

Career: Writer and editor.
Free-lance writer and editor of books and films, 1959-DATE; Editor, *Forgotten Fantasy*, October 1970-June 1971 (all issues published); co-Editor, Newcastle Publishing Company, Inc., 1971-DATE; co-Editor, Forgotten Fantasy Library, 1973-DATE; co-Editor, Arno Press Science Fiction reprint series, 1975; co-Editor, Arno Press Supernatural and Occult Fiction reprint series, 1976.

Agent: Jay Richards, 9265 Holcomb St., Los Angeles, CA 90035.

Interests: Collecting and reading books on films, science fiction, and fantasy; attending films and plays; classical music.

* * * * *

JUDITH MERRIL

Full Name: Josephine Judith Merril.
Born January 21, 1923, at New York, New York. Daughter of Samuel S. Grossman (a writer) and Ethel Hurwich (a social worker). Married Daniel A. Zissman, 1940 (divorced 1947); married Frederik Pohl (the science fiction writer), 1948 (divorced, 1953); married Daniel W. P. Sugrue, 1960 (divorced, 1975). Two children: Merril (daughter, born 1942), Ann Pohl (born 1950).

Education: Attended City College of New York, 1939-40.

Career: Writer and editor.
Full-time writer, editor, broadcaster, radio documentarist, 1946-DATE.

First Professional Sale: Fact articles for western and mystery magazines edited by Robert A. W. Lowndes in 1946.

Member:
Rochoale College Faculty Underground Club; Red, White & Black, Toronto; Toronto Free Clinic Senior Advisory Board; Town Hall Jazz Committee; St. Lawrence Center, Toronto; Hydra Club; Institute for 21st Century Studies; Elves, Gnomes and Little Men Chowder and Marching Society.

Merril was Book Editor of *The Magazine of Fantasy & Science Fiction* from May, 1965-June, 1969. She is best known for her series of 12 annual volumes of *The Year's Best SF*.

* * * * *

JEAN MERRILL

Full Name: Jean Fairbanks Merrill.
Born January 27, 1923, at Rochester, New York. Daughter of Earl Dwight Merrill and Elsie Almetta Fairbanks.

Education: B.A., Allegheny College, 1944; M.A., Wellesley College, 1945; Fulbright Scholar, University of Madras, 1952-53.

Agent: McIntosh & Otis, 475 Fifth Avenue, New York, NY 10017.

Career: Writer.
Feature Editor, Scholastic Magazines, 1945-50; full-time writer, 1950-DATE. Member: Authors Guild.

Awards: Fund for the Republic Award, 1956, for one-hour TV drama, "The Claws in the Cat's Paw."

* * * * *

ROY MEYERS

Full Name: Roy Lethbridge Meyers.
Born November 17, 1910, at Hounslow, Middlesex, England. Son of Percy F. C. and Maud Meyers. Married Mary Leasor, February 14, 1941. One child: C. J. L. Meyers.

Education: Attended University College; internship at St. Bartholomew's Hospital.

Career: Physician.
Licentiate, the Royal College of Physicians, 1939; Member, Royal College of Surgeons, 1940; physician, 1939-74, serving at Mill Hill Hospital, London, Wellhouse Hospital, and others; Deputy Commissioner of Medical Service, Southwest Region; Chairman of M.S.S. Medical Boards; general practioner, Stogumber, Taunton, Somerset, in conjunction with his wife, who is also a doctor. Died there February 13, 1974.

First Professional Sale: *The Man They Could Not Kill*, Blackfriars Press, 1945.

* * * * *

BARBARA MICHAELS

Full Name: Barbara Mertz.
Born September 29, 1927, at Canton, Illinois. Daughter of Earl D. Gross (a printer) and Grace Tregallas. Married Richard R. Mertz (a professor of history), June 18, 1950. Two children: Elizabeth Ellen, Peter William.

Education: Ph.B., University of Chicago, 1947; M.A., 1950; Ph.D., 1952.

Career: Author and historian.
Has been a full-time writer under the names Barbara Michaels, Barbara Mertz, and Elizabeth Peters, since 1964. Member: Egypt Exploration Society; American Research Council in Egypt.

Agent: Theron Raines, 244 Madison Avenue, New York, NY 10016.

* * * * *

SCOTT MICHEL

Full Name: Milton Scott Michel.
Born 1916. Son of Isidore Michel and Esther Good. Married Rita White. Two children: Claire, James.
Education: Attended New York University, 1935-41.

Career: Writer.
Technician at a diagnostic X-ray laboratory, New York, 1940-44; full-time writer, 1944-DATE.

Member:
Authors League of America; Dramatists Guild.

SANDRA MIESEL

Full Name: Sandra Louise Miesel.
    Born November 25, 1941, at New Orleans, Louisiana.
Daughter of Louis Schwartz (a dentist) and Dorothy
Sciele (a nurse). Married John Miesel, June 20, 1964.
Three children: Marie-Louise (born 1965), Anne-Louise
(born 1968), Peter (born 1969).

Education: B.S., College of St. Francis, 1962;
M.S., University of Illinois, 1965; A.M., 1966.

Career: Sales coordinator.
    Part-time sales coordinator, Editions Limited Gal-
lery, 1973-DATE.

First Professional Sale: "Poul Anderson: Maker
    of Universes," in SF Archives, 1973.

Honors: Nomination for Best Fanwriter, 1973, in the
    annual Hugo competition; various fantasy art prizes.

Member: Indiana Science Fantasy Association; Fantasy
Association.

Interests:
    Art history, comparative mythology, history of reli-
gion, archeology, medieval studies, collecting art
and antiquities, cooking, sewing, needlework (design
and executing original embroideries for sale).

    "I enjoy reading SF because it stimulates the imagi-
nation and intellect. It complements my overall interest in alien historic civilizations. I enjoy writing about SF because this is one activity that unites
the humanistic and scientific halves of my education.
My goal as a critic is to provide specialized information for the reader's assistance, not to formulate
sweeping literary theories."

* * * * *

JOSEPH MILLARD

Full Name: Joseph John Millard.
    Born January 14, 1908, at Canby, Minnesota. Son
of Frank Earnest Millard (a rancher) and Alice Lake.
Married Lee Harrington, February 14, 1931. One son,
Michael Harrington (born 1939).

Education: Graduated from Canby High, 1925.

Career: Writer.
    Has worked as an editor, advertising agent, salesman,
and at other miscellaneous jobs; full-time writer,
1936-DATE; former Publisher of National Mortician.

First Professional Sale: "Washington at Valley
    Forge," in Portal, 1927.

Interests: Stamps, U.S. history.

Millard writes:
    "After 33 years of full-time writing, it's a love-
hate relationship, I guess. Just finished another
55,000-word book in five weeks. Have done one in as
little as twelve days. What more can I say?
    "Regarding SF, I'd say that for once, real science
has outraced the field, making the old plots obsolete.
The new SF, in my mind, is the threshold of involvement with people as people--their problems and needs
and urges. I'd say that today Watergate and Nixon

are more SF than Skylab."

* * * * *

MARJORIE MILLER

Full Name: Marjorie Miller.
    Born May 28, 1922, at La Porte, Indiana. Daughter
of Warren Mithoff (in advertising) and Helen Hyde Modrall (an artist). Married William Eldridge Miller,
Jr., January 2, 1943. Five children: Margaret Ann
(born 1943), Warren Eldridge (born 1945), David Jameson (born 1952), Paul Modrall (born 1954), Stephen
Mithoff (born 1957).

Education:
    B.A., University of Texas, 1943; M.A., University of
Maryland, 1969; M.S.L.S., Catholic University, 1973.

Career: Librarian.
    Promotion Assistant, Amer-Aviation Relations, 1965-
66; English Teacher, Prince George's County Schools,
1967-68; Librarian, Prince George's County Library,
Maryland, 1970-DATE.

First Professional Sale: Isaac Asimov: A Check-
    list, Kent State University Press, 1972.

Interests: Backyard bird-watching, needlepoint, col-
    lecting Christopher Morley first editions, genealogy.

Member:
    Science Fiction Research Association; American Associ-
ation of University Women; Audobon Society; Common
Cause; Phi Beta Kappa; Alpha Chi; Phi Kappa Phi.

"My master's thesis at the University of Maryland was
'The Machine in the Future: Man and Technology in the
Science Fiction of Isaac Asimov.'"

* * * * *

P. SCHUYLER MILLER

Full Name: Peter Schuyler Miller.
    Born February 21, 1912, at Troy, New York. Son of
Philip Schuyler Miller (a chemist) and Edith May Figgis
(a teacher).

Education:
    B.S., Union College, Schenectady, NY, 1931; M.S. in
Chemistry, 1932.

Career: Technical writer.
    Laboratory assistant, General Electric Research La-
boratory, 1933-34; Supervisor of Adult Education, New
York State Education Dept., 1934-37; in adult education, public relations, and Director of Schenectady
Museum, Schenectady Dept. of Education, 1937-52; Technical Writer, Fisher Scientific Company, Pittsburgh,
1952-74; critic for Analog, beginning in 1945, and
with his own monthly column, October, 1950-January,
1975 (called "The Reference Library" beginning in
October, 1951). Died at Blenerhasset Island, West
Virginia, October 13, 1974.

First Professional Sale: "The Red Plague," in
    Wonder Stories, July, 1930.

Awards: Special Plaque, 21st World Science Fiction
    Convention (DisCon I), Washington, 1963, for "The

P. SCHUYLER MILLER (Cont.)

Reference Library."

Member:
  Research Associate, Section of Man, Carnegie Museum; Eastern States Archeological Society; Van Epps-Hartley Chapter of the New York Archeological Association; Society for American Archeology; Adirondack Mountain Club; Forest Preserve Association of New York State; Sierra Club; Delta Chi.

Miller was a descendant of General Philip Schuyler, and as a result was very much interested in the early history of New York State. He was also noted for his research on the Iroquois Indians. His one surviving relative, Mary Drake (his sister), kindly provided the following remarks:

"He had an unquenchable thirst for knowledge, and could speak with authority on most everything that had to do with life on this earth--the stars, the birds, conservation, American history, archaeology, Indians, plus his science fiction. And in all these fields he bought books, so that I find myself the owner of an estimated 15,000 volumes, not to mention correspondence and manuscripts. Part of the collection I shall probably donate to the Carnegie Museum, Section on Man. At this writing, I have not decided what to do with the rest."

* * * * *

WALTER M. MILLER JR.

Full Name: Walter Michael Miller, Jr.
  Born January 23, 1923, at New Smyrna Beach, Florida. Son of Walter Michael Miller and Ruth Adrian Jones. Married Anna Louise Becker, May 1, 1945. Four children: Margaret Jean (born 1945), Walter Michael III (born 1947), Cathryn Augusta (born 1949), Alys Elaine (born 1951).

Education: Attended University of Tennessee, 1940-42, and University of Texas, 1947-49.

Career: Writer.

First Professional Sale: "MacDougal's Wife," in *American Mercury*, 1950.

Awards: Hugo Award, Best Novelette, 1954 (1955), "The Darfstellar"; Hugo Award, Best Novel, 1960 (1961), *A Canticle for Leibowitz*.

* * * * *

MARLYS MILLHISER

Full Name: Marlys Joy Millhiser.
  Born May 27, 1938, at Charles City, Iowa. Daughter of Harold Henry Enabnit and Doris Britton. Married David Ralph Millhiser (a mechanical engineer), June 25, 1960. Two children: Jay David, Joy Marie.

Education: B.A., University of Iowa, 1960; M.A., University of Colorado, 1963.

Career: Writer.
  Junior high school teacher of history in Boulder, Colorado, 1963-65; full-time writer, 1972-DATE.

ALFRED L. MILLIGAN

Full Name: Alfred Lee Milligan.
  Born August 26, 1893, at Attica, Indiana. Son of Alfred A. and Charlotte Milligan. Married Beulah D. Milligan, November 10, 1926 (died 1943). Three children: Beulah, Charles, Arthur.

Career: Postmaster.
  With the Railway Mail Service; spent 34 years as an Assistant Postmaster in Attica, Indiana; now retired.

* * * * *

ROBERT P. MILLS

Full Name: Robert Park Mills.
  Born 1920, at Missoula, Montana. Married and divorced. Two children: Alison, Frederic.

Education: B.A., Rutgers University, 1942.

Career: Literary agent.
  Managing Editor, *The Magazine of Fantasy and Science Fiction*, Fall, 1949-August, 1958; Editor, September, 1958-March, 1962; Consulting Editor, April, 1962-Feb., 1963, and December, 1964-December, 1966; Literary Agent, as Robert P. Mills Ltd., September, 1959-DATE; free-lance editor. Editor, *Venture Science Fiction*, January, 1957-July, 1958.

First Professional Sale: "The Last Shall Be First," in *The Magazine of Fantasy and Science Fiction*, August, 1958.

Agent: Robert P. Mills Ltd., 156 E. 52nd St., New York, NY 10022.

Member: Society of Authors' Representatives.

* * * * *

SAMUEL MINES

Full Name: Samuel Mines.
  Born October 4, 1909, at New York, New York. Son of Israel Mines and Augusta Bloom. Married Rose Suzanne Wanderman, August, 1936. One daughter, Madeline (born 1943).

Education: Attended Columbia University, 1931-34.

Career: Writer and editor.
  Editor, Better Publications, 1942-54, including: *Startling Stories*, November, 1951-Fall, 1954; *Thrilling Wonder Stories*, December, 1951-Summer, 1954; *Wonder Story Annual*, 1952-53; *Space Stories*, October, 1952-June, 1953; *Fantastic Story Magazine*, Winter, 1952-Fall, 1954. Articles Editor, *Collier's*, 1955-56; science writer, American Cyanamid Company, 1956-61; Senior Science Writer, Pfizer Inc. (a pharmaceutical company), 1961-DATE; free-lance writer, 1941-DATE.

First Professional Sale: *Coyote Gulch*, Henry Holt, 1941.

Agent: Collins-Knowlton-Wing, 60 E. 56th St., New York, NY.

Interests: Camping, mountain climbing, classical music, nutrition, consumer standards.

SAMUEL MINES (Cont.)

Member:
    Sierra Club; Wilderness Society; Environmental Defense Fund; Audobon Society; Save-the-Redwoods League; Nature Conservancy; American Forestry Association; Association for Indian Affairs; National Parks Association.

Mines comments about modern science fiction.
    "I think a great deal of the current writing is far more mature than it was in the Fifties, and this is all to the good. The so-called 'New Wave'--unless it is already obsolete--turned me off completely. I considered it a cop-out--writers could splatter words around in any incoherent fashion they liked instead of undergoing the tough discipline necessary to be understandable. I thought it would not last, but that while it lasted it would do science fiction no good. The best work being written today is on a par with the best anywhere, and this is very encouraging for the future of science fiction."

* * * * *

STEPHEN MINOT

Full Name: Stephen Minot.
    Born May 27, 1927, at Boston, Massachusetts. Son of William Minot (a real estate manager) and Elizabeth Chapman. Married his second wife, Virginia Stover. Three children: Stephen Reid, Nicholas William, Christopher Bailey.

Education: A.B., Harvard University, 1953; M.A., Johns Hopkins University, 1955.

Career: Professor of English.
    Instructor, Bowdoin College, 1955-57; Asst. Professor of English, 1957-58; Visiting Assistant Professor of English, University of Connecticut, 1958-59; Associate Professor of English, Trinity College, 1959-DATE; writer-in-residence, Johns Hopkins University, 1974-75.

Agent: Curtis Brown Ltd., 60 E. 56th St., New York, NY 10022.

Awards:
    Atlantic First Award, 1962, for short story, "Sausage and Beer"; Saxton Memorial Foundation Fellowship, 1963-64; "Mars Revisited" was included in the anthology, O. Henry Prize Stories, 1971.

Member:
    Authors Guild; American Civil Liberties Union; National Association for the Advancement of Colored People; National Committee for an Effective Congress; American Association of University Professors; American Veterans Committee.

* * * * *

ADRIAN MITCHELL

Full Name: Adrian Mitchell.
    Born October 24, 1932, at London, England. Education: Attended Oxford University, 1952-55.

Career: Writer, poet, playwright.
    Reporter, Oxford Mail, 1955-57, and Evening Standard, 1957-59; instructor at writers workshops.

NAOMI MITCHISON

Full Name: Naomi Mary Margaret Mitchison.
    Born November 1, 1897, at Edinburgh, Scotland. Daughter of Professor John Scott Haldane (a physiologist and philosopher) and Louisa Kathleen Trotter. Married Gilbert Richard Mitchison, M.P. (now Baron Mitchison of Carradale), 1916. Five children: Professor Denis Anthony Mitchison (born 1919), Professor John Murdoch Mitchison (born 1922), Sonja Lois Godfrey, Professor Nicholas Avrion Mitchison (born 1928), Valentine Harriet Isobel Dione Arnold-Forster.

Career: Writer.
    Full-time writer, 1920-DATE, with over 70 book credits. "Much involved in increasingly left-wing politics In Highland local government, elected or nominated for some 25 years. At present farming and writing books and articles. I am also Mother of the baKgatla baKgafela tribe in Botswana, under the name Mmalinchwe, where I go every year; my regiment is Matshego."

First Professional Sale: The Conquered, Jonathan Cape, 1920.

Agent: David Higham Associates, John Street, Golden Square, London WC1, England.

Awards: Palmes de Académie Française.

Member: Southern Tenant Farmers Union of Arkansas.

Mitchison writes:
    "Since reading H. G. Wells as a child, and later, Stapledon, I have always enjoyed good SF, though I can't do with a great deal of it, especially when it is just bloodthirsty. Growing up in a scientific atmosphere, and working on guinea pig genetics with my brother, J. B. S. Haldane, I have always been interested in biology. My three sons are all professors of biology in some form, either in London or Edinburgh, and my grandchildren are going the same way. I could hardly escape. What I sometimes do is to ask one of them, 'What would happen if....' They say 'It couldn't happen.' I say, 'Yes, but if it did...?' Thus a book or part of a book is born. I get ideas from journals such as the New Scientist, from conversations with people, and from observations, especially of animals; but basically what I am doing is what any good novelist does: putting a character into an unfamiliar and uncertain or difficult situation, and seeing what they do. As I am a woman, I find it easier to know or feel what another woman would do (as Erif Der in The Corn King and Spring Queen, Cleopatra in Cleopatra's People, Kirstie in The Bull Calves, Lienor in To the Chapel Perilous, and so on). I also find myself faintly irritated by the role that women characters play in so much SF. In Solution Three, my new SF novel, there are several main women characters, though there are several men as well. I think it is probable that in time some rather new kinds of scientific thought, and perhaps SF as well, will come from writers with an African background. I am much interested also in Russian SF."

* * * * *

HERBERT MITGANG

Full Name: Herbert Mitgang.
    Born January 20, 1920, at New York, New York. Son of Benjamin Mitgang and Florence Altman. Married Shirley Kravchick, May 13, 1945. Three children: Esther, Lee, Laura.

HERBERT MITGANG (Cont.)

Education: LL.B., St. John's University.

Career: Editor.
Admitted to the New York Bar, 1942; Sports Stringer, *Brooklyn Eagle*, 1938-39; with Universal Pictures, 1945; Writer, Critic, Editor, *New York Times*, 1945-63; Member of Editorial Board, 1963-64, 1967-DATE; Executive Editor and Assistant to the President, CBS, 1964-67.

Member:
Authors League of America; Authors Guild; New York Newspaper Guild; Society of American Historians.

* * * * *

RUTHERFORD GEORGE MONTGOMERY

Full Name: Rutherford George Montgomery.
Born April 12, 1894, in North Dakota. Son of George Y. Montgomery and Matilda Procter. Married Eunice Opal Kirks, February 14, 1930. Three children: Earl, Polly, Marylin.

Education: Attended Western State College of Colorado.

Career: Writer.
Teacher in various Colorado schools, 1921-27; County Judge, State of Colorado, Gunnison County, 1931-36; Budget Commissioner, 1932-38; free-lance writer, 1939-DATE. Member: Society of Authors; Western Writers of America; Writers Guild of America, West.

Awards:
Commonwealth Club of California Juvenile Silver Medal, 1953, for *Wapiti the Elk*; New York Herald Tribune Children's Spring Book Festival Award, 1956, and Boys' Clubs of American Junior Book Award, 1957, both for *Beaver Water*.

* * * * *

SHEILA MOON

Full Name: Sheila Elizabeth Moon.
Born December 25, 1910, at Denver, Colorado. Daughter of Harry E. Moon (an engineer) and Jessie Jones.

Education: A.B., University of California, Los Angeles, 1940; M.A., 1942; Ph.D., University of California, Berkeley, 1955.

Career: Psychotherapist.
Self-employed psychotherapist (Jungian), in Los Angeles and San Francisco, 1945-DATE; Associate Professor of Psychology, Sonoma State College, 1965-70. Member: American Psychological Association; California Psychological Association; Phi Beta Kappa.

Awards: Bollingen Foundation Grant, 1956, for work on Navaho mythology.

* * * * *

MICHAEL MOORCOCK

Full Name: Michael John Moorcock.
Born December 18, 1939, at Mitcham, Surrey, England. Son of Arthur Moorcock (an engineer) and June (Nellie) Taylor (a company director). Married Hilary Denham Bailey (a journalist), September 29, 1962. Three children: Sophie Elizabeth (born 1963), Katherine Helen (born 1964), Max Edward (born 1972).

Education: Attended Pitmans College, 1951-55.

Career: Writer and editor.
Editor, *Tarzan Adventures*, 1957-58; Editor, Sexton Blake Library, 1958-61; Editor, *Current Topics* (a Liberal Party publication), 1962; Editor, *New Worlds*, May/June, 1964-March, 1971; Editor, *New Worlds (Quarterly)*, #1-6, 1971-73; free-lance author, 1957-DATE; composer and performer of popular music.

First Professional Sale: "Sojan the Swordsman," in *Tarzan Adventures*, May, 1957.

Agent: Wallace, Aitken & Sheil, 118 E. 61st St., New York, NY 10021.

Awards:
Nebula Award, Best Novella, 1967 (1968), "Behold the Man" (shorter version); August Derleth Award, Best Novel, 1974 (1975), *The Sword and the Stallion*; British Fantasy Award, 1967.

Member:
Science Fiction Writers of America; Authors Guild; National Union of Journalists.

Interests:
Book collecting (late 19th century and early 20th centuries, primarily), fell-walking, music of all kinds, painting.

Moorcock writes:
"All my books are linked--through continuing characters, situations, scenes, etc.--because they all explore the same themes--some metaphysically, some metaphorically, some realistically. Some are more sophisticated or ambitious than others, of course. Even my record work is linked. I couldn't work properly if it were not."

Regarding modern SF, he comments:
"I think the barriers between SF and ordinary modern fiction have already broken down. SF as a category form still exists--and will doubtless continue to exist. But the SF which no longer works within the conventions but merely makes use of some of the conventions can no longer easily be categorised save simply as 'modern fiction.' In much of my own work, I write a completely personal story or novel, utilising what I have learned from writing SF, but not producing what a purist would call 'true SF'--*The Final Programme* and *A Cure for Cancer* are examples. SF has been an invaluable training ground, and has provided considerable discipline to a number of writers--Ballard, Aldiss, Disch, Jones, M. John Harrison, etc., whose current work is no longer what an enthusiastic reader of, say, *Galaxy*, would be willing to distinguish as SF, and yet which contains much of the virtues of the best science fiction. I tend to hold the view (also expressed by Ballard) that magazine SF of the Forties was a 'naive' form--a 'primitive' literary movement--and I tend to prefer the unsophisticated work that appeared in *Astounding Stories*, *Planet Stories*, *Super Science Stories*, *Startling Stories*, etc., to the pseudo-sophisticated work that began to appear in *Galaxy* and *The Magazine of Fantasy and Science Fiction* in the early '50s."

He adds: "I lead a quiet life keeping 3 households."

BRIAN MOORE

Full Name: Brian Moore.
  Born August 25, 1921, at Belfast, Northern Ireland.
Son of James Brian Moore and Eileen McFadden.

Education: Attended St. Malachy's College.

Career: Writer.
  Reporter, *Montreal Gazette*, 1948-52; full-time
writer, 1952-DATE.

Awards:
  First Novel Award, Authors Club, 1956; Governor
General's Award for Fiction, 1960, for *The Luck of
Ginger Coffey*; Quebec Literary Prize, 1958.

* * * * *

C. L. MOORE

Full Name: Catherine Lucile Moore.
  Born January 24, 1911, at Indianapolis, Indiana.
Daughter of Otto Newman Moore and Maude Estelle
Jones. Married Henry Kuttner (the science fiction
writer), June 7, 1940 (died 1958); married Thomas
Reggie, June 13, 1963.

Education: B.A., University of Southern California,
  1956; M.A., 1964.

Career: Writer.
  With the Fletcher Trust Company, Indianapolis, 1930-
40, becoming President; Instructor of Writing and
Literature, University of Southern California, 1958-
61; free-lance author and script writer, 1933-DATE.

First Professional Sale: "Shambleau," in *Weird
  Tales*, November, 1933.

Agent: Harold Matson Agency, 22 E. 40th St., New
  York, NY 10016.

Member: Science Fiction Writers of America; Writers
  Guild of America, West; Mystery Writers of America;
  Phi Beta Kappa; Phi Kappa Phi.

* * * * *

PATRICK MOORE

Full Name: Patrick Alfred Moore.
  Born March 4, 1923, at Pinner, Middlesex, England.
Son of Capt. Charles C. Moore, M.C. and Gertrude
White.

Career: Writer.
  Has been Director of Armagh Planetarium, Armagh,
Northern Ireland; free-lance author, 1957-DATE.

First Professional Sale: "I think around 1946,
  but I am frankly not sure."

Agent: A. P. Watt & Son, 26/28 Bedford Row, London
  WC1R 4HL, England.

Awards:
  Order of the British Empire, 1968; D.Sc., Lancaster
University, 1974; Guido Horn d'Arturo Gold Medal,
Bologne, 1969; Boys Club Prize, 1968; Lorimer Gold
Medal, Edinburgh, 1964; Goodacre Gold Medal, 1970.

Member:
  British Astronomical Association (Director, Lunar
Section); International Astronomical Union; Royal Astronomical Society (Fellow); Astronomical Society of
the USSR (honorary member); various foreign scientific
societies.

Interests: Music (wrote and produced an opera in
  Brighton, 1974); cricket; chess.

"Too much to do; too little time...."

* * * * *

RAYLYN MOORE

Full Name: Raylyn Thyrza Moore.
  Born January 5, 1928, at Waynesville, Ohio. Daughter
of James Byrl Crabbe (a teacher) and Ethelyn Coverston
(a teacher). Married Ward Moore (the science fiction
author), June 14, 1967. Four children: Beth Penney
(born 1955), Jeanne Penney (born 1956), John Penney
(born 1956), Sara Rivkeh Moore (born 1965).

Education: B.A., Ohio State University, 1949; M.A.,
  San Jose State University, 1971.

Career: Writer and instructor.
  Reporter for various newspapers, 1949-64; Editor,
Executive Housekeeping, 1966-68; part-time instructor
in fiction writing at Monterey Peninsula College, 1969-
DATE; free-lance author, 1954-DATE.

First Professional Sale: "Death Is a Woman," in
  Esquire, 1954.

Moore notes: "Although I've been working for the
past four years almost exclusively in the SF and fantasy genres, all my published work during those years
has been in the short story form."

* * * * *

WARD MOORE

Full Name: Ward Moore.
  Born August 10, 1903, at Madison, New Jersey. Son
of Samuel Ward Moore ("a dreamer") and Stella Adelaide
Lemlein (a dress buyer). Married Lorna Lenzi, Sept.,
1942 (divorced); married Raylyn Thyrza Penney, June 14,
1967. Seven children: Frederica Margaret (born 1924),
Rebekah (deceased), David (deceased), Samuel (born
1947), Benyamin Haninah (born 1953), Hannah Rachel
(born 1955), Sara Rivkeh (born 1965).

Education: "None--and a good thing too."

Career: Writer.
  "Bum, in the Nixonian sense: that is, I have no certain income. I have done all sorts of things, raised
chickens, clerked in bookstores, built houses, contract
gardened, ghosted books, copy-edited, been a book-
review editor, proofreader, on relief and welfare."
Died January 29, 1978.
First Professional Sale: A poem to *New York Call*,
  1920.

Agent (for both Ward and Raylyn Moore): Virginia Kidd,
  Box 278, Milford, PA 18337.

Honors: "There has been no hero in my family for
  generations."

WARD MOORE (Cont.)

Member:
   Founder, Past President, Grand Exalted Master, Society Unalterably Opposed to All Progress; Charter and Only Member, Society for Burning Down Schools and Hanging Teachers.

Interests:
   "A writer is a writer, not someone who wastes time playing games. My only interest, outside my children, is in women. I adore them, without regard to race, color, creed, age, or national origin."

Moore writes:
   "It used to offend me when my ID cards or some other internal passport read Ward (NMI) Moore. What is this fantastic insistence that two names are insufficient? There was a time when one name was enough (Adam, Charlemagne, Nebuchadnezzar who suffered from emmerods, Rachel, the actress, Homer, Vercingetorix). I once knew a good man whose name was Cyril Robert Lionel James. He was a fine Trotskyist theoretician, but a lousy poker-player. He was (possibly is--I've long lost sight of him; saw a pamphlet by him in an obscure Village bookshop some years back) a possibly great man, but did his string of names make him better than I? Call me Ishmael: my legal name is Ward Moore.
   "My son's name is Benyamin Hanina Moore. The Y is there for purposes of proper pronunciation, since the Hebrew Yod is frequently pronounced Jay in English, giving rise to such absurdities as Jehovah. His middle name is after Hanina ben Dosa (not Hanina ben Tarydon), one of the few Jewish mystics. He prayed, 'Lord, thy servant is getting wet, stop the rain,' and the rain stopped. He returned to his house and prayed, 'Lord, thy servant's field is parched,' and the rain began again. I would have named him Hanina Benyamin, but looking ahead to the agony of American 'education'....
   "As for the French phrase so barbarously garbled by me [mais, je vous avoue, je ne pas couché avec une japonaise], I read it some years ago is some forgotten body's autobiography (I think), and the wistfulness of it, and my own deep regret at never having enjoyed this most desirable of conjunctions, made me write it down to use as the epigraph for my autobiography, I. The memorandum was lost, the autobiography never got beyond some fragments, and I regret I cannot cite the author of that nostalgic statement.
   "May I say as an aside that I deplore the segregation of imaginative writing under the phoney label of 'science fiction.' It was a sad day when Hugo Gernsback was plucked untimely from his mother's womb. (Any day would be untimely.) The surgery was fatal. 'Mainstream' survived, but 'science fiction' atrophied. The label has been an albatross around my neck."

He adds: "It's a mug's game."

* * * * *

DIGHTON MOREL

Full Name: Kenneth Lewis Warner.
   Born April 10, 1915, at Gosport, Hampshire, England. Son of Frederick George Warner (a shoemaker) and Caroline Weedon. Married Elfriede Krawatzo, October 24, 1953. Four children: Jennifer, Susan, Gabriele, Isabel. Education: Teaching Diploma, Nelson Hall Training College, 1947.

Career: Writer and editor.
   Teacher in Gosport, England, 1933-36; Education Officer, British Army, 1936-45, 1948-52, becoming a Captain; Literary Advisor and Editor of English-language publications, Ernst Klett (educational publishers), Stuttgart, West Germany, 1954-DATE; novelist, 1960-DATE.

Agent: Curtis Brown Ltd., 60 E. 56th St., New York, NY 10022.

* * * * *

AL MORGAN

Full Name: Albert Edward Morgan.
   Born January 16, 1920, at New York, New York. Son of Albert Edward Morgan (a businessman) and Julia Britt. Married Martha Falconer Jones (an actress), December 19, 1945. Three children: Allen, Martha Jo, Amy Jane.

Education: Attended New York University, 1937-41.

Career: Writer and playwright.
   Senior Editor of "Home Show," NBC, 1954-56; screenwriter, Universal International, 1956; Editor, Show Business Illustrated, 1960-61; Producer of "Today Show," NBC, 1961-69; full-time writer and playwright, 1969-DATE. Member: Authors Guild; Dramatists Guild.

Awards:
   Ohio State Award for Journalism, 1953; Academy of Television Arts and Sciences Emmy Award, 1968, for contribution to television programming, for his work on the "Today Show."

Agent: Roberta Pryor, International Famous Agency, 1305 Avenue of the Americas, New York, NY 10009.

* * * * *

DAN MORGAN

Full Name: Dan Morgan.
   Born December 24, 1925, at Holbeach, Lincolnshire, England. Son of Cecil Morgan (a tailor) and Lilian Kate Morley. Married Jean Morgan, 1949 (divorced); married Georgina Evelyn Morgan. One son, Glenn Dan (born 1951).

Career: Businessman and writer.
   Has been a professional guitarist, a soldier in the Royal Army Medical Corps; Managing Director, Dan Morgan Ltd. (retail menswear), 1958-DATE; part-time writer, 1952-DATE.

First Professional Sale: "Alien Analysis," in New Worlds, January, 1952.

Agent: Robert P. Mills Ltd., 156 E. 52nd St., New York, NY 10022.

Member: Science Fiction Writers of America; Society of Authors.

Interests: Spanish and plectrum guitars: author of a highly successful handbook on the instrument titled Guitar.

Morgan writes:
   "After four years as a full-time writer, I have been

DAN MORGAN (Cont.)

"forced by a combination of circumstances to resume
full-time management of my menswear business, but intend to get back to writing, at least on a part-time
basis at the earliest opportunity. One of the difficulties about being a full-timer is the fact that the
rewards here, in the U.K., are very meagre, and I'm
not a crust and garret type by nature. I love writing,
but I have been forced to recognise that I can earn
a great deal more money with a great deal less mental
strain by devoting the major part of my time to business.
    "What do I think of the material currently being
published in the field? Well, there's no doubt that
Sturgeon's Law still applies, as much as it ever did.
The rubbish makes me impatient, more impatient than
it would have twenty years ago, when I still had to
read something all the way through because I couldn't
believe that it would *all* be that bad. Now, if it
doesn't grab me in the first page or so--well, there
just isn't time, is there?
    "Without the shadow of a doubt the most impressive
and enjoyable book I have read recently is T. J. Bass's
The Godwhale--so much so that I had to write and tell
him so. I am a consistent admirer of Bob Silverberg--
his *Dying Inside* was most impressive, a novel in the
literary sense, as well as being good SF about a subject which has always fascinated me--see the Sixth
Perception series [now consisting of four volumes].
    "I found *The Gods Themselves* unreadable--although
in the old days I was a great admirer of Asimov--may-
be one of us changed. I find Heinlein self-indulgent
to an increasing extent, garrulous and tiresome. I
have very little time for any of my contemporaries on
this side of the pond, apart from John Brunner, whose
fault lies in over-production and consequent patchi-
ness. For the pretensions of the New Wavers I have
no time at all. Science fictionwise my models have
always been Americans, with the single exception of
Eric Frank Russell.
    "My interest in the guitar may show up here and
there in my fiction, but its main, and most profitable
appearance has been in the book *Guitar*, which I mentioned above. It may be a kind of oblique judgment
on the professional writing situation when I say that
this book, which was the easiest and quickest to write
of any of my books, has earned me more money than all
the rest of them put together."

* * * * *

NIGEL MORLAND

Full Name: Nigel Morland.
    Born June 24, 1905, at London, England. Son of
John and Gertrude Morland. Married Peggy Barwell (di-
vorced); married Pamela Hunnex (divorced); married
Jill Harvey. Three children: Terence, John, Ruth.

Career: Writer.
    Began his career as a crime reporter at age fifteen;
has since worked variously as a feature editor, managing editor, or editor, of a number of publications,
including *News Review*, *Doctor*, *Edgar Wallace Mystery
Magazine*, *Shanghai Sports*; was also a wartime correspondent; adviser on crime and detection to various
publications in England and the U.S.; full-time writer,
1930-DATE.

Member: Crime Writers Association (co-founder); Fo-
    rensic Science Society; Medico-Legal Society.

JOHN MORRESSY

Full Name: John Morressy.
    Born December 8, 1930, at Brooklyn, New York. Son
of John Emmett Morressy (a commissioner) and Jeanette
Geraghty. Married Barbara Turner, August 11, 1956.

Education: B.A., St. John's University, 1953; M.A.,
    New York University, 1961.

Career: Professor of English.
    Contract drafter and reviewer, Equitable Life, New
York, 1957-59; Instructor of English, St. John's University, 1962-66; Assistant Professor of English, Mon-
mouth College, 1966-67; Professor of English, Franklin
Pierce College, 1968-DATE.

First Professional Sale: "Don't Count Your Tigers,"
    in *Esquire*, 1955.

Agent: James Brown Associates, 22 E. 60th St., New
    York, NY 10022.

Awards:
    Fellowship in Prose to the Bread Loaf Writers' Con-
    ference, 1968; Fellowship in Speculative Fiction to
    the University of Colorado Writers' Conference, 1970.

Interests: Reading of all sorts; walking; leisurely
    travel in civilized places; good conversation.

Member: Science Fiction Writers of America; Authors
    Guild.

Morressy comments:
    "Most of my life has been spent in and around schools,
as student and teacher; understandably, the problems
of education loom large in my books. I am concerned
with what one must know to be truly human, and how this
is to be learned, and how taught.
    "The human race has amassed a great deal of knowledge,
much of it pernicious. After six or seven thousand
years of history, we still settle our ideological con-
flicts by killing one another. Our advances have been
technical, not humane. The differences between the
stone ax and the H-bomb lie in their relative effici-
ency; the mentality behind them is the same.
    "Our moralizing convinces us we are moral; our ra-
tionalizing persuades us we are rational. But our history proves that we are not to be trusted with sharp
instruments and things that blow up. Science fiction
gives me a chance to speculate on what the future will
be like. I believe there *will* be a future, but I expect it to be bleak and tough.
    "So that's why I write science fiction, and what I
try to write about. When I began to write, I knew exactly what I wanted to tell the world; now, I write in
order to find out what I really want to say. Fortunately, the reward is worth the effort. Writing is a pleasure to me, and the fact that it presents difficulties
that increase with experience does not diminish the
pleasure. There is a Puritan streak in me that makes
me suspect easy ways."

* * * * *

A. REYNOLDS MORSE

Full Name: Albert Reynolds Morse.
    Born October 20, 1914, at Denver, Colorado. Son of
Bradish P. Morse and Anna Reynolds Garrey. Married
Eleanor Reese (Secretary-Treasurer, IMS Company), March
21, 1942. One son, Brad G.

A. REYNOLDS MORSE (Cont.)

Education: B.A., University of Colorado, 1938;
M.B.A., Harvard University, 1939.

Career: Corporation executive.
President, IMS Company, Cleveland, 1949-DATE; art
collector, owning the world's largest single collection
of Salvador Dali's works, and operator of the Dali
Museum (housed in a wing of the IMS Building); Curator
of the George Elbert Burr Collection, Denver Public
Library; Member of Economic Development Board, University of Colorado. Member: Phi Beta Kappa; Shaker
Heights Country Club.

* * * * *

SAM MOSKOWITZ

Full Name: Sam Moskowitz.
Born June 30, 1920, at Newark, New Jersey. Son of
Harry Moskowitz (a shopkeeper) and Rose Gerber. Married Christine Elizabeth Haycock (a physician), July
6, 1958.

Education: Attended Central Commercial and Technical High School, Newark, New Jersey.

Career: Publisher and editor.
Literary agent, 1941-42; Managing Editor, *Frosted
Food Field*, April, 1945-September, 1955; Managing
Editor, *Science Fiction +*, March-December, 1953 (all
issues published); Editor, Cahners Publishing Company,
September, 1955-May, 1972 (editing *Quick Frozen Foods*);
Editor, Magazines for Industry, June, 1972-January,
1974; Editor and Co-Publisher, *Quick Frozen Foods*
(Harcourt Brace Jovanovich), 1974-DATE; Editor, *Weird
Tales*, Summer, 1973-Summer, 1974; Editor, Hyperion
Press Science Fiction Classics reprint series, 1973-
DATE.

First Professional Sale: "The Way Back," in
Comet Stories, January, 1941.

Honors and Awards:
Special Plaque, 13th World Science Fiction Convention (Clevention), Cleveland, 1955, for *The Immortal
Storm*; Big Heart Award, 18th World Science Fiction
Convention (Pittcon), Pittsburgh, 1960; Award of
Distinction, Eastern Science Fiction Association,
1962; Guest of Honor, Burroughs Bibliophiles, Cleveland, 1969; The Rebel Award, Southern Fandom, Atlanta,
1970; Hall of Fame, First Fandom, 1974.

Member:
Science Fiction Writers of America; Eastern Science
Fiction Association (founder and past President);
Fantasy Amateur Press Association; First Fandom;
Burroughs Bibliophiles.

Interests: Frozen foods, boxing, City of Newark.

Moskowitz writes:
"Science fiction is both my hobby and avocation.
There have been short periods in my life when it has
been my vocation. I began writing science fiction in
1940 out of utter desperation, since during the Depression it was virtually impossible to get work of any
type. I sold the second story I wrote, "World of
Mockery," to *Planet Stories* (Summer, 1941), but a
later story, "The Way Back," was placed and printed
in the January, 1941 *Comet* first. "The Way Back"

"was originally submitted as a 6,000-word short, but
F. Orlin Tremaine said he would buy it if I would double the length. I did and he did. "Man of the Stars,"
a novelette for *Planet Stories* (Winter, 1941), was the
best-received work of fiction I ever did. Most people
are not aware that I ever wrote and sold fiction, but
I have also had stories in *Amazing Stories, Fantastic
Universe, The Saint's Mystery Magazine, Info*, etc.,
as well as some anthology appearances. I quit writing
in 1942. I was agenting at the time, specializing in
science fiction, and handled the work of Harry Walton,
John Victor Peterson, Graph Waldeyer, Thomas S. Gardner, William Lawrence Hamling, among others. Believe
it or not, it was more difficult to get authors to
give me stories to sell than to sell them.

"I was placed in the 610th Tank Destroyer Division
when drafted in 1942, and when I got out, Malcolm Reiss
of *Planet Stories* tried to get me to write again, even
outlining plots for me, but I had lost all desire for
it. Jobs were easy to get, and I took a position with
a wholesale grocery firm, first as a truck driver, and
then as a salesman. During most of that time I treated
science fiction as a hobby, built up my collection, did
a great deal of background research in the field, wrote
The Immortal Storm and many scholarly articles for *Fantasy Commentator* and others. I had done several 'View-
points' columns for Alden H. Norton's *Astonishing Stories* in 1941 and 1942, and when *Fantastic Novels* was
revived, he asked me to do some science fiction reviews
for him.

"I had been running a science fiction club in Newark,
N.J., known as the Eastern Science Fiction Association,
and I succeeded in getting Hugo Gernsback to speak at
a meeting. He was impressed by the proceedings, and
he offered me the editorship of *Science Fiction +*, a
slick science fiction magazine he was about to launch,
partially, I suspect, as a tax write-off. While with
him I made professional connections that resulted in
my first hardcover science fiction anthology, *Editor's
Choice of Science Fiction*. When the magazine was abandoned after seven issues (I use the word 'abandoned'
advisedly, because there were several offers to continue, since it had almost doubled its circulation from
a low point with the third issue, to its peak with its
seventh and last issue). The science fiction field
was in a state of collapse, so since I was very expert
in the food business, I moved into the trade journal
field with *Frosted Frozen Field*, a frozen food magazine.

"*Quick Frozen Foods*, then, as today, the world's
leading frozen food magazine, and rated among the very
top trade journals in America, made me an offer to come
over to them. I did, in 1955, starting as an Associate
Editor, and through 17 years moving up progressively
to Managing Editor, Editor, Vice President, and Associate Publisher (April, 1970). In addition to QFF, I
was responsible for *Quick Frozen Foods Retailing, Quick
Frozen Foods International*, and two directories. All
departments in three offices, New York, Chicago, and
Los Angeles, including editorial, advertising, circulation, production, and directories, reported to me,
and were my responsibility.

"In 1972, a pattern occurred which is all too common
in big corporation management. The Cahners Publishing
Company, which had bought the magazine from E. W. Williams Publishing Company, decided to change not only
the methods of selling advertising, but the editorial
handling of the magazine. I fought these trends (which
had been in progress for several years), but at the
end of April, 1972, I was fired for resisting progress.
By December of that year, the magazine, which had been
in business for 34 years, took such devastating losses
under the unhampered new policy that it had to be sold
to Harcourt Brace Jovanovich, the big trade book, text

SAM MOSKOWITZ (Cont.)

"book, and magazine publishers.

"I took a position as Editor of *Beverage Industry Magazine* for Magazines for Industry, a publication appealing primarily to the carbonated soft drink industry; I also edited the magazine's annual Manual, a basic directory, and did extremely well there.

"Losses continued so staggering at *Quick Frozen Foods* that Harcourt Brace Jovanovich asked me if I would come back under special agreement, and see if I could save the publication from extinction. I returned on January 17, 1974, as Associate Publisher, and then was promoted to Co-Publisher in September, 1974, when it became obvious the magazine would break even by the end of the year.

"As an aside, my growth in the business field very closely resembles that in science fiction. Through conducting 30 or more surveys a year for 30 years, I am probably the world's leading authority on the frozen food industry, contributing to the major texts on the subject, including the definitive four-volume work, *The Freezing Preservation of Foods*, in which I present the only history of the prepared foods industry. I personally compile the basic statistics of the industry used by the government, as well as the business community. I lecture on the technology and merchandising of frozen foods at universities, and act as a consultant to many of the major firms, including DuPont, Minnesota Mining, American Can, Campbell Soup, General Mills, McCormick Spices, etc.

"My interest in the hardcover end of science fiction began in 1947, when the science fiction specialty presses flourished, including Fantasy Press, Gnome Press, Fantasy Publishing Company, Inc., Prime Press, and others. I organized The Avalon Company, and edited and published one book, *Life Everlasting and Other Tales of Science, Fantasy and Horror*, by David H. Keller, M.D., in a limited edition of 1200 numbered and signed copies. Despite my lack of knowledge of book publishing, I made money on the book, because of my basically sound grounding and education in business (I took four years of business in school), but also realized that it was not a practical operation when balancing time against income, so did not continue. The introduction to the Keller book, a life of that author, set the format for the popular profiles I was later to write for the science fiction magazines.

"I moved further into books in 1954, when McBride approached Hugo Gernsback to edit an anthology to be titled *Editor's Choice in Science Fiction*. I was about to be let go, but Gernsback suggested to Robert M. McBride that I do the job, and then permitted me to use his offices as a base of operation, paying me a partial salary for clean-up work. He offered me the magazine, *Science Fiction +*, and the distributor agreed to advance me enough to finance the magazine, but Gernsback changed his mind, saying he might resume it himself; .but after months of dickering with the distributor, he dropped it cold, and the time lag destroyed my opportunity, if opportunity it was, to take over.

"I got along so well with the editor at McBride, Otto v. St. Whitelock, that a series of anthologies were lined up (most not science fiction), and one which appeared in 1954, *Great Railroad Stories of the World*, had the best advance sale of any McBride book on that list; but evil days struck the firm, and they published very few new books after that, and paid for fewer than they published. For a short time, there were two McBrides, the old man splitting off and forming another company, but now both seem to be out of business.

"Within the science fiction fan world, my project which was greeted with the greatest enthusiasm was the hardcover publication of *The Immortal Storm*, a history of science fiction fandom, which was collected, revised (and 15,000 words added), and published by the Atlanta Science Fiction Association. The Association was made up of Ian MacCauley, Jerry Burge, and Carson Jacks. The man who did most of the work, and is responsible for the handsome appearance of the volume, in its time the most attractive semi-professional effort to appear in book form, was Jerry Burge. Absorbing the brunt of the financing was Carson Jacks, today virtually unknown. Though I had the book copyrighted in my name, and limited the printing to one edition, I eschewed all profits, leaving whatever there might be to be divided up entirely among the producers of the book. The book eventually sold out, and did make a profit. I never inquired how much, but none of the gentlemen involved has yet retired. The personal acclaim I received was worth far more than money. Before a switch of editors at World, a new trade edition of the book was seriously considered, with 15-20,000 words of new material.

"*The Immortal Storm* took about seven years to write, was done with extreme care, and I am now glad I did it, because no one else would have been able to piece together the thousands of personal and bibliographical bits that makes it an increasingly valuable reference as many of the old science fiction fans become well-known authors, editors, and artists, and as scores of the amateur publications become sought-after collector's items. If a publisher decides to bring out another edition in the future, I would bring the volume up to the onset of World War II. I have all the materials in superb order.

"From late 1953 to early 1955, I taught the first college-level course in science fiction writing in history at the City College of New York. Dr. Thomas S. Gardner had told me about a friend of his, Robert Frazier, who had been trying to get CCNY to let him teach a course on writing the popular science article. Strangely enough, they wanted a course on science fiction writing, for which he was not qualified. I got in touch with him, and the school supervisor at that time, Dr. Simon Lissim, who decided that my qualifications were satisfactory; but since I did not have a degree in science fiction writing, he would accept Robert Frazier's degree in science, and let the two of us teach the class together. I, understandably, did most of the work, but Frazier was able to secure classes on other subjects. I had as guest lecturers Robert A. Heinlein, John W. Campbell, Isaac Asimov, Lester del Rey, Robert Sheckley, Algis Budrys, and many others of similar stripe. I had to drop the class in 1955 when my editorial position required I be available nights. As a text, we used L. Sprague de Camp's *Science Fiction Handbook*.

"In compiling lists of Guests of Honor of the World Science Fiction Convention, my name is never shown. It has been forgotten, but I was 'Mystery Guest of Honor' at the 13th World Science Fiction Convention in Cleveland in 1955, and I have the handsome plaque presented to me by Anthony Boucher to prove it. A year-long guessing game was carried on by the committee of the Cleveland convention, highly publicized at the time, as to the Mystery Guest of Honor; the man who had, in their opinion, done the most for science fiction conventions up to that date. I planned, raised finances for, and conducted the First World Science Fiction Convention in 1939, when I was only 19 years old. That fact is well known, but what has been forgotten was that I did a heavy portion of the work on a very large percentage of the world conventions right through to 1955, in addition to presenting possibly several hundred small

SAM MOSKOWITZ (Cont.)

"conferences and meetings. I saved a half dozen conventions from economic disaster, auctioning non-stop
for interminable hours, until the committee would finally tell me I had covered expenses. Frequently,
hours before the convention, I would be called upon
to arrange almost the entire program, as their initial
plans fell through at the last moment.

"For nearly a score of years, I had worked free of
charge for clubs, conventions, and fan magazines, and
finally I had my fill. I would do exhaustive research
on science fiction, and sometimes have a fan magazine
editor hold it for three or five years. Frequently,
there were editing hatchet jobs on priceless bibliographies as they encountered space problems. Blatant
errors were edited into my copy. I decided that I
would only give material in special cases. The next
research article I did on "How Science Fiction Got
Its Name." I suggested to Robert W. Lowndes, who had
been publishing a series of articles in his magazines
on science fiction, including one I had written as a
thesis for Robert A. Madle (which got him an A Plus),
that he publish it. He couldn't use it at the time,
so I sent it to The Magazine of Fantasy and Science
Fiction, then edited by Anthony Boucher. I enclosed
first class postage, but when it was returned air
mail special delivery, I was so furious I didn't open
it for two days, because I imagined that this was
Boucher's way of expressing contempt for the material.
(We had engaged in a couple of disputes previously.)
When I did open it, I found that he merely wanted a
segment removed, and was eager to run it. The appearance of the article in the February, 1957 issue
of the magazine was actually the beginning of a continuous series which resulted in my later books.

"During the summer of 1956, Leo Margulies was a
guest speaker at the Eastern Science Fiction Association. After the meeting, he came up to my home with
a group of club members. He was so impressed by the
library (being an extraordinary bibliophile himself)
that he asked me to do the book review column for his
new magazine, Satellite. Some months later, he asked
me where I thought he could get a good article on
earth satellites. I made many suggestions which were
not quite satisfactory. Finally, I told him that no
one had ever done an article on the true father of
the earth satellite, Edward Everett Hale, who had
written "The Brick Moon" for the Atlantic Monthly in
1869, and its sequel "Life on the Brick Moon" for the
same publication in 1870. He became very excited
about the idea, and I cast it into article form, including material on other earth satellite stories.
It was very popular, even being quoted at length by
nationally syndicated columnists. While he was at
my home, he had noted my unusually fine run of old
interplanetary books. I told him I intended to write
a history of the interplanetary story, and was collecting books toward that end. He remembered that,
and suggested that I write the book in complete chapters, and run it in Satellite. The appearance of
Into Other Worlds by Roger Lancelyn Green in 1957
anticipated me, so I decided to write a history of
science fiction instead. The format I selected, an
author for each article, was the best for magazine
publication, which was the primary reason it was
written in that fashion.

"As a by-product of my research on the articles,
I was producing various literary tit-bits and little-
known delicacies for Satellite to reprint. When an
unwise change in format and frequency forced the
magazine to cease publication, I started a series on
interplanetary travel for Hans Stefan Santesson's

"Fantastic Universe, and also supplied pictorial material from old books. The closing down of that magazine
found me offering my wares to The Magazine of Fantasy
and Science Fiction, where Robert Mills decided against
it. Henry Morrison, who was then working for the
Scott Meredith Literary Agency, said that Amazing and
Fantastic were trying to change their image as action
pulps, and might be receptive to such 'prestige' pieces. They ordered five, and placed them in Fantastic,
which was declining badly in circulation. The effect
was a sharp and admitted circulation gain attributable
directly to the articles. They were willing to buy
24 a year, 12 for each magazine, but I told them that
since I was employed full-time, I could only research
and write about six. They decided to switch the articles to Amazing, which was higher budgeted, so they
could pay me more. They also asked me to select reprints and write introductory matter for them for both
magazines. These also had salutory circulation results.

"When I had written enough articles for a book, I
revised them, and began to look for a book publisher.
No one was standing in line waiting for a book on the
history of science fiction, and the volume may have
been rejected by as many as 18 publishers. One day,
I was approached by Jerome Fried, an editor for the
World Publishing Company, to assist a friend of his,
Noel Keyes, to assemble an anthology of future war
stories on a fee basis. That book fell through, but
Keyes asked me to assist him on an anthology titled
Contact, later published by Paperback Library. Fried
knew me from the time when, on the recommendation of
Virgil Finlay, he had commissioned me to do a supple-
ment to The Complete Book of Space Travel, by Albro
Gaul, a portfolio of early space ships, 1638-1929 (1956).
Later portions of this were plagerized by the Hearst
Features Syndicate in their Sunday papers throughout
the country, but World would not assign me the copyright to sue them for fear it would hurt their subsidiary sales. I gave him a carbon of the introduction
of my book, several chapters, and an outline. He submitted it to William Targ, executive editor, who decided to take a chance on the volume. Initial sales
were only fair, but the book got some 40 reviews, many
of them very long and complimentary. I made appearances on radio and television, and the sales continued
to come in. Not at any flood-level rate, but not at
a trickle either. As year followed year, the book refused to stop selling.

"By 1965, I had accumulated enough articles to put
together a second book on the moderns, Seekers of Tomorrow. In the meantime, World had been bought out by
Times-Mirror Press; both Targ and Fried had left, and
World decided they were only going to publish books of
a reference nature. After considerable editorial debate, they decided that my books filled the bill, particularly as sales on the first book continued to move
in. I had been submitting around to many publishers a
prospectus for a four-volume anthology of science fiction, taking it from the very beginnings up to the present. Wallace Exman, the new editor at World, thought
it might be a good idea if this notion was combined
with my histories, and a companion volume with a story
written by each of the authors written about was issued
with each nonfiction collection. Seekers and Modern
Masterpieces of Science Fiction were published simultaneously, but both sold out before publication. The
set received extraordinary reviews in the newspapers
across the country, and many of the reviewers mentioned
my previous book. I went to work on a companion to
Explorers of the Infinite called Masterpieces of Science Fiction. This also sold out before publication,
and for some reason received unusual reception behind
the Iron Curtain.

SAM MOSKOWITZ (Cont.)

"Fred Pohl had been following my articles in *Amazing*, and I was into a new series on serious aspects of science fiction, including religion, birth control, and Forteanism, and when Ziff-Davis sold the magazines, he made it clear that I would be welcome in his publications. I continued the series in *Worlds of Tomorrow* and *Worlds of If* for several years, but one day at an Eastern Science Fiction Association open meeting he said he would prefer that I do more articles on modern, young developing writers, and fewer on the old. I was two-thirds of the way through my next book, and if I had acceded to his request, with the limited time available to me I would have been unable to finish my book; so having no urgent need for the money, I decided I would forego the magazine sale of the remaining articles, and complete the book. It later developed that I had put too stringent an interpretation upon his suggestions, and that an accomodation could have been worked out.

"It had been my hope that with the direction pointed by my books, serious researchers would emerge who would move into the unexplored areas of science fiction for popular books and articles, academic reviews and the amateur press. It is a startling indictment, but only the collectors working for the amateur press have made a contribution of any true significance. What works did appear from the academics pretended that science fiction existed in a vacuum. They were unable to relate it to the times, to the publishing world of that period, and most unfortunate of all, they were unable to link what had gone in the past with what is being published presently.

"I had hoped with the immense amount of information I had, that others would slowly fill in the unexplored areas, offering me a springboard to move on to much more advanced aspects of science fiction. It soon became increasingly apparent that this was not going to happen, and except in the case of veteran bibliophiles who had spent a lifetime accumulating data, it was not likely to happen. It then became apparent, if the history of science fiction was to emerge with any semblance of coherency, I would have to personally move into the unknown areas myself, and clarify them. This was done with *Science Fiction by Gaslight*, published by World in 1968. It was a pivotal chapter in the history of science fiction, its growth in the popular magazines of the 1890s and the first decade of the 20th century, which obviously could not be explored because no bibliographies existed. No one was aware that it should be investigated, and if they were, no basic book on the history of the magazines involved as a unified phenomenon existed.

"*Under the Moons of Mars*, a history and anthology of science fiction in the Munsey magazines, dealt with a period that was known to most collectors, and of which several bibliographies had been done, but since there was no unified history of the early pulps, and complete confusion as to where and how science fiction entered the scene, added to the fact that the early pulps were even more difficult to locate than the earlier slick popular magazines (runs of which were preserved in a few of the larger libraries), the willing researcher could not even find a jumping-off point. I was able to put this period into perspective with desirable clarity, when the book appeared from Holt, Rinehart & Winston in 1970.

"*The Crystal Man*, by Edward Page Mitchell, which contained a 25,000-word preface revising the history of American science fiction, caused a sensation when it appeared in October, 1973. I had discovered a hitherto unknown American author, who was unquestion-

"ably a pivotal figure in the thematic history of science fiction. He was Edward Page Mitchell, who had spent 50 years as Associate Editor, Editor, and Publisher of the *New York Sun* from 1874 to 1924, and had anticipated even H. G. Wells on such themes as a time machine, invisible man, matter transmission, mechanical freezing for suspended animation, child mutations, friendly aliens, faster-than-light travel, computers, personality changes through brain surgery, and many others. He had been syndicated across the United States and overseas anonymously, so his true influence had not been realized.

"I have the research completed, waiting for the time and publisher, of a discovery that far transcends even Edward Page Mitchell, and its publication will write a completely new and unexpected chapter into the history of science fiction.

"*Strange Horizons* (Scribner) will be a combination of more fundamental data on science fiction through basic research, and advancing evaluation of it to a higher level than has previously been possible, because more essential background has been secured.

"I had been a friend of Leo Margulies for a long time, and had twice dissuaded him from reviving *Weird Tales* magazine during the late Fifties and early Sixties, because I couldn't see it economically viable. He came to me in late 1973 with an arrangement with a distributor and printer that appeared to minimize his chances for loss. I finally agreed to edit the magazine as a spare-time project, with an agreement that in addition to a small retainer, I would be entitled to a share of the profits, if any. The publication saw four issues, which were an outstanding success with the readership, but fell below the break-even point. The amount of loss per issue would have been negligible for a large publisher, but for Margulies, whose other publications were not too profitable, it was chancy. For me, it was just plain unprofitable. Packaged as a paperback, I could have gotten more for the stories I put together than what I had received from Margulies, and with about one-quarter of the work, so I asked out, and the magazine was not continued.

"The Hyperion Press of Westport, Connecticut, approached me in regard to editing a group of classic science fiction reprints in 1973. When they agreed to make certain changes in their standard operating procedure so the proposed set would be sold on both a library and trade basis, I accepted their offer to edit the series. A first group of 29 books, including six reissues of my own work, proved so successful that a second series was published several years later. The success of both series was due not only to the selections, but to the fact that myself and Hyperion had very considerable experience in the technical and business aspects of publishing which were complementary.

"Over the years, I have also edited a great many individual anthologies, including some ghost jobs. As the extent of my ghost editing becomes evident, it has been quite reasonably asked why I bother. I do virtually no ghost editing at all presently. At the best, I will consent to a job of collaboration or work by special arrangement as a consultant. It must be understood that not only do I have one of the world's larger collections of science fiction, but possible the best in the world for research purposes. It is a balanced collection--all the magazines, one of the world's largest fan magazine accumulations, most of the important hardcovers, including close to all reference works, and hundreds of extremely rare titles, thousands of letters, thousands of non-science fiction pulps and slicks which have carried or are in some fashion related to fantasy, and rows of filing cabinets with everything from notes and clippings to fan magazines about

SAM MOSKOWITZ (Cont.)

"the field filed in apple pie order. Given the subject, I can put an anthology together in a weekend or two, that will not duplicate any that have ever been published. I have the most intimate knowledge of how to go about securing rights, what is a fair price for the material, and how to secure additional copies of the needed work so that I can split the fee for an anthology, and yet make it profitable to all concerned because my reference material and know-how minimizes the work required. Furthermore, because my wife, who is an outstanding surgeon, has as one of her hobbies photography, a studio, darkroom, and equipment are on hand to supply any type of illustrative matter in black and white, or color.

"Another reason I took the ghost jobs is that I was so busy as an associate publisher of my company that I did not have the time to contact editors and seek out projects. With very few exceptions, most of the anthologies, historical pieces, and special consultant work that I have done has been the result of publishers or editors coming to me. One man I have ghosted for had already secured the contract and payment, as well as an agreement on the basic idea of the work. That is a bigger part of the job than most realize.

"I am at heart a collector and researcher. I exult in the thrill of discovery, and delight in talking books with other collectors. I intend to do some more fiction in the future, but will not take up full-time writing or free-lancing unless I should be unfortunate enough to lose my position, and not be able to obtain another good one.

"Aside from science fiction people, most of my personal and social life is occupied with my wife, Christine E. Haycock, M.D., an absolutely extraordinary achiever in her profession, whose firsts for a woman in her profession are legion, who in 1970 became the youngest woman ever given the coveted 'Woman of the Year' Award by the New Jersey Women's Medical Association branch of the American Medical Association, for her work past and present. In addition to private practice as a surgeon, she is Associate Professor of Surgery at the New Jersey College of Medicine and Dentistry, and a Col. and command officer in the 320th U.S. Medical Division of the Army Reserve. She was and is an avid reader of science fiction. Our miniature Schnauzer Impy, now close to 12 years old, is defeating the notion that you can't teach an old dog new tricks by winning awards in obedience and utility so numerous that they require an entire cabinet. He is one of only a handful of Schnauzers that have ever succeeded at tracking, and is quite obviously smarter than either one of us. Our new French poodle, Amy, has just won a first prize in obedience."

* * * * *

WALTER F. MOUDY

Full Name: Walter Frank Moudy.
  Born December 19, 1929, at Cassville, Missouri. Son of Ernest and Maxine Moudy. Married Marguerite Moudy, 1952. Three children: Tony, Chris, Jenny.

Education: A.B., University of Missouri, 1955; LL.D., 1957.

Career: Lawyer., 1957-73. Died April 13, 1973, in Kansas City, Missouri. Member: Phi Beta Kappa; Order of the Coif.

First Professional Sale: *No Man on Earth*, Berkley, 1964. Agent: Virginia Kidd, Box 278, Milford, PA.

* * * * *

SLAWOMIR MROZEK

Full Name: Sławomir Mrozek.
  Born June 26, 1930, at Borzecin, Poland. Son of Antoni Mrozek (a post office clerk) and Zofia Keozior. Married Maria Obremba, 1959.

Education: Studied architecture, oriental culture, and painting in Krakow, Poland.

Career: Writer.
  Has also been a caricaturist for various Polish newspapers and magazines, and a journalist in Krakow; now a full-time writer.

* * * * *

A. N. L. MUNBY

Full Name: Alan Noel Latimer Munby.
  Born December 25, 1913, at London, England. Son of Alan Munby (an architect) and Ethel Greenhill. Married Joan Edelsten, 1939 (died 1945); married Sheila Crowther-Smith, 1946. One son, Giles (born 1954).

Education: B.A., King's College, Cambridge University, 1935; M.A., 1947; Litt.D., 1962.

Career: Librarian.
  In the antiquarian book trade, with Bernard Quaritch, 1935-35; with Sotheby & Co., 1937-39, 1945-47; Fellow and Librarian, King's College, Cambridge University. Died December 27, 1974. Munby served as a Captain in the Queen Victoria Rifles during World War II, and was a prisoner of war from 1940-45.

Honors: Honorary Fellow, Pierpont Morgan Library, New York.

Member: Bibliographical Society (past President); British Museum (trustee); British Library Board.

Interests: Book collecting and shooting; author of a number of books on the history of libraries and the book trade.

* * * * *

H. WARNER MUNN

Full Name: Harold Warner Munn.
  Born November 5, 1903, at Athol, Massachusetts. Son of Edward Emerson Munn (a painter) and Jessica Anne Lemon (a musician). Married Malvena Ruth Beaudoin, January 14, 1930 (died 1972). Four children: John Warner (born 1930), James Edward (born 1936), Gerald Douglas (born 1942), Robin Shaun (born 1947).

Education: Attended Athol High School, 1917-21.

Career: Officer manager and writer.
  Has been a toolmaker, brakeman on the New York Central Railroad, deckhand on a Hudson River riverboat, carpenter ("built my own house"), bakery route salesman, ice cream salesman, vacuum cleaner salesman, planer

H. WARNER MUNN (Cont.)

man and rip saw operator in West Coast lumber mills; currently Office Manager, Stoker Lad Heating Company, Tacoma, Washington; free-lance writer, 1925-DATE.

First Professional Sale: "The Werewolf of Ponkert," in *Weird Tales*, July, 1925.

Awards: Henry Broderick Play Award, Northwest Writers Conference.

Member: Tacoma Writers Club (President); Ascension Lutheran Church (Council member); Washington Poets Association.

Interests:
Writing, theatre, good food, travel, pretty girls (!), photography, witchcraft and demonology, speculative fantasy, poetry, ancient and mediaeval history.

Munn writes:
"I lost my mother when two years old, and was brought up by my grandmother, who was a piano-teacher and artist, and possessed of an insatiable curiosity (which rubbed off on me). She corresponded with Jules Verne and H. G. Wells, and taught me to look at the world with wonder. I had read 100 books, at least, by the time I was seven--including the *Bible*, Burton's *Anatomy of Melancholy*, and *Les Miserables*. No idea now what I appreciated at this age, except acquiring a taste for rotund eloquence, and a love of quality in writing--which I have tried to emulate (still working at it). I was writing poetry about this time, and from then onward. Nothing remarkable, of course--just for fun. Then fiction, sporadically, stopping for a time after *Weird Tales* and *Unknown* folded. Began again as a hobby in 1965 with a book-length verse study of Joan of Arc's life.
"I was mentioned in Bernard de Voto's section in the *Atlantic Monthly* as 'the only active student of witchcraft and demonology alive' at that time, 'in Massachusetts.' I was pleased and flattered, being only a collector. Now I am more interested in historical fiction with a weird and a fantasy slant, and probably most of my future writing will be of this type, or science fiction with a sound historical basis. It is my belief that the surface of this earth, its interior and its seas, its future and its past, can yet contribute much to science fiction, without the necessity to voyage in imagination through space. I hope to be able to prove this."

* * * * *

ROBERT MURPHY

Full Name: Robert William Murphy.
Born August 27, 1902, at Ridley Park, Pennsylvania. Son of William Robert Murphy (an engineer) and Mary Elizabeth Bryant. Married Jean Warfield Whittle, March 22, 1946. Two children: Robert Shane, Molly Jean. Education: Attended Washington & Lee University.

Career: Editor and writer.
Senior Editor, *Saturday Evening Post*, 1942-62; instructor in writing at various colleges and writing conferences; free-lance author, 1938-71. Died July 13, 1971. Member: Explorers Club, New York.

Award: Dutton Animal Book Award, 1964, for *The Pond*.

JOE MUSSER

Full Name: Joseph L. Musser.
Born August 15, 1936, at Chicago, Illinois. Son of Joseph R. Musser and Nellie Weathers. Married Nancy Green, July 29, 1956. Five children: Kerry, Kevin, Bruce, David, Laurinda.

Career:
Member, Board of Directors, FourMost Productions, Wheaton, IL, 1965; Director of Creative Services, 1968-DATE; Assistant Director, Bedford Center for Creative Study, Glen Ellyn, IL, 1968-DATE. Member: Fellowship of Christians in the Arts, Media, and Entertainment.

Awards:
First Prize in Radio Competition, Festival of Arts in Birmingham, Alabama, 1966, for his radio drama, "Dawn at Checkpoint Alpha."

* * * * *

JOHN MYERS MYERS

Full Name: John Myers Myers.
Born January 11, 1906, at Northport, Long Island, New York. Son of John Caldwell Myers and Alice McCorry. Married Charlotte Shanahan, 1943. Two children: Anne Caldwell, Celia. Education: Attended St. Stephens College, Middlebury College, University of New Mexico.

Career: Writer.
Has worked as a newspaperman, copywriter for an advertising agency, farmer, special lecturer at the University of Arizona, director of a writers' conference, organizer of a collection of Western Americana for a library; full-time writer, 1941-DATE.

Agent: Ned Brown, 315 South Beverly Dr. Beverly Hills, CA.

* * * * *

VLADIMIR NABOKOV

Full Name: Vladimir Vladimirovich Nabokov.
Born April 23, 1899, at St. Petersburg, Russia. Came to the U.S. in 1940, and became a U.S. citizen in 1945. Son of Vladimir Dmitrievich Nabokov (a jurist and statesman) and Elena Ivanovna Rukavishnikova. Married Vera Evseevna Slonim, April 15, 1925. One son, Dmitrii Vladimirovich (a translator of his father's work).

Education: Attended Prince Tenisher School, St. Petersburg, 1910-17; B.A., Trinity College, Cambridge University, 1922.

Career: Writer.
Left Russia in 1919, settling in Berlin, where he taught English and tennis, and composed crossword puzzles in Russian (the first ever devised in that language) for the newspaper *Rul*, 1922-37; lived in Paris, 1937-40; Lecturer in Russian, Wellesley College, 1941-48; Research Fellow in Entomology, Harvard University, 1942-48; Professor of Russian Literature, Cornell University, 1948-59; writer of novels and stories, 1926-DATE. Member: Writers Guild.

Awards and Honors: Guggenheim Fellowships, 1943, 1952; National Institute of Arts & Letters Grant, 1951; Prize for literary achievement, Brandeis University, 1964.

MARY NASH

Full Name: Mary Nash.
  Born July 7, 1925, at Milwaukee, Wisconsin. Daughter of James Hurd Hughes (a lawyer) and Caroline Upham. Married and divorced. Three children: Norman, Hollister, Thomas.

Education: B.A., Radcliffe College, 1951; M.A., University of Washington, 1954.

Career: Writer, 1958-DATE. Agent: Russell & Volkening, 551 Fifth Avenue, New York, NY 10017.

* * * * *

ROBERT NATHAN

Full Name: Robert Gruntal Nathan.
  Born January 2, 1894, at New York. Son of Harold Nathan (a lawyer) and Sarah Gruntal. Married Joan Boniface Winnifrith.

Education: B.A., Harvard University, 1916.

Career: Writer.
  Screenwriter, Metro-Goldwyn-Mayer, 1943-50; freelance author, 1915-DATE.

First Professional Sale: A short story to *Smart Set* in 1915.

Agent: Swanson, 8523 Sunset Blvd., Hollywood, CA 90028.

Honors: Honorary degree from the University of Judaism; awards from the Los Angeles Library Association, and the Authors Club of Los Angeles.

Member:
  National Institute of Arts and Letters; Academy of American Poets (Fellow); Academy of Motion Picture Arts and Sciences; P.E.N.; Writers Guild of America, West; ASCAP.

Interests: "Staying alive."

"Almost all my books are fantasies, and many of them are more-or-less SF. The only books not fantastic--in the proper meaning of the word--are *Peter Kindred, Autumn, Road of Ages, The Seagull Cry, They Went On Together, Winter in April, The Orchid, Color of Evening.* I've published fifty-six volumes, including forty novels, and sixteen plays, poems, and other forms."

* * * * *

VICTOR S. NAVASKY

Full Name: Victor S. Navasky.
  Born July 5, 1932, at New York, New York. Son of Macy and Esther Navasky. Education: A.B., Swarthmore College, 1954; LL.B., Yale University, 1959.

Career: Writer and editor.
  Special assistant to the Governor, State of Michigan, 1959-60; Consultant, U.S. Civil Rights Commission, 1961; Editor & Publisher, *Monocle* (humor magazine), 1961-DATE.

Member: Phi Beta Kappa.

CLAIRE NECKER

Full Name: Claire Kral Necker.
  Born October 16, 1917, at Chicago, Illinois. Daughter of Joseph James Nemec (in publishing) and Josephine G. Kral. Married Walter L. Necker (a librarian), Aug. 21, 1939 (divorced, 1968).

Education: M.S., Northwestern University, 1938.

Career: Librarian.
  Curator, Field Museum of Natural History, Chicago, 1938-40; Physicist, Gaertner Scientific Corporation, 1944-49; Chemist, Commercial Testing and Engineering Company, 1949-52; Partner, Aardvark Books (antiquarian book business), 1942-59; Librarian, Lake County Public Library, Indiana, 1969-DATE.

First Professional Sale: *Cats and Dogs*, A. S. Barnes, 1969.

Interests: "Anything and everything connected with nature; cats; misc. handicrafts; and, of course, reading."

* * * * *

GLENN NEGLEY

Full Name: Glenn Robert Negley.
  Born November 5, 1907, at Indianapolis, Indiana. Son of Homer Samuel Hanway Negley (a building contractor) and Myrtle Rhoades. Married Julia Henderson, July 7, 1939.

Education: A.B., Butler University, 1930; M.A., 1934; Ph.D., University of Chicago, 1939.

Career: Professor of Philosophy.
  Instructor in Philosophy, University of Oklahoma, 1937-38; Asst. Professor, University of Illinois, 1938-46; Professor of Philosophy, Duke University, 1946-DATE; visiting professor and lecturer at a number of colleges and universities.

Awards: Rockefeller Foundation Research Fellow, 1946; Ford Foundation Research Fellow, 1953-54.

Member:
  American Philosophical Association; American Political Science Association; American Association of University Professors; Greenlands Association.

* * * * *

RAY NELSON

Full Name: Radell "Ray" Faraday Nelson. [name pronounced Ray-dell]. Born October 3, 1931, at Schenectady, New York. Son of Walter Huges Nelson (an electronics engineer) and Marie Reed (a school teacher). Married Perdita Lilly, 1951 (divorced, 1955); married Lisa Mullikin, 1955 (divorced, 1958, died 1966); married Kirsten Enge, 1958. One son, Walter Trygve (born 1958).

Education:
  B.A., University of Chicago, 1960; attended Art Institute of Chicago, 1954; Programmer's Certificate, Automation Institute, Oakland, California, 1961.

RAY NELSON (Cont.)

Career: Full-time writer.

First Professional Sale: "Turn Off the Sky," in
The Magazine of Fantasy and Science Fiction, August,
1963.

Agent: Adrienne Martine, 5816 Alameda Avenue #1,
Richmond, CA 94802.

Honors: Hugo nomination in 1964 for "Turn Off the
Sky" (the story was removed from the ballot amid
great controversy).

Member: Science Fiction Writers of America; Little
Men.

Interests:
First century history, cartooning, fanzines, waltz
collecting, chess, gardening, unitarianism, Atlantis,
Berkeley Free University, Egypt, ecology, crafts,
walking, Victorianism, art nouveaux, reincarnationism,
song writing, films, sex.

Nelson writes:
"My first published work, "Turn Off the Sky," was
hailed by Harlan Ellison as 'the first New Wave SF
story,' and hounded by controversy to the point where
it was underhandedly (or fearfully) removed from the
Hugo ballot before the voting. It is the best thing
I ever wrote. I've spent the rest of my life since
then trying, without success, to write a better one.
It's rough to start at the top, and work down."

* * * * *

JOSEF NESVADBA

Full Name: Josef Nesvadba.
Born June 19, 1926, at Praha [Prague], Czechoslova-
kia. Son of Josef and Ludmila Nesvadba. Married
Libuje Nesvadba, September 25, 1968.

Education: M.D., Charles University.

Career: Psychiatrist and group psychotherapist in
Prague. Member: P.E.N.

First Professional Sale: "The Einstein Brain,"
in The Magazine of Fantasy and Science Fiction,
May, 1962 ("Pirate Island" appeared in the February,
1962 issue).

Agent: Dilia, Vyjehradska 88, Praha 2, Czechoslovakia.

Nesvadba notes: "My work oscillates between psychotherapy, fiction writing, and script writing. I am
trying to develop a form of psycho-fiction, with stress
on new developments in this field."

* * * * *

JOHN NEUFELD

Full Name: John Arthur Neufeld.
Born December 14, 1938, at Chicago, Illinois. Son
of Leonard Carl Neufeld (a manufacturer) and Rhoda
Padway.

Education: B.A., Yale University, 1960.

Career: Editor.
Currently a staff member, Golden Press, New York;
novelist, 1968-DATE.

Agent: William Morris Agency, 151 El Camino, Beverly
Hills, CA 90212.

* * * * *

KRIS NEVILLE

Full Name: Kris Ottman Neville.
Born May 9, 1925, at Carthage, Missouri. Son of
Gilbert Ottman Neville (various blue & white collar
jobs) and Ethyl Mae Peters (a waitress). Married Lil
Johnson, September 28, 1957. Two children: Nieson
Ottman (born 1962), Helen Arleen (born 1964); three
step-children: Lois Tyus, Freddie Marie Tyus, Leonard
Tyus.

Education: B.A., University of California, Los Angeles, 1960.

Career: Writer
Various jobs in the plastics and chemistry industries,
including positions with The Conveyor Company, Rocketdyne, and Epoxylite (1955-66, and part-time in the late
1960s); currently a full-time writer.

First Professional Sale: "The Hand from the Stars,"
in Super Science Stories, July, 1949.

Interests: Bridge, conversation.

Neville has published books on epoxy resins, linear
polymers, biomedical plastics, adhesive dental restora-
tive materials, and insulation for industrial motors.
He comments:

"I got involved with the field originally through
fandom. I read the stuff avidly in high school in
Carthage, Missouri, and after World War II, when I
came out here to Los Angeles, I looked up the LASFS,
became a member, and was active in the club--or that
offshoot of it which consisted of the beer-drinking
veterans of the war--for a couple or three years. After I got out of college, I kind of drifted away from
the club, although I still view it fondly, and occasionally get involved in its affairs.
"Barry Malzberg and I have hasseled back and forth
in correspondence for a number of years the state of
SF, and I kind of have an opinion on the subject, but
not a rigorous one. I seldom read the magazines, although I still subscribe to F&SF. Every year or two
I check out a copy of Galaxy or Analog. Most of the
stuff I've read--including a representative selection
of all the magazines in 1973, a couple or three issues
of each--in the last few years has not appealed to me,
and the magazines seem rather horrible overall. The
material appearing in the original anthologies is
often a lot better, and I'll occasionally find a short
story that I can genuinely admire. I'm not too much
up on the novels, but I'm kind of disappointed by them,
too.
"Having said all that, though, it seems to me that
the best work being done today is a lot better than
the best that was done when I was writing, or that was
being done during the earlier Golden Ages. The field
is such a mishmash, though, of juveniles and experimental stuff and hard-core SF and who knows what all, that
I'm not even qualified to have an opinion, since I
don't keep up. My own personal taste is for the experimental stuff, and I steer pretty clear of hard-core SF."

P. H. NEWBY

Full Name: Percy Howard Newby.
Born June 25, 1918, at Crowborough, Sussex, England. Son of Percy Newby and Isabel Bryant. Married Joan Thompson, 1945. Two children: Sarah Jane, Katharine Charlotte.

Education: Attended St. Paul's College, 1936-38.

Career: Broadcasting executive.
Lecturer in English Literature, Fouad I University, Cairo, 1942-46; free-lance novelist, 1946-49; Producer in Talks Department, BBC, London, 1949-58; Chief of Third Programme, 1958-DATE.

Agent: David Higham Associates, 76 Dean St., London W1, England.

Awards:
Atlantic Award of Rockefeller Foundation, 1946; Somerset Maugham Prize, 1948, for *A Journey to the Interior*. Member: Society of Authors; Royal Society of Literature (Fellow).

* * * * *

JACK NEWFIELD

Full Name: Jack Newfield.
Born February 18, 1939, at New York, New York. Education: B.A., Hunter College, 1961.

Career: Editor.
Assistant Editor, *Village Voice*, New York. Member: Southern Christian Leadership Conference.

Agent: Lynn Nesbit, Time Life Building, Rockefeller Center, New York, NY 10020.

* * * * *

HOWARD NEWMAN

Full Name: Howard Newman.
Born December 22, 1911, at New York, New York. Son of Samuel Newman (a college professor) and Gussie Halpern. Education: Attended City College of New York, 1929, and Columbia University, 1930.

Career: Publicist.
Office boy for Dwight Deere Wiman Productions, 1929; worked as a press agent assistant on various theatre productions, 1930-46; free-lance film publicist for over 40 films, 1946-DATE; Head of Publicity, Samuel Bronston Studios, Madrid, 1961-64; Director of Publicity, Twentieth Century-Fox, 1964-67; Director of Publicity, Paramount Pictures, 1968-70; Director, Howard Newman Public Relations (film publicists), 1970-DATE. Member: Motion Picture Academy of Arts and Sciences; Publicists' Guild of America.

* * * * *

ROBERT NEWMAN

Full Name: Robert Howard Newman.
Born June 3, 1909, at New York, New York. Son of Samuel Jerome Newman and Nance Ortman. Married Dorothy Crayder, 1936. One daughter, Hila. Education: Attended Brown University, 1927-38.

Career: Writer.
Chief of Radio Output Division, Office of War Information, 1942-44; writer, particularly in radio and TV, 1936-DATE. Member: Radio Writers Guild; Writers Guild of America, East.

Agent: Harold Ober Associates, 40 E. 49th St., New York, NY 10017.

* * * * *

RUTH NICHOLS

Full Name: Joanna Ruth Nichols.
Born March 4, 1948, at Toronto, Ontario, Canada. Daughter of Edward Morris Nichols (a clergyman) and Vilas Ruby Smith. Married William Norman Houston, September 21, 1974.

Education:
B.A., University of British Columbia, 1968; M.A., McMaster University, 1972; Ph.D., 1975.

Career: Teacher and writer.
Teaching Assistant, McMaster University, 1970-74; sessional Lecturer, Carleton University, 1974.

First Professional Sale: *A Walk Out of the World*, Harcourt, Brace & World, 1969.

Honors & Awards:
Woodrow Wilson Fellowship, 1969-70; Doctoral Fellowship from the Canada Council, 1971-74; Canadian Association of Children's Librarians Award for best English language children's book published in Canada in 1972.

Interests:
History and manners of the Renaissance; medieval music; psychology; theory of the novel; yoga. "My Ph.D. thesis was on 'The Incarnational Theology of Charles Williams.'"

* * * * *

HAROLD NICOLSON

Full Name: Harold George Nicolson.
Born November 21, 1888, at Tehran, Persia. Son of Arthur Nicolson (a diplomat, First Baron Carnock) and Catharine Rowean-Hamilton. Married Victoria Sackville-West (a poet and author), October 1, 1912 (died 1962). Two sons: Lionel Benedict, Nigel.

Education: Attended Wellington College, and Balliol College, Oxford University.

Career: Politician, author, and journalist.
Diplomat for the British Diplomatic Service, 1909-29, serving in Madrid, Constantinople, Tehran, Berlin; Member of Parliament from West Leicester, 1935-45; Governor, BBC, 1941-46; Chairman of Committee of London Library, 1952-57; Trustee, National Portrait Gallery, 1948-64. Died 1968.

Honors & Awards:
Companion of St. Michael & St. George, 1920; Knight Commander of Royal Victorian Order, 1953; Commander of the Legion of Honor; numerous honorary doctorates; Honorary Fellow, Oxford University. Member: Royal Society of Literature (Fellow); Classical Association; New York Academy; Travellers' Club; Beefsteak Club.

MARJORIE NICOLSON

Full Name: Marjorie Hope Nicolson.
Born February 18, 1894, at Yonkers, New York. Daughter of Charles Butler Nicolson (a newspaper editor) and Lissie Hope Morris.

Education: A.B., University of Michigan, 1914; A.M., 1918; Ph.D., Yale University, 1920.

Career: Professor of English.
Asst. Professor of English, University of Minnesota, 1920-23; Asst. Professor, Goucher College, 1923-26; Professor of English and Dean, Smith College, 1927-41; Professor of English, Columbia University, 1941-62; Visiting Professor, Claremont Graduate School, 1962-63; Member, Institute for Advanced Study, 1963-68; Member of Committee on Awards, Guggenheim Foundation, 1930-37; Member of Advisory Board, 1937-66; lecturer at colleges and universities.

Awards:
Guggenheim Fellowship, 1926-27; Rose Crawshay Prize of British Academy, 1937; Distinguished Scholar Award ($10,000) from the American Council of Learned Societies, 1962; recipient of 16 honorary degrees from various institutions; Pilgrim Award, 1971.

Member:
Modern Language Association; Renaissance Society of America; History of Science Society; United Chapters of Phi Beta Kappa (President, 1940-46).

* * * * *

LARRY NIVEN

Full Name: Laurence Van Cott Niven.
Born April 30, 1938, at Los Angeles, California. Son of Waldemar Van Cott Niven (a lawyer) and Lucy Estelle Doheny (breeds Keeshond dogs). Married Marylin Wisowati, September 6, 1969.

Education: B.A., Washburn University, 1962.

Career: Writer, 1964-DATE.

First Professional Sale: "The Coldest Place," in *Worlds of If*, December, 1964.

Agent: Robert P. Mills Ltd., 156 E. 52nd St., New York, NY 10022.

Awards:
Nebula Award, Best Novel, 1970 (1971), *Ringworld*; Hugo Award, Best Short Story, 1966 (1967), "Neutron Star"; Hugo Award, Best Novel, 1970 (1971), *Ringworld*; Hugo Award, Best Short Story, 1971 (1972), "Inconstant Moon"; Hugo Award, Best Short Story, 1974 (1975), "The Hole Man"; Hugo Award, Best Novelette, 1975 (1976), "Borderland of Sol"; Ditmar Award (Australian), 1971, for best foreign SF, for *Ringworld*.

Member:
Science Fiction Writers of America.

Interests:
Sailing, backpacking, poker, Scrabble, attending fan groups of science fiction, Georgette Heyer literature.

Work in Progress: *The Ringworld Engineers*.

GUIDO NIZZI

Full Name: Guido "Skipper" Nizzi.
Born May 7, 1900, at Fiumalbo, Italy. Son of Carlo Nizzi and Gaetana Cesari.

Education: Studied for the priesthood, specializing in languages; never took his vows.

Career: Theatre manager. Member: Albuquerque Philatelic Society.

Interests: Philately.

* * * * *

STERLING NOEL

Full Name: Sterling Noel.
Born March 28, 1903, at San Francisco, California. Son of Joseph Jefferson Noel (a writer and playwright) and Rosalie Mahon (a writer). Married Harriet Xanders, March 28, 1964.

Education:
"Dropout from the University of California (Berkeley), Columbia University, and University of Paris. No degrees, honors, or anything else except unpleasant memories."

Career: Writer.
Newspaper writer since 1921; Managing Editor, *New York Journal*, 1937-42, when he went into the Navy; Sunday Editor of same from 1945-51; Managing Editor and later Executive Editor, *Baltimore News American*, 1956-69; at present columnist for the Hearst Newspapers; has also been Copy Editor for the Paris edition of the *Chicago Tribune*, 1931-34, and was a Naval liaison officer with the French Navy, attached to the admiral commanding cruiser division, 1943-44.

First Professional Sale: *I Killed Stalin*, Farrar, Straus, 1951.

Agent: Robert P. Mills Ltd., 156 E. 52nd St., New York, NY 10022.

Awards: Croix de Guerre; Silver Star.

Member:
Mason; Dramatists Guild; Authors League of America; Society of Professional Journalists; Sigma Delta Chi; various conservation groups.

Interests: "Nothing to speak of. Horse race handicapping, women, teaching writing occasionally."

Noel writes:
"Writing is a family vice. My early education was engineering, but I abandoned that in time. I was of the so-called Lost Generation in Paris, and knew most of 'em. I've contributed to Dr. Tom Wood's *Lost Generation Journal*, and still do. I've been living in Mexico for the past four years, but am ready to abandon that.
"For a while in the newspaper columns, I concentrated on ecology, and built up somewhat of a reputation as a conservationist, but people don't care much about that any more. The problem will always be with us, but readers get bored."

He also notes: "At one time, I was married to Catherine Littlefield; she died in November, 1951."

WILLIAM F. NOLAN

Full Name: William Francis Nolan.
Born March 6, 1928, at Kansas City, Missouri. Son
of Michael Cahill Nolan (an insurance adjuster) and
Bernadette Mariana Kelly. Married Marilyn Kam Seal
(a writer), March 6, 1970.

Education: Attended Kansas City Art Institute, 1946-
47; San Diego State College, 1947-48; Los Angeles
City College, 1953.

Career: Writer.
"I began as a professional artist with Hall Bros.
in Kansas City, as a greeting-card designer. Have
also worked in aircraft, acted in films and TV, been
a professional magazine and book editor, etc." Managing Editor, *Gamma*, #1-3, 1963-64.

First Professional Sale: "The Joy of Living,"
in *Worlds of If*, August, 1954.

Agent: Adams, Kay & Rosenburg, 9220 Sunset Blvd.,
Los Angeles, CA 90069.

Honors & Awards:
Adventure on Wheels was selected by the American
Library Association as one of 12 top books for young
adults in 1960; Edgar Special Award, 1970, for
Dashiell Hammett: A Casebook; Edgar Special Award,
1971, for *Space for Hire* (also named one of the year's
five best original paperbacks by the Mystery Writers
of America).

Member:
Science Fiction Writers of America; Mystery Writers
of America; Writers Guild of America, West; First
Printings of American Authors (Member, Advisory Board).

Interests:
"Collecting Hemingway, pulps, old comics, and sports
car racing (in which I participated and won a trophy
driving an Austin-Healey 100-M)."

Nolan writes:
"I've been involved in every aspect of science fic-
tion--as a fan (co-founder of the San Diego Science
Fantasy Society; co-chairman of the 1952 Worldcon),
letter writer (to *Famous Fantastic Mysteries*, *Planet
Stories*, etc.), artist and amateur publisher (*Ray
Bradbury Review*), fanzine editor (*Rhodomagnetic Digest*), book editor (seven science fiction anthologies),
magazine editor (the first three issues of *Gamma*),
actor-narrator (*Dream of the Stars*), lecturer (at
UCLA and Pasadena City College), critic (science fiction book reviewer for the *Los Angeles Times*), novelist (*Logan's Run*, *Space for Hire*), script writer
(films and TV), and short story writer (beginning with
If).
"I don't limit myself to science fiction; I work
the full range of writing, from novels to short stories, from profiles to full-length biographies, essays,
articles, film scripts, book reviews, literary criti-
cism--whatever turns me on most at a given time. I
jump around like a sand flea, never limiting myself
to a single field; I scatter my work over a hundred
markets. People tend to label writers, but I don't
fit any label.
"I wrote my first poem at nine, my first short story
at ten, my first novel at fifteen. Of course they
were all dreadful, but I was writing them only for
myself.
"For years I doubted that I could ever make a living

"at writing, since it seemed to require a type of super-
intelligence I lacked. I equated writing with total
scholastic brilliance; it took a long while to realize
that I didn't need to be a super-person to write, that
I just needed to be myself, know myself, and learn to
know other people.
"A published checklist of my work prepared by Charles
E. Yenter (Tacoma, Washington, 1974) reveals that I
have sold and/or had printed some 765 items. These
include 30 books in the main genres in which I work:
science fiction, auto racing, mystery/suspense, and
show business. In 1975, M.G.M. will produce my collaborative novel, *Logan's Run*, and I am currently very
active in television and film scripting. 1975 will
mark my 21st year as a professional writer, and I
wouldn't trade it for any other job in the world!"

* * * * *

JOHN NORMAN

Full Name: John Frederick Lange, Jr.
Born June 3, 1931, at Chicago, Illinois. Son of
John Frederick Lange, Sr. and Almyra D. Taylor. Married Bernice L. Green, January 14, 1956. Three children: John, David, Jennifer.

Education: B.A., University of Nebraska; M.A., University of Southern California; Ph.D., Princeton
University.

Career: Professor of Philosophy.
Has worked as a radio and continuity writer, a story
analyst at Warner Brothers Motion Pictures, a film
writer for the University of Nebraska, a technical editor and special materials writer for Rocketdyne (a division of North American Aviation specialized in the
production of rocket engines); served several years
in the U.S. Army, reaching the rank of Sergeant, and
an MOS of 1290, which is that of personnel management
specialist; currently Professor of Philosophy, Queen's
College, City University of New York.

First Professional Sale: "A radio script to a
station in Lincoln, Nebraska, for ten dollars, when
I was in high school or thereabouts."

* * * * *

JOAN NORTH

Full Name: Joan North.
Born February 15, 1920, at Hendon, London, England.
Daughter of Frank Wevil Gordon North (a metallurgist)
and Gladys May Paybody. Married C. A. Rogers (Astor
Professor of Mathematics at University of London),
February 24, 1952. Two children: Jane Petronelle,
Petra Nell.

Education:
Attended schools in England prior to 1932, in China,
1932-35; Lowther College, Wales, 1935-36; King's College, University of London, 1938-39.

Career: Writer.
Has been a nurse, social worker, with the BBC, and
in the publications department of the Tate Gallery,
London; now a full-time writer.

Member: Society of Authors; Buddhist Society; College
of Psychic Science; Churches Fellowship for Spiritual
and Psychic Studies.

STERLING NORTH

Full Name: Sterling North.
    Born November 4, 1906, at Edgerton, Wisconsin. Son of David Willard North (in real estate) and Elizabeth Nelson (a biologist & linguist). Married Gladys Dolores Buchanan, June 23, 1927. Two children: David Sterling, Arielle.

Education: B.A., University of Chicago, 1929.

Career: Writer and editor.
    Literary Editor, *Chicago Daily News*, 1929-43; Literary Editor, *New York Post*, 1943-49; Literary Editor, *New York World Telegram & Sun*, 1949-56; Founder and General Editor of North Star Books, 1957-74; writer. Died December 22, 1974.

Awards:
    Witter Brynner Poetry Award; *Poetry* Magazine's Young Poet Award; Dutton Animal Book Award, Dorothy Canfield Fisher Award, Aurianne Award, runner-up for Newbery Award, all for *Rascal*.

Member: Authors League.

* * * * *

ALDEN H. NORTON

Full Name: Alden Holmes Norton.
    Born July 23, 1903, at Lynn, Massachusetts. Son of Charles A. Norton (a musician) and Katherine White. Married Margaret Acheson, October 12, 1942.

Education: Ph.B., Brown University, 1925.

Career: Editor.
    With Popular Publications, Inc., New York, 1935-73; positions there included Editor of *Argosy*, Editor of *Super Science Stories* (November, 1941-May, 1943), Editor of *Astonishing Stories* (November, 1941-April, 1943), Supervisory Editor of all Popular Publications magazines, Head of Releases and Foreign Sales Dept.; now retired.

First Professional Sale: "Ten Minutes to Death," in *Detective Fiction Weekly*, 1932.

Agent: Lurton Blassingame, 60 E. 42nd St., New York, NY 10017.

Member: American Contract Bridge Association (Life Master).

* * * * *

ANDRE NORTON

Full Name: Andre Alice Norton [originally Alice Mary Norton]. Born 1912, at Cleveland, Ohio. Daughter of Adalbert Freely Norton (owned a rug company) and Bertha Stemm. Education: Attended Case Western Reserve University for two years.

Career: Writer.
    Children's Librarian, Cleveland Public Library, 1934-50; Editorial Reader, Gnome Press, 1950-58; full-writer, 1958-DATE.

First Professional Sale: *The Prince Commands*, D. Appleton-Century, 1934.

Agent: Larry Sternig Literary Agency, 2404 N. 44th St., Milwaukee, Wisconsin 53510.

Awards:
    Boys' Clubs of America Certificate, 1965, for *Night of Masks*; Plaque from the Netherlands Government, 1946, for *The Sword Is Drawn*; Chiana Library Honorable Mention; Headliner Award, Theta Sigma Phi, 1963; Invisible Little Man Award.

Member:
    Science Fiction Writers of America; Penwomen; League of American Authors; Swords-and-Sorcery Guild of America.

Interests: Reading history and archaeology, cats, needlework.

Norton writes:
    "My first book was accepted and published when I was quite young--in fact it was accepted before I was 21--so I have had a long writing career.
    "I began writing when I was in high school, and had written three full books before the third was published. I then went back and revised my first book (written in high school), and that was the second title I had published.
    "Until 1950, SF was very difficult to sell in the book trade. I worked in adventure-spy-historical-and mysteries. I really broke into the field as a writer after having edited some SF anthologies for World Publishing--though I had written early books on the subject, but had not discovered any publisher interested in them until that date.
    "SF appeals to me, as I have always enjoyed reading it, and it is a purely imaginative exercise--though one does have to do a lot of research for each book. I find that sword-and-sorcery has the greatest appeal for myself--and it is the most fun to write.
    "Most of my contributions in the field have been for teenagers, and my one rule is that one must never simplify--which is an insult to the readers' intelligence--and most SF readers tend to be in the upper third of their classes in school.
    "Because of health, I now lead a very quiet life, and have done so since 1952. I am now owned and operated by six cats, and live in semi-rural Florida. I would like to travel, but health prevents, so I do my travelling via books and TV."

    "The Witch World books grew of themselves--I never intended to make a series in the beginning. Part of *Witch World* was taken from separate scenes I had done years ago for a novel on the Crusaders who had settled in Outremer. And the background of most of the books is based on Celtic and early English legends and folklore. *Warlock of the Witch World* is a retelling of *Childe Roland*, and *Year of the Unicorn* of Beauty and the Beast.
    "The division of the books is according to continents on that world. Estcarp corresponds roughly to Europe, and High Hallack to America. The Estcarpian stories largely have the same family as characters--the High Hallack do not. *The Atlas of Fantasy* has a map of Witch World; however, since that was drawn quite a few more towns and important sites have been added.
    "As I mentioned, the Verlaine segment in *Witch World* was developed from a fragment I did about one of the knights of Outremer--those who settled in the Near East during the Crusades, and built up petty kingdoms there. I never wrote the historical tale, but used it as part of the fantasy. I switched to High Hallack with *Year of the Unicorn*, and then wrote several short stories and novelettes laid in the dales--which are founded on

ANDRE NORTON (Cont.)

"the Yorkshire dales of England, with their wild Vi-king-invader backgrounds. I then did the two novels, *The Crystal Gryphon* and *The Jargoon Pard*, taking up various dates before, during, and after the invasion.

"The Estcarp books are: *Witch World, Web of the Witch World, Three Against the Witch World, Warlock of the Witch World,* and *Sorceress of the Witch World.* The High Hallack series includes: *The Crystal Gry-phon, Spell of the Witch World, Year of the Unicorn,* and *The Jargoon Pard.*

"As for what I write--well, I write the kind of tales I like to read myself. There is a great deal of re-search which goes into each book--I use archaeology, ancient history, history of the middle ages, folklore, legends, natural history, and the occult for my back-grounds. When I use such a definite occult matter as psychometry, the tarot, etc., in a book, I have a definite demonstration by an expert in order to get the material correct."

* * * * *

VICTOR NORWOOD

Full Name: Victor George Charles Norwood.
   Born March 21, 1920, at Scunthorpe, Lincolnshire, England. Son of Elmer William Norwood (an Army major) and Alice Austen. Married Elizabeth McKie, October 31, 1937. Two children: Russell Paul (born 1942), Shane Victor (born 1955).

Education: B.A., Sheffield College, 1939; Dip.Lit., Bennett College, 1947.

Career: Writer.
   Has been a truck driver, blacksmith, prizefighter, bank guard, wrestler, opera singer, head croupier at a gambling establishment, gold and diamond prospector, private detective; author and lecturer, 1945-DATE; served in the British Merchant Marine, 1939-44, being mined or torpedoed on three different occasions.

First Professional Sale: *The Untamed*, Scion Ltd., 1951.

Agent: S. E. Porcelain, Box J, Rocky Hill, NJ.

Honors & Awards:
   American Historical, 1959; Bellamann, 1960; L.A.C.S., 1963; Special War Medal, British Merchant Marines; Africa Star; Italy Star; France & Germany Star; Atlan-tic Star; 1939/45 Star.

Member: Royal Society of Literature (Fellow); North Lincolnshire Writers' Circle (1st Chairman); Zoolo-gical Society (Fellow).

Interests: Shooting, sea fishing, movie making, karate, golf.

Norwood has made numerous television appearances in Australia, the U.S., and Britain; he is an authority on gold, opal, sapphire, and diamond prospecting, and on the aboriginal tribes of South America. He com-mented: "I have made no less than seven trips to the Amazon basin, the first in 1951, prospecting for dia-monds, and collecting pics and material for travel books, shooting color movies for lectures, etc. I got the idea for the Jacaré books from seeing an enor-mous Indian/Negro from Manaos wrestling with a live

"alligator (for tourists). His muscular development was superb, but he was dumb."

* * * * *

ALAN E. NOURSE

Full Name: Alan Edward Nourse. [Pronouced "Nurse"]
   Born August 11, 1928, at Des Moines, Iowa. Son of Benjamin Chamberlain Nourse (an electrical engineer) and Grace Ogg (a teacher). Married Ann Jane Morton, June 11, 1952. Four children: Benjamin Chamberlain (born 1958), Rebecca Stevens (born 1960), Jonathan Alan (born 1961), Christopher Ogg (born 1962).

Education: B.S., Rutgers University, 1951; M.D., University of Pennsylvania, 1955.

Career: Writer.
   Owner and Manager, Chamberlain Press, 1953-55; Intern, Virginia Mason Hospital, 1955-56; free-lance writer, 1956-58; general practice of medicine, North Bend, Wash-ington, 1958-64; free-lance author, 1964-DATE; one-time owner of Tradewinds Travel Bureau, North Bend.

First Professional Sale: "High Threshold," in *As-tounding Science Fiction*, March, 1951.

Agent: Brandt & Brandt, 101 Park Avenue, New York, NY 10017.

Awards:
   Junior Book Award, Boys Clubs of America, 1963, for *Raiders of the Rings*; Washington State Governor's Award, Governor's Festival of the Arts, 1966, 1974.

Member:
   Science Fiction Writers of America (President, 1968-69); Seattle Free Lances; American Medical Association; Washington State Medical Association; King County Medi-cal Association.

Interests: Hiking, backpacking, fishing, hunting.

Nourse writes:
   "Although I have been writing in the fields of sci-ence fiction and fantasy continuously since 1951, I have also written extensively in such diverse fields as mystery and detective, popularization of science, career guidance, popularization of astronomy, and health care. Only about 13 of my 33-odd books have been science fiction.
   "The organization of Chamberlain Press resulted from our attempt to buy out Prime Press. We did one book under the CP imprint, Richard Matheson's first collec-tion, *Born of Man and Woman*, published in 1954. Ac-tually, we didn't do too badly with that, thanks to an awfully good paperback sale to Bantam, but I was the only one in the organization who could do any of the work (the others merely provided funds), and this was in my third year of medical school; I made the dis-covery that publishing, even a book a year, is a like a full-time job. It was too much for me to try to juggle. With full time to devote, capital backing of around 100 grand (instead of 4), and reasonable pros-pects for an initial year's list of 10 titles, I might go it again, except that writing is more profitable. Mostly, I learned that shoestring publishing isn't the way to do it, Jack Chalker to the contrary notwithstan-ding. The amount of work involved is just staggering, the negative inertia you face equally staggering, if possible. To say nothing of getting books distributed.

ALAN E. NOURSE (Cont.)

"I think we sold almost a thousand, which (in retrospect) was probably incredibly good, but not a good foundation for going on to a second book. If we could have bought out Prime on our terms, I might be a publisher today instead of a doctor/writer...but there you are!"

* * * * *

CHARLES NUETZEL

Full Name: Charles Alexander Nuetzel.
  Born November 10, 1934, at San Francisco, California. Son of Albert Augustus Nuetzel (an artist) and Betty Stockberger. Married Brigitte Marianne Winter, Oct. 13, 1962.

Education: Attended San Fernando Valley State
  College for one term.

Career: Writer.
  Has been a pop music singer, film technician, and Editor/Packager of the Powell Books science fiction line (1969-70); free-lance author, 1960-DATE.

First Professional Sale: A story to *Cocktail*
  magazine, 1960.

Agent: Forrest J Ackerman, 2495 Glendower, Hollywood,
  CA 90027.

Nuetzel writes:
  "I met Ray Bradbury in a second-hand bookstore, and thus learned about science fiction fans and Forrest J Ackerman. In my fan years, I became a very close personal friend of E. Everett Evans, and have many manuscripts signed by him to 'my no. 1 fan.' Through his help I learned something about writing: a story should also have a sub-plot. I did for a while publish a fanzine better forgotten. Was a great Edgar Rice Burroughs fan, and have what was called by his secretary, Miss Jennings, the last books he autographed; no other proof other than the shaky handwriting.
  "My grandfather, on my mother's side, was John Stockberger, who edited what is now known as the *Valley Green Sheet* (a large circulation newspaper in the San Fernando Valley) during the time ERB had his Tarzana ranch. I'm told they knew each other in a casual manner.
  "My father, Albert Nuetzel, was a commercial artist all his life, working for the motion picture industry. To please his son, he did several SF covers in the Fifties for such magazines as F&SF, *Amazing*, and *Fantastic*, some of which were reprinted overseas.
  "All of which might seem to have little to do with myself as a writer. Not so!
  "Like Forry Ackerman is now saying (probably to please me), 'Ray Bradbury burned his first two million words of unpublished manuscripts; Charles Nuetzel *sold* his.' To which I silently add: maybe I should have burned mine too.
  "But the point is, a writer can do one of several things: write just for the fun of it, and never even try to get published; write and write and write until you get good enough to get published, destroying all the work in between; or write and write until you are just good enough to be published in the lowest crummy market possible, and keep on writing as fast as you can, learning on the job.

"My father taught me the following: an artist can sit up in an attic and paint for himself--and starve-- or he can use what talents and abilities and tricks he knows, and direct them to a commercial market, and make his living doing so.
  "Every good writer and fan has heard Ray Bradbury say over and over again in public, 'Write, write, write, until you get all the bad words out of your system... don't slant...write about what you hate and love violently....' A quote, I must state in Mr. Bradbury's defense, coming from a very weak human memory. I'll add another clause: 'Write all the bad plots out of your system!'
  "Thus, the first year of my professional writing was done in the following manner: I took a title, put it on the top third of the page, picked a penname, and then started writing until the story was finished. Most of the time I never read what I'd written, but sent it directly to Ackerman, who suffered through something like 100+ manuscripts during his first year of agenting for me. Needless to say, the agent didn't make much money, even though he gave me a pretty fair sales record for a first year pro writer.
  "I was told by Forry not to bother with sci-fi. Thus the stories were on subjects I'd sooner say nothing about. I used over a dozen pennames.
  "Being a great lover of the way Edgar Rice Burroughs made a lot of money, to say nothing about people like Erle Stanley Gardner, and lovingly calling them 'hacks,' I consider myself a professional 'hack,' and wish to God I could be as much of a 'hack' as the two above-mentioned rich writers. Not that I expect this to happen, but we all have our dreams.
  "While I admire the Ray Bradbury type of artist-writer, I disagree with him about one basic point: do slant and do write to sell as much as possible, using pennames to hide behind when the writing and/or subject matter is something you don't want to be credited for. Save your own name for things you wish to think of as 'quality.'
  "My father wanted me to become a singer. I must have been good enough at it, because I had some very important people helping me put an act together--and they were doing it for free! In the middle of this, I sold my first story.
  "In science fiction, I like the adventure-romance (ERB) and social satire. I am very strong on the first three words of a story. For example, 'the beautiful mountain' is not at all as interesting as 'if the beautiful....' Words like 'if,' 'but,' etc., are far more 'grabbing' than words like 'the,' 'a,' or 'an.'
  "I do believe, of course, that the next few words are also important, right until the last two saying 'The End.' And what they say must have plot, sub-plot, theme, conflict--in other words, it should be a damn good story! But those first few words will cause the reader to start reading, and any intelligent writer hopes and prays he will continue right to the end, and say, 'that's one hell of a story!'
  "My future plans are, of course, to be successful and make a lot of money. I would like to do more than simply write and package books for publishers. I have nothing against cutting out the middle man, and making more money. I enjoy seeing books filled with words that came off my typewriter--for a few moments, at least. I enjoy seeing translations of my work. Like all writers, I have a big ego in that direction.
  "It's pleasant to receive a note from Robert Bloch, saying that he had read a copy of *Swordmen of Vistar*, and that it was an enjoyable way to kill a rainy Sunday afternoon. That's the kind of response all writers need and crave."

CLAUDE NUNES

Full Name: Claude Nunes.
    Born April 14, 1924, at Johannesburg, Transvaal,
South Africa. Son of Manoel Nunes and Patricia Ina
Rose Ellis. Married Rhoda Gwylleth Williams-Foxcroft,
May 2, 1959. Children: Michael Manuel (born 1961),
David Owen (born 1966), Andrew Jonathan (born 1968).

Education: B.Com., University of South Africa,
    1946.

Career: Statistician.
    Statistician, Chamber of Mines of South Africa,
1942-DATE.

First Professional Sale: "The Problem," in *Science Fantasy*, April, 1962 (with Rhoda Nunes).

Member: Science Fiction Society of South Africa;
    Associate, Cost and Works Accountants.

Interests: Reading (heavily), photography, gardening, yoga, swimming, stamps.

Nunes writes:
    "As for how it feels to be one of the few in this
part of the world [South Africa], I hardly noticed it.
Naturally anti-social, because I have been deaf since
the age of 11 (meningitis), I doubt whether I would
have been a shining light in the SF world of America.
As it is, my wife is the one who takes the lead in
the local SF society.
    "As things are at the moment, my writing has dwindled to nothing because of family responsibility. My
children take up a great deal of my time, even at
night, and my father is ill, and has been so for nearly four years. This means that I have to act as 'the
man about the house' for my mother as well as in my
own home. Frankly, I never seem to have a moment to
myself.
    "As you know, the political situation in South Africa is distinctly 'Black' at the moment. There is
plenty of scope here for a shocker about the future
of my country, but I haven't the heart (or time) to
try to write it."

* * * * *

RHODA NUNES

Full Name: Rhoda Gwylleth Nunes.
    Born October 12, 1938, at Johannesburg, Transvaal,
South Africa. Daughter of Stanley Garth Williams-
Foxcroft (an inventor) and Hyldred Nosworthy Brick-
nell (a bookkeeper). Married Claude Nunes, May 2,
1959. Three children: Michael Manuel (born 1961),
David Owen (born 1966), Andrew Jonathan (born 1968).

Education: B.A., University of South Africa, Pre-
    toria, 1969.

Career: Housewife.
    "Short spell as a clerical worker just before mar-
riage"; writer.

First Professional Sale: "The Problem," in *Science Fantasy*, April, 1962 (with Claude Nunes).

Awards: CNA prize for English, 1955.

Member: Science Fiction Club of Johannesburg.

Interests:
    "Graphology, music, painting, psi (attempts at culti-
vating same, extensive reading), playing encyclopaedia
to my young, writing letters (long and many), designing
gadgets."

Rhoda Nunes writes:
    "I was the daughter of one of Churchill's WW2 'toy-
makers,' who invented a phototypesetting machine. I'm
attracted to SF because of its scope for new ideas,
and its breakaway from kitchen sink literature. Appal-
led at prevailing overseas idea that South Africa is
all backveld, without SF fans. My husband has been a
fan since 1936.
    "You asked how a collaboration works in practice. In
our case, in the two books and various short stories
we wrote together, it was a yin-yang proposition: each
supplied what the other lacked. I'm good at starting
things, while Claude's good at ending them; I begin a
story with verve and gusto, and peter out halfway, just
as Claude is getting into his stride. The beginning
of *Inherit the Earth*, for instance, was mostly mine.
I get general ideas which he elaborates into detailed
plot structures. Differences of ideas concerning plot
do not as a rule arise, because we act (or acted, rather) in writing in much the same way as we do when
planning a holiday: he decides route and destination,
while I provide the human touches en route, the warmth
and characterisation and bits of humour (like the story
of the small boy Ephraim in *Recoil* who developed a
cross between telepathy/clairvoyance and astral travel
as a game, to the bewilderment of his straitlaced aunt
and the befuddlement of the aliens). Claude's strong
point is his sheer persistence; he'd type solidly,
three pages per evening, come hell or high water or
colds in the head; I'd get flashes of enthusiasm or
inspiration to help when the going got tough, and I'd
help him rewrite and polish and type. He, you see,
could not always visualise human reactions and dialogue, being totally deaf; I could. And I've studied
psychology. So the fields of activity of each of us
meshed nicely. It's possibly significant that of the
five novels he's written, only the two in which we
collaborated have been published--plus one or two of
our short stories (collaborations and solo short stories). I also write a fair amount of humorous poetry
(with an underlying seriousness), for which there's
not much market, either in or out of SF.
    "As Claude said, there's much scope for 'a shocker'
SF book on this country...but then, that's true of almost anywhere today. Trouble is, by pointing out how
things might happen, one might help to bring them a-
bout. Which is a fearful responsibility. One advantage of SF in general is that it's verbal exploration
of alternative possibilities for redemption/destruc-
tion, without the practical risks of real-life action--
though it might provide a fuse. It's humbling to re-
alise that this is what SF might carry on its shoulders."

* * * * *

BJÖRN NYBERG

Full Name: Björn Emil Oscar Nyberg.
    Born September 11, 1929, at Stockholm, Sweden. Son
of Holger J. Nyberg (a businessman) and Margit E. Lar-
sson (a civil servant). Married Anne-Marie Jönson,
February 12, 1954. One daughter, A. Camilla (born 1956).

Education: Graduate, Stockholm School of Business,
    1961.

Interests: Reading, hunting, travel.

BJÖRN NYBERG (Cont.)

Career: Controller.
Officer, Supply and Administration, Swedish Air Force, 1951-60; Assistant Vice President, Bonnier Group, Sweden, 1960-70; Assistant Vice President, Sundstrand International Corporation, France, 1970-72; Group Controller-International, Litton Industries MTS Group, France, 1972-DATE.

First Professional Sale: *The Return of Conan*, Gnome Press, 1957.

Member: Order of Arla Coldin, Sweden (Master of Ceremonies, 1969-70).

* * * * *

PHILIP OAKES

Full Name: Philip Barlow Oakes.
Born January 31, 1928, at Burslem, Staffordshire, England. Son of Sam Oakes (a traveller) and Constance Barlow (a teacher). Married Stella Fleming (a librarian), September 9, 1950. Two children: Susan Jill, Toby Alan. Education: Attended school in Darwen, England.

Career: Writer.
Reporter, Eric R. Sly's Reporting Service, London, 1945-46, 1949-55; Reporter and author of column "The World I Watch," *Daily Express*, London, 1955-56; Film Critic, Granada Television Film Unit, 1956-58; Scriptwriter for Granada, 1959-61; Editor of "Coming On," a column in the *Sunday Times*, London, 1965-DATE.

Agent: Curtis Brown Ltd., 60 E. 56th St., New York, NY 10022.

* * * * *

FLANN O'BRIEN

Full Name: Brian O Nuallain.
Born October 5, 1911, at Strabane, County Tyrone, Northern Ireland; moved to Dublin as a child. Son of Michael Victor O Nuallain and Agnes Gormley. Married Evelyn McDonnell, 1949.

Education: M.A., University College, Dublin, 1929.

Career: Writer.
Senior civil servant, Government of the Republic of Ireland, serving four successive Ministers for Local Government, 1937-53; Columnist, *Irish Times*, Dublin, writing "Cruiskeen Lawn" (sometimes in Latin, German, or Irish) under the pseudonym Myles na Gopaleen, 1940-66. Died April 1, 1966.

* * * * *

ELLIOTT O'DONNELL

Full Name: Elliott O'Donnell.
Born February 27, 1872, at Clifton, Bristol, England. Son of Henry O'Donnell (a clergyman) and Elizabeth Sarah Harrison. Married Ada Caroline William, January 5, 1905 (deceased). Education: Attended Clifton Collge, Bristol; Queen's Service Academy, Dublin; and Neville Dramatic Academy, London.

Career: Writer.
Was an actor on stage and in films; writer, mainly about the supernatural, 1910-65; lecturer and broadcaster on similar subjects in England and the U.S.

Member: Society of Authors; Royal Commonwealth Society. Died May 8, 1965.

* * * * *

ANDREW OFFUTT

Full Name: Andrew Jefferson Offutt V.
Born August 16, 1934, at Louisville, Kentucky. Son of Andrew Jefferson Offutt IV (a sanitary engineer) and Helen J. Spaninger (a school teacher). Married Jodie McCabe, October 19, 1957. Four children: Christopher John (born 1958), Andrew Jefferson VI (born 1961), Mary Scott (born 1962), Melissa Joe (born 1964).

Education: A.B., University of Louisville, 1955.

Career: Writer.
Salesman, Foods Division, Procter & Gamble, 1955-62; Life Insurance Salesman, National Executive Life, 1962-63; Life Insurance Salesman, Coastal States Life, 1963-68; Manager of three life and health insurance agencies, Andrew Offutt Associates, 1968-71; full-time writer, 1971-DATE.

First Professional Sale: "And Gone Tomorrow," in *Worlds of If*, December, 1954 (as Andy Offutt).

Awards and Honors:
First Prize, *If* magazine's 1954 college science fiction contest ($1000); Master of Ceremonies, 32nd World Science Fiction Convention (Discon 2), Washington, 1974.

Member: Science Fiction Writers of America (Treasurer, 1973-76; President, 1976-1977).

Interests: History, psychology, women.

* * * * *

JACK OLECK

Full Name: Jack Oleck.
Born March 1, 1914, at New York, New York. Son of Richard Oleck (a clothier) and Yetta Lerner. Married Dorothy Feldman, February 1, 1941. Three children: Dennis Alan (born 1943), Jory Sean (born 1951), Sherry Beth (born 1953).

Education: "I am completely self-educated."

Career: Writer.
Editor and Publisher, *Interior Decorators News*, 1957-67; full-time writer, 1967-DATE.

First Professional Sale: *Messalina*, Lyle Stuart, 1959.

Member: "I have never found any literary organization to be of any real value to a writer, and accordingly resigned many years ago from the Writers Guild, and have never joined any other organization.

Interests: History, photography, the occult.

CHAD OLIVER

Full Name: Symmes Chadwick Oliver.
Born March 30, 1928, at Cincinnati, Ohio. Son of Symmes Francis Oliver (a physician) and Emma Winona Newman (a nurse). Married Betty Jane Jenkins, Nov. 1, 1952. Two children: Kimberly Frances (born 1955), Glen Chadwick (born 1968).

Education: B.A., University of Texas, Austin, 1951; M.A., 1952; Ph.D., University of California, Los Angeles, 1961.

Career: Professor of Anthropology.
Professor of Anthropology, University of Texas, Austin, 1955-DATE; Chairman of the Department of Anthropology, 1967-71; Chairman, Graduate Studies Committee, 1972-73.

First Professional Sale:
"The Boy Next Door," in The Magazine of Fantasy and Science Fiction, June, 1951 ("The Land of Lost Content," in Super Science Stories, November, 1950, was actually published first).

Agent: Collins-Knowlton-Wing, 60 E. 56th St., New York, NY 10022; Scott Meredith, 580 Fifth Avenue, New York, NY 10036.

Awards: Spur Award, Best Western Novel, 1967, for The Wolf Is My Brother.

Member:
Science Fiction Writers of America; Western Writers of America; American Anthropological Association; Trout Unlimited.

Interests: Fly fishing for trout, wildlife conservation, tennis, history of the American West.

Oliver writes:
"I was hooked on science fiction long before I ever heard of anthropology--and I was reading SF before I knew what it was. I read Jules Verne in grammar school. I was an outdoors-oriented kid, though an avid reader, until I became ill with rheumatic fever at 12. I then read omnivorously. One of my favorites was, of course, Edgar Rice Burroughs. I bought my first SF magazine (Amazing) because it had a Burroughs story in it. I read the other stories. One was "Treasure on Thunder Moon," by Edmond Hamilton. That ruined my life. I bought every SF magazine I could find, began firing off letters to editors, bought myself a second-hand typewriter, and began to try to write fiction. When I moved to Texas (1943), and recovered my health sufficiently to play football, etc., I kept at it. I wrote something every week until Tony Boucher bought my first story.
"Anthropology came later. I took my first anthro courses as a freshman at the University of Texas (1946), but did not seriously consider it as a career until I came under the influence of a great teacher, Dr. Gilbert McAllister, in my senior year. Although I went on to take an M.A. in English, with a minor in anthropology, and even taught English briefly, I had been converted. My major influence in graduate school at UCLA was Dr. Walter Goldschmidt, with whom I later participated in the Culture and Ecology of East Africa Project.
"I feel that anthropology and SF are very close in spirit, and tackle many of the same questions, albeit in different ways. There is an intellectual interplay between the two. Sometimes, I am not sure which hat "I am wearing when.
"However, it might be noted that less than half of my published fiction is oriented toward anthropology. A writer writes about what he knows and what interests him, but I hope that my scope is not limited to mixing anthropology and science fiction. It is a bigger world than that--and a bigger universe."

* * * * *

JANE OLIVER

Full Name: Helen Christina Easson Rees.
Born October 12, 1903. Daughter of Rufus Easson Evans (a physician) and Rose Alice Vassie. Married John Llewelyn Rees (a writer), March 25, 1939 (killed on active duty with the RAF in 1940).

Education: Attended University of Lausanne, 1922-23, and Bedford Training College, 1923-26.

Career: Writer.
Has worked in a bookstore, hospital, taught gymnastics and games, and has served as a secretary to several authors; drove an ambulance during the London blitz, 1940-43; active in the British Red Cross; writer, 1932-DATE. Member: Society of Authors; P.E.N.

* * * * *

ROSS R. OLNEY

Full Name: Ross Robert Olney.
Born April 9, 1929, at Lima, Ohio. Son of Ross Nelan Olney and Elizabeth Bowers. Married Patricia Wilson. Three sons: Ross David, Scott Hunter, Eric Paul.

Education: Attended University of Wisconsin, 1948-53, through U.S. Armed Forces Institute courses.

Career: Writer.
With U.S. Air Force, 1947-53, in Korea and elsewhere; Managing Editor, Science and Mechanics, 1962-63; freelance author, 1958-DATE.

Member:
Authors Guild; American Auto Racing Writers and Broadcasters Association; Society of Magazine Writers; Society of Children's Book Writers; Greater Los Angeles Press Club; Science Fiction Writers of America.

* * * * *

WALTER O'MEARA

Full Name: Walter Andrew O'Meara.
Born January 29, 1897, at Minneapolis, Minnesota. Son of Michael O'Meara (a logger) and Mary Wolfe. Married Esther Molly Arnold, August 18, 1922. Four children: Donn, Ellen, Deirdre, Wolfe.

Education: B.A., University of Wisconsin, 1920.

Career: Advertising director.
Reporter in Duluth, Minn., 1918-20; Copywriter, J. Walter Thompson Co. (advertising), Chicago, 1920-31; Creative Director, Benton & Bowles, New York, 1932-40; Creative Director, J. Walter Thompson Co., New York, 1940-50; Creative Consultant, Sullivan, Stauffer, Colwell, & Bayles, New York, 1951-69; Chief of Planning

WALTER O'MEARA (Cont.)

Staff, Office of Strategic Services, 1942-43; Deputy Price Administrator for Information, Office of Price Administration, Washington, 1943-44; Director, National Conference of Christians and Jews; writer, 1947-DATE.

Awards:
   American Association for State and Local History Award, 1951, for *The Grand Portage*; Citation for Distinguished Services to Journalism, University of Wisconsin, 1957.

Member: Phi Beta Kappa; Sigma Delta Chi; Deadline Club, and The Players, both in New York.

* * * * *

DENNIS O'NEIL

Full Name: Dennis Joseph O'Neil.
   Born May 3, 1939, at St. Louis, Missouri. Son of Joseph O'Neil (a grocer) and Ruth Noonan. Married Anne Heaney, January 8, 1966. One son, Lawrence (born 1966).

Education: B.S., St. Louis University, 1961.

Career: Writer.
   Has been a reporter, newspaper editor, and teacher; Managing Editor, *Newsfront*, 1970-71; Editor, National Comics, 1972-DATE.

First Professional Sale: "The Iconoclasts," in *Fantastic Stories*, April, 1971.

Member: Science Fiction Writers of America; Academy of Comic Book Arts (Board Member).

* * * * *

BEN ORKOW

Full Name: Ben Harrison Orkow.
   Born January 9, 1896, in Russia. Moved to the United States in 1906. Son of Abe and Anita Orkow. Married his third wife, Ruby Orkow, April 14, 1932. One daughter, Miriam (born 1933).

Career: Writer.
   "Author of a number of plays produced on Broadway. Wrote about 16 screenplays for major studios and stars; credits include about 20 TV plays. Currently writing novels (not SF) and a stage play."

First Professional Sale: "Milgrim's Progress," a play, 1924.

* * * * *

PAUL ORR

Full Name: Paul Wright Orr.
   Born January 22, 1904, at Walnut, Kansas. Son of Peter Perry Orr (a farmer) and Estelle Maude Jane Heard. Married Violet May Balcomb, June 19, 1926.

Education: A.B., Stanford University, 1925; M.A., Columbia University, 1928.

Career: Teacher.
   Student Secretary, YMCA, New York, 1926-28; English Teacher in Moscow, USSR, 1928-30; Science Teacher, Yamhill, Oregon school district, 1946-49; Teacher, Lebanon, Oregon, 1949-50; now retired.

Member: Sierra Club; American Civil Liberties Union; Audobon Society; Desert Protective Council.

Interests:
   Hiking, desert study, writing on social and ecological subjects, birding, volunteer work at San Bernardino County Museum's Calico dig, student of health and nutrition.

* * * * *

VIOLET ORR

Full Name: Violet May Orr.
   Born May 28, 1904, at San Francisco, California. Daughter of Jean Bart Balcomb (an engineer) and Rose Gibbs (a pianist). Married Paul Wright Orr, June 19, 1926.

Education: A.B., Stanford University, 1925; M.A., Columbia University, 1928.

Career: Teacher.
   Asst. Instructor, Stanford University, 1923-25; Asst. Instructor, Columbia University, 1927-28; English Teacher, Moscow, USSR, 1928-30; Teacher, Yamhill, Oregon, 1946-49; Teacher, Lebanon, Oregon, 1949-50; Teacher of emotionally disturbed children, Los Angeles, 1953; now retired.

Member: Phi Beta Kappa; Sierra Club; Women's International League for Peace and Freedom; Wilderness Society; Audobon Society; Desert Protective League.

Interests:
   Hiking, nature study, birding, writing, volunteer at San Bernardino County Museum's Calico dig, health and nutrition.

* * * * *

ANDREW OSMOND

Full Name: Andrew Osmond.
   Born March 16, 1938, in England. Son of Kingsford Richard Osmond and Doreen Pearson. Married Stuart Baldwin (an American), January 4, 1964. Two children: Matthew, Louise.

Education: B.A., Brasenose College, Oxford University, 1961.

Career: Writer.
   Founder and Publisher, *Private Eye* magazine, London, England, 1961-62; Officer with the British Diplomatic Service, 1962-67, with posts in France, London, West Africa, and finally as Second Secretary in Rome; full-time writer, 1967-DATE; served in the British Army as a Second Lieutenant with the Gurkha Rifles, Malaya, 1956-58.

Agent: Curtis Brown Ltd., 60 E. 56th St., New York, NY 10022. Interests: painting, acting, photography, riding, tennis, billiards, beagles.

MABLY OWEN

Full Name: Mably Ceredig Owen.
Born March 17, 1912, in Wales. Son of Edward Owen and Sarah Welsh. Married Daphne Owen, 1942.

Education: Honour's Degree in English, Swansea University College, 1934.

Career: Teacher.
With the RAF in World War II as an Education Officer and Flight Lieutenant; English master after the War, his final position being Lecturer in English, Normal College of Education, Bangor, North Wales, 1964-69. Died June 26, 1969.

Honors: Frank Treharne James Welsh Prize, Glamorgan County Welsh Exhibition, 1932. Member: Schools Council Committees.

* * * * *

MAURICE OWEN

Full Name: Maurice Leslie Lloyd Owen.
Born December 11, 1925, at Sydney, New South Wales, Australia. Son of Oswald Owen (a patrolman) and Mabel Brown. Married Joy Clark. Four children: Clark Lloyd (born 1951), Marion Julie (born 1952), Stephen (born 1954), Jacqueline Ann (born 1957).

Education: Attended Hutt Valley High, New Zealand, 1938-42.

Career: Company manager.
Wholesaler, Burns Philp & Co., Brisbane, Australia, 1943-DATE.

First Professional Sale: The White Mantle, Robert Hale, 1967.

Interests: Gardening.

* * * * *

MARK OWINGS

Full Name: Mark Samuel Owings.
Born January 3, 1945, at Baltimore, Maryland. Son of Harry Owings (a miller) and Elizabeth Theresa Schmidt.

Career: Employment security clerk.
"Have been a pricing clerk, bookkeeper, warehouseman, toy repairman, offset printing machine operator, and some less mentionable things"; currently Senior Employment Security Clerk, New York State Department of Labor, Bronx; Editorial Director, Croatan House, 1973-DATE.

First Professional Sale: "James Blish: Bibliography," in The Magazine of Fantasy and Science Fiction, April, 1972.

Member:
Science Fiction Research Association; Eastern Science Fiction Association (Director, 1972); National Fantasy Fan Federation (Director, 1967); Baltimore Science Fiction Society (Chairman, 1963-67); Washington Science Fiction Association (Vice-President, 1965-66).

Interests: Library research, book-finding, talking.

Owings comments:
"I feel that bibliography and general research in the field have improved in the last few years, and will continue to do so, simply because more information is available. I feel that the SFRA should accept no credit for this whatever.... Most of what has been produced always has been good, and the only real problem bibliographers face is encroaching academic obscurantism."

* * * * *

THOMAS PAGE

Full Name: Thomas Walker Page IV.
Born July 16, 1942, at Washington, D.C. Son of Thomas Walker Page and Susan Barbour. Married Monika Plank, November, 1971.

Education: B.A., Elon College, 1966; M.F.A., Columbia University, 1968.

Career: Writer.
Advertising copywriter, PhotoTechnical Advertising and Publicity Corporation (technical ads for camera and motion picture equipment), 1967-68; Copywriter, Diener Hauser Greenthal Agency (motion picture advertising), 1971-73; full-time writer, 1973-DATE.

First Professional Sale: The Hephaestus Plague, G. P. Putnam's Sons, 1973.

Agent: Roberta Kent, WB Agency, 156 E. 52nd St., New York, NY 10022.

Member: Authors Guild, Writers Guild of America, East.

Interests: Model building.

* * * * *

LAURAN PAINE

Full Name: Lauran Bosworth Paine.
Born February 25, 1916, at Duluth, Minnesota. Married Esther Conklin, July 5, 1938. Two sons: Lauran Bosworth Jr. (born 1944), Robert T. (deceased).

Education: Attended private schools in California and Illinois.

Career: Writer.
Has been a full-time writer all of his adult life.

* * * * *

BERNARD PALMER

Full Name: Bernard Palmer.
Born November, 1914, at Central City, Nebraska. Son of Ben H. Palmer (in the monument business) and Stella Jarvis. Married June Berger, June 20, 1934 (died 1939); married Marjorie Matthews (a writer), December 12, 1940. Four children: James Barrett (deceased), Morris Jay, Bonnie Lou, Janice Kay. Education: Attended Kearney State College, 1933, and Hastings College, 1940.

BERNARD PALMER (Cont.)

Career: Writer.
Stonecutter and shop foreman, Palmer Brothers Monument Company, Holdrege, Nebraska, 1957-67; Vice-President, 1962-74; President, 1974-DATE; Chairman of the Board of Directors, 1974-DATE; full-time writer, 1967-DATE; Member of the Board of Directors, Tyndale Foundation, 1963-DATE. Member: Gideons International; Kiwanis.

* * * * *

WILLIAM PALMER

Full Name: William J. Palmer.
Born August 20, 1890, at Le Roy, Minnesota. Son of George W. Palmer and Mary Grattan. Married Margaret Willis, July 22, 1915. Two children.

Education: A.B., University of Southern California; J.D., University of Southern California.

Career: Judge.
Attorney in California until 1932; Judge of the Superior Court of California for Los Angeles County, 1932-62; now retired.

Member:
Conference of California Judges; Los Angeles County Bar Association; California State Bar; Hollywood Masonic Club; U.S.C. Alumni Association; Westwood Camera Club; Sierra Club; United Methodist Church; ASCAP.

* * * * *

EDGAR PANGBORN

Full Name: Edgar Pangborn.
Born February 25, 1909, at New York, New York. Son of Harry Leroy Pangborn (a journalist) and Georgia Harriet Wood (a writer).

Education: Attended Harvard University, 1924-26, and the New England Conservatory of Music, 1927.

Career: Writer.
Free-lance writer, 1930-76. Died February 1, 1976.

First Professional Sale: A-100, E. P. Dutton, 1930 (as Bruce Harrison).

Agent: Robert P. Mills Ltd., 156 E. 52nd St., New York, NY 10022. Interests: Painting.

Award: International Fantasy Award, 1955, for A Mirror for Observers. Member: Authors Guild.

* * * * *

ALEXEI PANSHIN

Full Name: Alexis A. Panshin.
Born August 14, 1940, at Lansing, Michigan. Son of Alexis John Panshin (Professor of Wood Technology) and Lucie Elizabeth Padget. Married Cory Seidman, June 4, 1969.

Education: B.A., Michigan State University, 1965; M.A., University of Chicago, 1966.

Career: Writer.
"Sometime soldier, laborer, librarian, proofreader, and college teacher"; now a full-time writer.

First Professional Sale: "A Piece of Pie," in Seventeen, November, 1960.

Awards: Hugo Award, Best Fan Writer, 1966 (1967); Nebula Award, Best Novel, 1968 (1969), Rite of Passage.

Member: Science Fiction Writers of America; Institute for Research on the Dissemination of Human Knowledge.

Panshin notes: "My father was born in Russia; my mother's family is English-American, dating in this country from 1620. All present and future work is being done in collaboration with my wife, Cory Panshin."

* * * * *

RICHARD PAPE

Full Name: Richard Bernard Pape.
Born March 17, 1916, at Leeds, Yorkshire, England. Son of Richard Bernard Pape (an artist and soldier) and Elizabeth Fieldhouse. Married Stephanie Helen Prouting (a barrister), June 26, 1966.

Education: Attended Clare College, Cambridge University, 1938-40.

Career: Writer.
Principal Publications Officer, Dept. of Information, Port Moresby, Papua New Guinea, 1964-73; since 1973 has been employed by the Australian Department of Aboriginal Affairs at Canberra to write the book, The Australian Aboriginal; Literary Consultant, Papua New Guinea Government Literature Bureau; has had various editorial positions with a half dozen international newspapers.

First Professional Sale: Boldness Be My Friend, Elek Books, 1953.

Literary Agent: David Higham Associates, Golden Square, London, England.

Honors:
British Military Medal, Polish Air Force Eagle, and Dutch Order of Merit, for wartime activities in German occupied Europe [Pape was a P.O.W. for three years after being shot down during a Berlin raid on September 7, 1941].

Interests: Golf, music, painting, fly fishing.

Pape writes:
"During the war I operated in Intelligence units in Holland, Czechoslovakia, Germany, Poland, Hungary, and Lithuania. Perhaps one of my greatest achievements was writing a prison camp newspaper of 30,000 words called The Kriegie Edition. Every word was hand-printed (much of it in code), relating German/Russian troop movements. It was secretly smuggled back to the U.K. from East Prussia in 1944, and was publicly acclaimed by Sir Winston Churchill. It was later reproduced in facsimile form by the distinguished Yorkshire newspaper, the Yorkshire Post.
"My motoring records include: first man alive to drive from North Arctic Cape across two-thirds of the

RICHARD PAPE (Cont.)

"world to Cape Town, 17500 miles, including Norway, Sweden, Germany, Holland, France, Spain, North Africa, Sahara, French Equatorial Africa, Congo, the Rhodesias, South Africa. The official world endurance record was certified by all international motoring bodies.

"I drove the first car to cross from Vancouver to Toronto via the Rockies in 1956, 2000 miles in 56 hours. I broke the Alaska Highway Record (5000 miles in four and a half days of nonstop driving). I made a complete encirclement of the United States in a small, four cylinder British car at 600 miles per day. I broke various records at Daytona Beach in a small British car."

* * * * *

EDITH PARGETER

Full Name: Edith Mary Pargeter.
Born September 28, 1913, at Horsehay, Shropshire, England. Daughter of Edmund Valentine Pargeter and Edith Hordley.

Career: Writer.
Chemist's (pharmacist's) assistant and dispenser, Dawley, England, 1933-40; full-time writer, 1945-DATE. Served in the Women's Royal Navy Service, 1940-45, becoming a Petty Officer.

Awards: Edgar Award, Best Mystery Novel, 1961, *Death and the Joyful Woman* (as Ellis Peters); British Empire Medal, 1944.

Agent: Joyce Weiner, 127 Eyre Court, London NW8.

Member: Society of Authors; Authors Guild; P.E.N.

* * * * *

MICHEL PARRY

Full Name: Michel Patrick Parry.
Born October 7, 1947, at Brussels, Belgium. Son of Arthur Glyn Parry and Lucille Decoen. Married and divorced. One daughter, Kirsten Marianne (born 1971).

Career: Editor.
Story Editor, American International Films, 1969-70; Outside Editor, Sphere Books Ltd., 1970-73; European Editor, *Castle of Frankenstein*, 1964-DATE; free-lance editor, 1973-DATE.

First Professional Sale: "The Last Bus," in *Tandem Horror 2*, Tandem Books, 1968.

Agent: Jon Thurley, Kavanagh Entertainments, 170 Piccadilly, London, England.

Member: British Fantasy Society.

Interests:
"I'm very interested in films, with a particular fondness for fantasy films; have worked on my own 16mm films; also very interested in magic and the occult; collect fantasy/SF/comics, etc. I've written several film scripts which have been bought, but none have been filmed at the present date. Fantasy titles include 'The Blood of Berenice' and 'Sweeney Todd.'"

Parry writes:
"You ask me why the weird tale is so popular in Britain as compared to the United States. Well, to be honest, I'm not sure that the weird tale is more popular in Britain; there are far more books of this nature published in the United States, and appreciation of them is more apparent and better organised. I think probably that fantasy of the supernatural kind is more a part of American culture than European culture, because Americans are exposed to horror movies on TV from an early age, whereas in Britain children cannot see these films in theatres until they are 16 or 18; it is only recently that "Dracula" and "Frankenstein" have begun to make appearances on late-night TV. I'm sure this has created a greater tolerance and acceptance of fantasy in the States than over here.

"Of course, Britain does have a tradition of this kind of literature, the Gothic novel being the obvious antecedent. As far as popularity of the weird tale in England goes, I think the Gothic school's sensationalised offspring--the "Penny Dreadful"--has been more influential in shaping popular appeal. The British seem to favour stories of violence and cruelty more than any other kind of weird tale. Exactly why this should be, I cannot imagine, and I'm sure there is no simple explanation. In the last six or seven years, however, the mystical and magical fantasy genre has grown in popularity--largely, I believe, as the result of the emergence of a drug culture amongst the younger middle class (yes, we still have a class system over here!). This influential minority with its drug-induced mysticism has led to an observable increase in the popularity of "softer" fantasies, and of the Lovecraftian type of weird tale, with its suggestions of cosmic depths. This development is probably even more apparent in the States. In Britain, however, I'm sure this trend has to some extent eroded the appeal of the hardcore horror story, or gruesome weird tale."

* * * * *

M. E. PATCHETT

Full Name: Mary Osborne Elwyn Patchett.
Born December 2, 1897, in Australia. Daughter of Herbert Fraser Elwyn and Jean Stratham. Widow.

Career: Writer.
Was a journalist before becoming a full-time writer in 1953. Member: Royal Zoological Society (Fellow); Society of Australian Writers.

Agent: David Higham Associates, 76 Dean St., London, W.1, England.

* * * * *

J. MAX PATRICK

Full Name: John Max Patrick.
Born November 14, 1911, at Mineral, Washington. Son of John Richard Patrick and Edith Araminta Taylor.

Education: B.A., University of Toronto, 1934; B.Litt., Balliol College, Oxford University, 1937; D.Phil, 1952.

Career: Professor of English.
Senior History Master, St. Edward's School, Oxford, 1937-40; Lecturer in English, University of Manitoba, 1940-42; Asst. Professor of English, University of

J. MAX PATRICK (Cont.)

Buffalo, 1942-47; Associate Professor of English, Emory University, 1947-48; Professor of English, University of Florida, Gainesville, 1948-51; Professor of English, Queens College, 1951-54; Professor of English, New York University, 1954-DATE; has been a lecturer at University of Poitiers, Princeton University, University of Algiers, and Claremont Graduate School.

Awards: Fund for the Advancement of Education Fellow, 1955-56; Newberry Library Fellow, 1956.

* * * * *

JOSEPH F. PATROUCH JR.

Full Name: Joseph Francis Patrouch, Jr.
Born May 23, 1935, at Allentown, Pennsylvania. Son of Joseph Francis Patrouch (a businessman) and Ruth May. Married Ruth Sweitzer (a registered nurse), Sept. 6, 1958. Four children: Joseph Francis III, Katherine, Denise, Jean.

Education: B.A., University of Cincinnati, 1958; M.A., 1960; Ph.D, University of Wisconsin, 1965.

Career: Professor of English.
Assistant Professor of English, University of Dayton, 1964-70; Associate Professor, 1970-DATE. Member: Science Fiction Writers of America.

* * * * *

HUGO PAUL

Full Name: Paul H. Little.
Born February 5, 1915, at Chicago, Illinois. Son of Israel Isaac Litwinsky (a linen merchant) and Ida Marie Demont. Married Helen Mary McGrew (teacher and designer), April 3, 1941.

Education: B.S., Northwestern University, 1937.

Career: Writer.
Has been a radio announcer in San Francisco, an advertising manager for two food chains, and an assistant advertising manager for Armour & Co.; full-time writer, 1964-DATE.

Agent: A. C. Fierst, 630 Ninth Avenue, New York, NY 10036.

* * * * *

DONALD GORDON PAYNE

Full Name: Donald Gordon Payne.
Born January 3, 1924, at London, England. Son of Francis Gordon Payne (a mining consultant) and Evelyn Rogers. Married Barbara Back, August 20, 1947. Five children: Christopher Geoffrey (born 1950), Nigel David (born 1953), Adrian John (born 1955), Alison Bridget (born 1958), Robin Keith (born 1962).

Education: B.A., Corpus Christi College, Oxford University, 1949.

Career: Writer. Has been Editor, C. Johnson Pub-

lishers, 1950-53; Head of Editorial Department, Robert Hale (publishers), London, 1953-57; full-time writer, 1958-DATE.

First Professional Sale: The Midnight Sea, Hutchinson, 1958.

Agent: David Higham Associates, 76 Dean St., London.

Awards: Knight of Mark Twain, 1968; Meilleur Livre, Loisirs Jeunes, 1968.

Interests: Tennis, gardening, photography, bridge.

* * * * *

ROBERT PAYNE

Full Name: Pierre Stephen Robert Payne.
Born December 4, 1911, at Saltash, Cornwall, England. Son of Stephen Payne (a naval architect) and Mireille Antoinette Dorey.

Education: Attended University of Capetown, 1931-32; University of Liverpool, 1933-36; University of Munich, 1937; University of Paris, 1938.

Career: Writer, 1936-DATE.
Shipwright's apprentice, Liverpool, 1932-33, and at Singapore Naval Base, 1939-41; Armament Officer, Singapore Naval Base, 1941; with British Ministry of Information, 1941-42; Professor of English, Fuhtan University, China, 1942-43; Professor of English, Lienta University, 1943-46; came to U.S. in 1946; Head of English Department, Alabama College, 1949-54.

Honors: M.A., Asia Institute, 1951.

Agent: International Literary Agency, 71 Park Avenue, New York, NY 10016.

* * * * *

MERVYN PEAKE

Full Name: Mervyn Laurence Peake.
Born July 9, 1911, at Kuling, Central China. Moved to England in 1923. Son of Ernest Cromwell Peake (a doctor) and Elizabeth Powell. Married Maeve Gilmore (a painter). Three children: Sebastian, Fabian, Clare.

Education: Attended Eltham College and Royal Academy Schools in England.

Career: Writer, poet, painter, illustrator.
Was Britain's official artist sent to the liberated German concentration camp at Belsen; published his first book of poems in 1940; contracted encephalitis in 1956, and was finally hospitalized in 1964; survived in this limbo state until his death, on November 18, 1968.

Awards: Heinemann Award for Literature, 1951, for Gormenghast and The Glassblowers.

Agent: David Higham Associates, 76 Dean Street, Soho, London W.1, England.

Member:
Royal Society of Literature (Fellow).

A. PHILIPPA PEARCE

Full Name: Ann Philippa Pearce.
  Born at Great Shelford, Cambridgeshire, England.
Daughter of Ernest Alexander Pearce and Gertrude Rams-
den. Married Martin Christie (a fruitgrower), May 9,
1963.

Education: B.A., Girton College, Cambridge Univer-
    sity; M.A., 1942.

Career: Editor and writer.
  Civil servant, 1942-45; script writer and producer,
School Broadcasting Dept., BBC, 1945-58; Editor,
Education Department, Oxford University Press, 1959-
60; part-time producer in sound-radio, BBC, 1960-63;
Editor of Children's Books, Andre Deutsch Ltd., 1960-
DATE. Member: Society of Authors.

Awards: Carnegie Medal, 1959, for *Tom's Midnight
  Garden*; *New York Herald Tribune* Children's Spring
  Book Festival Award, 1963, for *A Dog So Small*.

* * * * *

JACK PEARL

Full Name: Jacques Bain Pearl.
  Born September 12, 1923, at Richmond Hill, New York.
Son of Harold H. Bain (an inventor) and Ada Swales.
Married June Hewes, September 14, 1947. Two children:
Jill, Janet.

Education: A.B., Columbia University, 1949; M.A.,
  1950.

Career: Writer.
  Part-time advertising copywriter, 1947-50; Editor,
"Gangbusters" TV show, 1952-53; Editor, *Saga* magazine,
1953-60; free-lance author, 1961-DATE. Member: Writers Guild of America, East.

Agent: Scott Meredith, 580 Fifth Avenue, New York,
  NY 10036.

* * * * *

DREW PEARSON

Full Name: Drew Pearson.
  Born December 13, 1897, at Evanston, Illinois. Son
of Paul Martin Pearson and Edna Wolfe. Married Countess Felicia Gizycka, 1925; married Luvie Moore,
November 12, 1936. One daughter, Ellen.

Education: A.B., Swarthmore College, 1919.

Career: Correspondent.
  Instructor in Industrial Geography, University of
Pennsylvania, 1921-22; Lecturer in Commercial Geogra-
phy, Columbia University, 1924; staff member, *United
States Daily*, 1926-33; staff member, *Baltimore Sun*,
1929-32; syndicated columnist, "Washington Merry-Go-
Round," 1931-69; radio broadcaster, 1935-69; Director,
American Friends Service Committee in Serbia, Monte-
negro, Albania, 1919-21; organized Friendship Train
to Europe, 1947-48; interviewed Premier Khrushchev,
Tito, King Paul of Greece, Premier Fanfani of Italy,
President Kennedy. Died September 1, 1969.

Member: International Platform Association; Overseas

Writers; National Press Club; Kappa Sigma; Delta Sigma
Rho; Phi Beta Kappa; Cosmos Club, Washington.

Awards:
  LL.D., Harding College, 1945, and William Jewell Col-
lege, 1948; Sigma Delta Chi National Award for Best
Washington Journalism, 1942; Father of the Year, 1948;
Knights of Columbus International Gold Medal, 1948;
French Legion of Honor; First Order, Star of Solidarity
(Italian Republic); Heart of Gold Award, Variety Club,
1963.

* * * * *

EDWARD PEARSON

Full Name: Edward Max Pearson.
  Born April 7, 1908, at Axminster, Devonshire, England.
Son of Max Von Guilleaume (an engineer) and Katherine
Letitia Paramore. Married Florence Rosemary Kettlewell,
August 18, 1933. One daughter, Penelope Ferelith (born
1935).

Education: M.A., Queens' College, Cambridge University, 1928.

Career: Gardener.
  Insurance agent, farmer, and land agent, 1928-33;
farmer, 1933-47; horticulture gardener, 1947-52; now
retired.

First Professional Sale: A book on bulb growing
  to Macdonald, 1953.

* * * * *

MICHAEL PEARSON

Full Name: Michael Edward Pearson.
  Born October 5, 1941, at Crosby, Lancashire, England.
Son of Edward Mansell Pearson (a draper) and Doris
Evelyn O'Brien. Married Lucy Rees, February 10, 1967.

Education: B.Sc., University of Leeds, 1965; D.Phil.,
  University of Sussex, 1970.

Career: Farmer, editor, writer.
  Farm labourer, Brookhouse Farm, 1961-62; Research
Fellow, University of Sussex, Feb.-Sept., 1970; Pro-
duction Office Assistant, Caliban Films, 1970-71; far-
mer, 1971-DATE. Sub-Editor, *Mountain Magazine*, 1968-
DATE.

First Professional Sale: "A Word in the Layman's
  Ear," in *Mountain Magazine*, November, 1969.

Member: British Society of Animal Production; British Society of Animal Behaviour.

Interests:
  "Deeply interested in problems of correlating agricultural exploitation of land with maintenance of aesthetic values of 'countryside.' Currently attempting
to explore possibilities on a small hill farm in North
Wales."

Pearson comments:
  "Constant awareness of aims not fulfilled, and projects not brought to completion. Family avowal most
commonly bandied about seems to be: 'Right! Well
next year we'll....'"

KIT PEDLER

Full Name: Christopher Magnus Howard Pedler.
Born June 11, 1927, at London, England. Son of
Hubert Pedler (a physician) and Mary Johnson (a pain-
ter). Married Una Freeston, 1949. Four children:
Carol, Mark, Lucy, Justin.

Education: Ph.D., University of London; Attended
the Institute of Ophthalmology, and trained at Westminster Hospital, London.

Career: Physician.
Qualified in medicine (M.B.B.S.), London, 1953;
qualified pathologist (M.C.Path.); spent twelve years
doing research on the eye and retina (author of 38
papers on the subject); Head of Anatomy Dept., London
University, for eight years.

Agent: Harvey Unna, 14 Beaumont Mews, Marylebone,
London W1N 4HE, England.

Interests: Sculpting, painting, beer brewing.

* * * * *

MARIO PEI

Full Name: Mario Andrew Pei [pronounced Pay].
Born February 16, 1901, at Rome, Italy. Son of
Francesco Pei (a hotel room service director) and
Luisa Ferri. Married Pearl Glover, June 25, 1924.

Education: A.B., City College of New York, 1925;
Ph.D., Columbia University, 1932.

Career: Professor of Romance Philology.
Instructor in Latin and Romance Languages, City
College of New York, 1923-37; Professor of Romance
Philology, Columbia University, 1937-70. Associate
Editor, *United America*, 1920-25. Died March 1978.

First Professional Sale: "A Universal Language
Can Be Achieved," in *Town & Country*, Sept., 1944.

Awards:
First Regional Award, Ziff-Davis Peace Plan Contest,
1945, for *The American Road to Peace*; George Washington Honor Medal, Freedom Foundation at Valley Forge,
1957, for *Free Will; the Third Philosophy*; Cavaliere
Ufficiale of the Order of Merit of the Italian Republic, 1958; Oscar for Literature, Unico National, 1959;
Author's Award, New Jersey Association of Teachers of
English, 1965, for *The Story of Language* and *The Story
of English*; also 1966, for *How to Learn Languages*;
and 1968, for *The Many Hues of English*; Townsend Harris Medal, CCNY Alumni, 1968; David McKay Humanities
Award, Brigham Young University, 1970; Xavier Hall
of Fame, 1972; D.H.L., Fort Lauderdale University,
1973.

Member:
Modern Language Association; American Association
of Teachers of French; American Association of Teachers
of Spanish; American Association of Teachers of Italian; Phi Beta Kappa; Linguistic Circle of New York;
New York Grand Jury Association; American Society of
Geolinguistics (Honorary President).

Interests: Travel, table tennis, bridge, chess.

Pei writes: "It is difficult to answer your query
"about the use of invented languages in science fiction
and fantasy, partly because I have only partial knowledge of such languages, but even more because there
is really no such thing as following linguistic principles in constructing an imaginary language.
"Natural languages do not subscribe to any definite
typology, which means that they go from the extreme of
monosyllabism and a grammatical structure based exclusively on syntax and word order (as in Chinese) to the
morphological complexity and richness of endings conveying all sorts of subsidiary notions of original Indo-
European (Latin, Greek, and modern Russian are fair
examples), then further on into the polysynthetism of
Basque and some American Indian languages, where the
word really has no separate existence, but has to be
extracted from a compound form that represents what to
us is an entire sentence.
"In the case of constructed languages, of which over
1,000 have been devised, not for purposes of science
fiction, but to be vehicles of international communication, there are two possibilities: the *a posteriori*,
where elements are taken from existing languages and
blended together in varying proportions (as in Esperanto), and the *a priori*, which exclude all connection
with existing languages and are purely arbitrary, both
as to vocabulary and as to structure (like Ro and Suma,
both American creations). A science fiction writer
who wishes to present an imaginary language has his
choice of using either method. What he comes up with
can be individually evaluated and judged, or even cri-
ticized, but there is no way of lumping them together
and passing judgment on them as a group.
"If you look into the final chapter of my *The Many
Hues of English*, you will see that I myself have succumbed to the temptation of prophesying the future
course of English, thereby making myself liable to
criticism. What I have never attempted to do is to
construct my own constructed language; this primarily
because many of the ones already offered could easily
serve the purpose of world communication, and there
is no need for me to add to the confusion that besets
the problem."

* * * * *

DON PENDLETON

Full Name: Donald Eugene Pendleton.
Born December 12, 1927, at Little Rock, Arkansas.
Son of Louis Thomas Pendleton (a machinist) and Drucy
Valentine. Married Marjorie Williamson, February 4,
1947. Six children: Stephen M. (born 1948), Gregory
L. (born 1949), Rodney A. (born 1952), Melinda L. (born
1957), Jennifer E. (born 1961), Derek C. (born 1963).

Career: Writer.
U.S. Navy Radioman, 1942-47, 1952-54; Railroad Telegrapher, Southern Pacific, 1948-57; Air Traffic Controller, Federal Aviation Administration, 1957-60; Aerospace Engineer, Aerospace Systems Engineering, 1961-67;
full-time novelist, 1971-DATE; Senior Editor, *Orion
Magazine*, 1967-71.

First Professional Sale: "Boomerang Peep Show,"
in *Ace Magazine*, 1958.

Agent: Scott Meredith, 580 Fifth Avenue, New York,
NY 10036. Member: Authors League; Authors Guild;
International Platform Association.

Interests: "My consuming interest in life lies in
the field of metaphysics. All of my writing is an
outpicturing of that interest."

WALKER PERCY

Full Name: Walker Percy.
  Born May 28, 1916, at Birmingham, Alabama. Son of Leroy Pratt Percy and Martha Phinizy. Married Mary Townsend. Two children: Ann Boyd, Mary Pratt.

Education: B.A., University of North Carolina, 1937; M.D., Columbia University, 1941.

Career: Writer.
  Intern, Bellevue Hospital, New York, 1942; retired from medicine after contracting tuberculosis; writer, 1961-DATE. Awards: National Book Award for Fiction, 1962, for *The Moviegoer*.

Agent: McIntosh & Otis, 475 Fifth Avenue, New York, NY 10017.

* * * * *

W. D. PEREIRA

Full Name: Wilfred Dennis Pereira.
  Born November 16, 1921, at London, England. Son of Ernani Horace Pereira (an export agent) and Helen Elizabeth Gonsalves. Married Irene Elizabeth Crawford, June 12, 1948. One daughter, Helen Elizabeth (born 1950).

Education: Honours Diploma, College of Aeronautical Engineering, London, 1948.

Career: Advertising agent.
  Technical writer, De Havilland Aircraft Company, 1948-50; technical writer, Rotol (Rolls-Royce, Bristol), 1950-58; Press Officer, Dowty Group, 1958-61; Publicity Manager, Daniels/Unochrome International, 1961-73; Director of his own advertising agency, Cheltenham, England, 1973-DATE.

First Professional Sale: *Time of Departure*, Robert Hale, 1956.

Interests: People, places, writing.

Pereira notes: "I write as a hobby, and, apart from eleven books published, have had four television plays produced, plus many short stories and articles sold. *Aftermath 15* was my first SF book, and I have become so fascinated with the medium that I intend to produce a series. Being an aviation engineer and technical writer by profession, my first books had an aeronautical background. My publisher then suggested that I try science fiction, and I sold my first book. The science side of the genre interests me as much as the completely free fiction side."

* * * * *

MICHAEL PERKINS

Full Name: Michael Perkins.
  Born November 3, 1942, at Lansing, Michigan. Son of William Perkins and Virginia Davis. Married Renie McCune, June 20, 1960 (died, 1968). Children: Leslie.

Education: B.A., Ohio University, 1963.

Career: Teacher.
  Case Worker, Department of Welfare, New York, 1963-66; Corrective Reading Teacher, Board of Education, New York, 1966-DATE; Editor, Tompkins Square Press.

* * * * *

LUDEK PESEK

Full Name: Ludek Pesek [pronounced Peshek].
  Born April 26, 1919, at Prague, Czechoslovakia. Son of Ludvik Pesek and Anna Cihakova. Married Beatrice [Bozena] Raymannova (a secretary), August 22, 1953.

Education: Attended Academy of Arts in Prague.

Career: Writer and painter.
  Full-time writer and painter, 1945-DATE, with many book and story credits, exhibitions in several countries of his paintings, and numerous photo credits; has also illustrated many of his own books and articles.

First Professional Sale: *Lide v Kameni [People Among the Stones]*, 1946.

Awards:
  Honorary Mention, European Literary Club, Prague, 1947, for *Lide v Kameni*; First Prize, European Literary Club Competition, 1948, for *Drazba [The Auction]*; Der Deutsche Jugendbuchpreis, 1971, for *Die Erde Ist Nah [The Earth Is Near]*; Honorary Mention, International Biennale of Illustrations, Bratislava, 1967, for *Die Planeten des Sonnensystems*.

* * * * *

HARRY PESIN

Full Name: Harry Pesin.
  Born October 16, 1919, at New York, New York. Son of Abraham Pesin (a businessman) and Lena Bachman. Married Betty Klein, February 20, 1944. Three children: Arthur, Alan, Richard.

Education: B.B.A., City College of New York, 1942.

Career: Director of advertising agency.
  Public Relations Director, Lester L. Wolff Advertising, New York, 1947; Vice-President and Creative Director, Rockmore Co., New York, 1948-60; Senior Vice-President and Creative Director, David J. Mendelsohn, New York, 1961-63; President and Creative Director, Pesin, Sydney & Bernard Advertising, Inc., 1963-DATE. Member: American Society of Magazine Photographers; Copy Club.

* * * * *

EMIL PETAJA

Full Name: Emil Theodore Petaja.
  Born April 12, 1915, at Milltown, Montana. Son of John Petaja (a lumberman) and Hanna Koski. Education: Attended Montana State University, 1936-38.

Career: Writer and publisher.
  Officer worker, 1938-41; Film Technician, Technicolor Corporation, Hollywood, 1941-46; Self-employed professional photographer in Sausalito and San Francisco, 1948-63; full-time writer, 1963-DATE; Chairman, Bokanalia Memorial Foundation; Publisher, Sisu Publishers, 1972-DATE.

EMIL PETAJA (Cont.)

First Professional Sale: "Time Will Tell," in *Amazing Stories*, June, 1942.

Agent: Forrest J Ackerman, 2495 Glendower Avenue, Hollywood, CA 90027.

Awards: Minor poetry and photography awards.

Member: Science Fiction Writers of America; Mystery Writers of America.

Interests:
   Music, gardening, old silent movies (collects prints of the films of Lon Chaney, Sr.), book collecting, print collecting, collecting fantasy art (especially works by Hannes Bok).

Petaja notes:
   "The source of five of my fantasy novels is the Finnish epic poem, *The Kalevala*. This is one of the newest of the great world epics, having been collected from folk sources and tales in Finland in the early part of the twentieth century by Elias Lonnrot. It has a wealth of fine stories about the gods and heroes of Suomi and Lapland (not to be confused with or identified with the Nordic-Teutonic gods and heroes, who are entirely different), and their fabulous wonders and incredible adventures. It is difficult to read in parts, although in 1960 Harvard University Press put out a prose edition with much factual material in an appendix about the bards who originally sang these songs. There are at least five English translations, my favorite being the W. F. Kirby rendition (poetry), published by Dent/Dutton, and available in the Everyman Library."

* * * * *

JERZY PETERKIEWICZ

Full Name: Jerzy Pietrkiewicz.
   Born September 29, 1916, at Fabianki, Poland. Son of Jan Pietrkiewicz and Antonina Politowska). Married Christine Brooke-Rose (the writer), 1948.

Education: M.A., University of St. Andrews, 1944; Ph.D., King's College, University of London, 1947.

Career: Teacher.
   Lecturer in Polish Language and Literature, University of London, 1950-64; Reader, 1964-DATE. Member: P.E.N.

Agent: Christy & Moore, 52 Floral St., London WC2.

* * * * *

GILBERT PHELPS

Full Name: Gilbert Henry Phelps.
   Born January 23, 1915, at Gloucester, Gloucestershire, England. Son of Gilbert Henry Phelps (a clerk) and Mary More Wilks. Married Dorothy Elizabeth Coad, 1939 (divorced); married Dorothy Kathleen Batchelor. Two children: John David (born 1941), Jean Hazel (born 1943); three step-children: Sebastian Barnes, Bartholomew Barnes, Julian Wesley.

Education: B.A., St. John's College, Cambridge

University, 1937; M.A., 1940.

Career: Author, lecturer, broadcaster.
   Research student and Assistant Supervisor, English Studies, St. John's College, Cambridge, 1937-40; also Lecturer and Tutor, Cambridge University Board of Extra-Mural Studies; Lecturer, British Council, Lisbon, 1940-42; Senior English Master, Blundell's School, 1943-45; Talks Producer, BBC, West Region, 1945-49; BBC Supervisor of Educational Talks and Third Programme Producer, 1949-60; Chief Instructor, BBC Staff Training, 1960-64; full-time author, lecturer, and broadcaster, 1964-DATE.

First Professional Sale:
   Poems sold in 1939; first story sale: "I Have Lived a Hundred Years," in *The Faber Book of West Country Stories*, 1951.

Agent: Elaine Green Ltd., 31 Newington Green, London N16 9PU, England.

Awards: Arts Council of Great Britain Award, 1966, for the body of his work.

Member: Society of Authors; BBC Club; Savile Club; Royal Commonwealth Society; P.E.N.

Interests: History, painting and music, gardening, sport of all kinds, psychology, Latin America.

Phelps writes:
   "I do a vast amount of miscellaneous writing, chiefly BBC scripts and series, mostly for the External Services, Home Radio, Schools Television & Further Education; I also do reviewing, introductions to new editions, literary criticism, and a good deal of lecturing, mostly to Adult Education audiences, though I tutored for a spell at University College, Oxford University last year.
   "*The Winter People* is a lost race novel. If the field is dying out, I suppose the main--and very understandable--reason is the romance of actual space exploration. I think writers in the lost race genre must do their homework on the scientific and anthropological aspects--as I tried to do in this book (everything in it is plausible, in the sense that it is based on research--including a study of hypothermia in order to get the symptoms of hibernation right!). I think this genre will return, because it is bound to be relevant to our present predicament--and because, like so many other lines in science fiction, it is imaginative and full of poetry."

* * * * *

JOHN T. PHILLIFENT

Full Name: John Thomas Phillifent.
   Born November 10, 1916, at Durham, England. Son of John Thomas Phillifent (a coal miner) and Mary Ann Phillifent. Married Barbara Mary Phillifent (divorced); married Joyce Isabel Phillifent. Two daughters: Sarah Joan (born 1952), Katherine Anne (b.1954).

Education: "University entrance."

Career: Engineer.
   Assistant Planning Engineer, Central Electricity Generating Board, London, through 1976; writer, 1954-76; served in the Royal Navy, 1937-47. Died in England December 16, 1976.

JOHN T. PHILLIFENT (Cont.)

First Professional Sale: *Space Puppet*, Tit-Bits SF Library, 1954.

Agent: Virginia Kidd, Box 278, Milford, PA 18337.

Member: Science Fiction Writers of America; Mensa.

Phillifent wrote for many years under the pseudonym John Rackham, and only started using his real name on his science fiction novels in 1972. He commented:

"Biographically, I do not rate much. Son of a coal miner, reasonably well educated, a spell with the Navy, then virtually the rest of my life in electricity generation. Very little of it shows in my work. Engineering backgrounds are as authentic as I can make them, and Navy experience helps to depict space-ship operation when called for, but direct drawings aren't there at all. One new trend seems to be showing. All my life I have been curious about the paranormal, open-minded, but, I hope, critical; I am delighted therefore at the current interest in this field, and am building some of my own observations into the fiction I am writing. I believe we are on the edge of a great breakthough into understanding more about the mind and its unused potential. If I had to name a favourite among my own books it would be *Watch on Peter*, a juvenile published here by Jonathan Cape (under Rackham) in 1964, and which has done well in French, Italian, and Portuguese editions. Next to that would be the three Man from U.N.C.L.E. novels, in my own name, in paper, from Ace and Souvenir Press, which were great fun to write (*The Mad Scientist Affair*, *The Corfu Affair*, *The Power Cube Affair*). I have no message. I write for fun. If it isn't fun to write, it won't be fun for anyone to read."

* * * * *

MICKEY PHILLIPS

Full Name: Alan Meyrick Kerr Phillips.
  Born October 21, 1916, at Punjab, India. Son of Alan Andrew Phillips (associated with the Indian State Railways) and Lucy Osborn. Married Janet Lockyer, September 21, 1946. Three children: Andrew, David, Jessica. Education: Attended Wellington College, 1930-34, and Royal Air Force College, 1934-36.

Career: Government official.
  With Royal Air Force, 1936-68, becoming a Wing Commander; now a British civil servant. Agent: Brandt & Brandt, 101 Park Avenue, New York, NY 10017.

* * * * *

ROG PHILLIPS

Full Name: Roger Phillips Graham.
  Born 1909, at Spokane, Washington. Education: A.B., Gonzaga University; graduate study at the University of Washington.

Career: Writer.
  Full-time writer, 1945-65. Died 1965.

First Professional Sale: "Let Freedom Ring," in *Amazing Stories*, December, 1945.

Agent: Forrest J Ackerman, 2495 Glendower Avenue, Los Angeles, CA 90027.

Member: Los Angeles Science Fantasy Society; Elves, Gnomes, and Little Men's Science Fiction and Chowder Marching Society.

Forrest J Ackerman, Phillips' agent, provided the following comments: "Rog Phillips edited "The Club House," a feature in *Amazing Stories* devoted to fanzines and fanews, for a number of issues (1948-53). He was on the Shaver side of the controversial Shaver mystery. Phillips taught a writing course in escape literature to prisoners at San Quentin penitentiary."

* * * * *

ROBERT M. PHILMUS

Full Name: Robert Michael Philmus.
  Born September 3, 1943, at New York, New York. Son of Herman Philmus (a jewelry designer) and Lillian Jurmark (a jewelry designer). Married Maria Rita Rohr, June 12, 1967.

Education: B.A., Brown University, 1964; Ph.D., University of California, San Diego, 1968.

Career: Professor of English.
  Teaching and Research Assistant, University of California, San Diego, 1964-66; Instructor, Carleton College, 1967-68; Associate Professor of English, Loyola College, Concordia University, Montreal, 1968-DATE. Member, Editorial Board, *Science-Fiction Studies*, 1972-DATE.

First Professional Sale: "Was Wells Anti-Wellsian?" in *Carleton Miscellany*, 1968.

Awards: Miscellaneous poetry prizes.

Member: Phi Beta Kappa; Science Fiction Research Association (Member, Editorial Board, 1972-73); Modern Language Association.

* * * * *

JOAN PHIPSON

Full Name: Joan Margaret Fitzhardinge.
  Born November 16, 1912, at Warrawee, New South Wales, Australia. Married Colin Hardinge Fitzhardinge. One son, one daughter.

Career: Writer, 1952-DATE. Member: Australian Society of Authors. Agent: A. P. Watt & Son, 26/28 Bedford Row, London WC1R 4HL, England.

Awards: Children's Book Council of Australia Book of the Year Award, 1953, for *Good Luck to the Rider*; 1963 for *The Family Conspiracy*; Boys' Clubs of America Junior Book Award, 1963, for *The Boundary Riders*.

* * * * *

MARGE PIERCY

Full Name: Marge Piercy.
  Born at Detroit, Michigan. Daughter of Robert Piercy and Bert Bunnin. Married Michel Schiff, 1957 (divorced); married Robert M. Shapiro (a systems analyst), Feb. 11, 1962.

MARGE PIERCY (Cont.)

Education: A.B., University of Michigan, 1957; M.A., 1958.

Career: Writer.
Full-time writer and poet, 1966-DATE. Awards: Avery & Jule Hopwood Award of University of Michigan for poetry and fiction.

Agent: Harold Matson Co., 22 E. 40th St., New York, NY 10016.

* * * * *

CHAPMAN PINCHER

Full Name: Henry Chapman Pincher.
Born March 29, 1914, at Ambala, Punjab, India. Son of Richard Chapman Pincher (a major in the British Army) and Helen Foster (an actress). Married Constance Sylvia Wolstenholme, 1965. Two children: Patricia Chapman, Michael Chapman.

Education: Attended King's College, University of London, 1932-36.

Career: Editor and correspondent.
On staff, Liverpool Institute, 1936-40; Technical Supply Officer, Rocket Division, Ministry of Supply, 1943-46; joined the London Daily Express, serving successively as Defence Editor, Science Editor, Medical Editor, and now Assistant Editor and Chief Defence Correspondent, 1946-DATE.

First Professional Sale: Breeding of Farm Animals, 1946.

Awards & Honors: Carter Medallist, London, 1934; B.Sc., 1935; Granda Award, Journalist of the Year, 1964; Reporter of the Decade, 1966.

Interests: Fishing, shooting, natural history, country life, ferreting in Whitehall, and bolting politicians.

* * * * *

DAVID PIRIE

Full Name: David Tarbat Pirie.
Born December 4, 1946, at West Pennard, Somersetshire, England. Son of H. B. Pirie (a businessman) and Joyce Pirie.

Education: B.A., University of York, 1968; studied at University of London, 1971-DATE.

Career: Writer.
Free-lance author, 1970-DATE; Contributing Editor and Film Critic, Time Out Magazine, 1972-DATE.

First Professional Sale: "Dracula Meets R. D. Laing," in Time Out Magazine, Summer, 1970.

Member: National Union of Journalists.

Interests: Video tennis, rock music (especially singles), landscape games.

Pirie notes: "Although I have primarily worked as "a critic (both of film and music) up to now, I intend to try very hard in the next few years to move into fiction and script writing. It seems to me that no matter how alert and lively the critic, criticism will eventually become a sterile exercise unless it is accompanied by creative work."

* * * * *

DORIS PISERCHIA

Full Name: Doris Elaine Piserchia.
Born October 11, 1928, at Fairmont, West Virginia. Daughter of Dewey Leslie Summers and Viola Crihfield. Married Joseph John Piserchia, August 25, 1953. Five children: Linda Elizabeth (born 1954), John Joseph (born 1957), James Anthony (born 1958), Dewey Leslie (born 1961), Patricia Jane (born 1962).

Education: A.B., Fairmont State College, 1950; graduate study at the University of Utah, 1963-65.

Career: Writer.
Lieutenant/jg, U.S. Navy, 1950-54; housewife, 1954-DATE; free-lance author, 1966-DATE.

First Professional Sale: "Rocket to Gehenna," in Fantastic Stories, September, 1966.

Interests: Swimming, diving, horseback riding, coin collecting.

* * * * *

CHARLES PLATT

Full Name: Charles Nathaniel Platt.
Born May 9, 1943, in England. Parents unknown. Married Jemima Gerrold (divorced). Two sons: William (born 1972), Wilbur (born 1973).

Education: Attended Cambridge University, 1962; Higher Diploma in Printing Management, London College of Printing, 1964.

Career: Writer and editor.
Has been an organist in a pop group, a free-lance photographer, designer of New Worlds magazine, free-lance designer of book jackets, writer of sex novels for Gold Star Publications, London; Editor, New Worlds, 1969-70; Science Fiction Editor, Avon Books, 1972-74; Instructor in Science Fiction, New School, New York, 1971-DATE.

First Professional Sale: "One of Those Days," in Science Fantasy, December, 1964/January, 1965.

Agents:
(Science fiction) Kirby McCauley, 220 E. 26th St., New York, NY 10010; (other) William Morris Agency, 151 El Camino, Beverly Hills, CA 90212.

Awards: Cambridge Society for Furtherment of Literature Award for poetry.

Member: Cambridge Science Fiction Society (Founder); Royal Astronomical Society.

Interests: "Drawing obscene pictures, making lampshades, sewing shirts, renovating buildings, watching daytime TV."

CHARLES PLATT (Cont.)

Platt writes:

"Small amounts of effort have yielded vast amounts of free time in which to do nothing. I would like to have been an astronaut. Otherwise, I wouldn't change a thing.

"I was not aware that anyone had ever described *Garbage World* as the most disgusting book ever written. They must be very naive and protected from life.

"The original title of the book was to have been *Turd from the Sun*, ruled out on grounds of poor taste and plagiarism. I wanted to write an anal fantasy, and at the same time comment on the anality of science fiction readers such as myself hoarding vast amounts of elaborately indexed rubbish. I've always had a weakness for shit fetishism; there it is. The novel originally appeared as a novelette in *New Worlds*, in two episodes; it suffered greatly from my expanding it into a book, and its style is as turgid as the swamps of shit it describes. Damon Knight carries credit or blame for commissioning me to do the expansion.

"*Planet of the Voles* was an attempt to go from the anal stage to the pubescent stage; it's a story about men who go around killing women, really, and I hoped it would appeal to the repressed desires of adolescent readers. Judging from sales, it didn't. It suffered as a book from having been written in 5 days. I suffered too, and continue to do so as a result from having written such nonsense."

He adds: "If you compare my entry in *Who's Who in America* with the answers on *your* form, you'll find discrepancies. This is because I lied to them." In *Who's Who in America*, Platt is listed as Charles Michael Platt, born April 19, 1949, in Tehran, Iran, the adopted son of Robert Morriah Platt; his wife is given as Leah Wallach, and his son is Joseph Richard. In *Contemporary Authors*, Platt is just Charles Platt, born April 26, 1945, son of Maurice Platt and Marjorie Hubbard. In *Contemporary Science Fiction Authors, First Edition*, the listing reads: Charles Platt, born October 25, 1944 in Hertfordshire, England, the son of Michael Platt and Elaine Bertha Hubbard. *Caveat emptor.*

* * * * *

FREDERIK POHL

Full Name: Frederik Pohl.
    Born November 26, 1919, at New York, New York. Son of Fred George Pohl (a businessman) and Anna Jane Mason (a secretary). Married Doris Baumgardt, 1940 (divorced, 1944); married Dorothy LesTina, 1945 (divorced, 1947); married Judith Merril (the writer), 1949 (divorced, 1952); married Carol Metcalf Ulf, September 15, 1952. Five children: Ann (born 1950), Karen (born 1952), Frederik III (deceased), Frederik IV (born 1956), Kathy (born 1958).

Education: Attended Brooklyn Technical High School.

Career: Writer, editor, lecturer.
    Editor, *Astonishing Stories*, February, 1940-September, 1941; Assistant Editor, November, 1941-April, 1943; Editor, *Super Science Stories*, March, 1940-August, 1941; Assistant Editor, November, 1941-May, 1943; Copywriter, Thwing and Altman, Inc., 1946; Book Editor and Assistant Circulation Manager, *Popular Science*, 1946-49; directed his own literary agency,

1949-53; free-lance author, 1953-59; Editor, *Star Science Fiction*, January, 1958 (only issue); Feature Editor, *Worlds of If*, July, 1959-January, 1961; Managing Editor, May, 1961-July, 1962; Editor, September, 1962-May, 1969; Editor Emeritus, July, 1969-July/August, 1970; Managing Editor, *Galaxy*, June, 1961-June, 1962; Editor, August, 1962-May, 1969; Editor Emeritus, July, 1969-June, 1970; Editor, *Worlds of Tomorrow*, April, 1963-May, 1967; Editor, *International Science Fiction*, November, 1967-June, 1968; Managing Editor, *Worlds of Fantasy*, #1, 1968; Executive Editor, Ace Books, Inc., 1971-72; Science Fiction Editor, Bantam Books, 1973-DATE.

First Professional Sale: "Elegy to a Dead Planet: Luna" (poem), in *Amazing Stories*, October, 1937 (as Elton V. Andrews).

Agent: Robert P. Mills Ltd., 156 E. 52nd St., New York, NY 10022.

Awards:
    Guest of Honor, 30th World Science Fiction Convention (L.A.Con), Los Angeles, 1972; Hugo Award, Best Professional Magazine, *Worlds of If*, 1965 (1966), 1966 (1967), 1967 (1968); Hugo Award, Best Short Story, 1972 (1973), "The Meeting" (a posthumous collaboration with C. M. Kornbluth).

Member:
    Science Fiction Writers of America (President, 1974-76); American Astronautical Society; British Interplanetary Society; New York Academy of Sciences; American Federation of Television and Radio Artists.

Interests:
    Singing, folk dancing, travel, science, politics [former committeeman for the Democratic Party]. "Although I have no formal training in science (except for Air Force meteorological training), and indeed little formal education in anything, I am deeply interested in all branches of science as a spectator sport. My interest in science was aroused by reading science fiction, and now my science fiction flows largely from what I have learned about science."

* * * * *

EDWARD POHLMAN

Full Name: Edward Wendell Pohlman.
    Born 1933, at Chuchokee Malyan, India. Married Julia Mae Denlinger, September 2, 1956. Two children: Douglas, Sharon.

Education: Ph.D., Ohio State University, 1960.

Career: Professor of Counseling Psychology.
    Professor of Counseling Psychology, University of the Pacific, 1960-DATE; Visiting Professor, Central Family Planning Institute, New Delhi, India, 1967-69; presented a series of programs on population and birth control on KCRA-TV, Sacramento, 1970; consultant to the World Health Organization and to the National Institute of Child Health and Human Development.

Honors and Awards:
    Series of grants from Planned Parenthood/World Population, 1962-66, from Carolina Population Center, 1967-69, and from U.S. Dept. of Health, Education, and Welfare, 1971, for abortion counseling materials. Member: American Psychological Association.

MAURICE PONS

Full Name: Maurice Pons.
Born September 14, 1927, at Strasbourg, France. Son of Émile Pons (a teacher) and Jeanne Dole.

Education: Licencie és Lettres, Sorbonne, University of Paris, 1946; Diplôme d'Études Supérieures de Philosophie, 1947.

Career: Writer, 1951-DATE. Award: Grand Prix de la Nouvelle, 1955, for *Virginales*.

* * * * *

JOSEPHINE POOLE

Full Name: Josephine Poole.
Born February 12, 1933, at London, England. Daughter of Charles Graham Cumpston (managing director of an engineering firm) and Astrid Walford (an artist). Married Timothy Ruscombe Poole (a driving instructor), July 14, 1956. Four children: Theodora Mary, Emily Josephine, Katherine Virginia, Isabel Beatrice.

Career: Writer.
Solicitors' secretary in Portugal, Spain, Italy, and Belgium, 1950-54; Secretary in Features Dept., BBC, 1954-56; free-lance author. Member: Society of Authors.

Agent: A. P. Watt & Son, 26/28 Bedford Row, London WC1R 4HL, England.

* * * * *

MELINDA POPHAM

Full Name: Melinda Popham.
Born April 25, 1944, at Kansas City, Missouri. Daughter of Arthur C. Popham (a lawyer) and Mary C. Hawn. Married John H. Benton (Chairman of the Board, Encyclopaedia Britannica Educational Corporation), January 9, 1971.

Education: B.A., University of Chicago, 1966; M.A., Stanford University, 1967.

Career: Writer.
Teacher, Crystal Springs School for Girls, Hillsborough, CA, 1967-69; Foreign Correspondent, *Oui* magazine, 1972-73.

Agent: Curtis Brown Ltd., 60 E. 56th St., New York, NY 10022.

Awards: Marjorie Fisher Winston Award for Fiction, 1963; Paul Shorey Short Story Prize, 1965; National Foundation for the Arts Grant, 1966.

* * * * *

J. B. POST

Full Name: Jerry Benjamin Post.
Born November 17, 1937, at Rochester, New York. Son of Donald Post (a boxer and shipping supervisor) and Kathryn Shippy. Married Joyce Arnold, April 15, 1967. One son, Jonathan Edward (born 1968).

Education: A.B., University of Rochester, 1960;

M.S.L.S., Columbia University, 1961.

Career: Librarian.
Map Librarian, Free Library of Philadelphia, 1961-DATE; served in the U.S. Army, 1962-63; Issue Editor, *Drexel Library Quarterly*, October, 1973.

Member:
Science Fiction Research Association; American Library Association; Special Libraries Association; Private Libraries Association; Dark Brotherhood; Philadelphia Science Fiction Society (President, 1965-66; Secretary, 1967).

Interests:
"Survival--when not surviving, book collecting, hiking, travel, wine tasting, talking with friends."

* * * * *

JOYCE POST

Full Name: Joyce Post.
Born January 10, 1939, at Harrisburg, Pennsylvania. Daughter of L. W. Arnold (a sheet metal worker) and Edna Stutz (a bank teller). Married J. B. Post (a map librarian), April 15, 1967. One son, Jonathan Edward (born 1968).

Education: A.B., Susquehanna University, 1960; M.S. L.S., Drexel University, 1961.

Career: Librarian, bibliographer, indexer.
Librarian, Foreign Trade Library, City of Philadelphia, 1963-65; Assistant Law Librarian, Pennsylvania State Law Library, 1965-67; Librarian in Charge of Technical Processing, Reader Development Program, Free Library of Philadelphia, 1967-68; Research Associate, Drexel University School of Library Science, 1972-73.

Member: American Library Association; American Society of Indexers; Beta Phi Mu.

Interests: Traveling, music, knitting.

* * * * *

JERRY POURNELLE

Full Name: Jerry Eugene Pournelle.
Born August 7, 1933, at Shreveport, Louisiana. Son of E. "Doc" Pournelle (a radio and TV station owner) and Ruth Lewis. Married Roberta Jane Isdell, July 18, 1959. Four children: Alexander Craig (born 1960), Francis Russell (born 1965), Phillip Eugene (born 1967), Richard Stefan (born 1970).

Education:
B.S., State University of Iowa, 1955; M.S., University of Washington; Ph.D., University of Washington.

Career: Writer.
Spent fifteen years in the aerospace industry in advanced planning, operations research, and space systems design; former Professor of History and Political Science, Pepperdine University; former Executive Assistant to the Mayor of the City of Los Angeles; former political campaign manager; now a full-time writer.

First Professional Sale: "Don't remember." First novel: *Red Heroin*, Berkley, 1965 (as Wade Curtis).

JERRY POURNELLE (Cont.)

Agent: Lurton Blassingame, 60 E. 42nd St., New York, NY 10017.

Awards:
Bronze Medal, American Security Council, 1965; Award of Honor, Republic of Estonia, 1968; John W. Campbell Award for Best New Writer, 1972 (1973).

Member:
Science Fiction Writers of America (President, 1973-74); Mystery Writers of America; American Security Council; Institute for Strategic Studies; American Rocket Society; American Association for the Advancement of Science (Fellow); Society for Creative Anachronism, Inc. (Knight Marshal).

Interests: Sailing, Go, Boy Scouts, backpacking ("with Larry Niven").

Pournelle comments: "I tell stories, rather than painting mood pictures, and consider the science fiction writer the modern equivalent of the chap who used to wander from campfire to campfire, and upon arrival saying, 'Hey fellows, if you'll give me a drink and some of that stew, I'll tell you a story about a virgin and a bull that you just wouldn't believe....'"

* * * * *

BRUCE POWE

Full Name: Bruce Powe.
Born June 9, 1925, at Edmonton, Alberta, Canada. Son of Wilbur Powe (an accountant) and Lillian Barr. Married Alys M. Brady, June 30, 1949. Two children: Bruce William, Kathleen.

Education: B.A., University of Alberta, 1949; M.A., 1951.

Career: Director of Public Relations.
Special assistant to the Minister of Mines and Technical Surveys, Government of Canada, 1951-57; Editorial Assistant, Imperial Oil Ltd., Toronto, 1957-60; Executive Director, Ontario Liberal Association, 1960-63; Vice-President in Public Relations, Baker Advertising Ltd., 1964-66; Director of Public Relations, Canadian Life Insurance Association, Toronto, 1966-DATE.

Member: Canadian Public Relations Society; Toronto Men's Press Club.

* * * * *

TALMAGE POWELL

Full Name: Talmage Powell.
Born October 4, 1920, at Hendersonville, North Carolina. Son of Dewitt Talmage Powell and Cora Lamb. Married Mildred Morgan. One son, Paul Talmage.

Career: Writer.
Has been a full-time, free-lance author of short stories and mystery novels since 1942.

Agent: Scott Meredith, 580 Fifth Avenue, New York, NY 10036.

JOE POYER

Full Name: Joseph John Poyer.
Born November 30, 1939, at Battle Creek, Michigan. Son of Joseph John Poyer (a salesman) and Eileen Powell (a hospital administrator). Married Susan Pilmore. Two children: Joseph John (born 1962), Geoffrey Robert (born 1965).

Education: A.A., Kellogg Community College, 1959; B.A., Michigan State University, 1961.

Career: Writer.
Free-lance author, 1964-DATE.

First Professional Sale: "TB in Cattle," in Science Newsletter, November, 1962.

Interests: Photography, motorcycles, travel, reading, design/inventing.

* * * * *

HUGH PRATHER

Full Name: Hugh Prather.
Born January 23, 1938, at Dallas, Texas. Son of Hugh Edmondson Prather, Jr. (a real estate developer) and Virginia Russ (a sculptress and painter). Married Gayle Plante (a writer), July 23, 1965. One son, Perry Scott.

Education: B.A., Southern Methodist University, 1966; graduate student, University of Texas, 1967.

Career: Writer, 1970-DATE. Agent: International Literary Agency, 130 E. 40th St., New York, NY 10016.

* * * * *

FLETCHER PRATT

Full Name: Murray Fletcher Pratt.
Born April 25, 1897, at Buffalo, New York. Raised in upstate New York on an Indian reservation. Married his second wife, Inge Marie Stephens (who, after his death, married Dr. John D. Clark, and died in January, 1970; she was a well-known illustrator).

Career: Writer.
Sometime newspaper man, librarian, and flyweight boxer (simultaneously); correspondent during World War II; gourmet cook; raised marmoset monkeys; free-lance author, 1928-56. Died June 10, 1956.

First Professional Sale: "The Octopus Cycle," in Amazing Stories, May, 1928 (with Irvin Lester).

Agent: Dr. John D. Clark, Green Pond Road at Jacob's Ladder, R.D.2, Newfoundland, NJ 07435.

Honors:
Distinguished Public Service Award and Medal, U.S. Navy, 1957 (posthumous).

Member:
Baker Street Irregulars; Lotus Club; Civil War Round Table; Authors Club; Trap Door Spiders (Founder); American Rocket Society (one of several founders).

Dr. Clark notes: "Pratt spoke seven languages besides English."

THEODORE PRATT

Full Name: Theodore Pratt.
   Born April 26, 1901, at Minneapolis, Minnesota. Son
of Thomas Pratt and Emma Hineline. Married Belle J.
Jacques, 1929. Education: Attended Colgate University and Columbia University for four years.

Career: Writer.
   Worked for several years as a playreader for a
Broadway producer; film reviewer for Variety; occasion-
al lecturer at the University of Florida and Univer-
sity of South Florida; free-lance author, 1933-70.
Died February, 1970.

Awards: Huntingdon Hartford Foundation Fellow, 1958.

Member: Phi Kappa Psi; Palm Beach County Historical
   Association (Governor); Gold Coast Press Club.

* * * * *

E. HOFFMANN PRICE

Full Name: Edgar Hoffmann Price.
   Born July 3, 1898, at Fowler, California. Son of
Murtilah Elijah Price (a horticulturist) and Maria
Theresa Hoffmann. Married Helen Price, 1928 (divorced
1931); married Wanda Price, 1934 (divorced, 1945);
married Loriena Price, 1959. Two children: Theresa,
Dan.

Career: Writer.
   Soldier, U.S. Army, 1917-24; Plant Supervisor, Union
Carbide, 1924-32; free-lance author, 1924-52, 1968-
DATE; Microfilm Technician, County of San Mateo, and
self-employed, 1952-68; occasional assistant to Farns-
worth Wright, Editor of Weird Tales, as a reader.

First Professional Sale: "Triangle with Variations," in Droll Stories, circa May, 1924.

Member: American Legion; American Federation of
   Astrologers; National Rifle Association; Theosophical Society in America.

Interests:
   "Professional photography, collecting Oriental rugs,
casual linguistics, honorary member and/or English
lecturer in various Buddhist and Taoist temples, astrology (professional), vegetable cuisine, Chinese,
Indian, and Mexican cuisine, wines & liquors, motoring, do-it-yourself car maintenance, sour dough bread."

Price writes:
   "While working with Karl Edward Wagner at Carcosa
House in selecting stories for my collection, Far
Lands, Other Times, I was not amazed at noting how
much trash I had sold; I was pleased by the number
of stories I could re-read without regret, and by
the number I am glad I wrote. In trying to stage a
comeback, in fantasy and SF, it seemed that I was
and am off the beam. Contemporary stuff: (a) wish
I could do it that way, but can't; (b) a lot of dri-
vel-trash-stupidity-ideology, and I'm glad I can't.
Writing is a great way of life. My favorite associates are soldiers and writers, Chinamen and other
orientals, and comparable off-trail folks.
   "The fan world is necrophiliac. I once had an informal group of very congenial fans at "The Lamasery"
(my home in the hills for more than 39 years), talking
about H. P. Lovecraft and Robert E. Howard. Someone

"finally dropped a brick by asking, "What's wrong with
E. Hoffmann Price?" "Oh---nothing---he's OK---BUT HE
ISN'T DEAD YET....""
   "Groups devoted to immortalizing deceased "greats,"
near greats, un-greats, pop up like mushrooms in well-
manured fields. These outfits range from serious-minded
operators, to juveniles concentrating on "in" gags and
chatter.
   "The researchers are unmitigated pests. When I was
contributing to Weird Tales, and later, when I advanced
to the "real" fiction fields of adventure, crime, and
western writing, there were very few fan letters. Fans
were busy buying and reading fiction. Today, I kill
hour after hour answering mail from folks who buy nothing except ancient pulps at $5 or $25 a copy. Money
thus spent on antiques and dead men's bones could, despite extortionate postal rates, be used to buy current
materials direct from the publishers.
   "Dr. Harry K. Brobet and I meet at long intervals to
re-hash and re-share our memories of our good friend,
H. P. Lovecraft. We have long been fed up with the
psychology buffs (Harry's Ph.D. is in psychology; he's
retiring after thirty years at a university position)
who have been analyzing and explaining HPL. Was he a
homosexual or only a "latent homosexual?" Gradually,
they're nibbling away at Howard.
   "The newly-discovered, never-before-published yarns
by this and that dead hero, stuff which neither the
deceased could sell during his lifetime, nor his agent
and heirs, until a "cult" developed, are now being published. It must be trash, else the big name could have
sold it years ago.
   "Hence my policy: I give no information, and I am
leaving no unpublished Mss., nor unfinished Mss. If
I can't sell it, it is not worth publishing later. I
have destroyed at least 45 duds--i.e., 10%, more or
less, of my total output. A lot of published stuff
is bound for destruction. What they, the fans and
gravedigger publishers, are doing to my deceased comrades, is warning enough! Not being dead yet, I am
still immune--but no one is so lowly as to escape the
ghouls once he's dead!"

   "Edmond Hamilton has suggested that writing for WT
was something like belonging to a fraternity, and
I know of no expression more felicitous or meaningful.
My Jade Pagoda series contains many references to the
"fraternity spirit," and specific examples of the travels of WT writers, with visiting stops along the way,
to see old friends or to meet a "member" one had read
often, but never had met.
   "Robert E. Howard wired me in June, 1932, that HPL
was in New Orleans, and gave me the hotel address. At
once, I went to locate him, and began a friendship.
In New York, 1933, I located Casket & Sunnyside in the
phone book, talked to its editor, Seabury Quinn, and
met him at his home that evening. HPL wrote from Providence, RI, to tell me (during my Irvington, NY so-
journ) that Frank Belknap Long would be happy to guide
me to the Paterson, NJ Municipal Museum, to meet James
Ferdinand Morton, HPL's distant kinsman.
   "Being a regular contributor to Weird Tales was a
way of living, a life style; so, of course, was being
a full-dress pulp writer in the "regular" or "real"
magazines of those days, but with the WT clique, it
was more so. I arrived in California in mid-April,
1934, and within 30 days I had driven to Auburn to see
Clark Ashton Smith, with whom I had corresponded for
a couple of years (I liked his work). En route to
California, I stopped in Cross Plains, Texas, to meet
Robert E. Howard--we'd corresponded since 1928, each
liking the other's stories. Jack Williamson and Edmond Hamilton and Otis Adelbert Kline and Robert Spencer

E. HOFFMANN PRICE (Cont.)

"Carr were "clubmembers" I met at the editorial rooms of WT, and, after reading "Shambleau" in typescript, I lost little time meeting C. L. Moore."

* * * * *

ROGER PRICE

Full Name: Roger Damon Mainwaring Price.
Born August 25, 1941, at Southport, Lancashire, England. Son of Norman Price (a journalist) and Jeramie Paiton (a novelist). Married Beryl Anne Ridgeway, 1966. Two children: Jane Catherine Julie (born 1969); Jacqueline Lucy (born 1972); two step-children: Paul Ross Price (born 1963), Justine Maria (born 1966).

Career: TV Producer/Director, author.
Soldier, H.M. Forces (a parachute regiment), 1958-61; Scriptwriter, ATV Ltd., 1961-63; Writer/Director, R.H.R. Productions, 1963-66; Writer/Director, BBC Television, 1966-70; Producer/Director, Writer, Granada TV, and then Thames TV Ltd., 1970-DATE.

First Professional Sale (Book): *The Tomorrow People in The Visitor*, Piccolo, 1973 (with Julian R. Gregory).

Agent: Alfred Davies & Associates, Eagle House, Jermyn St., London, England.

Member: Society of Film and Television Arts.

Interests: Reading SF, watching TV, his family, sports cars, four-wheel drive vehicles.

Price writes:
"Because my father and mother were both writers, the last thing I wanted to do was write. I tried to enter TV as a cameraman, but was put instead to writing documentary commentaries. My English teacher had told me I'd be a writer, but I didn't think it likely. Since then, I've built a career as a TV producer/director of drama and documentary (mainly for or about kids), and have written when forced to, either by a persistent boss or a fat cheque or both.
"*The Tomorrow People* was something I was asked to create for Thames TV to answer the BBC's *Dr. Who* series. I had always been keen on science fiction, and once or twice thought I might try and write some. The TV series, which is about psionic kids, the next stage of human evolution, who are active in our time and use their powers for the good of humanity, was a success. That lead to a second series of shows, and the first book. The second series took all my time to write, so I got Julian R. Gregory to write the book from my storyline. I wrote the next book myself, and am now working on the third TV series, and the third book. Thames TV allow me three months a year free from duties as a producer to write 13 half-hour dramas and the book.
"Regarding science fiction and televison in Great Britain, I think it's pretty well served. *The Tomorrow People*, although only a nationally networked (not international) children's show, gets a bigger budget than many adult dramas, and twice the budget of an afternoon drama serial. We have two home-grown science fiction series, mine, and the BBC's *Doctor Who*, which has run for more than ten years, and has built up a great following. The BBC also show science fic-

"tion for adults: *Star Trek* (and even *Dr. Who*) is at a time when adults can watch. Our science fiction is aimed purely at children. We transmit *The Tomorrow People* at a time (4:50 P.M.) when only kids are watching. In the same time slot, we also transmit the best we can buy of American sci-fi, *Voyage to the Bottom of the Sea*, *Time Tunnel*, and *The Wild Wild West*. From which, I suppose you can tell, our SF for kids is American sci-fi for adults. *The Tomorrow People* would probably be considered too deep for American child audiences.
"Often I think it would be nice to have more time to spend on the writing than I am allocated. But then, I am first a TV producer. I write for the people who employ me only on their insistence."

* * * * *

ROGER PRICE

Full Name: Roger Taylor Price.
Born March 6, 1921, at Charleston, West Virginia. Son of Roger T. Price (a coal operator) and Mary Presley. Married and divorced. Two children: Roger Taylor III, Sandi Hope.

Education: Attended University of Michigan, 1937, and American Academy of Art, 1939.

Career: Writer and publisher.
Has been a television and club comedian and actor; Partner, Price/Stern/Sloan (publishers), Los Angeles; free-lance author, 1951-DATE.

* * * * *

CHRISTOPHER PRIEST

Full Name: Christopher McKenzie Priest.
Born July 14, 1943, in England. Son of Walter Priest and Millicent Haslock. Married Christine Merchant.

Career: Writer.
Full-time author, 1968-DATE; part-time lecturer at the University of London; Reviews Editor, *Foundation*, 1973-DATE.

First Professional Sale: "The Run," in *Impulse*, May, 1966.

Agent: Virginia Kidd, Box 278, Milford, PA 18337.

Honors: Third Place, John W. Campbell Memorial Award for Best Science Fiction Novel of the Year, 1972, for *Fugue for a Darkening Island*.

Member: Science Fiction Writers of America; Society of Authors; Science Fiction Foundation (Vice-President).

* * * * *

J. B. PRIESTLEY

Full Name: John Boynton Priestley.
Born September 13, 1894, at Bradford, Yorkshire, England. Son of Jonathan Priestley (a schoolmaster). Married Patricia Tempest (died 1925); married Mary Holland Wyndham Lewis (divorced 1952); married Jacquetta Hawkes (the writer). Four daughters, one son. Education: M.A., Trinity Hall, Cambridge University.

J. B. PRIESTLEY (Cont.)

Career: Writer.
Began writing for newspapers at age sixteen, and has been writing steadily ever since; critic, reviewer, and essayist for various periodicals in London, 1922; first play produced in 1932; Director, Mask Theatre, 1938-39; lecturer on U.S. tour, 1937; has written for stage, screen, radio, and TV; President, Screenwriters Association, 1944-45; U.K. delegate to two UNESCO conferences, 1946-47; one of the originators of the Campaign for Nuclear Disarmament (CND); Chairman, International Theatre Conferences at Paris, 1947, and Prague, 1948; Chairman, British Theatre Conference, 1948, and International Theatre Institute, 1949; Member, National Theatre Board, 1966-67; Former Chairman, Council on London Philharmonic Orchestra; former Director, *New Statesman* and *Nation*. Member: Savile Club, London.

Honors & Awards:
James Tait Black Prize for Fiction, 1930, for *The Good Companions*; Ellen Terry Award for Best Play of 1947, for "The Linden Tree"; LL.D., St. Andrews University; D.Litt., University of Colorado, Birmingham University, Bradford University.

* * * * *

ANN PRIOR

Full Name: Ann Prior.
Born September 12, 1949, at Christchurch, New Zealand. Daughter of Arthur Norman Prior (a Professor of Philosophy at Oxford) and Mary Wilkinson.

Career: Writer, 1967-DATE. Agent: David Higham Associates, 76 Dean St., Soho, London W.1, England.

* * * * *

ROLAND PUCCETTI

Full Name: Roland Peter Puccetti.
Born August 11, 1924, at Oak Park, Illinois. Son of George Puccetti (a salesman) and Marie McKane. Married Jeanne Marie-Rose Maroun, November 7, 1959. Two children: Maïa Clara (born 1962), Peter Harry (born 1966).

Education: B.A., University of Illinois, 1948; M.A., University of Toronto, 1950; D. de l'U., University of Paris, 1952.

Career: Professor of Philosophy.
Associate Professor, American University of Beirut, 1954-65; Professor and Head of the Dept. of Philosophy, University of Singapore, 1965-71; Professor of Philosophy, and Chairman of the Department of Philosophy, Dalhousie University, 1971-DATE.

Agent: Harold Ober Associates.

Member: American Philosophical Association; Canadian Philosophical Association; Society for the Philosophy of Psychology.

Interests: Fiction writing, chess, field archery, tennis.

Puccetti notes: "I got into fiction-writing only

"in 1969, when I was already 45 years old, and an established professional philosopher. By the time I wrote *The Death of the Fuhrer*, my philosophical interests had shifted towards problems of the mind-brain relationship. I find medicine-fiction writing helps my philosophical thinking, and vice-versa."

* * * * *

CAROL PUGNER

Full Name: Wanda Carol Pugner.
Born August 1, 1943, at San Diego, California. Daughter of Ottis Lee Ligon and Margaret Melithia Boyd. Married Paul Edward Pugner, August 19, 1967. One son, Anders Lee Edward Pugner (born 1973).

Education: B.A., San Diego State College, 1965.

Career: Editor.
Teacher, Sweetwater Union School District, in the English, Journalism, and Drama Departments, 1968-72; free-lance editor, 1973-DATE; "mother."

First Professional Sale: *A Science Fiction Reader*, Charles Scribner's Sons, 1973.

Interests:
Politics, needlecraft, good books, good music, good friends. "I am currently following my husband around as he moves from school to school. He is presently enrolled at Humboldt State University, but will enter the master's program at Utah State University shortly. My own time is largely taken up with raising my first child, an experience which both enriches and debilitates."

* * * * *

TOM PURDOM

Full Name: Thomas Edward Purdom.
Born April 19, 1936, at New Haven, Connecticut. Son of Orlando Jackson Purdom (in U.S. Navy) and Inez Antoninette Tigna. Married Sara Jeanne Wescoat, November 19, 1960. Purdom's wife is a development writer and office manager for Presbyterian-University of Pennsylvania Medical Center. One son, Christopher William (born 1964).

Education: Attended Lafayette College, 1952-54.

Career: Writer.
"From 1954-68, I worked at various office and clerical jobs, mainly for United Airlines, part-time from 1963 while continuing my writing career"; Science Writer, University of Pennsylvania, 1968-70; Script Writer, Moore School of Electrical Engineering, University of Pennsylvania, 1968-70; Visiting Professor of English, Temple University, 1970-71; free-lance writer, 1963-DATE.

First Professional Sale: "Grieve for a Man," in *Fantastic Universe*, August, 1957.

Agent: Scott Meredith, 580 Fifth Avenue, New York, NY 10036.

Awards: One of ten winners in *New Republic* essay contest for young writers under 26 in 1958, for "In Praise of Science Fiction"; Top Story, Atlantic Young

TOM PURDOM (Cont.)

Writers contest, 1952; Fourth Prize, Scholastic National contest, 1950.

Member:
Science Fiction Writers of America (Vice-President, 1970-72); Philadelphia Science Fiction Society (past President and Vice-President); World Future Society; American Civil Liberties Union; H. C. Lea School Open Classroom Parents Group.

Interests:
History, science, city planning, military history, wargaming with military miniatures, bicycling, politics (active in most Philadelphia elections), soccer (Philadelphia Atoms fan), parenthood, the City of Philadelphia, learning things.

Purdom writes:
"I started reading SF in 1950 when I pulled a copy of *Adventures in Time and Space* off a library shelf in Tampa, Florida. I had already gotten interested in space travel by reading Willy Ley's book on rockets, and that led me to the SF anthologies. I was a very intense reader--and a real space travel fanatic--for about five years, and then some of my interest waned, as it seems to with most people. I've always thought those five years were a big event in my life, however, and that the time I spent reading three or four magazines and a couple of SF books per month was well spent. And I'm happy I still find enough SF to keep me reading the stuff. Even if you get tired of it after five or six years, anybody who goes through a period like that will be a lot richer in many different ways for the rest of his life. Most of my close friends have several things in common. They are all people engaged in some kind of professional or scholarly occupation, and they are all people with wide-ranging, lively minds that are interested in almost every subject a human being can be interested in--and they all read SF for at least one period in their lives, and still read it at least a little. I tend to feel there's some connection.

"Most of my basic feelings about fiction can probably be summed up by two quotes. One is Tolkien's comment that he loathed allegory, but loved history, real or feigned, with its infinite applicability. I like stories, true or untrue, and read *The Guns of August* for much the same reasons I read *War and Peace*. I think this is a basic human appetite, and I feel that people who like stories are generally the kind of people I like to live with.

"The other quote is from a poet--Yeats, I think-- who said young men sometimes asked him if they should become poets, and he always asked them why they wanted to pursue such a career. They would usually say they had some great idea or vision they wanted to communicate to the world, and in that case he would always tell them they should do something else. Now and then, however, one of them would say he wanted to write poetry because he loved words, and the sound of words, and liked to roll them around on his tongue, and play with them, and so on. And in that case Yeats would say, "You may be a poet." I would substitute stories for words in talking to would-be fiction writers, but the principle is the same.

"I have mixed feelings about the academic interest in science fiction. On the one hand, it's probably bringing in lots of new readers, and college SF courses should provide a lucrative market for the writers whose works get on the reading lists. And I'm all for SF courses and the reading of SF works in academic areas such as sociology, science, government, etc.

"SF English courses are something else, however. As I've indicated elsewhere, I think of fiction as essentially an emotional and aesthetic experience. The important thing about a work of fiction is the things that happen to the reader while he is reading it. If English students were merely given a list of books, and given grades for reading them, I wouldn't have any reservations at all about SF courses. But, as Silberman points out in his book, *Crisis in the Classroom*, school is always evaluative. The student must do something the teacher can evaluate--write essays about the work, discuss it in class, etc. And the teacher must do things that can be evaluated, too. He must give lectures, write papers, and so on. The result is a tendency to exaggerate the aspects of fiction that can be talked about and written about. And eventually, the tail begins to wag the dog. Aspects of fiction such as the author's worldview and philosophic opinions are thought of as the "point" of the work, and students start approaching novels and stories as if they were philosophic and sociological treatises disguised--for some obscure reason--behind pages of narration.

"Most of the English majors I've met seem to be preoccupied with two questions: how do you "judge" a story, and what does it mean. I've even seen readers for fourth graders in which they were told that the theme of a story is "What the author is trying to say," and were given the impression authors write stories because they want to communicate "themes." But I personally doubt if anybody would ever read any work of fiction with either question in mind if somebody hadn't stood up in front of a classroom and told them they should. People read fiction to satisfy a number of emotional needs--some of them very profound--and I tend to suspect that most of this bull about themes and judging stories is just another way of keeping our emotions at arms length.

"I once tried to explain this to an English teacher, and he nodded profoundly, and said, "I see. The medium is the message." But that isn't it at all. The medium is words. The message is the story. And the point of the story--its essential reason for being--is the emotional satisfaction it gives the reader and the writer. Writers do have worldviews, and the author's worldview is certainly one of the things many of us get from fiction, and one of the reasons we read it. But it isn't the main thing we usually read fiction for, and I get very annoyed at people who think a philosophy or an opinion is more important than a profoundly moving narrative. One tear for Charlie Morgan is worth any number of philosophic opinions.

"I have no reservations about courses that tell students something about the history and development of science fiction, brief them on some of its special conventions and traditions, and introduce them to a good cross-section of its literature, chosen by somebody who is familiar with the field. Courses like that merely shorten the process we all went through when we first started reading SF, and I gather that many SF writers teach such courses when they're given a chance to handle the SF offering. The whole thrust of academia, however, is toward the type of thing I'm complaining about, and I tend to think there isn't much you can do about it.

"I don't know what contribution I've made to the field, but I know the contribution I would like to make. I would like to write stories that will make my readers feel the way I felt when I first read science fiction-- and still feel when I read any of the current stuff I really like."

[The section on SF and academe was written in response to direct questions on the subject.]

RICHARD PURTILL

Full Name: Richard L. Purtill.
  Born March 13, 1931, at Chicago, Illinois. Son of
Joseph T. Purtill (a businessman) and Bertha Walker.
Married Elizabeth Banks (a statistician), June 20,
1959. Two sons: Mark, Timothy.

Education: B.A., University of Chicago, 1958;
  M.A., 1960; Ph.D., 1965.

Career: Professor of Philosophy.
  Instructor, Western Washington State College, 1962-
65; Assistant Professor, 1965-68; Associate Professor,
1968-72; Professor of Philosophy, 1972-DATE; Visiting
Lecturer, San Francisco State College, 1968-69.

Awards: National Endowment for the Humanities Summer
  Grant, 1970. Member: American Philosophical Association; American Association of University Professors; Sierra Club.

* * * * *

RODNEY QUEST

Full Name: Rodney Quest.
  Born in England, circa 1895 (?). Agent: John Cushman Associates, 24 E. 38th St., New York, NY 10016.

Career: Writer.
  Served in the British Army, 1914-19, receiving the
military cross, and in the Royal Air Force, 1939-45;
writer, 1933-DATE.

* * * * *

GILBERT A. RALSTON

Full Name: Gilbert Alexander Ralston.
  Born January 5, 1912, at Los Angeles, California.
Son of Alexander Gilbert Ralston and Jeannette John-
ston. Married Mary Katherine Hart, December 20, 1938.
Two children: Michael Gilbert, David Hart.

Education: Attended Pasadena College, 1929-32, and
  American Academy of Dramatic Arts, 1935.

Career: Writer.
  Actor and stage manager, 1931-35; writer and direc-
tor of radio shows for NBC, 1936-38; Production Super-
visor, Compton Advertising, 1939-42; successively
Organizer and Manager of Radio Department, and then
Executive Producer of Incorporated Television Division,
Proctor & Gamble, 1943-50; free-lance producer of
television films, 1950-55; Executive Producer in
Charge of Television Drama, CBS, 1955-57; free-lance
writer, 1958-DATE; Chairman, School of Communicative
Arts, Tahoe Paradise College, 1968; Dean, School of
Communicative Arts, Sierra Nevada College, 1969-73;
President of the College, 1973-DATE; President, Ral-
ston School of Communicative Arts, 1971-DATE; Vice-
President, Rule of Three Productions, 1973-DATE; lec-
turer on many college campuses.

Agent: Reese Halsey, 8733 Sunset Blvd., Los Angeles,
  CA 90069.

Member: American Society of Composers, Authors &
  Publishers; Writers Guild of America, West; Western
  Writers of America; Authors League.

AYN RAND

Full Name: Ayn Rand [first name pronounced like
  "pine"]. Born February 2, 1905, at St. Petersburg,
Russia. Came to the U.S., 1926, and naturalized 1931.
Married Frank O'Connor (an artist), 1929. Education:
Attended private school in St. Petersburg; graduate
in history, University of Leningrad, 1924.

Career: Writer and lecturer.
  Movie extra and junior screenwriter, Cecil B. De
Mille Studio, Hollywood, 1926-28; Head of Wardrobe
Dept., RKO Pictures, New York, 1929-32; screenwriter
for various Hollywood studios, 1932-34; free-lance
script reader, 1934-35; writer, 1935-41; script reader,
Paramount Pictures, 1941-43; part-time screen writer,
Hal Wallis Productions, 1944-49; full-time writer and
lecturer, 1951-DATE; visiting lecturer at many colleges
and universities.

Awards: D.H.L., Lewis & Clark College, 1963. Agent:
  Curtis Brown Ltd., 60 E. 56th St., New York, NY 10022.

* * * * *

FLORENCE ENGEL RANDALL

Full Name: Florence Engel Randall.
  Born October 18, 1917, at Brooklyn, New York. Daughter of Stewart Engel (an attorney) and Rachel Selig-
man. Married Murray Charles Randall (a sales executive)
November 5, 1939. Three children: Susan, Laurel,
Stewart. Education: Attended New York University,
1937.

Career: Writer.
  Sold her first story at age eighteen, but only became a full-time novelist in 1967.

Awards: *The Almost Year* was an American Library Association Notable Book in 1971. Member: Authors
  League; Science Fiction Writers of America.

* * * * *

RICK RAPHAEL

Full Name: Rick Raphael.
  Born February 20, 1919, at New York, New York. Son
of Louis Nevin Raphael and Viola Louise Felix. Married
Elizabeth L. Van Schaick, July 1, 1958. Six children:
Christopher Michael, Patricia Antoinette, Melanie Lou-
ise, Karen Sue, Teresa Frances, Stephanie Monique.

Education: B.A., University of New Mexico, 1948.

Career: Businessman.
  Captain, U.S. Army, 1936-46; reporter, 1946-59, writing for various political and scientific newspapers,
and for radio and TV; Press Secretary for Senator Frank
Church, 1965-69; executive with J. C. Penney Company,
1969-DATE; Assistant News Director, radio station KBOI,
Boise, Idaho, 1959-65.

Raphael writes:
  "In going through my abbreviated biography, I remembered something from a fear-ridden night a quarter of
a century ago. I was lying in the bed of a French
farmhouse, listening to the German artillery shells
landing ever closer to the building. I was convinced
that within moments, one would score a direct hit.

RICK RAPHAEL (Cont.)

"I was less concerned about dying than I was about
the fact that the man that killed me wouldn't know
who I was. If you're going to kill, at least know
me, look at me, I'm a human being like you; I live,
make love, have bowel movements, frighten easily.
My name is.... What I guess I'm trying to say is
that I should really be very grateful for your biography, for it is another small imprint of ME on human consciousness, and even, for a fleeting moment,
on human history. Understand?"

* * * * *

CARL HENRY RATHJEN

Full Name: Carl Henry Rathjen.
  Born August 28, 1909, at Jersey City, New Jersey.
Son of Carl Martin Henry Rathjen (a retail and whole-
sale food dealer) and Agnes Liechtenstein. Married
Olive Minerva Stretch (now an osteopathic physician),
May 14, 1958. One step-daughter, Barbara Joy.

Education: B.C.S., New York University, 1931.

Career: Writer.
  Has been a copywriter for an advertising agency,
laborer, counselor at a boys' camp, cutter in the
rubber industry; full-time author, 1932-DATE. Member: California Writers Guild.

Awards:
  Honorable Mention, *Boys' Life*-Dodd, Mead Writing
Award, 1954, for *Smoke-Eater*; "Runaway Rig" named
one of the twenty best *Saturday Evening Post* stories,
1957; Rotary International Service Award, 1965, for
conspicuous service to youth.

Agent: Larry Sternig, 2404 N. 44th St., Milwaukee,
  WI 53510.

* * * * *

HERMAN RAUCHER

Full Name: Herman Raucher.
  Born April 13, 1928, at New York, New York. Son of
Benjamin Brooks Raucher and Sophie Weinshank. Married
Mary Kathryn Martinet, April 20, 1960. Two children:
Jacqueline Leigh, Jennifer Brooke.

Education: B.S., New York University, 1949.

Career: Writer.
  Advertising writer, Twentieth Century-Fox, 1950-54;
with Walt Disney, 1954-55; with Calkins & Holden, New
York, 1956-57; Vice-President, Creative Director,
and Member of the Board of Directors, Reach, McCluton
(advertising), New York, 1957-63; Vice-President and
Creative Director, Maxon (advertising), New York,
1963-64; Vice-President and Creative Director, Gardner (advertising), 1964-65; consultant, Benton &
Bowles (advertising), New York, 1965-67; full-time
author, 1967-DATE, writing screenplays, teleplays,
and novels.

Agent: William Morris Agency, 151 El Camino, Beverly Hills, CA 90212. Member: Writers Guild of
  America; Dramatists Guild.

FRANCIS G. RAYER

Full Name: Francis George Rayer.
  Born June 6, 1921, in Worcestershire, England. Son
of Harry Rayer and Florence Nellie Shepherd. Married
Tessa Elizabeth Platt, February 23, 1957. Two sons:
William Francis (born 1961), Quintin George (born 1965).

Career: Technical journalist and equipment designer.
  Self-employed technical and electronic engineer,
1945-DATE.

First Professional Sale: "Juggernaut," Link
  House Publications, 1944.

Agent: E. J. Carnell Literary Agency, 17 Burwash Rd.,
  Plumstead, London SE18 7QY, England.

Member: Institution of Electronic & Radio Engineers
  (Associate); Chartered Engineering Institutions
  (Technical Engineer).

Interests: Amateur radio operator, G3OGR.

* * * * *

CLAIRE RAYNER

Full Name: Claire Berenice Rayner.
  Born January 22, 1931. Married Desmond Rayner (in
advertising), June 23, 1957. Three children: Amanda,
Adam, Jason.

Career: Writer.
  Former nurse in London; full-time writer, 1960-DATE;
presents regular TV broadcasts for "Town and Around,"
London, 1965-DATE.

Agent: Ursula Winant, Winant Towers, 1 Furnival St.,
  London EC4, England.

* * * * *

WILLIAM READY

Full Name: William Bernard Ready [pronounced Reedy].
  Born September 16, 1914, at Cardiff, Glamorgan,
Wales. Came to the U.S., 1948. Son of John Ready
and Nora Hart. Married Bessie Dyer, April 24, 1945.
Six children: Patrick, Vincent, Liam, Thomas, Mary,
Nora.

Education:
  B.A., University of Wales, 1937; Diploma in Paleo-
graphy and Archives, 1938; Associate of the Library
Association of Great Britain, 1938; B.A., Cl. II, Uni-
versity of Wales, 1939; Diploma in Education, Balliol
College, Oxford University, 1946; M.A., University of
Manitoba, 1948; Diploma in Advanced Library Adminis-
tration, Rutgers University, 1956; Diploma in Archival
Management, Radcliffe University, 1958; M.L.S., Univer-
sity of Western Ontario, 1970.

Career: Writer and librarian.
  Library Assistant, Cardiff Public Library, 1933-39;
Lecturer, University of California, Berkeley, 1950-51;
Assistant Director of Libraries, Stanford University,
1951-56; University Librarian, Marquette University,
1956-63; University Librarian and Professor of Bibliography, Sacred Heart College, 1963-66; University Librarian, McMaster University, 1966-DATE.

WILLIAM READY (Cont.)

First Professional Sale: "Barring the Weight,"
in Atlantic Monthly, 1948.

Agent: Russell & Volkening, New York.

Honors & Awards:
$1000 short story award, Atlantic Monthly, 1948;
Honor Roll of the American Short Story, 1952; Thomas
More Award ($500) and Citation, 1960; American Library
Association Clarence Day Award, for Library of the
Year, 1961.

Member:
American Association of Archivists; American Library
Association; Canadian Library Association; Institute
of Professional Librarians of Ontario; Library Associ-
ation of Great Britain; Ontario Library Association;
Royal Society of Canada (Fellow).

Interests: Walking, cinema, TV.

Ready has been Chairman of the Gromlech Press since
1970.

* * * * *

CLIFFORD C. REED

Full Name: Clifford Cecil Reed.
Born May 13, 1911, at Durban, South Africa. Son
of Clifford and Marion Phyllis Reed. Married Dorothy
Mary Reed, October 8, 1940. One son, Jeremy Clifford
(born 1943).

Career: Accountant.
Was a salesman and civil servant in South Africa
until 1939; in the South African Army, 1939-45; emigrated to Britain after the War; now an accountant
with the Housing Authority, London.

First Professional Sale: "Jean-Gene-Jeanne," in
Authentic Science Fiction, November, 1954.

Agent: E. J. Carnell Literary Agency, 17 Burwash
Road, Plumstead, London SE18 7QY, England.

Member: Chartered Institution of Secretaries.

* * * * *

KIT REED

Full Name: Lillian Craig Reed.
Born June 7, 1932, at San Diego, California. Daughter of John Rich Craig (an officer in the U.S. Navy)
and Lillian Hyde. Married Joseph Wayne Reed, Jr.
(a professor), December 10, 1955. Three children:
Joseph McKean (born 1959), John Craig (born 1961),
Katherine Hyde (born 1967).

Education: B.A., College of Notre Dame of Maryland,
1954.

Career: Writer and lecturer.
Reporter, St. Petersburg Times, Florida, 1954-55;
Reporter, New Haven Register, Connecticut, 1956-59;
free-lance author, 1959-DATE; visiting Professor of
English, Wesleyan University; regular book reviewer
for New Haven Register and Choice.

First Professional Sale: "The Wait," in The Magazine of Fantasy and Science Fiction, April, 1958.

Agent: Brandt & Brandt, 101 Park Avenue, New York,
NY 10017.

Honors & Awards:
Guggenheim Fellow, 1964-65; first American recipient,
five-year literary grant from Abraham Woursell Foundation, 1965-70; New England Newspaperwoman of the Year,
1958, 1959; Best Catholic Short Story of the Year, 1969.

Member: Authors Guild; P.E.N.

* * * * *

JAMES REEVES

Full Name: James Reeves.
Born July 1, 1909, at London, England. Son of Albert
John Reeves and Ethel Mary Blench. Married Mary Phil-
lips, 1936. Three children: Stella, Juliet Mary,
Gareth Edward.

Education: M.A., Cambridge University, 1931.

Career: Author and editor.
Teacher in state schools and teachers' training colleges, 1933-52; free-lance author and editor, 1952-DATE;
broadcaster and lecturer.

Agent: Sterling Lord Agency, 75 E. 55th St., New York,
NY 10022.

* * * * *

R. REGINALD

Full Name: Michael Roy Burgess.
Born February 11, 1948, near Fukuoka, Kyushu, Japan.
Son of Roy Walter Burgess (formerly a Major in the U.S.
Air Force; now Director, Medford School District Trans-
portation Office, in Oregon) and Betty Jane Kapel (a
library assistant). Married Mary Alice Wickizer Rogers,
October 15, 1976. Two step-children: Richard Albert
Rogers, (Mary) Louise Rogers.

Education: A.B. (Honors), Gonzaga University, 1969;
M.S. in L.S., University of Southern California, 1970.

Career: Publisher, author, and librarian.
Periodicals Librarian, California State College, San
Bernardino, 1970-76; Assistant Library Bibliographer,
1976-DATE; Associate Editor, Forgotten Fantasy Magazine,
October, 1970-June, 1971 (all issues published); Joint
Editor (with Douglas Menville), Newcastle Publishing
Company, Inc., North Hollywood, July, 1971-DATE; Editor
(with Douglas Menville), Forgotten Fantasy Library,
1973-DATE; Advisory Editor (with Douglas Menville),
Arno Press Science Fiction Series, 1975; Advisory Edi-
tor (with Douglas Menville), Arno Press Supernatural
and Occult Fiction Series, 1976; Advisory Editor (with
Douglas Menville), Arno Press Lost Race and Adult Fan-
tasy Series, 1977; Publisher and Editor, R. Reginald,
The Borgo Press, 1975-DATE; President and Chairman of
the Board of Directors, Lynwyck Realty and Investment
Company, Inc., San Bernardino, California, 1976-DATE;
Editor (with Douglas Menville), Forgotten Futures
Series, 1977-DATE; free-lance author, editor, and
bibliographer, 1968-DATE. Published his first book in
1970 under his own imprint, Unicorn & Son, Publishers.

R. REGINALD (Cont.)

Contributing Editor, *Contemporary Authors*, 1977-DATE.

First Professional Sale: *Cumulative Paperback Index, 1939-1959*, Gale Research Company, 1973.

Agent: The Borgo Press, P.O. Box 2845, San Bernardino, CA 92406.

Honors & Awards: Title II Fellowship, University of Southern California, 1969-70; miscellaneous scholarships and academic awards and prizes.

Member:
Science Fiction Writers of America; Science Fiction Research Association; Mythopoeic Society; Fantasy Association; William Morris Society & Kelmscott Fellowship.

Interests:
The mass market paperback, science fiction, popular culture, chronology, monarchs and monarchies, Assyriology and the Akkadian language, classical Greek, Chinese cuisine (Mandarin style), trivia, Woody Allen movies, ancient and Near Eastern history, books.

"I've often been asked why I use a pseudonym. It's difficult to provide an answer that makes much sense, even to myself. I'm not the kind of person who sits around musing about his past, and whenever I've taken the time to review some part of my personal history, I've often found it difficult to recall exactly just how things occurred. I couldn't tell you, for example, precisely when or where I first met my wife. Anything older than yesterday is a long time ago.

"I was shy and rather secretive as a kid, and I rather relished the thought of publishing something under an assumed name. And so, when I became an editor on our high school newspaper, I published an article under a pseudonym which was a translation of my legal name into Spanish. Later, in college, I did a short article on science fiction for *Charter*, Gonzaga University's literary magazine, and that's the first place 'R. Reginald' actually appeared.

"As for the name itself, I'm not really certain where it came from, but my standard story runs something like this: I was reading Saki (H. H. Munro) at the time; one of his favorite characters was a debonair Briton named Reginald, who was featured in many of the individual tales, and in two of the book titles. Since Saki had borrowed his *nom de plume* from Fitzgerald's *Rubaiyat*, I felt it was only fair that someone play the same trick on him. At first, it was just 'R. Reginald,' but naturally I started getting questions about the 'R' part of it, so I adopted as my given name 'Robert,' which I had always fancied as a child. When I started work on my first book, *Stella Nova: The Contemporary Science Fiction Authors*, I used the pseudonym exclusively in my correspondence and mailings (and my brother Steve used the name A. Stephens as distributor); once started, it's impossible to go back.

"Another factor was the discovery, in late 1964, that Noel Gerson had appropriated my real name for use on a series of semi-pornographic non-fiction studies for Monarch Books. It was rather shocking to find my name staring up at me from the local newsstand. He later used the name on some fictional crap from Midwood. I abandoned the use of my full name, and began signing just my surname and initials, a practice which I have since modified even further to just the surname. Out of fifteen books, my real name

has appeared just once, as co-author with 'Reginald,' in deference to my parents, who wanted one to show.

"Using a pseudonym creates a lot of complications that are probably not worth the trouble. I have a joint bank account with myself. Half of my correspondents know me under one name, and half under the other, and a few under both. Most of my contacts in the publishing world know me only as Reginald, which is probably just as well: trying to change my professional name at this point would be terribly confusing to everyone concerned, and would destroy whatever measure of professional recognition I've managed to build up over the years. On the other hand, neither am I as reticent as I used to be, and I no longer mind if people know. I have confidence in my own abilities and talents, and they're not dependent on the name I use."

*   *   *   *   *

LOUIS AARON REITMEISTER

Full Name: Louis Aaron Reitmeister.
Born February 2, 1903, at New York, New York. Son of Nathan Reitmeister and Jennie Crane. Married Betty Richmond, January, 1931 (divorced, 1956).

Career: Writer.
Writer and lecturer, 1923-75. Associate Editor, Lewis Copeland Publishing Company, 1928-31; Associate Editor, *Esthete*, 1928-31; Director, Childville (home for disturbed and retarded children), 1938-75; Member, Founders Society, Einstein College of Medicine, 1959-75; American Director and Member of Honorary Committee, Keren Or Institute for the Blind, Jerusalem, 1967-75; Sponsors' Council Chairman, Kfar Zvi Sitrin of Israel, 1971-75. Died August 20, 1975.

Member:
International Oceanographic Foundation; American Academy of Political and Social Sciences; Center for the Study of Democratic Institutions; American Humanist Association; Association on American Indian Affairs; National Geographic Society; National Audobon Society; Defenders of Wildlife; Committee for Humane Legislation; Bide-A-Wee Home Association; Friends of Animals; Oceanic Society; Project Jonah; Friends of the Sea Otters; Phi Beta Kappa; Long Key Fishing Club.

*   *   *   *   *

J. ALAN RENNIE

Full Name: James Alan Rennie.
Born January 29, 1899, in Scotland. Married Elizabeth Claire MacWalter Silander, April 28, 1931. One daughter, Elizabeth Pamela (deceased). Education: Attended Glasgow School of Art, 1919-22.

Career: Writer.
Ran away from school at age fifteen, and joined the British Army, serving from 1914-19; was wounded three times, and mentioned in dispatches; after World War I, worked as a sugar planter in Mozambique, as a cowboy in Alberta, Canada, and as an explorer in the Canadian Arctic; theatrical manager and impresario in London's West End during the late 1920s and early 1930s; full-time writer, 1935-41, 1944-69; served in the RAF during World War II, and retired as a Flying Officer (invalided out). British Legion Delegate to Highland and Islands Area Council, 1954-69. Died September 14, 1969. Member: Society of Authors; Radiowriters Association.

ED EARL REPP

Full Name: Edward Earl Repp.
  Born May 22, 1900, at Pittsburgh, Pennsylvania.
Son of Charles Edward Repp (an engineer) and Mary
Caroline Dunham. Married Margaret Louise Smith,
October 17, 1925. One son, Edward Earl, Jr. (born
1927; died in Vietnam, 1971).

Career: Writer.
  Full-time writer, 1919-DATE; has also been a screenwriter for Warner Brothers, Columbia, and RKO studios
at various periods; sometime publicity director.

First Professional Sale: "Attacked by an Octopus," in *Wide World* (England), 1920.

Honors: Honorable Mention, Best Short Film Subject,
  1938/39, by the Motion Picture Academy.

Member: Writers Guild of America.

Repp notes: "I enjoyed a period as a press agent
for various film stars, theatres, and Warner Brothers
Pictures. Also enjoyed writing features for Hearst
papers in Los Angeles, and for the *Los Angeles Times*
and *Los Angeles Daily News*. I've had 19 books published, under various pseudonyms (Peter Field, John
Cody, Brad Buckner, etc.), as well as some 200 motion
picture screen credits for all the leading producers,
some TV plays for programs like *Arizona Rangers* and
Broken Arrow, and over 1500 magazine stories in all
the leading publications. Now semi-retired."

Interests: Archaeology, geology, paleontology.

* * * * *

MICHAEL D. RESNICK

Full Name: Michael Diamond Resnick.
  Born March 5, 1942, at Chicago, Illinois. Son of
William Resnick (a writer) and Gertrude Diamond (a
writer). Married Carol Cain, October 2, 1961. One
daughter, Laura (born 1962).

Education: Attended University of Chicago, 1959-61,
  and Roosevelt University, 1962-63.

Career: Writer and editor.
  File clerk, Santa Fe Railroad, 1962-65; Editor,
National Tattler, 1965-66; Editor, *National Insider*,
1966-69; Publisher and Editor, Oligarch Publishing
Company, 1969; free-lance writer and editor, 1969-DATE.

Agent: JoAnn Wood, 873 Tower Avenue, Hartford, CT
  06112.

Member: Science Fiction Writers of America.

Interests:
  "Collie breeder/speaker/judge. Nostalgix Collie
Kennels has been among the nation's winningest since
1969; all of our dogs are named after SF stories or
characters. Our current top winning champions are
Ch. Nostalgix Gully Foyle, Ch. Nostalgix Nightwings,
and Ch. Nostalgix The Gray Lensman."

Resnick notes: "I wrote no SF from 1969-74; instead,
I ground out about 8 million words of drivel, mostly
soft-core pornography and gothics, while securing my
finances. Now I'm back to SF, hopefully to turn out
at least a couple of books a year."

MACK REYNOLDS

Full Name: Dallas McCord Reynolds.
  Born November 12, 1917, at Corcoran, California.
Son of Verne LaRue Reynolds (a revolutionist) and
Pauline McCord. Married Helen Jeanette Wooley, Sept.,
1947. Three children: Emil Reynolds (born 1940),
L'Verne (born 1943), Dallas Mack (born 1945).

Education: Attended Army Transportation Corps Marine
  Officer's Cadet School, 1944.

Career: Writer.
  Editor, *Catskill Mountain Star*, 1936-194?; Editor,
Oneonta News, 1938-194?; Secretary in 1940 for Presi-
dential Candidate John Aiken, of the Socialist Labor
Party; free-lance author, 1946-DATE; Foreign Editor,
Rogue, 1955-65; supervisor for IBM, 1943.

First Professional Sale: "What Is Courage," in
  Esquire, December, 1946.

Agent: Scott Meredith, 580 Fifth Avenue, New York,
  NY 10036.

Interests: Socioeconomics; anthropology, particularly
  pre-Columbian Mexico; collecting pre-Columbian artifacts.

Reynolds writes:
  "I am a dedicated 'radical,' neither Communist nor
Socialist, who believes that in the immediate future,
great changes must be made in our socio-economic systems, or the race is fated to perish. I try to work
this into my fiction.
  "I was born into science fiction. My grandfather
was such a fan of Jules Verne that he named my father,
Verne L. Reynolds, after him. My father, in turn, was
so impressed by Bellamy's *Looking Backward*, the Utopian
novel, that he became a radical, and as a young man
joined the I.W.W., and later the Socialist Party in
the days of Eugene V. Debs. Later, he switched to the
Socialist Labor Party, and was its vice-presidential
candidate in 1924. In 1928, and again in 1932, he
ran for president. He didn't make it.
  "I was active on the school newspaper in Kingston,
New York, and my first job after graduation was as a
reporter on the *Catskill Mountain Star*. Later, I became its editor at the age of 19, and also editor of
the *Oneonta News*. Still later, I edited the magazine,
Catskill Mountain Digest.
  "Following the war, I began to write stories and articles, selling my first story to *Esquire*. After several other sales, largely detective, I decided to go
into it on a full-scale basis, my wife promising to
support me for two years. The bargain was that if I
wasn't making a living by that time, I was to return
to newspaper or IBM work, and forget about it.
  "We moved to Taos, New Mexico, where Fredric Brown
told me I was a fool to try writing detective stories
during the day, and then entertain myself in the even-
ings reading science fiction. That was in 1949. I
have been writing SF ever since. For a time, I became
Travel Editor of *Rogue*, and touched upon some seventy-
five countries in all. After ten years of that, always
writing SF on the side, I came here to Mexico, built
a house, and settled down.
  "I suppose I like the field because there are few
taboos. I can, and do, say just about anything I want
to say. And I feel I have a lot to say.
  "I think writers should write about things they know.
When I write yarns laid in the center of the Sahara,
Moscow, or Borneo, for that matter, the reader can be
assured that I've been on the scene."

PAMELA REYNOLDS

Full Name: Pamela Reynolds.
  Born June 6, 1923, at New York, New York. Daughter
of George Peter Stemler (an accountant) and Erma Cary.
Married John Corneilius Reynolds (an attorney). Three
children: Nora Dare (born 1949), Brian Drew (born
1955), Diana Putman (born 1961).

Education: B.A., Wells College, 1945; M.A., Teachers College, Columbia University, 1948.

Career: Writer and teacher.
  Substitute English teacher, Fox Lane High School,
1967-DATE; writer, 1965-DATE.

First Professional Sale: Horseshoe Hill, Loth-
  rop, 1965.

Agent: Bertha Klausner, New York.

Member: United States Pony Club; Goldens Bridge
  Hounds Pony Club.

* * * * *

ELMER RICE

Full Name: Elmer Leopold Rice [originally Reizen-
  stein]. Born September 28, 1892, at New York, New
York. Son of Jacob Reizenstein and Fanny Lion. Married Hazel Levy, June 16, 1915 (divorced 1942); married Betty Field (an actress), January 12, 1942 (divorced, 1955); married Barbara A. Marshall. Five
children: Robert, Margaret, John, Judith, Paul.

Education: LL.B., New York Law School, 1912.

Career: Playwright.
  Claims clerk, Samstag & Hilder Bros., New York,
1907; law clerk, 1908-12; admitted to the New York
Bar, 1913; Dramatic Director, University Settlement,
and Chairman, Inter-Settlement Dramatic Society;
scenarist, Samuel Goldwyn Pictures, 1918-20; free-
lance writer, 1920; organized the Morningside Players
in New York; purchased and operated David Belasco
Theatre, New York, 1934-37; Regional Director, Works
Progress Administration Federal Theatre Project, 1935-
36; Director and co-founder, Playwright's Producing
Co., 1937-59; lecturer in English, University of Michigan, Ann Arbor, 1954; Adjunct Professor, New York
University, 1957-58; writer, playwright, theatre director. Died 1967.

Awards: Pulitzer Prize, 1929, for "Street Scene";
  Canada Lee Foundation Award, 1954, for "The Winner";
  Litt.D., University of Michigan, 1961.

Member:
  Dramatists Guild (founding member; President, 1939-
43); Authors League of America (Dramatists Guild representative on the council; President, 1945-46);
P.E.N. (International Vice-President, New York); American National Theatre and Academy (on executive committee); League of British Dramatists; National Council on Freedom from Censorship (Chairman); National
Institute of Arts and Letters; American Civil Liberties Union (Board Member); American Arbitration Association; Writers War Board (on advisory council).

Rice has also written several screenplays.

GUY RICHARDS

Full Name: Guy Richards.
  Born May 18, 1905, at New York, New York. Son of
Guy Richards (a banker) and Alice Lydia Reese. Mar-
ried his first wife 1932 (divorced 1938); married Mary
Spence Francis, August 26, 1940. Two children: An-
tonia, Pamela.

Education: Ph.B., Yale University, 1927.

Career: Reporter.
  Member of Whitney South Sea Expedition to New Guinea
and the Solomon Islands for American Museum of Natural
History, 1927; worked as a reporter for New York Daily
News, New York Sun, and Newhouse Newspapers; worked
for the New York Journal-American, beginning as a re-
porter, and becoming City Editor; Member, Board of
Trustees, Graham Home for Children; free-lance author.

Awards:
  Received two Page One Awards from the New York Newspaper Guild; Order of Silurians Prize; Correction Officers' Benevolent Association Special Award; Free
Assembly of Captive European Nations Award.

Member:
  American Museum of Natural History (Associate); First
Marine Division, U.S. Naval Institute (Associate); Shef-
field Historical Society; Century Club.

* * * * *

ROBERT S. RICHARDSON

Full Name: Robert Shirley Richardson.
  Born April 22, 1902, at Kokomo, Indiana. Son of Joel
Howard Richardson (a salesman) and Arlene Moore. Mar-
ried Marjorie Engstead, May 1, 1942. One daughter,
Rae (born 1944).

Education: B.A., University of California, Los Angeles, 1926; Ph.D., University of California, Berkeley, 1931.

Career: Writer.
  Astronomer, Carnegie Institute of Washington, Dept.
of Hale Observatory, 1931-58; Associate Director, Griffith Observatory, Los Angeles, 1958-64; free-lance
author, 1964-DATE.

First Professional Sale: "Darkness Over Los Angeles," in Los Angeles Times Sunday Magazine, ca. 1936.

Agent: Scott Meredith, 580 Fifth Avenue, New York,
  NY 10036.

Awards: First Annual Children's Science Book Award,
  New York Academy of Sciences, 1971, for The Stars
  and Serendipity.

Member:
  Astronomical Society of the Pacific; American Association for the Advancement of Science; Pasadena Museum
of Modern Art; Excelsior Telescope Club (Honorary
Life Member); Los Angeles Astronomical Society; Pacific Rocket Society; Friends of Altadena Library; Cal-
tech Play Reading Group.

Interests: Play reading, amateur acting, boxing.

ROBERT S. RICHARDSON (Cont.)

Richardson comments:
"I majored in math at UCLA, and was captain of the track team in 1926. I was the first trackman at UCLA to break 10 seconds in the 100 yard dash. From my earliest age, I had a strong interest in astronomy, reading, and writing, all cultural subjects, but unfortunately with scant money involved.

"I doubt if science fiction has done much to stimulate interest in astronomy, except on the sensational side; most readers would consider astronomy *per se* dry and dull. Many SF stories are not *science* fiction, but *fantasy* fiction.

"Recent discoveries in astronomy and other fields have so far surpassed writers' most way-out ideas, that SF now makes greater demands on one's imagination and inventive ability.

"I consider my best short story to be "Kid Anderson," which was published in the Spring, 1957 issue of *Space Science Fiction*, and anthologized in *Great Science Fiction by Scientists*. The story is about a prize fighter; it has no connection with astronomy.

"Most of my fiction has appeared under the pseudonym Philip Latham, the non-fiction fact articles being published under my own name."

* * * * *

LEIGH RICHMOND

Full Name: Leigh Richmond.
Daughter of Royal K. Tucker (an Episcopal minister) and Juliet Luttrell. Married Walter F. Richmond. Three children: Tucker Loane Stoodley (born 1936), Rusty Porter (born 1940), Scott Tucker Richmond (born 1951).

Career: Writer.
Has been a reporter/photographer, editor, and managing editor on various newspapers throughout the country; currently Secretary-Treasurer, The Centric Foundation, Inc., Merritt Island, Florida.

First Professional Sale: "Prologue to an Analogue," in *Analog*, June, 1961.

* * * * *

WALT RICHMOND

Full Name: Walter F. Richmond.
Born December 5, 1922, at Memphis, Tennessee. Son of Walter Richmond (a physicist). Married Leigh Tucker. One son, Scott Tucker (born 1951).

Career: Writer.
Trained as a research physicist; now President and Executive Director, The Centric Foundation, Inc. Died April 14, 1977.

First Professional Sale: "Where I Wasn't Going," in *Analog*, serialized from October-November, 1963 (with Leigh Richmond).

Walt and Leigh Richmond write:
"The Centric Foundation is a brand new organization dedicated to basic research and education, and one of our primary aims is to clarify the interpretations of physical phenomena, differentiating between experimental data and speculation in the field of physics.

"One of our aims will be to show that the interpretation of physical phenomena is not completely embodied--or most easily seen--in relativity or the quantum theory.

"To that end we intend to show the application of relatively simply high school mathematics to the experimental phenomena determined in physics laboratories.

"We expect to have a book out in a couple of years which will give more details on the subject."

* * * * *

ANNE RIDLER

Full Name: Anne Barbara Ridler.
Born July 30, 1912, at Rugby, Warwickshire, England. Daughter of Henry Christopher Bradby (master at Rugby School) and Violet Alice Milford. Married Vivian Ridler (printer to Oxford University), 1938. Four children: Jane, Alison, Benedict, Colin.

Education: Diploma in Journalism, King's College, University of London, 1932.

Career: Writer and editor.
Secretary and reader, Faber & Faber Ltd., London, 1935-40; free-lance author and editor, 1940-DATE.

Awards: Oscar Blumenthal Prize, 1954, and Union League Civic and Arts Foundation Prize, 1955, both for poems published in *Poetry*.

* * * * *

ALAN RIEFE

Full Name: Alan Riefe.
Born May 18, 1925, at Waterbury, Connecticut. Son of B. H. C. Riefe (a businessman) and Beatrice Wise. Married Martha Daggett, June 10, 1948 (died 1949); married Barbara Dube, February 9, 1955. Four children: Martha, Leslie, Sidney, Jordan.

Education: B.A., Colby College, 1950.

Career: Writer.
Wrote 27 network television programs, 1951-65; full-time novelist, 1965-DATE.

Agent: Knox Burger Associates, 39 1/2 Washington Square South, New York, NY 10012.

* * * * *

ROBERT RIENOW

Full Name: Robert Rienow [pronounced Reno].
Born December 4, 1909, at Grafton, Wisconsin. Son of Charles Rienow (a printer) and Agatha Jaeger. Married Leona Train (a writer), April 8, 1931.

Education: A.B., Carthage College, 1930; M.A., Columbia University, 1933; Ph.D., 1937.

Career: Professor of Political Science.
School principal in Essex, Wisconsin, 1931-32; Instructor, Union College, 1934-35; Instructor, State University of New York, Albany, 1936-39; Asst. Professor, 1939-43; Professor of Political Science, 1947-DATE; Member of Publications Committee, 1966-DATE; consultant to New York Dept. of Education.

ROBERT RIENOW (Cont.)

Agent: Paul R. Reynolds, 599 Fifth Avenue, New York, NY 10017.

Awards & Honors:
George Washington Honor Medal, Freedoms Foundation, 1956; Litt.D., Carthage College, 1963.

Member:
American Political Science Association; National Council for the Social Studies; American Association of University Professors; Wilderness Society; National Grange; National Parks Association; Nature Conservancy; Defenders of Wildlife; New York State Political Science Association; State University Faculties Association; University Club of Albany; Masons; Sierra Club.

* * * * *

ROBERT H. RIMMER

Full Name: Robert Henry Rimmer.
Born March 14, 1917, at Dorchester, Massachusetts. Son of Frank H. Rimmer and Blanche Rochefort. Married Erma Richards. Two sons: Robert Henry Jr., Stephen King.

Education: B.A., Bates College, 1939; M.A., Harvard University, 1941.

Career: Printing executive.
President, Relief Printing Corporation, Boston, 1945-DATE; President, Rimmer Engraving Corporation, Boston.

* * * * *

TERE RIOS

Full Name: Marie Teresa Rios Versace.
Born November 9, 1917, at Brooklyn, New York. Daughter of Rafael Rios (with government of Puerto Rico) and Marie Dowd. Married Humbert Joseph Versace (a retired Colonel, U.S. Army), October 12, 1936. Four sons: Humbert Roque, Stephen Vincent, Richard Patrick, John Michael; one daughter, Teresa Dominique.

Education: Attended schools in the U.S., Bermuda, and Puerto Rico.

Career: Writer.
Has been an art museum assistant, hotel clerk, secretary in a cotton gin, bookkeeper, Gallup pollster, real estate salesperson, postal clerk, volunteer with Red Cross and Civil Air Patrol; began writing after World War II.

Awards:
Honorable Mention, *Atlantic Monthly*, 1948, for "The Freedman"; Doubleday Prize, 1948, for her short story, "Los Carilargos."

Member: Writers Sodality of America; Wisconsin Regional Writers Association.

Rios is fluent in Spanish, and can speak some French and German. Her interests include: horses, flying, sailing, and eating out.

ALAIN ROBBE-GRILLET

Full Name: Alain Robbe-Grillet.
Born August 18, 1922, at Brest, France. Son of Gaston Robbe-Grillet (an engineer) and Yvonne Canu. Married Catherine Rstakian, October 23, 1957.

Education: Ingénieur Agronome, Institut National Agronomique.

Career: Writer.
Charge de Mission, Institut National des Statistiques, Paris, 1945-50; Engineer with Institut des Fruits et Agrumes Coloniaux, in Morocco, French Guinea, Martinique, and Guadeloupe, 1949-51; Literary Advisor, Editions de Minuit, Paris, 1954-DATE; free-lance author, 1953-DATE.

Awards: Fenelon Prize, 1954, for *Les Gommes*; Prix des Critiques, 1955, for *Le Voyeur*; Prix Louis Delluc, 1963, for *L'Immortelle*.

* * * * *

CECIL ROBERTS

Full Name: Cecil Edric Mornington Roberts.
Born May 18, 1892, at Nottingham, England. Son of John Godber Roberts and Elizabeth Roberts. Education: Attended University College, Nottingham.

Career: Author.
Literary Editor, *Liverpool Post*, 1915-18; official war correspondent with British forces, 1916-18; examining officer to Civil Liabilities Commission, 1919; Editor, *Nottingham Journal*, 1920-25; Member of the British Mission to the U.S., 1939-45; author, 1912-DATE; lecturer. Member: Society of Authors.

Agent: Curtis Brown Ltd., 60 E. 56th St., New York, NY 10022.

Awards: Honorary citizen of Alassio, Italy; LL.D., Washington & Jefferson College, 1927; Gold Medal and Diploma of City of Rome.

* * * * *

JANE ROBERTS

Full Name: Jane Roberts Butts.
Born May 8, 1929, at Albany, New York. Daughter of Delmar Hubbell Roberts and Marie Burdo. Married Robert F. Butts, December 27, 1954. Education: Attended Skidmore College, 1947-50.

Career: Writer.
Free-lance writer, 1957-DATE.

First Professional Sale: "The Red Wagon," in *The Magazine of Fantasy and Science Fiction*, December, 1956.

Roberts notes: "Much of my work is in the psychic and psychology fields. *The Education of Oversoul Seven* is the first of a novel series. I am presently working on the second book in the set, *The Further Education of Oversoul Seven*, and expect to do maybe seven books in all."

KEITH ROBERTS

Full Name: Keith John Kingston Roberts.
   Born September 20, 1935, at Kettering, Northamptonshire, England. Son of Lance John Kingston Roberts
(a cinema projectionist) and Laura Ellen Wells (a
nurse).

Education: National Diploma in Design, Northampton
   School of Art, 1956; attended Leicester College of
   Art, 1956-57.

Career: Advertising visualizer & copywriter; author.
   Animator and background artist, Nicholas Cartoon
   Films, Ltd., 1958-62; variety of jobs with provincial
   advertising agencies; Associate Editor, *Science Fantasy*, 1965-February, 1966; Managing Editor, *SF Impulse*,
   March, 1966-February, 1967 (all issues published);
   free-lance writer and illustrator, 1972-DATE.

First Professional Sale: "Boulter's Canaries,"
   in *New Writings in SF 3* (an anthology edited by John
   Carnell), Dobson, 1965 [several other stories were
   actually published earlier].

Agent: Giles Gordon, Anthony Sheil Associates, 52
   Floral St., London WC2 9DE, England.

Keith Roberts writes:
   "You asked about my story-cycle, *Pavane*. Dealing
with your last question first, a pavane (or pavan, or
pavanne--there seem to be various spellings) was the
stateliest of the mediaeval Court dances, and was often performed masked, and in fancy dress; hence its
name, which is simply Old French for a peacock. I
thought it would be a very apt title for a book in
which Church and State perform a continuous formal
'dance' in order to keep stable a basically artificial
society. I don't think there's any more direct connection with music than this. In the early stage, I
carried the device a stage further by subtitling the
various stories 'First Measure,' 'Second Measure,"
etc., but later dropped this as being perhaps a little
affected.
   "Unravelling the strands of the book a little, obviously the main influence was the real history of
the Isle of Purbeck, the little peninsula to the west
of Poole Harbour in Dorset still dominated by the
enormous ruin of Corfe Castle. 'Ceorfen' in Anglo-
Saxon carried the notion of something cut or carved,
and describes well the steep hill pass in which the
castle stands. The ground was rich in history before
William the Conqueror built the existing keep there
in the late eleventh century. From then on till the
seventeenth century the castle figured in no major
siege; a fact that goes a long way to illustrate its
great strength and impregnability. By the seventeenth
century, however, Corfe and the surrounding lands had
passed to the hands of the Bankes family, still one
of the great landowning families of Dorset. With the
outbreak of the Civil War, the Lord Bankes of the
time, a prominent Royalist and a member of King
Charles' Privy Council, placed the defence of Corfe
in the hands of his wife, a local woman still known
in the district as 'Brave Lady Mary.' In the two-
year siege that followed, her courage and resource-
fulness so earned the respect of her enemies that at
the termination of hostilities (Lord Bankes himself
had not survived the war), the keys of Corfe were returned to her, and she was allowed to retain her lands.
The castle itself was destroyed. At other places,
this 'slighting' amounted to little more than demili-
tarization; breaching of outer walls, removal of doors,

"etc. But Corfe was mined till no two walls stood in-
tact; a measure, I think, of the fear and terror the
place had inspired.
   "I had known the region for a number of years before
writing *Pavane*, and had always wanted to do a book on
the area, incorporating the story of the Great Siege.
What I didn't want to do, however, was simply to produce an historical novel. Something more seemed needed; I wanted to get across of little of the present-
day feel of Dorset and its inhabitants. For a long
time these requirements seemed irreconcilable; but the
problem was finally solved for me by accident. I happened to overhear a local girl retell the story of the
siege with great spirit. Afterwards, complimenting her
on her local knowledge, I merely remarked that she
supposed she must be a reincarnation of Brave Lady Mary;
and it seemed the thing resolved itself in a flash.
I realized that by using an alternate history device--
something I hadn't contemplated before--I could make
the siege happen in the twentieth century. This was
the germ for "Corfe Gate"; and "Corfe Gate" was the
start of *Pavane*.   .
   "The real siege had begun in a bizarre and ludicrous
fashion. At the outset of the war, the Castle owned
a small ceremonial cannon; something no bigger than a
punt gun by all accounts, but that deeply offended the
local Parliamentarians. A message was sent to Lady
Mary demanding the surrender of the piece; when she
sent back a dusty answer, fifty layabouts were hired
in Wareham--about five miles inland--plied with strong
drink, and set on to 'attack' the castle after dark.
Lady Mary and her helpers--a handful of serving maids--
kept the rabble at bay for some time by dumping hot
ashes on their heads when they tried to climb the bailey walls; then, tiring of the sport, she discharged
the cannon through the gateway. Nobody was in fact
hurt; but the fifty drunks were so alarmed by the noise
they are said to have run non-stop back to Wareham. I
decided to re-use the incident; but as it was to come
at a peak of the story, something more lethal°and effective was required. I accordingly borrowed a happening from your own history. Just before the Battle of
the Alamo, Santa Anna in similar fashion demanded the
surrender of a field piece from one of the little 'Tex-
ican' towns. When his messengers arrived, they found
the cannon loaded, primed, and esconced behind a make-
shift barrier. A placard hung from the muzzle invited
them to come and fetch it. It was this much more dramatic and effective story that formed a basis for the
high point of "Corfe Gate"; Eleanor's firing of the
cannon through the portcullis at the Lord of Rye and
Deal.
   "The story "Corfe Gate" was completed in rough form
in about ten days. It was this rough that formed the
basis of the first version of the story, the version
that appeared in the first British serial outing in
pulp, though it was subsequently considerably changed
for novel publication, and the little Coda added. I
hadn't at the start thought in terms of a novel at all,
"Corfe Gate" being originally intended as a one-off
novella; but during the writing I had 'discovered,' as
it were, a great deal about my postulated alternative
society. "The Lady Margaret," originally called "The
Lady Anne," with its story of steam haulage and high-
waymen, seemed a natural opening for the new novel,
and "The Signaller" was written soon after. It was
this story, as it happened, that was the first to see
print. Kyril Bonfiglioli at Oxford was at that time
engaged in changing the title of the old *Science Fantasy* magazine to *SF Impulse*, and had commissioned stories from a variety of authors on the theme of human
sacrifice. In "The Signaller," of course, I had such
a story ready-written; and it was finally printed in

KEITH ROBERTS (Cont.)

"the badly-circulated *Impulse* #1. Afterwards, discovering I had a novel-length cycle under way, Bon began a process of harrassment that was extremely good for me. To bulk out the book, I had already realized I needed a story about the operations of the Church. Visiting Dorset again in the vague hope of inspiration, I was rewarded with a full-scale hurricane, one of the few to hit Britain since the war. The scene at Kimmeridge Bay, a mile or so from Corfe Castle, was outside my previous experience; I used it as a climax to "Brother John," and the story, like the novel, was back-constructed from it. I only then needed to add "Lords and Ladies," written deliberately to tie up the several loose ends I had found myself with, and the cycle was complete. It finished its run in *Impulse* in July, 1966, and was rapidly contracted for by Lawrence Ashmead at Doubleday. Later publications included the Ace Special, and hardback and paperback outings in Britain, where the book is still in print.

"The Ace printing contained an additional story, "The White Boat." This was written nearly a twelve-month after the rest at the instigation of Mike Moorcock, then editing *New Worlds*. It wasn't included in the British publications, partly from considerations of length, partly because several editors over here felt that in mood and feeling it didn't really belong to the rest of the stories. I think there's probably something in this; *Pavane* was conceived largely as a 'wonder tale,' and to express something I felt about the Dorset people at the time; a wonderful blend of honesty, loyalty, and dourness. If you think back to the stories, I think you'll find they all take loyalty of one sort or another as a secondary theme; the loyalty of Jesse Strange to his ideals, Rafe Bigland to the Guild of Signallers, John to his visions, Eleanor to her liege sovereign. Becky, of "The White Boat," is the odd girl out; she's not really interested in anything further than the womblings of her own adolescent stomach. But I think for me this was a most important story; a sort of psychological breakthrough that has influenced much of what I've done since.

"So there 'tis; a book written back to front after years of puzzling, and triggered by a stray remark by a Dorset tourist. Of all the novels I've done it's still the one that rouses most interest and about which I get most letters; which is curious, because commercially it was a lead balloon. So bad were the British sales that I eventually changed publishers. I've done vastly better with everything else since; but nothing seems to have quite the same 'jizz.' I'd like to write another *Pavane* sometime; but since I don't know what I did in the first place to make the book so different, it's rather in the lap of the Gods. As you know, I recently published *The Chalk Giants*, a story about the same locale, and using very similar characters. I think it works quite well, and it's been generally much liked; but it's as different from *Pavane* as chalk from cheese."

* * * * *

TERENCE ROBERTS

Full Name: Ivan Terence Sanderson.
   Born January 30, 1911, at Edinburgh, Scotland. Son of Arthur Buchanan Sanderson (a whiskey manufacturer who founded the first game reserve in Kenya, and who was killed there by a rhinoceros while making a film with Martin Johnson in 1924) and Stella W. W. Robertson. Married Alma Viola Guillaume de Veil, February

18, 1934 (died, 1972); married Marion L. Fawcett (an editor and writer), May 4, 1972.

Education: M.A., Cambridge University, 1969.

Career: Writer and researcher.
   Began animal collecting, 1924; made a solo trip round the world, 1927-29, collecting for the British Museum; Leader of the Percy Sladen Expedition to Cameroon, on behalf of the British Museum and the Royal Society of London, 1932-33; did research at the University of London, 1933-35; collected animals in the West Indies, 1936-37; led a scientific expedition to Dutch Guiana, 1938; made an expedition into Jamaica, British Honduras, and Mexico, 1939-40; information and overseas press analyst for the British Government in New York, 1945-47; moved to the U.S., 1947; writer and lecturer on radio and TV, 1947-58; free-lance author, 1958-60, 1965-67; Senior Trade Editor, Chilton Book Co., 1961-65; Science Editor, *Argosy*, 1968-70; Trustee and Administrative Director, Society for the Investigation of the Unexplained, Columbia, NJ, 1970-73. Died Feb. 19, 1973.

Member: Royal Geographical Society (Fellow); Zoological Society (Fellow); Linnean Society (Fellow).

* * * * *

FRANK M. ROBINSON

Full Name: Frank Malcolm Robinson.
   Born August 9, 1926, at Chicago, Illinois. Son of Raymond Robinson (an artist and photographer) and Leona White.

Education: B.S., Beloit College, 1950; M.S., Northwestern University, 1955.

Career: Writer and editor.
   Asst. Editor, *Family Weekly*, 1955-56; Asst. Editor, *Science Digest*, 1956-59; Editor, *Rogue*, 1959-65; Managing Editor, *Cavalier*, 1965-66; Editor, *Censorship Today*, 1967; Staff Writer, *Playboy*, 1969-73; free-lance author, 1973-DATE. Member: Phi Beta Kappa; Sigma Delta Chi.

Agent: Curtis Brown Ltd., 60 E. 56th St., New York, NY 10022.

* * * * *

FRANK S. ROBINSON

Full Name: Frank Steven Robinson.
   Born September 7, 1947, at New York, New York. Son of Samuel Robinson (in garment industry) and Lotte Dreyfuss (a clothing designer).

Education: B.A., Queens College, 1967; J.D., New York University School of Law, 1970.

Career: Attorney.
   Staff Counsel, New York State Public Service Commission, 1970-DATE.

First Professional Sale: "Kerman Widens Lead in Poll," in *Worlds of Fantasy*, Spring, 1971.

Agent: Virginia Kidd, Box 278, Milford, PA 18337.

Honors: "Appointed by President Nixon to the U.S.

FRANK S. ROBINSON (Cont.)

"Assay Commission, 1972 (supposedly the youngest ever)."

Member: Albany Numismatic Society (Vice President); League of Women Voters; American Numismatic Association.

Interests: Numismatics, painting (surrealistic), sculpting, collecting autographs, politics.

"My novels generally avoid conventional forms or themes, and attempt to deal with such absurdly colossal matters as good vs. evil, epistemology, and the non-existence of God."

* * * * *

PHILIP BEDFORD ROBINSON

Full Name: Philip Bedford Robinson.
    Born December 10, 1926. Son of Frederick John Robinson (in insurance) and Lucy Bedford. Married Patricia Tryphena Chew, August 31, 1957.

Education: B.A., Corpus Christi College, Cambridge University, 1948.

Career: Computer programmer.
    Produce exporter in Bombay, Calcutta, and other cities in India, 1950-58; Computer Programmer and Team Leader, I.C.T., London, 1962-DATE. Member: British Astonomical Association; British Interplanetary Society.

* * * * *

ROSS ROCKLYNNE

Full Name: Ross Louis Rocklin.
    Born February 21, 1913, at Cincinnati, Ohio. Son of Francis Joseph Rocklin (a machinist) and Rose Lena Vandermullen. Married Frances Rosenthal, September 16, 1941 (divorced, 1947). Two sons: Keith Alan, Jeffrey David.

Career: Writer.
    Has worked as a story analyst for Warner Brothers, Hollywood, as a literary agent, a salesman and repairman of sewing machines, taxicab driver and dispatcher, lumberjack, sales clerk in an art shop, building manager; now a full-time writer.

* * * * *

CHARLES RODDA

Full Name: Charles Rodda.
    Born June 9, 1891, at Port Augusta, South Australia. Son of James Pascoe Rodda and Alvina Holtzmann.

Career: Writer.
    Trained for a career in music, but turned to journalism, working for newspapers in Adelaide and Melbourne, Australia; went to New York in 1919, becoming News Editor and Critic for *Musical America*, 1921-26; settled in England, 1939; full-time writer, 1926-DATE, primarily of mystery novels. Member: Society of Authors.

GENE RODDENBERRY

Full Name: Eugene Wesley Roddenberry.
    Born August 19, 1921, at El Paso, Texas. Son of Eugene Edward Roddenberry and Caroline Glen Golemon. Married Eileen Anita Rexroat, June 20, 1942 (divorced, 1969); married Majel Barrett, 1969. Three children: Darleen Anita (born 1948), Dawn Alison (born 1953), Eugene Wesley Jr. (born 197?).

Education: Attended Los Angeles City College, Miami University, University of California, Los Angeles, and Columbia University.

Career: Television producer, director, and writer.
    Served in the Army Air Force during World War II; after the war, became a professional pilot for Pan American Air Lines, surviving a plane crash in the Syrian desert in which 38 of 46 passengers were killed; went to Hollywood to become a television writer, then joined the Los Angeles Police Department when no openings were available; became a Sergeant in the police force, writing speeches for Chief William Parker, and walking a beat in Hollywood; sold several scripts in the mid-1950s to various television shows, and became a full-time TV writer; Head Writer, *Have Gun, Will Travel* series, 1957-59; created and produced MGM series, *The Lieutenant*; creator and producer, *Star Trek*, 1965-69; producer, creator, and writer of television programs and movie scripts.

First Professional Sale: A teleplay to the *Kaiser Aluminum Hour*, 1953.

Honors and Awards:
    Writers Guild of American Award, Best Teleplay of 1958, "Helen of Abiginian" (*Have Gun, Will Travel*); Golden Reels Awards, 1962, 1966; *Photoplay Magazine* Gold Medal, 1968; NAACP Brotherhood Award, 1967; Hugo Award, Best Dramatic Presentation, 1966 (1967), "The Menagerie" (*Star Trek*); Special Plaque, 26th World Science Fiction Convention (Baycon), Oakland, 1968, for *Star Trek*.

Member:
    Writers Guild of America, West; Science Fiction Writers of America; Television Academy of Arts and Sciences (Member of the Board of Governors); Association for Professional Law Enforcement; American Civil Liberties Union.

* * * * *

MARY RODGERS

Full Name: Mary Rodgers.
    Born January 11, 1931, at New York, New York. Daughter of Richard Rodgers (the composer) and Dorothy Feiner. Married Julian B. Beaty, Jr., December 7, 1951 (divorced, 1957); married Henry Guettel (vice-president of a motion picture company), October 14, 1961. Five children: Richard R. Beaty, Linda M. Beaty, Constance P. Beaty, Adam Guettel, Alexander Guettel.

Education: Attended Wellesley College, 1948-51.

Career: Composer and writer.
    Assistant Producer, New York Young People's Concerts, 1957-71; Member, Board of Trustees, Brearley School, 1973-DATE; free-lance writer, composer, and playwright.

Awards: *Book World* Spring Book Festival Award, 1972,

MARY RODGERS (Cont.)

and Christopher Award, 1973, both for *Freaky Friday*.

Member:
Dramatists Guild; American Federation of Television and Radio Artists; Screen Writers Guild; Cosmopolitan Club.

Agent: Shirley Bernstein, Paramuse Artists, Inc., 1414 Avenue of the Americas, New York, NY 10019.

* * * * *

ALVA ROGERS

Full Name: Alva C. Rogers.
Born January 17, 1923, at Silver City, New Mexico. Son of Alva and Anne Rogers. Married his wife, June 15, 1947. Three children: David, William Adrienne.

Education: Attended San Diego State College for two years.

Career: Writer. Member: First Fandom; Elves, Gnomes, and Little Men's Science Fiction, Chowder, and Marching Society.

First Professional Sale: *A Requiem for Astounding*, Advent: Publishers, 1964.

* * * * *

MICHAEL ROGERS

Full Name: Michael Rogers.
Born November 29, 1950, at Santa Monica, California. Son of Don Easterday Rogers (an engineer) and Mary Gilbertson.

Education: B.A., Stanford University, 1972.

Career: Writer and editor.
Contributing Editor, *Rolling Stone*, 1973-DATE; Books Columnist, 1973-74. Member: Authors Guild; Amateur Astronomers.

Agent: Harold Matson Co., 22 E. 40th St., New York, NY 10016.

* * * * *

NICHOLAS ROLAND

Full Name: Arnold Robert Walmsley.
Born August 29, 1912, at Cotta, Ceylon [now Sri Lanka]. Son of A. M. Walmsley (an Anglican priest) and A. J. Murgatroyd. Married Frances Councell de Mouilpied, 1944.

Education: M.A., Hertford College, Oxford University, 1935.

Career: Writer.
Private secretary in Vienna, 1935-38; with British Foreign Office, 1939-45; with British Diplomatic Service, 1946-70, serving in Jerusalem, Khartoum, and Lebanon; writer, 1970-DATE. Awards: Order of the British Empire, 1946; Order of St. Michael & St. George, 1963 (Companion).

DEANE ROMANO

Full Name: Deane Louis Romano.
Born January 4, 1927, at El Paso, Texas. Son of Frank Romano (a writer, song-writer, and telegrapher for Western Union) and Margaret Elinor Mallory (a horse player). Married Margaret Mary Robert, 1950 (divorced, 1953); married Alyce Virginia Morrow, 1954 (divorced, 1959). Two sons: Paris Robert (born 1950), David Deane (name originally Cairo Deane; born 1955).

Education: Attended Art Institute of Chicago, New York University, University of California, Los Angeles, University of California, Berkeley.

Career: Writer.
Licensed Radio Officer, Merchant Marine, 1945-52; Division Manager for Classified Sales, *Los Angeles Times*, 1956-58; full-time writer, 1959-DATE.

First Professional Sale: "Angels Flight," a screenplay, 1962.

Member: Science Fiction Writers of America; Writers Guild of America, West.

Louis Charbonneau's science fiction novel, *The Sensitives*, was based on Romano's screenplay of the same name.

* * * * *

BRUCE W. RONALD

Full Name: Bruce Walton Ronald.
Born August 1, 1931, at Dublin, Indiana. Son of James Hall Ronald (an attorney) and Dorothey Walton (a teacher). Married Virginia Ludwick, February 20, 1954. Four children: Roger C. (born 1955), Amy V. (born 1958), Kenneth D. (born 1961), Nora Katherine (born 1964).

Education: B.A., Miami University, 1953.

Career: Advertising copywriter.
Copywriter, McCann Erickson, New York, 1956-58; Copywriter and Creative Director, McCann Erickson, Montreal, 1959-62; Copywriter and Creative Supervisor, Kircher, Helton & Collett, Dayton, 1962-72, 1973-DATE; Creative Director, Coffman Associates, Cincinnati, 1972-73. Also edits a local house organ, *The Gem City Saver*.

First Professional Sale: "Some 2M puzzle thing, Harle, 1957."

Honors: Best of Show, Dayton Ad Club, 1972.

Interests: Acting, model RR, music, Minoan civilization, early Roman Empire (especially Otho), history and ethnology, Long Island.

Ronald collaborated with John Jakes and Claire Strauch in writing the humorous musical play, "Dracula, Baby" (Dramatic Publishing Company, 1970). He comments:

"John and I were working in the same office, and he agreed to play a part for me in a one-act I had written, "Last Train to Cliche Junction." Afterwards, we decided it might be fun to write and produce a musical. Three weeks later we had the first act, and three or four songs, but no music (another co-worker had agreed to write it, but, after reading what we had, looked up

BRUCE W. RONALD (Cont.)

"and said, 'But why do we *care* about these people?'
Which leads me to two confessions. One, I think theater criticism should be kept from the impressionable,
and Two, I never fail to mention the royalty checks
every time I see this man.) Anyway, Claire Strauch
literally wandered into a theater meeting, and mentioned that she wrote music. John and I handed her
a lyric, and fifteen minutes later, the basic melody
for the first song was 80% set.

"'Dracula, Baby' was first produced by the Town Hall
Players of Centerville, Ohio. John Jakes played Van
Helsing; Claire, her husband and I were in the opening
chorus number; I directed the show, and my wife did
the principal's choreography. The original was about
70 minutes long, and we added three scenes and four
songs to the published version.

"Dramatic told John that D,B was their best-selling
non-Broadway musical, which makes us feel good. Within the month, I was able to see a production of the
piece. Except for the original, this was the first
time I had seen it...and the first time ever for the
new material. It plays well, I think, and the cast
seemed to enjoy working in it. Since one of our
goals was to write an 'amateur' musical (unlike Broadway, where the songs and other good stuff goes to one
or two stars), this was gratifying."

* * * * *

ALBERT ROOT

Full Name: Albert Waldo Root.
    Born June 19, 1891, at Ireland, Indiana. Son of
John Wetzel Root and Flora Belle Corn. Married Maude
Ariel Dugan, December 30, 1916 (died, 1968). Two
children: Mary, Lillian.

Education: Attended college for two years.

Career: Poultry farmer.
    Has been a cost analyzer and a hatcheryman; now a
poultry farmer in Birdseye, Indiana.

* * * * *

DANIEL ROSELLE

Full Name: Daniel Roselle.
    Born August 11, 1920, at Brooklyn, New York. Son
of Saul Roselle and Malvina Escoll. Married Lois Jane
Mitchell, August 30, 1954. Three children: David
(born 1956), Lynn (born 1954), Ann (born 1965).

Education: B.S.S., City College of New York, 1940;
    M.A., Columbia University, 1947; Ph.D., 1950.

Career: Editor.
    Chairman, Department of History and Social Studies,
Mannheimer High School, Miami Beach, FL, 1941-42; Instructor in the Teaching of Social Studies, Teachers
College, Columbia University, 1947-48; Professor of
History, State University of New York, Fredonia, 1950-
68; Editor of *Social Education* magazine, and Director
of Publications for the National Council for the Social Studies, 1968-DATE.

First Professional Sale: "Charlemagne and the
    Whisperer," in *Ellery Queen's Mystery Magazine*,
    1946.

Honors & Awards:
    Fulbright Research Fellow, France, 1952-53; Winner of
"Distinguished Achievement Award for Editorial Writing,"
Editorial Press Association of America, 1972; "Eleanor
Fishburn Award," 1972, for "*Social Education* magazine's
outstanding contribution to international understanding."

Member: American Historical Association; National
    Council for the Social Studies; Society for French
    Historical Studies.

Interests: Reading, tennis, and travel (especially
    to Paris).

* * * * *

ETHEL ROSENBERG

Full Name: Ethel Clifford Rosenberg.
    Married David Rosenberg (a publisher), October 15,
1941. One daughter, Ruthanne.

Career: Writer and editor.
    Editor, David-Stewart Publishing Company, Indianapo-
lis, 1959-DATE; writer, 1959-DATE. Awards: Honorable
Mention, Indiana Authors' Awards, 1960, for Arizona
Highways Nature-Adventure Books.

Agent: Scott Meredith, 580 Fifth Avenue, New York,
    NY 10036.

* * * * *

MORDECAI ROSHWALD

Full Name: Mordecai Marceli Roshwald.
    Born May 26, 1921, at Drohobycz, Poland. Son of
Abraham Leib Roshwald (a merchant and public servant)
and Sidonia Feuer. Married Miriam Wyszynski, August,
1945. One son, Aviel Isaiah (born 1962).

Education: M.A., Hebrew University of Jerusalem,
    1942; Ph.D., 1947.

Career: Professor of Social & Political Philosophy.
    Moved to Israel, 1934; Teacher in the public schools
in Palestine and Israel, 1942-48; Lecturer on Political
Theory, Israel Institute of Public Administration, 1947-
51; Lecturer on Political Theory, Hebrew University of
Jerusalem, 1951-55; moved to the U.S., 1955; Instructor
of Philosophy and Political Theory, Brooklyn College,
1956-57; Professor of Social and Political Philosophy,
University of Minnesota, 1957-DATE; visiting appointments at University of Bath, England, Technion (Israel),
Simon Fraser University (Canada).

First Professional Sale: *Humanism in Practice*
    (Hebrew version), Am Oved, Tel-Aviv, 1947.

Awards: Two McKnight Foundation Awards at the Univer-
    sity of Minnesota; United Nations Award for essay
    competition, 1954.

Roshwald notes:
    "I wrote *Level 7* out of concern for the future of hu-
manity. The extinction of mankind described there is
an educational ploy. The automation and dehumanization
at Level 7 is the expression of another concern. *A
Small Armageddon* deals with a similar concern in a far-
cical manner: I was still concerned writing it, but I
needed a relaxation."

HARRY ROSITZKE

Full Name: Harry August Rositzke.
   Born February 25, 1911, at Brooklyn, New York. Son of Emil H. Rositzke and Anna Brockman. Married Barbara Bourgeois, May 11, 1942. Two children: John Brockman, Anne Elizabeth.

Education: A.B., Union College, 1931; Ph.D., Harvard University, 1935.

Career: Writer.
   Tutor in English, Harvard University, 1936-37; Instructor in English, University of Omaha, 1937-38; Instructor in English, University of Rochester, 1938-42; Foreign Intelligence Officer, Central Intelligence Agency, Washington, 1947-70, working in Munich, Germany, and New Delhi, India; free-lance writer, 1970-DATE; also owns his own farm in Virginia, where he raises Angus cattle.

* * * * *

HARRY ROSKOLENKO

Full Name: Harry Roskolenko.
   Born September 21, 1907, at New York, New York. Son of Barnett Roskolenko (a tailor, presser and farmer) and Sara Goldstein. Married Diana Chang, May 10, 1948 (divorced, 1955). One daughter, Deborah.

Career: Writer.
   Worked in a factory at age nine; at age 13, in 1920, shipped as a seaman on an oil tanker bound for Mexico, and worked as a sailor for seven years; employed by the WPA Writers Project during the Depression; has been a law clerk, patent researcher, second mate in the Merchant Marine, drawbridge operator; correspondent in China, Japan, Indochina, and East Asia, 1946-47; has travelled extensively for material for his books; full-time writer. Member: P.E.N.

* * * * *

JOSEPH ROSS

Full Name: Joseph Henry Wrzos [pronounced Vi-shus].
   Born September 9, 1929, at Newark, New Jersey. Son of Joseph Wrzos (a machinist) and Aniela Szugan. Married Anita Laufer, June 13, 1952. Two sons: Michael Geoffrey (born 1958), Kenneth Stephen (born 1963).

Education: B.A., Rutgers University, 1952; graduate student, Columbia University, 1952-53.

Career: English teacher.
   Assistant Editor, Gnome Press, 1953-54; Librarian, Roselle Park High School, Roselle Park, NJ, 1956-57; English teacher and Chairman of the English Department, Millburn Senior High School, Millburn, NJ, 1957-DATE (Chairman since 1969); Managing Editor, *Amazing Stories*, August, 1965-October, 1967; Managing Editor, *Fantastic Stories*, September, 1965-September, 1967.

First Professional Sale: "Gull" (poem), in *Hawk and Whippoorwill*, Spring, 1962.

Awards: Award for Excellence in the Study of English Literature, 1952.

Member: National Education Association; New Jersey Association of Teachers of English; Association of Secondary School Supervisors and Department Heads of New Jersey; Millburn Education Association; Eastern Science Fiction Association (Director).

Interests:
   "I have read and collected science fiction and fantasy (in all its forms, from pulps to slicks to hardcover and paperback 'classics'), and intend to do so until such matters are out of my hands."

Ross writes:
   "When--in 1965--I accepted the position of Managing Editor of both *Amazing Stories* and *Fantastic Stories*, I was then (as I still am now) teaching English full time at Millburn Senior High School here in New Jersey. So editing the two magazines--which task turned out to be killing but still exciting--was done exclusively in spare time and hours stolen from sleep. Right at the outset, I used the last name "Ross" rather than Wrzos, my legal name, because (from extensive past experience), I tended to find that typesetters just couldn't believe "Wrzos" in the copy, and invariably misspelled it. To avoid that headache, "Ross" was interested and did the trick, and I stayed with it for the two-plus years I edited the magazines, and for the *Best of Amazing* anthology that Doubleday put out. Since then, however, I have dropped "Ross" entirely, and use my legal name Wrzos exclusively. And that's how it will be in the future (so typesetters beware!)."

* * * * *

T. J. ROSS

Full Name: Theodore John Ross.
   Born 1924, at Boston, Massachusetts. Son of Samuel Ross and Rita Newman. Married Rhoda Pollack. Three sons: Richard, Jonathan, Laurence.

Education: B.A., Clark University; M.A., Columbia University.

Career: Professor of English.
   Professor of English, Fairleigh Dickinson University.

First Professional Sale: "Passion--Moral and Otherwise," an essay on Mary McCarthy, in *New Republic*, August 18, 1958.

Interests: Chess.

* * * * *

PHILIP ROTH

Full Name: Philip Milton Roth.
   Born March 19, 1933, at Newark, New Jersey. Son of Herman Roth and Bess Finkel. Married Margaret Martinson, 1959 (divorced, 1966).

Education: A.B., Bucknell University, 1954; M.A., University of Chicago, 1955.

Career: Writer.
   Instructor, University of Chicago, 1956-58; Visiting Lecturer, University of Iowa, 1960-62; Writer-in-Residence, Princeton University, 1962-64; Writer-in-Residence, University of Pennsylvania, 1965; full-time writer, 1962-DATE. Agent: Candida Donadio, 551 Fifth Avenue, New York, NY. Member: Phi Beta Kappa.

PHILIP ROTH (Cont.)

Honors & Awards:
First Prize, *Paris Review* short story contest, 1958; National Book Award for Fiction, 1960, for *Goodbye, Columbus*; Daroff Award, Jewish Book Council of America, 1960, for *Goodbye, Columbus*; grant from the National Institute of Arts and Letters, 1960; Guggenheim Fellowship, 1960; O. Henry Second Prize Award, 1960; Ford Foundation Grant in Playwrighting, 1965.

* * * * *

ABRAHAM ROTHBERG

Full Name: Abraham Rothberg.
Born January 14, 1922, at New York, New York. Son of Louis Rothberg and Lottie Drimmer. Married Esther Conwell (a physicist), September 30, 1945. One son, Lewis.

Education: B.A., Brooklyn College, 1942; M.A., University of Iowa, 1947; Ph.D., Columbia University, 1952.

Career: Writer.
Has worked as a professional singer, waiter, and as a worker with an electronics firm; Instructor in English and Humanities, Hofstra College, 1947-51; Instructor in Creative Writing, Columbia University, 1948; Editor-in-Chief, Free Europe Press and *East Europe* magazine, 1952-59; Managing Editor, George Braziller (publishers), 1959; Managing Editor, *New Leader*, 1960-61; roving correspondent for *National Observer* and *Guardian* in Europe, 1962-63; Senior Editor, Bantam Books, 1966-67; full-time writer, 1967-DATE. Member: Authors League; P.E.N.

Honors & Awards: Ford Foundation Fellow, 1951-52; John H. McGinnis Award for Short Story, 1969.

* * * * *

WILLIAM ROTSLER

Full Name: William Rotsler.
Born July 3, 1926, at Los Angeles, California. Son of Charles Golden Rotsler (a rancher) and Sarah Flynn. Married Marian Abney, October 10, 1953 (divorced, 1958). One daughter, Lisa Araminta (born 1954).

Education: Attended Ventura Junior College, 1946, and Los Angeles County Art Institute, 1947-50.

Career: Writer.
Rancher in Camarillo, California, 1943-44, 1946, 1954-58; sculptor in Los Angeles, 1950-60; photographer, 1958-DATE; motion picture director, producer, and writer (with 26 film credits), 1965-73; free-lance author, 1970-DATE.

First Professional Sale: "Ship Me Tomorrow," in *Galaxy*, June, 1970.

Agent: Richard Curtis, 156 E. 52nd St., New York, NY 10022.

Honors & Awards: Fan Guest of Honor, 31st World Science Fiction Convention (Torcon 2), Toronto, 1973; Hugo Award, Best Fan Artist, 1974 (1975).

Member: Science Fiction Writers of America.

Interests:
Photography, ancient civilizations, art, fast cars, handguns, drawing. "I have always worked for myself--not counting Uncle Sam and the family ranch and a few months at odd jobs when I was young. Can't stand the idea of a 9-to-5, though I have and do take various assignments. I am in many ways a hedonist."

* * * * *

FRANZ ROTTENSTEINER

Full Name: Franz Rottensteiner.
Born January 18, 1942, in Austria.

Education: Ph.D., University of Austria, 1968.

Career: Librarian, editor, and literary agent.
"I am employed as a librarian and documentalist with the American Institute for Building Research, and also am a free-lance SF editor with Insel Verlag in Germany, and occasionally act as SF consultant with Seabury Press in New York. I am editor/publisher of a one-man fanzine, *Quarber Merkur* (which is what got me my posts in SF publishing), and have a couple of books published in Germany (anthologies), and an illustrated history of SF, *The Science Fiction Book*. I am a member of the editorial boards of *Extrapolation* and *Science-Fiction Studies*." Also an agent for Stanislaw Lem and others.

Agent: Franz Rottenstein, Felsenstrasse 20, 2762 Ortmann, Austria.

Rottensteiner comments:
"There probably are basic differences between American and European science fiction, but such continental or national differences aren't so important as differences between individual writers. The bulk of science fiction is poor wherever you look, and while in the U.S. writers have achieved at least a higher level of mediocrity, the mass of European SF is much more clumsy. What matters is the highest achievements, and there the U.S.A. has yet to produce a figure comparable to H. G. Wells, Olaf Stapledon, Karel Capek, or Stanislaw Lem. What seems significant to me is that all these men developed apart from the SF field and its debilitating effects. What determines the worth of a writer, I think, is his philosophical substance, not the tricks of the trade, that men like Robert Silverberg, Roger Zelazny, or Barry Malzberg have learned well enough; but from a literary point of view they are just producing travesties of fiction, and I doubt that you would find literary critics of stature anywhere in the world who would bother even to read them--as Wells, Capek, Lem, and to some extent Stapledon are read and discussed. I should like to add that the more popular American writers are even worse: Asimov is a typical non-writer, and Heinlein or Anderson are just banal. And what today is praised as the maturity of modern SF and contemporary prose in forewords to SF anthologies, and press releases masquerading as criticism, is just impotent scribbling, of no consequence as prose, and even lacking the gusto and narrative vigour of some of the older and less skilled SF."

Rottensteiner mentions that "English I learned first in school, and later by reading; but my spoken English is atrocious."

BERTON ROUECHE

Full Name: Berton Roueche.
Born April 16, 1911, at Kansas City, Missouri. Son of Clarence Berton Roueche and Nana Mossman. Married Katherine Eisenhower, October 28, 1936. One son, Bradford.

Education: B.J., University of Missouri, 1933.

Career: Reporter.
Reporter, *Kansas City Star*, 1934-41; *St. Louis Globe-Democrat*, 1941-42; *St. Louis Post-Dispatch*, 1942-44; Staff Writer, *New Yorker*, 1944-DATE; faculty member at various writing conferences.

Awards:
Albert Lasker Medical Journalism Award, 1950, 1960; Mystery Writers of America Award, 1954; Annual Award, National Council of Infant and Child Care, 1956; Annual Award, American Medical Writers Association, 1963.

Member:
Kansas City Academy of Medicine (Fellow); Sigma Alpha Epsilon; Devon Yacht Club; Coffee House Club.

* * * * *

DONALD S. ROWLAND

Full Name: Donald Sydney Rowland.
Born September 23, 1928, at Great Yarmouth, Norfolk, England. Son of Arthur Rowland (a carpenter) and Beatrice Rix. Married Jessie Robinson, June 24, 1950. Three children: Donna Janita (born 1954), Donald Arthur (born 1960), Janita Ellen (born 1963).

Career: Writer.
Lance Sergeant, British Army, 1945-50; various jobs from 1950-57, including film projectionist, fruit canner, fish curer; Senior Clerk and Local Government Officer, Great Yarmouth, Britain, 1957-63; full-time writer, 1964-DATE.

First Professional Sale: *The Battle Done*, Digit Books, 1958.

Member: Society of Authors.

"I am totally dedicated to writing, working seven days a week. I've had one holiday in 24 years. Have written, to date, five war novels, 150 westerns, two thrillers, 105 romantic novels, three gothic novels, and fourteen science fiction novels, under about 55 pseudonyms."

* * * * *

FLORENCE WIGHTMAN ROWLAND

Full Name: Florence Wightman Rowland.
Born January 2, 1900, at Newark, New Jersey. Daughter of William Henderson Wightman and Florence Fairbanks. Married L. Vernon Rowland (an electrician), March 8, 1924. Three children: Madge, Jayne, Joyce.

Education: A.B., University of Southern California, 1923; General Secondary Teaching Certificate, University of California, Los Angeles, 1938.

Career: Writer, 1950-DATE.

* * * * *

KATHERINE ROY

Full Name: Katherine Roy.
Born December 4, 1907, at Sosua, San Domingo, West Indies. Daughter of William Augustine Morris (a doctor) and Rose Kennedy. Married Pio Ethier, 1926 (deceased); married Philippe Roy, 1943 (deceased). One daughter, Simonne.

Education: Attended Northwestern University, 1926-28, and University of Berlin, 1929-30.

Career: Writer.
Editor, *Beau Magazine*, Montreal, 1938-40; Member of Women's Auxiliary, Royal Victoria Hospital, Montreal; now a full-time writer. Member: Authors Guild; P.E.N.

Agent: McIntosh & Otis, 475 Fifth Avenue, New York, NY 10017.

* * * * *

BERTA RUCK

Full Name: Amy Roberta Ruck.
Born August 2, 1878, at Murree, India. Daughter of Arthur Ashley Ruck (a colonel) and Eleanor D'Arcy. Married Oliver Onions (a novelist who changed his name to George Oliver, but continued to write under his original name), 1909 (died, 1961). Two sons, Arthur, Bill.

Education: Studied art at Lambeth School of Art, Slade School of Art, and Colarossi's, Paris.

Career: Writer, 1914-DATE. Member: Forum, London.

* * * * *

DANE RUDHYAR

Full Name: Daniel Chenneviere.
Born March 23, 1895, at Paris, France. Came to the U.S., 1916. Married Malya Contento, 1930; married his second wife, Eya Fechin, 1945 (divorced, 1954); married his third wife, Gail Tana Whittall, March 27, 1964.

Education: Studied at the Sorbonne, University of Paris, and at the Paris Conservatory, 1912.

Career: Writer and composer.
Once secretary to the French sculptor Rodin; composer during his early years; writer and painter; his orchestral works "Poèmes Ironiques" and "Vision Végétale" were performed at the New York Metropolitan Opera Festival, 1917; did scenic music for Hollywood pilgrimage plays, 1920 and 1922; has written other orchestral and piano works; lecturer for fifty years in the U.S. and Europe.

Member: International Composers Guild; American Composers Alliance.

Awards: Received $1000 prize of Los Angeles Philharmonic, 1922, for his symphonic poem, "Soul Fire."

CHARLES W. RUNYON

Full Name: Charles West Runyon.
Born June 9, 1928, at Sheridan, Missouri. Son of Monte C. Runyon (a school teacher) and Nina West (a school teacher). Married Ruth Phillips, January 29, 1955. Two sons: Mark Charles (born 1958), Matthew G. (born 1967).

Education: Attended University of Missouri, 1948-50, 1952-55; Munich University, 1950-51; Indiana University, 1951-52.

Career: Writer.
Editor, *Sinclair Pipe Line*, 1955-57, and *Standard Oil*, 1957-60; full-time writer, 1960-DATE.

Agent: Scott Meredith, 580 Fifth Avenue, New York, NY 10036.

Awards:
Missouri Writers Guild Best Book of the Year Award, 1973, for *Power Kill*; Edgar nominee, 1973, for the same book.

Member:
Science Fiction Writers of America; Mystery Writers of American; Missouri Writers Guild; St. Francois Writers Society, Farmington, Missouri.

Interests: Pipe carving, canes, gardening, yoga.

* * * * *

JOANNA RUSS

Full Name: Joanna Russ.
Born February 22, 1937, at New York, New York. Daughter of Evarett I. Russ (a high school teacher) and Bertha Zinner (an elementary school teacher). Married Albert Amateau, 1963 (divorced, 1967).

Education: B.A., Cornell University, 1957; M.F.A., Yale Drama School, 1960.

Career: Professor of English.
Lecturer, Queensborough Community College, 1960-67; Instructor in English, Cornell University, 1967-70; Assistant Professor, 1970-72; Assistant Professor of English, State University of New York, Binghamton, 1972-DATE; visiting lecturer at various Clarion SF writing workshops, and at Tulane University, 1971, and the University of Washington, 1971 and 1973; freelance writer, 1959-DATE.

First Professional Sale: "Nor Custom Stale," in *The Magazine of Fantasy and Science Fiction*, September, 1959.

Agent: Curtis Brown Ltd., 60 E. 56th St., New York, NY 10022.

Awards:
Nebula Award, Best Short Story, 1972 (1973), "When It Changed"; Nebula finalist, 1971, "Poor Man, Beggar Man"; and 1968, *Picnic on Paradise*; N.E.H. Junior Humanist Fellowship for study of science fiction, 1974-75; participant in the seminar, Science, Technology, and the Humanities, Cornell University, 1974-75.

Member: Science Fiction Writers of America; Modern Language Association. Interests: "Survival."

BERTRAND RUSSELL

Full Name: Bertrand Arthur William Russell.
Born May 18, 1972, at Trelleck, Monmouthshire, England. Son of Lord John Russell and Katherine Stanley. Married Alys Whitall Pearsall Smith, 1894 (divorced, 1921); married Dora Winifred Black, 1921 (divorced, 1935); married Patricia Helen Spence, 1936 (divorced, 1952); married Edith Finch, 1952. Three children: John Conrad, Katharine Jane, Conrad Sebastian Robert.

Education: M.A., Trinity College, Cambridge University, 1894.

Career: Writer, lecturer, instructor.
Honorary attache at the British Embassy in Paris, 1894; Fellow and Lecturer at Trinity College, Cambridge, 1894-1916 (dismissed for his opposition to World War I, and sentenced to four and one-half months in prison); temporary professor, Harvard University, 1914; Professor of Philosophy, National University of Peking, 1920-21; co-founder and Director, of Beacon Hill School, Sussex, England, 1927-32; succeeded his brother as 3rd Earl Russell, 1931; Lecturer, University of Chicago, 1938; Professor of Philosophy, University of California, Los Angeles, 1939-40; appointed William James Lecturer in Philosophy at Harvard, and Professor of Philosophy at City College of New York (withdrawn over controversy surrounding his beliefs); Lecturer on History of Culture, Barnes Foundation, 1941-42; candidate for Parliament, 1907, 1922, 1923. Member: Royal Society (Fellow), Athenaeum Club. Died 1970.

Honors & Awards:
Nicholas Murray Butler Medal, 1915; Sylvester Medal of Royal Society, 1934; British Order of Merit, 1949; Nobel Prize for Literature, 1950; Kalinga Prize, 1957; Sonning Foundation Prize, Denmark, 1960.

* * * * *

ERIC FRANK RUSSELL

Full Name: Eric Frank Russell.
Born January 6, 1905, at Sandhurst, Surrey, England. One daughter, Erica (born 1934).

Education: Educated at military schools in England.

Career: Writer.
Technical representative for a Liverpool steel firm in the 1930s; writer, 1937-78. Died February 28, 1978.

First Professional Sale: "The Saga of Pelican West," in *Astounding Stories*, February, 1937.

Awards: Hugo Award, Best Short Story, 1954 (1955), "Allamagoosa."

* * * * *

RAY RUSSELL

Full Name: Ray Robert Russell.
Born September 4, 1924, at Chicago, Illinois. Son of William James Russell and Margaret Anna Otto. Married Ada Beth Szczepanski, September 5, 1950. Two children: Marc Antony (born 1951), Amanda (born 1957).

Education: Attended Chicago Conservatory of Music, 1947-48, and Goodman Memorial Institute, 1949-51.

RAY RUSSELL (Cont.)

Career: Writer and editor.
  Associate Editor, *Playboy*, 1954-55; Executive Editor, 1955-60; Contributing Editor, 1968-DATE; freelance writer and editor, 1953-DATE.

First Professional Sale: "The Lesser Sin," in *Esquire*, 1953.

Agent: H. N. Swanson, 8523 Sunset Blvd., Los Angeles, CA 90069.

Member: Writers Guild of America, West.

Interests:
  "Music: serious listener to symphonies, operas, chamber works, all other so-called 'classical' music. Own 6 or 700 records. Am a composer of minor works for piano, songs, etc. Music plays a strong role in many of my stories (see "Comet Wine," "Rational Moments," and "The Smiling Mandarin")."

Ray Russell is *Playboy* magazine's most popular living writer, based on statistics compiled twice a year by the publication's Reader Service Department. He comments:

  "Though not primarily a science fiction and fantasy writer, I have appeared in *F&SF*, *If*, *Amazing*, *Fantastic*, *Weird Tales*, *Gamma*, *Imagination*, and in many SF anthologies. Most of my SF&F work has appeared in 'slick' magazines, however. I have done motion picture work in the science fiction, fantasy, and horror fields for most of the major studios (MGM, Columbia, Warner Brothers, AIP, et al.)
  "I think the best, most enduring works of SF and fantasy are written by writers who are not specialists in these genres, writers to whom fantasy is but one bright ribbon of a broader literary spectrum. H. G. Wells and Aldous Huxley provide good examples, as does C. S. Lewis, with his powerful interplanetary trilogy, and Anthony Burgess, with *A Clockwork Orange* and *The Wanting Seed*. Two of my favorite short fantasies are "The Monkey's Paw," by erstwhile humorist W. W. Jacobs, and "The Secret Miracle," by Jorge Luis Borges. None of these writers ever attended an SF convention, or received a Hugo or Nebula. A great deal of my own writing is spangled with fantasy (even my comic novel of Hollywood, *The Colony*, contains a ghost story, in the form of Chapter 13), but it's not always recognized as such because it doesn't wear the official genre livery, doesn't ring the familiar Pavlovian bells. Thus, while I've appeared in numerous SF anthologies and magazines, my best fantasy work has found acceptance in mainstream publications such as *Playboy*, *The Paris Review*, et al."

* * * * *

FRED SABERHAGEN

Full Name: Fred Thomas Saberhagen.
  Born May 18, 1930, at Chicago, Illinois. Son of Frederick Augustus Saberhagen and Julia Agnes Moynihan. Married Joan Dorothy Spicci, June 29, 1968. Three children: Jill Ann (born 1969), Eric (born 1970), Thomas (born 1972).

Education: Attended Wright Junior College, 1956-57.

Career: Writer. Enlisted man, U.S. Air Force,

1951-55, operating electronic gear aboard B-36 aircraft; electronics technician, Motorola, Inc., Chicago, 1956-62; free-lance author, 1962-67, 1973-DATE; Assistant Editor, *Encyclopaedia Britannica*, 1967-73.

First Professional Sale: "Volume Paa-Pyx," in *Galaxy*, February, 1961.

Agent: Virginia Kidd, Box 278, Milford, PA 18337.

Member: Science Fiction Writers of America.

* * * * *

HENRY SACKERMAN

Full Name: Henry Claude Sackerman.
  Born March 24, 1940, at Paris, France. Son of Otto Sackerman (a jeweler) and Mirelle Dupont (a pianist).

Education: B.A., Sorbonne, University of Paris, 1962.

Career: Writer.
  Assistant Editor, Éditions Planètes, 1963-65; now a full-time writer.

First Professional Sale: *The Crowded Bed*, Bantam Books, 1967.

Member: Société Anonyme des Monteurs d'Avignan, France.

Interests: Science fiction, travel, cuisine, American history, steamships, French-American relations, "and several hundred more."

* * * * *

ARTHUR W. SAHA

Full Name: Arthur William Saha.
  Born October 31, 1923, at Hibbing, Minnesota. Son of William Saha (a carpenter) and Henriika Remes (a domestic). Married Taimi Elizabeth Leith, 1958. Two children: Heidi Elizabeth (born 1959), Matthew William (born 1965).

Education: A.B., Columbia University, 1947.

Career: Chemist.
  Research chemist, Interchemical Corporation, 1948-64; Senior Chemist, Alcan Metal Powders, 1964-DATE.

First Professional Sale: *The 1972 Annual World's Best SF*, DAW Books, 1972 (an anthology edited with Donald A. Wollheim). Interests: Philately, wildlife.

Member:
  First Fandom (Vice-President, East Coast); American Chemical Society; Mensa; served as Convention Secretary, 14th World Science Fiction Convention (Newyorcon), 1956.

* * * * *

MARGARET ST. CLAIR

Full Name: Margaret St. Clair.
  Born February 17, 1911, at Hutchinson, Kansas. Daughter of George A. Neeley (an attorney) and Eva M. Hostetler (a teacher). Married Eric St. Clair, 1932.

Education: M.A., University of California, 1934.

MARGARET ST. CLAIR (Cont.)

Career: Writer.
Has been a full-time writer since 1945.

First Professional Sale: "Current History," in
Detective Story, March, 1945.

Agent: McIntosh & Otis, 475 Fifth Avenue, New York,
NY 10017.

Member:
American Civil Liberties Union; Dramatists Guild;
Phi Beta Kappa; Society for Hellenic Studies; Science
Fiction Writers of America.

Interests:
"I am a passionate gardener, and I like cooking. I
make most of my clothes: I like to use my hands.
For about thirty years I have had a strong emotional
attachment to Quakerism, though I am in no sense a
Christian, and have no desire to be. My religious
beliefs are otherwise."

St. Clair writes:
"I expect the easiest way to describe my personality
and temperament would be to say that I have the sun in
Aquarius, the moon in Libra, Venus in Pisces, Mars in
Capricorn, Uranus in Capricorn, and Jupiter in Scorpio.
The ascendant in Aries (very important). An astrological friend tells me that I have a grand trine, adding
that I'm the only person he has ever known with that
configuration who amounted to anything. I thought
this over for a while, and then said, 'I don't think
I amount to anything especially.' As a writer, I
think I am very much better with short stories than
novels, but the wretched rates paid in the field have
almost forced me into the longer lengths, where I do
at least get a considerable sum all at once. There
is something very depressing at being paid the same
rates for short fiction that I got when started writing so many years ago. I like my amusing stories
a little better than the serious ones, I suppose because I have more fun writing them. I am a very slow
and painstaking writer; I consider two typewritten
pages a very good day's work. I have written two un-
performed plays, and once had a short article in *The
Psychoanalytic Quarterly*. I suppose the strongest
influences on my work have been Greek authors, English
and Celtic folklore, and a few writers whose work I
particularly admire, like Boccaccio. I like weather,
soap bubbles, opals, champagne, some rock music, a
good many perfumes, and fireworks."

* * * * *

RICHARD SALE

Full Name: Richard Bernard Sale.
Born December 17, 1911, at New York, New York. Son
of Richard Bernard Sale and Frances Topinka. Married
Mary Anita Loos (the writer), December 17, 1946 (di-
vorced). Three children: Lindsey (daughter), Richard
Townsend, Edward Clifford.

Education: Attended Washington & Lee University,
1930-33.

Career: Writer.
Free-lance writer for magazines, 1930-44; writer for
Paramount Pictures, 1944; writer/director for Republic
Pictures, 1945-48, for Twentieth Century-Fox, 1948-52,

for British Lion Pictures, 1953-54, for United Artists,
1954, and for Columbia Pictures, 1956; television writer, director, and producer, CBS, 1958-59; free-lance
author; composer of music for several motion pictures.

Agent: Paul R. Reynolds, 599 Fifth Avenue, New York,
NY 10017.

Member:
Authors League; Writers Guild of America; Directors
Guild of America; Academy of Motion Picture Arts and
Sciences; National Academy of Television Arts; Delta
Upsilon; Sigma Delta Chi; Balboa Angling Club; Shark
Island Yacht Club.

* * * * *

GEORGIA SALLASKA

Full Name: Georgia Myrle Sallaska.
Born October 15, 1933, at Erick, Oklahoma. Daughter
of George Herbert Stagner (a physician and surgeon)
and Myrtle Madden (a nurse). Married Jack W. Sallaska
(a TV program manager), August 2, 1963. Two sons:
George Allen Williams, Jack Patrick Sallaska.

Education: B.A., Central State University, 1954.

Career: Writer.
Advertising copywriter for twelve years; now a full-
time writer.

First Professional Sale: "Sit by the Fire," in
Fantastic Universe, May, 1958 (as Myrle Benedict).

Awards: Tepee Award (Best Novel by an Oklahoman),
1969, for *Three Ships and Three Kings*; Award of Merit,
Friends of American Writers, 1969, for the same book.

Member: Authors Guild.

Interests: Needlework, particularly needlepoint;
reading; dieting; drawing and painting; cats.

Sallaska writes:
"I write primarily to entertain myself, for few can
tell me a story as well as I can. That others are
likewise entertained always comes as a delightful surprise.
"My novels have been earnest attempts to re-create
the Classic times as lived. Fabulous elements? Mythos
abounds in same; however, I have tried to show that
fable is strongly rooted in reality; mystical subjective
experience also accounts for a lot of the mumbo-jumbo.
Pegasus 'flies,' for example, because he is a natural-
born jumper, and nobody has ever seen a horse take off
like that with somebody aboard him. The Trojan Horse
is a satirical song, because Poseidon (Earth-Shaker,
Horsefather) sent an earthquake to tumble down the
walls of Troy (Poseidon had been expelled from the Trojan pantheon because of an old quarrel, and nothing
could have been more easy to assume than that he was
getting some of his own back at last). Heracles' pro-
digious labors are a form of sympathetic magic, designed
to win Graecoi city-states to Eurystheus' side in order
to repel the Dorial incursion, and also to win the
approval of Heaven, which matched each city-state to
each of its thirteen links. Belt of Heaven, I meant
to say. Which, incidentally, and if anybody care besides myself, explains why Heracles kills two lions;
both Thebes and Mycene were Lion Cities. The Horse
(Sagittarius) is Thessaly, the Twins (Gemini) is Sparta

GEORGIA SALLASKA (Cont.)

"with its Dioscuri-cult, the Water-Pourer (Aquarius) is Orchomenus and the draining of clogged Lake Copais, and so on through the Zodiac. The magic being performed, however, is strictly wishful thinking, for poor old Heracles sweats and sweats and turns out loser in the end anyway. What Greek story ever ended any other way?

"I am closer in philosophy to Mary Renault than anybody else except Robert Graves, but whereas Renault's characters are all gold and white and shining, mine sweat, and there isn't a clean one in the lot, though some of them keep trying."

* * * * *

JAMES SALLIS

Full Name: James Sallis.
   Born December 21, 1944, at Helena, Arkansas. Son of Chappelle H. Sallis (a clerk) and Mildred Liming. Married Jane Rose (an artist), February 21, 1964. One son, Dylan Anthony.

Education: Attended Tulane University, 1962-64.

Career: Writer.
   Has been a college instructor, publisher's reader, and magazine editor; now a full-time writer.

* * * * *

JOSEPH SAMACHSON

Full Name: Joseph Samachson.
   Born October 13, 1906, at Trenton, New Jersey. Son of David Louis Samachson (a businessman) and Anna Roshansky. Married Dorothy Mirkin (a pianist and writer), December 12, 1937. Two children: Michael, Miriam.

Education: B.S., Rutgers University, 1926; Ph.D., Yale University, 1930.

Career: Chemist.
   Research chemist, Atlantic Refining Co., 1930-33, and with American Molasses Co., 1937-38; free-lance science writer, 1938-53; Biochemist, Brooklyn Jewish Hospital, 1953-55; Chief Chemist, Metabolic Laboratory, Montefiore Hospital, Bronx, 1955-61; Chief Chemist, Metabolic Research, Hines Veterans Administration Hospital, Illinois, 1961-73; Asst. Professor of Biochemistry, University of Illinois, 1961-68; Assoc. Clinical Professor, Loyola University, 1968-73; now retired.

Member: American Chemical Society; American Association for the Advancement of Science; American Association of Clinical Chemists; New York Academy of Sciences.

* * * * *

WILLIAM SAMBROT

Full Name: William Anthony Sambrot.
   Born December 17, 1920, at Pittsburgh, Pennsylvania. Son of Anthony Sambrot and Nancy Ciccetti. Married Marina Dianda, January 19, 1948. Two children: Steven, Shellie.

Education:
   "I haven't the faintest recollection of ever having attended the University of Biarritz--although I know I did for a short time in the winter of '45. I'd been stationed in Germany after the war (which I won for us singlehandedly), and we were told we'd be there until the War with Tibet, in '60. Meanwhile, Switzerland or Biarritz were up for grabs. I took the U. at Biarritz. Screen documentaries. Many famous Hollywood writers and directors were lecturing (at least, they told us they were famous; they were all colonels). Utter confusion. I spent most of the time trying to get something to eat. On detached duty. No outfit. No one would feed me. I didn't even get my regular pay. I wasn't on anyone's list. One sergeant even tried to claim I was a kraut. In Jan. '46 I learned my outfit was moving out--for the States. I rolled my kit (one blanket, one pair of sox, three battered contraceptive devices), and simply left for Le Havre. I learned a lot tho--I learned I should have gone to Switzerland.

   "Attended U.C. Berkeley under exactly similar circumstances: G.I. Bill. 50,000 ex-G.I.s under one squad tent, listening to canned lectures. 1947. Decided to specialize; courses in journalism, short story, etc., offered at Cal. extension in San Francisco. Took these during '47, '48 at night, and worked in a Brewery days. Learned a lot. Beer is beautiful before being pasteurized. Just dead water afterward. Made a big sale, thereby confounding prof who'd never made even one, and dropped out of school. No degree. Self taught. I also attended the Institute D'Allende, in Mexico, but that's even more confusing."

Career: Writer.
   Has been a bouncer in a night club, physical education instructor, brewery quality control man, script consultant, advertising copywriter, idea man; now a full-time writer.

First Professional Sale: "The Strong Man," in *Esquire*, June, 1951.

Agent: Curtis Brown Ltd., 60 E. 56th St., New York, NY 10022.

Awards:
   Freedom Foundation George Washington Gold Medal Award, 1951, for "Of Those Who Came," an article in the *Kiwanis*. "Basis for a radio series on Mutual. Given award in March, '52, at Palace Hotel, San Francisco. Others also present were Stanford University, Bank of America, and Standard Oil of California. Herbert Hoover was also there--a traumatic beginning for any writer--but all that was a long time ago, and not even worth recording. All I know is I should have stayed in the brewery. Who ever gave a rejection slip to a cool tall beer?"

Sambrot writes:
   "In answer to your question,'why do you seem to prefer shorter lengths in your writing,' it's just a matter of finances. I'm fairly well known with the editors of many of the generals here and abroad. I've had well over 200 published short stories in all the top-paying markets, and can earn with a short story sale the equivalent of what the book markets--say Ballantine, could offer for an advance. The hardback markets aren't even in it, from what I'm told. From my own experience with Pocket Books, the advance they gave me ($2000) about equalled what I got for each of some seven or eight of the stories in the collection of mine (14 stories) they published. Many of those stories are still selling--one just this month is out in a new Houghton

WILLIAM SAMBROT (Cont.)

"Mifflin textbook. So, even though that SF collection sold some 385,000 plus here, and went into two printings in England (Mayflower, 1964 and 1966), each of over half of the stories therein had earned me well over the total earning for the whole schmear.

"I'd love to come up with a 75,000 word novel and have it hit big--but realistically it seems virtually nil. As for prestige--who's to say? In the same mail delivered by my agent--along with yours came one from Cambridge Press, in English, requesting bio material for yet another *World's Who's Who of Authors* (really). I'm in the 38th edition of *Who's Who in America* (a 'pointer' telling where to look in other bios), *Who's Who in the West* (14th edition), *Personalities of the West and Midwest* (1972), *Bluebook of Magazine Writers*, *Working Press of the Nation* (Feature Writer--don't ask me why), *Men of Achievement* (1973), and *Dictionary of International Biography* (11th Ed.). Solely, in all, as a writer.

"A book can come out, sell (hardback especially) a handful, and die the death only a book can--total oblivion. A short story once sold can, literally, go on for years--an initial audience of millions, then, if one is fortunate, a readership in textbooks, or anthologies, or collections--in hardback, which never disappear from the library shelves.

"If you question the millions of initial readership, my latest SF sale (Ben Bova would not consider it such--SF, I mean), was "The Toast," in the January 1974 issue of *Girl Talk*. This magazine is a beautiful slick job, six colors, put out by Donovan Communications (an affiliate of ABC), which is sent gratis to every beauty shop in America and Canada. It has a guaranteed circulation of four million. This is my 40th SF sale, and will be (is) included in a second collection of SF making the rounds right now. Nongenre fiction which makes it fairly unacceptable--nevertheless--so was the first.

"I'd prefer to write SF above all others; the market for it in the generals is limited (he said dryly), and I'm forced to mine other fields--nevertheless, I dote on SF, and want nothing but the best for it as a genre.

"I grieve, for example, when Kenneth Rexroth (surely one of our finest litterateurs) says of SF: 'After Wells (H.G.), it seems as though most of SF is written by precocious schoolboys.'

"Why is this? I think mainly because the science part--the hard science most of the fans are so insistent on (and is so anathema to the 'mainstream' markets) is not in the least congenial to the truly creative literate mind. I daresay Bradbury is surely the most widely known of all SF writers--in France he's considered a poet. But of science--hard science--you'll find nothing in any of his work.

"I personally believe in miracles--and I also go firmly along with Augustine who said of miracles: 'Miracles are not contrary to nature--merely contrary to what we know of nature.' Scientists in the main are exactly opposite to Augustine. Helmholtz (who was also wrong about his contraction theory re the source of the sun's energy) is a beautiful example: 'All the fellows of this scientific society will be unable to convince me of ESP because it is clearly impossible.'

"Another lovely example of scientific flexibility is G. R. Price, a very eminent man: 'Not one thousand experiments with ten million trials, and by a hundred separate investigators giving total odds against chance of ten to the thousandth power, would make me accept ESP.' Freud termed all the paranormal pheno-

"mena 'that tide of occult mud.' How they fear the mind's hidden powers; the wild talents the top-brain is developing--anything, for that matter, incapable of being isolated, stained, and put under a microscope.

"Most scientists (and a helluva lot of Academics) are intensely specialized. In the main, they're self-protective, bureaucratic, double-talk, double-think, jargon-spewing individuals incapable of an over-view so necessary to humanize them. Most of them are totally stratified and locked into the system. The 'knowledge' they gather--scholars and scientists alike--is according to rules and methodology that often displaces human users. Pseudo-knowledge actually, which is mechanistic in the extreme: dehumanizing and categorizing 'facts.' There is no time nor indeed desire to examine the immensely diversified dynamic inner consciousness that is the active creative process.

"'A mechanistic view of life,' says Alistair Hardy, 'takes us out of the stream of life.' And thereby hangs the sad tale, I believe, of why so much of hard SF is irritating and virtually unreadable to so many mature individuals; ideas but no life. Action but no love--no tenderness.

"If one were to ask me specifically what is the absolutely greatest lack in most of the SF published since Wells (and why he should be the criterion beats me--I don't particularly dig him either), I'd have to say--LOVE. Why is there so little genuine tenderness in SF?

"What is there in SF that enables a 17-year-old high-school kid to turn out successful and salable material that wouldn't get past the first reader of any of the 'mainstream' magazines?

"Yet many writers have written successfully for the mainstream--SF I mean--and even though Harlan Ellison characterized the old *Post* and *Collier's* as 'dinosaurs,' never forget that the likes of Faulkner, Steinbeck, Hemingway, and further back, Jack London, all wrote for them, competing with every knowledgeable and good writer on the globe for the top dollar those markets paid. If one could sell SF to those markets in the face of that competition, then it must have had a universality that the genre magazines (then and today) lacked, and badly. A study of some of those authors who sold those markets might be instructive today: Bradbury, Gerald Kersh, Heinlein (of *The Green Hills of Earth* days), Stephen Vincent Benet, Philip Wylie, Conrad Richter, Will F. Jenkins, Ward Moore, Kurt Vonnegut, Jr.

"Well, I say again that SF is potentially the most exciting and fertile field for the genuinely creative literary writer--but until we take the hard science out and put a little humanity in, I doubt it'll attract many of them. To term a book or story 'Science Fiction' seems a pejorative today. Which is, perhaps, why the most successful practitioner of it divorced himself from it as soon as he hit the top (The Academy of Arts and Sciences, to be exact).

"I hope to live to see the day the term will become the hallmark of the best writing in America. I do what I can to hasten that glorious day."

* * * * *

THOMAS E. SANDERS

Full Name: Thomas Edward Nippawanock Sanders. Born April 30, 1926, at Picher, Oklahoma. Son of John Allen McAlister (a miner and mule skinner) and Grace Jewel Layne. Married Alberta Louise Halley, 1946 (divorced, 1962).

Education: B.A., University of Denver, 1950; M.A.,

THOMAS E. SANDERS (Cont.)

1951; graduate student, University of Colorado, University of Missouri, Barry College.

Career: Professor of English.
Asst. Professor of English, University of South Florida, 1968; Instructor, Kansas City (Mo.) Junior College, 1955-60; Teacher, Ida Fisher Junior High School, Miami Beach, 1961-63; Assistant Professor, Miami-Dade Junior College, 1963-68; Teacher, Hebrew Academy of Greater Miami, 1965-68; currently with University of South Florida Department of English.

First Professional Sale: "I Walked Last Night With Evil," in *The Arrowhead*, March, 1948.

Awards: McAnally Medal for Creative Research, University of Missouri, 1953.

Member:
National Council of Teachers of English; College Conference on Composition and Communication; National English Association; Missouri Historical Society; Florida English Association; Southeast Modern Language Association; Buckskin Council (elected, 1969).

Interests: American Indian jewelry, porcelains, oils, research on Native Americans.

Sanders writes:
"An avid reader of science fiction from a very early age, I was raised by a traditional Cherokee father, and in my Native American heritage I found much in common with science fiction writers who, more than anyone else, seemed to understand and empathize with the American Indian. Simultaneously with the publication of *Speculations* (my science fiction anthology), *Literature of the American Indian* (co-authored by Walter W. Peek, my blood brother) was published! In addition to these two works, I have edited *The Discovery of Poetry* and *The Discovery of Drama* (1967 and 1968), and books in the field of freshman composition. My science fiction classes average 150 students per quarter at the University of South Florida, and it is pretty marvelous to have students who have read the material! Much of the assigned reading in traditional classes is too onerous, it seems, for them, but they not only read the science fiction assignments, they also read beyond the requirements, and keep me rather busy suggesting more and more works. They are always a little amazed that the literature of science fiction is not trivial, escape, pulp fiction. That such names as Mary Shelley, Graham Greene, Stephen Vincent Benet, Howard Fast, Herman Melville, Edgar Allan Poe, and Nathaniel Hawthorne share literary quarters with such stylists as Theodore Sturgeon, Ray Bradbury, and R. A. Lafferty also delights them, for the knowledge supplies them the material with which to refute the arbitrary and provincial attitudes of many of the mainstream literature teachers whose limitations are a constant irritation to such students."

* * * * *

JIMMY SANGSTER

Full Name: Jimmy Sangster.
Born December 2, 1927, in North Wales. Son of Dudley Sangster (in real estate) and Ruth Bowlden. Married Monica Hustler (an artist), August 26, 1950. One son, Mark James.

Career: Writer and film producer.
Free-lance assistant film director, 1948-50; film production manager, 1950-55; free-lance author and film producer, 1957-DATE. Member: Screen Writers Guild of Great Britain; Association of Cine and Allied Technicians; Directors Guild of America.

Agent: Ashley Famous Artists, 45 New Bond St., London W.1, England.

* * * * *

WILLIAM SANSOM

Full Name: William Sansom.
Born January 18, 1912, at London, England. Son of Ernest Brooks Sansom and Mabel Clark. Married Ruth Grundy, 1954. Two sons: Sean, Nicholas.

Career: Writer.
Has worked in a bank, for an advertising agency, as a fireman in London during World War II, as a script writer of motion pictures; full-time writer, 1943-76. Died April 20, 1976.

Awards: Society of Authors Travel Scholarship, 1946; Literary Bursary, 1947. Member: Royal Society of Literature (Fellow).

* * * * *

HANS STEFAN SANTESSON

Full Name: Hans Stefan Santesson.
Born July 8, 1914, at Paris, France. Son of Nils Santesson and Astrid Medeus.

Career: Author and editor.
Editor, Unicorn Mystery Book Club, 1945-52; Editorial Director, *Fantastic Universe*, September, 1956-September, 1959; Editor, October, 1959-March, 1960; Editorial Director, *The Saint Mystery Magazine*, September, 1956-September, 1959; Editor, October, 1959-1967; Editor, *New Worlds* (American version), March, 1960-July, 1960; free-lance author and editor, 1967-75. Died February 18, 1975.

Awards: Edgar Award, 1963, Best Mystery Critic of the Year.

Member:
Science Fiction Writers of America; Mystery Writers of America; Crime Writers Association; Hydra Club; Society for the Investigation of the Unexplained; American Oriental Society; Booksellers League of New York; National Association of Book Editors.

Santesson was actively interested in Indo-Pakistani affairs, and was a member of the American Oriental Society from the mid-1930s.

* * * * *

ROGER SARAC

Full Name: Roger Andrew Caras.
Born May 24, 1928, at Methuen, Massachusetts. Son of Joseph Jacob Caras (an insurance executive) and Bessie E. Kasanoff. Married Jill Langdon Barclay, September 5, 1954. Two children: Pamela Jill (born 1956), Barclay "Clay" Gordon (born 1959).

ROGER SARAC (Cont.)

Education: A.B., University of Southern California,
1954.

Career: Author and naturalist.
   With Columbia Pictures, 1955-65, as an Executive
Assistant to the Vice-President, National Director
of Merchandising for the U.S. and Canada, and Casting
and Story Department Executive; Vice-President, Hawk
Films Ltd. and Polaris Productions Inc., during the
production of *2001: A Space Odyssey*, 1965-68; free-
lance author, broadcaster, and lecturer, 1968-DATE;
commentator, radio series "Pets and Wildlife," CBS
Network, 1969-72, 1973-DATE; commentator, radio series
"Report from the World of Animals," NBC Network,
1972-73; frequent appearances on television shows,
including *Today Show, Tonight Show, Dick Cavett, Mike
Douglas*; lecturer on college campuses.

Member:
   Royal Society of Arts (Fellow); Cleveland Museum
of Natural History (Associate Curator of Rare Books);
Humane Society of the United States (Vice-President);
Zoo and Wildlife Committee, Morris Animal Foundation
(Vice-President); Holy Land Conservation Fund (Presi-
dent and Member of the Board); Zero Population Growth
(Member of Advisory Board); Elsa Wild Animal Appeal
(Member, Board of Directors); Boy Scouts of America
(Member-at-Large, National Council); National Wild-
life Health Foundation (Honorary Trustee); North
American Wildlife Park (Member, Advisory Board); Ari-
zona-Sonora Desert Museum (Member, Advisory Council);
Institute for Child Development (President, Advisory
Council); Mensa; Outdoor Writers; Writers Guild of
America, West; Authors Guild.

First Professional Sale: *Antarctica: Land of
Frozen Time*, Chilton, 1962.

Agent: Roberta Pryor, International Famous Agency,
1301 Avenue of the Americas, New York, NY 10019.

Interests: Photography, antique collecting, book
collecting, art, bonsai, travel.

* * * * *

PAMELA SARGENT

Full Name: Pamela Sargent.
   Born March 20, 1948. Education: B.A., State University of New York, Binghamton, 1968; M.A., 1970.

Career: Author.
   Saleswoman and model, Honigsbaum's, Albany, NY, 1965-
66; assembly line worker, Endicott Coil Company, Bing-
hamton, 1966; saleswoman, Towne Distributors, Bing-
hamton, 1966; typist in the Cataloging Dept., SUNY
Binghamton Library, 1966-67; office worker, Webster
Paper Co., Albany, 1969; Teaching Assistant, SUNY
Binghamton, 1969-71; free-lance author, 1971-DATE.

First Professional Sale: "Landed Minority," in
The Magazine of Fantasy and Science Fiction,
September, 1970.

Member: Science Fiction Writers of America.

Sargent comments:
   "Compared to most science fiction writers, I was a
late-comer to the field. I have talked with SF writers
"who have been reading science fiction regularly and
compulsively since early childhood; my own habitual
reading of SF did not begin until I was in college.
Before that, the only science fiction novels I had read
were *Man of Many Minds*, by E. Everett Evans, *The Stars
My Destination*, by Alfred Bester, and a few novels by
H. G. Wells.
   "In retrospect, however, it seems that an interest
in science-fictional matters, however latent, was present all along. I was entranced by the SF I had read,
and chose to write my senior high school English paper
on H. G. Wells. I was a regular viewer of the *Twilight
Zone* television series (although *The Outer Limits* was
a show that, at that time, was beyond my comprehension).
While in college, between classes, studying, and working, I made up for lost time. I read SF compusively,
everything from E. E. Smith's Lensmen Series to J. G.
Ballard. I read Robert Heinlein's SF novels for young
people while recovering from bronchitis, and thus remember the illness as a pleasant interlude. I read
Kurt Vonnegut while recovering from pneumonia. I gob-
bled up books by John Brunner, Arthur C. Clarke, Philip
K. Dick, and Isaac Asimov. I discovered writers such
as Thomas M. Disch, R. A. Lafferty, and Ursula K. Le
Guin.
   "I had always loved writing, and reading, for as long
as I can remember. I wrote plays in grade school, and
autobiographical short stories modeled on the work of
J. D. Salinger during adolescence. I even attempted
a science-fictional short story while in my teens; it
concerned a 'Euthanasia Corps' in pursuit of a suicidal
man who had decided, too late, that he wanted to live
after all. Mercifully, the story died in my wastebas-
ket. Much later, while in college and attempting to
finish a paper on Aristotle, I took a break and began
to write a story which had been gnawing at me for a
few days, the first story I had written since high
school. It became 'Landed Minority,' my first published SF story.
   "Writing science fiction is a demanding art. The
author must not only pay attention to style, character,
plot, and other such essentials, but must also develop
ideas which are interesting in themselves. The idea
may be entirely new, or an old one used differently,
but even a completely original idea is not enough for
a truly successful SF novel. It is too easy to approach
such an idea in the obvious way; more difficult to
think it through to conclusions and consequences which
may not be so obvious.
   "The wonder of science fiction is the number of ways
in which it allows the writer to develop his or her
faculties. It is not enough simply to be a good sty-
list, to have original concepts, to plot well. The
writer must be learning new things constantly. Not
only must one be a student of literature in all its
forms, but one must also seek out ideas in the sciences,
anthropology, philosophy, sociology, economic theory,
psychology, history, futurology, and in the contempla-
tion of art and music, as well as in one's own experience. One must make these ideas live and breathe in
a fictional context of characters and societies that
also live and breathe. One of the benefits of writing
science fiction is that one becomes aware of new things,
is forever engaged in the adventure of intellectual
and artistic discovery, and is therefore truly alive
in the fullest sense of the word. Yet there are problems along the way that can affect the writer badly,
even fatally, insofar as his or her art is concerned.
In a field where so much is asked, it is easy to settle
for a less ambitious achievement; to be simply a sty-
list, a 'yarn-spinner,' an 'idea person,' or a personality admired as much for one's *persona* as for one's
writing. There is the commercial temptation of settling

PAMELA SARGENT (Cont.)

"into a successful niche, endlessly repeating past work. And the ambitious writer, striving for more, has to contend with the almost certain knowledge that the writing of a truly great work of science fiction is beyond almost all of us."

* * * * *

JEAN-PAUL SARTRE

Full Name: Jean-Paul Sartre.
  Born June 21, 1905, at Paris, France. Son of Jean-Baptiste Sartre (a naval officer) and Anne-Marie Schweitzer.

Education: Agrégé de Philosophie, École Normale Supérieure; further study under Edmund Husserl and Martin Heidegger.

Career: Writer.
  Professor of Philosophy, Lycée du Havre, 1931-32, 1934-36; at Institut Français, Berlin, 1933-34; at Lycée de Laon, 1936-37; at Lycée Pasteur, 1937-39; at Lycée Condorcet, 1941-44; full-time writer, 1944-DATE; founder-Editor, *Les Temps Modernes*, 1945-DATE; lecturer on college campuses.

Awards:
  French Popular Novel Prize, 1940, for *La Nausée*; French Legion d'Honneur, 1945 (refused); New York Drama Critics Award for Best Foreign Play of the Season, 1947, for *No Exit*; French Grand Novel Prize, 1950, for *La Nausée*; Omegna Prize, Italy, 1960; Honorary Fellow, Modern Language Association of America; Nobel Prize for Literature, 1964 (refused).

Member: American Academy of Arts and Sciences.

* * * * *

GEORGE BRANDON SAUL

Full Name: George Brandon Saul.
  Born November 1, 1901, at Shoemakersville, Pennsylvania. Adopted son of Daniel Brandon Saul (a mail clerk) and Mary E. Stamm. Married Dorothy Mae Ayers, 1925 (died, 1937); married Eileen Sarah Lewis, 1937. Three children: George Brandon II (born 1928); Michael Brandon (born 1938); Barbara Brigid Brandon (born 1942).

Education: A.B., University of Pennsylvania, 1923; A.M., 1930; Ph.D., 1932.

Career: Professor of English.
  Professor of English, University of Connecticut, 1924-72; now retired; assistant in English, University of Pennsylvania, 1922-23.

Awards:
  Prizes for verse from *Contemporary Verse, The Lyric, Poet Lore*; two awards from University of Connecticut Research Foundation for research in Ireland, 1967-70; Harrison Scholar in English, University of Pennsylvania, 1930-31.

Member: American Committee for Irish Studies; Poetry Society of America; Modern Language Association.
  Interests: Piano and composition.

JOSEPHINE SAXTON

Full Name: Josephine Mary Saxton.
  Born June 11, 1935, at Halifax, Yorkshire, England. Daughter of Ernest Howard (a dentist) and Clarice Lavinia Crowther. Married Geoffrey Banks (an artist), 1958 (divorced, 1960); married Colin Saxton (an artist), September, 1961. Three children: Simon Howard Banks, Matthew Colin Saxton, Naomi Josephine Saxton.

Education: Intermediate Degree, Halifax College of Art and Craft.

Career: Writer.
  Has also been a teacher, and has worked at various odd jobs and trades; now a full-time writer.

First Professional Sale: "The Wall," in *Science Fantasy*, November, 1965.

Agent: Virginia Kidd, Box 278, Milford, PA 18337.

Interests:
  "Several, everything, nothing. I am my own genre of fiction, which the SF world occasionally adopts to itself, because it is not easily labelled in any other category. I invented a new form for the novel in *Vector for Seven*."

* * * * *

JOHN M. SCHEALER

Full Name: John Milton Schealer.
  Born July 5, 1920, at Boyertown, Pennsylvania. Son of Roy F. Schealer (a dentist) and Helen Kern.

Education: B.A., University of Pennsylvania, 1943.

Career: Writer.
  Founder and past Executive Vice-President, Sound and Light Corporation of America.

* * * * *

JAMES H. SCHMITZ

Full Name: James Henry Schmitz.
  Born October 15, 1911, at Hamburg, Germany. Son of Joseph Henry Schmitz (a businessman) and Catherine Davis. Married Betty Mae Chapman, January 11, 1957.

Education:
  Realgymnasium obersekunda, Germany. "Realgymnasium is, or was then, the German equivalent of upper grade school, high school, and a year or two of college in this country. The 'real' part means that modern languages were taught in that branch of school rather than Latin or Greek. I went to both branches, at different times and places. The 'obersekunda' means the 'upper second' or third-to-last school year, which would make it the equivalent of the last or next-to-last year of high school here; I don't recall which now. Anyway, that's where I quit. I went to Chicago for a year of business school then. That would have been 1929 or 1930."

Career: Writer.
  "My first job was working for the International Harvester Company in Germany, starting, I think, in 1932, and ending when World War II began in Europe. I came

JAMES H. SCHMITZ (Cont.)

"to the States then, tried my hand at writing fiction, and got one story sold before I was drafted into the Army Air Force. After the war, I went into partnership with a brother-in-law, building automobile trailers and other items. I think it was in 1949 that we dissolved the partnership. I picked up writing again, got a few stories sold, but became involved in so many distracting activities that I didn't get much accomplished either in the writing area, or in anything else that you could call gainful employment, for almost ten years. In 1961, I cut out the distractions completely, and have been writing full-time since."

First Professional Sale: "Greenface," in *Unknown Worlds*, August, 1943.

Agent: Scott Meredith, 580 Fifth Avenue, New York, NY 10036.

Awards: Invisible Little Man Award, 1973.

Member: Science Fiction Writers of America.

Interests: Physical fitness, gardening, cookery.

Schmitz writes:
"Many of my stories and novels are set in a megacivilization called the Federation of the Hub. The Hub story characters are contemporaries, and tend to become variously involved with one another, and probably more than half of the fiction I've written in the past ten years has used the Hub background.
"That wasn't so much a planned development as a kind of self-perpetuating process which went on for a considerable while. I'd touched on the Hub in three earlier stories in the Fifties; then, in *A Tale of Two Clocks*, which I wrote in 1959, I developed the Hub background in some detail, because the story required it. Later, I had one of the Clock characters become the protagonist of a novelette called "Lion Loose," because he fitted the role exactly; and a few comments in "Lion Loose" led to other Hub stories, because I became curious about what they seemed to imply. One of the comments was a statement that a group of minor characters were on their way to go 'on a safari on Jontarou.' I wondered what sort of world could induce sportsmen to make a lengthy interstellar trip for the privilege to go hunting on it.
"So Jontarou shaped up gradually, and it appeared there was a situation there. That brought in Telzey Amberdon for the first time. I hadn't planned her as a character; she showed up because the situation I'd been working around with called for someone who thought and acted as she did to solve it. The story was called "Novice," and it appeared in the June, 1962 issue of *Analog*. A year later, I wrote a sequel called "Undercurrents," and Ace subsequently published both stories together as *The Universe Against Her*.
"It was primarily John Campbell who was responsible for the rest of the Telzey series. I'd written two more stories about her, which he published, but then ran into so much difficulty with her that I decided there'd been enough of Telzey. However, a few years later, Campbell told me, 'The boys keep asking for more Telzey stories.' So I brought her back for another set of adventures.
"Yes, I have been rather surprised by her continuing popularity. It isn't universal, of course. I've also heard from readers who simply detest her."

LAWRENCE SCHOONOVER

Full Name: Lawrence Lovell Schoonover.
Born March 6, 1906, at Anamosa, Iowa. Son of George Lawrence Schoonover (a farmer and banker) and Grace Lovell. Married Gertrude Bonn, May 29, 1938. Four children: Judith, Mary Elizabeth, Caroline, Virginia.

Education: Diploma, Shattuck School, 1923; attended University of Wisconsin, 1923-26.

Career: Writer.
Reporter, *Collier's*, 1927-28; advertising copywriter, Barton, Durstine & Osborn, 1928-31; Advertising Manager, Underwood & Underwood, 1931-41; Copy Chief, Gotham Advertising Co., 1943-45; Account Executive, Batten, Barton, Durstine & Osborn, 1947-47; full-time writer, 1947-DATE.

First Professional Sale: *The Burnished Blade*, Macmillan, 1946.

Agent:
"I have no agent. Literary agents, like real estate agents, tell their prospects that you're tops, but tell you that you're absolutely unsaleable."

Member: Chi Phi.

Schoonover notes: "*Central Passage* was the only SF book I ever wrote, and I've no intention of writing another--but it sticks in my mind that eldering authors, like Shakespeare in *The Tempest*, do sometimes produce delightful fantasies."

* * * * *

MARK SCHORER

Full Name: Mark R. Schorer.
Born May 17, 1908, at Sauk City, Wisconsin. Son of William Carl Schorer (a manufacturer) and Anna Walser. Married Ruth Tozier Page, August 15, 1936. Two children: Page, Suzanne.

Education: A.B., University of Wisconsin, 1929; Ph.D., 1936; M.A., Harvard University, 1930.

Career: Professor of English.
Instructor in English, Dartmouth College, 1936-37; Instructor in English, Harvard University, 1937-40; Instructor, Briggs-Copeland Faculty, 1940-45; Associate Professor of English, University of California, Berkeley, 1945-47; Professor of English, 1947-77; Head of the Department of English, 1960-65; Visiting Professor at Harvard University, 1952; Visiting Professor, University of Tokyo, 1956; Fellow, School of Letters, Bloomington, Indiana, 1947-77; Fulbright Professor, University of Pisa, 1952-53; Fulbright Professor, University of Rome, 1964; with Institute for Creative Arts, University of California, 1966-67; Director, Christian Gauss Seminar, Princeton University, 1949. Died August 11, 1977.

Awards:
Guggenheim Fellow, 1941-42, 1943, 1948; Fellow, Center for Advanced Study in the Behavioral Sciences, 1958-59; Bollingen Fellow, 1960; D.Litt., University of Wisconsin, 1962.

Agent: Brandt & Brandt, 101 Park Avenue, New York, NY 10017.

MARK SCHORER (Cont.)

Member:
Modern Language Association; Authors Guild; National Institute of Arts and Letters; American Academy of Arts and Sciences; American Council of Learned Societies; Phi Beta Kappa; Harvard Club; Century Association; Arts Club.

* * * * *

F. H. P. SCHUCK

Full Name: Frederick Hugh Paul Schuck.
Born January 18, 1916, at Brighton, Trinidad, West Indies. Son of Joseph G. Schuck, Sr. and Mary D. Nilger. Education: Attended Harvard University, Northeastern University, Florida Southern College.

Career: Air Force officer.
Former weather observer and forecaster, and a commercial pilot after World War II; presently a member of the 9329th Air Force Recovery Squadron, Tampa, FL.

Member:
Air Force Association; International Oceanography Society; American Museum of Natural History; Florida Sheriffs Association (honorary member); American Association for the United Nations.

* * * * *

L. M. SCHULMAN

Full Name: Lester Martin Schulman.
Born September 3, 1934, at Brooklyn, New York. Son of David Schulman and Rose Tirnauer. Married Janet Schuetz (an editor), May 19, 1957. One daughter, Nicole.

Education: B.A., Antioch College, 1955.

Career: Editor and author.
Editor, Popular Library, 1963-65; Editor, Bantam Books, 1966-67; Editor, Dell Publishing Co., 1967-69; free-lance author and editor, 1969-DATE.

Agent: Russell & Volkening, 551 Fifth Avenue, New York, NY 10017.

* * * * *

GEORGE H. SCITHERS

Full Name: George Harry Scithers [pronounced Sithers]. Born May 14, 1929, at Washington, D.C. Son of George Randall Scithers (an Army officer) and Ruth Smith McKelway (a teacher).

Education: B.S., U. S. Military Academy, 1950; M.S., Stanford University, 1954.

Career: Engineer.
With the U.S. Army, 1946-73, retiring as Lt. Colonel; Staff Engineer I, City of Philadelphia Transit Dept., 1973-DATE; Publisher and Editor, Amra, 1959-DATE; founder and Editor, Owlswick Press.

First Professional Sale: "The Faithful Messenger," in Worlds of If, March, 1969.

Awards:
Hugo Award, Best Amateur Publication, 1963 (1964), Amra; Hugo Award, Best Amateur Publication, 1967 (1968), Amra.

Member:
Science Fiction Writers of America; The CULT (Official Arbiter); Los Angeles Science Fantasy Society (Corporal-at-Arms); Elves, Gnomes, and Little Men's Science Fiction, Chowder, and Marching Society (Honorary Member); Washington Science Fiction Association (President); World Science Fiction Society (Chairman, 1963).

* * * * *

THOMAS N. SCORTIA

Full Name: Thomas Nicholas Scortia.
Born August 29, 1926, at Alton, Illinois. Son of Thomas Nicholas Scortia (in real estate) and Estella Lee Byerley. Married Irene Baron, 1960 (divorced, 1968).

Education: A.B., Washington University, 1949; graduate student, 1950.

Career: Writer.
Chemist, 1954-61; Assistant Branch Manager, United Aircraft, Sunnyvale, California, 1961-70; full-time writer, 1970-DATE.

First Professional Sale: "The Prodigy," in Science Fiction Adventures, February, 1954.

Agent: Curtis Brown Ltd., 60 E. 56th St., New York, NY 10022.

Member: Science Fiction Writers of America; Mystery Writers of America (Section Treasurer, 1972); Writers Guild of America, West.

Interests:
Painting, art collecting. "Science fiction has always been fascinating to me, and one may treat many themes in SF which cannot be adequately handled in any other form. Trite but true."

* * * * *

SEA-LION

Full Name: Geoffrey Martin Bennett.
Born June 7, 1909, in England. Son of Martin Gilbert Bennett (a rear admiral in the Royal Navy) and Esme Geraldine Hicks. Married Rosemary Alys Bechervaise, July 29, 1932. Two sons: Rodney Martin Dumaresq, Richard Hugh Hamilton Geoffrey.

Education: Attended Royal Naval College, Dartmouth, 1923-36, and Royal Naval College, Greenwich, 1929-30.

Career: Writer.
In the Royal Navy, 1923-58, becoming a Commander; Lord Mayor's Esquire, London, 1958-60; Secretary to the Lord Mayor of Westminster, 1960-74; Visiting Lecturer, University of New Brunswick, 1973; free-lance author, 1946-DATE. Member: Royal Historical Society (Fellow); Royal United Services; Institute for Defence Studies; Naval Records Society. Honors: Distinguished Service Cross, 1943; Order of the Orange Nassau, 1972; Gold Medal and Trench-Gascoigne Prize of Royal United Service Institution, 1935, 1941, 1942.

HANK SEARLS

Full Name: Henry Hunt Searls, Jr.
   Born August 10, 1922, at San Francisco, California.
Son of Henry Hunt Searls. Married Berna Ann Cooper.
Three children: Courtney, Henry, Peter.

Education: B.S., U. S. Naval Academy, 1944.

Career: Writer.
   With U. S. Navy, 1941-54, becoming a Lt. Commander;
writer for Hughes Aircraft, Culver City, California,
1955-56; with Douglas Aircraft, 1956-57; with Warner
Brothers, 1959; free-lance author, 1959-DATE. Member:
Authors League; Writers Guild of America, West.

Agent: Scott Meredith, 580 Fifth Avenue, New York,
   NY 10036.

* * * * *

ELIZABETH HOUGH SECHRIST

Full Name: Elizabeth Hough Sechrist.
   Born August 31, 1903, at Media, Pennsylvania. Daugh-
ter of Willard Graham Hough and Mary Parker. Married
Walter Levere Sechrist, October 6, 1930 (died 1968).

Education: Attended University of Pittsburgh and
   Carnegie Library School.

Career: Writer.
   Assistant Children's Librarian, Carnegie Library,
Pittsburgh, 1924-25; Head of Children's Dept., Bethlehem, Pennsylvania, Public Library, 1925-31; full-time
writer, 1931-DATE; now retired.

First Professional Sale: *Christmas Everywhere*,
   Macrae Smith, 1931.

* * * * *

GEORGE SELDEN

Full Name: George Selden Thompson.
   Born May 14, 1929, at Hartford, Connecticut. Son
of Hartwell Green Thompson (a doctor) and Sigrid
Johnson.

Education: B.A., Yale University, 1951.

Career: Writer. Awards: Fulbright Scholarship to
   Italy, 1951-52; Newbery Award runner-up, 1961, for
   The Cricket in Times Square.

* * * * *

CON SELLERS

Full Name: Connie L. Sellers, Jr.
   Born March 1, 1922, at Shubuta, Mississippi. Son
of Connie L. Sellers, Sr. (a farmer and repairman)
and May Menasco. Married Mary F. Raineri, June 16,
1943. Two sons: Leonard L. (born 1944), Shannon E.
(born 1946).

Education: A.A., Monterey Peninsula College, 1958.

Career: Writer and rancher.
   With U.S. Army, 1949-54, editing during that period

several newspapers, including *Ft. Lewis Warrior, Ft.
Jackson Journal, Zamagram* (Japan), *Taro Leaf* (Korea);
combat correspondent, Korea, 1950-51; now a full-time
writer and rancher in Wilderville, Oregon.

First Professional Sale: "Business Girls of Japan,"
   in *Mr. Magazine*, 1957.

Member: "Various horse clubs, national and regional;
   presently President, Border Horsemen of Oregon.

"I'm one of the few self-supporting free-lancers around;
no rich wife, no outside income. I have 95 books under
some 40 pennames, and at last count, more than 700
shorts and articles sales. Few of the books have SF
or fantasy; had a series at Pyramid, and a movie tie-in."

* * * * *

ARTHUR SELLINGS

Full Name: Arthur Gordon Ley.
   Born May 31, 1911, at Tumbridge Wells, Kent, England.
Son of Kent Ley and Stella Grace Sellings. Married
Gladys Pamela Judge, August 18, 1945.

Career: Scientist.
   Did scientific research for the British government;
free-lance writer, 1955-68. Died September 24, 1968,
at Worthing, Sussex, England.

First Professional Sale: "The Mission," in *A.D.
   2500; the Observer Prize Stories, 1954*, an anonymous
   anthology published by Heinemann, 1955.

Agent: E. J. Carnell Literary Agency, 17 Burwash Rd.,
   Plumstead, London SE18 7QY, England.

Interests: Printing, antiquarian book-dealing.

* * * * *

RICHARD SELTZER

Full Name: Richard Warren Seltzer, Jr.
   Born February 23, 1946, at Clarksville, Tennessee.
Son of Richard Warren Seltzer (a superintendent of
schools) and Helen Isabella Estes. Married Barbara
Anne Hartley, July 28, 1973.

Education: B.A., Yale University, 1969; M.A., University of Massachusetts, 1972.

Career: Writer and editor.
   Instructor, University of Massachusetts, 1973; Asst.
Editor, Benwill Publishing (publisher of electronics
magazines), 1973-DATE; free-lance translator of Russian.

First Professional Sale: *The Lizard of Oz: An
   Adult Fable*, B. & R. Samizdat Express, 1974.

Agent: B. & R. Samizdat Express, Box 161, West Roxbury, Massachusetts 02132.

Member: Modern Language Association; Committee of
   Small Magazine Editors & Publishers; New England
   Small Press Association.

Seltzer comments: "For me, writing and publishing
are two aspects of the same creative process. To write,
you have to dive down into yourself in search of an-

RICHARD SELTZER (Cont.)

"swers. To publish, you have to got out into the world--meeting and confronting and discovering. Writing brings you in touch with yourself. Publishing brings you in touch with the world."

* * * * *

ANYA SETON

Full Name: Anya Seton.
  Born 1916?, at New York, New York. Daughter of Ernest Thompson Seton (an author and naturalist) and Grace Gallatin. Three children.

Education: Attended Oxford University.

Career: Writer, 1941-DATE. Member: P.E.N.; Authors League; Pen & Brush Club; National League of American Pen Women.

* * * * *

IRVING SETTEL

Full Name: Irving Settel.
  Born November 21, 1916, at New York, New York. Son of Joseph Settel and Dora Settel. Married Gertrude Schulman (a writer), September 23, 1941. Two children: Kenneth, Joanne.

Education: B.A., Brooklyn College, 1951; M.S., New York University, 1955.

Career: Professor of Marketing.
  Professor of Marketing, Pace College, 1946-DATE; Vice-President, Popular Library; author and writer for radio and television; creator of TV programs, *Who's the Boss?* and *Who Pays?*; co-producer of program, *Where Have You Been?*; consultant to education TV.

* * * * *

DAVID SEVERN

Full Name: David Storr Unwin.
  Born December 3, 1918, at London, England. Son of Sir Stanley Unwin (the publisher) and Alice Mary Storr. Married Periwinkle Herbert, July 31, 1945. Two children: Phyllida Mary, Richard Corydon.

Career: Editor and author.
  Editorial Assistant, League of Nations Secretariat, Geneva, 1938-39; Art Editor, George Allen & Unwin (Publishers), London, 1940-43; publisher's reader for Allen & Unwin and other publishers; writer, 1942-DATE. Member: P.E.N.; Authors Society; Screenwriters Guild. Award: Authors Club First Novel Award, 1955, for *The Governor's Wife*.

* * * * *

ELIZABETH SEWELL

Full Name: Margaret Elizabeth Sewell.
  Born March 9, 1919, at Coonoor, India. Daughter of Robert Beresford Seymour Sewell (a marine biologist) and Dorothy Dean. Married Anthony C. Sirignano (a university lecturer), January 2, 1971.

Education: B.A., Newnham College, Cambridge University, 1942; M.A., 1945; Ph.D., 1949.

Career: Professor of English.
  Professor of English, Fordham University, 1954-55, 1958-59; Tougaloo College, 1963-64; Fordham University, 1967-69; Hunter College, 1971-74; Member of Faculty of the Dept. of Religious Studies, University of North Carolina, Greensboro, 1974-DATE.

Agent: Harold Ober Associates, 40 E. 49th St., New York, NY 10017.

Awards: Litt.D., St. Peter's College, 1963; Litt.D., Fordham University, 1968.

Member: P.E.N.; American Association of University Professors; Lewis Carroll Society.

* * * * *

ALAN SEYMOUR

Full Name: Alan Seymour.
  Born June 6, 1927, at Perth, West Australia. Son of Herbert Augustus Seymour (a seaman) and Louisa Mary Warren.

Career: Writer.
  Has been a radio announcer, director of an art school, film critic for the Australian Broadcasting Commission, director of chamber operas, television producer, script editor with BBC Television, radio and TV writer, literary critic; now a full-time novelist and playwright.

Agent: Film Rights Ltd., 113 Wardour St., London W.1, England.

Awards:
  "Swamp Creatures" was a finalist in the *London Observer* world-wide play competition, 1957; Sydney Journalist Club Play Competition Prize, 1961, for "Donny Johnson." Member: Society of Authors; Writers Guild.

* * * * *

STEPHEN C. SHADEGG

Full Name: Stephen C. Shadegg.
  Born December 8, 1909, at Phoenix, Arizona. Son of Jacob C. Shadegg and Katherine Barden. Married Eugenia Kehr, February 14, 1939. Four children: Cynthia, Eugenia, Stephen David, John Barden.

Career: Businessman.
  Director, S-K Research Laboratories, Phoenix, 1940-DATE; campaign director for a number of candidates for the Senate, House, and state governor. Awards: Freedoms Foundation Award; Phoenix Man of the Year. Member: American Academy of Political and Social Science.

* * * * *

DORIS SHANNON

Full Name: Doris Shannon.
  Born August 7, 1924, at Elmira, New York. Daughter of Edwin Giroux (an engineer) and Elizabeth Graham. Married Frank Shannon (a customs officer), August 1, 1947. Two children: Patricia Anne, Deborah Elizabeth.
Education: Attended Napanee Collegiate Institute.

DORIS SHANNON (Cont.)

Career: Writer.
Bank teller, Royal Bank of Canada, Napanee, Ontario, 1942-47; in Vancouver, B.C., 1948-49; writer, 1969-DATE. Member: Science Fiction Writers of America.

Agent: Kirby McCauley, 220 E. 26th St., New York, NY 10010.

Awards: *Writer's Digest* Creative Writing Award, 1969, for "And Then There Was the Youngest."

* * * * *

JACK SHARKEY

Full Name: John Michael Sharkey.
Born May 6, 1931, at Chicago, Illinois. Son of John Patrick Sharkey and Mary Luckey. Married Patricia Walsh, Bastille Day, 1962. Four children: Beth, Carole, Susan, Michael.

Education: B.A., St. Mary's College, 1962.

Career: Writer and Editor.
Free-lance author, 1952-DATE; Editor, *Good Hands* Magazine, for Allstate Insurance Corporation; playwright. Member: Alpha Psi Omega.

First Professional Sale: "The Case of the Frosty Fiend," in *A. D. Magazine*, 1952.

Awards: A.A.I.E. Best Editorial of 1967, "Stop or I'll Shoot...Unless We're in a Hospital Zone," in *Good Hands*.

Sharkey comments:
"A good yarn is a good yarn. I consider myself a good yarn-spinner, not a literary great. If I can give a reader a pleasant hour or so, I'm succeeding in my vocation."

* * * * *

DOLPH SHARP

Full Name: Dolph Sharp.
Born April 4, 1914, at Hempstead, New York. Son of Benjamin L. Sharp (a businessman) and Lillian Cooper. Married Roslyn Bernstein (a piano teacher), November 1, 1940. Four children: Miriam, Deborah, Naomi, Elizabeth Eve.

Education: A.B., University of Michigan, 1936.

Career: Advertising writer.
Has been a reporter, advertising copywriter, and special assignment writer for the *Reader's Digest*; free-lance writer, 1940-DATE. Agent: Ann Elmo, 52 Vanderbilt Avenue, New York, NY 10017.

* * * * *

MARGERY SHARP

Full Name: Margery Sharp.
Born 1905. Daughter of J. H. Sharp. Married Geoffrey L. Castle (a major in the Royal Army), 1938. Education: B.A., London University.

Career: Writer.
Worked for the Armed Forces Education Program during World War II; now a full-time professional writer (1930-DATE).

* * * * *

BOB SHAW

Full Name: Robert Shaw.
Born December 31, 1931, at Belfast, Northern Ireland. Son of Robert William Shaw (a policeman) and Elizabeth Megaw. Married Sarah Gourley, July 4, 1954. Three children: Alisa Claire (born 1956), Robert Ian (born 1962), Elizabeth Denise (born 1964).

Education: Attended Technical High School, Belfast, 1945-47.

Career: Publicity Officer.
Constructional draftsman, 1947-59, working in Canada, 1956-58; aircraft draftsman, 1959-60; public relations man, 1960-66; journalist, *Belfast Telegraph*, 1966-69; free-lance author, 1969-70; Press Officer, Short Bros. & Harland, Belfast, 1970-73; Publicity Officer, Vickers Shipbuilding Group, England, 1973-DATE.

First Professional Sale: "The Trespassers," in *Nebula Science Fiction*, December, 1954 ("Aspect" was actually published earlier, in the August, 1954 issue).

Agent: E. J. Carnell Literary Agency, 17 Burwash Rd., Plumstead, London SE18 7QY, England.

Member: Science Fiction Writers of America.

Interests:
Archery (twice represented Northern Ireland). "My aim in writing is to renew the vigour of traditional SF themes by combining them with, if it is within my powers, the same degree of characterisation that one finds in the general novel."

* * * * *

FREDERICK L. SHAW JR.

Full Name: Frederick Lincoln Shaw, Jr.
Born July 3, 1928, at Providence, Rhode Island. Son of Frederick Lincoln Shaw, Sr., and Lillian Thomas. Married his wife, December 19, 1966.

Education: B.A., University of California, Los Angeles, 1954; M.A., 1960.

Career: Author, editor, publisher.
"Have had five plays produced at UCLA, one being on a science fiction theme. Served a hitch in medical journalism (five years), rising to the position of Science Editor of *Drug Topics*. Quit to found my own publishing/printing firm (in Jamaica, New York), and to do free-lance writing."

First Professional Sale: *Envoy to the Dog Star*, Ace, 1967.

Member: Science Fiction Writers of America; American Educational Theater Association; American Association for the Advancement of Science.

FREDERICK L. SHAW JR. (Cont.)

Shaw comments:
"My only argument with organized fandom is the tendency it has to become 'clique-ish' and dictatorial as to taste standards it expects from its members. The recent 'everybody be down on Bradbury' trend is a case in point. Bradbury couldn't give less of a shit, especially since he won't even admit to being a sci-fi writer, and, like most creative artists, hates being categorized even that much. He weeps all the way to the bank over all this antagonism. My only other criticism with organized fandom is that it is organized, but I'm hopelessly anti-social anyway, and in my calmer moments, I'll admit that the fans seem to have a good time with their hobby, which is worthwhile. I suppose."

* * * * *

LARRY T. SHAW

Full Name: Lawrence Taylor Shaw.
Born November 9, 1924, at Schenectady, New York. Son of Welborn Taylor Shaw (a laborer) and Marie Gertrude Becker. Married Lee [Shirley Bell] Hoffman, 1956 (divorced, 1959); married Noreen Mary Kane, July 17, 1959. Two sons: Michael Evan (born 1960), Stephen Lawrence (born 1961).

Education: Attended New York University, 1946-47.

Career: Editor.
"After high school graduation, I went to work immediately as a copy boy for the New York Times, but returned to Schenectady to work for a year as a trainee-machinist in the General Electric Company. Then back to NYC, and an Assistant Editor's job with a trade magazine named Hat Life. Except for a short stint as a merchant seaman (Army Transport Service), I've been in publishing ever since. Other employers included Scott Meredith Literary Agency, Topics Publishing Co., Atlas Comics, etc." Associate Editor, If, Worlds of Science Fiction, May, 1953-March, 1954; Editor, Infinity Science Fiction, November, 1955-November, 1958 (all issues published); Editor, Suspect Detective Fiction, November, 1955-October, 1956; Editor, Science Fiction Adventures, December, 1956-June, 1958 (all issues published); Editor, Science Fiction Adventures (U.K.), March, 1958-November, 1958; Editor, Auto Age, February, 1953-April, 1953; Editor, Complete Road Tests, 1955 and 1956; Editor, Rodding and Re-Styling, April, 1955-March, 1957; November, 1960-December, 1962; July-September, 1964; Editor, Customs Illustrated, November, 1960-December, 1962; July-September, 1964; Editor, Custom Rodder, May, 1957-July, 1960; Editor, Car Speed and Style, December, 1957-July, 1960; Editor, Cars, December, 1959-November, 1960; Editor, Hop-up, May-December, 1962; Editor, Speed Mechanics, May-December, 1962; Editor, Car Model ("I created the idea for this specialized magazine; it was the first in its field, and is still being published today"), July, 1962-February, 1964; Managing Editor, Untamed, January, 1959-July, 1960; editor at various times for trade journals in the food, drug, and clothing industries; associate editor of various comic books; Editor, Regency Books, Evanston, Illinois, October, 1962-June, 1963; Editor, Lancer Books, New York, July, 1963-Oct., 1968 ("I developed for publication in paperback such best-selling characters as The Man from O.R.G.Y. and Conan the Barbarian; I was also largely responsible for the introduction and early development in paper-

back form of the modern Gothic mystery, and occult subjects"); Senior Editor, Dell Books, October, 1968-July, 1969; Senior Editor, American Art Enterprises, Chatsworth, California, August, 1969-May, 1975, editing three paperback imprints, and founding Canyon Books and Major Books; literary agent as Larry T. Shaw Literary Agency, Van Nuys, California, 1975-DATE; free-lance author and editor.

First Professional Sale: "Secret Weapon," in Fantasy Book, #3, 1948 (as Terry Thor).

Honors: Guest of Honor, Lunacon, 1970.

Member:
Science Fiction Writers of America; Mystery Writers of America (Editor of March of Crime newsletter); First Fandom; Praed Street Irregulars; West 35th Street Irregulars; Under 200 Club; The Petard Society; The Pinckard Salon.

Interests:
Science fiction, mystery fiction, aviation, comics, George Orwell, Lewis Carroll, Joseph Mitchell, A. J. Leibling, newspaper history, G. K. Chesterton, E. C. Large, Mervyn Peake, lighter-than-aircraft, Sherlock Holmes, old pulps, pipe smoking and collecting, Chinese food, writers and writing in general, SF fan activity, solving double-crostics and difficult crossword puzzles, politics, automobiles, squirrels.

Shaw notes:
"I am constantly gratified by the number of friends I've made, people who say I've helped them, and a small shelf of books dedicated to me, in the writing/publishing world. Am extremely proud of my wife and sons, who are good-looking, talented, and who among the three of them know everything in the world, thus relieving me of the necessity of knowing anything."

* * * * *

ROBERT SHECKLEY

Full Name: Robert Sheckley.
Born July 16, 1928, at New York, New York. Son of David Sheckley (an insurance broker) and Rachel Helen Feinberg. Married Barbara Scadron, 1951 (divorced, 1956); married Ziva Miri Kwitney, 1957 (divorced, 1972); married Abby Schulman, 1972. Three children: Jason William (born 1952), Alissa (born 1965), Anya (born 1974).

Education: B.A., New York University, 1951.

Career: Writer.
"Various minor jobs for short periods of time before 1951; free-lance since then."

First Professional Sale: "Final Examination," in Imagination, May, 1952.

Agent: Sterling Lord Agency, 660 Madison Avenue, New York, NY 10021.

Awards: Jupiter Award, Best Short Story, 1973 (1974), "A Supplicant in Space."

Interests: "In past years I've been seriously interested in chess, sailboats, motorcycles, short wave radio, philosophy, psychology, travel, photography, bicycling, tennis, and others."

ROBERT SHECKLEY (Cont.)

Sheckley writes:
  "You asked me why I prefer shorter lengths. I suppose it is because they seem most natural to me, which isn't really an answer at all. Let me try it this way: for many years, the ideas I got were, for the most part, just right for short stories, and incapable of expansion (at least by me) into longer lengths. I always get five or six novel ideas a year, but write rather few of them (though nowadays this is beginning to change). I've always been impatient, and have enjoyed writing in short, highly concentrated bursts--a mode best suited for short story work.
  "In the last several years, I've become much more interested in the novel form, am working in it now, and expect to go on. A new novel of mine, *Options*, was published by Pyramid in June of 1975. I'm writing a novel (presently untitled) under contract for Bantam, and have planned out several others. Also a collection of stories taken from other anthologies of mine, but not the same stories as in the *Robert Sheckley Omnibus*, will be published by Bantam.
  "My main hobby has always been travelling--a fact reflected in many of my stories and novels. I've finally settled down on the island of Ibiza, where I've lived for the past five years, and hope to go on living for some time to come. Ibiza is paradise. That's why I live there."

* * * * *

VINCENT SHEEAN

Full Name: James Vincent Sheean.
  Born December 5, 1899, at Pana, Illinois. Son of William Charles Sheean and Susan MacDermot. Married Diana Forbes-Robertson, August 24, 1935. Two children: Linda, Ellen.

Education: Attended University of Chicago, 1916-20.

Career: Writer.
  Reporter, *Chicago Daily News*, 1920; reporter, *New York Daily News*, 1920-22; Correspondent in Europe, *Chicago Tribune*, 1922-25; free-lance political journalist, correspondent, and author, 1925-75. Died March 15, 1975, in Italy.

* * * * *

LEE SHELDON

Full Name: Wayne Cyril Lee.
  Born July 2, 1917, at Lamar, Nebraska. Son of David Elmer Lee (a farmer) and Rosa Deselms. Married Pearl May Sheldon, March 17, 1948. Two sons: Wayne Sheldon (born 1950), Charles Lester (born 1952).

Education: Correspondent courses from University of Nebraska.

Career: Rural mail carrier.
  Farmer, 1935-51; rural mail carrier, U.S. Postal Service, Lamar, Nebraska, 1951-DATE; free-lance author, 1944-DATE.

First Professional Sale: "Gunsmoke in Paradise," in *Lariat Story Magazine*, January, 1945.

Member: Western Writers of America (President, 1970-

71); Nebraska Writers Guild (President).

Interests: Travel, truck gardening, orchard gardening.

Sheldon notes: "I've sold over 575 short stories and serials, plus some articles and plays, and more than 25 books. Several of the short stories were science fiction, so I tried one book, and it sold. I would like to write more, but commitments in my established fields have taken all my time. If time and market opportunities present themselves, I will write more SF."

* * * * *

WILLIAM R. SHELTON

Full Name: William Roy Shelton.
  Born April 9, 1919, at Rutherfordton, North Carolina. Son of William R. Shelton and Virginia H. Shelton. Married Helene Shelton, November 7, 1943. Children: Dana.

Education: B.A., Rollins College, 1948; graduate student, State University of Iowa, 1950.

Career: Writer.
  Scenario Writer, U.S. Air Force, Orlando, FL, 1954-58; Bureau Chief and Correspondent, *Time*, 1958-62; Contributing Editor, *Saturday Evening Post*, 1962-63; free-lance author, 1963-DATE.

Awards:
  Atlantic Monthly "First" Award, 1947, for short story, "The Snow Girl"; O. Henry Prize Stories Award, 1948; Eugene F. Saxton Fellow, 1950; Rollins College Medal of Honor, 1962.

* * * * *

ZOA SHERBURNE

Full Name: Zoa L. Sherburne.
  Born September 30, 1912, at Seattle, Washington. Daughter of Thomas Joseph Morin and Zoa Webber. Married Herbert Newton Sherburne, June 5, 1935 (died, 1966). Eight children: Marie A., Norene Y., Zoa May, Herbert Newton Jr., Thomas Morin, Philip G., Anne D., Robert A.

Career: Free-lance author, 1947-DATE.

First Professional Sale: A short story to *Pen Magazine*, October, 1947.

Agent: Ann Elmo, 52 Vanderbilt Avenue, New York, NY 10017.

Awards: Child Study Association Award, 1959, for *Jennifer*.

Member: Culver Alumni Fictioneers; Seattle Free Lance Writers.

Sherburne comments: "With eight children, and sixteen grandchildren, my interests are child-oriented. I work with scouts of both sexes, attend track meets and Little League ball games, and frequently speak at school and library meetings about my writing. I love to travel, and do a great deal of that these days.
  "Before starting on books, I wrote extensively for the short story markets. Have had over 300 stories

ZOA SHERBURNE (Cont.)

"stories published in such magazines as *Redbook, Collier's, Seventeen, American, Chatelaine, Woman's Home Journal*, and various juvenile markets. I've also had short stories and some of the books published in Germany, France, Sweden, Norway, England, Italy, and once in South Africa. Six of my books are in paperback."

* * * * *

GEORGE E. SHIRLEY

Full Name: George Ernest Shirley.
Born November 8, 1898, at Phelps, Missouri. Son of James E. and Lepha May Shirley. Married, with six children.

Career: Real estate broker.
With the U.S. Marines in France and Germany, 1918-19; produce work and sales, 1920-27; professional wrestler, 1925-30; rancher, 1928-34; Senior Heating Engineer, Holland Furnace Company, 1935-37; Branch Manager, 1937-42; real estate broker and developer, 1944-DATE.

* * * * *

LOUIS SHORES

Full Name: Louis Shores.
Born September 14, 1904, at Buffalo, New York. Son of Paul Shores (a painter) and Ernestine Lutenberg. Married Geraldine Urist, November 19, 1931.

Education:
A.B., University of Toledo, 1926; M.S., City College of New York, 1927; B.S. in L.S., Columbia University, 1928; Ph.D., George Peabody College, 1934.

Career: Librarian and instructor.
Library Assistant, New York Public Library, 1926-28; Library Director and Professor, Fisk University, 1928-33; Library and Library School Director, George Peabody College, 1934-46; Dean and Professor, School of Library Education, Florida State University, 1946-67; Editor, *Compton's Pictorial Encyclopedia*, 1935-41; Editor, *Collier's Encyclopedia*, 1946-59; Editor-in-Chief, 1959-DATE.

Honors & Awards:
Legion of Merit, U.S. Air Force, 1946; Mudge Citation in Reference, 1967; International Beta Phi Mu Award in Library Education, 1967; Library-Colleges Award, 1971; D.H.L., Dallas Baptist College, 1970; many others.

Member:
Southeastern Library Association (past President); Florida Library Association (past President); Association of College and Research Libraries (Member, Board of Directors); many other library associations and organizations.

Interests: Swimming, book collecting, psychic research, travel.

Shores writes:
"My autobiography *Quiet World* (published by Shoe String Press) reports, among other things, my mystical

"commitment to quiet, my life-long allergy to 'telling it like it is,' my preference for 'Once Upon a Time' and 'They Lived Happily Ever After' in books, music, philosophy, and religion. I predict, in *Looking Forward to 1999*, that the scientific method will modulate into psychical introspection by the year 2000, and that computers will become museum pieces/relics of the electronic age when telepathy becomes universal, and proves so much faster and more valid.
"My 26th book (to follow *Quiet World*) is titled *FOWST*, spelled differently, because the contract is not with the Devil, as in Goethe, Marlowe, and other Faust variations; the contract in *FOWST* is with an Angel, sent by God, to extend the hero's destined life for another year so that he may complete his highest commitment on Earth before passing on to the next of the planets on which his soul must exist on the way to DESTINY."

* * * * *

JACKSON SHORT

Full Name: unknown.
Born September 7, 1939, at New York, New York. Education: A.B., Antioch College.

Career: Advertising writer.
Newspaper reporter and editor, 1960-63; advertising writer, 1963-DATE; now a Vice-President in charge of the copy department of a major New York advertising firm; served in the U.S. Army Reserve National Guard, 1962-67.

Agent: Henry Morrison, 76 W. 10th St., New York.

* * * * *

SANDRA SHULMAN

Full Name: Sandra Dawn Shulman.
Born December 15, 1944, at London, England. Daughter of Alfred Shulman (a textile merchant) and Gladys Davis. Education: Attended North London Collegiate School, 1954-60; Diploma, St. Godrics College, 1962.

Career: Journalist.
Secretary and personal assistant to the Fiction Editor of Children's Magazines, Longacre Press, London, 1962-63; free-lance journalist and film researcher; novelist, 1966-DATE.

Agent: Free Lance Presentations Ltd., 63-67 Rosoman St., London EC 1, England.

* * * * *

EDWIN SILBERSTANG

Full Name: Edwin Silberstang.
Born January 11, 1930, at New York, New York. Son of Louis Silberstang (a lawyer) and Fay Berkowitz. Three children: Julian, Joyce, Allan.

Education: B.A., University of Michigan, 1950; J.D., Brooklyn Law School, 1957.

Career: Writer and attorney.
Private practice of law, Brooklyn, 1958-67; free-lance author, 1967-DATE. Member: Authors Guild.

WILLIAM T. SILENT

Full Name: John William Jackson, Jr.
  Born November 30, 1945, at Los Angeles, California. Son of John William Jackson. Married Sherry Jackson (a travel agent).

Education: A.B., Indiana University, 1967; M.A., University of California, 1969.

Career: Writer and designer.

First Professional Sale: *Lord of the Red Sun*, Walker & Co., 1971.

Member: Science Fiction Writers of America.

Interests:
  Game, costume, clothing, furniture design, board games, karate, sports, music. "Universal interests. I'm a thorough-going libertarian--a fact which strongly influences everything I have written in the last several years. My first book and some short stories appeared under the penname, William T. Silent, but my more recent work is under my real name."

* * * * *

ALAN SILLITOE

Full Name: Alan Sillitoe.
  Born March 4, 1928, at Nottingham, England. Son of Archibald Sillitoe (a tannery labourer) and Sylvina Burton. Married Ruth Fainlight (an author and poet), November 19, 1957. Two children: David Nimrod (born 1962), Susan (adopted; born 1960).

Career: Writer.
  Has worked in a bicycle plant, plywood mill, and as a lathe operator; Editorial Adviser, W. H. Allen (publishers), London; free-lance author.

First Professional Sale: *The General*, W. H. Allen, 1960.

Agent: Rosica Colin, 4 Hereford Square, London SW7.

Awards: Hawthornden Prize for Literature, 1960.

Member: Society of Authors; Writers Action Group.

Interests:
  Travel and maps. "I try to write science fiction or fantasy when it has some social or political content. I am a great admirer of that master of science fiction, Mack Reynolds--an American author."

* * * * *

ROBERT SILVERBERG

Full Name: Robert Silverberg.
  Born January 15, 1935, at New York, New York. Son of Michael Silverberg (a certified public accountant) and Helen Baim (a teacher). Married Barbara H. Brown, August 26, 1956.

Education: A.B., Columbia College, 1956.

Career: Writer.
  Has been a full-time, free-lance author since 1953;

Associate Editor, *Amazing Stories*, January, 1969; Associate Editor, *Fantastic Stories*, February-April, 1969; Editor, *New Dimensions* series of anthologies, 1970-DATE.

First Professional Sale:
  "Fanmag," an article in *Science Fiction Adventures*, December, 1953; First Story: "Gorgon Planet," in *Nebula Science Fiction*, February, 1954.

Agent: Scott Meredith, 580 Fifth Avenue, New York, NY 10036.

Awards:
  Co-Guest of Honor, 28th World Science Fiction Convention (Heicon '70), Heidelberg, Germany, 1970; Nebula Award, Best Short Story, 1969 (1970), "Passengers"; Nebula Award, Best Novel, 1971 (1972), *A Time of Changes*; Nebula Award, Best Short Story, 1971 (1972), "Good News from the Vatican"; Nebula Award, Best Novella, 1974 (1975), "Born with the Dead"; Jupiter Award, Best Novella, 1973 (1974), "The Feast of St. Dionysus"; Hugo Award, Most Promising Author, 1955 (1956); Hugo Award, Best Novella, 1968 (1969), "Nightwings."

Member: Science Fiction Writers of America (President, 1967-68; Western Regional Director, 1974-75).

Interests: Travel, collecting rare books, gardening, contemporary music and literature.

Silverberg writes:
  "I think that the state of SF has never been healthier, that we are in the midst of an incredibly fertile period, and that the trend will continue upward as new writers are attracted by the new freedoms of the medium. Until a few years ago, most SF was fundamentally juvenile in style and content: simple sentences, avoidance of material likely to unsettle the reader's emotions (such as erotic material), etc. There were some honorable exceptions, of course. Now SF is catching up with the outer world, at least to the extent that literary techniques used by the best mainstream writers since the 1920s are now acceptable in science fiction books. One can write the slam-bang kind of SF if one pleases, but markets now exist for a richer, more moving kind of fiction. Almost nothing that I've written since 1966 could have found a publisher when I began writing professionally in 1953; and yet I'm by no means an extremely experimental writer, nor is my material radical in content.
  "I view my current position in SF as that of a consolidator as much as an innovator. The 'new wave,' by which I mean chiefly the group of writers contributing to *New Worlds*, has imported into science fiction the experimental techniques of the avant-garde, leaning heavily on Joyce and Beckett; I find much of this fascinating as a reader, but feel no impulse to make use of those techniques in my own work. I think SF must be brought to a state of functional literacy before we go bounding off into avant-gardery. In my writing, I have two chief goals: to attain the sort of stylistic proficiency that is demanded of any writer in non-category fiction, and to transform the standard material of science fiction through an emphasis on emotion, intensity of incident, and complexity of character. I think my most successful attempt in these efforts was *The Masks of Time*, though I'm pleased with the flamboyant imagery of *Thorns*, and the stylistic level of the book version of *The Man in the Maze*. Much of my recent work has had a strong erotic content; I see this as a useful corrective to the innocence of nearly all SF of the past, and I expect to keep mining this particular lode as long as it yields fresh ore for me. It seems

ROBERT SILVERBERG (Cont.)

"preposterous to me that there should even be a debate on the place of sex in science fiction. (Would there be a debate on the appropriateness of sex in one's life?) I don't intend to write pornography that is incidentally SF, not because of moral objections, but simply because it seems like a boring thing to do; but where I can employ erotic themes to heighten the SF element of a novel, I'll do so unhesitatingly. Again, I think I was most successful at this in *The Masks of Time*, and if I sound defensive about that book's sexual content, it's because I've been attacked for it several times by fans, and even by writers of the old guard.

"I believe that when the current revolutionary movement in SF has run its course, we'll emerge with a vastly more interesting literature than we've had before, and that present controversies will seem astonishingly puerile to tomorrow's readers. I feel that SF will survive the injection of literacy that it's had lately, even if some old-line readers will be driven away by the transformation of their favorite genre, and I'm eager to be a part of the emerging new SF, standing as I do between the pulp-oriented writers of the past, and the literature-oriented writers of the past few years.

"My favorite among my own works? It varies from day to day, but I think I have a special place for *Son of Man*."

Since writing these words, several years ago, Silverberg has announced his retirement from writing fiction.

* * * * *

CLIFFORD D. SIMAK

Full Name: Clifford Donald Simak.
  Born August 3, 1904, at Millville, Wisconsin. Son of John Lewis Simak and Margaret Wiseman. Married Agnes Kuchenberg, April 13, 1929. Two children: Scott, Shelley (daughter).

Education: Attended University of Wisconsin.

Career: Reporter.
  Reporter with *Minnesota Star* and *Minnesota Tribune*, 1939-DATE, serving as News Editor from 1949-62, and Editor of the Science Reading Series from 1962-DATE; free-lance author, 1931-DATE.

First Professional Sale: "The World of the Red Sun," in *Wonder Stories*, December, 1931.

Agent: Robert P. Mills Ltd., 156 E. 52nd St., New York, NY 10022.

Honors & Awards:
  Guest of Honor, 29th World Science Fiction Convention (Noreascon), Boston, 1971; International Fantasy Award, Fiction, 1953, for *City*; Hugo Award, Best Novelette, 1958 (1959), "The Big Front Yard"; Hugo Award, Best Novel, 1963 (1964), *Way Station*; Minnesota Academy of Science Award, for Distinguished Service to Science, 1967.

Member: Science Fiction Writers of America; Minnesota Academy of Sciences; Sigma Delta Chi.

Simak writes:
  "Many of my stories have been placed in what may

"seem to be the mythical town of Millville. It is not. I was born in the township of Millville, Wisconsin, in the southwestern corner of the state. My grandfather's farm house, where I was born, sits on the end of a high ridge from which can be seen the confluence of the Wisconsin and Mississippi rivers. Millville itself is a wide place in the road in one of the deep hollows of that rugged country. When I last saw it, it had a gas station, an old-time general store, a church and school and a few residences. It probably has fewer buildings now. The rough, picturesque country in that area is the kind of land a man can easily fall in love with, and I have been in love with it all my life, although I only get to visit it occasionally.

"Bridgeport, which is used as a locale in *Time and Again*, is in the same part of Wisconsin. Willow Grove or Willow Bend, which I have also used, is an entirely mythical place.

"Regarding science fiction, I don't even pretend to know where the field is headed. I do think that the status of science fiction has improved. At one time, it was sneered at as a pulp paper fiction even lower than westerns, whodunits, and love stories. It was thought of in terms of ray guns and bug-eyed monsters. Today, it is widely accepted as a legitimate literature. It is hard for a man to stand off and view his own work objectively. It does seem to me that I, along with others, back in the late '30s and early '40s, may have made a contribution to naturalism in science fiction. The work done in that period relegated the mad scientist, the beastly alien invader, and many other old cliches to the past, and introduced believable characters and normal backgrounds. I recall that I wrote about Iowa farmers on Venus, a football team, an old soldier going to Mars for a reunion of the veterans of the Earth-Mars war. Other people did much the same thing. This was a revolution of considerable importance in the field, and to think that I may have had some small hand in it is gratifying.

"I have no opposition to the so-called new wave. It does pain me somewhat to see a small group of people, some of them good friends of mine, who proclaim that the new wave is the only way in which science fiction should be written. I think that the new wave does have something to offer to the field, but I do not think that it will dominate the field; at the moment, it has less dominance, perhaps, than it had a couple of years ago. It has a viewpoint and a technique which will be taken into the field as a part of the overall pattern of writing and of thought, and in that way it will contribute. When it disappears as a separate entity, which I am sure it will do in time, it will leave the field richer and more significant. It will have contributed; it will not have taken over. After all, all literature is in a certain sense 'escape literature,' in which the reader can momentarily identify with another character than his own, and the good story line still remains the backbone of all writing."

* * * * *

EDITH SIMON

Full Name: Edith Simon.
  Born May 18, 1917, at Berlin, Germany. Daughter of Walter Frederick Simon and Grete Goldberg. Married E. C. R. Reeve (a research geneticist), August 8, 1942. Three children: Antonia Mary, Simon Raynold, Jessica Carolyn.

Career: Artist, writer, historian.
  Has had seven one-person shows of pictures and sculptures in many media, 1971-74; writer, 1940-DATE.

D. N. SIMS

Full Name: Denise Natalie Sims.
   Born January 25, 1940, at Newquay, Cornwall, England.
Daughter of John Gwynffryn Davies (a lorry driver)
and Theodora Lillian Jacobs. Married Richard Leslie
Sims (a university lecturer), December 19, 1964.
Two sons: Guy Rohan (born 1968), Keir Alan (born 1970).

Education: B.A., University College, London University, 1962.

Career: Housewife and writer.
   Has been an English teacher in Japan from 1962-68,
a waitress, a shop assistant, a clerk for the Ministry
of Education; writer, 1973-DATE.

First Professional Sale: *A Plenteous Seed*,
   Robert Hale, 1973.

Member: British Labour Party.

Interests: Socialism, animals, Japan, reading in
   science and history, swimming, badminton, walking
   the English countryside with children in tow, and
   reading SF.

* * * * *

ANDREW SINCLAIR

Full Name: Andrew Annandale Sinclair.
   Born January 21, 1935, at Oxford, England. Son of
Stanley Charles Sinclair and Hilary Nash-Webber. Mar-
ried Miranda Seymour, October 18, 1972.

Education: B.A., Trinity College, Cambridge University, 1958; Ph.D., Churchill College, Cambridge,
   1963.

Career: Publishing director.
   Commonwealth Fellow, 1959-61; Director of Historical
Studies, Churchill College, Cambridge University,
1961-63; Fellow, American Council of Learned Studies,
1963-65; Lecturer in American History, University
College, University of London, 1965-67; Managing Director, Lorrimer Publishing, London, 1967-DATE; Managing Director, Timon Films, 1969-DATE.

Agent: Elaine Greene, 31 Newington Green, London
   N16, England.

Awards: Somerset Maugham Literary Prize, 1967. Member: Royal Society of Literature (Fellow).

* * * * *

UPTON SINCLAIR

Full Name: Upton Beall Sinclair.
   Born September 20, 1878, at Baltimore, Maryland.
Son of Upton Sinclair (a travelling salesman) and
Priscilla S. Harden. Married Meta H. Fuller, 1900
(divorced, 1911); married Mary Craig Kimbrough, April
21, 1913 (died, 1963); married Mary Elizabeth Willis,
October 14, 1961 (died, 1967). One son, David.

Education: A.B., City College of New York, 1897;
   graduate student, Columbia University, 1897-1901.

Career: Writer. Supported himself while an undergraduate by writing jokes and doing other hackwork;
wrote nearly 100 "nickel novels" while studying at Columbia; established a theater company for the performance of Socialist plays; assisted the government in
a Chicago stock yard investigation, 1906; founded Heli-
con House Colony, Englewood, NJ, 1906; founded Inter-
collegiate Socialist Society, now the League for Industrial Demoncracy; Socialist congressional candidate,
1906 and 1920, and senatorial candidate, 1922; candidate
for California governor, 1926, 1930, 1934; formed End
Poverty in California League; full-time writer, 1898-
68. Died November 25, 1968.

First Professional Sale: *Saved by the Enemy*,
   Street & Smith, 1898.

Awards: Pulitzer Prize, 1943, for *Dragon's Teeth*;
   Award of American Newspaper Guild, and United Automobile Workers, 1962.

Member: Authors League (founder); American Institute
   of Arts and Letters; American Civil Liberties Union.

* * * * *

ISAAC BASHEVIS SINGER

Full Name: Isaac Bashevis Singer.
   Born July 14, 1904, at Radzymin, Poland. Son of Pin-
chos Menachem Singer (a rabbi and author) and Bathsheba
Zylberman. Came to U.S., 1935. Married Alma Haimann,
1940. One son, Israel.

Education: Attended Tachenioni Rabbinical Seminary.

Career: Writer.
   Worked in Poland for the Yiddish press; Member of the
staff of *Jewish Daily Forward*, 1935-DATE; writer, 1935-
DATE. Member: P.E.N.; National Institute of Arts and
Letters.

Awards:
   Louis Lamed Prize (twice); Grant from National Institute of Arts and Letters, 1959; $10,000 grant from Na-
tional Council on the Arts, 1966.

* * * * *

KURT SINGER

Full Name: Kurt Deutsch Singer.
   Born August 10, 1911, at Vienna, Austria. Son of
Ignatius Singer (a businessman) and Irene Deutsch.
Married Hilda Tradelius, 1932 (divorced, 1954); married
Jane Sherrod (an author). Two children: Marian Birgit
(born 1940); Kenneth Walt (born 1945).

Education: Attended University of Zürich, 1932-33;
   Ph.D., University of Indiana, 1950.

Career: President of newspaper syndicate.
   Has been a reporter, book reviewer, film critic, editorial writer, editor-in-chief, and editorial director
of various publications; free-lance author, 1934-DATE;
President, BP Singer Features, Inc. (a newspaper syndicate), 1955-DATE; Vice President, International Platform Association.

First Professional Sale: "Hitler Unmasked," in
   People, 1934. Agent: BP Singer Features, 3164 Tyler
   Avenue, Anaheim, CA 92801.

KURT SINGER (Cont.)

Member: "I am not a joiner."

Interests:
"Collect art, books, documents, letters and autographs; have made four world trips."

"I wish I had a carbon copy of everything I wrote in
my younger years. A writer needs a second job in order to survive. A writer will always be his own best
agent.
"As to why ghost and weird stories are more popular
overseas, my guess is that there is more of a tradition for it in old England, in French literature,
and in Germany (E. T. A. Hoffmann and the Black Forest
stories). I also believe that the majority of readers
in the U.S.A. are women, and few women read ghost,
weird, and science fiction stories."

* * * * *

CURT SIODMAK

Full Name: Curt [originally Kurt] Siodmak.
Born August 10, 1902, in Dresden, Germany. Son
of Ignatz "Ike" Siodmak and Rose Siodmak. Married
Henrietta De Perrot, 1931. One son, Geoffrey Curt
De Perrot (born 1933).

Education: Ph.D., University of Zürich, 1927; attended Technische Hochschule, Dresden & Stuttgard,
1929-30.

Career: Film writer and director.
"Drove a steam engine for the German railway, and
worked in factories in Germany before Hitler; moved
to England, 1933, and worked for Gaumont British, 1933-
37; came to the U.S., 1937; film director and writer
in U.S. (35 credits) and abroad (18 credits); free-
lance author, 1925-DATE, with 18 novels published in
German, and many others published in English (some
translated)."

First Professional Sale: "The Eggs from Lake
Tanganyika," in *Amazing Stories*, July, 1926 (translated from the German original).

Agent: Paul R. Reynolds, 599 Fifth Avenue, New York,
NY 10017.

Awards: Bundespreis, 1964, for movie "Feuerschiff"
("Lightship"). Member: Writers Guild of America;
Screen Directors Guild; P.E.N.

Interests: Raising Black Angus cattle on his California ranch.

* * * * *

OSBERT SITWELL

Full Name: Sir Francis Osbert Sacheverell Sitwell.
Born December 6, 1892, at London, England. Son of
Sir George Reresby Sitwell, 4th Baronet, and Lady
Ida Emily August Denison. Brother of Dame Edith
Sitwell and Sacheverell Sitwell. Education: Studied
at Eton.

Career: Author.
Succeeded to the title and family estate as fifth
baronet, 1943; served as justice of the peace in Derbyshire, 1939; Trustee, Tate Gallery, 1951-58; writer,
1916-69. Died in Florence, Italy, May 4, 1969.

Honors & Awards:
Received the first *Sunday Times* Gold Medal for English Literature, 1947; Commander of the Order of the
British Empire, 1956; Companion of Honour, 1958; Companion of Literature, 1967; LL.D., University of St. Andrews, 1946; D.Litt., University of Sheffield, 1951.

Member:
Society of Authors; Royal Society of Literature (Fellow); Royal Institute of British Architects (Fellow);
American Institute of Arts and Letters (Honorary Associate); St. James's Club.

* * * * *

JOHN SLADEK

Full Name: John Thomas Sladek.
Born December 15, 1937, at Waverly, Iowa. Son of
Victor B. Sladek (a tailor) and Elsie Lynch. Education: Attended St. Thomas College, 1955-56, and University of Minnesota, 1956-59.

Career: Writer and Editor.
Engineering Assistant, University of Minnesota, 1959-
61; Technical Writer, Technical Publications, St. Louis,
1961-62; free-lance author; editor of *Ronald Reagan,
the Magazine of Poetry*, 1968-DATE.

Agent: Scott Meredith, 580 Fifth Avenue, New York,
NY 10036.

* * * * *

FRANK G. SLAUGHTER

Full Name: Frank Gill Slaughter.
Born February 25, 1908, at Washington, D.C. Son of
Stephen Lucius Slaughter (a farmer, sawmill operator,
and rural mail carrier) and Sallie Nicholson Gill.
Married Jane Mundy, June 10, 1933. Two sons: Frank
Gill Jr., Randolph M.

Education: A.B., Duke University, 1926; M.D., Johns
Hopkins University, 1930.

Career: Writer.
Intern, assistant resident, resident surgeon, Jefferson Hospital, Roanoke, VA, 1930-34; physician specializing in surgery, Jacksonville, FL, 1934-42; free-lance
author, 1946-DATE.

Agent: Brandt & Brandt, 101 Park Avenue, New York,
NY 10017. Member: American College of Surgeons (Fel-
low); American Medical Association; Authors Guild;
Phi Beta Kappa; Florida Yacht Club.

* * * * *

WILLIAM SLEATOR

Full Name: William Warner Sleator III.
Born February 13, 1945, at Havre de Grace, Maryland.
Son of William Warner Sleator, Jr. (a professor) and
Esther Kaplan.

Education:
B.A., Harvard University, 1967.

WILLIAM SLEATOR (Cont.)

Career: Writer and musician.
  Studied piano for twelve years, the cello for five,
and worked for several years as an accompanist for
ballet classes, with one year at the Royal Ballet
School in London; composer of scores for ballets and
amateur films and plays; free-lance author, 1970-DATE.

* * * * *

BARBARA SLEIGH

Full Name: Barbara Sleigh.
  Born January 9, 1906, in Worcestershire, England.
Daughter of Bernard Sleigh (an artist) and Stella
Phillp. Married David Davis (a free-lance broadcas-
ter, January 29, 1936. Three children: Anthony,
Hilary (daughter), Fabia. Education: Attended art
school, 1922-25, and art teachers college, 1925-28.

Career: Writer.
  Art teacher, Smethwick High School, England, 1928-
30; Lecturer, Goldsmiths' College, London, 1930-33;
Assistant on radio program "Children's Hour," BBC,
1933-36; writer.

Agent: Harvey Unna, 79 Baker St., London W.1, England.

* * * * *

LOUIS SLOBODKIN

Full Name: Louis Slobodkin.
  Born February 19, 1903, at Albany, New York. Son
of Nathan Slobodkin (an inventor) and Dora Lubin.
Married Florence Gersh (an author), September 27, 1927.
Two sons: Laurence B., Michael E.

Education: Attended Beaux Arts Institute of Design,
  New York, 1918-22.

Career: Writer and illustrator.
  Sculptor in studios in France and the U.S., 1931-35;
Head of Sculptor Division, New York City Art Project,
1941-42; executor of statues and panels for government buildings in Washington, D.C., New York, and
other cities; exhibitor and lecturer at museums; free-
lance author, 1944-75. Died 1975.

Awards: Winner of various sculptor competitions;
  Caldecott Medal, 1944, for illustrations in *Many
  Moons*, by James Thurber.

Member:
  Sculptors Guild; National Sculpture Society; American Institute of Graphic Arts; Authors Guild.

* * * * *

GEORGE EDGAR SLUSSER

Full Name: George Edgar Slusser.
  Born July 14, 1939, at San Francisco, California.
Son of Raymond Leroy Slusser (a salesman) and Edlo
Mildred Raerth. Married Daniele Genevieve Chatelain,
July 2, 1965.

Education: A.B., University of California, Berkeley, 1961; Diplôme d'Études, Université de Poitiers,

1962; Ph.D., Harvard University, 1974.

Career: English professor and writer.
  With the U.S. Army, serving in the Intelligence Corps
in Germany, 1963-65; Assistant Professor of English,
California State College, San Bernardino, 1971-75; free-
lance author and critic, 1975-DATE; free-lance translator from German and French, 1975-DATE.

First Professional Sale: *Robert A. Heinlein: Stranger in His Own Land*, Borgo Press, 1976.

Honors: Fulbright Fellow, Tüburgen; Fulbright Fellow,
  1975-76, Université de Paris (Nauterre).

Interests: Beer brewing, organic gardening.

* * * * *

CORDELIA TITCOMB SMITH

Full Name: Cordelia Meda Titcomb Smith.
  Born November 6, 1902, at Bath, Maine. Daughter of
Fred Evans Titcomb (a barber and musician) and Katrina
Beals. Married James Ambler Smith, 1930 (died, 1948).
Two children: Sally Jean (born 1934), Margaret L.
(born 1936).

Education: B.L.S., Simmons College, 1926; Certificate in Library Work with Children, Western Reserve
  University, 1929.

Career: Librarian.
  Director of Young Adult Work in Ohio libraries until
1970; now retired.

First Professional Sale: A short story in 1941.

Member: American Library Association; Pan Pacific
  and Southeast Asia Association. Interests: Reading,
  travel, book discussion.

* * * * *

CORDWAINER SMITH

Full Name: Paul Myron Anthony Linebarger.
  Born July 11, 1913, at Milwaukee, Wisconsin. Son of
Paul Myron Wentworth Linebarger and Lillian Bearden.
Married Genevieve Cecilia Collins, 1950. Two children:
Johanna Lesley, Marcia Christine.

Education:
  Attended University of Nanking, 1930, and North China
Union Language School, 1931; A.B., George Washington
University, 1933; graduate study at Oxford University,
1933, at American University, 1934, at University of
Chicago, 1935; M.A., Johns Hopkins University, 1935;
Ph.D., 1936; graduate study at University of Michigan,
1937 and 1939; Certificate in Psychiatry, Washington
School of Psychiatry, 1955; attended Universidad Inter-
americana, 1959-60.

Career: Professor of Asiatic Studies.
  Instructor, Harvard University, 1936-37; Associate
Professor, Duke University, 1937-46; Professor of Asiatic Studies, School of Advanced International Studies
of Johns Hopkins University, 1946-66; Visiting Professor, University of Pennsylvania, 1955-56; Visiting Professor, Australian National University, 1957; helped
found Office of War Information during World War II as

CORDWAINER SMITH (Cont.)

a member of the Operations Planning and Intelligence
Board; U.S. Army consultant to British land forces
in Malaya, 1950, and to Eighth Army in Korea, 1950-52;
with the U.S. Army Intelligence Service, 1942-66, becoming a Lt. Colonel; awarded Bronze Star; served in
Washington, D.C., and at the China-Burma-India Theater
Headquarters, Chungking, China, 1942-46; lecturer at
various colleges and universities; free-lance author,
1937-66. Died in Australia, August 6, 1966.

First Book Publication:
 The Political Doctrines of Sun Yat-sen, Johns Hopkins
Press, 1937; First SF Sale: "Scanners Live in Vain,"
in *Fantasy Book*, #6, 1950.

Member:
 American Peace Society (President); American Politi-
cal Science Association; American Society of Interna-
tional Law; Council on Foreign Relations; American
Association for Asian Studies; American Philatelic
Society; Psywar Society; American Legion; Reserve
Officers Association; Association of the U.S. Army;
Phi Beta Kappa; Pi Gamma Mu; Southern Political Sci-
ence Association; Masonic Order; Cosmos Club, Washing-
ton; D. C. Political Science Association; Science
Fiction Writers of America.

Smith was fluent in Chinese, German, French, Spanish,
and was able to read Russian, Portuguese, and Dutch;
he travelled around the world six times.

* * * * *

DODIE SMITH

Full Name: Dorothy Gladys Smith.
 Born at Whitefield, Lancashire, England. Daughter
of Ernest Walter Smith and Ella Furber. Married Alec
Macbeth Beesley, 1939. Education: Attended Royal
Academy of Dramatic Art, London.

Career: Writer and playwright.
 Actress, 1915-22, appearing first at Tottenham
Palace in "Playgoers," then touring with various
repertory companies; left the stage to become a buyer
at Heal & Son, London; wrote a screenplay, "Schoolgirl
Rebels," under the pseudonym Charles Henry Percy,
while still a student at the Royal Academy; left her
business career with the success of her first professionally produced play, "Autumn Crocus," 1931; full-
time writer and playwright, 1931-DATE.

* * * * *

EDWARD E. SMITH

Full Name: Edward Elmer Smith.
 Born May 1, 1890, at Sheboygan, Wisconsin. Son
of Fred Smith (a ship's first mate) and Caroline
Mills. Married Jeannie MacDougall. Two children:
Verna Jeannie, Roderick.

Education: Ph.D., George Washington University.

Career: Organic chemist.
 Worked successively as a western ranch hand, lumberjack, silver miner, surveyor, engineer, junior chemist, assistant chemist, senior chemist, chief chemist,
cereals technologist, explosives expert; free-lance

author, 1927-65. Died August 31, 1965, at Seaside,
Oregon.

First Professional Sale: "The Skylark of Space,"
 serialized in *Amazing Stories*, August-October, 1928.

Agent: Scott Meredith, 580 Fifth Avenue, New York,
 NY 10036.

Honors & Awards:
 Guest of Honor, 2nd World Science Fiction Convention
(Chicon I), Chicago, 1940; first recipient of First
Fandom Hall of Fame award, 1964.

Member: First Fandom; Science Fiction Writers of
 America.

Verna Smith Trestrail, "Doc" Smith's only daughter,
mentions that both Harvard University and Syracuse
University have asked for Smith's holographs, diaries,
letters, personal papers, manuscripts, and pictures.
She adds: "It is common knowledge that the U.S. military has adopted and adapted many of Doc's 'brain
children'--Admiral Nimitz picked up his CIC sub-nano-
second computer system from the Lensman flagship *Z9M9Z*,
and used it for the Battle of the Coral Sea. Harvard
honored him in their alumni magazine for November 30,
1957, and George Washington University is doing a profile on him as one of their most honored alumni."

* * * * *

GEORGE H. SMITH

Full Name: George Henry Smith.
 Born October 27, 1922, at Vicksburg, Mississippi.
Son of George Henry Smith and Maria Eve Poche. Married
M. Jane Deer (a writer), February 10, 1950.

Education: B.A., University of Southern California,
 1950.

Career: Writer.
 "Writing is the only work I've ever done; free-lance
author since 1950. Although most of my work has been
outside the SF field, I started my professional career
almost exclusively in SF, and many of my early short
story sales were to SF pulps. Since then, I've written
and sold more material in other fields, men's magazines,
nonfiction books dealing with the occult, political
and biographical subjects."

First Professional Sale: "The Last Spring," in
 Startling Stories, August, 1953.

Agent: Scott Meredith, 580 Fifth Avenue, New York,
 NY 10036. Member: Science Fiction Writers of America.

Interests: Military miniatures and history. "Writing
 is the worse job in the world except for all the other
 jobs that have ever existed."

* * * * *

GEORGE O. SMITH

Full Name: George Oliver Smith.
 Born April 9, 1911, at Chicago, Illinois. Son of
Henry Robert Smith (a factory superintendent) and Mary
Jane Twigg. Married Helen Kunzler, 1936 (divorced,
1948); married Dona Louise Stebbins, 1949 (died, 1974).
Three children: Diana Helen (born 1939), George Oliver
Jr. (born 1943), Douglas Stewart (born 1952).

GEORGE O. SMITH (Cont.)

Education: Attended University of Chicago, 1929-30.

Career: Radio engineer.
    Radio service and repair, Chicago, 1932-35; radio
engineer, General Household, 1935-38; with Wells-Gar-
diner, 1938-40; with Philco, 1940-42; with Crosley,
1942-44; Editorial Engineer, Office of Scientific
Research and Development, National Defense Research
Council, 1944-45 ["this was a crash writing program
to get sonar maintenance manuals to the fleet; the
OSRD-NDRC jointly awarded a contract to the University
of California, which promptly set up a writing factory
high in the Empire State Building in New York, because
that's where the writers could be found; somewhere
along my checkered path there is, mouldering, a 'Certificate of Merit' award for having been a part of
this program"]; radio engineer, Philco, 1946-51; Manager, Components Engineering, Emerson Radio, New York,
1951-57; "intermission--heart attack," 1958-59; Senior
Technical Information Analyst, ITT Defense Communications, 1959-74; now retired.

First Professional Sale: "QRM--Interplanetary,"
    in Astounding Science Fiction, October, 1942.

Agent: Lurton Blassingame, 60 E. 42nd St., New York,
    NY 10017.

Interests: Boating, photography, wood and metal
    working.

Smith writes:
    "On 1 May 1974, I retired from the rat race after
some 40 years in the electronics whirlpool, and began
to relax and tamper with the typewriter again. We'd
disposed of our last income tax dependent in July of
1972, when he graduated with an Associate in Applied
Science degree from a strange joint called the Fashion
Institute of Technology in New York. None of this
ding-busted calculus for Douglas, with odd-ball terms
such as 'dielectric constant,' and 'permeability,'
and the Greek alphabet spattered all over the page.
He went in for interior design, and took to Arizona
where the action is. So Dona, my wife, suggested
in November, 1973, that we inquire about the Social
Security and the ITT Pension Plan, and take the money
and run--to some climate that does not drizzle all
spring, steam all summer, and make us run the furnace
all winter; and where we aren't faced with the second-
highest per-capita school tax in these here United
States.
    "Well, all I can say is that we missed a silver an-
niversary by three months and three days, and enjoyed
12 days of my retirement. Dona entered Riverview
Hospital on 13 May with a set of ugly complications
that ended with a rapid decline; she died on the 25th."

    "You asked me about the current trends in science
fiction. One of the popular topics for discussion
during the Post-War years was 'Has science caught up
with science fiction?'
    "The answer to that one is that science not only
caught up with SF, but passed it in a cloud of dust,
and emitted spare parts that the average writer could-
n't identify, let alone use. I couldn't resist the
remark in the Campbell memorial anthology about we-all
using 'old-hat stuff like vacuum tubes and thermionic
devices such as wide-band klystrons and travelling
wave tubes to operate Venus Equilateral.'
    "One could, in what we loftily call the 'good old
days,' get along with a flair for style, a talent for

"scribbling readable dialog, and a wide spattering of
scientific knowledge; compounded by an ability to argue
in sheer sophistry with a straight face--the 'what would
happen if...' game that made a lot of us regular contributors to the John W. Campbell school of science
fiction.
    "But science didn't catch up with science fiction.
Science came a-roaring along behind like Bobby Unser
or A. J. Foyt overtaking a Model T--and ran science
fiction right into the ground. To go on....
    "How can one write a good old-fashioned space opera
when we have sound scientific evidence that no form of
viable life can even exist on any of the Solar planets
except Earth? I forget which of the old Campbell classics it was (I think it was "Uncertainty"), in which one
of their problems in developing a 'ray gun' was that
one must pack umpty-skillion watts into a beam so that
enough power gets to the target--and that one required
a perfect reflector, otherwise the gun crew would get
more radiation than the target. They didn't know about
(I should have said 'he,' but it was also true that
'they' didn't) coherent wave fronts. Now with what I
hope is amused disdain, NASA is working with lasers
called 'death rays.'
    "More years back than I care to admit to, I conceived
the idea of doing a space opera in which the big grand
wind-up was to take place when the Outer Planets were
all more or less in line. This idea came because most
writers of space opera ignored the true geography (that
ain't at all right, dammit) geometry (and that isn't
either!) and I sure hate to use that overworked word
'configuration,' but you get the idea. Well, anyway,
while I was concocting the plot, the U.S. Printing
Office offered an inch-thick volume entitled The Positions of the Five Outer Planets from 1653 to 2060, and
I said that this was IT; I was going to plot the planetary positions, and write it as it had to be.
    "But then, space opera died a sudden death with the
demise of the Standard Magazines, and John W's growing
interest in Hubbard's 'New Science of the Mind' killed
that market, and the only place I've ever used it was
to illustrate that diagram in the Campbell anthology.
    "Then, some not-too-many years back, we were greeted
by a TV show called Star Trek, and I was prepared to
accuse it of one of the troubles with science fiction.
To wit:
    "The technical problem of creating an authentic-look-
ing set for a science fiction show is tremendous, primarily because it must appeal to the guy who doesn't
really care for science fiction but wants entertainment,
and one of the problems of science fiction is that it
especially appeals to a rather limited scope of thinking minds (when it is done right). Science fiction
movie sets abound with flashing neon tubes, the spark-
ladder, meters of strange design, steam whistles, and
air gauges, and other oddball hardware.
    "The alternative to this is to change the idea from
hardware to oddball people. So Captain Kirk and his
merry men went from one oddball planet to another,
peopled with normal-looking humans or near-humans, who
lived in strange and dangerous ways.
    "John W. wouldn't have given this kind of story house-
room; he called it 'travelogue,' and preferred to skip
it. The idea behind the travelogue story is to get to
Mars in a super-speed rocket, and then ride a thoat
across the sea bottoms of Barsoom for three thousand
haaads, having adventures. So now we read about faraway places full of bird people, cultures that live
under water, and the like.
    "Where is the science fiction of "The Roads Must Roll"
days? Gone, unhappily. The plan of those days was to
introduce some new device, and then write about how
normal men and women lived and coped with the culture

GEORGE O. SMITH (Cont.)

"it introduced. For example, read "Counter Foil" in Bob Silverberg's anthology. With some pride, I cooked up the answer to the transportation problem by inventing the teleport transit system (Teleportransit, Inc.) and writing about the average citizen and how it affected his life when he could get from one place to another in a flash by simply paying fare, and dialing his destination in a small booth.

"Now, there may be argument that Hal Clement's *Mission of Gravity* is travelogue--and possibly it is-- but here we read about a planet with a strange environment caused by its rapid revolution, and human beings coping with the technical details of operating on it, with the help and sometimes hindrance of a life form that had evolved there. The latter, I suspect, was installed in the story to show by contrast how the two different planetary environments were adapted to their own planets."

* * * * *

H. ALLEN SMITH

Full Name: Harry Allen Smith.
Born December 19, 1907, at McLeansboro, Illinois. Son of Henry Smith and Adeline Allen. Married Nelle Simpson, February 14, 1927. Two children: Allen Wyatt, Nancy Jean.

Career: Writer.
After finishing eighth grade, Smith worked as a chicken picker in a poultry house, a shoeshine boy in a barber shop, a newspaper reporter in Indiana, Kentucky, Florida, Oklahoma, and Colorado; with the United Press, New York, 1929-34; rewrite man, *New York World-Telegram*, 1936-41; full-time writer, 1941-76. Died February 24, 1976. Member: Society of the Silurians; Authors Guild.

Agent: Harold Matson Co., 22 E. 40th St., New York, NY 10016.

* * * * *

MARTIN SMITH

Full Name: Martin Smith.
Born 1942. Son of John Smith (an engineer and designer) and Louisa Lopez (a teacher). Married Emily Arnold (a researcher). Two children: Ellen, Luisa.

Education: B.A., University of Pennsylvania, 1964.

Career: Writer.
Has been a reporter for the Associated Press and the *Philadelphia Bulletin*, and an editor for Magazine Management; full-time writer, 1968-DATE.

Agent: Knox Burger, New York.

Member: Authors Guild.

Martin Smith writes:
"Since 1968, I have been a full-time writer, which leaves no time for anything else. At the moment, I am working on a Russian novel, but that project has been going on so long it has become a condition, like saying 'at present I live in New York!' As for my SF novels, *The Analog Bullet* was a complete screw-up.

"*The Indians Won* had a genuinely good idea and intentions which did not reach success, but of which I can be content." Smith writes thrillers as "Simon Quinn."

* * * * *

W. J. SMITH

Full Name: Walter James Smith.
Born April 7, 1917, at West Bromwich, England. Son of Thomas Dawes Smith (a clerk) and Elizabeth Ann Evans. Married Catherine Mary Kerr, August 12, 1953. Three children: Andrew James (born 1954), Robert James (born 1955), Margaret Mary (born 1958).

Career: Certificate, Alsager Teachers Training College, 1950.

Career: Headmaster.
Has been a salesman, and a drama tutor for various English schools; currently Deputy Headmaster in Twickenham, England.

First Professional Sale: "Gadget," in *Hobbies*, 1952.

Honors: L.R.A.M., acting.

Interests:
"Modelling historical figures, raising a family. I have the strongest interest in SF, into which I try to introduce two features I find generally lacking, but of universal interest: light romance, and the puzzle element. Feel I might even be trying to break newish ground here. Find Wells still the top SF man."

* * * * *

WILBUR SMITH

Full Name: Wilbur Addison Smith.
Born January 9, 1933, at Broken Hill, Northern Rhodesia. Son of Herbert James Smith and Elfreda Lawrence. Married Jewell Slabbert, August 28, 1964.

Education: Bachelor of Commerce, Rhodes University, 1954.

Career: Writer.
With Goodyear Tire and Rubber Company, Port Elizabeth, South Africa, 1954-58; with H. J. Smith & Sons Ltd., Salisbury, Rhodesia, 1958-63; full-time writer, 1964-DATE. Member: Chartered Institute of Secretaries; Rhodesian Wildlife Conservation Association; British Sub Aqua Club.

Agent: Monica McCall, 667 Madison Avenue, New York, NY 10021.

* * * * *

VIRGINIA DRIVING HAWK SNEVE

Full Name: Virginia Driving Hawk Sneve.
Born February 21, 1933, at Rosebud, South Dakota. Daughter of James H. Driving Hawk (an Episcopal priest) and Rose Ross. Married Vance M. Sneve (a teacher of industrial arts), July 14, 1955. Three children: Shirley Kay, Paul Marshall, Alan Edward. Education: B.S., South Dakota State University, 1954; M.Ed., 1969.

VIRGINIA DRIVING HAWK SNEVE (Cont.)

Career: Editor and teacher.
   Teacher of English in public schools, White, SD,
1954-55, and Pierre, SD, 1955-56; Teacher of English
and Speech, Flandreau Indian School, Flandreau, South
Dakota, 1965-66; Guidance Counselor, 1966-70; Editor,
Brevet Press, Sioux Falls, South Dakota, 1972-DATE;
member of Rosebud Sioux Tribe; Member, Board of Directors, United Sioux Tribes Cultural Arts, 1972-73.

Awards: Manuscript Award in American Indian category,
   Interracial Council for Minority Books for Children,
   1971, for *Jimmy Yellow Hawk*.

Member: National League of American Pen Women; South
   Dakota Press Women.

* * * * *

C. P. SNOW

Full Name: Charles Percy Snow.
   Born October 15, 1905, at Leicester, England. Son
of William Edward Snow (a shoe factory clerk) and Ada
Sophia Robinson. Married Pamela Hansford Johnson (a
novelist and critic), July 14, 1950. One son, Philip
Charles Hansford.

Education: B.Sc., University College, Leicester,
   1927; M.Sc., 1928; Ph.D., Christ's College, Cambridge
University, 1930.

Career: Physicist, writer, lecturer.
   Fellow, Christ's College, Cambridge University, 1930-
50; Commissioner, British Civil Service, 1945-60; Physicist and Director, English Electric Company, London,
1947-64; Director, Educational Film Centre, London,
1961-64; Parliamentary Secretary, Ministry of Technology, 1964-66; lecturer at various colleges and universities; free-lance author, 1932-DATE; served as
Director of Technical Personnel for the Ministry of
Labour during World War II, and was placed on the list
prepared by Himmler of people to be taken into custody
after Germany occupied Great Britain.

Honors & Awards:
   James Tait Black Memorial Prize, 1955, for *The Masters* and *The New Men*; LL.D., University of Leicester,
1959; from University of Liverpool, 1960; from St.
Andrews University, 1962; from Polytechnic Institute
of Brooklyn, 1962; from University of Bridgeport, 1966;
D.Litt., Dartmouth College, 1960; from Bard College,
1962; from Temple University, 1963; from Syracuse University, 1963; from University of Pittsburgh, 1964;
D.H.L., Kenyon College, 1961; from Washington University, 1963; from University of Michigan, 1963; Doctor
of Philological Sciences from Rostov State University,
1963; D.Sc., Pennsylvania Military College, 1966;
Commander of the British Empire, 1943; knighted by
Queen Elizabeth II, 1957; created Baron Snow, 1964.

* * * * *

E. V. SNYDER

Full Name: Eugene Vincent Snyder.
   Born January 1, 1943, at New York, New York. Son
of Eugene Vincent Snyder and Mary Farrell. Married
Nancy Leonhardt, May 12, 1968. One daughter, Laura
Jean (born 1971).

Education: B.A., Hofstra University, 1964; M.A.,
   1970; Ph.D., New York University, 1975.

Career: Professor.
   With U.S. Army, 1967-69, serving in Germany and Viet-
nam; awarded Bronze Star, Presidential Unit Citation,
Vietnam Service Medal; retired as Captain; Assistant
Professor, Brookdale Community College, 1970-DATE.

First Professional Sale: *Ecodeath*, Doubleday &
   Co., 1972 (with William Jon Watkins).

Member: Alpha Psi Omega; American College Theatre
   Association.

Interests:
   Golf, tennis, karate, reading science fiction. "SF
is fast moving from avocation to vocation with me. I
have been reading it since high school, and have seen
too many things read come true, to take it all lightly."

* * * * *

GUY SNYDER

Full Name: Guy Eugene Snyder, Jr.
   Born May 3, 1951, at Columbus, Ohio. Son of Guy Eugene Snyder (a sales representative for an oil company)
and Rita Clair Brown.

Education: B.A., Wayne State University, 1973.

Career: Writer and editor.
   Has been a parks and recreation department laborer
and a garbageman; Construction Reports Editor, *Michigan
Contractor & Builder*, 1974-DATE.

First Professional Sale: *Testament XXI*, DAW Books,
   1973.

Member: Science Fiction Writers of America.

Interests:
   "I'm a collector of classical music recordings, a member of various local science fiction fan organizations,
and an advocate for an increase in the quality of contemporary science fiction.
   "I tend to be a loner. I also tend to write uncon-
ventional stories, and get letters from editors protes-
ting that my works don't fit the demands of their mar-
ketplaces. But I'm confident I will succeed someday.
   "The original title of *Testament XXI* was *The Well
Tempered Woman's Waist*; the publisher did not like my
title, and suggested the change."

* * * * *

ZILPHA KEATLEY SNYDER

Full Name: Zilpha Keatley Snyder.
   Born May 11, 1927, at Lemoore, California. Daughter
of William Solon Keatley (a rancher) and Dessa Jepson
(a teacher). Married Larry Alan Snyder, June 18, 1950.
Three children: Susan Melissa (born 1954), Douglas
Clark (born 1956), Benton Lee (foster son; born 1954).

Education: B.A., Whittier College.

Career: Writer.
   Teacher in California, New York, Washington, and Alaska for nine years between 1949-63; Master Teacher,

ZILPHA KEATLEY SNYDER (Cont.)

University of California, Berkeley, 1959-61; full-
time writer, 1964-DATE.

First Professional Sale: *Season of Ponies*,
Atheneum, 1964.

Honors & Awards:
The Egypt Game (1967) was a Newbery Honor Book,
won a prize in the Spring Book Festival, New York,
received the Lewis Carroll Shelf Award, and was awarded the George Stone Recognition of Merit, 1973; *The
Changeling* (1970) received the Christopher Medal,
and was a Junior Literary Guild choice; *The Headless
Cupid* (1971) was a Newbery Honor Book, a Junior Guild
choice, was on the Hans Christian Andersen International Honors List, and received the Christopher Medal and the William Allen White Award, 1974; *The
Witches of Worm* (1972) was a Newbery Honor Book.

* * * * *

ROBERT SOBEL

Full Name: Robert Sobel.
Born February 19, 1931, at New York, New York. Son
of Philip Sobel (an artist) and Blanche Levinson.
Married Carole Ritter (a teacher), June 30, 1958.
One son, David.

Education: B.S.S., City College of New York, 1951;
M.A., New York University, 1952; Ph.D., 1957.

Career: Professor of History.
Instructor, New York University, 1956; Associate
Professor of History, Hofstra University, 1957-DATE;
Consulting Editor, Year, Inc. Member: American His-
torical Association; American Economic Association;
American Association of University Professors; Phi
Alpha Theta.

* * * * *

JERRY SOHL

Full Name: Gerald Allan Sohl, Sr.
Born December 2, 1913, at Los Angeles, California.
Son of Fred J. Sohl (a pharmacist) and Florence Wray
(an artist). Married Jean Gordon, October 28, 1943.
Three children: Gerald Allan, Jr. (born 1944), Mar-
tha Jane (born 1947), Jennifer (born 1949).

Education: Attended Central College, 1933-34.

Career: Writer.
Was a newspaperman for many years before turning
to writing; Reporter and Editor, *Daily Pantagraph*,
1945-58; free-lance novelist, 1952-DATE ["let Bob
Tucker talk me into writing my first book, and I've
been unable to stop writing since"]; screenwriter
for various television shows, including *Star Trek,
The Invaders, The Outer Limits, Twilight Zone, G. E.
Theatre, Alfred Hitchcock Presents*, etc., 1958-DATE.
Instructor (English), Moorpark College, 1974.

First Professional Sale: "A Work of Art," in
Chicago Daily News, 1935.

Agent: Scott Meredith, 580 Fifth Avenue, New York,
NY 10036.

Member:
Screenwriters Guild; Writers Guild of America, West;
Science Fiction Writers of America; Mystery Writers of
America.

Interests: Pianist, printer, psychiatry (research,
not practice), hiking, golf, travelling, sociology,
anthropology, ethics.

Sohl writes:
"My principal goal in writing is to try to show that
each person is an individual, and is valuable in himself no matter who he is, and that irresponsible people
who do not recognize human worth get only what is coming
to them, whether it is such a minor thing as the mis-
eries, or a major thing like a lifetime jail sentence.
"As to whether or not science fiction will ever become as lucrative as general fiction or nonfiction, I
would have to say no, I don't think it will.
"For *The Lemon Eaters* (Simon & Schuster), for example, I earned in excess of $100,000. Of course, as
has been noted, this was a mainstream novel, and as
such had more exposure and general appeal.
"On the other hand, my science fiction classic, *Cos-
tigan's Needle*, has yet to earn more than $5000, inclu-
ding all editions, both foreign and domestic, and the
SF book club notwithstanding.
"Is it any wonder then that I have turned away from
science fiction?
"I must add what I see as the truth, and that is that
most adult science fiction readers seem hung up on an
adolescent level somewhere, for I find little in it
these days that appeals to me. The writing is, for
the most part, atrocious, and the old guard has become
so conservative that they are ridiculous.
"For that reason, I am frankly depressed, because
I think something may have gone out of my own life,
which is that wonderful 'what if...?' feeling that I
once felt reading Hugo Gernsback and Eando Binder. I
think those at the forefront of science fiction tend
to regard themselves as gurus, with the rest of the
world far behind them somewhere. Believe me, they're
not. It is they who are far, far behind. The future
is not in the nuts and bolts of SF, but in the exploration of inner space of individuals, the brain and the
genes.
"Adult science fiction is not well received by the
rank and file of SF aficionados."

* * * * *

DAVID A. SOHN

Full Name: David A. Sohn.
Born November 28, 1929, at Columbus, Ohio. Son of
Albert Edward Sohn and Margaret Crittenden. Married
Elizabeth Manning, October 15, 1954. Four children:
Matthew, Elizabeth, Jennifer, Andrew.

Education: A.B., Wabash College, 1950; A.M., Indiana
University, 1952.

Career: Instructor.
Instructor in English, Middlesex Junior High School,
Darien, Connecticut, 1952-67; Curriculum Consultant
in Language Arts, School District 65, Evanston, Ill.,
1968-DATE; Asst. Supervisor of Study Skills, Yale University, 1957-66; consultant to Bantam Books.

Member: International Reading Association; National
Council of Teachers of English; National Education
Association; National Reading Conference.

IVAN SOUTHALL

Full Name: Ivan Francis Southall.
   Born June 8, 1921, at Canterbury, Victoria, Australia. Son of Francis Gordon Southall (in insurance) and Rachel Elizabeth Voutier. Married Joyce Blackburn, September 8, 1945. Four children: Andrew John, Roberta Joy, Elizabeth Rose, Melissa Frances.

Education: Attended Melbourne Technical College, 1937-41.

Career: Writer.
   Process engraver, *Melbourne Herald and Weekly Times*, 1936-41, 1947; full-time author, 1948-DATE; past president, Community Youth Organization, Victoria; Foundation President, Knoxbrooke Training Centre for the Intellectually Handicapped, Victoria. Member: Australian Society of Authors.

Awards:
   Australian Children's Book of the Year awards, 1966, *Ash Road*; 1968, *To the Wild Sky*; 1971, *Bread and Honey*; Australian Picture Book of the Year Award, 1969, for *Sly Old Wardrobe*; Japanese Government's Children's Welfare and Culture Encouragement Award, 1969, for *Ash Road*.

* * * * *

STEVEN M. SOUZA

Full Name: Steven Michael Souza.
   Born November 3, 1953, at New Bedford, Massachusetts. Son of Arthur A. Souza and Helen Macedo.

Education: Attended Stonehill College, 1971-DATE.

Career: Student. Member: American Chemical Society.

First Professional Sale: *The Espers*, Lenox Hill Press, 1972.

Interests:
   Electronics, horror and sci-fi films, art, comic collecting. "After finishing school, I hope to get into an active branch of chemistry, although I do intend to continue writing. A distinct possibility for my career would be technical writing."

* * * * *

LEWIS SOWDEN

Full Name: Lewis Sowden.
   Born March 24, 1903, at Manchester, England. Son of Jacob Sowden or Soden (a businessman) and Anna Mofson. Married Dora Leah Levitt (a music and ballet critic), 1936.

Education: M.A., University of the Witwatersrand, 1928.

Career: Journalist.
   Journalist, 1928-74; Assistant Editor and Drama Critic, *Rand Daily Mail*, Johannesburg, South Africa, 1951-66; Staff Editor, *Encyclopaedia Judaica*, 1966-71; Foreign Correspondent, South African Morning Newspaper Group, 1971-74. Died August 1974.

First Professional Sale: *The Union of South Africa*, Doubleday, Doran, 1943.

Agent: A. P. Watt & Son, 26/28 Bedford Row, London WC1R 4HL, England.

Awards:
   U. S. State Department Grant for touring U.S., 1961-62 ["made protest against South African Foreign Minister at the U.N. General Assembly, November, 1961"].

Member:
   South African Society of Journalists (Chairman); South African P.E.N. Club (past chairman); Sigma Delta Chi.

Sowden notes: "On returning to South Africa in 1962, I was deprived of my passport by the South African Government, but allowed to leave on a one-way exit permit in March of 1966."

* * * * *

ROBERT SPEAIGHT

Full Name: Robert William Speaight.
   Born January 14, 1904, at St. Margaret's Bay, Kent, England. Son of Frederick William Speaight (a company director) and Emily Isabella Elliot. Married Esther Evelyn Bowen, 1935; married Bridget Laura Bramwell Bosworth-Smith, May 28, 1951. Three children: Patrick William Ellis, Teresa Clara Davison, Crispin John.

Education: M.A., Lincoln College, Oxford University, 1925.

Career: Actor, author, lecturer.
   Started his theatrical career with the Liverpool Repertory Theatre, 1926; toured Egypt with Shakespearina Company, 1927; played leading Shakespearian roles at Old Vic, 1931-32; has appeared in dozens of roles in England, the U.S., Canada, France, and Scotland; lecturer for British Council on tours abroad; broadcaster and recording artist for English poetry; free-lance author, 1932-76. Member: Royal Society of Literature (Fellow); Beefsteak Club; Garrick Club. Died April 4, 1976.

Honors: Commander of the Order of the British Empire, 1958; Legion of Honour, 1969.

* * * * *

ROBERT DONALD SPECTOR

Full Name: Robert Donald Spector.
   Born September 21, 1922, at New York, New York. Son of Morris Spector (a salesman) and Helen Spiegel (a bookkeeper). Married Eleanor Luskin, August 19, 1945. Two children: Stephen Brett (born 1948), Eric Charles (born 1951).

Education:
   B.A., Long Island University, 1948; M.A., New York University, 1949; Ph.D., Columbia University, 1962.

Career: Professor of English.
   Instructor, Long Island University, 1948-58; Asst. Professor, 1958-61; Associate Professor, 1961-65; Professor of English, and Chairman, Dept. of English, 1965-DATE; series editor, Johnson Reprint Corporation, 1967-74. Honors: Travel Grant, Swedish Government, 1966; Fellow, Huntington Library, 1974.

ROBERT DONALD SPECTOR (Cont.)

First Professional Sale: "The Year 1939," in *Upward Magazine*, 1940.

Member: On Board of Trustees, Long Island University, 1969-70; American Scandinavian Foundation.

"I have combined interests in 18th century English literature and contemporary comparative literature. My work in Gothic and science fiction covers the subject from the 18th century on."

* * * * *

J. E. SPERRY

Full Name: Jane Eisenstat.
Born March 2, 1920, at New York, New York. Daughter of Frank Madison Sperry (an artist) and Olga Sperry. Married Benjamin Eisenstat (an artist), August 23, 1940. Two children: Kathryn Sperry, Alice Amanda. Education: Attended Pennsylvania Academy of Fine Arts.

Career: Art teacher.
Drawing teacher, Fleisher Art Memorial, Philadelphia, for eight years; Instructor in Drawing and Painting, Philadelphia Museum College of Art, 1957-DATE.

Awards: Mary Smith Prize, Philadelphia Water Color Club, 1958.

* * * * *

NORMAN SPINRAD

Full Name: Norman Richard Spinrad.
Born September 15, 1940, at New York, New York. Son of Morris and Ray Spinrad.

Education: B.S., City College of New York.

Career: Writer.
Has been a literary agent and a television writer; full-time author, 1963-DATE.

First Professional Sale: "The Last of the Romany," in *Analog*, May, 1963.

Member: Science Fiction Writers of America (Vice President, 1972-74); Writers Guild of America, West.

Awards: Jupiter Award, Best Novella, 1974 (1975), "Riding the Torch."

* * * * *

PATRICIA SQUIRES

Full Name: Patricia Sylvia Ball.
Born September 18, 1936, at Yapton near Arundel, Sussex, England. Daughter of George Richard Henry Deegan (a maintenance and decorating contractor) and Lillian Talbot. Married Eric Ball, December 17, 1955. Two children: Sandra Patricia, Jacqueline Anne.

Career: Writer.
Employed on a small farm in tasks concerned with fruits and vegetables, 1951-53; welder of wire products,

1953-55; writer.

Interests: Gardening, decorating, needlework, historic places, reading, country walking.

* * * * *

BRIAN M. STABLEFORD

Full Name: Brian Michael Stableford.
Born July 25, 1948, at Shipley, Yorkshire, England. Son of William Ernest Stableford (an aircraft designer) and Joyce Wilkinson (a school teacher). Married Vivien Owen, September 3, 1973.

Education: B.A., University of York, 1969; Graduate student working on his doctorate, 1972-DATE.

Career: Writer.

First Professional Sale: "The Earth and the Moon" (a poem), in *Manchester Evening News*, 1957.

Agent: Janet Freer, 118 Tottenham Court Rd., London, W1, England

Interests:
Gambling, word games. "Have webbed toes. Eyesight very poor. Allergic to dust and miscellaneous things. Was transplanted from working-class Catholic school to middle-class Anglican school at age of seven--this remains only actual experience of entering an alien world, but may be not unconnected with present occupation."

* * * * *

DAVID STACTON

Full Name: David Derek Stacton.
Born April 25, 1925, near Minden, Nevada. Son of David Stacton and Dorothy Green. Education: Attended Stanford University, 1941-43; B.A., University of California, 1950; student, Stanford Radio and Television Institute, 1955.

Career: Writer.
Glasgow Visiting Professor, Washington & Lee University, 1965-66; Guggenheim Fellow, 1960-61; full-time writer, 1954-68. Died February 20, 1968.

Agent: Paul R. Reynolds, 599 Fifth Avenue, New York, NY 10017.

* * * * *

BEN STAHL

Full Name: Benjamin Stahl.
Born September 7, 1910, at Chicago, Illinois. Son of Benjamin Franklin Stahl (in real estate) and Grace Meyer. Married Ella Lehocky, December 19, 1936. Four children: Benjamin F., Gail, Regina, David F. A.

Career: Artist and writer.
Artist and illustrator, 1933-DATE; co-founder and adviser, Famous Artists School, Westport, Conn., 1949-DATE; has taught painting at School of the Art Institute of Chicago, and American Academy of Art; Member, Florida State Art Commission; author, 1965-DATE; has had numerous exhibitions of his paintings.

BEN STAHL (Cont.)

Honors & Awards:
Saltus Gold Medal of National Academy of Design,
1949; Sequoia Award, Best Children's Book, 1965, for
Blackbeard's Ghost; 27 other awards.

Member:
Society of Illustrators; Artists and Writers, New
York; Players, New York; Sarasota Art Association;
Westport Artists (founder/the first president).

* * * * *

J. K. STANFORD

Full Name: John Keith Stanford.
Born April 29, 1892, at Bromley, Kent, England. Son
of Edward Stanford and Caroline Fraser. Married Evelyn
Lushington, 1919; married Eleanor Davies, 1927. Two
sons, two daughters.

Education: M.A., St. John's College, Oxford University, 1919.

Career: Writer.
With Indian Civil Service, 1919-38; Director, Edward
Stanford Ltd. (map publishers), 1937-50; Chairman of
the Board, 1944-50; Member of the Vernay-Cutting Expedition into northeast Burma, 1938-39; explored the bird
life of Cyrenaica, 1952; writer, 1944-71. Member: British Ornithologists Union (Vice President, 1951-52); Kipling Society (past Chairman). Died September 24, 1971.

Agent: A. P. Watt & Son, 26/28 Bedford Row, London
WC1R 4HL, England.

* * * * *

OLAF STAPLEDON

Full Name: William Olaf Stapledon.
Born May 10, 1886, at Wallasey, Cheshire, England.
Son of William Clibbett Stapledon (a shipping manager)
and Emmeline Miller. Married Agnes Zena Miller, July
16, 1919. Two children: Mary Sydney (born 1920),
John David (born 1923).

Education: M.A., Liverpool University, 1909?; Ph.D.,
1910?.

Career: Writer and teacher.
"After spending a year on the staff of the Manchester Grammar School, and eighteen months in shipping in
Liverpool and Port Said, Egypt, he lectured extramural-
ly for Liverpool University, in English literature,
industrial history, and psychology. He served in
France with the Friends Ambulance Unit from 1915-18,
and married his cousin, Agnes Miller, from Australia
in 1919. At the time of his death, on September 6,
1950, at Caldy Wirral, Cheshire, England, Olaf Stapledon had only one grandson. He now has five grandchildren, and three great-grandchildren."

Agnes Stapledon writes about her husband:
"When Olaf Stapledon wrote his first imaginative
history of the human race, which he called *Last and
First Men*, he thought of it as 'philosophical fantasy.'
He was unaware at that time (1930) of the term 'science fiction,' and was amazed at the interest which it
evoked in America among science fiction enthusiasts."

ARTHUR D. STAPP

Full Name: Arthur Donald Stapp.
Born December 26, 1906, at Seattle, Washington. Son
of Orrill V. Stapp (a piano teacher) and Frances Bailey.
Married Eleanor Blakkestad (a children's librarian),
August 6, 1949. One daughter, Marilyn.

Education: Attended New York University, 1945-46,
and Rand School, 1947-48.

Career: Writer.
Co-Publisher, *North Central Outlook*, 1923-41; writer,
primarily of juvenile books, 1946-DATE. Member:
Authors Club; Washington Alpine Club. Died 1972.

* * * * *

CHRISTINA STEAD

Full Name: Christina Ellen Stead.
Born July 17, 1902, at Rockdale, Sydney, Australia.
Daughter of David George Stead and Ellen Butters. Mar-
ried William James Blake (an author; surname originally
Blech; died 1968). Education: Teacher's Certificate,
Teachers' College, Sydney University.

Career: Writer.
Worked as a public school teacher, teacher of abnor-
mal children, and a demonstrator in a psychology lab,
in Australia; grain company clerk, London, 1928-29;
bank clerk, Paris, France, 1930-35; lived in U.S. in
late 1930s and 1940s; senior writer, Metro-Goldwyn-Mayer, 1943; Instructor, Workshop in the Novel, New York
University, 1943-44; full-time writer, 1934-DATE.

Agent: Cyrilly Abels, 597 Fifth Avenue, New York, NY
10017.

Awards: Aga Khan Prize, 1966; Arts Council of Great
Britain grant, 1967; Australian National University
fellowship in the creative arts, 1969.

* * * * *

BYRON STEEL

Full Name: Francis Steegmüller.
Born July 3, 1906, at New Haven, Connecticut. Son
of Joseph F. Steegmuller and Bertha R. Tierney. Married Beatrice Stein, July 1, 1935 (died 1961); married
Shirley Hazzard, December 22, 1963.

Education: B.A., Columbia University, 1927; M.A.,
1928.

Career: Author, 1930-DATE. Member: National Institute of Arts and Letters; Phi Beta Kappa; Century Club.

Awards: Red Badge Mystery Prize, 1940; National Book
Award, 1971, for *Cocteau: A Biography*.

* * * * *

MARY Q. STEELE

Full Name: Mary Quintard Steele.
Born May 8, 1922, at Chattanooga, Tennessee. Daughter
of Gilbert Eaton Govan (a librarian) and Christine
Noble. Married William O. Steele (a writer), June 1,
1943. Children: Mary Quintard, Jenifer Susan, Allerton.

MARY Q. STEELE (Cont.)

Education: B.S., University of Chattanooga, 1943.

Career: Writer, 1958-DATE. Awards: Aurianne Award
of the American Library Association, 1966, for *Big
Blue Island*.

* * * * *

ANDREW JACOB STEIGER

Full Name: Andrew Jacob Steiger.
  Born July 1, 1900, at Pittsburgh, Pennsylvania.
Son of August Jacob Steiger (a florist) and Mary Bre-
thauer. Married Alexandra M. Chibirnova, June 6, 1939.
Education: M.A., Columbia University, 1931; attended
Union Theological Seminary, 1930-31.

Career: Reporter and correspondent.
  Secretary of Moscow Bureau, *New York Times*, 1938-39;
Foreign News Editor, CBS, 1941-45; Reports Officer,
U.N. Relief and Rehabilitation Mission, Minsk, 1946-
47; Moscow correspondent, McGraw-Hill World News,
1947-49; Moscow correspondent, Reuters News Agency,
1950-54; news writer, Universal Trade Press Syndicate,
New York, 1956-DATE.

Member: Authors League; Overseas Press Club; American Association of Translators; American Association
  for the Advancement of Science; English-Speaking
  Union.

* * * * *

BRAD STEIGER

Full Name: Eugene E. Olson.
  Born February 19, 1936, at Bode, Iowa. Son of
Erling E. Olson (a farmer) and Hazel Jensen. Married
Marilyn Gjefle. Four children: Bryan, Steven, Kari,
Julie. Education: Attended Luther College, 1953-57,
and University of Iowa, 1963.

Career: Writer.
  High school teacher in Clinton, Iowa, 1957-63; in-
structor of literature and creative writing, Luther
College, 1963-67; President, Other Dimensions Inc.,
Decorah, Iowa, 1970-DATE; lecturer at colleges and
for private groups; conducts syndicated radio program,
The Strange World of Brad Steiger, and co-hosts *Thres-
hold*, a radio interview program; writer, 1964-DATE.
Member: American Society for Psychical Research;
Authors Guild.

Agent: Jay Garon-Brooke Associates, 415 Central
  Park West, New York, NY 10025.

* * * * *

JOHN STEINBECK

Full Name: John Ernst Steinbeck.
  Born February 27, 1902, at Salinas, California.
Son of John Ernst Steinbeck (a county treasurer) and
Olive Hamilton (a school teacher). Married Carol
Henning, 1930 (divorced, 1943); married Gwyn Conger,
1943 (divorced, 1949); married Elaine Scott, 1950.
Two sons: Tom, John IV. Education: Special student
at Stanford University, 1919-25.

Career: Writer.
  Has been a hod-carrier, apprentice painter, laboratory assistant, ranch hand, fruitpicker, construction
worker at Madison Square Garden, and reporter; writer,
1929-68. Died 1968.

Honors & Awards:
  Three-time winner of the Commonwealth Club of Cali-
fornia General Literature Gold Medal for Work by a
California author, 1936, for *Tortilla Flat*; 1937, for
In Dubious Battle; 1940, for *The Grapes of Wrath*; New
York Drama Critics Circle Silver Plaque, 1938, for
play version of "Of Mice and Men"; Pulitzer Prize for
Literature, 1940, for *The Grapes of Wrath*; Nobel Prize
for Literature, 1962.

Agent: McIntosh & Otis, 475 Fifth Avenue, New York,
  NY 10017.

* * * * *

CHRIS STEINBRUNNER

Full Name: Peter Christian Steinbrunner.
  Born December 25, 1933, at New York, New York. Son
of Josef and Maria Steinbrunner.

Education: M.A., Fordham University.

Career: Film manager.
  Producer and film manager of *Journey to Adventure*,
a syndicated travel show; writer, 1971-DATE.

Member:
  Mystery Writers of America (past Vice President);
Science Fiction Writers of America; Baker St. Irregulars;
Sons of the Desert; Fantasy Film Club; Knights of Co-
lumbus.

* * * * *

DANIEL STERN

Full Name: Daniel Stern.
  Born January 18, 1928, at New York, New York. Son
of Morris S. Stern (a foreman) and Dora Stern. Education: Attended New School for Social Research.

Career: Advertising copywriter.
  Cellist, Indianapolis Symphony Orchestra, 1948-49;
free-lance magazine writer, New York, 1955-58; currently an advertising copywriter. Awards: Huntington
Hartford fellow, 1955, 1957.

* * * * *

PHILIP VAN DOREN STERN

Full Name: Philip Van Doren Stern.
  Born September 10, 1900, at Wyalusing, Pennsylvania.
Son of I. U. Stern and Anne Van Doren. Married Lillian
Diamond, 1928. One daughter, Marguerite Louise.

Education: Litt.B., Rutgers University, 1924.

Career: Author and editor.
  Worked in advertising, 1924-26; worked as a designer
for Alfred A. Knopf, Simon & Schuster; part-time Editor
of Pocket Books in the 1940s; Editor and member of the

PHILIP VAN DOREN STERN (Cont.)

planning board of the U.S. Office of War Information, 1941-43; General Manager, Editions for the Armed Forces, 1943-45; Vice-President in Change of Editorial Work, Pocket Books, 1945-46; free-lance writer and editor, 1932-DATE.

Honors & Awards:
  Litt.D., Rutgers University, 1940, and from Lincoln College, 1958; Fletcher Pratt Award of the New York Civil War Round Table, 1958, for *An End to Valor*; Guggenheim Fellow, 1959-60.

Agent: Marie Rodell, 141 E. 55th St., New York, NY 10022.

* * * * *

CLIFFORD STEVENS

Full Name: Clifford Stevens.
  Born March 27, 1926, at Brattleboro, Vermont. Son of Clarence Frederick Stevens and Agnes Murray. Education: Attended Creighton University, 1945-46, 1959-60, and New Melleray Abbey Seminary, 1946-52, and Conception Seminary, 1954-56.

Career: Priest.
  Worked in a California shipyard for a year before studying for the priesthood; ordained Roman Catholic priest in Omaha, 1956; parish priest, Omaha Diocese, 1956-61; Chaplain, U.S. Air Force, 1961-69; with the Institute of Man and Science, Rensselaerville, NY, 1969.

* * * * *

D. E. STEVENSON

Full Name: Dorothy Emily Stevenson.
  Born 1892, at Edinburgh, Scotland. Daughter of David Alan Stevenson (a civil engineer) and Anne Roberts. Married James Reid Peploe (a major in the British Army), 1916. Three children: Robert, Rosemary, John.

Career: Writer, 1929-DATE; President, Dumfriesshire Girl Guides Association. Died December 30, 1973.

Honors: Boston University created a D. E. Stevenson Room in their library, and several of her books were made selections of the Christian Herald Family Bookshelf.

Agent: Curtis Brown Ltd., 60 E. 56th St., New York, NY 10022.

* * * * *

BRUCE STEWART

Full Name: Bruce Stewart.
  Born April 9, 1927, at Auckland, New Zealand. Son of Robert Stewart (a taxi driver) and Esther Walsh. Married Helen Noonan, October 16, 1951. Six children: Mark, Catherine, Christopher, Clare, Dominic, Susannah.

Education: B.A., Auckland University, 1948.

Career: Writer and actor, working mainly in British

television.

First Professional Sale: "Shadow of a Pale Horse," a teleplay shown on Granada TV, London, 1959.

Agent: Harvey Unna, London, England.

Awards: Edgar Award, 1961; Charles Henry Foyle Award, 1966. Member: Writers Guild of Great Britain; British Film Institute.

* * * * *

FRED MUSTARD STEWART

Full Name: Fred Mustard Stewart.
  Born September 17, 1936. Son of Simeon Stewart (a banker) and Janet Mustard. Married Joan Richardson (a theatrical agent), March 18, 1968.

Education: A.B., Princeton University, 1954.

Career: Writer.
  Served in the U.S. Coast Guard, 1955-58, retiring as a Lieutenant j.g.; free-lance author. Member: P.E.N.

Agent: William Morris Agency, 151 El Camino, Beverly Hills, CA 90212.

* * * * *

GEORGE R. STEWART

Full Name: George Rippey Stewart.
  Born May 31, 1895, at Sewickley, Pennsylvania. Son of George Rippey Stewart (an orange grower) and Ella May Wilson (a teacher). Married Theodosia Burton, May 17, 1924. Two children: Jill Stewart (born 1925), John Harris (born 1928).

Education:
  A.B., Princeton University, 1917; M.A., University of California, Berkeley, 1920; Ph.D., Columbia University, 1922.

Career: Professor.
  Instructor, University of Michigan, 1922-23; Professor, University of California, Berkeley, 1923-62; now retired.

First Professional Sale: A short poem to *Judge*, 1919.

Honors & Awards:
  International Fantasy Award, Fiction, 1951, for *Earth Abides*; Hillman Award; Wagner Medal (for his books on California history); Commonwealth Club of California medals for *Ordeal by Hunger* and *East of the Giants*; L.H.D., University of California, Berkeley.

Member:
  Phi Beta Kappa; American Name Society; Bohemian Club, San Francisco; Faculty Club of University of California.

Interests: Bookbinding, fly-fishing.

Stewart comments: "*Earth Abides* was my only SF book. Some people say it is not science fiction at all, but I am not concerned about classification. It has a strangely intense effect upon many people--one that I cannot altogether explain. People tell me, 'It changed

GEORGE R. STEWART (Cont.)

"my life.' Thornton Beach State Park recently dedicated their nature trail to me, and at their dedica-
tion, a ranger read from the ending of the book, with
considerable effect upon the audience. The power of
the book may be that it escapes from the mechanistic
trap (which ruins so much science fiction), and becomes
humanistic."

* * * * *

MARY STEWART

Full Name: Mary Florence Elinor Stewart.
   Born September 17, 1916, at Sunderland, Durham,
England. Daughter of Frederick Albert Rainbow (a
clergyman for the Church of England) and Mary Edith
Matthews. Married Frederick Henry Stewart, 1945.

Education: B.A., University of Durham, 1938; M.A.,
   1941.

Career: Writer.
   Head of English and Classics, Abbey School, Malvern
Wells, England, 1940-41; Lecturer, University of Durham, 1941-45; part-time lecturer, 1948-55; full-time
writer, 1955-DATE.

Agent: Curtis Brown Ltd., 60 E. 56th St., New York,
   NY 10022.

Awards: Edgar Award, 1964, for *This Rough Magic*;
   British Crime Writers Association Award, 1960, for
   My Brother Michael.

* * * * *

RAMONA STEWART

Full Name: Ramona Stewart.
   Born February 19, 1922, at San Francisco, California.
Daughter of James Oliver Stewart and Theresa Waugh.
Education: Attended University of Southern California,
1938-41.

Career: Writer, 1945-DATE. Agent: William Morris,
   151 E. Camino, Beverly Hills, CA 90212.

* * * * *

CATHERINE R. STIMPSON

Full Name: Catherine Roslyn Stimpson.
   Born June 4, 1936, at Bellingham, Washington. Educa-
tion: A.B., Bryn Mawr College, 1958; B.A., Newnham
College, Cambridge University, 1960; M.A., 1965; Ph.D.,
Columbia University, 1967.

Career: Professor of English.
   Lecturer, Barnard College, 1963-64; Instructor,
1964-67; Assistant Professor of English, 1967-DATE;
first Acting Director of the Women's Center and its
Executive Committee; lecturer for colleges and clubs;
consultant to Affirmative Action Institutes.

Awards: Woodrow Wilson Fellow, 1958; Fulbright Fellow for study in England, 1958-60.

Agent: Gloria Safier, 667 Madison Ave., New York,
   NY 10021.

HANK STINE

Full Name: Henry Eugene Stine.
   Born April 13, 1945, at Sikeston, Missouri. Married
Cristine Annette Kindred, June, 1966 (divorced, 1968).
Children: Eden Rain (born 1966).

Career: Writer.
   Has been a film director and editor, and a magazine
editor; now a full-time writer. Member: Science Fiction Writers of America.

"Reality fascinates me. I keep looking for it. Father
in service. Moved from town to town. I keep looking
for something real. Structure has become my all-con-
suming passion: not style or plot. I can handle them.
But structure. Like a song is structured or a film.
If something must be said about me, let it be this:
I'm a 'Citizens for Boysenberry Jam' fan."

* * * * *

PEG STOKES

Full Name: Peg Stokes.
   Born at Walkerton, Indiana. Daughter of Sid C. Ewing
and Marie Mikesell. Married Lyall N. Stokes, 1941.
Education: Studied music privately for 12 years, and
spent two years at the South Bend Conservatory of Music,
in Indiana; studied drama for two years.

Career: Writer.
   Has been CCA Director for WFBM-TV, Indianapolis, lecturer for the Redpath Bureau of Chicago, and Director
of the Lakeland Humane Society; writer, 1951-DATE.

Member:
   Theta Sigma Phi; National League of American Pen Wo-
men; Women's National Book Association; Christophers;
Brown County Art Gallery Association; International
Platform Association; Indianapolis Press Club; National
Federation of Press Women.

* * * * *

GRAHAM BRICE STONE

Full Name: Graham Brice Stone.
   Born January 7, 1926, at Norwood, South Australia.
Son of Nelson Brice Stone and Jeannie Campbell McAnna.
Married Joy Anderson, 1956 (divorced, 1965); married
Patricia Cowper, 1965. Two children: Timothy Nicholas
(born 1961), Dorinda Dawn (born 1968).

Education: B.A., University of Sydney, 1962; Associate, Library Association of Australia.

Career: Librarian.
   Served in the Royal Australian Air Force; Librarian,
Public Library of New South Wales, 1953-63; Librarian,
National Library of Australia, 1963-DATE.

Member:
   Library Association of Australia; Australia and New
Zealand Association for the Advancement of Science;
Futurian Society of Sydney (life member); Australian
Science Fiction Association.

First Professional Sale: Articles or reviews in
   1948/49, journalistic work for various trade publications, and much unpaid work for minor club publications.

GRAHAM BRICE STONE (Cont.)

Stone writes:
"I have been compiling data on science fiction books for many years. It is disgraceful that there is no general bibliography, which should have been done before any of the (mostly quite worthless) commentary and marginalia that has been produced. Forty years of associated activities, thousands of little magazines and trivial sheets, and no bibliography of science fiction books--and no complete and reliable magazine index either. My own efforts have been done out of sheer desperation. I have reached the point where my information on books is close enough to being complete to think about publication, and I am almost persuaded to undertake it, beginning with installments.
"I deplore most of the activities supposedly in support of science fiction. I think it is significant that those involved allow themselves to be called 'fans,' a 'fan' being commonly understood as a half-wit who makes a nuisance of himself at a public entertainment; no one claiming to have a serious interest in any other subject would tolerate the word being applied to him. The development of private jargon, the habit of meaningless titles for publications, the general ignorance and lack of background that makes possible the association of 'fantasy' with science fiction, the general treating of the whole movement as a joke, have contributed to the weakness and lack of progress of the field."

* * * * *

IDELLA PURNELL STONE

Full Name: Idella Purnell Stone.
  Born April 1, 1901, at Guadalajara, Jalisco, Mexico. Daughter of George Edward Purnell (a dentist) and Carrie Idella Braga. Married Remington Stone, Sept. 10, 1932 (died 1969). Three children: Marijane (born 1934), Remington (born 1938), Carrie (foster child, born 1945).

Education: B.A., University of California, Berkeley, 1922.

Career: Writer and editor.
  Secretary, American Consulate at Guadalajara, Mexico, 1922-24; Founder, Editor, and Publisher, poetry magazine Palms, 1923-30; founded and was Dean of the first summer session at the University of Guadalajara, 1932; riveter, Douglas Aviation, during World War II; reviewed books for the Los Angeles Daily News in the late 1940s; ran a Dianetics center in Pasadena, 1951-57; free-lance author and editor.

First Professional Sale: "My first sale was in my late teens, but I don't recall details."

Awards: Miscellaneous poetry awards and prizes.

Member: Science Fiction Writers of America; Poetry Society of America.

Interests: Travel, gardening, hiking.

Idella Stone comments: "I have had a very interesting life, and as I have had very long-lived parents, feel that I'm good for 15 or 20 more years, which I hope to cram with books! And hope to sell the few SF stories I've done, and do more. At present I'm reviewing books for a local paper, The View."

LESLIE F. STONE

Full Name: Leslie Frances Stone.
  Born June 8, 1905, at Philadelphia, Pennsylvania. Daughter of George Stone (a merchant) and Lillian Spellman (a writer and poet). Married William Silberberg (an editorial reporter), July 17, 1927 (died 1957). Two sons: Donald (born 1934), William (born 1942). Education: Attended William & Mary College.

Career: Author; now retired.

First Professional Sale: "Men with Wings," in Air Wonder Stories, July, 1929.

Agent: Robert P. Mills Ltd., 156 E. 52nd St., New York, NY 10022.

Member: Science Fiction Writers of America.

* * * * *

JACK TREVOR STORY

Full Name: Jack Trevor Story.
  Born March 20, 1917, at Bengeo, England. Son of James Storey (a house painter and cook) and Rhoda Dyball. Eight children: Jacqueline, Christine, Peter, Jennifer, Caroline, Lee, Lindsay, Lorel.

Career: Writer, 1949-DATE. Agent: Dina Lom, 6A Maddox St., London W.1, England.

* * * * *

REX STOUT

Full Name: Rex Todhunter Stout.
  Born December 1, 1886, at Noblesville, Indiana. Son of John Wallace Stout and Lucetta Elizabeth Todhunter. Married Fay Kennedy, December 16, 1916 (divorced); married Pola Hoffman (a textile designer), December 21, 1932. Two children: Barbara, Rebecca.

Career: Writer.
  Worked as a cook, salesman, bookkeeper, pueblo guide, bellhop, hotel manager, architect, and cabinetmaker, 1908-12; free-lance magazine writer in New York, 1912-16; created and managed Educational Thrift Service, a school banking system eventually enrolling over two million children, 1916-27; writer in Paris, 1927-29; novelist, 1927-75; founder and former Director, Vanguard Press; radio broadcaster; Chairman, Writers War Board, 1941-46, and Writers Board for World Government, 1949-75; President, Friends of Democracy, 1941-51; Treasurer, Freedom House, 1957-75. Died 1975.

Awards: Silver Dagger, Crime Writers Association, 1970, for The Father Hunt.

* * * * *

ADRIEN STOUTENBURG

Full Name: Adrien Pearl Stoutenburg.
  Born December 1, 1916, at Darfur, Minnesota. Daughter of Lace Kendall Stoutenburg (a barber) and Madeline Christy (a beauty parlor operator).

Education: Attended Minneapolis School of Arts, 1936-38.

ADRIEN STOUTENBURG (Cont.)

Career: Writer.
Darkroom assistant, Health Clinic, Minneapolis, 1936-39; Librarian, Hennepin County, Minnesota, 1951-52; Political Reporter, *Richfield News*, Minnesota, 1951-53; Editor, Parnassus Press, Berkeley, 1956-58; free-lance author, 1940-DATE.

First Professional Sale: "Patched Wings," in *Young People's Weekly*, 1939 or 1940.

Agent: Curtis Brown Ltd., 60 E. 56th St., New York, NY 10022.

Awards:
Michael Sloan Award and Edwin Markham Award, Poetry Society of America, 1961; Lamont Award, American Academy of Poets, 1964 for *Heroes, Advise Us*; Silver Medal of the Commonwealth Club of California, 1969, for *Short History of the Fur Trade* (poetry); Borestone Mountain Awards, 1957, 1960, 1962, 1965, 1966, 1967, 1968, 1970, 1972; six Junior Literary Guild selections, 1956 (2), 1958 (2), 1962, 1963.

Interests:
Camping, bird watching, painting, guitar, politics, conservation. "I have lived for varying periods in Iowa, Wisconsin, Long Island, Mexico, Colorado, New Mexico, California; and, of course, Minnesota. Met Clifford Simak several times in Writers Workshop, Minneapolis. Poetry readings at San Francisco State, and University of California, Berkeley. Among odd jobs not listed are machinist's helper in World War II, making oil flow units for Naval guns, peach packing in Colorado for five days; was, in Berkeley, a friend of Reginald Bretnor."

* * * * *

LEON E. STOVER

Full Name: Leon Eugene Stover.
Born April 9, 1929, at Lewistown, Pennsylvania. Son of George Franklin Stover (a professor) and Helen Elizabeth Haines. Married Takeko Kawai, October 12, 1956.

Education: Diploma, George School, 1947; B.A., Western Maryland College, 1950; M.A., Columbia University, 1952; Ph.D., 1962.

Career: Professor of Anthropology.
Instructor, American Museum of Natural History, 1955-57; Instructor in Anthropology, Hobart & William Smith Colleges, 1957-63; Asst. Professor, Hobart & William Smith Colleges, 1963-64; Visiting Assistant Professor of Cultural Anthropology, Tokyo University, 1963-65; Associate Professor of Anthropology, Illinois Institute of Technology, 1964-74; Professor of Anthropology, 1974-DATE. Science Editor, *Amazing Stories*, February, 1968-September, 1969; Science Editor, *Fantastic Stories*, March, 1968-October, 1969.

First Professional Sale: Four articles on China and Southeast Asia to *The American Oxford Encyclopedia*, 1961.

Agent: Robert P. Mills Ltd., 156 E. 56nd St., New York, NY 10022.

Member: Science Fiction Writers of America; Science Fiction Research Association; Association for Asian Studies; American Association for the Advancement of Science; Associate of Current Anthropology.

Interests: Sinology (two books published in this field, and a third in progress).

Stover writes:
"When I began teaching SF in 1965, the second person to do so in the United States at the college level, I had no idea academic interest would swell. Now that it has, I can only suppose that it foretells the absorption of SF into the mainstream. Because the university is a custodial institution, its objects of study are by definition museum pieces. SF will probably survive for a time as a publisher's category, but not as a distinctive genre with anything more than marginally differentiated content. Note that I speak of academic interest as a symptom of this change, not its cause."

* * * * *

RANDOLPH STOW

Full Name: Julian Randolph Stow.
Born November 28, 1935, at Geraldton, Western Australia. Son of Cedric Ernest Stow (a barrister and solicitor) and Mary Sewell.

Education: B.A., University of Western Australia, 1956.

Career: Novelist and poet.
Has worked on a mission for aborigines in northwest Australia, and as an assistant to the governmental anthropologist in New Guinea; has lived in England, Scotland, and Malta, teaching English in between times in at the University of Adelaide, 1957, the University of Western Australia, 1963-64, and in England at the University of Leeds, 1962, 1968-69; Harkness Fellow of the Commonwealth Fund, 1964-66.

* * * * *

A. G. STREET

Full Name: Arthur George Street.
Born April 7, 1892, at Wilton, Salisbury, England. Son of Henry Street (a farmer) and Sarah Anne Butte. Married Vera Florence Foyle, 1918. One daughter, Pamela.

Career: Writer.
Emigrated to Canada, 1911, and worked there as a farm laborer in Manitoba, 1911-14; farmer with his father at Wilton, 1914-17; took over farm in 1918; free-lance writer and journalist (and sometime farmer), 1932-66. Died July 21, 1966. Member: Edinburgh University Agricultural Society; Savage Club; Farmers Club; Salisbury Club.

* * * * *

JEREMY STRIKE

Full Name: Thomas Edward Renn.
Born November 8, 1939, at Welch, West Virginia. Son of Ernest Edward Renn and Dorothy Strike. Education: B.A., University of Toledo, 1962.

Career: Advertising writer. Director of Radio-Tele-

JEREMY STRIKE (Cont.)

vision Advertising, Flournoy & Gibbs, Toledo, Ohio, 1962-66; Director of Advertising, Savage Communcations, Inc., Toledo, 1966-69; free-lance writer in Europe, 1969-DATE.

* * * * *

ARKADII STRUGATSKII

Full Name: Arkadii Natanovich Strugatskii.
   Born August 28, 1925, at Batumi, Georgian SSR, Soviet Union. Son of Natan Strugatskii (a bibliographer) and Aleksandra Litvinchova (a teacher). Married Elena Oshanina, 1955. One daughter, Mariia (born 1955); one step-daughter, Natalia (born 1951).

Education: Attended State Institute of Foreign Languages, 1943-49; Interpreter of Japanese, and 2nd Class Interpreter of English.

Career: Writer and translator.
   Has been an Army officer; employee of Goslitisdat Publishing House, Moscow, 1959-61, and of Detgis Publishing House, 1961-64; free-lance writer and translator, with his brother Boris, 1964-DATE.

First Professional Sale: *The Country of the Purple Clouds*, Detgis Publishing House, 1959 (with Boris Strugatskii).

Awards: 2nd Award of Ministry of Education, 1959, for *The Country of the Purple Clouds*.

Member: Union of Soviet Translators; Union of Soviet Writers.

Interests:
   History, sociology, literature in general, Japanese medieval literature. "I've loved SF since childhood. Consider H. G. Wells, Karel Capek, and A. N. Tolstoi the founders of contemporary SF. The best SF writers of today, in my opinion, are Ray Bradbury, Robert Sheckley, Stanislaw Lem, Ivan Efremov, Kobo Abe. I think very much of Bulgakov's *The Master and Margarita*."

* * * * *

BORIS STRUGATSKII

Full Name: Boris Natanovich Strugatskii.
   Born April 15, 1933, at Leningrad, Russian Soviet Federated Socialist Republic, USSR. Son of Natan Strugatskii (a bibliographer) and Aleksandra Litvinchova (a teacher). Married Adelaida Karpeliuk, 1957. One son, Andrei Borisovich (born 1958).

Education: Attended State University of Leningrad, 1951-56, receiving a degree in astronomy.

Career: Writer.
   Astronomer, State Observatory of Pulkovo, 1956-64; free-lance author, with his brother Arkadii, 1964-DATE.

First Professional Sale: *The Country of the Purple Clouds*, Detgis Publishing House, 1959.

Awards: 2nd Award of the Ministry of Education,

1959, for *The Country of the Purple Clouds*.

Member: Union of Soviet Writers.

Interests: Sociology, and some special branches of astronomy.

* * * * *

FRANCIS STUART

Full Name: Francis Stuart.
   Born April 29, 1902, at Townsville, Australia. Son of Henry Irwin Stuart and Elizabeth Montgomery. Married, with one son and one daughter.

Career: Writer, 1923-DATE. Member: Irish Academy of Letters (founder). Awards: Royal Irish Academy Award.

* * * * *

HARALD STÜMPKE

Full Name: Gerolf Steiner.
   Born March 22, 1908, at Strasbourg, Alsace-Lorraine, Germany (later restored to France). Son of Karl Theodor Steiner and Katharina Frick. Married Renate du Mesnil de Rochemont, November 27, 1954. Seven children: Ursula, Friederike, Alfred, Berthold, Irmtrud, Wolfram, Dietrich.

Education: Dr. in Sciences, University of Heidelberg, 1931.

Career: Professor of Zoology.
   Assistant in zoology laboratory, University of Heidelberg, 1931-35; scientific collaborator, Food Cold Storage Investigating Laboratory, Karlsruhe, Germany, 1935-39; Asst. Professor of Zoology, Darmstadt Institute of Technology, 1939-47; Professor of Zoology, University of Heidelberg, 1950-62; Professor of Zoology and Director of the Zoology Laboratory, Baden Institute of Technology, 1962-DATE.

Member: German Zoologists Association; Deutscher Kaltetech Verein (German refrigeration engineers association); Gesellschaft Deutscher Naturforscher und Aerzte.

* * * * *

THEODORE STURGEON

Full Name: Theodore Hamilton Sturgeon [originally, Edward Hamilton Waldo]. Born February 26, 1918, at Staten Island, New York. Son of Edward Waldo (in oil production) and Christine Dicker (a writer, artist, musician). Married Wina Golden, April 16, 1969. One son, Andros.

Education: Attended Overbrook High School, in Philadelphia (did not graduate).

Career: Writer.
   Has been an apartment house manager, and a Class A heavy equipment worker (earth moving); now a full-time writer. Contributing Editor, *Galaxy*, May/June, 1972-DATE; Contributing Editor, *Worlds of If*, July/August, 1972-November/December, 1974. Sometime book reviewer for *Venture Science Fiction* and *New York Times*.

THEODORE STURGEON (Cont.)

First Professional Sale: [See comments below.]
"Ether Breather," in *Astounding Science Fiction*,
September, 1939.

Awards & Honors:
Guest of Honor, 20th World Science Fiction Conven-
tion (Chicon III), Chicago, 1962; Nebula Award, Best
Novelette, 1970 (1971), "Slow Sculpture"; Internation-
al Fantasy Award, 1954, for *More Than Human*; Hugo
Award, Best Short Story, 1970 (1971), "Slow Sculpture."

Member: Writers Guild of America, West; Science
Fiction Writers of America.

Interests: Music, painting, mechanics, alternative
life-styles.

J. Michael Reaves, who interviewed Sturgeon to obtain
the information for this sketch, had these additional
comments: "Sturgeon was adopted quite early by his
step-father, William Sturgeon, the head of the Romance
Department at Drexel Institute. Hence the name change.
(Seems that he is still catalogued by libraries under
the name 'Waldo.') His *first* professional sale was
not "Ether Breather," as given above--it was several
short-shorts to a syndicated newspaper in the late
1930s, for the total sum of $5, and he recalls being
so happy about it that he quit his job. He can't
remember the names of any of them, however, so I stuck
with his first SF sale." Sturgeon himself had this
remark: "Get rid of the fossil fuels!"

* * * * *

KATHLEEN SULLY

Full Name: Kathleen M. Sully.
Born April 14, 1910, at London, England. Daughter
of Albert Coussell (a mathematical engineer) and Kate
Bown. Has three children. Education: Studied dress
design at Barrett Street Trade School, art at Taunton
Art College and St. Alban's Art College, and attended
various night colleges before receiving a teaching
certificate at Gaddesden Teacher Training College.

Career: Writer.
Has been a domestic, teacher of art and English,
a dress model, professional swimmer and diver, cinema
usherette, tracer in the Admiralty, free-lance artist,
bus conductor, owner of an antique shop, dress manufacturer; now a full-time novelist.

* * * * *

C. L. SULZBERGER

Full Name: Cyrus Leo Sulzberger II.
Born October 27, 1912, at New York, New York. Son
of Leo Sulzberger Sulzberger Kahn and Beatrice Jose-
phi. Married Marina Tatiana Lada, January 21, 1942.
Two children: Marina Beatrice, David Alexis.

Education: B.S., Harvard University, 1934.

Career: Correspondent.
Reporter and rewrite man, *Pittsburgh Press*, 1934-35;
reporter, United Press, 1935-38; foreign correspondent, *London Evening Standard*, 1938-39; reporter for
various news services, 1939-40; correspondent with

London bureau of *New York Times*, 1940-44; Chief of
Foreign Service, based in Paris, 1944-54; Foreign Af-
fairs Columnist, 1954-DATE. Member: Phi Beta Kappa;
Metropolitan Club, Washington; Morfontaine, Paris.

Awards: Overseas Press Club Award, 1941, for best
reporting on the German-Russian front.

* * * * *

ROSEMARY SUTCLIFF

Full Name: Rosemary Sutcliff.
Born December 14, 1920, at West Clanden, Surrey,
England. Daughter of George Ernest Sutcliff (in the
Royal Navy) and Nessie Elizabeth Lawton. Education:
Attended Bideford Art School in Devonshire.

Career: Writer, 1950-DATE. Member: P.E.N.; National
Book League; Society of Authors.

Awards:
Carnegie Medal, 1959, for *The Lantern-Bearers*; placed
on the Honours List of the Hans Christian Andersen
Award, 1959, for *Warrior Scarlet*; *New York Times* Spring
Book Festival Prize, 1962, for *Dawn Wind*.

* * * * *

JAMES SUTHERLAND

Full Name: James Edward Sutherland.
Born August 25, 1948, at Greenwich, Connecticut.
Son of Hector H. Sutherland (a college instructor) and
Martha Scofield.

Education: A.A.S., Rochester Institute of Technology,
1968; B.S., 1970; graduate student, State University
of New York, 1974-DATE.

Career: Student of environmental science and forestry. Peace Corps volunteer in South Korea, 1971.

Honors & Awards:
First prize for best editorial in a high school newspaper from American Newspaper Publishers Association,
1966; Ford Foundation grant.

* * * * *

DAVID A. SUTTON

Full Name: David Ambrose Sutton.
Born October 5, 1947, at Birmingham, Warwickshire,
England. Son of James Edward Sutton (a tool-maker)
and Rose Ayling. Married Sandra Carroll, July 11, 1970.

Career: Free-lance editor.
Editor, *New Writings in Horror and the Supernatural*,
1971-DATE; editor and publisher of the fanzine *Shadow*,
January, 1968-DATE.

Member:
British Fantasy Society (past Editor of the *Bulletin
of the British Fantasy Society*, and former Vice-President of the organization).

Interests:
Film-going, rock music, astronomy, Fortean research.

HENRY SUTTON

Full Name: David Rytman Slavitt.
   Born March 23, 1935, at White Plains, New York. Son
of Samuel Saul Slavitt (an attorney) and Adele Rytman.
Married Lynn Meyer, August 27, 1956. Three children:
Evan Meyer (born 1957), Sarah Rebecca (born 1960),
Joshua Rytman (born 1963).

Education: B.A., Yale University, 1956; M.A., Columbia University, 1957.

Career: Writer.
   Instructor in English, Georgia Institute of Technology, 1957-58; writer and editor for *Newsweek*, 1958-
65; free-lance author, 1965-DATE.

First Professional Sale: "Warning" (a poem),
   in *Kenyon Review*, 1955.

Agent: William Morris Agency, 151 El Camino, Beverly
   Hills, CA 90212.

* * *.* *

JEAN SUTTON

Full Name: Eugenia Geneva Sutton.
   Born July 5, 1917, at Denmark, Wisconsin. Daughter
of Christopher Hansen and Mary Honora Baumgart. Married Jefferson Howard Sutton (a science fiction writer
under the name Jeff Sutton), February 1, 1941. Two
children: Chris (son, born 1946), Gale (born 1952).

Education: B.A., University of California, Los Angeles, 1940; M.A., San Diego State College, 1956.

Career: Teacher.
   Secretary, San Diego City Council, 1948-52; Social
Studies Teacher, Grossmont Union High School District,
La Mesa, California, 1952-7?. Now retired.

First Professional Sale: *The Beyond*, G. P. Putnam's Sons, 1968 (with Jeff Sutton).

* * * * *

JEFF SUTTON

Full Name: Jefferson Howard Sutton.
   Born July 25, 1913, at Los Angeles, California.
Son of Thomas Shelley Sutton (a newspaper editor) and
Sarah Elizabeth King. Married Eugenia Geneva Hansen,
February 1, 1941. Two children: Chris (son, born
1946), Gale (born 1952).

Education: B.A., San Diego State College, 1954;
   M.A., 1956.

Career: Editorial consultant.
   Prior to World War II, was a newspaper reporter,
a public relations man, and a staff member and photographer for International National News Photos; Research Engineer, Convair Division of General Dynamics,
1956-58; Communications Specialist with Convair, 1958-
60; free-lance editorial consultant for the aerospace
industry, 1960-DATE; free-lance author, 1954-DATE.

First Professional Sale: "The Third Empire," in
Spaceway Science Fiction, February, 1955.

Interests:
   "Nature in whatever form, but especially astronomy
and the seas and the timeless Southwest deserts."

Sutton comments: "Writing, with me, has always been
an avocation rather than a vocation, probably because
I write what I like to write rather than with an eye
on the market. My preference has always been science
fiction, because of its lack of bounds in time and space,
and in the challenge of making the seemingly implausible
plausible. It is, to me, The Big Arena in the writing
world. If you wish to people it with unpeople, from
this galaxy or the next, there are no limitations except those self-imposed."

* * * * *

LEE SUTTON

Full Name: Homer Lee Sutton.
   Born September 24, 1916, at Redondo Beach, California.
Son of Elmer T. Sutton (a house painter) and Nellie E.
Cole. Married Mildred Robinowitz, August 10, 1938.
Two children: Blake M. (born 1943), Beth (born 1954).

Education: A.B., Kenyon College, 1952; M.L.S., Columbia University, 1953; graduate student, University
   of Iowa, 1957-58.

Career: Professor of English.
   Assistant Librarian, City College of New York, 1953-
55; Librarian, Parsons College, 1955-67; Associate
Professor of English, John F. Kennedy College, 1967-
DATE.

First Professional Sale: "Headquarters Soldier"
   (poem), in *Harper's Magazine*, 1945.

Agent: Robert P. Mills Ltd., 156 E. 52nd St., New
   York, NY 10022.

Awards: Phelan Award for Literature, 1948, for his
   unpublished volume of verse. *Venus Boy* was cited by
   The Magazine of Fantasy and Science Fiction as the
   best juvenile SF novel of the year, 1955.

Member:
   Science Fiction Writers of America; Phi Beta Kappa;
Beta Phi Mu; American Association of University Professors; Iowa Library Association (President, 1965-66);
American Library Association (President, College Section, Association of College and Research Libraries,
1965-66). Interests: Theater, painting, sculpture.

Sutton notes: "Outside of the SF field, I have published verse, short stories, and essays in *Caper*, *Poetry*, *Harper's*, *Saturday Review*, *Colorado Quarterly*,
Common Sense, *Library Journal*. "Soulmate," in F&SF
for June, 1959, was republished in *The Best of Fantasy
and Science Fiction*, and in the anthology *Other Worlds,
Other Gods*, Doubleday, 1971."

* * * * *

DARKO SUVIN

Full Name: Darko R. Suvin.
   Born 1930, at Zagreb, Yugoslavia. Married, with no
children. Currently a landed immigrant in Canada.

Education: Has B.A., M.Sc., and Ph.D., all from
   Zagreb University; has also studied at the Sorbonne,

DARKO SUVIN (Cont.)

University of Paris, and Yale University.

Career: Professor of English.
   Lecturer, Faculty of Philosophy, Zagreb University, 1959-67; Vice-President, Union Internationale des Théâtres Universitaires, Zürich, 1962-65; Member, Croat National Theatre Board, 1962-64; on National Library Board, Yugoslavia, 1963-65; Art Director, International Student Theatre Festival, Zagreb, 1967; Visiting Lecturer, University of Massachusetts, 1967-68; Visiting Associate Professor, Comparative Literature, Indiana University, 1968; Member, Executive Board, Inter-University Center for Para-Literature, Montreal, 1969; Canada Council research grantee, 1969 and 1972; Programming Co-Chairman, Science Fiction Research Association Secondary Universe 4 Conference, Toronto, 1971; Chairman, International Symposium on H. G. Wells and Science Fiction, McGill University, October, 1971; co-Editor, *Science-Fiction Studies*; Member of Editorial Board, *Brecht Today*, the yearbook of the International Brecht Society; Chairman, Graduate Faculty Committee for Research into Para-Literature, McGill University; Canada Council leave grantee, 1973-74; Ford Foundation Fellow, 1965-66; currently, Associate Professor of English, McGill University, Toronto, Canada.

Interests: Theatre, drama, science fiction, utopian fiction. Reads Serbo-Croatian, English, French, Italian, German, Russian, and Spanish.

Member: Science Fiction Research Association (Member of Executive Committee, 1970-73).

* * * * *

DWIGHT V. SWAIN

Full Name: Dwight Vreeland Swain.
   Born November 17, 1915, at Rochester, Michigan. Son of John Edgar Swain (a railroad telegrapher) and Florence Marietta Vreeland. Married Margaret Reaves Simpson, August 6, 1942 (divorced, 1968); married Joye Raechel Boulton, February 12, 1969. One son, Thomas McCray (born 1946). Also, Rocio Mendez Garcia (born 1959), "a non-adopted Mexican orphan who lives with us, but who for all practical intents and purposes has become our child."

Education: A.A., Jackson Junior College, 1935; B.A., University of Michigan, 1937; M.A., University of Oklahoma, 1954.

Career: Writer.
   Newspaper writer and editor prior to World War II; Editorial Assistant, *Flying Magazine*, 1941; "officially on disability retirement due to bronchial asthma, so no present employer. Last post was as professor (professional writing), School of Journalism, University of Oklahoma, where I entered employment as a film script writer in September, 1949. Joined the academic faculty in 1952"; Consultant, Palmer Writers School, 1966-DATE ("I supervised the preparation of an entire new fiction course for them"); writer, 1935-DATE.

First Professional Sale:
   "Hard to say on this. First sale I recall was to *Target Magazine* about 1935. First big sale, *True*, about 1939. First science fiction sale, 'Henry Horn's

Super-Solvent,' *Fantastic Adventures*, November, 1941."

Honors:
   "An annual scholarship given in my name, and in recognition of my services, to top undergraduate Professional Writing student by the School of Journalism, University of Oklahoma; first awarded, June, 1974."

Member:
   American Medical Writers Association; Science Fiction Writers of America; University Film Association (former member of the Editorial Board for its *Journal*); National Cowboy Hall of Fame and Western Heritage Center (former judge).

Interests: Harmonica, violin, swimming, travel, reading, psychology, archaeology, sociology, economics, esoterica.

Swain writes:
   "My general approach both to life and to writing are summarized in my book, *Techniques of the Selling Writer*, University of Oklahoma Press, 1974. I'm one of those rare birds who's equally at home in film and print, fact and fiction. I particularly love the film script form, have scripted more than 50 fact and feature films (a good many dealing with science-oriented subjects), and would like nothing better than to have a go at more of the same, if my health permitted, since film work provides the human contact ordinarily lacking in print fiction.
   "Most of my print science fiction consisted of magazine novels (25,000-40,000 words), of the space opera variety--Lord knows how many I did. I feel there's still a place for adventure and strong story lines in the field, and am unhappy to see so many books coming out which are, in effect, more word photography and/or introspection. The field was infinitely more fun back in the days when Ray Palmer edited *Amazing Stories/Fantastic Adventures* (where I broke in), with heavy emphasis on action/conflict/humor.
   "Incidentally, Ray and Bill Hamling (for whose *Imagination/Imaginative Tales* I later wrote dozens of novels) both spurred writers on by giving them illustrations around which to write stories on assignment--a nice gimmick save for those unhappy times when a picture later would be changed without notifying the author, with the result that the cover scene wouldn't appear in the story!"

* * * * *

THOMAS BURNETT SWANN

Full Name: Thomas Burnett Swann, Jr.
   Born October 11, 1928, at Tampa, Florida. Son of Thomas Burnett Swann (a banker) and Margaret Gaines.

Education: A.B., Duke University, 1950; M.A., University of Tennessee, 1955; Ph.D., University of Florida, 1960.

Career: Writer.
   In the U.S. Navy, 1950-54; Instructor and Professor of English at various Florida colleges, 1960-69; full-time writer, 1969-76. Died at his parents' home of cancer, May 5, 1976.

First Professional Sale: A poem to *The Wall Street Journal*, 1954; first science fiction sale: "Winged Victory," in *Fantastic Universe*, July, 1958.

THOMAS BURNETT SWANN (Cont.)

Honors: Hugo Award nominations for *Day of the Minotaur*, "The Manor of Roses," and "Where Is the Bird of Fire?"

Member:
Science Fiction Writers of America; Phi Beta Kappa; Unitarian Church.

Interests:
Collecting miniature figurines, preferably copied after those of classical antiquity; collecting dictionaries of mythology in many languages; writing poetry.

Swann writes:
"One of my characters says, 'Dream high and half is enough.' I wanted to be a writer, and I wanted a wife and at least three children. I got the first half.
"My contribution to the fantasy field has been slight. I think of myself as writing domestic rather than epic fantasies--stories in which the focus is on the daily lives of a very small group of people or humanized beasts. Someone once called my stories too bland. I prefer to call them microcosmic.
"The effect I strive for (but often miss) is literate entertainment, with sometimes a wisp of allegory or enlightenment which the reader can take or leave. I hate books which set out to be allegories, like *Pilgrim's Progress* (dreadful book!).
"I don't think any of my books will last twenty years, but if they do, Olympus preserve me from the scholars! By the way, I didn't plague my students, I learned from them more than they learned from me, and they often show up in my books.
"One of the reasons why I was so glad to retire from teaching was that I was being pressured to write more literary criticism. Publish or perish is sadly true, and fantasy doesn't count, unless against you.
"I'm not really qualified to judge the current state of science fiction, since I don't get to read very much. As for fantasy, I think it has, and always will have, an important place, because the best of it is true, even if fanciful. It is our dreams verbalized, and who can live without dreams? Or deny their ultimate truth?"

* * * * *

LESLIE KAY SWIGART

Full Name: Leslie Kay Swigart [pronounced Swĩgart].
Born September 23, 1948, at Van Nuys, California. Daughter of Leland Swigart (a parts department manager for a Ford dealership) and Orpha Alice Greene.

Education: B.A., University of Southern California, 1970; M.L.S., University of California, Los Angeles, 1971; graduate student, California State University, Long Beach, 1973-DATE.

Career: Librarian.
Student assistant, University of Southern California Library, 1967-70; private secretary to Harlan Ellison (the science fiction writer), 1971; Assistant Humanities Librarian, California State University, Long Beach, 1971-DATE.

Member:
Pi Delta Phi; Beta Phi Mu; California Library Association; Modern Language Association; Science Fiction

Research Association (Member, Committee on Library Resources; Member, Executive Board, 1974-76).

Interests:
Bibliography (especially in the SF and fantasy fields), needlepoint, music (especially medieval and Renaissance, and Mozart), reading, reading, reading.

Swigart notes: "I use the elongated form of my name because in high school, when I was applying for college (architecture school), all of the applications came back addressed to Mr. LKS! In those pre-feminism days, girls just didn't apply to architecture school, and a name like Leslie is ambiguous at best, so they assumed I was a Mr., and I got mad and started using Kay as a subtle fight against chauvinism, even before I knew what it was. Even the Navy and Marines thought I was a guy, and wanted me to join...."

* * * * *

PAUL TABORI

Full Name: Paul [originally, Pál] Tábori.
Born May 8, 1908, at Budapest, Hungary. Son of Cornelius Tabori (an author and journalist) and Elsa Ziffer. Married Katherine Elizabeth Barlay, February 16, 1933. One son, Peter (born 1934).

Education: Ph.D., University of Berlin, 1930; Doctor of Economics & Political Science, University of Budapest, 1932.

Career: Writer.
Has been a writer, correspondent and editor for various European and British magazines, newspapers, and news agencies, director of literary agencies in Budapest and London, an Assistant Editor for *World Review*, producer for a TV series, story editor for a theatre, editorial consultant; Film Critic, *London Daily Mail*, 1942-44; Korda Contract Writer, 1943-48; Director, Telewriters Ltd., 1951-58; Visiting Professor at several American colleges, 1966-67, 1969-70; Co-Editor, International P.E.N. Books; Counsulting Editor, Paul Raymond Publications; free-lance author, 1927-74. Died November 9, 1974.

First Professional Sale: *Uj Buda*, Ludwig Vaggenreiter (Berlin), 1927.

Member:
P.E.N. (active on many committees and boards; currently, Acting Chairman, International Writers in Prison Committee); Society of Authors; Crime Writers Association; Critics Circle; Science Fiction Writers of America; Authors Guild.

Interests: Travel.

Awards: Medal of the City of Paris, 1961; Special Award, Writers Guild of Great Britain, 1964; Special Award, International Writers Guild, 1967.

Tabori writes:
"I have written in three different languages, beginning with Hungarian, then switching to German, and now for the last four decades writing almost exclusively in English. I wrote a science fiction novel in my teens which was called *Death of Sleep*, and which envisioned a world in which sleep had been abolished. I wrote a number of short stories in all three languages, but I feel that my own contribution, if any, has been in science fiction satire, as a very humble follower

PAUL TABORI (Cont.)

"of Swift and Orwell. I am at the moment working on a short study called "Sex and Utopia," which will be a brief analysis of the treatment of this problem in various classical and modern works of science fiction, and which will be published shortly in *Men Only* magazine.

"As for the current state of science fiction, I am afraid I do not read enough of it to be a qualified judge. It does seem to me that the frontiers of general fiction and science fiction are being rapidly abolished, and the distinction is becoming increasingly blurred. I think the best science fiction is the sort which takes a fantastic or out-of-way idea, and treats it with complete factual realism--exploring all possibilities to their logical ends. I don't very much like Westerns, soap opera, or detective stories disguised as science fiction, and I believe as in connection with every other form of writing, that excessive pre-occupation with form, and experimentation for experimentation's sake, are always a cover-up for a lack of ideas, an absence of real content."

* * * * *

ROBERT LEWIS TAYLOR

Full Name: Robert Lewis Taylor.
Born September 24, 1912, at Carbondale, Illinois. Son of Roscoe Aaron Taylor (a land developer) and Mabel Bowyer. Married Judith Martin, February 3, 1945. Two children: Martin Lewis (born 1945), Elizabeth Ann (born 1948).

Education: A.B., University of Illinois, 1933.

Career: Author.
Reporter, *St. Louis Post-Dispatch*, 1936-39; Profile Writer, *New Yorker*, 1939-63; free-lance author, 1934-DATE.

First Professional Sale: Several pieces to *American Boy Magazine*, 1934.

Awards:
Pulitzer Prize for Fiction, 1959, for *The Travels of Jaimie McPheeters*; runner-up in general reporting division, annual awards of Delta Sigma Chi, 1939.

Member: Delta Tau Delta; Down East Yacht Club; Centro Náutico la Floresto.

"*Adrift in a Boneyard* was my first novel, a fantasy, and it was written purely to entertain. This may be said also of my more recent books, several fiction, and three biographies. I have had no 'message' for the reader, unless it's to urge him to enjoy life."

* * * * *

WILLIAM F. TEMPLE

Full Name: William Frederick Temple.
Born March 9, 1914, at Woolwich, London, England. Son of William James Temple (an engineer) and Doris Beatrice Jackson. Married Joan Gertrude Streeton (a rare book dealer), September 16, 1939. Two children: Anne Katharine (born 1940), Cliff Geoffrey (born 1947).

Education: Attended Woolwich Polytechnic, 1930.

Career: Author.
Stock Exchange Official, London Stock Exchange, 1930-40, 1946-50; field artillery gunner in the British Army, 1940-46; cataloguer and quoter of scientific and medical journals, William Dawson & Sons Ltd., 1969-DATE; Editor, *Dan Dare Space Annual*, 1951.

First Professional Sale: "The Kosso," in *Thrills*, an anonymous anthology published by Philip Allan & Co., 1935.

Agent: Scott Meredith, 580 Fifth Avenue, New York, NY 10036.

Member: British Interplanetary Society (Editor of its *Journal*, 1938-39).

Interests:
Classical music (listening), classic films (viewing and collecting), book collecting, money collecting, watching his wife gardening, cat collecting and maintenance ("five at present"), beer-brewing and drinking.

Temple writes:
"My own favourite (pardon my English) book among my books? That's tough. Maybe a crime-thriller, *The Dangerous Edge*, a 90,000-worder hardcover, published here by John Long Ltd. in 1950. The high-spot was a terrific car chase through the streets of London (subway stations, etc.), and out into the country. I thought it would make a grand action film sequence, and tried to persuade several film producers so. No dice. Twenty years later came "The French Connection," "Bullitt," "The Italian Job," and God knows how many more carbon copies. Another high-spot was a detailed description of a break-in into a jeweler's shop (your spelling this time) through the ceiling. Much, much later came the film "Riffifi," almost identically similar.

"My largely ignored novel (though it sold well enough here and in German translation) was before its time. But it was turned down by American publishers because it was passé ('reminiscent of the old *Shadow*!'). Timing was never my strong point.

"Another 'favorite' (damn Yankees!) was my nonfiction *The True Book About Space-Travel* (Frederick Muller here--and *The Prentice-Hall Book About Space-Travel* over there). Circa 1954 it anticipated so much of what came to pass. But then, I wasn't alone in that. One of my two oldest SF friends, Arthur C. Clarke, did as much--or more. (The other oldest is Forry Ackerman, who stays with us here every time he visits England. Arthur rings me every time he's in London. He did a fortnight ago, ere returning to Ceylon. But he never rings me from Ceylon. But Forry does from Hollywood.)

"I suppose my real favourite is *Four-Sided Triangle*, if only from the travail caused me in writing it, as a British Eighth Army gunner/signaler in the War. I had to write it three times. The first ms. was lost in action in a skirmish with Rommel's tanks in Tunisia. The second version disappeared during a bombardment on the Anzio beachhead. The third version (which was filmed) set me free from the hated Stock Exchange after the War.

"But freedom didn't last all that long. Eventually, I was back in the office cage. *Shoot at the Moon* set me free again--to buy a very large house in a very large, olde-worlde garden here in Folkestone, where I always wanted to live, because my literary hero wrote all his best SF here (i.e., H. G. Wells). I might have remained free if Warner Bros. and later EMI/MGM had taken up their film options on that novel (why that

WILLIAM F. TEMPLE (Cont.)

"all went wrong is a long story--it was all a matter of bad timing again), but back I am in the office cage, hating it, with a bulging notebook of germ-ideas and outlines for and of stories/novels, SF and otherwise, which remind me of the children in Maeterlinck's *The Bluebird*, in Limbo, waiting to be born. But the years are running out...time for writing (or even thinking) there is not.

"I've had nearly 100 published short stories, mostly SF. A good many have been anthologized--but far more have gone with the wind. In the long run, don't they all go that way? It'll happen to the Works of Shakespeare--eventually."

* * * * *

M. B. TEPPER

Full Name: Matthew Bruce Tepper.
  Born September 23, 1953, at Los Angeles, California. Son of Harry William Tepper (an orthodontist) and Anne Drucker (a legal secretary).

Education: Attended West Los Angeles College, 1970, Santa Monica College, 1970-73, San Francisco State University, 1973-DATE.

Career: Student.
  Music Librarian, Santa Monica College, 1972-73; self-employed percussionist.

First Performed Work: "Sonatina for Harpsichord, Op. 32," performed March 27, 1974, Tina Digesti Woods, harpsichordist.

Awards: Gordon Durfee Music Scholarship, 1973.

Member:
  Pacific Palisades Science Fiction Society (founder); Santa Monica Strategic Games Club; Los Angeles Science Fantasy Society (past Secretary; impeached).

Interests:
  Music performance (voice, piano, percussion, conducting), composition, philately, numismatics, geology, book collecting, record collecting, science fiction fandom, nudism, criticism.

"I find much of my serious work falls into the category of music composition or privately-published, free-lance reviews of science fiction and related material. This does not rule out the possibility of future work in the field of science fiction and fantasy, however; indeed, I hope to unite SF and opera in a series of important works starting with *Planetfall*, an opera in one act after a short story by John Brunner."

* * * * *

ERIC THACKER

Full Name: Eric Lee Thacker.
  Born September 29, 1923, at Leeds, Yorkshire, England. Son of George Ernest Thacker and Jane Lee. Married Doreen Mary Smith, August 11, 1956. Four children: Andrea Mary (born 1960), Miles David (born 1963), Clinton Roger (born 1965), Deborah Clare (born 1965). Education: Attended Hartley Victoria Methodist College (theological), 1952-55.

Career: Minister.
  Clerk in a department store in Leeds, 1937-38; with a shopfitter's firm, 1938-39; billposter's assistant, 1939; with an engraving firm, 1939-44, 1947-52; in the British Army, 1944-47; Methodist Minister, 1955-DATE, in Derbyshire, Lancashire, South India, and Yorkshire.

First Professional Sale: *Musrum*, Jonathan Cape, 1968 (with A. Earnshaw).

Thacker writes:
  "My writing activity has largely been in the areas of poetry and jazz criticism. No collection of poems has been published; individual poems have appeared in English and Indian magazines; and the long poem "Dongdeath and Jazzabeth" was produced in mimeo, non-professionally, by Cavan McCarthy, whose occasional magazine specializes in concrete poetry. ("Dongdeath" is not a concrete poem, but one which combines jazz imagery with mythology, real and invented, together with verbal techniques which employ the heavy use of puns and the occasional use of chance and automation.)
  "*Musrum* is not SF, but belongs, I suppose, to the 'super-genre.' It invents the category of the 'musroid,' which is virtually limitless in its possibilities, excluding only the self-containedly mundane. The book depends on the interaction of the verbal and the visual. Drawings are as important as text, and are numerous--drawn by both authors in their differing but related styles. 'Strong' humour is the pervading genius, sparked by extravagant paradox and violent shifts of meaning and imagery. Surrealism is perhaps the strongest influence. Both authors admire the best in SF, but are unaware of definite influence here.
  "My long friendship with Anthony Earnshaw is rooted in our common interest in jazz, and in the art and literature of the fantastic. We write largely for the sake of mutual entertainment."

* * * * *

ELSWYTH THANE

Full Name: Elswyth Thane.
  Born May 16, 1900, at Burlington, Iowa. Married William Beebe (a naturalist and writer), September 22, 1927 (deceased).

Career: Writer, 1925-DATE. Formerly a newspaper reporter and a writer for films.

* * * * *

ROBERT THEOBALD

Full Name: Robert Theobald.
  Born June 11, 1929, at Madras, India. Son of Raymond Theobald and Irene Pulleins. Education: M.A., Cambridge University, 1952.

Career: Self-employed socio-economist.

* * * * *

ROBERT THOM

Full Name: Robert Thom [originally, Robert Flatow].
  Surname changed legally at age seven. Born July 2, 1929, at New York, New York. Son of Julius Flatow (an accountant) and Lily Pendlebury. Married Millie Perkins, December 24, 1964. Three children: Kate, Elizabeth, Lille.

ROBERT THOM (Cont.)

Education: B.A., Yale University, 1951; graduate
student, Cambridge University, 1951-52.

Career: Writer.
Full-time author, 1949-DATE, primarily of screenplays and teleplays.

Awards: Emmy Award, Best Dramatic Show of 1963, for
"The Madman," an episode on the CBS series, *The
Defenders*.

* * * * *

DAN THOMAS

Full Name: Leonard M. Sanders, Jr.
Born January 15, 1929, at Denver, Colorado. Son of
Leonard M. Sanders (a purchasing agent) and Jacqueline
Thomas. Married Florine Cooter (a writer), August
21, 1956.

Education: Attended University of Oklahoma.

Career: Reporter.
Reporter in Texas and Oklahoma; free-lance magazine
writer; Book Page Editor and Fine Arts Editor, *Fort
Worth Star-Telegram*, 1958-DATE.

First Professional Sale: "Race to the Frozen
Sea," in *True*, May, 1952.

* * * * *

MARTIN THOMAS

Full Name: Thomas Hector Martin.
Born June 29, 1913, at Bristol, England. Son of
Charles Thomas (a British soldier killed on active
duty in Iraq in 1921) and Helen Josephine Butcher.

Education: Attended St. George Grammar School,
Bristol.

Career: Writer.
Has earned his living as a free-lance author since
the age of 17, when he embarked upon a career as a
cartoonist, commercial artist, and writer; after service in World War II, he branched out into fiction
writing, selling a series of occult short stories,
newspaper serials in the detective and SF genres,
a hundred short stories, and several dozen crime novels under five pseudonyms.

First Professional Sale: A series of occult
shorts syndicated to Mirror Features, 1946-47.

Interests: Riding, reading psychology and philosophy, satirical comedy, listening to good music.

* * * * *

THEODORE L. THOMAS

Full Name: Theodore L. Thomas.
Born April 13, 1920, at New York, New York. Married
Virginia Kent Paton, July 18, 1947. Three children:
Lenore Webster, Jefferson Webster, Alexandra Webster.
Education: S.B., Massachusetts Institute of Technolo-
gy; J.D., Georgetown University, 1953.

Career: Patent lawyer.
Chemical engineer, American Cyanamid Company, Stam-
ford, Conn., 1947-50; patent lawyer in Washington,
1950-55; Patent Lawyer, Armstrong Cork Co., Lancaster,
Penn., 1955-DATE; Chairman, Lancaster Zoning Board of
Adjustment, 1966-70; Chairman, Lancaster Narcotics and
Dangerous Drugs Committee, 1970-71.

Member:
Science Fiction Writers of America; American Association for the Advancement of Science; American Bar Association; American Patent Law Association; Philadelphia
Patent Law Association; Underwater Explorer's Club.

* * * * *

HARLAN THOMPSON

Full Name: Harlan Howard Thompson.
Born December 25, 1894, at Brewster, Kansas. Son of
William Lewis Thompson (a rancher) and Clare Cornelia
Shultz. Married Gertrude Elizabeth Friend, May 31,
1961. Three children: Charlotte Faith, Harlan Tren-
holm, Barbara Lorraine.

Education: Attended University of Southern California, 1917-18.

Career: Writer.
Was a rancher for many years in Alberta, Canada (the
famous T.X Ranch; writer, 1946-DATE.

First Professional Sale: *The Wild Palomino*, Longmans, Green (New York), 1946.

Agent: McIntosh & Otis, 475 Fifth Avenue, New York,
NY 10017.

Awards:
Gold Medal, Boys' Clubs of America, 1947, for *Prairie
Colt*; Commonwealth Club of California Silver Medal,
1956, for *Spook, the Mustang*.

Member: P.E.N.; California Writers Guild; Western
Writers of America; Westerners, Los Angeles Corral.

Interests: Breeder of exotic cattle (Chianinnis
from Italy); travel.

* * * * *

ROSEMARY TIMPERLEY

Full Name: Rosemary Kenyon Timperley.
Born March 20, 1920, at London, England. Daughter
of George Kenyon Timperley (an architect) and Emily
Mary Lethem (a teacher). Married James McInnes Cameron
(a teacher), March, 1952 (died, 1968).

Education: B.A., King's College, London University,
1941.

Career: Writer.
Teacher, South-East Essex County Technical School,
1941-49; Journalism, *Reveille Magazine*, 1950-59; free-
lance author, 1956-DATE; Editor, *Ghost Book* series,
Barrie & Jenkins, 1969-73.

First Professional Sale: *The Listening Child*,
Barrie, 1956. Agent: Harvey Unna, 14 Beaumont Mews,
London W1N 4HE, England.

ROSEMARY TIMPERLEY (Cont.)

Member: Society of Authors; Crime Writers Association.

Interests:
   Psychiatry, medicine, languages (Russian, Italian, Arabic, Chinese), history, novels, music, travel to Moscow, Morocco, Italy, and Greece ("but can't afford to travel anymore").

Timperley writes:
   "Writing has helped me to get through life--I don't know how I'd have managed without it. So far it's always been there as an escape, something to do. I hope to die before I 'dry up.'
   "You ask why I think the ghost story is so popular in Great Britain. It wasn't all that popular until there was a sort of boom in ghosts about five years ago; and within the past twelve months there's been a flurry of paperbacks and magazines with supernatural material. I suppose it's about the only escape material left, except for science fiction. People don't believe in the formal religions anymore, so they've lost their miracles and angels there. The 'carnal knowledge' syndrome has rather knocked romance on the head, as love stories are dull without the frustration content. Increased bureaucracy, although it's necessary and essentially beneficial in an overcrowded country, is rather crushing to the spirit--so I guess we look for other spirits, and turn to ghosts. It's the appeal of the irrational, the old unconscious gasping for breath in an age when we're all supposed to be educated and conscious, and to make our minds control our emotions, rather than the other way around. Having had so much explained and rationalised, people are hungry for mystery. There are fewer ghosts in Roman Catholic countries, where they have saints instead. C. G. Jung talks a lot of sense about it all. Symbols of mystery, such as ghosts, are a religious need, so when the spirits walk out, the spectres walk in. This is only my personal opinion, of course. I don't move in circles where these topics are discussed; I only write the bloody things!"

* * * * *

JAMES TIPTREE JR.

Full Name: Alice Hastings Sheldon.
   Born 1916, near Chicago, Illinois. Daughter of Herbert Edwin Bradley (the explorer and naturalist) and Mary Wilhelmina Hastings (a writer of mysteries and travel books). Married Huntington Denton Sheldon (a physician), 1955. Two children.

Education: Ph.D., George Washington University, 1967.

Career: Psychologist.
   Has been a government employee, businessperson, and college instructor; currently an experimental psychologist and writer.

First Professional Sale: "Birth of a Salesman," in Analog, March, 1968.

Agent: Robert P. Mills Ltd., 156 E. 52nd St., New York, NY 10022.

Awards:
   Nebula Award, Best Short Story, 1973 (1974), "Love

Is the Plan, the Plan Is Death"; Hugo Award, Best Novella, 1973 (1974), "The Girl Who Was Plugged In."

Member: Science Fiction Writers of America.

Tiptree was the B. Traven of the science fiction world until her identity was revealed by Charles N. and Dena Brown, in their publication Locus. Tiptree accompanied her parents on expeditions to the Belgian Congo to study Gorillas in 1921-22 and 1924; she also travelled to Sumatra in 1925, and back to Africa in 1930-31. Her mother, Mary Hastings Bradley, wrote several books about their travels in which Tiptree was the featured character, including Alice in Jungleland (1927), and Alice in Elephantland (1929). Tiptree herself comments:
   "When all the mystery about me is dissolved to reveal the short grey figure in the 2-button suit complete with writer's meaningless random features out of which peers hopefully--something; when I do wander out clutching the curtains, everyone is going to have a good laugh. Truly, if I had known how much interest would be generated by my recessiveness, I never would have started it. I just thought the writing is the thing, you know? And I never expected it to go like this. Well, look at my published interviews. You'll see. My secret is that there really isn't one. And I certainly AM NOT anybody you ever heard of--unless you're a Polish student of rat behaviour--and above all I am not anybody 'official,' nor connected with any machinery of what we laughingly refer to as government, including the Park Police. My closest approach is turning on Bill Moyers and cheering. My time is spent shovelling work into cartons, and unshovelling them again six months later, as I rush harriedly by. It's not B. Traven, it's more Caspar Hauser. But...as I've begged over and over and over to everyone I know--and some I count my best of friends--may I beg off from your spotlight for the time being? There is, really, no good reason; there's only that I--I'm up to here with life in some odd way, one more thing I can't. If this sounds more than a bit psycho, it is.
   "I was born in the Chicago area a long time back, trailed around places like colonial India and Africa as a kid (and, by the way, I knew in my bones that they weren't going to stay 'colonial' any more than I was going to stay a kid, but nobody ever asked me). I'm one of those for whom the birth and horrendous growth of Nazism was the central generation event. From it I learned most of what I know about politics, about human life, about good and evil, courage, free will, fear, responsibility, and What to Say Goodbye To... and, say it again, about Evil. And Guilt. If one of the important things to know about a person is the face in his nightmares, for me that face looks much like my own. In some ways, it is easier to live with a Devil who is clearly different, black or white or yellow, old, young, female or male or such. Them, the baddies; Me (wholly a different animal), the good guy. Easier, but maybe not so instructive.
   "At any event, by the time I had finished the decade's worth of instruction in How Things Are provided by this event--you know, joining organisations, getting in the Army, milling around in the early forms of American left-wing sentiment, worrying about Is It Going to Happen Here--an occupation I haven't given up--getting out of the Army, doing a little stint in government, trying a dab of business, etc., etc., I realised that my whole life, my skills and career, such as they were, my friends, everything had been shaped by this event, and rather derailed from what I'd intended to be in a vague way. So ensued a period of more milling (I'm a slow type), including some dabblings in academe. And now the story grows even vaguer for the time being,

JAMES TIPTREE JR. (Cont.)

"since I'm against lying on principle. (Life's too short, it takes all one's time to get a finger on some truth.)

"But y'know, the other day it came to me, all I write is one story. There's this backward little type, and he's doing some grey little task, and believing like they tell him, and one day he starts to vomit, and rushes straight up a mountain, usually to his doom. Human or alien, mountain or rocket, it's all the same. Next year I'm trying a real departure: there's this *girl*, see, and she rushes *down* a salt mine. But they always vomit. The amount of sheer puke in my stories is staggering.

"Let me tell you how all this got started. Couple of years back, under a long siege of work and people pressure, I set down four stories, and sent 'em off literally at random. Then I forgot the whole thing. I mean, I wasn't rational; the pressure had been such that I was using speed (VERY mildly), and any sane person would have grabbed sleep instead. Obviously, one more activity was sheerly surreal. So some time later I was living, as often happens, out of cartons and suitcases, and this letter from Condé Nast (who the hell was Condé Nast?) turned up in a carton. Being a compulsive, I opened it. Check. John W. Campbell. About three days later I came to in time to open one from Harry Harrison.

"Now, you understand, this overturned my reality-scene. I mean, we know how writers start. Years, five, ten years, they paper a room with rejection slips. It never occurred to me anyone would buy my stuff. Never. I figured I had the five years to get my head together. I had a list of the places I was going to rotate the things through. (Methodical, even when stoned, see above.)

"And I still haven't got it together. The thing has gone on and on, 21 as of now, and I still don't believe it. I don't deny I love it, but I deny being happy. It's too weird. As I told David Gerrold, if these guys only knew it, I'd have paid them for their autographs. I mean, years, years, and years, I've been the kind of silent bug-eyed Rikki-Tikki-Mongoose type fan who thinks those guys who wrote them walk around six inches off the ground with private MT channels in their closets, step in and Flick!--Gal Central.

"As to why, ah indeed, why? Somewhere Freud is said to have observed that every action is over-determined, that is, that there is usually more than one sufficient cause, that acts occur at convergence points where many causes meet. (I wish I could locate this quote, since I may be over-interpreting; it's a very useful concept.)

"At any event, I could give you a set of plausible reasons, like the people I have to do with include many specimens of prehistoric man, to whom the news that I write *ugh, science fiction* would shatter any credibility that I have left. (Sometimes I think SF is the last really dirty word.)

"Or that I'm unwilling to tarnish my enjoyment of this long-established secret escape route by having to defend it to hostile ears. (Coward!). Or, conversely, that my mundane life is so uninteresting that it would discredit my stories. Probably the real reason is partly inertia, it started like this, I don't yet really believe it, let it be till it ripens. That too.

"But basically, maybe I believe something about the relation of writers to their stories, that the story is the reallest part of the story-teller. Who cares about the color of Coleridge's socks? (Answer,

"Mrs. C.). Of course, I enjoy reading a writer's auto-biography--or rather SOME writers! A few. By far the most of them make me nervous, like watching a stoned friend driving a crowded expressway. For Chrissakes, stop!

"I told this to Harlan Ellison, but I don't think he understood, because he is one of the few who can reveal all he wants to without spoiling his stories. But there's the catch. When you're reading Harlan's wonderfully natural, candid, human-all-too-human accounts of Harlan Living, *are you really looking behind the scenes?* You are not. You are looking at more of Harlan's writing, not because Harlan is being deceptive, or being less than candid, but because Harlan belongs to that human type, Homo logensis, the Talking Man, like Mailer, like Thomas Wolfe, whose life forms into narrative as it is being lived, so that at every act of unveiling, of putting the naked squirm of the inmost flesh into words, another level of reality forms behind and beneath in which the living Harlan exists just one jump ahead of the audience.

"Those of us who are not so blessed are very rightly dubious about the value of straight autobiographical writing. For example, the poet Auden offers as his autobiography a collection of cherished quotations and notations, his commonplace book. (I'm reading it now, it's great.) And he's right; if you want a terrible instance of suicide by autobiography, try Cordwainer Smith. One of the greats. If only I'd never read that perishing introduction in which he blathers on about his household, and how his cook or somebody is really almost human. Jesus.

"You'll notice I left a 'partly' dangling a few paragraphs ago. Well, the last remaining part of my secretiveness is probably nothing more than childish glee. At last I have what every child wants, a secret life. Not an official secret, not a polygraph-enforced, bite-the-capsule-when-they-get-you secret, nobody else's damn secret but MINE. Something THEY don't know. Screw Big Brother. A beautiful secret REAL world, with real people, fine friends, doers of great deeds, and speakers of the magic word, Frodo's people if you wish, and they write to me and accept my offerings, and I'm damned if I feel like opening the door between that magic reality and the universal shitstorm known as the real (sob) world ...when all the more cogent reasons are done, it's probably that simple.

"So, how reconcile that with honesty? Well, who is honest? You? Or you? Don't tell me, man. You know as well as I do we all go around in disguise. The halo stuffed in the pocket, the cloven hoof awkward in the shoe, the X-ray eye blinking behind thick lenses, the two midgets dressed as one tall man, the giant stooped in a pinstripe, the pirate in a housewife's smock, the wings shoved into sleeveholes, the wild racing, wandering, raping, burning, bleeding, loving pulses of reality decorously disguised as a roomful of human beings. I know goddam well what's out there, under all those masks. Beauty and Power and Terror and Love. So who the fuck cares whether the mask is one or two millimetres thick? Does THAT convey?

"There is always a learning. For some people named Joseph Conrad, it seems to have been just living in a noticing way. For Tiptree, hidden years of writing crap headed MEMO, SUBJECT, TO,...PROBLEM, CONCLUSIONS, RECOMMENDATIONS. And then trying to do it like they said, and then discovering that when I really did do it like they said---nobody could read it. Not even me.

"So then more effort imploring the reader-fish to bite, to *read* about my goddam problem. I even tried putting dirty stories in footnotes, somewhere they're still there stamped Swallow Before Reading...above all it was cut, cut, *cut*...starting with that gorgeous

JAMES TIPTREE JR. (Cont.)

"line you like best. And I wrote a little, well, I guess it was poetry; one began: 'Sitting on a fruit-crate in the abandoned tractor park...'

"Also, I once worked briefly on a paper, the good old crazy *Chicago Sun*, where a bloat-eyed scotch-sodden frog from Texas called a Feature Editor kept a big pair of shears by his bottle; and when you handed him your hot and beating prose he eyed it in silence with the reds of his eyes shining over the bags, and then...took up the shears...and cut off the last third, which was where the point was...A learning experience. (Also instructive was the fact that every time you wrote about the school board stealing the slum kids' money it came out in pied type...anybody ever hear what they had there *before* Daley?)

"Learning how to write is the big thing with me. I don't have any illusions of genius. Nobody writes for me, what's printed is what *I* wrote (aside from a little cleaning-up of words unsuitable for I guess Mom), but I'm very eager for critical reaction, and very willing to put it back in the oven. For example, Harry Harrison has twice pushed stories back at me for fix-ups, one being the original "And I Have Come Across This Place by Lost Ways," which He bought for *Nova 2* (notice the Freudian slip in capitalising 'He' back there; Harry really is one of my gods). It had too much social chitchat at first, and the doom wasn't spelled out clear enough at the end. (I tend to make all my points indirectly, you know, somebody just mutters that the world ended yesterday.) Sure enough, he was right; I spent a week of nights revising. Again, that wolf story from *Venture*, "The Snows Are Melted, the Snows Are Gone," when he bought it for the *Best SF* anthology, he objected to the wolf's showing no sign of strain, being a mutant and all. So I tried him with an epileptic episode and that was right, too. But Christ, it's agony. I don't see how these one-draft wonders do it. What I send out is about Draft X.

"All this by way of starting to talk about the real thing, the stories. For the most part, my stuff has been gestated privately, some germ working around in its own terms, which I then finish up in the style it seems to demand. Some are *Gee, that's interesting* germs, like the *Analog* one about the haploid people, where I got brooding over what people would have been like if the alternating generation system had survived, and how essentially doomed it was, as a system.

"Others arise out of a loving interest in the endless foul-ups of daily life, how the poor bastard behind some desk or title copes all day long with the throng of wild Indians, crackpots, active idiots, weirdos of all descriptions which we call the General Public. How do you run a race-track--a matter-transmitter system--a hatchery--a research lab--extrapolated into interstellar terms? (Strong biographical aroma here--yeah, yea verily, I have coped.) Others arise by analogy; for example, some of the side-repercussions of the civil rights movement, some time back, started "Happiness Is a Warm Spaceship," where the happy 'liberal' hero runs into some aliens that don't want to get integrated. (Like most old-line liberals, who started off with a general sense of Righting Injustice, I've gone through a long educative process in which the Black Brother changes from being a featureless object of sympathy to a bunch of real people.)

"One story no one seems to have noticed or liked represents a scream from deep inside. If you have time and want to know most of what makes Tiptree tick, look in *Galaxy*, April, 1969, for "Beam Us Home." I take a little sad credit too; recall that was written

"in 1968, and check the social-prediction scene. It'll also show you that I'm a bit of a Trekky, enough so I sent Roddenberry a dedicated copy, and got this beautiful letter back.

"Another big hunk of Tiptree is in "The Last Flight of Dr. Ain," which I wanted to call "Dr. Ain's Love Story." That is screaming from the heart as good as I could do it in 1968. (By the way, only a couple people noticed that Ain's first name is Charles, (C.?) Tiptree's a furtive bastard.)

"I want to cut to the bone ALWAYS. The question is, what is bone? Sometimes it's in the bare events, sometimes in the tone, sometimes in the minutiae--oh hell, that's no good. The question remains, each time answered differently.

"You see, my aim really is not to bore. I read my stuff with radar out for that first dead sag, the signal of oncoming *boredom*, the onset of crap, stuffing, meaningless filler, wrongness. And don't *repeat* at me, you bastard...Bleeding Sebastian, how I have been bored in my life, the interminable, unforgivable, life-robbing information-less timelost entropy-triumphant stagnant retching BOREDOM I have suffered...I won't do it to anyone else. If I can help it. And yet I want to communicate, and I'm prolix, right? Do you get the picture of Tiptree agonisingly contorted between his gabbling tongue and his saber-wielding ear? Do you?

"I want to say a word about influences. Who one admires and who one is influenced by aren't the same. For example, sometimes you learn a trick from a guy who has nothing but that trick. (Even that guy with the shears 'influenced' me, ah oui!) You learn from a myriad people, *and* from their mistakes. But there's a feeling that your list of 'influences' is your list of greats. NOT SO. And here's the important thing to me:

"Who do I admire in SF? You and you and you as far as eye and memory reach, Sir and Madam. Some for this, some for that. All different. But more than that--

"I love the SF world. And I don't love easy. Out of SF I wouldn't spare one, from the dimmest two-neurone dreamer to the voice from the heart of the sun...maybe to you on the inside it's not as clear as to me out here. What *is* SF?

"What but a staggering, towering, glittering, mad, lay cathedral? Built like the old ones by spontaneous volunteers, some bringing one laborious gargoyle, some a load of stone, some engineering a spire. Over years now, over time the thing has grown, you know? To what god? Who knows. Something different from the gods of the other arts. A god that isn't there yet, maybe. An urging saying Up, saying Screw it all. Saying Try. To...be...more? We don't know. But *everyone* has made this. Limping, scratching, wrangling, clowning, goony, sauced, hes, shes, its, thems, beemies for all I know, swooping glory, freaked out in corners, ridiculous, noble, queerly vulnerable in some way others aren't-- totally irrelevant, really--

"These are the nearest to winged people that we have, and I would shut up forever rather than hurt one of them. Dead or alive."

* * * * *

J. R. R. TOLKIEN

Full Name: John Ronald Reuel Tolkien [pronounced like dóll-keen]. Born January 3, 1892, at Bloemfontein, Orange Free State, South Africa. Son of Arthur Reuel Tolkien (a bank manager) and Mabel Suffield. Married Edith Mary Bratt, March 22, 1916 (died, 1971). Four children: John Francis Joseph Reuel (born 1917), Michael Hilary Reuel (born 1921), Christopher John Reuel (born 1924), Priscilla Mary Reuel (born 1929).

J. R. R. TOLKIEN (Cont.)

Education: Attended King Edward VI School, Birmingham; B.A., Exeter College, Oxford University, 1915; M.A., 1919.

Career: Professor of English.
Assistant, *Oxford English Dictionary*, 1918-20; Reader in English, University of Leeds, 1920; Professor, 1924-25; Rawlinson and Bosworth Professor of Anglo-Saxon, Oxford University, 1925-45; Merton Professor of English Language and Literature, 1945-59; Fellow of Pembroke, College, 1926-45; retired in 1959. Died at Bournemouth, England, September 2, 1973.

Member: Science Fiction Writers of America (Honorary Member).

Awards: International Fantasy Award, 1957, for *The Lord of the Rings* Trilogy; Gandalf Award, 1974.

* * * * *

WALKER A. TOMPKINS

Full Name: Walker Allison Tompkins.
Born July 10, 1909, at Prosser, Washington. Son of C. E. Tompkins and Bertha A. Tompkins. Married Grace Spear, 1941. Three children: Reid, Joyce, Pamela.
Education: Attended Modesto Junior College, University of Washington, Columbia University, University of California, Oxford University.

Career: Writer.
Newspaper reporter, 1927-31; free-lance author, 1931-DATE.

Agent: Lenniger Literary Agency, 11 W. 42nd St., New York, NY 10036.

Member:
Western Writers of America; California Writers Guild; Writers Guild of America, West; Sierra Club; Westerners, Los Angeles Corral.

* * * * *

ROBERT E. TOOMEY JR.

Full Name: Robert Emmett Toomey, Jr.
Born September 5, 1945, at Hartford, Connecticut. Son of Robert Emmett Toomey (a golf pro) and Adelaide Reilly. Married and divorced. One daughter, Elizabeth Margaret (born 1966).

Career: Writer.
Journalist and reporter, *Holyoke Transcript*, Massachusetts, 1966-67; Films Editor, *Springfield Area Life and Times*, Massachusetts, 1971-73; free-lance writer, 1969-DATE.

First Professional Sale: "Pejorative," in *New Worlds*, July, 1969.

Agent: Henry Morrison, 311 1/2 W. 20th St., New York, NY.

Member: Science Fiction Writers of America.

Interests: Film and literary criticism, chess, travel, lecturing.

Toomey writes:
"Like most writers, I have worked at a variety of jobs, from turret lathe machinist to civil engineer to golf course landscaper. I've been in and out of the military and a number of institutions of higher education, and if I've learned a lesson from all of this, it's that human beings are a durable lot, and writing about them is more fun than anything. Too bad it pays so poorly. Oh well. *C'est la vie.*"

* * * * *

ANTHONY TOWNE

Full Name: Anthony Towne.
Born February 14, 1928, at Haverhill, Massachusetts. Son of Edwin G. Towne, Jr., and Margaret Anthony.

Education: B.A., Yale University, 1951.

Career: Writer (first book published in 1967).

* * * * *

POLLY TOYNBEE

Full Name: Polly Mary Louisa Toynbee.
Born December 27, 1946, at Ventnor, Isle of Wight, Great Britain. Daughter of Theodore Philip Toynbee (a writer, and son of Arnold Toynbee) and Anne Barbara Denise Powell (a social worker). Married Peter George James Jenkins (a journalist). Two children: Amy (born 1963), Millie (born 1971).

Education: Attended Holland Park Comprehensive, and St. Annes College, Oxford University.

Career: Writer.
Currently a feature writer for the *London Observer*.

Agent: A. D. Peters Ltd., 10 Buckingham St., London W.1, England.

Member: Labour Party.

* * * * *

DON TRACY

Full Name: Donald Fiske Tracy.
Born August 20, 1905, at New Britain, Connecticut. Son of Wilbur Clinton Tracy and Charlotte Fuller. Married Carolyn Boyd Herring, June 14, 1929.

Career: Writer.
Reporter in New Britain, 1926-28, in Baltimore, 1929-34; rewrite man, *Radio News*, 1935-41; free-lance writer, 1941-DATE; summer Instructor in Fiction, Syracuse University, 1955-59. Member: Authors Guild; Clearwater Country Club.

* * * * *

ROBERT TRALINS

Full Name: Sandor Robert Tralins.
Born April 28, 1926, at Baltimore, Maryland. Son of Emanuel Tralins (a shipbuilder) and Rose Miller. Married Sonya Lee Mandel, September 2, 1945. Two sons: Myles Jay (born 1947), Alan Harvey (born 1951).

ROBERT TRALINS (Cont.)

Education: Attended Johns Hopkins University, 1946-48.

Career: Writer.
Has been a full-time writer since 1947.

First Professional Sale: A story or article in 1948; first book: *The Aenidians*, Classic Books, 1954.

Interests:
Chess, sailing (owns a 33 foot Classic clipper rigged ketch, a Luders design built by Cheoy Lee of Hong Kong, 1971).

Tralins notes: "I'm the author of 194 published books and novels. I've had more than 1500 magazine stories and articles published, but have concentrated only on books during the past decade. Some screenplays as well."

* * * * *

JACOB TRANSUE

Full Name: Joan Matheson.
Born January 29, 1924, at East Stroudberg, Pennsylvania. Daughter of William Transue (an engineer, farmer, and artist) and Helena Keller (a musician). Married David Matheson, December 1, 1941. One daughter, Hedda (born 1955).

Career: Writer.
Feature columnist, *Easton Express*, 1962-65; Editor, *The Minisink Bull*, 1966-70.

First Professional Sale: *First Vice President*, Doubleday & Co., 1952.

Agent: Virginia Kidd, Box 278, Milford, PA 18337.

Transue writes:
"My ancestors were carried away by the Shawnee, and Americanized during long years of captivity before the Revolution, and we have had no use for Europe ever since. I must be the first member since that time to see Europe without a uniform. Lived in France for four years. Loved it, but the Indians are right.
"Started out early as a serious voice student, and was a performing prodigy at ten. At thirteen, that career climaxed with a performance with a symphony orchestra. The following month, my father died intestate, the legal-financial establishment divvied up the estate, and my mother and I were cast adrift. I moved to Washington, D.C., a place I have detested ever since. Won a national poetry contest in school, and was immediately accused of plagiarism by a teacher. When that was settled in my favor, I left public school, and moved to the Corcoran Art School, so 'formal' education was a short adventure.
"Lived in New York five years working on radio and early TV, plus the usual number of strange employments (night-club swami, model, publicity writer). My first book was published while I was in Hawaii. *The Advertiser* sent a reporter who (I later learned) had just emerged from a prefrontal lobotomy. She made me sound like the patient. The interview cooled plans for a lit-tea and sale. Something strange happens to everything I write. Sold my first short story

"to the *Saturday Evening Post* just before it threw in the sponge.
"Again in Washington, D.C., I amused myself sending funny letters to the *Washington Post*. They finally asked me to write them ten sample columns as a try-out for a feature. When I turned them in, they discovered I wasn't a Liberal Anglophile. Back to the Reservation.
"My second novel was about Hawaii, and yielded nothing but an interminable and very funny correspondence with Viking Press. It was never published, and is now passé.
"From 1957 to 1970, I was fully occupied helping to found the Delaware Valley Conservation Association, and trying to expose the power combines determined to rip off the Delaware River. During that time, I edited *The Minisink Bull*, which a local official called 'scurrilous,' but which Senator Metcalf called 'the most delightful paper (if I can call it that) that has ever crossed my desk.' *Twilight of the Basilisks* was written to help keep the *Bull* going, and is about Indians and conservation, and addresses the puzzle of the roots of Empire and how to rip them out.
"Lack of credentials has never bothered me. I worked for two years with a psychologist from the Pennsylvania Department of Education testing helpless children. In France, I translated case histories for a French psychoanalyst. Those two experiences convinced me that, like most Christian theology, the Freudian ideology leads inevitably to an imperialistic worldview. I suspect that formal education does the same thing. I once showed my boss, by comparing Szondi, Rorschach, MMP, and other readings with the leading aptitude tests, that we were sifting obsessives into administrative and executive positions. He agreed. It's still going on.
"I probably have known more people 'when' than anyone else of equal obscurity. A Jonah in reverse. 'Eat at Transue's table for a year, and get famous.' It's a magic that, apparently, I can only give away. Many have made it big in showbiz, writing, and politics. One became the FBI's 'most wanted.'
"Indians, conservation, and music remain the big pegs of my lifeline. I would like to write more about Scrim Shaw because I like comparing the native worldview with that of the ageless empire, but *Twilight* fell down the usual well after Berkley welched on my galleys and hard cover contract. The book was a mess. Par for the course.
"Following our expropriation from the Delaware by the Corps of Engineers, for half the value of our place, we moved to Nebraska where we are now farming a little homestead. It's a great place to write."

* * * * *

HENRY TREECE

Full Name: Henry Treece.
Born 1911, at Wednesbury, Staffordshire, England. Son of Richard Treece and Mary Mason. Married Mary Woodman, 1939. Two children: Jennifer Elizabeth, Gareth Richard.

Education: B.A., Birmingham University, 1933; Diploma in Education, 1934; Diploma, University of Santander, 1933.

Career: Writer.
English Master, The College, Shropshire, 1934-35; English Master, Tynemouth School, Northumberland, 1935-39; English Master, The Grammar School, Barton-on-Humber, 1939-59; professional writer, 1959-66. Died June 10, 1966.

HENRY TREECE (Cont.)

Agent: Ann Elmo, 52 Vanderbilt Avenue, New York, NY 10017.

Awards: Art Council Play Prize, 1955. Member: Barton Drama Club; Barton Cricket Club.

* * * * *

S. J. TREIBICH

Full Name: Stephen John Treibich.
Born March 8, 1936. Education: Master's degree.

Career: Writer. Died April 14, 1972.

First Professional Sale:
Haelstrom Manor, Lancer Books, 1966 ["First Context," a story co-authored with Laurence M. Janifer, actually was published first, in *The Magazine of Fantasy and Science Fiction*, August, 1965].

Laurence M. Janifer, who collaborated with Treibich on many of his books, had the following comments:
"He was the finest storyteller I've ever known. Everyone who knew him tried to push him to get those stories down on paper, but there wasn't enough time, and there was always the distraction of doctors, and hospitals, and operations, and recoveries. Most of the stories didn't get told. A very few of those that did, got down on paper. He was a kind and generous and electric man, a good friend."

* * * * *

MAX TRELL

Full Name: Max Trell.
Born September 6, 1900, at New York, New York. Son of Salomon Trell and Sophia Levine. Married Bluma L. Popkin (a professor of classics), September 6, 1926. One son, Max Jr.

Education: B.A., Columbia University, 1923; studied at the Sorbonne, University of Paris, 1929-30.

Career: Film producer and director.
Reporter, *Zits Theatrical Weekly*, 1924; for the *New York Daily News*, 1925-27; Story Editor, Warner Brothers, 1927-32; Associate Editor, *Pictorial Review*, 1934-39; producer and director of films for Columbia Pictures; free-lance author, 1930-DATE. Member: Screen Writers Guild, West.

Awards:
Academy Award for story and narration, 1947, for "Climbing the Matterhorn," a short movie; Freedoms Foundation Award, 1948, for story and continuity of "Dick's Adventures," a syndicated cartoon feature based on American history.

* * * * *

ELIZABETH BORTON de TREVINO

Full Name: Elizabeth Borton de Treviño.
Born September 2, 1904, at Bakersfield, California. Daughter of Fred Ellsworth Borton (a lawyer) and Carrie Christensen. Married Luis Treviño Gomez, August 10, 1935. Two children: Luis Frederico, Enrique Ricardo.

Education: B.A., Stanford University, 1925; studied violin at the Boston Conservatory of Music.

Career: Writer and journalist.
Former reviewer of performing arts for *Boston Herald*; now a professional writer and journalist; honorary lecturer, American Institute for Foreign Trade.

Agent: McIntosh & Otis, 475 Fifth Avenue, New York, NY 10017.

Awards & Honors: Honorary Citizen of Texas; Medal of Kansas City Woman's Organization; Newbery Medal, 1966, for *I, Juan de Pareja*.

Member:
Women in Communications; Hispanic Society; Phi Beta Kappa; Pan American Round Tables; Altrusa Clubs.

* * * * *

ELLESTON TREVOR

Full Name: Elleston Trevor [originally, Trevor Dudley-Smith]. Born February 17, 1920, in England. Son of Walter Smith and Florence Elleston. Married Jonquil Burgess (her husband's literary manager), 1947. One son, Peregrine Scott.

Career: Writer.
Apprentice racing driver for two years prior to World War II; in the Royal Air Force, 1940-46; full-time writer, 1946-DATE.

Awards: Edgar Award, 1966, for *The Quiller Memorandum*.

* * * * *

MERIOL TREVOR

Full Name: Lucy Meriol Trevor.
Born April 15, 1919, at London, England. Daughter of Arthur Prescott Trevor and Lucy Dimmock. Education: B.A., St. Hugh's College, Oxford University, 1942.

Career: Writer.
Relief worker, U.N. Relief and Rehabilitaion Administration, Italy, 1946-47; full-time writer, 1947-DATE.

Agent: Harold Ober Associates, 40 E. 49th St., New York, NY 10017.

* * * * *

ANTONY TREW

Full Name: Antony Francis Trew.
Born June 5, 1906, at Pretoria, South Africa. Son of Harry Trew (an army officer and police commissioner) and Florence Dixon. Married Nora Houthakker, July 10, 1931. Three sons: Peter, Robert, Antony.

Career: Writer.
Left Diocesan College in 1922 to join the Merchant Navy, and spent five years at sea, qualifying as an officer; Sub-Lieutenant, South African Navy, 1927-31; Divisional Secretary of the Automobile Association of South Africa, Transvaal, 1932-36; Joint General Manager of the Head Office in Johannesburg, 1936-39; with the

ANTONY TREW (Cont.)

South Africa Navy and Royal Navy, 1939-45, serving
at Tobruk Naval Base and with the Anti-Submarine Group
in the Mediterranean, 1941; later was Technical Deputy
Director of South African Naval Forces at Capetown,
and Commander of the *H.M.S. Walker*, a destroyer on
convoy duty to North Russia; became a Lt. Commander,
receiving the Distinguished Service Cross; Director-
General, Automobile Association of South Africa, 1946-
66, resigning to devote full time to his writing.
Long-time member of the South African Road Safety
Council, and other national, state, and local bodies
in South Africa devoted to roads and traffic.

* * * * *

JACQUELYN TRIMBLE

Full Name: Jacquelyn Trimble.
   Born October 21, 1927, at Portland, Oregon. Daughter of Frederick Willis Whitney (a civil engineer)
and Naomi Agnes Groll. Married Louis Preston Trimble
(the writer), November 21, 1952 (divorced). One step-
daughter, Victoria Rosemary (born 1939).

Education: B.A., University of Washington, 1951;
   M.L.S., 1959.

Career: Writer.
   Librarian and Secretary to the Microbiology Dept.,
University of Pennsylvania, 1955-56; Buyer of Children's Books, Hartman's Bookstore, 1956-58; Reference
Librarian, King County Public Library, 1962-67; Editor, *Pacific Northwest Needle Arts Guild Newsletter*,
1973-74; free-lance author, 1967-DATE.

First Professional Sale: *The Whisper of Shadows*,
   Ace Books, 1964 (as Phyllis A. Whitney).

Agent: Scott Meredith Literary Agency, 580 Fifth
   Avenue, New York, NY 10036.

Member: Embroiderers' Guild; Pacific Northwest
   Needle Arts Guild; National Council of American
   Embroiderers; Science Fiction Writers of America.

Interests: Needle arts, gardening.

Jacquelyn Trimble comments: "My collaborator
was my ex-husband, who has done a great deal more
successful writing than I. In practice, he would
generally do the first draft--he would always do the
first draft. I'd do the second, and we'd argue out
the third. I did assist on two other of his books,
but not to a degree sufficient to merit credit as a
collaborator. On one occasion, we did attempt to
work from my first draft--but this was completely
unsuccessful."

* * * * *

LOUIS TRIMBLE

Full Name: Louis Preston Trimble.
   Born March 2, 1917, at Seattle, Washington. Son of
Charles Louis Trimble (an artist) and Rose Alice Pot-
ter. Married Jacquelyn Whitney (a librarian and
author), November 21, 1952 (divorced). One daughter,
Victoria Rosemary (born 1939).

Education: B.A., Eastern Washington State College,

1950; Ed.M., 1953; also attended University of Washington, 1952-53, 1955, 1956-57, and University of Pennsylvania, 1955-56.

Career: Professor of Social Studies.
   High school teacher of English, Bonners Ferry, Idaho,
1946-47; Instructor in Spanish and English, Eastern
Washington State College, 1950-54; Instructor, University of Washington, 1956-59; Assistant Professor, 1959-
67; Associate Professor of Humanities and Social Studies, 1967-DATE; free-lance author, 1938-DATE.

First Professional Sale: *Sports of the World*,
   Golden West Publishers, 1938.

Agent: Scott Meredith, 580 Fifth Avenue, New York,
   NY 10036.

Member: Science Fiction Writers of America; Western
   Writers of America.

Interests: Golf, studying languages, travel.

"I'm currently involved in Yugoslavia, writing a text
on scientific English to help Yugoslav technical school
students *read* scientific and technical English--am
doing this on a one year sabbatical leave from my university."

* * * * *

DALTON TRUMBO

Full Name: Dalton Trumbo.
   Born December 9, 1905, at Montrose, Colorado. Son
of Orus Bonham Trumbo and Maud Tillery. Married Cleo
Beth Fincher (a photographer), March 13, 1939. Three
children: Nikola, Christopher, Melissa.

Education: Attended University of Colorado, 1924-25,
   and University of Southern California, 1928-30.

Career: Writer.
   Has been a car washer, section hand, a bread-wrapper,
an estimator on the night shift for Divis Perfection
Bakery (Los Angeles), reader at Warner Brothers, Managing Editor of *The Hollywood Spectator*, Founding Editor of *The Screenwriter*, 1945; screenwriter, 1936-DATE;
war correspondent, 1945; served as National Chairman,
Writers for Roosevelt, 1944. Trumbo was blacklisted
after refusing to testify before the House Committee
on Un-American Activities, and between 1947-60 turned
out a variety of film scripts under pseudonyms for
low-budget Mexican and Hollywood film companies; he
won an Academy Award in 1957 for one of these movies,
"The Brave One," written under the penname Robert Rich.

Agent: Shirley Burke, 370 E. 76th St., New York, NY
   10021. Award: National Booksellers Award, 1939, for
   Johnny Got His Gun. Member: Screenwriters Guild.

* * * * *

THOMAS TRYON

Full Name: Thomas Tryon.
   Born January 14, 1926, at Hartford, Connecticut. Son
of Arthur Lane Tryon (a clothier) and Elizabeth Lester.
Education: B.A., Yale University, 1949.

Career: Writer, 1971-DATE; actor, 1960-DATE. Agent:
   International Famous Agency, 1301 Avenue of the Americas, New York, NY 10019.

E. C. TUBB

Full Name: Edwin Charles Tubb.
   Born October 15, 1919, at London, England. Son of Edwin Margrie Tubb (an engineer) and Marie Francois Bonzec (a dress designer). Married Iris Kathleen Smith, 1944. Two children: Jennifer Evelyn (born 1948), Linda Edwina (born 1954).

Career: Writer.
   Has been a welfare officer, catering manager, and advisory consultant; free-lance author, 1950-DATE; Editor, *Authentic Science Fiction*, February, 1956-October, 1957; Editor, *Eye @ Vector*, 1958-60.

First Professional Sale: "No Short Cuts," in *New Worlds*, Summer, 1951.

Agent: E. J. Carnell Literary Agency, 17 Burwash Road, Plumstead, London SE18 7QY, England.

Honors & Awards:
   Co-Guest of Honor, 28th World Science Fiction Convention (Heicon '70), Heidelberg, Germany, 1970; Cytricon Literary Award, Best British SF Author, 1955; Special Award, Eurocon 1, Trieste, 1972, for best short story, "Lucifer."

Tubb is best known for his long series of books featuring Earl Dumarest, who roams the Galaxy looking for traces of the lost planet Earth. He had these comments:
   "Dumarest will, one day, find Earth and so end the series. As to how I conceived of the character, well, he just grew--probably from my subconscious, as these things usually happen."

* * * * *

DONALD H. TUCK

Full Name: Donald Henry Tuck.
   Born December 3, 1922, at Launceston, Tasmania, Australia. Son of Harry Playford Tuck (an associate professor of electrical engineering) and Beatrice May Norsworthy. Married Audrey Jean Cranston, May 1, 1954. One son, Marcus Jonathan (born 1960).

Education: B.Sc., University of Tasmania, 1948.

Career: Superintendent.
   War service with the A.I.F., 1942-45; Technical Editor, Defence Research Laboratories, 1948-50; Technical Editor, C.S.I.R.O., Melbourne, 1951; Assistant Librarian, Electrolytic Zinc Company, Risdon, Tasmania, 1952-57; Publicity Officer, 1957-72; Assistant Superintendent of the Industrial Services Department, 1972-DATE.

Honors & Awards:
   Fan Guest of Honor, 33rd World Science Fiction Convention (Aussiecon), Sydney, 1975; Special Plaque, 20th World Science Fiction Convention (Chicon III), Chicago, 1962, for *The Handbook of Science Fiction*.

Interests: Philately, good music, cricket, Australian Rules football (soccer).

Tuck writes:
   "I am essentially a collector and bibliographer, with reading unfortunately a side-line. Bibliography takes time, and my main wish would be for a halt in "publishing so that I can catch up on my reading. Still, the flow of new material does show that science fiction is still quite virile. My grumble with the field is the trend away from magazines to paperbacks. A magazine is a much more friendly publication, with a form of 'togetherness,' especially when expressed in good letter columns. Post-war enthusiasts will remember the letters in *Thrilling Wonder* and *Startling* in the late 1940s, which gave these magazines a flavour all of their own. Today, only Ted White endeavors to reach his audience in this fashion.
   "Today's science fiction is better written. We'll all admit this, but there is too much pointless material or gobbledygook to my way of thinking. There are, of course, no new plots, but some of today's writers make very creditable efforts with new twists and the like--and the power of their writing can at times grip one. Probably the main addition to the field in the last decade is the addition of sex, and excluding the sheer porn from a few specialist publishers, it has been added reasonably well. Though I must confess I still have a soft spot for the Weinbaum-type of light romance of 30 years or so ago. My sense of wonder then was ripest--the fantastic adventures of Burroughs, the space epics of Edward Smith--and they have lost nothing in re-reading a few years back.
   "However, I hope I'm not too much biased on the past, as the Kubrick/Clarke film "2001: A Space Odyssey" renewed my sense of grandeur in science fiction. I'm optimistic enough to want more, and hope that authors like Farmer, Heinlein, and Silverberg, and others, will renew that all-important sense of wonder for at least myself, if not the rest of the science fiction reading public."

* * * * *

WILSON TUCKER

Full Name: Arthur Wilson "Bob" Tucker.
   Born November 23, 1914, at Deer Creek, Illinois. Son of James Ira Tucker (a stage manager) and Marie Ross. Married Mary Joesting (divorced, 1942); married Fern Delores Brooks, November 3, 1953. Five children: Judith Marie (born 1938), Robert Arthur (born 1940), David Roger (born 1954), Brian Arthur (born 1957), Bruce Wesley (born 1960).

Career: Writer and electrician.
   Has worked as a projectionist in about ten theatres, an electrician for Twentieth Century-Fox Studios, and as a stage electrician for the University of Illinois at Urbana, and the University of Illinois at Normal; now retired. Free-lance author, 1941-DATE; Reporter and local Editor, *Bloomington-Normal Labor News*, a division of the *Peoria Labor News*, 1942-45; Editor and Publisher, *Science Fiction News Letter*, 1949-53.

First Professional Sale: "Interstellar Way-Station," in *Super Science Novels*, May, 1941.

Agent: Curtis Brown Ltd., 60 E. 56th St., New York, NY 10022.

Honors & Awards:
   Fan Guest of Honor, 25th World Science Fiction Convention (NyCon 3), New York, 1967; Hugo Award, Best Fan Writer, 1969 (1970); John W. Campbell Memorial Award for Best Science Fiction Novel of the Year, Retrospective Award, 1976, for *The Year of the Quiet Sun*.

Member: Science Fiction Writers of America; Mystery Writers of America.

WILSON TUCKER (Cont.)

Interests:
   Travelling, public speaking. "Have attended about fifty regional and world science fiction conventions, frequently as a speaker, or panelist, or guest of honor, or toastmaster."

Tucker writes:
   "About my start in writing: about 1927 I originated our local school newspaper in an accidental way. One of my teachers caught me making carbon-copy 'newspapers' in study hall, and passing them around to nearby students. She suggested my enterprise be put to better use, and arranged for the principal's secretary to mimeograph my work. About a hundred copies were struck off, and for the next two years I was writer and editor of that paper. Out of school, I bought a very-much-used typewriter for $11, and decided to be a big name author. About ten years later, I finally made it with my first sale to Fred Pohl. He remembered that sale, only a week ago, when we met at the world convention. He even quoted the title correctly.
   "I'm not good at short stories; I've never mastered them, and so I turned to books in 1946, selling the first one I ever wrote. Have been doing that ever since, with perhaps a half dozen short stories scattered over the intervening thirty-odd years.
   "I think I invented the habit (at least in the science fiction world) of including the names of fans and friends in my books. I usually use only one of their two or three names, most often a surname, and the practice began with my first book, The Chinese Doll, which was a murder mystery involving fans. Now they call it 'tuckerizing,' and several people do it.
   "I've been interested in science fiction since I learned to read, I think. Ray Cummings's serial Brand New World in a 1929 Argosy was my first plunge, although I had read the Burroughs and Rockwood books earlier without knowing they were science fiction— if you'll stretch a point. I picked up my first copy of Weird Tales in 1930 in a theater, and after that quickly discovered the Clayton and Gernsback magazines."

* * * * *

CATHERINE TURNEY

Full Name: Catherine Turney.
   Born December 26, 1906, at Chicago, Illinois. Daughter of George Turney (a manufacturer) and Elizabeth Blamer. Married and divorced.

Education: Attended Columbia School of Journalism, and the Pasadena Playhouse School of the Theatre.

Career: Writer.
   First play, "Bitter Harvest," produced in London in 1936; Contract Writer, Warner Brothers, 1943-48.
Agent: Shirley Burke, 370 E. 76th St., New York 10021.

* * * * *

JOSEPH TUSIANI

Full Name: Joseph Tusiani.
   Born January 14, 1924, at Foggia, Italy. Came to the U.S., 1947, and naturalized in 1956. Son of Michael Tusiani and Maria Pisone. Education: Ph.D., University of Naples, 1947.

Career: Instructor in Italian Literature.
   Teacher of Latin and Greek, Liceo Classico, San Severo, Italy, 1944-47; Lecturer in Italian, Hunter College, 1950-63; Lecturer in Italian Literature, New York University, 1956-63; Chairman of the Italian Dept., College of Mount Saint Vincent, 1948-71; Instructor in Italian Literature, Herbert H. Lehman College, City University of New York, 1971-DATE.

Awards & Honors:
   Greenwood Prize, Poetry Society of England, 1956; Silver Medal for Latin Poetry (Rome), 1962; Alice Fay di Castagnola Award, Poetry Society of America, 1968; Spirit Gold Medal of the Catholic Poetry Society of America, 1969; Outstanding Teacher Award, College of Mount Saint Vincent, 1969; Litt.D., College of Mount Saint Vincent, 1971.

Member:
   Poetry Society of America; P.E.N.; Catholic Poetry Society of America; Dante Society of America; American Association of University Professors.

* * * * *

AMOS TUTUOLA

Full Name: Amos Tutuola.
   Born 1920, at Abeokuta, Nigeria. Son of Charles Tutuola (a cocoa farmer) and Esther Aina. Married Alake Victoria, 1947. Three children: Olubunmi, Oluyinka, Erinola.

Career: Writer and government worker.
   Employed by the Nigerian Government Labor Dept., Lagos, Nigeria, and the Nigerian Broadcasting Corp., Ibadan, Nigeria; free-lance author, 1952-DATE. Member: Mbari Club (Nigerian authors; founder).

* * * * *

THEODORE TYLER

Full Name: Edward William Ziegler ["a ziegl is a tile"]. Born July 12, 1932, at New York, New York. Son of Vinton E. Ziegler and Beatrice Skelton. Married Sally McIntosh, June 15, 1957. Three children: Andrew, Matthew, Sally.

Education: B.A., Duke University, 1955.

Career: Writer and editor.
   Writer and editor for Reader's Digest.

First Professional Sale: Men Who Make Us Rich, Macmillan, 1962 (as Edward Ziegler).

* * * * *

JAMES RAMSEY ULLMAN

Full Name: James Ramsey Ullman.
   Born November 24, 1907, at New York, New York. Son of Alexander F. Ullman and Eunice Ramsey. Married Ruth Fishman, 1930; married Elaine Luria, 1946; married Marian Blinn, 1961. Two sons: James Ramsey Jr., William A.

Education: Attended Phillips Academy, Andover, 1922-25; B.A., Princeton University, 1929.

JAMES RAMSEY ULLMAN (Cont.)

Career: Writer.
  Newspaper reporter and feature writer, 1929-32; theatrical producer, New York, 1933-37 (co-producer of
Sidney Kingsley's "Men in White," a Pulitzer Prize
play, 1934); executive of the Works Progress Administration Federal Theater Project, 1938-39; full-time
writer, 1939-71. Died June 20, 1971.

Member: P.E.N.; Overseas Press Club; Authors Guild;
  American Alpine Club; Princeton Club; St. Botolph
  Club.

Agent: Harold Matson, 22 E. 40th St., New York, NY
  10016.

* * * * *

LOUIS UNTERMEYER

Full Name: Louis Untermeyer.
  Born October 1, 1885, at New York, New York. Son of
Emanuel Untermeyer (a jeweler) and Julia Michael.
Married Jean Starr (a poet), 1907 (divorced); married
Virginia Moore (a poet), 1926 (divorced); married
Esther Antin (a lawyer), 1933 (divorced); married
Bryna Ivens (an editor of children's books), 1948.
Four children: Richard (deceased), John Moore, Lauren
S., Joseph Louis.

Career: Writer.
  Jewelry manufacturer with his father and uncle,
Untermeyer-Robbins Co., and Charles Keller & Co.,
1902-23, becoming Vice-President and Manager of the
factory at Newark; resigned 1923, to devote his time
to writing, editing, and lecturing. Lecturer at vari-
ous colleges and universities; Publications Editor,
U.S. Office of War Information, 1942; Editor, Armed
Forces Editions, 1944; Consultant in English Poetry,
Library of Congress, 1961-63; U.S. representative at
conferences in India, 1961; conducted seminars in
American poetry in Japan in 1962. Member: National
Institute of Arts and Letters; Phi Beta Kappa. Died
December 18, 1977.

Awards: Gold Medal, Poetry Society of America, 1956,
  for services to poetry.

* * * * *

JOHN UPDIKE

Full Name: John Hoyer Updike.
  Born March 18, 1932, at Shillington, Pennsylvania.
Son of Wesley Russell Updike (a teacher) and Linda
Grace Hoyer. Married Mary Entwistle Pennington, 1953.
Four children: Elizabeth Pennington, David Hoyer,
Michael John, Miranda.

Education: A.B., Harvard College, 1954; attended
  Ruskin School of Drawing and Fine Art, Oxford, England, 1955.

Career: Writer.
  Reporter, "Talk of the Town" column, *New Yorker*
magazine, 1955-57; full-time writer, 1958-DATE. Member: National Institute of Arts and Letters.

Awards:
  Guggenheim fellowship in poetry, 1959; Richard and
Hinda Rosenthal Award of National Institute of Arts

and Letters, 1960, for *The Poorhouse Fair*; National
Book Award in Fiction, 1963, for *The Centaur*; Prix de
Meilleur Livre Étranger, 1966, for *The Centaur*.

* * * * *

MAE URBANEK

Full Name: Mae Urbanek.
  Born September 10, 1903, at Denver, Colorado. Daugh-
ter of Boyd Byron Bobb and Sarah Hotze. Married Jerry
Urbanek (a rancher), December 15, 1928.

Education: B.S., Northwestern University, 1927.

Career: Rancher and writer.
  Rancher at Lusk, Wyoming, 1928-DATE; free-lance aut-
hor, 1958-DATE. Member: Wyoming Federation of Garden
Clubs; Wyoming Press Women; Rebekah Lodge; Alpha Gamma
Delta; Delta Kappa Gamma.

* * * * *

JACK VANCE

Full Name: John Holbrook Vance.
  Born August 28, 1916, at San Francisco, California.
Son of Charles Albert Vance (a rancher) and Edith
Hoefler. Married Norma Ingold, August 24, 1946. One
son, John Holbrook II (born 1961).

Education: B.A., University of California, Berkeley,
  1942.

Career: Writer.
  Has been a screen writer for Twentieth Century-Fox;
full-time writer, 1946-DATE.

First Professional Sale: "The World-Thinker," in
  Thrilling Wonder Stories, Summer, 1945.

Agent: Scott Meredith, 580 Fifth Avenue, New York,
  NY 10036.

Awards:
  Nebula Award, Best Novella, 1966 (1967), "The Last
Castle"; Jupiter Award, Best Novelette, 1974 (1975),
"The Seventeen Virgins"; Hugo Award, Best Short Fiction,
1962 (1963), "The Dragon Masters"; Hugo Award, Best
Novelette, 1966 (1967), "The Last Castle."

Member: Science Fiction Writers of America.

Vance comments: "I was born in San Francisco, and
spent my childhood on a ranch in the San Joaquin Valley
in California. Re *Trullion: Alastor 2262*: I like baseball and (college) football myself, and so it simply
seemed automatic to consider what new type of games
might be possible. Hence, *hussade* [the planetary sport
of Trullion]."

* * * * *

MARK VAN DOREN

Full Name: Mark Van Doren.
  Born June 13, 1894, at Hope, Illinois. Son of Charles
Lucius Van Doren (a physician) and Dora Butz. Married
Dorothy Graffe, September 1, 1922. Two sons: Charles,
John. Education: A.B., University of Illinois, 1914;
A.M., 1915; Ph.D., Columbia University, 1920.

MARK VAN DOREN (Cont.)

Career: Professor of English.
  Professor of English, Columbia University, 1920-59;
Literary Editor, *The Nation*, 1924-28; Lecturer, St.
John's College, 1937-57; Visiting Professor of Eng-
lish, Harvard University, 1963. Died 1972.

Member: National Institute of Arts and Letters;
  American Academy of Arts and Letters.

Honors & Awards:
  Pulitzer Prize for Poetry, 1940, for *Collected Poems*;
Litt.D., Bowdoin College, 1944; from University of
Illinois, 1958; from Columbia University, 1960; from
Knox College, 1966; from Harvard University, 1966;
L.H.D., Adelphi University, 1957; from Mount Mary
College, 1965; Fellowship, St. John's College, 1959;
Honorary Degree in Medicine, Connecticut State Medi-
cal Society, 1959; Sarah Josepha Hale Award of the
Richards Free Library, Newport, New Hampshire, 1960;
Emerson-Thoreau Award, American Academy of Arts and
Letters, 1963.

* * * * *

SYDNEY VAN SCYOC

Full Name: Sydney Joyce Van Scyoc [pronounced Sy-
  ock]. Born July 27, 1939, at Mt. Vernon, Indiana.
Daughter of John William Brown (a postal employee)
and Geneva Alberta Blanche Curry. Married Jim R.
Van Scyoc, June 23, 1957. Two children: Sandra Kirsten (born 1965), John Scott (born 1967).

Career: Writer.
  "Graduated from high school in 1957, and married
an Air Force officer immediately thereafter. Attended
college-level classes here and there, but never got
as far as a degree. Also did a little flying, and
studied Japanese briefly." Free-lance writer, 1962-
DATE.

First Professional Sale: "Shatter the Wall," in
  Galaxy, February, 1962.

Agent: Adrienne Martine, 5816 Alameda Avenue #1,
  Richmond, CA 94802.

Member:
  Science Fiction Writers of America; Mystery Writers
of America; Alameda County Association for Retarded
Children; Starr King Unitarian Church; League of
Women Voters.

Interests: Gardening, stamp collecting, swimming,
  reading.

"Why are so few women involved in science fiction,
either as readers or writers? This has puzzled me
since I first realized I had to find male companions
to discuss Heinlein. Of course, women have long been
greeted by large and bristly UNWELCOME mats when they
ventured too near the male strongholds of science and
technology, and this has naturally discouraged very
many from interest in science fiction as well. Then,
given the heavy preponderance of male authors and
readers in the field, a woman has consistently had
the choice of identifying herself almost exclusively
with male protagonists, or hunting elsewhere for reading material. For myself, I have found it difficult
to create strong female protagonists, simply from the

"lack of real-life prototypes. Worse, I have found it
difficult to create myself--from the same lack. Now
I see around me a whole generation of women who must
create themselves from a non-existent mold--but, thank
goodness, that creation *is* finally going forward, and
unless my eyes deceive me, we are already experiencing
an influx of women into science fiction. I expect that
as the genre matures, and more importantly, as our society matures, we will see a larger and larger percentage of women writing science fiction--and doing it
well. Quite a change--but isn't change what science
fiction is supposed to be all about?"

* * * * *

HERBERT van THAL

Full Name: Herbert Maurice van Thal.
  Born March 30, 1904, at London, England. Married
Phyllis Bayler. No children.

Education: Attended St. Pauls College.

Career: Author, editor, literary agent.
  Director, London Management (a literary agency),
London, England; free-lance author and editor.

Agent: London Management, 235/241 Regent St., London,
  W1A 2JT, England.

* * * * *

ZAARA VAN TUYL

Full Name: Rosealtha Van Tuyl.
  Born November 3, 1901, at Lynch, Nebraska. Daughter
of Charles Cornell and Leora MacGinitie. Married
Harold Heuer Van Tuyl, October 27, 1919 (died 1929).
Three children: Andrew, Barbara, Carol.

Education: A.B., Fresno State College, 1932.

Career: Writer.
  Grade school teacher until 1955; also has been a real
estate agent and a farmer; now spends most of her time
doing occult research and investigation.

* * * * *

A. E. van VOGT

Full Name: Alfred Elton van Vogt [pronounced Vōt].
  Born April 26, 1912, near Winnipeg, Manitoba, Canada.
Son of Henry van Vogt (a barrister and solicitor) and
Aganetha Buhr. Married Edna Mayne Hull, May 9, 1939
(died 1975).

Education: Attended Kelvin Technical High School,
  Winnipeg, and Morden High School; honorary B.A. from
  Golden State College.

Career: Author, 1932-DATE.

First Professional Sale: A true confession story
  to *True Story Magazine*, 1932.

Agent: Forrest J Ackerman, 2495 Glendower Avenue,
  Hollywood, CA 90027.

Honors & Awards: Co-Guest of Honor, 4th World

A. E. van VOGT (Cont.)

Science Fiction Convention (Pacificon I), Los Angeles, 1946; Manuscripters Literature Award, 1948; Ann Radcliffe Literature Award, Count Dracula Society, 1968.

Member:
  Science Fiction Writers of America; Authors Guild; Academy of Science Fiction, Fantasy, and Horror Films; Count Dracula Society.

Interests:
  "I make studies. I have studied the type of person you have to be to make money, the violent male, Red China, exercise, the human mind and behavior (for 15 years I ran a dianetic center [1950-65]), hypnotism, dream therapy, and (more recently) learning many languages. Some of these avocations have already been written up as books."

van Vogt notes: "Recently, I wrote a three-act play sequel to Molière's 'Le Malade Imaginaire.' The title of the play: 'The Invalid's Wife.'"

* * * * *

HUGH VENNING

Full Name: Hubert Van Zeller [originally, Claud Van Zeller]. Born April 3, 1905, at Suez, Egypt. Son of Francis Van Zeller (a government official) and Monique van de Velde.

Career: Benedictine monk.
  Became a Benedictine monk, Downside Abbey, Bath, England, 1924; ordained to the priesthood, 1930; chief work is preaching and giving retreats in England and America.

* * * * *

GORE VIDAL

Full Name: Eugene Luther Vidal, Jr.
  Born October 3, 1925, at the U.S. Military Academy, West Point, New York. Son of Eugene Luther Vidal (an Army Instructor of Aeronautics, and later Director of Air Commerce under President Roosevelt) and Nina Gore. Education: Graduate of Phillips Exeter Academy, 1943.

Career: Writer.
  Worked as an editor for E. P. Dutton & Co. during the 1940s; full-time writer, 1944-DATE; lived in Guatemala, 1946-47, and in Europe and North Africa, 1947-49; began writing for TV in 1953; appears frequently on TV and radio talk shows. Member: Dramatists Guild; New York Athletic Club.

Award: Edgar Award, Best Teleplay, 1955.

* * * * *

HARL VINCENT

Full Name: Harold Vincent Schoepflin.
  Born 1893, at Buffalo, New York. Married, with one daughter.

Career: Engineer (steam power generation).
  Part-time writer, 1928-68. Died in Los Angeles, May 5, 1968.

First Professional Sale: "The Golden Girl of Munan," in *Amazing Stories*, June, 1928.

Agent: Forrest J Ackerman, 2495 Glendower Avenue, Hollywood, CA 90027.

Forrest J Ackerman, Vincent's agent at the time of his death, provided these additional comments: "Harl Vincent was the subject of a biographical sketch in the December, 1938 *Amazing Stories*. His first story was "The Golden Girl of Munan"; he befriended Ackerman the next year, and gave him the original manuscript. Had a novel, "Venus Liberated," in *Amazing Stories Quarterly*, Summer, 1929, and a sequel, "Faster Than Light," in the Fall/Winter, 1932 issue. Vincent had over 75 SF stories published altogether; probably the best known was "Prowler of the Wastelands" (*Astounding Stories*, April, 1935). He collaborated with his then-agent, Charles Roy Cox, on "Sky Cops," published in *Amazing*, December, 1931. He died of emphysema in 1968."

* * * * *

VERNOR VINGE

Full Name: Vernor Steffen Vinge [pronounced Vĭn-jē]. Born October 2, 1944, at Waukesha, Wisconsin. Son of Clarence Lloyd Vinge (a professor of geography) and Ada Grace Rowlands (a geographer). Married Joan Carol Dennison, January 17, 1972.

Education: B.S., Michigan State University, 1966; M.A., University of California, San Diego, 1968; Ph.D., 1971.

Career: Professor of Mathematics.
  Assistant Professor of Mathematics, San Diego State University, 1972-DATE.

First Professional Sale: "Apartness," in *New Worlds*, June, 1965.

Member: Science Fiction Writers of America; American Mathematical Society.

Interests: Astronomy.

* * * * *

ROBERT VITARELLI

Full Name: Robert Francis Vitarelli.
  Born September 21, 1940, at Waterbury, Connecticut. Son of Romeo Anthony Vitarelli (a carpenter) and Eva Cynthia Cicchetti. Married Jo-Ann Frances Calabrese, February 20, 1965. Three sons: Douglas Robert (born 1965), Jonathan Robert (born 1966), Gregory Robert (born 1969).

Education: A.B., Clark University and the School of the Worcester Art Museum, 1962; graduate student at the University of Hartford.

Career: Author.
  Teacher in Connecticut and Massachusetts, 1962-66; Editor, Xerox Educational Publications, 1966-73; freelance author, 1973-DATE.

First Professional Sale:
  The Haunted Spacesuit, American Educational Publications, 1970 (an anthology).

ROBERT VITARELLI (Cont.)

Interests: Piano, painting, tennis, solitude.

Vitarelli notes: "I have accidentally written science fiction stories because of their tremendous ability to deal with the provable side of fantasy. A kind of writing that presents the opportunity to dream and yet consider the truth in dreams. Plus the fact that I am *very* superstitious."

* * * * *

FRANCIS VIVIAN

Full Name: Arthur Ernest Ashley.
   Born March 23, 1906, at East Retford, Nottinghamshire, England. Son of Arthur Ernest Ashley (a photographer) and Elizabeth Hallam. Married Dorothy Wallwork (a school teacher), December 26, 1940. One daughter, Susan Elizabeth.

Career: Writer and editor.
   Free-lance author and short story writer, 1932-52; Assistant Editor, *Nottinghamshire Free Press*, 1952-71; now retired. Member: British Legion; Nottingham Writers Club.

Agent: John Farquharson Ltd., 15 Red Lion Square, London W.C.1, England.

* * * * *

E. VOISKUNSKII

Full Name: Evgenyi Lvovich Voiskunskii.
   Born April 9, 1922, at Baku, Azerbaijan S.S.R., Soviet Union. Son of Lev Solomonovich Voiskunskii (a teacher of Latin) and Vera Solomonovna Rosengauz. Married Lidia Vladimirovna Voiskunskaia, 1944. One son, Aleksandr Evgenevich (born 1947).

Education: Diploma of Specialist in Literature, Gorky Institute of Literature, Moscow, 1952.

Career: Writer.
   With the Soviet Navy, 1940-56, serving in the Baltic Sea, and taking part in the defense of Leningrad; full-time writer, 1956-DATE; correspondent and editor of a number of Naval newspapers, 1943-51.

First Professional Sale: "The Sixteen-Year-Old Brigade Leader," in *Almanack Molodaia Gvardiia*, 1955.

Awards: Prize in the All-Russian Competition, 1957, for his play "Submarina."

Member: Union of Soviet Writers. Interests: Philately.

* * * * *

WERNHER von BRAUN

Full Name: Wernher von Braun.
   Born March 23, 1912, at Wirsitz, Germany. Came to the U.S., 1945, and naturalized, 1955. Son of Baron Magnus von Braun and Emmy von Quistorp. Married Maria Louise von Quistorp, March 1, 1947. Three children: Iris Careen, Margrit Cecile, Peter Constantine.

Education: B.S., Berlin Institute of Technology, 1932; Ph.D., University of Berlin, 1934.

Career: Rocket engineer.
   Assistant to Hermann Oberth in liquid-fuel, small rocket motor experiments in Germany, 1930; Liquid Fuel Expert, German Ordnance Dept., Kummersdorf Army Proving Grounds, 1932-37; Research and Development Service, Liquid Fueled Rocket and Guided Missile Center, Peenemuende, Germany, 1937-45; involved in the beginnings of American rocket development and research, at White Sands Proving Grounds, Redstone Arsenal in Alabama, and the George C. Marshall Space Flight Center, Huntsville, Alabama, 1945-77. Died June 16, 1977.

Awards:
   Astronautics Award, 1955; Space Flight Award, 1957; Distinguished Civilian Service Award, U.S. Dept. of Defense, 1957; Decoration for Exceptional Civilian Service, 1957; Award for Great Living Americans, U.S. Chamber of Commerce, 1958; Robert H. Goddard Memorial Trophy, 1958; Distinguished Federal Civilian Service Award, 1959; Hamilton Holt Gold Medal, 1959; Gold Medal Award of the British Interplanetary Society, 1961; Greek Fellowship Award, 1961; Hermann Oberth Award, 1961; Order of Merit for Research and Invention, 1962; Elliott Cresson Award, 1962; many other awards and honorary degrees for his work in pioneer rocketry and astronautics.

Member:
   American Institute of Aeronautics and Astronautics (Fellow); American Astronautical Society (Fellow); Hermann Oberth Society; British Interplanetary Society; German Rocket Society; International Academy of Astronautics; Explorers Club; many others.

* * * * *

KURT VONNEGUT JR.

Full Name: Kurt Vonnegut, Jr.
   Born November 11, 1922, at Indianapolis, Indiana. Son of Kurt Vonnegut and Edith Lieber. Married Jane Marie Cox, 1945. Three children: Mark, Edith, Nanette. Legal guardian of his deceased sister's children: James, Steven, and Kurt Adams.

Education:
   Attended Cornell University, 1940-42; Carnegie Institute of Technology, 1943; University of Chicago, 1945-47.

Career: Writer.
   Police Reporter, Chicago City News Bureau, 1947; public relations man, General Electric Co., Schenectady, NY, 1947-50; free-lance author, 1950-DATE; lecturer at the University of Iowa Writers Workshop, 1965-DATE. Member: Authors League; Barnstable Yacht Club; Delta Upsilon; Barnstable Comedy Club.

* * * * *

JOHN ROYAL VORHIES

Full Name: John Royal Harris Vorhies.
   Born March 25, 1920, at Dallas, Texas. Son of Oscar William Vorhies (a salesman) and Bessie Lu Harris. Married Jessie Alice Nettleton, October 7, 1944. Four children: John Royal Harris, Jr. (born 1945), Gordon Arthur Nettleton (born 1948), Peter Oscar William (born 1950), Bettie Lu Fulks (born 1952).

JOHN ROYAL VORHIES (Cont.)

Education: LL.B., University of Texas, Austin, 1944.

Career: Lawyer.

First Professional Sale: *Pre-empt*, Regnery, 1967.

Interests: Skiing, backpacking.

Vorhies writes:
"Your question: 'Do you think the possibility of
an actual episode of this (*Pre-empt*'s) type has increased with the passing of seven years?'
"Seven years ago, about 100 men were in positions
of responsibility where they could be Captain Hawks.
Today, perhaps 400 men, American and Russian, are in
similar positions. In that sense, it's more likely,
but I never thought it probable that a nuclear sub-
marine commander would take off on his own the way
my unflawed hero, Hawk, did.
"I wrote the book to demonstrate how easily two
knot-headed, leather-balled national leaders could
destroy the world--an act for which there is no jus-
tification.
"Robert Kennedy's *Thirteen Days* had not yet been
published, so I used my imagination as to what went
on in JFK's and Khrushchev's minds. If you carefully
read *Thirteen Days*, you will see the point. JFK was
acting the role of a leather-balled knot-head, although he wasn't that; but he did make the decision
to allow the confrontation to go to its full nuclear
conclusion. All that remained was for Khrushchev to
be equally leather-balled and knot-headed. But he
wasn't. We say he broke and ran, and his people called
him a coward. I say that he had too much heart and
feeling to kill the multitudes.
"In *Pre-empt*, I shifted all that heart and feeling
over to our side, and installed it in the President.
For the President's Russian counterpart, I left only
naked fear.
"The first indication that I had about how people
would feel about my Presidential character came from
the printer or typesetter who worked on the book. After the climax came and went, and the General who was
with the President realized that all was safe again,
I had him say, 'Thank you, Mr. President.' But the
galley proofs had it, 'Thank you, *Mrs.* President.'
"If the book is prophecy, it really does mean that
we shall quickly rid ourselves of any President who
backs down in a nuclear confrontation. What happened
to Khrushchev is a fine lesson for Russian leaders.
Both sides currently strive to avoid confrontation,
but it will happen one day. Perhaps tomorrow.
"One little aspect of my prophecy has happened. In
Pre-empt, I used imaginary 'White House tapes' made
for 'historical purposes' to tell much of the story,
and my character, Secretary of Defense Homer Brass,
used them to convict the President of cowardice.
"I wonder if the idea of Mr. Nixon's White House
tapes made for historical purposes can be traced to
Pre-empt, or did I merely prophesy a coming event?
I would write and ask Mr. Nixon about that, but I
doubt that he has the time or the staff to open and
read his mail these days.
"P.S. My newfound friend, a psychiatrist, wanted
to know how I could approve of a President who backed
away from confrontation. Any lawyer who has done
much criminal defense work knows the answer to that.
When you have no factual or legal defense for your
client, and the State's case is too simple and straight
to confuse, then you get down on your knees before
the jury, and plead for mercy."

EDWARD WAGENKNECHT

Full Name: Edward Charles Wagenknecht.
  Born March 28, 1900, at Chicago, Illinois. Son of
Henry Ernest Wagenknecht and Mary Erichsen. Married
Dorothy Arnold, 1932. Three sons: Robert, David, Wal-
ter.

Education: Ph.B., University of Chicago, 1923; M.A.,
  124; Ph.D., University of Washington, 1932.

Career: Professor of English.
  Assistant, University of Chicago, 1923-25; Associate
Professor of English, University of Washington, 1925-
43; Associate Professor of English, Illinois Institute
of Technology, 1943-47; Professor of English, Boston
University, 1947-65; now retired. Literary Editor,
Seattle Post-Intelligencer, 1935-40.

* * * * *

KARL EDWARD WAGNER

Full Name: Karl Edward Wagner.
  Born December 12, 1945, at Knoxville, Tennessee.
Son of Aubrey Joseph Wagner (Chairman, Tennessee Valley
Authority) and Dorothea Johanna Huber.

Education: A.B., Kenyon College, 1967; M.D., University of North Carolina, 1974.

Career: Writer and psychiatrist.
  Resident in Psychiatry, John Umstead Hospital, Butner,
North Carolina, 1974-DATE; free-lance author, 1970-DATE.
Editor-in-Chief, Carcosa (publishing company), 1972-
DATE.

First Professional Sale: *Darkness Weaves...*,
  Powell, 1970.

Agent: Kirby McCauley, 220 E. 26th St., New York,
  NY 10010.

Award: August Derleth Award, Best Short Story, 1974
  (1975), "Sticks." Member: Science Fiction Writers of
America. "My major work as a writer has been on my
Kane series. Began work on this in 1960, slowly developing the character and his world. Have only in
the last few years made a serious effort to market the
series. The Kane books are not being published in
chronological order."

* * * * *

SHARON WAGNER

Full Name: Sharon B. Wagner.
  Born December 16, 1936, at Wallace, Idaho. Daughter
of Moses Ross Wagner (a drilling contractor) and Dorothy A. Stephens.

Education: Attended Colorado Woman's College, 1955-
  56, and Mesa Community College, 1967; Diploma in Fic-
Tion, Famous Writers School, 1965.

Career: Writer.
  Clerical worker in Shelby, Montana, 1957-58; secretary in Cheyenne, Wyoming, 1958-62, and in Denver, 1962-
63; clerk, Arizona State University, 1966-68; full-time
writer, 1968-DATE.

H. RUSSELL WAKEFIELD

Full Name: Herbert Russell Wakefield.
    Born May 9, 1888 in Kent, England. Son of Henry
Russell Wakefield and Emily Dallaway. Education:
Attended Marlborough College, Oxford University, re-
ceiving a degree in history.

Career: Writer.
    Publisher in London, 1920-30; full-time writer,
1930-51; civil servant in London, 1951-65. Died August 2, 1965. Member: Oxford and Cambridge Golfing
Society; Vincent's Club.

* * * * *

DALE L. WALKER

Full Name: Dale Lee Walker.
    Born August 3, 1935, at Decatur, Illinois. Son of
Russell Dale Walker (a career soldier) and Eileen M.
Guysinger. Married Alice McCord, September 30, 1960.
Five children: Dianne, Eric, Christopher, Michael,
John.

Education: B.A., University of Texas at El Paso,
    1962.

Career: Publicity officer.
    Reporter, KTSM-TV, El Paso, 1962-66; Director of
News-Information Office, University of Texas at El
Paso, 1966-DATE.

Member:
    National Historical Society; Society of WWI Aero
Historians; Western Writers of America; El Paso Coun-
ty Historical Society; El Paso Westerner's Corral;
Sigma Delta Chi.

* * * * *

DAVID WALKER

Full Name: David Harry Walker.
    Born February 9, 1911, at Dundee, Scotland. Son of
Harry Giles Walker and Elizabeth Bewley Newsom. Married Willa Magee, 1939. Four children: Allan Giles,
Barclay James, David Clibborn, Julian Harry. Education: Attended Royal Military College at Sandhurst,
1929-30.

Career: Writer.
    In the British Army (The Black Watch), 1931-47,
serving in India, Sudan, Canada, France; prisoner of
war, 1940-45; Instructor, Staff College, Camberley,
1945-46; Comptroller to the Viceroy of India, 1946-47;
retired with rank of Major; full-time writer, 1947-
DATE; Member, Canada Council, 1957-61.

Awards: Member of the Order of the British Empire;
    D.Litt., University of New Brunswick; Governor Gener-
    al's Prize, 1952, for The Pillar; 1953, for Digby.

Member:
    Royal Society of Literature (Fellow); Royal and
Ancient Golf Club, St. Andrews (Scotland).

Interests:
    Skiing, bird-watching. Agent: Russell & Volkening,
551 Fifth Avenue, New York, NY 10017.

DOREEN WALLACE

Full Name: Dora Eileen Agnew Wallace.
    Born June 18, 1897, at Lorton, Cumberlandshire, Eng-
land. Daughter of Robert Brure Agnew Wallace and
Mary Elizabeth Peebles. Married Rowland Rash (a farmer
and landowner), October 4, 1922. Three children: Laura
(born 1925), Moray (son, born 1926), Stella (born 1929).

Education:
    B.A., Saverville College, Oxford University, 1919;
M.A., 1925 ("Oxford did not give degrees for women until then").

Career: Novelist and journalist.
    Teacher of English, co-educational grammar school,
Diss, Norfolk, 1919-22; free-lance author and journalist, 1922-DATE.

First Professional Sale: A Little Learning, Ernest
    Benn, 1931.

Agent: David Higham Associates, 76 Dean St., London,
    W.1, England.

Member: P.E.N.; Authors Society.

Interests: Painting, gardening, politics, teaching
    painting.

Wallace writes: "I've had to compromise between
writing and family life. Luckily, farming gave me a
subject. I have always known that duty comes first:
for a woman, husband, children, cooking, washing, household slutting. My writing talent has had to be fitted
in."

* * * * *

IAN WALLACE

Full Name: John Wallace Pritchard.
    Born December 4, 1912, at Chicago, Illinois. Son of
William Arthur Pritchard (in advertising) and Hallie
Kohlhas. Married Elizabeth Brown Paul, 1938. Two sons:
John William (deceased), Alan Paul (born 1950).

Education: B.A., University of Michigan, 1934; M.A.,
    1939; Ed.D., Wayne State University, 1957.

Career: Director of Publications; writer.
    Divisional Director of Publications, Detroit Board
of Education, 1934-74; part-time lecturer in educational
philosophy, Wayne State University, 1955-73; full-time
writer, 1974-DATE.

First Professional Sale: Every Crazy Wind, Dodd,
    Mead, 1952 (as John Wallace Pritchard).

Agent: Scott Meredith, 580 Fifth Avenue, New York,
    NY 10036.

Member:
    Science Fiction Writers of America; American Psycho-
gical Association; Sigma Delta Chi; American Association
of School Administrators; Philosophy of Education Society; Authors Guild; Authors League.

Interests:
    Archaeology, astrophysics, philosophy of religion,
metaphysics. "Quoted from the front matter of Croyd:

IAN WALLACE (Cont.)

"'In fiction, a just-possible hypothesis can burgeon as vital reality; and we can watch its consequences developing in all kinds of experience--hard, sweet, bitter, droll, aspirational, fantastic, human.' (Purports to be quoted from C. Ansata, *Fantasy and Inquiry*, World Copyright Union, 1992.)

"Croyd appears in *Croyd, Deathstar Voyage, A Voyage to Dari*. Claudine St. Cyr appears in *Dr. Orpheus* and *The Purloined Prince*. Pan Sagittarius appears in *Pan Sagittarius, A Voyage to Dari*, and is foreshadowed in *Deathstar Voyage*."

* * * * *

WILLIAM WALLING

Full Name: William Herbert Walling.
Born November 25, 1926, at Denver, Colorado. Son of Herbert E. Walling (an electrician) and Sopia Helen Keinath (a secretary). Married Judith Ruth Malone, September 6, 1952. Three children: Elizabeth Anne (born 1955), Julia Susan (born 1957), Jill Kathleen (born 1961).

Education: Bachelor of Engineering, University of California, Los Angeles, 1951.

Career: Engineer.
Aviation cadet, U.S. Air Force, 1944-45; engineer, with various companies in the Los Angeles area, 1951-DATE; Design Specialist, Lockheed Missiles & Space Company, 1960-DATE.

First Professional Sale: *No One Goes There Now*, Doubleday, 1971.

Agent: Adrienne Martine, 5816 Alameda Avenue #1, Richmond, CA 94802.

Member: Science Fiction Writers of America; Authors Guild.

Interests:
Classical music, history (especially early Roman Empire), astronomy. "I like 'hard' SF, with heavy technical background. Most admire Robert Heinlein, Walter M. Miller, Jr., and Frederik Pohl."

* * * * *

G. McDONALD WALLIS

Full Name: Geraldine June McDonald Wallis.
Born June 17, 1925, at Seattle, Washington. Daughter of Howard Roswell McDonald and Genevieve Talbott. Married Charles Wallis. Two sons: Christopher McDonald (born 1951), John Talbott (born 1963).

Education:
Attended Punahou School, Hawaii; Shanghai American School, China; and various California high schools.

Career: Writer.
Formerly an actress on radio, TV, and in stock, under the name Cathy McDonald; last performance in the West Coast Company of "Sabrina Fair," Geary Theatre, San Francisco; free-lance author, 1960-DATE.

First Professional Sale: "Men May Age," sold to

Eve, but the magazine folded before the story was published.

Agent: Hy Cohen, Candida Donadio & Associates, 111 W. 57th St., New York.

Member: Authors Guild.

Interests: Travel, art, music, hiking, swimming, boats (especially freighters to anywhere).

* * * * *

CHAD WALSH

Full Name: Chad Walsh.
Born May 10, 1914, at South Boston, Virginia. Son of William Ernest Walsh and Katie Wrenn. Married Eva May Tuttle, 1938. Four children: Damaris Wrenn, Madeline, Sarah-Lindsay, Alison Elise.

Education: A.B., University of Virginia, 1938; A.M., University of Michigan, 1939; Ph.D., 1943.

Career: Professor of English.
Research Analyst, U.S. Army Signal Corps, Arlington, Va., 1943-45; Professor of English, Beloit College, 1945-DATE; ordained priest in the Episcopal Church, 1949; assistant at St. Paul's Church in Beloit, Wisconsin; Fulbright lecturer at Turku, Finland, 1957-58, and at Rome, 1962; Visiting Professor, Wellesley College, 1958-59.

Honors & Awards:
Major Hopwood Award for playwrighting, 1939; "Spirit" Medal, Catholic Poetry Society of America, 1964; First Award, Council for Wisconsin Writers, 1965; Golden Anniversary Poetry Award, Society of Midland Authors, 1965.

Member:
American Association of University Professors; Modern Language Association; National Association for the Advancement of Colored People; International Association of University Professors of English; Phi Beta Kappa; Raven Society.

* * * * *

ELIZABETH WALTER

Full Name: Elizabeth Walter.
Born in England.

Career: Editor, Collins Publishers, London, 1961-DATE.
Awards: Scott Moncrieff French Translation Prize for *A Scent of Lilies*, by Claire Gallois.

* * * * *

WILLIAM GREY WALTER

Full Name: William Grey Walter.
Born February 19, 1910, at Kansas City, Missouri. Son of Karl Walter (an editor and banker) and Margaret Hardy (a journalist). Married Vivian Joan Dovey, 1947 (divorced, 1973). One son, Timothy (born 1949).

Education: M.A., King's College, Cambridge University, 1934; Sc.D., 1947; Hon. M.D., Université d'Aix-Marseille, 1949.

WILLIAM GREY WALTER (Cont.)

Career: Physiologist.
Physiologist, Burden Institute, Bristol, England, 1939-77; scientific consultant to various firms and organizations; on the editorial boards of several biomedical and neurophysiological journals. Died May 6, 1977.

First Professional Sale: *The Living Brain.*

Awards: Ambrose Fleming Premium, I.E.E., 1942; John Snow Medal, 1950; honorary degree from the Université de Liège, 1967.

Member:
Physiological Society; EEG Society (founder); International Brain Research Organisation; Electrophysiological Technologists Association (President); Institute of Biology (Fellow).

Interests:
Tennis, swimming, gliding, writing poetry. "A classical education in Greek and Latin gave me a love of languages--and also a pedantic feeling about etymology and semantics. My father was a music critic--so I learned something of that too."

* * * * *

HUGH WALTERS

Full Name: Walter Llewellyn Hughes.
Born June 15, 1910, at Bilston, Staffordshire, England. Son of Walter Martin Hughes and Kate Latham. Married Doris Higgins, 1933 (deceased). Two children: Walter Fred, Gillian Doris.

Education: Attended Wednesbury Technical College, 1928, and the Birmingham College of Advanced Technology.

Career: Engineer and company director.
Managing Director, Bradsteds Ltd., Bilston, England, 1938-DATE; Justice of the Peace, Bilston, 1947-DATE.

First Professional Sale: *Blast-Off at Woomera*, Faber & Faber, 1957.

Agent: Paul R. Reynolds, 599 Fifth Avenue, New York, NY 10017.

Member: Institute of British Engineers; British Interplanetary Society; Bilston Rotary Club; Ancient Order of Foresters.

* * * * *

BRYCE WALTON

Full Name: Bryce Walton.
Born May 31, 1918, at Blythedale, Missouri. Son of Paul Dean Walton and Golda Powers. Married Ruth Arschinov (a photographer), January 1, 1954. One daughter, Krissta Kay. Education: Attended Los Angeles Junior College, 1939-41, and California State College, Los Angeles, 1946-47.

Career: Writer.
Has been a sailor, migrant farmer, gold miner, railroad section hand, 1938-41; free-lance writer, 1945-DATE. Award: Alfred Hitchcock Best Short Story of the Year Award, 1961.

LUKE WALTON

Full Name: Bill Henderson.
Born April 5, 1941, at Philadelphia, Pennsylvania. Son of Francis L. Henderson and Dorothy Galloway. Married Nancy Sodeman (a writer), December 27, 1967.

Education: B.A., Hamilton College, 1963; graduate student, University of Pennsylvania, 1965-66.

Career: Editor.
Newspaper reporter for *Main Line Times* and *Camden Courier Post*, New Jersey, 1962-65; Editor, Doubleday & Co., 1972-DATE.

Awards: Citation from the New Jersey Association of Teachers of English, 1972, for *The Galapagos Kid.*

Agent: Phil Spitzer, 111-25 76th Avenue, Forest Hills, NY 11375.

* * * * *

SU WALTON

Full Name: Su Walton.
Born November 27, 1944, at Edinburgh, Scotland. Daughter of Peter Walton (a surgeon) and Rosemary Murray-Kerr. Education: Attended Cheltenham Ladies' College, 1958-62, and St. Hilda's College, Oxford University, 1963-65.

Career: Writer, 1967-DATE.

* * * * *

SANDOL STODDARD WARBURG

Full Name: Sandol Stoddard Warburg.
Born December 16, 1927, at Birmingham, Alabama. Daughter of Carlos French Stoddard and Caroline Harris. Married Felix M. Warburg, April 2, 1949 (divorced, 1963); married Frank Drew Dollard (a Professor of English Literature), June 19, 1966. Four sons: Anthony, Peter, Gerald, and Jason Warburg.

Education: A.B., Bryn Mawr College, 1959.

Career: Writer, 1960-DATE. Awards: *The Thinking Book* was chosen as one of ten best picture books of 1960 by *New York Herald Tribune*; *Saint George and the Dragon* was named a distinguished book in 1963 by the American Library Association.

* * * * *

LYND WARD

Full Name: Lynd Kendall Ward.
Born June 26, 1905, at Chicago, Illinois. Son of Harry F. Ward (a minister) and Daisy Kendall. Married May McNeer (a writer), June 11, 1926. Two children: Nanda Weedon, Robin Kendall.

Education: B.S., Teachers College, Columbia University, 1926; student, National Academy for Graphic Arts, Leipzig, Germany, 1926-27.

Career: Artist and illustrator.
Full-time illustrator and graphic artist, 1927-DATE; Director, Graphic Arts Division, Federal Art Project,

LYND WARD (Cont.)

New York, 1937-39; has exhibited his wood engravings in most national print shows; his prints are in permanent collections of the Library of Congress, Smithsonian Institution, Neward Museum, Metropolitan Museum, Victoria & Albert Museum, and others.

Awards & Honors:
   Zella de Milhau Prize, 1947; Library of Congress Award for wood engraving, 1948; National Academy of Design Award, 1949; Caldecott Medal, 1953, for *The Biggest Bear*; Silver Medal of the Limited Editions Club, 1954; John Taylor Arms Memorial Award, 1962; Samuel F. B. Morse Medal, 1966; Rutgers Award, 1970; Silver Medallion from the University of Southern Mississippi, 1973.

Member:
   Society of American Graphic Artists (past president); Society of Illustrators; National Academy of Design; P.E.N.

* * * * *

ERIC WARMAN

Full Name: William Eric Warman.
   Born September 23, 1904, at London, England. Son of William Warman and Margaret Dent. Married and divorced. One daughter, Jean.

Career: Publisher.
   Director, Books for Pleasure Group, London, 1949-60; Managing Director, 1960-DATE; Partner, Consortium Publications, London, 1960-DATE; Director, Theo Cowan Ltd. (public relations), London, 1962-DATE; Chairman, Soundguide Ltd., London, 1963-DATE. Member: Society of Authors; Crime Writers Association; P.E.N.; Savile Club.

* * * * *

HARRY WARNER JR.

Full Name: Harry Backer Warner, Jr.
   Born December 19, 1922, at Chambersburg, Pennsylvania. Son of Harry Backer Warner (an accountant) and Margaret Caroline Klipp.

Career: Editor.
   Clerical worker, Pennsylvania Railroad Company, 1942; with *Hagerstown Herald and Mail*, Maryland, beginning as a reporter; currently Feature Editor.

First Professional Sale: "Cold War," in *Future Science Fiction*, March, 1953.

Honors & Awards:
   Fan Guest of Honor, 29th World Science Fiction Convention (Noreascon), Boston, 1971; Hugo Award, Best Fan Writer, 1968 (1969); 1971 (1972).

Member:
   National Fantasy Fan Federation (Director); Fantasy Amateur Press Association (has been President, Vice-President, and Secretary-Treasurer); Futurian Federation of the World; Institute for Specialized Literature (Director).

Interests: Music, record collecting, baseball.

SYLVIA TOWNSEND WARNER

Full Name: Sylvia Townsend Warner.
   Born December 6, 1893, at Harrow, Middlesex, England. Daughter of George Townsend Warner and Eleanor Mary Hudleston.

Career: Writer and editor, 1926-78. Member: Royal Society of Literature (Fellow); American Academy of Arts and Letters; Rachel Carson Trust (sponser). Died May 1, 1978.

* * * * *

R. WARNER-CROZETTI

Full Name: Ruth G. "Lora" Warner Crozetti.
   Born May 18, 1913, at Indianapolis, Indiana. Daughter of Harry William Warner (a stairbuilder and cabinetmaker) and Evelyn D. Morgan. Married Jay Crozetti, October 16, 1937. One daughter, Janice L. (born 1938).

Education: Educated by a private tutor, G. W. Harvey of the University of Adelaide, South Australia.

Career: Writer.
   Has been an office clerk, typist, secretary, bookkeeper, and office manager; full-time writer, 1960-DATE.

First Professional Sale: "The Seven Thousand Steps," in *Spaceway Science Fiction*, December, 1954 (as J. M. Loring, with Atlantis Hallam).

Agent: Forrest J Ackerman, 2495 Glendower Avenue, Hollywood, CA 90027.

Member: Los Angeles Science Fantasy Society.

Interests: Painting, drawing, costume design.

* * * * *

PATRICIA S. WARRICK

Full Name: Patricia Scott Warrick.
   Born February 6, 1925, at La Grange, Indiana. Daughter of Ross B. Scott (a beekeeper) and DeEtte Ulman. Married James E. Warrick, 1965. Three children: Scott McArt, David McArt, Kristin McArt.

Education: B.S., Indiana University, 1946; B.A., Goshen College, 1964; M.A., Purdue University, 1965; doctoral candidate, University of Wisconsin.

Career: Professor of English.
   With Office of Development, Long Island University, 1946-48; Director of Technicians, Medical Laboratory, St. Elizabeth's Hospital, Indianapolis, 1948-52; Instructor in English, Lawrence University, 1965-66; Instructor, University of Wisconsin, Fox Valley, 1966-71; Assistant Professor of English, 1971-74; Associate Professor, 1974-DATE.

* * * * *

WILLIAM JON WATKINS

Full Name: William Jon Watkins.
   Born July 19, 1942, at Coaldale, Pennsylvania. Son of Charles William Joseph Watkins (a crane operator) and Edna Pearson (a secretary). Married Sandra Lee Preno (an R.N.), July 25, 1961. Three children: Tara Lee (born 1962) Wade William (b. 1963), Chadom C. (b. 1964).

WILLIAM JON WATKINS (Cont.)

Education: B.S., Rutgers University, 1964; M.Ed., Rutgers Graduate School of Education, 1965.

Career: Professor of Humanities.
Instructor, Delaware Valley College, 1965-68; High School Teacher, Asbury Park, New Jersey, 1968-69; Associate Professor of Humanities, Brookdale Community College, 1969-DATE.

First Professional Sale: *Ecodeath*, Doubleday, 1972 (with E. V. Snyder).

Agent: Scott Meredith Literary Agency, 580 Fifth Avenue, New York, NY 10036.

Awards: Per Se Award for One-Act Plays, 1969, for "Judas Wheel."

Member: Science Fiction Writers of America; World Future Society.

Interests: Karate, hermetics, string sculptures, concrete poetry.

Watkins writes:
"Whoever runs things stopped sending me memoes when I was five years old, so I assume everything is vital, especially contradictions. I think things are predestined, but I also think we get to stop the Game and discuss alternative futures before we choose one. I think revenge is futile but inevitable. I think Time is infinite in all directions, and that nothing ever stops happening. I think death is a form of sensory incompetence that stops us from noticing that all things are still going on. I think life can become a form of sensory incompetence too if we don't pay an awful lot of attention to it.
"I think Science sees us as small, inefficient, chemical reactors constantly bubbling, fuming, stinking; fit only as a servo-mechanism for the deodorant industry. I think Science has discovered less about being alive than about being dead. Still, I think Science has allowed man to fulfill his sole purpose, the evolution of technology. I believe the machines are likely to treat us about as well as we treated the apes. I doubt that they'll understand us or even try. I don't blame them; WE never understood us all that well.
"I think a lot of things we always assumed were dead will turn out to be alive, and a lot of things we always thought were alive will turn out to have been dead after all. That's probably why so much of what I write leans toward the mystical and the occult instead of the technological. What we think of as science will seem ludicrous in a hundred years; the occult may not.
"I have heard that there is a legendary bird that flies in smaller and smaller concentric circles until it flies up its own anus and disappears. I am trying to write novels like that. When I succeed, I believe *I* will disappear."

* * * * *

IAN WATSON

Full Name: Ian Watson.
Born April 20, 1943, at Tyneside, England. Son of John William Watson (a postmaster) and Ellen Cowe Rowley. Married Judith Jackson, September 1, 1962. One daughter, Jessica Scott (born 1973).

Education: B.A., Balliol College, Oxford University 1963; B.Litt., 1965; M.A., 1966.

Career: College lecturer.
Lecturer in Literature, University of Tanzania, 1965-67; Invited Foreign Lecturer, English Dept., Tokyo University of Education, and Keio University, Tokyo, 1967-70; Temporary Lecturer, English Dept., Japan Women's University, Tokyo, 1968-69; Lecturer in Complementary Studies, Birmingham Polytechnic Art and Design Centre, School of History of Art and Complementary Studies, 1970-DATE.

First Professional Sale: "Soyinka's Dance of the Forests," in *Transition*, #27, 1966 (Uganda).

Awards: Runner-up for the John W. Campbell Memorial Award for Best Science Fiction Novel of the Year, 1974, for *The Embedding*.

Member: Science Fiction Foundation (Council Member)

Watson writes:
"I first started writing SF in Japan as the only san reaction to the place. A survival strategy. The contradiction between the English literature I was nominally teaching and the environmental message from outside was too great. In a sense, Japan propelled me into the future. And I see SF now as a survival strategy generally--a metaphorical tool for thinking about the future flexibly and boldly. Which was also why I started running a course on SF and Futures Studies when I got back to England in 1970, as well as writing SF increasingly.
"The type of SF I work with, both in teaching and writing, could loosely be called Social Science SF, I suppose--somewhere at the intersection of Linguistics, Philosophy, Social Anthropology, Epistemology: though with as solid a factual base in terms of 'hard science' as I can provide. I'm particularly interested, too, in exploring the extent to which our knowledge of the Universe reflects an 'actual' Universe--or is delimited by our own thought structures. Which brings in the question of the nature of the 'Alien' and of possible alien viewpoints--since I'm not 'opposed' to outer space as such (quite the opposite), only to the idea that human destiny involves strip-mining the Galaxy."

* * * * *

TONY RUSSELL WAYMAN

Full Name: Tony Russell Wayman.
Born March 3, 1929, at Branksome, Dorsetshire, England. Son of Russell James Wayman and Amy Ivy Whiteman. Married Norah Wayman, 1950 (divorced, 1969).

Career: Writer.
"Became an apprentice Optometrist in 1945, joined the Royal Navy 1946, served in Hong Kong and Singapore till 1954, went into advertising in Singapore till 1957, quit in disgust, wrote articles and features for Malaysian media, broadcast for Australian Broadcasting Commission, wrote stories, treatments, scenarios, and shooting scripts for Malay movies, helped produce Indian-Malaysian and Indonesian-Malaysian movies, managed a snake-show, did movie and stage PR work, etc., until 1963, when I came to the U.S." Malaysian movie credits include: "Jula Juli Bintang Tujoh," "Siti Zubaidah," "Aladin Burok," "Pedang Hikmat," "Wily Delilah."

TONY RUSSELL WAYMAN (Cont.)

First Professional Sale:
"Somewhere back in 1955, I guess. Wrote Malay fairy-fantasies and myth-type movies in 1959 or so. Published an article on all this in *Hollywood Monsters* in 1961."

Member: Science Fiction Writers of America; Singapore Recreation Club; National Travel Club; Cosmopolitan Club, Kuala Lumpur, Malaysia.

Wayman writes:
"I don't particularly regard myself as a 'science fiction' or 'fantasy' writer. Nor, for that matter, do I regard myself as a writer of *books*, necessarily. My philosophy is that the subject chooses its form, and when I have an idea, it might work out to a short story, an article, a novel, a play, a movie, or whatever. My novel, *World of the Sleeper*, was originally a Malay movie I wrote called "Pedang Hikmat"; what I did was to supply a science fiction framework within which I could use the plot, though not the intent, of the original fantasy. By the same token, New Wave, Old Style, Black Humor, or whatever are used by me as the story dictates.
"There is very little 'speculative fiction' written or published, today or in any time, that might not as easily be mainstream writing, none at all if one excludes the science-gadgetry yarns beloved of John W. Campbell. I was led into writing by 1) a natural aptitude for telling of the fantastic ("Diary of a Snail" at age 10); 2) an interested English teacher at age 11 who turned me on to LITERATURE; 3) desire at 13 to be a newspaper columnist; 4) winning of a short story competition at age 15; 5) being turned on to the fascinations of Harry Stephen Keeler at age 9; 6) being put down at age 16 by John Creasey, a patron of the Boys' Club I was in; 7) being cursed with a facile talent for sales-writing; 8) an inborn detestation for an honest day's work."

* * * * *

A. C. WEBB

Full Name: Augustus Caesar Webb.
Born April 9, 1894, at Montgomery, Alabama. Son of Joshua Webb and Martha Jones. Education: B.Ph., Brown University, 1918; attended Northwestern University, 1924.

Career: Pathologist.
Has been a pathologist for Provident Hospital, Chicago, 1942-45; Asst. Professor of Pathology, Howard University; Deputy Coroner and Pathologist, Cook County Coroner's Office, Chicago, 1948-60; now retired.

First Professional Sale: "Clue of the Missing Dog," in *Master Detective Stories*, ca. 1929. Member: Chicago Pathological Society; New York Academy of Science; American Association for the Advancement of Science.

* * * * *

JEAN FRANCIS WEBB

Full Name: Jean Francis Webb III.
Born October 1, 1910, at White Plains, New York. Son of Jean Francis Webb, Jr. (an electrical engineer) and Ethel Morrison. Married Nancy Bukeley (a writer and public relations worker), May 27, 1936. Four sons: Jean Francis IV, Rodman B., Morrison DeSoto, Alexander Henderson.

Education: B.A., Amherst College, 1931.

Career: Writer, 1931-DATE.
Has also been a teacher of adult courses in professional writing, University of Hawaii, 1940; guest lecturer at various colleges and universities; President, Lewisboro School League, 1947-48; Secretary of Trustees, South Salem Library, New York, 1946-DATE.

Agent: McIntosh & Otis, 475 Fifth Avenue, New York, NY 10017.

Awards: *New York Herald Tribune* Honor Book Award, 1962, for *Kaiulani, Crown Princess of Hawaii*.

Member: Sons of the Revolution; Phi Delta Theta.

* * * * *

NELL WISE WECHTER

Full Name: Nell Wise Wechter.
Born August 6, 1913, at Stumpy Point, North Carolina. Daughter of Enoch Raymond Wise (a fisherman) and Edith Casey Best. Married Robert William Wechter (a U.S. Navy officer and teacher), March 12, 1943. One daughter, Marcia Michele.

Education: B.S., East Carolina College, 1951; M.A., 1952; M.A., University of North Carolina, 1964.

Career: Writer and teacher.
Public school teacher in North Carolina, 1933-64; free-lance feature writer for various N.C. newspapers, 1943-68; Associate Editor, *Hyde County Herald*, 1948-50; Teacher of Creative Writing and English, College of the Ablemarle, 1972; writer, 1937-DATE.

Awards:
George Washington Gold Medal from Freedoms Foundation, 1950, for play "All Aboard for Freedom"; First Place awards from Guildford Fine Arts Festival, 1955, 1956; Franklin McNutt Award, 1956; American Association of University Women Award, 1957, for *Taffy of Torpedo Junction*; National Teacher's Medal for N.C., Freedoms Foundation, 1958. Member: National Education Association; North Carolina Education Association; Outer Banks Woman's Club.

* * * * *

ROBERT WEINBERG

Full Name: Robert Edward Weinberg.
Born August 29, 1946, at Newark, New Jersey. Son of David Weinberg (an accountant) and Dorothy Weinberg (a secretary). Married Phyllis Horsky, May 27, 1973.

Education: B.S., Stevens Institute of Technology, 1968; M.S., Fairleigh Dickinson University, 1970; Ph.D. candidate, Illinois Institute of Technology.

Career: Author and editor.
Free-lance author, 1969-DATE; Associate Editor, FAX Books, West Linn, Oregon, 1973-DATE; Publisher and Editor of Robert Weinberg editions, Oak Lawn, Illinois.

First Professional Sale: "Destroyer," in *Worlds of If*, May, 1969.

SOL WEINSTEIN

Full Name: Sol Weinstein.
  Born July 29, 1928, at Trenton, New Jersey. Son of Samuel E. Weinstein (a junk dealer) and Clara Sara Sherman. Married Ellie Eisner, May 29, 1955. Two children: David Meyer, Judith Miriam. Education: Attended Washington Square College and New York University.

Career: Writer.
  Newspaperman, *Trentonian*, New Jersey, 1952-60; reporter, *Camden Courier-Post*, 1960-62; comedy writer, *Jerry Lester Show* (TV), 1962; comedy writer, *That Was the Week That Was* (TV show), 1964; writer of nightclub material for various comedians; television writer of comedy material; free-lance author, 1962-DATE.

Member: American Society of Composers, Authors, and Publishers; American Guild of Authors and Composters; Writers Guild of America, West.

* * * * *

REX WELDON

Full Name: Duane Weldon Rimel.
  Born February 21, 1915, at Asotin, Washington. Son of Pearl Guy Rimel (a painter) and Florence Wilsey. Married Ruth McClure (a program clerk), September 2, 1944. Four children: Duane Weldon, Jr., William L., Kay, James Arthur.

Career: Writer.
  Has been a professional jazz pianist, bartender, liquor store clerk, salesman, proofreader, night clerk in a hotel; reporter, *Clarkston Herald*, Washington, 1942-47; Editor, *Valley News*, Lewiston, Idaho, 1954; former Commissioner, Federal Housing Committee, Asotin County, Washington; President, Lewiston Central Labor Council, 1952-53; writer, 1945-DATE. Member: Elks.

* * * * *

JAMES WELLARD

Full Name: James Howard Wellard.
  Born January 12, 1909, at London, England. Son of James Hitchen Wellard and Frances Massey. Married Mary Higgins, June 3, 1944. Two children: John, Julia.

Education: B.A., University College, London University, 1932; Ph.D., University of Chicago, 1934.

Career: Writer.
  Rockefeller Fellow, 1933-34; journalist on various American and British newspapers, 1940-56; war correspondent, 1941-45; visiting lecturer, University of Illinois, 1955-56; Asst. Professor, Longwood College, 1957-61; Fulbright lecturer, University of Tehran, Iran, 1959-60. Member: Society of Authors; Writers Guild; Royal Geographical Society.

* * * * *

EDWARD WELLEN

Full Name: Edward Paul Wellen.
  Born October 2, 1919, at New Rochelle, New York. Son of Hyman Levy (a tailor) and Lillian Welinsky (a shopkeeper and office worker).

Education: Attended Shrivenham American University, 1945, and City University of New York, 1951-53.

Career: Writer.
  Dispatcher, Pelham Oil Company, 1937-42; soldier in the U.S. Army, 1942-45; self-employed stamp dealer, 1947-52; free-lance author, 1952-DATE.

First Professional Sale: "Origins of Galactic Slang," in *Galaxy*, July, 1952.

Awards: First Prize, Birmingham Festival of the Arts, 1964, for his television script, "*The* Hubert Otis."

Member: Science Fiction Writers of America; Mystery Writers of America. Interests: Psychosomatosemantics.

Wellen comments:
  "My mother's father's true surname was Harris, but an Ellis Island mixup resulted in his taking the name Welinsky. My mother divorced my father, and resumed her maiden name, copying her brother in shortening it to Wellen.
  "In the mystery field, pseudonyms are Paul Felder, Lew Gellert, Larry Killian. I admire Joyce and Twain, the former for wordforming, the latter for the lions' point of view. (In *Tom Sawyer Abroad*, our heroes escape the lions. 'And when they see we was really gone and they couldn't get us, they sat down on their hams and looked up at us so kind of disappointed that it was as much as a person could do not to see *their* side of the matter.')"

* * * * *

MANLY WADE WELLMAN

Full Name: Manly Wade Wellman.
  Born May 21, 1903, at Kamundongo, Angola. Son of Frederick Creighton Wellman (a doctor, artist and author) and Lydia Isely. Brother of Paul I. Wellman, the author. Married Frances Obrist, June 14, 1930. One son, Wade (born 1937).

Education: A.B., Wichita University, 1926; B.Litt., Columbia University, 1927.

Career: Writer.
  Worked as a reporter, reviewer, and feature writer for various Kansas newspapers, 1927-34; free-lance author, 1934-DATE; Instructor in Creative Writing, Elon College, 1962-69; Instructor in Creative Writing, University of North Carolina, 1964-71.

First Professional Sale: "Back to the Beast," in *Weird Tales*, November, 1927.

Agent: Kirby McCauley, 220 E. 26th St., New York, NY 10010.

Honors & Awards:
  World Fantasy Award, Best Single Author Collection or Anthology, 1973/74 (1975), *Worse Things Waiting*; Ellery Queen Award, 1946, for *Star of a Warrior*; Edgar Award, Best Nonfiction Study of Crime, 1955 (1956), *Dead & Gone*; Award of Merit, American Association of Local Historians, 1973, for *The Kingdom of Madison*.

Member: Science Fiction Writers of America.

Interests: Hiking, studying history & folklore, talking to people, the North Carolina mountains, folk music.

MANLY WADE WELLMAN (Cont.)

Wellman writes:
"I've worked long and hard for more than 40 years; fantasy and SF have changed in approach by writers, but never in the important impact of wonder, to reader and writer both. I have been gratified to see this genre accepted at last as worth and important literature. I will go on writing as long as anyone wants to read me.

"You ask for my best work in this field. I would suppose the stories about John the wandering guitar-picker in *F&SF*, published as *Who Fears the Devil?* by Arkham House in 1963. At least, I liked doing them best, and I like them best to reread, and the great response to this book, not only by SF readers, but by folklorists generally, must mean something."

* * * * *

BASIL WELLS

Full Name: Basil Eugene Wells.
Born June 11, 1912, at Springboro, Pennsylvania. Son of Carl Wells (a grocer and miller) and Gertrude Worden (an artist). Married Margaret Hughes, June 10, 1935. Two sons: Hugh Duane (born 1936), William Carl (born 1938).

Education: Attended Houghton College, 1931-32.

Career: Machine operator.
Operator of a machine making zippers, Talon Division of Textron, 1939-74; now retired.

First Professional Sale: "Rebirth of Man," in *Super Science Stories*, September, 1940.

Interests: Gardening, carpentry, book collecting, cooking.

Wells comments: "I'm more interested in reaching and entertaining readers than in the *immediate* financial gain obtainable. Once reader recognition comes so does the rest, hopefully! One story, published, can do the trick. Sold, but unpublished, there's no way!"

* * * * *

JOEL WELLS

Full Name: Joel Freeman Wells.
Born March 17, 1930, at Evansville, Indiana. Son of William Jackson Wells (an engineer) and Edith Strassell. Married Elizabeth Hein, June 5, 1952. Five children: William, Eugenia, Susan, Steven, Daniel.

Education: B.A., University of Notre Dame, 1952; graduate student, Northwestern University, 1963.

Career: Editor.
Promotion Director, Thomas More Association, Chicago, 1955-64; Editor, *Critic* magazine, 1964-DATE; Editor, Thomas More Press, 1971-DATE; Vice-President and Director. Rosary College, River Forest, Illinois, lecturer, 1963-DATE; served in the U.S. Navy, 1952-55, becoming a Lieutenant j.g. Free-lance editor of anthologies with Dan Herr.

ROBERT WELLS

Full Name: Frank Charles Robert Wells.
Born January 31, 1929, at London, England. Son of Sydney Frank Wells (a lawyer) and Violet Tomlinson. Married Alice Secker, May 14, 1955. Two sons: Robert Jeremy (born 1957), Nicholas Secker (born 1958).

Education: School Certificate, Pontllanfraith Education Institute, 1945; attended Goldsmiths College, University of London, 1951-53.

Career: Bank manager.
Clerk and Assistant Manager, Banco Español en Londres, 1953-67; Manager, Exporters Refinance Corporation, 1968-72; Manager (Export Finance), Lloyds Bank Ltd., London, 1973-DATE.

First Professional Sale: "The Desolate," in *Points* (Paris), 1953.

Agent: E. J. Carnell Literary Agency, 17 Burwash Rd., Plumstead, London SE18 7QY, England.

Awards: Runner-up Prize, *Observer* Short Story Competion, 1954, "The Machine That Was Lovely" (winners and runners-up were included in the anthology *A.D. 2500*, published by Heinemann).

Member: British Science Fiction Association.

Interests:
"Boating (powered canal-boat operator), Oriental woodcarving, H. G. Wells first editions collecting (although H. G. Wells is not traceably related in any way to my family).

"The gap in educational dates represents a long hospitalization (tubercular spine), 1946-50, including around three years horizontal life in a plaster cast, during which time I taught myself Spanish, typing and stenography."

* * * * *

FREDRIC WERTHAM

Full Name: Fredric Wertham [originally, Frederick Ignace Wertheimer]. Born March 20, 1895, in Bavaria, Germany.

Education:
M.D., University of Würzburg; also studied at Kings College, London University; Erlangen, Paris, London, Vienna; Johns Hopkins University.

Career: Psychiatrist.
Assistant Psychiatrist, Kraepelin Clinic, Munich, 1921; psychiatrist at various hospitals and clinics in the U.S., 1921-47; Associate in Psychiatry, Johns Hopkins Hospital and Medical School; Senior Psychiatrist, New York City Dept. of Hospitals; Fellow, National Research Council, Washington; Co-Editor, *American Journal of Psychotherapy*; currently, Consulting Psychiatrist, Queens Hospital Center, New York, New York.

Awards & Honors:
Gutheil Memorial Award of the Association for the Advancement of Psychotherapy, 1968; Sigmund Freud Award, American Society of Psychoanalytic Physicians, 1971; Chicago Books Clinic Award, 1974, for *The World of Fanzines*.

MARY WESLEY

Full Name: Mary Wesley.
Born June 24, 1912, at Englefield Green, England. Daughter of Mynors Farmar (a colonel) and Violet Dalby. Married Lord Swinfen, January, 1937 (divorced, 1944); married Eric Siepmann (a writer), April 22, 1951. Three children: Roger Eady, Toby Eady, William Siepmann. Education: Attended Queens College, University of London, 1928-30, and London School of Economics and Political Science, 1931-32.

Career: Writer.
Member of staff, War Office, London, 1939-41. Member: London Library.

* * * * *

ANTHONY WEST

Full Name: Anthony Panther West.
Born August 4, 1914, at Hunstanton, Norfolk, England. Came to the U.S., 1950. Son of Herbert George Wells (the science fiction author) and Rebecca West (the author). Married Lily Dulaney Emmet, December 20, 1952. Two children: Caroline, Edmund.

Career: Writer.
Roamed the world for four years before resettling in England; worked as a dairy farmer and breeder of Guernsey cattle, 1937-43; with the BBC, 1943-47, working with the Far Eastern Division and the Japanese Service; free-lance author, 1947-50; on the staff of the New Yorker, 1950-DATE. Member: Century Association, New York.

Awards: Houghton Mifflin Literary Fellowship, 1950, for The Vintage.

* * * * *

JESSAMYN WEST

Full Name: Jessamyn West.
Born 1907, in Indiana. Married H. M. McPherson. Education: A.B., Whittier College; also studied at the University of California, and in England.

Career: Writer, 1945-DATE.
Has taught and lectured at various colleges and universities. Awards & Honors: Honorary degrees from Whittier College, Mills College, Swarthmore College, Indiana University, Western College for Women; Indiana Authors' Day Award, 1956, for Love, Death & the Ladies' Drill Team; Thormod Monsen Award, 1958, for To See the Dream.

* * * * *

PAUL WEST

Full Name: Paul West.
Born February 23, 1930, at Eckington, Derbyshire, England. Son of Alfred Massick West and Mildred Noden. Married. One daughter, Amanda Klare.

Education: B.A., University of Birmingham, 1950; M.A., Columbia University, 1953.

Career: Professor of English.
Associate Professor of English, Memorial University

of Newfoundland, 1957-62; Associate Professor, Pennsylvania State University, University Park, 1963-69; Professor of English and Comparative Literature, 1969-DATE; Senior Fellow of the Institute for Arts and Humanistic Studies, 1970-DATE; Visiting Professor, University of Wisconsin, 1956-66; Crawshaw Professor of English, Colgate University, 1972; Melvin Hill Distinguished Visiting Professor of Humanities, Hobart & William Smith Colleges, 1974. Member: P.E.N.; Authors Guild.

Awards & Honors:
Canada Council Senior Fellow, 1959; Guggenheim Fellow, 1962; listed in "Books of the Year" by the New York Times, 1969, 1970, 1971; Paris Review Aga Khan Prize for Fiction, 1974.

* * * * *

REBECCA WEST

Full Name: Cecily Isobel Andrews.
Born December 25, 1892, in County Kerry, Ireland. Daughter of Charles Fairfield (an army officer and editor) and Isabella Mackenzie (a musician). Married Henry Maxwell Andrews (a banker), November 1, 1930. One son by H. G. Wells: Anthony Panther West (born 1914).

Education: Attended Royal Academy of Dramatic Art, and George Watson's Ladies' College.

Career: Writer.
Novelist, critic, and journalist from age 19 (after a brief period on the stage); started as a reviewer of books for Freewoman, a feminist magazine; joined Clarion in 1912 as a political writer; was the book editor of New Statesman & Nation in the 1920s; became an advocate of Socialism, and was active for a time in the Fabian Society; during World War II, supervised BBC broadcasts to Yugoslavia; covered the post-war treason trials of Lord Haw-Haw and others for New Yorker; free-lance author, 1912-DATE.

Honors & Awards:
Order of St. Sava, 1937; Chevalier of the Legion of Honor, 1957; Commander in the Order of the British Empire, 1957; Dame of the British Empire, 1959. Member: American Academy of Arts and Sciences; Oxford and Cambridge Club; Lansdowne Club.

* * * * *

WALLACE WEST

Full Name: George Wallace West.
Born May 22, 1900, at Walnut Hills, Kentucky. Son of Colonel William West and Anna Pauline Scott. Married Claudia M. Weyant, October, 1928.

Education: A.B., Butler University, 1924; LL.B., Indiana Law School, 1925.

Career: Pollution control expert.
Has been a farmer, barber, press telegrapher, journalist for the United Press, publicity officer for Paramount Pictures, editor of ROTO, Voice of Experience, Song Hits, and Movie Mirror; with the publicity department of CBS; news writer and commentator for ABC, NBC, and Mutual; air and water pollution control expert, American Petroleum Institute, 1947-68; consultant on air pollution for the Air Pollution Control Administra-

WALLACE WEST (Cont.)

tion, U.S. Public Health Service, Department of Health, Education, and Welfare, Washington, D.C.; now retired.

First Professional Sale: "Static," in Street & Smith's Sea Stories, September, 1926.

Member: Phi Kappa Phi; Science Fiction Writers of America.

"I started writing at age 13, when I won Honorable Mention in a McCall's Magazine short story contest. At about the same time, I wrote a lost worlds SF novel. This manuscript was destroyed when my home burned. Started writing extensively in the early twenties after taking a short story course at the University of Wisconsin."

* * * * *

DAVID WESTHEIMER

Full Name: David Westheimer.
Born April 11, 1917, at Houston, Texas. Married Doris G. Rothstein, 1945. Two sons: Frederick, Eric.

Education: B.A., Rice Institute, 1937; also studied at Columbia University.

Career: Writer.
Asst. Amusement Editor, Houston Post, 1939-41, 1945-46; in the U.S. Air Force, 1941-46, 1950-53; worked in radio-television and Sunday magazine editing, 1953-60; Editor, Literary Projects Co., Beverly Hills, CA, 1960-62; free-lance author, 1962-DATE.

Awards: McMurray Bookshop Award, Texas Institute of Letters, 1948, for Summer on the Water.

Member: Writers Guild of America, West; Authors League; Texas Institute of Letters.

* * * * *

ROBERT WEVERKA

Full Name: Robert Weverka.
Born November 17, 1926, at Los Angeles, California. Son of Lloyd J. Weverka (an executive) and Blanche McPhee. Married Ethel Gough, July 7, 1956. Four children: Peter, Thomas, Anne, Robert Philip.

Education: B.A., University of Southern California, 1950.

Career: Writer.
Salesman, Gough Industries, 1950-55; Advertising Director, Huddle Restaurants, 1956-57; President, We-verka & Associates (advertising agency), Beverly Hills, 1957-68; free-lance author, 1968-DATE. Member: Writers Guild of America, West.

* * * * *

DENNIS WHEATLEY

Full Name: Dennis Yeats Wheatley.
Born January 8, 1897, at London, England. Son of Albert David Wheatley and Florence Baker (Lady Newton). Married Nancy Madelaine Leslie Robinson, 1923; married

Joan Gwendoline Johnstone, August 8, 1931. One son, Anthony Marius.

Career: Writer.
With British Army, 1914-19; with Wheatley & Son (wine merchants), London, 1916-31; free-lance writer, 1932-77; Member, National Service Recruiting Panel, 1940-41; Member, Joint Planning Staff of War Cabinet, 1941-44; Wing Commander, Winston Churchill's staff, 1945; received U.S. Bronze Star. Died November 11, 1977.

Member: Royal Society of Literature (Fellow); Royal Society of Arts (Fellow); St. James' Club; Paternoster Club; Old Comrades Association.

Wheatley writes:
"For the past few years I have been very fully occupied in selecting for Sphere Books Ltd. a series which they began to publish in May of 1974. It is called The Dennis Wheatley Library of the Occult, and consists not only of fiction titles by the most famous authors from the earliest times up to the present day, but also books on palmistry, astrology, faith healing, etc. We published 6 books to start with, and are following up with two new ones each month. I write an introduction to each title.
"I have never personally attended any magical ceremony because I believe it dangerous to do so, and I very definitely believe in supernatural powers. I feel very strongly that any association with them could prove most dangerous, because in the first place, it is such a fascinating subject that one may become so engrossed in it as to neglect one's family and career; secondly, if one is at all weak-minded one may well land up in a lunatic asylum.
"As I entered the family wine business in Mayfair on my return from the First World War, and worked in it for the best part of 10 years, I did acquire a very considerable knowledge about wine, and after selling my business in 1933, I transferred my personal connections to Messrs. Justerini & Brooks. I certainly use my knowledge of wine now and again when the occasion offers in my books, and I have a very large cellar of fine wines of my own.
"I also have a library of some 4,000 books, about half of which are modern first editions, the majority having been autographed to me by their authors, and it is said to be one of the finest collections in this country."

* * * * *

HARVEY WHEELER

Full Name: John Harvey Wheeler Jr.
Born October 17, 1918, at Waco, Texas. Married Mimi Arnold, 1941; married Norene Burleigh (a nurse), March 26, 1971. Two sons: David Carroll, John Harvey III.

Education: B.A., Indiana University, 1946; M.A., 1947; Ph.D., Harvard University, 1950.

Career: Political scientist.
Asst. Professor of Political Science, Johns Hopkins University, 1950-54; Professor of Political Science, Washington & Lee University, 1954-60; Senior Fellow-in-Residence, Center for the Study of Democratic Institutions, 1960-DATE; Visiting Scholar, 1961-63, and Program Director, 1969-72; Consultant, Fund for the Republic, 1958-DATE. Member: American Political Science Association; Pi Sigma Alpha. Agent: Zeigler & Ross, 9255 Sunset Blvd., Los Angeles CA 90069.

PAUL WHEELER

Full Name: Paul Wheeler.
Born May 23, 1934, in Jamaica, British West Indies. Son of William Alfred Wheeler (a civil servant) and Ives Baker. Married Alexandra Martinez, March 26, 1964. Two children: Lara, Sacha.

Education: B.A., Exeter College, Oxford University, 1959; M.A., University of Chicago, 1960.

Career: Research Assistant.
Research Assistant, British Foreign Office, London, 1963-DATE; with British Army, 1953-55. Member: Crime Writers Association.

Agent: A. D. Peters, 10 Buckingham St., London WC2.

* * * * *

DAVID WHITAKER

Full Name: David Whitaker.
Born April 18, 1930, at Knebworth, Hertfordshire, England. Son of Richard Archer Whitaker (an accountant) and Helen Nicholas. Married June Barry (an actress), June 8, 1963.

Career: Writer.
Became a writer in England after successful surgery for a bone disease that had rendered him an invalid for much of his youth; full-time author, 1957-DATE, with more than 150 television and film credits since 1967; worked as a story consultant and editor for the BBC for several years. Member: Writers Guild of Great Britain (past Chairman, 1966-68).

Agent: A. L. S. Management, 9 Orme Court, London W.2, England.

* * * * *

JAMES WHITE

Full Name: James White.
Born April 7, 1928, at Belfast, Northern Ireland. Parents unknown. Married Margaret Sarah Martin (a housewife and auxiliary nurse), May 17, 1955. Three children: Patricia Mary (born 1957), Martin James (born 1959), Peter Gerard (born 1962).

Career: Publicity officer.
Salesman, John Collier (clothing store), Belfast, 1943-59; Manager, Tailoring Department, Belfast Co-op (department store), 1959-65; Technical Clerk, Shorts (aircraft company), 1965-66; Publicity Officer, 1966-DATE; part-time science fiction writer, 1951-DATE.

First Professional Sale: "Assisted Passage," in *New Worlds*, January, 1953.

Agent: E. J. Carnell Literary Agency, 17 Burwash Rd., Plumstead, London SE18 7QY, England.

Awards: Europa Special SF Award, 1972, for *All Judgment Fled*.

Member: Science Fiction Writers of America; Knights of St. Fantony.

White writes: "I am a non-racist, non-sectarian, non-violent person, and an optimist, despite living in Belfast's Andersonstown district; and at my age I am too old or too stubborn to change any of these sentiments. I believe that the best stories are those which face ordinary characters (not necessarily human characters) with extraordinary situations, which is what I try to do.

"The three books in the 'Sector General' series are *Hospital Station*, *Star Surgeon*, and *Major Operation*. I am not sure whether *Major Operation* should be listed as a collection or a novel because, although published as five separate novelettes in the UK *New Writings in SF* series (Nos. 7, 12, 14, 16, & 18), it was originally planned as a serial novel. Other 'Sector General' stories are 'Countercharm,' a short which appeared in *The Aliens Among Us* collection, and 'Occupation: Warrior,' reprinted in the same book. The latter story was originally written with the same background as the SG stories, but Ted Carnell, who was then editor of the UK *New Worlds* SF magazine, *and* my agent, said that it was a bit too violent and satirical to be linked with the 'Sector General' series; he asked me to make a few changes, namely, replacing the SG species classification system with planets of origin--instead of DBLF, FGLI, etc., using Kelgian, Illensan, and so on--and calling the organisation which sorted the mess out in the end the Guardsmen instead of the Monitor Corps. The original title of the story was 'Classification: Warrior,' and not 'Occupation: Warrior.' Only Ted Carnell and myself knew about this 'Occupation/Classification: Warrior' business, and I think he was probably right in wanting the change, because the story was not really part of the SG series, even though it had the same background, and despite the fact that the main character in the story turns up as Fleet Commander Dermod in *Star Surgeon* and *Major Operation*. Another SG story, 'Spacebird,' appeared in *New Writings in SF 22* in 1974."

* * * * *

TED WHITE

Full Name: Theodore Edwin White.
Born February 4, 1938, at Washington, D.C. Son of Edwin Paul White (a photographer) and Dorothea Belz. Married Sylvia Dees, November 30, 1958; married Robin Postal (now her husband's secretary), February 26, 1966.

Career: Writer and editor.
Head of Foreign Dept., Scott Meredith Literary Agency, 1963; Assistant Editor, *The Magazine of Fantasy and Science Fiction*, November, 1963-67; Associate Editor, 1967-May, 1968; Associate Editor, Lancer Books, 1966; Managing Editor, *Amazing Stories*, March, 1969-November, 1969; Editor, January, 1970-DATE; Managing Editor, *Fantastic Stories*, April, 1969-December, 1969; Editor, February, 1970-DATE; free-lance author, 1963-DATE.

First Professional Sale: "The Detroit Convention," in *Fantastic Universe*, January, 1960 (with Forrest J Ackerman, Belle C. Dietz, John Magnus, and Burnett R. Toskey).

Awards: Hugo Award, Best Fan Writer, 1967 (1968).

Member:
Chairman, 25th World Science Fiction Convention (NyCon 3), New York, 1967; Fantasy Amateur Press Association; Science Fiction Association; New York Futurians; Science Fiction Writers of America; New York Fanoclasts (founder).

ROBERT WHITEHEAD

Full Name: Robert John Whitehead.
Born January 21, 1928, at Logansport, Indiana. Son of William B. Whitehead (a plumber) and Kathleen O'Morrow. Married Mary Ellen Leffert, November 23, 1950. Two sons: Mark, Kevin.

Education: B.S., Ball State University, 1951; M.A., 1954; Ed.D., Indiana State University, 1960.

Career: Professor of Education.
Public school teacher, Logansport, Indiana, 1951-56; Teacher, Burris Laboratory School, Ball State University, 1956-58; Instructor in Elementary Education, Indiana University, 1958-60; Professor of Education, Sacramento State College, 1960-DATE.

* * * * *

LESLIE H. WHITTEN

Full Name: Leslie Hunter Whitten.
Born February 21, 1928, at Jacksonville, Florida. Son of Leslie Hunter Whitten and Linnora Harvey. Married Phyllis Webber (a teacher), November 11, 1951. Three children: Leslie Hunter III (born 1953), Andrew Cassius (born 1956), Daniel Lee (born 1965).

Education: B.A., Lehigh University, 1950.

Career: Newspaper writer and columnist.
News Editor, Radio Free Europe, 1952-57; Desk Editor, International News Service, 1957-58; Newsman, United Press International, 1958; Reporter, *Washington Post*, 1958-62; Reporter, Hearst Newspapers, 1962-69; Chief Associate, Jack Anderson (the columnist), 1969-DATE.

First Professional Sale: *Progeny of the Adder*, Doubleday, 1965.

Agent: Curtis Brown Ltd., 60 E. 56th St., New York, NY 10022.

Member: American Civil Liberties Union. Interests: "Translate Baudelaire."

* * * * *

LEONARD WIBBERLEY

Full Name: Leonard Patrick O'Connor Wibberley.
Born April 9, 1915, at Dublin, Ireland. Son of Thomas Wibberley (an agricultural scientist) and Sinaid O'Connor (a teacher). Married Katherine Hazel Holton (a teacher). Six children: Kevin, Patricia, Anabella, Christopher, Rory, Cormac.

Education: Attended El Camino Junior College, 1968-69.

Career: Writer.
Has been a street fiddler, ditch digger, cook; book publisher's apprentice, Collins, London, 1931-32; reporter and editor for various British papers, 1932-36; Editor, *Trinidad Evening News*, West Indies, 1936-38; free-lance author.

First Professional Sale: *The King's Beard*.

Agent: McIntosh & Otis, 475 Fifth Avenue, New York, NY 10017.

Member: Dramatists Guild; Authors League.

Interests: Long distance sailing, violin making, violin playing, reading, listening to music, boat building.

Wibberley comments:
"About half of my books are out of print--not through the failure of the books, but through failure of the publishers--the juvenile department of Funk & Wagnalls, for instance, and also Ives Washburn.
"I think this is the result of the determination of the government to abolish novelists by cutting off funds for libraries of every kind. Novelists are actually very dangerous to governments, so I don't blame them."

* * * * *

DON WIDENER

Full Name: Donald Widener.
Born March 13, 1930, at Holdenville, Oklahoma. Son of Carl James Widener and Lucile Cole. Married Veda Rose Pannell, June 13, 1953. Two sons: Jeffrey Scott, Christopher Neil.

Education: A.A., Compton Junior College, 1950.

Career: Business executive.
Newspaper reporter and editor, *Los Angeles Herald-Examiner*, 1954-58; Proposal Writer, Bendix Corporation, 1958-60; Assistant to the President, Rocket Power Inc., 1960-63; Press Relations Officer and Producer/Writer, NBC, 1964-70; President, Widener & Productions, Los Angeles, 1970-DATE.

Member: California Museum Foundation; Museum of the Sea Committee; National Academy of TV Arts and Sciences; Greater Los Angeles Press Club.

Awards:
Chicago International Film Festival Hugo Award, 1967, for "Tijuana Revolution: The New Brass"; Emmy Award, Best Single TV Program, and Best Documentary in Public Interest, 1969, for "The Slow Guillotine"; Alfred I. du Pont-Columbia University Broadcast Journalism Award for investigative reporting; Silver Award of the New York Film and TV Festival, 1969; Emmy Award, Best News Documentary, 1970, "Timetable for Disaster."

* * * * *

KATE WILHELM

Full Name: Katie Wilhelm.
Born June 8, 1928, at Toledo, Ohio. Daughter of Jesse Thomas Meredith (a millwright) and Ann McDowell. Married Joseph B. Wilhelm, 1947 (divorced, 1962); married Damon Francis Knight (the science fiction author), February 23, 1963. Three children: Douglas Wilhelm (born 1949), Richard Wilhelm (born 1953), Jonathan Knight (born 1966).

Career: Writer.
Co-Director, Milford Science Fiction Writers Conferences, 1963-72; lectured at Clarion Science Fiction

KATE WILHELM (Cont.)

Writers Workshop, 1968-70.

First Professional Sale:
  "The Mile-Long Spaceship," in *Astounding Science
Fiction*, April, 1957 ["The Pint-Sized Genie," in *Fantastic Stories*, October, 1956, was actually published
first].

Agent: Brandt & Brandt, 101 Park Avenue, New York,
  NY 10017.

Awards: Nebula Award, Best Short Story, 1968 (1969),
  "The Planners."

* * * * *

MILDRED WILDS WILLARD

Full Name: Mildred Wilds Willard.
  Born October 11, 1911, at New Kensington, Pennsyl-
vania. Daughter of John Michael Wilds (a grocer) and
Emma Miller. Married Kester T. Willard (with the Uni-
ted Air Lines sales department), October 13, 1934.
Two sons: John Michael, Thomas Gordon.

Education: A.B., Northwestern University, 1932.

Career: Writer.
  High school teacher, Lancaster, Wisconsin, 1932-34;
Reporter, *Chicago Tribune*, 1935-43; secondary and ele-
mentary school teacher in Illinois, 1956-62; writer,
1967-DATE. Awards: First Prize for short story,
Midwest Writers Conference, 1950.

* * * * *

CHARLES WILLEFORD

Full Name: Charles Ray Willeford III.
  Born January 2, 1919, at Little Rock, Arkansas.
Son of Charles Ray Willeford II and Aileen Lowey.
Married Mary Jo Norton (an English professor), July
1, 1951.

Career: Professor of English.
  With the U.S. Army, 1936-56, retiring as a Master
Sergeant; Instructor in Humanities, University of
Miami, Coral Gables, 1964-67; Asst. Professor, Miami-
Dade Junior College, 1967-68; Chairman of the Depart-
ments of English and Philosophy, 1968-70; Associate
Professor of English, 1970-DATE.

Education: A.A., Palm Beach Junior College, 1960;
  A.B., University of Miami, 1962; M.A., 1964.

Awards & Honors:
  Silver Star, Bronze Star, Purple Heart, Luxembourg
Croix de Guerre; Beacon Fiction Prize, 1956, for *Pick-
Up*. Member: Mystery Writers of America; Authors
League; Vorpal Blades.

* * * * *

E. C. WILLIAMS

Full Name: Eric Cyril Williams.
  Born July 22, 1918, at Peckham, London, England.
Son of Charles John Williams (a wholesale chemist)
and Mabel Grace Wellington. Married Mona Winifred

Jones, April 28, 1962. One daughter, Rosemary Monica
(born 1965).

Career: Shipping manager.
  Civil Service photographer, 1933-40; soldier in the
Signals Corps, 1940-46; Bookseller, Foyles, Books &
Careers, 1947-61; engineers contract clerk, 1961-65;
Shipping Manager, Stone Platt Industries, Sussex, 1965-
DATE.

First Professional Sale: "The Garden of Paris,"
  in *Weird Shadows from Beyond* (an anthology edited
  by John Carnell), Corgi, 1965.

Agent: E. J. Carnell Literary Agency, 17 Burwash Rd.,
  Plumstead, London SE18 7QY, England.

Interests:
  Astronomy, listening to classical music. "It can't
be money, it can't be fame that keeps me writing--or
the expectation of either--it must be the hope that
one day I will write something that I will like."

* * * * *

JAY WILLIAMS

Full Name: Jay Williams.
  Born May 31, 1914, at Buffalo, New York. Son of
Max Jacobson and Lillian Weinstein. Married Barbara
Girsdansky, June 3, 1941. Two children: Christopher
(born 1943), Victoria (born 1952).

Education: Attended University of Pennsylvania, 1931-
  32, and Columbia University, 1933-34.

Career: Writer.
  Comic and MC in vaudeville shows, 1935-37; press agent,
1937-41; full-time writer, 1942-78. Died July 12, 1978.

First Professional Sale: *The Stolen Oracle*, 1942.

Agent: Russell & Volkening, 551 Fifth Avenue, New
  York, NY 10017.

Honors & Awards:
  Guggenheim Fellowship, 1949; Young Readers Choice
Award, 1961, for *Danny Dunn and the Homework Machine*,
and 1963, for *Danny Dunn on the Ocean Floor*; Boys' Clubs
of America Award, 1949, for *The Roman Moon Mystery*;
Lewis Carroll Shelf Award, 1973, for *The Hawkstone*.

Member: Authors League of America; Society of Authors.

Interests: Field archery, Japanese and Chinese art,
  ship modelling, modern graphic art.

Williams writes:
  "I don't consider myself to be a science fiction
author, specifically, or a children's author, although
I have written a great deal for children, and have also
written a good deal of science fiction. As a professional writer, I've tried a great many forms, according
to the demands the stories themselves have made on me.
But I must confess that I am greatly drawn to fantasy
and to science fiction, which seem to me ideal vehicles
for the expression, not only of serious contemporary
problems, but allegorical statements about our time as
well. I like children, and enjoy writing for them; and
the Danny Dunn books, particularly, allow me to say a
great deal about society, morality, and the philosophy
of science without getting solemn or losing my own

JAY WILLIAMS (Cont.)

"pleasure in the writing. It is very challenging, for example, to try to deal with the morality of using a computer to do one's homework, without getting pompous about it. And I feel sure that every author who has tried fantasy has succumbed to a certain extent to use the form as allegory; one need only remember Lewis's Narnia books.

"The differences between writing for children and writing for adults are vast, but in general one may say that children are a little more intelligent than adults, a little readier to use their imagination, a little more eager to meet an author halfway. They are also more critical, being quick to recognize a patronizing tone or sham wisdom. So that while one can be more subtle and more complex in an adult work, both the challenge and the response are greater when writing for children."

* * * * *

JOHN A. WILLIAMS

Full Name: John Alfred Williams.
 Born December 5, 1925, at Jackson, Mississippi. Son of John Henry Williams (a laborer) and Ola Mae Williams. Married Carolyn Clopton (divorced); married Lorrain Isaac, October 5, 1965. Three sons: Gregory D., Dennis A., Adam J.

Education: A.B., Syracuse University, 1950.

Career: Writer.
 Public relations man with Doug Johnson Associates, Syracuse, 1952-54; staff member for radio and TV special events programs, CBS, 1954-55; Publicity Director, Comet Press, 1955-56; Publisher and Editor, *Negro Market Newsletter*, 1956-57; Assistant to the Publisher, Abelard-Schuman, 1957-58; Director of Information, American Committee on Africa, 1958; European Correspondent, *Ebony* and *Jet*, 1958-59; Special Events Announcer, station WOV, New York, 1959; Correspondent in Africa, *Newsweek*, 1964-65; Lecturer in Writing, City University of New York, 1968; Lecturer in Afro-American Literature, College of the Virgin Islands, 1968; Guest Writer, Sarah Lawrence College; Regents Lecturer, University of California, Santa Barbara, 1972; Distinguished Professor of English, La Guardia Community College, 1973-74; free-lance writer, lecturer, 1960-DATE.

Awards: National Institute of Arts & Letters Award, 1962; Centennial Medal, Syracuse University, 1970.

Member: Authors Guild; Black Academy of Arts and Letters (Member, Board of Directors); Rabinowitz Foundation; New York State Council on the Arts.

* * * * *

NICK BODDIE WILLIAMS

Full Name: Nick Boddie Williams.
 Born August 23, 1906, at Onancock, Virginia. Son of John F. Williams (a lawyer) and Anne McKown (a teacher). Married Elizabeth Rickenbaker, 1931 (died 1973); married Barbara Steele, June 29, 1973. Four children: Susan (born 1933), Nick (born 1935), Elliott (daughter, born 1946), Elizabeth (born 1948).

Education: A.B., University of Texas, 1929.

Career: Newspaper writer and editor.
 With the *Fort Worth Star Telegram*, 1927-29, and the *Nashville Tennessean*, 1929-31; began working for the *Los Angeles Times* in 1931 as a copy editor, and became, successively, Telegraph Editor, Picture Editor, News Editor, Assistant Managing Editor, Managing Editor, and finally, for eleven years, Editor; retired in 1972.

First Professional Sale: A short story published under a pseudonym (title and name forgotten), to *Weird Tales*, ca. 1927.

Honors: D.C.L, University of the South, 1973.

Interests: Gardening.

Williams writes:
 "Before I wrote *The Atom Curtain*, I'd had a science fiction story ("The Terrible Morning") published in *Collier's Magazine*, about 1946--it made the cover. It had to do with the effects of a supernova's explosion on the people of Los Angeles (and by implication on the rest of the world). Created a suicidal impulse, followed by universal coma. Excessive cosmic radiation. And before that, I had a story in *Weird Tales*. But most of my slick fiction was southern colloquial, some boy-meets-girl in slick and pulp. Also a novel serially in *Adventure Magazine*.
 "About 1949 or so, I was promoted to Assistant Managing Editor of the *Times*--and simultaneously ran dry as a writer. Nothing since then except the one SF novel, and a series of columns in the *Times* after my retirement.
 "I do read, and have always read, a great deal of science fiction, usually in paperback. But also detective novels, a lot of current fiction, archeology, history, books on art, biography--in fact, a whopping lot of stuff from the Bible to Shakespeare to Dickens to Wolfe, Faulkner, Hemingway, Fitzgerald--and on and on and on."

* * * * *

ROBERT MOORE WILLIAMS

Full Name: Robert Moore Williams.
 Born June 19, 1907, at Farmington, Missouri. Son of John Browning Williams and Ida May Moore. "I am an eleventh generation descendent of Robert and Elizabeth Williams, who settled in Roxbury, Massachusetts, in 1638." Married Margaret Jelley, 1938 (divorced, 1952). One daughter, Sarah Browning (born 1944).

Education: B.A., University of Missouri ("graduate of the first School of Journalism ever established on planet Earth").

Career: Writer.
 Full-time writer, 1937-72. Died February, 1977.

First Professional Sale: "Zero As a Limit," in *Astounding Stories*, July, 1937 (as Robert Moore).

Robert Moore Williams writes:
 "Writing a piece on writing I find very difficult. In truth, I find it more than usually difficult in this case simply because the letter requesting it referred to writing as a discipline. Writing is one of the most difficult of the arts. I have scant sympathy for anyone who refers to it as a discipline. Certainly discipline is needed, but the usual meaning of the word cannot be used to describe writing. You don't disci-

ROBERT MOORE WILLIAMS (Cont.)

"pline writing, it disciplines you. You don't write, you are written. You don't go to school to learn how to write, you bring it with you.

"Probably both the psychologists and the professors of literature will disagree with me. I couldn't care less if they do. You don't learn how to write by listening to psychologists or to professors of literature. You learn to write by writing. Then, if the It so chooses, or if She so wills, and if you have brought something with you, perhaps you become a writer.

"What is *It*, and who is *She*? Dig the answers out of some of the world's great books, out of George Groddeck's *Book of the It*, out of Erich Neumann's *The Great Mother*, dig them out of Raynor C. Johnson's *Nurslings of Immortality*, dig them out of Robert Graves' *The White Goddess*. Most important, if you want to be a writer, dig them out of yourself. They're all in you. If you would find them, all you have to do is go looking, and when you find your answers, to face the consequences of discovery.

"After the rules of grammar and spelling are half-way learned, writing becomes a process of exploring your own emotional world, and the history that is contained therein. This history is longer and deeper than most people realize, and the real roots of fiction writing lie in it. From it they emerge as vague impulses in the patterns of the archetypes, as hunches to go in this direction and to avoid that direction, to use this idea as a major theme, and to avoid that one, to use the episode at the river crossing--which just 'happened' to pop into your mind--as part of the story. From the whole history of the human race--it's your history too, and it's all within you--you select those bits that you wish to use to tell your story.

"And this above all, this first and foremost, this the beginning and the ending, *that you love it!* Love *what*? The whole wide world and all that's in it, the lady of your choice, and the meaning of the word *story*. Where do you get this kind of love? You bring it with you from a thousand lifetimes! How do you find out if you have it? You get a typewriter, and start pointing it in some direction. If you don't have it, the knocks you get on the noggin will send you into some other activity. If you do have it, it will give you the ability to withstand those knocks. Whether you have it or don't have it, the knocks are coming. Love helps you rise above them.

"What I am talking about here is a particular kind of way of being in love. Since love is a flow toward the opposite sex (but is not necessarily restricted to sex, all the psychoanalysts on earth to the contrary!), if you are a boy type, it comes out as a way of seeing every woman not only as herself, and as being worth loving for herself, but also as a representative of the Goddess, of the entire feminine side of nature.

"Individual women have a way of being around for a time, then of going on. The Goddess was with you in the beginning, She will be with you in the ending; pour your love for Her into the story you are writing.

"If you are a girl type, you reverse this, of course.

"I have needed about thirty years of the hardest kind of work to dig this out of my inner world. I give it to you for free, but, speaking bluntly, I doubt if many of you will be able to use it. I suspect this is something that does not come down from the Olympian heights of schools of writing, or from courses in literature in our universities, but which you have to learn for yourself the only way that matters, the hard way. Maybe not. It seems to me that the kids I see coming into the world today have talents "and gifts that simply were not in the world when I was young. Perhaps they will not have to learn the hard way.

"My advice to all writers everywhere is--*be in love!* And, no matter what happens--*stay in love!*

"I would give the same advice to plumbers and carpenters and to the wet-backs working in the orange grove across the road--except they don't seem to need it as much as writers. For writers, however, it is the essence and the secret of existence."

*　*　*　*　*

TENNESSEE WILLIAMS

Full Name: Tennessee Williams [originally, Thomas Lanier Williams]. Born March 26, 1914, at Columbus, Mississippi. Son of Cornelius Coffin Williams (a travelling salesman) and Edwina Dakin.

Education: A.B., University of Iowa, 1938; attended play writing seminar, New School for Social Research, 1940.

Career: Writer and playwright.
Free-lance author and playwright, 1928-DATE: first used the name Tennessee Williams in 1939; clerical worker and manual laborer, International Shoe Company, St. Louis, 1934-36; went to New Orleans, 1939, where he was a waiter and hotel elevator operator; worked on a pigeon ranch in California, 1940; underwent eye surgery in 1940, and moved to Florida, where he worked as a teletype operator; had two further eye operations in 1941-42; went to New York, 1942, working at odd jobs as a poet and waiter in a Greenwich Village night club, and an usher in a movie theater; worked for MGM for six months; underwent eye surgery a fourth time in 1945; settled in Chapala, Mexico, in 1945 to work on "A Streetcar Named Desire"; has travelled much since.

First Professional Sale: "The Vengeance of Nitocris," in *Weird Tales*, August, 1928 (as Thomas Lanier Williams).

Honors & Awards:
Third Prize, *Smart Set* contest, 1930; Group Theatre Award, 1939, for "American Blues"; Rockefeller Foundation Fellowship, 1940; grant from American Academy and National Institute of Arts and Letters, 1943; New York Drama Critics Circle Award, Donaldson Award, and Sidney Howard Memorial Award, 1945, all for "The Glass Menagerie"; New York Drama Critics Circle Award, and Pulitzer Prize, 1948, for "A Streetcar Named Desire"; New York Drama Critics Circle Award, and Pulitzer Prize, 1955, for "Cat on a Hot Tin Roof"; National Institute of Arts and Letters Gold Medal, 1969.

Member: Dramatists Guild; National Institute of Arts and Letters; American Society of Composers; ASCAP; Alpha Tau Omega.

*　*　*　*　*

URSULA MORAY WILLIAMS

Full Name: Ursula Moray Williams.
Born April 19, 1911, at Petersfield, Hampshire, England. Daughter of A. Moray Williams (an archaeologist) and Mable Unwin. Married Peter Southey John, September 28, 1935. Four sons: Andrew, Hugh, Robin, James.

Education: Year of art school at Winchester, England.

URSULA MORAY WILLIAMS (Cont.)

Career: Writer, 1931-DATE.
   Has also been Justice of the Peace, Worcestershire-Evesham Bench, Governor of County School, Evesham, and Manager of Beckford Junior School. Member: National Book League; P.E.N.; Cheltenham Literary Festival Society.

Agent: Curtis Brown Ltd., 60 E. 56th St., New York, NY 10022.

* * * * *

AMABEL WILLIAMS-ELLIS

Full Name: Lady Mary Amabel Nassau Williams-Ellis.
   Born May 10, 1894, at Newlands Corner, near Guildford, England. Daughter of J. St. Loe Strachey (Editor of *The Spectator*) and Amy Simpson (an author). Married Sir Clough Williams-Ellis (the author, architect, and founder of Portmeirion Village), 1915. Three children: Christopher (deceased), Susan, Charlotte.

Career: Author and editor.
   Has also been Literary Editor of *The Spectator*.

Interests: History, science, folk-lore, and fairy-tales for children.

Lady Amabel's husband, Sir Clough Williams-Ellis, designed the Welsh village and resort Portmeirion, at Penrhyndeudraeth, Merionethshire, where the television series *The Prisoner* was filmed. She had these additional comments:

   "I am working on a book probably to be called *Pills to Purge Melancholy* or *Escape from Melancholy*. This is especially addressed to young 'drop-outs' of my acquaintance, and includes an account of a Meditation Course that I went to at Kathmandu, on the instructions of a Buddhist grand-daughter.
   "The fact that it was a grand-daughter who packed me off to Nepal and her lamas, and the new book, afford 'sidelights.' The new book will explain much else, such as a brief discussion of the latest ideas about Homo sapiens as a biological entity, a living creature possibly in need of a 'new species' classification. (See Chomsky and other linguistic fellows.)
   "There is also section suggesting (via 'Black Pages' consisting of quotations from such works as *Catch-22*) that it is a good idea to do what Wordsworth and Bunyan so eloquently recommended, that is, to try to behave a little better.
   "I hazard that happy people don't commit atrocities, and suggest that history shows that we do not live in exceptionally evil times, as the 'dropping-out' young seem to suppose. (There were a lot of 'dropped-out' Americans at the Kathmandu Mediation Course.)
   "All that is nothing to do with SF? Yes, I think it's quite relevant. To read 'good' SF (i.e., the sort of tales in the anthologies we've done) is to get ideas about certain very strong human drives, and to be helped in distinguishing which drives are harmful, and which are life-enhancing. Also, of course, SF discusses assorted social values, all things that the young would jib at, and would not read in sermons or political pamphets.
   "With regards to the anthologies, I have editorial control--often with difficulty, but I've got the argument that it's silly of them to pay a cat and

"catch their own mice. With my collaborators, it's a matter of give and take. Both are, or were, much to be listened to. One as a teacher-trainer in English literature, and Dr. Pearson as a biologist who has contact with SF readers of a slightly different kind-- i.e., more or less young scientists at universities. I specialize in teenagers because of my grandchildren, I suppose."

* * * * *

JACK WILLIAMSON

Full Name: John Stewart Williamson.
   Born April 29, 1908, at Bisbee, Arizona Territory. Son of Asa Lee Williamson (a farmer and rancher) and Lucy Betty Hunt. Married Blanche Slaten Harp, August 15, 1947. Two step-children: Keigm Harp (born 1930), Adele Harp (born 1928).

Education: B.A. & M.A., Eastern New Mexico University, 1957; Ph.D., University of Colorado, 1964.

Career: Writer; Professor of English.
   Free-lance author, 1928-DATE; served in the U.S. Army during World War II as an Air Force weather forecaster; Wire Editor, *Portales News Tribune*, 1947; wrote comic strip *Beyond Mars* for *New York Sunday News*, 1952-55; Instructor, New Mexico Military Institute, 1957-59; Instructor, University of Colorado, Boulder, 1960; Professor of English, Eastern New Mexico University, 1960-DATE.

First Professional Sale: "The Metal Man," in *Amazing Stories*, December, 1928.

Agent: Scott Meredith, 580 Fifth Avenue, New York, NY 10036.

Honors & Awards:
   Nebula Award, Grandmaster Award, 1976; Pilgrim Award, Science Fiction Research Association, 1973; First Fandom Science Fiction Hall of Fame Award, 1968.

Member:
   Science Fiction Writers of America; Science Fiction Research Association; National Council of Teachers of English; Modern Language Association; Teachers of English to Speakers of Other Languages.

Interests: Travel, photography, astonomy.

Williamson writes:
   "About academic science fiction research, it's true that I have been promoting it, and I do believe that SF is worth serious intellectual attention. To re-state the basic argument for it: our world is changing rapidly in many ways under the impact of applied technology. Being about change, about the consequences of technological innovation, about all sorts of alternative possibilities, science fiction has been able to grapple with aspects of reality neglected in most other fiction.
   "Perhaps that's not the best argument. Science fiction is literature. It's a way of artistic response to experience. Like other sorts of art, it can be good or bad, true or false, obscure or universal. But, at its best, it can be as good as any other sort of literature. If you look back at literary history, you find no prejudice against fantasy through most of the centuries. For various reasons, science fiction has been identified as a subliterate pulp genre. That was

JACK WILLIAMSON (Cont.)

"particularly true through the years 1926-1945, when there was no book market for it at all. Since World War II, it has been steadily recovering its lost intellectual recognition.

"I don't think this academic attention will hurt the field as a whole. I think science fiction has become highly diversified; it exists at a good many levels for different sorts of readers.

"I do think that individual writers have been too much influenced by the wrong sort of critical attention. But that's only a personal reaction. I'm glad that we have no public censors of science fiction. I like science fiction because it gives the writer more freedom, I think, than any other contemporary literary form--including necessarily the freedom to write bad science fiction."

* * * * *

DONALD C. WILLIS

Full Name: Donald Chalmers Willis.
   Born September 18, 1947, at Santa Barbara, California. Son of Howard Chalmers Willis (an auditor) and Dolores Medalen.

Education: A.A., Sacramento City College, 1967; B.A., University of California, Los Angeles, 1969.

Career: Clerk.
   Clerk typist, Los Angeles Public Library, 1971-DATE.

First Professional Sale: *Horror and Science Fiction Films: A Checklist*, Scarecrow Press, 1972.

Interests: Filmgoing, baseball, reading (favorite writers: Henry James, Dostoevsky, Tolstoy, H. P. Lovecraft, James Agee).

* * * * *

ANGUS WILSON

Full Name: Angus Frank Johnstone Wilson.
   Born August 11, 1913, at Bexhill, Sussex, England. Son of William Johnstone Wilson and Maude Caney.

Education: B.A., Merton College, Oxford University, 1936.

Career: Writer.
   Has worked as a tutor, secretary, caterer, co-manager (with his brother) of a restaurant, social organiser; Member of the Staff of the Department of Printed Books, British Museum, 1936-42, 1947-55; full-time writer, 1955-DATE; part-time lecturer at various colleges and universities. Member: Arts Council of Great Britain; Society of Authors; P.E.N. Awards: James Tait Black Memorial Prize, 1959, for *The Middle Age of Mrs. Eliot*; Meilleur Roman Étranger Prix, 1960.

* * * * *

COLIN WILSON

Full Name: Colin Henry Wilson.
   Born June 26, 1931, at Leicester, England. Son of Arthur Wilson (a shoe operative) and Anetta Wilson. Married Dorothy Betty Troop, 1951 (divorced, 1952);

married Pamela Joy Stewart (a librarian), 1960. Four children: Roderick, Sally Elizabeth (born 1960), John Damon (born 1965), Christopher Rowan Mark (born 1971).

Education: Attended Gateway School, Leicester, 1941-47.

Career: Writer.
   Has been a laboratory assistant, tax collector, ditch digger, hospital porter, worker in a plastics factory; free-lance author, 1956-DATE; Writer-in-Residence, Hollins College, 1966-67; Visiting Professor, University of Washington, 1967-68; Visiting Professor, Rutgers University, 1974; Editor, Aldus Books Occult Series, 1975.

First Professional Sale: *The Outsider*, Victor Gollancz, 1956.

Agent: Bolt & Watson Ltd., 8 Storeys Gate, London SW1, England.

Awards: Ford Foundation grant, 1961.

Interests: Music, mathematics, wine.

* * * * *

EDMUND WILSON

Full Name: Edmund Wilson.
   Born May 8, 1895, at Red Bank, New Jersey. Son of Edmund Wilson (a lawyer) and Helen Mather Kimball. Married Mary Blair, 1923; married Margaret Canby, 1930; married Mary McCarthy, 1938; married Elena Thornton, 1946. Three children: Rosalind, Reuel, Helen.

Education: A.B., Princeton University, 1916.

Career: Writer and critic.
   Reporter, *New York Evening Sun*, 1916-17; Managing Editor, *Vanity Fair*, 1920-21; Associate Editor, *New Republic*, 1926-31; Book Reviewer, *New Yorker*, 1944-48; free-lance author, 1922-72. Died 1972. Member: Charter Club, Princeton Club.

Awards: Guggenheim Fellow, 1935; National Institute of Arts and Letters Gold Medal, for essays and criticism, 1955.

* * * * *

HAZEL WILSON

Full Name: Hazel Emma Wilson.
   Born April 8, 1898, at Portland, Maine. Daughter of Fred Linwood Hutchins (a real estate broker) and Emma Jones. Married William Jerome Wilson, September 16, 1930 (died 1963). One son, Jerome Linwood (born 1931).

Education: A.B., Bates College, 1919; B.S. in Library Science, Simmons College, 1920.

Career: Writer.
   Librarian in various cities in the U.S. and France, 1920-30; teacher at various schools in the U.S. and France, and at George Washington University; reviewed juveniles for the *Washington Sunday Star* for many years; free-lance author, 1939-DATE.

First Professional Sale: *The Red Dory*, Little, Brown, 1939.

HAZEL WILSON (Cont.)

Agent: McIntosh & Otis, 475 Fifth Avenue, New York, NY 10017.

Honors & Awards:
Honorary M.A. degree, Bates College; Boys' Clubs of American Award, for *Thad Owen*; Ohioana Award, for *Island Summer*; Edison Foundation Award, for *His Indian Brother*; Cumberland County 200th Anniversary Award for literary accomplishment.

Member: Children's Book Guild; Women in Communication; American Newspaper Women's Club.

Interests:
Gardening, travel, reading, visiting art museums, speaking to groups of children. "I've devoted much time and effort to almost anything concerning children. Have had 20 juveniles published, done volunteer work at children's hospitals, spoken to children at book fairs and at individual schools, and was active in getting school libraries in the District of Columbia. Am also a devoted grandmother."

* * * * *

RICHARD WILSON

Full Name: Richard Wilson.
Born September 23, 1920, at Huntington Station, New York. Son of Richard Wilson (a clerk) and Felicitas Minna Krause (a writer). Married Jessica Gould, 1941 (divorced, 1944); married Doris Owens, 1950 (divorced 1967); married Frances Daniels, 1967. One son, Richard David (born 1951); three step-children: Margot Owens (born 1946); James B. Daniels (born 1955); Stephen W. Daniels (born 1957).

Education: Attended Brooklyn College, 1935-36, and University of Chicago, 1947-48.

Career: Public relations agent.
Reporter, copyreader, assistant drama critic, Fairchild Publications, 1941-42; Chief of Bureau, Transradio Press, 1946-51; reporter, deputy to editor, Reuters Ltd., New York, 1951-64; Director, News Bureau, Syracuse University, 1964-DATE; free-lance author, 1940-DATE.

First Professional Sale: "Murder from Mars," in *Astonishing Stories*, April, 1940.

Awards: Nebula Award, Best Novelette, 1968 (1969), "Mother to the World."

Member: Science Fiction Writers of America; Syracuse Press Club; American College Public Relations Association.

Wilson writes:
"My wife and I collect American oil paintings, preferably landscapes and seascapes of the 19th century. I collect old ink fountain pens, and have to be restrained from buying every old workable standard or portable nonelectric typewriter I see.
"But my chief avocation since my teens has been reading, writing, and collecting science fiction. The Sunday children's section of the *Long Island Daily Press*, Jamaica, N.Y., published my juvenilia when I was 12 or 13. Later, I edited and published science fiction fan magazines, including *The Atom, Science*

Fiction News Letter, and *Escape*.
"My work as a professional newsman is reflected in many of my 100-odd published stories in which the protagonist is a reporter or editor with a background paralleling my own. I try to write about what I know, and a work in progress is about a writer at a flea market (such as my wife and I frequent) who writes stories about his customers.
"I encouraged the George Arents Research Library of Syracuse University to begin collecting SF books, magazines, mss., and memorabilia; it now has a notable collection which includes the papers of Hugo Gernsback, Frederik Pohl, Will F. Jenkins (Murray Leinster), Damon Knight, Robert Silverberg, Hal Clement, Donald A. Wollheim, Andre Norton, Anne McCaffrey, Keith Laumer, Piers Anthony, Larry Niven, Roger Zelazny, and Richard Wilson. The collection includes papers of the Galaxy Publishing Corporation (*Galaxy* and *If*), and Mercury Press (*The Magazine of Fantasy and Science Fiction*)."

* * * * *

ROBIN SCOTT WILSON

Full Name: Robin Scott Wilson.
Born September 19, 1928, at Columbus, Ohio. Son of J. Harold Wilson (a teacher) and Louise Walker. Married Patricia Van Kirk (a graphic designer), January 20, 1951. Four children: Kelpie (born 1956), Leslie (born 1959), Kerry (born 1961), Andrew (born 1963).

Education: B.A., Ohio State University, 1950; M.A., University of Illinois, 1954; Ph.D., 1959.

Career: College instructor.
With the Central Intelligence Agency, 1959-67; Professor of English, Clarion State College, 1967-70; Associate Director, Committee on Institutional Cooperation, 1970-DATE.

First Professional Sale: "Third Alternative," in *Analog*, March, 1964 (as Robin Scott).

Agent: Robert P. Mills Ltd., 156 E. 52nd St., New York, NY 10022.

Member: Science Fiction Writers of America; Modern Language Association; American Association for Higher Education. Interests: Sailing.

Wilson founded the annual Clarion Science Fiction Writers Workshop, now permanently resident at Justin Morrill College, Michigan State University.

* * * * *

RUSS WINTERBOTHAM

Full Name: Russell Robert Winterbotham.
Born August 1, 1904, at Salina, Kansas. Son of Jonathan Harvey Winterbotham (a doctor) and Gertrude Bond. Married Nadine Schick, November 25, 1932. One daughter, Ann (born 1936).

Education: B.A., University of Kansas, 1927.

Career: Writer.
Reporter and writer for various Midwest newspapers, 1928-43; comic strip writer, Newspaper Enterprises Association, Cleveland, 1943-69. Died June 9, 1971, at Lakewood, Ohio.

RUSS WINTERBOTHAM (Cont.)

First Professional Sale: *Lindbergh: Hero of the Air*, Haldeman-Julius Co., 1928.

Agent: Scott Meredith, 580 Fifth Avenue, New York, NY 10036.

Member: Western Writers of America; Mystery Writers of America; Sigma Delta Chi.

Before his death in 1971, Winterbotham commented: "I'm now retired, and devoting my entire time to loafing, with the exception of doing the script for one comic strip (newspaper comic). The science fiction market doesn't seem to demand my talents, whatever they are, and I need the rest."

* * * * *

ARTHUR WISE

Full Name: Arthur Wise.
Born January 12, 1923, at York, England. Son of Arthur Wise and Edith Mary Hobson. Married Lilian Nanette Gregg, September 6, 1947. Three children: John Christopher, Susan, Julia.

Education:
Diploma in Speech and Drama, Central School of Speech and Drama, 1949; Diploma in Dramatic Art, University of London, 1949; Certificate, International Phonetics Association.

Career: College instructor and writer.
Fighter pilot, Royal Air Force, 1941-46; has been Chief Examiner of Spoken English, University of Durham, and University of London; Lecturer in Speech Education at the University of Leeds; and consultant on technical weapons; full-time writer, 1969-DATE; Director, Swords of York, Ltd., 1963-DATE.

First Professional Sale: *Days in the Hay*, Cassell, 1960.

Member: Society of Teachers of Speech and Drama; Society of Arms and Armour; Society of Authors; Association of University Teachers; York Society of Speakers.

* * * * *

ELLEN WOBIG

Full Name: Ellen Wobig.
Born April 18, 1911, at Janesville, Wisconsin. Daughter of J. A. Forrest. Married Harold Wobig, September 4, 1940, Two sons: Gerald C., Harold A.

Career: Housewife and writer. First Professional Sale: *The Youth Monopoly*, Ace Books, 1968.

* * * * *

P. G. WODEHOUSE

Full Name: Pelham Grenville Wodehouse.
Born October 15, 1881, at Guildford, Surrey, England. Son of Henry Ernest Wodehouse (a civil servant and judge) and Eleanor Deane. Married Ethel Rowley, Sept. 30, 1914. One step-daughter, Leonora (deceased).

Education: Attended Dulwich College, 1894-1900.

Career: Writer.
Became U.S. citizen, 1955. Worked as a bank clerk in England, 1901-03; writer of "By the Way" column, *London Globe*; writer for *Vanity Fair*, under various pseudonyms, 1915-19; novelist and playwright, 1902-75. Died February 14, 1975.

Honors & Awards: Litt.D., Oxford University, 1939; knighted by Queen Elizabeth II, January, 1975.

Member: Dramatists Guild; Old Alleynian Association; Coffee House, New York.

* * * * *

BARBARA H. WOLF

Full Name: Barbara Herrman Wolf.
Born April 28, 1932, at Rochester, New York. Daughter of Roy F. Herrman (a physician) and Estelle Chappel. Married Jack C. Wolf (a writer and professor).

Education: B.S., Northwestern University, 1954; M.A., State University of New York, Brockport, 1969.

Career: Instructor in Creative Writing.
Foreign TV correspondent in Africa, the Middle East, and elsewhere for United Press-Movietone Television, 1958-62; co-owner, Wolf Gallery, Rochester, NY, 1963-67; Instructor in Creative Writing, State University of New York, Brockport, 1970-DATE.

* * * * *

JACK C. WOLF

Full Name: Jack Clifford Wolf.
Born May 25, 1922, at Omaha, Nebraska. Married Barbara Herrman (an instructor).

Education:
B.S., Creighton University; M.A., State University of New York, Brockport; Ph.D., State University of New York, Buffalo; has also studied at the University of Vienna, University of Florence, and University of Grenoble.

Career: Professor of English.
Co-owner, Wolf Gallery, Rochester, NY, 1963-67; Professor of English, State University of New York, Brockport, 1967-DATE; Associate Editor, *Modern Language Studies*; former Foreign Correspondent for UPI-Fox Movietone Television in Africa and the Middle East.

Awards: SUNY faculty research fellowship, 1973, to complete a volume of original poetry, *A Moon for Icarus*. Interests: Writing, photography.

* * * * *

BERNARD WOLFE

Full Name: Bernard Wolfe.
Born August 28, 1915, at New Haven, Connecticut. Son of Robert Wolfe and Ida Gordon. Education: B.A., Yale University, 1935; graduate student, 1935-36.

Career: Writer, 1946-DATE; screen writer. Member: Phi Beta Kappa; Sigma Xi.

GENE WOLFE

Full Name: Gene Rodman Wolfe.
  Born May 7, 1931, at Brooklyn, New York. Son of
Roy Emerson Wolfe (a restaurateur and shopkeeper) and
Mary Olivia Ayres. Married Rosemary Dietsch, November
3, 1956. Four children: Roy Emerson II (born 1958),
Madelaine (born 1960), Therese Georgeanne (born 1963),
Matthew Dietsch (born 1966).

Education: B.S.M.E., University of Houston, 1956.

Career: Editor.
  Project Engineer, Procter & Gamble, 1956-72; Senior
Engineering Editor, *Plant Engineering*, 1972-DATE.

First Professional Sale: "Mountains Like Mice,"
  in *Worlds of If*, May, 1966.

Agent: Virginia Kidd, Box 278, Milford, PA 18337.

Awards: Nebula Award, Best Novella, 1973 (1974),
  "The Death of Dr. Island."

Member: American Institute of Plant Engineers; American Society of Business Press Editors.

"Raised in Texas. Fundamentally a Texan and an outsider. Got Combat Infantry Medal in Korean War."

* * * * *

LOUIS WOLFE

Full Name: Louis Wolfe.
  Born June 29, 1905, at Bound Brook, New Jersey.
Son of William Wolfe (a merchant) and Charlotte Kas-
netz. Married Adele Wolfe (a teacher), 1958.

Education: B.Litt., Rutgers University; graduate
  work at Columbia University, New York University,
  New School for Social Research, City College of
  New York, Colorado University.

Career: Writer and editor.
  Has been a teacher and radio broadcaster in New York;
a professional storyteller at camps, recreation cen-
ters, and on the air; an editor for the Bureau of Curriculum Research, New York; an editor for G. P. Putnam's Sons in New York; free-lance author, 1951-DATE.
Member: Authors Guild.

* * * * *

DONALD A. WOLLHEIM

Full Name: Donald Allen Wollheim.
  Born October 1, 1914, at New York, New York. Son
of J. L. Wollheim (a doctor) and Rose Grinnell. Married Elsie Balter, June 25, 1943. One daughter, Elizabeth.

Education: B.A., New York University.

Career: Writer and editor.
  Editor, Albing Publications, 1941-42; Editor, Ace
Magazines, 1942-47; Editor, Avon Books, 1947-52; Edi-
tor, Ace Books, 1952-67; Vice-President, Editorial,
1967-71; Publisher and Editor, DAW Books, 1971-DATE;
Editor, *Stirring Science Stories*, February, 1941-
March, 1942 (all issues published); Editor, *Cosmic
Stories*, March, 1941-July, 1941 (all issues published);
Editor, *Avon Fantasy Reader*, #1-18, 1947-52; Editor,
Out of This World Adventures, July, 1950-December, 1950
(all issues published); Editor, *10 Story Fantasy*,
Spring, 1951 (only issue published); Editor, *Avon Sci-
ence Fiction Reader*, #1-3, 1951-52; Editorial Consul-
tant, *Saturn*, March, 1957-March, 1958 (all issues pub-
lished); free-lance author, 1934-DATE; Editor, *World's
Best Science Fiction*, 1965-71 (with Terry Carr); Editor, *Annual World's Best SF*, 1972-DATE (with Arthur W.
Saha).

First Professional Sale: "The Man from Ariel,"
  in *Wonder Stories*, January, 1934.

Awards:
  Hugo Award, Best Book Publisher, 1963 (1964), Ace
Books; Special Plaque, 33rd World Science Fiction Convention (Aussiecon), Sydney, 1975, for "the fan who
has done everything."

Member:
  Science Fiction Writers of America; Mystery Writers
of America; Western Writers of America; American Rocket
Society; Aviation Space Writers Association; National
Association of Book Editors; British Model Soldier
Society; Burroughs Bibliophiles; Miniature Figure Col-
lectors of America.

Interests: Collecting model soldiers.

* * * * *

ROBERT WOOD

Full Name: Robert Williams Wood.
  Born May 2, 1868, at Concord, Massachusetts. Son of
Robert Wood (a doctor and pioneer sugar grower in Haw-
aii) and Lucy Jane David. Married Gertrude Hooper
Ames, April 19, 1892 (died 1958). Three children:
Margaret (born 1893), Robert (born 1894), Elizabeth
(born 1898).

Education: B.A., Harvard University, 1891; graduate
  student, Johns Hopkins University, 1891-92.

Career: Professor of Physics.
  Research Professor of Physics, Johns Hopkins University, 1901-51. Died August, 1955, at East Hampton, NJ.

First Professional Sale: *How to Tell the Birds
  from the Flowers*, Paul Elder, 1904.

Honors & Awards:
  Royal Society of Arts Medal, for defraction grating
process of color photography; Franklin Institute John
Scott Medal; J. Traill Taylor Medal for photography
by invisible rays; Gold Medal of the Italian Society
of Science; Frederic Ives Optical Society Medal; Rum-
ford Medal; Draper Gold Medal; numerous honorary degrees; many other awards.

Member:
  Royal Society (Fellow); Optical Society; Physical
Society; National Academy; American Academy; Royal
Microscopic Society; London Optical Society; Royal
Institute; London Physical Society; many others.

Interests: Painting, photography. "When Vice President of the American Physical Society, at a meeting
  in Berkeley, he wrote 'Throttlebottom' on his ID but-
  ton--typical Woodism!"--Elizabeth Wood Bogert.

MARTIN WOODHOUSE

Full Name: Martin Woodhouse.
  Born August 29, 1932, at Romford, Essex, England.
Son of Robert Arnold Woodhouse (a physician), and Jose-
phine Fielding.

Education: B.A., Cambridge University, 1954; M.A.,
  1958; M.B. and B.Ch., St. Mary's Hospital Medical
  School, University of London, 1957.

Career: Writer.
  Earned spending money during college by writing
science fiction stories for American pulp magazines
under various pseudonyms; after completing military
service, and a year as a research scholar with the
Medical Research Council Applied Psychology Unit at
Cambridge, he began writing for TV, beginning with
a children's TV series, and eventually becoming the
lead writer for *The Avengers* for four years; full-
time novelist, 1966-DATE. Member: Institute of
Electrical Engineers (Medical Division).

Agent: Terence Baker, Richard Hatton Ltd., 17A Curzon St., London W.1, England.

* * * * *

CORNELL WOOLRICH

Full Name: Cornell George Hopley-Woolrich.
  Born December 4, 1903, at New York, New York. Son
of Genaro Hopley-Woolrich and Claire Tarler. Education: Attended Columbia University, 1921-25.

Career: Full-time writer, 1926-68. Died September
  25, 1968.

Awards:
  $10,000 First Prize, College Humor and First Nation-
al Pictures, 1927, for *Children of the Ritz*; Edgar
Award, 1949; Edgar Award, Best Motion Picture, 1950,
for "The Window"; Screen Writers Guild Award, 1954,
for "Rear Window"; French Mystery Prize, 1954, for
short story, "One Foot in the Grave"; First Prize in
Ellery Queen Short Story Contest, 1962.

* * * * *

JANETTE WOOLSEY

Full Name: Janette Woolsey.
  Born December 11, 1904, at Livingston Manor, New
York. Daughter of George Samuel Woolsey and Nellie
Dodge.

Education: A.B., Middlebury College, 1925; B.S.,
  Pratt Institute, 1926; M.S., Columbia University,
  1931.

Career: Librarian.
  Assistant Children's Librarian, Pratt Institute,
1926-27; Children's Librarian, Ohio University, 1927-
36; Director of Children's Work, Martin Memorial Library, York, Pennsylvania, 1936-67; Elementary School
Librarian, York City School District, 1936-67; now
retired.

First Professional Sale: *New Plays for Red Letter Days*, Macrae Smith, 1953.

Honors: Life membership in the Pennsylvania Parent-
  Teachers' Association for outstanding work with children.

Member:
  American Library Association; Pennsylvania Library
Association; York Historical Society; College Club of
York County; York County League of Women Voters; Delta
Delta Delta.

Interests:
  "My avocation has been writing. I started by writing
plays for marionettes, which were used for our Marionette Theatre sponsored by the Library. And my hobby
has been a life-long interest in books and reading.
  "Although I had been interested in writing for many
years, it wasn't until I began to collaborate with Elizabeth Hough Sechrist in 1952 that I knew I had a real
avocation. Our writing partnership has proved to be a
most happy one. Altogether, we have written 9 books.
Four of these were about holidays, one a book of plays,
two on Brotherhood, and two were anthologies, one a
collection of our favorites for Story Hours, and the
other *Terribly Strange Tales*.
  "This was a joy to do. Both of us enjoy mysteries,
but we decided the stories in our anthology should dif-
fer from the average mystery tale. These must be tales
that end in strange ways. We read through collection
after collection of short stories--choosing, eliminat-
ing, and finally making the final decision. Tracking
down copyright owners and elusive authors in some cases
turned out to be almost as strange as the tales themselves.
  "Writing with someone can be a very stimulating and
enjoyable experience. Although Mrs. Sechrist and I
decide in advance who is going to write what, we exchange ideas, and when we read each other's work, both
criticize and accept criticism freely. Writing can
be lonely. But it's not when you're working with a
good friend."

* * * * *

HELEN WRIGHT

Full Name: Mary Helen Wright.
  Born December 20, 1914, at Washington, D.C. Daughter
of Frederick E. Wright (a geophysicist) and Kathleen
Finley. Married John F. Hawkins, 1946 (divorced); married Rene Greuter, 1967.

Education: B.A., Vassar College, 1937; M.A., 1939.

Career: Writer.
  Assistant, Mt. Wilson Observatory, Pasadena, 1937;
Junior Astronomer, U.S. Naval Observatory, Washington,
1942-43; free-lance author and editor, 1943-DATE. Mem-
ber: American Astronomical Society; History of Science
Society; International Astronomical Union.

* * * * *

LAN WRIGHT

Full Name: Lionel Percy Wright.
  Born July 8, 1923, at Watford, Hertfordshire, England.
Son of Percy Robert Wright (a railway official) and
Frances Ethel Fothergill. Married Betty Foster, May 7,
1949.

Education: Cambridge Certificate, Watford Centre
  School, and Pupil Teacher Centre, 1940.

LAN WRIGHT (Cont.)

Career: Group electrical buyer.
   Various purchasing positions, British Railways, 1940-67; Deputy Company Buyer, Haden Young Ltd. (an electrical firm), 1967-DATE; served in the Royal Navy, 1942-46.

First Professional Sale: "Operation Exodus," in *New Worlds*, January, 1952.

Agent: E. J. Carnell Literary Agency, 17 Burwash Road, Plumstead, London SE18 7QY, England.

Member: Royal Society of Arts (Fellow); Institute of Purchasing and Supply.

Interests: Cricket, philately, reading, book collecting, wine and food.

Wright writes:
   "My present full-time occupation involves considerable travel and personal involvement. The ideas still come, and, one day, may be set down on paper. All my novels have been published in France, Italy, Spain, Germany, and several in Portugal, Holland, and Brazil. My own favorite of my own books is *The Pictures of Pavanne*. My favorite authors: C. S. Forester, Douglas Reeman (and as Alexander Kent), and Isaac Asimov."

* * * * *

PATRICIA WRIGHTSON

Full Name: Patricia Wrightson.
   Born June 19, 1921, at Lismore, New South Wales, Australia. Daughter of Charles Radcliff Furlonger and Alice Dyer. Married and divorced. Two children: Jennifer Mary, Peter Radcliff. Education: Attended St. Catherine's College and State Correspondence School, Australia.

Career: Editor and author.
   Has been a hospital administrator; Editor, *School Magazine*, Sydney, 1970-DATE; free-lance author, 1955-DATE. Member: Australian Society of Authors; Authors Guild of America.

Honors & Awards:
   Book of the Year Award, Australian Children's Book Council, 1956, for *The Crooked Snake*; American Library Association notable book, 1963, *The Feather Star*; *Book World* Spring Award, 1968, and Hans Christian Andersen Honors List, 1970, for *A Racecourse for Andy*.

* * * * *

STEFAN WUL

Full Name: Pierre Pairault.
   Born March 27, 1922, at Paris, France. Son of Henri Pairault (a factory director) and Graziella Le Creurer. Married Jeanne Brault (a personal secretary), January 8, 1951.

Education: Baccalauréat Philo-Lettres, College Rocroy-Saint-Léon, 1940; Chirurgien-Dentiste F.M.P, Ecole Dentaire de Paris, 1945.

·Career: Dentist and writer.
   Dentist in private practice, Ivry-la-Bataille,

France, 1945-DATE; free-lance author, 1956-DATE.

Awards: Grand Prix du Roman Science-Fiction, 1956, for *Retour à "O"*.

* * * * *

PHILIP WYLIE

Full Name: Philip Gordon Wylie.
   Born May 12, 1902, at Beverly, Massachusetts. Son of Edmund Melville Wylie (a Presbyterian minister) and Edna Edwards (an author). Married Sally Johanna Ondeck, April 17, 1928 (divorced, 1937); married Frederica Ballard, April 7, 1938. One daughter, Karen (born 1932).

Education: Attended Princeton University, 1920-22.

Career: Writer.
   Staff Member, *New Yorker*, 1925-27; Advertising Manager, Cosmopolitan Book Company, 1927-28; Writer, Paramount Pictures Corporation, 1931-33, and for Metro-Goldwyn-Mayer, 1936-37; was also consultant to the Civil Defense Administration; full-time writer, 1937-71. Died October 21, 1971, at Miami, Florida.

Agent: Harold Ober Associates, 40 E. 49th St., New York, NY 10017.

Honors & Awards:
   Litt.D., University of Miami, and Florida State University. Gold Medal of the Freedom Foundation, 1953; Henry H. Hyman Memorial Trophy, 1959.

* * * * *

JOHN WYNDHAM

Full Name: John Wyndham Parkes Lucas Beynon Harris.
   Born July 10, 1903, at Knowle, Warwickshire, England. Son of George Beynon Harris and Gertrude Parkes. Married Grace Isabel Wilson, July 26, 1963.

Education: Attended Bedales School.

Career: Writer, 1931-69. Died at Petersfield, England, March 11, 1969.

First Professional Sale: "Worlds to Barter," in *Wonder Stories*, May, 1931.

Member: Society of Authors; P.E.N.; Science Fiction Writers of America.

* * * * *

ESMÉ WYNNE-TYSON

Full Name: Esmé Wynne-Tyson.
   Born June 29, 1898, at London, England. Married L. C. Wynne-Tyson (a wing commander in the Royal Air Force), June 22, 1918. One son, Timothy Jon Lynden.

Career: Writer.
   Was a child actress on the London stage, making her first appearance at age 12; later wrote plays with Noel Coward, and novels with J. D. Beresford; Editor, *World Forum*, 1961-DATE. Awards: Special Prize, Millenium Guild of New York, 1957; Freshel Award, 1962, for *The Philosophy of Compassion*.

CHELSEA QUINN YARBRO

Full Name: Chelsea Quinn Yarbro.
 Born September 15, 1942, at Berkeley, California. Daughter of Clarence Elmer Erickson (a statistical cartographer) and Lillian Chatfield (an artist and teacher). Married Donald Paul Simpson (an artist and inventor), November 3, 1969.

Education: Attended San Francisco State University, 1960-63.

Career: Writer.
 Statistical Cartographer, C. E. Erickson & Associates, 1963-70; has also been a counsellor and vocal coach; free-lance author, 1970-DATE.

First Professional Sale:
 "The Posture of Prophecy," in *Worlds of If*, September, 1969 [a play, "The Crook-Backed King," was actually performed earlier, by the Mirthmakers, in August, 1964].

Agent: Kirby McCauley, 220 E. 26th St., New York, NY 10010.

Awards: Mystery Writers of America Scroll Winner, 1973, for "The Ghosts at Iron River"; National Thespian Scholarship, 1960, for studies at SF State.

Member: Mystery Writers of America; Science Fiction Writers of America (Secretary, 1970-72).

Interests:
 "Music, particularly opera, and composition. Cooking and gardening (herbs and vegetables as well as house plants). Riding when I can afford it. Live theatre. Some art exhibits. Travel. Fishing."

Yarbro writes:
 "Most writing is a lot of work, and dull, but that's part of the demands if one actually does writing as a self-supporting profession. On the other hand, if you have to write or go crazy, I feel you should learn to be as professional as possible, so that you can get some appreciation, as well as money, to show for the personal effort writing requires. The creating of fiction is fun. The pure copying part is a bore.
 "You wanted to know why women writers are rare in science fiction. I've got a few ideas on that. For one thing, a great many men resent women in the field, and refuse to take women writers seriously, or accept them as legitimate professionals. This is not terribly good for the self-esteem, and makes the women who would be contributors, but who are lacking in a conviction of their own worth, shy away from the field. And since women account for 15% of the professionals, they don't have a lot of support from other women, simply because there aren't a lot of other women around. Also, as I am sure you're aware, the schools tend to push women into domestic, supportive, and non-technical roles, assuming that a woman who is going to get married and have a family cannot possibly give a damn about physics. Part of this stems from a general male desire not to be shown up by a mere female, but that rivalry comes in later. Most of the damage is done by second grade.
 "Women writers are expected to write nurse novels and gothics, and occasionally a best-seller about how crazy women are. If I sound resentful, it's because I am. Mind you, I do not want to be a man, but I'm very tired of being penalized for being a woman. Also,

"there's no earthly use in wanting expiation or restitution from the male half of the race. For one thing, such gestures are truly futile, and for another, we have to learn to live together. Women have spent so much time on their knees, I doubt if any of us would want to see another creature have to assume that posture.
 "There is also the circular argument put forth in a fanzine not long ago that since science fiction is not about women, women are not interested in it, and since they are not interested in it, science fiction is not about women, etc., ad ridiculum. That is a defensive male attitude I can do without, although it is annoyingly prevalent in the field."

* * * * *

LAURENCE YEP

Full Name: Laurence Michael Yep.
 Born June 14, 1948, at San Francisco, California. Son of Thomas Gim Yep (a postal clerk) and Franche Lee.

Education: B.A., University of California, Santa Cruz, 1970; Ph.D. candidate, State University of New York at Buffalo.

Career: Writer, 1968-DATE. Member: Science Fiction Writers of America; Modern Language Association.

First Professional Sale: "The Selchey Kids," in *Worlds of If*, February, 1968.

Agent: Lurton Blassingame, 60 E. 42nd St., New York, NY 10017.

* * * * *

JANE YOLEN

Full Name: Jane Hyatt Yolen.
 Born February 11, 1939, at New York, New York. Daughter of Will Hyatt Yolen (a journalist and public relations man) and Isabelle Berlin (a social worker). Married David W. Stemple, September 2, 1962. Three children: Heidi Elisabet (born 1966), Adam Douglas (born 1968), Jason Frederic (born 1970).

Education: B.A., Smith College, 1960; Ph.D. candidate, University of Massachusetts.

Career: Writer.
 Mss. Clerk, Gold Medal Books, 1961-62; Associate Editor, Rutledge Books, 1962-64; Assistant Editor, Alfred A. Knopf juvenile books, 1964-66; free-lance author.

First Professional Sale: Articles to the *Bridgeport Sunday Herald*, 1958.

Agent: Curtis Brown Ltd., 60 E. 56th St., New York, NY 10022.

Awards: *Emperor and Kite* was a Caldecott Honor Book; Chandler Medal; many other junior book awards.

Member:
 Society of Children's Book Writers (Member, Board of Directors); Pioneer Valley Ballet Co. (Member, Board of Directors); Little Book House Museum (Member, Board of Incorporators); Delegate to the Democratic National

JANE YOLEN (Cont.)

Convention, 1972.

Interests: Politics, folklore, folksinging, ballet.

Yolen comments: "Though I have written many different kinds of books--nonfiction and realistic novels, picture concept books and musical plays, I consider myself basically a fantasy writer for young people. It comes as no shock that my nonfiction sells faster than my fiction, since 90% of children's book sales are to schools and libraries, and we are still in the grip of the terror that came from the Russians getting Sputnik in the air first. But it always makes me sad to think that some children will be getting short-changed on fantasy."

* * * * *

MIRIAM YOUNG

Full Name: Miriam Young.
Born February 26, 1913, at New York, New York. Daughter of Frank A. Burt (an actor) and Myrtle McKenley. Married Walter Young (an artist), September 7, 1934. Three children: Peter, Nancy, Barry. Education: Attended Columbia University.

Career: Writer, 1944-74. Died September 12, 1974.

Agent: Russell & Volkening, 551 Fifth Avenue, New York, NY 10017.

* * * * *

ROBERT F. YOUNG

Full Name: Robert Franklin Young.
Born June 8, 1915, at Silver Creek, New York. Son of Franklin B. Young (a postal worker) and Edna Baker. Married Regina M. Sadusky, October 7, 1941. One daughter, Roberta Jean (born 1942).

Career: Inspector in a non-ferrous foundry.

First Professional Sale: "The Black Deep Thou Wingest," in Startling Stories, June, 1953.

Agent: Raines & Raines, 244 Madison Avenue, New York, NY 10016.

Member: Science Fiction Writers of America.

* * * * *

GEORGE ZEBROWSKI

Full Name: George T. Zebrowski [pronounced Zebrov-ski]. Born December 28, 1945, at Villach, Austria. Son of Anthony Zebrowski and Anna Popovicz.

Education: Attended State University of New York, Binghamton, 1964-69.

Career: Writer and editor.
Has worked as a copy editor, mss. reader, interviewer, pool operator; has also lectured at SUNY Binghamton on science fiction; free-lance author, 1970-DATE.

First Professional Sale: "The Water Sculptor," in Infinity One (an anthology edited by Robert Hoskins), Lancer Books, 1970.

Awards: Runner-up for a Nebula Award, 1971, for "Heathen God."

Member:
Science Fiction Writers of America (Editor, SFWA Bulletin, 1970-75); World Future Society.

Interests: Chess, classical music, futuristics, films.

* * * * *

ROGER ZELAZNY

Full Name: Roger Joseph Zelazny.
Born May 13, 1937, at Euclid, Ohio. Son of Joseph Frank Zelazny (a pattern maker) and Josephine Sweet. Married Sharon Steberl, December 5, 1964 (divorced, 1966); married Judith Callahan, August 20, 1966. Two sons: Devin Joseph (born 1971), Jonathan Trent (born 1976).

Education: B.A., Western Reserve University, 1959; M.A., Columbia University, 1962.

Career: Writer.
Claims Representative, Social Security Administration 1962-65; Claims Policy Specialist, 1965-69; full-time writer, 1969-DATE.

First Professional Sale: "Passion Play," in Amazing Stories, August, 1962.

Agent: Henry Morrison, 58 W. 10th St., New York, NY 10011.

Honors & Awards:
Guest of Honor, 32nd World Science Fiction Convention (Discon 2), Washington, 1974; Nebula Award, Best Novella, 1965 (1966), "He Who Shapes"; Nebula Award, Best Novelette, 1965 (1966), "The Doors of His Face, the Lamps of His Mouth"; Nebula Award, Best Novella, 1975 (1976), "Home Is the Hangman"; Hugo Award, Best Novel, 1965 (1966), And Call Me Conrad [published in book form as This Immortal]; Hugo Award, Best Novel, 1967 (1968), Lord of Light; Hugo Award, Best Novella, 1975 (1976), "Home Is the Hangman"; Prix Apollo, 1972, for Isle of the Dead.

Member:
Science Fiction Writers of America (Secretary-Treasurer, 1967-68); Authors Guild; Authors League.

"With respect to your question regarding the period of time involved in the writing of the Amber Series, the delay is because of the fact that I like to take a break between Amber books, and do something else--i.e., other novels--for a change of pace. Otherwise, it would be an awfully long spell of writing about nothing but Amber. As to the source of the idea, too many things went into it for me to be able to say with any precision."

The Amber Series now consists of four volumes: Nine Princes in Amber, The Guns of Avalon, Sign of the Unicorn, and The Hand of Oberon. Zelazny served in the Ohio National Guard, 1960-63, and the U.S. Army Reserve, 1963-66.

CHLOE ZERWICK

Full Name: Chloe Zerwick.
   Born February 13, 1923, at Cincinnati, Ohio. Daughter of Meyer and Corinne Greenwold. Married Jacob L. Fox, Jr., 1943; married M. B. Zerwick, 1959. Two children: Jay Fox, Phoebe Zerwick.

Education: B.A., University of Chicago, 1943.

Career: Writer and editor.
   Associate Editor, *Common Cause*, 1948-50, and *American Exporter*, 1953-55.

First Professional Sale: Magazine articles, dates unknown.

* * * * *

ROSE A. ZIMBARDO

Full Name: Rose Abdelnour Zimbardo.
   Born May 29, 1932. Daughter of Albert J. Abdelnour (a clerk) and Angela Lombardi. Married Philip Zimbardo (a professor of psychology), July 13, 1957. One son, Adam.

Education: A.B., Brooklyn College, 1956; M.A., Yale University, 1957; Ph.D., 1960.

Career: Professor of English.
   Assistant Professor of English, City University of New York, 1960-69; Associate Professor of English, and Director of Master of Arts Programs in English, State University of New York, Stony Brook, 1969-DATE.

First Professional Sale: *Wycherley's Drama*, Yale University Press, 1965.

Zimbardo writes:
   "As I tried to prove in a paper that I delivered at the Modern Language Association Conference in December, 1974, on "The Medieval-Renaissance Vision of *The Lord of the Rings*," I do not consider Tolkien a science fiction writer. In fact, especially when one considers his conception of Saruman, the great technologist, I am confident that he did not think of himself as a 'science' anything. I'm also a bit uneasy about thinking him a writer of 'fantastic' literature, because that implies that any literature that does not follow the aesthetic principles of 19th century realism is 'fantastic,' and I rather think that Ortega was right in thinking the 19th century 'an aberration in taste.'"

* * * * *

LLOYD ZIMPEL

Full Name: Lloyd Zimpel.
   Born September 2, 1929, at Princeton, Minnesota. Son of George Zimpel (a truckdriver) and Erna Kuether. Married Nina Youkelson, June 16, 1956. Three sons: Benjamin, Jason, Aaron.

Education:
   B.A., University of Minnesota, 1954; graduate student, State University of Iowa, 1956-57, and San Francisco State College, 1960-61.

Career: Education officer.
   Advertising Director, West Coast Life Insurance Company, San Francisco, 1959-63; Education Officer, California Fair Employment Practice Commission, 1963-DATE; free-lance author.

Agent: Max Gartenberg, 331 Madison Avenue, New York, NY 10017.

Awards: Quill Awards from the *Massachusetts Review*, 1964 and 1969.

Afterword

This book was five years in the making, a far longer period than I anticipated when I started, and now that it is finished, I feel that a few readers might appreciate having some idea of how the book was constructed, and just what it contains.

At first, the proposal seemed easy. I planned to base the project on several large science fiction collections available locally. I was fortunate in having the help of my good friend Douglas Menville, whose knowledge of early science fiction and fantasy is encyclopedic in scope and in having access to a collection which had recently been purchased by the University of California at Riverside from the estate of Dr. J. Lloyd Eaton, one of the major contributors to the Day *Supplemental Checklist*. Eaton had collected actively into the late 1950s, and his 8,000-book collection was very strong in early materials. Menville's own collection filled in many of Eaton's gaps, and a third collection, assembled by Barry Levin, and later used by him to start his science fiction dealership, also helped. To these I could add my personal library of 17,500 volumes, which is very strong in modern materials, especially British and American paperbacks.

I quickly ran into problems. While my own collection was easy to index and categorize, the Eaton books, most of which were published before SF became a recognizable genre, were much more difficult to handle. Many contained trace elements of the supernatural, requiring close reading to determine each book's qualifications. Adding to my difficulties was the fact that approximately one quarter of Eaton's holdings were collections or anthologies. I had already determined that I would list such works only when at least one third of the stories included had science fiction or fantasy content, or when one long story occupied more than a third of the pages in the book. Each of these books required extensive examination, and what had appeared to be the work of several months slowly became several years. Every evening I would drive the fifteen miles to Riverside, and spend two to four hours going through books that often crumbled away in my hands. Many had to be read from cover to cover, an excruciating task at best. I could average no more than thirty books a night. The bibliographical data for each book were written down in a spiral notebook, keyed with the notations "SF," "Not SF," or "Borderline," where I failed to make a decision (these books were reexamined at a later date). In this way, the bibliography was put together piece by piece, like some huge mosaic. The information in the notebook was transcribed onto cards, and the cards filed into two sections, one for books marked "SF," and another for those marked "Not SF." Each card was also labeled "E" for the Eaton Collection. Similarly, I spent several weeks going through Menville's collection, skipping any books already encountered, and using his extensive knowledge of the subject as a rough guide to the others. Barry Levin typed out a complete list of his collection, and I only looked at the books unique to his library. At the end of this process, my file of verified SF titles filled nine drawers with about 19,000 cards, of which 15,884 were actually first editions, another 2,000 being retitlings, and the remainder see references. The second file, those books verified "Not SF," totaled more than 4,000 cards in two drawers.

Simultaneously, I had begun mailing questionnaires to active science fiction and fantasy authors, requesting biographical data for *Contemporary Science Fiction Authors II*, the new version of *Stella Nova*. I sent out close to 2,000 forms during the next year and a half, eventually getting 1,443 biographies, including some supplemental material from Gale's *Contemporary Authors* series. Generally, only those writers already listed in the bibliography were included, plus a handful of contributors. For the first time, I also listed deceased writers, whenever I could contact estates, agents, or relatives of the biographees.

Roughly 93 percent of the books listed in this work were actually seen and evaluated personally. Three other persons were allowed to contribute material: Douglas Menville read, evaluated, and summarized about 5 percent of the entries; Mary Burgess, my wife, read and evaluated perhaps 2 to 3 percent of the books; Gordon Johnson, a librarian in Scotland, hunted down some 50 modern British titles I was unable to locate elsewhere, and provided plot summaries. In each case, I examined the contributor's material thoroughly, and where I felt a description was vague or uncertain, asked to see the book myself, requested a second evaluation, or excluded the work. In addition, a handful of items were included on the basis of published plot descriptions in dealers' catalogs and annotated bibliographies.

All of the entries have been checked twice through the *National Union Catalog* and the *British Museum Catalogue* or the *British National Bibliography;* books not listed in these sources were verified in other publications, including the *Cumulative Book Index*, the *United States Catalog*, the national bibliographies of Canada, Australia, and South Africa, various university catalogs, *Whitaker's*, my own *Cumulative Paperback Index* (and the unpublished material I compiled for its sequel), *Book Publishing Record*, and various author bibliographies. Information on authors' complete or real names, dates of birth and death, and pseudonyms has been tracked through a wide variety of sources, including *The New York Times Obituary Index*, *Who Was Who*, *Who Was Who in America*, *Catalog of Copyright Entries* and other records in the Copyright Office, and many author dictionaries and directories. In searching for possible SF titles, I have gone through dozens of dealers' catalogs, read the entire file of *Library Journal*, *School Library Journal*, and *Booklist* for the past twenty years, examined all appropriate entries in the *Fiction Catalogue*, spent many hours in bookstores, and pursued every possible lead in tracking down elusive titles. Many of the scarcer books were obtained through interlibrary loan from other institutions, courtesy of California State College, San Bernardino. As a result, this bibliography is the most complete book of its kind ever published, listing an estimated 95 to 98 percent of all science fiction and fantasy books actually published through 1974, the remaining 2 to 5 percent being unverified or unmentioned in any available source.

From the beginning, I have limited the scope of this work to prose fiction, excluding verse, drama, comics, or fiction in which more than half of the book consists of illustrations. Science fiction has always seemed to me essentially a prose genre, but the decision was pragmatic--the number of fantasy plays in particular seems endless, and there are few sources available for such materials. Originally, the book covered through the end of 1973, but I extended it a year when the work dragged out. I had no bottom time limit at first, but later removed publications released before 1700. This was about the time that the prose novel was establishing itself as a distinct literary form in England, and was also the period when the first genre of fantastic literature, the imaginary voyage, came into vogue. It provided a convenient (if arbitrary) cut-off date. The only book that I regretted leaving out was Cyrano de Bergerac's story of a voyage to the Sun and the Moon published originally in the 1680s.

I include books packaged as science fiction or fantasy, tales set in a definite future (books set in the indefinite near future are excluded unless specific dates are mentioned or implied), stories of the supernatural, alternate histories, fiction dealing with the exploration of outer space (except those relating actual events), imaginary wars, fantasy utopias and dystopias, travels in time, heroic or mythic fantasy, tales set in completely imaginary worlds or on mythical islands which do not actually exist, lost race novels, stories in which God or the devil are real and actual beings, tales about men with superhuman or psychic powers, stories of sentient animals, and other fantastica. I exclude occult works purporting to be nonfiction, suspense stories using fictional locales in a present-day setting (unless the fictional regions imply changes in the Earth's physical appearance), nonfiction flying saucer accounts, gothics (unless a supernatural element is clearly and unambiguously present), present-day utopias, collections or anthologies in which less than a third of the stories included have fantastic elements (rounded off to the nearest third), Salem witch trial stories (unless the witches have clear supernatural powers), and stories in which supernatural elements are presented by the author in a purposely ambiguous way. Nonfiction works about science fiction and fantasy are included, but I have not listed biographical or critical studies of individual authors, except where the author is regarded primarily as a science fiction or fantasy writer, or where the work in question deals specifically with the author's science fiction or fantasy *oeuvre*. Also included are a small number of items which are not in themselves fantastic, but which use science fiction and fantasy as background settings; typical of these works are Anthony Boucher's *Rocket to the Morgue*, a mystery novel, and Barry Malzberg's *Herovit's World*, which deals with a neurotic science fiction writer. Horror stories with no supernatural elements (for example, Gaston Leroux's *Phantom of the Opera*) are excluded. Certain series, such as Doc Savage and The Shadow, are included in their entirety because background material in the series contains fantastic elements, even though individual novels may not actually qualify. The Shadow, for example, seems to rely on occult powers to help keep him from being seen at night, although in many of his adventures these powers are scarcely mentioned or used. Other series characters, including The Avenger, have no evident superhuman abilities, and their adventures have been judged individually.

In each instance, it is important to consider the intent of the writer. To be listed, a story must include events or happenings of a fantastic nature which could not actually occur in real life, but which are made real in the context of the story. Hence, dream tales are listed if some possibility exists within the story that the events are real; they are excluded if the author's intent is to deny the possibility of such things ever happening. Juvenile books were a problem from the beginning. At first, I thought to exclude them completely, but immediately ran into the problem of the Robert Heinlein and Andre Norton juveniles, which were released in hardcover for the adolescent market, and reprinted in paperback as adult books. These had to be included. As I read further, it became obvious to me that the distinctions between "adult" and "juvenile" books were largely the creation of the publishing houses, and did not often exist in reality. At the same time, I did not want to include volumes aimed at the very young. Ultimately, the cut-off date was set at around grade five, or about the age of eleven, each book being judged individually on content, size of type, number of pages, and other such factors.

As with all such books, *Science Fiction and Fantasy Literature* could not have been completed without the help of many others. Seven of these people have been given title page credit. Douglas Menville shared his vast knowledge and experience, qualities which made this work much better than it otherwise would have been. He also supplied me with an unending stream of cards, notes, and reviews, and these, combined with a knack for finding what must surely be the most obscure fantasies ever published, added immeasurably to the book's completeness. My wife, Mary, has been a constant source of support since our marriage in October, 1976, providing encouragement when the project seemed interminable, and helping with evaluations, bibliographical checking, and filing. George Locke, owner of Ferrett Fantasy Ltd. of London, handled all United Kingdom mailings of the questionnaires for *Contemporary Science Fiction Authors II*. Michael Grainey, now a government attorney in Salem, Oregon, checked a great many records at the Copyright Office in Washington, D.C. Gordon Johnson, a librarian in Glasgow, found and read a number of recent British titles unobtainable in the United States. Barry Levin typed out a complete list of his extensive collection, and provided copious and wise advice on many different matters. Doris Illes copied the card index of the Eaton Collection, giving me, in effect, a master list to use as a guide to more than 8,000 volumes.

Others who helped in various ways include: Holly Sullivan, Al Germeshausen, Bill and Margaret Crawford, Barry McGhan, Peter Briscoe, George Slusser, Poul Anderson, Brian W. Aldiss, Alan E. Nourse, Charles Platt, Science Fiction Writers of America, E. W. Ball and the Fantasy Centre in England, Bond Street Bookstore, Lyn Young, Collector's Bookstore of Hollywood, the late, lamented Sunset-Vine Bookmart, Al Saunders, Larry Shaw, Joe Gores, California State College at San Bernardino, Ken Slater and his Fantast (Medway) Ltd., Neil Barron, Sherry Gottlieb and her Change of Hobbit Bookstore in Westwood, R. Lionel Fanthorpe, H. W. Hall, Charles N. Brown and *Locus*, Mark Owings, Bruce Robbins, Leslie Kay Swigart, and Donald H. Tuck. A special word of thanks should go to the University of California at Riverside Library, and especially to Clifford Wurfel, Special Collections Librarian, his able assistant, Greg Robbins, and Abigail Dahl-Hansen, University Librarian during the period I was working in the Eaton stacks. Thanks also to the long-suffering staff at Gale Research Company, and particularly to James M. Ethridge, Editorial Vice President, and my editor, Dedria Bryfonski, for all their help, patience, and willing support. I could not imagine a better group of people to work with. The responsibility for any errors, omissions, or misstatements is solely my own, as is the burden for typographical mistakes, since I typed the book myself.

This is not, of course, the final word on the subject--no bibliography ever is. But it does represent a major step towards providing bibliographical control over a particularly difficult field. I have already started an addendum file, and will shortly be starting work on a supplemental volume, to cover the years 1975-1979 inclusive, with *Contemporary Science Fiction Authors III*. I currently plan to produce supplements at five-year intervals, with complete revisions of the book every ten years. Corrections and additions are welcome, and should be sent to the author at P.O. Box 2845, San Bernardino, California 92406. Please provide complete bibliographical data for corrections, and plot summaries or descriptions for additions.

Robert Reginald
San Bernardino, California
22 December 1978

www.ingramcontent.com/pod-product-compliance
Lightning Source LLC
Chambersburg PA
CBHW081645280326
41928CB00069B/2924